AFRICA SINCE 1914

A Historical Bibliography

Clio Bibliography Series No. 17

Gail A. Schlachter, Editor
Pamela R. Byrne, Executive Editor

1. The American Political Process (1972)
2. Afro-American History (1974)
3. Indians of the United States and Canada (1974)
4. Era of the American Revolution (1975)
5. Women in American History (1979)
6. The American and Canadian West (1979)
7. European Immigration and Ethnicity in the United States and Canada (1983)
8. Afro-American History, Volume II (1981)
9. Indians of the United States and Canada, Volume II (1982)
10. The History of Canada (1983)
11. Urban America (1983)
12. Religion and Society in North America (1983)
13. Social Reform and Reaction in America (1984)
14. American Popular Culture (1984)
15. The American Presidency (1984)
16. Latin American Politics (1984))
17. Africa since 1914 (1984)
18. Labor in America (1984)
19. The Middle East in Conflict (1984)

AFRICA SINCE 1914

A Historical Bibliography

ABC-Clio Information Services

Santa Barbara, California
Denver, Colorado
Oxford, England

Library of Congress Cataloging in Publication Data
Main entry under title:

Africa
(Clio bibliography series; no. 17)
Includes index.
1. Africa—Bibliography. I. ABC-Clio Information
Services.
Z3501.S9 1985 [DT351] 016.967 83-27153
ISBN 0-87436-395-0

ABC-Clio Information Services, Inc.
2040 Alameda Padre Serra
Santa Barbara, California

ABC-Clio Information Services, Inc.
The Consulate
700 East Ninth Avenue
Denver, Colorado

Clio Press Ltd.
55 St. Thomas St.
Oxford 0X1 1JG, England

Printed and bound in the United States of America

ISBN 0-87436-395-0

TABLE OF CONTENTS

PREFACE

It was scarcely two decades ago that Hugh Trevor-Roper, Regius Professor at the University of Oxford, characterized African history as the "unrewarding gyrations of barbarous tribes in picturesque but irrelevant corners of the globe." He suggested that the historical study of the continent was a passing media fad, and that there existed only the history of Europeans in Africa: "the rest is darkness. . .and darkness is not a subject for history." He might well have concluded with a line from Hegel: "Africa is not a historical continent, it shows neither change nor development."

Few historians today would accept these pronouncements. Since 1960, a watershed year in which more than a dozen African states achieved independence and the *Journal of African History* began publication, there has been a rapid growth in research and scholarship on the history of Africa. A flood of dissertations, books, and articles has revealed the diverse past of Africa and its peoples, and has introduced new research methods and theoretical concepts. The rapid expansion of information has caused textbooks to become quickly dated, particularly those works dealing specifically with modern Africa. More European documents have become available and historians are now evaluating them with greater critical skill. Additionally, a generation of young scholars, armed with the techniques of collecting oral history, has contributed new insights into our understanding of colonialism, liberation, and independence. Ironically, European and American historians now often turn to Africanists and their studies for methodological and theoretical conceptions. African history has come of age.

The new prominence of African studies has stimulated a prolific body of periodical literature. Every aspect of the political, economic, and social environment of each African country has been analyzed, it would seem, as well as the complex international relations among African states and between African states and major world powers and international organizations. Much of this immense body of scholarship has now been made accessible in this one-volume bibliography that contains abstracts representing a decade (1973-1982) of journal literature on modern Africa since 1914. Its entries are drawn from the vast history data base of ABC-Clio Information Services, covering more than 2,000 periodicals published in almost 90 countries. In order to create this unique bibliographic volume, the editor reviewed the many thousands of abstracts of articles published during 1973-1982 and selected every abstract that related to Africa. Thus, this volume offers an in-depth representation of the scholarship published in the world's periodical literature on this subject and far exceeds what one could expect to find through an online search of the data base or even through a manual search of the subject index for the ABC-Clio Information Services' history data base as a whole.

The arrangement of the volume is geographical, organized by country, with the first chapters covering studies of more than one nation. These multi-country studies are useful for their analysis of international relations, economic and development policies, political ideologies and movements, military development, and efforts at regional or continental integration of the many diverse states that form this complex and dynamic region. The specific country studies provide an in-depth look at the political, social, and economic dynamics of each nation. The variance in the size of the chapters represents not any predisposition on the part of the editors, but rather the amount of scholarship on each topic that was published in the journal literature during the decade covered by this volume.

Africa since 1914 utilizes ABC-SPIndex, one of the most advanced and comprehensive indexing systems yet developed. ABC-SPIndex allows fast, analytical, and pinpoint access by linking the key subject terms and historical period of each abstract to form a composite index entry that provides a profile of the journal article. Each set of index terms is rotated so that the complete profile appears in the index under each of the subject terms. Thus, the number of subject access points is increased severalfold over conventional hierarchical indexes, and irrelevant material can be eliminated early in the search process. The explanatory note at the beginning of the subject index provides more information about ABC-SPIndex.

Care has been taken to eliminate inconsistencies that might have appeared in the subject index as a result of combining a decade of data base material. The subject profile index thus reflects a highly labor-intensive effort, the product of many hours of editing and reediting, and allows easy access to the materials included in this volume. Additional cross-references have been included to ensure fast and accurate searching. The result is a bibliography that is extremely thorough in its treatment of the modern periodical literature on Africa.

This volume represents the collaboration of a skilled and diverse group. Pamela R. Byrne, Executive Editor of the Clio Bibliography Series, directed the development and production of this volume and provided guidance essential to its creation. Assistant Editor Lance J. Klass, who has published on African archaeology and ethnology, served as project coordinator and had responsibility for conceptualizing this volume, selecting and organizing the entries from the ABC-Clio data base, and editing the subject index. He also designed the cover for the book. Historian-editor and Africanist Terry H. Elkiss, formerly of the African Studies Center at Michigan State University and now on the staff at ABC-Clio, was a key collaborator. Assistant Editor Susan K. Kinnell provided essential editorial support at crucial stages of the project and saw it through the final phases of production. The Data Processing Services Department, under the supervision of Ken Baser, Director, and Deborah Looker, Production Supervisor, ably manipulated the data base to meet editorial specifications.

Appreciation is extended, most especially, to the worldwide community of scholars who provided the abstracts that form this volume and without whose work this contribution to African scholarship and research would not have been possible.

LIST OF ABBREVIATIONS

A. .... Author-prepared Abstract
Acad. .... Academy, Academie, Academia
Agric. .... Agriculture, Agricultural
AIA .... Abstracts in Anthropology
Akad. .... Akademie
Am. .... America, American
Ann. .... Annals, Annales, Annual, Annali
Anthrop. .... Anthropology, Anthropological
Arch. .... Archives
Archaeol. .... Archaeology, Archaeological
Art. .... Article
Assoc. .... Association, Associate
Biblio. .... Bibliography, Bibliographical
Biog. .... Biography, Biographical
Bol. .... Boletim, Boletin
Bull. .... Bulletin
c. .... century (in index)
ca. .... circa
Can. .... Canada, Canadian, Canadien
Cent. .... Century
Coll. .... College
Com. .... Committee
Comm. .... Commission
Comp. .... Compiler
DAI .... Dissertation Abstracts International
Dept. .... Department
Dir. .... Director, Direktor
Econ. .... Economy, Econom-.
Ed. .... Editor, Edition
Educ. .... Education, Educational
Geneal. .... Genealogy, Genealogical, Genealogique
Grad. .... Graduate
Hist. .... History, Hist-.
IHE .... Indice Historico Espanol
Illus. .... Illustrated, Illustration
Inst. .... Institute, Institut-.
Int. .... International, Internacional, Internationaal, Internationaux, Internazionale
J. .... Journal, Journal-prepared Abstract
Lib. .... Library, Libraries
Mag. .... Magazine
Mus. .... Museum, Musee, Museo
Nac. .... Nacional
Natl. .... National, Nationale
Naz. .... Nazionale
Phil. .... Philosophy, Philosophical
Photo. .... Photograph
Pol. .... Politics, Political, Politique, Politico
Pr. .... Press
Pres. .... President
Pro. .... Proceedings
Publ. .... Publishing, Publication
Q. .... Quarterly
Rev. .... Review, Revue, Revista, Revised
Riv. .... Rivista
Res. .... Research
RSA .... Romanian Scientific Abstracts
S. .... Staff-prepared Abstract
Sci. .... Science, Scientific
Secy. .... Secretary
Soc. .... Society, Societe, Sociedad, Societa
Sociol. .... Sociology, Sociological
Tr. .... Transactions
Transl. .... Translator, Translation
U. .... University, Universi-.
US .... United States
Vol. .... Volume
Y. .... Yearbook

Abbreviations also apply to feminine and plural forms.
Abbreviations not noted above are based on *Webster's Third New International Dictionary* and the *United States Government Printing Office Style Manual.*

1. GENERAL

1. Asiwaju, A. I. NEW TRENDS IN COLONIAL AFRICAN HISTORIOGRAPHY: FRANCE AND BRITAIN IN AFRICA. *J. of the Hist. Soc. of Nigeria [Nigeria] 1974 7(3): 563-569.* Prosser Gifford and Roger Louis's *France and Britain in Africa* (New Haven: Yale U. Pr., 1971) and T. L. Gann and P. Duignan's *Colonialism in Africa, 1870-1960* (Cambridge U. Pr.) are almost exclusively written by US or European scholars and tend to neglect African oral tradition.

2. Bernardi, Bernardo. I CINQUANT'ANNI DELL'INTERNATIONAL AFRICAN INSTITUTE (1926-1976) [The fifty years of the International African Institute, 1926-76]. *Africa [Italy] 1976 31(2): 159-169.* A measure of where the International African Institute has gone in its 50 years of existence can be seen by the fact that its first president was Lord Lugard, first British governor-general of Nigeria while the present president is the distinguished Nigerian scholar J. F. Ade Ajayi. The Institute has contributed greatly to the studies of African social, political, religious, and economic institutions and to the knowledge of African linguistics. J. C. Billigmeier

3. Bernstein, Henry. MARXISM AND AFRICAN HISTORY: ENDRE SIK AND HIS CRITICS. *Kenya Hist. Rev. [Kenya] 1977 5(1): 1-21.* Outlines the Marxist concept of dialectical materialism, assesses the value of Hungarian writer Endre Sik's *The History of Black Africa,* 4 vols. (1966, 1974), and asserts that Sik's understanding of dialectical materialism is undermined by theoretical and methodological errors and is inapplicable to African realities.

4. Blackey, Robert. FANON AND CABRAL: A CONTRAST IN THEORIES OF REVOLUTION FOR AFRICA. *J. of Modern African Studies [Great Britain] 1974 12(2): 191-209.* Revolutionary theories must be adapted to the land in question. Frantz Fanon (Algeria) and Amilcar Cabral (Guinea-Bissau) presented Africa with two distinctive ideologies. Compares their ideas on revolution, violence, class, culture, and political parties. Although Fanon and Cabral differed in temperament and scope, their writings are complementary. 64 notes. H. G. Soff

5. Bradlow, Frank R. AN AFRICANA RESEARCHER IN IRELAND AND THE UNITED KINGDOM. *Q. Bull. of the South African Lib. [South Africa] 1973 27(3): 73-84.* Describes the author's travels in Great Britain and Ireland in connection with his research on Major Richard Wolfe and Thomas Baines. To this end he visited Forenaghts (Wolfe's home) in Ireland and the Livingstone Museum at Blantyre. 3 photos, 22 notes. J. A. Casada

6. Brokensha, David. AFRICA, WHITHER NOW? *J. of African Studies 1974 1(1): 101-112.* An essay review of two groups of books which treat Africa, one series popular and misleading, the other academic and ponderous. The popular group consists of Stanislav Andreski, *The African Predicament* (London: Michael Joseph, 1968); Leonard Barnes, *African Renaissance* (London: Gollancz, 1969); Leonard Barnes, *Africa in Eclipse* (London: Gollancz, 1971); John Biggs-Davidson, *Africa—Hope Deferred* (London: Johnson, 1972); Rene Dumont, *False Start in Africa* (New York: Praeger, 1969); Ely J. Kahn, Jr., *The First Decade: A Report on Independent Africa* (New York: W. W. Norton, 1972); James Mayall, *Africa: The Cold War and After* (London: Elek, 1971); Erik Robins and Blaine Littell, *Africa: Images and Realities* (New York: Praeger, 1971); and V. G. Solodovnikov, *Africa Fights for Independence* (Moscow: Novasti, 1970). The academic group consists of: Frederick S. Arkhurst, ed., *Africa in the Seventies and Eighties: Issues in Development* (New York: Praeger, 1970); Peter Lloyd, *Classes, Crises and Coups: Themes in the Sociology of Developing Countries* (London: MacGibbon and Kee, 1971); Michael Lofchie, ed., *The State of Nations: Constraints on Development in Independent Africa* (U. of California Pr., 1971); Jacques Maquet, *Power and Society in Africa* (New York: McGraw-Hill, 1971); Jacques Maquet, *Africanity, The Cultural Unity of Black Africa* (New York: Oxford U. Pr., 1972); Donald G. Morrison, et al., *Black Africa: A Comparative Handbook* (New York: Free Pr., 1972); John N. Paden and Edward W. Soja, eds., *The African Experience* (Northwestern U. Pr., 1970). V. L. Human

7. Brunschwig, Henri. AFRIQUE NOIRE (IMPÉRIALISME) [Black Africa: imperialism]. *Rev. Hist. [France] 1977 258(2): 457-484.* Resumé of collective works, histories, and monographs concerning Black Africa and imperialism. Treats geographical areas and discusses recurrent themes. Classifies works on imperialism by theories of motivation. Table. G. H. Davis

8. Brunschwig, Henri. BULLETIN HISTORIQUE: AFRIQUE NOIRE (1976-1979) [Historical bulletin: Black Africa, 1976-79]. *Rev. Hist. [France] 1980 263(1): 149-194.* Review article of 43 books, of which 10 works on general African history published between 1976 and 1979 emphasize non-Eurocentric approaches, but colonialism is still an important feature of the literature. Reviews of works in German, French, and English encourage further research. Topics discussed include West Africa, East Africa, German colonization, and Southern Africa. G. H. Davis

9. Brunschwig, Henri. HISTOIRE DE L'AFRIQUE NOIRE (1970-1975) [History of black Africa, 1970-75]. *Rev. Hist. [France] 1976 256(1): 171-205.* Describes and evaluates 42 works on the history of black Africa published between 1970 and 1975. Includes a discussion of general works and geographical subdivisions of Africa. G. H. Davis

10. Caplan, Gerald L. REVIEW ARTICLE—THE USE OF AFRICAN HISTORY. *African Rev. [Tanzania] 1974 4(1): 127-135.* Reviews Walter Rodney's *How Europe Underdeveloped Africa*(London: Panther House, 1972). European intervention prevented the fulfillment of Africa's potential for centuries, and Africans have been misled to believe that development means Westernization. 11 notes. H. G. Soff

11. Carter, Gwendolen M. AFRICAN STUDIES IN THE UNITED STATES: 1955-1975. *Issue 1976 6(2-3): 2-4.* Examines African studies departments at colleges and universities, surveying the various agencies offering grant allocations for extended study, 1955-75.

12. Curtin, Philip D. AFRICAN HISTORY. Kammen, Michael, ed. *The Past Before Us: Contemporary Historical Writing in the United States* (Ithaca, N.Y.: Cornell U. Pr., 1980): 113-130. Serious study of African history in American universities is limited and has a short history. Just when the field began to gain interest, universities suffered losses of students and of academic positions for trained historians. Contributions to historical writing by nonhistorians—anthropologists and linguists, for example—have been important, especially in studies based on oral history and non-European languages. Economic history has been slow in developing among Africanists. The brain drain from Europe and Africa has accounted for many of the scholars now teaching and researching African history in the United States. 54 notes. S

13. Curtin, Philip D. THE BLACK EXPERIENCE OF COLONIALISM AND IMPERIALISM. *Daedalus 1974 103(2): 17-29.* Two traditions in Western historiography discourage concern about Africa, especially colonial Africa—an ethnocentrist bias and elitism. Narrower definitions of "imperialism" and "colonialism" and the demographical studies of colonial Africa now provide the key to the variables in the kinds of colonial experiences. Strains in the New World societies were among racial groups with minor cultural differences; in North Africa, among cultural groups with minor racial differences; in sub-Saharan Africa, among groups with cultural and racial differences. Based on secondary sources; 18 notes. E. McCarthy

14. Depelchin, Jacques. TOWARD A PROBLEMATIC HISTORY OF AFRICA. *J. of Southern African Affairs 1977 2(1): 5-10.* Discusses primary resistance and nationalism as a theme in 20th-century African history in response to the work of T. O. Ranger and from a Marxist perspective. Africans were fighting against the expropriation of their land. Ranger's discussion contains no analysis of the class nature of colonial society. Unlike Ranger the Russian historian A. B. Davidson was talking about liberation movements, not nationalist movements. "The task of a problematic history is to forge tools of analysis and develop a methodology which leaves absolutely no room for subjectiv-

ism, idealism, or any other form of mystification." 11 notes.
E. P. Stickney

15. Diop, Louise-Marie. LE SOUS-PEUPLEMENT DE L'AFRIQUE NOIRE [Underpopulated black Africa]. *Bull. de l'Inst. Fondamental d'Afrique Noire [Senegal] 1978 40(4): 718-862.* Analyzes why Africa south of the Sahara is underpopulated. Africa compared favorably with the monsoon areas of Asia and with Europe, 10th-16th centuries. Slave trading over four centuries, colonial penetration, and lack of industrial development led to a decrease in population rather than an increase as in other parts of the world. 2 maps, 6 tables, 3 charts, 313 notes, biblio., 2 appendixes. H. L. Calkin

16. Eriken, Tore Linné. MODERN AFRICAN HISTORY: SOME HISTORIOGRAPHICAL OBSERVATIONS. *Scandinavian J. of Hist. [Sweden] 1979 4(1): 75-97.* Examines in the light of recent trends in African history and especially of the influence of Basil Davidson, whose books stress both the central place of Africa itself and the place of Africa in the global context, the historiographical debate over selected themes in African history: the ecological and political transformation during the first phase of the colonial period, African forms of resistance and collaboration, and the ideological foundations of the nationalist movement. In particular, Davidson's *Africa in Modern History* (London, 1978) has been important not just in indicating the way history has influenced present developments but also in stimulating historiographical debate. Mainly secondary sources, especially the writings of Davidson; 39 notes. P. J. Beck

17. Filesi, Teobaldo. UN PROBLEMA INSOLUTO: LA PERIODIZZAZIONE DELLA STORIA DELL'AFRICA [An unsolvable problem: the periodization of history in Africa]. *Africa [Italy] 1978 33(1): 53-66.* Africa is atypical because of its structural peculiarities. For purposes of periodization it cannot be subjected to traditional Western models or to generalizations on the continental level. As a result historical treatment of the African continent must be flexible. J/S

18. Frank, Genevieve. BIBLIOGRAPHIE SUR L'ÉVOLUTION DU SYNDICALISME EN AFRIQUE DANS LES PAYS AU SUD DU SAHARA [Bibliography on the development of labor unions in Africa south of the Sahara]. *Genève-Afrique [Switzerland] 1974 13(1): 101-118, (2): 98-117.* A bibliography of general and comparative studies dealing with the development of labor unions and organizations in Africa south of the Sahara.

19. Garaudy, Roger. WE CAN LEARN FROM AFRICA. *Center Mag. 1973 6(2): 38-41.*

20. Goncharov, L. V. and Il'in, Iu. M. AFRIKANISTIKA V SSSR (70E GODY) [African studies in the USSR in the 1970's]. *Narody Azii i Afriki [USSR] 1980 (1): 137-147.* Presents the research carried out by various organizations and institutes devoted to the study of African problems under the direction of the Institute of Africa of the Academy of Sciences of the USSR, established in 1959. In the late 1950's, after the success of the liberation movements and the fall of colonialism, the Soviet Union increased its relations with the new states and encouraged research into African problems, dealing in particular with the socioeconomic aspect, Soviet-African cooperation, neocolonialism, South Africa, the history of the national liberation movements, ethnography, and geography. Note. C. Pichelin

21. Gromyko, A. A. LENIN I AFRIKA [Lenin and Africa]. *Aziia i Afrika Segodnia [USSR] 1980 (5): 2-4.* V. I. Lenin investigated the Western countries' colonial policy in Africa, their contradictions, and the national liberation movement on the continent. Life has testified to the correctness of his scientific forecast that the oppressed peoples of Africa would win their independence. His concept of national liberation revolutions developing into social ones and of an accelerated development of backward countries toward socialism bypassing capitalism have materialized in the social life of the socialist-oriented countries, whose number has been constantly growing. J

22. Haeffner, Gerd. PHILOSOPHIE IN AFRIKA [Philosophy in Africa]. *Stimmen der Zeit [West Germany] 1978 196(12): 795-806.* Since World War II, Western European philosophy has been increasingly replaced by ethnic philosophy in African universities.

23. Hecht, Robert. THE RISE OF RADICAL AFRICAN STUDIES. *J. of Development Studies [Great Britain] 1978 15(1): 120-126.* Review essay of *African Social Studies: A Radical Reader,* edited by Peter C. W. Gutkind and Peter Waterman (Heinemann Educational Books, 1977); *The Political Economy of Contemporary Africa,* edited by Peter C. W. Gutkind and Immanuel Wallerstein (Sage Publ., 1976); and *Nigeria: Economy and Society,* edited by Gavin Williams (Rex Collings, 1976). All deal with African politics and economy from a leftist point of view, late 19th-20th centuries.

24. Henige, David. AFRICAN CHRONOLOGY. *African Affairs [Great Britain] 1976 75(298): 104-108.* A scorching condemnation of G. S. P. Freeman-Grenville, *Chronology of African History* (Oxford, 1973). This volume of significant dates in African history from ca. 1000 B.C. to 1971 is filled with incorrect names and dates and is generally unusable. H. G. Soff

25. Henige, David. THE ARCHIVES OF THE MILL HILL FATHERS. *African Res. and Documentation [Great Britain] 1980 (22): 18-20.* The major area of activity of the St. Joseph's Society for the Missions (Mill Hill Missionaries) was Africa, but 181 classifications of archives are located at the society headquarters in London at St. Joseph's College.

26. Henige, David. A COMPREHENSIVE BIBLIOGRAPHY OF CATHOLIC MISSIONARY MATERIALS RELATING TO AFRICA: THE BIBLIOTHECA MISSIONUM. *African Res. and Documentation [Great Britain] 1978 (18): 20-22.* Discusses the *Bibliotheca Missionum,* a bibliography of the published writings of Catholic missionaries, six volumes of which deal specifically with Africa from 1053 to 1940.

27. Hopkins, A. G. IMPERIAL BUSINESS IN AFRICA. *J. of African Hist. [Great Britain] 1976 17(2): 267-290.* Continued from a previous article (see abstract 559). Assesses the quality of African company histories and suggests ways to improve business history writing. 69 notes. H. G. Soff

28. Jewsiewicki, Bogumil. ÉTUDE BIBLIOGRAPHIQUE: NATION, ETHNIE ET CLASSE: CONSTRUCTION NATIONALE EN AFRIQUE ET COMMUNAUTÉ INTERNATIONALE [Bibliographical essay: nation, ethnicity and class: nation building in Africa and the international community]. *Études Int. [Canada] 1981 12(1): 201-206.* Review article on seven works on colonialism, political thought, decolonization, ethnicity, and international relations in Africa in the 19th and 20th centuries. J. F. Harrington

29. Leigh, Carol. PERIODICALS AND ARTICLES OF INTEREST. *Rhodesiana [Zimbabwe] 1976 (35): 60-62.* Lists articles published in 1976 on the history of central and southern Africa.

30. Lemon, Anthony. FEDERALISM AND PLURAL SOCIETIES: A CRITIQUE WITH SPECIAL REFERENCE TO SOUTH AFRICA. *Plural Soc. [Netherlands] 1980 11(2): 3-24.* Notes efforts to create a federation in South Africa since the 1850's, focusing on the 20th century, and examines the attempts at federation in the Central African Federation and Nigeria.

31. Lot, G. ARKHIVNYE ISTOCHNIKI V GDR PO ISTORII STRAN AFRIKI IUZHNEE SAKHARY [Archival sources in East Germany on the history of African countries south of the Sahara]. *Narody Azii i Afriki [USSR] 1974 (5): 233-236.* Describes the valuable documents on sub-Saharan African history contained in East Germany's Central State Archives in Potsdam, particularly on the anticolonial and anti-imperialist movement of the 19th century.

32. Luben, Dusan. TENSIONS ET CONFLITS DU CONTINENT AFRICAIN [Tensions and conflicts of the African continent]. *Etudes Polémologiques [France] 1982 (25-26): 99-130.* A general chronology of African events since 1945 and analyzes zones of confrontation and instability within sectoral chronologies. Article to be continued. J/S

33. McCall, Daniel F. RADCLIFFE-BROWN VS. HISTORICAL ETHNOLOGY: THE CONSEQUENCE OF AN ANTHROPOLOGICAL DISPUTE FOR THE STUDY OF AFRICA'S PAST. *Int. J. of African Hist. Studies 1980 13(1): 95-102.* The functionalist school of anthropology led by A. R. Radcliffe-Brown, dominated both the British and Americans during the 1920's through the 1940's. Their antihistorical views severely hurt the collecting and writing of the history of African peoples. 25 notes. R. T. Brown

34. Motani, Nizar A. THE EXPANDING FRONTIER OF AFRICAN HISTORY: FROM OLIVER AND ATMORE TO ROBIN HALLETT. *African Studies Rev. 1975 18(2): 134-139.* Reviews Roland Oliver and Anthony Attmore's *Africa since 1800,* 2d ed., (Cambridge U. Pr., 1972); J. D. Omer-Cooper, E. A. Ayandele, A. E. Afigbo, and R. J. Gavin's *The Making of Modern Africa, vol. 1, The Nineteenth Century and the Partition*(Humanities Pr., 1972); E. A. Ayendale, A. E. Afigbo, R. J. Gavin, and J. D. Omer-Cooper's *The Making of Modern Africa, Vol. 2, The Late Nineteenth Century to the Present* (Humanities Pr., 1972); Evelyn John Rich and Immanuel Wallerstein, eds., *Africa: Tradition and Change* (Random House, 1972); and Robin Hallett's *Africa since 1875: A Modern History* (Ann Arbor: U. of Michigan Pr., 1974).

35. Negash, Girma. THE POLITICS OF LIBERATION: BASIL DAVIDSON HERALDS THE EMERGENCE OF AN AFRICAN POLITICAL IDEA. *UMOJA: A Scholarly J. of Black Studies 1979 3(2): 115-128.* A review article on Basil Davidson's *Let Freedom Come: Africa in Modern History* (Boston: Atlantic-Little, Brown, 1978).

36. Obichere, Boniface I. THE CONTRIBUTIONS OF AFRICAN SCHOLARS AND TEACHERS TO AFRICAN STUDIES, 1955-1975. *Issue 1976 6(2-3): 27-32.* Discusses scholarly studies by Africans aimed at discovering black interpretations of African history and then teaching these interpretations to the remainder of the world of scholars and students; exhorts African scholars to change their perspectives from those of anthropology to those of sociology, so that old stereotypes may be destroyed, philosophies formalized, and the dissemination of scientific and objective findings facilitated.

37. Orhonlu, Cengiz. AFRÍKA ÍLE ÍLGÍLÍ TÚRKÇE YAYINLAR VE KAYITLAR [Turkish publications and records concerning Africa]. *Tarih EnstitúsúDergisi [Turkey] 1976-77 7-8: 145-156.* A bibliography of works in modern and Ottoman Turkish concerning Africa, subdivided into topics, covering the period from the 14th century to the present, with a strong emphasis on the North African territories formerly under Ottoman rule. F. A. K. Yasamee

38. Perinbaum, B. Marie. *HOMO AFRICANUS: ANTIQUUS OR OECONOMICUS?* SOME INTERPRETATIONS OF AFRICAN ECONOMIC HISTORY. *Comparative Studies in Soc. and Hist. [Great Britain] 1977 19(2): 156-178.* Examines varying interpretations of African economic history, 19th-20th centuries, focusing on the *antiquus* argument (economic process in a so-called promotive society) and the *oeconomicus* argument (the extent to which traditional economic studies can be applied to African economic history) offered in the 1950's-60's.

39. Prins, Gwyn. THE END OF THE BEGINNING OF AFRICAN HISTORY. *Social Hist. [Great Britain] 1979 4(3): 495-508.* A review article which examines: R. Palmer and N. Parsons ed., *The Roots of Rural Poverty in Central and Southern Africa*(Heinemann, 1977), in which the use of colonial archival material unsupported by field data emphasizes the difficulty of applying general theoretical notions such as "underdevelopment" on any smaller scale than the regional; J. Vasina's *The Children of Woot* (Madison: U. of Wisconsin Pr., 1978), which, by contrast, inspires confidence in its conclusions about the Kuba people of Zaire through a critical discussion of source materials; and J. M. Janzen with the collaboration of M. D. Arkinsall *The Quest for Therapy in Lower Zaire* (U. of California Pr., 1978) which uses specific case histories to illustrate the interaction between Western and traditional medicine. The reviewer asserts that these three books indicate that there are grounds for hoping that the present crisis in African historical research may be overcome. 30 notes. A. P. Oxley/S

40. Randles, W. G. L. LA CIVILISATION BANTOU, SON ESSOR ET SON DÉCLIN [Bantu civilization: its takeoff and its decline]. *Annales: Économies, Sociétés, Civilisations [France] 1974 29(2): 267-281.* Analysis of the conditions which led to the "takeoff" of Bantu civilization and its subsequent decline. Among the diverse consequences of the contacts established with Europe was the dislocation of the "homeostatic equilibrium" which constituted the traditional management systems of the Africans. 98 notes. R. Howell

41. Ranger, Terence. WHITE PRESENCE AND POWER IN AFRICA. *J. of African Hist. [Great Britain] 1979 20(4): 463-469.* An African Study Association of the United Kingdom conference on Whites in Africa—Past, Present and Future (September, 1978) illustrates a trend toward greater sophistication among scholars. Many papers questioned myths of the stability and significance of various white groups; many saw whites in Africa as agents of metropolitan ideology or as victims along with blacks of international capitalism. The claim to expertise was an essential part of the colonial white self-image in Africa. "This return to the subject of the whites in Africa has been an occasion for humility rather than a renewed pink pride." Also published in *African Research and Documentation* 1979 (19). A. W. Novitsky

42. Ranger, Terence. WHITES IN AFRICA. *African Res. and Documentation [Great Britain] 1979 (19): 2-7.* Summarizes the proceedings of the 1978 conference of the African Studies Association of the United Kingdom on white settlers in Africa, primarily during the 20th century.

43. Salmon, Pierre. HISTOIRE DES SOCIÉTÉS AFRICAINES [History of African societies]. *Cahiers de Clio [Belgium] 1981 (65): 15-23.* A brief study of African history.

44. Seidman, Ann. MODERN AFRICAN HISTORY AND ITS ROOTS. *Monthly Rev. 1979 31(7): 56-63.* Review article on Basil Davidson's *Let Freedom Come: Africa in Modern History* (Boston: Atlantic-Little, Brown, 1978).

45. Semi-Bi, Zan. L'HISTOIRE AFRICAINE ÉCRITE PAR DES AFRICAINS: REFLEXIONS À PROPOS DU LIVRE DE JOSEPH KI-ZERBO [African history written by Africans: reflections on the book of Joseph Ki-Zerbo]. *Rev. Française d'Études Pol. Africaines [France] 1973 (92): 77-85.* Reviews the first general history of Black African people, *History of Black Africa Yesterday and Today* (Paris, 1973) by Joseph Ki-Zerbo of Senegal.

46. Shepperson, George. THE AFRO-AMERICAN CONTRIBUTION TO AFRICAN STUDIES. *J. of Am. Studies [Great Britain] 1974 8(3): 281-301.* Discusses the extensive writings about Africa by American Blacks. Beginning in the 1830's, the writers were notably defensive in treating their African antecedents and, to a small degree, remain so today. Since 1900, their studies of Africa have become increasingly erudite and professional. Carter Woodson (1875-1950) and W. E. B. Du Bois (1868-1963) especially encouraged American Blacks to improve and professionalize their studies on a wide variety of African topics. 76 notes. H. T. Lovin

47. Simensen, Jarle. DEN RADIKALE RETNING I U-LANDSSTUDIENE OG DENS TOLKNING AV AFRIKANSK HISTORIE [The radical direction in the study of underdeveloped countries and its interpretation of African history]. *Hist. Tidsskrift [Norway] 1977 56(4): 365-397.* The radical trend in Third World studies since the mid-1960's is divided between the American underdevelopment and dependency school and a mainstream European Marxist school that concentrates on class relations. The author analyzes the contributions of radical social scientists to the study of modern African history. Radical theories must be seen primarily as value-based models for the analysis of rich and poor country relations. Broadly applied, they may foreclose important questions of causality by their assumption that capitalism and colonialism are necessary and sufficient conditions of current Third World underdevelopment and poverty. The author examines and dismisses the relevance of Thomas Kuhn's theories of paradigmatic change in explaining the rise of the radicals in Third World studies. J/S

48. Smith, Daniel R. SUB-SAHARAN AFRICA: RECENT LITERATURE. *Trends in Hist. 1979 1(2): 117-131.* Surveys scholarly periodical literature of 1978 which pertains to major episodes and

personalities in sub-Saharan Africa during the 1960's, in addition to material which investigates the region's more remote past.

49. Smith, Van Mitchell. MARXISM AND AFRICAN STUDIES. *Social Sci. J. 1982 19(1): 133-144.* Reviews *Forced Labour in Colonial Africa* (1979) by A. T. Nzula et al., No Sizwe's *One Azania, One Nation: The National Question in South Africa* (1979), Bernard Makhosezwe Magubane's *The Political Economy of Race and Class in South Africa*(1979), Baruch Hirson's *Year of Fire, Year of Ash* (1979), and John S. Saul's *The State and Revolution in Eastern Africa*(1979).

50. Solodovnikov, V. SOVETSKAIA AFRIKANISTIKA MEZHDU XXIV I XXV SEZDAMI KPSS [Soviet African studies between the 24th and 25th Congresses of the CPSU]. *Narody Azii i Afriki [USSR] 1976 (2): 8-19.* The 24th Party Congress foretold the events that took place in Africa: the further development of national liberation movements into social revolutions and the crash of the colonial system. The author describes the research which has been done between the two Party Congresses by the Institute of Africa at the Academy of Sciences of the USSR, whose research tries to answer such questions as how to overcome economic backwardness and how to use Africa's resources and productive forces. The researchers also point out the detrimental effect of foreign monopolies on the economies of the new states and the advantages of state control over them. The institute is also studying sociopolitical and ideological processes and social and class changes in contemporary African society. Also mentions some of the research done by other institutes and institutions of higher education. Primary sources; 5 notes. L. Kalinowski

51. Strayer, Robert. MISSION HISTORY IN AFRICA: NEW PERSPECTIVES ON AN ENCOUNTER. *African Studies Rev. 1976 19(1): 1-16.* A close parallelism exists between development and change in missionary history in Africa and African history itself in sub-Saharan Africa, 1950-60.

52. Sullivan, Jo. RECENT TRENDS IN AFRICAN HISTORY. *Social Educ. 1982 46(7): 508-515.* Discusses the contributions of recent historical research on Africa, advances in the study of early history and oral traditions, economics, African women, and the reevaluation of the colonial period.

53. Tedeschi, Salvatore. IL III CONGRESSO INTERNAZIONALE DEGLI AFRICANISTI [The third International Congress of Africanists]. *Africa [Italy] 1974 29(1): 87-94.* A report on this congress held at Addis Ababa in December 1973, followed by a title list of all the papers delivered on the political, social, economic, and historical aspects of Africa, résumés of which are intended for publication. R. O. Khan

54. Thion, Serge. AFRICA: WAR AND REVOLUTION. *Dissent 1979 26(2): 213-225.* Traces political developments in Africa since the revolution in Mozambique in 1974 and gives a brief background history of South Africa since colonization by the Dutch in the 17th and 18th centuries.

55. Turri, Eugenio. UN ITINERARIO INTELLETTUALE: PELLEGRINO IN AFRICA [An intellectual itinerary: pilgrim in Africa]. *Comunità [Italy] 1980 34(182): 171-225.* Reflects on 20 years of events in Africa since his first research trip to Darfur in the late 1950's.

56. Ursu, D. P. STANOVLENIE NATSIONAL'NOI ISTORIOGRAFII V STRANAKH TROPICHESKOI AFRIKI [The emergence of national historiography in tropical Africa]. *Voprosy Istorii [USSR] 1979 (8): 70-84.* Discusses a number of topical methodological problems concerning the emergence of national historiography in tropical Africa known as the decolonization of history. The birth of modern historical science in the newly independent countries of sub-Saharan Africa is an event of great importance. The Africans are beginning to write their own history, as well as to create it as subjects. An important factor in the struggle for social cohesion and national consolidation are the rehabilitation and new interpretation of history. This paper is an attempt to examine the origins, evolution, and periodization of modern African historiography as well as its methodological trends. J

57. Waterman, Peter. ON RADICALISM IN AFRICAN STUDIES. *Politics and Society 1973 3(3): 261-281.* A bibliographical and methodological analysis of radicalism in recent African historical, sociological, economic, and political studies. Examines radicalism as a "commitment" by Africanists; as an "approach," in which a differentiation between reformist and radical assumptions is made (including varieties of Marxist approaches); and as an "interest," whereby the disciplines ask new questions. Based on published and unpublished works; 117 notes. D. G. Nielson

58. Weinstein, Warren. HUMAN RIGHTS IN AFRICA: A LONG-AWAITED VOICE. *Current Hist. 1980 78(455): 97-101, 130-132.* Evaluates political and economic developments in Africa, reviews the accomplishments of several African conferences on human rights, and assesses human rights in African countries during the 1970's.

59. Wright, D. R. VISUAL IMAGES IN GEOGRAPHY TEXTS: THE CASE OF AFRICA. *Geography [Great Britain] 1979 64(3): 205-210.* Analyzes photographs of tropical Africa in 12 British school textbooks published between 1951 and 1977, showing no marked "traditional" or "Western" emphasis in the books, except where the writer deliberately emphasizes either a village case study or the so-called New Africa.

60. —. A BIBLIOGRAPHY OF BOOKS AND KEY ARTICLES ON AFRICA PUBLISHED IN POLISH, ENGLISH, OTHER LANGUAGES, IN POLAND SINCE 1960, WITH AN INTRODUCTORY ESSAY ON AFRICAN STUDIES IN EASTERN EUROPE AND THE SOVIET UNION. *Munger Africana Lib. Notes 1976 33: 1-65.* A bibliography on Africa which includes over 400 entries in addition to an author and geographical index prepared by the Center of African Studies of the University of Warsaw, with an essay on African Studies in Eastern Europe and the USSR.

61. —. [THE PERIODIZATION OF BLACK AFRICAN DEPENDENCY]. *Cahiers d'Études Africaines [France] 1976 16(1-2): 7-74.*

Coquery-Vidrovitch, Catherine. LA MISE EN DÉPENDANCE DE L'AFRIQUE NOIRE. ESSAI DE PÉRIODISATION HISTORIQUE [The creation of dependency for Black Africa: an essay in historical periodization], *pp. 7-58.* An application of Marxist dependency theory to the history of colonial Africa. Asserts the primacy of economic factors and that the colonizers, practitioners of a capitalist mode of production, overwhelmed black Africans, who had a tributary mode of production. Proposes four periods for the process: installation of the trade economy, 1800-50; precolonial incubation, 1850-80; predatory colonization, 1890-1930; and colonial imperialism, 1936-52. 28 notes, biblio.

Brunschwig, Henri. UNE AUTRE CONCEPTION DE L'HISTOIRE? [A different notion of history?], *pp. 59-68.* Criticizes Coquery-Vidrovitch's Marxist approach for its exclusively economic concern and lack of erudition. 3 notes.

Coquery-Vidrovitch, Catherine. L'HISTOIRE VIVANTE [Living history], *pp. 67-74.* The author defends her use of Marxist categories as a means of promoting explanatory rather than narrative history. 4 notes. B. S. Fetter

2. PAN-AFRICAN INTEGRATION AND COOPERATION

62. Agyeman, Opoku. KWAME NKRUMAH AND TOM MBOYA: 'NONALIGNMENT' AND PAN-AFRICAN TRADE UNIONISM. *Pan-African J. [Kenya] 1977 10(1): 51-71.* Kwame Nkrumah, the Pan-African leader, named Thomas Mboya, his Kenyan *protégé,* chairman of the All-African Peoples Conference in Accra in 1958. By the end of this conference, the beginnings of disagreement had developed between the two leaders, as Nkrumah sought to establish a single All-African Trade Union Federation. This federation (AATUF) was to be strongly opposed by Mboya and his supporters. The AATUF gained influence, and 37 national unions were represented at the AATUF's Second Congress at Bamako in 1964. Based on newspaper reports and periodical articles; 89 notes. F. P. Tudor

63. Agyeman, Opoku. THE OSAGYEFO, THE MWALIMU, AND PAN-AFRICANISM: A STUDY IN THE GROWTH OF A DYNAMIC CONCEPT. *J. of Modern African Studies [Great Britain] 1975 13(4): 653-675.* A comparison of the Pan-African policies of Kwame Nkrumah and Julius Nyerere. Nkrumah wanted immediate African unity; Nyerere argued for a gradual approach. The two national leaders quarreled over this difference until it colored their other policies and actions. Nkrumah was overthrown in 1966; the same year witnessed a change in Nyerere's thinking. He became a stronger proponent of immediate unity, thereby contradicting many of his former arguments. 77 notes. V. L. Human

64. Ahmad, Muhammad. TOWARD PAN AFRICAN LIBERATION. *Black Scholar 1974 5(7): 24-31.* The black people of the world must realize that their oppression is of an international order, and they must organize to destroy and overthrow it internationally. The formation of a world state that represents and works for the benefit of the world's majority, the black underclass, becomes the ultimate focus of Pan-Africanism, Black Nationalism, or Black Power. M. M. McCarthy

65. Ajala, Adekunle. THE RISING TIDE OF PAN-AFRICANISM, 1924-1963. *Tarikh [Nigeria] 1980 6(3): 35-46.* Examines the development of Pan-Africanism, emphasizing the gradual shift in leadership from Afro-Americans and Africans living outside of Africa to native Africans.

66. Akindele, R. A. REFLECTIONS ON THE PREOCCUPATION AND CONDUCT OF AFRICAN DIPLOMACY. *J. of Modern African Studies [Great Britain] 1976 14(4): 557-576.* Classifies the foreign policy resolutions of the Organization of African Unity (OAU) in order to identify the major preoccupations of African diplomacy during 1963-73. A study of varying issues suggests broad agreement, although African diplomacy continues to operate under the major constraints of military weakness, economic backwardness, and technological underdevelopment. 65 notes. R. V. Ritter

67. Akinsanya, Adeoye. THE AFRO-ARAB ALLIANCE: DREAM OR REALITY. *African Affairs [Great Britain] 1976 75(301): 498-510.* In 1963 the Organization of African Unity was established with high hopes. It is now seen as little more than a talking shop, with few accomplishments. Divisiveness among African states has been caused partially by the Arab-Israeli conflict; many African states have been loathe to choose sides. The author examines Arab commitments to Pan-Africanism. 63 notes. H. G. Soff

68. Akinyemi, A. Bolaji. AFRICA—CHALLENGES AND RESPONSES: A FOREIGN POLICY PERSPECTIVE. *Daedalus 1982 111(2): 243-254.* Given the plurality of perspectives among African states the Organization of African Unity, formed in 1963 and consisting of 47 members, has given some measure of success to African foreign policy objectives.

69. Akinyemi, A. Bolaji. THE ORGANISATION OF AFRICAN UNITY AND AFRICAN IDENTITY. *Africa Q. [India] 1981 20(3-4): 5-18.* Defines the objectives of the Organization of African Unity and examines whether they are congruent with resolutions made by the organization about six crises: 1) the Congolese crisis of 1964, 2) the Nigerian crisis, 1967-70, 3) the crisis over dialogue, 1971, 4) the issue of irredentism and boundary adjustments, 5) the crisis over unconstitutional changes of government, and 6) the crisis over Angola. Concludes that there has been no widespread defiance of OAU consensus by its member states.

70. Alimov, Y. OAU: TEN YEARS OF EXISTENCE. *Int. Affairs [USSR] 1973 (7): 59-64.* Analyzes the role of the Organization of African Unity in national liberation movements of developing nations of Africa against neocolonialism, 1963-73.

71. Asante, S. K. B. AFRICA IN WORLD POLITICS: THE CASE OF THE ORGANIZATION OF AFRICAN UNITY AND THE MIDDLE EASTERN CONFLICT. *Int. Problems [Israel] 1981 20(2-4): 111-128.* Discusses the attitudes of the Organization of African Unity toward Israel and the Arab-Israeli conflict since 1958.

72. Binaisa, Godfrey L. ORGANIZATION OF AFRICAN UNITY AND DECOLONIZATION: PRESENT AND FUTURE TRENDS. *Ann. of the Am. Acad. of Pol. and Social Sci. 1977 (432): 52-69.* Although colonialism is now buried in most parts of Africa, its ghost still haunts us in the unnecessarily large number of states. The drive for independence in Africa was first propounded by blacks in America in the philosophies of Pan-Africanism, African personality, and negritude in the early part of this century. Africans derived moral support from the Atlantic Charter and the weakening by World War II of the two European empires. The demise of the Indian Empire was the final nail in the coffin of British imperialism. The most important meeting leading to the formation of the Organization of African Unity was the Conference of Independent African States in April 1958. In the same year, an East African group (PAFMECA) was formed, and by 1963 membership included 18 countries. In 1960-62, 23 states achieved independence. On 25 May 1963, the OAU charter was signed, uniting 47 independent black and Arab nations to promote solidarity among member states. One of the most important objectives of the OAU has been decolonization of Africa, but even after this is achieved, the OAU will still be united in facing the numerous problems of political, economic, and social development in Africa. J

73. Bissell, Richard. AFRICAN UNITY TWELVE YEARS LATER. *Current Hist. 1975 68(405): 193-196.* How stable are the new states of Africa? What economic and political problems do they face? In this issue, African specialists discuss recent events in the African states in the light of historic and social trends. The Organization of African Unity, established 12 years ago, "produces a consensus usually supported by a majority of its members. Thus the OAU has not failed some part of African expectations." J

74. Canada, Afroman. ROY INNES: PAN-AFRICANISM AND BLACK NATIONALISM ARE ONE. *Africa Report 1973 18(1): 34-35.* Interview with Congress of Racial Equality leader. S

75. Cervenka, Zdenek. L'O.U.A. CONTRE VENTS ET MARÉES [The OAU against the winds and the tides]. *Rev. Française d'Études Pol. Africaines [France] 1973 8(93): 61-79.* Studies the political problems and crises faced by the Organization of African Unity (OAU) during its 10-year existence, including internal conflicts, border differences, territorial conflicts, and language and cultural differences among its 41 member independent African states (1963-73).

76. Cervenka, Zdenek. THE OAU AND THE QUEST FOR UNITY, 1963-1976. *Tarikh [Nigeria] 1980 6(3): 47-59.* Examines the record of the Organization of African Unity in effectively dealing with Africa's political and economic dilemmas.

77. Cervenka, Zdenek. OAU OG BETYDNINGEN AV DEN NYE ARABISK-AFRIKANSKE SOLIDARITET [The Organization of African Unity and the meaning of the new Arab-African solidarity]. *Internasjonal Politikk [Norway] 1974 (1): 5-17.* Discusses "the tenth

OAU Summit which opened in Addis Ababa on 25 May 1973. The most significant outcome of this anniversary meeting was the emergence of a new kind of Arab-African solidarity. This has been the culmination of the trend which was clearly evident already at the 1972 OAU Summit in Rabat, and which constitutes one of the major shifts in the OAU policy during its 10 years of existence. The author makes an analysis of this Arab-African development and his conclusion is that although it is too early to assess fully the Arab-African solidarity and its impact on Africa's plight against the white supremacy in Southern Africa, there is no doubt that the Arab-African alliance has already profoundly changed the African political scene and, if further developed, it could play a decisive role in attaining both political and economic objectives of the Organisation of African Unity in its second decade." J

78. Chartrand, Philip E. THE ORGANIZATION OF AFRICAN UNITY AND AFRICAN REFUGEES: A PROGRESS REPORT. *World Affairs 1975 137(4): 265-285.* Discusses the efforts of African nations and the Organization of African Unity (OAU) in taking care of refugees, 1960's-70's. S

79. Chrisman, Robert. ASPECTS OF PAN-AFRICANISM. *Black Scholar 1973 4(10): 2-8.* Chronicles the growth of Pan-Africanism, 1880-1973, highlighting the growth of black consciousness and the first Pan-African Congress in 1900.

80. Copson, Raymond W. AFRICAN INTERNATIONAL POLITICS: UNDERDEVELOPMENT AND CONFLICT IN THE SEVENTIES. *Orbis 1978 22(1): 227-245.* Relations between the new states of Africa in the course of the 1970's have been very unstable, marked by ethnic, territorial, ideological and personal conflicts. None of the larger states are secure and prosperous enough at home to exercise regional leadership or hegemony; the result has been international chaos. Each state lacks a unifying ethnic majority. African states, like African economies, are underdeveloped, and conflict has been the unavoidable consequence. 32 notes. J. C. Billigmeier

81. Diate, Ibou. L'O.U.A., L'ONU ET LE RÈGLEMENT PACIFIQUE DES CONFLITS INTERAFRICAINS [The Organization of African Unity(OAU), the UN, and the peaceful settlement of inter-African conflicts]. *Ann. Africaines [Senegal] 1975: 9-34.* Unlike the League of Nations, the UN specifically allows and supports the formation of regional groups to preserve peace and mediate disputes before the involvement of the UN Security Council. One such group is the Organization of African Unity. However, the UN Charter is not clear as to when and how regional groups surrender jurisdiction to the UN. The author discusses the role of the Organization of African Unity, showing the African preference for keeping an African framework in settling disputes and incipient wars. The UN is called in if the problem is too big for the OAU to handle, e.g., Congo, 1964. Though the OAU is not always effective, it does preserve Africa from its major fear—outside intervention. 102 notes. R. Garfield

82. Drake, St. Clair. THE BLACK DIASPORA IN PAN-AFRICAN PERSPECTIVE. *Black Scholar 1975 7(1): 2-13.* Discusses the dispersal of black Africans throughout the world during the last 10,000 years and the more recent Pan-African movements.

83. Duffield, Ian. PAN-AFRICANISM, RATIONAL AND IRRATIONAL. *J. of African Hist. [Great Britain] 1977 (4): 597-620.* Reviews Immanuel Geiss's *The Pan-African Movement* (London: Methuen, 1974). Originally published in German in 1968, this is a new and fresh interpretation of Pan-Africanism. The author analyzes the role of Pan-Africanists in various aspects of African development, including railways, shipping, aircraft, commodity trading, and banking. From the 19th century, economic development was a major consideration for Pan-Africanists. Geiss explores both the rational and irrational aspects of Pan-Africanism, and though he has neglected some important areas of inquiry, he has suggested some new interpretations which are useful and welcome. 110 notes. H. G. Soff

84. Ekpo, Smart A. THE OAU AND THE SECESSION ISSUE. *Africa Report 1975 20(6): 33-36, 52.* Though the charter of the Organization of African Unity maintains respect for the independence of nations and stresses noninterference in domestic disputes, the secessionist movement in Eritrea, 1963-75, had caused a split in unity in several cases.

85. El-Ayouty, Yassin. O.A.U. MEDIATION IN THE ARAB-ISRAELI CONFLICT. *Genève-Afrique [Switzerland] 1975 14(1): 5-29.* Describes and analyzes the 1971 attempt by African presidents in the Organization of African Unity to mediate in the Arab-Israeli conflict and its immediate aftermath.

86. El-Khawas, Mohamed A. SOUTHERN AFRICA: A CHALLENGE TO THE OAU. *Africa Today 1977 24(3): 25-41.* Summarizes the support provided by the Organization of African Unity for anticolonial movements. Legitimizing the anticolonial forces, financing liberation movements, and reconciling contending factions are the three channels of support. The OAU has been partially successful in each area but has been hampered by disagreements among member states and their failure to provide financial support. Based on secondary sources; 61 notes. G. O. Gagnon

87. Esedebe, P. Olisanwuche. THE GROWTH OF THE PAN-AFRICAN MOVEMENT, 1893-1927. *Tarikh [Nigeria] 1980 6(3): 18-34.* Discusses the development of the Pan-Africanism in the Americas and Africa, emphasizing the roles of such leaders as Edward Wilmot Blyden and Marcus Garvey.

88. Esedebe, P. Olisanwuche. PAN-AFRICANISM: ORIGINS AND MEANING. *Tarikh [Nigeria] 1980 6(3): 3-17.* Attempts to present a clear definition of Pan-Africanism by examining its history and the ideas of its major spokesmen.

89. Esedebe, P. Olisanwuche. WHAT IS PAN-AFRICANISM? *J. of African Studies 1977 4(2): 167-187.* Contends that the concept of Pan-Africanism has often received inadequate definition by recent scholars and that the roles of W. E. B. DuBois and George Padmore in fostering it have been emphasized to the exclusion of those of others, especially Edward Wilmot Blyden (1832-1912). Surveys the history of Pan-Africanism and concludes that it centers around the notion of a distinct "African personality," as discerned by Blyden. Argues that Pan-Africanism is a practical idea and movement aiming at African political and cultural unity and race solidarity. 67 notes. L. W. Truschel

90. Etinger, Ia. OKAM [Organization of African and Malagasy States]. *Voprosy Istorii [USSR] 1974 (2): 214-219.* Describes steps leading to the creation in 1965 of this organization, as part of the Organization of African Unity (OAU), and successor to the Brazzaville group of independent French-speaking countries. In 1975 its membership included the Ivory Coast, Upper Volta, Dahomey, Gabon, Niger, Senegal, Togo, Central African Republic, Mauritius, and Rwanda (several others having withdrawn). Describes its political programs in support of African liberation movements to 1973. 21 notes. N. Frenkley

91. Etinger, Ia. ORGANIZATSIIA AFRIKANSKOGO EDINSTVA NA SOVREMENNOM ETAPE [The present stage of the Organization of African Unity]. *Aziia i Afrika Segodnia [USSR] 1981 (2): 22-24.* Creation in 1963 of the Organization of African Unity mirrored an objective necessity for the unification of the newly free states on an anti-imperialist footing, for strengthening their political independence, and achieving Africa's full decolonization. The African leaders held it that economically backward countries would strengthen their positions in the face of imperialism only by acting within a united Pan-African organization. The work of the OAU confirms the centripetal tendencies overcoming the centrifugal ones, in spite of all the inner contradictions and controversies. On the whole, its members act as a united front in the international arena. J/S

92. Eze, Osita C. OAU FACES RHODESIA. *African Rev. [Tanzania] 1975 5(1): 43-62.* The Organization of African Unity (OAU) has been ineffective in dealing with the Unilateral Declaration of Independence by Southern Rhodesia because of inherent organizational and continental weaknesses. 3 tables, 60 notes. R. T. Brown

93. Fredland, Richard A. THE OAU AFTER TEN YEARS: CAN IT SURVIVE? *African Affairs [Great Britain] 1973 72(288): 309-318.* Questions of sovereignty, ideological differences, imperialist interests, the failure of intra-African activities, the division between black and

Arab Africa, the location of headquarters in Ethiopia, introspection, the diversion of international attention, and apathy have frustrated the effectiveness of the Organization of African Unity. 3 notes.
H. G. Soff

94. Gitelson, Susan Aurelia. THE OAU MISSION AND THE MIDDLE EAST CONFLICT. *Internat. Organization 1973 27(3): 413-419.* The Organization of African Unity (OAU) began to take an active role in the Middle East conflict at the June 1971 summit meeting in Addis Ababa. Four representatives were chosen for a fact-finding mission, which was accepted by both Israel and Egypt, and in which president Leopold Senghor of Senegal played the most prominent role. Discusses the UN General Assembly debate, the OAU summit meeting at Rabat, and the accomplishments and limitations of the OAU mission. "The OAU mission... has served as an interesting test case of the possibilities for states at the periphery of the international system to help resolve conflicts among other small states." 12 notes. E. P. Stickney

95. Golden, L. GARVI I GARVIIZM [Garvey and Garveyism]. *Mirovaia Ekonmika i Mezhdunarodnye Otnosheniia [USSR] 1980 (10): 130-138.* Examines the philosophy of Marcus Garvey and its influence on national movements in Africa, Latin America and the United States.

96. Ijere, M. O. PROBLEMS OF POST-INDEPENDENCE INTEGRATION MOVEMENT IN AFRICA. *Pan-African J. [Kenya] 1972 5(3): 331-346.* The economy of most African states is at a low level. To change into a thriving economy, states must develop regional integration. The rationale behind integration, examples of integration, and some problems that East Africa encountered in the East African Community are emphasized. 14 notes. H. Soff

97. Iqbal, Mehrunnisa H. THE ORGANISATION OF AFRICAN UNITY—1969-73. *Pakistan Horizon [Pakistan] 1973 26(4): 50-60.* Reviews the accomplishments and weaknesses of the Organization of African Unity. The organization serves primarily as a forum for an exchange of ideas and opinion on mutual problems. 32 notes.
H. M. Evans

98. Kamal, Humayun Akhtar. ORGANIZATION OF AFRICAN UNITY. *Pakistan Horizon [Pakistan] 1973 26(1): 36-47.* Discusses the establishment of the Organization of African Unity in 1961, its administration, aims, failures, and achievements; also considers how it has successfully overcome former colonial rivalries.

99. Kannyo, Edward. HUMAN RIGHTS IN AFRICA. *Bull. of the Atomic Scientists 1981 37(10): 14-19.* With the preparation of a charter on human rights by the Organization of African Unity, the first major step in the establishment of an African regional human rights mechanism has been taken. However, its successful operation will largely depend on the pace and degree of regional integration achieved by the OAU.

100. Kapitsa, L. M. INTEGRATSIONNYE PROTSESSY V RAZVIVAIUSHCHEMSIA MIRE (NA PRIMERE GOSUDARSTV TROPICHESKOI AFRIKI) [Processes of integration in the developing world: the example of tropical African countries]. *Narody Azii i Afriki [USSR] 1980 (3): 96-104.* Unlike other forms of economic cooperation, economic integration is linked to social structure and is applicable only between countries with analogous socioeconomic systems and means of production. Some intra-African unions are viable, others faltered due to tribalism and unbridgeable differences in levels of development. Association with the European Economic Community carries the danger of neocolonial exploitation. As the state sector controls the economy in most developing countries, cooperation with Comecon countries is the most logical alternative. Table, 8 notes. N. Frenkley

101. Kossakowski, Ireneusz. THE LINES OF ACTIVITY OF THE ORGANIZATION OF AFRICAN UNITY. *Studies on the Developing Countries [Poland] 1977 (8): 83-107.* Reviews the aims (strengthening the unity and solidarity of the African states, creating better living conditions for African peoples, defending territorial sovereignty and independence, eliminating colonialism, protecting human rights, etc.) and achievements of the Organization of African Unity from 1963 to 1974.

102. Kunig, Philip. DIE ORGANISATION DER AFRIKANISCHEN EINHEIT UND DER PROZESS DES NATION BUILDING: DIE VÖLKERRECHTLICHEN RAHMENBEDINGUNGEN [The Organization of African Unity and the process of nation building: the framework of international law]. *Archiv des Völkerrechts [West Germany] 1982 20(1): 40-57.* Although the Organization of African Unity, founded in 1963, has become the strongest regional organization with 50 member states, it cannot issue binding decrees or orders under international law, but it can suggest, mediate, and discuss solutions to the domestic and foreign problems of its members.

103. Legum, Colin. THE ORGANISATION OF AFRICAN UNITY—SUCCESS OR FAILURE. *Internat. Affairs [Great Britain] 1975 51(2): 190-207.* Discusses the Organization of African Unity (OAU) since its inception in 1963. Pan-Africanism has grown from aspiration into political-economic reality. P. J. Beck

104. Maina-Wa-Kinyatti. DIALECTICAL REALITY OF THE AFRICAN REVOLUTION. *Black Scholar 1973 4(10): 20-23.* Discusses the political and socioeconomic position of persons of African descent in the world today. Offers a critique of Pan-Africanism, suggesting shortcomings which, if amended, might prove the beginning of the liberation of Africa.

105. Mariñas Otero, Luis. LA DIFÍCIL RUTA DE LA INTEGRACIÓN AFRICANA (DE LA EXPLOTACIÓN A LA COOPERACIÓN) [The hard path of African integration: from exploitation to cooperation]. *Rev. de Politica Int. [Spain] 1976 (146): 27-51.* Surveys Pan-Africanist policies from precolonial times to the 1975 Lomé Convention, the most important attempt yet to rid Africa of the effects of colonialism.

106. Mariñas Otero, Luis. LA OCAM, EVOLUCIÓN DE UNA ORGANIZACIÓN AFRICANA DE INTEGRACIÓN [OCAM: the evolution of an organization for African unity]. *Rev. de Política Int. [Spain] 1975 (138): 165-179.* Examines independence movements in Africa with particular reference to the Organisation Commune Africaine et Malgache (OCAM).

107. Mathews, K. THE ORGANIZATION OF AFRICAN UNITY. *India Q.: J. of Int. Affairs [India] 1977 33(3): 308-324.* Traces the development and principal achievements of the Organization of African Unity. In April 1958, President Kwame Nkrumah of Ghana called the first conference of independent African states in Accra. Subsequently, a moderate faction for concerted black nationalist activities was organized by Nigeria, Ivory Coast, and several Francophone countries. Later a more militant group led by the Congo, Cameroon, Chad, Gabon, and Upper Volta organized. In May 1963, most of the nations of Africa joined the Organization of African Unity's effort to build Pan-Africanism. The OAU is one of the largest multinational organizations, but its membership is drawn from among the poorest countries in the world. The original 32 members in 1963 were joined by 16 additional countries by 1977. Analyzes 20 major conflicts within Africa dealt with by the OAU. Based on secondary sources; 49 notes. S. H. Frank

108. Mazov, S. V. NATSIONAL'NYI KONGRESS BRITANSKOI ZAPADNOI AFRIKI (1920-30): IDEINYE I ORGANIZATSIONNYE OSNOVY [The National Congress of British West Africa, 1920-30: ideological and organizational principles]. *Narody Azii i Afriki [USSR] 1978 (6): 58-68.* Studies the ideology and organization of the National Congress of British West Africa whose formation reflected important changes at the beginning of the 20th century in the life of West African nations. The author discusses the Pan-African movement as led by M. Garvey, B. Washington, W. Du Bois, and K. Hefford. The Congress became the first political organization in tropical Africa, uniting the new social forces of the English West African colonies. Delegates to the Congress condemned racial discrimination, and discussed municipal and administrative reform, education, trade, government policy, and the right of nations to self-determination. Biblio.
S. R. Gudgin

109. Mazrui, Ali A. BLACK AFRICA AND THE ARABS. *Foreign Affairs 1975 53(4): 725-742.* Briefly recounts 12 centuries of Afro-Arab relations, examining why radical Africans in the 1960's moved toward a closer relationship with the Arab states. Israel was regarded as

too closely aligned with the West, and South Africa, Portugal, and Southern Rhodesia all had close Israeli connections. Black Africans today are trying to consolidate their political alliance with the Arab world with an economic partnership. The Organization of African Unity (OAU) serves as "a mechanism by which the Arabs can politically influence black Africans. On the other hand, it is also evolving into a mechanism through which black Africans might seek economic concessions from the Arabs." 9 notes. C. W. Olson

110. Meyers, B. David. INTRAREGIONAL CONFLICT MANAGEMENT BY THE ORGANIZATION OF AFRICAN UNITY. *Internat. Organization 1974 28(3): 345-373.* "Examines the intraregional conflict management activities of the Organization of African Unity (OAU). Three traditional regionalist claims are tested and suggestions concerning the future role of such organizations are provided. The findings indicate that in a number of cases the OAU was not an effective agent for conflict management; its limitations were clearest in internal disputes and those international conflicts involving allegations of subversion. Evidence from this study does not convincingly support the proposition that similarities of interests, problems, and loyalties found at the regional level make it more likely that attempts at settlement will be forthcoming and successful. Other findings indicate that the organization was able to isolate intraregional conflicts from entanglement in more complex global disputes; this ability was, however, highly dependent on the desire of the great powers to remain uninvolved. The OAU was able to relieve the UN of the potential burden of numerous local conflicts, but this too sometimes proved dependent on policy decisions made by the United States or the Soviet Union. It is suggested that regional organizations may assist the superpowers in avoiding unwanted involvement in local disputes, but that unless the conflict management capacity of such organizations is increased, the result may be that many conflicts will remain unsettled." J

111. Mubako, Simbi. THE QUEST FOR UNITY IN THE ZIMBABWE LIBERATION MOVEMENT. *Issue 1975 5(1): 6-17.* Outlines the difficulties the Organization of African Unity has faced in the attempt to unite anti-colonialist movements in Southern Africa during the last 15 years. S

112. Mytelka, Lynn K. A GENEALOGY OF FRANCOPHONE WEST AND EQUATORIAL AFRICAN REGIONAL ORGANISATIONS. *J. of Modern African Studies [Great Britain] 1974 12(2): 297-320.* Following the independence of French Africa, many states merged into federations. Most federations were short-lived, and memberships continued to alter. Discusses the Mali Federation, the Equatorial Customs Union, and the West African Custom Union. Table, 26 notes, biblio. H. G. Soff

113. Neuberger, Benjamin. RACIAL NATIONALISM IN BLACK AFRICA. *Wiener Lib. Bull. [Great Britain] 1975 28(35-36): 50-56.* Describes the origins of African nationalism and Pan-Africanism, rooted in the ideas of black scholars in the United States, which emphasized racial identity and solidarity.

114. Neuberger, Benyamin. NATURAL AND ARTIFICIAL BORDERS: THE AFRICAN VIEW. *Int. Problems [Israel] 1978 17(1): 95-102.* Discusses the concepts of natural and artificial national boundaries in European and African political theory. A general consensus exists among African leaders about the artificiality of current borders and a belief that European imperialism destroyed natural geographic, cultural, linguistic, and ethnic boundaries of Africa.

115. Nowicka, Ewa. HISTORIA PANAFRIKANIZMU A RUCHY UMYSŁOWE WŚRÓD CZARNEJ LUDNOŚCI STANÓW ZJEDNOCZONYCH AP [History of Pan-Africanism and the intellectual movements among the black population of the United States of America]. *Kultura i Społeczeństwo [Poland] 1980 24(3-4): 271-290.* Adekunle Ajala, an African scholar, suggests three stages of the movement: a) the discovery of unity among African peoples, b) nationalization of Pan-Africanism and, c) the rise of independent African nations. There were two primary aims of the movement: to bring one faith to the peoples of Africa and to return all Africans back to Africa. Discusses the roles of Martin R. Delany, Alexander Crummell, Edward W. Blyden, Henry McNeal Turner, and W. E. B. DuBois. Based on the works of the founders and leaders of the movement and numerous secondary sources; 53 notes. D. S. Lloyd

116. Nwafor, Azinna. LIBERATION AND PAN-AFRICANISM. *Monthly R. 1973 25(6): 12-28.* Reviews the failure of Pan-Africanism while arguing for socialist revolution as the means for national liberation movements to overcome neocolonialism. S

117. Nworah, Dike. THE AFRICAN GROUP IN THE UNITED NATIONS, 1963-1966: THE ABSENCE OF A MECHANISM FOR CO-OPERATION. *Int. Studies [India] 1975 14(4): 633-641.* The formation of one coherent group was among the most challenging tasks of the new Organization of African Unity. A widespread demand for an idealistic set of rules of procedure to govern the group at the UN spread through the OAU Council of Ministers. Later, opposition from various states grew until the matter was deleted from the agenda of its November 1966 meeting. Lack of discipline among the states, the demands for individual sovereignty, inadequate funding, and membership overlap with other organizations were the principal problems. The dream did not emerge, but the group did register some successes in increased visibility and influence. Based on published official and unofficial sources; 51 notes. R. E. Stack

118. Nworah, Dike. THE INTEGRATION OF THE COMMISSION FOR TECHNICAL CO-OPERATION IN AFRICA WITH THE ORGANIZATION OF AFRICAN UNITY: THE PROCESS OF THE MERGER AND THE PROBLEMS OF INSTITUTIONAL RIVALRY AND COMPLEMENTARITY. *African Rev. [Tanzania] 1976 6(1): 55-67.* A history of the merger of an imperial bureaucracy with an independent African bureaucracy, which went smoothly and efficiently without duplication of efforts, 1950-68. 26 notes. R. T. Brown

119. Nworah, Dike. THE ORGANISATION OF AFRICAN UNITY AND THE INTERNATIONAL LABOUR ORGANISATION, 1963-1973: A DECADE OF INTERNATIONAL CO-OPERATION. *Africa Q. [India] 1977 16(4): 27-34.* Surveys the participation of African states, particularly through the Organization of African Unity, in the workings of the International Labor Organization. Emphasizes their efforts to present a united front on African affairs, especially in opposition to South Africa.

120. Nyang, Sulayman Sheih. ISLAM AND PANAFRICANISM. *Afrique et L'Asie [France] 1975 (104): 42-50.* The Pan-Africanists can be divided into three groups. The first consists of those who identify intellectually with all other blacks; the second, those who seek the emergence of Africa and the Caribbean as a power in world affairs; the third, those who favor the political unification of the African continent. Islam has influenced black Africa for several centuries, and now it can promote Pan-Africanism by providing the bridge which links the Arab north and sub-Saharan Africa. The common historical experience, defeat and exploitation by Europe, should promote their mutual understanding. 20 notes. J. S. Gassner

121. Nyerere, Julius. ADDRESS TO THE SIXTH PAN-AFRICAN CONGRESS. *African Rev. [Tanzania] 1974 4(2): 181-188.* The purpose of the Congress is to serve human liberation and voice opposition to racism, colonialism, oppression, and exploitation everywhere. Noting that this Pan-African Congress was the first one ever held in Africa, the author traces the history of the Congress from 1900 and the contributions of its many leaders. A speech made by the president of Tanzania on 19 June 1974. H. G. Soff

122. Nyerere, Julius. BLACK UNITY AND HUMAN FREEDOM. *Africa Report 1975 20(5): 2-6.* Opening address to the Sixth Pan-African Congress by Nyerere, describing the roots of the Pan-African movement and the struggle against racism. S

123. Nyerere, Julius. JULIUS K. NYERERE'S SPEECH TO THE CONGRESS. *Black Scholar 1974 5(10): 16-22.* Tanzania's president notes the Pan-African movement's accomplishments toward real human liberation since the first Pan-African Congress in London in 1900. Speech to the Sixth Pan-African Congress, Tanzania, June 1974.

124. Oded, Aryeh. SLAVES AND OIL: THE ARAB IMAGE IN BLACK AFRICA. *Wiener Lib. Bull. [Great Britain] 1974 27(32): 34-47.* Describes the criticism of the Arab oil producers by the

Organization of African Unity (OAU), for their refusal to sell oil to the OAU countries at discount prices, underlining Afro-Arab hostility.

125. Ofari, Earl. A CRITICAL REVIEW OF THE PAN-AFRICAN CONGRESS. *Black Scholar 1974 5(10): 12-15.* Cites the numerous failures of the Sixth Pan-African Congress, held in Tanzania, June 1974. Although the Congress was hailed a "historical event," its organizational weaknesses, its failure to critically discuss the political and economic differences which divide African nations, and especially the absence of serious socialist strategies and plans made the Congress significant more for its lost potential than its scant achievements.

126. Ofoegbu, Mazi Ray. "AFRICAN PERSONALITY," "AFRICAN SOCIALISM," AND "AFRICAN DEMOCRACY" AS PAN-AFRICAN CONCEPTS. *Tarikh [Nigeria] 1980 6(3): 60-69.* Surveys the social, economic, and political concepts expressed by Pan-Africanism as unique to the needs and aspirations of Africans.

127. Okolo, Julius Emeka and Langley, Winston E. THE ORGANIZATION OF AFRICAN UNITY AND APARTHEID: CONSTRAINTS ON RESOLUTION. *World Affairs 1974/75 137(3): 206-232.* The OAU has not realized its 1965 objective to eradicate apartheid in South Africa because of lack of monetary support and the priorities of individual national interests. S

128. Oyedeji, Olalekan. INTELLECTUAL ORIGINS OF PAN-AFRICANISM AND BLACK STUDIES AS A CRUCIAL STEP TOWARDS ITS REALIZATION. *Pan African J. [Kenya] 1974 7(1): 29-38.* Analyzes issues connected with the founding and purpose of Pan-Africanism. Black studies programs help to fill the educational void which is a major obstacle to Pan-Africanism. Various ideologies are discussed including those of W. E. B. Du Bois, Marcus Garvey, and Julius Nyerere. 18 notes. H. G. Soff

129. Person, Yves. L'O.U.A. OU UNE DÉCENNIE D'ÉPREUVES POUR L'UNITÉ [The OAU or a decade of trial for unity]. *Rev. Française d'Études Pol. Africaines [France] 1973 8(93): 29-58.* Outlines the formation and the 10-year existence of the Organization of African Unity (OAU), 1963-73, especially the contribution of Ghanaian President Kwame Nkrumah in working toward economic freedom from colonial ties and the reconstruction of African culture.

130. Polhemus, James H. THE PROVISIONAL SECRETARIAT OF THE O.A.U., 1963-64. *J. of Modern African Studies [Great Britain] 1974 12(2): 287-295.* The Organization of African Unity was formed in May 1963 and was operated by a Provisional Secretariat until August 1964. Assesses the effectiveness of the Provisional Secretariat and the administrative patterns created. 25 notes. H. G. Soff

131. Provizer, Norman W. THEMES, IMAGES AND MODES: A NOTE ON PAN-AFRICANISM. *Southern Q. 1977 16(1): 59-66.* An examination of the diversity and commonality of views concerning Pan-Africanism. Such themes and modes as freedom, dignity, unity, and race awareness are referenced. 33 notes. R. W. Dubay

132. Romero, Patricia W. W. E. B. DU BOIS, PAN-AFRICANISTS, AND AFRICA 1963-1973. *J. of Black Studies 1976 6(4): 321-336.* Modern scholarship lacks a definitive account of Pan-Africanism prior to 1956, especially the part played by Ras Makonnen. A new interpretation of Africa's conception of early Pan-Africanists, particularly W. E. B. DuBois, is also called for. Primary and secondary sources; notes, biblio. D. C. Neal

133. Rossi, Gianluigi. THE OAU: RESULTS OF A DECADE. *Int. J. of Pol. 1974-75 4(4): 15-34.* Although the principles of national sovereignty and noninterference in internal affairs have represented a major obstacle to its effectiveness, the Organization of African Unity has been an important forum for cooperation on issues of decolonization and economic and social growth in 1963-73.

134. Segre, Dan V. COLONIZATION AND DECOLONIZATION: THE CASE OF ZIONIST AND AFRICAN ELITES. *Comparative Studies in Soc. and Hist. [Great Britain] 1980 22(1): 23-41.* Compares Zionism and Pan-Africanism and their relationship to the West.

135. Shaw, Timothy. ORGANIZATION OF AFRICAN UNITY: PROSPECTS FOR A SECOND DECADE. *Int. Perspectives [Canada] 1973 (Sept-Oct): 31-34.* Chronicles the growth and success of the Organization of African Unity, 1963-73.

136. Smith, Earl. PAN-AFRICANISM—A POLITICAL, ECONOMIC & SOCIAL PHILOSOPHY. *Freedomways 1980 20(1): 27-35.* Criticizes Imanuel Geiss's *The Pan-African Movement* (New York: Africana Publ. Co., 1974) in its approach to Pan-African history, since it does not take into account "capitalist development worldwide, the relationship between classes and certain social groups and their importance in a social formation fostered by colonial-imperialism."

137. Stoklitskaia, L. TROPICHESKAIA AFRIKA V POISKAKH FORMULY SOTRUDNICHESTVA [Tropical Africa in search of economic cooperation]. *Aziia i Afrika Segodnia [USSR] 1982 (4): 28-30.* Describes benefits, possibilities, and problems of economic integration, for multilateral cooperation on a regional and subregional level is the only way to resolve the contradiction of the economic development of tropical Africa.

138. Touré, Sekou. SEKOU TOURÉ'S SPEECH TO THE CONGRESS. *Black Scholar 1974 5(10): 23-29.* The president of Guinea traces the accomplishments of African civilization and the oppression by the European colonialists during the 19th century, and emphasizes the liberation struggle of Pan-Africanism in the 20th century. Speech to the Sixth Pan-African Congress, Tanzania, June 1974.

139. Tsomondo, Micah S. FROM PAN-AFRICANISM TO SOCIALISM: THE MODERNIZATION OF AN AFRICAN LIBERATION IDEOLOGY. *Issue 1975 5(4): 39-46.* Discusses the ideological evolution of Pan-Africanism and its recent relationship to socialism, 1945-75.

140. Ugonna, Nnabuenyi. THE RISE OF CREATIVE ETHIOPIANISM: THE PAN-AFRICANIST LITERARY INFLUENCE. *Pan-African J. [Kenya] 1973 6(1): 1-13.* Records the rise of creative Ethiopianism in the United States, and the writing of fiction to perpetuate Ethiopianist ideas. Also traces the infuence of early Afro-American novelists on the development of African literature.

141. Ukpabi, S. C. THE O.A.U. AND THE PROBLEMS OF AFRICAN UNITY. *Africa Q. [India] 1976 15(4): 25-55.* Examines the development, problems, and objectives of the Organization of African Unity, 1963-75, in the context of the Pan-African movement, 1829-1975.

142. Umozurike, U. O. THE DOMESTIC JURISDICTION CLAUSE IN THE OAU CHARTER. *African Affairs [Great Britain] 1979 78(311): 197-209.* Reviews the aims and achievements of the Organization of African Unity (OAU), 1963-73, concentrating on the domestic jurisdiction charter. Since the latter maintains respect for the independence of nations and stresses noninterference in internal disputes, it has been an obstacle to the promotion of peace and justice and the protection of human rights in Africa. International law demands that the OAU should address itself more to these issues. Primary sources; 43 notes. S. Lakhan

143. Watson, Denton L. THE NAACP AND AFRICA: AN HISTORICAL PROFILE. *Crisis 1977 84(4): 131-138.* W. E. B. DuBois was responsible for bringing Pan-Africanism to the consciousness of many Americans. He advocated that America support the end of colonialism in Africa. He publicized the richness of the history and culture of the subject peoples. He encouraged the NAACP to finance the first two Pan-African Congresses. DuBois kept the NAACP actively interested in African affairs, especially as a pressure group during the formative years of the UN. There is a binding relationship between the NAACP and anticolonialism in Africa. A. G. Belles

144. Welch, Claude E., Jr. THE O. A. U. AND HUMAN RIGHTS: TOWARDS A NEW DEFINITION. *J. of Modern African Studies [Great Britain] 1981 19(3): 401-420.* African governments have a record of opposing and evading international human rights groups and their campaigns by asserting and exercising claims to domestic jurisdiction. The Organization of African Unity was founded in 1963; only in 1979 did it agree to the formation of the African Commission on Human

Rights. Domestic law in most African states seems to contravene rights listed in international covenants that their governments have begun to accept and ratify. In the light of recent African history, the outlook for widespread observance of human rights there is not promising. Based on UN and Amnesty International documents and the *African Research Bulletin;* 39 notes. L. W. Truschel

145. Woronoff, Jon. L'ORGANIZATION DE L'UNITÉ AFRICAINE ET LA PROBLÈME DES RÉFUGIÉS [The Organization of African Unity and the problem of refugees]. *Rev. Française d'Études Pol. Africaines [France] 1973 8(93): 80-97.* Studies the lack of internal stability and the concern for refugees which led to the Organization of African Unity's studying the problem and passing recent resolutions offering assistance and guidance to refugees, 1973.

146. Yadi, Melchiade. PROMOTION DU DÉVELOPPEMENT INDUSTRIEL ÉQUILIBRÉ DES PAYS-MEMBRES DE L'UDEAC ET DE LA CAE [Promotion of the balanced industrial development of member countries of the Central African Customs and Economic Union (UDEAC), and the East African Community (EAC)]. *Études Int. [Canada] 1975 6(1): 66-102.* Discusses the function of UDEAC and EAC in promoting equal industrial development among the member states of their respective organizations. Makes extensive use of tabular and statistical information, 1964-70, to examine the relative industrialization of each of the African member states. Discusses in detail the specific means used by each organization to protect and promote native industry and to harmonize industrial production by the equitable division of industry. Primary and secondary sources; 11 tables, 4 charts, 41 notes. J. F. Harrington, Jr.

147. Yimenu, Shibabaw. PAN-AFRICANISM AND AFRICAN ECONOMIC DEVELOPMENT. *Black Scholar 1975 6(8): 32-40.* Discusses nation-by-nation African economic, agricultural, and population development, 1961-73, and current priorities for the Pan-Africanism movement.

148. —. EXCLUSIVE INTERVIEW WITH OAU CURRENT CHAIRMAN: GENERAL GOWON. *Afriscope [Nigeria] 1973 3(7): 10-22.* General Yakubu Gowon assesses the accomplishments of the Organization of African Unity. Illus. G. O. Gagnon

3. AFRICAN POLITICS

The Colonial Era

149. Ageron, Charles-Robert. L'IDÉE D'EURAFRIQUE ET LE DÉBAT COLONIAL FRANCO-ALLEMAND DE L'ENTRE-DEUX-GUERRES [The concept of Eurafrica and the Franco-German colonial dialogue between the wars]. *Rev. d'Hist. Moderne et Contemporaine [France] 1975 22(3): 446-475.* The concept of a unified international administration of all the African colonies by a Franco-German partnership or by a united Europe originated toward the end of the 19th century, especially among the Socialists, and was later promoted by Count Richard de Coudenhove-Kalergi. After 1920, German colonialists supported Eurafrica as a means of recovering Germany's colonial role, a position taken also by French leftists. After 1930, the need to end the economic depression kept the Eurafrica concept alive. Until the outbreak of World War II, revisionists and appeasers argued for various international solutions of the colonial problem. One of Adolf Hitler's war aims was the establishment of Eurafrica. The decolonization of Africa ended the debate. Primary and secondary sources; 68 notes. J. S. Gassner

150. Almeida-Topor, Hélène d'. CRISE COMMERCIALE ET CRISE DU SYSTÈME COLONIAL EN AFRIQUE NOIRE [Commercial crisis and crisis of the colonial system in Black Africa]. *Rev. Française d'Hist. d'Outre-Mer [France] 1976 63(3-4): 538-543.* The Great Depression began in Black Africa with a commercial slump which soon extended to other sectors of African economic life. The prosperity of the colonies had rested on a fragile equilibrium which was broken. The plunge in the prices of raw materials affected the Africans especially because agricultural production and the export of such products was their only means of raising cash for taxes and consumer goods. The government made matters worse by increasing direct taxes on the African population to make up for the drop in customs revenues. 15 notes. J. C. Billigmeier

151. Almeida-Topor, Hélène d'. INTERPRÉTATION GRAPHIQUE: INTRODUCTION À UNE ÉTUDE GRAPHIQUE DE LA CRISE [Interpretation in graphs: introduction to a graphic study of the crisis]. *Rev. Française d'Hist. d'Outre-Mer [France] 1976 63(3-4): 713-776.* Presents 127 graphs of economic and trade statistics for French colonies in Africa and Indochina for 1924-38, together with a methodological introduction. Part of a special issue on Africa and the Depression.

152. Andrew, C. M. and Kanya-Forstner, A. S. FRANCE AND THE REPARTITION OF AFRICA, 1914-1922. *Dalhousie Rev. [Canada] 1977 57(3): 475-493.* Discusses the work of the *parti colonial* and such men as Gaston Doumergue, minister of colonies, 1914-17, Albert Duchêne, head of the African department, August Terrier, secretary-general of the Comité de l'Afrique Française, and Henri Simon, colonial minister, 1918. The acceptance by Clemenceau of the mandate principle was a blow to the expansionist dreams of the group but they attempted to make the best of a bad situation. Based on a paper given as part of the opening ceremonies for the Center for African Studies at Dalhousie University, November, 1975. 91 notes. C. H. Held

153. Anyanwu, K. Chukwulozie. AFRICAN POLITICAL ASPIRATIONS AND THE WESTERN POLICY OF RESISTANCE. *Pan-African J. [Kenya] 1977 10(1): 85-105.* World War II marked a watershed in the history of African political aspirations. The collapse of the Western colonies and empires was accompanied by the collapse of liberal democracy and the growing acceptance of socialist ideology. In December 1960, the UN General Assembly demanded that independence should be granted to all colonized territories, without any conditions or reservations. Despite this resolution, political aspirations in Africa have met with resistance from the Western democratic nations. Secondary sources; 49 notes. F. P. Tudor

154. Bennett, Norman Robert. AFRICA AND EUROPE. *Int. J. of African Hist. Studies 1980 13(4): 690-698.* Reviews 11 volumes in French and English concerning imperialism and imperial administration. R. T. Brown

155. Borneman, Ernest. AUS DEN GRÜNDERJAHREN DES NEUEN AFRIKA [The early years of the new Africa]. *Zeitgeschichte [Austria] 1979 6(7): 240-245.* Personal memoirs of the Student Movement House in Russell Square in London and the people met there and in private lodgings shared with Cyril Lyonel Richard James of Trinidad, where radical Africans debated the future of their countries. Many of them, including Nnamdi Azikiwe and Jomo Kenyatta, were to take leading parts in that future. G. Herritt

156. Brionne, Bernard. LE DÉCHIREMENT DE L'AFRIQUE PORTUGAISE [The break-up of Portuguese Africa]. *Défense Natl. [France] 1974 30(7): 63-83.* Analyzes the history of each Portuguese African territory in highlighting the problems General António de Spinola faces in creating a viable community.

157. Brunschwig, Henri. DE LA RÉSISTANCE AFRICAINE A L'IMPÉRIALISME EUROPÉEN [African resistance and European Imperialism]. *J. of African Hist. [Great Britain] 1974 15(1): 47-64.* Current African liberation movements did not have their origins in the resistance movements led by traditional leaders against the European imperialists. Local leaders usually led the resistance in defense of a belief or economic interest essential and particular to an ethnic group. The adoption of imported ideologies common to different ethnic groups serves as the basis for current independence movements. Primary and secondary sources; 32 notes. C. Hopkins

158. Brunschwig, Henri. L'IMPÉRIALISME EN AFRIQUE NOIRE [Imperialism in black Africa]. *R. Historique [France] 1973 249(1): 129-142.* A bibliographic essay and critical analysis of recent historiographical studies on imperialism in Black Africa. Considers, among other things, reinterpretations on colonial doctrines, European expansion and the problems it caused in the area of international relations, the forms of exploitation, types of colonial administrators, decolonization, and independence. Poses questions for further research. R. C. Alltmont

159. Buijtenhuijs, R. "MESSIANISME" ET NATIONALISME EN AFRIQUE NOIRE: UNE REMISE EN QUESTION [Messianism and nationalism in Black Africa: a reexamination]. *African Perspectives [Netherlands] 1976 (2): 25-44.* Reconsiders Balandier's thesis of messianic religious movements as early forerunners of African nationalism. These movements detached themselves from the "normal" political scene. Secondary accounts; notes, biblio. L. W. Truschel

160. Camara, Ahmad. CABRAL'S MURDER. *Afriscope [Nigeria] 1973 3(3): 13-19.* Describes the assassination of Amilcar Cabral (1973) as part of the colonial counteroffensive. Summarizes the liberation struggle in Angola, Mozambique, Zimbabwe, South Africa, and South-West Africa. Illus. G. O. Gagnon

161. Cell, John W. ON THE EVE OF DECOLONIZATION: THE COLONIAL OFFICE'S PLANS FOR THE TRANSFER OF POWER IN AFRICA, 1947. *J. of Imperial and Commonwealth Hist. [Great Britain] 1980 8(3): 235-257.* A study of the transfer of power in Africa in 1947 as local governments were established, centering on the role of the Arthur Creech Jones's circular dispatch in February 1947. With the end of World War II, the Colonial Office in London sought new ways of gaining African cooperation not only for the welfare of the Africans but to maintain the prestige and very survival of the British Commonwealth. Regrettably this attempt failed and African national leaders continued to be jailed as "agitators." Based on printed sources and Colonial Office documents in the Public Record Office; 33 notes. M. C. Rosenfield

162. Coquery-Vidrovitch, Catherine. COLONISATION OU IMPÉRIALISME: LA POLITIQUE AFRICAINE DE LA FRANCE ENTRE LES DEUX GUERRES [Colonization or imperialism: French African policy between the wars]. *Mouvement Social [France] 1979 (107): 51-76.* From Albert Sarraut's scheme in the early twenties to the beginning of the Second World War, France's economic policy in Africa remained fundamentally identical, whatever domestic politics were in favor, because it always thought of integrating the African countries into the Western capitalist economy in keeping with state-oriented economic

planning and an infrastructure which would be partially financed by metropolitan interests and for their profit. The short era of the Popular Front showed however one major difference: a social and labor policy, which, despite limited achievements, paved the way for growing nationalist movements. J

163. Coquery-Vidrovitch, Catherine. L'AFRIQUE COLONIALE FRANÇAISE ET LA CRISE DE 1930: CRISE STRUCTURELLE ET GENÈSE DU SOUS-DÉVELOPPEMENT [The French colonies in Africa and the 1930 crisis: structural crisis and the genesis of underdevelopment]. *Rev. Française d'Hist. d'Outre-Mer [France] 1976 63(3-4): 386-424.* Many of the problems of contemporary underdevelopment go back to the Great Depression; 1928-35 marked a premature and lasting reversal of trends toward development in French colonial Africa. Reeling from the world economic crisis, metropolitan nations like France fell back on their colonies and exploited them more thoroughly, while binding them ever more closely to themselves. The results in the colonies included rapid urbanization and increasing class differentiation, as well as flow of wealth toward the metropolis. These are also the features of contemporary underdevelopment. 154 notes.
J. C. Billigmeier

164. Coquery-Vidrovitch, Catherine. MUTATION DE L'IMPÉRIALISME COLONIALE FRANÇAISE DANS LES ANNÉES 30 [Mutations in French colonial imperialism in the 1930's]. *African Econ. Hist. 1977 (4): 103-152.* Traces the impact of the Great Depression as a key to understanding the genesis of current underdevelopment in former French African colonies. After reviewing sources and methods, discusses the chronology of the development of crisis in imports and exports, trade, investment, changes in taxes, prices, wages, and in the operation of financial institutions. Examines the contrasting relationship between foreign economic activity and the level and nature of colonial activity. In the French African colonies, the depression was longer and deeper due to structural factors such as the organization of trade and the investment policies of both public entities and private companies. Increased tax burdens contributed to the erosion of traditional institutions. The author also views the profound internal social crisis brought on by the Depression, which resulted in the birth of a local bourgeoisie, rapid growth in urbanization, and the fall in income among native agricultural producers. Summarizes the conclusions of a colloquium fully published in the *Revue Française d'Histoire d'Outre-Mer* 1976 63(3-4). 15 tables, 42 graphs, 121 notes. S. Sevilla

165. Davidson, Basil. AFRICAN PEASANTS AND REVOLUTION. *J. of Peasant Studies [Great Britain] 1974 1(3): 269-290.* The last 13 years have seen important peasant uprisings in Angola, Guinea-Bissau, and Mozambique, conflicts which must be judged to some extent within the context of traditional colonial wars. Although the influence of events in neighboring countries and urban notions of freedom and nationalism are undeniable, these struggles reveal the rising trend of modern resistance and its final dependence on mass participation by local communities conscious of their particular oppressions and fighting together to overcome them. The role of such revolutionary movements as the MPLA has been to organize and guide rebellions which would have occurred spontaneously if less successfully without them. J

166. Davidson, Basil. INTRODUCTION: COLONIALISM ON THE CHEAP: THE PORTUGUESE IN AFRICA UP TO C. 1921. *Tarikh [Nigeria] 1980 6(4): 1-4.* Portugal pursued a poor man's colonialism, depriving Africans not only of independence but also of any aspect of citizenship: in 1921 over 99% of the entire populations of Angola, Guinea-Bissau, and Mozambique, defined as natives, could possess no civic rights.

167. Dianoux, Hugues Jean de. RÉSISTANCES EN AFRIQUE PORTUGUAIS: TROIS OUVRAGES DE RENÉ PÉLISSIER [Resistance in Portuguese Africa: three works by René Pélissier]. *Genève-Afrique [Switzerland] 1981 19(1): 147-159.* Reviews Pélissier's monographs *Les Guerres Crises: Résistance et Révolte en Angola (1845-1941)* and *La Colonie du Minotaure: Nationalismes et Révoltes en Angola (1926-1961)*and *Le Naufrage des Caravelles: Etudes sur la Fin de l'Empire Portuguaise (1961-1975),* a collection of previously published articles. B. S. Fetter

168. D'Souza, Henry. EXTERNAL INFLUENCES ON THE DEVELOPMENT OF EDUCATIONAL POLICY IN BRITISH TROPICAL AFRICA FROM 1923 TO 1939. *African Studies Rev. 1975 18(2): 35-44.* Shows the political and financial reasons for Great Britain's introduction of a new educational policy, known as "adaptation," in Africa in 1923 and British involvement with similar organizations in Europe and the United States.

169. Du Bois, Shirley Graham. TOGETHER WE STRUGGLE, TOGETHER WE WIN. *Black Scholar 1975 6(7): 36-41.* Report presented at the fifth anniversary celebration of *The Black Scholar* (March 1975) on the struggle of African countries for liberation, 1970-75.

170. Ekoko, A. Edho. THE BRITISH ATTITUDE TOWARDS GERMANY'S COLONIAL IRREDENTISM IN AFRICA IN THE INTER-WAR YEARS. *J. of Contemporary Hist. [Great Britain] 1979 14(2): 287-307.* Germany was very dissatisfied with the colonial settlement of the Paris Conference after World War I. Both the Weimar Republic and the early Hitler regime viewed the mandate system as provisional. The colonies could have been used as a sop to Hitler before 1936, but Great Britain always hesitated. After the German occupation of the Rhineland on 7 March 1936, it was too late to give Hitler a colonial pacifier. He then had other ambitions. Based on the Official Journal of the League of Nations and other primary sources; 49 notes.
M. P. Trauth

171. Ernst, K. ZU DEN WECHSELBEZIEHUNGEN ZWISCHEN SOZIALÖKONOMISCHER UND BEVÖLKERUNGSENTWICKLUNG UNTER DEN BEDINGUNGEN KOLONIALER UND NEOKOLONIALER ABHÄNGIGKEIT UND AUSBEUTUNG (AM BEISPIEL DES SUBSAHARISCHEN AFRIKA) [On the interrelation of the development of socioeconomic factors and population under the conditions of colonial and neocolonial dependency and exploitation: the example of sub-Saharan Africa]. *Wissenschaftliche Zeitschrift der Karl-Marx U. Leipzig [East Germany] 1976 25(3): 257-262.* As a result of the export of capital and the need for cheap labor in the colonial areas, sub-Saharan population development was stabilized and a minimum of social progress was guaranteed in the beginning of the 20th century and especially after World War II.
R. Wagnleitner

172. Ferreira, Eduardo de Sousa. THE PRESENT ROLE OF THE PORTUGUESE RESETTLEMENT POLICY. *Africa Today 1974 21(1): 47-55.* Describes the extensive efforts of Portugal to encourage Portuguese settlement in Africa thereby cementing the colonies to the metropolis and neutralizing the guerrilla movements. Secondary sources; 3 tables, 25 notes. G. O. Gagnon

173. Fields, Karen. POLITICAL CONTINGENCIES OF WITCHCRAFT IN COLONIAL CENTRAL AFRICA: CULTURE AND THE STATE IN MARXIST THEORY. *Can. J. of African Studies [Canada] 1982 16(3): 567-593.* Examines the question of "legitimacy" of a colonial state, which is based neither on the consent of the people nor on continuous terror. Critically analyzes relevant Weberian and Marxist concepts to show that they do not necessarily apply to a colonial situation and that cultural factors and mental and behavioral routines play a large part in the maintenance of a political order. British colonial administration, while imbued with a belief in its civilizing mission, had to find support in local customs and ally itself with indigenous cultures, including magic and sorcery. 62 notes. J. V. Coutinho

174. Grigor'ev, V. M. ISTORIOGRAFIIA PORTUGAL'SKOGO KOLONIALIZMA [The historiography of Portuguese colonialism]. *Voprosy Istorii [USSR] 1973 (12): 174-179.* Portugal's is the only colonial empire surviving today which remains practically the same size as it was in the 19th century. This makes it an especially interesting subject for historians of colonialism. At the same time, the evolving national liberation movements in the strategic regions of Angola, Guinea, and Mozambique have attracted considerable attention from historians of African decolonization. The main recent works on both themes are considered, especially those of N. Harris, P. Wesley, and J. Duffy. Secondary sources; 28 notes.

175. Henderson, Ian. WAGE-EARNERS AND POLITICAL PROTEST IN COLONIAL AFRICA: THE CASE OF THE COPPERBELT. *African Affairs [Great Britain] 1973 72(288): 288-299.* An exploratory study of the relationship between African labor (11 percent of the total population) and political movements. It is suggested that existing theories, such as the "convergence theory" are not accurate and more historical studies are needed on the pre-trade union labor force. Particular emphasis is given to Kenya and the copperbelt strikes in Zambia during 1935 and 1940. A major conclusion is that trade unions originated many methods subsequently developed by political movements, not vice-versa. 28 notes. H. G. Soff

176. Henderson, Robert D'A. PORTUGUESE AFRICA: MATERIALS IN ENGLISH AND IN TRANSLATION. *African Res. and Documentation [Great Britain] 1977 (12): 15-19.* Continued from a earlier article *[African Research and Documentation,* (11)]. Lists materials pertaining to Portuguese Africa, written between 1937 and 1976.

177. Henriksen, Thomas H. LESSONS FROM PORTUGAL'S COUNTER-INSURGENCY OPERATIONS IN AFRICA. *J. of the Royal United Services Inst. for Defence Studies [Great Britain] 1978 123(2): 31-35.* Discusses what may be learnt from the Portuguese response to insurgency in Angola, Mozambique, and Guinea-Bissau, 1961-74.

178. Henriksen, Thomas H. NAMIBIA: A COMPARISON WITH ANTI-PORTUGUESE INSURGENCY. *Round Table [Great Britain] 1980 (278): 184-194.* Draws comparisons and distinctions between insurgency in South-West Africa (Namibia) since 1966 and liberation movements in Angola, Guinea-Bissau, and Mozambique between 1961 and 1975.

179. Henriksen, Thomas H. PEOPLE'S WAR IN ANGOLA, MOZAMBIQUE, AND GUINEA-BISSAU. *J. of Modern African Studies [Great Britain] 1976 14(3): 377-400.* A comparative study of successful insurgencies in Angola, Mozambique, and Guinea-Bissau. These peoples' wars must be redefined in an African environment, and involve more sophistication than might at first be apparent. In this redefinition the author considers likely zones of guerrilla warfare operations; preparations for insurgency; terrain and sanctuaries; insurgent-held zones; international aid; ideological influences; politicization and factionalism; and level of warfare. 41 notes. R. V. Ritter

180. Henriksen, Thomas H. PORTUGAL IN AFRICA: COMPARATIVE NOTES ON COUNTERINSURGENCY. *Orbis 1977 21(2): 395-412.* For 13 years Portugal conducted counterinsurgency operations in Africa. Although those operations have received little notice, there were definite similarities between them and other better known counterinsurgency operations. Although the Portuguese military efforts were largely successful, the Portuguese still lost, primarily because the Portuguese government eventually lost the support of its own armed forces, which eventually not only jettisoned the overseas empire but overthrew the government itself. Primary and secondary sources; 36 notes. A. N. Garland

181. Henriksen, Thomas H. SOME NOTES ON THE NATIONAL LIBERATION WARS IN ANGOLA, MOZAMBIQUE, AND GUINEA-BISSAU. *Military Affairs 1977 41(1): 30-36.* The wars for national liberation against the Portuguese in Angola, Mozambique, and Guinea-Bissau were in some ways similar to preceding models and in other ways very new and different. They represent the first successful guerrilla wars in sub-Sahara Africa. The leaders of the three main revolutionary movements—MPLA, FRELIMO, and PAIGC—adapted and improvised in guerrilla warfare and proved that revolutionary wars need not occur in a society of predetermined levels of economic or social development. As part of their success in Africa, the wars imposed a tremendous drain on Portugal's human and material resources. 22 notes. A. M. Osur

182. Hopkins, A. G. REVIEW ARTICLE: THE BURDENS OF EMPIRE. *African Affairs [Great Britain] 1978 77(306): 108-120.* A critical review of L. H. Gann and Peter Duignan, eds. *Colonialism in Africa, 1870-1960, Vol IV: The Economics of Colonialism* (Stanford: Hoover Inst. Pr., 1967), focusing on the defense of colonial rule. 53 notes. H. G. Soff

183. Isaacman, Allen and Isaacman, Barbara. RESISTANCE AND COLLABORATION IN SOUTHERN AND CENTRAL AFRICA, C. 1850-1920. *Int. J. of African Hist. Studies 1977 10(1): 31-62.* Focuses on four neglected themes in the discussion of African resistance to imperialism: the impact of African expansionist activities on the scramble, the diversity of response to imperialism among the different strata of a given society, localized protests against the imposition of a capitalist economy, and collaboration. The Afrocentric approach to the subject of resistance argues that African initiative, adaptation, and choice played a dominant role both in the scramble and in the process of decolonization. Based on case studies from central and southern Africa; 142 notes. M. M. McCarthy

184. Ivanov, Iu. M. OSOBENNOSTI RAZVITIIA KAPITALIZMA V TROPICHESKOI AFRIKE V PEROVI POLOVINE XX VEKA [The distinctive features attending the development of capitalism in tropical Africa in the first half of the 20th century]. *Voprosy Istorii [USSR] 1973 (10): 47-63.*

185. Kennedy, Dane. CLIMATIC THEORIES AND CULTURE IN COLONIAL KENYA AND RHODESIA. *J. of Imperial and Commonwealth Hist. [Great Britain] 1981 10(1): 50-66.* Traces the climatic fears of the Europeans in Kenya and Southern Rhodesia and the effect of the fears of the harmful sun's rays on the white settler culture. While the first decade appears to be free of such fears, as the ideal and healthful climate is praised, by the early 20th century the idea was developing that the climate was "unhealthy" and white settlers needed trips to the coast to recover from the effects of highland living. Based on Colonial Office Papers at Public Record Office, London, and the National Archives of Rhodesia and secondary sources; 72 notes. M. C. Rosenfield

186. Khapoya, V. B. AFRICAN AND VIETNAMESE LIBERATION MOVEMENTS: A COMPARATIVE STUDY. *Pan-African J. [Kenya] 1977 10(1): 23-37.* Examines the historical origins of resistance to colonial rule in Indochina and Portuguese Africa. Vietnamese opposition to French colonial control began in the 1860's, whereas anticolonial resistance in Portuguese Africa began after 1950. In both areas the initial armed resistance against the colonizing powers ended in defeat and the colonizing powers exercised economic exploitation and suppressed political activity among the local population. Based on secondary sources and a film on the Frelimo revolutionary struggle in Mozambique; 53 notes. F. P. Tudor

187. Khazanov, A. THE PEOPLES OF AFRICA IN THE STRUGGLE AGAINST COLONIALISTS. *Int. Affairs [USSR] 1974 (4): 28-34.* Discusses Portuguese colonialism in Africa, its dependence on assistance from other imperialist powers, and its conflicts with the national liberation movements during the years 1969-74.

188. Kirk-Greene, A. H. M. THE BRITISH COLONIAL GOVERNOR IN THE LITERATURE. *African Res. and Documentation [Great Britain] 1977 (12): 10-13.* Briefly describes the biographical and autobiographical literature on British Colonial governors in Africa, published between 1930 and 1976.

189. Kirk-Greene, A. H. M. DAMNOSA HEREDITAS: ETHNIC RANKING AND THE MARTIAL RACES IMPERATIVE IN AFRICA. *Ethnic and Racial Studies [Great Britain] 1980 3(4): 393-414.* Discusses the *damnosa hereditas* or fatal legacy of the "British officers' commitment to the concept of martial races" which has imposed constraints on independent African governments, and reduced chances for establishing national identity and political stability.

190. Kirk-Greene, A. H. M. THE THIN WHITE LINE: THE SIZE OF THE BRITISH COLONIAL SERVICE IN AFRICA. *African Affairs [Great Britain] 1980 79(314): 25-44.* The concept of the "steel frame" of British colonial administration—the iron rule of the District Commissioner and administrative strait jacket—is both imprecise and unsupported by statistical data. The number of white administrators was always small, but their power was undoubtedly perceptible and effective, for reasons of coercion, collaboration, confidence, and competence. Essentially, the District Commissioners ruled with an authority erected

upon their own self-confidence. The administration of the Empire was a confidence trick played by the officials upon themselves as much as on others. 14 tables, 33 notes. J. V. Coutinho

191. Kirk-Greene, A. H. M. TOWARDS A HISTORY OF COLONIAL ADMINISTRATORS IN AFRICA: SOURCES AND PROBLEMS. *African Res. and Documentation [Great Britain] 1982 (29): 16-18.* Discusses the literature on British colonial government in Africa, 1937-57, especially various stages in the career of a colonial administrator, including family provenance, education, recruitment, the job, relationships, promotion and honors, hobbies, and retirement occupations.

192. Kosmin, Barry A. COLONIAL CAREERS FOR MARGINAL FASCISTS—A PORTRAIT OF HAMILTON BEAMISH. *Wiener Lib. Bull. [Great Britain] 1973/74 27(30/31): 16-23.* A biographical account of Henry Hamilton Beamish's political career in Africa as a British fascist. Brief mention of Major L. M. Hasting's influence on Beamish is also included. 30 notes. T. H. Bauhs

193. Libera, Anna. THE NEW SLAVE TRADE: PORTUGUESE COLONIALISM IN AFRICA. *Internat. Socialist R. 1973 35(2): 18-23.* Portugal's policies in Angola, Mozambique, and Guinea (Bissau) have been racist and exploitative. S

194. Loth, H. DIVERSION GEGEN ANTIKOLONIALE EINHEIT. DOKUMENTE ZU "ANTIKOMMUNISTISCHEN AKTIVITÄTEN" DES DEUTSCHEN IMPERIALISMUS ZWISCHEN DEN BEIDEN WELTKRIEGEN [Diversion against anticolonial unity: documents on "anticommunist activities" of German imperialism between the wars]. *Wissenschaftliche Zeitschrift der Karl-Marx U. Leipzig [East Germany] 1976 25(6): 539-547.* Publication of 12 reports from German diplomats in Africa between 1929 and 1937 which blamed the growth of the political consciousness of the black population on Communist propaganda and subversion. Documents from Zentrales Staatsarchiv der DDR, Potsdam. R. Wagnleitner

195. Mährdel, Christian. DAS DEMOKRATISCHE BÜNDNIS VON PROLETARISCH-SOZIALISTISCHEN UND REVOLUTIONÄR-DEMOKRATISCHEN POLITISCHEN KRÄFTEN IM KAMPF UM NATIONALE UND SOZIALE BEFREIUNG (AM AFRIKANISCHEN BEISPIEL) [The democratic unity of proletarian-socialist and revolutionary-democratic political tendencies in the national and social liberation struggle: the African example]. *Archív Orientální [Czechoslovakia] 1978 46(2): 112-127.* National liberation movements in Africa have increasingly taken on a socialist bias during the 1970's.

196. Manning, Patrick. NOTES TOWARD A THEORY OF IDEOLOGY IN HISTORICAL WRITING ON MODERN AFRICA. *Can. J. of African Studies [Canada] 1974 8(2): 235-253.* Examines thoughts on historiography of modern Africa dealing specifically with the evaluation of the colonial period in Africa and the study of African domestic slavery, 19c-1960's.

197. Marchand, Jean. LA FIN DE L'EMPIRE PORTUGAIS [The end of the Portuguese empire]. *Écrits de Paris [France] 1974 (340): 3-15.* Describes the disintegration of the Portuguese empire in Africa and discusses its consequences for other African countries still under white rule.

198. Marchand, Jean. LA REVANCHE DU MONDE ARABE SUR L'EUROPE OCCIDENTALE EN AFRIQUE NOIRE [The revenge of the Arab world on Western Europe in Black Africa]. *Écrits de Paris [France] 1976 (356): 11-22.* Shows how following World War II, the Arab world of northern Africa encouraged rebellions in the still colonial Black African territories.

199. Martens, J.; Verdaasdonk, A.; van Rijen, J.; van Kampen, A.; and Tielemans, J. DIARY OF INHAMINGA. *Issue 1974 4(2): 62-73.* Diary by five Dutch missionaries of the last days of Portugal's empire in Guinea, Angola, and Mozambique. S

200. Mazrui, Ali A. GANDHI, MARX AND THE WARRIOR TRADITION. *J. of Asian and African Studies [Netherlands] 1977 12(1-4): 179-196.* African resistance movements have taken three forms in the 20th century: masculine warrior in active resistance, feminine passive resistance, and in the modern era, Marxist revolutionary ideology which both sexes employ. Secondary sources; 23 notes. R. T. Brown

201. McCormack, Robert. AIRLINES AND EMPIRES: GREAT BRITAIN AND THE "SCRAMBLE FOR AFRICA": 1919-1932. *Can. J. of African Studies [Canada] 1976 10(1): 87-105.* Studies a new dimension of British imperialism in Africa between the two world wars. After 1919 civil air transport began to play a more important role in European political decisions in Africa. The airlines opened a new era in rapid communication which hastened the development of Africa. The "scramble" which followed was not different than that which had taken place with regard to territories. Nevertheless, this rivalry assisted the development of African aviation. Based on Public Record Office records of Britain, other government documents, newspapers, unpublished airline reports, and secondary sources; 117 notes. J

202. McCormack, Robert. IMPERIAL MISSION: THE AIR ROUTE TO CAPE TOWN 1918-32. *J. of Contemporary Hist. [Great Britain] 1974 9(4): 77-97.* On 20 January 1932, Imperial Airways launched its Cape Town-Cairo-Paris route, fulfilling Cecil Rhodes' vision dating from 1876. The political situation in Egypt was the chief cause of delay from World War I to the early 30's. Impetus for the air route came with Sir Samuel Hoare's (1880-1959) leadership in 1926. Six years later, the proponents of empire had triumphed. Based on archival and published primary sources; 70 notes. M. P. Trauth

203. Mitchell, Louis D. THE PORTUGUESE IN AFRICA. *Crisis 1973 80(10): 335-338.* Presents an overview of Portugal's 450-year history in Africa, including the course of imperialism, the slave trade, and modern foreign relations. S

204. Mosley, Paul. AGRICULTURAL DEVELOPMENT AND GOVERNMENT POLICY IN SETTLER ECONOMIES: THE CASE OF KENYA AND SOUTHERN RHODESIA, 1900-60. *Econ. Hist. Rev. [Great Britain] 1982 35(3): 390-408.* Finds little statistical support for the idea that colonial policy crippled indigenous African agriculture. Before 1945, land scarcity created by government policy, consistent with the Boserup model of agricultural development, appears to have stimulated modernization of African agricultural techniques, although in areas where much land had been allocated to Europeans innovation in African agriculture was clearly inhibited by fears of confiscation. After 1945 the Boserup model loses much of its explanatory value. Access to high value cash crops became the most important determinant of interdistrict differences in African agricultural prosperity. 6 tables, appendix entitled "A Note on the Data." B. L. Crapster

205. Natsoulas, Theodore. RACE RELATIONS IN PORTUGUESE AFRICA: A BIBLIOGRAPHIC INQUIRY. *J. of African Studies 1981 8(2): 79-84.* Prior to the early 1960's and the beginning of the colonial war in Angola in 1961 in particular, writers on the subject of Portuguese colonialism generally agreed on the notion of the nonracist nature of Portugal's tropical empire, a concept reflected in the extension of Gilberto Freyre's lusotropicality from Brazil to the African colonies. While writers like Basil Davidson and James Duffy began to attack this view in the 1950's, the historian Charles R. Boxer was the first to systematically critique the history of Portuguese racial policies as the long-term development of a racial caste system. The past 20 years have seen an outpouring of writings debunking the myth of multiracialism and nondiscrimination all through the history of Portuguese colonialism in the tropics. Secondary works; 4 notes. L. W. Truschel

206. Newbury, Colin W. and Newbury, Gertrude E. LABOR CHARTERS AND LABOR MARKETS: THE ILO AND AFRICA IN THE INTERWAR PERIOD. *J. of African Studies 1976 3(3): 311-327.* Assesses the influence of the indigenous labour conventions adopted by the International Labour Conference between 1930 and 1936. The International Labor Organization's method of publicity was most effective in regulating conditions of labor in backward areas. A good deal of diplomacy was required to secure support for the Forced Labour Convention of 1930. The author considers the reformed labor legislation and labor stabilization and recruitment policies of the colonial powers. 36 notes. E. P. Stickney

207. Newbury, M. Catharine. *UBUREETWA* AND *THANGATA*: CATALYSTS TO PEASANT POLITICAL CONSCIOUSNESS IN RWANDA AND MALAWI. *Can. J. of African Studies [Canada] 1980 14(1): 97-111.* Examines the political impact of two traditional labor requisition institutions. In Rwanda, native chiefs backed by the colonial government used *ubureetwa* to impose on their subjects new calls for work or to increase old requirements. In Malawi, the European colonists transformed a precolonial device called *thangata* into an effectual instrument of exploitation. In spite of substantial differences in social and political contexts, the polarizing effects of the transformation were similar. 31 notes. J/S

208. Ntalaja, Nzongola. PEASANTS AND NATIONALISM: AN AFRICAN OVERVIEW. *Pan-African J. [Kenya] 1974 7(3): 263-268.* African peasants are the backbone of nationalist and independence movements. They never ceased to resist colonial rule and they still have a responsibility to free South Africa. 27 notes. H. G. Soff

209. Nwafor, Azinna. IMPERIALISM AND REVOLUTION IN AFRICA. *Monthly Rev. 1975 26(11): 18-30.* Analyzes Amilcar Cabral's essay on imperialism in Africa, "Foundations and Objectives of National Liberation in Relation to Social Structure," in *Liberation in Guinea* (London: Stage I, 1969).

210. Nwanunobi, C. Onyeka. WAGE LABOUR AND THE POLITICS OF NIGERIA AND KENYA: A COMPARATIVE STUDY. *African Studies Rev. 1974 17(1): 77-104.* Labor unions and organizations played a secondary role in Nigerian politics, 1939-66, whereas in Kenya politics were merged with the traditional concerns of the labor union.

211. Obukhov, Lev. SOME ASPECTS OF THE IDEOLOGICAL ACTIVITY OF REVOLUTIONARY DEMOCRATS IN AFRICA. *Archív Orientální [Czechoslovakia] 1978 46(2): 128-140.* African national liberation movements have become more adept at using public education and mass media to raise class awareness, 1960's-70's.

212. Odetola, Olatunde. WHAT IS AFRICAN LIBERATION. *Studies in Comparative Int. Development 1974 9(3): 103-110.* Critical review of Richard Gibson's *African Liberation Movements* (Oxford: Oxford U. Pr., 1972) and Leonard Barnes's *Africa in Eclipse* (New York: Int. Publications Service, 1971), noting the inadequacies of their hypotheses, problem-solving attempts, and general approach. Concludes that "Gibson's work provides no new ideas... on the subject of African liberation" and "Barnes's work makes for sloppy and morbid reading." The latter work, on the whole, is the better of the two. S. A. Farmerie

213. Offiong, Daniel A. THE CHEERFUL SCHOOL AND THE MYTH OF THE CIVILIZING MISSION OF COLONIAL IMPERIALISM. *Pan-African J. [Kenya] 1976 9(1): 35-54.* Ernest W. Lefever's *Spear and Scepter* argues that colonial imperialism had a civilizing mission. By placing the barbaric rites cited by Lefever into their context, the author refutes the claim that precolonial Africa had an Iron Age level of culture and condemns the exploitative nature of British policy in Nigeria. Secondary sources; 62 notes. M. Feingold

214. Ojo, Michael A. HOW THE TRUSTEESHIP COLONIES BECAME INDEPENDENT. *Africa Q. [India] 1977 16(4): 99-119.* Traces the progress to independence of former German and Italian colonies in Africa (Tanganyika, Togoland, the Cameroons, Ruanda-Urundi, and Somaliland) which, after coming under British, French, or Belgian administration, became UN trust territories after World War II.

215. Ojo, Michael A. U.N. AND FREEDOM FOR PORTUGUESE COLONIES. *Africa Q. [India] 1976 16(1): 5-28.* Studies the decolonization of Portuguese Africa, analyzing events, policies, and UN actions and the stance of sympathetic non-Africans and the African liberation movements during the 1950's and 1960's.

216. Pearce, R. D. THE COLONIAL OFFICE IN 1947 AND THE TRANSFER OF POWER IN AFRICA: AN ADDENDUM TO JOHN CELL. *J. of Imperial and Commonwealth Hist. [Great Britain] 1982 10(2): 211-215.* Supplements an earlier article by John W. Cell (see entry 161). Refers to Cell's description of the establishment of local governments and the attempt, centered in Arthur Creech Jones's dispatch of February 1947, to check the growth of African nationalism. Rejects the idea of local reform apart from the reform of the central legislature and emphasizes the "new breed" of Colonial Office officials who were trying to deal with the new nationalist realities. Based on Colonial Office papers at Public Record Office, London and secondary sources; 16 notes. M. C. Rosenfield

217. Pegushev, A. M. UCHENYE SOTSIALISTICHESKIKH STRAN O PROBLEMAKH NATSIONAL'NOGO DVIZHENIIA V AFRIKE [Scholars of the socialist countries on problems of national liberation movements in Africa]. *Narody Azii i Afriki [USSR] 1980 (5): 169-179.* The 3d Symposium of Historians and Africanists of Socialist Countries entitled History of the National Liberation Movement in Africa: The Problem of Leadership and the fourth meeting of the working group History of Africa and the National Liberation Movement in Africa took place in September, 1979 in Leipzig. Participants came from Czechoslovakia, East Germany, Hungary, Poland, and the USSR. These meetings served to increase the collaboration among Africanists from the Socialist countries. Cites previous symposiums on similar subjects (Budapest in 1977 and Varna in 1975), publications resulting there from, and other primary sources; 9 notes. S. J. Talalay

218. Pélissier, René. CONSÉQUENCES DÉMOGRAPHIQUES DES RÉVOLTES EN AFRIQUE PORTUGAISE (1961-1970): ESSAI D'INTERPRÉTATION [Demographic consequences of the revolts in Portuguese Africa, 1961-70: an interpretive essay]. *Rev. Française d'Hist. d'Outre-Mer [France] 1974 61(222): 34-73.* For propaganda purposes, the guerrillas of Portuguese Africa have grossly exaggerated the size of populations under their control. At the end of 1973, the majority of people living in Guinea-Bissau, Angola, and Mozambique were still under Portuguese rather than African nationalist rule. Based on the Portuguese censuses of 1950, 1960, 1970, and secondary works; 3 maps, 19 tables, 42 notes. L. B. Chan

219. Pirouet, Louise. ARMED RESISTANCE AND COUNTER-INSURGENCY. *J. of Asian and African Studies [Netherlands] 1977 12(1-4): 197-214.* Examination of the response of the mass of citizens to revolution and counterinsurgency in Kenya, Sudan, and Zimbabwe shows that the tactics of counterinsurgency are self-defeating. 46 notes, biblio. R. T. Brown

220. Pomeroy, Willim J. OPPRESSORS ARE NEVER DIVIDED BY COLOR. *World Marxist R. [Canada] 1974 17(2): 119-124.* Reviews Henry Winston's *Strategy for a Black Agenda; a Critique of New Theories of Liberation in the United States and Africa* (New York: New Outlook, 1972). S

221. Porter, Andrew. THE DEVELOPMENT OF COLONIAL RULE IN AFRICA. *African Res. and Documentation [Great Britain] 1981 (27): 3-8.* Traces the three periods of colonization of Africa by European nations: 1) 1875-1910, 2) 1914-40's, and 3) decolonization, 1948-70's. A combination of war, depression, and demands for development weakened the foundations of colonial government, and political independence and self-government resulted.

222. Rensburg, A. P. J. van. A BOOK SHAKES LISBON. *Historia [South Africa] 1974 19(2): 117-120.* Review article on António de Spinola's *Portugal and the Future* (1974), commenting favorably on Portuguese racial tolerance in their colonies as compared to other European colonizers.

223. Rimmer, Douglas. THE ECONOMICS OF COLONIALISM IN AFRICA. *J. of African Hist. [Great Britain] 1978 19(2): 265-273.* Reviews *Colonialism in Africa 1870-1960: Volume 4, The Economics of Colonialism* (London: Cambridge U. Pr., 1975), edited by Peter Duignan and L. H. Gann. Supports the general theme of the book: colonial administration throughout the period reflected metropolitan concepts of political economy; it did not reflect exploitation of the populace and resources, as radicals and Marxists assert, which paved the way for contemporary underdevelopment. For many Africans, colonialism was an economically liberating force and provided opportunities previously denied by political disorder and lack of transport, communications, skills, and knowledge. The benefits are most clearly seen in demographic trends. 16 notes. A. W. Novitsky

224. Robinson, Ronald. THE MORAL DISARMAMENT OF AFRICAN EMPIRE 1919-1947. *J. of Imperial and Commonwealth Hist. [Great Britain] 1979 8(1): 86-104.* Discusses the moral aspects of colonialism and trusteeship in Africa. Nationalism caused self-government to replace good government. Based on Colonial Office records at the Public Record Office, London; 75 notes. M. C. Rosenfield

225. Rodrigues de Areia, M. L. LA SÉCURITÉ SOCIALE DANS LES INSTITUTIONS TRADITIONELLES DE L'AFRIQUE CENTRALE ET L'INTRODUCTION DES SYNDICATS [Social security in the traditional institutions of Central Africa and the introduction of labor unions]. *Rev. de l'Inst. de Sociologie [Belgium] 1974 (1): 149-164.* Discusses the reactions of traditional social institutions in Central Africa, mainly Zaire, Zambia, and Northern Angola, to colonialism and labor unions and organizations, illustrating the process of cultural dualism which developed as European institutions were imposed on traditional societies.

226. Sabatier, Peggy R. "ELITE" EDUCATION IN FRENCH WEST AFRICA: THE ERA OF LIMITS 1903-1945. *Int. J. of African Hist. Studies 1978 11(2): 247-266.* Explores the educational opportunities available to French West Africans during the pre-World War II period, describing the nine elite schools located in Senegal, Mali, the Ivory Coast, and Algeria. The limitations on education for elites were: the number of students educated, the curriculums and diplomas, and in the careers that awaited graduates. 2 tables, 48 notes. M. M. McCarthy

227. Sanderson, Lilian. EDUCATION AND ADMINISTRATIVE CONTROL IN COLONIAL SUDAN AND NORTHERN NIGERIA. *African Affairs [Great Britain] 1975 74(297): 427-441.* Discusses the role of education in Muslim states resistant to western ideas and religion. Nigeria and the Sudan faced similar educational problems, and their similar problems led to civil war in each country. The author discusses the development of education in the 20th century. In both countries, political considerations have determined educational development. 56 notes. H. G. Soff

228. Sanger, Clyde. THE PORTUGUESE COLONIES IN AFRICA. *Can. Labour 1974 19(1): 2-4, 50.* Portugal's African colonies can look forward only to continued war. S

229. Sharevskaia, B. I. K VOPROSU O TIPOLOGII ANTIKOLONIAL'NYKH RELIGIOZNO-POLITICHESKIKH DVIZHENII V TROPICHESKOI AFRIKE [The typology of anticolonial religious-political movements in tropical Africa]. *Narody Azii i Afriki [USSR] 1974 (4): 16-26.* Distinguishes three degrees of importance of the traditional or Afro-Christian religious element in the anticolonial movements of preindependence tropical Africa, concluding that such movements were essentially political.

230. Smyth, Rosaleen. THE DEVELOPMENT OF BRITISH COLONIAL FILM POLICY, 1927-1939, WITH SPECIAL REFERENCE TO EAST AND CENTRAL AFRICA. *J. of African Hist. [Great Britain] 1979 20(3): 437-450.* Since 1920, British officials saw the cinema as a propaganda tool for imperial interests. American films were viewed as a threat to British commercial and political interests, leading to strict censorship. South African policies of racial discrimination in censorship and segregation in theaters were precedents adopted throughout East and Central Africa. By 1935, the educational potential of film was developed when the Carnegie Foundation funded the International Missionary Council's Bantu Educational Kinema Experiment, which lasted only two years. Neither financial nor government support was available. The Colonial Film Unit was created in 1939 to provide war propaganda, but later turned to the production of instructional films. 91 notes. A. W. Novitsky

231. Spivey, Donald. THE AFRICAN CRUSADE FOR BLACK INDUSTRIAL SCHOOLING. *J. of Negro Hist. 1978 63(1): 1-17.* Industrial education was utilized in the maintenance of subordination and exploitation of black people in the US South and in Africa. It was a negative aspect of the Pan-African movement. Both white Europeans and white Southerners put industrial schooling to effective use in pursuing a world order based upon white rule. Based upon primary materials in the Rockefeller archives and domestic and foreign secondary materials; 82 notes. N. G. Sapper

232. Taddia, Irma. PROBLEMI DI STORIA DEL COLONIALISMO FRANCESE NELL'AFRICA TROPICALE [Historical problems of French colonialism in tropical Africa]. *Storia Contemporanea [Italy] 1978 9(3): 549-567.* Points out the need to rewrite the history of French expansion in Africa, taking into account the reaction of the colonized societies. Few accounts present reliable economic data. In the balance of payments Africa showed always a deficit, except for Algeria. French expansion in Africa was the expression of nationalistic sentiments of poor whites. Secondary sources; 49 notes. A. Sbacchi

233. Vedovato, Giuseppe. L'AFRICA ITALIANA VERSO L'INDIPENDENZA [Italian Africa on the way to independence]. *Riv. di Studi Pol. Int. [Italy] 1981 48(1): 75-82.* Reviews Gianluigi Rossi's *L'Africa Italiana verso l'Indipendenza (1941-1949)* which discusses the negotiations at the United Nations for the independence of Libya, Eritrea, and Somalia, in the context of the political, economic and strategic factors involved and worsening East-West relations.

234. Wheeler, Douglas L. AFRICAN ELEMENTS IN PORTUGAL'S ARMIES IN AFRICA (1961-1974). *Armed Forces and Soc. 1976 2(2): 233-250.* Discusses the political and social consequences of Portugal's use of African troops in its armies in Africa, 1950's-70's.

235. Whitehead, Clive. EDUCATION POLICY IN BRITISH TROPICAL AFRICA: THE 1925 WHITE PAPER IN RETROSPECT. *Hist. of Educ. [Great Britain] 1981 10(3): 195-203.* In 1925 the British government published a White Paper entitled *Education Policy in British Tropical Africa* which has traditionally been accepted as a landmark of imperial policy in the 20th century. The main significance of the White Paper lay in the official recognition that it accorded to the Christian missions as partners of state in the provision of schooling in the colonies. It failed to make any significant impact on the policy and practice of colonial education before the war, partly because of the shortages of skilled personnel, but mainly because the Depression meant that colonial governments were preoccupied with maintaining existing services and would not experiment with new educational ideas. Based on International Missionary Council Archives and Minutes of the Advisory Committee on Education in the Colonies and secondary sources; 40 notes. G. L. Neville

236. —. [POLITICAL CHANGE IN SOUTHERN AFRICA]. *Pan-African J. [Kenya] 1973 6(2): 248-251.* Reviews Gerard Chaliand's *Armed Struggle in Africa: with the Guerrillas in "Portuguese" Guinea* (New York: Monthly Rev. Pr., 1967), Donn Barnett's and Roy Harvey's *The Revolution in Angola, MPLA, Life Histories,and Documents* (Indianapolis: Bobbs-Merrill, 1972), John Sykes's *Portugal and Africa: the People and the War* (London: Hutchinson, 1971), and Christian P. Potholm's and Richard Dale's *Southern Africa in Perspective*(New York: Free Pr., 1972), all concerned with guerrilla warfare and the liberation movements in southern Africa. S

Politics after Independence

237. Adelman, Kenneth L. THE CENTRAL AFRICAN STATES. *Current Hist. 1979 76(445): 115-118, 132-134.* Discusses the conflict between Zaire, Angola, and Zambia in 1976-77, and its resolution in 1978.

238. Ake, Claude. EXPLANATORY NOTES ON THE POLITICAL ECONOMY OF AFRICA. *J. of Modern African Studies [Great Britain] 1976 14(1): 1-23.* The salient features of Africa's contemporary political economy are intense ethnic conflict, the single party system, brutal political efficiency, repression, and recurring military coups. These features are explained by the material base of underdeveloped, state-dominated economies that are still dependent on former colonial powers. Africa's natural ethnic consciousness has been turned into conflict by imperialism and by struggles among native bourgeois factions. These factions exploit the masses through the single party system and its variant of military rule. W. R. Hively

239. Alexandre, Pierre; Ellington, John; and Miller, Gerald. THE POLITICS OF LANGUAGE. *Africa Report 1973 18(4): 16-25.*

240. Anise, Ladun. AFRICA: CHALLENGE OF THE UNFINISHED REVOLUTION. *Black Scholar 1974 5(7): 2-9.* The African revolution has abandoned its original intent, beguiled and immobilized by the concealed arms of foreign exploitation. The encounter between black and white in Southern Africa reveals a profound moral depravity. Secondary sources; 7 notes. M. M. McCarthy

241. Anise, Ladun. DEVELOPMENT AND DEPENDENCY IN THE NEW REVOLUTIONARY AFRICAN STATES. *Black Scholar 1980 11(5): 2-13.* Surveys the character and development of revolutionary socialist regimes in Africa and assesses their continuing dependency on Western economic interests and the constant threat of destabilization.

242. Anise, Ladun. TRENDS IN LEADERSHIP SUCCESSION AND REGIME CHANGE IN AFRICAN POLITICS SINCE INDEPENDENCE. *African Studies Rev. 1974 17(3): 507-523.* Examines, classifies, and quantifies the various successions of leaders and regimes which have occurred in 40 African states since 1952.

243. Atimomo, Emiko. MIDDLE EAST: THE WAR'S IMPLICATIONS FOR AFRICA. *Afriscope [Nigeria] 1973 3(12): 25-30.* The Middle Eastern conflict is indicative of the major problems of Africa: lack of military power, disunity, and control by superpowers (USA, USSR) of Third World nations. Africa will remain an ineffective pawn until it solves its problems. G. O. Gagnon

244. Ayandele, E. A. AFRICAN STUDIES AND NATION-BUILDING. *African Historical Studies* (Totowa, N.J.: Frank Cass, 1979): 286-305. African states, notably Liberia, that adopted Western cultures and political systems in the 19th century, failed to achieve the goals of a global culture and rapid modernization. African national development in the 20th century depends on an educational system that reflects African history, culture, values, and visions for the future.

245. Barbag, Anna. THE ROLE OF THE ENGLISH LANGUAGE IN THE DEVELOPMENT OF AFRICAN NATIONALISM. *Africana Bull. [Poland] 1976 24: 35-42.* Although it was not the intention of the colonial powers, English became a significant factor in the nation-building process and in facilitating communications among black Africans, 1710-1975. Nevertheless, some newly independent countries wished to abolish English as an unwelcome reminder of colonialism.

246. Barnes, Sandra T. POLITICAL TRANSITION IN URBAN AFRICA. *Ann. of the Am. Acad. of Pol. and Social Sci. 1977 (432): 26-41.* Political change in Africa has not met the expectations of preindependence analysts. Civil wars, military coups, and the demise of multiparty states weigh heavily on the performance of public authorities and the smooth functioning of the body politic. At the local level, political and demographic changes also exceed expectations. Administrators are unprepared to deal with the vast numbers of migrants who are attracted to the burgeoning cities. At the same time, agencies are constantly reorganized and bureaucratic continuity is minimal. The result is that residents are forced to meet political needs through their own efforts. To these ends there has been an increasing Africanization of the polity, as seen in the proliferation of traditional authority figures who adapt their roles as chiefs or patrons to the modern urban marketplace, and a proliferation of organizations and networks that serve as interest groups or dispute settlement mechanisms in place of formal governmental institutions. Although unanticipated, these features can no longer be considered deviations from a prescribed norm. They are an organic part of the political process. Today they account for much of the stability and continuity that are to be found in Africa's urban political systems. J

247. Barrows, Walter L. COMPARATIVE GRASSROOTS POLITICS IN AFRICA. *World Pol. 1974 26(2): 283-297.* Review article of Nicholas S. Hopkins's *Popular Government in an African Town: Kita, Mali* (Chicago and London: U. of Chicago Press, 1972), Maxwell Owusu's *Uses and Abuses of Political Power: A Case Study of Continuity and Change in the Politics of Ghana* (Chicago and London: U. of Chicago Press, 1970), and Joan Vincent's *African Elite: The Big Men of a Small Town* (New York and London: Columbia U. Press, 1971). Each of the books investigates politics in an African town—Kita in Mali, Gondo in Uganda, and Swedru in Ghana. Comparison of the three reveals remarkably similar patterns of local politics. Each community is characterized by an instrumental, materially oriented style of politics in which the ambitions of leaders for prestige and the desire of followers for tangible benefits lead to groupings which cut across ethnic lines. Communalism, "tribalism," and traditionalism are inadequate and misleading in the three cases considered here. The point of departure adopted by each author, which emphasizes rational actors pursuing their separate goals, reveals a politics based on utility-maximization rather than on the evocation of collective identities. Factions emerge as the characteristic expression of utilitarian politics in two of the local communities, but in the third (Gondo), intra-elite unity is emphasized in order to close ranks in the face of a political environment which historically has been hostile. J/S

248. Barrows, Walter L. ETHNIC DIVERSITY AND POLITICAL INSTABILITY IN BLACK AFRICA. *Comparative Pol. Studies 1976 9(2): 139-170.* Discusses ethnic diversity, civil wars, political instability, and social change in Black African nations in the 1960's and 70's.

249. Bates, Robert H. ETHNIC COMPETITION AND MODERNIZATION IN CONTEMPORARY AFRICA. *Comparative Pol. Studies 1974 6(4): 457-484.*

250. Bernardi, Bernardo. LA VIOLENZA NEL CONTINENTE AFRICANO [Violence on the African continent]. *Problemi di Ulisse [Italy] 1978 14(86): 50-57.* Decolonization in Africa brought with it a continent-wide wave of violence. The new regimes have proved worse "colonialists" in dealing with dissident ethnic groups than the Europeans ever were.

251. Braginski, M. RABOCHII KLASS AFRIKI V GODY NEZAVISIMOSTI [The working class of Africa in the years of independence]. *Aziia i Afrika Segodnia [USSR] 1977 (5): 15-16.* The political activity of the African working class has been increasing in the last decade. Though small enterprises abound on the continent, the greater part of the proletariat is concentrated at the few big plants and mines. The number of industrial workers in the total of hired labor has increased. All this is a factor in heightening the role of the African proletariat in the revolutionary process. J

252. Brionne, Bernard. NOUVEAUX FACTEURS DE DÉSÉQUILIBRE EN AFRIQUE [New factors of unrest in Africa]. *Défense Natl. [France] 1975 31(4): 65-79.* Examines decolonization in Africa, precipitated by the Algerian doctrine on development, the oil crisis, and the collapse of the Portuguese Empire.

253. Buijtenhuijs, Rob. THE REVOLUTIONARY POTENTIAL OF BLACK AFRICA: DISSIDENT ELITES. *African Perspectives [Netherlands] 1978 (2): 135-146.* Examines the revolutionary potential among black elites in Africa, 1960-78. The potential of the lower classes for revolution is weak as a result of a passive acceptance of the status quo, but they can be influenced and organized by a revolutionary elite. It is these elite groups that need identification. They will be among those not now in power, and include African students presently excluded from entrance into governmental positions, and those unable to satisfy middle-class ambitions because of economic stagnation. Unemployed intellectuals often undertake subversive activities, and ethnic and linguistic discrimination can also be a cause of dissidence.
R. V. Ritter

254. Callaghy, Thomas M. THE RISE OF THE AFRICAN STATE. *Problems of Communism 1980 29(5): 54-60.* Reviews six studies on the African state system. With the emergence of an African state system, interstate conflict and outside intervention have increased, and broader notions such as Pan-Africanism have declined. 5 notes.
J. M. Lauber

255. Carter, Marshall. CONSTITUTIONAL LAW AND PRACTICE IN THE COMMONWEALTH STATES OF AFRICA. *Africa Today 1980 27(4): 47-49.* A review of B. O. Nwabueze's *Constitutionalism in the Emergent States* (1973), *Presidentialism in Commonwealth Africa* (1975), and *Judicialism in Commonwealth Africa: The Role of the*

Courts in Government (1977). The three volumes are a major contribution to understanding the governmental failures of Africa and provide sound remedial recommendations. G. O. Gagnon

256. Cefkin, J. Leo. AFRICAN DEVELOPMENT STRATEGIES AND THE WHITE RULED STATES OF SOUTHERN AFRICA. *Africa Today 1973 20(4): 29-37.* Examines various policies of majority-rule nations toward colonial and minority-rule governments. Concludes that these nations will be able to support liberation movements more completely as alternative sources of development funds are found and as internal pressures build within isolated, minority-ruled southern African nations. Secondary sources; 11 notes. G. O. Gagnon

257. Chalendar, Pierrette and Chalendar, Gérard. LES CHEMINS DE LA NEGRITUDE [The paths of negritude]. *Esprit [France] 1978 (2): 75-89.* Traces the history of the concept of negritude and attempts to explicate its underlying political ideology.

258. Charlton, Roger. DIFFUSION AND POLITICAL CHANGE IN POST-COLONIAL AFRICA: PERSPECTIVES ON UNIPARTISM AND MILITARY INTERVENTION. *Cultures et Développement. Rev. Int. des Sci. du Developpement [Belgium] 1979 11(3): 439-456.*

259. Chazan, Naomi. AFRICAN VOTERS AT THE POLLS: A RE-EXAMINATION OF THE ROLE OF ELECTIONS IN AFRICAN POLITICS. *J. of Commonwealth and Comparative Pol. [Great Britain] 1979 17(2): 136-158.* Examines the functions, substance, results, and trends of elections in sub-Saharan Africa. Election results have not always adequately reflected the contents or directions of public opinion as expressed in the campaigns. Based on published documents and secondary works; 46 notes, appendix. D. J. Nicholls

260. Chazan, Naomi. THE NEW POLITICS OF PARTICIPATION IN TROPICAL AFRICA. *Comparative Pol. 1982 14(2): 169-189.* Discusses the participation explosion in the politics of tropical Africa, tracing patterns of development over the past two decades. There is much evidence to indicate that group-based voluntary political participation has been prevalent in African politics for a number of years. Participation is analyzed according to both formal and informal networks. Informal participation allowed only indirect group involvment, while formal participation allowed direct individual involvement. In the present political climate, there is a trend toward formal participation, but the trend is seen as an integration of both formal and informal mechanisms. 69 notes. M. A. Kascus

261. Chrétien, Jean-Pierre. L'ALIBI ETHNIQUE DANS LES POLITIQUES AFRICAINES [The ethnic alibi in African politics]. *Esprit [France] 1981 (7-8): 109-115.* Analyzes the political issues derived from or related to ethnic groups in Africa.

262. Collier, Ruth Berins. PARTIES, COUPS AND AUTHORITARIAN RULE: PATTERNS OF POLITICAL CHANGE IN TROPICAL AFRICA. *Comparative Pol. Studies 1978 11(1): 62-93.* Maintains that the different types of authoritarian regimes that have emerged in tropical Africa have been determined by the manner in which each country was introduced to competitive party politics, from the end of World War II to the present.

263. Czirkin, W. E. ISTOTA, TREŚĆ, FORMA PAŃSTWA O ORIENTACJI SOCJALISTYCZNEJ [The nature, essence, and characteristics of socialist oriented states]. *Państwo i Prawo [Poland] 1973 28(6): 47-57.* A Marxist-Leninist analysis of the development and characteristics of African states with a socialist orientation, 1963-73.

264. Davidson, Basil. THE MOVEMENTS OF NATIONAL LIBERATION. *Tarikh [Nigeria] 1980 6(4): 5-19.* The independence of Portuguese colonies in Africa followed longtime efforts by indigenous independence movements, and the new democratic states represented a complete reversal of colonial concepts of elite classes.

265. Doornbos, Martin R. A NOTE ON TIME HORIZONS AND INTERPRETATIONS OF AFRICAN POLITICAL CHANGE. *African Rev. [Tanzania] 1974 4(4): 557-564.* A growing call for political order in developing nations by political scientists is based on deceptive perspectives of nationalism, independence, and nationbuilding. If, however, the observer used a more logical time perspective, it would be seen that the processes that created independence could not cease with the passing of the colonial order but would continue to effect change. 7 notes. R. T. Brown

266. Dudley, Billy. POWER AND PROGRAMS IN AFRICA. *Afriscope [Nigeria] 1975 5(1): 6-9.* Examines the structural violence which has characterized many African government policies, 1964-74. Nations devoted to violence cannot produce beneficial change, as political theorist Ali Mazrui hypothesizes, in fact the violence dehumanizes black Africa and prevents any moral challenge of the equally dehumanized posture of South Africa and Zimbabwe. Based on current events. G. O. Gagnon

267. Duvall, Raymond and Welfling, Mary. DETERMINANTS OF POLITICAL INSTITUTIONALIZATION IN BLACK AFRICA. *Comparative Pol. Studies 1973 5(4): 387-417.* Assesses the importance of "hypothesized determinants of party system institutionalization in new nations." S

268. Duvall, Raymond and Welfling, Mary. SOCIAL MOBILIZATION, POLITICAL INSTITUTIONALIZATION, AND CONFLICT IN BLACK AFRICA: A SIMPLE DYNAMIC MODEL. *J. of Conflict Resolution 1973 17(4): 673-702.* "A simple model involving five concepts—social mobilization, party system institutionalization, turmoil, internal war, and elite conflict—is specified and its structural parameters are estimated for 28 black African nations. The model is fully reciprocal, involving each concept as a function of each of the others, and the concepts are measured for two time periods, 1960-1964 and 1965-1969. Two-stage least-squares regression is utilized to generate parameter estimates. The resulting model structure is evaluated according to 1) its correspondence with extant scholarly theorizing, 2) its ability to account for variance in the concepts, 3) the systematic character of the residual, or error, terms, and 4) its predictions for the future. The major conclusions are that: forms of conflict interrelate in complex ways and are not simply different aspects of a single phenomenon; conflict affects the mobilization of society and the development of political institutions; social mobilization has little, if any, effect on conflict; and, the institutionalization of party systems as linkages between publics and governments has a real impact on the mobilization of society and on the level of conflict in society." J

269. Ekeh, Peter P. COLONIALISM AND THE TWO PUBLICS IN AFRICA: A THEORETICAL STATEMENT. *Comparative Studies in Soc. and Hist. [Great Britain] 1975 17(1): 91-112.* There are two public realms in post-colonial Africa: one "in which primordial groupings, ties, and sentiments influence..* . public behavior" and another "which is historically associated with the colonial administration" and which has "no moral linkages with the private realm." S

270. Elaigwa, J. Isawa. THE NIGERIAN CIVIL WAR AND THE ANGOLAN CIVIL WAR. *J. of Asian and African Studies [Netherlands] 1977 12(1-4): 215-235.* Discusses the links between domestic struggles and the international alignments which result, the role various foreign nations played in both the Nigerian and Angolan civil wars, and the splits within the Organization of African Unity over both. 54 notes. R. T. Brown

271. Eppstein, John. THE FATE OF PORTUGUESE AFRICA. *World Survey [Great Britain] 1975 (83): 1-17.* Discusses the Communist Party's assumption of power in Guinea and Mozambique and its struggle to control Angola following the revolution in Portugal in 1974.

272. Fauré, Yves-A. CÉLÉBRATIONS OFFICIELLES ET POUVOIRS AFRICAINS: SYMBOLIQUE ET CONSTRUCTION DE L'ÉTAT [Official ceremonies and African powers: symbols and construction of the state]. *Can. J. of African Studies [Canada] 1978 12(3): 383-404.* Inherited from colonization and built on the occidental model, official ceremonies in Black Africa have resisted the will for cultural liberation and policies for authenticity. As symbolic practices they reflect the major problem of the official society, for they contribute actively to the construction of the state. Their structural invariance and institutional universality, while explaining their nonautonomy in relation to the state, can also shed light on the latter's relative autonomy in Black Africa. 49 notes. J

273. Folami, Toni. AFRICA AFTER INDEPENDENCE. *Contemporary Rev. [Great Britain] 1975 227(1317): 198-200.* Surveys the political directions followed by African states since independence.

274. Gadau, Alhaji Abdulkadir Dafuwa. DECOLONIZATION AND RACIALISM IN AFRICA: THE PRESENT STAGE. *Pakistan Horizon [Pakistan] 1975 28(1): 3-8.* Discusses the European colonization of Africa, the development of African political consciousness, the growth of independence movements since 1956, and racism which emerged during decolonization.

275. Gerold-Scheepers, Thérèse J. THE POLITICAL CONSCIOUSNESS OF AFRICAN URBAN WORKERS: A REVIEW OF RECENT PUBLICATIONS. *African Perspectives [Netherlands] 1978 (2): 83-98.* Explores theories on the political consciousness of African urban workers. Beginning with literature on the labor aristocracy thesis, covers objections to the thesis, and discusses studies of political consciousness among urban workers, workers' organizations, and workers' action. R. V. Ritter

276. Gutkind, Peter C. W. CHANGE AND CONSCIOUSNESS IN URBAN AFRICA: AFRICAN WORKERS IN TRANSITION. *Cahiers d'Études Africaines [France] 1981 21(1-3): 289-346.* Describes the antagonisms, especially since 1950, between the workers of Africa's so-called rising nations and the owners of the means of production, who represent the vestiges of colonialism. Explores possibilities for a rising and better organized political consciousness among all strata of Africa's working class.

277. Hanne, William G. THEORIES OF POLITICAL POWER WITHIN AFRICA. *Military Rev. 1974 54(10): 52-57.* Identifies four theories of political power in Africa, based respectively on African personality, Negritude, Pan-Africanism, and African unity.

278. Hastings, Adrian. CHURCH-STATE RELATIONS IN BLACK AFRICA, 1959-1966. *Kyrkohistorisk Årsskrift [Sweden] 1978 78: 402-407.* Despite the tension between Christianity and the independence movements, the relationship between church and state in black African nations has been benign, in part because political leaders have needed the churches' technological and educational expertise and desired to gain the allegiance of their followers.

279. Henriksen, Thomas E. END OF AN EMPIRE: PORTUGAL'S COLLAPSE IN AFRICA. *Current Hist. 1975 68(405): 211-215.* Can the revolutionary leadership of Portugal's former colonies escape the inefficiency, corruption and elitism of the colonial rulers and the governments of some of the former French and British territories? Will the new governments succeed in hammering out an authentic national culture? J

280. Howard, Rhoda. THE DILEMMA OF HUMAN RIGHTS IN SUB-SAHARAN AFRICA. *Int. J. [Canada] 1980 35(4): 724-747.* Addresses the issue of human rights in the Third World by examining English-speaking African countries in a historical and comparative context since 1948. English-speaking African countries have a common colonial heritage, sharing an official language and institutional structure. They resemble Western democracies, yet are not able to attain the degree of civil and political liberty to which they ostensibly aspire, because of social, economic, and historical impediments. Secondary sources; 47 notes. J. Powell

281. Huff, David L. and Lutz, James M. THE CONTAGION OF POLITICAL UNREST IN INDEPENDENT BLACK AFRICA. *Econ. Geography 1974 50(4): 352-367.*

282. Hussain, Arif. THE EDUCATED ELITE: COLLABORATORS, ASSAILANTS, NATIONALISTS: A NOTE ON AFRICAN NATIONALISTS AND NATIONALISM. *J. of the Hist. Soc. of Nigeria [Nigeria] 1974 7(3): 485-497.* Illustrates the problems imposed upon the study of African nationalism, 1945-74, by the use of subjective definitions, and attempts to formulate a clearer understanding and series of definitions of African nationalism.

283. Iordanski, V. TROPICHESKAIA AFRIKA: KONFLIKT ARKHAIKI I "MODERNIZMA" [Tropical Africa and its conflict between the archaic and the modern]. *Mirovaia Ekonomika i Mezhdunarodnye Otnosheniia [USSR] 1982 (4): 107-115.* Examines the revival of sorcery and paganism as a quest for participation in political life in tropical Africa, 1980-81.

284. Jacomy-Millette, Annemarie. IS THE INSTITUTION OF THE OMBUDSMAN APPLICABLE TO AFRICA? LEGISLATION AND FIRST RESULTS. *Can. J. of African Studies [Canada] 1974 8(1): 145-153.* Although the office of ombudsman in Tanzania, Ghana, Sudan, and Mauritius has been an adjunct of the executive power rather than the legislature since the 1960's, a new institution is emerging which will provide protection of individuals' civil rights.

285. Janke, Peter. INTELLECTUAL OBSOLESCENCE: THE SURVIVAL OF MARXIST STATECRAFT IN AFRICA. *Contemporary Rev. [Great Britain] 1978 233(1351): 57-65.* Discusses the role of Marxism-Leninism in African politics since 1960.

286. Jewsiewicki, Bogumil. L'EXPERIENCE D'UN ETAT-PROVIDENCE EN AFRIQUE NOIRE [The experiment of one welfare state in black Africa]. *Hist. Reflections [Canada] 1976 3(2): 79-103.* Totalitarianism is not an exclusively European phenomenon. Among former colonial states in Africa, European powers created the totalitarian framework, and these new states kept their structure and ethos after independence. There is no two-party political system in these states, but, rather, one party which consists of the rising middle class whose ties are interwoven with the new military and civil servant castes. Colonial rule, therefore, fastened distortions on political life in Africa that have yet to be overcome. P. Travis

287. Jinadu, L. Adele. SOME COMMENTS ON FRANTZ FANON AND THE HISTORIOGRAPHY OF AFRICAN POLITICS. *J. of Developing Areas 1973 7(2): 287-298.*

288. Johns, Sheridan and Riley, Richard. LOCAL AND DISTRICT COUNCILS—SHOULD THEY BE FORGOTTEN? *J. of Modern African Studies [Great Britain] 1975 13(2): 309-332.* A study of the varied ways in which self-rule in developing African nations has affected the subnational councils in policymaking and governmental administration. Especially in some military governments, local councils as well as parties have lost significance. However, "even if local and district councils are not of primary importance in Commonwealth Africa today, they will continue to be significant institutions and should not be neglected in research." The increasing attention to the dynamics of political change may bring new attention to all institutions and phenomena at the local level. 62 notes. R. V. Ritter

289. Kasfir, Nelson. DEPARTICIPATION AND POLITICAL DEVELOPMENT IN BLACK AFRICA. *Studies in Comparative Int. Development 1974 9(3): 3-25.* Examines departicipation, the process of curtailing mass political involvement, and characterizes it as a striking feature of postindependence black Africa. The problems of measuring departicipation are discussed as are the characteristics, patterns, and desirability of this tendency. Primary and secondary sources; 12 notes, biblio. S. A. Farmerie

290. Kobishchanov, Iu. RELIGII I ETNICHESKIE PROBLEMY V AFRIKE [Religion and ethnic problems in Africa]. *Aziia i Afrika Segodnia [USSR] 1981 (3): 55-56, 59.* Examines the multireligious structure of Africa and its influence on political life and relationships between ethnic groups.

291. Kofele-Kale, Ndiva. THE POLICY OF NONALIGNMENT IN AN AGE OF ALIGNMENT POLITICS: AFRICA TWENTY YEARS AFTER BANDUNG. *Civilisations [Belgium] 1978 28(3-4): 251-266.* Examines the policy of nonalignment of African states, 1955-76, and the difficulty in maintaining it when dealing with the Great Powers.

292. Krasuski, Jerzy. STRUKTURA POLITYCZNA WSPÓLNOTY FRANCUSKIEJ 1958-1970 [The political structure of the French Community, 1958-70]. *Przegląd Zachodni [Poland] 1980 36(2): 32-59.* French colonies in Africa obtained their independence against the wishes of De Gaulle. In the plebiscite of 1958 the colonial peoples overwhelmingly supported the constitution creating the French Community, which resulted in a measure of independence resembling home rule for the colonies. Guinea seceded immediately, and as the constitution balkan-

ized Africa, tendencies to unify territories arose. Demands for independence increased and were met first for Madagascar, followed by Mali. In two years a complex structure developed: 1) France with overseas dependencies; 2) overseas French-administered territories; 3) independent member-states of the French Community; 4) independent states tied by treaties to the Commonwealth; and 5) the joint British-French Condominium of New Hebrides. In later years African states entered into groupings: pro-Western, anti-Western, and into the Organization of African Unity. By and large former French colonies retain a pro-French attitude. M. Krzyzaniak

293. Laidi, Zaki. CONTRADICTIONS AFRICAINES ET SYSTÈME INTERNATIONAL [African contradictions and the international system]. *Défense Natl. [France] 1980 36(2): 85-98.* Analyzes the internal contradictions of African states since 1960 as they try to adjust to the logic of the modern state and how foreign interventions have given those contradictions an international dimension.

294. Lawler, James. CONFLICT-AVOIDANCE IN AFRICA. *Peace Res. Rev. [Canada] 1976 7(1): 1-163.* Gives an overview of problems of managing discontent and identity and examines the limits of conflict avoidance across the whole of sub-Saharan Africa since independence.

295. Lebedeva, E. TROPICHESKAIA AFRIKA: KRIZIS SOTSIAL'NO-POLITICHESKICH STRUKTUR [Tropical Africa and crisis of sociopolitical structures]. *Aziia i Afrika Segodnia [USSR] 1981 (10): 21-24.* Analyzes the social and political systems of capitalist countries in Africa, 1970-80.

296. Lemarchand, René. AFRICAN POWER THROUGH THE LOOKING-GLASS. *J. of Modern African Studies [Great Britain] 1973 11(2): 305-314.* A highly critical review of Jean Ziegler's *Le Pouvoir africain* (Paris, 1971). The book is condemned for inaccuracy, shoddy research, false assumptions, stereotyping, and doing more harm than good to African studies. 14 notes. H. G. Soff

297. LeVine, Victor T. AFRICAN PATRIMONIAL REGIMES IN COMPARATIVE PERSPECTIVE. *J. of Modern African Studies [Great Britain] 1980 18(4): 657-673.* An analysis of the features and types of personalist governments in modern Africa. Most African rulers in recent years have headed highly traditionalist neopatrimonial regimes or, more commonly, modern patrimonial governments, which nonetheless incorporate, in varying degrees, political and cultural symbols and forms evident in Africa's precolonial past. African patrimonial regimes suffer from instability, as the rulers exceed the limits prescribed by traditional political mores and face deadly competition from political arrivals. Based on secondary accounts and analyses of recent African governments; 29 notes. L. W. Truschel

298. LeVine, Victor T. LEADERSHIP TRANSITION IN BLACK AFRICA: ELITE GENERATIONS AND POLITICAL SUCCESSION. *Munger Africana Lib. Notes 1975 30: 1-67.*

299. Lonsdale, John. STATES AND SOCIAL PROCESSES IN AFRICA: A HISTORIOGRAPHICAL SURVEY. *African Studies Rev. 1981 24(2-3): 139-225.* A review of the literature concerning the growth of African states and of the role played by those states in the major processes of change, prepared for the American Council of Learned Societies and the Social Science Research Council. 14 notes, biblio. R. T. Brown

300. Maguire, Kevin. AFRICAN ELITES. *Rocky Mountain Social Sci. J. 1973 10(2): 141-146.* Reviews six works on modern African political and social organization and development. S

301. Mair, Lucy. STRENGTHS & WEAKNESSES. *Encounter [Great Britain] 1977 48(1): 69-74.* Discusses political conditions and military events in Africa, since 1961, emphasizing their depiction in a variety of primary and secondary books.

302. Manchkha, P. I. KOMMUNISTY, REVOLIUTSIONNYE DEMOKRATY I NEKAPITALISTICHESKII PUT' RAZVITIIA V STRANAKH AFRIKI [Communists, revolutionary democrats and the noncapitalist path of development in countries of Africa]. *Voprosy Istorii KPSS [USSR] 1975 (10): 57-69.* An analysis of postcolonial black Africa. By their political, economic, cultural, and social policies, revolutionary democratic parties in Africa now represent the bulk of the population, striving toward a noncapitalist development. Despite difficulties created by repression and socioeconomic backwardness, Communist parties do exist in Africa as the vanguard of anti-imperialist and anticapitalist efforts. Communists must deal with anticommunism in the guise of theories of "special African socialism" or "specific black psychology." Based on published primary sources and V. I. Lenin's *Collected Works;* 15 notes. L. E. Holmes

303. Marenin, Otwin. REVIEW ESSAY: CLASS ANALYSIS IN AFRICAN STUDIES. *J. of African Studies 1976 3(1): 133-138.* An analysis of the views of Michael Lofchie as expressed in: "The Political Origins of the Uganda Coup" in the *Journal of African Studies* (see abstract 3257), and "Class Action by the Military," in the *Journal of Modern African Studies.* Lofchie is arguing for the importance of the term, "class," as being crucial to understanding the Uganda coup. Even though the term is descriptively imprecise he considers it productive of more meaningful analysis. This, however, only reflects the limitations of the present means of explanation of phenomena with a pluralistic base and for which Marxist economic determinism is inadequate. 7 notes. R. V. Ritter

304. Martin, Denis. LE STICK ET LE DERRICK [The stick and the derrick]. *Rev. Française de Sci. Politique [France] 1975 25(6): 1062-1076.* It may seem at first as though no political régimes in contemporary Black Africa are "democratic" in the sense meant by western political science. It could be deduced from this that the "development" stage is almost automatically accompanied by an authoritarian situation. It is important in the first place to consider the meaning of the notion of "authority" in Africa; but it is essential to look at the circumstances surrounding this supposed "development." The result of Africa's integration in the capitalist world market is to build up a network of contradictions around the development of the productive forces. Under these circumstances, authoritarianism can appear to be a way of limiting, or even hiding, the effects of this. J

305. Martyshin, O. O NEKOTORYKH IDEINYKH TECHENIIAKH V SOVREMENNOI AFRIKE [Ideological trends in modern Africa]. *Aziia i Afrika Segodnia [USSR] 1978 (4): 23-25.* Detailed study of the main trends of non-Marxist sociopolitical thought in relation to Africa. The author singles out three main trends: the ideology of national democracy, national-bourgeois reformism, and petty-bourgeois utopian socialism. In the 1970's national democracy and scientific socialism are drawing closer together. The growing revolutionary movement in Africa and in the whole world is a guarantee of the triumph of the truly socialist tendencies. J

306. Mazrui, Ali A. CHRISTIAN POWER AND MUSLIM CHALLENGE IN AFRICA'S EXPERIENCE. *Indian J. of Pol. [India] 1978 12(3): 129-145.* Discusses the conflicting claims of Christianity and Islam in Africa, emphasized in the contemporary period by the rise in oil power and the emergence of Arab leadership in the developing nations. The political resurrection of Islam was heralded by the growing importance of the OPEC countries during the 1970's. Christianity, which spread under European hegemony in Africa, has suffered from the decline of imperialism. J/S

307. Mazrui, Ali A. MARXIST THEORIES, SOCIALIST POLICIES, AND AFRICAN REALITIES. *Problems of Communism 1980 29(5): 44-53.* A review article on eight studies of problems related to the application of Marxism to Africa. There are important social and economic conditions that make Africa inhospitable for Marxism. 9 notes. J. M. Lauber

308. Mazrui, Ali A. NATIONALISTS AND STATESMEN: FROM NKRUMAH AND DE GAULLE TO NYERERE AND KISSINGER. *J. of African Studies 1979-80 6(4): 199-205.* A comparative typological analysis of four modern leaders. Distinguishes nationalists from statesmen and identifies Charles de Gaulle and Kwame Nkrumah as nationalists and Henry A. Kissinger as a statesman, while fitting Julius Nyerere into both categories. While both Nkrumah and Nyerere are ranked highly as assertive Pan-Africanist leaders, neither succeeded in achieving economic or political integration of their respective regions in West or East Africa or in uniting Africa as a whole. L. W. Truschel

309. McCain, James A. IDEOLOGY IN AFRICA: SOME PERCEPTUAL TYPES. *African Studies Rev. 1975 18(1): 61-87.* African socialism has been the predominant ideology of Africa, 1960-70's, and Julius Nyerere of Tanzania the ideal type of African socialist leader.

310. Mel'nikov, E. POLITICHESKIE PREOBRAZOVANIIA V AFRIKANSKIKH STRANAKH SOTSIALISTICHESKOI ORIENTATSII [Political changes in African countries of socialist orientation]. *Mirovaia Ekonomika i Mezhdunarodnye Otnosheniia [USSR] 1981 (12): 121-126.* Examines recent changes in political and governmental institutions of African socialist-oriented countries.

311. Mittelman, James H. POLEMICS AND AFRICAN STUDIES. *Issue 1974 4(1): 2-5.* Two recent conferences in Africa demonstrated that intellectual and academic freedom have ceased to take precedence over values such as national liberation and self-determination. S

312. Neuberger, Benyamin. HAS THE SINGLE-PARTY STATE FAILED IN AFRICA? *African Studies Rev. 1974 17(1): 173-179.* Minimum stability, economic competency, and unity of the population have been achieved by the one-party state systems in Africa, 1960-67.

313. Neuberger, Benyamin. STATE AND NATION IN AFRICAN THOUGHT. *J. of African Studies 1977 4(2): 198-205.* Surveys the major historic schools of thought on the connection of state and nation. Concludes that African problems of building nations closely resemble the "classical" circumstances of 19th-century Europe. With the exceptions of Nigeria and Somalia, Africa's leaders currently face the essential task of building unified nations on the basis of artificially devised states. Based on secondary works and published interviews; 24 notes. L. W. Truschel

314. Neuberger, Benyamin. THE WESTERN NATION-STATE IN AFRICAN PERCEPTIONS OF NATION-BUILDING. *Asian and African Studies [Israel] 1976 11(2): 241-261.* Advocates comparative analysis of African nationalism with that of Western Europe. Africa's solutions to national questions depended on balancing acceptance with rejection of Western models, precedents, associations, connotations, and analogies. The African experience combined intercontinental learning with the specific needs of nationalism. Secondary sources; 99 notes. J. M. Sanderson

315. Nkemdirim, Bernard A. THE FORMATION OF NATIONAL STATES AND COLLECTIVE VIOLENCE IN AFRICA. *Africa Q. [India] 1977 17(2): 65-77.* Surveys the violence accompanying and following the independence of African states, especially the Congo, Zanzibar, Nigeria, and Benin, which is seen as an inevitable and even beneficial stage in the emergence of new nations.

316. Nkemdirim, Bernard A. REFLECTIONS ON POLITICAL CONFLICT, REBELLION, AND REVOLUTION IN AFRICA. *J. of Modern African Studies [Great Britain] 1977 15(1): 75-90.* In the past decades Africa has been beset with numerous rebellions, wars, and other forms of violent political action. The author reviews new conclusions and analyses, intended to help students better understand social change and political conflict in Africa. 2 tables, 37 notes. H. G. Soff

317. Nnoli, O. SOCIO-ECONOMIC INSECURITY AND ETHNIC POLITICS IN AFRICA. *African Rev. [Tanzania] 1974 4(1): 1-23.* The term ethnic is used in order to avoid the phrase tribalism. There has been an increase in hostilities between ethnic groups in Africa 1950-73, as witnessed in Nigeria, Kenya, Uganda, Sudan, and Zaire. Such unrest is caused by the socioeconomic insecurity of the individual and can only be eliminated by the creation of an egalitarian and democratic society. 102 notes. H. G. Soff

318. Nwosu, Humphrey N. STRATEGIES OF STATE BUILDING: AFRICAN EXPERIENCE RECONSIDERED. *Civilisations [Belgium] 1978 28(1-2): 31-50.* Discusses two strategies—revolutionary and progressive—in the problems of building government institutions and leadership in Africa.

319. Ola, Opeyemi. THE ECONOMIC FOUNDATIONS OF THE CRISIS OF PARLIAMENTARY DEMOCRACY IN AFRICA. *African Studies R. 1973 16(2): 233-254.* Deteriorating economies and the impact of economic deprivation on significant groups causes parliamentary democracy to fail in Africa. S

320. Park, Sang-Seek. POLITICAL SYSTEMS IN BLACK AFRICA: TOWARD A NEW TYPOLOGY. *J. of African Studies 1977 4(3): 296-318.* Existing typologies of political systems in Black African states have proven inadequate to describe the essence of internal political conditions in these countries. Political scientists have overemphasized relations between political parties and governments in Black Africa. The author offers new typologies that stress relations of governments to bureaucracies, party elites, and military establishments. Secondary sources; 3 tables, 40 notes. L. W. Truschel

321. Pastore, Paola. L'EVOLUZIONE DEL SOCIALISMO AFRICANO: AL DI LÀ DEL MITO [The evolution of African socialism: beyond the myth]. *Affari Esteri [Italy] 1974 6(23): 110-119.* African socialism remains in a state of flux, is highly diverse, and is opposed by strong traditions of nationalism which have emerged in the postcolonial era. 7 notes. A. R. Stoesen

322. Patrzałek, Aleksander. ZAGADNIENIE INSTYTUCJONALIZACJI PARTII POLITCYZNYCH W CZARNEJ AFRYCE [The question of institutionalization of political parties in black Africa]. *Państwo i Prawo [Poland] 1974 29(4): 56-68.* Examines the development of the institutionalization of political parties, 1958-74, which is linked with constitutionalism, the African presidential system, the legalization of one-party systems, and the identification of the state with a single party.

323. Rogge, John R. AFRICA'S RESETTLEMENT STRATEGIES. *Int. Migration Rev. 1981 15(1-2): 195-212.* Examines the options for African asylum states in their attempts to support large refugee communities.

324. Ross, Marc Howard. COMMUNITY FORMATION IN AN URBAN SQUATTER SETTLEMENT. *Comparative Pol. Studies 1974 6(3): 296-328.* Explores the political integration of African squatter settlements, small communities populated by rural outcasts and urban misfits. S

325. Rubin, Neville. AFRICA AND REFUGEES. *African Affairs [Great Britain] 1974 73(292): 290-311.* Traces the problem of defining and placing refugees since 1951. In 1964 the OAU began to deal specifically with refugees in Africa. There are over a million refugees in Africa with the majority originating in Angola and residing in Zaire. Discusses asylum, movement, education, settlement, and employment of refugees. 3 tables, 40 notes. H. G. Soff

326. Saul, John S. LIBERATION AND THE SOCIAL STRUCTURE: PORTUGUESE AFRICA: LIBERATION MOVEMENTS PROVIDE STRUCTURE FOR EMERGING STATES. *Int. Perspectives [Canada] 1974 (6): 34-38.* Events in Portuguese Africa from 1956 to the present have shown that only in resorting to violence have Africans in that region been able to win independence and begin social revolutions.

327. Schaffer, Bernard. ADMINISTRATIVE LEGACIES AND LINKS IN THE POST-COLONIAL STATE: PREPARATION, TRAINING AND ADMINISTRATIVE REFORM. *Development and Change [Netherlands] 1978 9(2): 175-200.* Discusses the postindependence continuation in Anglophonic Africa of links with Western administrative practices which have blocked reform.

328. Small, N. J. CITIZENSHIP, IMPERIALISM, AND INDEPENDENCE: BRITISH COLONIAL IDEALS AND INDEPENDENT AFRICAN STATES. *Civilisations [Belgium] 1977 27(3-4): 289-312.* Continued from a previous article. Discusses efforts by Kwame Nkrumah in Ghana in 1951-66 and by Julius Nyerere in Tanzania in the 1960's to overcome the gap between the interpretation of official doctrine and the daily experience of citizens by forging a common national consciousness.

329. Sylla, Lanciné; Goldhammer, Arthur, transl. SUCCESSION OF THE CHARISMATIC LEADER: THE GORDIAN KNOT OF AFRICAN POLITICS. *Daedalus 1982 111(2): 11-28.* Examines political authority in African states in the light of Max Weber's analysis of

charismatic leadership, with special attention to the problems encountered in finding a successor for a charismatic leader.

330. Terray, Emmanuel. TECHNOLOGIE, ÉTAT ET TRADITION EN AFRIQUE [Technology, state, and tradition in Africa]. *Ann.: Économies, Sociétés, Civilisations [France] 1973 28(5): 1331-1338.* Critical analysis of Jack Goody, *Technology, Tradition, and the State in Africa* (Oxford U. Press, 1971). Despite some shortcomings, it is a significant and valuable book, both for its methodology and for its conclusions. 6 notes. R. Howell

331. Thomas, Dani B. POLITICAL DEVELOPMENT THEORY AND AFRICA: TOWARD A CONCEPTUAL CLARIFICATION AND COMPARATIVE ANALYSIS. *J. of Developing Areas 1974 8(3): 375-390.*

332. Tordoff, William. RESIDUAL LEGISLATURES: THE CASES OF TANZANIA AND ZAMBIA. *J. of Commonwealth and Comparative Pol. [Great Britain] 1977 15(3): 235-249.* Examines the declining role of parliament in the one-party governments introduced in Tanzania in 1965 and Zambia in 1973, by considering the electoral system, the background of elected ministers, and parliament's critical role in both states. The Zambian parliament remains critical of government policy, while the Tanzanian parliament has come to agree with ruling party policy. This difference is explained by the greater heterogeneity of Zambian politics and the influence of ministers elected in 1973. The reason for maintaining parliament, and not rule by presidential decree or by amalgamating parliamentary and party structures, is the legitimacy it lends to the government. 53 notes. S. G. Jackson

333. Toscano, Lorenzo M. AFRICA NERA OGGI [Black Africa today]. *Affari Esteri [Italy] 1973 5(18): 122-132.* Examines changes in black Africa since 1960. The new nations of Africa are experiencing the same growing pains that most Western nations have known in the past. The African future as one of diversification rather than unity.
A. R. Stoesen

334. Tunteng, P. Kiven. GEORGE PADMORE'S IMPACT ON AFRICA: A CRITICAL APPRAISAL. *Phylon 1974 35(1): 33-44.* To George Padmore "the necessity of a global overthrow of capitalism seemed no less important than the goal of black emancipation itself." The author discusses his relation with Kwame Nkrumah, who had been his student in London, and who appointed Padmore his adviser on African affairs when he became prime minister in Ghana. It was Padmore who assumed the major burden of organizing the 1958 Accra conferences. Both Nkrumah and Padmore were the targets of disparaging attacks since "they misjudged the extent to which Africans were ready to undertake collective work for the purpose of continental development." 40 notes. E. P. Stickney

335. Tunteng, P. Kiven. TOWARD A THEORY OF ONE-PARTY GOVERNMENT IN AFRICA. *Cahiers d'Études Africaines [France] 1973 13(4): 649-663.* Official claims about the democratic nature of one-party governments in Africa have not been substantiated by the actual operation of such regimes. African uniparties are really political machines; whereas the object of political parties is to mobilize public opinion in support of definite programs, the political machine seeks only to win and retain power at any cost. One-party government in Africa could only be democratic if it had a knowledgeable and committed leadership, allowed for leadership mobility, allowed for meaningful contact between the leaders and the masses, and maintained a sense of proportion in avoiding cults of personality. 36 notes.
J. C. Billigmeier

336. Turner, Thomas and Weinstein, Warren. INTRODUCTION TO PEASANTS REBELLION AND ETHNIC CONFLICT IN AFRICA. *Pan-African J. [Kenya] 1974 7(3): 185-192.* Introduction to a special issue on peasant rebellion. Peasants live on the fringe of society, and are not always a cultural part of the whole. The author discusses peasants and rebellions in Burundi, Zaire, and Ethiopia. The leadership variable is critical in rebellions. 21 notes. H. G. Soff

337. Twumasi, Patrick. ETHNIC POLITICS IN AFRICA: A REVIEW ARTICLE. *J. of Asian and African Studies [Netherlands] 1979 14(3-4): 292-296.* A review of Crawford Young's *The Politics of Cultural Pluralism* (1976), Ugbana Ukpu's *Ethnic Minority Problems in Nigerian Politics* (1977), Nelson Kasfir's *The Shrinking Political Arena* (1976), and Enid Schildkrout's *People of the Zogo: The Transformation of Ethnic Identities in Ghana* (1978). Each stresses the role of ethnic politics in modern Africa. R. T. Brown

338. Wasserman, Gary. THE POLITICS OF CONSENSUAL DECOLONIZATION. *African Rev. [Tanzania] 1975 5(1): 1-15.* A study of the processes involved in "agreed upon" decolonization which resulted in "the integration of an indigenous leadership into colonial political, social and economic patterns." 41 notes. R. T. Brown

339. Welch, Claude E., Jr. THE RIGHT OF ASSOCIATION IN GHANA AND TANZANIA. *J. of Modern African Studies [Great Britain] 1978 16(4): 639-656.* The right of association is considered a second order right to consolidate newly achieved independence, maintain national unity in multiracial regions, and lessen linguistic fragmentation and religious division. In Ghana and Tanzania the right of association was tolerated in the economic sphere but not in the political. In Ghana the right of association was restricted on ethnic grounds to prevent the Frante from playing a major role, while in Tanzania the restriction reflected the government's fears that economic inequalities between Africans and Asians would breed division. Based on government published documents and secondary sources; 41 notes.
A. Sbacchi

340. Wires, Richard. TURBULENT NORTHEAST AFRICA. *Indiana Social Studies Q. 1977 30(2): 44-55.* General discussion of political, economic, and social affairs in Ethiopia and Egypt, 1970's.

341. Wiseberg, Laurie S. HUMAN RIGHTS IN AFRICA: TOWARD THE DEFINITION OF THE PROBLEM OF A DOUBLE STANDARD. *Issue 1976 6(4): 3-13.* Discusses patterns of racism and human rights violations in developing nations of Africa in the 1970's. Considers the hypocrisy of some African leaders, such as Uganda's Idi Amin, who accuse other nations of racism yet who are themselves guilty of it.

342. Woodward, Peter. ETHIOPIA AND THE SUDAN: THE INTER-STATE OUTCOME OF DOMESTIC CONFLICT. *Contemporary Rev. [Great Britain] 1977 230(1336): 231-234.* Discusses the 1977 war between Ethiopia and the Sudan in the context of national and international politics since 1945.

343. Woronoff, Jon. REFUGEES: THE MILLION-PERSON PROBLEM. *Africa Report 1973 18(1): 29-33.* Decolonization throughout Africa has caused the migration of refugees. S

344. Zolberg, Aristide R. TRIBALISM THROUGH CORRECTIVE LENSES. *Foreign Affairs 1973 51(4): 728-739.* Discusses and criticizes the Western idea of the uniform savagery of Black African government and society. Reflecting the savage within the Westerners themselves, the idea forms the basis for many Western assumptions about the contemporary political scene in Black Africa, seemingly confirmed by the troubles of the 1960's. "Tribalism" is the most important Western concept with respect to Africa; through it, some believe they can explain the seeming African proclivity toward violence. The author questions whether Westerners, who have such expertise at impersonal violence, are in a position to criticize. Moreover, he notes that some ethnic arrangements are of quite recent origin, deriving from the impact of colonization, and black rulers of today face more severe problems than their colonial predecessors, both because of the greater degree of democracy and the higher expectations of both rulers and ruled. While African leaders may not have all the answers, their knowledge and skill may provide answers to the problems their people face. 2 notes. J. A. Kicklighter

345. —. [AFRICA AFTER INDEPENDENCE]. *Esprit [France] 1980 (2): 13-27.*

Chaliand, Gérard. L'AFRIQUE SANS RÉVOLUTION [Africa without revolution], *pp. 13-23.* Examines the political conditions of Africa south of the Sahara since independence, finding that there has been little movement to revolution primarily because government leaders have favored the former parent states.

Bureau, Jacques. IRRÉDUCTIBILITÉ AFRICAINE [African irreducibility], *pp. 24-27.* Chaliand's analysis is too pessimistic and does not give enough consideration to Africa's diversity.

The New African Military

346. Adekson, J. 'Bayo. THE BRAWN VERSUS BRAIN CONFLICT IN CONTEMPORARY AFRICAN CIVIL-MILITARY HISTORY AND THOUGHT. *Plural Soc. [Netherlands] 1979 10(3-4): 3-20.* A comparative study of military education during the 1960's in Sir Abubakar Balewa's Nigeria, Kwame Nkrumah's Ghana, and Milton Obote's Uganda, focusing on the traditional conflict between book-learning and soldierly qualities and the consequences for civil-military relations.

347. Adekson, J. 'Bayo. ETHNICITY AND ARMY RECRUITMENT IN COLONIAL PLURAL SOCIETIES. *Ethnic and Racial Studies [Great Britain] 1979 2(2): 151-165.* Discusses the organization and control of the colonial military in sub-Saharan African states according to the ideas of Frederick Lugard and practiced by the British, French, and Belgian governments. Table, 57 notes.

348. Adekson, J. 'Bayo. PAY, PROMOTION, AND OTHER SELF-INTERESTS OF MILITARY INTERVENTION IN POLITICS. *Military Affairs 1981 45(1): 18-22.* Investigates the major self-interests, motivations, and internal organizational issues orienting soldiers of selected sub-Saharan African countries to political action, 1966-76, and analyzes the personal, economic, bureaucratic, technical, and institutional influences on the armies. Many armies showed signs of restlessness and even outright opposition in relation to the progress, development, or modernization of their societies, if they meant demands which included a cutback in the size of the military or a reduction of pay, privilege, procurement, and power. 23 notes. A. M. Osur

349. Auma-Osolo, Agola. OBJECTIVE AFRICAN MILITARY CONTROL: A NEW PARADIGM IN CIVIL-MILITARY RELATIONS. *J. of Peace Res. [Norway] 1980 17(1): 29-46.* Examines military intervention in African governments. Focusing on Nigeria, the author determines that military coups d'etat have occurred despite professionalization of the army and large socioeconomic benefits for military service. Traditional African warriorism and the desire to defend society against corruption have caused African armed forces to impose military governments. 11 tables, fig., 24 notes, biblio. S

350. Baynham, S. J. THE MILITARY IN BLACK AFRICAN POLITICS. *Army Q. and Defence J. [Great Britain] 1975 105(3): 304-312.* Discusses why the military has gained increasing control over domestic politics in several African nations since the 1960's.

351. Bienen, Henry. AFRICAN MILITARIES AS FOREIGN POLICY ACTORS. *Int. Security 1980 5(2): 168-186.* Examines the diversity of African military regimes and their formulation and conduct of foreign policy.

352. Charlton, Roger. PLUS ÇA CHANGE... ? A REVIEW OF TWO DECADES OF THEORETICAL ANALYSES OF AFRICAN COUPS D'ETAT. *Cultures et Développement [Belgium] 1981 13(1-2): 27-62.* Reviews the literature of military studies and political science on African coups d'état since 1960. The explanation for the frequent failure of the military governments ushered in by coup is commonly inadequate in both kinds of writing.

353. Churchill, Ward. U.S. MERCENARIES IN AFRICA: THE RECRUITMENT NETWORK AND U.S. POLICY. *Africa Today 1980 27(2): 21-46.* US policy tacitly permits military recruitment of mercenary troops as the only means of supporting American interests in the Third World because American advisers and direct intervention are politically inexpedient. Describes the function of *Soldier of Fortune* as illustrative of the impunity with which mercenary recruitment occurs despite laws precluding such activities in the United States. Predicts increasingly blatant recruitment during the 1980's. Secondary sources and personal experience; 72 notes. G. O. Gagnon

354. Crocker, Chester A. MILITARY DEPENDENCE: THE COLONIAL LEGACY IN AFRICA. *J. of Modern African Studies [Great Britain] 1974 12(2): 265-286.* Africa's military forces have not been seriously studied because colonial forces were basically police, without involvement in international affairs; independence was generally nonviolent; most African military forces have insignificant power and capability. Discusses military decolonization and compares Anglophone and Francophone Africa. 47 notes. H. G. Soff

355. Decale, Samuel. MILITARY COUPS AND MILITARY REGIMES IN AFRICA. *J. of Modern African Studies [Great Britain] 1973 11(1): 105-127.* A review article on recent studies of military coups and military regimes in modern Africa. Most works discussed are not considered adequate. Emphasis has been on the prerequisites for military intervention and the military as rulers. Sierra Leone, Central African Republic, Uganda, Algeria, Dahomey, and Ghana are the states most often discussed. 68 notes. H. G. Soff

356. Decale, Samuel. PRAETORIANISM, CORPORATE GRIEVANCES AND IDIOSYNCRATIC FACTORS IN MILITARY HIERARCHIES. *J. of African Studies 1975 2(2): 247-274.* A comparative study of military governments in Africa, shifting attention from a scholar's fixation on the systemic weaknesses of African states and the application of organization theory "to the internal dynamics of African military hierarchies, their officer cliques and the corporate and personalist ambitions therein." Claims a validation of the negative image of military elites in office. Personal motives for intervention have often been camouflaged, and once the new leaders are in power, they have not been able to resolve the socioeconomic and political issues they face. 58 notes. R. V. Ritter

357. Eleazu, Uma O. THE ROLE OF THE ARMY IN AFRICAN POLITICS: A RECONSIDERATION OF EXISTING THEORIES AND PRACTICES. *J. of Developing Areas 1973 7(2): 265-286.* Examines explanations of military intervention in African politics and discusses military aid. S

358. Francis, P. G. THE NEW AFRICAN OFFICER CORPS. *Army Q. and Defence J. [Great Britain] 1975 105(4): 433-439.* Discusses the differences between senior and junior African army officers in the 1970's.

359. Jackman, Robert W. THE PREDICTABILITY OF COUPS D'ÉTAT: A MODEL WITH AFRICAN DATA. *Am. Pol. Sci. Rev. 1978 72(4): 1262-1275.* A model of the structural determination of coups d'etat for the new states of black Africa in the years from 1960 through 1975. Results indicate that both social mobilization and the presence of a dominant ethnic group are destabilizing (these effects are additive); multipartyism is destabilizing while electoral turnout in the last election before independence is stabilizing; multipartyism is particularly destabilizing where a dominant ethnic group exists; the presence of such a group reduces (but does not eliminate) the stabilizing effect of turnout; and multipartyism has no pronounced effect on elite instability where turnout is high. Taken together, these patterns account for over four-fifths of the variance in coups d'etat in black Africa in the period. J

360. Lacina, Karel. ÚLOHA ARMÁDY V SOUDOBÉM AFRICKÉM POLITICKÉM ŽIVOTĚ [The role of the army in the political life of contemporary Africa]. *Československý Časopis Hist. [Czechoslovakia] 1978 26(6): 801-820.* Surveys and classifies the military coups d'etat in sub-Saharan Africa, 1963-77. Describes the chief types as conservative stabilization (Zaire, 1965), reactionary retreat (Ghana, 1966), and revolutionary democratic change (Ethiopia, 1974). New, socialist-oriented governments set up by progressive army officers accentuate Africa's polarization but also point the way to the future. 18 notes. R. E. Weltsch

361. Lemarchand, Rene. AFRICAN ARMIES IN HISTORICAL AND CONTEMPORARY PERSPECTIVES: THE SEARCH FOR CONNECTION. *J. of Pol. and Military Sociol. 1976 4(2): 261-275.* In their treatment of the military in Africa historians and political scientists proceed from different perspectives and make widely divergent assumptions about the relationships of the military to society. The author seeks to clarify a number of epistemological issues which stand in the way of a

more fruitful interdisciplinary dialogue. It focuses on problems of conceptualization and explanation, and goes on to explore the levels at which interdisciplinary research on the military is likely to generate the most promising theoretical breakthroughs. An attempt is made to identify those areas of research which lend themselves most readily to a sustained collaborative effort between historians and political scientists. J

362. Martin, Michel L. LES RÔLES EXTRA-MILITAIRES DES FORCES ARMÉES DANS LES SOCIÉTÉS AFRICAINES NON-INDUSTRIALISÉES [The extramilitary roles of armed forces in nonindustrial African societies]. *Afrique et l'Asie [France] 1974 (101): 21-34.* The conditions of the armies of the developing states of Africa and the lack of causes of war among them are conducive to civic action by these armies. In addition to alleviating unemployment, civic action has several objectives. These include basic and vocational education, political indoctrination, public works, and agricultural development. Such projects require considerable foreign technical aid. Civic action by the army is open to criticism as a form of forced labor and it may have adverse effects not only on the behavior of the military but also on the relation of the military to political authority. Biblio. J. S. Gassner

363. Mazrui, Ali A. PHALLIC SYMBOLS IN POLITICS AND WAR: AN AFRICAN PERSPECTIVE. *J. of African Studies 1974 1(1): 40-69.* A discussion of objects which represent both male sexual virility and military or political power. The bull, cock, sword, and spear are widespead examples, both in Africa and elsewhere. War dances often are sexual dances as well; military and sexual conquest are seen as one and the same. Christianity proved to be counter-phallic, as was Gandhianism. Both have played a large role in the politics of Africa, but both declined rapidly when military weaknesses were replaced by strength and virile male images could viably replace symbols of feminine weakness. 32 notes, 2 appendixes. V. L. Human

364. Mazrui, Ali A. THE RESURRECTION OF THE WARRIOR TRADITION IN AFRICAN POLITICAL CULTURE. *J. of Modern African Studies [Great Britain] 1975 13(1): 67-84.* A study of the warrior tradition as a cultural phenomenon in African society. The tradition goes back to before the intrusion of the white man in Africa and relates to basic tribal values. Manhood was linked to both sexual virility and valor in war. Ruthlessness and brutality became associated with manliness. Illustrations of the tradition and its relation to sex may be seen in the case of the precolonial Shaka of Zululand, the Mau-Mau, and the contemporary Ugandan Idi Amin Dada. In all these instances there is the "impulse to power in human affairs." 24 notes. R. V. Ritter

365. Mazrui, Ali A. SOLDIERS AS TRADITIONALIZERS: MILITARY RULE AND THE RE-AFRICANIZATION OF AFRICA. *World Pol. 1976 28(2): 246-272.* On the basis of evidence mainly from West Africa, many scholars in the 1960's made predictions about likely trends in Africa as a whole on such issues as one-party states. On the basis of data from Eastern Africa, can we now risk predictions about likely performance of military regimes in Africa as a whole? There is evidence from Eastern Africa that African soldiers may be agents of retraditionalization. The bulk of the army in most countries is recruited from some of the most rural and least acculturated sectors of society. Contemporary African soldiers may be traditionalists in charge of modern armies with modern technology. What happens when a modern organization is manned mainly by rural recruits? It may be that both modernization and retraditionalization are taking place under military leadership in Africa. The cultural revivalist role of sub-Westernized or non-Westernized African soldiers is beginning to manifest itself in places like Uganda under Idi Amin and Zaire under Mobutu Sese Seko. The political decline of Westernized intellectuals and the rise of soldiers may herald a partial re-Africanization of Africa, but with some painful costs. J

366. McKown, Roberta. DOMESTIC CORRELATES OF MILITARY INTERVENTION IN AFRICAN POLITICS. *J. of Pol. and Military Sociol. 1975 3(2): 191-206.* The military coup is examined because of its prevalence, its potential international implications, and the possible insights such an examination might provide for developing a comprehensive theoretical framework. The political process in most African states suggests that a focus on elite political behavior will prove more fruitful than viewing the coup d'état merely as a reaction to economic or other societal conditions. Three dimensions of elite political behavior were analyzed: the ability to govern effectively, intra-elite cohesion, and the position of the military vis-à-vis other coercive forces and the state. Event data collected for elite and "mass" instability and coercion in 14 countries provided strong evidence for the usefulness of examining elite cohesion per se. J

367. Ogueri, Eze, II. THEORIES AND MOTIVES OF MILITARY COUPS D'ETAT IN INDEPENDENT AFRICAN STATES. *Civilisations [Belgium] 1973-1974 23-24(3/4): 262-288.* Discusses reasons for coups d'etat in Africa: desire for change of government; violation of the constitution by civilian political elites; extravagance on the part of government; slowness in overcoming poverty; tribalism; foreign ideologies; capitalistic versus communistic economic systems; the contagion of coups; lust for power; power vacuum; unattractive conditions in military service; social stratification; and divine inspiration. There is hope for African political systems that will ultimately provide enduring peace and stability. 37 notes. H. L. Calkin

368. Patrzałek, Aleksander. RZADY WOJSKOWE A INSTYTUCJE PRAWNE I POLITYCZNE W CZARNEJ AFRYCE [Military governments, and the legal and political organizations in Black Africa]. *Państwo i Prawo [Poland] 1979 34(6): 36-47.* Analyzes the impact of coups d'etat on legal, political, and social institutions in Africa.

369. Pinkney, Robert. THE THEORY AND PRACTICE OF MILITARY GOVERNMENT. *Pol. Studies [Great Britain] 1973 21(2): 152-166.* Inadequacies and unwarranted generalizations and assumptions abound in many of the existing studies of military rule in tropical Africa. The author analyzes the conditions necessary for a military government to operate as compared to a civilian government. M. Harrison

370. Pirro, Ellen B. and Zeff, Eleanor E. A NEW LOOK AT MILITARY-CIVILIAN GOVERNMENTS. *J. of Strategic Studies [Great Britain] 1979 2(2): 206-227.* The development of analytic thinking about military and civilian regimes in Africa has moved through a phase of analysis of the political system and the nature of military governments, to a performance phase, examining how military and civilian governments differ in their governmental operations. Another method—policy analysis—focuses on the similarities and differences between the policies and goals articulated in each government. This method can detect differences among regimes and possibly predict future policy and performance trends. 14 tables, 2 fig., 2 notes, biblio. A. M. Osur

371. Potapov, V. I. NAEMNIKI: ORUDIE IMPERIALIZMA [Mercenaries: a weapon of imperialism]. *Voprosy Istorii [USSR] 1979 (2): 84-94.* The practice of recruiting mercenaries has been engendered by an antagonistic society and was often resorted to in ancient times, in the Middle Ages, and in the contemporary period. Already in those remote times attempts were made to condemn this vile practice as a phenomenon inimical to the cause of peace. The voice of protest against the recruitment of mercenaries was raised with particular intensity after World War II by the peoples of the colonial, dependent and developing countries, for it was used by imperialism as an instrument for suppressing the national liberation struggle. Citing examples from the contemporary history of Africa, the author convincingly shows that the practice of recruiting mercenaries is a crime and highlights the struggle waged by mankind's progressive forces for condemning the recruitment of mercenaries in international law and for its liquidation in practice. Secondary sources; 40 notes. J

372. Ravenhill, John. COMPARING REGIME PERFORMANCE IN AFRICA: THE LIMITATIONS OF CROSS-NATIONAL AGGREGATE ANALYSIS. *J. of Modern African Studies [Great Britain] 1980 18(1): 99-126.* Analyzes the difference in performances of Third World regimes, and the role played by the military and civilians. With scarce available data the hypothesis is that military governments have performed comparatively well. Based on government published documents and secondary sources; 6 tables, 52 notes. A. Sbacchi

373. Shabtai, Sabi H. ARMY AND ECONOMY IN TROPICAL AFRICA. *Econ. Development and Cultural Change 1975 23(4):*

687-701. Examines the contributions of the army to the economies of the Tropical African nations, with special reference to the Ivory Coast. Discusses the military's efficiency and technical orientation, the cost of military establishments in Africa, the technical capabilities of the military, and the transferability of military skills to nonmilitary employment. Secondary sources; table, 26 notes. J. W. Thacker, Jr.

374. Weinstein, Warren. MILITARY RULE IN AFRICA. *Africa Today 1973 20(4): 77-80.* Reviews five studies of military governments in Africa: Edward Feit's *The Armed Bureaucrats* (Houghton Mifflin, 1973); Robert Pinkney's *Ghana Under Military Rule* (London: Methuen and Co., 1972); Anton Bebler's *Military Rule in Africa: Dahomey, Ghana, Sierra Leone and Mali* (Praeger, 1973); *The Arms Trade with the Third World* (Humanities Press, 1971) published by the Stockholm International Peace Research Institute, and *Arms and African Development* (Praeger, 1972), edited by Frederick Arkhurst. G. O. Gagnon

375. Welch, Claude E. LES COUPS D'ETAT MILITAIRES EN AFRIQUE [Military coups d'etat in Africa]. *Afrique et l'Asie Modernes [France] 1975 3: 29-40.* Since independence, African armies have become deeply politicized and many coups have occurred; the unity of these armies is precarious and they have generally not brought stability to their countries.

376. Welch, Claude E. WARRIOR, REBEL, GUERRILLA, AND PUTSCHIST. *J. of Asian and African Studies [Netherlands] 1977 12(1-4): 82-98.* Analyzes the development of four types of political violence in Africa. Includes a list of military coups in Africa to 1975. Table, 35 notes. R. T. Brown

377. Welch, Claude E., Jr. CONTINUITY AND DISCONTINUITY IN AFRICAN MILITARY ORGANISATION. *J. of Modern African Studies [Great Britain] 1975 13(2): 229-248.* Precolonial African societies varied greatly in their forms of military organization. In some cases military training became an integrating force amidst an ethnically diverse society. The colonial intrusion broke the organic ties that existed between military and social organizations and introduced tensions between society and the military. African governments must revise the patterns of civil-military relations which they have inherited from colonial rule and find means of using the military as a means of national integration rather than allowing it to arrogate self-perpetuating power to itself. Civilian control through the dominant party system is most feasible. 45 notes. R. V. Ritter

378. Wells, Alan. THE COUP D'ETAT IN THEORY AND PRACTICE: INDEPENDENT BLACK AFRICA IN THE 1960S. *Am. J. of Sociol. 1974 79(4): 871-887.* "Attempts have been made to explain coups d'état by reference to macro social and economic variables, structural features of the military in general, and, more commonly, of military elites, or by reference to the individual psychological qualities of the coup participants. Such theories are often held to be mutually exclusive and competing. This paper examines these theories and then tests them against data for 35 independent countries in sub-Sahara Africa, a region for which it has been widely argued that only 'micro' explanations of coup activity are possible. Each country is first assigned a score on a coup activity scale which provides an interval measure of the dependent variable. Colonial background, contagion, and temporal hypotheses do not explain differences in coup activity. The data are then subjected to multiple-regression analysis using sets of socioeconomic and military variables. Although no single independent variable is conspicuously related to coups, multivariate analysis does explain some variance in coup activity. An explanation of coup activity that integrates the three levels usually employed by social scientists is suggested. This takes into account societal conditions conducive to coups, the relative dominance of military institutions, and, for residual variance, the personal characteristics of military officers and external influences on them." J

379. —. [CRITICISMS OF ALAN WELLS' ANALYSIS OF COUPS D'ETAT]. *Am. J. of Sociol. 1976 82(3): 674-685.*

Morrison, Donald George and Stevenson, Hugh Michael. THE PRACTICE AND EXPLANATION OF COUPS D'ETAT: MEASUREMENT OR ARTIFACT?, *pp. 674-683.* A critique of Alan Wells' earlier article on coups d'etat in independent Black Africa in the 1960's (see abstract 378). Given the public nature of the coup, it is not surprising that Wells' model is generally accurate. Nevertheless, it is certainly not wholly accurate. Wells fails to cite sources for certain data, and complains that data is lacking when it is not. Submission of his problem to regression analysis using such data as is available results in substantially modified conclusions. 6 tables, note, biblio.

Phillips, John and Ba-Yunus, Ilyas. COMMENT ON ALAN WELLS' "THE COUP D'ETAT IN THEORY AND PRACTICE: INDEPENDENT BLACK AFRICA IN THE 1960S," *pp. 684-685.* Wells' analysis is better than most, but statistical error prevents wholehearted acceptance of it, and results in findings less predictable than Wells suggests. Statistical error also permits the possibility of upward bias in the model analysis conclusions. Table, note. V. L. Human

4. INTERNATIONAL RELATIONS, AID, AND TRADE

General

380. Anise, Ladun. AFRICAN ATTITUDES TOWARD AMERICA. *Issue: A Q. J. of Opinion 1980 10(1-2): 3-8.* Biased and unrealistic American attitudes toward Africa have negatively influenced African feelings toward America.

381. Eze, Osita C. PROSPECT OF INTERNATIONAL PROTECTION OF HUMAN RIGHTS IN AFRICA. *African Rev. [Tanzania] 1974 4(1): 79-90.* Human dignity is not protected in Africa and until economic development is attained, governments will continue to place more emphasis on economy than on civil rights. Development of human rights is traced from the US Bill of Rights to the UN Declaration on Human Rights (1948), and to the African Lagos Conference (1961). Economic inequality is given as the cause for unequal enjoyment of human rights. 34 notes. H. G. Soff

382. Goldblatt, Murray. THE UN'S CONCERN FOR HUMAN RIGHTS AS MIRRORED IN RESOLUTIONS ON AFRICA. *Internat. Perspectives [Canada] 1973 (2): 31-33.* During its 27th session, the UN considered such problems as "territories under Portuguese administration, the status of Rhodesia under Ian Smith, the policies of the apartheid of the government of South Africa, and the future of Namibia." L. S. Frey

383. Gould, W. T. S. INTERNATIONAL MIGRATION IN TROPICAL AFRICA: A BIBLIOGRAPHICAL REVIEW. *Int. Migration Rev. 1974 8(3): 347-365.* Discusses political, economic, and labor aspects of international migration in tropical Africa in the 1960's and 70's, with a bibliography.

384. Gouraige, G. J. Eddy. THE UNITED NATIONS AND DECOLONIZATION. *Black Scholar 1974 5(7): 16-23.* Resolutions accepted by the UN 1946 to 1960 established the issue of decolonization as a top priority in UN affairs and gave the General Assembly tools with which to bring about the end of colonialism. But the UN can do more than it has to bring about the end of Portuguese colonialism in Africa. Primary and secondary sources; table, 15 notes. M. M. McCarthy

385. Greenfield, Richard. REFUGEES IN NORTH-EASTERN AFRICA: THE SITUATION IN 1979. *Round Table [Great Britain] 1980 (277): 39-52.* By far the largest number of refugees in the world, nearly 50%, are in the countries bordering Ethiopia. The author surveys the development of the problem in the 1970's, focusing on the often appalling conditions in Djibouti, the Sudan, Kenya, and Somalia.

386. Nyerere, Julius K. HUMANITY WILL NOT BE DENIED. *African R. [Tanzania] 1973 3(3): 341-346.* A speech by the President of Tanzania to the UN General Assembly on its 25th anniversary in 1970. Nyerere emphasized that a major role of the UN is to combat evil, and the greatest evil today is apartheid in South Africa and Portuguese colonialism. H. G. Soff

387. Osipov, Iu. EKONOMICHESKAIA SITUATSIIA V AFRIKE [The economic situation in Africa]. *Aziia i Afrika Segodnia [USSR] 1981 (10): 12-16.* Discusses the development of collective measures among young African states as an economic defense against imperialist economic domination.

388. Preiswerk, Roy. NEOKOLONIALISMUS ODER SELBSTKOLONIALISIERUNG? [Neo-colonialism of self-colonialization?]. *Europa Archiv [West Germany] 1973 28(24): 845-853.* The failure of the emancipating character of the policy of assimilation in the francophone countries in Africa since World War II proves that the export of European culture is only another form of colonialism.

389. Wallerstein, Immanuel. AFRICA IN A CAPITALIST WORLD. *Issue: A Q. J. of Opinion 1980 10(1-2): 21-31.* Examines the gradual integration of Africa into the capitalist world system from circa 1500 to the present.

Foreign Relations

390. Adamolebun, Ladipo. CO-OPERATION OR NEOCOLONIALISM: FRANCOPHONE AFRICA. *Africa Q. [India] 1978 18(1): 34-50.* Examines the relations between France and tropical Africa in the late 1950's and early 1960's, which began as a cooperative effort and later became neocolonialism.

391. Adebisi, Busari. NIGERIA'S RELATIONS WITH SOUTH AFRICA: 1960-1975. *Africa Q. [India] 1977 (3): 67-89.* Examines Nigeria's foreign relations with South Africa since Sharpeville, through civilian rule and two successive military governments, and finds Nigeria's anti-apartheid stance hampered until recently by economic ties.

392. Albright, David E. SOVIET POLICY. *Problems of Communism 1978 27(1): 20-39.* Discusses the priorities, general approach, objectives, and operating style that have shaped Soviet policy toward Africa in recent years. The author feels that there has been a basic continuity in Moscow's broad outlook and approach, and that the escalation of Soviet activities on the continent since 1975 reflects an increase in opportunities rather than a change in approach. 86 notes. J. M. Lauber

393. Avriel, Ehud. SOME MINUTE CIRCUMSTANCES. *Jerusalem Q. [Israel] 1980 (14): 28-40.* Israel's first ambassador to Ghana, Ehud Avriel, recollects his relationship with Kwame Nkrumah and later with President William Tubman of Liberia and discusses the difficulties inherent in Israel's relations with African states.

394. Baatz, Wolfgang. ZUR MILITÄRISCHEN INFILTRATION DES BRD-IMPERIALISMUS IN AFRIKA [On the military infiltration in Africa by West Germany]. *Militärgeschichte [East Germany] 1980 19(4): 402-413.* Within the NATO framework, West Germany sought by diverse means to strengthen its influence in Africa. Describes particularly military and military-economic aspects of neocolonialist policy, whose components are military support of the remaining colonial regimes in southern Africa and military aid to new national states. 81 notes. J/T (H. D. Andrews)

395. Benaerts, Pierre. NOUVEAU PARTAGE OU GRAND AFFRONTEMENT EN AFRIQUE [A new division or great confrontation in Africa]. *Écrits de Paris [France] 1976 355: 38-49.* Surveys the political situation in Africa, emphasizing the determining role of the United States, the USSR, and China.

396. Ben-Shalom, Arye. APARTHEID'S ARAB FRIENDS. *Patterns of Prejudice [Great Britain] 1977 11(2): 17-19, 22.* Briefly examines the growing collaboration between Arabs and South Africa, the calculated political and economic interests of Arab states and the sources of friction.

397. Bermingham, Jack and Clausen, Edwin G. REVOLUTION AND FOREIGN POLICY: SINO-AFRICAN RELATIONS 1949-1976. *Munger African Lib. Notes 1981 (59-60): 9-40.* Examines the economic and ideological relations between China and the developing nations of Africa from 1949 to 1976 in the context of Mao Zedong's worldview, the realities of Africa, and the goals of Africans and suggests that China's successes in Africa are largely due to its ability to present itself as a viable alternative to what many Africans regard as the imperialist hegemony of the USSR and the United States.

398. Bienen, Henry. U.S. FOREIGN POLICY IN A CHANGING AFRICA. *Pol. Sci. Q. 1978 93(3): 443-464.* Analyzes interests in southern Africa in relation to the nation's interest in Africa as a whole. Argues that Africa has become too differentiated, and relations between

African states too complex, for the United States to have a single African policy. J

399. Bon, Daniel L. and Mingst, Karen. FRENCH INTERVENTION IN AFRICA: DEPENDENCY OR DECOLONIZATION. *Africa Today 1980 27(2): 5-20.* Pragmatic French intervention in former colonies has maintained a modified dependency, but the relationships are more akin to Great Power-client relationships than to colonial dependency. The colonial legacy merely provided the initial entree. Assessing the relationship between former imperial powers and their recent colonies in decolonization or dependency terms is a misleading exercise. 47 notes. G. O. Gagnon

400. Brayton, Abbott A. SOVIET INVOLVEMENT IN AFRICA. *J. of Modern African Studies [Great Britain] 1979 17(2): 253-269.* Reviews different interpretations of the USSR's involvement in African states between 1960 and 1977 and tests the geopolitical hypotheses put forward by some writers. Those states deliberately "penetrated" by the Soviets, without the benefit of a Russian-supported preindependence liberation movement or an unstable pro-Soviet leader, have been among the poorest and most politically unstable on the continent: Benin, Congo (Brazzaville), Ethiopia, Mali, Somalia, and Uganda. There is no evidence to suggest that the Soviet Union is following a particular geopolitical strategy, but rather is seeking easy, quick victories, taking advantage of available opportunities. Based on published sources, principally US government, World Bank and UN agencies, 5 tables, 10 notes, appendix. D. J. Nicholls

401. Butler, Shannon R. and Valenta, Jiri. EAST GERMANY IN THE THIRD WORLD. *US Naval Inst. Pro. 1981 107(9): 58-64.* East Germany is the Soviet Union's main East European ally in Africa, and since the early 1960's has increased its military activities on that continent as elsewhere. Today, the East Germans are militarily involved in Mozambique, Angola, Zaire, South Yemen, Ethiopia, and Namibia. They are also active in Latin America, where East Germany is presently increasing its medical and economic assistance to the Nicaraguan government. 17 notes, 5 photos, map, table. A. N. Garland

402. Chang Ya-chün. PEIPING'S AFRICAN POLICY IN THE 1970'S. *Issues & Studies [Taiwan] 1981 17(2): 44-58.* Before the 1970's, China's activities in Africa followed from its pursuit of Third World leadership, but, tempered by internal circumstances, were inconsistent. By the 1970's, however, China was turning to practical politics without dropping its ideological goals. African leaders were invited to Peking, and trade agreements, propaganda, and economic, technological, and military assistance were emphasized, with general success. China's self-reliance model of economic development appealed to the Africans. China could not, however, compete with the USSR in financial or other resources. 42 notes. J. A. Krompart

403. Chazan, Naomi. ISRAEL IN AFRICA. *Jerusalem Q. [Israel] 1981 (18): 29-44.* Discusses resumption of Israeli-African diplomatic relations since the rupture following the 1973 October War.

404. Cherkasov, P. P. POLITIKA FRANTSII V AFRIKE (70-E GODY XX V.) [French policy in Africa in the 1970's]. *Voprosy Istorii [USSR] 1981 (8): 49-64.* Discusses French policy in the African continent in the 1970's, its aims and main directions in the West and Equatorial Africa, in the Maghreb countries, in the region of the Horn of Africa and in the South of the continent. French policy is studied in the context of the global foreign policy of the Fifth Republic and its course in the developing countries. J

405. Chhabra, Hari Sharan. THE COMPETITION OF ISRAEL AND THE ARAB STATES FOR FRIENDSHIP WITH THE AFRICAN STATES. *India Q.: J. of Int. Affairs [India] 1975 31(4): 362-370.* Analyzes the competition between Israel and the Arab States for friendship with independent African states. Arab contacts in Africa go back a thousand years. Although Jewish and Ethiopian exchanges date from the days of King Solomon and the Queen of Sheba, there was no significant African support for Zionism except in South Africa. Since its establishment in 1948, however, Israel has sent sizeable amounts of foreign, military, and technical aid to Africa. By the late 1960's and early 1970's the Organization of African Unity was largely pro-Arab. Arab dominance in the supply of petroleum was of great importance in guiding the attitudes and policies of African nations. Secondary sources; 9 notes. S. H. Frank

406. Coker, Christopher. ADVENTURISM AND PRAGMATISM: THE SOVIET UNION, COMECON, AND RELATIONS WITH AFRICAN STATES. *Int. Affairs [Great Britain] 1981 57(4): 618-633.* Discusses the interests of the USSR's Eastern European allies in southern Africa, and the degree to which these interests have brought these countries into conflict with the Soviet Union since 1960.

407. Crocker, Chester A. THE AFRICAN DIMENSION OF INDIAN OCEAN POLICY. *Orbis 1976 20(3): 637-668.* Events in sub-Saharan Africa since the early 1960's have caused the military roles and relationships enjoyed by European powers to be either adjusted or eliminated entirely. As that happened, the USSR has begun to take a greater military interest in the area and has actively sought to foster military relationships with many of the sub-Saharan African countries. A primary reason for the Soviet Union's action has been its development of an Indian Ocean military strategy, which seems to be both political and diplomatic in nature. On the other hand, the United States has shown only minor interest in maintaining any strategic presence in Africa, although the Angolan conflict may cause tremendous changes in southern Africa's power relationships. Still, any US administration is going to meet with great difficulty in trying to solve the region's many and diverse political and military conflicts. 66 notes. A. N. Garland

408. Decalo, Samuel. AFRICA AND THE U.N. ANTI-ZIONISM RESOLUTION: ROOTS AND CAUSES. *Cultures et Développement [Belgium] 1976 8(1): 89-117.* Traces Afro-Israeli foreign relations, 1958-73, and highlights some reasons for the African anti-Israeli majority in the UN on 10 November 1975.

409. Decraene, Philippe. IS THE ROMANCE WITH ISRAEL OVER? *Africa Report 1973 18(3): 20-24.* Since the Six-day War, diplomatic relations between Israel and former African allies have been steadily deteriorating. S

410. Deshpande, G. P. CHOU EN-LAI'S AFRICAN SAFARI. *China Report [India] 1975 11(5-6): 77-103.* Gives a country-by-country account of Chou En-Lai's 1963-64 venture to identify African nationalism with the need for Afro-Asian solidarity against imperialism and neocolonialism. Against the backdrop of the Sino-Soviet split, the eight-country visit established China as an international power relevant to Africa which shared a similar historical background of Western domination. In broad terms, Chou gained some support for Afro-Asian unity, though other Chinese doctrinal objectives were less successful. 101 notes. S. F. Benfield

411. Durch, William J. THE CUBAN MILITARY IN AFRICA AND THE MIDDLE EAST: FROM ALGERIA TO ANGOLA. *Studies in Comparative Communism 1978 (1-2): 34-74.* Cuba's military intervention in Angola follows the pattern of its past activities. Castro has developed over the past 15 years a policy of aiding colonial liberation movements. Cuba has intervened with combat troops in Algeria, Syria, and Angola from 1961 to 1976 and sent training detachments to many African states. Construction workers often are in the military reserve and might well be military men. In sending troops to Angola, Cuba was not acting as proxy for the USSR but acting independently. Ultimately 15-18,000 Cubans fought in Angola. Cuba's actions have won it great esteem in Third World countries. 147 notes. D. Balmuth

412. Etinger, Y. AFRICAN COUNTRIES: ANTI-IMPERIALIST FOREIGN POLICIES. *Int. Affairs [USSR] 1973 (8): 75-81.* Discusses the neutrality and anti-imperialist foreign policy of developing nations in Africa as a means of developing economic independence, 1960's-70's.

413. Fessard de Foucault, Bertrand. INDÉPENDANCES NATIONALES ET COOPÉRATION FRANCO-AFRICAINE [National independence and Franco-African cooperation]. *Études [France] 1973 338(4): 535-558.* The system of cooperation between France and its excolonies in Africa, launched by General Charles de Gaulle, proves to be obsolete today. African countries tend to have more and more adult relations with France and are asking for modifications in the judicial

systems relating them to France. Based on official documents; 26 notes.
C. Collon

414. Franceschini, Paul Jean. LA POLITICA AFRICANA DELLA FRANCIA [The African politics of France]. *Affari Esteri [Italy] 1977 9(35): 434-447.* France openly proclaimed its sympathies and became directly involved in African affairs in 1977 by supporting President Mobutu Sese Seko in Zaire; this, however, did not represent a change in French foreign policy but rather a continuation of a long-term commitment to its old colonies and areas of special interest.

415. Freeman, Linda. CANADA AND AFRICA IN THE 1970'S. *Int. J. [Canada] 1980 35(4): 794-820.* Canada's involvement with Africa in the 1970's has operated in concert with its major allies, Great Britain and the United States. It has included efforts to contain the expansion of Soviet and Chinese influence on the continent, maintain a political and economic environment receptive to open economic relations with the developed capitalist world, and support regimes that are genuinely pro-West in their orientation. Secondary sources; 3 tables, 58 notes.
J. Powell

416. Gareau, Frederick H. THE IMPACT OF THE UNITED NATIONS UPON AFRICA. *J. of Modern African Studies [Great Britain] 1978 16(4): 565-578.* Balance sheet of UN activities in Africa. On one side countries were helped to gain independence and receive financial aid from the UN. Conversely the UN failed to abolish apartheid in South Africa and to give independence to Namibia. Based on UN documents and secondary sources; 60 notes. A. Sbacchi

417. Gitelson, Susan Aurelia. AFRICA'S RUPTURE WITH ISRAEL. *Midstream 1974 20(1): 29-41.* The effect of the Yom Kippur War (October 1973) on Israel's relations with the Black African states. S

418. Gitelson, Susan Aurelia. THE LINKAGE BETWEEN EXTERNAL AND DOMESTIC POLICIES: ISRAEL'S EXPERIENCE WITH GHANA AND NIGERIA. *Jewish Social Studies 1980 42(2): 95-118.* Examines Israel's relations with Ghana and Nigeria as a case study demonstrating that bilateral relations between a small or middle power from one regional subsystem with a small or middle state from another regional subsystem depend mainly upon four major variables: the state's domestic situation; its general foreign policy orientation; its leadership; and the perceived timeliness, quality, and relevance of the programs offered by the donor country. Ghana's and Nigeria's general foreign policy orientations had the greatest impact on diplomatic relations, while leaders had the most immediate impact. Social pressures and leaders' perceptions of the timeliness and quality of aid affected relations from time to time. Based on interviews, newspaper accounts, and other primary and secondary sources; fig., table, 65 notes.
J. D. Sarna

419. Gitelson, Susan Aurelia. UNFULFILLED EXPECTATIONS: ISRAELI AND ARAB AID AS POLITICAL INSTRUMENTS IN BLACK AFRICAN UNITED NATIONS VOTING BEHAVIOR. *Jewish Social Sci. 1976 38(2): 159-175.* A quantitative analysis of the correlation between technical assistance offered by Israel to Black Africa and the support by the latter of Israel on votes in the General Assembly indicates some correlation in those issues of great importance to the donor state. Although it is difficult to differentiate between cause and consequence, about half of the states aided by Israel tended to support the latter on a significant number of occasions. The relationship between Israel and Black Africa on General Assembly voting patterns became more tenuous when political pressures within and outside the United Nations were brought to bear on Black Africa, as in the case of voting following the Yom Kippur War. The correlation between Arab aid to Black Africa and voting behavior in the UN on the part of the latter is less positive than in the Israeli-Black Africa case. Based on a systematic aggregate analysis of the relationship between aid and voting behavior in the United Nations between 1958 and 1972. N. Lederer

420. Guelke, Adrian. SOUTHERN AFRICA AND THE SUPERPOWERS. *Int. Affairs [Great Britain] 1980 56(4): 648-664.* Increasing tensions between the USSR and the United States have inspired Soviet interest in African countries and have left the United States (continually more disenchanted with African nationalism) in embarrassed partnership with South Africa despite its attitude on human rights and strict adherence to apartheid.

421. Gupta, Anirudha. INDIA AND AFRICA SOUTH OF THE SAHARA. *Int. Studies [India] 1978 17(3-4): 639-653.* In 1947 India's prestige in colonial Africa was high because of its own liberation from Britain, and because of Jawaharlal Nehru's policy of nonalignment. During the 1960's, however, India's influence in Africa waned, while China's influence became more pronounced. However, India's involvement in the liberation of Bangladesh restored much of the prestige lost during the 1960's. Indian diplomacy acquired a new dynamism under Indira Gandhi, a dynamism that the Desai government pursued after Gandhi left office. 29 notes. T. P. Linkfield

422. Hannam, Harry. THE COMMONWEALTH SECRETARIAT. *African Res. and Documentation [Great Britain] 1977 (12): 1-9.* Describes the development of the Commonwealth Secretariat, an international body at the service of all Commonwealth members, since 1965, its structure and functions, and its involvement in African affairs.

423. Harshe, Rajen. FRENCH NEO-COLONIALISM IN SUB-SAHARAN AFRICA. *India Q. [India] 1980 36(2): 159-178.* French neocolonialism remains an important factor in the affairs of several African states. France exercises considerable control over the economic and political institutions of its past colonies through negotiating treaties, loans, and currency arrangements. French military intervention has occurred as well. Changing conditions cast doubt on France's ability to retain its powerful influence among the sub-Saharan African states. Based on government documents and secondary sources; 2 tables, 49 notes. W. R. Johnson

424. Houser, George M. MEETING AFRICA'S CHALLENGE: THE STORY OF THE AMERICAN COMMITTEE ON AFRICA. *Issue 1976 6(2-3): 16-26.* Examines the scholarly and political development of the American Committee on Africa, 1950's-70's.

425. Howe, Russell Warren. UNITED STATES POLICY IN AFRICA. *Current Hist. 1979 76(445): 97-100, 130-131.* From 1885 to the late 1950's the US foreign policy toward Africa was vague; following growing independence from colonial powers in the 1950's and 60's when the United States was a major provider of aid, the administration of Jimmy Carter has further improved relations with Africa.

426. Hull, Galen. THE FRENCH CONNECTION IN AFRICA: ZAIRE AND SOUTH AFRICA. *J. of Southern African Studies [Great Britain] 1979 5(2): 220-233.* French economic, political, and military ties to Zaire and South Africa provide a defense for American and European economic interests in these mineral-rich countries. French aid and military assistance to Zaire and arms trade with South Africa serve a Western need to safeguard major sources of vital raw materials, rather than advancing the interests of European-African solidarity as proclaimed by France. Based on newspapers and secondary sources; 24 notes. L. W. Truschel

427. Hutchison, Alan. CHINA IN AFRICA: A RECORD OF PRAGMATISM AND CONSERVATISM. *Round Table [Great Britain] 1975 (259): 263-271.* Examines China's foreign policy in Africa since the early 1960's, the two strands of policy known as the united front from above, or legitimate relations, and the united front from below, or support for dissidents, and the record of their implementation and success. Argues that the latter policy was promoted by the desire to play out the Sino-Soviet split in Africa, while the policy as a whole was promoted by the need to divert the United States from its policy of containing China. The period of the Cultural Revolution formed a watershed in China's relations with African countries, countries which, disappointed by apparent American indifference and disillusioned by Soviet action in Czechoslovakia, were searching for a true major power friend. China launched a new diplomatic offensive, disavowing the united front from below and concentrating on the establishment of relations with legitimate governments. China has maintained this policy, from which it has derived considerable success. C. Anstey

428. Johnson, Willard R. AFRICANS AND ARABS: COLLABORATION WITH CO-OPERATION, CHANGE WITHOUT CHALLENGE. *Int. J. [Canada] 1980 35(4): 766-793.* In March 1977 a

summit meeting of 60 African and Arab states attempted to institutionalize a joint economic and diplomatic agreement. As it completes its first years of active diplomacy, African-Arab relations have yet to achieve a clear identity. In terms both of its rhetoric and the promise of the financial and natural resources available to the Program of Cooperation, a real alliance of significant import to the existing regional if not world economic and perhaps political and security order could have developed. But the changes the collaboration has achieved thus far do not challenge the existing order. They do not and will not disrupt the ties that the Arabs and the Africans have to the industrial world. Both groups will continue their dependency on that world, perhaps in preference to a new dependency on each other. Secondary sources; table, 9 notes.
J. Powell

429. Jundanian, Brendan F. GREAT POWER INTERACTION WITH AFRICA: AN AFRICANIST'S PERSPECTIVE. *Studies in Comparative Communism 1973 6(3): 319-325.* Comments on Bruce D. Larkin's *China and Africa, 1949-1970*(Berkeley: University of California Press, 1971), and Helen Desfosses Cohn's *Soviet Policy Toward Black Africa: The Focus on National Integration* (New York: Praeger, 1972); following a background discussion of the relationship of the Great Powers to the newly independent African nations. Both the USSR and China have increased ties with the elites of African countries and have exhibited a marked degree of pragmatism by recognizing the exceeding complexity of African politics. 4 notes. D. Balmuth

430. Kaczyński, Bogusław. AFRICAN-ARAB COOPERATION AND THE EVOLUTION IN THE POSITION OF THE ORGANIZATION OF AFRICAN UNITY ON THE MIDDLE EAST CONFLICT. *Studies on the Developing Countries [Poland] 1978 (9): 29-47.* Examines the attitudes of black African nations toward the Arab world and Israel from 1955 to 1977 and concludes that black sympathy for the Jewish state and Israel's clever policies in the region kept many African states from openly stating solidarity with Arab States against Israeli aggression until tentative expressions of opposition toward Israel's relations with the Arabs began in 1967 and have since grown ever stronger and clearer.

431. Kanet, Roger E. and Morris, William. DIE SOWJETUNION IN AFRIKA [The Soviet Union in Africa]. *Osteuropa [West Germany] 1978 28(11): 978-985.* The USSR could not compete with the United States in Africa, 1945-60's, because of its strategic inferiority, but since the late 1960's the Soviet government has been able to support pro-Soviet parties and movements in Africa.

432. Kanet, Roger E. THE SOVIET UNION, THE FRENCH COMMUNIST PARTY AND AFRICA, 1945-1950. *Survey [Great Britain] 1976 22(1): 74-92.* During 1945-50, the USSR had no direct contacts with Africa. While following an essentially Maoist policy of appealing to all patriotic elements in a struggle against the imperialists, it was forced to work through the Communist Party of France, which for reasons of its own, supported the Rassemblement Democratique African, a bourgeois-nationalist organization. When the Soviet Union tried to pursue a strictly Communist policy, the bourgeois-nationalists broke away and Soviet policy ended in failure. Secondary sources; 75 notes.
R. B. Valliant

433. Khazanov, A. BELYI DOM I "CHERNYI KONTINENT" [The White House and the "Dark Continent"]. *Aziia i Afrika Segodnia [USSR] 1981 (9): 14-16.* Examines US attitudes toward the nations of Africa from 1978 to 1981, focusing on the dealings of Secretary of State Alexander Haig and National Security Adviser Richard Allen with African countries, and discusses the relationship between the United States and South Africa.

434. Kosukhin, N. RASPROSTRANENIE IDEI NAUCHNOGO SOTSIALIZMA V AFRIKE [Spreading the idea of scientific socialism in Africa]. *Aziia i Afrika Segodnia [USSR] 1981 (7): 2-5.* Examines the methods of spreading socialism in Africa, 1960-80.

435. Kraus, Jon. AMERICAN FOREIGN POLICY IN AFRICA. *Current Hist. 1981 80(464): 97-100, 129, 138.* Explores the Carter administration's policies in Africa and the results of their implementation and examines the validity of the criticism of US conservatives.

436. Kraus, Jon. ISLAMIC AFFINITIES AND INTERNATIONAL POLITICS IN SUB-SAHARAN AFRICA. *Current Hist. 1980 78(456): 154-158, 182-184.* Discusses religious and racial cleavages in Sub-Saharan Islamic countries and their relations with the newly wealthy oil-producing Arab states; 1960's-70's.

437. Lancaster, Carol. UNITED STATES POLICY IN SUB-SAHARAN AFRICA. *Current Hist. 1982 81(473): 97-100, 132-135.* Examines the limited US economic ties with sub-Saharan Africa, and argues that greater involvement is needed if the United States hopes to maintain or advance its security interests in the region.

438. Legum, Colin. THE AFRICAN ENVIRONMENT. *Problems of Communism 1978 27(1): 1-19.* Analyzes the spectrum of African political attitudes toward the USSR and changes in the character of those attitudes, 1970-78. Judged in terms of overall Soviet strategic objectives, Africa has not afforded the USSR any conspicuous successes. Nevertheless, Moscow has recently committed increased resources there and assigned the continent a much higher priority than have Western powers. The key to success or failure is likely to depend more on the degree to which the economic and military assistance offered by Moscow is perceived by Africans to be relevant to their aspirations and interests. Map, 31 notes. J. M. Lauber

439. Legum, Colin. BRITAIN TILTS TOWARD BLACK AFRICA. *Africa Report 1973 18(5): 14-15.* Britain now leans toward independence for African colonies, especially those of Portugal. S

440. Lellouche, Pierre and Moisi, Dominique. FRENCH POLICY IN AFRICA: A LONELY BATTLE AGAINST DESTABILIZATION. *Int. Security 1979 3(4): 108-133.* France's foreign policy toward former French colonies and Africa, 1960-79, evolved from cooperation, 1960-63, and disengagement, 1963-74, to combatting destabilization, 1974-79. The last phase has included a military presence and conflict intervention and encouraged multilateral military and economic links with the West.

441. Lhuisard, A. LA CHINE ET L'AFRIQUE [China and Africa]. *Défense Natl. [France] 1974 30(6): 89-105.* Examines the influence of China on the African continent ca. 1958-70's and discusses China's success in formulating a foreign policy which is sensitive to the aspirations of the developing nations of Africa.

442. Lin Bih-jaw. COMMUNIST CHINA'S FOREIGN POLICY IN AFRICA: A HISTORICAL REVIEW. *Issues & Studies [Taiwan] 1982 18(2): 31-53.* Communist China has had some successes in gaining influence and closer relations with African nations. Cultural differences and Africa's political diversity and preoccupation with domestic issues, however, limit China's foreign policy accomplishments there. Based on Mainland English language publications; 40 notes. J. A. Krompart

443. Marchand, Jean. LA CHINE POPULAIRE ET L'AFRIQUE NOIRE [China and black Africa]. *Rev. Militaire Générale [France] 1973 (3): 419-433.* Examines the growth of friendly foreign relations between China and several developing African countries, 1955-71.

444. Marchand, Jean. LA PENETRATION SOVIETIQUE EN AFRIQUE [Soviet penetration in Africa]. *Écrits de Paris [France] 1977 371: 5-14.* Shows the extent to which the USSR has infiltrated Africa in recent months, particularly Mozambique, Zaire, Ethiopia, and the Sudan, while assessing the US reaction.

445. Marchand, Jean. LES INCERTITUDES DE LA COOPÉRATION EN AFRIQUE NOIRE ET À MADAGASCAR [Uncertainties concerning cooperation in Black Africa and Madagascar]. *Écrits de Paris [France] 1974 (335): 9-24.* The cooperative structures developed between France and its former African colonies during the 1950's and 1960's continue to be threatened by those who fear for their countries' autonomy and independence.

446. Masi, Fernando Luis. PARTICULARISMO VERSUS GLOBALISMO: LA POLÍTICA EXTERIOR NORTEAMERICANA EN ÁFRICA (1977-1981) [Particularism versus globalism: North American foreign policy in Africa, 1977-81]. *Foro Int. [Mexico] 1981 22(2): 180-202.* Examines US foreign policy in Africa, especially southern Africa and the Horn of Africa, noting the Carter administration's initial

application of "particularism" and its 1979 return to "globalism" under the impact of domestic political changes. Secondary sources; 53 notes.
D. A. Franz

447. Matthews, Robert O. CANADA'S RELATIONS WITH AFRICA. *Int. J. [Canada] 1975 30(3): 536-568.* Examines the ambivalence in Canada's foreign aid and trade relations with Africa, 1970-75; 4 tables, 27 notes.
R. V. Kubicek

448. Mayall, James. THE MALAWI-TANZANIA BOUNDARY DISPUTE. *J. of Modern African Studies [Great Britain] 1973 11(4): 611-628.* Although the differences between the states of Malawi and Tanzania include other elements this study focuses on the boundary problem. Presents and explains the Tanzanian claims and Malawi's response under the leadership of President Hastings Banda. There is conflicting evidence in the early maps; the *Annual Colonial Reports* on Nyasaland before the establishment in 1953 of the Central African Federation all show a shoreline boundary. It seems likely the *status quo* will persist. "A substantive settlement... will have to wait on a more general political *détente* between the two states." Map, 44 notes.
R. V. Ritter

449. Mazrui, Ali A. THE BOLSHEVIKS AND THE BANTU: FROM THE OCTOBER REVOLUTION TO THE ANGOLAN CIVIL WAR. *Survey [Great Britain] 1976 22(3-4): 288-306.* Contacts between African nationalists and the USSR often resulted from dissatisfaction with the West. Nevertheless, it was the Western revolutionary tradition, embodied in France and the United States which legitimized African rebellion against colonial powers. Among Africans Marxism and pan-Africanism were often linked; however, Marxists such as George Padmore argue that Africa must be free to "Africanize Marxism." Although US leaders view themselves as pragmatists and Soviet leaders as ideologists, the Soviets were more successful in dealing with the nonaligned nations of Africa. Soviet involvement in Angola may well mark a new phase in African-Soviet relations. Secondary sources; 9 notes.
D. R. McDonald

450. Ménudier, Henri. L'ALLEMAGNE ET L'AFRIQUE [Germany and Africa]. *Défense Natl. [France] 1981 37(Aug-Sept): 21-33.* Discusses West and East German policies toward Africa, 1949-81, showing how West Germany has developed a real African policy supporting stability.

451. Metzler, John J. PEIPING IN AFRICA: PROSPECTS AND PORTENTS FOR COMMUNIST CHINA'S ROLE IN THE SUBSAHARAN ZONE. *Issues and Studies [Taiwan] 1978 14(8): 72-84.* A history of Chinese contacts with Africa from 1949 to 1975, and prospect for Chinese-African relations in the future.

452. Miller, Jake C. AFRICAN-ISRAELI RELATIONS: IMPACT ON CONTINENTAL UNITY. *Middle East J. 1975 29(4): 393-408.* Considers both historical and current events in determining the impact upon continental unity of African-Israeli relations. The Arab cause won support from the Organization for African Unity. Until 1973 African nations were reluctant to lend their support to the Arab cause, but since the most recent war African states have joined with other developing nations to isolate Israel in international organizations. Analyzes why many African states terminated relations with Israel in 1973. Few African states, however, followed severance with tangible support for the Arabs. Based on newspaper accounts; 62 notes.
E. P. Stickney

453. Miller, Jake C. BLACK LEGISLATORS AND AFRICAN-AMERICAN RELATIONS, 1970-1975. *J. of Black Studies 1979 10(2): 245-261.* The 18 black members of Congress in 1975 have had little impact on American foreign policy in Africa because of their concentration on domestic programs, Congress's limited role in foreign affairs, and the State Department's bias in favor of Europe. Black legislators have sought to influence US policy by attending conferences and fact-finding missions, cooperation and conflict with the president, filing suits in federal courts, regular legislative means, appealing to other groups and the American public, and working collectively through the Congressional Black Caucus. Based on periodicals and published statements.
R. G. Sherer

454. Mulira, James. THE ROLE OF THE SOVIET UNION IN THE DECOLONIZATION PROCESS OF AFRICA: FROM LENIN TO BREZHNEV. *Mawazo [Uganda] 1976 4(4): 26-35.* The policies of the Soviet bloc toward decolonization in Africa have generally been guided by Leninist principles, but modified with changing conditions by subsequent Soviet leaders. The assumption that Soviet socialism would provide a viable base for future international communism did not apply to Africa until the end of World War II. Stalin gave limited diplomatic support to anticolonial movements but had no pragmatic policy toward Africa, 1945-53. African nationalism of the mid-1950's indicated to the USSR a potential power vacuum when African colonies threw off the colonial rule, with the implication that Soviet aid was as good if not better than that of the West. The author sees a change in Soviet foreign policy toward Africa in the material and diplomatic support that Khrushchev gave to bourgeois nationalist movements. Kosygin and Brezhnev tended to continue this by supporting the Organization for African Unity (OAU). Based on secondary sources; 21 notes.
J. J. N. McGurk

455. Nadelmann, Ethan A. ISRAEL AND BLACK AFRICA: A RAPPROCHEMENT? *J. of Modern African Studies [Great Britain] 1981 19(2): 183-219.* Reviews Israel's relations with black Africa. Between 1956 and 1973 Israel established and maintained extensive bilateral ties to many African countries, but they began to erode with the 1967 war, and after the 1973 war, 21 black African states joined nine others that had earlier broken diplomatic relations with Israel, while only four retained them. By 1980, however, Africa had accepted large numbers of Israeli advisers and technicians and considered reestablishing formal diplomatic relations, despite the threat of Arab states' withholding oil and aid, a substantial growth of Israeli-South African ties since 1973, and Prime Minister Begin's intransigence. Based on newspapers, memoirs, and secondary sources; 4 tables, 121 notes.
L. W. Truschel

456. Natufe, O. Igho. NIGERIA AND SOVIET ATTITUDES TO AFRICAN MILITARY REGIMES, 1965-1970. *Survey [Great Britain] 1976 22(1): 93-111.* The USSR welcomed coups d'etat in the pro-Western states of Africa and believed that in pro-Soviet countries the armies, the last protectors of the masses against corruption and oppression, would not revolt. The coups in Ghana and Mali upset Soviet calculations. The most important Soviet victory came when the pro-Soviet side won in Nigeria. Based on contemporary periodicals, personal experiences, and secondary sources; 47 notes.
R. B. Valliant

457. Neffe, Dieter. DIE MILITÄRPOLITIK FRANKREICHS GEGEN DIE FRANCOPHONEN SUBSAHARISCHEN LÄNDER IN DEN SIEBZIGER JAHREN [The military policy of France against the francophone sub-Saharan countries in the 1970's]. *Militärgeschichte [East Germany] 1982 21(6): 667-677.* Divides French policy in sub-Saharan Africa in the 1970's into two periods. In the early 1970's France attempted to achieve its aims in this region with new, less disreputable methods. Although military action moved to the background, the mechanism of armed intervention was further developed. In the later 1970's France strengthened its military intervention potential and secured its bases. Map, 33 notes.
J/T (H. D. Andrews)

458. Neffe, Dieter. DIE MILITÄRPOLITIK FRANKREICHS GEGEN DIE FRANCOPHONEN SUBSAHARISCHEN LÄNDER IN DEN SECHZIGER JAHREN [The military policy of France toward the Francophone sub-Saharan countries in the 1960's]. *Militärgeschichte [East Germany] 1982 21(2): 185-196.* Investigates the military policy of France toward its former African colonies. France's military engagement continued, based on national armies it built up and controlled, forces it stationed in the region, and intervention with troops from metropolitan France. Divides the period into the period of the buildup of a military instrument of French imperialism, 1960-63, and that of its neocolonial employment, 1964-70. Table, map, 30 notes.
J/T (H. D. Andrews)

459. Nixon, Richard M. UNITED STATES FOREIGN POLICY FOR THE 70'S: SHAPING A DURABLE PEACE (AFRICA). *Africa Today 1973 20(2): 3-10.* An excerpt from President Nixon's "State of the World" speech to Congress in May 1973. Promises that America will support African nations' economic development, avoid interference in domestic politics, and continue seeking evolutionary change in Rhodesia and South Africa.
G. O. Gagnon

460. Njoya, Adamou Ndam. THE SOCIOLOGY OF AFRICAN DIPLOMACY. *Mawazo [Uganda] 1975 4(3): 7-22.* Seeks a sociology of African diplomacy based on the diplomatic experience of African nations since 1962. The functions of African diplomats do not differ from those of other nations. But they have advanced from amateurism in diplomacy toward a more scientific approach, led by the body of diplomats trained in centers such as the International Institute of Public Administration (Paris) and the Carnegie Endowment for International Peace. The author describes the functions and ambitions of the International Relations Institute of Cameroon (IRIC) as a center for research and training of all cadres in the diplomatic service at consular, chancellery, and diplomatic levels. 6 notes. J. J. N. McGurk

461. Noer, Thomas J. "NON-BENIGN NEGLECT": THE UNITED STATES AND BLACK AFRICA IN THE TWENTIETH CENTURY. Haines, Gerald K. and Walker, J. Samuel, ed. *American Foreign Relations: A Historiographical Review*(Westport, Conn.: Greenwood Pr., 1981): 271-292. Surveys the literature on the United States and its relationship with black Africa, lamenting its scarcity due to the perception that Africa is a geographically remote area of little economic or strategic importance. Secondary sources; 62 notes. J. Powell

462. Nworah, Dike. NATIONALISM VERSUS COEXISTENCE: NEO-AFRICAN ATTITUDES TO CLASSICAL NEUTRALISM. *J. of Modern African Studies [Great Britain] 1977 15(2): 213-237.* Neutralism is very similar to coexistence and in the present decade the Afro-Asian world faces decisions on neutrality and national sovereignty. The author discusses African response at various conferences including the Bandung Conference and the Organization of African Unity. As late as the Colombo Conference of 1976, African states maintained the right to control their foreign affairs. 87 notes. H. G. Soff

463. Nyang, Sulayman S. AFRICAN OPINIONS AND ATTITUDES TO THE PALESTINE QUESTION. *Search: J. for Arab and Islamic Studies 1980 1(3-4): 218-245.* Newly independent African states during the 1960's tended to support Israel, perceived as an underdog. Israel's decisive victory in the 1967 war and subsequent refusal to relinquish Sinai, Anwar Sadat's success in unifying the Arab states, and Israel's diplomatic relations with South Africa all persuaded the African states to support Egypt and the Palestinians.

464. Nzongola-Ntalaja. AFRICA AND THE QUESTION OF PALESTINE. *Search: J. for Arab and Islamic Studies 1982 3(1): 1-18.* Examines the progressive awakening of African states to the centrality of the Palestine question from 1947 to 1979.

465. O'Ballance, Edgar. THE CUBAN FACTOR. *J. of the Royal United Services Inst. for Defence Studies [Great Britain] 1978 123(3): 46-51.* Discusses Cuban military power in contemporary Africa in the light of Cuban history since 1959.

466. Obichere, Boniface. AMERICAN DIPLOMACY IN AFRICA: PROBLEMS AND PROSPECTS. *Pan African J. [Kenya] 1974 7(1): 67-80.* Analyzes US policy toward Africa since 1787, with emphasis on the post-1960 years. Among the aspects covered are AID missions, consular offices, and millionaire ambassadors. Although Africa is not a US priority, in the current energy crisis the African states and the United States may draw closer together and plan usable projects for the future. 25 notes. H. G. Soff

467. Oded, Aryeh. AFRIKAH BEIN HA'ARAVIM LEVEIN YISRAEL [Africa between the Arabs and Israel]. *Hamizrah Hehadash [Israel] 1975 25(3): 184-208.* Arab refusal to sell oil cheaply to Africa was considered a poor return for African severance of diplomatic relations with Israel. The Arabs had an advantage in Africa because of the large Muslim populations there, and through Arab and Muslim influence in the Organization of African Unity. However, the African nations' long-standing fear of Arabs outweighs their influence. 120 notes, 2 appendixes. T. Sassoon

468. Ogunbadejo, Oye. CONSERVATISM AND RADICALISM IN INTER-AFRICAN RELATIONS: THE CASE OF NIGERIA AND TANZANIA. *Jerusalem J. of Int. Relations [Israel] 1979 4(1): 23-33.*

469. Ogunbadejo, Oye. SOVIET POLICIES IN AFRICA. *African Affairs [Great Britain] 1980 79(316): 297-325.* Outlines the USSR's coherent policy toward Africa and the interconnections of its political, economic, and strategic aspects. Its aim is to advance the USSR's national interests. Moscow has sought to maximize those interests while changing some of its methods as circumstances demanded. 102 notes. J. V. Coutinho

470. Ohaegbulam, Festus Ugboaja. AFRICA AND SUPERPOWER RIVALRY: PROSPECTS FOR THE FUTURE AND POSSIBLE REMEDIES. *J. of African Studies 1981-82 8(4): 163-175.* Assesses the history and the diplomatic, economic, and military components of American and Soviet involvement in independent Africa after 1960. Moves by both superpowers to obtain African diplomatic support have irritated African governments. The United States has established far stronger economic ties to Africa than has the Soviet Union, which seeks primarily to deny African resources to the West. Militarily, the USSR has gone far beyond American involvment in Africa by supporting armed revolutionary struggles. It seeks to gain African port facilities for its long-range navy and as a stepping-stone to Latin America. The superpower rivalry is detrimental to long-range African interests because it promotes conflict and loss of independence. Secondary sources; 39 notes. L. W. Truschel

471. Ojo, Olusola. THE ROLE OF THE ARAB WORLD IN THE DECOLONIZATION PROCESS OF BLACK AFRICA. *Int. Problems [Israel] 1981 20(2-4): 73-84.* Divides the role of the Arab states in the decolonization of Africa into three periods, the decade of noninvolvement, 1945-55, gradual involvement, 1955-73, and frustrated expectations, 1973-78.

472. Oudes, Bruce. THE CIA AND AFRICA. *Africa Report 1974 19(4): 49-52.* Describes Central Intelligence Agency operations in Africa, based on *The CIA and the Cult of Intelligence* (Knopf, 1974) by Victor Marchetti and John Marks. S

473. Oudes, Bruce. U.S.-AFRICA RELATIONS: KAUNDA'S DIPLOMATIC OFFENSIVE. *Africa Report 1975 20(3): 41-43.* President Kenneth Kaunda of Zambia has attempted to force a change in US-African relations. S

474. Owen, David. APARTHEID. *Contemporary Rev. [Great Britain] 1980 236(1372): 225-232.* Describes the circumstances surrounding a decisive shift in British foreign policy in 1977 as a result of the realization that British interests would henceforth lie with Black Africa.

475. Paris, Henri. L'ACTION RÉCENTE DES SOVIÉTIQUES EN AFRIQUE [Recent Soviet activity in Africa]. *Défense Natl. [France] 1980 36(10): 41-52.* The USSR's activity in Africa since the 1920's and particularly in the 1970's indicates that its main objective there is to improve its position in Europe.

476. Park, Sang-seek. AFRICA AND TWO KOREAS: A STUDY OF AFRICAN NON-ALIGNMENT. *African Studies Rev. 1978 21(1): 73-88.* A study of African foreign policy on Cold War questions, 1960-75, particularly as they relate to diplomatic recognition of North and South Korea. African countries have exhibited different policies at different times. 4 tables, 9 notes, biblio. R. T. Brown

477. Pope, Ronald R. INTRODUCTION: SOVIET VIEWS ON BLACK AFRICA. *Int. J. of Pol. 1976-77 6(4): 3-11.* Introduces four recent articles from specialized Soviet publications and gives an overall view. Increased Soviet interest in Black Africa stems from growing Chinese involvement, African desire to assert independence from the West, the emergence of pro-Soviet regimes in Angola and Somalia, the USSR's desire to underline its great power status, and its belief in the inevitable progressive evolution of African politics. The articles promote traditional Soviet goals for developing nations: decreasing ties with the West, increasing cooperation with the Soviet bloc, expanding the state sector of the national economies, and collectivizing agriculture. Secondary sources; 8 notes. R. E. Noble

478. Rainero, Romain. DIECI ANNI DI POLITICA ESTERA DELL'AFRICA INDIPENDENTE [Ten years of foreign policy in independent Africa]. *Nuova Rivista Storica [Italy] 1974 58(5/6): 610-617.* From 1963 to 1973 independent Africa had no common foreign policy because of its wide range of regimes. Within Islam there is the socialism of Algeria and the conservatism of Morocco; the totalitari-

anism of Ethiopia contrasts with the specifically African ideology of Julius Nyerere's socialism in Tanzania. Border disputes, the African leaders' struggles for hegemony and prestige, and the meddling of major powers have hampered African diplomacy. C. Bates

479. Rossi, Gianluigi. GUERRA FREDDA E QUESTIONE DELLE EX COLONIE ITALIANE NEL 1947 [The Cold War and the question of former Italian colonies in 1947]. *Africa [Italy] 1978 33(4): 509-524.* The growing embitterment of East-West relations in 1947 had a noticeable effect on the attitude of Britain and the United States for the disposition of the former Italian colonies in Africa, given new strategic importance by the Cold War. The Americans no less than the British opposed the restoration of Italian control over Libya and Eritrea in addition to Somalia. The main reason for such opposition came from the uncertainty as to the final standing of Italy in the Cold War. Based on British and American diplomatic sources; 38 notes. J

480. Rossi, Gianluigi. TRIESTE E COLONIE ALLA VIGILIA DELLE ELEZIONI ITALIANE DEL 18 APRILE 1948 [Trieste and the colonies on the eve of the Italian elections of 18 April 1948]. *Riv. di Studi Pol. Int. [Italy] 1979 46(2): 205-231.* Discusses the positions of the Italian political forces toward the African colonies following World War II. Examines the USSR's initiatives toward Italy's East African ex-colonies and the responses of Western nations, most specifically in the form of a declaration, 20 March 1948, on the status of Trieste.

481. Rubin, Leslie. AFRICA: THE REDUCED LAAGER. *Freedom at Issue 1976 (34): 29-30.* Attacks African UN delegations for their vote in 1975 equating Zionism with apartheid as racist doctrines.

482. Rubio García, Leandro. AFRICA NEGRA Y ESTADOS ARABES: PETROLEO Y MUNDO POBRE [Black Africa and Arab States: oil and a poor world]. *Rev. de Politica Int. [Spain] 1976 (145): 127-151.* Studies changes in the political attitudes of black African states toward the Middle East problem after the October War, resulting from the possibility of receiving foreign aid from the Arab states.

483. Sawant, Ankush Balaji. RIVALRY BETWEEN EGYPT AND ISRAEL IN AFRICA SOUTH OF THE SAHARA, 1956-1970. *Int. Studies [India] 1978 17(2): 299-329.* When Israel, through Egyptian efforts, found itself isolated in the Middle East, it attempted to win friends in Africa by offering nations economic and technical assistance. Israel achieved notable success in Africa, but Egypt applied steady pressure to counterbalance Israeli moves. The turning point in this Egyptian-Israeli rivalry in Africa was the Six-Day War (1967) which caused many non-Arab African nations to shift their support from Israel. 2 tables, 138 notes. T. P. Linkfield

484. Selcher, Wayne A. BRAZILIAN RELATIONS WITH PORTUGUESE AFRICA IN THE CONTEXT OF THE ELUSIVE "LUSO-BRAZILIAN COMMUNITY." *J. of Interam. Studies and World Affairs 1976 18(1): 25-58.* The Brazilian government has shown a willingness to work with and assist newly independent African states that formerly belonged to Portugal, but it has refused to deal with extreme left-wing governments. Brazil has sent ambassadors to the new nations and some technical aid and relief assistance has been furnished. In return, Brazil expects to enhance its foreign trade through commercial agreements with Portuguese-speaking Africa. Based on Brazilian public documents, newspapers, and magazines; 5 notes, biblio. J. R. Thomas

485. Servranckx, Jacques. LES ACTIONS RÉCENTES DE LA FRANCE EN AFRIQUE [Recent French activities in Africa]. *Défense Natl. [France] 1980 36(10): 32-40.* French military activity in Africa from the military program laid down under the law of 19 June 1976 to 1980 indicates that France has kept faith with its allies.

486. Shaw, Timothy M. THE POLITICAL ECONOMY OF AFRICAN INTERNATIONAL RELATIONS. *Issue 1975 5(4): 29-38.* Analyzes the current international political economy of Africa, emphasizing the factors of nationalism and race relations.

487. Skinner, Elliott P. AFRICAN STATES AND ISRAEL: UNEASY RELATIONS IN A WORLD OF CRISIS. *J. of African Studies 1975 2(1): 1-23.* A review of diplomatic relations between Israel and the nations of black Africa. Early cordiality resulted from Israel's need for friends and Africa's desire to receive aid and win official support. Differences soon manifested themselves and have progressively worsened. Israel came to be viewed as an agent of Western imperialism; Israelis began to regard the African nations as ingrates who accepted money but withheld support. In point of fact, Israel and black Africa have little in common, and their early friendship was based on a series of myths which eventually had to be exposed. 54 notes. V. L. Human

488. Slonim, Shlomo. ISRAEL AND THE NEW SCRAMBLE FOR AFRICA. *Midstream 1977 23(9): 30-35.* Attempts to influence control of the Red Sea have led the Soviet Union (whose relations with Egypt have deteriorated recently) to offer aid to Ethiopia (risking the antagonism of Somalia), while Israel is also becoming more heavily involved in Africa in order to counteract both Arab and Soviet influence over essential waterways in the mid-1970's.

489. Smolansky, O. M. SOVIET POLICY IN THE MIDDLE EAST AND AFRICA. *Current Hist. 1978 75(440): 113-116, 127-128.* In October 1977 the USSR and the United States made public a joint foreign policy statement on the Middle East which recognized the rights of Palestinians and called for Israeli withdrawal from land occupied in 1967, but detente has not excluded Soviet activity in Africa.

490. Solodovnikov, V. G. POBEDA NAD FASHIZMOM I NATSIONAL'NO-OSVOBODITEL'NOE DVIZHENIE V AFRIKE [The victory over fascism and the national liberation movement in Africa]. *Narody Azii i Afriki [USSR] 1975 (5): 6-19.* The defeat of fascist Germany and militarist Japan facilitated the rise of the national liberation movements and the destruction of the colonial system of imperialism. The victory of the Soviet people in World War II assured the victory of socialism. The war experience has given Africans a sense of self-awareness and has readied them for the national liberation struggle. The author cites statements by African leaders that the USSR was their inspiration. For independent African states, the USSR is an example of a progressive socialist state that is providing them with foreign aid to help overcome economic dependence, liquidate all forms of capitalist exploitation, and strengthen their sovereignty. Based on a report to a conference of the Scientific Council of the Institute of Africa and the Soviet Association of Friendship with the People of Africa, 23 April 1975; 31 notes. L. Kalinowski

491. Suret-Canale, Jean. DIFFICULTÉS DU NÉO-COLONIALISME FRANÇAIS EN AFRIQUE TROPICALE [Difficulties of French neocolonialism in tropical Africa]. *Can. J. of African Studies [Canada] 1974 8(2): 211-233.* Despite its economic hegemony in the area, French neocolonial rule in tropical Africa, 1960-72, is being challenged by economic competition of the United States, European Economic Community members, and by nationalist sentiments within African governments that previously supported French colonial policy.

492. Suret-Canale, Jean. L'AFRIQUE MAL EN POINT [Africa in a bad state]. *Civilisations [Belgium] 1979 29(3-4): 236-250.* Decolonization of France's former empire has often been replaced by neocolonialism in the classical economic pattern, with direct control now held by multinational corporations in the franc zone, and spawning ultranationalism and socialism as the African reaction.

493. Tarabrin, E. AFRIKA V GLOBAL'NOI STRATEGII IMPERIALIZMA [Africa in the global strategy of imperialism]. *Mirovaia Ekonomika i Mezhdunarodnye Otnosheniia [USSR] 1982 (2): 25-37.* Imperialism attempts by direct and indirect means to involve the newly independent African countries in the preservation of capitalism and promotion of anti-Communism. US policies are of particular danger for African independence, especially its rapprochement with Egypt and the creation of a military bridgehead in Northeastern Africa. J/S

494. Thompson, W. Scott. THE COMMUNIST POWERS AND AFRICA. *Orbis 1973 16(4): 1066-1069.* Reviews Bruce Larkin's *China and Africa 1949-1970*(University of California Press, 1971) and Robert Legvold's *Soviet Policy in West Africa* (Harvard U. Press, 1970). S

495. Tomlin, Brian W. and Buhlman, Margaret A. RELATIVE STATUS AND FOREIGN POLICY: STATUS PARTITIONING AND THE ANALYSIS OF RELATIONS IN BLACK AFRICA. *J. of*

Conflict Resolution 1977 21(2): 187-216. A revision of the status-field theory, applied to foreign relations of 32 black African states in the middle 1960's, permits an analysis of their foreign policy as determined by their power and degree of economic development.

496. Torre, Serrando de la. ASPECTOS DE LA POLÍTICA CHINA EN LAS LUCHAS DE LIBERACIÓN DE AFRICA [Aspects of Chinese policy toward the liberation struggles of Africa]. *Rev. de Politica Int. [Spain] 1977 (149): 147-173.* Discusses the principles behind China's early African policies, and the growth of a more pragmatic Chinese approach to African problems.

497. Tunteng, P. Kiven. FRANCE-AFRICA: PLUS ÇA CHANGE... *Africa Report 1974 19(4): 2-6.* French foreign policy toward Africa remains unchanged from the days of de Gaulle. S

498. Utete, Charles M. B. CHINA'S AFRICAN POLICY. *African Rev. [Tanzania] 1975 5(1): 100-106.* A review of Alaba Ogunsanwo, *China's Policy in Africa, 1958-1971* (Cambridge: Cambridge U. Pr., 1974) which is one of the very few studies available. 2 notes. R. T. Brown

499. Valenzuela-Fuenzalida, Juan J. INDIFERENCIA, ESTEREOTIPO Y COOPERACION HORIZONTAL: OBSTACULOS PARA LA COOPERACION ENTRE AFRICA Y AMERICA LATINA [Indifference, stereotyping, and mutual cooperation: obstacles in the cooperation between Africa and Latin America]. *Estudios de Asia y Africa [Mexico] 1981 16(1): 124-160.* Describes Juan J. Valenzuela-Fuenzalida's Proyecto Gondwana, which was begun in 1974 at Ahmadu Bello University, Zaria, Nigeria to ascertain the African perception of Latin Americans. Results of a survey showed the lack of accurate knowledge regarding Latin America. These are obstacles in the Third World to mutual international cooperation and growth. Based on a work presented at the 1st meeting of the Latin American Association of Afro-Asian Studies, Mexico City, 16 July 1978; biblio., 2 appendixes, 27 notes, 7 charts. N. A. Newhouse

500. Valkenier, Elizabeth Kridl. GREAT POWER ECONOMIC COMPETITION IN AFRICA: SOVIET PROGRESS AND PROBLEMS. *J. of Int. Affairs 1980-81 34(2): 259-268.* Describes the extent of the USSR's economic relations with Africa from 1955 to 1980, commenting on its political aims. The relative failure of Soviet policies in Africa provides opportunities for Western nations to expand their influence.

501. Vedovato, Giuseppe. I PROBLEMI POSTI ALLA NATO DALLA PENETRAZIONE SOVIETICA IN AFRICA [The problems posed for NATO by the Soviet penetration in Africa]. *Riv. di Studi Pol. Int. [Italy] 1979 46(3): 389-395.* Soviet penetration in Africa in the 1960's-70's, has further eroded the position of Europe in Africa, where NATO had already failed to assert leadership.

502. Vengroff, Richard. NEO-COLONIALISM AND POLICY OUTPUTS IN AFRICA. *Comparative Pol. Studies 1975 8(2): 234-250.* A comparative study based on statistical data from the 1960's of the attempts of France and Great Britain to maintain internal control of their African ex-colonies, the French through trade control and the British, adapting more to the growing world imperialist system, through multinational corporations.

503. Vukadinović, Radovan. KINESKI CILJEVI I INTERESI U AFRICI [China's aims and interests in Africa]. *Politička Misao [Yugoslavia] 1981 18(3): 299-309.* Analyzes Chinese policy toward Africa in the past 20 years. In the main it has been directed toward winning recognition from newly independent states in order to foster general international standing and thwarting Soviet interests.

504. Weinstein, Warren. AFRICA'S APPROACH TO HUMAN RIGHTS AT THE UNITED NATIONS. *Issue 1976 6(4): 14-21.* Discusses African developing nations' interest in the UN Commission on Human Rights' attempts to deal with racism and human rights violations, 1966-70's; considers violations in Southern Africa, Ghana, Rwanda, Burundi and Uganda.

505. Weissman, Stephen R. CIA COVERT ACTION IN ZAIRE AND ANGOLA: PATTERNS AND CONSEQUENCES. *Pol. Sci. Q. 1979 94(2): 263-286.* Describes the Central Intelligence Agency's intervention in the Third World through case studies of "covert action" in Zaire and Angola. The varying degrees of success of covert action depended upon collateral use of overt diplomacy, the internal organization of targeted groups, and the nature of the Soviet and Chinese responses. J

506. Yakemtchouk, R. LA RECONNAISSANCE D'ÉTAT ET DE GOUVERNEMENT EN AFRIQUE [The recognition of state and of government in Africa]. *Bull. des Séances de l'Acad. Royale des Sci. d'Outre-Mer [Belgium] 1973 (2): 170-196.* Analyzes the problem of diplomatic recognition of states in newly independent Africa. Historical precedents offer no guidelines. An accord for the transfer of power was the means to extend recognition to some countries. Other African states and governments failed to receive recognition where their competence to govern and the representation of citizens were questioned. The Estrada Doctrine allows for recognition of the state but not the internal government: international relations are thus maintained despite coups d'état. The integration of Africa into the international order remains difficult. 25 notes. H. D. Nycz

507. Yeh Po-t'ang. PEIPING'S POLICY TOWARDS AFRICA AS VIEWED FROM THE INDEPENDENCE OF GUINEA-BISSAU AND MOZAMBIQUE. *Issues and Studies [Taiwan] 1974 10(15): 2-12.* Discusses China's diplomacy and foreign aid policy toward African nations in light of recent independence movements in Guinea-Bissau and Mozambique, 1960's-70's.

508. Young, Crawford. SOVIET DIPLOMACY IN AFRICA. *Orbis 1982 25(4): 1053-1062.* Presents a review of Dan C. Heldman, *The USSR and Africa: Foreign Policy under Khrushchev* (1981) and David and Marina Ottaway, *Afrocommunism* (1981). Compares the failures of the Khrushchev era with the moderate gains made by the Soviets since the Portuguese and Ethiopian collapse. 12 notes. J. W. Thacker, Jr.

509. Yu, George T. CHINA'S IMPACT. *Problems of Communism 1978 27(1): 40-50.* Examines overall Chinese activities on the African continent, the image that the USSR has sought to project in Africa, and Moscow's perceptions of how Chinese behavior tarnishes that image. Discusses Peking's critique of the USSR's intentions and actions in Africa, and the impact that China has apparently had on Soviet policy toward the continent. 3 tables, 37 notes. J. M. Lauber

510. Yu, George T. CHINA'S ROLE IN AFRICA. *Ann. of the Am. Acad. of Pol. and Soc. Sci. 1977 (432): 96-109.* Over two decades have passed since China made its first formal presence in Africa in 1955, and since then China has become a major actor with vital interests in the continent. The greater part of Chinese-African interaction occurred from 1960-65—a high point of African decolonization and a time of Sino-Soviet conflict. From 1965-70 Chinese-African interaction coincided with the Great Proletarian Cultural Revolution. It was a time of Chinese retreat. Since 1970, China has reemerged as a major actor in Africa. There are three major components of China's role in Africa: the Chinese model, the superpowers, and China's Third World policy. The call to liberation struggles has long been a hallmark of Chinese policy. The Chinese model also relates to China's developmental experience. China has stressed struggle against the superpowers, the US and Soviet Union, identifying with the Third World against them. There can be no doubt that Africa occupied a central place in Chinese foreign policy and the United States and Soviet Union were important factors in it. China can expect to retain its presence in Africa if it responds to Africa's changing situation.

511. —. [BRAZILIAN FOREIGN POLICY IN SOUTHERN AFRICA]. *Munger Africana Lib. Notes 1974 23: 4-37.*

Glasgow, Roy. PRAGMATISM AND IDEALISM IN BRAZILIAN FOREIGN POLICY IN SOUTHERN AFRICA, *pp. 4-20.* From a paper given at the 1973 African Studies Association meeting, Syracuse, New York.

Spitzer, Manon L. COMMENT, *pp. 21-23.*

Glasgow, Roy. REPLY, *p. 24.*

Sanders, Thomas. COMMENT, *pp. 25-26.*

Glasgow, Roy. REPLY, *pp. 27-28.*

—. INTERVIEW, *pp. 29-37.*

512. —. MIDDLE EAST WAR: AFRICAN REACTION. *Afriscope [Nigeria] 1973 3(12): 8-10.* Catalogs the reactions of the African states which severed diplomatic relations with Israel following the October War (1973). G. O. Gagnon

Foreign Aid

513. Arnold, Guy. AID AND AFRICAN DEVELOPMENT. *Contemporary Rev. [Great Britain] 1982 240(1394): 113-119.* Surveys the international dimensions of foreign aid to Africa, 1950-81.

514. Bailey, Martin. FREEDOM RAILROAD. *Monthly Rev. 1976 27(11): 32-44.* Made possible by a $400 million loan from the People's Republic of China, the recently completed Uhuru (Freedom) Railroad forms a vital link between the Zambian Copperbelt and the Tanzanian port of Dar es Salaam. The benefits afforded both nations are numerous, e.g., the abandonment of reliance on Rhodesian transport facilities, the creation of new jobs and skills, and the development of important trade connections. The evidence does not suggest that Tanzania and Zambia have sold out to the Chinese; China seems determined to help progressive African nations help themselves and thus prevent their affiliation with either Washington or Moscow. M. R. Yerburgh

515. Baskin, V. S. TEKHNICHESKAIA POMOSHCH' KAPITALISTICHESKIKH GOSUDARSTV STRANAM AFRIKI [Technical aid by capitalist countries to the countries of Africa]. *Narody Azii i Afriki [USSR] 1981 (5): 15-25.* Traces the sharp growth of Western technical assistance during the 1960's and 1970's. Examines the importation and confirmation of Western norms through technical education of specialists, but draws attention to the corresponding drawbacks of brain drain and insufficient cadres. Stresses the negative effects of the presence of Western specialists: cost, effect on prices and jobs, interference in internal politics, remoteness of many local projects, and subordination to the interests of donor countries. English summary. F. A. K. Yasamee

516. Berman, Edward H. AMERICAN PHILANTHROPY AND AFRICAN EDUCATION: TOWARDS AN ANALYSIS. *African Studies Rev. 1977 20(1): 71-85.* The American financial contribution to education in Africa has been increasing steadily since the 1920's.

517. Berman, Edward H. THE FOUNDATIONS' INTEREST IN AFRICA. *Hist. of Educ. Q. 1978 18(4): 461-470.* Review article of Kenneth James King's *Pan-Africanism and Education: A Study of Race Philanthropy and Education in the Southern States of America and East Africa* (Oxford: Clarendon Press, 1971) and E. Jefferson Murphy's *Creative Philanthropy: Carnegie Corporation and Africa, 1953-1973* (New York and London: Teachers College Press, 1976). King examines the education for blacks promoted by American industrialists through their philanthropic organizations. The educational philosophy and goals were based on racism. Education was designed to fit the black for labor by providing an agricultural education, simple manual training, and some character education. Murphy deals with the more modern period and the Carnegie Corporation. 7 notes. R. V. Ritter

518. Cervenka, Zdenek. THE PRAGMATIC APPROACH. *Africa Report 1975 20(1): 37-41.* Examines West Germany's economic relations with Africa 1966-74. S

519. Cotter, William R. U.S. AID: HOW AFRICA IS SHORTCHANGED. *Africa Report 1974 19(6): 2-8, 54.* Foreign aid to Africa decreases annually, despite Africa's growing development needs and growing US dependence on Africa's raw materials. S

520. Diggs, Charles C., Jr. THE DROUGHT IN THE SAHEL. *Black Scholar 1974 5(10): 37-42.* Describes the devastation of the Sahel drought, 1968-74, and the slow progress of efforts to relieve the approximately 25 million inhabitants of the six countries of the arid belt south of the Sahara Desert: Mauritania, Senegal, Mali, Upper Volta, Niger, and Chad.

521. Dow, Thomas E., Jr. FAMINE IN THE SAHEL: A DILEMMA FOR UNITED STATES AID. *Current Hist. 1975 68(405): 197-201.* It seems clear that any effort that treats the Sahel food shortage as simply an emergency... will only result in a still larger population sharing in current levels of misery. Because the current United States approach defines the food shortage in this way, it will serve only to maintain the problem and, in a quantitative sense, to make it worse. J

522. Gitelson, Susan Aurelia. ARAB AID TO AFRICA. *Midstream 1976 22(8): 22-28.* Examines the extent, nature, and problems involved in Arab economic aid to African nations during the 1970's.

523. Gitelson, Susan Aurelia. ARAB AID TO AFRICA: HOW MUCH AND AT WHAT PRICE? *Jerusalem Q. [Israel] 1981 (19): 120-127.* Outlines the hardships that increased oil prices, imposed by the Organization of Petroleum Exporting Countries, have caused for the development of African nations, 1973-80, and demonstrates the Africans' conflict between acceptance of foreign aid from Arab states and regional political independence.

524. Gribbin, Robert E. TWO RELIEF CRISES: BIAFRA AND SUDAN. *Africa Today 1973 20(3): 47-59.* The Sudan and Biafra cases suggest that private agencies are the best vehicles for relief, that donor nations must be aware of Third World sensitivities, and that the UN and a sympathetic press are helpful. Biblio. G. O. Gagnon

525. Houndjahoue, Michel. ESSAI SUR L'ETUDE DE LA COOPERATION BILATERALE ENTRE LE CANADA ET L'AFRIQUE FRANCOPHONE, 1961-1981 [The study of bilateral cooperation between Canada and French-speaking Africa, 1961-81]. *Etudes Int. [Canada] 1982 13(2): 263-282.* Divides the period into three phases: in the years 1961-68 Canadian aid was slight and discontinuous; 1969-75 saw a remarkable increase in foreign aid under the influence of the Trudeau and Chevrier missions and Canada's changing foreign policy; 1975-81 there was industrial cooperation, that is, cooperation between "project-countries" and "program countries." 65 notes. J. F. Harrington, Jr.

526. Howard, Rhoda. THE CANADIAN GOVERNMENT RESPONSE TO AFRICA'S REFUGEE PROBLEM. *Can. J. of African Studies [Canada] 1981 15(1): 95-116.* Canada's main response to the problem of African refugees has been financial contributions. The Canadian representatives of the United Nations High Commission for Refugees (UNHCR) have insisted on the necessity of assuring the refugees legal protection. Canadian politics in this domain are motivated by both humanitarian reasons and a desire to maintain political stability in Africa. Primary sources; 73 notes. J. Powell

527. Il'in, Iu. NAUCHNOE SOTRUDNICHESTVO SSSR S AFRIKANSKIMI STRANAMI [Scientific cooperation of the USSR with the countries of Africa]. *Aziia i Afrika Segodnia [USSR] 1977 (5): 18-20.* Provides numerous examples of growing Soviet-African scientific cooperation. J/S

528. Janke, Peter. MARXISM IN AFRICA: THE CUBAN CONNECTION. *Midstream 1978 24(7): 3-10.* The Marxist-Leninist African states, Angola, Ethiopia, and Mozambique, are far from reaching their objectives but have depended since 1975 on the military forces or a small support staff of political commissars and media persons from Cuba and East Germany.

529. Kheir, A. M. SOVIET POLICY BOOMERANGS IN AFRICA. *Eastern Horizon [Hong Kong] 1978 17(9): 40-43.* Summarizes the USSR's assistance to Africa, its goals, and its failures, emphasizing assistance to Egypt, Sudan, and Somalia during the 1950's-70's.

530. Miller, Jake C. THE HOMELESS OF AFRICA. *Africa Today 1982 29(2): 5-30.* Analyzes and describes the causes of the African refugee problem and summarizes efforts to address the problem by the UN, the Organization of African Unity, and other agencies. Calls for more international effort to aid African refugees and to eliminate the causes of homelessness. Based on UN, OAU, and secondary sources; 77 notes. G. O. Gagnon

531. Rettman, Rosalyn J. THE TANZAM RAIL LINK: CHINA'S "LOSS-LEADER" IN AFRICA. *World Affairs 1973/74 136(3): 232-258.*

532. Sircar, Parbati K. THE GREAT UHURU (FREEDOM) RAILWAY: CHINA'S LINK TO AFRICA. *China Report [India] 1978 14(2): 15-24.* Following Rhodesia's Unilateral Declaration of Independence in 1965, its northern neighbor, Zambia, cut off all trade. Zambia thus hampered severely its own trade with the outside world, and the idea of a railway linking Dar-es-Salaam with Zambia's copper-mining region assumed critical importance. China, which imports more than half its copper, was another interested party, and the result was the Tanzam Railway project, financed by an interest-free loan from China to the two African nations. Work began in 1970, and the line was officially opened in 1975, having been completed two years ahead of schedule. Discusses the project's economic significance, and its place in China's foreign policy. 5 tables, 25 notes. L. W. Van Wyk

533. —. [THE DROUGHT]. *Africa Report 1974 19(5): 11-16.*
—. REFUGEES FROM AFRICA'S FAMINES, *pp. 11-12.*
—. EASING THE TRANSPORT BOTTLENECK, *pp. 13-16.* UNICEF provides food to refugee camps in West Africa and Ethiopia; poor transportation and storage facilities hinder food distribution to West Africa's interior. S

534. —. [U.S. FOREIGN POLICY AND AMERICAN FOUNDATION INTERVENTION IN AFRICAN EDUCATION, 1945-75]. *Harvard Educ. Rev. 1979 49(2): 145-184.*
Berman, Edward H. FOUNDATIONS, UNITED STATES FOREIGN POLICY, AND AFRICAN EDUCATION, 1945-1975, *pp. 145-179.* Examines the shaping of African educational policy from 1945 to 1975 with the aid of American foundations and US foreign policy decisions, which have been implemented in the political and economic interests of American corporations.
Pifer, Alan; Sutton, Francis X.; and Stifel, Laurence D. RESPONSES TO EDWARD H. BERMAN, *pp. 180-184.* Responses from representatives of the Carnegie Corporation and the Ford and Rockefeller foundations.

International Trade

535. Akinsanya, Adeoye. THE EUROPEAN COMMON MARKET AND AFRICA. *Int. Problems [Israel] 1977 16(1-2): 99-117.* Examines the origins of the European Economic Community (EEC), its goals and aspirations, the effect of Great Britain's entry, the nature and purpose of African dealings with the EEC, and African attitudes to it.

536. Akinsanya, Adeoye. THE EUROPEAN COMMON MARKET AND AFRICA. *Pan-African J. [Kenya] 1976 9(4): 415-430.* Reviews the aims and origins of the European Economic Community (EEC), and discusses how and why many African nations have become associated with it and the benefits and disadvantages of this association, 1957-76. Despite the short-term economic advantages of African links with the EEC, this association has really been between the producers of raw materials and the highly industrialized West and it has meant a continuation of Africa's postcolonial dependence. 39 notes. R. D. Black

537. Akinsanya, Adeoye. THE EUROPEAN COMMON MARKET AND AFRICA. *Pakistan Horizon [Pakistan] 1975 28(3): 38-55.* Traces the history of the European Economic Community and examines the implications of Africa's association with it. 40 notes. H. M. Evans

538. Amvrosova, M. SKANDINAVSKAIA SOTSIAL-DEMOKRATIIA I AFRIKA [Scandinavian social democracy and Africa]. *Aziia i Afrika Segodnia [USSR] 1981 (2): 24-27.* Describes the attempts of some Western countries, Scandinavian among them, to integrate the newly-free African states more firmly into the world capitalist economic system, to preserve their control over them. J

539. Avery, William P. and Picard, Louis A. PULL FACTORS IN THE TRANSFER OF CONVENTIONAL ARMAMENTS TO AFRICA. *J. of Pol. and Military Sociol. 1980 8(1): 55-70.* An empirical examination of "pull factors" (conditions associated with a recipient country's domestic situation) in the arms trade to Africa indicates that the availability of economic resources is the primary influence on levels of arms transfers to Africa during the period 1965-71. The proximity of the Middle East conflict has a significant impact on North African calculations of arms needs. An unexpected finding is the apparent absence of a significant relationship between regional conflict in the South and arms imports. On the political level, civil strife and military influence in government are significant factors in decisions to import arms. Based on data from the U.S. Arms Control and Disarmament Agency; 3 tables; 13 notes, 42 ref. J

540. Baregu, Mwesiga L. MULTINATIONAL CORPORATIONS IN AFRICA. *Taamuli [Tanzania] 1977 7(2): 19-31.* Multinational corporations began penetrating African nations in force during the postcolonial era, and tended to concentrate their African investments in mining and processing industries. This concentration had a distorting effect on the economies of their host nations. 25 notes. D. S. Rockwood

541. Bono, Salvatore. RAPPORTI COMMERCIALI E DI LAVORO FRA L'ITALIA E L'AFRICA [Trade and labor relations between Italy and Africa]. *Africa [Italy] 1976 31(2): 291-294.* Commercial and labor relations between Italy and Africa have increased greatly in the postwar era. In 1963, Italy exported as much to Africa as it did to South America; in 1975 it was twice as much. Italy exports more to Africa (minus South Africa) than it does to Asia (minus Japan, Israel, and China). Africa's share of Italy's trade is just over nine percent. Italy trades more with Africa than with any single nation of the European Community except France. J. C. Billigmeier

542. Chinua, Alex. MULTINATIONAL COMPANIES GROW NEW WINGS. *Afriscope [Nigeria] 1974 4(6): 29-35.* Outlines the exploitation of Africa by "giant monopolies." Provides extensive examples of mergers such as Standard Bank and Chartered Bank which have solidified foreign control of Africa. Concludes for "Africa's multinational companies, it is super profits, for the Africans it is a never ending toil and poverty." G. O. Gagnon

543. Clarke, Michael. EVALUATING LOMÉ. *J. of Common Market Studies [Great Britain] 1982 20(3): 287-292.* Reviews six books which discuss the relationship between the European Communities and the African, Caribbean, and Pacific states.

544. Colitti, Marcello. I RAPPORTI FRA L'ITALIA E I PAESI AFRICANI [The relations between Italy and the African countries]. *Affari Esteri [Italy] 1974 6(23): 93-109.* Trade and commercial relations between Italy and the nations of Africa increased markedly during the 1960's bringing closer ties with many of the nations south of the Sahara. In the 1970's Italy has sought to gain an even closer connection. While a number of problems remain, Italy stands ready to work with the nations of Africa in every way possible. A. R. Stoesen

545. Cooper, Frederick. AFRICA AND THE WORLD ECONOMY. *African Studies Rev. 1981 24(2-3): 1-86.* A review of the literature and of the academic debate concerning the relation of the African economy to the world economy prepared for the American Council of Learned Societies and the Social Sciences Research Council. 181 notes, biblio. R. T. Brown

546. Coquery-Vidrovitch, Catherine. L'IMPÉRIALISME FRANÇAIS EN AFRIQUE NOIRE: IDÉOLOGIE IMPÉRIALE ET POLITIQUE D'ÉQUIPEMENT, 1924-1975 [French imperialism in black Africa: imperial ideology and investment policy, 1924-75]. *Relations Int. [France] 1976(7): 261-282.* Examines the increase of productive forces in Africa. They do not seem to have risen and fallen in concert with political development or events. During the period between the wars when the French Empire and imperial ideology were basically intact, foreign investments were low; after World War II, when nationalism was sweeping black Africa, they were on the average four times higher. French economic power in Africa did not stop with the granting of an often only nominal independence in 1958-60. 3 tables, 6 graphs, 71 notes. J. C. Billigmeier

547. Curry, Robert, Jr. and Rothchild, Donald. ON ECONOMIC BARGAINING BETWEEN AFRICAN GOVERNMENTS AND MULTI-NATIONAL COMPANIES. *J. of Modern African Studies [Great Britain] 1974 12(2): 173-189.* Large corporations that deal with Africa are the primary contact between Africa and the industrialized world. Analyzes this relationship and notes the crucial variables

affecting bargaining and economic relations. African nations possess advantages not yet exercised. 27 notes. H. G. Soff

548. Dobosiewicz, Zbigniew. POLAND AND WEST AFRICAN COUNTRIES. *Studies on the Developing Countries [Poland] 1979 (10): 121-129.* Examines Poland's trade and scientific cooperation with the nations of West Africa.

549. Dzidzienyo, Anani and Turner, L. Michael. RELACIONES ENTRE AFRICA Y BRASIL: UNA RECONSIDERACION [Africa-Brazil relations: another look]. *Estudios de Asia y Africa [Mexico] 1981 16(4): 651-674.* In the last seven years Brazil has adopted a policy of expansion of its interests in West Africa, and this policy has been characterized by Brazilians themselves as "conquest." The authors analyze the extent of Brazil's commercial ties with Nigeria, Angola, and Gabon and its historical and cultural ties with those countries. Given Africa's colonial experience and the importance of the racial question in both national and international politics, Africans would be well advised to look closely into any attempts at foreign penetration of their markets. 61 notes. J. V. Coutinho

550. Engberg, Holger L. THE OPERATIONS ACCOUNT SYSTEM IN FRENCH-SPEAKING AFRICA. *J. of Modern African Studies [Great Britain] 1973 11(4): 537-545.* A study of the monetary relationships between France and its former African colonies in the light of current unrest and the desire for greater economic freedom by the African states. Although there have been some changes, two principles have been repeatedly reaffirmed: the free convertibility between the C. F. A. franc and the French franc and the French treasury guarantee of the external value of the African currency. This is equivalent to saying that the Operations Account system must be maintained. The price paid for this unique relationship consists of other constraints: monetary dependence on France and fixed exchange rates among the overseas members of the franc zone. The political significance will probably take on increasing importance as the states proceed in their development efforts. 9 notes. R. V. Ritter

551. Falegan, S. B. AFRICA AND THE DOLLAR. *Afriscope [Nigeria] 1973 3(4): 23-26.* The world monetary crises of the 1960's adversely affected Africa's monetary reserves, aggravated an unfavorable balance of trade, and facilitated debt payment. Illus. G. O. Gagnon

552. Faroqui, Hossain Shahid. THE ACP-EC PHENOMENON: THE LOMÉ CONVENTION IN PERSPECTIVE. *Dacca U. Studies Part A [Bangladesh] 1977 (26): 117-129.* On 28 February 1975, the representatives of the nine member-countries of the European Economic Community (EEC) and the 46 African, Caribbean, and Pacific (ACP) nations assembled in Lomé, Togo, and signed a five-year economic trade and aid pact, the Lomé Convention. It created a special relationship between the EEC and ACP countries: the EEC granted the ACP countries duty-free access to its own market on a nonreciprocal basis, agreed to help implement an export stabilization scheme for the ACP countries, and agreed to provide substantial economic assistance. 88 notes.

553. Fouguet, David. AFRICAN UNITY—IN EUROPE. *Africa Report 1975 20(4): 7-9.* African states have united in tough bargaining with the European Economic Community to forge trade agreements. S

554. Gnevushev, N. A. EES I STRANY AFRIKI [The EEC and African countries]. *Narody Azii i Afriki [USSR] 1979 (6): 12-23.* Criticizes dealings of the European Economic Community with African countries as attempts to impose economic policies which suit only West European enterprises. Reviews advantages and disadvantages stemming from the Lomé Convention in 1975, citing economic data showing effects of nationalizing multinational corporations such as Lonrho. The opposition to foreign intervention is aided by socialist countries, but success depends more on the skill of a given state's foreign policy. 33 notes. V. A. Packer

555. Goncharov, L. AFRIKA V BOR'BE ZA NOVYI MEZHDUNARODNYI EKONOMICKESKII PORIADOK [Africa in the struggle for the New International Economic Order]. *Mirovaia Ekonomika i Mezhdunarodnye Otnosheniia [USSR] 1982 (6): 49-62.* Considers the major issues of African economic development, which are closely interwoven with the reshaping of the unequal economic relations existing between newly independent African countries and the developed capitalist countries. J/S

556. Gruhn, Isebill V. THE LOMÉ CONVENTION: INCHING TOWARD INTERDEPENDENCE. *Int. Organization 1976 30(2): 241-262.* The European Economic Community and 46 African, Caribbean, and Pacific States (ACP) signed a trade and aid convention in February 1975. The negotiations leading to the Lomé Convention and its provisions constitute an instructive vehicle for an examination of North-South bargaining. The organization, tenacity, and skill of the ACP states, as well as some rethinking regarding their own situation on the part of European states produced some innovative and groundbreaking moves toward more equitable trade and aid relations. But even the most innovative components of the Lomé Convention are perhaps less significant for their short-term economic effects than they are for a general understanding regarding the structure of North-South relations. J

557. Grzybowski, Antoni. WCZORAJ I DZIŚ TURYSTYKI AFRYKAŃSKIEJ [The past and present in African tourism]. Szymański, Edward. *Tradycja i Współczesność w Azji, Afryce i Ameryce Łacińskiej* (Warsaw: Polska Akademia Nauk Zakład Krajów Pozaeuropejskich, 1978): 239-266. Examines European stereotypes of Africa and their effect on increasing tourist traffic to Africa following the advent of independence.

558. Harriss, Barbara. GOING AGAINST THE GRAIN. *Development and Change [Netherlands] 1979 10(3): 363-384.* Examines state intervention in the food grains marketing system of the Sudano-Sahelian states, 1960's-70's.

559. Hopkins, A. G. IMPERIAL BUSINESS IN AFRICA. *J. of African Hist. [Great Britain] 1976 17(1): 29-48.* Research on expatriate firms in colonial Africa is inadequate. The author surveys existing secondary sources on foreign companies in Africa, especially company histories. In a subsequent article he will attempt to judge the quality of these studies. 86 notes. Article to be continued (see abstract 27). H. G. Soff

560. Iudanov, Iu. ZAPADNOEVROPEISKII KAPITAL V AFRIKE [Western European capital in Africa]. *Mirovaia Ekonomika i Mezhdunarodnye Otnosheniia [USSR] 1978 (10): 23-38.* Analyzes the level and distribution of foreign investment in Africa and shows that the involvement of Western European companies still far exceeds that of either Japanese or American business.

561. Jepma, Catrinus. AN APPLICATION OF THE CONSTANT MARKET SHARES TECHNIQUE ON TRADE BETWEEN THE ASSOCIATED AFRICAN AND MALAGASY STATES AND THE EUROPEAN COMMUNITY (1958-1978). *J. of Common Market Studies [Great Britain] 1981 20(2): 175-192.* Measures the structure and growth of trade flows between the European Economic Community and its associated states in Africa, showing that the treaty commitment to development for all the associated states has not been fulfilled.

562. Johnson, Willard R. and Wilson, Ernest J., III. THE "OIL CRISES" AND AFRICAN ECONOMIES: OIL WAVE ON A TIDAL FLOOD OF INDUSTRIAL PRICE INFLATION. *Daedalus 1982 111(2): 211-241.* Discusses the ability of African economies to absorb the shocks caused by the oil prices fluctuations of the 1970's and especially the inability of less developed countries to meet their energy needs in a period of increased oil prices and continuing recession in the industrial markets.

563. Kaviraj, Sudipta. MULTI-NATIONAL FIRMS IN AFRICA. *Africa Q. [India] 1977 16(3): 54-66.* Reviews, in Marxist-Leninist terms, a collection of essays published under this title in Uppsala, 1975: the reviewer finds many contributions valuable but ideologically unsound and unduly pessimistic about the future.

564. Kennedy, Paul. AFRICAN BUSINESSMEN AND FOREIGN CAPITAL: COLLABORATION OR CONFLICT. *African Affairs [Great Britain] 1977 76(303): 177-194.* Focuses on African businessmen in private enterprise in Africa, and examines the question of how far

they can be said to fulfill the "comprador" role allotted to them by dependency theory. Indicates the weakness of dependency theory with regard to the relationship between local business groups and foreign investments. Among the changes taking place in the Third World is "the rise of new groups including local capitalists and the proletariat which is linked to them and to the multinational state corporations." Discusses in some detail the situation in Ghana. 27 notes. E. P. Stickney.

565. Kirkpatrick, Colin and Nixson, Frederick. TRANSNATIONAL CORPORATIONS AND ECONOMIC DEVELOPMENT. *J. of Modern African Studies [Great Britain] 1981 19(3): 367-399.* Assesses the role of Western multinational corporations in the development of national economies among African less developed countries, with emphasis on the mining and manufacturing sectors. Radical dependency theory fails to explain the intricacies of the "symbiotic relationships" between multinationals and developing nations. African states, in their dealings with the multinationals have tended to acquire large revenues, as well as structural growth and change in their economies. These result from host governments' taxing and increasing their involvement or share of control in the new industries. Multinationals have reinvested profits in local manufacturing enterprises, while transferring technology and introducing new consumer tastes. Based on published UN and World Bank reports and secondary sources; 5 tables, 119 notes.
L. W. Truschel

566. Magyar, Karl P. UNITED STATES TRADE WITH AFRICA: A CRITICAL PERSPECTIVE. *J. of African Studies 1981 8(3): 121-125.* After 1973 the American trade surplus with Sub-Saharan Africa became a trade deficit. This was not entirely due to the rise in price of Nigerian petroleum, since American imports have exceeded exports with 14 of 17 leading trade partners in the region. The United States is certain to increase imports of African energy resources and cash crops. Nonetheless, an activist role by Washington facilitating private business investments to sell American products and to foster African development can succeed because Africans have become disillusioned with the repeated failures of socialist policies and programs for economic growth. L. W. Truschel

567. Mariñas Otero, Luis. EL ACUERDO DE LOMÉ [The Lomé Convention]. *Rev. de Política Int. [Spain] 1975 (139): 53-71.* Discusses the background to the Lomé negotiations, and their importance, both for the European Economic Community and for developing nations.

568. Ndongko, Wilfred A. THE ECONOMIC ORIGINS OF THE ASSOCIATION OF SOME AFRICAN STATES WITH THE EUROPEAN ECONOMIC COMMUNITY. *African Studies R. 1973 16(2): 219-232.* Examines French colonial economic policy and the origins of French West African states' association with the European Economic Community. S

569. Nevski, A. ORUDIE NEOKOLONIALIZMA V AFRIKE [An instrument of neocolonialism]. *Aziia i Afrika Segodnia [USSR] 1982 (9): 12-15.* Discusses the efforts of the countries of tropical Africa to come to terms with multinational corporations and their influence on the world economic system.

570. Rivers, Patrick. UNWRAPPING THE AFRICA TOURIST PACKAGE. *Africa Report 1974 19(2): 12-16.* Effects of tourism on national development in Africa in the seventies. S

571. Robinson, Randall. GULF OIL'S STRATEGY TO APPEASE AND OPPRESS. *Black Scholar 1973-74 5(4): 51-55.* Gulf Oil's domestic publicity campaign to appease the American Black community conceals its oppressive policies in Africa. S

572. Rood, Leslie L. FOREIGN INVESTMENT IN AFRICAN MANUFACTURING. *J. of Modern African Studies [Great Britain] 1975 13(1): 19-34.* The host governments in the developing nations welcome foreign investment but are concerned about outside exploitation. The first comprehensive figures on private foreign direct investment in the developing world make possible this analysis of 1) the nature and amount of such investment in black Africa; 2) the influence of the size of the market; and 3) the risks of nationalization, Africanization, and indigenization. Investment in manufacturing by multinational corporations is relatively safe. 3 tables, 32 notes. R. V. Ritter

573. Rood, Leslie L. FOREIGN INVESTMENT IN AFRICAN DEVELOPMENT. *J. of African Studies 1978 5(1): 18-33.* A comparative analysis of alleged beneficial and detrimental effects of foreign investments on developing countries in black Africa since 1945. Compares the findings of a number of case studies and overall assessments with the author's observations with respect to extractive and manufacturing enterprises. Based on personal observations, United Nations documents, and secondary sources; 31 notes.
L. W. Truschel

574. Rubinshtein, G. I. RAZVIVAIUSHCHIESIA STRANY AFRIKI V MEZHDUNARODNOI TORGOVLE [The developing nations of Africa in international trade]. *Narody Azii i Afriki [USSR] 1974 (3): 8-19.* Surveys trends in the foreign trade carried on by developing African states since 1960, noting their lessening dependence on capitalist countries and growing exchange with the USSR.

575. Sakarai, Lawrence J. THE IMPERIALISTS IN AFRICA. *Africa Q. [India] 1976 16(1): 29-59.* Studies the bonds between Africa and imperialist economies and capitalist control of traditional African social organization.

576. Schatz, Sayre P. PERSPECTIVES ON TRANSNATIONAL CORPORATIONS AND AFRICA. *African Studies Rev. 1981 24(4): 23-28.* Reviews five books published in 1979-80 which present both favorable and antagonistic views of the roles of multinational corporations in modern African states. 3 notes. R. T. Brown/S

577. Seidman, Ann. POST WORLD WAR II IMPERIALISM IN AFRICA: A MARXIST PERSPECTIVE. *J. of Southern African Affairs 1977 2(4): 403-425.* Outlines the factors driving multinational corporations to compete in devising new techniques to extract surplus value from the divided politically independent African states, and the implications for Africa of the general crisis of capitalism in the 1970's. The new nations have found it difficult after a century of colonial rule to carry out the transition to socialism. In the period 1965-75, US multinationals took out of Africa (excluding South Africa) about 25% more than they invested there. 2 tables, 64 notes. E. P. Stickney

578. Smith, Keith. WHO CONTROLS BOOK PUBLISHING IN ANGLOPHONE MIDDLE AFRICA? *Ann. of the Am. Acad. of Pol. and Social Sci. 1975 421: 140-150.* Book publishing in anglophone middle Africa must be interpreted against a background of illiteracy, an emphasis on achievement reading, and other social and infrastructural elements. International market forces acting through metropolitan publishers determine general and non-fiction publishing, whereas the major market governing African creative writing is found in African schools and universities. The actions of British publishing multinationals only diverge slightly from the pattern of multinational action in less developed countries. Educational publishing is dominated by these multinationals who, through localization and because of the barriers to African educational publishing, have generally retained their position. State publishing, retarded by problems, has not yet proved very successful. Only limited government action has been taken to adjust the balance in favor of indigenous publishing because a symbiotic relationship exists between the educational system, multinational publishers, bureaucrats and transnationalism. J

579. Smith, S. US CAPITAL IN AFRICA. *Int. Affairs [USSR] 1974 (4): 52-56.* Discusses US capital penetration in Africa, the pattern of US foreign investments and profits in Africa, the concentration of US capital in the Republic of South Africa, and the increasing difficulties US monopolies are confronting in Africa.

580. Sundiata, I. K. PRELUDE TO SCANDAL: LIBERIA AND FERNANDO PO, 1880-1930. *J. of African Hist. [Great Britain] 1974 15(1): 97-112.* Examines the economic relations between Fernando Póo and Liberia. The switch to cocoa cultivation on Fernando Póo in the 1870's brought about a dependence on migrant labor from Liberia. European economic competition in the early 20th century led to the detention of laborers, the nonpayment of contracts, and other abuses. A League of Nations investigation in 1929-30 unfairly placed the blame on Liberia rather than on the Spanish authorities on Fernando Póo. Primary and secondary sources; 71 notes. Map. C. Hopkins

581. Vinogradova, L. EES I RAZVIVAIUSHCHIESIA STRANY: SUSHCHNOST' LOMEISKIKH KONVENTSII [Relations of the European Economic Community (EEC) with developing nations and the Lomé conventions]. *Mirovaia Ekonomika i Mezhdunarodnye Otnosheniia [USSR] 1981 (6): 125-131.* Examines economic relations of the EEC with African, Caribbean, and Pacific states regulated by the Lomé conventions, 1976-80.

582. Wassermann, Ursula. AFRICAN TRADE AND THE COMMODITY PRICE BOOM. *J. of World Trade Law [Switzerland] 1975 9(2): 224-225.* Comments on the fact that African terms of trade, in spite of increased earnings from the rise in price of exports of certain primary commodities, still suffer from import competition and have not improved. J

583. Whiteman, M. K. THE LOMÉ CONVENTION. *World Survey [Great Britain] 1975 (82): 1-17.* Traces the diplomatic negotiations, 1957-75, which led to the Lomé Convention of 1975 on economic relations between developing nations and the European Economic Community.

584. Wills, K. B. TO ENGLAND BY FLYING BOAT. *Soc. of Malawi J. [Malawi] 1980 33(1): 33-38.* In 1950, the author and his family traveled from Blantyre, Malawi to England via several forms of transportation. Much of the trip took place on the *City of Salisbury,* a wartime Sunderland Flying Boat, which had been converted to civilian use. 2 photos. L. S. Guyotte

585. Zartman, I. William. LES TRANSFERTS D'ARMEMENTS EN AFRIQUE [The transfer of arms to Africa]. *Etudes Int. [Canada] 1977 8(3): 478-486.* Discusses the reasons for Africa's armament needs. Notes that France is the major supplier of weapons to African nations, followed at a considerable distance by the USSR, Great Britain, and the United States. Leading buyers include South Africa and Nigeria. The multiple suppliers reflect the polycentric nature of African power; each supplier services the needs and thereby controls the aspirations of a clique of nations. The author mentions possible problems including the impact of nuclear weapons in Africa. Biblio. J. F. Harrington, Jr.

586. —. THE STRANGE CASE OF LONRHO. *Africa Report 1974 19(2): 40-45.* Discusses controversial political involvement of a British mining and trading company in Africa. S

Development Strategies and Programs

587. Adepoju, Aderanti. MIGRATION AND DEVELOPMENT IN TROPICAL AFRICA: SOME RESEARCH PRIORITIES. *African Affairs [Great Britain] 1977 76(303): 210-225.* Shows that migration is not an undesirable phenomenon but that "what is needed is a concerted effort to channel the energy of migrants into productive activities." Discusses the pertinent areas of future research and their policy significance. These areas include 1) geographic mobility and nonmobility; 2) the interrelations between migration, fertility, and population growth; 3) the role of migrants as agents of diffusion of techniques and material objects; 4) urban-rural transfer of earning and rural development; 5) return migration and its role in the development of the origin area; 6) the development of medium-size towns; and 7) the brain drain. Table, 59 notes. E. P. Stickney

588. Akpan, M. B. ECONOMIC DEVELOPMENT IN LIBERIA AND TANZANIA: 1960-1972. *Africa Q. [India] 1977 16(3): 42-53.* Compares Tanzania's economic development on the 'Chinese model' with that of Liberia on the 'Brazilian model,' and finds the former preferable on egalitarian grounds.

589. Aleksandrovskaia, L. AFRICA: SOME TENDENCIES IN ECONOMIC DEVELOPMENT. *Int. Affairs [USSR] 1974 (7): 64-71.* Discusses economic development and industrialization in developing nations in Africa in the 1960's and 70's, emphasizing the exploitation of natural resources.

590. Aleksandrovskaia, L. and Matsenko, I. EXPERIENCE AND PROBLEMS OF NATIONALIZATION IN AFRICAN COUNTRIES. *Int. J. of Pol. 1976-77 6(4): 66-86.* African countries have had almost 20 years' experience with nationalization. The goals are to weaken or eliminate foreign control and to concentrate economic levers in state hands in the interest of structural reorganization. The methods are diverse: total or partial nationalization, gradual or rapid, with or without compensation. African states have to strike a balance between the need to nationalize and the need to attract foreign capital and allow time to develop organizational and technical skills; therefore nationalization is usually partial and gradual, with compensation to foreign owners. African experience largely refutes Western arguments against nationalization. Translated from *Mirovaia Ekonomika i Mezhdunarodnye Otnosheniia* 1975 (7): 48-59. Based on UN documents and secondary sources; table, 19 notes. R. E. Noble

591. Aleksandrovskaia, L. and Matsenko, I. OPYT I PROBLEMY NATSIONALIZATSII V STRANAKH AFRIKI [The experience and problems of nationalization in Africa]. *Mirovaia Ekonomika i Mezhdunarodnye Otnosheniia [USSR] 1975 (7): 48-59.*

592. Aleksandrovskaia, L. RAZVITIE PROMYSHLENNOSTI V AFRIKE: PODKHODY I PRIORITETY [The development of industry in Africa: approaches and priorities]. *Mirovaia Ekonomika i Mezhdunarodnye Otnosheniia [USSR] 1980 (4): 97-108.* Analyzes issues such as the general conditions of African industrial development, neocolonialism, regional strategies of industrialization, and national programs of industrial development. Recommends fully independent national industrial policies, greater cooperation with the socialist countries, and better use of internal resources.

593. Amin, Samir. UNDERDEVELOPMENT AND DEPENDENCE IN BLACK AFRICA. *Social and Econ. Studies [Jamaica] 1973 22(1): 177-196.* Divides African economic history into four periods and traces economic development through each of these periods. Because of the impact of colonialism, there no longer exist any traditional societies in Africa. 19 notes. E. S. Johnson

594. Anifowose, Remi. INDIGENISATION POLICIES IN AFRICA: A COMPARATIVE VIEW. *Genève-Afrique [Switzerland] 1980 18(1): 7-30.* In Nigeria indigenization was first implemented in 1972 under the federal military government, which required Nigerian participation in a number of previously foreign-controlled firms. The policy is somewhat older in Kenya, whose economy in colonial times was dominated by white settlers. Despite these efforts to transfer ownership to African entrepreneurs, management of the most important industries has remained in foreign hands. 58 notes, 7 appendixes. B. S. Fetter

595. Baier, Stephen. ECONOMIC HISTORY AND DEVELOPMENT: DROUGHT AND THE SAHELIAN ECONOMIES. *African Econ. Hist. 1976 (1): 1-16.* Analyzes the historical interdependence between the economies of the Hausa and Tuareg and the ecological environment of the Sahel in order to understand and offer recommendations for the current problems of arid lands in Africa.

596. Baker, Jonathan. OIL AND AFRICAN DEVELOPMENT. *J. of Modern African Studies [Great Britain] 1977 15(2): 175-212.* African oil production since World War II has increased at a phenomenal rate. The author outlines the current oil situation in Africa and analyzes the future effects of high oil prices. 2 maps, 9 tables, 122 notes. H.G. Soff

597. Banks, F. E. MULTINATIONAL FIRMS AND AFRICAN ECONOMIC DEVELOPMENT. *J. of World Trade Law [Switzerland] 1975 9(3): 347-354.* The contention that African economic development has been wrongly biased by the failure of multinational corporations to train African technicians in the industrial sector is presented with the suggestion that African governments might remedy this shortage through judicious regulation of MNC operations. J

598. Belloncle, Guy. STRUCTURES VILLAGEOISES ET STRATÉGIES DE DÉVELOPPEMENT: PROJETS COOPÉRATIFS ET PROJETS ÉDUCATIFS EN AFRIQUE NOIRE [Village structures and development strategies: cooperative and educational projects in Black

Africa]. *Communautés: Arch. Int. de Sociologie de la Coopération et du Développement [France] 1981 (56): 61-104.*

599. Bellot, Jean-Marc and Bellot-Couderc, Béatrice. SÉCHERESSE ET ÉLEVAGE AU SAHEL [Drought and sheep raising in the Sahel]. *Cultures et Développement [Belgium] 1979 11(1): 47-67.* Considers the consequences of the droughts in the Sahel, 1969-74, and pays particular attention to the transformation in the system of sheep raising during and since this period.

600. Bobrie, François. L'INVESTISSEMENT PUBLIC EN AFRIQUE NOIRE FRANÇAISE ENTRE 1924 ET 1938: CONTRIBUTION MÉTHODOLOGIQUE [Public investment in French Black Africa, 1924-38: a methodological contribution]. *Rev. Française d'Hist. d'Outre-Mer [France] 1976 63(3-4): 459-476.* Analyzes public investment in the French colonies of Black Africa, 1924-38. Most of the investment was in railways, ports, wharves, bridges, and roads, and to a far lesser degree, health and welfare. Education did not seem to figure; investments concentrated on things valuable to economic development in the narrow sense. Statistics show public investment rising to 1931, dropping 1932-36, to rise again slightly 1937-38. Public investment helped introduce wage labor and modern economic practices to Africa. 11 tables, 2 graphs, 29 notes. J. C. Billigmeier

601. Brown, LaVerne. JAMES H. ROBINSON'S UNFINISHED TASK. *Crisis 1973 80(5): 159-161.* Discusses Operation Crossroads Africa, the organization established in 1958 by James H. Robinson, which enabled US and Canadian students to work and learn in Africa. S

602. Brown, Robert Wylis. AFRICA'S GIANT OILFIELDS. *Africa Report 1975 20(2): 50-54.* Surveys Africa's various giant oilfields discovered in the last 15 years and, while optimistic, does not expect discoveries of such magnitude in the near future. S

603. Canal, Carlos M. BUSINESS: AMERICAN BANKS IN BLACK AFRICA. *Africa Report 1975 20(5): 15-16.* Discusses loans by US and European banks to African countries during 1972-74 and why US banks wish to do business in Africa.

604. Carsen, John. LOMÉ-KONVENTIONS BETYDNING FOR INDUSTRIUDVIKLINGEN I AFRIKA [The importance of the Lomé Convention for industrial development in Africa]. *Økonomi og Politik [Denmark] 1978 52(3): 220-248.* The Lomé Convention, signed in 1975 by nine European Economic Community countries and 43 African states, initiated a policy of trade stabilization and improvement, with financial and technical assistance and industrial cooperation from the Common Market. The convention replaces bilateral agreements and emphasizes the industrial development of the African countries. Provisions were made for a Center for Industrial Development and a Committee for Industrial Cooperation. There is a desire for greater activity since African productivity remains low. R. E. Lindgren

605. Chauleur, Pierre. DÉVELOPPEMENT ET PROBLÈMES DÉMOGRAPHIQUES AFRICAINS [Development and demographic problems in Africa]. *Études [France] 1981 354(4): 437-449.* Discusses Africa's current problems of underdevelopment, food shortages and malnutrition, unemployment, and rapidly decreasing self-sufficiency due to drought, wars, overpopulation, and urbanization. Stresses Africa's need to exploit more thoroughly its own alimentary resources.

606. Chodak, Szymon. PEASANTS AND AGRICULTURAL CHANGE. *Can. J. of African Studies [Canada] 1980 14(3): 531-533.* Review article of Kenneth R. M. Anthony, Bruce F. Johnston, William O. Jones, and Victor Uchendu's *Agricultural Change in Tropical Africa* (Ithaca: Cornell U. Pr., 1979) and David K. Leonard's *Reaching the Peasant Farmer: Organization Theory and Practice in Kenya* (Chicago: U. of Chicago Pr., 1977).

607. Cohn, Theodore. THE SAHELIAN DROUGHT: PROBLEMS OF LAND USE. *Int. J. [Canada] 1975 30(3): 428-444.* Explores overpopulation, water resources, nomadic customs and transportation as aspects of land use which governments must act upon to deal with drought in the area between the Sahara and the savannah. 39 notes. R. V. Kubicek

608. Dalby, David. DROUGHT IN SUDANIC AFRICA: THE IMPLICATIONS FOR THE FUTURE. *Round Table 1974 (253): 57-64.* Analyzes the calamitous drought of 1973 affecting a belt of territory stretching 4,000 miles from Senegal to Ethiopia. Both climatic change and man's mismanagement are causes of the catastrophe, and the consequences and political repercussions of the drought are examined. The slow international response to the crisis is deplorable, and radical improvements in communications in Africa are needed. Africa's subsistence economies should now be closely observed and a thorough inquest held to prevent the disaster's recurrence. African governments face enormous difficulties in dealing with drought and their success, and survival, "will depend on the degree to which rural populations can be involved in decisions affecting their own future." R. G. Neville

609. Due, Jean M. ALLOCATION OF CREDIT TO UJAMAA VILLAGES IN TANZANIA AND SMALL FARMERS IN ZAMBIA. *African Studies Rev. 1980 23(3): 33-48.* A statistical analysis of the repayment rates on agricultural loans granted to two groups of African farmers who had been selected on a political basis and who were living in regions of high political consciousness. Based on field research; 6 tables, 10 notes, biblio. R. T. Brown

610. Due, John F. THE PROBLEMS OF RAIL TRANSPORT IN TROPICAL AFRICA. *J. of Developing Areas 1979 13(4): 375-393.* African railroad construction began around the turn of the century, primarily for military and political rather than economic reasons. The railroads were with light rails and with a narrower gauge than in Western Europe or North America. The railroads were not integrated as a system. When African nations gained independence many non-Africans left, and road construction and use increased rapidly, partially in reaction to the colonial railroads. In several Commonwealth nations passenger traffic was unimportant as a revenue source, and railroad efficiency, rates, and even bulk traffic declined. African railroads deteriorated due to lack of trained personnel following independence, management failure to adapt to changing conditions, government neglect, time-caused physical deterioration, increase of road transport, and inadequate communications. 4 tables, 2 fig., 31 notes. O. W. Eads, Jr.

611. Eicher, Carl K. FACING UP TO AFRICA'S FOOD CRISIS. *Foreign Affairs 1982 61(1): 151-174.* The food crisis in sub-Saharan Africa arose from agricultural policies that were not suited to the area's needs. Food policy should deal with the causes of the crisis: inadequate food production and poverty. Remedial measures should be long-term and include: increased incentives to farmers, location-specific research on staple food production, graduate training programs in agriculture, and the realization that achieving a reliable food surplus is a prerequisite for national development. Foreign nations that donate food should coordinate their activities to help attain these goals. Based on studies by the USDA, UN, World Bank, OAU, and FAO, and other sources; 3 fig., 13 notes. A. A. Englard

612. Eisemon, Thomas Owen. THE IMPLEMENTATION OF SCIENCE IN NIGERIA AND KENYA. *Minerva [Great Britain] 1979 17(4): 504-526.* The achievements of Nigerian and Kenyan science are primarily quantitative and in the sphere of construction of an institutional framework for scientific research. Although many scientific organizations have been formed, scientific research, in a more substantial sense, has not been much advanced because of unfulfilled predictions of a weakening of the ties to international scientific work resulting from policies favoring Africanization and the equation of scientific activity with national development.

613. Eisemon, Thomas Owen. SCIENTISTS IN AFRICA. *Bull. of the Atomic Scientists 1980 36(2): 17-22.* Scientists in Nigeria and Kenya find it difficult to realize their full potential in their fields because of the lack of facilities and infrastructure, 1960's-70's.

614. Esseks, John D. THE FOOD OUTLOOK FOR THE SAHEL: REGAINING SELF-SUFFICIENCY OR CONTINUING DEPENDENCE ON INTERNATIONAL AID? *Africa Today 1974 22(2): 45-56.* Sahelian prospects include recurring famine unless 1) the countries can develop sufficient storage, 2) foreign aid provides predictive and developmental capacity, and 3) increased food production

allows the countries to hedge against future droughts. Based on UN and agricultural studies; illus., table, 47 notes. G. O. Gagnon

615. Gibbons, R. Arnold. PROBLEMS OF EDUCATIONAL TECHNOLOGY IN AFRICA. *Black Scholar 1973 5(1): 15-19.* The introduction of Western technology into African education which began in the 1960's must be balanced by a maintenance of traditional culture; otherwise the inevitable result will be an uncontrolled cultural colonialism.

616. Glantz, Michael H. THE SAHELIAN DROUGHT: NO VICTORY FOR ANYONE. *Africa Today 1975 22(2): 57-61.* Places the Sahel disaster in the context of man's historical propensity to create deserts and famine, then to return to the same destructive forms of land use once balance is partially restored. The Sahel disaster may convince Sahelian and international leadership of the need for conservation of resources. Secondary sources; 17 notes. G. O. Gagnon

617. Gordon, David F. DECOLONIZATION AND DEVELOPMENT IN KENYA AND ZIMBABWE: A COMPARATIVE ANALYSIS. *Issue: A Q. J. of Opinion 1981 11(3-4): 36-40.* Compares the development strategies that have resulted from decolonization in Zimbabwe and Kenya, from 1950 to 1981, with special attention to Zimbabwe's economic model, drawing from both capitalism and socialism.

618. Gromyko, A. A. AFRIKA V MIROVOM RAZVITII I PROBLEMY SOVETSKOI AFRIKANISTIKI [Africa and global development: problems of Soviet African studies]. *Narody Azii i Afriki [USSR] 1980 (3): 3-13.* Research and study programs conducted at the Academy of Sciences' Africa Institute in the 1970's are primarily concerned with combatting the anti-Soviet premises of Western imperialist propaganda in the Third World. Western capital investments and monopolies lead to neocolonial control and exploitation endangering independence of African developing countries. A socialist ideological and political orientation strengthens the state sector, assures development of natural resources and their use for national economic growth, and introduces socioeconomic and agrarian reforms benefiting large segments of the native population. Based on the author's report to the Third All-Union Conference of Africanists, 15-17 October 1979; 11 notes. English summary. N. Frenkley

619. Grove, A. T. DESERTIFICATION IN THE AFRICAN ENVIRONMENT. *African Affairs [Great Britain] 1974 73(291): 137-151.* Describes desert encroachment resulting from human activity or climatic change. Man's role includes burning fields and overgrazing animals. The local inhabitants must be educated to the advantages of countermeasures. This is particularly difficult with pastoralists who refuse to acknowledge their association with a state. 26 notes. H. G. Soff

620. Guyer, Jane I. FOOD, COCOA, AND THE DIVISION OF LABOUR BY SEX IN TWO WEST AFRICAN SOCIETIES. *Comparative Studies in Soc. and Hist. [Great Britain] 1980 22(3): 355-373.* Examines the development of the division of labor by sex among the Yoruba of western Nigeria and the Beti of south central Cameroon as cocoa was introduced as a cash crop.

621. Hayward, Fred M. POLITICAL PARTICIPATION AND ITS ROLE IN DEVELOPMENT: SOME OBSERVATIONS DRAWN FROM THE AFRICAN CONTEXT. *J. of Developing Areas 1973 7(4): 591-612.* Hypothesizes the role of political participation in economic development in Africa since the 1960's. S

622. Heisel, Donald. FOOD AND POPULATION IN AFRICA. *Current Hist. 1975 68(406): 258-261.*

623. Hopkins, Nicholas S. THE SMALL URBAN CENTER IN RURAL DEVELOPMENT: KITA (MALI) AND TESTOUR (TUNISIA). *Africa [Great Britain] 1979 49(3): 316-328.* The major contrast in Kita is between town and country; in Testour the cleavage follows class lines within the town. Unlike Mali, a creation of the colonial period, Tunisia's long history provides a background of continuity. Kita, a town formed in 1881, is a center for the development of agriculture, but is little affected by centrally organized socialism, and the surrounding countryside tends to political indifference. Testour is also an agricultural center and is more open to the influences of civil politics. In both towns the influence of Islam, once so important, has diminished, 1950's-78. R. L. Collison

624. Hougham, David. THE SPATIAL COMPONENTS OF ANGLO-AFRICAN DEVELOPMENT PLANS, 1943-1956. *Can. J. of African Studies [Canada] 1981 15(3): 527-538.* Spatial, as distinguished from sectoral, planning is concerned with the overall geographical imprint of development. It did not become a significant feature of long-term development planning in Africa or the Third World in general until the 1960's. But inspection of Colonial Development and Welfare plans for British colonial territories in Africa from the early 1940's to the mid-1950's suggests that, although sectoral considerations were predominant, the plans included spatial objectives and policies which were innovative and foreshadowed concepts that have since become standard. 55 notes. J. V. Coutinho

625. Huybrechts, A. L'INDUSTRIE EN AFRIQUE [Industry in Africa]. *Bull. des Séances de l'Acad. Royale des Sci. d'Outre-Mer [Belgium] 1977 (2): 95-107.* Africa is the least industrialized area of the Third World. Almost half the industry is located in North Africa. Despite abundant natural resources several problems constrain industrial development: a weak agricultural base, poor general economic development, poor transportation, and lack of capital and skilled labor. Governmental support of small and medium enterprises could ameliorate the situation. Based on UN and other statistics; 4 tables, biblio. M. Schumacher

626. Hveem, Helge. AFRIKA I VERDENSØKONOMIEN: UTVIKLING OG UNDERUTVIKLING [Africa in the world economy: development and underdevelopment]. *Internasjonal Politikk [Norway] 1976 (3B): 729-746.* Surveys the economic and social patterns in Africa today, including the effects of recent economic crises. There has been no economic development as far as the great majority is concerned; economic dependence on outside countries has increased. The author discusses development in new centers within Africa, such as resource-rich states like Nigeria, Zaire, and South Africa. The creation of a *New International Economic Order* may well remove some obstacles to development, but only mass mobilization, greater self-reliance, and emphasis on rural development can bring hope to the great majority of Africa's people. J/S

627. Ijere, M. O. THE PARADOX OF COLONIAL HERITAGE IN AFRICAN DEVELOPMENT. *Pan-African J. [Kenya] 1974 7(3): 269-280.* Although many Africans disclaimed colonialism, they have clung to colonial ideas since independence. The states that complained the most have, paradoxically, retained the most from colonialism. 14 notes. H. G. Soff

628. Jansen, Eirik G. FISKERIENE PÅ VICTORIASJØEN OG NORSK NAERINGSLIV [The fisheries of Lake Victoria and Norwegian commerce]. *Samtiden [Norway] 1977 86(10): 594-601.* In establishing which criteria Norwegian authorities should follow in investment projects in developing nations, the author examines a Lake Victoria fishing project, 1965-75, financed by the UN Development Program.

629. Jinadu, L. Adele. SOME AFRICAN THEORISTS OF CULTURE AND MODERNIZATION: FANON, CABRAL AND SOME OTHERS. *African Studies Rev. 1978 21(1): 121-138.* Africans have tended to reject Western models of modernization, 1950-75, and have slowly developed their own cultural models, which go beyond immediate pragmatic needs. 15 notes, biblio. R. T. Brown

630. Jursa, Paul E. and Winkates, James E. TOURISM AS A MODE OF DEVELOPMENT. *Issue 1974 4(1): 45-49.* Discusses advantages and disadvantages of promoting tourism in developing nations in Africa. S

631. Katsman, V. Ia. and Nikolaeva, O. L. PROTSESSY NEKAPITALISTICHESKOGO RAZVITIIA STRAN AFRIKI [The process of the noncapitalist development of African countries]. *Narody Azii i Afriki [USSR] 1977 (5): 172-175.* Reports on a symposium, held at the African Institute of the Soviet Academy of Sciences, on the noncapitalist development of African countries. The main points at issue were the concepts "national democratic revolution," "socialist orientation," and "noncapitalist development." The speakers divided the transitory period

of noncapitalist development into a series of phases marking the transformation from revolutionary democracy toward socialism. Particular attention was paid to Angola and Mozambique, and special reference was made to the measures undertaken in Algeria toward a Socialist state. E. R. Sicher

632. Keyes, Gene and Seymour, Scott. THE SAHARA FOREST AND OTHER SUPERORDINATE GOALS. *Peace Res. Rev. [Canada] 1975 6(3): 1-62.* Reviews proposals for grandiose engineering and welfare proposals that might now serve the world community as unifying "superordinate goals," efforts so beneficial as to be compelling to the nations involved and so big as to require international cooperation—epitomized by the notion of reforestation of the Sahara, first proposed by Charles Fourier in 1808.

633. Kiva, A. V. TROPICHESKAIA AFRIKA: NEKOTORYE PROBLEMY REVOLIUTSIONNO-DEMOKRATICHESKIKH PREOBRAZOVANII V DEREVNE ("UDZHAMAA" V TANZANII) [Tropical Africa: some problems with revolutionary-democratic transformations in the village: *ujamaa* in Tanzania]. *Narody Azii i Afriki [USSR] 1974 (5): 15-25.* Discusses the failure of traditional village communities to satisfy the social and agricultural needs of present-day tropical African countries. The author makes a qualified recommendation of the adoption of the Tanzanian system of *ujamaa* agricultural cooperatives.

634. Korovikov, V. URANOVYE KLADOVYE KONTINENTA [Uranium store-rooms of the continent]. *Aziia i Afrika Segodnia [USSR] 1982 (5): 13-15.* Examines the African uranium industry from the 1940's to 1982, discussing its impact on the political and economic lives of South Africa, Zaire, Namibia, Niger, and Gabon, and its role in Western economies and foreign policies.

635. Kraus, Jon. AFRICAN TRADE UNIONS: PROGRESS OR POVERTY? *African Studies Rev. 1976 19(3): 95-108.* Reviews Anthony Clayton and Donald S. Savage's *Government and Labour in Kenya, 1895-1963* (London: Frank Cass, 1974); Richard Sandrook's *Proletarians and African Capitalism: The Kenya case, 1960-1972* (Geneva: Int. Labor Organization, 1972); Robin Cohen's *Labour and Politics in Nigeria* (London: Heineman, 1974); Wogu Ananaba's *The Trade Union Movement in Nigeria* (New York: Africana, 1970); R. D. Grillo's *African Railwaymen: Solidarity and Opposition in an East African Labor Force* (Cambridge: Cambridge U. Pr., 1975); and Robert Bates's *Unions, Parties and Political Development: A Study of Mine-Workers in Zambia* (New Haven: Yale U. Pr., 1971).

636. Krylov, V. NEKOTORYE ASPEKTY AGRARNOGO RAZVITIIA AFRIKI [Some aspects of African agrarian development]. *Aziia i Afrika Segodnia [USSR] 1981 (3): 29-33.* The peasant-agrarian question in the developing Afro-Asian countries must be viewed in the light of regional and world developments which have made neocolonialism the main form of capitalist oppression and have made the solution of agrarian problems dependent on the struggle of these countries against it.

637. Kupriianov, P. I. RAZVITIE KAPITALIZMA V SEL'SKOM KHOZIAISTVE STRAN TROPICHESKOI AFRIKI (MEZHDUNARODNYI SEMINAR V DAKARE) [The development of capitalism in agriculture in tropical African countries: an international seminar in Dakar]. *Narody Azii i Afriki [USSR] 1974 (4): 235-237.* Summarizes the proceedings of a conference on the development of capitalism in agriculture in tropical African countries organized by the UN's African Institute for Economic Development and Planning in Dakar 3-12 December 1973, whose participants examined tropical Africa's dependence on the world capitalist system.

638. Laidlaw, Karen A. and Stockwell, Edward G. TRENDS IN THE RELATIONSHIP BETWEEN URBANISATION AND DEVELOPMENT IN AFRICA. *J. of Modern African Studies [Great Britain] 1979 17(4): 687-694.* The process of economic development in the Third World should be reflected by a rise in productivity and real incomes and a reduction in fertility, and historically these have been closely associated with urbanization. Although it is clear that urbanization is a major aspect of social change in Africa since 1965, it has not had a determining effect on productivity, incomes, or fertility and can therefore not be considered an unequivocal index that African societies are becoming more modern. Based on UN and Population Reference Bureau data; 3 tables, 11 notes. D. J. Nicholls

639. Lea, John P. and Wu, Chung-tong. DECENTRALIZATION AND DEVOLUTION: A REVIEW OF THE UNITED NATIONS CONFERENCE ON HUMAN SETTLEMENTS, NAIROBI, 1978. *J. of Modern African Studies [Great Britain] 1980 18(3): 533-540.* A sharp critique of proposals made at the UN Conference on Human Settlements for developing nations to create new geographical growth centers for their economies and populations and localize authority for planning development. Such new growth centers are not inevitably effective means of development and local governments in Africa are too weak and understaffed to carry out developmental plans. Based on the report of the 1978 Nairobi Conference and secondary sources; 2 tables, 20 notes. L. W. Truschel

640. Legassick, Martin. PERSPECTIVES ON AFRICAN "UNDERDEVELOPMENT." *J. of African Hist. [Great Britain] 1976 17(3): 435-440.* Reviews three volumes about the economic history of Africa: Walter Rodney, *How Europe Underdeveloped Africa* (London, 1972); E. A. Brett, *Colonialism and Underdevelopment in East Africa: The Politics of Economic Change, 1919-1939* (London, 1973); and S. E. Katzenellenbogen, *Railways and the Copper Mines of Katanga* (Oxford, 1973). Brett and Rodney have made important contributions to economic historiography of Africa. 11 notes. H. G. Soff

641. Levkovsky, Aleksei and Safari, Hamid. NATURE OF STATE STRUCTURE IN ASIAN AND AFRICAN COUNTRIES. *World Marxist R. [Canada] 1973 16(10): 18-25.* Communists in Asia and Africa support a strong public sector for economic development and growth. S

642. Lewis, Shelby. AFRICAN WOMEN AND NATIONAL DEVELOPMENT. Lindsay, Beverly, ed. *Comparative Perspectives of Third World Women: The Impact of Race, Sex, and Class* (New York: Praeger, 1980): 31-54. Rejects various existing views about the concept of African development and women's place in it, focusing on women's role in society, their contributions to development, why women have been excluded from development programs, and the commitment of African states to change the economic, social, and political situation to improve women's status.

643. Leys, Colin. AFRICAN ECONOMIC DEVELOPMENT IN THEORY AND PRACTICE. *Daedalus 1982 111(2): 99-124.* Criticizes the dependency theory of peripheral capitalism with respect to economic growth in Africa; viable alternatives to economic relationships with more developed countries did not exist.

644. Lisowski, Andrzej. MINING AS A TOWN-FORMING FACTOR IN COUNTRIES OF TROPICAL AFRICA. *Africana Bull. [Poland] 1978 (27): 105-126.* Analyzes the demography, economic growth, and position in the settlement system of mining cities in tropical Africa, showing the extent of the role of mining in their development.

645. Lofchie, Michael F. POLITICAL AND ECONOMIC ORIGINS OF AFRICAN HUNGER. *J. of Modern African Studies [Great Britain] 1975 13(4): 551-567.* Studies of famine in Africa have almost universally blamed the situation on drought. The two are not necessarily synonymous. African domestic food production was down before the drought. The real causes are political. Agricultural exports are booming while people starve. Government policies favor export producers; communal ownership of land frees workers to plant and harvest the crops of the giant exporters. The system has been in effect so long that change may be difficult; alternatives are matters of the past. 16 notes. V. L. Human

646. Mabogunje, Akin L. MANUFACTURING AND THE GEOGRAPHY OF DEVELOPMENT IN TROPICAL AFRICA. *Econ. Geography 1973 49(1): 1-20.*

647. Mazrui, Ali A. THE AFRICAN UNIVERSITY AS A MULTINATIONAL CORPORATION: PROBLEMS OF PENETRATION AND DEPENDENCY. *Harvard Educational R. 1975 45(2): 191-210.* "Describes the symbiotic relationship between education and economic development, and then outlines strategies for changing the university so

it will foster cultural as well as economic independence in African nations." S

648. Mazrui, Ali A. and Locke, Rovan. THE CHINESE MODEL AND THE SOVIET MODEL IN EASTERN AND SOUTHERN AFRICA. *Asian Forum 1977 9(1): 1-15.* Discusses the application to Africa of the Soviet and Chinese models for the theory and strategy of liberation and economic and technological development. Whether the Chinese or the Russian models are transferable to Africa or not hinges on whether Africa has the type of leadership, the level of organization, and quality of cultural coherence to make them work. The author concludes that there is no link between influencing an African country's internal policy and influencing its foreign policy or vice versa. Based on secondary sources; 15 notes. R. B. Orr

649. McGowan, Patrick J. ECONOMIC DEPENDENCE AND ECONOMIC PERFORMANCE IN BLACK AFRICA. *J. of Modern African Studies [Great Britain] 1976 14(1): 25-40.* Contrary to the assumptions of many black African policymakers and theorists, there seems to be no relationship between neocolonial economic dependence and poor economic performance. The author correlates three measures of economic dependence developed by Barbara Stallings with 23 indicators of economic performance, and with the percentage of foreign trade in the total gross national product of 30 black African states. Further analysis reveals that neither the type of colonial heritage nor the region within Africa is related to poor economic performance. Based on data from secondary sources; 3 tables, 9 notes. W. R. Hively

650. Morgan, W. B. FOOD SUPPLY AND STAPLE FOOD IMPORTS OF TROPICAL AFRICA. *African Affairs [Great Britain] 1977 76(303): 167-176.* Studies the food supply in 35 tropical African countries, only three of which recorded an excess of supply, analyzes food imports by countries, and discusses causes of the failure to increase farm production per worker. The drought of the late 1960's and early 1970's underlined the precariousness of the agricultural situation for several countries. Both Rhodesia and Madagascar were net food exporters in 1969-71, especially of sugar and maize. Despite various efforts of governments to eliminate food imports, in many cases they have increased. Rice is the chief foodstuff imported by the countries most dependent on imports. 13 notes. E. P. Stickney

651. Morgenthau, Ruth Schachter. THE DEVELOPING STATES OF AFRICA. *Ann. of the Am. Acad. of Pol. and Social Sci. 1977 (432): 80-95.* The colonial era, with its monopoly of wealth by whites, is over. None of the withdrawing colonial powers were very good at preparing the African nations for independence. It took a decade for the invisible structures of empire to start giving way. Most African countries inherited insufficient administrative and economic infrastructures, borders that made little economic sense, and small markets. As a result, they were vulnerable, at independence, to fluctuating world prices and feast or famine conditions, making economic planning almost impossible. The economies of African states are governed by forces largely out of their control, and growth does not bring development for many because of lopsided distribution. There is, however, industrial potential, and manufacturing, though limited by low purchasing power, is growing. With the oil crisis, a few African states may hope to catch up soon with industrialized states in living standards, but meanwhile producing resources does not ensure equal distribution. Multinationals also weaken some African states by making them dependent. If they are to gain a sense of shared stake, they must cease to feel like horses driven by jockeys from the industrialized states. J

652. Mullings, Leith. WOMEN AND ECONOMIC CHANGE IN AFRICA. Hafkin, Nancy J. and Bay, Edna G., eds. *Women in Africa: Studies in Social and Economic Change*(Stanford, Ca.: Stanford U. Pr., 1976): 239-264. Precolonial African villages were characterized by sexual equality and equal access to the means of production. However, the acceleration of class stratification under colonialism resulted in the deterioration of the position of women relative to men, as evidenced in Labadi, a Ga town in Ghana. The introduction of large-scale production for exchange, and the transfer of production resources into private property, disrupted the reciprocal division of labor. Women have found themselves in a money economy where the products of their labor are considered inferior and they are denied access to resources. On the other hand, in Mozambique and Guinea-Bissau, where postcolonial societies are committed to the eradication of class stratification, the liberation of women has been declared a major step in the social revolution. Field work and secondary sources; 26 notes. S. Tomlinson-Brown

653. Mushkat, Marion. SOUS-DÉVELOPPEMENT EN AFRIQUE: UNE SITUATION IMPOSÉE PAR DES ÉLÉMENTS EXTÉRIEURS? [Underdevelopment in Africa: a situation caused by external factors?]. *Africa [Italy] 1975 30(1): 39-45.* Examines the theory of "peripheric capitalism" which has been formulated under the influence of the Marxist doctrine on imperialism. Colonialism and imperialism were practiced in Africa long before the advent of the Europeans and it is not always possible to establish a clear relationship between colonialism and underdevelopment. The fact of having been colonized is not in itself an immunity against the effects of underdevelopment. The author concludes that the key to development is offered by the possibility for African countries of organizing themselves on an inter-African basis. J

654. Nivosu, Emmanuel J. CASE FOR SPECIAL SCHOOLS FOR THE DISTRIBUTIVE TRADES IN AFRICA. *African Studies R. 1973 16(3): 437-442.* State-sponsored corporations designed to benefit domestic producers and consumers should take precedent over the random distribution of private groups. S

655. Nowlan, David M. THE FORMATION OF DEVELOPMENT STRATEGY IN TROPICAL AFRICA. *Co-Existence [Great Britain] 1973 10(1): 34-56.* Discusses the formulation of economic development strategy in the countries of tropical Africa (1950's to present), including goals for African nations on the national, international, and global levels.

656. Ogbu, John U. SEASONAL HUNGER IN TROPICAL AFRICA AS A CULTURAL PHENOMENON. *Africa [Great Britain] 1973 43(4): 317-332.* Refutes the notion that expected seasonal hunger can be countered by enough hard work to prevent a food shortage. Uses evidence gathered, 1964-70, from two widely separate African communities, the Chakaka Pola of Northern Malawi and the Onicha Ibo of Eastern Nigeria.

657. Panarin, S. PAUPERIZATSIIA SEL'SKOGO NASELENIIA V RAZVIVAIUSHCHIKHSIA STRANAKH AZII I AFRIKI [Pauperization of peasants in the developing countries of Asia and Africa]. *Aziia i Afrika Segodnia [USSR] 1982 (7): 29-32.* The growing poverty-stricken village populations in Asia and Africa place an enormous burden on national resources and seriously impede socioeconomic development.

658. Parker, Ian. PROBLEMS OF ECONOMIC DEVELOPMENT. *Africa Today 1973 20(4): 45-49.* Reviews Thomas De Gregori's *Technology and the Economic Development of the Typical African Frontier* (Cleveland: Case Western Reserve U. Press, 1969) and *Africa: Problems in Economic Development* (Free Press, 1972), edited by J. S. Uppal and Louis Salkever. Each examines the broad issues of African development. G. O. Gagnon

659. Pastore, Paolo. PROBLEMI DELLO SVILUPPO DEI PAESI AFRICANI [Problems of the development of African countries]. *Affari Esteri [Italy] 1976 8(31): 512-525.* Evaluates the general economic conditions of Africa and discusses the possible benefits its unexploited resources could provide for both industrialized countries and African nations given a rational international division of labor.

660. Pickett, James. POPULATION, LABOUR FORCE, AND ECONOMIC GROWTH. *J. of Modern African Studies [Great Britain] 1973 11(4): 591-610.* A study of certain basic features of African demography, considering how these relate to sectoral increases of output and employment, and the implications of a conscious effort to provide more jobs than might normally be expected from industrial expansion. Most remedial policies suggested—population control, agricultural development, expansion of employment in the nonagricultural sector—are difficult and slow. In the meantime developed countries might join with a number of African countries in the search for short-term public works programs which would enhance long-term development and provide a stop-gap measure while more significant remedial policies are developed. 8 tables, 38 notes. R. V. Ritter

661. Poursin, Guy. A PROPOS DES OSCILLATIONS CLIMATIQUES: LA SÉCHERESSE AU SAHEL [Concerning climatic fluctuations: drought in the Sahel]. *Ann.: Économies, Sociétés, Civilisations [France] 1974 29(3): 640-647.* The Sahel, the area south of the Sahara constituting in effect the shoreline of the desert, is in the process itself of being transformed irreversibly into desert. Although a number of theories of a biogeographical and demographic nature have been advanced for this phenomenon, the principal cause is purely climatic and the present state of technology precludes effective counteraction. 2 maps, 3 tables, graph, 7 notes. R. Howell

662. Raichur, Satish. IMPLEMENTATION PROBLEMS OF ECONOMIC DEVELOPMENT PLANS. *Africa Today 1973 20(2): 67-75.* Reviews the *Proceedings of the Conference on the Implementation Problems of Economic Development Plans and Government Decisions in the Countries of Black Africa* 3 vol. (Budapest, 1973), edited by Jozef Bognar, which contains 31 papers and 17 abstracts on economic problems of development (vol. 1), international economic relations (vol. 2), and implementation problems in selected African Countries (vol. 3). The papers were presented by socialist economists. G. O. Gagnon

663. Roemer, Michael. ECONOMIC DEVELOPMENT IN AFRICA: PERFORMANCE SINCE INDEPENDENCE, AND A STRATEGY FOR THE FUTURE. *Daedalus 1982 111(2): 125-148.*

664. Rood, Leslie L. NATIONALISATION AND INDIGENISATION IN AFRICA. *J. of Modern African Studies [Great Britain] 1976 14(3): 427-448.* Studies the concept of nationalization and the related concepts of expropriation, indigenization, and Africanization, and analyzes the returns on foreign investments in Black Africa, 1960-75, in the mining industry, services, and manufacturing. Compensation varies greatly, and the standards of law by which profits are to be judged is in process of reinterpretation. The law certainly plays less than a commanding role. Indigenization relates more particularly to small- and medium-scale businesses. Table, 31 notes. R. V. Ritter

665. Rothchild, Donald. REALIST PERSPECTIVES ON AFRICAN MODERNIZATION. *Africa Today 1973 20(4): 38-44.* Reviews Henry Bretton's *Power and Politics in Africa*(Chicago: Aldine, 1973), René Dumont and Marcel Mazoyer's *Socialisms and Development* (Praeger, 1973), and Robert Solo and Everett Rogers, eds. *Inducing Technological Change for Economic Growth and Development* (East Lansing: Michigan State U. Press, 1973). Each volume focuses on possible options available to developing nations. 2 notes. G. O. Gagnon

666. Samoff, Joel. UNDERDEVELOPMENT AND ITS GRASS ROOTS IN AFRICA. *Can. J. of African Studies [Canada] 1980 14(1): 5-36.* Examines case studies of the local politics of underdevelopment. The early 20th-century Gezira cotton-growing scheme in the Sudan and the introduction of coffee in the Kilimanjaro (Tanzania) and Murang'a (Kenya) districts of East Africa were relatively successful. But agricultural development in the Kigoma region (Tanzania) resulted in the disintegration of social organization, a conservative political system, and conversion of a regional power to a labor reservoir. The Zambian copperbelt is part of a complex international operation of dominant multinational corporations. The African miners remain in subordinate positions socially and economically despite the government's commitment to Zambianization. The author also examines major areas of debate on the political economy of developing nations. Table, 46 notes. S

667. Seidman, Robert B. LAW, DEVELOPMENT, AND LEGISLATIVE DRAFTING IN ENGLISH-SPEAKING AFRICA. *J. of Modern African Studies [Great Britain] 1981 19(1): 133-161.* Great Britain's former colonies in independent sub-Saharan Africa have generally retained the verbose legalese and drafting procedures of British and British colonial laws. Both these features are depicted here as devised to advance the interest of the propertied middle classes in Britain and the British colonial officials who ruled in African colonies. The drafting of statutes using British legalese and favoring an alleged principle of equality before the law is outmoded in African countries mobilizing to attain socioeconomic development. Based on British and African statutes, official reports and documents, and secondary sources; 98 notes. L. W. Truschel

668. Shafer, Michael. CAPTURING THE MINERAL MULTINATIONALS: ADVANTAGE OR DISADVANTAGE? *Int. Organization 1983 37(1): 93-119.* Nationalization of the Zairian and Zambian copper industries failed to deliver the hoped-for benefits and pushed some still further beyond reach. It did so because nationalization entailed the loss of insulation, that is, the wide range of unperceived risk management and custodial functions fulfilled by the multinational mining corporation. Without this insulation these two governments, their copper industries, and their citizens' welfare all suffered. Looking beyond Zaire and Zambia, it appears that the loss of insulation has negative effects in all cases of mining industry nationalization. The size of the costs are mitigated by the strength of the nationalizer's political system. J

669. Shaw, Timothy M. and Grieve, Malcolm J. DEPENDENCE AS AN APPROACH TO UNDERSTANDING CONTINUING INEQUALITIES IN AFRICA. *J. of Developing Areas 1979 13(3): 229-246.* Viewing inequality, transnational class linkages, the state, and development strategies (state capitalist *vs.* state socialist), the authors observed the second decade of independence, the failure of optimistic solutions and predictions in Africa. To avoid isolation, ruling classes often continue to rule through collaboration with such external economic interests as multinational corporations. African failure to develop an independent form of capitalism is blamed on dominance of multinational corporations in the global economy. Authors recommend socialism in Africa as a viable alternative to perpetual dependence. 54 notes. O. W. Eads, Jr.

670. Shen, T. Y. MACRO DEVELOPMENT PLANNING IN TROPICAL AFRICA: TECHNOCRATIC AND NON-TECHNOCRATIC CAUSES OF FAILURE. *J. of Development Studies [Great Britain] 1977 13(4): 413-427.* Unrealistic planning, political instability, and disadvantageous trade relationships frustrated national economic development in 22 African countries in the 1960's.

671. Solodovnikov, V. and Gavrilov, N. AFRICA: TENDENCIES OF NON-CAPITALIST DEVELOPMENT. *Int. Affairs [USSR] 1976 23(3): 31-39.* The continuing expansion of socialism underscores the growing weakness of capitalism in Africa. Although admittedly there exists periodic backsliding by some countries, there is, nonetheless, a persistent revolutionary process which seeks to transform the African precapitalist and primitive capitalist society to socialism through revolutionary Leninism, i.e., the fostering of national-democratic revolutions led by revolutionary democrats and supported by the progressive elements among the peasants, workers, petite bourgeoisie, and national intelligentsia. 14 notes. D. K. McQuilkin

672. Southall, Roger J. and Kaufert, Joseph M. CONVERGING MODELS OF UNIVERSITY DEVELOPMENT: GHANA AND EAST AFRICA. *Can. J. of African Studies [Canada] 1974 8(3): 607-628.* Ghana and East Africa, due to their common experience with British colonial rule, are similar in the formation of institutions of higher education, whose development rested on specialization in technical education and regional-local jurisdiction according to the number of students a given area could produce, 1945-67.

673. Srinivasan, Padma. HISTORICAL AND SOCIOLOGICAL CONSTRAINTS OF THE ECONOMIC DEVELOPMENT OF AFRICA. *Africa Q. [India] 1976 15(4): 67-89.* Describes the sociological and historical constraints on African economic development, paying special attention to the effects of colonial rule since 1865.

674. Stefański, Bogdan. NATIONALIZATIONS OF FOREIGN-OWNED ASSETS IN AFRICA. *Africana Bull. [Poland] 1975 23: 47-80.* Examines the extent, methods, and results of nationalization in African countries, 1956-75, showing the foreign owners' means of resistance and the forms of nationalization most advantageous to the African host countries.

675. Stephens, Hugh W. ADMINISTRATION IN AFRICAN DEVELOPMENT: A CONTINUING NEGLECT. *J. of Comparative Administration 1973 5(3): 383-391.* Review essay of Michael Lofchie, ed. *The State of the Nations: Constraints on Development in Independent Africa* (U. of California Press, 1971) and Philip Foster and Aristide

Zolberg, eds. *Ghana and the Ivory Coast: Perspectives on Modernization*(U. of Chicago Press, 1971).

676. Stoklitskaia, L. OB EKONOMICHESKOI EVOLIUTSII NAIMENEE RAZVITYKH STRAN AFRIKI [The economic evolution of the least developed countries of Africa]. *Aziia i Afrika Segodnia [USSR] 1980 (9): 33-36.* Discusses the socioeconomic evolution of the least developed African countries. Their condition is too dramatic even by the standards of the developing world, their development prospects seem too alarming, just as their special problems and difficulties. During the 1970's the rates of growth of the per capita GNP in the least developed countries did not even reach 1%, export dynamics were negative, the targets of the UN Second Decade far below the mark. The mechanism that could bring these countries into the orbit of steady and dynamic development should be created by radical, progressive reorganization of socioeconomic structures. J

677. Suret-Canale, J. SÉCHERESSE ET FAMINE DANS LE SAHEL [Drought and famine in the Sahel]. *Cultures et Développement [Belgium] 1976 8(2): 327-334.* Reviews several publications on the nature and consequences of the 1968-73 drought and famine in Africa's Sahel, highlighting the role of socioeconomic conditions.

678. Suret-Canale, Jean. SÉCHERESSE ET FAMINE DANS LE SAHEL... ET AILLEURS [Drought and famine in the south border of the Sahara..* . and elsewhere]. *Cultures et Développement [Belgium] 1980 12(1): 137-141.* Reviews several books and reports dealing with drought and famine in the Sahara and Sahel regions and some other parts of Africa.

679. Svanidze, I. EKOLOGICHESKAIA SITUATSIIA NA KONTINENTE [Ecological situation on the continent]. *Aziia i Afrika Segodnia [USSR] 1981 (5): 33-35.* Discusses the economic and ecological impact of soil erosion and desertification in Africa in 1981. Supports the reconstruction of African agricultural techniques and describes desertification prevention methods and the problems caused by pollution.

680. Svanidze, I. A. TROPICHESKAIA AFRIKA: KREST'IANSKAIA OBSHCHINA I SOTSIAL'NIE PEREMENI [Tropical Africa: the peasant commune and social changes]. *Narody Azii i Afriki [USSR] 1979 (1): 16-26.* A detailed study of communal land ownership in contemporary tropical Africa. Analyzes the organization of the commune, the role of European colonization in tropical Africa, and the hierarchical structure found within the commune. Assesses the African commune from the point of view of economic and social progress, and, in particular, noncapitalist development on the continent. Biblio. S. R. Gudgin

681. Tosh, John. THE CASH-CROP REVOLUTION IN TROPICAL AFRICA: AN AGRICULTURAL REAPPRAISAL. *African Affairs [Great Britain] 1980 79(314): 79-94.* Recent work in African agricultural history has aimed at the recovery of African initiatives in the past. It focuses not on the politics of the chieftain but the labor of the peasants. However, little awareness is shown of the circumstances in which cash crops were actually grown on African smallholdings. The author attempts to replace the African peasant in his natural environment and within the established complex of food crops and to show how the peasants' commitment to subsistence farming affected production for the market. 72 notes. J. V. Coutinho

682. Vilakazi, Absolom. AFRICA'S ROUGH ROAD: PROBLEMS OF DEVELOPMENT. *Issue 1974 4(3): 43-50.* Exposes influence of European imperialism and capitalism on political and economic development of Africa, and the cultural imperialism of Western scholars who separate African history from world history. S

683. Wallerstein, Immanuel. DEPENDENCE IN AN INTERDEPENDENT WORLD: THE LIMITED POSSIBILITIES OF TRANSFORMATION WITHIN THE CAPITALIST WORLD ECONOMY. *African Studies Rev. 1974 17(1): 1-26.* Shows how the structure of the international economic system, 1968-74, has made it difficult for developing nations, especially in Africa, to achieve a policy of self-reliance or choose an alternative economic policy.

684. Waters, Alan Rufus. UNDERSTANDING AFRICAN AGRICULTURE AND ITS POTENTIAL FOR CHANGE. *J. of Modern African Studies [Great Britain] 1974 12(1): 45-56.* Many modern African governments, not understanding the nature of small scale farming, have tried to replace the small farmer with large agricultural units. Suggests studies of African agriculture and small landholders in order to avoid inappropriate governmental decisions. Table, diagram, 45 notes. H. G. Soff

685. Wet, J. M. J. de. DOMESTICATION OF AFRICAN CEREALS. *African Econ. Hist. 1977 (3): 15-32.* Summarizes botanical evidence concerning the origins and distribution of indigenous African cereals from 7,000 B.C. to the 1970's.

5. AFRICA IN THE WORLD WARS

World War I

686. Almeida-Topor, Hélène d'. LES POPULATIONS DAHOMÉENNES ET LE RECRUTEMENT MILITAIRE PENDANT LA PREMIÈRE GUERRE MONDIALE [The Dahomeans and military recruitment during the First World War]. *R. Française d'Hist. d'Outre-Mer [France] 1973 60(219): 196-241.* When World War I began, Dahomey was directly concerned because it bordered on German-ruled Togo. French recruitment for military service outside of Dahomey generally was met by Dahomean aversion, fear, and armed resistance. Opposition to the French levies reached its peak in 1916. Based on documents in the national archives of Dahomey and France and secondary works; 100 notes, 2 appendixes. L. B. Chan

687. Andrew, C. M. and Kanya, Forstner, A. S. FRANCE, AFRICA AND THE FIRST WORLD WAR. *J. of African Hist. [Great Britain] 1978 19(1): 11-23.* During World War I, French aims in Africa were determined by colonialists and Africanists, not by the cabinet. These men wanted to acquire German territories in Africa and were greatly disappointed when they became mandates. The French government underestimated the value of Africa in the war effort. French losses were made up by the recruitment of over 450,000 African soldiers. Moroccans were the most valued, and a Moroccan regiment was the most highly decorated unit in the French army. World War I demonstrated both great military and economic potential for French Africa. Before the war, the empire provided very little to the French economy. The war, although it did not increase trade with the colonies, provided the stimulus for future investment. After the war, Africa was suddenly popular, thought to be a source of unlimited raw materials and labor. This mistaken idea of its economic value was made clear in 1940. 49 notes. H. G. Soff

688. Brown, John Sloan. OF BATTLE AND DISEASE: THE EAST AFRICAN CAMPAIGN OF 1914-18. *Parameters 1982 12(2): 16-24.* Disease has been a little studied but important element in warfare. In the 1914-18 East African Campaign during World War I a medically well-prepared German army held off a numerically superior British force partly due to the latter's susceptibility to local diseases such as smallpox, malaria, sleeping sickness, dysentery, and pneumonia. Some of the most serious blows to the Germans themselves occurred from disease late in the war when they were running short of medical supplies and were forced to move into unfamiliar country. Based on the campaign history by the German commander Paul von Lettow-Vorbeck and secondary sources; 41 notes. L. R. Maxted

689. Burke, Edmund. MOROCCAN RESISTANCE, PAN-ISLAM AND GERMAN WAR STRATEGY, 1914-1918. *Francia [France] 1975 3: 434-464.* When World War I broke out in August 1914, the Moroccans of the Atlas and Rif mountains had been resisting the French for years. The withdrawal of numerous French units to France encouraged the chieftains to renew their attacks on the colonizers. Led by such famous figures as Abd-el-Krim and the Raisuli, the Moroccans were given arms and other aid by Germany and the Ottoman Empire as part of their policy of using Pan-Islamism against the Allies. The Arab revolt in 1916 was a crucial blow to this policy. The contacts between the Central Powers and the Moroccan rebels probably helped the latter more. The greatest service performed by German and Turkish agents was to bring the various leaders into contact with one another, which permitted coordination of strategy and helped the rise of nationalist feeling. 89 notes. J. C. Billigmeier

690. Contamin, Robert. LA PRISE DE COCO-BEACH (21 SEPTEMBRE 1914) [The capture of Cocobeach, 21 September 1914]. *Rev. Hist. des Armées [France] 1981 (2): 82-97.* In order to prevent the Germans at Cocobeach on Gabon's north coast from carrying out an attack upon Libreville, the colonial capital, only a few miles south of Cocobeach, the French sent the gunboat *Surprise* with 250 riflemen from Libreville to Cocobeach. There the *Surprise* sailed back and forth along the coast, shelling German buildings while the gunboat's steam launch towed boats carrying the riflemen to the shore where they attacked the Germans' left flank. The outnumbered Germans were defeated and the threat to Libreville was ended. Eyewitness account written in 1920; 4 photos, map. J. S. Gassner

691. Du Bois, W. E. B. THE AFRICAN ROOTS OF WAR. *Monthly R. 1973 24(11): 28-40.* Reprints a 1915 article which sees the causes of World War I in European imperialism and racism in Africa. S

692. Forster, Kent. THE QUEST FOR EAST AFRICAN NEUTRALITY IN 1915. *African Studies Rev. 1979 22(1): 73-82.* Colonial officials of both British and German East Africa tried to avoid being drawn into the European conflict because they feared the disruption of their fledgling societies and the potential dangers of African uprisings. These local interests were rejected by their home governments. Based on contemporary East African newspapers; 2 notes, biblio. R. T. Brown

693. Garson, N. G. SOUTH AFRICA AND WORLD WAR I. *J. of Imperial and Commonwealth Hist. [Great Britain] 1979 8(1): 68-85.* South Africa entered World War I as a subordinate part of the British Empire, but as the war progressed it became clear that there would be considerable political impact as a result of its nonparticipation in prewar British foreign policy. Secondary sources; 35 notes. M. C. Rosenfield

694. Grove, Eric J. THE FIRST SHOTS OF THE GREAT WAR: THE ANGLO-FRENCH CONQUEST OF TOGO, 1914. *Army Q. and Defense J. [Great Britain] 1976 106(3): 308-323.* Discusses Great Britain and France's joint armed invasion of the German colony of Togo as a prelude to World War I in 1914, emphasizing aspects of military strategy.

695. Hodges, G. W. T. AFRICAN MANPOWER STATISTICS FOR THE BRITISH FORCES IN EAST AFRICA, 1914-18. *J. of African Hist. [Great Britain] 1978 19(1): 101-116.* Gives tentative figures on how many Africans served in the British forces in East Africa, and how many died. Over 50,000 were soldiers and a million were followers. Fatalities numbered over 20%. Desertions were most frequent when far from home and during an offensive maneuver. German East Africa, forced to supply men to both sides, suffered considerably. Table, 78 notes. G. H. Soff

696. Jaques, Robert. THE MAN WHO FOUGHT RICHTHOFEN... AND LIVED! *Manuscripts 1980 32(1): 61-63.* When the newly commissioned Southern Rhodesian pilot, D. G. "Tommy" Lewis flew out on a mission with his squadron of the Royal Flying Corps, 20 April 1918, he became Baron Manfred von Richthofen's 80th victim. After being shot down Lewis returned to Southern Rhodesia to a legal career. But he never flew another airplane. D. A. Yanchisin

697. Killingray, David and Matthews, James. BEASTS OF BURDEN: BRITISH WEST AFRICAN CARRIERS IN THE FIRST WORLD WAR. *Can. J. of African Studies [Canada] 1979 13(1-2): 7-22.* While several studies have been made of East African carrier service during the First World War, relatively little has been written about the military role of West African porters during this period. The collective economic, social, and political impact of carrier service was understandably greater in East Africa than in British West Africa. However, the recruitment of tens of thousands of British West Africans during World War I represented for West Africa a mobilization of its labor force on a scale unknown until that time. J

698. Killingray, David. REPERCUSSIONS OF WORLD WAR I IN THE GOLD COAST. *J. of African Hist. [Great Britain] 1978 19(1): 39-59.* Ghana was on the periphery of World War I, yet the first British military operation of that war was set in motion from there. Ghana remained relatively quiet with only scattered disturbances, but economic conditions were deeply affected by the war. Trade suffered due to a shortage of barter items, former business with German companies halted, and a coin shortage led to inflation of as much as 50%. Unlike France, Britain resisted the temptation of conscription from Africa for Europe, and used Africans only in the African campaigns. 100 notes. H. G. Soff

699. Lewis, George Edward. AN EAST AFRICAN WAR DIARY, 1916. *Q. Bull. of the South African Lib. [South Africa] 1973 27(4): 98-119.* The author's diary kept from 10 January to 24 August 1916 during his service as a member of the fourth Battery of the South African Field Artillery in the German East Africa campaign of 1916. He ceased writing owing to an attack of blackwater fever. The diary describes camp life, incidents in the field, and battle action. A brief background setting is provided as an introduction. Photo, map, 9 notes.
J. A. Casada

700. Matthews, James K. CLOCK TOWERS FOR THE COLONIZED: DEMOBILIZATION OF THE NIGERIAN MILITARY AND THE READJUSTMENT OF ITS VETERANS TO CIVILIAN LIFE, 1918-1925. *Int. J. of African Hist. Studies 1981 14(2): 254-271.* Nigerian veterans of World War I were treated shamefully, receiving few rewards, benefits, or recognition. Even demobilization was poorly handled, with little attention paid to the needs of the troops. This poor record of reward for services rendered was a natural result of the "differences between colonizer and colonized." Based on Colonial Office records; map, 75 notes.
R. T. Brown

701. Osuntokun, Akinjide. ANGLO-FRENCH OCCUPATION AND THE PROVISIONAL PARTITION OF THE CAMEROONS 1914-1916. *J. of the Hist. Soc. of Nigeria [Nigeria] 1975 7(4): 647-656.* Examines the issues at stake in the Cameroons as a result of the outbreak of World War I. Both Great Britain and France justified their activities in the region on the basis of imperial security but the author sees it as "imperial covetousness" and suggests that differences over the Cameroons severely strained the Anglo-French alliance. Particular attention is devoted to the attitudes and policies of the British Foreign Office toward the Cameroons. Based on manuscript materials, mainly from the Public Record Office, and published sources; 44 notes.
J. A. Casada

702. Osuntokun, Jide. ANGLO-SPANISH RELATIONS IN WEST AFRICA DURING THE FIRST WORLD WAR. *J. of the Hist. Soc. of Nigeria [Nigeria] 1974 7(2): 291-301.* Examines questions of Allied security and strategy in West Africa during World War I from the perspective of Anglo-Spanish relations. In particular, the Spanish-ruled island of Fernando Póo had strategic importance, and West Africa was vital to the Allies as a source of raw material and as potential pawns in the bargaining which was certain to follow the war. In essence, Spanish authorities went beyond the limits of strict neutrality in their relations with Great Britain in West Africa. Based on printed and manuscript sources, most notably Colonial Office papers; 49 notes.
J. A. Casada

703. Osuntokun, Jide. NIGERIA'S COLONIAL GOVERNMENT AND THE ISLAMIC INSURGENCY IN FRENCH WEST AFRICA, 1914-1918. *Cahiers d'Études Africaines [France] 1975 15(1): 85-93.* Having made peace with Muslim leaders in Nigeria, local British officials were able to aid their French counterparts against a Muslim revolt during World War I. Most of the early opposition had been local, but in 1916-17 pro-Turkish Senusi forces crossed the Sahara, being defeated only with British aid. Based on materials in the French Archives d'Outremer, the Public Records Office, and published materials; 36 notes.
B. S. Fetter

704. Osuntokun, Jide. THE RESPONSE OF THE BRITISH COLONIAL GOVERNMENT IN NIGERIA TO THE ISLAMIC INSURGENCY IN THE FRENCH SUDAN AND THE SAHARA DURING THE FIRST WORLD WAR. *Odu: a J. of West African Studies [Nigeria] 1974 (10): 98-107.* The alliance of the Ottoman Empire with the Central Powers caused Allied authorities to suspect the involvement of Pan-Islamic agents in every outbreak of local opposition. The resistance was actually rooted in opposition either to European rule or to demands for African military service. Opposition to French rule was due to the French colonial policy of overcentralization. The British involvement was motivated by an interest in keeping the insurgents from disturbing the British hold on their Islamic territories in West Africa, particularly Nigeria. Based on French and British documents; 36 notes.
M. M. McCarthy

705. Osuntokun, Jide. THE RESPONSE OF THE BRITISH COLONIAL GOVERNMENT IN NIGERIA TO THE ISLAMIC INSURGENCY IN THE FRENCH SUDAN AND THE SAHARA DURING THE FIRST WORLD WAR. *Bull. de l'Inst. Fondamental d'Afrique Noire [Senegal] 1974 36(1): 14-24.* Muslim opposition to French rule in the Sudan and Sahara during World War I arose because of the centralization of administration and political power in French hands and the military conscription of unwilling desert people. The British cultivated the friendship and alliance of the Northern Nigerian ruling class, and the Muslims had an interest in maintaining the status quo with the British, under whom they had come to enjoy enormous power and wealth. British efforts were directed toward keeping Islamic insurgents from threatening the British hold in Nigeria and West Africa. 36 notes.
H. L. Calkin

706. Osuntokun, Jide. WEST AFRICAN ARMED REVOLTS DURING THE FIRST WORLD WAR. *Tarikh [Nigeria] 1977 5(3): 6-17.* There were numerous armed revolts by Black Africans against colonial powers, especially Great Britain and France, 1914-18, because of massive military conscription for the European front in French West Africa, the economic depression that followed the outbreak of war, and the coincidence of the war's beginning with the African peoples' full realization of colonialism's impact.

707. Page, Melvin E. THE GREAT WAR AND CHEWA SOCIETY IN MALAWI. *J. of Southern African Studies [Great Britain] 1980 6(2): 171-182.* Chewa resistance to wartime labor service took a passive but nonetheless effective form in the Central Region of Great Britain's Nyasaland Protectorate during World War I. While the chiefs cooperated with the colonial authorities in recruiting laborers, the *nyau* secret society hid its members to avoid labor service. This resistance was most effective in the Dedza District, where the *nyau* society was strongest in its membership and influence. Based on Malawi National Archives, British Colonial Office documents, field interviews and questionnaires, newspapers, and secondary sources; table, 35 notes.
L. W. Truschel

708. Page, Melvin E. THE GREAT WAR IN MALAWIAN MEMORY. *Centennial Rev. 1977 21(3): 321-332.* The World War I experience affected the cultures of those nations peripherally involved as well as those near the battlefield. A fifth of the population of Malawi, then a British protectorate, served as soldiers or laborers in the war. Memories of the time still color artistic, literary, rhetorical, and political forms there. Recruiting raids (reminiscent of the slave trade), discriminatory treatment in the military, battlefield experiences, and popular resentment at being forced into a distant conflict sparked bitterness and pride which sired Malawian nationalism. Later, veteran-dominated organizations provided the basis for the independence movement.
T. L. Powers

709. Page, Melvin E. MALAWIANS AND THE GREAT WAR: ORAL HISTORY IN RECONSTRUCTING AFRICA'S RECENT PAST. *Oral Hist. Rev. 1980 49-61.* Oral history is a valuable methodological tool for interpreting 20th-century African history. The use of oral history and comparison with traditional documentation provides an interesting case study in evaluating the impact of World War I on the history of the Nyasaland Protectorate, present-day Malawi. 51 notes.
D. A. Yanchisin

710. Page, Melvin E. THE WAR OF *THANGATA:* NYASALAND AND THE EAST AFRICAN CAMPAIGN, 1914-1918. *J. of African Hist. [Great Britain] 1978 19(1): 87-100.* The people of Malawi called World War I the war of *thangata,* referring to European demands for African labor for which Africans gain no benefit. First demands were for soldiers to protect the border with German East Africa, and the role of soldiers fit well into the desire to be warriors. Demands for carrier service were met with reluctance and resistance, particularly from preacher John Chilembwe. The government used tricks and deception to induce volunteers, and growing resentment was channeled into secret religious societies particularly among the Chewa. In addition to working without benefit, the men were poorly fed and housed and suffered greatly. Several thousand died. The war became a watershed for later independence movements. 54 notes
H. G. Soff

711. Page, Melvin E. "WITH JANNIE IN THE JUNGLE": EUROPEAN HUMOR IN AN EAST AFRICAN CAMPAIGN, 1914-1918. *Int. J. of African Hist. Studies 1981 14(3): 466-481.* There was a well-developed sense of self-deprecating humor among the white troops of the World War I East African campaign as well as a deep sense of loyalty to their favorite commander, Jan Smuts. In addition there was an

"underlying negative view of Africans." Based on primary sources; 4 illus., 22 notes. R. T. Brown

712. Picciola, André. QUELQUES ASPECTS DE LA CÔTE D'IVOIRE EN 1919 [Some aspects of the Ivory Coast in 1919]. *Cahiers d'Études Africaines [France] 1973 13(2): 239-274.* From 1914 to 1918, France, constrained to use all its resources for the war effort, relied heavily on its overseas possessions. In increasing numbers, both fighting men and raw materials found their way from colony to metropolitan France. In the case of the Ivory Coast, these demands caused the colony, under the authoritarian rule of Governor Angoulvant, to enjoy a real economic development. 44 notes, biblio. J. C. Billigmeier

713. Pirouet, M. Louise. EAST AFRICAN CHRISTIANS AND WORLD WAR I. *J. of African Hist. [Great Britain] 1978 19(1): 117-130.* A critical view of the widely held claim that World War I was injurious to the Christian cause because Africans were denied European leadership. On the contrary, Africans played a positive role and examples are given from Kigezi, Uganda, where Africans took responsibilities and carried them out. Catholics and Anglicans did best since they had trained an African clergy, but other missions found Africans who rose to the occasion. The greatest injury to the missions caused by World War I was the European failure to see that Africa did not require a return to prewar methods. 53 notes. H. G. Soff

714. Quinn, Frederick. AN AFRICAN REACTION TO WORLD WAR I: THE BETI OF CAMEROON. *Cahiers d'Études Africaines [France] 1973 13(4): 722-731.* The Beti of the Yaoundé region in Cameroon prospered under the German colonial administration, so when World War I broke out, they remained loyal to Berlin. When Allied forces took Yaoundé, the Beti leaders went into exile in Spanish (Equatorial) Guinea and Spain itself. When the French received the League of Nations mandate to govern Cameroon, the Beti leadership led by Karl Atangana, argued successfully that they would serve France as loyally as they had Germany. 26 notes. J. C. Billigmeier

715. Rathbone, Richard. WORLD WAR I AND AFRICA: INTRODUCTION. *J. of African Hist. [Great Britain] 1978 19(1): 1-9.* Introduction to papers presented at a conference on World War I and Africa at the School of Oriental and African Studies, London, April 1977. Outlines the significance of inflation, the great influenza epidemic, labor recruitment, and the growth of European business. 11 notes. H. G. Soff

716. Scholler, Heinrich. GERMAN WORLD WAR I AIMS IN ETHIOPIA: THE FROBENIUS-HALL MISSION. Tubiana, Joseph, ed. *Modern Ethiopia, from the Accession of Menilek II to the Present* (Rotterdam: Balkema, 1980): 303-326. Discusses four periods in which Germany has had close connections with Ethiopia since the reign of Menelik II in 1889, resulting in military programs of various types and with different strategic aims.

717. Summers, Anne and Johnson, R. W. WORLD WAR I CONSCRIPTION AND SOCIAL CHANGE IN GUINEA. *J. of African Hist. [Great Britain] 1978 19(1): 25-38.* An analysis of the impact of French mobilization on Guinea during World War I. It was originally intended that Africans would man the garrisons in Africa to free French soldiers for Europe. To conscript sufficient forces, they had to rely on the power of persuasion of chiefs, who were promised more authority when the war ended, so that military conscription actually restored the power of chiefs. Upon their return to Guinea from Europe, some conscripts led resistance to the inequalities that existed in Guinea. They never fully reentered the colonial situation but remained a special social group who threatened political stability. 32 notes. H. G. Soff

718. Thomas, Roger. MILITARY RECRUITMENT IN THE GOLD COAST DURING THE FIRST WORLD WAR. *Cahiers d'Études Africaines [France] 1975 15(1): 57-83.* Questions the prevailing opinion that recruitment in British West Africa was strictly voluntary during World War I. Demonstrates that most recruitment occurred in Northern Ghana, where Great Britain had appointed chiefs over previously acephalous groups, and in two eastern areas, where loyalist chiefs actively encouraged enlistment. Based on materials in the National Archives of Ghana (Accra, Kumasi, Tamale), the Public Records Office, and published materials; 109 notes. B. S. Fetter

719. Willan, B. P. THE SOUTH AFRICAN NATIVE LABOUR CONTINGENT, 1916-1918. *J. of African Hist. [Great Britain] 1978 19(1): 61-86.* The South African Native Labor Contingent (SANLC) was created in 1916. Never intended to bear arms in World War I, they were sent to France where they were of particular value in unloading supply ships. White South African opposition to sending blacks to Europe was strong; widespread recruitment began in 1916 through newspapers, meetings, and churches, but to a generally poor response. The SANLC was led by a white colonel and was divided into battalions. There was some African dissatisfaction, and incidents did occur, including the sinking of the *Mendi* with the loss of 600 Africans. 93 notes. H. G. Soff

720. Yonge, B. T. THE STRANDING OF THE SYBIL. *Tanzania Notes and Records [Tanzania] 1974 (75): 29-35.* Relates the sinking of the HMS *Sybil*, a converted cargo boat, inLake Victoria in November 1914. The *Sybil* hit an uncharted rock while searching for the German gunboat *Heinrich Otto* near Bujaga on the eastern side of the lake. Her captain beached the *Sybil* near Bujaga Point. British authorities refloated her the next year, and she remained in service on Lake Victoria until 1966. Map. C. Hopkins

World War II

721. Ageron, Charles Robert. LES POPULATIONS DU MAGHREB FACE À LA PROPAGANDE ALLEMANDE [Population groups of the Maghreb in the face of German propaganda]. *Rev. d'Hist. de la Deuxième Guerre Mondiale [France] 1979 29(114): 1-39.* Before 1939 National Socialist propaganda relating to Africa stressed good relations with Arabs and German anticolonialism. To preserve relations with Italy, anticolonialism was kept mild. During the North African campaigns, German propaganda reached its height. The themes were constant: the invincible power of Germany, denunciation of Jews and their connections with Anglo-Saxons and Bolsheviks, alleged affinities between Islam and National Socialism, the struggle against Anglo-American capitalism, dissension among the Allies, denunciation of Giraud and de Gaulle. Although German victory over France greatly stimulated Maghreb nationalism, Nazi propaganda failed to promote this theme. 71 notes. G. H. Davis

722. Aran, Esther. REDIFAT YEHUDEY LUV (KEFI SHEHI MISHTAKEFET BEDIVUHEY HAKONSULIYA HAGERMANIT BETRIPOLI) [The persecution of the Libyan Jews: reports of the German consulate of Tripoli]. *Yalkut Moreshet Periodical [Israel] 1982 (33): 153-156.* Several hundred Libyan Jews were sent to concentration camps in 1940. The German army entered in 1941, and foreign nationals were expelled and the Italian authorities introduced measures against the Jews in 1942. In his reports, the German consul Dr. Gebhard Walter summed up anti-Jewish legislation adopted in Libya. 2 notes. R. Hetzron

723. Auphan, Admiral. UN MENSONGE INCREVABLE: "LES ALLEMANDS À DAKAR" [A persistent lie: "the Germans at Dakar"]. *Écrits de Paris [France] 1974 (332): 11-15.* Shows that the Germans were not present in Dakar on 22 September 1940, contrary to statements in the recent edition of *Souvenirs de Guerre* by Admiral Thierry d'Argenlieu.

724. Azéma, Jean-Pierre. LE DRAME DE MERS EL-KEBIR [The tragedy of Mers el-Kebir]. *Histoire [France] 1980 (23): 15-25.* Reopens the discussion of the complex and controversial question of the Royal Navy's torpedoing of the French fleet on 3 July 1940 in the roads of Mers el-Kebir, shortly after the collapse of France in World War II.

725. Beecher, Lloyd, Jr. THE SECOND WORLD WAR AND U.S. POLITICO-ECONOMIC EXPANSION: THE CASE OF LIBERIA, 1938-45. *Diplomatic Hist. 1979 3(4): 391-412.* Before World War II American relations with Liberia were primarily sentimental. As war approached the US military understood Liberia's strategic value and promoted the country's development for military reasons. As the security of the region improved, the military's interest in the country declined, but the State Department became more active, promoting economic development to benefit the United States and planning reform

measures. Based on archival and published primary sources; 53 notes.
S

726. Béthouart, Emile and Gromand, Roger. LE DÉBARQUEMENT ALLIÉ AU MAROC 8 NOVEMBRE 1942 [Allied landing in Morocco 8 November 1942]. *Nouvelle Rev. des Deux Mondes [France] 1977 (4): 39-76.* Two personal accounts of the Allied landing in Morocco and the victory over German forces in North Africa, stressing the 8 November battle as a decisive one and a turning point in World War II.

727. Blanc, Marcel. LA LEGION ÉTRANGÈRE DANS LA CAMPAGNE DE NORVÈGE EN 1940 [The Foreign Legion in the Norwegian campaign of 1940]. *Rev. Hist. des Armées [France] 1981 (1): 142-165.* The 13th Demi-Brigade of the Foreign Legion, formed in Morocco, participated in the successful attack on Narvik in conjunction with Polish and Norwegian troops supported by British naval units. The demi-brigade's convoy sailed from Brest to Greenock, Scotland, whence it proceeded to Ballangen, where the demi-brigade established its base. The first phase of the operation was an amphibious assault landing to capture Bjervik. In the second phase, the demi-brigade made another landing just east of Narvik resulting in the capture of Narvik and the pursuit of the remaining German troops almost to the Swedish border. At the same time, the British government decided to evacuate all Allied forces from Norway. Accordingly, the demi-brigade returned to Great Britain and eventually back to North Africa. In part an eye-witness account; 6 photos, 5 maps, note.
J. S. Gassner

728. Bouche, Denise. LE RETOUR DE L'AFRIQUE OCCIDENTALE FRANÇAISE DANS LA LUTTE CONTRE L'ENNEMI AUX CÔTÉS DES ALLIES [The return of French West Africa to the struggle against the enemy on the side of the Allies]. *Rev. d'Hist. de la Deuxième Guerre Mondiale [France] 1979 29(114): 41-68.* The Anglo-American invasion of North Africa (8 November 1942) caused a break in the loose ties of French West Africa with the Vichy government. French West Africa under the leadership of Pierre Boisson had acknowledged Vichy but hoped to be treated as a neutral by the British. The Free French agitated from London against the Vichy alignment, and the invasion of North Africa forced a realignment and a change of personnel. At first General Henri Giraud was recognized and under him Boisson and others were dismissed. There were also significant changes in Senegal and Ivory Coast. Archival and secondary sources; 125 notes.
G. H. Davis

729. Buffotot, Patrice. LES FORCES AÉRIENNES FRANÇAISES LIBRES EN AFRIQUE: L'ESCADRILLE "TOPIC" DU G. R. B. 1 À KOUFRA EN FÉVRIER 1941 [The Free French Air Force in Africa: the "Topic" squadron of Bomber Reserve Group 1 at Al-Kufrah in February 1941]. *Rev. Hist. des Armées [France] 1980 (2): 171-188.* Extracts from the log of the "Topic" squadron, which was found half charred among the debris of a Blenheim that crashed near Khartoum. They illustrate the beginnings of the Free French Air Force. The squadron was formed of inexperienced and diverse personnel and assorted and obsolete material. It had to prove itself thousands of miles away from Europe. Composed of 12 aircraft, the squadron lost five pilots and six planes after it was sent to Sudan. The leader crashed near Khartoum. 4 photos, map, 4 notes.
J. V. Coutinho

730. Candlin, A. H. S. WAR IN ETHIOPIA (1941): COORDINATED IRREGULAR AND REGULAR CAMPAIGNS. *Army Q. and Defence J. [Great Britain] 1974 104(5): 580-589.* Great Britain seized Ethiopia from Italy during World War II through coordination of army offensives with a guerrilla campaign.

731. Caravaglios, Maria Genoino. LA SANTA SEDE E L'INGHILTERRA IN ETIOPIA DURANTE IL SECONDO CONFLITTO MONDIALE [The Holy See and Great Britain in Ethiopia during World War II]. *Africa [Italy] 1980 35(2): 217-254.* Describes relations between the British military government in Ethiopia and the Vatican over the disposition of Italian Catholic missions and missionaries, 1941-43. The Vatican tried to induce the British to allow the Italians to remain until they could be replaced, but the military authorities evacuated them all in 1942. Based mostly on upublished documents.
J/S

732. Ceva, Lucio. MONOGRAFIE DELL'UFFICIO STORICO DELL'ESERCITO SULLA GUERRA IN AFRICA SETTENTRIONALE (1940-1943) [Monographs of the Historical Section of the Army: the war in North Africa, 1940-43]. *Italia Contemporanea [Italy] 1975 26(119): 105-129.* Between 1949 and 1974 the Historical Section of the Army published eight separate studies dealing with the military operations in North Africa, 1940-43. This is a monumental collective effort (3069 pages, 206 maps, and 472 documents). Lucio Ceva pays tribute to the high quality of the presentation, especially of the last three volumes, but deplores the lack of analytical indices and adequate bibliographical information. The volumes of this series did not appear in chronological order, and there are several methodological as well as material deficiencies. Volumes I and III receive special attention, and some errors are brought to the attention of the reader.
H. W. L. Freudenthal

733. Ceva, Lucio. POLIVALENZA E ATTUALITA DEL MINCULPOP [Polyvalence and actuality of the Minculpop]. *Risorgimento [Italy] 1982 34(2): 149-158.* In the winter of 1941 British troops occupied the Italian North African territories of Cyrenaica. In July of the same year the Italian Ministry of Popular Culture (Minculpop) published a dossier of alleged British atrocities and vandalism as part of the war propaganda effort. Two anonymous documents found in the state archives disprove the accusations, but, curiously, passages from the dossier have been recently quoted by the independent government of Libya at a UN-sponsored seminar on war wreckage and minefields still existing in that country almost 40 years after the end of the war. Based on *Che Cosa Hanno Fatto gli Inglesi in Cirenaica*[What the English did in Cyrenaica] (1941) and two documents in the archive of the Italian Army General Staff.
J. V. Coutinho

734. Compagnon, Jean. LA LEGION ÉTRANGÈRE DANS LA CAMPAGNE DE TUNISIE 1942-1943 [The Foreign Legion and the Tunisian campaign, 1942-43]. *Rev. Hist. des Armées [France] 1981 (1): 185-216.* In order to support the Allied forces engaged in a see-saw campaign against Axis troops, the Foreign Legion sent six infantry battalions from Morocco and Algeria to Tunisia, where they were gradually reorganized to form the 1st and 3d Foreign Legion Provisional Infantry Regiments and an armored cavalry group of the 1st Foreign Legion Cavalry Regiment. Toward the end of the Tunisian campaign, two independent Legion battalions came from Libya as part of the 1st Free French Division. All of the Foreign Legion units were battle-experienced and highly effective, despite the inferiority of their weapons and equipment. They suffered many casualties but inflicted heavy losses upon the enemy and received the surrender of the Hermann Goering Division. Based on original combat records of the Foreign Legion units; 4 photos, 10 maps, 24 notes, biblio.
J. S. Gassner

735. Dougherty, James J. LEND-LEASE AND THE OPENING OF FRENCH NORTH AND WEST AFRICA TO PRIVATE TRADE. *Cahiers d'Études Africaines [France] 1975 (3): 481-500.* With French possessions in West and North Africa separated from France during World War II, new mechanisms for the supply of consumer goods to those regions had to be developed. At first the American administration favored government-to-government assistance (Lend-Lease) rather than private trade, but toward the end of the war American private companies pressed the government for a resumption of private trade. This the French resisted until 1946, in the hope of reestablishing their own merchants' dominance. Based on materials in the US National Archives, the private papers of American war leaders, and published sources; 64 notes.
B. S. Fetter

736. Driss, Rachid. LA TUNISIE AU DÉBUT DE LA SECONDE GUERRE MONDIALE (1939-1940) [Tunisia in the beginning of World War II, 1939-40]. *Cahiers de Tunisie [Tunisia] 1979 27(107-108): 213-275.* Recalls political and military events in Tunisia at the beginning of World War II, up to the Franco-German armistice of June 1940.

737. Driss, Rachid. LA TUNISIE SOUS L'OCCUPATION ALLEMANDE (NOVEMBRE 1942-MAI 1943) [Tunisia under the German occupation, November 1942-May 1943]. *Cahiers de Tunisie [Tunisia] 1979 27(109-110): 455-471.* Recalls political and military events in Tunisia under the German military occupation, up to the entrance of Allied troops in May 1943.

738. Ethell, Jeff. "LIGHTNING OVER AFRICA": THE STORY OF AMERICA'S VERSATILE AND DURABLE P-38 DURING WW-II ACTION OVER NORTH AFRICA. *Aviation Q. 1979 5(1): 88-104.* Traces the history of the P-38 campaigns over North Africa during World War II and discusses the plane's characteristics.

739. Facon, Patrick. LE PLAN VII (1943-1944) [Plan VII (1943-44)]. *Rev. Hist. des Armées [France] 1979 (3): 185-204.* In July 1943 the French air force units in Africa were reorganized as an independent entity, excluding naval flying units, under the command of General René Bouscat. Since a principal objective of the reorganization was to make as many French air force units as possible available for use by the Allies, a major problem was the control of units which were on detached duty with the Allies. Another problem was the unification of Free French units with those of the various French African forces. The new French air force was to be equipped by the British, Americans, and Soviets according to a schedule known as Plan VII, supervised by a Joint Air Commission at Algiers. Despite some delays, the plan was carried out so effectively that a year later the French air force had 600 aircraft and 33,000 men. Its most serious problem was no longer a lack of matériel but of personnel. 2 tables, 2 charts, 8 photos, 32 notes.
J. S. Gassner

740. Fol, Jean-Jacques. LE TOGO PENDANT LA DEUXIÈME GUERRE MONDIALE [Togo during World War II]. *Rev. d'Hist. de la Deuxième Guerre Mondiale [France] 1979 29(115): 69-77.* Unlike the French colony Dahomey, Togo was legally a mandate of the League of Nations divided in administration between Great Britain and France. French administrators attempted to combine the Dahomey and Togo structures. By the time World War II began, Togo was divided geographically, nationally (between elements loyal to the old German colonial system and those who supported French controls), and between those who opposed all colonialism and those who did not. During the war imports declined with resulting shortages of food, fuel, and other items. The fall of France stimulated pro-German sentiment which continued even after the balance changed with the Anglo-American landings in North Africa in 1942. Based on administrative archives and Radio Accra archives.
G. H. Davis

741. Gazin. LE DÉBARQUEMENT DES ALLIÉS EN AFRIQUE DU NORD (ALGER, 8-13 NOVEMBRE 1942) [The Allied landing in North Africa, Algiers, 8-13 November 1942]. *Nouvelle Rev. des Deux Mondes [France] 1979 (10): 79-87.* Analyzes the events connected with the Allied landing in North Africa during World War II, stressing the action of French General Alphonse Pierre Julin's army when confronted by the Allied forces.

742. Glen, Lawrence. THE KUFRA CONVOY. *Army Q. and Defence J. [Great Britain] 1979 109(1): 37-41.* Describes the Kufra convoy operation to transport supplies across 700 miles of desert from Wadi Halfa on the East bank of the Nile River to the Kufra Oasis where the Long Range Desert Group, part of the Sudan Defence Force, was sabotaging operations behind enemy lines during 1940.

743. Goldsmith, R. F. K. THE EIGHTH ARMY AT BAY—JULY 1942. *Army Q. and Defence J. [Great Britain] 1974 104(5): 552-560, 1975 105(1): 67-75.* Part I. FROM THE JAWS OF DEFEAT. Discusses General Claude Auchinleck's assumption of command of Great Britain's Eighth Army as it retreated from Axis forces toward El Alamein, Egypt, between May and June of 1942, and describes the first battle near El Alamein in early July. Part II. A NEW DEFENSIVE SYSTEM. Describes Auchinleck's direction of the British Eighth Army's defense against the Axis forces at El Alamein in July 1942.

744. Graeme-Evans, Alex. FIELD-MARSHALL BERNARD MONTGOMERY: A CRITICAL ASSESSMENT. *Army Q. and Defence J. [Great Britain] 1974 104(4): 412-426.* Aims to "substantiate the argument that Montgomery was not of the same mettle as his German and British counterparts of equal fame" by examining his military leadership qualities in the 1942-43 North African campaign and the European campaign, 1944-45. In the former, the difficulties of Montgomery's task had been much reduced before El Alamein, and his failure to destroy the German army after the battle directly reflects on his generalship. His conduct of the battle itself merits considerable criticism. On the European Front he displayed similar and other inadequacies. Controversy over Montgomery derives from his character; 56 notes.
D. H. Murdoch

745. Hallo, Jean-Pierre. LE RÉGIMENT DE MARCHE DE LA LÉGION ÉTRANGÈRE 1943-1945 [The Foreign Legion *régiment de marche* of 1943-45]. *Rev. Hist. des Armées [France] 1981 (1): 217-241.* A regiment of the Foreign Legion was organized in Algeria with survivors of the Tunisian campaign and consisted mainly of French and Germans, with some Jewish refugees and Spanish civil war veterans. Equipped with American tanks and half-tracks, it was transformed into an armored infantry regiment and became part of the 5th Armored Division. After training, it was shipped from Oran to France, moved north, and participated in the piercing of the Belfort gap, the reduction of the Colmar pocket, and the final victorious penetration into Germany, when the unit crossed the Siegfried line and passed through Baden and Württemberg. By the end of hostilities, the regiment had penetrated into Austria. 4 illus., 3 maps, 14 notes.
J. S. Gassner

746. Halstead, Charles R. and Halstead, Carolyn J. ABORTED IMPERIALISM: SPAIN'S OCCUPATION OF TANGIER 1940-1945. *Iberian Studies [Great Britain] 1978 7(2): 53-71.* Examines the motives behind Spain's actions in Tangier in World War II when, hoping to reconstruct an empire in Africa, the Spanish government undertook a political and military occupation of the International Zone, 1940-45. 162 notes.
M. Smith

747. Headrick, Rita. AFRICAN SOLDIERS IN WORLD WAR II. *Armed Forces and Soc. 1978 4(3): 501-526.* Disputes the prevailing thesis that African soldiers developed anticolonial attitudes while serving in European Allied armies during World War II. The war was a modernizing experience which raised expectations, thereby leading to revolution. Few African revolutionary leaders, except for those in the Gold Coast and Kenya, ever served in the military. But thousands of veterans became educated, learned skills, and acquired materialistic ambitions associated with modern societies. Based on primary sources, interviews, and African secondary literature; 70 notes.
J. P. Harahan

748. Kaddache, Mahfoud. L'OPINION POLITIQUE MUSULMANE EN ALGÉRIE ET L'ADMINISTRATION FRANÇAISE (1939-1942) [Muslim political opinion concerning Algeria and French administration, 1939-42]. *Rev. d'Hist. de la Deuxième Guerre Mondiale [France] 1979 29(114): 95-115.* French propaganda portrayed Muslim Algerians as loyal before and after the defeat of France in 1940. The facts depart from this view in subtle ways. Muslim leaders remained faithful but desertion was common. A new spirit of recalcitrance arose among Muslims, especially since they had no interest in fighting against Germany. The French arrested the leaders of the Parti du Peuple Algérien (PPA) as well as the Communists and the ulemas. Those who escaped undertook clandestine nationalist activities. The Germans' effective radio propaganda, popular songs, poems, and school and recreational activities stressed nationalist themes among Muslims. Based on French and Arabic archival and published sources; 78 notes.
G. H. Davis

749. Kam'a N'dumbe III, Alexandre. LES BUTS DE GUERRE DE L'ALLEMAGNE HITLÉRIENNE EN AFRIQUE [The war aims of Hitler's Germany in Africa]. *Rev. d'Hist. de la Deuxième Guerre Mondiale [France] 1977 27(106): 37-60.* Adolf Hitler had definite plans for North Africa, black Africa south of the Sahara, and South Africa. He announced these in his first two books. Major German political parties, colonial associations, and powerful capitalists supported a strong African policy before World War II, and the military sought posts there. Nazi racial theory was applied as a pseudoscience to African conditions and colonial policy. The defeat of Nazi Germany weakened the color line by demonstrating that white people *per se* are not invincible and encouraged colonial people to fight for liberty after the war against imperialist powers as they had done against the dictators during the war. Based mostly on German archives; 51 notes.
G. H. Davis

750. Killingray, David. THE IDEA OF A BRITISH IMPERIAL AFRICAN ARMY. *J. of African Hist. [Great Britain] 1979 20(3): 421-436.* Britain consistently maintained small colonial armed forces in African territories for internal security and local defense. Propaganda

for use of African troops in extra-continental imperial affairs arose on four occasions when the Empire faced a shortage of manpower. Such propaganda gained support as India increasingly opposed the use of the Indian army for Imperial defense in Asia and the Middle East. The Colonial Office rejected the propaganda in 1916-18 and 1919-21. Policy changed in 1939-42, and African troops were used in the East African campaign, against Italy, as labor troops in the Middle East, and after 1943 as combatants in Asia. After World War II, the Colonial Office wished to maintain a sizeable African army but was frustrated by extensive postwar military retrenchment. 78 notes. A. W. Novitsky

751. Killingray, David. MILITARY AND LABOUR RECRUITMENT IN THE GOLD COAST DURING THE SECOND WORLD WAR. *J. of African Hist. [Great Britain] 1982 23(1): 83-95.* Over seventy thousand men drawn mainly from Ghana (primarily the Northern Territories) served in the armed forces, and about half of these served overseas in Asia. Though nominally volunteers, many of them were recruited by a system of levies on individual districts, or through misunderstanding of what they were required to do. Of those who went overseas, the initial drafts served in East Africa (1939-40); the second period (1941-42) was devoted to containing the Vichy threat; and the last period was spent in Southeast Asia. The returning soldiers were healthy, better clothed and fed, and had acquired new skills. They expected better employment and education, both of which were difficult to provide. Published sources; 59 notes. R. L. Collison

752. Marchelli, Alfredo. LA BATTAGLIA DEI TRASPORTI MARITTIMI NELLA CAMPAGNA DI LIBIA [The battle over marine transport in the Libyan campaign]. *Movimento di Liberazione in Italia [Italy] 1973 25(112): 55-81.* The main activity of the Italian navy during World War II was to escort the merchant fleet from the Italian ports to the North African landing places of Tripoli, Tobruk, and Bengasi. British submarines, aircraft, and light surface units attacked the supply line to Libya and its battlefields. For Great Britain the security of the short route to the Far East through the Mediterranean and the Suez Canal was essential. The Italian maritime power was at a disadvantage because of a technology gap; there were errors in evaluating the situation before the war, and a lack of strategic planning resulted in small tactical actions but no attempt at a full blockade of Malta. Based on official histories and other secondary sources; biblio. E. Makino

753. Moritz, Erhard. PLANUNGEN FÜR DIE KRIEGFÜHRUNG DES DEUTSCHEN HEERES IN AFRIKA UND VORDERASIEN [Plans for the German army's warfare in Africa and the Middle East]. *Militärgeschichte [East Germany] 1977 16(3): 323-333.* Five documents from the Army's Supreme Command dated from April to July 1941 provide evidence of the origins of plans for military campaigns in Afghanistan and North Africa after the defeat of the Soviet Union. These plans were designed to challenge Great Britain in India and to prepare for conflict with the United States by control of West African territory. 5 documents, 4 notes. H. D. Andrews

754. Nofi, A. A. THE DESERT FOX: ROMMEL'S CAMPAIGN FOR NORTH AFRICA, APRIL 1941-DECEMBER 1942. *Strategy & Tactics 1981 (87): 4-15.* Describes the North African campaign fought by General Erwin Rommel in Egypt and Libya during World War II. Of tremendous strategic importance, it was the last honorably conducted campaign in modern times.

755. Nofi, A. A. PANZERARMEE AFRIKA AND THE WAR IN THE DESERT JUNE 1940—DECEMBER 1942. *Strategy & Tactics 1973 (40): 4-19.* Describes the military campaign between the Axis powers and Great Britain in North Africa during World War II.

756. Nouschi, André. LE GOUVERNEMENT D'ALGER: NOTES ET REFLEXIONS [The Algiers government: remarks and observations]. *Storia e Pol. [Italy] 1975 14(1-2): 21-34.* After June 1943, Algiers became "the capital of the France in war" until the provisional government moved to Paris. In this period Charles de Gaulle (1890-1970) won power, depriving Henri Honoré Giraud (1879-1949) of his authority. The life of the Algiers government was not easy. Churchill wanted to be its guardian, and Roosevelt disliked de Gaulle. But after the liberation of Paris (1944) and de Gaulle's visit to the United States, Roosevelt recognized de Gaulle's government as the legal French government. 34 notes. A. Canavero

757. Ohlinger, John F. INCIDENT AT FOUL BAY. *Aerospace Hist. 1976 23(2): 71-74.* Memoir of a World War II experience piloting a C-47 on a mapping mission along the ferry route from Africa to China. All went well to Foul Bay, a Red Sea inlet in Egypt. A salt flat that looked like a suitable landing site from the air turned out to be pock-marked with underground voids, into one of which the plane fell while taxiing. The aircraft was slightly damaged, but the crew was able to radio for help. An RAF transport arrived the next day with equipment to get the C-47 back into the air. 2 photos. C. W. Ohrvall

758. Olorunfemi, A. EFFECTS OF WAR-TIME TRADE CONTROLS ON NIGERIAN COCOA TRADERS AND PRODUCERS, 1939-45: A CASE STUDY OF THE HAZARDS OF A DEPENDENT ECONOMY. *Int. J. of African Hist. Studies 1980 13(4): 672-687.* A history of the impact of World War II economic controls in southwestern Nigeria. After the war, the Cocoa Marketing Board was created, and it dominated the cocoa economy of West Africa for 20 years. Based on British and Nigerian records; 69 notes. R. T. Brown

759. Pearce, R. D. MORALE IN THE COLONIAL SERVICE IN NIGERIA DURING THE SECOND WORLD WAR. *J. of Imperial and Commonwealth Hist. [Great Britain] 1983 11(2): 175-196.* "During the Second World War the Colonial Service in Africa was strained to breaking point and morale amongst the British officers slumped to its nadir." This study deals with this problem in Nigeria and the various attempts made to deal with the worst aspects of the problem: poor pay and living conditions. At the same time some of the privileges of the Europeans in the Colonial Service were being removed, and by war's end the Colonial Service had found its mission: to be self-liquidating. Based on Colonial Office papers, London; the Walker Papers and the Crocker Papers at Rhodes House; the Ibadan Archives and various printed secondary materials; 129 notes. M. C. Rosenfield

760. Pirrone, Giorgio. LA BRIGATA CORAZZATA SPECIALE IN AFRICA SETTENTRIONALE [The special armored brigade in North Africa]. *Riv. Militare [Italy] 1979 102(3): 105-112.* The confection, from units on hand and certain additional forces, of a special armored brigade in Libya in November-December 1940 was the Italian reply to British armored strength in Egypt.

761. Pitt, Barrie. TOBRUK. *British Heritage [Great Britain] 1982 3(2): 38-51, (4): 36-47.* Continued from an earlier article (see following entry). Part 4. Focuses on Rommel's Afrika Korps' raid on the Tobruk fortress in 1942, which resulted in defeat for the British under Major-General H. B. Klopper. Part 5. Focuses on the plan under the command of Lieutenant Colonel John Haselden, Operation Daffodil, which started with a small group of men whose mission was to blow up the main fuel storage tanks in Tobruk but soon became a bigger operation whose "success was negligible while its cost, especially to the Navy, was disastrous."

762. Pitt, Barrie. TOBRUK. *British Heritage [Great Britain] 1981 2(6): 20-31; 1981-82 3(1): 32-45.* Continued from an earlier article (see following entry). Part 2. Describes the 1941 siege of Tobruk during World War II, focusing on defense of the port by Australian troops under Major-General Leslie Morshead and the operations of assorted British and Indian troops against German and Italian forces under General Erwin Rommel. Part III. Describes the June 1942 battle of Tobruk, in which General Erwin Rommel defeated the British forces, taking the fort which had resisted attack for more than a year.

763. Pitt, Barrie. TOBRUK. PART I. *British Heritage [Great Britain] 1981 2(5): 34-45.* History and significance of Tobruk, Libya, and the fighting there during World War II, 1939-43. Article to be continued (see preceding entry).

764. Queuille, Pierre. LA DIPLOMATIE ANGLO-AMÉRICAINE EN VUE D'UN DÉBARQUEMENT ALLIÉ EN AFRIQUE [Anglo-American diplomacy with a view to the Allied landing in Africa]. *Bull. de la Soc. d'Hist. Moderne [France] 1980 79(5): 7-12.* Discusses Anglo-American diplomacy and behind-the-scenes machinations in Algiers with the French in an effort to rally the French army in Africa to the Allied cause before the German Afrika Korps arrived.

765. Richards, Pamela Spence. INFORMATION FOR THE ALLIES: OFFICE OF WAR INFORMATION LIBRARIES IN AUSTRALIA, NEW ZEALAND, AND SOUTH AFRICA. *Lib. Q. 1982 52(4): 325-347.* In 1942 the U.S. Office of War Information (OWI) was created by the federal government to increase domestic understanding of America's war effort and to facilitate the flow of American information overseas. As part of this operation, 14 information libraries were established throughout Allied and neutral territory. The OWI librarians sent to Australia, New Zealand, and South Africa arrived in those countries at critical periods in their library development, since all three nations were in the process of reevaluating their library services in the light of recent critical Carnegie Commission reports. By offering strong models of modern information service and by energetically supporting emerging local movements for tax-supported public libraries, three OWI librarians in particular made contributions to library development in Australia, New Zealand, and South Africa that endure to this day. J

766. Sairigné, Gabriel de. BIR HAKEIM [Bir Hacheim]. *Rev. Hist. des Armées [France] 1981 (1): 166-184.* Diary of a company commander of the 13th Demi-Brigade of the Foreign Legion, which, as part of the 1st Free French Brigade, moved into Libya in January 1942 and took up a fortified position at Bir Hacheim, guarding the left flank of the British Eighth Army facing the Afrika Korps of General Erwin Rommel. For three months the demi-brigade was engaged in patrolling and skirmishing, until Rommel mounted a major offensive toward Egypt. The demi-brigade's position at Bir Hacheim came under intense artillery fire and aerial bombardment; it was attacked and surrounded by Rommel's forces. After two weeks of resistance against superior forces, it was ordered to withdraw and it succeeded in breaking through the encirclement, having suffered 800 casualties. 4 photos, 2 maps, 15 notes. J. S. Gassner

767. Spencer, Ian. SETTLER DOMINANCE, AGRICULTURAL PRODUCTION AND THE SECOND WORLD WAR IN KENYA. *J. of African Hist. [Great Britain] 1980 21(4): 497-514.* European settlers had had indifferent success in farming during the 1930's. During World War II the farmers saw their best contribution to the war effort to be increased production of wheat, maize, and dairy products. Agricultural credit was obtained from the British government in 1940. Guaranteed prices and a rapidly increasing population brought prosperity to the farmers and rescued many who had been burdened by debts in the 1930's. Generous loans were made available in 1944 from the Land and Agricultural Bank for the extension of acreage and a machinery pool was created. Conscripted African labor never provided more than 10% of the total African work force. Based on public records and published sources; 95 notes. R. L. Collison

768. Stanley, Clifford R. NEAR TO GREATNESS. *Army Q. and Defence J. 1974 104(2): 185-192.* A personal account of the fierce fighting during the first half of 1943 on the Allied front at Beja in northern Tunisia. Based on correspondence of participants and military and press reports. R. G. Neville

769. Tlili, Béchir. DU FRONT ANTIFASCISTE ET ANTIHITLÉRIEN DE TUNISIE. LE GROUPEMENT DU *IL GIORNALE* (1939) [The Tunisian antifascist and anti-Hitler front: the *Il Giornale* organization, 1939]. *Cahiers de Tunisie [Tunisia] 1979 27(109-110): 163-300.* Description and analysis of the composition, program, goals, policy, methods, and activities of the antifascist organization in Tunisia that published from March to September 1939, under the direction of Giorgio Amendola, the daily *Il Giornale.*

770. Van Crefeld, M. ROMMEL'S SUPPLY PROBLEM, 1941-42. *J. of the Royal United Services Inst. for Defence Studies [Great Britain] 1974 119(3): 67-73.* Historians have tended to assume that Adolf Hitler's refusal to support Rommel in a thrust from Libya to the Persian Gulf was based on strategic considerations. Doubts can be raised about the feasibility of such an objective in terms of supply problems. An analysis of Rommel's difficulties indicates that the central issue was the length of his supply line rather than simply inadequate supplies of fuel. North Africa was lost to the Axis because of Rommel's "impossibly long lines of communication inside Africa," not the Axis failure to win the air-naval struggle on the Mediterranean, nor Hitler's failure to support him since "Rommel in fact got all the forces that could be maintained in Africa." Based on German military sources; 111 notes. D. H. Murdoch

771. Woolford, J. V. SOUTH AFRICA AND THE WAR. *Hist. Today [Great Britain] 1974 24(7): 481-488.* Focuses on General Jan Smuts's part in South Africa's decision to enter World War II in 1939.

772. —. FIELD-MARSHAL VISCOUNT MONTGOMERY OF ALAMEIN—OBITUARY. *Army Q. and Defence J. [Great Britian] 1976 106(2): 154-160.* Discusses the life, career, and military strategy of British Field Marshall Bernard Montgomery (1887-1976), including his role at the battle of El Alamein during World War II, 1930's-45.

6. AFRICAN SOCIETY AND CULTURE

773. Abate, Yohannis. POPULATION GROWTH AND URBANIZATION IN AFRICA. *Current Hist. 1980 78(455): 102-106, 132-133.* Discusses Africa's unrestrained population growth in spite of poor nutrition and disease, and the corresponding decline in economic growth; 1960's-70's.

774. Achebe, Chinua. THOUGHTS ON THE AFRICAN NOVEL. *Dalhousie R. 1973/74 53(4): 631-637.* One of 10 papers read at the Conference on African Literature, Dalhousie U., 1973. S

775. Adepoju, Aderanti. MIGRATION AND SOCIOECONOMIC CHANGE IN AFRICA. *Int. Social Sci. J. [France] 1979 31(2): 207-225.* Discusses migration in tropical Africa: patterns, characteristics and determinants, socioeconomic change in rural areas, policy measures taken, and the needs of research for the advancement of knowledge and for planning.

776. Alexandre, Pierre. SUR QUELQUES FORMES DE RÉSISTANCE À LA DÉPENDANCE CULTURELLE EN AFRIQUE NOIRE [Some forms of resistance to cultural dependence in black Africa]. *Afrique et l'Asie [France] 1974 (102): 4-13.* After gaining their independence, the new African states did not restore their precolonial cultures. Instead, they have retained some of the elements of the cultures of their former European rulers, such as language, educational system, and religion. While science, by its nature, cannot by "Africanized," other features of a culture may be peculiar to a particular nation or continent. Africans are uncertain how to deal with the European cultural elements which remain from the era of colonialism. They have reacted in various ways, such as absolute rejection, syncretism, assimilation, and the revival of the indigenous culture. At the same time, Africa is also affected by the worldwide diminution of intercultural difference. J. S. Gassner

777. Amadi, Adolphe O. THE EMERGENCE OF A LIBRARY TRADITION IN PRE- AND POST-COLONIAL AFRICA. *Int. Lib. Rev. [Great Britain] 1981 13(1): 65-72.* Efforts to create modern libraries and achieve universal literacy in Africa have failed and probably will continue to fail because the impetus behind these efforts has been external.

778. Anderson, Gwen. BRINGING THE BIBLE TO AFRICA. *African Res. and Documentation [Great Britain] 1981 (26): 1-4.* Surveys the problems associated with translating the Bible into African languages and traces the history of the British and Foreign Bible Society's efforts to bring the scriptures to the African people.

779. Andrade, Mario de. COMMUNICATION FOR CULTURAL DECOLONIZATION IN AFRICA. *Cultures [France] 1982 8(3): 15-25.* Focuses on the preservation of cultural identity in the former Portuguese colonies of Cape Verde Islands, Guinea (now Guinea-Bissau) and Mozambique, independent since 1974-75; stresses the accomplishments since the 1950's and particularly during the 1970's, of the African Party for Independence of Guinea and Cape Verde (PAIGC), the African Linguistic Seminar, the Integrated Education Center (CAPI), Radio Libertacão broadcasts, and films.

780. Anise, Ladun. THE AFRICAN REDEFINED: THE PROBLEMS OF COLLECTIVE BLACK IDENTITY. *Issue 1974 4(4): 26-32.* The goals of revolutionary black Americans do not necessarily represent black African interests. S

781. Aref'ev, A. L. POLITIKA AFRIKANSKIKH GOSUDARSTV V OTNOSHENII MOLODEZHI [The policy of African states on youth]. *Narody Azii i Afriki [USSR] 1980 (5): 131-139.* In the majority of African states programs are being developed to deal with problems of youth and to try to guarantee their well-being. The programs are examined against the background of poverty, illiteracy, and unemployment faced by the younger generation. Significant improvement in the situation for the young can be achieved only through revolutionary democratic and anticapitalist reforms. 5 tables, 36 notes. S. J. Talalay

782. Aseto, D. O. and Cosminsky, S. A MODEL OF SLUM GENERATION IN AFRICA. *Pan-African J. [Kenya] 1976 9(1): 17-34.* Examines the growth of urban slums in Africa, constructing a model which takes account of the consequences of free enterprise and the economic system, poverty, racial discrimination, and traditional kinship obligations. The cases of Southern Rhodesia, Zambia, South Africa, and Nigeria show that this model can be used for studying other developing nations in Africa. 5 tables, 52 notes. M. Feingold

783. Ault, David E. and Rutman, Gilbert L. THE DEVELOPMENT OF INDIVIDUAL RIGHTS TO PROPERTY IN TRIBAL AFRICA. *J. of Law and Econ. 1979 22(1): 163-182.* Survey of the origin and evolution of individual rights in African traditional law finds that as commercial agriculture and population grew, law evolved toward greater appreciation of individual rights, a change which post-World War II independence leaders failed to appreciate, opting instead for communal agricultural projects generally antithetical to ethnic life, 20th century.

784. Awoonor, Kofi. TRADITION AND CONTINUITY IN AFRICAN LITERATURE. *Dalhousie R. 1973/74 53(4): 665-671.* Defines the ritualistic structure informing African literature. One of 10 papers read at the Conference on African Literature, Dalhousie U., 1973. S

785. Axelson, O. E. HISTORICAL NOTES ON NEO-AFRICAN CHURCH MUSIC. *Zambezia: the J. of the University of Rhodesia [Zimbabwe] 1974 3(2): 89-102.* Relates some of the conflict between missionary-educated Africans and a number of Christian sects over the inappropriateness of the acculturation process in African composition, instruments, and style in church ritual. The interaction has resulted in African music's increased use within the church since 1960. Based on secondary sources; 51 notes. O. B. Pollak

786. Ayandele, E. A. and Ade Ajayi, J. F. WRITING AFRICAN CHURCH HISTORY. *African Historical Studies* (Totowa, N.J.: Frank Cass, 1979): 230-252. Scholars of African church history have long denied the authenticity of churches that broke away from mission churches, thus contributing to their ambiguous position in African society; yet the imprinting of national characteristics of Christianity is valid.

787. Bascom, William. FOLKLORE AND THE AFRICANIST. *J. of Am. Folklore 1973 86(341): 253-259.* A discussion of the methodology of African folklore stressing that folklore is more than verbal art: it is "folk learning." S

788. Bassani, Ezio. LA SCULTURA DELL'AFRICA NERA E LA CULTURA EUROPEA [The sculpture of black Africa and European culture]. *Africa [Italy] 1981 36(2): 167-182.* Examines the relationship between European culture and African sculpture during the last five centuries. African art, first appreciated in the Kunstkammer by princes and rich European merchants, was later considered the product of an inferior civilization. Only after the discoveries made by the artists of the Ecole de Paris and by the German Expressionists in the early 20th century, did African sculpture come to be considered as art. Reports on the stages of this recognition and on the publications and exhibitions that have supported and accompanied its progress. J/S

789. Bebey, Francis. BLACK AFRICAN ANCESTRAL MUSIC FOR A NEW WORLD. *Cultures [France] 1973 1(3): 221-225.* An introduction to the traditional music of Black Africa, its composers, performers, instruments, and religious and ethnic themes. African music is profoundly about man. R. K. Adams

790. Beidelman, T. O. SOCIAL THEORY AND THE STUDY OF CHRISTIAN MISSIONS IN AFRICA. *Africa [Great Britain] 1974 44(3): 235-249.* Examines some basic theoretical issues involved in the study of Christian missions in Africa. Six broad themes are related to sociological theories and proposed as fruitful areas of future study: the secular attributes of missionaries; the relation of religious beliefs, organization, and character of missionary activities; missionary views on the process of conversion; the routinization of missionary careers; missionaries' inconsistent use of the concept of a total society; and the

impact of colonial and bureaucratic structures on missions. The author deplores the lack of attention paid by anthropologists to the study of colonial groups such as administrators, missionaries, and traders and claims the history of missionary enterprise would illustrate fundamental dilemmas of modern social organization. Based on study of Church Missionary Society in Ukaguru, Tanzania, primary and secondary sources; 17 notes. C. Fry

791. Bennetta, Jules-Rosette. BAPOSTOLO RITUAL: AN AFRICAN RESPONSE TO CHRISTIANITY. *Can. J. of African Studies [Canada] 1975 9(1): 89-102.* The independent African churches are one of the principal sources of cultural transformation. In these churches the customary rituals and the Christian beliefs intertwine. One area of examination is the Bapostolo ritual (the apostolic church of John Maranke) and their main ritual event, the Sabbath *kerek*.This participation prepares them for their daily life. *Kerek* has three distinct components: prayer, preaching and songs of praise. They rely heavily on their own feelings about the ordering of events as the ritual progresses. The ritual itself provides an account of the practical and spiritual concerns of the participants. Based on theses, tracts, personal observation, and secondary works; 25 notes. J

792. Berman, Edward H. AFRICAN RESPONSES TO CHRISTIAN MISSION EDUCATION. *African Studies Rev. 1974 17(3): 527-540.* Studies African attitudes to Christian Mission education, from the 19th century to 1974.

793. Berman, Edward H. AFRICANS AND THEIR SCHOOLS. *Hist. of Educ. Q. 1977 17(2): 209-221.* Review essay on David R. Morrison, *Education and Politics in Africa: The Tanzanian Case* (Montreal: McGill Queen's Pr., 1976), J. M. Mwanakative, *The Growth of the Education in Zambia since Independence* (Lusaka: Oxford U. Pr., 1968), John E. Anderson, *The Struggle for the School: The Interaction of Missionary, Colonial Government and Nationalist Enterprise in the Development of Formal Education in Kenya* (London: Longman Group Ltd., 1970). 18 notes. L. C. Smith

794. Binet, Jacques. URBANISM AND ITS EXPRESSION IN THE AFRICAN CITY. *Diogenes [Italy] 1976 (93): 81-104.* Discusses the double life of modern African cities, with traditional village characteristics in the quarters and modern European characteristics, such as monuments and public buildings, in the center.

795. Blumenthal, Susan. THE WORLD'S BEST TRAVELED ART. *Africa Report 1974 19(1): 4-10.* International art collectors have drained the African continent, leaving African museums nearly devoid of native art. S

796. Booth, Newell S. CIVIL RELIGION IN TRADITIONAL AFRICA. *Africa Today 1976 23(4): 59-65.* Emphasizes the unity of religion and politics in traditional Africa through an analysis of selected Baluba social customs. Contemporary African states must devise a replacement to legitimatize civil religions because the precolonial experience emphasized unitary society and not a pluralistic state. Secondary sources; 21 notes. G. O. Gagnon

797. Borrmans, Maurizio. L'ISLAM AFRICANO [African Islam]. *Problemi di Ulisse [Italy] 1977 14(83): 51-61.* Islam has been in Africa since the 7th century and continues to show great vitality in the 20th.

798. Bosworth, William. THE RIGID EMBRACE OF DEPENDENCY: FRANCE AND BLACK AFRICAN EDUCATION SINCE 1960. *Contemporary French Civilization 1981 5(3): 327-345.* The post-independence African educational system has led to a new type of dependency on French culture and language that hinders genuine independent national development.

799. Bray, Mark. POLICIES AND PROGRESS TOWARDS UNIVERSAL PRIMARY EDUCATION. *J. of Modern African Studies [Great Britain] 1981 19(4): 547-563.* Education ministers of African states met at a UNESCO sponsored conference in Addis Ababa in 1961 and resolved that Africa would attain "universal, compulsory, and free" primary education by 1980. Some African states, representing a wide spectrum of political ideology, have met this goal, while most have not. Financial constraints and rapid population growth have been major obstacles to achieving universal primary education in Africa, which has also been affected by qualitative factors, such as the lack of teacher training and variations in dropout rates. Based on published reports and statistics by African governments and international organizations, especially UNESCO; table, 46 notes. L. W. Truschel

800. Clignet, Remi. SOCIAL CHANGE AND SEXUAL DIFFERENTIATION IN THE CAMEROUN AND THE IVORY COAST. *Signs: J. of Women in Culture and Soc. 1977 3(1): 244-260.* A comparison of the rates of social change and sexual differentiation in Cameroon and Ivory Coast, societies which have contrasting histories and ethnic structures. Examines the interrelation of changes in women's status as affected by complexity of social structures and by past and present cultural models and stereotypes. 9 tables, 25 notes. L. M. Maloney

801. Condé, Maryse. NON-SPÉCIFICITÉ DE LA CRITIQUE LITTÉRAIRE "AFRICANE" [Nonspecification in African literary criticism]. *African Perspectives [Netherlands] 1977 (1): 35-41.* There are two types of literature existing in modern Africa: that written in non-African languages and the oral literature in "national" languages. The author discusses the reputations of African authors and offers some definitions dealing with African literary development. G. E. Pergl

802. Crowley, Daniel J. TOWARD INTERNATIONAL ARCHIVES OF AFRICAN ART AND FOLKLORE. *J. of African Studies 1975 2(1): 108-117.* A plea for the creation of international archives to house African art and folklore materials. Extensive materials are available, though scattered; others no doubt are being regularly and forever lost. Many African nations have expressed interest in preserving their heritage. Expense is not a prohibitive factor. The primary task is to foment interest and to recruit competent persons who will act at once to get the project underway before other disciplines preempt it. 9 notes. V. L. Human

803. D'Aeth, Richard. TRADITIONAL AND MODERN ASPECTS OF EDUCATIONAL PLANNING IN AFRICA. *J. of Modern African Studies [Great Britain] 1974 12(1): 109-116.* Educational planning must consider the cultural history of the state, but there are many cultural traditions within any one African country, indigenous culture, Islamic culture, and Western culture. Education should consider the type of society the nation wishes to develop. Traditional and modern education must not be viewed as opposites. A social and cultural understanding of schools and education is required before planning can occur and human qualities must be considered on a par with logistics. H. G. Soff

804. Das, Man Singh. BRAIN DRAIN CONTROVERSY AND AFRICAN SCHOLARS. *Studies in Comparative Internat. Development 1974 9(1): 74-83.* Examines attitudes of African students attending American institutions of higher education toward returning home for employment. Since 84 percent plan to return there is little evidence for brain drain. 4 tables, 23 notes. S. A. Farmerie

805. Dozon, Jean-Pierre. LES METAMORPHOSES URBAINES D'UN "DOUBLE" VILLAGEOIS [Urban metamorphoses of a "twofold" villager]. *Cahiers d'Etudes Africaines [France] 1981 21(1-3): 389-403.* Concentrates on the town of Dobe to illustrate the societal breakdown of an African village and dislocation of its inhabitants as a result of colonialism and contact with larger urbanized centers, the result of which is a gradual disappearance of traditional norms and values.

806. DuToit, Brian M. MAN AND CANNABIS IN AFRICA: A STUDY OF DIFFUSION. *Africa Econ. Hist. 1976 (1): 17-35.* Examines the social use and diffusion of cannabis in Africa by using historical, archaeological, ethnographic, and linguistic evidence.

807. Egudu, R. N. AFRICAN LITERATURE AND SOCIAL PROBLEMS. *Can. J. of African Studies [Canada] 1975 9(3): 421-447.* African literature allows rapport between the writer and his society. At present, there is no split between the two, despite the social and political revolutions which have divided the continent since World War II. African literature developed in full during the colonial period; the writers then denounced colonialism. Now they attack the problems of the new independent Africa. At present, there is some balance between

the output of African literary and historical writing, and between creative and sociopolitical works. Based on speeches and secondary works; 54 notes. J

808. Fabre, Michael. RENE MARAN, THE NEW NEGRO AND NEGRITUDE. *Phylon 1975 36(3): 340-351.* Explores the role René Maran played as a cultural link between the English and French-speaking black universe between the two world wars. His significance is symbolized by his being awarded the Prix Goncourt in 1921 for his novel *Batouala,* hailed as a "black triumph in literature" achieved by one who held an administrative post in the French colony of Chad. His influence contributed toward the restoration of "a positive image of Africa as much as it perpetuated the image of France as a land of racial equality." He stands out as an artist, as denunciator of French colonial crimes, as mentor of various founders of negritude, as propagandist, and as having a major part in the relations which united Afro-American and black French authors. 46 notes. R. V. Ritter

809. Fernandez, James W. THE ETHNIC COMMUNION: INTER-ETHNIC RECRUITMENT IN AFRICAN RELIGIOUS MOVEMENTS. *J. of African Studies 1975 2(2): 131-147.* A study of the difficulties in the way of realization of the universalist ideals expressed by various African religious movements. Examines attempts made in this direction by the Bwiti cult of northern Gabon, the Amakhehleni [Old Man's Cult] of Natal, South Africa, the Church of God in Christ of Sydenham, South Africa, Christianisme Celeste of Porto Novo, Dahomey, and the Apostles' Revelation Society of the Volta region, Ghana. What superficially looks to be participatorily panethnic by virtue of Christian content actually is modified by an "affirmation of a paleogenealogical sense of cultural identity" including a covenant viewed as ethnic, "a reaffirmation of ancient ties." Table, 13 notes.
R. V. Ritter

810. Frenkel', M. Iu. AFRIKANSKIE ISTOKI TEORII NEGRITIUDA [African sources of the theory of Negritude]. *Narody Azii i Afriki [USSR] 1979 (1): 53-61.* Analysis of the genesis of the theory of Negritude as formulated by Leopold Senghor, a form of cultural nationalism, whose failings as an ideology are clarified by comparison of Senghor's views with those of Edward Blyden. Biblio. S. R. Gudgin

811. Golden, L. KINEMATOGRAFIIA STRAN TROPICHESKOI AFRIKI [Cinematography in the countries of tropical Africa]. *Narody Azii i Afriki [USSR] 1981 (3): 108-113.* Cinematography appeared in tropical Africa only in the 1960's, as a large number of the countries gained independence. During the colonial period Africans did not make their own films, but European filmmakers made films about them. After achieving independence, these countries began the building of a culture that included the introduction of cinematography, particularly documentary films. The socialist countries have greatly influenced the cinema industry in the countries of tropical Africa, which have, in turn, contributed new themes and subjects to world cinema. Largely secondary sources; note. S. J. Talalay

812. Golden, L. KINOISKUSSTVO SOVREMENNOI AFRIKI [Contemporary African cinema]. *Aziia i Afrika Segodnia [USSR] 1982 (12): 48-50.* Discusses the films of directors Rui Guerro of Mozambique, Mahmoud Dreze of Libya, and Suheilya ben Barki of Morocco, as well as other African directors.

813. Goody, Jack and Buckley, Joan. INHERITANCE AND WOMEN'S LABOUR IN AFRICA. *Africa [Great Britain] 1973 43(2): 108-121.* Examines the contribution of women to cultivation in pastoral as well as purely farming economies, tracing the correlates throughout Africa of the dominant part played by women in hoe cultivation; although women are excluded from ownership of the means of production there is social recognition of the key role they play.

814. Gray, Richard. CHRISTIANITY AND RELIGIOUS CHANGE IN AFRICA. *African Affairs [Great Britain] 1978 77(306): 89-100.* The introduction of Christianity to Africa had a great effect on the continent. Of particular value to Africans was the Christian view of life after death, an idea which was widely accepted and accounted for many converts. In other areas not so revolutionary, Christianity and traditional beliefs interacted and produced a new set of ideas. The author discusses French, British, and Belgian Catholics, and Protestants. 49 notes. H. G. Soff

815. Gray, Richard. CHRISTIANITY AND RELIGIOUS CHANGE IN AFRICA. *Kyrkohistorisk Årsskrift [Sweden] 1978 78: 345-352.* Examines the theological, political, and social transformation of Africa caused by the introduction of Christianity in the 19th and 20th centuries.

816. Grohs, Gerhard. DIFFICULTIES OF CULTURAL EMANCIPATION IN AFRICA. *J. of Modern African Studies [Great Britain] 1976 14(1): 65-78.* Emancipation means more than political freedom from foreign rule. As Immanuel Kant and Karl Marx observed, it also entails mature thinking without external guidance. The author analyzes the cultures of Tanzania, Senegal, and South Africa to illustrate three types of emancipation. Tanzania, with practically no native bourgeoisie, integrates cultural with political emancipation. Senegal, while independent, is still dominated externally by French cultural and economic power, and internally by a French-speaking elite. South African blacks, on the other hand, promote "black consciousness" to create the preconditions of emancipation. Based on African documents and other sources; 43 notes. W. R. Hively

817. Gstrein, Heinz. CHRISTLICHE UND ISLAMISCHE AFRIKA-MISSION—RIVALEN ODER PARTNER? [Christian and Muslim missions in Africa—rivals or partners?]. *Wort und Wahrheit [West Germany] 1973 28(5): 421-424.* Compares the achievements of Christian and Islamic missions in Africa. The basic doctrines of Islam are more acceptable to the African life-style; North Africa is a centuries-old example of this. Explains the messianic aspects and sectarian development of Islam. Secondary sources. G. E. Pergl

818. Guyer, Jane I. HOUSEHOLD AND COMMUNITY IN AFRICAN STUDIES. *African Studies Rev. 1981 24(2-3): 87-137.* A review of the literature on the changing concepts of African household, family, and community prepared for the American Council of Learned Societies and the Social Science Research Council. 15 notes, biblio.
R. T. Brown

819. Hastings, Adrian. CHRISTIANITY IN INDEPENDENT AFRICA. *African Affairs [Great Britain] 1974 73(291): 229-232.* A synopsis of several planned seminars designed to discuss the current status of Christianity in Africa. H. G. Soff

820. Hay, Margaret Jean. WOMEN'S STATUS, FEMINIST CONSCIOUSNESS, AND STUDIES ABOUT AFRICAN WOMEN. *Int. J. of African Hist. Studies 1980 13(4): 699-713.* Reviews Margaret Strobel's *Muslim Women in Mombasa, 1890-1975* (1979), Deborah Pellow's *Women in Accra: Options for Autonomy* (1977), Martin King Whyte's *The Status of Women in Preindustrial Societies* (1978), and Lois Beck and Nikki Keddie's *Women in the Muslim World* (1978). 20 notes. R. T. Brown

821. Helbling, Mark. AFRICAN ART: ALBERT C. BARNES AND ALAIN LOCKE. *Phylon 1982 43(1): 57-67.* Albert C. Barnes and Alain Locke met in Paris, France, in December 1923. From that friendship evolved a complex relationship that resulted in the promotion of African art. Barnes, a rich collector, responded to the ideas of John Locke and Charles S. Johnson. African art was understood not as artifact, but as the historical expression of the Afro-American artistic mind. A. G. Belles

822. Hill, Mildred A. COMMON FOLKLORE FEATURES IN AFRICAN AND AFRICAN AMERICAN LITERATURE. *Southern Folklore Q. 1975 39(2): 111-133.* Similarities are found in African and African American literature since the 17th century, notably in storytelling and folk sayings.

823. Ischinger, Barbara. NEGRITUDE: SOME DISSIDENT VOICES. *Issue 1974 4(4): 23-25.* Three African writers, Jean-Marie A. Ndengue, Marcien Towa and Stanislas Adotévei, claim that Léopold Sénghor, founder of the negritude movement, has been a servant of colonialism and that negritude has been detrimental to the African cause. S

824. Iyasere, Solomon O. ORAL TRADITION IN THE CRITICISM OF AFRICAN LITERATURE. *J. of Modern African Studies [Great*

Britain] 1975 13(1): 107-120. Through a strict attention to texture and structure, a more formal textual consideration, and the reexamination of how the content of a work is satisfactorily shaped into a perceivable *Gestalt,* African literature is at last receiving the serious treatment it has long deserved. A historical sense is necessary for its full appreciation and understanding, including both a knowledge of oral influences and an investigation into their place in the language and forms of contemporary fiction. When writing in English the African even "remodels the language to reflect the rhythms of his traditional speech patterns, and to carve into perceivable form the imaginative experience of his personal heritage." The author surveys the work of several modern African writers to illustrate these points. 25 notes. R. V. Ritter

825. Jakubowicz, Karol. AFRYKAŃSCY SŁUCHACZE POLSKIEGO RADIA [African audiences of Polish radio]. *Kultura i Społeczeństwo [Poland] 1978 22(3): 277-293.* The clubs of audiences of Polish radio, as well as the clubs of listeners to other radio stations, include the most active and alert members of the African community. These organizations are of supratribal nature and have attempted to draw their members into active participation in social life and international, social, and political events. Based on Don Smith's "Student Audiences for International Broadcasting," *J. of Broadcasting* 1971 and *Szkolnictwo w Kulturach Afryki* (1973).

M. Swiecicka-Ziemianek/S

826. Janosik, Robert J. RELIGION AND POLITICAL INVOLVEMENT: A STUDY OF BLACK AFRICAN SECTS. *J. for the Sci. Study of Religion 1974 13(2): 161-176.* "This study represents an effort to utilize some of the tools traditionally applied by political scientists in studies of secular organizations to deal analytically with the part religious organizations play in modernization." S

827. John, Magnus. LIBRARIES IN ORAL-TRADITIONAL SOCIETIES. *Int. Lib. Rev. [Great Britain] 1979 11(3): 321-339.* Discusses the problems and advantages of establishing libraries in oral traditional societies, focusing on the traditional cultures in sub-Saharan Africa, 1955-79.

828. Jose, Alhaji Babatunde. PRESS FREEDOM IN AFRICA. *African Affairs [Great Britain] 1975 74(296): 255-262.* There are only 179 daily newspapers in Africa, with a total circulation under four million. Several nations have no dailies. The masses do not look to newspapers for information. Nevertheless, papers are influential because most people believe whatever they read. This presents a problem for many governments and the press is not, therefore, really free in Africa. Based on a speech to the Royal African Society, 10 April 1975.

H. G. Soff

829. Jules-Rosette, Bennetta. THE CONVERSION EXPERIENCE: THE APOSTLES OF JOHN MARANKE. *J. of Religion in Africa [Netherlands] 1975 7(2): 132-164.* The Apostles of John Maranke are indigenous African Christians, independent of missions, who have had a personal conversion of the heart. John Maranke was founder of the church, which has 200,000 members. Visions and prophesies form a part of the acceptance needed to be a member, and baptism is the principal ceremony. Oral interviews with Apostles are outlined as well as the author's personal experiences leading to conversion as an Apostle. 26 notes. H. G. Soff

830. Kerr, David. DIDACTIC THEATRE IN AFRICA. *Harvard Educ. Rev. 1981 51(1): 145-155.* Examines how performing arts in Africa have been used as a tool for informal adult education, focusing especially on their history and dual nature, characterized both as spontaneous creations of the African masses and as plays whose messages did not emerge from a popular viewpoint but were imposed by an alien force.

831. Killam, G. D. AFRICAN LITERATURE AND CANADA. *Dalhousie U. 1973/74 53(4): 672-687.* Suggests comparisons between Canada and African countries in terms of literary studies. One of 10 papers read at the Conference on African Literature, Dalhousie U., 1973. S

832. Killam, G. D. MODERN BLACK AFRICAN WRITING IN ENGLISH: A SELECTED BIBLIOGRAPHY. *Can. J. of African Studies [Canada] 1975 9(3): 537-566.* The aim of this bibliography is to introduce readers to the large and significant amount of Black African creative writing in English. Selected lists of bibliographies, books of criticism and anthologies are included. Single stories, poems, critical articles and reviews are not. Instead readers are referred to the bibliographies of Barbara Abrash, Hans Zell, and Helene Silver for comprehensive listings of these materials. This bibliography is arranged alphabetically by country and by author within each section. Most of the titles listed are available in paperback. E. R. Campbell

833. Killingray, David. AFRICA: BOOKS FOR SCHOOLS. *J. of African Hist. [Great Britain] 1979 20(4): 573-577.* Reviews six survey texts on African history. During the colonial era, the clear purpose of education in Africa was to present an uncritical acceptance of the ruling colonial authority. At independence, African secondary schools remained tied to overseas examinations and syllabi. The decolonization of academic history occurred after the political process. It was inspired by the universities, especially through the Ibadan Workshop on the teaching of African history (1965) and the first conference for Tanzanian history teachers, Dar-es-Salaam (1967). Despite deficiencies, African texts on that continent have improved, as have texts used in British schools. 10 notes. A. W. Novitsky

834. Koehl, Robert. THE COMPARATIVE HISTORY OF AFRICAN EDUCATION. *Hist. of Educ. Q. 1973 13(1): 83-88.* Review article of Vincent M. Battle and Charles H. Lyon, eds., *Essays in the History of African Education* (Teachers College Press, Columbia University, 1970), a collection of student research papers of mixed value.

L. C. Smith

835. Koehl, Robert. EDUCATING BLACK AFRICANS. *Hist. of Educ. Q. 1977 17(4): 467-470.* Reviews Charles H. Lyons's *To Wash an Aethiop White: British Ideas About Black African Educability 1530-1960* (New York: Teachers College Pr., 1975). Racial stereotypes based on biology were present in the 16th century. Racial attitudes had much to do with ideas of education for black Africans. The situation was in some ways worse after the advent of mass education in Europe widened the gap between Africans and Europeans: it was easier to educate a small African elite to be the equal of a small European elite than to raise Africa's illiterate masses to approach the level of 19th and 20th century Europeans. The Europeans tried to educate the African to be a black European, instead of a learned African, an enterprise not always successful. Today's African elites are the products of this education; they are part European. J. C. Billigmeier

836. Kontro, Ari. THE FINNISH MISSION SOCIETY'S "POLITICAL IMAGE" OF AFRICA: POLITICAL DEVELOPMENTS IN SOUTH WEST AFRICA AND TANZANIA SINCE THE SECOND WORLD WAR, AS SEEN BY THE FINNISH MISSION SOCIETY. *Scandinavian J. of Hist. [Sweden] 1979 4(1): 35-45.* The Finnish Mission Society, which has taken a close interest in African affairs since 1868, has served as an important disseminator of information. This survey of the period 1945-75 illustrates the society's role in offering an insight into Scandinavian attitudes toward Africa, particularly Namibia and Tanzania. In most cases, the image has been one which would not harm the Mission Society's activities in the field. Based on the Society's records, and newspaper *Suomen Lähetyssanomat;* 36 notes.

P. J. Beck

837. Lambo, T. Adeoye. CHANGING PATTERNS OF MENTAL HEALTH NEEDS IN AFRICA. *Contemporary Rev. [Great Britain] 1973 222(1286): 146-154.* Discusses the present state of mental health problems in Africa in the light of changing patterns of need since 1955.

838. LeRoy, Étienne. L'ÉVOLUTION DE LA JUSTICE TRADITIONNELLE DANS L'AFRIQUE FRANCOPHONE [The evolution of traditional justice in Francophone Africa]. *Can. J. of African Studies [Canada] 1975 9(1): 75-87.* The legal dualism provoked by the introduction of French law into Africa during the colonial period is presently one of the causes of the paralysis of institutional reforms in many countries which got their independence in 1960. Since then two trends have been opposed to each other: the Senegalese trend is based on the institutional transformation of traditional justice; the Congolese trend emphasizes internal adjustment of traditional structures to modernity. The proposed reform will give a great role to arbitration and

will restrict the intervention of courts to exceptional forms of conflict settlements. Based on theses, speeches, and secondary sources; 21 notes. J

839. Lindfors, Bernth. POLITICS, CULTURE AND LITERARY FORM IN BLACK AFRICA. *Colby Lib. Q. 1979 15(4): 240-251.* Discusses African literature in English and French, which reflect and project the cultural revolution in Africa during the 20th century.

840. Long, Charles H. ORAL LITERATURE AND FOLKLORE IN AFRICA: A REVIEW ARTICLE. *Hist. of Religions 1974 14(1): 65-73.* Reviews recent trends in the study of African folklore and oral literature, noting the overlap of folklore and religious studies. Appraises Ruth Finnegin's *Oral Literature in Africa*(Oxford U. Press, 1970). T. L. Auffenberg

841. Lux, André. LE PROBLÈME DE LA STÉRILITÉ EN AFRIQUE ET SES IMPLICATIONS DE POLITIQUE DÉMOGRAPHIQUE: À PROPOS DE DEUX OUVRAGES RÉCENTS [The problem of sterility in Africa and its implications for demographic policy as shown in two recent works]. *Can. J. of African Studies [Canada] 1976 10(1): 143-155.* A review of works by B. Kwaku Adadevoh and Anne Retel-Laurentin which discuss the high infertility rate in Africa south of the Sahara, the highest rate in the world, 1950-76. The fertility problem is especially evident among black Africans, and is compounded by the infant mortality rate. These African countries are seeking medical means to overcome the problem. Table, 32 notes. E. R. Campbell

842. Maack, Mary Niles. LIBRARIES FOR THE GENERAL PUBLIC IN FRENCH-SPEAKING AFRICA: THEIR CULTURAL ROLE, 1803-1975. *J. of Lib. Hist. 1981 16(1): 210-225.* Discusses the underlying philosophy of library service as it evolved in French-speaking Africa from 1803 to 1975. The first purpose of the early colonial libraries was to transplant French civilization, commerce, and administration to Africa. Thus a demand arose for books to support French culture and thought, to sustain a limited amount of applied scientific research, and to aid in governing the colony. Initiatives to establish a coherent system of library service for general readers can be traced from the 1930's. These libraries had somewhat broader aims than the earlier ones, seeking to reach not merely the elite but the masses. Today they employ such modern techniques as audiovisual materials, closer to the oral traditions of many villagers, even capable of serving the illiterate. Primary sources; 36 notes. J. Powell

843. MacGaffey, Wyatt. AFRICAN IDEOLOGY AND BELIEF: A SURVEY. *African Studies Rev. 1981 24(2-3): 227-274.* A review of the literature concerning African religions and philosophies prepared for the American Council of Learned Societies and the Social Science Research Council. 20 notes, biblio. R. T. Brown

844. Malizia, Pierfranco. [NEGRITUDE]. *Civitas [Italy] 1977 28(1): 51-62, (2): 41-52.* Part I. LA "NEGRITUDINE": ANALISI DI UN MITO ["Negritude": analysis of a myth]. Examines the variety of meanings that the term "negritude" has had since its introduction in the late 1940's and analyzes some of the limits and prejudices that have surrounded it. Part II. IL SUPERAMENTO DELLA "NEGRITUDINE" [Overcoming "negritude"]. Considers negritude—the political-cultural nationalism conceptualized by Leopold Senghor of Senegal—which, because of its colonial context, was restricted to a Western image of Africans; overcoming the concept as part of the decolonization process has been facilitated by the emergence of "Africanism."

845. Marvin, Richard. THE SOCIAL GRADING OF OCCUPATIONS IN SUB-SAHARAN AFRICA, 1954-74. *J. of Developing Areas 1981 15(4): 621-637.* On the basis of an analysis of data on preference among male students for five middle-range occupations—three white-collar (secondary-school teacher, primary-school teacher and office clerk) and two manual occupations (truck driver and automobile mechanic)—presented in nine studies of social grading of occupations carried out by different scholars among African secondary-school pupils between 1954 and 1974, concludes that, in all the years they were rated, secondary-school teacher was the highest and truck driver the lowest, the relative position of the mechanic improved over the years, and, in the white-collar category, the primary-school teacher rates higher than the clerk in the more recent studies, reversing the earlier standings. A strong relationship is posited among overall occupational ratings and income and education of respondents, and evidence shows, contrary to the generally held views in the literature, that occupational hierarchies are neither universal nor stable over the years. Fig., 3 tables, 37 notes. V. Samaraweera

846. Marwick, M. G. HOW REAL IS THE CHARMED CIRCLE IN AFRICAN AND WESTERN THOUGHT? *Africa [Great Britain] 1973 43(1): 59-71.* Examines the validity of Karl Popper's dichotomy of open and closed societies from the perspective of social anthropology as part of an ongoing discussion of the relation between African traditional thought and Western concepts of causation.

847. Masolo, Dismas A. TOWARDS AUTHENTIC AFRICAN LITERATURE: LUO ORAL LITERATURE. *Africa [Italy] 1976 31(1): 57-72.* Describes the background and development of "Négritude" literature and music during the 20th century, emphasizing the contribution of the Luo peoples of Kenya and the diversity of approaches among African oral traditions. J/S

848. Mazrui, Ali A. ECLECTICISM AS AN IDEOLOGICAL ALTERNATIVE: AN AFRICAN PERSPECTIVE. *Alternatives [Netherlands] 1975 1(4): 465-486.* At least since the beginning of this century Africa has been an intellectual melting pot. The penetration of external intellectual influences, started earlier, gathered momentum more recently and assumed most diverse forms in the last 70 to 80 years. Both Islam and Christianity as systems of ideas came to Africa from their earliest days. Ethiopia has been Christian longer than many parts of Europe, including England, and North Africa was substantially Islamized in the first century of Muhammad's religion, which later spread to other parts of the continent. Each had ideas and values which have direct political implications. After examining the role of culture in imperialism, the entry of liberal and capitalist values in Africa, the rise of modern nationalism, the fascination of Marxism among black intellectuals, and the obstinate resilience of many traditional African values, the essay concludes that creative eclecticism (implying a genius for selectivity, for synthesizing disparate elements, and for ultimate independent growth in the intellectual field) is the only ideological alternative compatible with African autonomy in modern conditions. J

849. Medjigbodo, Nicole. AFRIQUE CINÉMATOGRAPHIÉE, AFRIQUE CINÉMATOGRAPHIQUE [Africa filmed, African films]. *Can. J. of African Studies [Canada] 1980 13(3): 371-387.* African cinema began under the very conditions that accompanied the birth of the cinema in the capitalist system. Since political independence, the emergence and development of African cinema has remained within the neocolonial context; conditions for the emergence of a real national cinema, answering particular needs of development and liberation, do not exist. The cinema could constitute for Africa a valuable tool for communication and education, especially a cinema geared to sharpen an awareness of the social, economic, and political realities. In the face of the powerful Euro-American trusts, which are opposed by the considerable though scattered efforts of a number of African screenwriters, there is a growing need for a parallel and militant cinema which, following the Latin American example, will gradually enable the peasants and workers to make the cinema their own instrument of expression. 41 notes. J

850. Mouralis, Bernard. L'INVITATION À L'ÉCRITURE: ÉTUDE DE QUELQUES TEXTES AFRICAINS PRODUITS DANS UN CADRE INSTITUTIONNEL EUROPÉEN [An invitation to writing: a study of some African texts produced in a European institutional framework]. *Cultures et Développement [Belgium] 1980 12(2): 271-294.* Analyzes African literature written by European colonizers and the role Europeans have played in promoting literature written by the Africans themselves.

851. Mphahlele, Es'Kia. AFRICA IN EXILE. *Daedalus 1982 111(2): 29-48.* Discusses the problem of exiled people of Africa from 1950 to 1982 with special emphasis on the exile literature.

852. Mudimbe-Boyi, Mbulamwanza. AFRICAN AND BLACK AMERICAN LITERATURE: THE "NEGRO RENAISSANCE" AND THE GENESIS OF AFRICAN LITERATURE IN FRENCH. Davis, Allen F., ed. *For Better or Worse: The American Influence in the World*(Westport, Conn.: Greenwood Pr., 1981): 157-169. Discusses

the history of the Harlem Renaissance, a US literary movement of the 1920's led by Arna Bontemps, Claude MacKay, Countee Cullen, and Langston Hughes, that displayed a pronounced racial awareness and ideological stance that caught the attention of French-speaking black writers in France and Africa, such as Léon Damas, Aimé Césaire, and Leopold Senghor, who adopted the techniques and aims of the American school. Comments on the role of the Parisian reviews, *La Revue du Monde Noir* and *Légitime Défense,* as conductors of American influence on Africans.

853. Murphree, Marshall W. WHITES IN BLACK AFRICA: THEIR STATUS AND ROLE. *Ethnic and Racial Studies [Great Britain] 1978 1(2): 154-174.* White Africans living in newly independent black nations have retained a relatively high socioeconomic status, but threats of expendibility, both in terms of African culture and economics, and loss of national identity have rendered them politically powerless, 1960's-70's.

854. Natsoulas, Theodore. PATRIARCH MCGUIRE AND THE SPREAD OF THE AFRICAN ORTHODOX CHURCH IN AFRICA. *J. of Religion in Africa [Netherlands] 1981 12(2): 81-104.* The African Orthodox Church was a forerunner of later black solidarity movements with the white community. George Alexander McGuire closely associated his movement with the Universal Negro Improvement Association of Marcus Garvey. Relies heavily on *The Negro Churchman: The Official Organ of the African Orthodox Church, 1921-1931,* 2 vols, Millwood, NY: Kraus-Thomson Organization, 1977. 76 notes. R. J. Jirran

855. Nicol, Davidson. ALIOUNE DIOP AND THE AFRICAN RENAISSANCE. *African Affairs [Great Britain] 1979 78(310): 3-11.* A biographical sketch of the Latinized African Alioune Diop, listing his achievements, 1947-77, in African arts, and his pioneer service in rediscovering and dewesternizing African culture and promoting black solidarity. As a poet, writer, and conference organizer, Diop has struggled, since 1947, to revitalize African culture and integrate it with the mainstream of world culture. S. Lakhan

856. Nicolas, Guy. L'EXPANSION DE L'INFLUENCE ARABE EN AFRIQUE SUDSAHARIENNE [The expansion of Arab influence in Subsaharan Africa]. *Afrique et l'Asie Modernes [France] 1978 (1): 23-46.* The spread of Arab influence in Africa south of the Sahara has been a long process, beginning in the 8th century. Today Islam and the influence of the conservative Arab states is a major bulwark against Marxism, the influence of the West having faded considerably.

857. Nicolas, Guy. VERS UNE RENAISSANCE DU PROCESSUS DE "GUERRE SAINTE" AU SUD DU SAHARA? [Is the process of the "holy war" to revive south of the Sahara? Part 2]. *Civilisations [Belgium] 1979 29(1-2): 108-126.* Continued from a previous article. Treats the growth of Islam in Subsaharan Africa in the 1970's.

858. N'Jie, M. D.; Mashabela, Harry; Meregini, Lawson; Paterson, Adolphus; Allen, Neil; Downs, Stephen; and Wepukhulu, Hezekiah. PEOPLE. *Africa Report 1973 18(6): 6-23.* Reports the lives of typical individuals in South Africa and West Africa. S

859. Nketia, J. H. Kwabena. THE MUSICAL HERITAGE OF AFRICA. *Daedalus 1974 103(2): 151-161.* Africa has a rich musical heritage. In addition to fulfilling the functions commonly associated with music, it generated social action and expressed social relationships. Current research is particularly anxious to preserve traditional materials both in the music itself and in musical instruments. Suggests a multidisciplinary approach to the complexities of this heritage. 12 notes. E. McCarthy

860. O'Brien, Rita Cruise. WHITE SOCIETY IN AFRICA: AN INTRODUCTION. *Tarikh [Nigeria] 1979 6(2): 1-12.* An introduction to an entire issue devoted to the presence of Europeans in Africa with particular attention to Senegal, Kenya, Algeria, Mozambique, Southern Rhodesia, and South Africa.

861. Obumselu, Ben. MARX, POLITICS AND THE AFRICAN NOVEL. *Twentieth Century Studies [Great Britain] 1973 (10): 107-127.* Evaluates the relevance of the literary application of Marxism in novels to social and political realities in developing nations of Africa in the 1960's and 70's; examines the works of Frantz Fanon, Ayi Kwei Armah, Sembene Ousmane, and Ngugi wa Thiong'o.

862. Odita, E. Okechukwu. AFRICAN ART: THE CONCEPT IN EUROPEAN LITERATURE. *J. of Black Studies 1977 8(2): 189-204.* Western Europe discovered Benin art in 1897. The members of the British landing squadrons were amazed to find bronze casting, ivory carvings, and other art objects which seemed too sophisticated to be purely African in origin. Describes how Benin art's functions are primarily commemorative, ritualistic, and ceremonial. The art is noted primarily for cast-bronze heads and plaques, and bronze animal figures such as leopards and cocks. Twentieth-century European art movements—the Fauves, Expressionists, and Cubists—were linked through African art. Quotes Gertrude Stein on the differing effects of African art on Henri Matisse and Pablo Picasso. 6 notes, refs. E. P. Stickney

863. Ofuatey-Kodjoe, W. EDUCATION AND SOCIAL CHANGE IN AFRICA: SOME PROPOSALS. *J. of African Studies 1976 3(2): 229-246.* A study of the social changes which came into African societies as a result of colonialism, and the largely unanticipated results of processes generated by the colonial system itself. When sovereignty was restored to the territories, power was handed back not to the traditional leaders but to the Western-educated elite. Education continues to be the "main criterion of status, the main basis for social differentiation, and the most important mechanism for individual advancement and social mobility." Yet the attempts at technical and agricultural education have failed. The author proposes more emphasis on the broader availability of education, and maintenance of a populist ideology, but with a differentiation in the nature of the education offered. 33 notes. R. V. Ritter

864. Ogude, S. E. IN SEARCH OF MISERY: A STUDY OF GRAHAM GREENE'S TRAVELS IN AFRICA. *Odu: a J. of West African Studies [Nigeria] 1975 (11): 45-60.* Examines the Africa which emerges out of the world of Graham Greene (b. 1904) and concentrates on his *Journey without Maps.*Africa represents the world as it should be. But there is another Africa which Greene also knew and which by and large is the Africa that Europe knew. Greene is constantly brought face to face with decay, with old age, with disease, and, above all, with ignorance and poverty. 13 notes. M. M. McCarthy

865. Ogundipe-Leslie, Omolara. TEN YEARS OF TUTUOLA STUDIES. *African Perspectives [Netherlands] 1977 (1): 67-76.* Surveys literary criticism of the works of Amos Tutuola (b. 1922) and elaborates on the major critical articles focusing on the oral tradition in Tutuola's work. In the fifties, the reaction to Tutuola was one of excitement, while in the sixties, Tutuola was seen as a visionary and a genius. From the late sixties specific aspects of his works have undergone close textual examination. While much requires to be done on Tutuola, he is generally accepted as a significant and historically important African writer. Secondary sources. S. Lakhan

866. Okeh, Peter Igbonekwu. LES ORIGINES ET LE DÉVELOPPEMENT DE LA LITTÉRATURE NÉGRO-AFRICAINE: UN REGARD CRITIQUE [The origins and development of Negro-African literature; a critical review]. *Can. J. of African Studies [Canada] 1975 9(3): 409-420.* "Negro-African literature" refers to the literature of Black writers in Africa and in America. The historical documentation of this literature is not something new. What is new and certainly very difficult is to write this type of history in such a manner as to place the various elements in their proper perspective and to give the appropriate emphasis to the various forms of this literature. This literature is essentially an oral one. In spite of this, it has taken a written form which has been developed in the past and will continue to be developed in the future. Based on secondary works; 14 notes. J

867. Onoge, Omafume F. THE CRISIS OF CONSCIOUSNESS IN MODERN AFRICAN LITERATURE: A SURVEY. *Can. J. of African Studies [Canada] 1974 8(2): 385-410.* Examines the development of African consciousness among literary figures, 1939-74; examines the effects of colonialism, socialism, and economic conditions.

868. Owomoyela, Oyekan. WESTERN HUMANISM AND AFRICAN USAGE: A CRITICAL SURVEY OF NON-AFRICAN RESPONSES TO AFRICAN LITERATURE. *Issue 1974 4(4): 9-14.*

869. Paluch, Andrzej K. URBANIZACJA I PRZEMIANY AFRYKAŃSKICH STRUKTUR SPOŁECZNYCH [Urbanization and the transformation of African social structures]. *Przeglad Socjologiczny [Poland] 1975 27: 137-158.* The pluralism of modern African urban societies interacts with traditional, kinship-oriented values. Social classes in the Marxist sense are only in the formative stage. Political stratification in Africa is quite complex and in flux, with the privileges of the modern, educated elite often underlaid by traditional divisions. The role of kinship is diminishing, while urban associations—professional, political, etc.—both ethnic and modern supra-ethnic groups, are becoming an important factor. Based on secondary sources; 67 notes.
L. A. Krzyzak

870. Pauw, B. A. ANCESTOR BELIEFS AND RITUALS AMONG URBAN AFRICANS. *African Studies [South Africa] 1974 33(2): 99-111.* Discusses the carryover of traditional religious beliefs and ceremonies from the time of tribal life into modern urban settings. There is little doubt that such beliefs persist, and the incidence of these is analyzed. However, these have been adapted and changed to suit a new social life and culture, particularly as regards application "of the idea that dead ancestors influence the living." Biblio. J. A. Casada

871. Peel, J. D. Y. *[AFRICA* AT 50]. *Africa [Great Britain] 1980 50(4): 335-340.* During the first fifty years of the publication of *Africa,* its columns reflected the changing interests of its readership. In the 1930's contributors dealt with practical problems, in the 1940's, with vernacular languages and literatures and with education. Anthropology achieved a commanding position in the 1950's, and the early 1960's, years of independence, marked a turning point in which new and more specialized journals were founded, and articles submitted extended far beyond the bounds of ethnography. The future policy of *Africa* offers new opportunities including developmental studies. R. L. Collison

872. Peil, Margaret. AFRICAN SQUATTER SETTLEMENTS: A COMPARATIVE STUDY. *Urban Studies [Great Britain] 1976 13(2): 155-166.* Squatter settlements, defined as housing erected without at least tacit permission of the owner of the land, appears to be less common in West than in Central or East Africa. This is due to a lower commitment to permanent urban residence, greater governmental flexibility in planning and tolerance of substandard housing, and to land tenure patterns in several West African countries. Most migrants prefer to rent a room rather than build because they intend to return home eventually and can afford the rents. Those who prefer to build in town can get legal access to land and are allowed to build a house they can afford. Increasing governmental control over the housing market seems to be detrimental to the interests of the poor and seems to cause an expansion of squatting. J

873. Perova, M. V POISKAKH RESHENIIA DEMOGRAFICHESKIKH PROBLEM [In search of solving population problems]. *Aziia i Afrika Segodnia [USSR] 1981 (5): 31-33.* Examines family planning policies in Botswana, Egypt, Ghana, Mauritius, and Morocco, noting the failure to limit population growth by purely medical means.

874. Pobee, John S. and Mends, Emmanuel H. SOCIAL CHANGE AND AFRICAN TRADITIONAL RELIGION. *Sociol. Analysis 1977 38(1): 1-12.* Analyzes the influence of Islam, Christianity, nationalism, and secularism on traditional African religions, especially on rites of passage, ceremonies, and celebrations, 1910's-70's.

875. Poulter, Sebastian. AN ESSAY ON AFRICAN CUSTOMARY LAW RESEARCH TECHNIQUES: SOME EXPERIENCES FROM LESOTHO. *J. of Southern African Studies [Great Britain] 1975 1(2): 181-193.* The study of African customary law is experiencing a rapid growth, and yet there is little consensus on methodology. Examines recent literature in the light of research undertaken in Lesotho, 1969-71. Based on field work and secondary sources; 44 notes. S. P. Carr

876. Prussin, Labelle. AN INTRODUCTION TO INDIGENOUS AFRICAN ARCHITECTURE. *J. of the Soc. of Architectural Hist. 1974 33(3): 183-205.* Reviews indigenous architecture of Sub-Saharan Africa in the light of social needs.

877. Raison, Jean-Pierre. L'ENCADREMENT DES COLONISATIONS ORGANISÉES: RÉFLEXIONS SUR QUELQUES EXEMPLES AFRICAINS [Infrastructure of organized settlements: remarks on some examples in Africa]. *Travaux & Mémoires de l'Inst. des Hautes Études de l'Amérique Latine [France] 1979 (32): 161-168.* An analysis of the various types of infrastrucure in zones of organized settlement in several countries of Africa and in Madagascar.

878. Roberts, Jack Storm. INTRODUCING AFRICAN POP. *Africa Report 1975 20(1): 42-45.* Discusses modern popular music trends in Africa. S

879. Schmidt, Nancy J. THE WRITER AS A TEACHER: A COMPARISON OF THE AFRICAN ADVENTURE STORIES OF G. A. HENTY, RENE GUILLOT, AND BARBARA KIMENYE. *African Studies Rev. 1976 19(2): 69-80.* The most popular African adventure stories from the 1870's to the 1970's consistently pay little regard to the realities of life in Africa.

880. Shurnik, W. A. E. FOREIGN NEWS COVERAGE IN SIX AFRICAN NEWSPAPERS: THE POTENCY OF NATIONAL INTERESTS. *Gazette: Int. J. for Mass Communication Studies [Netherlands] 1981 28(2): 117-130.* A study of African newspapers from Mali, the Ivory Coast, Senegal, Kenya, Guinea, and Tanzania refutes the theory that African media are dominated by non-African, Western news services. Among other results of the study, these findings emerge: 1) there is heavy emphasis on Third World news, 2) the world at large is presented as being more peaceful than turbulent, 3) the politics of the regime in power affects news coverage in that nation, and 4) among the regions of the world, Africa was the most favored in terms of amount of coverage, and the papers favored their own regions over other areas in the same nation. 6 tables, 9 notes. J. S. Coleman

881. Shvetsova, S. I. PROBLEMI SOTSIAL'NOGO OSVOBOZHDENIIA ZHENSHCHIN V TROPICHESKOI AFRIKE [The problems of social emancipation of women in tropical Africa]. *Narody Azii i Afriki [USSR] 1979 (1): 91-99.* Analyzes measures taken for the social liberation of women in Ethiopia, Congo, Guinea, Tanzania, and Angola. The All-African Organization of Women, founded in 1962, discusses the right to vote, activity in local and national governments, women in education, and medical services for women. Today in almost all states of tropical Africa, there are organs dealing with the position of women in society, either in the form of sections of ruling parties or as national women's organizations. Tables, biblio. S. R. Gudgin

882. Simoons, Frederick J. LACTOSE MALABSORPTION IN AFRICA. *African Econ. Hist. 1978 (5): 16-34.* An examination of lactose malabsorption offers insight into the great antiquity of dairying, the spread of peoples in Africa, and current nutritional problems associated with infant formula. Many Africans who do not use dairy products are physically unable to tolerate cow's milk. Secondary sources; table, 5 fig., biblio. W. D. Piersen

883. Sklar, Richard L. LA DOMINATION DE CLASSE SUR LE CONTINENT AFRICAIN [Class domination on the African continent]. *Esprit [France] 1978 (9): 4-34.* Critical analysis of the influences of socialism on the development of a dominant class in developing African countries today.

884. Sklar, Richard L. THE NATURE OF CLASS DOMINATION IN AFRICA. *J. of Modern African Studies [Great Britain] 1979 17(4): 531-552.* Discusses aspects of class formation, consolidation, identification, and action in Africa since independence to test the validity of a Marxist conception of class based solely on domination of the means of production and of the idea of the subordination of African ruling classes to foreign capitalist interests. Class relations in Africa are determined by relations of power, not production, and their formation, identification, and action are determined by a coming together of holders of different functions, including high-status occupation, high income, superior education, and a specific measure of power, notably the ability to control the means of consumption and compulsion. Based on printed sources; 59 notes. D. J. Nicholls

885. Sokro, N'Guessan A. REMARQUES SUR LE PROPHÉTISME ET LE MESSIANISME AFRICAINS [Prophets and messianism in Africa]. *Rev. d'Hist. et de Philosophie Religieuses [France] 1979*

59(3-4): 397-409. Surveys African syncretist prophetic religious sects of the 19th and 20th centuries in response to assertions of R. Bastide.

886. Solodovnikov, V. and Braginsky, M. THE WORKING CLASS IN THE AFRICAN COUNTRIES' SOCIAL STRUCTURE. *Int. Affairs [USSR] 1976 (10): 41-49.* Examines the importance of the proletariat in the social structure of recently independent and developing nations in Africa during the 1970's.

887. Southall, Aidan. PROBLEMS OF THE NEW MORALITY. *J. of African Studies 1974 1(4): 363-389.* Politics and economics force Africa to jettison its past, but that rejection also destroys the African identity whose soul, wounded by colonial exploitation, is in need of healing. The changing sex roles of men and women encapsulates this dilemma. The author investigates African attitudes toward nudity, education, economic advancement for women, and marriage. These have been changing since colonial times, and continue to change as cultural identity is sacrificed for self-sustaining growth. 39 notes.
W. R. Hively

888. Spencer, Paul. DROUGHT AND THE COMMITMENT TO GROWTH. *African Affairs [Great Britain] 1974 73(293): 419-427.* Examines the social causes of the severe drought in Africa in the 1970's. Rather than an arbitrary act of nature, the famine and drought are ramifications of man's aspirations for growth. This is a worldwide problem rooted in overpopulation. 20 notes. H. G. Soff

889. Sprinzak, Ehud. AFRICAN TRADITIONAL SOCIALISM—A SEMANTIC ANALYSIS OF POLITICAL IDEOLOGY. *J. of Modern African Studies [Great Britain] 1973 11(4): 629-648.* A study of the relationship of the language of ideology and language of social reality demonstrating the semantic incongruities that often exist in fact. It is evident that the usual assumption that African society having been traditionally communal some form of a socialist regime might be introduced very smoothly needs serious qualification both as a premise and as a conclusion. Traditionally society did not ideologize, it merely inherited and perpetuated. Modern African society does not share this simplicity. The ideologies have arrived, and the future is unpredictable as a result. 42 notes. R. V. Ritter

890. Steeves, Edna L. NEGRITUDE AND THE NOBLE SAVAGE. *J. of Modern African Studies [Great Britain] 1973 11(1): 91-104.* The concept of negritude emerged in the 1930's. Although it has changed and is interpreted differently by various blacks, negritude is still a literary movement that stresses that black is beautiful. Africans were "noble savages" to Europeans for centuries, yet by the time of the 18th-century slave trade, they were no longer curiosities but barbarians. Negritude is part of the struggle to remove that stereotype. In fact, the ancient primitive virtues of Africa may be preferable to the Western world's modern cultures. 9 notes. H. G. Soff

891. Stuart, Richard. RELIGIONS IN AFRICA. *Can. J. of African Studies [Canada] 1980 14(1): 178-181.* Review article of three collections comprising some 60 articles on African and Afro-American religious systems: Edward Fanshol é-Luke et al, *Christianity in Independent Africa*(London: Rex Collings, 1978), Newell D. Booth's *African Religions: A Symposium* (New York: NOK Publ., 1977), and *African Perspectives: Religious Innovations in Modern African Society* (1976-77).

892. Sudarkasa, Niara. AFRICAN AND AFRO-AMERICAN FAMILY STRUCTURE: A COMPARISON. *Black Scholar 1980 11(8): 37-60.* Analyzes African family structure and compares it with Afro-American family structure, which has evolved from the first Blacks brought to the United States from Africa.

893. Taylor, Elyseo J. FILM AND SOCIAL CHANGE IN AFRICA SOUTH OF THE SAHARA. *Am. Behavioral Scientist 1974 17(3): 424-439.*

894. Thomas, Louis-Vincent. ACCULTURATION ET NOUVEAUX MILIEUX SOCIO-CULTURELS EN AFRIQUE NOIRE [Acculturation and new sociocultural spheres in black Africa]. *Bull. de l'Inst. Fondamental d'Afrique Noire [Senegal] 1974 36(1): 164-215.* Surveys acculturation and discusses schools and cities as among the most significant loci of the social and cultural changes occurring in Black Africa as blacks and whites are brought closer together. 106 notes.
H. L. Calkin

895. Tsegah, Francis A. and Tiewul, S. Azadon. ARBITRATION AND THE SETTLEMENT OF COMMERCIAL DISPUTES: A SELECTIVE SURVEY OF AFRICAN PRACTICE. *J. of World Trade Law [Switzerland] 1975 9(4): 378-397.* Recourse to arbitration for the settlement of commercial disputes is a common practice in most African countries. In English-speaking African states, arbitration statutes reflect the general principles of arbitration applicable in the former period of European colonialism. The authors, both Ghanaians, treat a complexity of issues including various types of arbitration statutes, arbitration with national governments and parastatal agencies, and enforcement of arbitration awards. J

896. Tumanova, L. MELKAIA BURZHUAZIIA AFRIKANSKOGO GORODA [The petite bourgeoisie in African towns]. *Aziia i Afrika Segodnia [USSR] 1981 (11): 36-38.* Describes the growing influence of socialist ideas in African capitalist countries, and the role of the petite bourgeoisie, the working class, and the peasantry in implementing social progress.

897. Turner, H. W. AFRICAN INDEPENDENT CHURCHES AND EDUCATION. *J. of Modern African Studies [Great Britain] 1975 13(2): 295-308.* Studies the attitudes of the independent churches of Africa toward education. In general, membership is less educated than among the older churches of mission origin. The prophet-healing type is more African in orientation and less congruent with education, which implies some Westernization. Motives for education are mixed and hard to analyze, involving economic, nationalist, social, and religious implications. There is a movement to develop schools on a par with white education which would include a utilitarian emphasis. 20 notes.
R. V. Ritter

898. Turner, H. W. AFRICAN RELIGIOUS RESEARCH: NEW STUDIES OF NEW MOVEMENTS: SOME PUBLICATIONS ON AFRICAN INDEPENDENT CHURCHES SINCE 1973. *J. of Religion in Africa [Netherlands] 1980 11(2): 137-153.* Reviews 10 books: two each on West Africa, East Africa, Central Africa, and South Africa.
R. J. Jirran

899. Turner, H. W. THE APPROACH TO AFRICA'S NEW RELIGIOUS MOVEMENTS. *African Perspectives [Netherlands] 1976 (2): 13-23.* A call for utilization of many academic disciplines in examining new religious movements which have appeared in Africa. Offers two typologies of these movements. Based on recent assessments of such movements; 11 notes. L. W. Truschel

900. Uyanga, Joseph. AFRICAN MOBILITY: A SOURCE PAPER. *Int. Migration Rev. 1981 15(4): 707-736.* Bibliography of sources on migration in Africa published in Africa, the United States, and Great Britain, 1930's-70's.

901. Valenti, Suzanne. THE BLACK DIASPORA: NEGRITUDE IN THE POETRY OF WEST AFRICANS AND BLACK AMERICANS. *Phylon 1973 34(4): 390-398.* Negritude refers to "a special set of qualities, values, thoughts, and emotions" possessed by Blacks. It is examined in the poetry of diverse Black writers in West Africa and the United States, 1930-72. S

902. Van Allen, Judith. AFRICAN WOMEN: "MODERNIZATION," AND NATIONAL LIBERATION. Iglitzin, Lynne B. and Ross, Ruth, eds. *Women in the World* (Santa Barbara, Calif.: Clio Books, 1976): 25-54. Contrary to much social science literature, Western colonization of Africa has hindered equal rights for women. By supplying industrialized countries with raw material without developing industry of its own, Africa has become economically dependent on Western nations. The politicians and skilled and semiskilled workers who benefit economically from Western influences tend to adopt restrictive Western attitudes toward women. Under the system of "female farming," established before colonization, women had been responsible for the growth and sale of crops. Women traders had achieved some independence and formed political groups. The system broke down when colonialists passed on modern farming techniques exclusively to men and began controlling market prices. Although

progress toward equal rights is slow and hampered by economic dependence on the Western world in Kenya, Guinea, and Tanzania, political parties in the newly independent nations of Guinea-Bissau, Mozambique, and Angola incorporate women's rights issues in their party philosophies. Secondary sources; 60 notes. J. Holzinger

903. Van Allen, Judith. MODERNIZATION MEANS MORE DEPENDENCY. *Center Mag. 1974 7(3): 60-67.* Modernization in Africa is causing the women to become more dependent on men. S

904. Verhelst, T. G. COMMON LANDS IN SOME AFRICAN LEGAL SYSTEMS. *Rev. de l'Inst. de Sociologie [Belgium] 1973 (2): 399-438.* Surveys land law in Africa, south of the Sahara, discussing; 1) traditional land law, 2) British and French colonial legislation, and 3) property law in modern African states, which tends to reinforce the prerogatives of the state with regard to land resources.

905. Voll, John Obert. WAHHABISM AND MAHDISM: ALTERNATIVE STYLES OF ISLAMIC RENEWALS. *Arab Studies Q. 1982 4(1-2): 110-126.* Compares two Islamic revivalist movements; Wahhabism, founded by Muhammad ibn Abd al-Wahhab, and Mahdism, founded by Muhammad Ahmad al-Mahdi, movements which arose in the 19th and 20th centuries, focusing on their different ideologies, their use of the Koran, and their impact on the political and religious life of the Muslim world in the 1970's and 1980's.

906. Warner, Keith Q. NÉGRITUDE: A NEW DIMENSION IN THE FRENCH CLASSROOM. *J. of Negro Educ. 1974 43(1): 77-81.* Teachers of French should recognize the importance of writings in French by black authors of the West Indies and French Africa. These works can add a new dimension to the teaching of the French language, especially for black students. B. D. Johnson

907. Wästberg, Per. THEMES IN AFRICAN LITERATURE TODAY. *Daedalus 1974 103(2): 135-150.* Contemporary African literature is growing in significance. There is a deep sense of political obligation, and much literature is documentary. The novel, although alien to traditional patterns of African expression, has been widely adapted. Outstanding novelists are Simbane Ousmane of Senegal, Mongo Beti of Cameroon, and, above all, Chinua Achebe of Nigeria. Drama, influenced by oral literature, is best produced by Wole Soyinka of Nigeria. African poetry, written mainly in French, is exemplified in the poems of Leopold Sedar Senghor of Senegal. Primary and secondary sources; 17 notes. E. McCarthy

908. Wauthier, Claude. THE SITUATION OF THE AFRICAN WRITER IN POST-COLONIAL AFRICA. *Dalhousie R. 1973/74 53(4): 733-741.* Discusses the political position of critical African authors. One of 10 papers read at the Conference on African Literature, Dalhousie U., 1973. S

909. Weems, Luther X. THE RHYTHM OF BLACK PERSONALITY. *Southern Exposure 1975 3(1): 14-19.* While the Western definition of personality emphasizes the uniqueness of an individual, the African definition emphasizes "a universal oneness" often evidenced by the sense of rhythm which permeates the African's mind and world. Examples are cited of how rhythm is prevalent in the individual, kinship patterns, male-female relationships, and religion as a unifying life theme. Secondary sources; 2 illus., biblio. G. A. Bolton

910. Weiskel, Timothy C. NATURE, CULTURE AND ECOLOGY IN TRADITIONAL AFRICAN THOUGHT SYSTEMS. *Cultures [France] 1973 1(2): 123-144.* Traditional African cultures possess the equivalent of an ecological code, embodied in their myths and social customs, and they maintain the balance between nature and culture. Based on field work among the Mbuti Pygmies and Lele peoples of Zaïre and the Baoulé of Ivory Coast; 45 notes. R. K. Adams

911. Wekerle, Anton. MODERN AFRICAN CRIMINAL LAW AND PROCEDURE CODES. *Q. J. of the Lib. of Congress 1978 35(4): 282-287.* Traces the development in the legal systems of 19 sub-Saharan African countries from the criminal law and procedure codes inherited from France, Belgium, and Italy before independence to their modern equivalents. They have been updated in form and content, and some include provisions for the promotion of social evolution, political unity, and economic development. Based on African criminal law and criminal procedure codes in the Library of Congress; 45 notes. A. R. Souby

912. White, Landeg. LITERATURE AND HISTORY IN AFRICA. *J. of African Hist. [Great Britain] 1980 21(4): 537-546.* Reviews *Domination and Resistance,* edited by Werner Lange (East Lansing: Michigan State U., 1979), *Critical Perspectives on Chinua Achebe,* edited by C. L. Innes and Bernth Lindfors (London: Heinemann, 1979), and Dorothy S. Blair's *African Literature in French* (Cambridge U. Pr., 1976). These three studies examine the reflection of history in the oral and written literature of Nigeria, Ethiopia, and the former French colonies. 13 notes. R. L. Collison

913. Wilson, Monica. ZIG-ZAG CHANGE. *Africa [Great Britain] 1976 46(4): 399-409.* Discusses the Nyakusa-Ngonde peoples who live by the Songe river on the Malawi-Tanzania border and developments in their marriage procedures which have reflected social change. In precolonial times, cattle were paid for a bride, polygyny was accepted, divorce practically unknown, and levirate customary. With the introduction of Christianity, polygyny and divorce were discouraged. When cattle became scarce, poor men married by giving service but the proportion of cattle to people improved in the 1930's, making earlier marriages possible. In modern times, women have become more independent, rejecting arranged marriages, prepared to seek divorce if the marriage is not successful, and eschewing polygyny and levirate as bondage. Based on fieldwork; 13 notes, biblio. R. L. Collison

914. Winters, Christopher. URBAN MORPHOGENESIS IN FRANCOPHONE BLACK AFRICA. *Geog. Rev. 1982 72(2): 139-154.* The morphology of large cities in francophone black Africa is partly the result of cultural factors. French and Belgian colonialists laid out the cities according to turn-of-the-century Western European urban preferences, including geometrical order, racial segregation, and use of greenery. Many aspects of colonial urbanism continued after independence. Since 1960 immigrants from the countryside have increasingly brought elements of village morphology to the cities, and the practice of a laissez-faire economic system has resulted in an increasingly complicated urban fabric. The governing elites try to create geometrically regular cities with a European image. J

915. Young, Crawford. PATTERNS OF SOCIAL CONFLICT: STATE, CLASS, AND ETHNICITY. *Daedalus 1982 111(2): 71-98.* Discusses the role of colonialism in Africa as a moulder of concepts of class and ethnicity which were carried over into the period of independent states.

916. —. WOMEN IN AFRICA. *African Econ. Hist. 1978 (5): 62-69.*
Little, Kenneth, *pp. 62-64.*
Lawson, Rowena M., *pp. 65-66.*
Galbraith, Virginia, *pp. 66-69.* The 11 essays in Nancy J. Hafkin and Edna G. Bay, eds., *Women in Africa: Studies in Social and Economic Change*(Stanford U. Pr., 1976), are stronger as they move away from the contemporary era. Women's activities in Africa have helped sustain and change social systems although beginning with colonization women's status declined. East African women seem to have had more exotic outlets than the market women of West Africa. 2 notes. W. D. Piersen

7. NORTH AFRICA

General

917. Abu-Aziz, Yahya. ITTIHĀMĀT AL-FRANSIYĪN FĪ JANŪB AL-JAZĀ'IR WA-AL-SAHRĀ' MIN KHILĀLI MĀ KATABŪHU WA-MIN ISTIFĀDATIHIM MIN TURUQ AL-QAWĀFIL FĪ GHAZWIHĀ [French interests in southern Algeria and the Sahara from their writings and their use of the caravan routes in their conquest]. *Majallat Al-buhūth Al-Tārīkhiya [Libya] 1981 3(2): 357-384.* The earliest European explorers into the interior of Africa in the 18th century were followed by imperialist expansion in the 19th century by the French and British. France occupied Algiers in 1837 and expanded south toward Niger and Senegal. By the turn of the century they had crushed Tuareg opposition and controlled all of southern Algeria. Exploration of the area continued from the mid-19th century for military and colonialist purposes, with plans proposed for railways and grandiose designs to create an enormous interior lake in Algeria/Tunisia which were finally shelved only in 1953. Based on French official sources and published reports by explorers; map, 55 notes.
C. H. Bleaney

918. Adam, Andre. LE CHANGEMENT CULTUREL DANS LE MAGHREB INDÉPENDANT: ACCULTURATION OU RECULTURATION? [Cultural change in the independent Maghreb: foreign cultural influence or return to cultural tradition?]. *Rev. de l'Occident Musulman et de la Méditerranée [France] 1975 (19): 7-15.* Examines cultural developments in independent Tunisia, Morocco, and Algeria, and inquires whether there has been an increase in foreign influence with the ending of colonialism, or a return to precolonial Maghreb culture. Continued scientific and technological influences are inescapable, and the author considers intellectual, moral, and religious values, for these are less affected by science and technology in the Islamic world than in the Christian one. He also analyzes innovations in Moslem law, especially concerning marriage, birth control, and socialism, and emphasizes bilingualism, particularly the problem of developing education in written Arabic. 3 notes. R. O. Khan

919. Arkoun, Muhammad. THE ADEQUACY OF CONTEMPORARY ISLAM TO THE POLITICAL, SOCIAL, AND ECONOMIC DEVELOPMENT OF NORTHERN AFRICA. *Arab Studies Q. 1982 4(1-2): 34-53.* Examines social, economic, and demographic changes in North Africa and the role of Islam in the region's social and political development during the 20th century.

920. Arnaud, Jacqueline. LE ROMAN MAGHRÉBIN EN QUESTION CHEZ KHAÏR-EDDINE, BOUDJEDRA, TAHAR BENJELLOUN [The Maghreb novel called into question in the works of Khaïr-Eddine, Boudjedra, and Tahar Benjelloun]. *Rev. de l'Occident Musulman et de la Méditerranée [France] 1976 (22): 59-68.* Assesses the contribution of this generation of Maghreb novelists in abandoning set literary forms and taboos. Writing in French, they have violently transgressed sexual, religious, and political taboos, aiming to destroy set social forms, and exposing the stress imposed, especially on women, by the ancient established patriarchy. They have attacked the political use of religion and established leadership and power and have written in an accessible and attractive manner. R. O. Khan

921. Badran, Margot Farranto. MIDDLE EAST AND NORTH AFRICA: WOMEN. *Trends in Hist. 1979 1(1): 123-129.* Review essay of periodical literature published from 1973 to 1979, on the traditional and changing or modern worlds of Middle Eastern and North African women, primarily in the 19th and 20th centuries.

922. Basu, A. R. INTERACTION BETWEEN ELITES AND NATIONALIST MOVEMENT: STUDIES OF COLONIAL SITUATION IN MOROCCO, ALGERIA AND TUNISIA. *Indian Pol. Sci. Rev. [India] 1978 12(2): 217-226.* Describes elite relationships to nationalist movements in terms of three modes of consciousness: liberal assimilation, traditional anticolonialism, and radical anticolonialism. Morocco is an example of traditional anticolonialism. Different strata of Algerian society articulated all three phases simultaneously. Only in Tunisia did one mode succeed another in the colonial dialectic. J. C. English

923. Benani, Ahmed. SAHARA OCCIDENTAL ET AFFRONTEMENTS NATIONALITAIRES DANS LE MAGHREB [Western Sahara and nationalist confrontations in the Maghreb]. *Genève-Afrique [Switzerland] 1979 17(1): 89-111.* Although Moroccans have made claims on neighboring territories since independence in 1956, these territorial claims have intensified since 1971 to solidify bourgeois support for the regime. Moroccan efforts have been resisted by the Algerian rulers, the Mauritanians, and the Polisario guerrillas. Photo, 2 maps, 37 notes. B. S. Fetter

924. Berque, Jacque. TRADITION AND INNOVATION IN THE MAGHRIB. *Daedalus 1973 102(1): 239-250.*

925. Bessis, Juliet. CHEKIB ARSLAN ET LES MOUVEMENTS NATIONALISTES AU MAGHREB [Chekib Arslan and the nationalist movements in the Maghreb]. *Rev. Hist. [France] 1978 259(2): 467-489.* Chekib Arslan (1869-1946) was a Lebanese aristocrat who evolved into an influential proponent of pan-Arabism with strong influence in Tunisia, Algeria, and Morocco (Maghreb). 70 notes.
G. H. Davis

926. Bisson, Jean and Rognon, Pierre. ROBERT CAPOT-REY: TRENTE ANS DE GEOGRAPHIE SAHARIENNE [Robert Capot-Rey: 30 years of Saharan geography]. *Ann. de Géographie [France] 1978 87(479): 59-73.* Discusses the role of Robert Capot-Rey in the Institute for Saharan Research, 1935-70's, and his interest in the influence of winds on the desert, the relationship between man and nature, and his more flexible view of the Sahara as a geographical region.

927. Brett, Michael. THE COLONIAL PERIOD IN THE MAGHRIB AND ITS AFTERMATH: THE PRESENT STATE OF HISTORICAL WRITING. *J. of African Hist. [Great Britain] 1976 17(2): 291-305.* A review of recent essays dealing with Algeria, Morocco, and Tunisia and French control of those states. Most recent books deal with the question of where the French went wrong in North Africa. 43 notes. H. G. Soff

928. Brett, Michael. MUFTI, MURABIT, MARABOUT AND MAHDI: FOUR TYPES IN THE ISLAMIC HISTORY OF NORTH AFRICA. *Rev. de l'Occident Musulman et de la Méditerranée [France] 1980 (29): 5-15.* Historically, four types of politico-religious leader have been recognized in Moslem North Africa: *Mufti, Murabit, Marabout,* and *Mahdi.* In *The Green Book,* Libyan chief Colonel Muammar Qadhafi seems to see himself as a *Murabit,* but his recent actions characterize him more as a *Mahdi.* 9 notes. A. E. Standley

929. Brewer, William D. THE LIBYAN-SUDANESE "CRISIS" OF 1981: DANGER FOR DARFUR AND DILEMMA FOR THE UNITED STATES. *Middle East J. 1982 36(2): 205-216.* Suspicion between Libya and Sudan was long standing but became critical following the Libyan military presence in Chad, the flight of Prime Minister Hisserie Habre to Darfur, and the resultant border raiding. Darfur only became part of Sudan in 1916 and the Islamic fundamentalism of much of the population make it a politically sensitive frontier region, as was shown in 1976 when Madhists from Darfur entered Omdurman and Khartoum and attempted a coup. By late 1981 border raids had intensified resulting in Chadian troops and Libyan planes attacking Darfur border villages, and increased US aid for Sudan. However, the Sudan government will need to foster development in the province to maintain security of the frontier and to encourage Darfuri support for Sudan as an integrated nation. Based on western press reports and secondary sources; 33 notes. F. A. Clements

930. Brown, L. Carl. THE UNITED STATES AND THE MAGHRIB. *Middle East J. 1976 30(3): 273-290.* The American image of the Maghreb (North Africa) relies on music and drama which are historically inaccurate. Until the end of the Napoleonic Wars, North African developments accelerated the creation of the US navy. Since 1950, after an interlude of a century and a quarter, the United States has accelerated the Maghreb's move from colonialism to independence. "The new pattern is one of mutual discovery with an increasing number

of Maghribis gaining first-hand experience of the United States." 25 notes. E. P. Stickney

931. Burke, Edmund, III. TOWARDS A HISTORY OF THE MAGHRIB. *Middle Eastern Studies [Great Britain] 1975 11(3): 306-323.* For the English-speaking world, the reconstruction of the history of North Africa must begin with the only two books available: Charles André Julien's classic *History of North Africa from the Arab Conquest to 1830* and Jamil Abun-Nasr's *A History of the Maghrib.* Though differing in detail, both agree on "the anarchic state of pre-colonial Maghribi society, the inevitability of French domination, and the belief that France had a civilizing mission to fulfill." Revisionist objections to these views has not produced new works yet, but has stimulated new lines of inquiry, even while recognizing that "the dispute is basically a political one in which history serves as the chosen battlefield." Instead of continuing the older emphasis on the views of the urban and official classes, younger historians are looking at Arabic sources of the lower classes and the peasants, the social composition of elite groups, large-scale movement of populations (Berbers from 900 to 1800), histories of scholars and notable citizens of particular cities, juridical materials, records of Muslim pious foundations, land records, mosque or Zawiya library holdings, historical patrimonies, and oral materials. In addition, public health records, educational records, and statistics on legal interactions in European collections offer additional clues. Important interpretive questions remain to be answered: what is the nature of the Maghreb's backwardness vis-à-vis the West's "quantum leap forward" after 1500? Can a history of the Maghreb be written in the same manner as a history of France or England? Can a history of North Africa be written without inserting that history into the history of the Islamic world? K. M. Bailor

932. Cooke, James J. PAUL AZAN AND *L'ARMÉE INDIGÈNE NORD-AFRICAINE.Military Affairs 1981 45(3): 133-137.* Analysis of Colonel Paul Louis Azan's *L'Armée Indigène Nord-Africaine* (1925) and the reaction to it in France and North Africa. The book "remains as an example of the colonialist-associationist mentality which permeated large sections of the French military consecrated to service in the Maghrib. It was an attempt to systematize the recruiting of natives, especially in Algeria, in terms which would suit the colons of Algeria.... The value of native troops for the French army was never doubted, but to create a North African army was another matter which became mixed up with prevailing racial thought, colon politics, and great confusion within the French military in the interwar era, and with colonial politics." Based on French and other primary sources; 41 notes. A. M. Osur

933. Damis, John. THE FREE-SCHOOL PHENOMENON: THE CASES OF TUNISIA AND ALGERIA. *Int. J. of Middle East Studies [Great Britain] 1974 5(4): 434-449.* The free schools in Tunisia and Algeria have introduced European methods and values outside the structure of the official state educational systems. Primary and secondary sources; 2 tables, 45 notes. R. B. Orr

934. Dilger, Konrad. DIE STÄRKUNG DES ISLAMISCHEN RECHTS IN AFRIKA ALS FOLGE DER EMANZIPATION AFRIKANISCHER MITGLIEDSSTAATEN DER ARABISCHEN LIGA [The strengthening of Islamic law in Africa as a consequence of the emancipation of the African member states of the Arab League]. *Welt des Islams [Netherlands] 1978 18(3-4): 153-177.* Describes the development of civil law in Algeria and the Sudan after both countries gained independence. Based on a paper delivered at the annual meeting of the Society for African Law, held in Heidelberg, 8 November 1975. 133 notes, biblio. A. Menicant

935. Epalza, Miguel de. UN IMPORTANTE INSTRUMENTO DE TRABAJO: LA SECCIÓN 'ÁFRICA' DE LA BIBLIOTECA NACIONAL DE MADRID [An important research tool: the Africa section of the National Library in Madrid]. *Almenara [Spain] 1973 (4): 346-349.* Discusses the origins and contents of the Africa section of the National Library. Emphasizes its importance for the history of the Spanish Protectorate in Morocco, since it was organized around the legacy of Africanists who held important administrative posts during the Protectorate. A. G. (IHE 89435)

936. Gaha, Mohamed Kamel. LA LINGUISTIQUE ET LE PROBLÈME DES FORMES LITTÉRAIRES [Linguistics and the problem of literary forms]. *Cahiers de Tunisie [Tunisia] 1980 28(111-112): 255-272.* A linguistic structural approach to define literary forms and its application to research work on the study of figures in Maghrebian author Kateb Yacine's *Le Polygone Etoilé* (1980).

937. Gaudy, Georges. DEVANT L'HISTOIRE, EN AFRIQUE DU NORD [Before history, in North Africa]. *Écrits de Paris [France] 1975 (351): 56-60.* The disruptive forces of Islam continued to underlie the culture of Northern Africa during three hundred years of French domination and inevitably reasserted themselves in this century.

938. Gouletquer, Pierre and Kleinmann, Dorothée. STRUCTURE SOCIALE ET COMMERCE DU SEL DANS L'ÉCONOMIE TOUARÈGUE [Social structure and the salt trade in the Tuareg economy]. *Rev. de l'Occident Musulman et de la Méditerranée [France] 1976 (21): 131-139.* Examines the role of the salt trade among the Tuareg especially the expansion of the trade during the last century, when increased demand among the south Sahara groups coincided with increasing demand for grain among the Tuareg. Salt trading by nomads is presented as a relatively recent development, connected with changing dietary habits, economic structures, and social organization. Biblio. R. O. Khan

939. Graham-Brown, Sarah. MIDDLE EAST AND NORTH AFRICA: PROBLEMS OF RURAL HISTORY. *Trends in Hist. 1979 1(1): 116-122.* Review essay on periodical literature, published in 1975-78, on rural history in the Middle East and North Africa, a problem area because there is little documentation available for nonliterate or semiliterate societies, from the 16th to the 20th centuries.

940. Grosse, Scott D. THE POLITICS OF FAMILY PLANNING IN THE MAGHRIB. *Studies in Comparative Int. Development 1982 17(1): 22-48.* Explores the historical background of family planning in Algeria, Morocco, and Tunisia. Examines its chronology and the influence of political and nonpolitical elites. Tunisia was a pioneer, though not necessarily the most successful. Family planning is closely linked to the problem of labor absorption and is an instrument of both social and economic planning. Varying degrees of support for family planning are premised on the views of political and religious leaders and the socioeconomic philosophy of the times. Government policies in the three states indicate increasing antinatalist activity. Based mostly on primary sources; 5 notes, 81 ref. S. A. Farmerie

941. Gruner, Roger. PLACE DE L'ISLAM DANS LES CONSTITUTIONS DU MAGHREB [The place of Islam in the constitutions of the Maghreb]. *Afrique et l'Asie Modernes [France] 1981 (3): 39-54.* A comparative study of the constitutional regimes of Morocco, Algeria, Tunisia, and Libya, centering on their references to Islam.

942. Heggoy, Alf Andrew. THEY WRITE IN FRENCH, NOT IN ARABIC: SOME THOUGHTS ON NORTH AFRICAN AUTHORS. *Indiana Social Studies Q. 1977 30(2): 98-102.* Examines the impact of the French schools in colonial North Africa, 1830-1950's, on the authors of the area.

943. Hermassi, Elbaki. POLITICAL TRADITIONS OF THE MAGHRIB. *Daedalus 1973 102(1): 207-224.*

944. Keenan, Jeremy H. THE TUAREG VEIL. *Middle Eastern Studies [Great Britain] 1977 13(1): 3-13.* Briefly describes the origin, uses, symbolic significance, myths, and associated terminology of the veil. Seeks to clarify Robert Murphy's analysis of social interaction among the Southern Tuareg with respect to Kel Ahaggar [evil eye/evil mouth] mythology. Examines the impact of industrialization; tribal variations ("social distance"); the veil as status symbol, as courting component, and in social ritual. Based on field work, 1964-71, other primary sources, and secondary sources; 42 notes. R. B. Mendel

945. Komorowski, Zygmunt. CONTRIBUTION À L'ÉTUDE DES TRADITIONS CULTURELLES DU NORD-EST MAGHRÉBIN (LES CONFINS ALGÉRO-TUNISIENS) [A contribution to the study of the cultural traditions in the northeast Maghreb: the borders of Algeria and Tunisia]. *Africana Bull. [Poland] 1978 (27): 7-33.* Studies

traditional cultural bonds which unite the ethnic groups in areas near the border of Algeria and Tunisia.

946. Laroui, Abdallah and Manheim, Ralph, transl. THE RENASCENT MAGHRIB. *Int. J. of Pol. 1977 7(3): 5-28.* Analyzes the reactions of the indigenous society in Morocco, Algeria, and Tunisia to the experience of colonialism until the early 1930's. Examines political, economic, and social evidence to construct a model of the old and new Maghreb, the latter arising out of the colonial experience. After 1930 foreign colonization in North Africa was living on borrowed time. From *The History of the Maghrib: An Interpretive Essay* (Princeton U. Pr., 1977). Secondary material; 40 notes. R. E. Noble

947. Lewis, William H. NORTH AFRICA AND THE POWER BALANCE. *Current Hist. 1973 64(377): 30-32, 40.* Overcoming ethnocentrism, the West must learn that North African nations have a place in the international balance of power. S

948. Lewis, William H. NORTH AFRICA: STRUGGLE FOR PRIMACY. *Current Hist. 1979 76(445): 119-121, 131.* Discusses leadership crises in North Africa after the passing of the first generation of postindependence leaders, exemplified by the death of Algeria's Houari Boumedienne in December, 1978.

949. Ling, Dwight L. PLANNERS OF PROTECTORATES: CAMBON IN TUNISIA AND LYAUTEY IN MOROCCO. *Muslim World 1974 64(3): 220-227.* A comparison study of two architects of the French protectorates in North Africa, Pierre Paul Cambon (1843-1924) in Tunisia and Louis Hubert Gonzalve Lyautey (1854-1934) in Morocco. Though their careers, during the late 19th and early 20th centuries, were similar, their backgrounds, personalities, and regimes were not. Their regimes differed in their establishment, relations with the peoples, and economic policies. Although they added stability to the countries they governed, their policies, which were controversial, were altered after their departure. Based on French sources and secondary material; 28 notes. P. J. Mattar

950. Marshall, Susan E. ISLAMIC REVIVAL IN THE MAGHREB: THE UTILITY OF TRADITION FOR MODERNIZING ELITES. *Studies in Comparative Int. Development 1979 14(2): 95-108.* Compares and contrasts the uses of Islamic culture as a tool for modernization in Algeria and Tunisia, which have in common colonialism and cultural identity, coating the pill of socialism with Islam; and the resurrection of Islam in times of political crisis. Tradition has functioned as ideology. The author also analyzes Islamic resurgence in Iran, Pakistan, and Malaysia. Note, 46 ref. S. A. Farmerie

951. Marshall, Susan E. and Stokes, Randall G. TRADITION AND THE VEIL: FEMALE STATUS IN TUNISIA AND ALGERIA. *J. of Modern African Studies [Great Britain] 1981 19(4): 625-646.* National policy on the status of women in society has diverged since independence in Algeria and Tunisia. While the law and national leadership under Bourguiba in Tunisia have pioneered among Arab countries in the emancipation of women from traditional Islamic constraints, the political elite of the ruling FLN in Algeria has, despite its radical rhetoric, actually reintroduced such traditional practices as polygynous marriage by familial arrangement, and the husband's right to repudiate his spouse. Tunisia under Bourguiba has pursued Westernization, even to the point of openly challenging Islamic law and reputed statements of Mohammed on the status of women. The Algerians, suffering from a protracted crisis of political instability, elite fragmentation, and local ethnic revitalization, have retreated to a position of reaffirming Islamic tradition on the status of women. 2 tables, 42 notes. L. W. Truschel

952. Micaud, Charles A. BILINGUALISM IN NORTH AFRICA: CULTURAL AND SOCIO-POLITICAL IMPLICATIONS. *Western Pol. Q. 1974 27(1): 92-103.* Looks at the history of biculturism, Arabic and French, since the 19th century and examines the linguistic situation in modern North African schools. S

953. Murphy, Robert F. LA PARENTÉ TOUARÈGUE [Tuareg kinship]. *Rev. de l'Occident Musulman et de la Méditerranée [France] 1976 (21): 173-185.* Questions the assumption that a positive congruence exists between social structure and kinship terminology, and suggests that kinship terms may develop in contradiction to social organization and ultimately transform it. Analyzes Tuareg kinship terminology in relation to the tribe's social system since the 19th century and finds a discontinuity similar to that between Iroquois terminology and kinship endogamy. Asserts that a relationship exists between social organization and man's verbal system for expressing kinship, but the kin terms will negate and reorder the social system rather than reaffirm it. 2 diagrams, 3 notes, biblio. Translated from *American Anthropologist* 1967 (69): 163-170. R. O. Khan

954. N'Dumbe, Alexandre Kum'a, III. L'ALLEMAGNE NAZIE ET L'AFRIQUE DU NORD [Nazi Germany and North Africa]. *Cahiers d'Hist. [France] 1974 19(4): 319-341.* Reviews the attitudes and policy of Nazi Germany toward North Africa. Anti-Semitism and resistance to the imperialism of France and Britain were key ingredients in the Arab policy of Germany. The nature of Nazi propaganda in this regard and the obstacles to it are noted, as is the question of the independence of the Arab peoples in the face of German policy and actions. Based on German government archives and published sources; 56 notes. R. Howell

955. Nouschi, André. CRISE AU MAGHREB: REMARQUES DE MÉTHODE SUR LA VIE RURALE DE 1929 À 1936 [Crisis in the Maghreb: methodological remarks concerning rural life, 1929-36]. *Rev. Française d'Hist. d'Outre-Mer [France] 1976 63(3-4): 425-440.* The agricultural crisis connected with the Great Depression began at different times in different places and with different products in French North Africa (The Maghreb). For indigenous farmers the crisis meant severe dislocation; for European agriculturalists it led to centralization of properties and a halt to new settlement. The Great Depression also caused a revival of Maghrebine nationalism, for the Moslems there could see how much better the state took care of local Europeans than it did of them, and how France structured the local economy for its own benefit. 16 notes. J. C. Billigmeier

956. Parzymies, Stanislaw. LE CONFLIT DU SAHARA OCCIDENTAL ET LE CONTENTIEUX TERRITORIAL AU MAGHREB [The Western Sahara conflict and territorial conflict in the Maghreb]. *Africana Bull. [Poland] 1981 (30): 53-71.* Discusses the history of territorial disputes between Morocco, Tunisia, and Algeria. Includes the roles and policies of the governments and of transgovernmental bodies.

957. Perkins, Kenneth J. NORTH AFRICAN PROPAGANDA AND THE UNITED STATES, 1946-1956. *African Studies Rev. 1976 19(3): 65-78.* Since 1945, the North African states, particularly Morocco and Tunisia, have made attempts to familiarize Americans with their political, social, and economic climate and to make the US public sympathetic with their demands for independence.

958. Piazza, Calogero; Missori, Mario; and Filesi, Cesira. L'INVENTARIO DELLE FONTI MANOSCRITTE RELATIVE ALLA STORIA DELL'AFRICA DEL NORD ESISTENTI IN ITALIA: I FONDI DELL'ARCHIVIO CENTRALE DELLO STATO [The inventory of manuscript sources relative to the history of North Africa extant in Italy: the stocks of the Central State Archive]. *Africa [Italy] 1977 32(4): 557-565.* A brief survey of documents in the Italian State Archives dealing with North Africa, especially the Italian colonial possessions in Libya (Tripolitania), Eritrea, and Somalia. Many of these documents are from the private papers of leading Italian statesmen from Francesco Crispi and Agostino Depretis to Benito Mussolini and Pietro Badoglio. 4 notes. J. C. Billigmeier

959. Ponikiewski, Augustyn. AGRICULTURAL POLICY IN MAGHREB COUNTRIES. *Africana Bull. [Poland] 1977 (26): 25-56.* Analyzes the agrarian sector in Algeria, Libya, Morocco, and Tunisia during the 1960's and 1970's and concludes that agriculture in all of these countries is progressively varied in its nature and national role.

960. Provansal, Danielle. LE PHÉNOMÈNE MARABOUTIQUE AU MAGHREB [The marabout phenomenon in the Maghreb]. *Genève-Afrique [Switzerland] 1975 14(1): 59-77.* Analyzes maraboutism in the Maghreb from the first appearance of Sufism in the twelfth century to the present day, with particular reference to attitudes of marabouts toward rulers and the role of women.

961. Qazzaz, Ayad al-. MIDDLE EAST AND NORTH AFRICAN OIL. *Social Studies 1981 72(4): 171-176.* Analyzes history, function, and production value of the Middle East and North African oil industry and trade and Western nations' dependency on it. Biblio.
L. R. Raife

962. Reklajtis, Elżbieta. INTEGRACJA SPOLECZNA A POLITYKA JEZYKOWA W MAGHREBIE [Social integration and language policy in the Maghreb]. *Przegląd Socjologiczny [Poland] 1979 31(2): 163-182.* Developing a synthesis of colonial and Arabic cultural elements in newly independent Morocco, Algeria, and Tunisia was made difficult by the still popular stereotype associating the French language with effectiveness and modernity and Arabic with backwardness. In language policy "only radical decisions and actions can bring back the dynamics and the evolutionary character to the Arabic language and culture in the Maghreb countries."

963. Rondot, Pierre. DIE ROLLE DES ISLAMS IN DER PØLITIK DER MAGHREB-STAATEN [The role of Islam in the politics of the Maghreb states]. *Europa Archiv [West Germany] 1973 28(8): 283-290.* In the 1960's and early 1970's Islam has been used to promote nationalism, fraternity, state morals, and socialism in Morocco, Tunisia, Algeria, Mauritania, and Libya.

964. Rondot, Pierre. EGYPTE ET LIBYE: ACCORD DE PRINCIPE ET DISSENTIMENT AIGU [Egypt and Libya: agreement on principle and bitter disagreement]. *Rev. Française d'Études Pol. Africaines [France] 1973 (92): 10-13.* Offers an update on the persistent crisis between Egypt and Libya, which threatens the 1969 pact of Gamal Abdel Nasser and the path to Arab unity which could have important consequences for Cairo-Tripoli relations, accentuating the Arab-Israeli conflict.

965. Rondot, Pierre. GENÈSE ET PERSPECTIVES DU CONFLIT EGYPTO LIBYEN [Genesis of and perspectives on the Egypto-Libyan conflict]. *Défense Natl. [France] 1977 33(11): 71-89.* Explains the reasons behind the progressive deterioration in relations between Libya and Egypt in the years following the unitarian aspirations of both nations expressed in the Tripoli Pact (1969), ascribing the current state of hostility to the deeply divergent political stances of Anwar Sadat and Muammar Qadhafi.

966. Rosciszewski, Marcin M. TRADITIONAL SECTOR OF MAGHREB AGRICULTURE. *Hist. of Agric. [India] 1980 2(1): 66-116.* During the colonial period European influence disrupted the traditional agricultural system. Oasis farming and seminomadic livestock raising practices changed drastically as Europeans consolidated land holdings and plowed grazing lands. The native inhabitants were forced off the best lands or became part of a rural proletariat on the large estates. The economic and social structure of the Maghreb also changed with the influence of the Europeans. When the Maghreb countries gained their independence in the mid-20th century, European influence had disrupted traditional agricultural practices for such a long time that economic and social dislocation were major national problems. 5 tables, 53 notes.
R. D. Hurt

967. Sainte-Marie, Alain. LA CRISE DE 1929 EN AFRIQUE DU NORD [The crisis of 1929 in North Africa]. *Peuples Méditerranéans-Mediterranean Peoples [France] 1978 (5): 49-72.* Analyzes the economic crisis of 1929 in the Maghreb, in terms of economic development and decolonization.

968. Schoneweg, Egon and Henderson, George, transl. DIFFERENCES AND SIMILARITIES IN NORTH AFRICAN NATIONALISMS. *Int. J. of Pol. 1977 7(3): 29-64.* Although feeble roots are visible in the precolonial period, nationalism in Morocco, Algeria, and Tunisia was essentially a result of the colonial experience. Despite differences in detail, nationalist movements in all three countries developed in two stages: the first, to World War II, sought reforms within the system; the second demanded independence. Nationalism began with urban intellectuals and the bourgeoisie, spread to the urban proletariat, and finally to the rural population. French reform efforts, hampered by the opposition of French settlers, proved inadequate, and the policy of force became hopeless once nationalism had won the support of the rural masses. Translated from *Nationale Emanzipationsbewegung in Maghreb* (1969) Secondary material; 104 notes.
R. E. Noble

969. Souriau, Ch. LA CONSCIENCE ISLAMIQUE DANS OEUVRES RÉCENTS D'INTELLECTUELS DU MAGHREB [Islamic consciousness in the recent works of some intellectuals of the Maghreb]. *Rev. de l'Occident Musulman et de la Méditerranée [France] 1980 (29): 69-107.* The works of A. Laroui, H. Djait, M. Arkoun, and A. Bouhdiba illustrate the rejection by the Moslem world of Western models of leadership. These writers are aware of both cultures, particularly exemplified by their attitudes toward women and society. 2 diagrams, 15 notes.
A. E. Standley

970. Stoklitski, S. ALZHIR, MAROKKO, TUNIS: PUTI MOBILIZATSII VNUTRENNIKH NAKOPLENII [Algeria, Morocco, Tunisia: the mobilization of internal accumulation]. *Mirovaia Ekonomika i Mezhdunarodnye Otnosheniia [USSR] 1974 (6): 65-75.* Discusses the difficulties encountered by these countries in facilitating the accumulation of capital for independent economic development during the late 1960's and early 1970's with special reference to the Algerian experience.

971. Tardits, Claude. CONCLUSION (SUR LES ACTES DE COLLOQUE SUR L'ORGANIZATION SOCIALE CHEZ LES TOUAREGS, ABBAYE DE SENANQUE, JUIN 1974) [Conclusion: Concerning the papers delivered at the Colloquium on Tuareg Social Organization, Abbaye de Senanque, June 1974]. *Rev. de l'Occident Musulman et de la Méditerranée [France] 1976 (21): 163-171.* Surveys nine papers on the Tuareg given at the colloquium by André Bourgeot, Jeremy H. Keenan, Marceau Gast, Helene Claudot, Edmond Bernus, S. Bernus, Henri Guillaume, Pierre Gouletquer and Dorothée Kleinmann, and Pierre Bonte.
R. O. Khan

972. Tessler, Mark A. THE IDENTITY OF RELIGIOUS MINORITIES IN NON-SECULAR STATES: JEWS IN TUNISIA AND MOROCCO AND ARABS IN ISRAEL. *Comparative Studies in Soc. and Hist. [Great Britain] 1978 20(3): 359-373.* Examines factors which account for unnarrowed cultural distance between minorities and host cultures, and discusses perceived sociocultural identities among the minorities, 1972-75.

973. Tretiakov, P. AGRARNYE PREOBRAZOVANIIA V SEVERNOI AFRIKE [Agrarian reforms in northern Africa]. *Aziia i Afrika Segodnia [USSR] 1975 (3): 10-13.* The experience of agrarian transformations in the countries of the Maghreb show diverse solutions to the peasant question. Common to all countries is the natural connection among the nature of agrarian reforms, class composition of society, and their political regimes.
J/S

974. Wall, Michael. THE MAGHREB. *World Survey [Great Britain] 1974 (64): 1-17.* Discusses how Morocco, Tunisia, and Algeria achieved independence from France in the 1950's and 1960's, and describes economic development and politics in the three countries after independence.

975. Zartman, I. William. THE ELITES OF THE MAGHREB: A REVIEW ARTICLE. *Int. J. of Middle East Studies [Great Britain] 1975 6(4): 495-504.* Discusses four recent studies on Maghrebi elites, which provide information on elite backgrounds and structures and stability policies within these structures. The studies say little about policies of change within the structures or about policy or attitudinal relations with elite social background variables. 7 notes.
R. B. Orr

976. Zartman, I. William. THE SOUTHWEST SHORE. *Military R. 1973 53(4): 84-94.* Surveys the extent of "unity" of Morocco, Algeria, and Tunisia. Despite similar life styles, colonial divisions and the politics of independence have prevented North African unity from extending beyond careful institutionalized cooperation at the economic level and the assumption of common diplomatic positions. 3 illus., map. Reprinted from the *International Journal*, Autumn 1972.
J. K. Ohl

977. Zingg, Paul J. AMERICA AND NORTH AFRICA: A CASE IN UNITED STATES-THIRD WORLD RELATIONS. *Hist. Teacher 1979 12(2): 253-270.* Until recently this has been a neglected area in American-Third World studies. The author surveys the available material from the Barbary War to the present; the historiography of the field is on the "threshold of sophistication and definition." New work

needs to be done on economic, cultural, and ideological factors. Note, biblio. L. C. Smith

978. Zingg, Paul J. THE COLD WAR IN NORTH AFRICA: AMERICAN FOREIGN POLICY AND POSTWAR MUSLIM NATIONALISM 1945-1962. *Historian 1976 39(1): 40-61.* In the Cold War era those responsible for US foreign policy saw North Africa as part of the East-West conflict. This view blinded them to the reality of rising Third World nationalism. US policymakers confused North African Communism with genuine Muslim nationalism. M. J. Wentworth

979. Zingg, Paul J. THE UNITED STATES AND NORTH AFRICA: AN HISTORIOGRAPHICAL WASTELAND. *African Studies R. 1973 16(1): 107-117.*

Algeria

980. Aballea, François. DÉSTRUCTURATION ET RESTRUCTURATION DE L'ESPACE ALGÉRIEN [Destructuring and restructuring of Algerian land]. *Recherche Sociale [France] 1977 (63): 5-59.* Describes land use in Algeria and environmental changes, 19th-20th centuries.

981. Abun-Nasr, Jamil M. ISLAM UND DIE ALGERISCHE NATIONALIDENTITÄT [Islam and Algerian national identity]. *Welt des Islams [Netherlands] 1978 18(3-4): 178-194.* The penetration of reformed Islam into Algerian politics rehabilitated the Muslims spiritually, made a contribution to the political liberation of Algeria, and became a symbol of its unity and political identity. Secondary sources; 46 notes. A. Menicant

982. Adair, Philippe. MYTHES ET REALITES DE LA REFORME AGRAIRE EN ALGERIE: BILAN D'UNE DECENNIE [Myths and facts in Algerian land reform: an evaluation after 10 years]. *Etudes Rurales [France] 1982 (85): 49-65.* The Algerian land reform which became operational under state control in 1971 aimed at removing the dualist agrarian framework so as to increase output, reduce unemployment, and set up rural structures. Ten years later the results are disappointing. Extension of the agricultural public sector reproduces—in a different pattern—the previous dualism, land redistribution is limited and output almost stationary; the creation of new jobs, characterized by the development of salaried posts, is still insufficient and the fittings of rural structures have not gone beyond the blueprint stage. Failure to make the reform truly applicable is marked by the secondary role agriculture plays to industrialization. J/S

983. Arnaud, Jacqueline. KATEB YACINE ET LE THEÂTRE POLITIQUE SUR LE SOL ALGERIEN [Kateb Yacine and political theater in Algeria]. *Mediterranean Peoples [France] 1982 (19): 133-151.* Discusses the work of playwright Kateb Yacine, especially his period from 1970 to 1972 when he experimented with collective theater in dialectal Arabic with the Théâtre de la Mer's presentation of *Mohammed Prends ta Valise.*

984. Balta, Paul. [ALGERIA'S NATIONAL DEVELOPMENT, 1973-77]. L'ALGÉRIE AUJOURD'HUI: I-DE LA LÉGITIMITÉ RÉVOLUTIONNAIRE À LA LÉGITIMITÉ INSTITUTIONNELLE [Algeria today: I. from revolutionary legitimacy to institutional legitimacy]. *Défense Natl. [France] 1977 33(5): 89-102.* Examines the priority accorded by Algeria to the consolidation of an internal institutional structure to affirm its status as an independent and legitimate nation, 1975-77. LA POLITIQUE EXTÉRIEURE DE L'ALGÉRIE SUR LA BRÈCHE AFRICAINE [Algeria's foreign policy on the African breach]. *Défense Natl. [France] 1977 33(6): 87-98.* Surveys the factors which caused Algeria to reformulate its foreign policy, 1973-77, with reference to its increased focus on the problems facing African nations, particularly the struggle for decolonization.

985. Balta, Paul. PANORAMA DE L'ALGÉRIE MODERNE; UN TRIPLE DIALOGUE: EUROPÉEN, ARABE ET AFRICAIN [Panorama of modern Algeria: the triple dialogue of European, Arab, and African]. *Défense Natl. [France] 1974 30(12): 43-53.* Examines Algeria's mature and successful foreign policy, and assesses how successful it has been in achieving its goal of a triple dialogue, Arab-African, Euro-Arab, and Euro-Arab-African since 1962.

986. Balta, Paul. PANORAMA DE L'ALGÉRIE MODERNE: UNE TRIPLE RÉVOLUTION INDUSTRIELLE, AGRAIRE ET CULTURELLE [Panorama of modern Algeria: a triple industrial, agrarian, and cultural revolution]. *Défense Natl. [France] 1974 30(11): 37-50.* Underlines the particular traits of Algerian development arising from industrialization, land reform, and cultural progress, and discusses the ambitious objectives defined in the second quadrennial plan.

987. Bamya, Aïda. "L'AS" DE TAHAR OUATTAR *[L'as* by Attahar Wattar]. *Rev. de l'Occident Musulman et de la Méditerranée [France] 1976 (22): 131-136.* Assesses this novel's description of repression under colonialism and the activities of Algerian collaborators during the war of national liberation. Examines the author's aims, which are an extension of his communist ideology, and his experiences both in the war and in independent Algeria. 14 notes. R. O. Khan

988. Basu, Anup Ranjan. NATIONAL INTERESTS AND OBJECTIVES IN ALGERIAN FOREIGN POLICY. *African Q. [India] 1981 21(1): 39-60.* A military, political, and economic survey of postindependence Algeria.

989. Beckett, Paul A. ALGERIA *VS.* FANON: THE THEORY OF REVOLUTIONARY DECOLONIZATION, AND THE ALGERIAN EXPERIENCE. *Western Pol. Q. 1973 26(1): 5-27.* Outlines the development of Algeria's political system both during the revolutionary war (1954-62) and after independence (1962-69) in order to determine the validity of Frantz Fanon's theory of revolutionary decolonization as presented in his *The Wretched of the Earth* (New York: Grove Press, 1966). S

990. Benabdelkrim, Ahmed. THE AGRARIAN REVOLUTION IN ALGERIA. *World Marxist Rev. [Canada] 1976 19(10): 118-126.* Discusses the agrarian revolution in Algeria as a weapon against big landowners and proprietors, 1962-76.

991. Bennoune, Mah Foud. SOCIO-ECONOMIC CHANGES IN RURAL ALGERIA: 1830-1954: A DIACHRONIC ANALYSIS OF A PEASANTRY UNDER COLONIALISM. *Peasant Studies Newsletter 1973 2(2): 11-18.* Outlines "the nature and extent of French land colonization in Algeria" and the adjustments of the peasants to the colonial situation. S

992. Bennoune, Mahfoud. FRENCH COUNTER-REVOLUTIONARY DOCTRINE AND THE ALGERIAN PEASANTRY. *Monthly R. 1973 25(7): 43-60.* Describes French counterinsurgency techniques during the Algerian revolt, including forced resettlement of peasants and psychological warfare. S

993. Boals, Kay. THE POLITICS OF CULTURAL LIBERATION: MALE-FEMALE RELATIONS IN ALGERIA. Carroll, Berenice A., ed. *Liberating Women's Hist.* (Chicago: U. of Illinois Pr., 1976): 194-211. Establishes a framework for the systematic comparative analysis of the process of cultural liberation. There are six process-oriented types of consciousness which reflect the dialectic between dominant and oppressed groups on the external (economic, military, technological) and psychic (emotional, cultural) levels. These include traditional, traditionalist, assimilationist, reformist, revolutionary, and transforming consciousnesses, each of which is examined in terms of male-female and colonizer-colonized relationships in Algeria. In the areas of political rights, employment opportunity, and equal primary education, traditionalist attitudes toward male-female relations in Algeria have been bypassed under the pressure of commitment to development goals. In the more private realms, traditionalist consciousness has combined with Marxist ideology to stifle liberation in male-female relations. Primary and secondary sources; 36 notes. S

994. Boals, Kay and Stiehm, Judith. THE WOMEN OF LIBERATED ALGERIA. *Center Mag. 1974 7(3): 74-76.*

995. Bondy, François. FRANTZ FANON—"BLACK ORPHEUS" OF THE HOMELESS LEFT. *Encounter [Great Britain] 1974 43(2): 25-29.* A biography of doctor and psychiatrist Frantz Fanon

(1925-61), his revolutionary political thought on self-government and his active involvement in the Algerian struggle in the 1950's.

996. Bono, Salvatore. TESTIMONIANZE ORALI PER LA STORIA CONTEMPORANEA DELL'ALGERIA [Oral testimony about the contemporary history of Algeria]. *Africa [Italy] 1975 30(1): 104-106.* The National Library of Algeria undertook to tape-record detailed narrations of persons who took significant part in contemporary Algerian history. Begun in 1971, the enterprise was stimulated by the scarcity of written Algerian documentation for the colonial period and for the beginnings and development of the nationalist movement. Based on secondary studies and journals; 2 notes. L. R. Atkins

997. Bourgeot, André. CONTRIBUTION À L'ÉTUDE DE LA PARENTÉ TOUARÈGUE [A contribution to the study of Tuareg kinship]. *Rev. de l'Occident Musulman et de la Méditerranée [France] 1976 (21): 9-31.* Defines the kinship ideology and characterizes its lineal nature among the Imuhag Tuareg of the Ahaggar in Algeria. Suggests that matrilineal features were retained as patrilineal ones developed and argues that political power was linked to the *kasbab,* the institution which governed accession to the chieftaincy. Also examines several features of Tuareg social organization and emphasizes its strongly patrilineal nature and the influence of Islam. 2 tables, 9 diagrams, 28 notes. R. O. Khan

998. Burke, Edmund, III. FRANTZ FANON'S *THE WRETCHED OF THE EARTH.Daedalus 1976 105(1): 127-135.* While still a modern classic, Fanon's *Wretched of the Earth*(1961) now reveals more clearly its limitations as a work related to a particular period and set of circumstances. Fifteen years after its appearance, segments of the book appear shallow, shortsighted, and contradictory. Nevertheless, it also reveals the hopes and fears of that period expressed in an idealism which would be hard to duplicate today. Its two major myths, the liberating qualities of violence and the primacy of the peasant in liberation struggles, still have adherents. The book seems now to be a slice of that period when colonial peoples were filled with utopian visions. Primary and secondary sources; 10 notes. E. McCarthy

999. Chaliand, Gérard; Minces, J. and Henderson, George, transl. SOCIETY AND THE NATIONAL MOVEMENT. *Int. J. of Pol. 1977 7(3): 65-79.* Prior to the formation of the National Liberation Front (FLN), the principal Algerian nationalist groups were bourgeois in outlook and opposed to armed struggle. When the FLN, whose leaders had close peasant ties, initiated armed attacks in 1954, the peasants quickly gave it support. Leaders of other movements then joined the FLN and by 1956 transformed it into "a coalition dominated by a crushing petit bourgeois majority." At every stage in its development the Algerian revolutionary movement lacked a truly revolutionary avant-garde, never achieved a consistent doctrine, and achieved Algerian independence while manifesting contradictory aspirations. Translated from *L'Algérie Indépendante* (Paris, 1972). Secondary sources; 15 notes. R. E. Noble

1000. Cherkasov, P. P. KRAKH OAS [Collapse of the OAS]. *Voprosy Istorii [USSR] 1974 (9): 133-149.* The Organisation de l'Armée Secrète (OAS) was formed in April 1961 by ultra-rightist French underground groups to combat the Algerian Front de Libération Nationale. Arising during the Algerian war of 1954-62, the OAS defended the French colonial hold on Algeria and used terrorism to oppose General Charles de Gaulle's reversal of policy and his decision to grant independence to Algeria. The last important terrorist act of the OAS was the abortive assassination attempt on de Gaulle on 22 August 1962. 88 notes. N. Frenkley

1001. Cherkasov, P. P. PROVAL GENERAL'SKOGO PUTCHA V ALZHIRE (APREL' 1961 G.) [Failure of the generals' putsch in Algeria, April 1961]. *Voprosy Istorii [USSR] 1977 (9): 113-131.* An hour-by-hour account of the military and ultrarightist French settlers' insurrection which began in Algiers in the night of 21-22 April and was suppressed by French government troops in the night of 25-26 April 1961. The collapse of the putsch was due to a lack of support by the French civilian population, the large number of Communist cells in the army, and the moral isolation of the insurgents, whose goals were at odds with the national interests of France. Based mainly on published archives of the OAS (Organisation de l'Armée Secrète), trial protocols, and other primary sources; 105 notes. N. Frenkley

1002. Cherkasova, P. P. "NEDELIA BARRIKAD" V GORODE ALZHIRE [Barricades Week in Algiers]. *Voprosy Istorii [USSR] 1979 (1): 95-109.* Narrates the events surrounding the attempted military coup in Algiers from 12 January to 1 February 1960. The main issue dividing the ruling camp was acceptance of or opposition to the policies of Charles de Gaulle. The unresolved contradictions became more acute as it became clear that de Gaulle was moving toward granting self-determination to the indigenous population of Algeria. Barricades Week was the first act of a three-year political drama around this issue. Secondary sources; 92 notes. C. J. Read

1003. Cherniaev, V. OSVOBODITEL'NAIA VOINA ALZHIRSKO-GO NARODA [The Algerian people's war of liberation]. *Voenno-Istoricheskii Zhurnal [USSR] 1974 (11): 74-83.* Provides a history of Algeria from the outbreak of the War of Liberation in 1954 to its successful conclusion in 1962 and the establishment of the Republic.

1004. Chich, Pierre. LA PRESSE ÉCRITE EN ALGÉRIE [Written media in Algeria]. *Rev. Française d'Études Pol. Africaines [France] 1973 8(96): 49-63.* Describes the reorientation of existing colonial newspapers, or the emergence of new ones, in the trend for nationalization of the press in Algeria following the 1962 revolution and independence, 1963-73.

1005. Claudot, Hélène. ANALYZE SÉMANTIQUE DES TERMES DE PARENTÉ CHEZ LES TOUAREGS DE L'AHAGGAR [A semantic analysis of kinship terms among the Ahaggar Tuaregs]. *Rev. de l'Occident Musulman et de la Méditerranée [France] 1976 (21): 67-83.* Shows the internal logic of kinship terminology among the Tuareg and applies it to other institutional aspects of the society, especially the rules of inheritance, connubium, and conduct. Discusses the gap between kinship ideology and social practice, and the evolution of the vocabulary, particularly the recent borrowings of foreign words. 5 tables, 2 charts, diagram, 12 notes. R. O. Khan

1006. Collot, Claude. MOUFDI ZAKARIA, NATIONALISTE ALGÉRIEN ET CHANTRE DU MAGHREB ARABE [Moufdi Zakaria, Algerian nationalist and poet of the Arab Maghreb]. *Rev. de l'Occident Musulman et de la Méditerranée [France] 1978 (25): 139-141.* Provides an appreciation of Moufdi Zakaria who died in 1977, renowned as a major figure in the Algerian nationalist movement for both political and literary activities. In the period from the 1920's until independence in 1962 Zakaria was imprisoned and tortured several times, took part in the publishing of nationalist journals, served as an election candidate, and played an active role in various liberation organizations, including the Association of Moslem Students of North Africa, the Algerian People's Party, the Movement for the Triumph of Democratic Liberties, and the National Liberation Front. He also composed patriotic anthems including the hymn of the Algerian revolution in 1956. P. J. Taylorson

1007. Collot, Claude. TRADITION ET INNOVATION DANS L'ADMINISTRATION FRANÇAISE: L'EXPÉRIENCE ALGÉRIENNE DE 1955 À 1962 [Traditions and reforms in French administration: the experience in Algiers, 1955-62]. *R. Hist. de Droit Français Étranger [France] 1974 52(4): 628-657.* A precise critical history of the organization and methods of France's administration in Algeria, 1955-62. B. Altmann

1008. Cooke, James L. THE COLONIAL ORIGINS OF COLON AND MUSLIM NATIONALISM IN ALGERIA—1880-1920. *Indian Pol. Sci. Rev. [India] 1976 10(1): 19-36.* The historical process leading to the Algerian revolution of 1954-62 was set in motion during the period 1880-1920. The *colon* minority developed a siege mentality. It stifled political expression by the Algerian natives, expropriated sections of their land, and displayed both religious and cultural intolerance toward them. J. C. English

1009. Danziger, Raphael. ALGERIA AND THE PALESTINIAN ORGANIZATIONS. Ben-Dor, Gabriel, ed. *The Palestinians and the Middle East Conflict* (Ramat Gan, Israel: Turtledove Publ., 1978): 347-373. Considers Algerian influence on the Arab cause through the example of its revolutionary struggle and ideology and support for the Palestinians through the provision of guerrilla training and propaganda resources.

1010. DeChanterac, Arnaud. SOUVENIRS SUR L'ALGÉRIE ET L'O.A.S. (1957-1962) [Remembrances of Algeria and the OAS, 1957-62]. *Écrits de Paris [France] 1977 (370): 46-59.* Recounts a number of events crucial to the outcome of the Algerian War of the late 1950's and early 1960's and the important though ultimately futile role of the Secret Army Organization (OAS) on behalf of elements loyal to France.

1011. Déjeux, Jean. LE DEBAT CULTUREL EN ALGERIE (1979-1982) [The cultural debate in Algeria, 1979-82]. *Afrique et l'Asie Modernes [France] 1982 (2): 3-22.* Discusses the debate demanded by the 4th Congress of the Front de Liberation Nationale (FLN) to determine the place of the Berber language and culture in Algeria, and examines the results of several meetings discussing the total recognition of Berber culture and Berber as the second national language.

1012. Dejeux, Jean. LES RENCONTRES DE SIDI MADANI (ALGÉRIE) (JANVIER-FÉVRIER-MARS 1948) [The Sidi Madani meetings, Algeria, January, February, March 1948]. *Rev. de l'Occident Musulman et de la Méditerranée [France] 1975 (20): 165-174.* Describes a project by the French Service des Mouvements de Jeunesse to bring together the foremost French and Algerian intellectuals and artists at a hotel 37 miles south of Algiers. Lectures and discussions were held on various aspects of literature and the arts, including Algerian literature and Franco-Islamic relations. The residents were Albert Camus, Jean Sénac, Jean Cayrol, Mohammed Zerrouki, E. de Kermadec, Henri Calet, Louis Parrot, Jean Tortel, Pierre Minet, Louis Guilloux, Michel Leiris, Brice Parain, Francis Ponge, Marcel Damboise, Abbé Morel, and Nabahni Kouriba. 11 notes, appendix. R. O. Khan

1013. Dejeux, Jean. UN BANDIT D'HONNEUR DANS L'AURÈS, DE 1917 À 1921 [An honorable bandit in the Aurès, 1917-21]. *Rev. de l'Occident Musulman et de la Méditerranée [France] 1978 (26): 35-54.* Outlines the history of bandit heroes in Algeria during the 19th century and focuses on Messaoud Ben Zelmat who achieved renown as a Robin Hood figure in the Aurès region, 1917-21. With his gang he held out against the gendarmes and soldiers sent to capture him. After his death he was celebrated in song as a knightly hero, stalwart in his fight against authority and associated with the struggle against colonialism. 64 notes. P. J. Taylorson

1014. Dominique, Pierre. LES ÉVENEMENTS DE SÉTIF EN MAI 1945 [The Sétif incident, May 1945]. *Écrits de Paris [France] 1973 (323): 46-51.* Recounts events surrounding the insurrection in Sétif, Algeria in May 1945. Much responsibility for the slaughter of Frenchmen belongs to Charles de Gaulle.

1015. Etienne, Bruno. THE EUROPEANS OF ALGERIA. *Tarikh [Nigeria] 1979 6(2): 63-78.* Discusses the colonization of Algeria by France and the changing geographical patterns of settlement, employment, legal status, landownership, industrial control, and political factors affecting the Europeans from 1830 to their departure by 1962.

1016. Fiedler, Milan. THE AGRARIAN REFORM IN ALGERIA. *Archív Orientání [Czechoslovakia] 1976 44(2): 126-148.* Algerian agricultural reform since 1960 made use of traditional aspects of agrarian society as well as socialist techniques.

1017. Fitte, Albert. LE COMBATTANT ALGÉRIEN DE LA GUERRE D'INDÉPENDANCE D'APRÈS *EL MOUDJAHID* [The Algerian soldier of the war of independence according to *El Moudjahid]. Actes du 96ᵉ Congrès National des Sociétés Savantes* (Paris: Bibliothéque Nationale, 1976): 513-524. Examines the qualities and objectives of the Algerian fighting man of the Algerian war of independence, 1954-62 as presented in the pages of *El Moudjahid,* the journal of the Algerian National Liberation Front (FLN) of which all issues have not survived. The Algerian soldier had military, psychological, and political goals. The military successes of the National Liberation Army (ALN) were few, and *El Moudjahid* had to resort to wild exaggerations to hide ALN failures. But on the psychological and political plane, *El Moudjahid* formed part of the propaganda apparatus with which the Algerian nationalists won their independence. 23 notes. J. C. Billigmeier

1018. Forsythe, Dennis. FRANTZ FANON—THE MARX OF THE THIRD WORLD. *Phylon 1973 34(2): 160-170.*

1019. Gadant, Monique. LES FEMMES, LA FAMILLE ET LA NATIONALITÉ ALGÉRIENNE [Women, family, and Algerian nationality]. *Mediterranean Peoples [France] 1981 (15): 25-56.* Discusses the position of women in Algerian society since independence in 1962. Women's status remains tied to religious values, which consign them to the private sphere of the family. The authorities appeal to Islamic tenets and family solidarity in order to halt Algerian progress toward democracy.

1020. Gadant-Benzine, Monique. MOULOUD FERAOUN, UN ALGÉRIEN AMBIGU... ? [Mouloud Feraoun, an obscure Algerian?]. *Peuples Méditerranéens [France] 1978 4: 3-20.* The nationalist ideology in Algeria defines the nation as a monolithic block, perfectly homogeneous. It denies all social, political, or cultural differences. The nation, preexisting to 130 years of colonial domination (1830-1954) was secured by armed struggle and by the need to restore Arabo-Islamic values. Reality does not correspond to the myth which is meant to express it. A study of the *Journal* that Mouloud Feraoun wrote in secret, 1955-62, shows that national feeling in acculturated elites expressed itself as a double belonging, as a cleavage of the personality forced to choose between the culture and the value system taught in French schools and the culture and the value system inherited from the tribe, the family, and the nation. Mouloud Feraoun expressed through his own situation the feeling of the majority of Maghrebian intellectuals, whether or not engaged in political activities. Humanist and nonviolent, he was killed by members of the OAS on 15 March 1962 in Algiers. J/S

1021. Gast, Marceau. LES KEL RELA: HISTORIQUE ET ESSAI D'ANALYSE DU GROUPE DE COMMANDEMENT DES KEL AHAGGAR [The Kel Rela: historical outline and an attempt to analyze the dominant group of the Kel Ahaggar]. *Rev. de l'Occident Musulman et de la Méditerranée [France] 1976 (21): 47-65.* Analyzes the social organization, history, and matrimonial alliances of the Kel Rela, as presented by their genealogy since the founding ancestor of the matrilineage. Defines their principal characteristics through their system of kinship and alliance, which terminated with Algerian independence. Traces the system's evolution from the expulsion of the Imenânes, a foreign religious line of patrilinear descent, and notes the tendency to absorb offspring of patrilineal as well as matrilineal marriages with outsiders. Examines the role of the supreme chief, or *amenūhal,* the system of distributing economic resources, and the manipulation of the group's political and economic cohesion. Map, 2 tables, 5 diagrams, 7 notes, biblio. R. O. Khan

1022. Gellner, Ernest. THE UNKNOWN APOLLO OF BISKRA: THE SOCIAL BASE OF ALGERIAN PURITANISM. *Government and Opposition [Great Britain] 1974 9(3): 277-310.* Discusses the "near-socialism" of present-day Algeria, particularly exploring the relationship between the Algerian political regime and the puritanical Muslim faith which is the official religion.

1023. Gendzier, Irene L. PSYCHOLOGY AND COLONIALISM: SOME OBSERVATIONS. *Middle East J. 1976 30(4): 501-515.* Discusses Frantz Fanon's *A Dying Colonialism,* which singled out the impact of decolonization on the family, on relations between men and women in the family, and on medicine. The book is a eulogy of Algeria in revolt. Fanon attacked European doctors who withheld medical help for political reasons and contended that the voice of the radio is that of the oppressor. 28 notes. E. P. Stickney

1024. Gil Benumeya, Rodolfo. ARGELIA Y SUS SIGNIFICADOS VEINTE AÑOS DESPUÉS [Algeria and its importance 20 years after]. *Rev. de Política Int. [Spain] 1974 (136): 139-147.* Discusses developments in Algeria, 1954-74, pointing to the opportunities for close ties between that country and Spain.

1025. Gourmen, P. LES BATAILLONS DU TRAIN EN ALGÉRIE [Battalions of the Army Service Corps in Algeria]. *Rev. Hist. des Armées [France] 1978 5(3): 173-184.* After 1954, the underequipped

French Army Service Corps in Algeria were gradually enlarged and reequipped to serve additional French forces being sent from mainland. The author describes assistance to the civil population until August 1962, when the units were recalled to France. Based on official records, map, 5 illus., 7 notes. G. E. Pergl

1026. Groot, Cor de. PANORAMA VAN DE ALGERIJNSE OORLOG [Panorama of the Algerian war]. *Tijdschrift voor Geschiedenis [Netherlands] 1978 91(3): 518-522.* Review of Alistair Horne's *A Savage War of Peace: Algeria 1954-1962* (London, 1977), based mainly on published materials and interviews with various participants. The French settlers in Algeria, the *pieds noirs,* never wanted a French Algeria but an Algeria dominated by them and protected by France. French politicians failed to understand the problem while General de Gaulle's initial objectives were obscure and might have prolonged the war. European economic prosperity of the 1960's was more responsible for France's reemergence than the exit from Algeria. G. D. Homan

1027. Guellal, Cherif. THE ECONOMY: ALGERIA'S OIL STRATEGY. *Africa Report 1975 20(5): 41-44.* Discusses the development of the Algerian oil industry during 1965-75 and the political and economic leverage President Houari Boumedienne hopes to gain in conducting foreign policy with oil-consuming countries.

1028. Hadjeres, Sadeq. FROM LIBERATION FRONT TO CONSTRUCTION FRONT. *World Marxist R. [Canada] 1975 18(1): 127-138.* Discusses the anti-imperialist efforts of Algeria since 1954. S

1029. Hanley, David. FRANTZ FANON: REVOLUTIONARY NATIONALIST? *Pol. Studies [Great Britain] 1976 24(2): 120-131.* Examines Frantz Fanon as a modern political philosopher, tracing his preoccupation with the theory and idea of nation which presupposed his idea of nationalist doctrine, and the consequences this had for his political theory as a whole, 1950's-60's.

1030. Hansen, Emmanuel. FREEDOM AND REVOLUTION IN THE THOUGHT OF FRANTZ FANON. *Pan-African J. [Kenya] 1977 10(1): 1-22.* Summarizes the life of Frantz Fanon (1925-61) and examines the concepts of freedom and revolution in his thought. Fanon's philosophy was shaped by his observation of living conditions in Martinique, France, and Algeria, the intellectual currents of Caribbean protest literature, Sartrean existentialism, and Marxism. Fanon's call for revolution was intended as a means to achieve freedom. 49 notes. F. P. Tudor

1031. Harbi, Mohammed. ALGERIAN NATIONALISM AND BERBER IDENTITY. *Peuples Mediterranéens-Mediterranean Peoples [France] 1980 (11): 31-37.* Argues that Algerian nationalism, in reaction to French colonialism, postulated the existence of an Arabo-Islamic Algeria and that this has been incapable of accepting the Berbers, resulting in conflict since 1942.

1032. Heggoy, Alf A. THE EVOLUTION OF ALGERIAN WOMEN. *African Studies Rev. 1974 17(2): 449-456.* A research note on the small change in the role of women in Algerian society from the colonial era to the present. Biblio. R. T. Brown

1033. Heggoy, Alf Andrew. ALGERIAN WOMEN AND THE RIGHT TO VOTE: SOME COLONIAL ANOMALIES. *Muslim World 1974 64(3): 228-235.* Describes the plight of Algerian women during the French colonial period and during the first few years of independence. Although their husbands were granted the franchise in 1919, women were not allowed to vote until 1958. The French colonials had sought to maintain the existing religious limitations on women. The Algerian women were nonpersons not only politically, but legally and socially as well. It was not until the French reforms of the 1950's that women gained some rights. These gains were continued after Algeria became independent in 1962, because the nationalists, for a variety of reasons, accepted woman suffrage. Secondary French works; 9 notes. P. J. Mattar

1034. Heggoy, Alf Andrew. ARAB EDUCATION IN COLONIAL ALGERIA. *J. of African Studies 1975 2(2): 149-160.* An analysis of the stuggle between French dominated education, with its emphasis on French language and culture, and Islamic and national culture. The Algerians saw retention of the Arabic language as a significant key to the perpetuation of their culture. Not until 1947, when it was too late, did the French accept Arabic as the official language and incorporate it into the curriculum at every level of the public school system. The French wanted Algeria to be France, but were without the means to bring this about. The Algerian elites insisted on being themselves in Islamic and Arabic terms. By the time of the revolution it was too late for last minute changes and reforms to be effective. 3 notes. R. V. Ritter

1035. Heggoy, Alf Andrew. DEVELOPMENT OR CONTROL: FRENCH POLICIES AND ELITIST REACTIONS IN COLONIAL AND REVOLUTIONARY ALGERIA. *J. of African Studies 1978-79 5(4): 427-443.* A critique of the typology of Algerian elites presented by William B. Quandt in his *Revolution in Political Leadership: Algeria, 1954-1968.* Quandt failed to account for nonpolitical elites, including Islamic leaders and novelists, who nonetheless contributed to the Algerian revolution. Traces the creation of Moslem elites in French Algeria. The French failed to train an Algerian elite by modernizing the state, economy, and educational system in favor of Moslem Algerians. A revolutionary elite had come to oppose them by 1954, and French efforts after this date to create a friendly elite came too late to succeed. Primary documents and secondary sources; 43 notes. L. W. Truschel

1036. Heggoy, Alf Andrew and Zingg, Paul J. FRENCH EDUCATION IN REVOLUTIONARY NORTH AFRICA. *Int. J. of Middle East Studies [Great Britain] 1976 7(4): 571-578.* The French educational system, with its emphasis on the scientific method and affection for the French language and culture, collided with Muslim goals in Algeria which sought the cultivation of mental agility and the perpetuation of religious tradition. Algerian resistance centered on a determined refusal to become patriotic and cultured Frenchmen. Therefore meaningful educational reform could not be achieved within the colonial context. Primary and secondary sources; 23 notes. R. B. Orr

1037. Horne, Alastair. THE SAVAGE WAR. *Encounter [Great Britain] 1977 49(5): 76-84.* The author discusses the research for his *A Savage War of Peace: Algeria, 1954-62* (London: Macmillan, 1977).

1038. Karim, Ahmed. AGRARIAN CHANGES IN ALGERIA. *World Marxist R. [Canada] 1973 16(1): 89-95.* The Algerian government's agrarian reforms intended to help the people are being opposed by conservative large landholders and the wealthy bourgeoisie. S

1039. Kee, Robert J. ALGIERS—1957: AN APPROACH TO URBAN COUNTERINSURGENCY. *Military Rev. 1974 54(4): 73-84.* While the draconian tactics of Brigadier General Jacques Massu won the battle of Algiers for France, the monetary, political, and moral costs were too high.

1040. Keenan, Jeremy H. SOME THEORETICAL CONSIDERATIONS OF THE TEMAZLAYT RELATIONSHIP. *Rev. de l'Occident Musulman et de la Méditerranée [France] 1976 (21): 33-46.* Defines the contract of protection between the Tuareg warrior nobility, Ihaggaren, and vassals, Imrad, of the Kel Ulli region. The structure of this contract, inherited through matrilinear transmission and governing the economic infrastructure of both groups, is analyzed to reveal its effect on politics and economics. This contract remains the principal unit of authority in this society with its rigorous class divisions. However, a new kind of social ethic has resulted from the process of modernization in the Ahaggar area since 1965. 12 notes, biblio. R. O. Khan

1041. Kielstra, Nico. WAS THE ALGERIAN REVOLUTION A PEASANT WAR? *Peasant Studies 1978 7(3): 172-186.* Participants in the Algerian revolution of the 1950's-1960's were members of a proletariat created by French colonization, beginning in the 1800's, with urban aims and ambitions, rather than peasants.

1042. Klein, Jean. UN ÉPISODE DE LA DÉCOLONISATION: LA GUERRE D'ALGÉRIE (1954-1962) [An episode in decolonization: the Algerian War, 1954-62]. *Francia [France] 1978 6: 640-645.* Reviews Harmut Elsenhans's *Frankreichs Algerienkrieg 1954-1962. Entkolonisierung einer kapitalistischen Metropole. Zum Zusammenbruch der Kolonialreiche* (1974), a sociologist's presentation using neo-Marxist methods, of the 1954 Algerian insurrection against France. 2 notes. G. P. Cleyet

1043. Knauss, Peter. ALGERIA'S "AGRARIAN REVOLUTION": PEASANT CONTROL OR CONTROL OF PEASANTS? *African Studies Rev. 1977 20(3): 65-78.* Success of the Algerian political revolution in 1962 simply brought a change of masters for the peasants. Land control continues in the hands of an elite, and agricultural productivity continues to fall while capital investment in rural areas also declines. Table, chart, 14 notes, biblio. R. T. Brown

1044. Koerner, Francis. LES RÉPERCUSSIONS DE LA GUERRE D'ESPAGNE EN ORANIE (1936-1939) [The effects of the Spanish civil war upon Oran, 1936-39]. *Rev. d'Hist. Moderne et Contemporaine [France] 1975 22(3): 476-487.* The Spanish civil war polarized the population of Oran. Political parties campaigned on their positions favoring or opposing General Francisco Franco (1892-1975). Military supplies were shipped in great quantities from the port of Oran to the Spanish Republicans, and both sides recruited volunteers to fight in Spain. The extreme Right organized militant patriots, royalists, colonialists, fascists, and anti-Semites in order to mobilize support for the Franco regime, and Oran became more deeply involved in the Spanish war than any other part of France or of Algeria. Primary and secondary sources; 61 notes. J. S. Gassner

1045. Koerner, Francis. L'EXTRÊME DROITE EN ORANIE (1936-1940) [The extreme right in Oran, 1936-40]. *Rev. d'Hist. Moderne et Contemporaine [France] 1973 20(4): 568-594.* In the years prior to World War II, public opinion in Oran became more favorable to fascism. Public opinion is traced in newspapers, campaign literature, political coalitions, and election results. Primary and secondary sources; 103 notes. S. R. Smith

1046. Kukharev, A. N. SREDNIE GORODSKIE SLOI V SOTSIAL'NO-KLASSOVOI STRUKTURE ALZHIRA [Middle urban strata in the social and class structure of Algeria]. *Narody Azii i Afriki [USSR] 1981 (3): 75-86.* With the destruction of the structure of colonial society, the formation of a national state, and socioeconomic transformations accompanied by migration and shifts in village and city populations, the Algerian middle strata have undergone significant changes. The author discusses the criteria for discussing these strata. 2 tables, 46 notes. S. J. Talalay

1047. Landa, R. G. IZUCHENIE ALZHIRSKOI REVOLIUTSII V SSHA [The study of the Algerian Revolution in the United States]. *Narody Azii Afriki [USSR] 1975 (4): 175-187.* Studies US historiography on the Algerian revolution 1954-62, and suggests that although the Americans lacked the extensive first-hand knowledge available to the French, growing rivalry for influence in North Africa led to an improvement in American information.

1048. Landa, Robert Grigor'ievich. KHUARI BUMED'IEN: STANOVLENIE REVOLIUTSIONERA [Houari Boumédienne: the making of a revolutionary]. *Narody Azii i Afriki [USSR] 1981 (1): 117-129.* Biography of Algerian chief of state Boumédienne (1927-78) concentrating on the period 1946-62. Stresses the hero's character of quietude (mistaken by some for coldbloodedness) and steadfastness in face of tribulations. He had "the steel nerves and patience of the peasant" and was "modest but effective." His mistrust of everyone is noted. E. S. Kirby

1049. Landau, Jacob M. SOME SOVIET WORKS ON ALGERIA. *Middle Eastern Studies [Great Britain] 1981 17(3): 408-412.* Reviews a selection of the large number of Soviet books on Algeria covering attacks on French colonial policy in Algeria, the social development of Algeria after independence, and contemporary Algerian literature translated from the French. In some cases cited works are by non-Russian and non-Algerian authors. F. A. Clements

1050. Lee, Robert D. AUTONOMY AND DEPENDENCE IN FRENCH ALGERIA: FOUR APPROACHES TO A CASE STUDY. *Rev. de l'Occident Musulman et de la Méditerranée [France] 1977 (24): 141-167.* Attempts to discover whether Algerian policy was made in Paris or Algiers during the colonial period using the decisions of French ministers Morinaud and Régnier, 1934-35. Previous studies have failed to assess the real degree of political autonomy in the Algerian *départements.* 80 notes. M. Smith

1051. Leveau, Philippe. LE CHÉNOUA: DE LA COLONISATION AU VILLAGE DE REGROUPEMENT [Chénoua: from colonization to resettlement village]. *Rev. de l'Occident Musulman et de la Méditerranée [France] 1975 (19): 101-112.* Describes this mountainous region of Algeria and traces its history from the colonial period onward. The effect on the local people of the appropriation of much of the better land for extensive colonial properties is examined, together with the government's regrouping of the population of the area after independence. The author considers how the exploitation of the resources of the area continued but with the establishment of a communal infrastructure and how the chenouis were resettled on the plains. Based on documents from the Overseas Archives at Aix-en-Provence; 3 fig., 32 notes. R. O. Khan

1052. Lever, Évelyne. L'OAS ET LES PIEDS-NOIRS [The OAS and the *pieds noirs].Histoire [France] 1982 (43): 10-23.* A relation, with illustrations, a chronological table, and a short bibliography, of the political and military events that after 1954 led to Algeria's independence from France in July 1961, centering on the rebellion of the *pied noirs*(Algerian-born descendants of French settlers), and the terrorist actions of the Secret Army Organization (OAS).

1053. Lica, Guido. ALGERIA: NASCITA DI UNA NAZIONE [Algeria: birth of a nation]. *Riv. di Studi Politici Int. [Italy] 1973 40(1): 23-68.* Discusses French rule in Algeria, and the developments which followed independence, 1962-71.

1054. Madani, Ali. EXPÉRIENCE ALGÉRIENNE D'ENSEIGNEMENT MASSIF DE L'ARABE PAR LA RADIO [The Algerian experiment in mass teaching of Arabic by radio]. *Afrique et l'Asie Modernes [France] 1978 (4): 41-43.*

1055. Marseille, Jacques. LE COMMERCE DE L'ALGÉRIE DE 1924 À 1938: INTERPRÉTATION DES TERMES DE L'ÉCHANGE [Algeria's trade, 1924-38: interpretation of the terms of exchange]. *Rev. Française d'Hist. d'Outre-Mer [France] 1976 63(3-4): 529-537.* The Great Depression did not touch Algeria very deeply; one can speak there of a recession rather than of a depression. The terms of trade were highly favorable to Algeria, which was integrated almost fully into the metropolitan market and gave a much-needed stability in the face of the wild fluctuations in the world market during the 1930's. Products of France sold in Algeria were marketed by premonopolistic groups operating according to free market processes, so that the sales of these products remained constant while their prices fell by 50%. 10 notes. J. C. Billigmeier

1056. Miette, Roland. L'AGRICULTURE DANS LE DÉVELOPPEMENT ALGÉRIEN [Agriculture in the development of Algeria]. *Afrique et L'Asie [France] 1975 (104): 22-41.* The government of Algeria has instituted a massive industrial development program, but agriculture has not expanded at the same pace and cannot keep up with the growing population. In order to close this gap, the government is extending arable areas by constructing new irrigation systems, using greater amounts of fertilizers, and promoting the production of high-food-value commodities such as livestock and grain. Nevertheless, Algeria will continue to import more and more food, balancing its international payments by means of the export of manufactured goods. Based on government statistics; 4 tables. J. S. Gassner

1057. Miette, Roland. L'AUTOGESTION AGRICOLE EN ALGÉRIE [Self-management in Algerian agriculture]. *Afrique et L'Asie [France] 1974 (103): 19-31.* After independence, the new Algerian government was faced with a complex problem concerning land tenure. French colonial laws never took into consideration the traditional arrangements based on Muslim customs by which the greatest part of the land had been held communally by tribes or by families. After the departure of the French settlers, it was impossible to restore the land to its previous tenants. A collective farming system was therefore proposed. At first, a centralized administration headed by a government agency was established, but it failed because it was too bureaucratic and not adapted to natural and local conditions. Self-management was then instituted, and this may be the first phase of extensive agrarian reform, aimed at both the economic improvement of agriculture and the restructuring of rural society. The new program is offered as a true revolution for Algeria. J. S. Gassner

1058. Miette, Roland. LE PROBLÈME DE LA STEPPE EN ALGÉRIE [The problem of the Algerian steppe]. *Afrique et L'Asie [France] 1974 (100): 52-61.* The high plain of Algeria, with an area of about 12 million hectares, supports some eight million sheep in a good year. The problem of its optimum utilization has evoked two solutions. The steppe can be used either for the cultivation of cereal crops or exclusively for sheepraising and animals incidental to that activity, such as goats and donkeys. Because of the water shortage and the poor quality of the soil, the steppe could produce only about 4.5 million quintals of grain, which compares poorly with the steppe's potential capability of supporting 20 million sheep by proper management of the grazing lands, which the experience with grazing cooperatives has shown is possible.
J. S. Gassner

1059. Miette, Roland. LE SYSTÈME POLITIQUE ALGÉRIEN [The Algerian political system]. *Afrique et l'Asie Modernes [France] 1977 (3): 25-41.* Although political opposition has been restricted, Algeria's National Liberation Front has maintained many essential liberties while insuring political stability and social peace since 1962.

1060. Miette, Roland. LES COOPERATIVES POLYVALENTES EN ALGERIE [Multipurpose cooperatives in Algeria]. *Afrique et l'Asie [France] 1974 (102): 31-39.* The traditional Islamic system of agricultural land tenure has resulted in the division of the land into family farms too small for modern techniques. In order to modernize agriculture while simultaneously preserving the traditional family farm, the Algerian government in 1972 organized a national system of multiservice farm cooperatives based on the communes, with two objectives, agricultural development and integration of the peasantry into the national political party and the national system of public administration. Certain groups are obliged by law to join the cooperatives, while others, including the small farmers, are theoretically free to join or not. The government, however, expects all of them to enter the cooperatives, which will thus eventually provide the framework of all rural life in Algeria.
J. S. Gassner

1061. Miette, Roland. LES COOPÉRATIVES PASTORALES EN ALGÉRIE [Grazing cooperatives in Algeria]. *Afrique et l'Asie [France] 1974 (101): 35-40.* The agrarian revolution in Algeria seeks not only land reform but also the development of the rural economy through new institutions and the national integration of peasants and herders. These aims are being achieved for the nomadic shepherds of the high plains and the northern Sahara through the establishment of municipal communes and grazing cooperatives. There are 26 cooperatives already in existence and 30 more being organized. The system is expected to increase livestock production by at least 50 percent, to improve grazing land, and to reduce soil erosion.
J. S. Gassner

1062. Miette, Roland. RÉALITÉ ALGÉRIENNE [The Algerian reality]. *Afrique et l'Asie Modernes [France] 1977 (2): 52-56.* Discusses Algeria's economic plan of 1970 concerning the problems of rural exodus, energy, agricultural underproductivity, and industrialization.

1063. Miller, Mark J. RELUCTANT PARTNERSHIP: FOREIGN WORKERS IN FRANCO-ALGERIAN RELATIONS, 1962-1979. *J. of Int. Affairs 1979 33(2): 219-237.* Surveys the situation of Algerian workers in France, noting the many problems that their presence has caused both France and Algeria (especially during the Algerian struggle for independence, 1954-62) and calling attention to the parallels between Franco-Algerian relations and current concerns of Mexico and the United States.

1064. Mortimer, Robert. ALGERIA'S NEW SULTAN. *Current Hist. 1981 80(470): 418-421, 433-434.* On the whole, Algerian foreign policy has not changed significantly under President Bendjedid Chadli. Since his takeover in February, 1979, the structure of power—the government, the army, and the party—has not been altered in the transition to the post-Boumédienne era.

1065. Mortimer, Robert A. ALGERIA AND THE POLICIES OF INTERNATIONAL ECONOMIC REFORM. *Orbis 1977 21(3): 671-700.* Outlines the ideology and activities which brought about Algeria's rise to power among developing nations, 1962-76, and analyzes the impact which collective power wielded by developing nations has on international economic reform.

1066. Nagy, László. AZ ANTIIMPERIALISTA EGYSÉGFRONT ALGÉRIÁBAN (1935-1939) [United anti-imperialist front in Algeria, 1935-39]. *Párttörténeti Közlemények [Hungary] 1980 26(4): 109-131.* Independence from France was an issue not readily grasped by the newly established Communist Party in interwar Algeria, 80% of whose members were of European origin and showed little interest in problems of anticolonialism but were concerned only with social progress. Only after 1942 did the Algerian Communist Party learn from its past mistakes and move in the appropriate direction. 55 notes. T. Kuner

1067. Nagy, László J. GAZDASÁG ÉS TÁRSADALOM A GYARMATI ALGÉRIÁBAN [Economy and society in colonial Algeria]. *Századok [Hungary] 1982 116(2): 301-322.* European settlers, especially in the years 1870 and 1936, came to dominate the Algerian economy, based in part on the grant of land to them. Social classes did not develop properly among the Algerians, and the creation of an autonomous economy after independence was a serious challenge. Based on primary and secondary documents; 5 tables, 67 notes. R. Hetzron

1068. Nemoz, Emile. TÉMOIGNAGE SUR L'ALGÉRIE [Evidence on Algeria]. *Écrits de Paris [France] 1976 (356): 64-71.* Recounts the history of Algeria, emphasizing the civilizing effects of French colonialism over the past two centuries and expressing concern for its economic and political future.

1069. Nouschi, André. POUVOIR ET POLITIQUE EN ALGÉRIE [Power and politics in Algeria]. *Ann.: Écon., Soc., Civilisations [France] 1979 34(3): 590-598.* Reviews and comments on recent books about Algeria since 1830: J.-C. Vatin's *L'Algérie Politique: Histoire et Société*(Paris, 1974); J. Leca and J.-C. Vatin's *L'Algérie Politique: Institutions et Régime* (Paris, 1975); and B. Etienne's *L'Algérie, Culture et Révolution* (Paris, 1977). These basic works written by political scientists focus on politics and institutions and may be helpful to historians. Vatin deals with the colonial period and Etienne with Algeria since independence in 1962. Secondary sources; 7 notes.
G. P. Cleyet

1070. Nursey-Bray, Paul. RACE AND NATION: IDEOLOGY IN THE THOUGHT OF FRANTZ FANON. *J. of Modern African Studies [Great Britain] 1980 18(1): 135-142.* Discusses Frantz Fanon's ideology of race and national culture in terms of Third World revolutionary humanism. Racism in the colonial context is an ideology that justifies economic exploitation, oppression, domination, and the debasement of national culture. The colonial power instigates class antagonism in order to obfuscate national liberation ideals. In spite of the principle of divide and rule, under colonialism there is a rise in class solidarity rather than class struggle. Secondary sources; 33 notes.
A. Sbacchi

1071. Osterkamp, Rigmar. L'ALGERIE ENTRE LE PLAN ET LE MARCHE: POINTS DE VUE RECENTS SUR LA POLITIQUE ECONOMIQUE DE L'ALGERIE [Algeria between the plan and the marketplace: recent viewpoints on Algeria's economy]. *Can. J. of African Studies [Canada] 1982 16(1): 27-42.* Algeria's economic and social development in the last decade has been disappointing. This is the conclusion of the post-1979 public debate on Algerian economic and developmental policy. One main line of thought believes that the Algerian central planning mechanisms have been inefficient and proposes a decentralization of economic decisionmaking. A second school is convinced that market prices as allocative devices have not been used rationally. Both views are represented in the new Five-Year Development Plan, 1980-84. J/S

1072. Pervillé, Guy. GUERRE ÉTRANGÈRE ET GUERRE CIVILE EN ALGÉRIE 1954-1962 [Foreign war and civil war in Algeria, 1954-62]. *Relations Int. [France] 1978 (14): 171-196.* Contrasts the confusion of French objectives in the Algerian war with the clarity of the Algerian liberation movement's aims, which aided in the latter's victory. The French wavered between the contradictory goals of maintaining internal order during a war of foreign aggression, and Charles de Gaulle's concept of a civil war which prepared the defeated for independence. R. Stromberg

1073. Pervillé, Guy. LE SENTIMENT NATIONAL DES ÉTUDIANTS ALGÉRIENS DE CULTURE FRANÇAISE DE 1912 À 1962

[The national consciousness of the Algerian students of French culture, 1912-62]. *Relations Int. [France] 1974 (2): 233-259.* Defines the history of the Algerian students of French education from 1912 to Algerian independence (1962), as a French moral conquest paralleling the military conquest and ending in a rally to the Algerian nationalist movement. In 1919, the awakening of Islam put French preponderance in question and initiated a tension in Algerian students' minds. From 1943 on the nationalist ideology created a synthesis which integrated French cultural contributions into an Arabic Islamic personality. 51 notes. G. P. Cleyet

1074. Petrosov, Iu. A. VAZHNYI IDEOLOGICHESKII DOKUMENT ALZHIRSKOI REVOLIUTSIONNOI DEMOKRATII [An important ideological document in Algerian revolutionary democracy]. *Narody Azii i Afriki [USSR] 1977 (5): 153-161.* Discusses the historical and ideological background to the Algerian national charter, promulgated in 1976, which exemplifies those socialist concepts which developed relatively late in the Algerian revolution.

1075. Pozdorovkina, E. ALZHIR: NARODNOE PROSVESHCHENIE I PODGOTOVKA KADROV [Algeria: public education and the training of cadres]. *Aziia i Afrika Segodnia [USSR] 1979 (6): 25-28.* Highlights cultural construction in the developing countries. Dwells on the efforts and successes of the Algerian people in the abolition of the cultural backwardness inherited from the colonial regime. J

1076. Prochaska, David. LA SÉGRÉGATION RESIDENTIELLE EN SOCIETÉ COLONIALE: LE CAS DE BÔNE (ALGÉRIE) 1872-1954 [Residential segregation in colonial society: the case of Bône, Algeria, 1872-1954]. *Cahiers d'Hist. [France] 1980 25(2): 148-176.* A pervasive and thoroughgoing residential segregation is one of the chief characteristics of the colonial city. In the port city of Bône (now Annaba) in Algeria, an increasing residential segregation among the French, Muslims, Algerians, Jews, Italians, and Maltese can be traced. A quantitative study using the index of dissimilarity shows that segregation of Europeans from Muslims and Jews rose rapidly to 1911 and remained at a high level through 1954. Italians and Maltese were also segregated from the French. The results were counter to the French intention of increasing European assimilation of and association with Muslims. Based on the municipal archives of Annaba; map, 9 tables, 26 notes. R. Howell

1077. Ralston, Richard David. FANON AND HIS CRITICS: THE NEW BATTLE OF ALGIERS. *Cultures et Développement [Belgium] 1976 8(3): 463-493.* Examines the controversy surrounding the influence of Frantz Fanon's thought on, and his role in, Algerian events during the 1950's and his relevance today.

1078. Ray, Vanita. HOUARI BOUMEDIENNE: A TRIBUTE. *Africa Q. [India] 1979 18(2-3): 71-74.* Summarizes and assesses the political career of Algeria's President Houari Boumédienne (1927-78), with comments on Algerian problems highlighted by his death.

1079. Rémond, René. LE 13 MAI 1958: LA RÉPUBLIQUE EST MORTE, VIVE LA RÉPUBLIQUE! [13 May 1958: the Republic is dead, long live the Republic!]. *Histoire [France] 1978 (1): 26-34.* Feeling ran high in Algiers on 13 May 1958. The day began with a demonstration, continued with a riot, and ended with incipient secession which marked the advent of the Fifth Republic and the comeback of Charles de Gaulle. J

1080. Rioux, Albert. LA LEÇON DE L'ALGÉRIE [The lesson of Algeria]. *Action Natl. [Canada] 1976 65(6): 369-383.* For 3,000 years, Algeria has been subjected to waves of invaders. In 1830, France colonized the territory. The nation was saved from religious, ideological, and cultural assimilation by two factors: the Arabic language and Islam. With independence, Algeria retained a strong economic infrastructure developed by the French, but lost scientists and technologists. Since the coup d'etat of Houari Boumédienne (19 June 1965), Algeria has proceeded with a triple revolution: industrial, agricultural, and cultural. Of particular concern are land redistribution and modernization of rural living conditions, development of widespread technical education, assumption of a major role in international affairs, and attraction of investment capital from oil-producing states. A. W. Novitsky

1081. Rondat, Pierre. QUELQUES RÉFLEXIONS SUR L'EFFORT ALGÉRIEN [Some reflections on the Algerian effort]. *Défense Natl. [France] 1978 34(6): 85-98.* Analyzes the social, economic, and political structure of Algeria since 1962, assessing in particular the impact of legislation since 1971 (referring mainly to the agrarian revolution) on the objective of a true socialist democracy.

1082. Rondot, Pierre. L'ÉQUILIBRE POLITIQUE INTERNE DE L'ALGÉRIE [The internal political equilibrium of Algeria]. *Défense Natl. [France] 1980 36(5): 63-76.* A report on the political situation in Algeria in 1979-80 following the death of President Houari Boumédienne.

1083. Sanson, Henri. HOUARI BOUMEDIÈNE: ISLAM ET PERSONNALITÉ [Houari Boumedienne: Islam and personality]. *Afrique et l'Asie Modernes [France] 1979 (2): 56-65.* Studies the life of the late Algerian president, Houari Boumedienne, centering on his important personality as a revolutionist. Reviews the period up to the war for Algerian independence under Ben Bella (1954-65), and the revolutionary stage (1965-78), which he fought as a Muslim and a faithful believer in realities.

1084. Sari, DJ. L'ÉVOLUTION DE LA PRODUCTION AGRICOLE EN ALGÉRIE [The evolution of agricultural production in Algeria]. *Afrique et l'Asie Modernes [France] 1977 (3): 12-24.* Discusses the deficiencies and irregularities in food production in Algeria since 1966.

1085. Sari, Djilali. TENDANCES GENERALES DE L'ÉVOLUTION DE LA POPULATION AGGLOMERÉE EN ALGERIE (1966-77) [General tendencies of the evolution of the mass population in Algeria, 1966-77]. *Afrique et l'Asia Modernes [France] 1979 (1): 62-70.* Studies the growth of the mass population in Algeria, as well as the migratory movements, based on the census of 1966-77.

1086. Schlette, Heinz Robert. ALBERT CAMUS UND "DIE ARABER" [Albert Camus and the Arabs]. *Zeitgeschichte [Austria] 1974 2(1): 1-8.* Analyzes, criticizes, and rejects Conor Cruise O'Brien's *Albert Camus: of Europe & Africa* (Viking Press, 1970) interpretation of Camus' attitudes toward the Arabs and the conflict in Algeria. Argues that O'Brien's judgment that Camus was a leftist French intellectual incapable of understanding the Arabs is not substantiated by Camus' activities in Algeria in the 1930's, nor by Camus' subsequent novels. Camus took a position between French colonialists and supporters of a completely independent Algeria. Based on Camus' writings and secondary works; 47 notes. J. B. Street

1087. Schliesendinger, Odile. POLITIQUE DE L'ÉDUCATION EN ALGERIE [Educational policy in Algeria]. *Études [France] 1973 339(10): 371-382.* Analyzes Algeria's educational policy since independence and discusses the Arabization of social life and the effort to create a national culture. G. E. Pergl

1088. Shagal', V. E. ARABIZATSIIA KUL'TURY V ALZHIRE [Arabization of culture in Algeria]. *Narody Azii i Afriki [USSR] 1981 (3): 94-98.* In the first Algerian constitution (1963) the official languages of Algeria were both Arabic and French. However, in the 1976 constitution only Arabic was listed. In order to implement Arabization of all aspects of social and political life of Algeria, there must be a single national language. National Charter of Algeria, 1976 and other primary sources; 12 notes. S. J. Talalay

1089. Simeonova, Elena. ANTIIMPERIALISTICHESKIIAT KURS NA VUNSHATA POLITIKA NA ALZHIRSKATA DEMOKRATICHNA I NARODNA REPUBLIKA [The anti-imperialist foreign policy of the Algerian Democratic and Popular Republic]. *Izvestiia na Inst. po Istoriia na BKP [Bulgaria] 1976 35: 233-263.* Reviews Algeria's foreign policy since independence (1962), stressing its pursuit of nonalignment and peaceful coexistence, its support for Arab and African unity, its participation in the struggle against imperialism, and its cooperation with the USSR.

1090. Sivan, Emanuel. ANTI-COLONIALISM AT THE AGE OF THE POPULAR FRONT: ALGERIAN COMMUNISM. 1935-1939. *Asian and African Studies [Israel] 1977 11(3): 337-374.* Examines the colonial policy of the French Communist Party (PCF), as illustrated by its intervention in Algerian politics in the interwar period. In theory the PCF was suited to the Algerian situation, but the trial period was too short to show whether the party could improve its position in the Muslim community. The continued hostility of Muslim moderates and the exclusion of Communists from the new scheme for a native political alliance suggest its chances were small. Based on documents in the Centre d'Information d'Études, Algiers, the private archives of Colonel P. Schöen, and secondary sources; 157 notes. J. M. Sanderson

1091. Sivan, Emanuel. COLONIALISM AND POPULAR CULTURE IN ALGERIA. *J. of Contemporary Hist. [Great Britain] 1979 14(1): 21-53.* A survey of popular Algerian literature, 1891-1920, reveals the prevailing, disdainful stereotypes of the Arab. He was either nameless and generalized in an uncomplimentary way or given epithets more appropriately applied to animals. Based largely on contemporary literature; 144 notes. M. P. Trauth

1092. Sivan, Emmanuel. LEFTIST OUTCASTS IN A COLONIAL SITUATION: ALGERIAN COMMUNISM 1927-1935. *Asian and African Studies [Israel] 1975 10(3): 209-257.* Discusses the composition of the Algerian Communist Party, 1927-35, particularly noting its youthful leadership, and examines the party's position in France, Algeria, and the Comintern.

1093. Sivan, Emmanuel. 'SLAVE OWNER MENTALITY' AND BOLSHEVISM: ALGERIAN COMMUNISM, 1920-1927. *Asian and African Studies [Israel] 1973 9(2): 154-195.* Analyzes the political and nationalist beliefs of the Communist Party of Algeria, discussing the reasons why the Algerian Party's peculiar mixture of Leninism and racism, dubbed by the Comintern as a "slave owner mentality," should have survived.

1094. Sivers, Peter von. COLONIAL ELITES AND NATIONALIST POLITICS: THE ANALYSIS OF ALGERIAN POLITICAL AND SOCIAL CLASS STRUCTURES. *European J. of Sociol. [Great Britain] 1979 20(1): 142-148.* Reviews books by J.-C. Vatin and Jean Leca on Algerian politics and by F. Colonna on Algerian teachers. Independent Algeria is an administrative state, in which single-party rule conceals conflicts from the public. Its power is unthinkable without the rising lower middle class. Although not a "mediating elite," it was the temporary ally of the nationalists after 1962; teachers were recruited primarily from this class. R. Aldrich

1095. Smirnov, G. V. ROL' GOSUDARSTVA V RESHENII PROBLEMY NAKOPLENIIA V ANDR [The role of the government in solving problems of resources in the Algerian National Democratic and Popular Republic]. *Narody Azii i Afriki [USSR] 1973 (5): 13-22.* Examines the part played by the Algerian government in building up capital reserves to broaden the basis of the Algerian economy, 1962-73.

1096. Smith, Tony. THE FRENCH ECONOMIC STAKE IN COLONIAL ALGERIA. *French Hist. Studies 1975 9(1): 184-189.* France's economic stake in Algeria was not a major motivation for the Algérie française movement since French capitalism has historically adjusted well to political decolonization. Primary and secondary sources; 19 notes. H. T. Blethen

1097. Smith, Tony. MUSLIM IMPOVERISHMENT IN COLONIAL ALGERIA. *Rev. de l'Occident Musulman de la Méditerranée [France] 1974 17: 139-162.* Analyzes the 1954 Algerian revolution. In the 1920's and 1930's French capitalism began to exploit Algeria at the expense of the land and labor of the Muslim people. The result was the economic, political, social, and psychological disfranchisement of the Muslim community. In time the Algerian people, as part of a worldwide process of cultural trauma, revolted. Based on official published statistics and secondary sources; 2 charts, 59 notes. G. M. White

1098. Smith, Tony. THE POLITICAL AND ECONOMIC AMBITIONS OF ALGERIAN LAND REFORM, 1962-1974. *Middle East J. 1975 29(3): 259-278.* The Algerian Revolution was basically an affair of the peasantry. The massive exodus of the European population threatened a breakdown in the entire system of agricultural production; accordingly, the workers occupied the estates on which they had formerly been hired hands. The new government legitimized these seizures. The agrarian revolution of 1972-73 first expropriated large domains belonging to public organizations, and then privately held land. Local governments were created, leading to a limited decentralization of the state. "A more productively employed peasantry will provide some of the goods and much of the demand for a growing industrialist sector." The most crying need is for a strong party system. 51 notes. E. P. Stickney

1099. Spillmann, Georges. ALGÉRIE 1974 [Algeria in 1974]. *Afrique et L'Asie [France] 1974 (103): 3-18.* After 12 years of independence, Algeria is prosperous but faces the problem of rapid population growth which in turn creates problems concerning education and employment. The government is planning a massive program of industrial development, to be financed with the income derived from the export of oil and natural gas. On the other hand, Algeria is cautious in regard to urbanization. Unlike many other developing countries, the capital, Algiers, is not the only economic center; several industrial plants are being planned or built, not only along the coastal zone but also in the interior highlands in order to reduce the migration of the rural population. Because of this prospective industrial development and the concurrent agrarian reform, Algeria may achieve a measure of economic self-sufficiency. J. S. Gassner

1100. Stiehm, Judith. ALGERIAN WOMEN: HONOR, SURVIVAL, AND ISLAMIC SOCIALISM. Iglitzin, Lynne B. and Ross, Ruth, eds. *Women in the World* (Santa Barbara, Calif.: Clio Books, 1976): 229-241. Although Algerian women were granted equal rights with men in the constitution of 1963, the Arabic custom of secluding women from public life still prevails. Male honor has long been "closely linked to female purity." In order to insure women's fidelity, men traditionally segregated them from the rest of society. Although the 19th-century French colonialists tried to discourage female exclusion, polygamy, and the wearing of the veil, Algerians held fast to the old ways. Women participated in the fight for independence against the French, but after the emergency of war passed, women fell back into their submissive role. Moreover, after the constitution of 1963 was overthrown by Houari Boumedienne in 1965, women lost the small political power they had accumulated. Today, educational opportunities are greater for women than ever before and the female literacy rate has risen to 15 percent, but women are not trained for technical jobs with the result that "less than 3 percent of the labor force is female." Secondary sources; 10 notes. J. Holzinger

1101. Stora, Benjamin. LA BRÈVE EXISTENCE DU SYNDICAT MESSALISTE: L'USTA (1956-1959) [The brief existence of the Messalist union: the Federation of Unions of Algerian Workers (USTA), 1956-59]. *Mouvement Social [France] 1981 (116): 95-122.* Examines the history of an Algerian labor union that preceded the General Union of the Algerian Workers (UGTA). The USTA, which emerged on 14 February 1956, was led by militants of the Algerian National Movement (MNA) of Messali Hadj and was primarily active in France. It achieved a membership of 15,000 before its disappearance in 1962. J/S

1102. Sutton, Keith. THE INFLUENCE OF MILITARY POLICY ON ALGERIAN RURAL SETTLEMENT. *Geographical Rev. 1981 71(4): 379-394.* The rural settlement system of Algeria had long been characterized by a highly dispersed, poorly structured pattern until a large proportion of the rural population was resettled by the French army during the War of Independence, 1954-61. Evidence during the 1960's suggested that many of these temporary resettlement centers remained in existence. Data from the 1977 population census permitted a sample of the centers to be traced and an assessment to be made of their role in the rural settlement pattern. The acquisition of service functions by the permanent centers was a significant factor in the restructuring of several rural regions. J

1103. Sutton, Keith. POPULATION RESETTLEMENT—TRAUMATIC UPHEAVALS AND THE ALGERIAN EXPERIENCE. *J. of Modern African Studies [Great Britain] 1977 15(2): 279-300.* Gives a working definition of resettlement programs and analyzes the French policy of regroupment in Algeria, 1954-61. Discusses the effects of forced resettlements on the inhabitants and the national government. Table, 95 notes. H. G. Soff

1104. Svanidze, I. A. AGRARNYE PREOBRAZOVANIIA V ALZHIRE [Agrarian reforms in Algeria]. *Voprosy Istorii [USSR] 1980 (6):*

78-89. Characterizes the agrarian structure of Algeria in the period when the country won its independence and traces the progress made in restructuring its agriculture. In 1963 the farms belonging to the European colonists and companies were transformed into self-governing state farms and merged into bigger demesnes. The self-governing sector now accounts for two-thirds of the country's overall agricultural output in terms of value. Since 1971 a series of far-reaching measures have been carried out to reorganize the traditional sector of agriculture, including the distribution of publicly-owned lands among the fellahin, confiscating the landed estates belonging to the landlords who fled from the country, limiting the size of big landholdings and the number of cattle owned by big-time cattlebreeders, broad cooperation of the peasantry, and reconstruction of the forestry. J

1105. Talbott, John. THE STRANGE DEATH OF MAURICE AUDEN. *Virginia Q. Rev. 1976 52(2): 224-242.* On 11 June 1957, during the Battle of Algiers, French paratroopers arrested a young Communist university mathematics professor, Maurice Auden. On 21 June military authorities reported that he had escaped. "Maurice Auden vanished, never to be seen again." The author compares Auden's case to the Dreyfus Affair and traces the unsuccessful attempt of Auden's wife and friends both in Algiers and in France to find out what happened. O. H. Zabel

1106. Talbott, John E. THE MYTH AND REALITY OF THE PARATROOPERS IN THE ALGERIAN WAR. *Armed Forces and Soc. 1976 3(1): 69-86.* From their defeat at Dien Bien Phu in 1954, to the Battle of Algiers in 1958, French paratroopers were mythical heroes to the French press and the public. Known as having a special spirit, the *Esprit Para,* the leaders of these paratroopers created an ideology based on a rejection of materialism, exaltation of ascetism, violence, risk, and action for action's sake. After 1968, the paratroopers fell from grace as the French government deliberately reassigned all active special troops into the regular French armed forces. Drawn from contemporary periodicals, primary works, and secondary sources; 57 notes. J. P. Harahan

1107. Turin, Yvonne. LITTÉRATURE ENGAGÉE ET ANTI-COLONIALISME EUROPÉEN DANS L'ALGÉRIE DU CENTENAIRE: LE CAS SINGULIER D'ALBERT TRUPHÉMUS [Literature *engagée* and European anticolonialism in the Algeria of the centenary: the singular case of Albert Truphémus]. *Rev. d'Hist. Moderne et Contemporaine [France] 1976 23(4): 606-624.* At the time when the Europeans of Algeria were celebrating the centenary of the conquest of Algeria by France (1830-1930), Albert Truphémus appeared on the literary scene in Algiers with his first novel, *L'Hôtel du Sersou.* Others followed, but they did not celebrate *Algérie française.* Though of European origin himself, Truphémus sympathized with the indigenous Muslims and castigated the European *colons,* particularly those of recent and non-French origin. 51 notes. J. C. Billigmeier

1108. Villers, Gauthier de. L'ÉTAT ET LA RÉVOLUTION AGRAIRE EN ALGÉRIE [The state and the agricultural revolution in Algeria]. *Rev. Française de Sci. Pol. [France] 1980 30(1): 112-139.* Examines the state in Algeria and its agricultural revolution *(révolution agraire,* or RA), begun in 1963 with the nationalization of colonial land and the setting up of a self-managed system of nationalized farms. Discusses the major characteristics of the revolution, the state's administration, and its complex and contradictory relationship with the different social classes.

1109. Wright, M. Frank. FRANTZ FANON: HIS WORK IN HISTORICAL PERSPECTIVE. *Black Scholar 1975 6(10): 19-29.* Discusses the later writings of Negro revolutionary and psychiatrist Frantz Fanon, focusing on his class analysis of African society, in which he erred, and his brilliant critique of bourgeois theory in the behavioral sciences.

1110. Zlatorunski, A. ALZHIR: POSTUP' REVOLUTSII [Algeria: progress of the revolution]. *Aziia i Afrika Segodnia [USSR] 1981 (7): 41-42.* Examines the economic, cultural, and political achievements of Algeria, 1976-81.

1111. Zlatorunsky, A. ALGERIA'S HORIZONS. *Int. Affairs [USSR] 1973 (11): 80-85.* Discusses Algeria's economic growth, industrialization, agricultural reform, and cultural change, particularly in education, since 1967.

Egypt

General

1112. Balkovac-Kreškenji, Branka. L'ÉGYPTE DE SADATE À LA RECHERCHE DE SA VOIE; ČASOPIS: PROBLÈMES POLITIQUES ET SOCIAUX [Sadat's Egypt in search of its way: the journal *Problèmes Politiques et Sociaux*]. *Politička Misao [Yugoslavia] 1978 15(3): 498-501.* Reviews *Problèmes Politiques et Sociaux* [France] 1978 333, which is dedicated to a consideration of Anwar Sadat's Egypt.

1113. Boyd, Douglas A. DEVELOPMENT OF EGYPT'S RADIO: "VOICE OF THE ARABS" UNDER NASSER. *Journalism Q. 1975 52(4): 645-653.* After the overthrow of King Farouk in 1952, Egypt expanded its radio to become the dominant broadcaster in the Middle East. The Voice of the Arabs (Sawt al-Arab) became the most influential part of Egyptian propaganda and played a critical role in Middle Eastern events. But after 1958 it at first gradually lost impact as audiences became more sophisticated and later its credibility in the Six-Day War (1967). This and the death of Gamal Abdel Nasser changed the Voice of the Arabs. Primary and secondary sources; 42 notes. K. J. Puffer

1114. Friendly, Alfred. SEARCH FOR TOMB IN EGYPT UNCOVERS VAST ANIMAL CULT. *Smithsonian 1973 4(5): 66-73.* Discusses the findings, theories, and contributions of 20th-century British Egyptologist Walter Bryan Emery. S

1115. Fryzeł, Tadeusz. OPEN-DOOR POLICY OF EGYPT AND ITS DEVELOPMENT. *Studies on the Developing Countries [Poland] 1977 (8): 64-82.* Examines the history of Egypt from 1952—the year in which Colonel Nasser overthrew the monarchy—to 1976, showing discrepancies between Sadat's Open Door Policy (instituted in 1974) and Nasser's National Charter policies announced in 1962, and pointing out that the new policy is dangerously neocapitalist and has led to excessive Egyptian indebtedness to the West.

1116. Hanafi, Hassan. THE RELEVANCE OF THE ISLAMIC ALTERNATIVE IN EGYPT. *Arab Studies Q. 1982 4(1-2): 54-74.* Analyzes Islamic influence in Egyptian social and political life during the 20th century and discusses the potential for an Islamic revolution.

1117. Nowakowski, Stefan. WIEŚ I MIATSO WSÓŁCZESNEGO EGIPTU [Village and city in modern Egypt]. *Kultura i Społeczeństwo 1975 19(4): 99-111.* Contemporary Egypt is undergoing strong social, economic and cultural changes in an attempt to become like the developed countries. There is a deep contrast between the monuments of the past and elements of the modern that have arisen since the abolition of monarchy in 1952. Although a leader in the Arab world, Egypt still faces many economic and social difficulties which it has to overcome. M. A. J. Swiecicka-Ziemianek

1118. Rejwan, Nissim. EGYPT'S SEARCH FOR A NEW SELF-IMAGE. *Midstream 1974 20(6): 58-62.*

1119. Rodrik, Dani. RURAL TRANSFORMATION AND PEASANT POLITICAL ORIENTATIONS IN EGYPT AND TURKEY. *Comparative Pol. 1982 14(4): 417-442.* Discusses the lasting impact that the peasantry as a social class has had on the political structure of the Third World, focusing on the range of political action as a function of rural processes rather than elite preferences. Egypt and Turkey are compared with respect to the variables that affect the nature of the impact, since they both experienced a process of rural mobilization in the 1950's wherein the peasants served different purposes. In Turkey the peasants gave rise to a conservative party; in Egypt they formed the basis of a radical junta. 3 tables, 84 notes. M. A. Kascus

1120. Simiot, Bernard. SUEZ, RENDEZ-VOUS DE L'HISTOIRE [Suez, rendezvous of history]. *Nouvelle R. des Deux Mondes [France] 1975 (7): 38-49.* History of the Isthmus of Suez, from 1453 to the present reopening of the Suez Canal to world shipping, from the earlier political and military struggle for dominance in the Mediterranean to the

Indian Ocean policies of the USSR, and global trade and aid commitments. Illus., 2 tables, 3 notes. R. K. Adams

1121. Tahtinen, Dale R. ECONOMIC AND POLITICAL DEVELOPMENTS IN EGYPT. *Current Hist. 1975 68(402): 66-68, 85-86.*

1122. Tana, Fabio. LA FORMAZIONE DELL'EGITTO CONTEMPORANEO: 1945-1952 [The formation of contemporary Egypt: 1945-52]. *Comunità [Italy] 1976 39(176): 46-122.* Examines the transition toward modern and independent Egypt, begun in 1945 with the changes caused by World War II, and concluded in 1952 with the removal of the king and the emigration of the traditional political elite.

1123. Tsatsos, Jeanne. HEURES DU SINAÏ [Sinai diary]. *Nouvelle Rev. des Deux Mondes [France] 1982 (3): 533-542, (4): 15-23.* Part 1. Diary of a pilgrimage to Mount Sinai, Egypt, relating the trip through Cairo, Heliopolis, Giza, and Pharan. Part 2. Impressions of the monastery of St. Catherine on Mount Sinai and the perennial Hellenic character of the sanctuary.

1124. Warburg, Gabriel R. THE SINAI PENINSULA BORDERS, 1906-47. *J. of Contemporary Hist. [Great Britain] 1979 14(4): 677-692.* The Sinai Peninsula borders were delineated in 1841 as Suez-to-Rafah; in 1906 a British ultimatum forced the separating administrative line from Aqaba to Rafah. The Aqaba-to-Rafah line, making most of the Sinai peninsula Egyptian, was generally recognized until after World War II, although it was never legally established. Archival sources; map, 43 notes. M. P. Trauth

Economics

1125. Abdalla, Nazem. THE ROLE OF FOREIGN CAPITAL IN EGYPT'S ECONOMIC DEVELOPMENT: 1960-1972. *Int. J. of Middle East Studies [Great Britain] 1982 14(1): 87-97.* Analyzes the sources, size, and impact of foreign investment on Egypt's economic growth 1960-72. Foreign capital inflow to Egypt during this period came first from the United States and then primarily the USSR and Arab oil-exporting countries. Foreign capital contributed to the industrialization of the Egyptian economy, but also resulted in an increase in indebtedness. 8 tables, 36 notes. R. B. Orr

1126. Abdel-Khalek, Gouda. LOOKING OUTSIDE OR TURNING NORTHWEST? ON THE MEANING AND EXTERNAL DIMENSION OF EGYPT'S *INFITAH,* 1971-1980. *Social Problems 1981 28(4): 394-409.* Describes how Egypt, restructuring its economic relations and turning toward the United States and Europe, is developing a 19th-century type of specialization, centered on oil, the Suez Canal, and tourism, which will lead to a smaller share for labor in the GNP, a greater breach between rich and poor, possible social unrest, and a mounting political repression.

1127. Abed, George T. LABOUR ABSORPTION IN INDUSTRY: AN ANALYSIS WITH REFERENCE TO EGYPT. *Oxford Econ. Papers [Great Britain] 1975 27(3): 400-425.* The assumption that economic growth would solve unemployment problems in developing nations has proved erroneous. An analysis focusing on wage and price distortions in the industrial sector and developed by use of factor demand equations (linked with market conditions for industrial products) derived from neoclassical production theory provides employment growth equations. Applied to data for Egypt, 1952-67 (a period of intensive industrialization), analysis indicates the slow rate of labor absorption may in this case be due to a nonoptimal technology dictated by price distortions in the factor market and possible depression of demand by high rates of increase in industrial prices. 8 tables, appendix. D. H. Murdoch

1128. Abou-Zeid, Ahmed M. NEW TOWNS AND RURAL DEVELOPMENT IN EGYPT. *Africa [Great Britain] 1979 49(3): 283-290.* In 1961 the General Desert Development Organization (GDDO) was established as the organization responsible for developing desert areas, reclaiming lands, tapping underground and subterranean waters, and settling nomadic populations on reclaimed land. The GDDO's efforts to establish a number of sedentarization projects of this kind have met with great resistance from the Bedouin. The creation of new towns, 1961-78, has been only partially successful, but they have influenced other villages in their areas, to the extent that they are themselves developing into small industrial and trade centers. 2 notes. R. L. Collison

1129. Agwah, A. IMPORT DISTRIBUTION, EXPORT EXPANSION AND CONSUMPTION LIBERALIZATION: THE CASE OF EGYPT. *Development and Change [Netherlands] 1978 9(2): 299-329.* Discusses the possible link between import substitution policy and the lessening of controls over domestic consumption in Egypt. Based on statistics from 1954 to the early 1970's.

1130. Amin, Galal A. SOME ECONOMIC AND CULTURAL ASPECTS OF ECONOMIC LIBERALIZATION IN EGYPT. *Social Problems 1981 28(4): 430-441.* Discusses how Egypt's increasing dependence on foreign decisions and capital over the past two decades, especially since 1970, threatens traditional, national values essential to self-esteem, enthusiasm, and creativity.

1131. Baker, Raymond William. SADAT'S OPEN DOOR: OPPOSITION FROM WITHIN. *Social Problems 1981 28(4): 378-384.* Describes the politics of Egyptian President Anwar Sadat over the past decade, the failure of his open door policy and growing dissatisfaction with his blocked peace initiative, sparking a wide spectrum of opposition opinion, which may prove crucial in diminishing Sadat's ability to carry Egypt with him in his economic and foreign policy reorientations.

1132. Barkai, Haim. EGYPT'S ECONOMIC CONSTRAINTS. *Jerusalem Q. [Israel] 1980 (14): 122-144.* Discusses the economic conditions contributing to the direction of Egyptian foreign policy in the 1970's and leading up to the Camp David Agreement and the peace treaty with Israel.

1133. Benedick, Richard Elliot. THE HIGH DAM AND THE TRANSFORMATION OF THE NILE. *Middle East J. 1979 33(2): 119-144.* Summarizes the latest research about the Aswan Dam and Egypt's efforts to improve the standard of living of its growing population. The dam, built by the USSR between 1960 and mid-1975, did not cause the extensive damages, such as underground seepage and coastal erosion, that were predicted. The damage that it has caused is more than offset by the economic benefits, such as increased cultivation, hydroelectric power, and security from floods. Secondary works; 33 notes. P. J. Mattar

1134. Birks, J. S. and Sinclair, C. A. EGYPT: A FRUSTRATED LABOR EXPORTER. *Middle East J. 1979 33(3): 288-303.* Analyzes the implications of labor exportation for Egypt in the mid-1970's. About six percent of the Egyptian male labor force worked abroad in 1976 in oil rich countries. In contrast to the illiterate half of the population, most emigrant laborers were educated, causing a brain drain. Their remittances were often spent on consumption items, which fueled inflation. The unemployed in Egypt were too poor to finance emigration. The marked expansion of labor export has now subsided. Based on publications of Arab governments, and secondary works; 5 tables, fig., 18 notes. P. J. Mattar

1135. Block, Peter F. MARITIME EGYPT: AN ISLAND IN A SEA OF SAND. *US Naval Inst. Pro. 1979 105(8): 62-69.* Discusses the importance of maritime affairs for Egypt's economy in the 1970's and Egyptian and American naval cooperation. 6 photos, map. A. N. Garland

1136. Byres, T. J. AGRARIAN TRANSITION AND THE AGRARIAN QUESTION. *J. of Peasant Studies [Great Britain] 1977 4(3): 258-274.* Review of Mahmoud Abdel-Fadil's *Development, Income Distribution and Social Change in Rural Egypt 1952-1970: A Study in the Political Economy of Agrarian Transition* (Cambridge U. Pr., 1975), the first serious and adequate attempt to analyze the agrarian question in Egypt. The author posits that an agrarian transition did in fact take place between 1952 and 1970, and assesses the dimensions of that transition, considering the land reforms and agrarian policies in Nasser's Egypt. There is, however, some doubt whether an agrarian transition has occurred and whether the agrarian question has been solved. R. V. Ritter

1137. Cooper, Mark EGYPTIAN STATE CAPITALISM IN CRISIS: ECONOMIC POLICIES AND POLITICAL INTERESTS, 1967-1971.

Int. J. of Middle East Studies [Great Britain] 1979 10(4): 481-516. Analyzes the political basis and economic impact of policies between the Six-Day War of 1967 and the death of Nasser in September 1970. There was a fundamental continuity between the Nasser and Sadat regimes, and an understanding of the continuity is vital in order to comprehend the Egyptian political economy in the 1970's. Secondary sources; 12 tables, 2 fig., 71 notes. R. B. Orr

1138. Deeb, Marius. BANK MISR AND THE EMERGENCE OF THE LOCAL BOURGEOISIE IN EGYPT. *Middle Eastern Studies [Great Britain] 1976 12(3): 69-86.* The directors and supporters of the Bank Misr, founded in 1920 and now Egypt's largest commercial bank, were greatly outnumbered by the Federation of Industries and the local foreign minorities it represented, and they failed to achieve their goals of economic independence and the formation of a national bourgeoisie in the interwar period. However, their ideals were pursued by the Egyptian urban middle class; some of these aims were reflected in the 1947 joint-stock companies law, which required 51 percent of the capital, 40 percent of the board of directors, 75 percent of the employees, and 90 percent of the workers to be Egyptian. Based primarily on Bank Misr reports, import-export records, and other contemporary documents; 103 notes. K. M. Bailor

1139. Deeb, Marius. THE SOCIOECONOMIC ROLE OF THE LOCAL FOREIGN MINORITIES IN MODERN EGYPT, 1805-1961. *Int. J. of Middle East Studies [Great Britain] 1978 9(1): 11-22.* Examines the socioeconomic role played by local foreign minorities in Egypt, like the Greeks, the Armenians, the Italians, and other Europeans who emigrated to Egypt during the 19th and 20th centuries who kept their language and culture and were not assimilated into Egyptian society. Concludes that these local foreign minorities can be regarded as a major agent of change affecting the internal development of Egypt's social and economic history. Secondary sources; 50 notes. R. B. Orr

1140. Diatlov, V. I. GENEZIS I STRUKTURA KRUPNOI EGIPETSKOI BURZHUAZII (PERVAIA POLOVINA XX V.) [The genesis and structure of Egypt's upper middle class, 1900-50]. *Narody Azii i Afriki [USSR] 1977 (2): 61-70.* Fundamental change in the semicolonial socioeconomic structure of Egypt occurred during 1900-50, when the upper middle class had its genesis. This class concentrated its interests predominantly in joint-stock companies by which it created national companies able to compete with foreign enterprises. Members of the upper middle class came from the gentry. The author's analysis of the positions held by the gentry, prominent officials, and highly educated people shows that there was a degree of unity between the bourgeoisie and the gentry which permitted a unified class policy. Surveys the most important business groups in Egypt on the eve of the 1952 revolution. Based on biographies of chief actors in joint-stock companies; 2 tables, 20 notes. L. Kalinowski

1141. Efrat, Moshe. HA-SECHER HAG'VOAH B'ASWAN [The Aswan high dam]. *Hamizrah Hehadash [Israel] 1973 23(1): 61-65.* Discusses the expenses involved in building the Aswan Dam, the number of Egyptian and Soviet workers involved, the estimated increase in cultivated area, and the projected increase in agricultural production. By-products of the construction of the new dam will include better navigation of the Upper Nile, development of tourism and fishing around Lake Nasser as well as a possible increase of bilharzia, destruction of the delta sardine industry, and damage to dams and the coastline of Egypt proper. F. Rosenthal

1142. Gray, Albert L., Jr. EGYPT'S TEN YEAR ECONOMIC PLAN: 1973-1982. *Middle East J. 1976 30(1): 36-48.* Analyzes the reasons for the failure of the economic plans of the 1960's. Emphasizes foreign investment as the key to the success of the Ten-Year Plan, enumerating a number of countries that have promised financial aid. Speculates about the future use of the Suez Canal and notes the rebuilding of Port Said, Ismailia, and Suez. The government will have to tax the people more heavily, increase employment, and control population growth if the plan is to be fulfilled. 16 notes. E. P. Stickney

1143. Gudowski, Janusz. ORGANIZATION OF WATER SUPPLY AND USE FOR AGRICULTURAL NEEDS IN THE LIGHT OF THE EGYPTIAN LEGISLATION: THE EVOLUTION OF MODERN WATER LAW IN EGYPT. *Africana Bull. [Poland] 1980 (29): 17-36.* Traces the development of government policies and laws relating to agricultural water use in Egypt, providing a comprehensive list of Egyptian water legislation during the period 1881-1977.

1144. Guillot, Roger. QUEL AVENIR POUR LE CANAL DE SUEZ? [What is the future for the Suez Canal?]. *Défense Natl. [France] 1979 35(Feb): 85-92.* Analyzes Suez Canal traffic in the years before the closure of the canal in 1967 and the two years following its reopening in 1975 and studies the plans of the Egyptian government to regain the traffic in oil and petroleum products.

1145. Hamed, Osama. EGYPT'S OPEN DOOR ECONOMIC POLICY: AN ATTEMPT AT ECONOMIC INTEGRATION IN THE MIDDLE EAST. *Int. J. of Middle East Studies [Great Britain] 1981 13(1): 1-9.* Egypt's 1974 Law No. 43 contains many of the provisions meant to facilitate foreign, especially Arab, investment in Egypt. It created free zone areas in Port Said and other Suez Canal area cities, facilitated the repatriation of profits, relaxed exchange restrictions, gave the private sector access to the parallel market, curtailed the state monopoly in foreign trade, and abolished the state trading companies handling it. It failed, however, to attract the amounts of foreign capital its designers hoped for. Based on publications of the World Bank. J. Powell

1146. Hamman, Mona. WOMEN AND INDUSTRIAL WORK IN EGYPT: THE CHUBRA EL-KHEIMA CASE. *Arab Studies Q. 1980 2(1): 50-69.* Examines the role of women in the Egyptian industrial labor force since the early 19th century. Describes and analyzes a 1975 experimental literacy program at the Chubra El-Kheima industrial plant, in which the female success rate was much lower than the male.

1147. Hansen, Bent and Wattleworth, Michael. AGRICULTURAL OUTPUT AND CONSUMPTION OF BASIC FOODS IN EGYPT, 1886/87-1967/68. *Int. J. of Middle East Studies [Great Britain] 1978 9(4): 449-469.*

1148. Hansen, Bent. INCOME AND CONSUMPTION IN EGYPT, 1886/1887 TO 1937. *Int. J. of Middle East Studies [Great Britain] 1979 10(1): 27-47.* Estimates the per capita income and consumption for Egypt from 1886-87 to 1937 as a way of evaluating British colonial and economic policy. Examines indexes of rural and urban real value added per capita, the per capita consumption of cereals, legumes, coffee, tobacco, and sugar, and the level of railroad passenger travel. Based on official Egyptian publications; 10 tables, 6 notes, biblio. R. B. Orr

1149. Hansen, Bent and Tourk, Khairy. THE PROFITABILITY OF THE SUEZ CANAL AS A PRIVATE ENTERPRISE, 1859-1956. *J. of Econ. Hist. 1978 38(4): 938-958.* Computes internal rates of return and present values for capital in general and for particular investors (French shareholders and the British and Egyptian governments) from construction to nationalization of the canal. Terminal values at the nationalization had to be imputed. Compares rates of return with opportunity costs represented by the return on alternative investments. For capital generally, French shareholders, and the British government, rates of return were 8-9% against opportunity costs of 3-4%. For the Egyptian government, corresponding figures were 2-5% and 11%. American investment would not have been profitable. J

1150. Hillal Dessouki, Ali E. POLICY MAKING IN EGYPT: A CASE STUDY OF THE OPEN DOOR ECONOMIC POLICY. *Social Problems 1981 28(4): 410-416.* Deals with some aspects of the Egyptian policymaking process in relation to the open door economic policy and analyzes how economic liberalization during 1970-74 became a policy issue, emphasizing the role of external factors, especially the International Monetary Fund, in influencing and shaping the policy.

1151. Komzin, I. DAM OF HOPE. *Soviet Military Rev. [USSR] 1975 (8): 58-60, (9): 56-59.* Discusses the author's participation in the building of the Aswan Dam in Egypt, 1959. From *Believing in a Dream* (Moscow, 1973).

1152. Korany, Bahgat. DÉPENDANCE FINANCIÈRE ET COMPORTEMENT INTERNATIONAL [Financial dependence and international behavior]. *Rev. Française de Sci. Pol. [France] 1978 28(6): 1067-1092.* Discusses Egypt's foreign policy and international behavior, 1967-76, with special reference to its economic dependence on the conservative oil-producing countries.

1153. Korayem, Karima. THE RURAL-URBAN INCOME GAP IN EGYPT AND BIASED AGRICULTURAL PRICING POLICY. *Social Problems 1981 28(4): 417-429.* Shows how hidden taxes paid by the rural population in Egypt have been higher than the funds received through explicit subsidization, and how pricing policy, negatively biased against farmer income, has been the chief factor in the increasing rural-urban income gap over the past two decades.

1154. Kowark, Hannsjörg and Taylor, S. M. DIE RÄUMUNG DES SUEZ-KANALS [Clearing of the Suez Canal]. *Marine Rundschau [West Germany] 1974 71(12): 724-733.* Describes the clearing work in the Suez Canal, which was closed after the Six-Day War and did not open again until after the October War. Egypt's effort was supported by the navies of the United States, France, Great Britain, and the USSR. The British started in April 1974, and HMS *Maxton,* for the first time since 1967, sailed the Port Said-Suez route. 16 illus. G. E. Pergl

1155. Makaeev, D. A. IZ ISTORII RAZVITIIA SOVETSKO-EGIPETSKIKH EKONOMICHESKIKH SVIAZEI (1922-1939 GG.) [From the history of the development of Soviet-Egyptian economic ties, 1922-39]. *Narody Azii i Afriki [USSR] 1974 (3): 51-63.* Describes the growth of Soviet trade with Egypt from Egyptian independence in 1922 to World War II. The fairly low level of trade was due to Egypt's independence on Western capitalist markets and the USSR's lack of export goods.

1156. Moghira, Anouar. LA NOUVELLE VALLÉE OU L'ÉCHEC DE LA MISE EN OEUVRE D'UN PROJET DE DEVELOPPEMENT NASSÉRIEN [The new valley, or the failure of the implementation of a Nasser development project]. *Afrique et l'Asie Modernes [France] 1978 (4): 31-40.* Discusses the evolution and current status of the New Valley development and land reclamation project 300 kilometers west of the Nile delta in Egypt, begun by President Nasser in 1959 and wholly stalled by bureaucratic inefficiency since 1974.

1157. Osochowska-Rusak, Marlena R. THE LEVEL AND STRUCTURE DYNAMICS OF FOOD CONSUMPTION IN EGYPT IN THE YEARS 1959/60-1970/71. *Africana Bull. [Poland] 1976 24: 135-149.* Statistics indicate that a considerable consumption decrease of important foodstuffs took place in the second half of the 1960's; according to World Health Organization nutritional requirements, average nutrition in Egypt is insufficient, especially in the animal protein group.

1158. Prowizur, Edwin. QUELQUES NOTES RÉCAPITULATIVES À PROPOS DU BARRAGE D'ASSOUAN (R.A.E.) ET DES PROBLÈMES SOCIO-ÉCONOMIQUES QU'IL A ENGENDRÉS [The Aswan Dam in Egypt and the socioeconomic problems it has created]. *Civilisations [Belgium] 1978 28(3-4): 319-327.* Discusses how the social problems generated by the construction of the Aswan Dam between 1958 and 1970, notably the relocation of approximately 8,000 people, were resolved.

1159. Quintana Pali, Santiago. EL ALGODON EN EGIPTO 1805-1930 [Cotton in Egypt, 1805-1930]. *Estudios de Asia y Africa [Mexico] 1980 16(3): 436-465.* During the 19th and early 20th centuries Egypt's economic growth was predicated on the growth of an exclusively export-oriented agriculture, of which cotton constituted the main crop. This policy created conditions that prevented the emergence of modern sectors in the economy. The emphasis on cotton hindered the transition from an export economy to one of a more complex nature. Biblio., 26 notes. J. V. Coutinho

1160. Quintana Pali, Santiago. POLÍTICAS DE REFORMA AGRARIA EN EGIPTO E IRÁN: UNA COMPARACIÓN ENTRE DOS CASOS DE DESARROLLO CAPITALISTA [Agrarian reform policies in Egypt and Iran: a comparison of two cases of capitalist development]. *Estudios de Asia y África [Mexico] 1979 14(3): 405-465.* Agrarian reform cannot be understood except within the concept of development. In capitalism, redistribution of land is followed by the appearance of a capitalist-type agriculture and a rural proletariat. Redistribution of property rights does not imply redistribution of economic roles; these are maintained although in a less oppressive relationship. Against this theoretical background the author shows that the Iranian and Egyptian land reforms, even though they were carried out in different social and political conditions, had very similar effects. 135 notes, biblio. J. V. Coutinho

1161. Rakovski, N. S. MBRR I EGIPET [International Bank for Reconstruction and Development (IBRD) and Egypt]. *Narody Azii i Afriki [USSR] 1979 (5): 80-88.* Discusses credits and loans given to Egypt by the IBRD (World Bank) and the International Development Association, two UN bodies largely controlled by US capital. Stresses negative aspects of these economic aid programs. While helping Egypt to meet short-term financial obligations, they made Egypt economically and politically dependent on the imperialist donor-nations. 2 tables, 28 notes. N. Frenkley

1162. Richards, Alan. THE AGRICULTURAL CRISIS IN EGYPT. *J. of Development Studies [Great Britain] 1980 16(3): 303-321.* Examines the history of and current responses to Egypt's agricultural problems, including a brief description of Nasser's agrarian programs and emphasizing the more recent developments in such matters as crop patterns and mechanization.

1163. Richards, Alan. AGRICULTURAL MECHANIZATION IN EGYPT: HOPES AND FEARS. *Int. J. of Middle East Studies [Great Britain] 1981 13(4): 409-425.* Examines the effects of agricultural mechanization in Egypt today with emphasis on the following issues: the opportunity cost of land used to grow animal fodder, especially clover, the impact of mechanization on land yields, and the problem of excess demand for labor when using traditional techniques. Such an examination reveals considerable grounds for skepticism about the social benefits of agricultural mechanization in Egypt. Based on information gathered during three trips to Egypt in 1979 and 1980; 2 tables, 61 notes.
R. B. Orr

1164. Richards, Alan. AGRICULTURAL TECHNOLOGY AND RURAL SOCIAL CLASSES IN EGYPT, 1920-1939. *Middle Eastern Studies [Great Britain] 1980 16(2): 56-83.* Analyzes social and agricultural changes in Egypt, 1920-40. The rural economy recovered from the intensification of agriculture before World War I. The technical changes were a response to production difficulties and helped large landowners more than small ones, and prevented the further deterioration of the landless class. Secondary sources; 10 tables, fig., 89 notes.
P. J. Mattar

1165. Richards, Alan. LAND AND LABOR ON EGYPTIAN COTTON FARMS, 1882-1940. *Agric. Hist. 1978 52(4): 503-518.* In an effort to produce cotton for an organized export market, Egyptian large-scale landowners resorted to a two-tiered labor force called the *'izbah.* In this system a yearround worker, the *tamaliyya,* was employed by the landowner as a sharecropper under a variety of arrangements. The balance of the labor force was made up of the *tarahil,* an emergency labor force used only in periods of difficulty such as planting or harvesting. Based on primary and secondary sources; 55 notes.
R. T. Fulton

1166. Rycroft, Robert W. and Szyliowicz, Joseph S. THE TECHNOLOGICAL DIMENSION OF DECISION MAKING: THE CASE OF THE ASWAN HIGH DAM. *World Pol. 1980 33(1): 36-61.* Examines the role of technological variables in the decisions by Egypt, the World Bank, and the United States regarding the selection and financing of the Aswan Dam. Assesses decisionmaking models in their technological dimension, defined in terms of design, impact, and management issues. Shows the dominance of "muddling through" and "bounded rationality" behavior for each participant. The technological dimension, though important, is clearly secondary to politics. J/S

1167. Szymański, Edward. NASEROWSKA KONCEPCJA PRZEMIAN SPOŁECZNYCH W EGIPCIE [Nasser's conception of social changes in Egypt]. *Przegląd Socjologiczny [Poland] 1979 31(2): 21-36.* Studies the social and economic changes effected by Gamal Abdel Nasser's government after the army coup of 1952 brought it to power. By 1962, in keeping with the six objectives of the revolution, "Nasser had nationalized all large Egyptian enterprises, expanded land reform, and placed all important sectors of the economy under the control of socialist planners."

1168. Tignor, Robert. THE ECONOMIC ACTIVITIES OF FOREIGNERS IN EGYPT, 1920-1950: FROM MILLET TO HAUTE BOURGEOISIE. *Comparative Studies in Soc. and Hist. [Great Britain] 1980 22(3): 416-449.* Traces the economic activity of foreigners residing in Egypt and their efforts to create a self-conscious bourgeoisie. Despite such achievements as the diversification of the economy, they remained isolated from Egyptian society and separated from each other by ethnic and cultural traits that they would not relinquish.

1169. Tignor, Robert L. DEPENDENCY THEORY AND EGYPTIAN CAPITALISM, 1920 TO 1950. *African Econ. Hist. 1980 (9): 101-118.* The experience of Egypt, 1920-50, modifies the dependency hypothesis of developmental deformation in societies incorporated as peripheries to capitalist centers, since its artisanal occupations and local commerce continued and were modernized. Moreover, ownership and management of joint stock companies were Egyptianized while import-substitution industrialization was nearly completed. Even where British colonial control was predominant—overseeing state railways, hydraulic projects, and the tendering system—gains to Egypt were enormous. The Egyptian failure to develop industry and diversify agriculture was as much the result of internal as external factors. Primary sources; 39 notes. W. D. Piersen

1170. Tignor, Robert L. THE EGYPTIAN REVOLUTION OF 1919: NEW DIRECTIONS IN THE EGYPTIAN ECONOMY. *Middle Eastern Studies [Great Britain] 1976 12(3): 41-68.* Western-educated, strongly nationalistic landed families, led by such individuals as Ismāīl Sidqī, Yūsuf Nahās, Tal at-Harb, and 'Umar Lutfī, after 1919 created the three most important economic institutions in pre-Nasser Egypt: Bank Misr, Egypt's first national bank; the Egyptian Federation of Industries, created to encourage industrialization; and the Egyptian General Agricultural Syndicate, created to gain control over the marketing of Egyptian cotton. Together, these institutions helped to dismantle European control of Egypt's economy, but this should not be interpreted as evidence of an emerging Egyptian bourgeoisie. Based on works and speeches of the above individuals, British Foreign Office documents, and secondary works; 81 notes. K. M. Bailor

1171. Tignor, Robert L. NATIONALISM, ECONOMIC PLANNING, AND DEVELOPMENT PROJECTS IN INTERWAR EGYPT. *Int. of African Hist. Studies 1977 10(2): 185-208.* The program for economic development which emerged informally in interwar Egypt was similar to the one employed by many newly independent African states. The White Nile dam project and the electrification of the Aswan dam were two major development schemes which were stymied by a combination of nationalist suspicions and political rivalries. The two programs also serve as a background for the rise of Ahmad 'Abud. 50 notes. M. M. McCarthy

1172. Timm, Klaus. DER EINTRITT DER ÄGYPTISCHEN FRAU IN DIE MODERNE PRODUCTION [The entrance of the Egyptian woman into modern production]. *Wissenschaftliche Zeitschrift der Humboldt-Universität zu Berlin [East Germany] 1974 23(2): 147-154.* Against a general account of accelerating Egyptian industrialization, especially since 1952, the author discusses the nature of the slow movement of women into the labor market, the increasing need for their wages in urban families, and at the same time the Muslim religious factors and the family factors that stand strongly in the way of hiring women or giving them equality with male workers. Tables, 34 notes. M. Faissler

1173. Voll, Sarah P. EGYPTIAN LAND RECLAMATION SINCE THE REVOLUTION. *Middle East J. 1980 34(2): 127-148.* The Egyptian government has pursued a program of reclamation of land since the 1952 revolution, starting with the Agrarian Reform Law promulgated in September 1952. The government had two goals: to increase domestic agricultural production and to achieve food security for Egypt. The expenditure for the program has been high—723 million Egyptian pounds through 1982—but the results have been disappointing. Of the 1.5 million landless families, only 56,000 were given reclaimed lands through 1978, and agricultural production has been very poor. Based on UN and Egyptian government publications; table, 30 notes. P. J. Mattar

1174. Young, Warren L. HUMAN RESOURCES AND ECONOMIC DEVELOPMENT: MANPOWER, EDUCATION, AND THE "LEWIS MODEL" IN EGYPT, 1952-1967. *Genève-Afrique [Switzerland] 1975 14(1): 78-102.* Discusses the suitability of W. A. Lewis's model for an analysis of Egyptian economic development, 1952-67, and examines the Egyptian labor force, the educational system and traditional attitude to it, vocational training, and the lack of skilled labor.

1175. Zaki, Mokhlis Y. EGYPTIAN COTTON PRODUCERS' RESPONSE TO PRICE: A REGIONAL ANALYSIS. *J. of Developing Areas 1976 11(1): 39-58.* Egypt is divided into three agricultural regions: the lower Delta; the middle, from Cairo to Assiut along the Nile; and the upper to the Sudanese border. The author traces the connection between cotton price fluctuations and the land area devoted to cotton raising. While cotton remained relatively stable, 1944-66, areas which grew the highest-priced cotton had more land area devoted to that crop than areas which grew lower-priced varieties, sometimes exceeding the governmental limit placed on land that could grow cotton. Egyptian farmers are generally slow in adjusting crops as prices change. Opening of new cropland is an important method of adjusting crops and prices. 3 tables, 40 notes. O. W. Eads, Jr.

1176. Zvereva, L. S. INOSTRANNYI KAPITAL V EKONOMIKE ARE [Foreign capital in the economy of Egypt]. *Narody Azii i Afriki [USSR] 1980 (2): 26-38.* Analyzes the results of massive foreign investments in the economy of Egypt since the creation of free zones in 1971 to promote foreign and Arab investments and the subsequent departure of the Egyptian leadership from the socialist line, especially since 1974, which started an era of open doors and liberalization even more attractive to foreign investors. Underlines the negative aspect of this financial support and the close dependence of Egypt on foreign creditors and investors. Table, 39 notes. English summary. C. Pichelin

Politics

1177. Abdel-Malek, Anouar. THE OCCULTATION OF EGYPT. *Arab Studies Q. 1979 1(3): 177-199.* Surveys Egypt's historic importance as a center in the cause of Arab unity, emphasizing the negative impact of the government's peace agreement with Israel in 1979.

1178. Agrell, Wilhelm. STRATEGI PÅ FELAKTIG PREMISSER: EN STUDIE AV DET EGYPTISKE HÖGKVARTERET 1967 [Military strategy based on wrong premises: a study of the Egyptian headquarters, 1967]. *Kungliga Krigsvetenskaps Akademiens Handlingar och Tidskrift [Sweden] 1973 177(5): 133-150.* Describes Egypt's policy in the weeks before the Six Day War (1967). The main reasons for the Egyptian defeat were their failure to close the Strait of Tiran; their miscalculation concerning the timing of the Israeli attack; the Israelis' discovery of the Egyptian air raid plans, which enabled the former to attack first; and the Arabs' inability to offer any resistance to Israeli attacks on their air bases. Map, 28 notes, biblio. U. Bartels/S

1179. Agwani, M. S. RELIGION AND POLITICS IN EGYPT. *Int. Studies [India] 1974 13(3): 367-388.* Examines the role of Islamic tradition in the political system of Egypt in the 20th century, including attempts to adapt the Islamic perspective to the priorities of the modern age.

1180. Akhavi, Shahrough. EGYPT'S SOCIALISM AND MARXIST THOUGHT: SOME PRELIMINARY OBSERVATION ON SOCIAL THEORY AND METAPHYSICS. *Comparative Studies in Soc. and Hist. [Great Britain] 1975 17(2): 190-211.*

1181. Altman, Israel. ISLAMIC LEGISLATION IN EGYPT IN THE 1970S. *Asian and African Studies [Israel] 1979 13(3): 199-219.* Anwar Sadat encouraged the rise of Islamic fundamentalists in Egypt as a counterweight to Marxists. These groups, however, had little impact on national legislation. Contemporary Egyptian sources; 83 notes. R. T. Brown

1182. Ayubi, Nazih N. M. BUREAUCRATIC INFLATION AND ADMINISTRATIVE INEFFICIENCY: THE DEADLOCK IN EGYPTIAN ADMINISTRATION. *Middle Eastern Studies [Great Britain] 1982 18(3): 286-299.* A major problem for Egypt, especially in the economic sector, is that the government bureaucracy, which began inflating after 1973 has developed a momentum of its own while its performance has declined in quality and efficiency. The resulting deadlock has frustrated administrative personnel and possibly harmed society in general. The situation could have serious organizational and political implications in the immediate future. Based on primary and secondary Arabic sources; 4 tables, 24 notes. F. A. Clements

1183. Ayubi, Nazih N. M. LE RENOUVEAU POLITIQUE DE L'ISLAM. LE CAS DE L'ÉGYPTE [The political revival of Islam: the case of Egypt]. *Esprit [France] 1981 (12): 39-55.* Analyzes the importance of Islam as a religion and its revival in the political events of the Arab countries, focusing on the case of Egypt as a typical example, and underlines the political activities of Islamic organizations. A French translation of an article in *International Journal of Middle East Studies* [Great Britain] 1980 12(4): 423-453.

1184. Ayubi, Nazih N. M. THE POLITICAL REVIVAL OF ISLAM: THE CASE OF EGYPT. *Int. J. of Middle East Studies [Great Britain] 1980 12(4): 481-499.* Discusses the complex doctrinal and historical relationship in Islam between religion and politics, both domestically and internationally, and considers its possible political roles. These include use of Islam as an instrument of justification as in the case of the Saudi royal family, who are "protectors of the Two Sacred Mosques," and Islam as a catalyst for sociopolitical resistance or a revolutionary means to reconstruct society. Secondary sources; 53 notes. J. Powell

1185. Aziz, M. A. OCTOBER WAR AND INTERNATIONAL POLITICS. *Indian J. of Pol. [India] 1976 10(1): 91-94.* Presents a model of Egypt's foreign policy decisionmaking behavior preceding the 1973 October War. Failure to achieve a negotiated settlement led Egypt by logical steps to a limited military operation. D. K. Lambert

1186. Badeau, John S. NASSER. *Worldview 1973 16(3): 28-31.* A review article on three early reports about the political career of Gamal Abdel Nasser (1918-70), those of Mohamed Heikal, Robert Stephens, and Anthony Nutting.

1187. Baker, Raymond William. EGYPT IN SHADOWS: FILMS AND THE POLITICAL ORDER. *Am. Behavioral Scientist 1974 17(3): 393-423.*

1188. Baratelli, F. Micali. LA RIAPERTURA DEL CANALE DI SUEZ TRA POLITICA E STRATEGIA [The reopening of the Suez Canal from a political and strategic point of view]. *Riv. Marittima [Italy] 1975 108(7-8): 9-22.* Investigates the political-strategical consequences of the reopening of the Suez Canal, stressing the influence of and power competition between the two superpowers. Emphasizes the importance of the Arabian Sea and the Indian Ocean since the 19th century, which with the reopening of the Canal are rejoined to the Mediterranean. J/S

1189. Battle, Lucius D. ANWAR SADAT REMEMBERED. *SAIS Rev. 1981-82 (3): 41-48.* Examines the impact of Anwar Sadat from 1957 to 1981, discussing his position and activities during the administration of Gamal Abdel Nasser, 1956-70, and Sadat's contacts with the author, appointed US ambassador to Egypt in 1964.

1190. Battle, Lucius D. A HOUSE IN CAIRO. *Foreign Service J. 1974 51(11): 16-18.* Personal account (1964-67) of the property involved in a diplomatic transfer of land from the US government to Anwar Sadat. S

1191. Beeson, Irene. THE 'NASSERIZATION' OF EGYPT AND ITS REVERSAL UNDER SADAT. *Int. Perspectives [Canada] 1975 (4): 23-28.*

1192. Binder, Leonard. THE FAILURE OF THE EGYPTIAN LEFT. *Asian and African Studies [Israel] 1980 14(1): 20-34.* Both the Communist and socialist left have found themselves coopted by the basically conservative socialism of the Egyptian ruling elite. Their misunderstanding of the historical realities of the economic and political structure made them withhold their opposition too long. Based on Egyptian printed sources; 11 notes. R. T. Brown

1193. Bowie, Leland. CHARISMA, WEBER, AND NASIR. *Middle East J. 1976 30(2): 141-157.* Charisma is an antieconomic revolutionary force. Max Weber was correct in broadening the term to apply to political life. Charisma can both maintain and disrupt social order. Gamal Abdel Nasser was perceived as a charismatic figure by the Egyptian people who believed he brought about certain value transformations. Weber's concept of charisma remains a valid tool of political analysis but should not be used "until carefully scrutinized survey data are available." 67 notes. E. P. Stickney

1194. Bowie, Leland. THE COPTS, THE WAFD, AND RELIGIOUS ISSUES IN EGYPTIAN POLITICS. *Muslim World 1977 67(2): 106-126.* Analyzes the role of the Copts, the old Christian minority in Egypt, in Egypt's dominant party, the Wafd, between 1918 and 1942. The party, under the leadership of Sa'd Zaghlūl, sought an alliance of Muslims and Copts against the British. Zaghlūl won the confidence of the Copts by emphasizing the secular nature of Egyptian nationalism. The Copts showed their loyalty by joining the Muslims in protests and demonstrations, and in serving in high posts in the party and government, even after Zaghlūl's death in 1927. But this kind of cooperation prompted Wafd's opponents to accuse the Wafd of tolerating "Coptism" (anti-Muslim conspiracy). The Wafd reacted, in a clear demonstration of political opportunism, by appealing to Islamic sentiment, which resulted in a backlash against the Copts. While the Wafd showed courage in initially incorporating Copts in Egypt's political life, the party is also responsible for retarding such a development. 68 notes. P. J. Mattar

1195. Bozzo, Anna. SULLA STORIOGRAFIA ARABA CONTEMPORANEA: A PROPOSITO DI UN RECENTE LAVORO DI RIF'AT AS-SA'ĪD [On contemporary Arab historiography: the recent work of Rif'at as-Sa'īd]. *Oriente Moderno [Italy] 1977 57(9-10): 391-403.* Praises Rif'at as-Sa'īd's objective studies of the Egyptian leftism of the 1940's, especially his use of official documents.

1196. Camera d'Afflitto, Isabella. *AT-TAKFIR WA AL-HIGRAH* E L'INTEGRALISMO MUSULMANO IN EGITTO [At-Takfir wa al-Higrah and pan-Islamism in Egypt]. *Oriente Moderno [Italy] 1978 58(4-6): 145-153.* Describes the religious-political Moslem sect at-Takfir wa al-Higrah which flourished after President Sadat encouraged pan-Islamism rather than pan-Arabism in Egypt.

1197. Cantori, Louis J. EGYPT AT PEACE. *Current Hist. 1980 78(453): 26-29, 38.* Discusses political and economic developments in Egypt and its continued isolation from other Arab states after the 1979 peace treaty with Israel.

1198. Chernovskaia, V. V. INTELLIGENTSIIA I RABOCHIIK-LASS EGIPTA V PERVOI POLOVINE XX V. [The intelligentsia and the working class of Egypt, 1900-50]. *Narody Azii i Afriki [USSR] 1977 (3): 80-91.* Analyzes the development of closer relations between Egypt's intellectuals and the working class, 1900-50. Two political parties were active during the years of Egypt's occupation and of the protectorate state, 1882-1922: the National Party, whose main goals were the liberation of Egypt from colonialism and moderate constitutional reform; and the People's Party, whose main goals were the liberation of Egyptians from tradition and absolutism and the guarantee of constitutional rights. These two parties united into the Wafd Party, which led the national liberation movement against English imperialism during 1919-21. The intellectuals educated the working class and obtained its support through educational institutions and the formation of trade unions. Describes the split between the Right and the Left of the intellectuals and their influence on the working class. 35 notes. L. Kalinowski

1199. Chernovskaia, V. V. OFITSERSKII KORPUS EGIPTA KAK SOTSIAL'NAIA GRUPPA (1850-1952) [Egypt's officer corps as a social group, 1850-1952]. *Narody Azii i Afriki [USSR] 1975 (3): 67-79.* Describes the formation of Egypt's officers corps as a new group of the intelligentsia in the second half of the 19th century. By the time of English occupation, this group numbered 4,000 and had close ties with the ruling class. From 1849 to 1875, over half of the educated people in Egypt belonged to the officer corps. After Egypt's independence in 1922, the Egyptian army greatly increased in number. The army found itself in need of more specialists, and during 1939-45, hundreds of teachers, doctors, lawyers, and engineers joined. Under the influence of the growing internal crisis and political struggle in Egypt, 1936-49, young officers came to the conclusion that the monarchist system had to be overthrown. In 1949, the secret army organization, "free officers," was formed. Because of strict discipline, organization, and centralization, this group was much better prepared for revolutionary struggle than any organization or political party of the civil intelligentsia. This made the army, under the leadership of the "free officers," a real revolutionary power. Table, 45 notes. L. Kalinowski

1200. Cohen, Stephen P. and Azar, Edward E. FROM WAR TO PEACE: THE TRANSITION BETWEEN EGYPT AND ISRAEL. *J. of Conflict Resolution 1981 25(1): 87-114.* Israeli and Egyptian intellectuals meeting in Cairo in May 1979, agreed on the principle of self-determination for Palestine but differed on the key issues of security, interaction, and acceptance: Israelis insist on increased territory as necessary to their security whereas Egyptians only recognize the security needs of Israel's 1967 "core"; Israelis insist on a unique Jewish, non-Arab culture whereas Arabs would like to see the Arabization of Israel; and both Israelis and Arabs argue as to whether Anwar Sadat's "acceptance" of Israel represents an invitation to partnership or a threat to Israeli independence.

1201. Cooper, Mark N. THE DEMILITARIZATION OF THE EGYPTIAN CABINET. *Int. J. of Middle East Studies [Great Britain] 1982 14(2): 203-225.* Analyzes the military presence in Egyptian cabinets from 1952 to 1977. During this period the role of the military was reduced, but there was difficulty in finding a stable civilian pattern. Fig., 3 tables, 16 notes. R. B. Orr

1202. Crabbs, Jack, Jr. POLITICS, HISTORY, AND CULTURE IN NASSER'S EGYPT. *Int. J. of Middle East Studies [Great Britain] 1975 6(4): 386-420.* Discusses the efforts made to rewrite history by the regime of Gamal Abdel Nasser and the fate of various Egyptian historians who accepted or resisted government-imposed interpretations. Primary and secondary sources; 172 notes. R. B. Orr

1203. Crecelius, Daniel. SA'UDI-EGYPTIAN RELATIONS. *Int. Studies [India] 1975 14(4): 563-585.* Saudi Arabian-Egyptian relations were virtually nonexistent until the restoration of the Saud rulers after 1902. Due to British interference, relations between the wars were underdeveloped, yet strained. The foundation of the Arab League established an entente centered on opposition to Israel and British domination. Gamal Abdal Nasser's (1918-70) aggressive drive for Arab leadership destroyed this cooperation by 1962. Egypt's Anwar Sadat and Saudi Arabia's oil wealth and support for confrontation states led to a Cairo-Riyadh Axis, particularly after the October War. Although a permanent meaningful relationship could develop, there is still little more than an entente based on a few policy goals and tactics. Secondary sources; 12 notes. R. E. Stack

1204. Dawisha, A. I. PERCEPTIONS, DECISIONS AND CONSEQUENCES IN FOREIGN POLICY: THE EGYPTIAN INTERVENTION IN THE YEMEN. *Pol. Studies [Great Britain] 1977 25(2): 201-226.* Analyzes the decision of President Gamal Abdel Nasser of Egypt to intervene in the Yemen civil war in 1962. Reviews the background and Nasser's perceptions of it, and reconstructs the decision-making process. Explores the consequences of the policy decision and tests a number of general methodological hypotheses against the actual events. 5 figs., 5 tables, 60 notes. R. Howell

1205. Deeb, Marius. LABOUR AND POLITICS IN EGYPT, 1919-1939. *Int. J. of Middle East Studies [Great Britain] 1979 10(2): 187-203.* Analyzes the rise and development of a new labor movement in Egypt between 1919 and 1939. The Wafd Party dominated the labor scene in Egypt throughout most of the interwar period. The trade union movement was adversely affected by having strong ties with the Wafd. Whenever the Wafd was driven out of power the activities of trade unions were curbed and their power curtailed. Therefore there was no labor movement in Egypt independent of politics during the period. Based on British Foreign Office records and other primary sources; 139 notes. R. B. Orr

1206. Deeb, Marius. THE 1919 POPULAR UPRISING: A GENESIS OF EGYPTIAN NATIONALISM. *Can. Rev. of Studies in Nationalism [Canada] 1973 1(1): 106-119.* Understanding the anti-British Egyptian uprising of March-April 1919 is essential for comprehending the later stages of the Egyptian nationalist movement. The uprising was a spontaneous, popular, and intensely nationalistic outburst, later formally organized and controlled by the Wafdist Central Committee. This interpretation differs from other explanations in two main respects. Other observers either deny the nationalistic character of the uprising, or else confine it to the Western-educated intellectuals and officials. The masses, according to this view, were impelled only by religious considerations or economic hardships. In fact, the uprising materialized out of the cooperation of two leading traditional classes, the *effendiya* in the urban centers and the medium landowners in the countryside. 73 notes. T. Spira

1207. Dekmejian, R. Hrair. MARX, WEBER AND THE EGYPTIAN REVOLUTION. *Middle East J. 1976 30(2): 158-172.* Examines scholarly literature on Egypt. According to Weber, charismatic leadership exceeds that of a mere "popular" leader, Marx's analysis emphasizes class affiliations and loyalties of a leader. Examines the writing of Leland Bowie (see abstract 1193) and John Entelis (see abstract 1215) on the character of the political leadership of Gamal Abdel Nasser (1918-70). "Had Nasir ruled solely by charisma, the Egyptian political system would have been unable to sustain the protracted period of confrontation with Israel, especially in the face of repeated defeats." Suggests areas of future study and research respecting contemporary Egypt. 24 notes. E. P. Stickney

1208. Deshpande, G. P. STRATEGY OF THE UNITED FRONT AGAINST IMPERIALISM: A STUDY OF SINO-UAR RELATIONS, 1956-1959. *Int. Studies [India] 1975 14(3): 357-374.* China became deeply involved with Egypt and the United Arab Republic in an attempt to build a United Front. China began with immediate full support of Nasser's Suez Canal nationalization in 1956. China condemned imperialist "unequal treaties" and promoted the United States as Egypt's chief imperialist enemy. But in 1957 Egypt and the Arabs disappointed China in their reception of the Eisenhower Doctrine. In 1958 China, facing growing anticommunism from the newly-formed UAR, attempted to remain friendly. Attempts continued into 1959, in spite of Nasser's sharpening attacks over Iraq and Tibet, to no avail. Then, in October, China sponsored a Syrian Communist attack on the idea of the UAR. Secondary sources; 63 notes. R. E. Stack

1209. Divine, Donna Robinson. WHY THIS WAR... *Int. J. Middle East Studies [Great Britain] 1976 7(4): 523-543.* Analyzes the decision of Egypt's Anwar Sadat to initiate the October War of 1973. Discusses Sadat's decision to go to war in terms of Professor Graham T. Allison's three models for study of the decisionmaking process. Secondary sources; 84 notes. R. B. Orr

1210. Dogra, K. K. REOPENING OF THE SUEZ CANAL. *J. of the United Service Inst. of India [India] 1975 105(439): 163-173.* Analyzes the impact of the reopening of the Suez Canal. It cut travel times on some of the world's main shipping lanes and created a possible power struggle in the Indian Ocean. The Soviet Union acquired easy access to the area from the Mediterranean Sea with the canal's reopening. With bases in Somalia, Iraq, and South Yemen it has the capability to cut the oil supply to the West from the Persian Gulf. The United States has responded by planning a base on the island of Diego Garcia and by building strong ties with area nations like Iran. Most area nations agree that demilitarization of the ocean would be the best alternative, but that seems unlikely. Undocumented. L. R. Maxted

1211. Dooley, Howard J. SUEZ, 1956: COLLUSION AND COVER-UP. *Pro. of the Michiana Area Historians 1975 1(2): 1-15.* Examines the historiography, particularly the collusion controversy, of the Suez Crisis which holds that Great Britain, France, and Israel conspired to overthrow Egypt's President Nasser. S

1212. Duclos, Louis-Jean. LA "GUERRE D'USURE" EGYPTO-ISRAELIENNE, 1968-1970 [The Egyptian-Israeli war of attrition, 1968-70]. *Études Int. [Canada] 1979 10(1): 127-175.* From 8 March 1969, the Arab effort at restoration of the territories lost in 1967 took the form of a limited armed conflict. The evolution of this crisis depended not only on the capabilities of the belligerents nor on the intervention of the superpowers but also on the objectives of the principal actors. Analysis of these objectives confirms the radical nature of the hostility between Egypt and Israel and the both defensive and restitutional aspects of each country's goals. Above all, the object of the crisis was basically the occupied territories dispute, and the cease-fire has left a legacy of heightened disaffection in comparison with the period preceding the crisis. Secondary sources; 12 tables, 3 schemas, 5 annexes, 186 notes. J. F. Harrington

1213. El Hakim, Tewfiq. LIBERTÉ ET AUTOCRATIE DANS LE TIERS MONDE. LA CONSCIENCE RETROUVÉE [Liberty and autocracy in the Third World: conscience recovered]. *Esprit [France] 1973 (12): 812-835.* One of three articles on the problem of the exercise of power in recently decolonized Muslim societies. Discusses the regime of Gamal Abdel Nasser from the intellectuals' point of view, one that is filled with the disillusionment of the time. G. F. Jewsbury

1214. El-Ayouty, Yassin. EGYPT AND THE PALESTINIANS. *Current Hist. 1973 64(377): 9-12, 39.*

1215. Entelis, John P. NASSER'S EGYPT: THE FAILURE OF CHARISMATIC LEADERSHIP. *Orbis 1974 18(2): 451-464.*

1216. Fokeev, G. V. BOR'BA ZA LIKVIDATSIIU POSLEDSTVII AGRESSII PROTIV EGIPTA V 1956-1957 GODAKH [The struggle to eliminate the consequences of the 1956-57 aggression against Egypt.] *Voprosy Istorii [USSR] 1972 (8): 64-78.* "The article examines the events connected with the effort to eliminate the consequences of the Anglo-Franco-Israeli aggression launched against Egypt in 1956 and to secure the withdrawal of Israel's troops from the occupied Egyptian territory. These events and certain other problems directly resulting from the aggression have many features in common with the present-day problems created by Israel's aggression launched against Arab countries in 1967. It will be recalled that the withdrawal of Israel's forces after the 1956 aggression was delayed for three months and was effected only in March 1957. The sustained efforts to secure the withdrawal of these forces, which were further complicated by the Israeli government's stubborn attempts to annex part of the captured Egyptian territory, are examined by the author in conjunction with relevant problems of international, notably inter-Arab, relations in the Middle East and North Africa." J

1217. Forster, Peter. SADATS WAGNIS [Sadat's risk]. *Schweizer Monatshefte [Switzerland] 1978 58(6): 415-421.* Discusses the developments in the Middle East since the war of 1967 and the changes caused by Anwar Sadat's journey to Israel in 1977. R. Wagnleitner

1218. Freedman, Robert O. SOVIET POLICY TOWARD SADAT'S EGYPT—FROM THE DEATH OF NASSER TO THE FALL OF GENERAL SADEK. *Naval War Coll. R. 1973 26(3): 63-79.* "With the death of Gamal Abdel Nasser, the diplomatic efforts of the USSR in the Middle East received a severe blow. Begun in the early 1960's, the program had been predicated on the sale and finance of arms to a volatile leader in a hostile environment. Indeed, shortly after the succession of Anwar Sadat to power, this expensive attempt at influencing Arab politics became something of a nightmare for the Soviets. Internal Arab power struggles, an increasingly hostile Arab press, and ever more demanding requests on the part of Sadat culminated in the expulsion of Soviet forces from the UAR in July of 1972. The lessons of this long-term fiasco are apparent, for when a state seeks to 'purchase' allies the question of mutual exploitation is bound to lead to enmity." J

1219. Georges-Picot, Jacques. LE CANAL DE SUEZ [The Suez Canal]. *Rev. des Deux Mondes [France] 1982 (7): 53-63, (8): 364-371.* Part I. Recounts Gamal Abdel Nasser's nationalization of the Suez Canal, 1956-58, and the evolution of the Canal Company in the succeeding years as it sought ways to use its indemnity money. Part 2. Explores the Socialist government's 1982 decision to nationalize the Canal Company (Compagnie Financière de Suez) and the decision's origins in the Common Program of the French Left.

1220. Georgiev, A. A. KONTRREVOLIUTSIIA V EGIPTE I NEKOTORYE VOPROSY ARABSKOGO OSVOBODITEL'NOGO DVIZHENIIA [Counterrevolution in Egypt and the Arab liberation movement]. *Narody Azii i Afriki [USSR] 1980 (5): 140-150.* In the 1950's and 1960's the national liberation movement in the Arab East took on an anti-imperialist character, becoming a struggle for social liberation. In many countries, including Egypt, Iraq, Algeria, Libya, and South Yemen, progressive regimes were created and changed the socioeconomic orientation of these developing nations. In the 1970's, however, these movements encountered difficulties, and in Egypt a counterrevolution took place. The Arab community is convinced that despite the experience of countries where socialist orientation has been lost, their social and national problems can be resolved only by strengthening anti-imperialist Arab unity, a path leading eventually to socialism. 16 notes. S. J. Talalay

1221. Gershoni, Israel. HE'ACHDUT HA'ARAVIT B'TODEAH HALEUMIT MAMIZRIT B'SHELHAI SHANOT HASHLOSHIM [Arab unity in Egyptian national consciousness in the late 1930's. Part I]. *Hamizrah Hehadash [Israel] 1979 28(3-4): 182-194.* Describes the split in Egyptian national self-image. The particularist-territorialist perception developed through Ahmad Lufti as-Sayyid in the early 1920's. By the 1940's the pan-Arab or pan-Islam self-perception grew popular. In the late 1930's several organizations, including the Association for the Unification of Arab Culture, the Arab Union Association, and the Arab Medical Congress, came into being. Such groups were created by Egyptian intellectuals and professionals as vehicles for unification with their colleagues in the Middle East in the political, cultural, professional, and ideological arenas. 43 notes, 150 ref. T. Koppel

1222. Gershoni, Israel. HE'ACHDUT HA'ARAVIT B'TODEAH HALEUMIT MAMIZRIT B'SHELHAI SHANOT HASHLOSHIM, HALEK 2 [Arab unity in Egyptian national consciousness in the late 1930's, part 2]. *Hamizrah Hehadash [Israel] 1980 29(1-4): 1-31.* Continued from a previous article (see preceding entry). Examines the attitudes of the Egyptian ruling class toward Arab unity within a fully integrated pan-Arab political framework. Pan-Arabism is perceived as a morale booster, as the harbinger of another Islamic golden age, as a humane influence on mankind in general, and as a cultural stimulus to the revitalization of the Arabic language. Cultural unity is seen as a first step to political unity, implying the eventual establishment of a pan-Arab nation. This attitude, prevalent in the 1930's, declined by the 1970's. Based on Egyptian periodicals from the late 1930's, secondary sources; 113 notes. T. Koppel

1223. Gershoni, Israel. DAT U'LEUMIYUT B'MISHNATAN SHEL HATNU'OT HASALAFIYOT HAMITZRIYOT [Religion and nationalism in the teachings of the Salafi movements in Egypt]. *Hamizrah Hehadash [Israel] 1976 26(3-4): 181-202.* Discusses two Egyptian ideological movements that began in the 1920's. The Islamic nationalist movement Salafi felt that Islam must be the center of any nationalist movement. The Egyptian nationalist movement portrayed Islam as an obstacle. The author describes in detail three of the major Islamic nationalist movements: the Association of Islamic Guidance, the Young Men's Moslem Association, and the Society of Moslem Brothers and suggests that the success of the Salafi movement led to Egypt's prominence in the Arab world today. Based on books and journal articles; 74 notes. T. Koppel

1224. Gil Benumeya, Rodolfo. LA NACION EGÍPICA Y LA OBRA DE ANUAR EL SADAT [Egypt and the work of Anwar Sadat]. *Rev. de Política Int. [Spain] 1974 (133): 149-158.* Discusses Anwar Sadat's attempts, since he became Egypt's President in September 1970, to reconcile the two contradictory aims pursued by Nasser: the economic and social development of Egypt, and the creation of formal and spiritual ties with other Arab states.

1225. Gorelick, Robert E. ARTICLE VI OF THE ISRAEL-EGYPT PEACE TREATY AND THE ARAB LEAGUE DEFENCE PACT. *Int. Problems [Israel] 1981 20(1): 10-13.* Relates the basic discrepancies in Egyptian foreign policy with its membership in the Arab League, denoting a constant preparedness for war, and its recent treaty with Israel, denoting a sincere desire for peace.

1226. Hajjaj, Aref. DER BRUCH MIT DEM NASSERISMUS IN ÄGYPTEN [The break with Nasserism in Egypt]. *Europa Archiv [West*

Germany] 1974 29(20): 707-716. The stagnation of the political impetus of Nasserism after the Egyptian defeat in 1967 enabled Anwar Sadat in 1971 to start a critical discussion of the negative aspects of the Egyptian revolution of 1952, which led to the political end of such left-wing Nasserites as Ali Sabri.

1227. Harik, Iliya. THE SINGLE PARTY AS A SUBORDINATE MOVEMENT: THE CASE OF EGYPT. *World Pol. 1973 26(1): 80-105.* The single-party system under Nasser differed from the Soviet as well as the machine-politics model. The party was a collaboration movement comprised of a nationally dominant leader and local influentials of divergent social groups who formed a front within a party framework. It was transformed into a mobilization movement with a fair degree of discipline for nearly three years before it reverted to a collaboration movement in 1968. During all its different phases, the party remained politically most relevant and effective at subnational levels where it enjoyed an autonomy lacking on the national level. In short, the single party under Nasser was a mass organization whose powers were residual, community-bound, and nontransferable to national leadership roles, whereas locally it stimulated participation and involvement in community politics and contributed to intense political competition and to a high turnover rate of leaders. J

1228. Heikal, Mohamed Hassanein. EGYPTIAN FOREIGN POLICY. *Foreign Affairs 1978 56(4): 714-727.* Two rival systems struggle for control of Middle Eastern destinies, and this fact has affected Egyptian foreign policy since World War II. Under US leadership, the Middle Eastern system has been preoccupied with Soviet proximity to the region while the Arab system has considered the Middle East, exclusive of Israel, as a single, united confederation. Since the 1973 October War, Egypt has reversed its historical position and has become more closely identified with the Middle Eastern system.
M. R. Yerburgh

1229. Hentsch, Thierry. LA POLITIQUE ISRAÉLIENNE DE SADATE OU L'ÉNIGME DE LA STRATÉGIE ÉGYPTIENNE [Sadat's policy toward Israel or the enigma of the Egyptian strategy]. *Études Int. [Canada] 1980 11(4): 647-670.* Discusses Anwar Sadat's efforts to secure through negotiations with Israel, what Egypt has failed to achieve through combat. Examines Sadat's negotiating techniques which are unorthodox as he frequently initiates discussions from an apparently weak position. Notes that Egypt's success is often contingent on external forces beyond Sadat's control. 73 notes. J. F. Harrington, Jr.

1230. Hinnebusch, Raymond A. EGYPT UNDER SADAT: ELITES, POWER STRUCTURE AND POLITICAL CHANGE IN A POST-POPULIST STATE. *Social Problems 1981 28(4): 442-464.* Examines transformations in the Egyptian state, specifically in the political establishment, following movement into a new stage of economic liberalization and a westward political realignment in 1970, and assesses the relative strength and effect of forces pulling the political system toward liberalization on one side, and toward conservative authoritarianism on the other.

1231. Howard-Merriam, Kathleen. EGYPT'S OTHER POLITICAL ELITE. *Western Pol. Q. 1981 34(1): 174-187.* Studies post-1952 female public leadership in Egypt. Opportunities for female political leadership expand or contract with changing roles and national regimes. The individuals making the greatest impact upon the status of women have been those who have established their presence in the governing elite and exerted influence to promote programs benefiting women. Based on interviews with female public leaders in Egypt; 29 notes.
J. Powell

1232. Hurni, Ferdinand. VON NASSER ZU SADAT [From Nasser to Sadat]. *Schweizer Monatshefte [Switzerland] 1976 56(4): 293-306.* While President Gamal Abdel Nasser stressed socialism and nationalism in the 1950's and 1960's, President Anwar Sadat has adopted a more pragmatic policy for Egypt, which has taken into account the issues of pan-Arabism, relations with the Soviet Union, and the Arab-Israeli conflict.

1233. Hussein, Mahmoud. LIBERTÉ ET AUTOCRATIE DANS LE TIERS MONDE. NASSER ET LES ÉGYPTIENS [Liberty and autocracy in the Third World: Nasser and the Egyptians]. *Esprit [France] 1973 (12): 804-811.* One of three articles on the problem of the exercise of power in recently decolonized Muslim societies, surveying Gamal Abdel Nasser's impact on Egypt. Nasser was at the center of a deep democratic movement that was discovered and lost, realized and alienated. G. F. Jewsbury

1234. Ibrahim, Ibrahim A. SALAMA MUSA: AN ESSAY ON CULTURAL ALIENATION. *Middle Eastern Studies [Great Britain] 1979 15(3): 346-357.* As a member of Egypt's Coptic minority, Salama Musa (b. 1887) believed that Egypt should not associate with Arabic Islam. Egyptians were not Arabs and had nothing in common with the Semites. Instead Musa's nationalism would be associated with Pharaonism and Westernization; the latter was not only necessary but a natural process. Industrialization would free Egypt from British imperialism. Musa formed in 1930 the Jam'iyyat al-Misri li al-Misri to boycott English and European goods and encourage Egyptian products. Musa also advocated women's rights, education, and tried to form a socialist party. 91 notes. S

1235. Ibrahim, Saad Eddin. ANATOMY OF EGYPT'S MILITANT ISLAMIC GROUPS: METHODOLOGICAL NOTE AND PRELIMINARY FINDINGS. *Int. J. of Middle East Studies [Great Britain] 1980 12(4): 423-453.* In July 1977 Egypt witnessed a bloody confrontation between the government and the members of a militant Islamic group called the Repentance and Holy Flight group (RHF). The incident was triggered when the group kidnapped a former Minister for Religious Endowment, demanded the release of RHF members being detained by the government, and then carried out their threat to kill the former cabinet minister when the release did not materialize. Study of the RHF within the context of Islamic militantism, its ideology, structure, leadership, membership and recruitment, regional background, strategies, and motivations shows that such groups are attractive to deeply religious recruits who have been displaced from the countryside and find a strong sense of Muslim communion within the alienation of the city. Based on interviews with imprisoned members of the Repentance and Holy Flight group; table, 53 notes.

1236. Ibrahim, Saad Eddin. AN ISLAMIC ALTERNATIVE IN EGYPT: THE MUSLIM BROTHERHOOD AND SADAT. *Arab Studies Q. 1982 4(1-2): 75-93.* Analyzes the alternatives presented by the Muslim Brotherhood, an Islamic religious and political group founded in 1928, to the policy orientations of Anwar Sadat's regime during the period 1970-82, focusing on those parts of the Brotherhood's ideology that best represent an integrated critique of Sadat's policies.

1237. Israeli, Raphael. THE ROLE OF ISLAM IN PRESIDENT SADAT'S THOUGHT. *Jerusalem J. of Int. Relations [Israel] 1980 4(4): 1-12.* Egyptian President Anwar Sadat, as secretary of the Islamic Congress in the 1950's, gained firsthand experience of the power of Islam as an international force. On succeeding Nasser as president in 1970, he put international Islam to service in the conflict with Israel. Since his 1977 peace initiative, however, Sadat, without ever renouncing his commitment to an Islamic world view, has changed tactics and recovered the disputed sacred territory and won American goodwill, although he has also incurred the wrath of Muslim critics both within Egypt and without.

1238. Israeli, Raphael. SADAT'S EGYPT AND TENG'S CHINA: REVOLUTION VERSUS MODERNIZATION. *Pol. Sci. Q. 1980 95(3): 361-371.* Analyzes the processes of modernization and revolution, which displace each other in a cyclical fashion in non-Western societies. Uses case studies of Anwar Sadat's Egypt and Deng Xiaoping's (Teng Hsiao-p'ing) China to illustrate the theory and to argue that the transition from modernization to revolution and vice versa hinges on certain types of leaders. J

1239. Jankowski, James. EGYPTIAN RESPONSES TO THE PALESTINE PROBLEM IN THE INTERWAR PERIOD. *Int. J. of Middle East Studies [Great Britain] 1980 12(1): 1-38.* Examines the prevalent attitudes of informed Egyptians to events in Palestine in the period 1920-1940, concentrating on the years 1929-30 and 1936-39. With respect to both periods, the author focuses on public opinion in response to events in Palestine, and points out the dominant opinions expressed by the Egyptian press. Based on newspaper accounts and interviews; 215 notes. R. B. Orr

1240. Jankowski, James. THE GOVERNMENT OF EGYPT AND THE PALESTINE QUESTION, 1936-1939. *Middle Eastern Studies [Great Britain] 1981 17(4): 427-453.* Examines the growth of Egyptian government involvement in the Palestine question, the secret representations to Britain in 1936 and the detailed and lengthy negotiations over the British White Paper of 1939. Attempts an evaluation of this change from a policy of noninvolvement and assesses the consequences of involvement which are seen in relation to Egyptian influence on British policies, the effects on Egyptian domestic policies and its relations with the rest of the Arab World. Based on British Foreign Office Records, Egyptian official documents, contemporary Egyptian newspapers and secondary sources; 127 notes. F. A. Clements

1241. Kimche, Jon. THE RIDDLE OF SADAT. *Midstream 1974 20(4): 7-28.* Reviews Anwar Sadat's political life since the overthrow of King Farouk in 1952. S

1242. Koshelev, V. S. IZ ISTORII TAINYKH ANTIBRITANSKIKH ORGANIZATSII V EGIPTE (1870-1924 GG) [Excerpts from the history of the secret anti-British organizations in Egypt, 1870-1924]. *Narody Azii i Afriki [USSR] 1980 (1): 111-119.* Outlines the different stages in the history of a few anti-British movements in Egypt from the creation of the first societies in the 1870's. Describes the role of these political organizations, their activities in the struggle for independence, and sometimes irresponsible acts of terrorism which gave the British the opportunity to repress the liberation movement. The murder of Sir Lee Stack in Cairo in 1924 marked the end of the most active period of these secret societies. 43 notes. C. Pichelin

1243. Krása, Miloslav. RELATIONS BETWEEN THE INDIAN NATIONAL CONGRESS AND THE WAFD PARTY OF EGYPT IN THE THIRTIES. *Archiv Orientální [Czechoslovakia] 1973 41(3): 212-233.* Surveys the relationship between the Indian National Congress and the Egyptian Wafd party in the thirties in their common struggle against British rule. Indo-Egyptian contacts held promise for mutual support between the two key liberation movements in regions of the British Empire, but war intervened to alter the situation before they matured. 74 notes. G. E. Pergl

1244. Lacouture, Jean. ANOUAR EL-SADATE, PAYSAN DU NIL [Anwar Sadat, a Nile villager]. *Histoire [France] 1978 (4): 82-85.* Discusses Anwar Sadat's life as expressed in his autobiography, *À la recherche d'une identité: histoire de ma vie* (1978).

1245. Mauny, Michel de. POURQUOI L'EGYPTE VEUT LA PAIX [Why Egypt wants peace]. *Écrits de Paris [France] 1978 (385): 43-49.* Economic conditions in Egypt have made it a proponent of peace in the Middle East.

1246. Mayer, Thomas. ABBAS HILMI II AS REFLECTED IN SOME OF HIS PAPERS. *Asian and African Studies [Israel] 1980 14(3): 279-286.* An examination of a collection of the personal correspondence of the last khedive of Egypt shows him to have been at the center of a number of intrigues in the Middle East. These were encouraged by those in his pay as a means of ingratiating themselves. Based on the collection of Abbas Hilmi papers on loan to the University Library Durham and British Foreign Office Records; 36 notes. R. T. Brown

1247. Mayer, Thomas. EGYPT AND THE GENERAL ISLAMIC CONFERENCE OF JERUSALEM IN 1931. *Middle Eastern Studies [Great Britain] 1982 18(3): 311-322.* The 1931 Islamic Conference was seen by Mawlana Shaukat Ali, president of the Caliphate Society in India, as a means of turning Jerusalem into the new Islamic center where the next caliph would be nominated, while Muhammed Amin al-Husseini, the Mufti of Jerusalem, saw it as a vehicle for arousing Muslim opposition to the Zionist presence in Palestine. Initial Egyptian reaction was hostile because of the question of the caliphate, but this was dispelled by a visit from the Mufti. However, his discussions with opposition parties in Egypt antagonized the government, which then renewed the attack on the conference. Although the conference took place and may have heightened an awareness of the Zionist problem, it did not lead to greater Egyptian intervention, which only really emerged after the Arab Revolt of 1936. Based on primary Arabic sources, British Foreign Office Records, Israeli State Archives, Central Zionist Archives and secondary sources; 92 notes. F. A. Clements

1248. Merriam, John G. EGYPT AFTER SADAT. *Current Hist. 1982 81(471): 5-8, 38-39.* Analyzes the diplomatic and domestic problems confronting post-Sadat Egypt, including the possible development of a "strategic consensus" among Egypt, Israel, and Saudi Arabia, and the internal threat posed by Islamic fundamentalism.

1249. Merriam, John G. and Merriam, Kathleen H. EGYPT'S STRUGGLE TO MODERNIZE. *Int. Rev. of Hist. and Pol. Sci. [India] 1973 10(4): 65-89.* Great Britain's military occupation of Egypt was detrimental to Egypt's nation building efforts and modernization, 1919-33. British High Commissioner George Ambrose Lloyd successfully retarded the development of Egypt's military institutions, important to a nation's state building process, by politicizing military appointments. Egyptian nationalists acquiesced, realizing that modernization could only come through the conclusion of an Anglo-Egyptian treaty. Based on government documents and secondary sources; 48 notes. E. McCarthy

1250. Mikhailov, A. AN IMPORTANT MILESTONE IN EGYPT'S HISTORY. *Int. Affairs [USSR] 1977 (8): 46-53.* Review of Egypt's 1952 independence struggle. A band of unknown officers led by Gamal Abdel Nasser initiated a coup by which they took control of the country. Nasser immediately threw off imperialist shackles, drove the hated British from the country, and returned British-held properties to Egyptians. The Soviet Union resolutely supported these actions and actively led the opposition to the imperialist invasion of 1956. The United States then attempted to establish new forms of imperialism in place of the old, but Nasser steadfastly refused to join military alliances whose objective was to prepare for invasions of Soviet territory. V. L. Human

1251. Mitchell, Richard P. and Kepel, Gilles. LES FRÈRES MUSULMANS [The Muslim Brotherhood]. *Histoire [France] 1980 (26): 20-29.* Founded during the 1930's, the Muslim Brotherhood was based on political and religious principles and rejected the Westernization of Egypt. It was banned and brutally repressed by Gamal Abdel Nasser, but is today experiencing an unmistakable revival throughout the Muslim world. J

1252. Moore, Clement Henry. AUTHORITARIAN POLITICS IN UNINCORPORATED SOCIETY: THE CASE OF NASSER'S EGYPT. *Comparative Pol. 1974 6(2): 193-218.*

1253. Müller, Zdeněk. NASSERISM: THE SHAPING OF THE IDEOLOGY OF THE EGYPTIAN LEADERSHIP AFTER 1952. *Arch. Orientální [Czechoslovakia] 1982 50(1): 22-42.* Following the 1952 coup by Egypt's Free Officers group, intense ideological controversy emerged. Gamal Abdel Nasser's *Philosophy of the Revolution* blamed the decline of Egyptian society on foreign rulers and colonizers and called for a policy based on anticolonialism, Afro-Asian solidarity, opposition to great power military bases and interference, nationalism, and socialism. The 1962 National Charter was based on this philosophy, though there were vast differences of opinion concerning the road Egyptian socialism should take. The leftist trend included a school of Marxist socialism based on "scientific" principles and a school of non-Marxist socialism based on philosophers such as Sartre and Bergson. The rightist schools included one favoring Islamic socialism and one that advocated a nationalist socialism with a religious component. The leading spokesman of the left was Fouad Moursi. Secondary sources; 53 notes. J. Powell

1254. Muzikář, Josef. AVANTGARDNÍ POLITICKÉ STRANY V ARABSKÉM REVOLUČNÍM HNUTÍ (GAMÁL ABDANNÁSIR A JEHO VZTAH K POLITICKÝM STRANÁM) [Avant-garde political parties in the Arab revolutionary movement: Gamal Abdel Nasser and his relations with political parties]. *Československý Časopis Hist. [Czechoslovakia] 1979 27(4): 481-513.* In 1952 Gamal Abdel Nasser (1918-70) proclaimed Islamic socialism as a guiding principle of the Egyptian revolution. This movement tended to ignore class differences rather than emphasize them, and the requirements of Egyptian national unity also favored a single mass party over the proletarian vanguard party typical of scientific socialism. The composition of the Arab Socialist Union (1962-78) reflected its dependence on Egypt's bureaucracy and army, and spelled a heavy bourgeois preponderance in this socialist party. Similar trends have characterized Baathism in Iraq and

Syria and the National Liberation Front in Algeria. 104 notes.
R. E. Weltsch

1255. Muzikář, Josef. VANGUARD POLITICAL PARTIES AND THE ARAB REVOLUTIONARY MOVEMENT. *Arhív Orientální [Czechoslovakia] 1979 47(4): 225-259.* Examines the development and character of political parties in socialist Arab states, focusing on Egypt and the Arab Socialist Union.

1256. Narayan, B. K. SADAT AND THE PAN-ARAB MOVEMENT. *Indian J. of Pol. [India] 1976 10(2): 60-69.* President Anwar Sadat has not given up the pan-Arab ideal. He is a genuine nationalist with a pan-Arab outlook. His role is basically that of continuing Nasser's Arab revolution while accepting the coexistence of different systems within the Arab world. Egyptian leaders whether Nasser or Sadat have all along gauged that whatever importance the Arabs would have either in the West or in the East would be proportionate to their international influence either as political allies who had to be supported or potential enemies who had to be appeased. The Arabs had to build up an Arab potential first. Secondary sources. J

1257. Nasser, Gamal Abdel. MEMOIRS OF THE FIRST PALESTINE WAR. *J. of Palestine Studies [Lebanon] 1973 2(2): 3-32.* The first English translation of Nasser's memoirs which, written after the Israeli raid on Gaza, 28 February 1955, shed light on the military capability of the Egyptian army in 1948, as well as on the revolutionary influences of the Palestinians on Egyptian officers just prior to the downfall of the monarchy.

1258. Nicolle, David. THE EGYPTIAN ADVANCE. PART I: THE FALUJA POCKET. *Army Q. and Defence J. [Great Britain] 1975 105(4): 440-456.* Describes operations by the Egyptian army against the Israelis near Faluja, Palestine, in the First Palestine War of 1948. Article to be continued.

1259. Nicolle, David. UNEASY ALLIES. *Army Q. and Defence J. [Great Britain] 1979 109(4): 429-432.* Egyptian military forces in World War II supported the British until shortly before the end of the war, a fact which has been largely ignored until recently, when relations between the two countries began improving after postwar politics had destroyed the relationship between them.

1260. O'Ballance, Edgar. THE EGYPTIAN SITUATION. *Army Q. and Defence J. [Great Britain] 1979 109(4): 405-412.* Discusses Egyptian President Anwar Sadat's three-part peace plan from 1973 when the Egyptian army crossed the Suez Canal and broke through the Bar Lev Line, until October, 1979 when Sadat sent arms to Morocco, and briefly traces Egypt's economic and defense problems since 1948.

1261. Puaux, François. ANOUAR EL-SADATE. LA CONQUÊTE DU POUVOIR [Anwar Sadat: the conquest of power]. *Nouvelle Rev. des Deux Mondes [France] 1981 (11): 279-288.* An account of the career of Anwar Sadat (1918-81), centering on his ambitions, policies, attitudes, and activities concerning Egypt and the Arab world, Israel, and the Great Powers.

1262. Qureshi, Yasmin. A REVIEW OF SOVIET-EGYPTIAN RELATIONS. *Pakistan Horizon [Pakistan] 1982 35(1): 107-146.* Examines the changes in political leadership in the USSR and Egypt, and changing political relations between the two countries.

1263. Ra'anan, Uri. THE SOVIET-EGYPTIAN "RIFT." *Commentary 1976 61(6): 29-35.* Although numerous stories have flooded the West indicating a permanent break in Soviet-Egyptian relations since 1959, no such irreversible breach actually exists. Indeed, despite the much-publicized expulsion of Soviet experts from Egypt in 1972, from the Yom Kippur War in October 1973 to date, rather than embargoing arms, the Soviets have provided Egypt with a considerable quantity of weapons. It appears that Egypt and the USSR are de-emphasizing their relationship in order to encourage US attempts to gain Egyptian friendship, in the expectation that US tactics will include increased pressure on the Israelis to compromise in a Middle East settlement. Primary and secondary sources. S. R. Herstein

1264. Reed, Stanley F. DATELINE CAIRO: SHAKEN PILLAR. *Foreign Policy 1981-82 (45): 175-185.* Anwar Sadat's successor, President Hosni Mubarek inherits substantial domestic opposition. A significant source of discontent is the Egyptian perception of excessive US influence in Egyptian affairs. Managing domestic opposition is Mubarek's top priority. Helping to fulfill Sadat's domestic and foreign policies (through substantial economic aid, speeded up arms shipments, and realization of Palestinian autonomy) is the best assurance that the US can have that Mubarek's regime will surmount its difficulties.
M. K. Jones

1265. Reid, Donald M. FU'AD SIRAJ AL-DIN AND THE EGYPTIAN WAFD. *J. of Contemporary Hist. [Great Britain] 1980 15(4): 721-744.* Fu'ad Siraj al-Din belonged to the class of landed gentry of Egypt, traditionally supporters of the Palace. In 1936 he became a member of parliament, but unlike his father, as a member of the Wafd or Constitutional Liberal Party. In 1943, he became Minister of Agriculture; in 1948, Secretary General of Wafd; and in 1950, Minister of Finance. In order to stay in power, he courted King Faruq only to share his downfall in 1952. Brought to trial in 1953, Siraj received a fifteen-year sentence for corruption but was released in 1955 or early 1956. Briefly rearrested in 1961 and 1967, he later shared in Sadat's Thermidor of 1970. By 1977, Siraj was again a potentate. Based mainly on primary sources; 64 notes. M. P. Trauth

1266. Reid, Donald M. THE NATIONAL BAR ASSOCIATION AND EGYPTIAN POLITICS 1912-1954. *Int. J. of African Hist. Studies 1974 7(4): 608-643.* The Wafd Party made more effective use of the Egyptian National Bar Association than its opponents during the 20th century. The Wafdists enlisted the bar association to keep their party's activities visible not only to the legal profession and the politicians, but also to the general public. Primary sources; 73 notes, 2 appendixes. M. M. McCarthy

1267. Reid, Donald M. THE RETURN OF THE EGYPTIAN WAFD, 1978. *Int. J. of African Hist. Studies 1979 12(3): 389-415.* Describes the activities of Siraj al-Din and the New Wafd Party in Egypt in the context of President Anwar Sadat's liberalization program. 73 notes. M. McCarthy

1268. Rejwan, Nissim. THE EGYPTIAN MOOD ON THE EVE OF WAR. *Midstream 1973 19(10): 63-66.*

1269. Rejwan, Nissim. HANATSERIZM VEHA'ISLAM—HAMEIMAD HARA'AYONI [Nasserism and Islam: the ideological dimension]. *Hamizrah Hehadash [Israel] 1974 24(3): 161-174.* Analyzes the relationship between Islamic tradition and the nationalist socialist ideology of Nasser's Egypt. While the 1956 Egyptian constitution proclaimed Islam as Egypt's official religion, Nasserism was predominantly secular, and neither orthodox Muslims nor orthodox Marxists are willing to reconcile the two. Shaykh Mustafa al-Sibai, a Syrian theologian, tried to prove that Nasserist socialism was inherent in Islam, but the Egyptian Sayyid Qutb, executed for incitement, argued that socialism and nationalism were antagonistic and alien to Islam. 36 notes. T. Sassoon

1270. Rizvi, Nihal H. POLITICAL ORGANIZATION OF A REVOLUTIONARY REGIME: THE CASE OF EGYPT. *Hamdard Islamicus [Pakistan] 1981 4(4): 53-82.* Discusses the role of political organizations such as the National Union and the Arab Socialist Union in mobilizing mass support for the revolutionary regime in Egypt following the overthrow of the monarchy in 1952.

1271. Rogers, Glenn F., Jr. THE BATTLE FOR SUEZ CITY. *Military Rev. 1979 59(11): 27-33.* Discusses the Egyptian conquest of Suez City during the October War, 1973.

1272. Rondot, Pierre. ANOUAR AS SADAT ET L'ÉGYPTE (1970-1980) [Anwar Sadat and Egypt (1970-80)]. *Défense Natl. [France] 1981 37(1): 71-83.* A brief, general view of Anwar Sadat's policies as president of Egypt.

1273. Rondot, Pierre. ÉGYPTE: APRÈS LE "QUATRIÈME COMBAT" [Egypt: After the "Fourth Battle"]. *Rev. Française d'Études Pol. Africaines [France] 1973 8(95): 8-12.* Discusses the strategic results of the October War, its political implications (such as the moral degeneration of Arab partisans, danger to the strength of the Arab coalition, questionable reliability of international, including Soviet, support to Egypt), and the demonstration of inferior military techniques by Egypt.

1274. Rondot, Pierre. LE PRAGMATISME ÉGYPTIEN DANS LA CRISE ORIENTALE [Egyptian pragmatism in the Eastern crisis]. *Défense Natl. [France] 1975 31(6): 77-89.* Analyzes President Anwar Sadat's paradoxical position, contrasting the brilliance of his foreign political actions with the gloom of the day-to-day difficulties concerning internal economic development.

1275. Rondot, Pierre. TRAITS ORIGINAUX ET VOCATION ARABE DE L'EGYPTE [Original traits and Egypt's Arabic vocation]. *Défense Natl. [France] 1977 33(2): 25-39.* Interprets Egypt's foreign policy, 1957-77, in the light of its traditional historical and geographical background and Arabic culture.

1276. Rosen, Steven J. and Fukuyama, Francis. EGYPT AND ISRAEL AFTER CAMP DAVID. *Current Hist. 1979 76(443): 1-4, 39-41.* Discusses Egyptian President Anwar Sadat's 1977 trip to Jerusalem and the reactions of the United States, the Soviet Union, Israel, and the other Arab states, and describes the peace negotiations which followed through 1978.

1277. Rubin, Barry. AMERICA AND THE EGYPTIAN REVOLUTION, 1950-1957. *Pol. Sci. Q. 1982 97(1): 73-90.* American policy toward Egypt was transformed during this critical period from one oriented toward eventual Egyptian participation in an anti-Soviet collective security network to a belief that Gamal Abdel Nasser was the key force behind political upheaval and anti-Americanism in the Arab world. Chronicles the events leading up to Nasser's nationalization of the Suez Canal company and the creation of the Eisenhower Doctrine. Based on extensive interviews, newly released documents, and secondary sources; 67 notes. L. J. Klass

1278. Rubin, Barry. EGYPT AND THE PALESTINE QUESTION, 1922-1939. *Wiener Lib. Bull. [Great Britain] 1978 31(45-46): 18-28.* Egyptian interest in the Palestine question grew gradually in the 1920's and 1930's, aroused by a traditional concern for security on the northeast frontier, desire that the Muslim area remain Muslim; and an ambition to lead the Arab world. Some Egyptian leaders, however, felt sympathy for Zionist achievements and worked for cooperation with the Jews. Although these leaders did not prevail, Egyptian attitudes, compared to the attitudes of the rest of the Arab world, were relatively restrained. The exigencies of domestic politics help explain the gradual turn away from moderation and lack of interest, as politicians began to compete with each other in making capital out of the Palestine issue. Also at work was the Egyptian realization that the German and Italian threat to the status quo in the Middle East gave them a leverage in the area because of British fears for the security of their supply lines. 61 notes. R. V. Layton

1279. Rubinstein, Alvin Z. EGYPT SINCE THE OCTOBER WAR. *Current Hist. 1976 70(412): 14-17, 37, 38.* Discusses political and economic trends in Egypt, 1973-75, emphasizing President Anwar Sadat's changing foreign policy toward the United States and the USSR.

1280. Rubinstein, Alvin Z. EGYPT'S FOREIGN POLICY. *Current Hist. 1974 66(390): 53-56, 88.* Reviews the main elements of Egypt's diplomatic and military strategy, in view of the Yom Kippur War and the use of the oil weapon. From an issue on the Middle East, 1974. S

1281. Salem-Babikian, Norma. THE SACRED AND THE PROFANE: SADAT'S SPEECH TO THE KNESSET. *Middle East J. 1980 34(1): 13-24.* Examines the speech of Anwar Sadat delivered at the Knesset (Israeli parliament) in Jerusalem on 20 November 1977, to determine, among other things, whether the speech used religious terms for political functions. Sadat used religious themes for their rhetorical persuasive powers and for legitimating his peace initiative. He succeeded in legitimating his peace initiative in the West but not in the Arab world, because he could not achieve concrete results for the Arabs. Secondary works; fig., 29 notes. P. J. Mattar

1282. Saliba, Najib E. THE DECLINE OF NASIRISM IN SADAT'S EGYPT. *World Affairs 1975 138(1): 51-59.* President Anwar Sadat turned Egypt away from the leftist orientation of Nasserism toward traditional conservatism in 1970-74.

1283. Sawant, Ankush B. EGYPT'S FOREIGN POLICY. *Int. Studies [India] 1977 16(3): 411-430.* A bibliographical essay covering the main English language source material regarding the early Anglo-Egyptian relations and the radical changes in Egypt's foreign relations engendered by its emergence as an independent nation. 137 notes. R. V. Ritter

1284. Sawant, Ankush B. RECENT CHANGES IN EGYPT'S FOREIGN POLICY. *India Q. [India] 1979 35(1): 20-41.* Surveys events since Anwar Sadat became president of Egypt in 1970 as a means of understanding present Egyptian foreign policy. A watershed was Sadat's expulsion of the 20,000 Soviet military experts in 1972, followed by his limited victory in the 1973 offensive across the Suez Canal into the Israel-held Sinai. This opened the way to friendly relations with the United States in his moves to rebuild the shattered Egyptian economy. Sadat's initiative toward Israel was an even more unprecedented step. Despite extreme criticism by the rest of the Arab world he has persisted in this direction and has been rewarded by the return of the Sinai to Egypt. Primary sources; 75 notes. R. V. Ritter

1285. Schueftan, Dan. NASSER'S 1967 POLICY RECONSIDERED. *Jerusalem Q. [Israel] 1977 (3): 124-144.* Reviews Arab attitudes toward Israel 1948-67, and concludes that Gamal Abdel Nasser was forced into the Six-Day War with Israel against his will, chiefly by pressure from Syria.

1286. Schuetz, C. F. UN FOOD OFFICE IN CAIRO CLOSED BY ARAB PRESSURE. *Int. Perspectives [Canada] 1980 (Sept-Oct): 22-24.* By demanding the relocation of the Cairo regional bureau in some other city, the Arab countries have used the UN Food and Agricultural Organization (FAO) as a political weapon to punish Egypt for signing a peace treaty with Israel. The location of the office became a major issue which threatened the existence of the food agency until a compromise agreement resulted in the closing of the office "for the time being." The confrontation has serious implications as another example of nations getting their way by radicalizing minor aspects of international relations. Photo. E. S. Palais

1287. Semaan, Khalil I. DRAMA AS A VEHICLE OF PROTEST IN NĀSIR'S EGYPT. *Int. J. of Middle East Studies [Great Britain] 1979 10(1): 49-53.* Examines Arabic dramatists' political messages, using the play, *Ma'sāt al-Hallāj* by Salāh 'Abd al- Sabūr. The play appears to be a description of the regime of Gamal Abdel Nasser, whose miscalculations brought about suffering and loss of life and property. R. B. Orr

1288. Sen, Pradeep. PARTY SYSTEM UNDER SADAT—CHANGE OR CONTINUITY? *India Q. [India] 1981 37(3): 414-427.* A consideration of the nature and changes in the political party system in Egypt under the regime of Anwar Sadat. Like Nasser before him, Sadat acted swiftly to eliminate his enemies and consolidate his regime, and only then considered the desirability of political parties. Nasser seemed to favor the Left over the Right, but in reality he kept the two at odds with each other so they would not bother him. Anwar Sadat has retained that policy; his periodic forays into the realm of pluralistic politics are but smokescreens, devices to make the people think that they have a democratic society. 48 notes. V. L. Human

1289. Sfeir, Antoine. LENDEMAINS DE PAIX EN ÉGYPTE [Egypt after the peace settlement]. *Études [France] 1980 352(1): 9-20.* Egyptian president Anwar Sadat's power was greater in 1979 than it had been since his election in 1970, but he has met serious economic problems and some opposition to Egypt's peace treaty with Israel.

1290. Shamir, Shimon. EGYPT AFTER THE YOM KIPPUR WAR: A PROVISIONAL BALANCE-SHEET. *Wiener Lib. Bull. [Great Britain] 1975 28(35-36): 57-64.* Discusses the achievements of President Anwar Sadat's regime after the October War, whose main objectives were the restoration of Arab territories lost in 1967, and the establishment of Palestinian influence on the West Bank and in the Gaza Strip.

1291. Shamir, Shimon. THE INFLUENCE OF GERMAN NATIONAL-SOCIALISM ON RADICAL MOVEMENTS IN EGYPT. *Jahrb-*

uch des Inst. für Deutsche Geschichte [Israel] 1975 Beiheft 1: 200-209. In the 1930's political, economic, and social conditions all helped provide a climate in Egypt that encouraged the adoption of Nazi ideals and methods. Such radical organizations as the Society of Muslim Brethren, the Young Men's Muslim Association, the Blue Shirts, the Young Egypt Society with its Green Shirts, all borrowed much from the Nazis, although German Nazis offered them very little encouragement. Among the junta that overturned the Egyptian government in 1952 were Anwar Sadat and Gamal Abdel Nasser, who as young men had belonged to radical movements. 17 notes. M. Faissler

1292. Sheehan, Edward R. F. SADAT'S WAR. *IDOC Middle East Q. 1974 1(1): 53-59.* As a result of the 6 October 1973 military offensive against Israel, Egypt won diplomatic attention from the US that it might not have. S

1293. Shepard, William. THE DILEMMA OF A LIBERAL: SOME POLITICAL IMPLICATIONS IN THE WRITINGS OF THE EGYPTIAN SCHOLAR, AHMAD AMIN (1886-1954). *Middle Eastern Studies [Great Britain] 1980 16(2): 84-97.* Ahmad Amin was a liberal Egyptian intellectual, but his lack of faith in public opinion led him to a directive concept of political leadership. His view of public opinion explains the failure of liberal democracy in Egypt. Yet his way of thinking, which is prevalent, is not inconsistent with the recent process of liberalization, whose outcome remains to be seen. Based on Ahmad Amin's works; 55 notes. P. J. Mattar

1294. Shlaim, Avi. SADAT AND HIS CRITICS. *Contemporary Rev. [Great Britain] 1978 233(1352): 113-121.* Discusses relations between President Anwar Sadat of Egypt and other leaders of Arab states, 1973-78.

1295. Siverson, Randolph M. ROLE AND PERCEPTION IN INTERNATIONAL CRISIS: THE CASES OF ISRAELI AND EGYPTIAN DECISION MAKERS IN NATIONAL CAPITALS AND THE UNITED NATIONS. *Internat. Organization 1973 27(3): 329-346.* "Reports an exploration of the relationship between a decision maker's role and his perception during an international crisis. Research on the social and political processes of the United Nations suggests that a variety of factors, including communication patterns, nonnational roles, and learning experiences may produce a role orientation in delegates that would have an impact upon their perceptions even when their nation is involved in an international crisis. This proposition is explored using content analysis data from the 1956 Suez crisis. The decision makers whose perceptions furnish the data are the Egyptian and Israeli Permanent Representatives to the United Nations and the occupants of high foreign policy positions in the national capitals of Egypt and Israel. The initial analysis of the data indicates only very small differences in the perceptions. The analysis of the data does not support the original proposition. Finally, some caveats concerning the research are raised." J

1296. Slonim, Shlomo. AMERICAN-EGYPTIAN RAPPROCHEMENT. *World Today [Great Britain] 1975 31(2): 47-57.* The real turning point in US-Egyptian relations was the expulsion of the Russians from Egypt in July 1972. The Yom Kippur War simply accelerated a process already under way and the worldwide alert of US forces in October 1973 was not so much to rescue Israel as to save Egypt from a Soviet occupation that would have radically upset the balance of power. J

1297. Slonim, Shlomo. SADAT'S AMERICAN STRATEGY. *Midstream 1977 23(7): 27-31.* Chronicles diplomatic relations between Egypt and the US, 1971-77, maintaining that the current apparent turnabout from the USSR to the US can be traced back to 1971.

1298. Smith, Charles D. 4 FEBRUARY 1942: ITS CAUSES AND ITS INFLUENCE ON EGYPTIAN POLITICS AND ON THE FUTURE OF ANGLO-EGYPTIAN RELATIONS, 1937-1945. *Int. J. of Middle East Studies [Great Britain] 1979 10(4): 453-479.* Examines the causes and influence on Egyptian politics and the future of Anglo-Egyptian relations, 1937-45, of the event of 4 February 1942, when the British ambassador in Cairo threatened King Farouk I with forced abdication because he refused to appoint the leader of the Wafd party prime minister. Based on British Foreign Office documents and Egyptian primary sources; 93 notes. R. B. Orr

1299. Springborg, Robert. IN SEARCH OF EGYPT. *Politics [Australia] 1976 11(1): 85-89.* Reviews R. Hrair Dekmejian's *Egypt Under Nasser: A Study of Political Dynamics* (Albany: State U. of New York Pr., 1971); Iliya F. Harik's *The Political Mobilization of Peasants: A Study of an Egyptian Community* (Bloomington: Indiana U. Pr., 1974); James B. Mayfield's *Rural Politics in Nasser's Egypt: Quest for Legitimacy* (Austin: U. of Texas Pr., 1971); and Amos Perlmusser's *Egypt: The Praetorian State* (New Brunswick, N.J.: Transaction Books, 1974).

1300. Springborg, Robert. PATRIMONIALISM AND POLICY MAKING IN EGYPT: NASSER AND SADAT AND THE TENURE POLICY FOR RECLAIMED LANDS. *Middle Eastern Studies [Great Britain] 1979 15(1): 49-69.* A comparative study of political leadership in Egypt. A study of the land tenure policy for reclaimed lands of Gamal Abdel Nasser and Anwar Sadat provides a means of evaluating the diverse ways in which patrimonialism may function. Nasser's exclusivism led his power to ebb into the clientage network beneath him. Sadat's inclusivism likewise has led to a dilemma resulting from his inclusion of a large number of individuals in policymaking. Such dilemmas are inherent in patrimonialism. Primary sources; 49 notes. R. V. Ritter

1301. Springborg, Robert. PROFESSIONAL SYNDICATES IN EGYPTIAN POLITICS, 1952-1970. *Int. J. of Middle East Studies [Great Britain] 1978 9(3): 275-295.* Traces the history of professional syndicates in Egypt during the Nasser period, 1952-70, showing how the ups and downs of these syndicates reflected shifts of power within the inner core of the elite. It is unclear whether syndicates remained weak only because the government refused to allow them to grow stronger, or because of factors characteristic of Egyptian political culture, such as a preference for small, informal groups over large formal organizations. Professional syndicates have become more viable voluntary associations since 1952. 80 notes. R. B. Orr

1302. Springborg, Robert. SAYED BEY MAREI AND POLITICAL CLIENTELISM IN EGYPT. *Comparative Pol. Studies 1979 12(3): 259-288.* Traces the decline of clientelism in Egypt by observing the fortunes of Sayed Marei and his patronage system, 1920's-70's.

1303. Springborg, Robert. U.S. POLICY TOWARD EGYPT: PROBLEMS AND PROSPECTS. *Orbis 1981 24(4): 805-818.* Analyzes the motives, problems, and prospects for the United States-Egyptian relationship in the Middle East. Created in 1977 as a marriage of convenience between two weakened parties trying to avoid domestic and foreign problems, the relationship has met with only limited success. Anwar Sadat was not able to convince other Arabs to join in the peace process, and the United States was unable to get the Israelis to make major concessions. Both sides seem to have based their strategy on erroneous conceptions, and the future of the Egyptian-American relationship is not promising. J. W. Thacker, Jr.

1304. Stein, Janice Gross. MILITARY DECEPTION, STRATEGIC SURPRISE, AND CONVENTIONAL DETERRENCE: A POLITICAL ANALYSIS OF EGYPT AND ISRAEL, 1971-73. *J. of Strategic Studies [Great Britain] 1982 5(1): 94-121.* Examines the calculations of Egypt's leaders from 1971 to 1973, calculations that culminated in the successful deception of October 1973, and Israeli intelligence estimations and warnings during the same period. A comparative analysis shows which factors Egypt's leaders considered and which of these same factors Israel's leaders ignored. Leaders generally do not go to war for military objectives but for far broader economic, diplomatic, and political purposes. Israel's military intelligence in 1973 can be faulted for focusing too heavily on military and discounting Egyptian consideration of broader purposes. Based on Egyptian, Israeli, and other primary sources; 70 notes. A. M. Osur

1305. Stephens, Robert. NASSER. *Hist. Today [Great Britain] 1981 31(Feb): 17-21.* Questions the legacy of Gamal Abdel Nasser of Egypt.

1306. Tignor, Robert L. BANK MISR AND FOREIGN CAPITALISM. *Int. J. of Middle East Studies [Great Britain] 1977 8(2): 161-181.*

Discusses the problems facing the Egyptian Bank Misr, 1919-49. Shows how the bank evolved and began to modify its original nationalist, populist, and antiforeign character. Primary sources; 62 notes.
R. B. Orr

1307. Vasil'ev, A. and Perminov, P. EGIPET: REVOLIUTSIIA I KONTRREVOLIUTSIIA [Egypt's revolution and counterrevolution]. *Aziia i Afrika Segodnia [USSR] 1982 (7): 12-15.* Many of the issues leading to the revolution which overthrew the corrupt regime of King Farouk on 23 July 1952 persist today and are aggravated by newer problems such as inflation, isolation from the Arab world, and imbalanced economic development.

1308. Vernant, Jacques. RÉFLEXIONS SUR LA VISITE DU PRÉSIDENT SADAT [Reflections on President Sadat's visit]. *Défense Natl. [France] 1978 34(1): 89-95.* Suggests that Anwar Sadat's visit to Israel may be interpreted as a proposal for an alternative forum for negotiations to the Geneva Conference, one disengaged from the supervision of the Great Powers.

1309. Wakebridge, Charles. THE EGYPTIAN STAFF SOLUTION. *Military Rev. 1975 55(3): 3-11.* Describes the Egyptian preparation for the 6 October 1973 attack against the Bar-Lev Line, the Israeli position on the East Bank of the Suez Canal. Scientific research, sound planning, attention to detail, and deception and secrecy on the part of the Egyptians enabled them to mount a large-scale assault crossing of the Suez Canal, take the Israelis by surprise, and push them back. 5 illus.
J. K. Ohl

1310. Warburg, Gabriel. LAMPSON'S ULTIMATUM TO FARUQ, 4 FEBRUARY, 1942. *Middle Eastern Studies [Great Britain] 1975 11(1): 24-32.* The standard accounts of this attempt to force King Farouk's abdication give Great Britain all the credit; but with the official British records now available, it is clear that Nahas Pasha and the Wafd party made common cause with the British government prior to the ultimatum, and used the ultimatum to regain power in Egypt. Somewhat ironically, this led to the "Free Officers" revolt in 1952, whose leaders included Muhammad Najib, Gamal Abdel Nasser and Anwar Sadat. Based on foreign office documents and secondary works.
K. M. Bailor

1311. Warburg, Gabriel R. ISLAM AND POLITICS IN EGYPT: 1952-80. *Middle Eastern Studies [Great Britain] 1982 18(2): 131-157.* The Muslim Brotherhood had been a significant force in Egyptian politics before the 1952 coup and was associated with the Free Officer movement, which recognized that unless the Brethren could be persuaded to cooperate with the new regime they would have to be suppressed. Examines how, after 30 years of Western imported government and 25 years of Arab nationalism and socialism, Islam has again come to the fore. Discusses social and cultural factors, internal politics, external relations, and the movement's populist character. Based on secondary sources, some in Arabic and Hebrew; 97 notes. F. A. Clements

1312. Witte, Barthold. FÜNF JAHRE SADAT—EINE BILANZ [Five years of Sadat: a balance]. *Europa Archiv [West Germany] 1975 30(21): 671-678.* Anwar Sadat defeated the left-wing Nasserists, undertook a limited democratization, began a new economic policy that attracted foreign investment, and slowly developed a new foreign policy toward Israel, 1970-75.

1313. —. MAN OF THE MOMENT: ANWAR AL-SADAT. *Africa Report 1973 18(6): 24-25.*

1314. —. THE SUEZ CROSSING: AN INTERVIEW WITH MAJOR GENERAL MOHAMED ABDEL HALIM ABOU GHAZALA. *Military Rev. 1979 59(11): 2-7.* Mohamed Ghazala, commander of the artillery of the Egyptian Second Army, explains how his troops crossed the Suez Canal during the October War, 1973.

Society

1315. Allen, Roger. CONTEMPORARY EGYPTIAN LITERATURE. *Middle East J. 1981 35(1): 25-39.* Surveys the trends in Egyptian literature from 1967 until 1980. Defeat in the Six-Day War of 1967 caused a profound reexamination of beliefs and values in Egypt. This affected the quality and quantity of literature. The famous writers, such as Ihsan Abd al-Quddus and Yusif Idris, wrote little. New writers, such as Sanallah Ibrahim and Jamal al-Ghitani, are charting new territory. 43 notes. P. J. Mattar

1316. Aly, Abd al-Monein Said and Wenner, Manfred W. MODERN ISLAMIC REFORM MOVEMENTS: THE MUSLIM BROTHERHOOD IN CONTEMPORARY EGYPT. *Middle East J. 1982 36(3): 336-361.* The role of the Muslim Brotherhood in Egypt is used as a case study of developments that have taken place in modern Islamic reform movements, following a brief historical introduction to the growth and development of these movements. The position of the brotherhood in terms of political action, both covert and overt, is discussed, as is its relationship with the Free Officers movement prior to the coup. Its position under Gamal Abdel Nasser and Anwar Sadat is also discussed, as is the support received from Saudi Arabia as an ideological movement and as a counter to the Egyptian left. Based on press reports and secondary sources; 64 notes. F. A. Clements

1317. Billops, Camille. TAHIA HALIM. *Women's Studies 1978 6(1): 107-111.* Tahia Halim, an Egyptian artist in Cairo, was born in Sudan. She studied at the Academy of Fine Arts in Cairo and the Académie Julian in Paris. Halim's early paintings depict European subjects, but her mature works display Egyptian content and form, and her contemporary paintings depict Pharaonic and Arab fables in desert tones. She received a Guggenheim prize for her painting *Pietá* in 1958, and in 1960 received a gold medal for her Cairo exhibit. The Egyptian Ministry of Culture has granted her a lifetime stipend. 3 fig. S. P. Forgus

1318. Bresc, Henri. LES COPTES D'ÉGYPTE [The Copts of Egypt]. *Histoire [France] 1978 (5): 84-86.* Discusses the history, persecution, and adaptation of the Coptic Christian minority in a thoroughly Islamicized Egypt, 19th-20th centuries.

1319. Busool, Assad N. THE DEVELOPMENT OF TAHA HUSAYN'S ISLAMIC THOUGHT. *Muslim World 1978 68(4): 259-284.* Traces the development of Tāhā Husayn's thought from his early childhood and as a student at Al-Azhar University and the Egyptian University before World War I, until he became one of Egypt's most respected intellectuals in the 1950's. Until World War II, Husayn was a critic of orthodox Islam and a promoter of Westernization and pharaonism (Egyptian nationalism). After the War his ideas changed radically and he became religious, anti-Western, and a supporter of Arab unity. Based on Husayn's writings, and Arabic and English secondary works; 91 notes. P. J. Mattar

1320. Calabrese, Maria C. LA POLITICA DI PIANIFICAZIONE FAMILIARE IN EGITTO FINO AL 1977 [Family planning policy in Egypt, 1966-77]. *Oriente Moderno [Italy] 1978 58(1-3): 97-107.* Discusses the two plans to deal with overpopulation in Egypt by family planning since 1966, and asserts that their failure was partly due to religious teaching and the conservative attitudes of the uneducated classes.

1321. Charalampopoúlou, Charal D. O PNEUMATIKÓS TOÛ SINÂ ARCHIMANDRÍTES DANIÊL PAPAÏOÁNNOU (1852-1930) [The confessor of Sinai, Archimandrite Daniel Papaioannou (1852-1930)]. *Epetirís Etaireías Stereoelladikôn Meletôn [Greece] 1974-75 5: 427-434.* A biography of Archimandrite Daniel Papaioannou (1852-1930) of the Orthodox monastery on Mount Sinai.

1322. Chernovskaia, V. V. EGIPETSKAIA INTELLIGENTSIIA V PERVOI POLOVINE XX V. (CHISLENNOST', SOSTAV, STRUKTURA I SOTSIAL'NOE-KLASSOVOE POLOZHENIE) [Egyptian intelligentsia in the first half of the 20th century (its numerical strength, composition, structure, and social class position)]. *Narody Azii i Afriki [USSR] 1976 (3): 56-69.* From 1907 to 1947 the increase in the intelligentsia in Egypt was considerable. The author analyzes the growth in educational institutions, and the increase in number of students receiving diplomas from secondary and special schools and institutions of higher education. He gives statistics regarding the different fields of endeavor of the intelligentsia, particularly from 1927 to 1947. From the end of the 1940's, over 83 percent of the intelligentsia was employed by the government. The process of differentiation based on social standing and wealth in the intelligentsia also grew along with the social and political crisis which resulted in the revolutionary coup of 1952. The division among the intelligentsia into two opposing camps, the progressive and the reactionary, became even more evident after the revolution. 2 tables, 35 notes. L. Kalinowski

1323. Cooke, Miriam. YAHYĀ HAQQĪ AS CRITIC AND NATIONALIST. *Int. J. of Middle East Studies [Great Britain] 1981 13(1): 21-34.* The literary criticism of Yahyā Haqqī from 1920 through 1959 appeared at a time when Egyptian literature was abandoning traditional cliches and adopting Romantic and realist modes from the West. This era was also intensely nationalistic. The modern school from 1917 to 1925 called for an authentic Egyptian literature which should arise from the fact that Egypt—its peasants, bourgeoisie, and national rulers—was one. Literature then, served a social and political function. Haqqī's criticism took three forms: sociopolitical, with judicious criticism both of literature and of social progress, apologetic, compensating for what is bad in Egyptian literature by emphasizing the good, and exploratory. 111 notes. J. Powell

1324. Dajani, Karen Finlon. CAIRO: THE HOLLYWOOD OF THE ARAB WORLD. *Gazette [Netherlands] 1980 26(2): 89-98.* The Egyptian film industry, beginning in the 1930's, has been the principal supplier of films for the Arab world. The films are generally apolitical and geared for mass entertainment. Since 1975 government agencies have been set up to assist the film industry, which generates a good profit from film exports. Based on interviews and secondary sources; 3 tables, 18 notes, biblio. J. S. Coleman

1325. Dickie, James. SAYYID DARWISH: A BIOGRAPHICAL NOTE. *Islamic Q. [Great Britain] 1974 18(1-2): 8-10.* Born in Egypt in 1892, Sayyid Darwish rose from humble circumstances to be regarded as one of the greatest Arab composers of modern times. His life can be treated in three phases: a failed religious; a theatrical entertainer; and a brilliant composer from 1917. Following his death from a drug overdose in 1923, Sayyid Darwish's reputation increased throughout the Arab world. Secondary sources; 2 notes. P. J. Taylorson

1326. ElCalamawy, Sahair. THE AMERICAN INFLUENCE ON EDUCATION IN EGYPT. Davis, Allen F., ed. *For Better or Worse: The American Influence in the World*(Westport, Conn.: Greenwood Pr., 1981): 137-144. Discusses the vacuum created in Egypt in the 19th century by the decline of its educational system and the amelioration of this situation by the arrival of American missionaries and educational assistance. The latter manifested itself in the establishment of mission-run schools and the American University in Cairo, which, unlike their French and English counterparts, espoused no political or cultural propaganda for the founding country, offered all classes in Arabic, and practiced flexible methods that were adopted in Egyptian-sponsored schools when they began to appear in the 20th century.

1327. ElGuindi, Fadwa. VEILING *INFITAH* WITH MUSLIM MUSIC: EGYPT'S CONTEMPORARY ISLAMIC MOVEMENT. *Social Problems 1981 28(4): 465-485.* Describes the contemporary Islamic Movement in Egypt, with its two fundamental features of egalitarianism and sexual segregation, within which a new kind of Egyptian woman is emerging: educated, professional, nonelitist, and veiled, symbolizing the beginning of a synthesis between modernity and authenticity.

1328. Eliraz, Giora. THE SOCIAL AND CULTURAL CONCEPTION OF MUSTAFA SADIK AL-RAFII. *Asian and African Studies [Israel] 1979 13(2): 101-129.* The Egyptian poet, historian, and theologian, Mustafa Sadik al-Rafii, was a major apologist for traditional Islam who struggled against the encroachment of modernism and westernization. He is one of the founders of the concepts of militant Islam which led to the Muslim Brotherhood. Based on the writings of Rafii; 123 notes. R. T. Brown

1329. Eliraz, Giora. T'MUNAT HA'OLAM HAHEVRATIT V'HATARBUTIT SHEL MUSTAFA SADIQ AR-RAFAI [The social and cultural conception of Mustafa Sadiq ar-Rafai]. *Hamizrah Hehadash [Israel] 1978 27(3-4): 203-224.* Mustafa Sadik al-Rafii, ignored by most Western scholars, was a major figure in the struggle for Egyptian self-direction between the wars. Rafii considered Islam the absolute answer to all of the world's spiritual and material problems. He accepted the Koran as the acme of Arabic literary achievement, and objected to attempts to modernize the Arabic language. He warned against imitation of the West, yet acknowledged that science and technology could be adapted to the benefit of Islam. Rafii was blindly confident in his religion, diminishing his stature as an Egyptian leader. Based on Rafii's writings and historical works; 123 notes. T. Koppel

1330. Faksh, Mahmud A. THE CONSEQUENCES OF THE INTRODUCTION AND SPREAD OF MODERN EDUCATION: EDUCATION AND NATIONAL INTEGRATION IN EGYPT. *Middle Eastern Studies [Great Britain] 1980 16(2): 42-55.* Modern secular education, which was introduced during Mehemet Ali's rule (1905-48), rivaled but did not supplant the traditional religious system. The two systems perpetuated the differences between social classes and helped breed two distinct mentalities. Since the 1952 revolution mass education has contributed to the unification of cultural life. Secondary works; 3 tables, 48 notes. P. J. Mattar

1331. Garrison, Jean L. PUBLIC ASSISTANCE IN EGYPT: AN IDEOLOGICAL ANALYSIS. *Middle East J. 1978 32(3): 279-290.* Examines how Egyptian public welfare programs between 1946 and 1974 were used by the old and new regimes for ideological purposes. Public health was enacted as a reformist measure in response to political and economic turmoil, especially to help the village poor. But the government was unwilling to commit sufficient sums to it and the programs were no more than a token scheme. The revolutionary regime made minor changes until 1961, when socialism became a state philosophy. A new law was passed and expenditures were doubled. It fell far short of the projected needs, and public assistance still meets the minimal needs of Egypt's poor. It continues to be of rhetorical significance, because the government uses it to dmeonstrate its humanitarianism and progressiveness. Secondary works; table, graph, 41 notes. P. J. Mattar

1332. Gershoni, Israel. ARABIZATION OF ISLAM: THE EGYPTIAN SALAFIYYA AND THE RISE OF ARABISM IN PRE-REVOLUTIONARY EGYPT. *Asian and African Studies [Israel] 1979 13(1): 22-57.* It has been argued that Egypt's decision to join the Arab League in 1945 was a purely political decision, but in the 1920's the Association for Islamic Guidance, the Young Men's Moslem Association, and the Muslim Brotherhood succeeded in creating a fundamentalist Muslim and Arab identity among Egyptians that has not yet been fully satisfied. 102 notes. R. T. Brown

1333. Giladi, Avner. TAHANIM HEVRATI'IM V'LEUMI'IM B'TOHNIYOT-LIMUDIM B'SIFRAI-LIMUD MITZRI'IM [Some aspects of social and national content of Egyptian curricula and textbooks]. *Hamizrah Hehadash [Israel] 1979 28(3-4): 195-219.* The textbooks and educational system of a country are good indicators of the social, national, and political views of a country's leadership. Egyptian textbooks are examined as indicators of modernization. Two divergent trends are discernible in the 1960's, when political thought leaned toward Arab socialism. An external stratum states the purposes of Arab education in the context of Islam and other religious sources. The internal stratum uses the body of textbooks to explain or legitimize reforms made necessary by modernization. Social issues such as family planning are justified within the Islamic fundamentalist framework. After the 1973 war, *Al-Tammiya al-iqtisadiyya w'al-ijtimmaiyya* discussed Egypt's social problems with rare candor. This book is seen as a long-awaited step in introducing modernization to the Egyptian student through social and humanist education rather than technology and scientific curricula, as had formerly been the case. Primary sources and Egyptian and United Nations documents; 137 notes. T. Koppel

1334. Gilsenan, Michaël. L'ISLAM DANS L'ÉGYPTE CONTEMPORAINE: RELIGION D'ÉTAT, RELIGION POPULAIRE [State and popular Islam in contemporary Egypt]. *Ann.: Écon., Soc., Civilisations [France] 1980 35(3-4): 598-614.* There are different ideological discourses in Egyptian society which all manifest certain internal tensions and blockages. The relations of social reality and discourse are highly problematic. In the Nasserist period the nation state and the cult of the *za'im*, or leader, went hand in hand. Opposing forces were suppressed, but their social bases remained and no critical reading of history was generated. The crushing defeat of 1967 exposed the myth of the army and the *za'im* and discredited this form of nationalism and socialism. Islam remained as an unsullied language of refuge and of traditionalist calls for the recasting of social forms. There are many different currents of Islamic ideology, from the quasi-millenarian to the repressive versions of certain sections of the bourgeoisie. The state's current attempt to utilize religion seems rather to subvert itself and to encourage opposition in a religious idiom. J

1335. Jankowski, James. THE EASTERN IDEA AND THE EASTERN UNION IN INTERWAR EGYPT. *Int. J. of African Hist. Studies 1981 14(4): 643-666.* The Society of the Eastern Union was an organization of Egyptian intellectual elite which had as its goal the linking of all Asian and African peoples to carry out common beneficial programs. The society was a failure because of the ambiguities associated with the concept and with the role of Egypt in the whole program. At best it succeeded in creating the beginnings of a pan-Arab identity. Secondary sources; 106 notes. R. T. Brown

1336. Khalifa, A. M. A PROPOSED EXPLANATION OF THE FERTILITY GAP DIFFERENTIALS BY SOCIO-ECONOMIC STATUS AND MODERNITY: THE CASE OF EGYPT. *Population Studies [Great Britain] 1973 27(3): 431-442.* "Theoretically, three types of variables have been examined. The first type contains the structural variables such as socio-economic status; the second demographic variables, such as age at marriage; and the third those concerning contraceptive use. The last are considered as explanatory intervening variables. Contraceptive use varies with the structural and the demographic variables. Not all the variation, however, could be explained by the first two types. Using Egyptian data, it was found that there are clear differences in fertility behavior related to all the structural and demographic variables considered. The ideal or preferred family size did not show the same degree of variability; a relatively low family-size preference prevails among most couples in all socio-economic and modernization strata. This means that there is a gap between the behavioral and attitudinal dimensions of fertility. The width of this gap varies with different structural and demographic variables whether single or multiple indicators are used. Considering the frequency of use and use-effectiveness of contraceptives as intervening variables, these gaps can be explained. It was found that differences in use are associated with differences in the gap, although use-effectiveness differences do not conform to exactly the same pattern." J

1337. Khalil, Hasan Fathi. MAHMUD TIMOR RĀ'ID AL-QISSA AL-ARABIYAH AL-HADITHAH [Mahmud Timor, pioneer of the modern Arabic story]. *Al-Arabi [Kuwait] 1974 (183): 40-45.* Discusses Timor's career as an author, the formative influences on his work, and his philosophy of life.

1338. Khoury, R. G. ṬĀHĀ HUSAYN (1889-1973) ET LA FRANCE [Ṭāhā Husayn (1889-1973) and France]. *Arabica [Netherlands] 1975 22(3): 225-266.* Ṭāhā Husayn, after contact with European professors at the Egyptian University (doctorate 1914) and despite his blindness and through his persistence, was awarded a scholarship to study at the University of Paris. Here he finished his *doctorat d'université* (1916) and the same year married a French woman, who vastly improved his contact with life. He spent World War I in Paris and became the first Egyptian awarded the *doctorat d'état* (1919). Based on Husayn's memoirs and secondary sources; numerous notes. W. J. Wilson

1339. Lazarus-Yafeh, Hava. CONTEMPORARY RELIGIOUS ATTITUDES OF MUSLIM ARABS TOWARD THE KA'BA AND THE HAJJ. *Asian and African Studies [Israel] 1978 12(2): 173-201.* Surveys contemporary Egyptian writing on Islamic institutions which sees increasing fundamentalist orthodoxy at all levels encouraged by both the intellectual community and the secular government.

1340. Machut-Mendecka, Ewa. EUROPEAN AND ARAB ELEMENTS IN EGYPTIAN DRAMA. *Africana Bull. [Poland] 1980 (29): 109-121.* Examines the impact of the dramatic theories and themes of Arab and European theater on Egyptian drama, 19th-20th centuries, discussing the work of Marun an-Naqqash, Ahmad Shauqi, Taufig al-Hakim, and others.

1341. Machut-Mendecka, Ewa. SOCIAL CHANGES IN EGYPTIAN REALISTIC DRAMA. *Africana Bull. [Poland] 1981 (30): 147-158.* Illustrates how Egyptian realistic drama reflects the society of Egypt, and traces the social changes evident in both, in the periods 1919-52 and 1952-80.

1342. Nagi, Mostafa H. INTERNAL MIGRATION AND STRUCTURAL CHANGES IN EGYPT. *Middle East J. 1974 28(3): 261-282.* Examines the impact of internal migration to cities on the economic growth, labor force and social organization of Egypt, 1937-70's.

1343. Najjar, Fauzi M. STATE AND UNIVERSITY IN EGYPT DURING THE PERIOD OF SOCIALIST TRANSFORMATION, 1961-67. *Rev. of Pol. 1976 38(1): 57-87.* The university in developing countries is looked upon as the "cornerstone of equality of opportunity." During the period of socialist transformation the military elite in Egypt attempted by legislation to modernize the universities but were opposed by conservative intellectuals from the traditional elite. The result has been disastrous for Egyptian higher education and proves that "once the university becomes an arm of the government, this can only result in tragic diminution of its special functions." 57 notes. L. E. Ziewacz

1344. Nazarova, N. KOPTSKAIA TSERKOV' [The Coptic church]. *Aziia i Afrika Segodnia [USSR] 1981 (8): 58-60.* Discusses the Coptic Church in Egypt, its rites, involvement in the Monophysite controversy, and its role in Egyptian political disputes.

1345. Nelson, Cynthia. THE VIRGIN OF ZEITOUN. *Worldview 1973 16(9): 5-11.* Discusses the sociological significance of the apparition of Zeitoun (involving the Virgin Mary) in Egypt in 1968, including its possible relationship to the 1967 Six-Day War.

1346. Oliverius, Jaroslav. MUHAMMAD MANDŪR UND SEINE AUFFASSUNG DER LITERATURKRITIK [Muhammad Mandūr and his approach to literary criticism]. *Archív Orientální [Czechoslovakia] 1980 48(1): 50-59.* Muhammad Mandūr (1907-65) ranks among the outstanding representatives of modern Arab literary criticism. Due to his work, literary criticism in Egypt took shape as an independent branch within the framework of literary culture. Mandūr was able to link the best traditions of Arab classical criticism into a harmonious unity with the ideas and impulses of European literature, and in his own theoretical approach he devoted properly balanced attention to an overall aesthetic evaluation of a work of fiction as well as to its social message. J/S

1347. Pennington, J. D. THE COPTS IN MODERN EGYPT. *Middle Eastern Studies [Great Britain] 1982 18(2): 158-179.* Copts form the largest Christian community in the Middle East and could be 10% of the Egyptian population. The quality of their life has always depended on the regime in power. After the 1952 coup some of the large landowning Copts suffered from the land reforms, but the peasants profited. There was some loss of prestige, resulting in migration to North America and Australia. Nasser's control of the regime and the neutrality of the Patriarch resulted in little trouble between church and state. Under Sadat Islamic piety was stressed, but there was some official sympathy for the Copts. Nevertheless, they felt disadvantaged in terms of education and employment, particularly in the government sector. In the late 1970's tension rose; clashes between Islamic groups and the Copts were further complicated by the dismissal of the Patriarch and the assassination of Sadat. Based on Arabic and other secondary sources; 15 notes. F. A. Clements

1348. Reid, Donald M. EDUCATIONAL AND CAREER CHOICES OF EGYPTIAN STUDENTS, 1882-1922. *Int. J. of Middle East Studies [Great Britain] 1977 8(3): 349-378.* Discusses the educational and career choices open to Egyptian students, 1882-1922, including careers in law, medicine, engineering, and teaching. By 1922 a law degree was the best way to get to the top of Egyptian society; medicine, followed by engineering, also made great strides, but teaching remained an unpopular career despite improvements in salaries. Primary sources; 5 tables, 79 notes. R. B. Orr

1349. Reid, Donald M. THE RISE OF PROFESSIONS AND PROFESSIONAL ORGANIZATIONS IN MODERN EGYPT. *Comparative Studies in Soc. and Hist. [Great Britain] 1974 16(1): 24-57.*

1350. Rubin, Trudy. THE 500 SOULS: IN CAIRO AND ALEXANDRIA THEY LIVE ON THEIR MEMORIES. *Present Tense 1975*

3(1): 63-66. Discusses daily life in the small and dwindling Jewish communities of Cairo and Alexandria, Egypt, during the 1970's. S

1351. Sabat, Khalil. LES "MASS MEDIA" EN ÉGYPTE [The mass media in Egypt]. *Rev. de l'Occident Musulman et de la Méditerranée [France] 1979 (27): 135-156.* Traces the history of the press, theater, cinema, music and song, and radio and television in Egypt from the late 18th century until the 1970's, beginning with the shortlived journals established during Napoleon's Egypt expedition (1798-1801). The Comedy Theatre was inaugurated in 1868 and the first film was shown only a year after the invention of the cinematograph. The singer and composer Abduh al-Hamuli (1845-1901) made a major contribution to enriching Egyptian music, radio became popular in the 1930's, and television made its debut during the 1950's. Biblio., 4 notes. P. J. Taylorson

1352. Sestier, Camille. LA "MALÉDICTION" DE TOUTANKHAMON [The "curse" of Tutankhamen]. *Histoire [France] 1980 (19): 78-80.* Traces the history of the curse of Tutankhamen which followed those archaeologists, Howard Carter and the 5th Earl of Carnarvon, who discovered the ancient pharaoh's tomb in Egypt in 1922.

1353. Smith, Charles D. THE INTELLECTUAL AND MODERNIZATION; DEFINITIONS AND RECONSIDERATIONS: THE EGYPTIAN EXPERIENCE. *Comparative Studies in Soc. and Hist. [Great Britain] 1980 22(4): 513-533.* The career and writings of Muhammed Heikal (1888-1956) suggest that Western-oriented intellectuals are not necessarily willing agents of change in premodern societies; Heikal was separated by his intellectual elitism from the rest of society. He worked to prevent the process of modernization in its social as opposed to its intellectual aspects, thus proving less able to perceive and respond to Egypt's socioeconomic problems than the traditional religious Muslim Brotherhood.

1354. Szymański, Edward. WIELCY REFORMATORZY UNIWERSYTETU AL-AZHAR [The great reformers of the University of Al-Azhar]. *Kultura i Społeczeństwo [Poland] 1977 21(3): 97-109.* The great reforms in al-Azhar began in 1895-96 under Sheik al-Ahmadi az-Zawahiri and Sheik Muhammad Mustafa al-Maraghi. But al-Maraghi's great plan of reform presented to the government in 1929 failed because he demanded the closing of two other indispensable institutions, Dar al-Ulum and the School of Moslem Law, in order to create jobs for the graduates of al-Azhar, and al-Maraghi was forced to resign.
M. Swiecicka-Ziemianek

1355. Vatikiotis, P. J. THE MODERN HISTORY OF EGYPT ALLA FRANCA. *Middle Eastern Studies [Great Britain] 1974 10(1): 80-92.* A review article on Jacques Berque, *Egypt, Imperialism and Revolution* (London: Faber and Faber, 1972). Berque "sets out to restore the Egyptian's Islamic, or native, authenticity in the face of the disastrous consequences of his confrontation with Western civilization." The book begins with British occupation in 1882, and extends to the military coup of 1952 viewing the "process of decolonization" in immanentist, eschatological terms. The author's main argument is "that the British occupation caused the "denaturation' of the Egyptian, especially the peasant. It concealed and arrested his "authenticity' by a hypocritical veil of inadequate modernity." This approach is too much a single-theory dogmatism. 17 notes. R. V. Ritter

1356. Winter, Michael. HA"ASHRAF" VE"NIQABAT AL-ASHRAF" BEMITSRAYYIM BITKUFAT HA'OTTOMANIM UVAZMAN HEHADASH [*Ashraf* and the *Naqib al-Ashraf* in Egypt in Ottoman and modern times]. *Hamizrah Hehadash [Israel] 1975 25(4), 293-310.* The *Ashraf* were the descendants of Mohammed by his grandson Hasan, elder son of Fatima and Ali. In Egypt, they preserved their genealogical records carefully, and enjoyed the social and economic prerogatives of a religious aristocracy. The *Naqib al-Ashraf* was their doyen, who ascertained lineage. However, the *Ashraf* had by the 1950's ceased to be an elite, and no mention is found of the *Naqib al-Ashraf* after 1952. 135 notes. T. Sassoon

1357. Yadegari, Mohammad. THE IRANIAN SETTLEMENT IN EGYPT AS SEEN THROUGH THE PAGES OF THE COMMUNITY PAPER *CHIHRINIMI* (1904-1966). *Middle Eastern Studies [Great Britain] 1980 16(2): 98-114.* Reconstructs the history of the Iranian community in Egypt, with a population of 3,500 in 1938, by surveying the pages of *Chihrinimi,* an illustrated Persian language weekly founded in Alexandria in 1904, then published in Cairo, 1905-66. 78 notes.
P. J. Mattar

1358. Yadlin, Rivka. "THE EGYPTIAN PERSONALITY": TRENDS IN EGYPTIAN CHARACTER LITERATURE. *Asian and African Studies [Israel] 1980 14(1): 1-19.* A survey of Egyptian literature shows that contrary to a negative feeling toward the Arab personality in much of the Middle East, Egyptians have responded to adversity by asserting the productive value of national identity. Based on Arabic language literature; 45 notes. R. T. Brown

1359. Ye'or, Bat. ZIONISM IN ISLAMIC LANDS: THE CASE OF EGYPT. *Wiener Lib. Bull. [Great Britain] 1977 30(43-44): 16-29.* Some have denied that oriental Zionism ever existed, but Zionism was a greater success among the oriental Jewish masses than among their western coreligionists, if one thinks in terms of the massive collective emigration that emptied entire regions of their Jews. Modernization had a corrosive effect on Jewish life in Egypt, which had been patriarchal, traditionalist, and strongly influenced by Arab-Moslem customs. Zionism contributed answers to the questions of modernization, but at the same time Zionist methods sometimes indicated an inability to comprehend the special history and culture of Oriental Jewry. As Egyptian xenophobia grew more threatening in the 1930's and 1940's, Zionism had to function in the most difficult circumstances. It had to concentrate on the everyday requirements of the indigent Jewish population and attend to their religious, educational, and medical needs. Instruction in self-defense also took place, which proved extremely useful when pogroms broke out during and after the war. In the face of enormous pressures, the small Jewish community in Egypt showed a courageous spirit and a remarkable sense of solidarity. 48 notes. R. V. Layton

1360. Yusif, Niqola. AL-SHA'IR 'AZIZ ABAZA WA-MASRAHIATIHI [The poetry of Aziz Abaza, and his plays]. *al-Adib [Lebanon] 1974 33(2): 7-11.* Discusses the career of this Egyptian poet, reproducing some of his poems, and describing his major plays.

Libya

1361. Alessandrini, Adolfo. LIBIA 1949: TESTIMONIANZE D'UN DIPLOMATICO [Libya in 1949: testimony of a diplomat]. *Riv. di Studi Pol. Int. [Italy] 1981 48(2): 203-212.* The Italian ambassador to Lebanon during the negotiations at the United Nations for the independence of the Italian colonies in Africa comments on Gianluigi Rossi's *L'Africa italiana verso l'indipendenza (1941-1949)* at a round table held in January 1981.

1362. Alexander, Nathan. THE FOREIGN POLICY OF LIBYA: INFLEXIBILITY AMID CHANGE. *Orbis 1981 24(4): 819-846.* Foreign policy of Colonel Muammar Qadhafi, leader of Libya since 1969, has been "described as bizarre, unpredictable, and quixotic," but such characterizations mistake style for substance and underestimate the effect of history and geography on Libyan foreign policy. Qadhafi has built on the policies of his predecessor, and stressed freedom, socialism, Arab unity and Arab nationalism. The basis of this policy has been obscured by Qadhafi's flamboyant and mercurial personality. Based on published works and the author's experience as a businessman who has traveled widely in Libya (Nathan Alexander is a pseudonym); 36 notes.
J. W. Thacker, Jr.

1363. Alexander, Nathan. LIBYA: THE CONTINUOUS REVOLUTION. *Middle Eastern Studies [Great Britain] 1981 17(2): 210-227.* The prime objectives of the Revolutionary Command Council (RCC) in Libya were to ensure the survival of the revolution and the sociopolitical and economic development of the state. In 1969 the coup d'état replaced a traditional society in terms of political and administrative structure, and the first task of the RCC was to reduce tribal and regional power by installing new local leaders identified with the revolution. Early moves were a failure, as was the creation of the Arab Socialist Union Party, which could not respond to local needs while reflecting central policies. The result was a fresh impetus given by the creation of People's Committees on 15 April 1973 with a five-point program aimed at continuing the revolutionary process but also intended to serve as an adjunct to the security services. Further moves in this direction were the

establishment of the General People's Congress and revolutionary committees based on nongeographical structures. Based on Libyan and Western newspaper reports and secondary sources; 50 notes.
F. A. Clements

1364. Al-Harir, 'Abd-al-Muali Salih. MUNAZAMMAT TASHKILATI MAKHSUSA AL-SIRIYYA WA-ADWARAHA FI HARAKAT AL-NIDAL AL-WATANI 1911-1918 [The secret organization *Tashkilati Makhsusa* and its role in the national movement 1911-18]. *Majallat al-Buhūth al-Taikhiya [Libya] 1979 1(1): 14-50.* *Tashkilati Makhsusa* was a secret Ottoman organization officially aimed at countering foreign espionage but, as was discovered in 1918 when the organization's existence became publicly known, it also dealt with internal security. Its history can be divided into three stages: 1) 1911-12, when its main policy was to counter the spread of Italian influence in the Empire, and officers of the organization led the Libyans during the Italian invasion; 2) 1912-15, when relations between the organization and the Libyan national movement, under Ahmad 'Abdul Sharif, began to deteriorate; and 3) 1915-18, when a split occurred with the Libyans because the Ottomans wanted them to fight the British in the western desert of Egypt and the Libyans felt that this would weaken their efforts against Italy. Based on memoirs of Ottoman rulers and secondary sources; 59 notes.
Y. Sassoon

1365. Allan, J. A. and McLachlan, K. S. AGRICULTURAL DEVELOPMENT IN LIBYA AFTER OIL. *African Affairs [Great Britain] 1976 75(300): 331-347.* The government of Libya has a large income from oil. At the current rate of production, reserves will last another 33-45 years. Much of the oil income has been budgeted for agricultural development, and in this area the government has serious intentions. The scope of Libya's agricultural development is discussed including irrigation, livestock, and dryland farming. 31 notes, appendix. H. G. Soff

1366. Allan, J. A. DROUGHT IN LIBYA: SOME SOLUTIONS AVAILABLE TO AN OIL-RICH GOVERNMENT. *African Affairs [Great Britain] 1974 73(291): 152-158.* Drought is a permanent condition in almost all of Libya. Underground water is available in some areas but they are in danger of depletion due to overuse. The government, although aware of this critical situation, has passed no regulatory acts. Development schemes are planned for the south, with particular emphasis given to the Kufra Scheme which is keyed to sheep production. Although the project has fallen short of expectations, the technological problems of obtaining water have been solved. 17 notes.
H. G. Soff

1367. Anderson, Lisa. LIBYA AND AMERICAN FOREIGN POLICY. *Middle East J. 1982 36(4): 516-534.* Lack of understanding of the contemporary Libyan scene has led to an American policy that respects nothing of the historical background or the Libyan view of US-Libyan relations. Examines the history of Libya from the first half of the 20th century through the development of the present ruling ideology. Discusses factors determining Libyan foreign policy and its effects in the Arab and Islamic worlds and in relations with the United States. Secondary sources. F. A. Clements

1368. Barghathi, Yusuf Salim al-. AL-ADWĀR WA-ATHARUHĀ FĪ HARAKAT AL-JIHĀD AL-LĪBĪ [The *dors* and their influence on the Libyan jihad movement]. *Majallat Al-buhūth Al-tārīkhiya [Libya] 1981 3(2): 213-243.* Traces the political history and internal organizations of the *dors*, the regionally-based military units of the Libyan jihad movement that formed the popular resistance to the Italian invasion in 1911 until they were crushed in 1932. Turkish officers joined tribal sheikhs and leaders of religious orders to set up *dors* based on Turkish military structure. After Turkey signed the Treaty of Ouchy in 1912 and recalled its officers, the organization developed on a more tribal basis under Ahmad Al-Sharif and later Umar Al-Mukhtar as autonomous local guerrilla forces operating out of strongholds, particularly in the Jebel al-Akhdar and Barqa area. Based on Italian archival materials and conversations with veterans; 5 photos, 3 maps, 2 fig., 76 notes, biblio.
C. H. Bleaney

1369. Bleuchot, Hervé. KADHAFI. ELEMENTS POUR UN PORTRAIT [Qadhafi: elements for a portrait]. *Etudes [France] 1982 357(5): 437-450.* Recounts the life and career of Colonel Muammar Qadhafi, especially since 1974; discusses Libya's strained relations with Egypt and Israel.

1370. Decalo, Samuel. LIBYA'S QADDAFI. *Present Tense 1974 1(2): 50-54.*

1371. Farley, J. G. LIBYA. *World Survey [Great Britain] 1975 (79): 1-17.* Colonel Muammar Qadhafi's policies, 1971-75, have focused on restoring Islam to Libya and promoting Arab unity.

1372. Fathaly, Omar I. and Abusedra, Fathi S. THE IMPACT OF SOCIO-POLITICAL CHANGE ON ECONOMIC DEVELOPMENT IN LIBYA. *Middle Eastern Studies [Great Britain] 1980 16(3): 225-235.* When it achieved its independence in 1951, Libya was a poor country with ethnic, tribal, and regional conflicts, and with traditional institutions which were obstacles to economic progress. The first major oil discovery in 1959 stimulated development, but it was after the revolution of 1969 that traditionalism was attacked and a commitment to modernization began. When the existing bureaucracy was perceived by the revolutionary leaders as an obstacle to development, the "popular revolution" was launched to promote public participation in development. These sociopolitical changes have provided favorable conditions for economic development, though traditionalism still poses an obstinate barrier. Based on secondary sources; 4 tables; fig., 18 notes.
P. J. Mattar

1373. Filesi, Cesira. GIOVANNI AMENDOLA, MINISTRO DELLE COLONIE, E LA QUESTIONE CIRENAICA (FEBBRAIO-OTTOBRE 1922) [Giovanni Amendola, minister of colonies, and the Cyrenaic question, February-October 1922]. *Riv. di Studi Pol. Int. [Italy] 1977 44(1): 77-105.* Depicts the liberal colonial policy of Giovanni Amendola toward the people of Libya in 1921. His long-range plan was to ingratiate the colonial power with the Arabs through friendship, political progress, and cultural and economic development. In Cyrenaica he hoped to maintain a peaceful coexistence with the Sanusi without realizing the Arabs' feelings of independence. In Tripolitania he was compelled to use force to protect the local population and introduce order and justice. Based on the Historical Archives of the former Ministry of Italian Africa and secondary sources; 75 notes. A. Sbacchi

1374. Filesi, Cesira. LA TRIPOLITANIA NELLA POLITICA COLONIALE DI GIOVANNI AMENDOLA [Tripoli in the colonial policy of Giovanni Amendola]. *Africa [Italy] 1977 32(4): 517-542.* Reconstructs the history of Libyan events, February-October 1922, during which Giovanni Amendola held the Ministry of Colonies. To find a solution to the difficult situation in Tripoli, Amendola felt it opportune to seek the collaboration of Governor Giuseppe Volpi. The negotiations proved ineffective in stopping the rebels, which compelled Amendola to resort to military operations. Having driven back the rebels and led the Berbers to their natural settlements, his efforts were directed at preventing a Senussite expansion in Tripoli. During his last months in the Ministry of the Colonies, Amendola tried to contain the attacks of rebels, but all attempts were frustrated by the advent of fascism. Based on documents in the Historical Archives of the former Ministerio dell' Africa Italiana. J/S

1375. Folayam, Kola. THE RESISTANCE MOVEMENT IN LIBYA. *Tarikh 1973 4(3): 46-56.* Chronicles Libyan resistance to intervention and attempted colonization by Italy. S

1376. Folayan, Kola. ITALIAN COLONIAL RULE IN LIBYA. *Tarikh 1974 4(4): 1-10.*

1377. Fowler, Gary L. DECOLONIZATION OF RURAL LIBYA. *Ann. of the Assoc. of Am. Geographers 1973 63(4): 490-506.* "Italians held large areas of the better agricultural land in Libya in 1940. Although the colonists in Cyrenaica were evacuated prior to British occupation, the majority of those in Tripolitania remained to face an uncertain future under British and then Libyan administration. The pace of land transfers accelerated after the 1956 Italo-Libyan Accord and spread from planned settlements to private farms and estates. By 1964, Libyans controlled practically all former Italian lands." J

1378. Glukhov, Y. LIBYA: TIME OF CHANGE AND RENEWAL. *Int. Affairs [USSR] 1977 (2): 113-119.* On 1 September 1969, a military coup led by Muammar al-Qadhafi toppled the Libyan monarchy, in 1970 British and American bases were closed down, and soon thereafter the petroleum industry was nationalized. The government has been developing agriculture and industry. Illiteracy has already been reduced from 80 to 40%. Under the first five-year plan, which emphasizes infrastructure, the state sector is to account for 75% of the GNP. In foreign affairs, Libya has been actively anti-imperialist, giving substantial aid to Egypt and Syria in the October 1973 war, and strengthening ties with the socialist states. L. W. Van Wyk

1379. Goldberg, Harvey E. RITES AND RIOTS: THE TRIPOLITANIAN POGROM OF 1945. *Plural Soc. [Netherlands] 1977 8(1): 35-56.* Attempts to interpret the anti-Jewish riots of Tripolitania, Libya of 1945, observing parallels between collective behavior analyses and theories of ritual action and describing Muslim-Jewish relationships in Tripolitania from a social and symbolic viewpoint.

1380. Hajjar, Sami G. THE JAMAHIRIYA EXPERIMENT IN LIBYA: QADHAFI AND ROUSSEAU. *J. of Modern African Studies [Great Britain] 1980 18(2): 181-200.* Examines the political theory of Muammar Qadhafi as pronounced in the *Green Book* dealing with the issue of democracy and *jamahiriya* (the era of the masses and the practice of direct democracy). Demonstrates the marked conceptual similarities between Qadhafi's *Green Book* and Jean Jacques Rousseau's *Social Contract.*57 notes. A. Sbacchi/S

1381. Landau, Jacob M. SOME RUSSIAN PUBLICATIONS ON LIBYA. *Middle Eastern Studies [Great Britain] 1979 15(2): 280-282.* A bibliographic essay surveying a sampling of Soviet writings on Libya. Such writings have increased substantially during the 1960's and 1970's, reflecting Libya's growing importance as an oil producer and increased involvement in Arab and African affairs. Economic and historical studies get the most attention, but the titles include a general handbook of information, a travel guide, and a collection of poems translated from Arabic into Russian. Strangely, Soviet books have largely avoided Libya since Muammar Qadhafi's coup in 1969. R. V. Ritter

1382. Lenczowski, George. POPULAR REVOLUTION IN LIBYA. *Current Hist. 1974 66(390): 57-61, 86.* Elucidates the ideology of Colonel Muammar Qadhafi, Chairman of the Revolutionary Command Council (RCC). From an issue on the Middle East, 1974. S

1383. Mason, John P. PETROLEUM DEVELOPMENT AND THE REACTIVATION OF TRADITIONAL STRUCTURE IN A LIBYAN OASIS COMMUNITY. *Econ. Development and Cultural Change 1978 26(4): 763-776.* Employment opportunities in the oil industry and with the government, and opportunities to market surplus garden produce, have revitalized the fraternal joint family of Libya's Augila Oasis since the early 1960's. Based on a field trip to Libya in 1969-70 and published works; 7 tables, 9 notes. J. W. Thacker, Jr./S

1384. Mason, John P. QADHDHAFI'S "REVOLUTION" AND CHANGE IN A LIBYAN OASIS COMMUNITY. *Middle East J. 1982 36(3): 319-335.* Examines the effects of the Libyan revolution in the Arabized Berber oasis of Augila. Outlines the situation before 1969 and describes its transformation into a small town. Discusses changes in oasis life in relation to the socialist Islamic policy defined in Muammar Qadhafi's *Green Book.*Based on field research, 1969 and 1977-78, personal communications, and secondary sources; map, diagram, 27 notes. F. A. Clements

1385. Muzikář, Josef. ISLAM AND THE IDEOLOGY OF MU'AMMAR AL-QADHDHĀFĪ'S GREEN BOOK. *Arch. Orientální [Czechoslovakia] 1982 50(1): 1-21, (2): 105-121.* Part 1. Muammar Qadhafi's *Green Book* consists of three volumes published during the period 1976-79. They express his Third International (Universal) Theory of Arab Unity. According to this theory, the Islamic nations must unite in order to survive and perpetuate a society based on Islamic law. Nationalism and religion are the basic motivating forces of history. When these are united, when a nation is united under Islamic law, then it is invincible. Furthermore, *djamāhīrīya,* as instituted in Libya in 1973, is the most natural form of government. It attempts to do away with representative government, which is just another form of dictatorship, and is founded upon a direct democracy of people's congresses. There are many critics of the political and theological implications of Qadhafi's theory, but it has aroused considerable interest and controversy among Islamic nations. Part 2. Analyzes Qadhafi's economic theory. He rejects the wage system, whether from private or state sources, but offers no workable replacement and hardly mentions production problems. The work is primarily a statement of extreme leftist, even anarchic, ideals, which sound very good on paper but are unworkable in fact. It serves primarily to win the admiration of the masses and to suggest that a former colony might have some answers for the world. 124 notes. J. Powell/V. Human

1386. Neutze, Dennis R. THE GULF OF SIDRA INCIDENT: A LEGAL PERSPECTIVE. *US Naval Inst. Pro. 1982 108(1): 26-31.* On 19 August 1981, two United States Navy fighter aircraft from the USS *Nimitz* (CVN-68) shot down two Soviet-built SU-22 Libyan fighter planes at the northern end of the Gulf of Sidra, some 60 nautical miles from the coast of Libya. Since then, the affair has become a matter of great concern because of its international law implications. The United States and Libya have made conflicting claims about the incident. For the time being, and until the 3d UN Conference on the Law of the Sea can come up with a comprehensive treaty—expected this year or next—the United States must continue to claim certain legal rights in such disputed areas as the Gulf of Sidra so that the principles of freedom of navigation can be assured to all countries. Secondary sources; 5 notes, 2 photos, map. A. N. Garland

1387. Oren, Stephen. QADDAFI, ARAB UNITY, AND ISLAM. *Worldview 1974 17(4): 22-24.* Muammar Qadhafi, president of Libya, who has sought the unity of Islam and the destruction of Israel, nevertheless poses a barrier to the unity of the Arab states.

1388. Persegani, Italo. PER UN RIESAME DELLA POLITICA ECONOMICA ITALIANA IN LIBIA (1920-1940) [A reexamination of Italian economic policy in Libya, 1920-40]. *Nuova Riv. Storica [Italy] 1981 65(5-6): 572-587.* The origins and ultimate failure of Italian economic policies in Libya between the two wars are studied in official documents not intended for publication. They reveal a double and contrasting policy orientation, fostering free enterprise on the one hand and state control on the other. The problems and difficulties of these policies are studied in the history of the Unione Coloniale Italo-Araba (Italo-Arab Colonial Union), the first colonizing society to be established in Cyrenaica. Based on primary material in the archive of the Istituto Agronomico per l'Oltramare, Florence; 84 notes. J. V. Coutinho

1389. Rainero, Romain. LA CAPTURE, L'EXÉCUTION D'OMAR EL-MUKHTAR ET LA FIN DE LA GUÉRILLA LIBYENNE [The capture and execution of Omar el-Mukhtar and the end of the Libyan guerrillas]. *Cahiers de Tunisie [Tunisia] 1980 28(111-112): 59-73.* Narrates the political and military events in Libya from 1929 to 1931, centering on the colonial policy of Italy's Fascist government and the resistance led by Omar al-Mukhtar, whose capture and execution on 16 September 1931 marked the end of guerrilla warfare in Libya.

1390. Rochat, Giorgio. IL GENOCIDIO CIRENAICO E LA STORIOGRAFIA COLONIALE [The genocide in Cyrenaica and colonial historiography]. *Belfagor [Italy] 1980 35(4): 449-454.* Responds to a conservative critic of an earlier article by the author on the repression of the revolt of seminomadic populations in Cyrenaica in 1930-31, in which 50,000 of 120,000 people involved were massacred.

1391. Rochat, Giorgio. LA REPRESSIONE DELLA RESISTENZA ARABA IN CIRENAICA NEL 1930-31, NEI DOCUMENTI DELL'ARCHIVIO GRAZIANI [The crushing of Arab resistance in Cyrenaica, 1930-31, from documents in the Graziani Archives]. *Movimento di Liberazione in Italia [Italy] 1973 25(110): 3-39.* The conquest of Libya was slow and costly. For many years Italian rule was successfully challenged by the rebel Sanusi. Marshal Pietro Badoglio, governor of Tripoli and Cyrenaica, sought complete submission through contact with the revered chief Omar el-Muktar, but felt compelled to resort to repressive measures. Rodolfo Graziani, second in command and in charge of the military operations in Cyrenaica, represented the new Fascist style of waging war with utmost brutality. After the capture and execution of Omar el-Muktar, Arab resistance ceased for a time. During the critical year of 1930-31 the relationship between Badoglio and Graziani deteriorated. H. W. L. Freudenthal

1392. Romano, Sergio. LA GUERRE DE LIBYE: LES ITALIENS ET L'AFRIQUE [The Italians in Africa during the Libyan War]. *Histoire [France] 1978 (2): 42-49.* Italian efforts from 1911 to identify with imperial Rome resulted in the rise of Arab and Libyan nationalism, whose fulminating spokesman is Colonel Muammar Qadhafi. J

1393. Rondot, Pierre. LA LIBYE DU COLONEL GADDHAFI: UNITÉ ARABE ET RÉVOLUTION CULTURELLE [Colonel Qadhafi's Libya: Arab unity and cultural revolution]. *Défense Natl. [France] 1977 33(4): 37-53.* Assesses present day Libya in terms of its geographical, historical, and ethnic background, and in the context of the dominant influence exercised by the country's political leader, Muammar Qadhafi, 1969-76.

1394. Rondot, Pierre. LIBYE: DU COUP D'ÉTAT DU Ier SEPTEMBRE 1969 AU "GOUVERNEMENT DES MASSES" [Libya: from the coup d'état of 1 September 1969 to government by the masses]. *Défense Natl. [France] 1979 35(8-9): 69-85.* Traces the political changes in Libya 1969-79, and the character of Muammar Qadhafi.

1395. Rondot, Pierre. LIBYE: LA PHILOSOPHIE POLITIQUE DU COLONEL KADHAFI [Libya: the political philosophy of Colonel Qadhafi]. *Rev. Française d'Études Pol. Africaines [France] 1973 8(96): 15-20.* A detailed study of Colonel Muammar Qadhafi's philosophy of Arab unity, alliance with Egypt and Syria, the Arab-Israeli conflict, and the Libyan cultural revolution, 1973.

1396. Rossi, Gianluigi. ALLE ORIGINI DELL'INDIPENDENZA LIBICA: LA DICHIARAZIONE BRITANNICA DELL'8 GENNAIO 1942 SULLA CIRENAICA [The origins of Libyan independence: the British declaration of 8 January 1942 on Cyrenaica]. *Africa [Italy] 1977 32(4): 475-502.* Describes the origin of the statement on Cyrenaica, issued by British Foreign Minister, Anthony Eden, on 8 January 1942. This statement eventually influenced the talks between the Great Powers over the solution to the Libyan problem at the end of World War II. Soon after the Italian intervention in the conflict Idris el-Sanusi aimed at inducing the British authorities in Egypt to exert pressures on London to take a formal pledge on the future political status of Libya or Cyrenaica as a compensation for the military support provided by the Sanusi in the western desert. Reveals, on the one hand, the extreme prudence displayed by the British government in undertaking positive pledges over the postwar status of Libya during the conflict and, on the other, the continued curtailment of the original requests advanced by Idis, following a procedure, which was later to become a practice, to request of the British government no more than it was in a position to grant, postponing to more favorable times the realization of the goal of independence. Based on documents in the Public Record Office, London. J

1397. Said, Hakim Mohammed. 'UMAR AL-MUKHTÁR: PATHOLOGY OF LEADERSHIP. *Hamdard Islamicus [Pakistan] 1980 3(3): 61-69.* The history of the resistance in the Arab emirate of Cyrenaica toward the Italian advance in the Italian Sanusi War is typified by Sidi Omar al-Mukhtar, leader of the Sanusi who used guerilla tactics to effectively combat the Italian threat.

1398. St John, Ronald Bruce. LIBYA'S FOREIGN AND DOMESTIC POLICIES. *Current Hist. 1981 80(470): 426-429, 434-435.* The revolutionary change in Libya, 1969-81, under Muammar Qadhafi has destroyed or drastically modified the former social and economic structure beyond the possibility of reestablishment, regardless of future changes in the national leadership.

1399. Saint Robert, Philippe de. LORSQUE LA LIBYE PARAÎT [When Libya appeared]. *Défense Natl. [France] 1973 29(1): 65-73.* Reviews political change in Libya since Muammar Qadhafi's 1969 coup and the resultant opportunities for France.

1400. Sanger, Richard H. LIBYA: CONCLUSIONS ON AN UNFINISHED REVOLUTION. *Middle East J. 1975 29(4): 409-417.* Libya celebrated the fifth anniversary of the Republican takeover in 1974. Most of the successes of the revolution were internal and economic, while most of its failures were external and political. A quiet, goodhearted, feudal monarchy had changed into a tightly controlled semisocialist military dictatorship with strong pan-Arab tendencies and Third World leanings. Discusses friction with Egypt, growing military and naval strength, agricultural backwardness, and standard of living. The two great question marks were oil and Israel. E. P. Stickney

1401. Schlüter, H. NON-ARABIC REGIONAL BIBLIOGRAPHIES PERTAINING TO THE LIBYAN ARAB REPUBLIC. *Int. Lib. Rev. 1976 8(2): 201-216.* Covers general, regional, and subject bibliographies of Libya, 1866-1973.

1402. Taleyarkhan, Homi J. H. INDO-LIBYAN ECONOMIC COOPERATION: A PERSPECTIVE OF DEVELOPMENTS. *Africa Q. [India] 1979 19(1): 45-53.* Examines Libya's growing appreciation for India and the improvement in economic relations between the two countries.

1403. Velev, Zdravko. NIAKOI ASPEKTI OT PODGOTOVKATA I PROVEZHDANETO NA REVOLIUTSIIATA V LIBIIA [Some aspects of the preparation and implementation of the revolution in Libya]. *Izvestiia na Inst. po Istoriia na BKP [Bulgaria] 1980 43: 243-271.* Traces the state of political forces in Libya after its independence in 1951, the emergence of opposition against the monarchy, and the role of the Free Officers Organization in carrying out the coup in 1969, led by Muammar Qadhafi.

1404. VonMehren, Robert B. and Kourides, P. Nicholas. INTERNATIONAL ARBITRATIONS BETWEEN STATES AND FOREIGN PRIVATE PARTIES: THE LIBYAN NATIONALIZATION CASES. *Am. J. of Int. Law 1981 75(3): 476-552.* Discusses the nationalization by the Libyan government of nine international oil companies between 1971 and 1974 and the ensuing arbitration by international tribunals, providing a comparative analysis of litigation problems in international law and of the impact of arbitration awards on international law.

Morocco

1405. Abu-Lughod, Janet. DEPENDENT URBANISM AND DECOLONIZATION: THE MOROCCAN CASE. *Arab Studies Q. 1979 1(1): 49-66.* Discusses demographic changes in Morocco and their social and economic impact.

1406. Angelelli, J. P. OUFKIR... OU LE MAROC RÉEL [Oufkir—or the real Morocco]. *Écrits de Paris [France] 1978 (376): 48-56.* Discusses the role of the Moroccan military figure, Mohamed Oufkir, in the evolution of Morocco toward independence, 1940's-50's, a process which Oufkir aided greatly.

1407. Ayache, Germain. SOCIÉTÉ RIFAINE ET POUVOIR CENTRAL MAROCAIN (1850-1920) [Rif society and Moroccan central power, 1850-1920]. *Rev. Hist. [France] 1975 254(2): 345-370.* Earlier accounts of the social practices of the Moroccan Rif people present a view of constant blood feuds carried to the extent of anarchy. The extensive practice of killings between Rif people did exist, but can be understood only in the historical development of a primitive people, whose social practices became excessive as they interacted with the centralized Moroccan government of the sultan. These matters were further complicated by the pressure of European involvement in the 20th century. 36 notes. G. H. Davis

1408. BenBarka, Mehdi. THE LOST REVOLUTION. *Int. J. of Pol. 1977 7(3): 83-87.* A 1962 assessment of the independence movement in Morocco which passed through three stages, 1920-60, the first marked chiefly by propaganda among the petite bourgeoisie, the second by armed struggle of both urban and rural forces, the third by inclusion of the movement within the framework of North African revolution. Negotiations with France ended the Moroccan revolution just as an alliance between workers and peasants was emerging. The recognition of independence and the return of the Sultan should be seen as the compromise it was and not as a complete defeat of French colonialism. R. E. Noble

1409. BenBarka, Mehdi. MOROCCO AND AFRICAN LIBERATION MOVEMENTS. *Int. J. of Pol. 1977 7(3): 80-82.* Morocco's independence movement united all social classes except those which saw colonialism as the guarantor of their privileges, and has "offered a paradigm for Africa as a whole." Report to the Second Conference of African Peoples, Tunis, 25-29 January 1960. R. E. Noble/S

1410. Benoist-Méchin. LYAUTEY L'AFRICAIN [Lyautey, the African]. *Nouvelle Rev. des Deux Mondes [France] 1978 (11): 320-336.* Excerpt of the author's forthcoming *Lyautey l'Africain ou le rêve immolé* (Paris, Librairie académique Perrin) in which he relates the building up, the organization, and administration of Morocco as a French protectorate, 1912-25, by Marshal Louis-Hubert Lyautey.

1411. Bensimon, Doris. LES DÉBUTS DU MOUVEMENT SIONISTE AU MAROC: QUELQUES DOCUMENTS DES ARCHIVES SIONISTES DE JERUSALEM [The initial performance of the Zionist movement in Morocco: some documents from the Zionist Archives in Jerusalem]. *Michael: On the Hist. of the Jews in the Diaspora [Israel] 1978 5: 17-80.* Reproduces two groups of letters: 1) those written by the leaders of certain Zionist organizations in Morocco, describing their difficulties in founding the groups; and 2) correspondence exchanged between the World Zionist Organization and the French Zionist Organization to obtain permission from French authorities officially to create a Zionist Organization in Morocco. Based on documents in the Zionist Archives in Jerusalem; 30 notes. L. Makin

1412. Botoran, Constantin. VITEJII LUI ABD EL-KRIM [The brave deeds of Abd-el-Krim]. *Magazin Istoric [Rumania] 1976 10(3): 17-19, 21.* Describes the resistance of the Berber tribes of the Rif region in Morocco to Spanish colonialism, their establishment of the Rif republic in 1921 and its defeat by combined French and Spanish forces in 1926, from reports in a 1931 Bucharest journal.

1413. Boudroua, Ahmed. REFLEXIONES SOBRE LA IDEOLOGIA EN MARRUECOS [Reflections on ideology in Morocco]. *Estudios de Asia y Africa [Mexico] 1982 17(2): 216-224.* Morocco as a nation is a gift of Islam and a creation of Idris I, in the second century of the Hegira. Adopting the doctrine of the teacher Malik, Idris gave the Berbers a sense of identity and a territory. Malik taught that all norms for individual and social concerns in Islamic life are to be found in the Koran and the Sunna. Leadership is in the hands of the Commander of the Faithful, who is elected and has the power to appoint his successor. This ideology is real because it is active, all-embracing, practical and gives a group a sense of identity and homogeneity. 4 notes. J. V. Coutinho

1414. Braun, Frank H. MOROCCO: ANATOMY OF A PALACE REVOLUTION THAT FAILED. *Int. J. of Middle East Studies [Great Britain] 1978 9(1): 63-72.* Discusses the abortive military coup d'état in Morocco, July 1971, showing how the traditional system of patronage, manipulation, and institutionalized corruption revolving around the king was no longer workable. Therefore the king was isolated and forced to look for political support outside the traditional establishment. The most important outcome of this process so far has been the acceptance of a more democratic constitution. Secondary sources; 30 notes. R. B. Orr

1415. Brown, Kenneth; Henderson, George, transl. RESISTANCE AND NATIONALISM. *Int. J. of Pol. 1977 7(3): 100-106.* Analyzes the relationship between two aspects of the nationalist movement in Morocco: the Rif War, carried on by tribes in northern Morocco from 1921 to 1927, and the urban struggle touched off in 1930 by the *Dahir Barbère,* a law seen as threatening Moroccan unity. Despite differences in social structures and cultural values, both areas suffered poverty and discontent; the Rifis attempted to mobilize urban as well as rural opinion, and the struggle in the Rif inspired the earliest nationalists of the towns. Translated from "Résistance et nationalisme," in *Abd-el-Krim et la République du Rif,*(Paris, 1976). Secondary materials; 14 notes. R. E. Noble

1416. Cassell, Kay Ann. AN INTERNATIONAL WOMAN—ASSIGNMENT: MOROCCO. *Wilson Lib. Bull. 1973 47(10): 848-851.* Suggests goals for library education and administration in developing nations. S

1417. Castorino, Francesco G. NEL TRENTENNALE DELLA SCOMPARSA DI SAINT-EXUPÉRY: IL SAHARA VISTO ATTRAVERSO I SUOI "RAPPORTI" DA CAP JUBY 1928-1929 [The 30th anniversary of Saint-Exupéry's death: the Sahara as seen through his reports from Cape Juby 1928-29]. *Africa [Italy] 1974 29(4): 609-626.* Reviews reports written while Antoine de Saint-Exupéry (1900-44) was commanding the air base at Cape Juby. Describes desert life and the people, especially the Moors and the nomads, and discusses the problems of Franco-Spanish relations in the area. 33 notes, appendix. R. O. Khan

1418. Cohen, David. LYAUTEY ET LE SIONISME 1915-1925 [Lyautey and Zionism, 1915-25]. *Rev. Française d'Hist. d'Outre-Mer [France] 1980 67(3-4): 269-300.* After the Balfour Declaration, the Jews of Morocco felt that they had now to adhere to the Zionist movement. The request to set up Zionist organizations met a polite but firm refusal. Ultimately, the decision to oppose Zionist propaganda among the Jews of Morocco came from the desire of General Louis Hubert Lyautey to preserve the French position in the country from all foreign interference. Based on documents in the diplomatic archives of the Ministry of Foreign Affairs in Paris; 85 notes. D. G. Law

1419. Damis, John. MOROCCO: POLITICAL AND ECONOMIC PROSPECTS. *World Today [Great Britain] 1975 31(1): 36-42.* "The king has tried to shore up his authoritarian regime with some rudimentary reforms. Its chances of survival will depend largely on the success in attracting foreign investors, who stayed away after 1971 owing to the uncertain political outlook." J

1420. Damis, John. THE ORIGINS AND SIGNIFICANCE OF THE FREE SCHOOL MOVEMENT IN MOROCCO, 1919-1931. *Rev. de l'Occident Musulman et de la Méditerranée [France] 1975 (19): 75-99.* Examines the development of this system of indigenously sponsored private schools, mostly for elementary education. Considers the motives of the founders, the social origins and motivations of teachers, parents, and students, the institutional aspects of the schools, including their financial and administrative organization, the high rate of failure among the early schools, and the significance of the free schools in the late 1920's. Based on oral evidence; table, 40 notes. R. O. Khan

1421. Eastman, Harland H. NEW LIFE FOR THE OLDEST AMERICAN LEGATION. *Foreign Service J. 1977 54(6): 4, 6, 38.* Discusses the history, floor plans, and 1975 restoration project of the Tangier building, known primarily as the American Legation, which housed the US consular offices, 1821-1961, and is probably the oldest US real estate acquired abroad.

1422. Eickelman, Dale F. THE ART OF MEMORY: ISLAMIC EDUCATION AND ITS SOCIAL REPRODUCTION. *Comparative Studies in Soc. and Hist. [Great Britain] 1978 20(4): 485-516.* Presents alternatives to correspondence theory (which posits a correlation between imparted ideology and resultant social action) through description and analysis of Islamic cognitive style, institutions of higher education, and the social context of both, as they existed in Marrakech, Morocco, 1920's-30's.

1423. Eickelman, Dale F. IS THERE AN ISLAMIC CITY? THE MAKING OF A QUARTER IN A MOROCCAN TOWN. *Internat. J. of Middle East Studies [Great Britain] 1974 5(3): 274-294.* Studies the social organization and structure of one urban quarter of a Moslem city in Morocco. Applies the discipline of social analysis to the information uncovered by scholars versed in the language and history of Islam. Primary and secondary sources; table, 2 graphs, 41 notes. R. B. Orr

1424. Forst, Robert D. THE ORIGINS AND EARLY DEVELOPMENT OF THE UNION MAROCAINE DU TRAVAIL. *Int. J. of Middle East Studies [Great Britain] 1976 7(2): 271-287.* Traces the origins and early development of Morocco's labor movement, 1936-58, with emphasis on the Union Marocaine du Travail. Based on primary and secondary sources; 42 notes. R. B. Orr

1425. Gallissot, René. LE MAROC ET LA CRISE [Morocco and the crisis]. *Rev. Française d'Hist. d'Outre-Mer [France] 1976 63(3-4): 477-491.* The Great Depression was late in Morocco, but its impact when it came was substantial. Phosphate exports dropped; capital invested in Moroccan stock companies plunged, 1928-32; and agricultural production declined, especially wheat and wine, even though acreage devoted to them increased. The speculative boom came to a crashing halt and the inherent weaknesses of a colonial economy based on credit were exposed. Heavy taxation of the Moroccans, together with outbreaks of typhus and famine, led to social transformations among the native population and to the resurgence of nationalism. 2 tables, 3 graphs, 9 notes. J. C. Billigmeier

1426. Glaser, David M. MURDER IN THE CASBAH OR THE EFFECT OF MOROCCO'S RESERVATION TO THE VIENNA CONVENTION ON DIPLOMATIC RELATIONS. *New York U. J. of Int. Law and Pol. 1978 11(2): 299-321.* The United States violated Morocco's jurisdiction when it tried a US marine in a military court for murdering an American in Morocco, ignoring Morocco's right to attach a reservation to the 1969 Vienna Convention on the Law of Treaties, 1969-78.

1427. Hoffer, Wilfried. JÜDISCHE SCHICKSALE—IN MAROKKO [Jewish fates in Morocco]. *Frankfurter Hefte [West Germany] 1981 36(7): 37-42.* Although many Moroccan Jews emigrated to Israel after 1948 in the midst of increasing anti-Israeli propaganda and rural pauperization in Morocco, Moroccan Jews for hundreds of years had been treated favorably in Morocco; for example, during World War II King Mohammed V refused to adopt the anti-Semitic policies of the Vichy government.

1428. Hoisington, William A., Jr. CITIES IN REVOLT: THE BERBER DAHIR (1930) AND FRANCE'S URBAN STRATEGY IN MOROCCO. *J. of Contemporary Hist. [Great Britain] 1978 13(3): 433-448.* On 16 May 1930 the French and the Moroccan authorities signed a *dahir,* or agreement, transferring criminal justice to French courts. The Berbers felt the change to be the beginning of the end of their native customs. Demonstrations and minor violence in Morocco led the French to hand over responsibility for law and order to native rulers. The dahir was not revoked but the French promised to use it only with great discretion. Things then quieted down and "the revolt proved the success of France as educator and exemplar." Based on primary sources; 48 notes. M. P. Trauth

1429. Hoisington, William A., Jr. COMMERCE AND CONFLICT: FRENCH BUSINESSMEN IN MOROCCO, 1952-55. *J. of Contemporary Hist. [Great Britain] 1974 9(2): 49-68.* Seeks resolution of the debate between those who see the European community in Morocco as closed and homogeneous and those who see it as having been open to a variety of views. Recounts and analyzes the career of Lemaigre Dubreuil who headed one of the largest European firms in Morocco as an illustration of the difficulty of ascribing common interests to those liberals who were often regarded as political partners. It also demonstrates how difficult it is to generalize on the lines of division within the French business community. His motives were neither ideological nor economic and he was not a liberal in terms of prior commitment, but sought a resolution of conflict between the French interests and native nationalist interests. 35 notes. R. V. Ritter

1430. Jilali, El Miloudi. MAROC: QUEL "CONSENSUS NATIONAL"? [Morocco: which "national consensus"?]. *Esprit [France] 1981 (4): 157-163.* The present social conditions and political situation in Morocco are characterized by government repression, war in the Sahara, and political opposition movements.

1431. Kuuz, A. EKONOMIKA MAROKKO: TRUDNYE VREMENA [Economics of Morocco: difficult time]. *Aziia i Afrika Segodnia [USSR] 1982 (3): 38-40.* Examines causes of economic recession in Morocco.

1432. Kuuz, A. A. PRONIKNOVENIE AMERIKANSKOGO KAPITALA V MAROKKO [Penetration of American capital into Morocco]. *Narody Azii i Afriki [USSR] 1980 (3): 105-114.* Utilizes selected statistics, 1957-79, to examine the gradually increasing capital investments in Morocco's national economy by the US government and private sector. Though the United States has not supplanted traditional Franco-Moroccan ties, US-Moroccan trade has increased at the expense of the French, and US political influence and military aid to Morocco have risen dramatically since the mid-1970's. 7 tables, 14 notes. N. Frenkley

1433. Lainé, Serge. L'AÉRONAUTIQUE MILITAIRE FRANÇAISE AU MAROC 1911-1939 [French air forces in Morocco, 1911-39]. *Rev. Hist. des Armées [France] 1978 5(4): 107-119.* Presents a history of French military aviation in Morocco from the time of the Moroccan crisis and of the use of the air force in colonial pacification campaigns. Describes the air units' organizational system and equipment up to the outbreak of World War II. Based on official records; 5 illus., 14 notes. G. E. Pergl

1434. Landa, R. MAROKKANSKIE VSTRECHI [Meetings in Morocco]. *Aziia i Afrika Segodnia [USSR] 1981 (2): 40-43.* Discusses politics and economic conditions in Morocco based on a recent visit. J/S

1435. Landau, Jacob M. SOME EAST EUROPEAN WORKS ON MOROCCO. *Middle Eastern Studies [Great Britain] 1982 18(1): 116-200.* A review of a large number of East European books and pamphlets dealing with the geography, economy, politics, history, and literature of Morocco. 2 notes. F. A. Clements

1436. Miner, Horace M. TRADITIONAL MOBILITY AMONG THE WEAVERS OF FEZ. *Pro. of the Am. Phil. Soc. 1973 117(1): 17-36.* Analyzes the occupational mobility among the weavers of Fez, Morocco, against a substantial historical and economic background dating from the 14th century. With the end of the French protectorate in 1956, education was expanded, factories were introduced, and the civil service had numerous openings. The craft censuses of 1956 and 1967 show no trend of handicrafts being passed down from father to son and there seems to be a very slow decline in weaving. Based upon extensive interviews; 5 tables, fig., biblio. C. W. Olson

1437. Mniai, Hassan. INTRODUCTION A L'ÉTUDE DU ROMAN MAROCAIN D'EXPRESSION ARABE [Introduction to the study of the Moroccan novel in Arabic]. *Rev. de l'Occident Musulman et de la Méditerranée [France] 1976 (22): 49-57.* Surveys the Arabic novel in Morocco since World War II and its reflection of politics and cultural policy. R. O.Khan

1438. Moore, Clement Henry. THE BERBER MYTH AND ARAB REALITIES. *Government and Opposition [Great Britain] 1974 9(3): 384-394.* Reviews Robert Montagne's *The Berbers: Their Social and Political Organization* translated by David Seddon (London: F. Cass, 1973) and *Arabs and Berbers: From Tribe to Nation in North Africa,* edited by Ernest Gellner and Charles Micaud (London: Duckworth, 1973), discussing how the Berber myth perpetrated by French colonial administrators misrepresented the realities of the Arabs of Morocco, 1930-70's.

1439. Mourad, Kamal ed-Din; Henderson, George, transl. THE ORIGINS OF THE MOROCCAN BOURGEOISIE. *Int. J. of Pol. 1977 7(3): 88-99.* French colonial administration, by encouraging foreign capital to use Moroccans in its distribution networks, created the Moroccan middle classes. During World War II the bourgeoisie joined the Sultan in seeking greater political independence from the French; this phase of the independence movement led to the Sultan's deposition in 1953. Meanwhile radicalized peasants and workers had begun guerrilla operations. The bourgeoisie, realizing it was losing control of the masses, entered negotiations with France, which brought an end to guerrilla warfare, the return of the Sultan, and the recognition of Moroccan independence. Thus the bourgeoisie and traditional forces retained control and thwarted the popular revolution. Translated from *La Maroc à la recherche de la révolution*(Paris, 1972). 6 notes. R. E. Noble

1440. Oved, Georges. CONTRIBUTION A L'ÉTUDE DE L'ENDETTEMENT DE LA COLONISATION AGRICOLE AU MAROC [A contribution to the study of the indebtedness of agricultural colonization in Morocco]. *Rev. Française d'Hist. d'Outre-Mer [France] 1976 63(3-4): 492-505.* France pursued a policy in Morocco of colonizing the land with French settlers. These usually lacked agricultural experience and fell into debt to European traders. The Great Depression's falling prices and slackening demand worsened the situation of the European farmers. Under pressure the government stepped in with treasury loans to help pay off the traders. After 1934, the settlers and traders began to work more closely together, faced as they were by the twin threats of the rise of the leftist Popular Front in France and of Moroccan nationalism. 46 notes. J. C. Billigmeier

1441. Pennell, C. R. IDEOLOGY AND PRACTICAL POLITICS: A CASE STUDY OF THE RIF WAR IN MOROCCO, 1921-1926. *Int. J. of Middle East Studies [Great Britain] 1982 14(1): 19-33.* Examines the ideological aspects of the Rif War in Morocco, 1921-26, by looking at the policies adopted by the Rif leadership, together with their pronouncements. It is impossible to distinguish between the ideological and the practical aspects of the policy, both of the Rifi leadership and their opponents. 71 notes. R. B. Orr

1442. Pennell, Richard. THE RESPONSIBILITY FOR ANUAL: THE FAILURE OF SPANISH POLICY IN THE MOROCCAN PROTECTORATE, 1912-21. *European Studies Rev. [Great Britain] 1982 12(1): 67-86.* Analyzes Spain's loss of control of Morocco, which it governed as a protectorate from 1912 to 1921. Because of a lack of Spanish financial support, the Spanish army failed to rule militarily and also to effect a change in Moroccan economic life and education. Spanish military leaders failed to understand the Moroccan people, believing them incapable of organizing resistance. Unwittingly, they created a local leadership in eastern Morocco that capitalized on internal army rivalry and handed the Spaniards a series of defeats in July and August 1921, known as the Anual disaster. 50 notes. J. G. Smoot

1443. Price, David Lynn. MOROCCO: THE POLITICAL BALANCE. *World Today [Great Britain] 1978 34(12): 493-500.* In 1977 Morocco's King Hassan II created a unicameral Parliament, but conditions for its development were far from ideal because of debilitating economic problems and military expenditures in the war in the Moroccan Sahara; however, the king and political parties are determined to create institutions for change.

1444. Rivet, Daniel. ECOLE ET COLONISATION AU MAROC: LA POLITIQUE DE LYAUTEY AU DÉBUT DES ANNÉES 20 [School and colonization in Morocco: the policy of Lyautey at the beginning of the 1920's]. *Cahiers d'Hist. [France] 1976 21(1-2): 173-197.* Analyzes the educational policy of Hubert Lyautey (1854-1934), which juxtaposed contrasting intentions. As a result, education oscillated between anachronism, contemporary concerns, and future perspectives. Based on manuscript sources; 77 notes. R. Howell

1445. Rivet, Daniel. LYAUTEY L'AFRICAIN [Lyautey the African]. *Histoire [France] 1980 (29): 16-24.* Hubert Lyautey's hitherto unpublished correspondence shows how this French soldier was able to impose a regime in Morocco which preserved the honor and dignity of the Moroccans. The experiment ended with the Rif War in 1925. J

1446. Rivlin, Benjamin. THE UNITED STATES AND MOROCCAN INTERNATIONAL STATUS, 1943-1956: A CONTRIBUTORY FACTOR IN MOROCCO'S REASSERTION OF INDEPENDENCE FROM FRANCE. *Int. J. of African Hist. Studies 1982 15(1): 64-82.* World War II and US involvement in Moroccan affairs "internationalized" the question of Morocco's relations with France. Whether intended or not, this gave Moroccan nationalism room to grow. Based on Moroccan and American government documents; 40 notes. R. T. Brown

1447. Rockwell, Paul Ayres and Walker, Dale L., ed. MOROCCAN BOMBER: AMERICAN FIGHTERS IN THE RIF WAR, 1925. *Aviation Q. 1979 5(2): 108-135.* Memoir of the Escadrille de la Garde Cherifienne (Squadron of the Sultan's Guard), a group of American volunteers who flew missions against the revolting Berber tribes of Morocco.

1448. Rondot, Philippe. MAROC: LE DOUBLE PARI DU ROI HASSAN II [Morocco: the double gamble of Hassan II]. *Défense Natl. [France] 1981 37(1): 85-103.* Reflections on two aspects of the policies of King Hassan II of Morocco: the attempted occupation of the Western Sahara since the Green March of 1975, and internal social unrest, 1979-80.

1449. Rosen, Lawrence. EQUITY AND DISCRETION IN A MODERN ISLAMIC LEGAL SYSTEM. *Law & Soc. Rev. 1980-81 15(2): 217-245.* Drawing on a detailed study of a *qadi's* court in contemporary Morocco, shows how cultural assumptions give shape to the judge's modes of reasoning, factual assessments, and choice of remedies. Suggests that if careful attention is given to the broader cultural precepts within which judicial discretion is located, Max Weber's *Kadijustiz,* whether represented by an Islamic court official or a Western justice of the peace, will be seen to possess definite regularities. J

1450. Sabagh, Georges and Kim, Sun Bin. THE RELATIONSHIP BETWEEN MIGRATION AND FERTILITY IN AN HISTORICAL CONTEXT: THE CASE OF MOROCCO IN THE 1960S. *Int. Migration Rev. 1980 14(4): 525-538.* Hypothesizes that social mobility may account for lowered fertility among Moroccan women migrating from village to city following independence compared to fertility figures for preindependence migrants.

1451. Sánchez Pérez, Andrés. ABDELKRIM. *Rev. de Hist. Militar [Spain] 1973 17(34): 123-157.* A narrative of the life of Abd-el-Krim (1885-1963), leader of the Riff tribesmen who revolted against Spanish and French encroachments in Morocco, 1922-26. Born in the coastal town of Agadir, Abd-el-Krim grew up in close contact through his father with Spanish colonials. He took a position as a minor civil servant in Melilla and became a teacher in the Hispano-Arab School. Imprisoned in 1915 for his pro-German and anti-French views, he organized Riff revolts at the end of World War I. After amazing early successes, Abd-el-Krim's forces were overwhelmed and the French held him in comfortable confinement on Réunion Island and in France. He escaped to Cairo in 1947 and carried on a vociferous publicity campaign against French colonialism until his death. Secondary sources; 8 illus. K. W. Estes

1452. Sotto Montes, Joaquín de. NOTAS PARA LA HISTORIA DE LAS FUERZAS INDÍGENAS DEL ANTIGUO PROTECTORADO DE ESPAÑA EN MARRUECOS [Notes for the history of native forces in the former Spanish protectorate of Morocco]. *Rev. de Hist. Militar [Spain] 1973 17(35): 117-154.* The use of native troops in Spanish armies dates from the 14th-century use of Moorish auxiliaries in the Christian forces. Such utilization remained small until the Spanish penetration into North Africa began in earnest after Algeciras (1906). Native troops served in police, paramilitary, and regular combat units in Morocco. The author describes the major regiments and battalions, focusing on organizational characteristics, operational history through 1939, lists of commanding officers through 1964, and battle honors. Secondary works; 3 illus., 14 notes, biblio. K. W. Estes

1453. Spaak, Jean-Daniel. Y A-T-IL ÉQUILIBRE SOCIO-ÉCONOMIQUE DANS LE HAUT ATLAS OCCIDENTAL? [Social and economic stability in the western High Atlas]. *Afrique et L'Asie [France] 1974 (100): 22-51.* The western High Atlas mountains, constituting 5% of the area of Morocco, support a population of 551,000, or 4% of the total. The economy is based on agriculture and cattle raising, for both of which water is the critical resource. Because of the irregularity of precipitation, the economy is subject to great fluctuations. Thus an important objective is to regularize the water runoff at the highest possible elevations, a task complicated by deforestation. Forest management is required but cannot be accomplished without management of the grazing lands which provide almost all of the nourishment of the livestock, which in turn produce the fertilizer needed for the region's intensive agriculture. Based on personal observation and published works; 8 tables. J. S. Gassner

1454. Waterbury, John. ENDEMIC AND PLANNED CORRUPTION IN A MONARCHICAL REGIME. *World Pol. 1973 25(4): 533-555.* Analyzes political corruption in contemporary Morocco. Corruption is not necessarily unplanned and unwanted; in Morocco it serves to hold together conflicting ethnic and class elements, spread democracy, encourage capital formation, and permit minority participation. Patronage and dependency serve to perpetuate the survival of the ruling regime. Resources are wasted and the masses of people do not benefit from corruption. Corruption has so long been a part of the Moroccan government that it has become institutionalized. 32 notes. V. L. Human

1455. Weiner, Jerome B. THE GREEN MARCH IN HISTORICAL PERSPECTIVE. *Middle East J. 1979 33(1): 20-33.* Examines the conduct and historical context of Morocco's campaign in October and November of 1975 to acquire the Western Sahara. King Hassan II's successful campaign to annex the Sahara was not just to acquire the vast mineral deposits, especially phosphates. It was also to unify a divided country unsure about Hassan's leadership, and to defuse his opposition. He achieved his political goals, but it is uncertain how long this will last. Secondary works; table, 19 notes. P. J. Mattar

Sudan

1456. Abdel-Rahim, Muddathir. TRAINING: THE SUDANESE EXPERIENCE. *Philippine J. of Administration [Philippines] 1973 17(2): 210-226.* "Training for public service was generally aimed at the Sudanization of the bureaucracy and specifically directed toward (1) eliminating Egyptian influence, (2) achieving nationalist aspirations, and (3) substantially improving education and administration. It involved three phases: (a) training of junior district officers and professionals, (b) expansion of the localization policy, and (c) almost complete Sudanization of the civil service, judiciary and armed forces. The rapid localization of the bureaucracy, dictated by political necessity, brought about problems of administrative organization and efficiency. Measures were therefore adopted to remedy these; hence, the setting up of the 'School of Administration,' the Khartoum Institute of Public Administration, and the Department of Political Science at the University of Khartoum and similar bodies like the Local Government Training Academy. But Sudanese training, after 17 years of experiment, still has to contend with psychological, financial and political problems." J

1457. Adams, Martin. THE BAGGARA PROBLEM: ATTEMPTS AT MODERN CHANGE IN SOUTHERN DARFUR AND SOUTHERN KORDOFAN (SUDAN). *Development and Change [Netherlands] 1982 13(2): 259-289.* Discusses obstacles hindering attempts to modernize agricultural and livestock practices among the Baggara, a group of Arabic-speaking people in Sudan.

1458. Adams, Martin E. and Howell, John. DEVELOPING THE TRADITIONAL SECTOR IN THE SUDAN. *Econ. Development and Cultural Change 1979 27(3): 505-518.* Examines the prospects for the Economic Development Plan (1977-83) for the Sudan which is to be financed largely by Arab money and is the result of a study by the International Labor Organization (ILO). Past economic planning in the Sudan and the organizational and attitudinal problems of implementation lead to the conclusion that the plan is too optimistic, the priorities are misleading, and the government is uncertain about rural economic development. Based on government documents and published sources; 17 notes. J. W. Thacker, Jr.

1459. Adams, William Y. PARADIGMS IN SUDAN ARCHAEOLOGY. *Africa Today 1981 28(2): 15-24.* Identifies and explains four successive paradigms governing field archaeology in the Sudan since 1917: the extractive colonial, the enlightened colonial, the postcolonial, and the independent national. The paradigmatic changes mainly reflect evolving political circumstances. Technological advances, professionalization of archaeology, and changing attitudes of the West toward Africa and Africans also contributed to these changes. Secondary sources; 19 notes. G. O. Gagnon

1460. Ahmed, Abdel Ghaffar M. and Rahman, Mustafa Abdel. SMALL URBAN CENTRES: VANGUARDS OF EXPLOITATION; TWO CASES FROM SUDAN. *Africa [Great Britain] 1979 49(3): 258-271.* Small marketing centers, operated by diverse ethnic groups, have been a common feature of Africa for at least 500 years. In the colonial period they extended their domination over the surrounding countryside. They have now become administrative and trade centers, the changes contributing adversely to the development of the areas. The economy of these areas, remaining subsistence, generates limited purchasing power at the same time as prices increase. 4 fig., 12 notes. R. L. Collison

1461. Allum, Percy. THE SUDAN: NUMEIRY'S TEN YEARS OF POWER. *Contemporary Rev. [Great Britain] 1979 235(1366): 233-242.* Surveys the political development of the Sudan under President Jaafar Nemery, 1969-79, showing how the regime is less stable than it may appear.

1462. Askarova, D. A. RABOCHEE I PROFSOIUZNOE DVIZHENIE SUDANA (1956-1969) [The worker and trade-union movement in Sudan, 1956-69]. *Narody Azii i Afriki [USSR] 1975 (1): 147-156.* The worker and trade union movement in Sudan during 1956-69 was characterized by the development of class consciousness and the political maturity of the working class. The author describes how the workers under the leadership of the Sudan Workers' Trade Unions Federation struggled for a national economy free from the influence of foreign capital, industrialization, radical agrarian reforms, liquidation of tribal administrations, democratization of social life, worker participation in government, and for the acceptance of various workers' demands. 32 notes. L. Kalinowski

1463. Badal, R. K. THE RISE AND FALL OF SEPARATISM IN SOUTHERN SUDAN. *African Affairs [Great Britain] 1976 75(301): 463-474.* Animosity between the government, in the north, and the peoples of southern Sudan has been expressed through the south's demands for self rule, secession, or an end to the north's firm control. The author traces the variety of ethnic groups in the Sudan and the role of Islam as a divisive force in possible unification. Forced Islamization has further alienated the south. Table, 34 notes. H. G. Soff

1464. Barbour, K. M. THE SUDAN SINCE INDEPENDENCE. *J. of Modern African Studies [Great Britain] 1980 18(1): 73-97.* Assesses the degree of progress in the Sudan since independence. Among the achievements reported are the fast and extended rail service, the extension of radio and television networks, the expansion of health and education programs, and increased investments in agricultural schemes. All official policies are directed by the Sudanese Socialist Union. Based on government published documents and secondary sources; map, 3 tables, 39 notes. A. Sbacchi

1465. Barton, Nathalie. THE SUDAN: A BID TO BALANCE BETWEEN ARAB, AFRICAN WORLDS. *Internat. Perspectives [Canada] 1973 (3): 49-54.* Stresses the importance of the Addis Ababa Agreement (1972) and the role of President Jaafar Nemery in unifying the Sudan. L. S. Frey

1466. Bayoumi, A. MEDICAL RESEARCH IN SUDAN SINCE 1903. *Medical Hist. [Great Britain] 1975 19(3): 271-285.* Lists the personnel of and the medical research work done at the Wellcome Tropical Research Laboratories in Khartoum in the Sudan from 1903 to 1952. 37 notes, appendixes. M. Kaufman

1467. Bayoumi, Ahmed. MEDICAL ADMINISTRATION IN THE SUDAN, 1899-1970. *Clio Medica [Netherlands] 1976 11(2): 105-116.* At the end of the 19th century the British brought modern medical techniques to the Sudan. In the 20th century the Royal Medical Corps built hospitals and supervised vaccinations against smallpox and sleeping sickness, and in 1924 the British established the Kitchener School of Medicine in Khartoum. In the 1950's many English doctors, due to political changes, left the Sudan. The government is succeeding in expanding medical services to meet the needs of the Sudanese; 3 tables, 13 notes. A. J. Papalas

1468. Bechtold, Peter K. MILITARY RULE IN THE SUDAN: THE FIRST FIVE YEARS OF JA'FAR NUMAYRI. *Middle East J. 1975 29(1): 16-32.* The Democratic Republic of Sudan, established 1 January 1956, has experienced three major self-proclaimed revolutions, and the "format of government has twice changed between parliamentary democracy and military regimes." Examines the performance of the army rulers by concentrating on the major issues as perceived by the Nemery regime, the ways in which the junta attempted to resolve these issues, and its relationships to existing political groups. 25 notes. E. P. Stickney

1469. Bell, J. Bowyer. THE CONCILIATION OF INSURGENCY: THE SUDANESE EXPERIENCE. *Military Affairs 1975 39(3): 105-113.* Places the South Sudanese revolt in historical perspective and describes the events leading to the unexpected 1972 negotiated agreement which all concerned received enthusiastically. In the Sudan, as with any revolt, the critical moment is the simultaneous perception by both sides that there is no advantage in continuing the struggle. Primary and secondary sources; 19 notes. A. M. Osur

1470. Bell, J. Bowyer. THE SUDAN'S AFRICAN POLICY: PROBLEMS AND PROSPECTS. *Africa Today 1973 20(3): 3-12.* Examines the background of the Regional Autonomy Agreement (1972) which ended the Sudanese civil war. This signaled a de-emphasis of Arabist foreign policy and a beginning of an increasingly African foreign policy. An African orientation will most likely ensure Sudan's stability. 9 notes. G. O. Gagnon

1471. Berkley, Constance E. THE CONTOURS OF SUDANESE LITERATURE. *Africa Today 1981 28(2): 109-118.* Provides a narrative history of Sudanese literature stressing the challenges of oral traditions, Arab and African culture, and the problems of an emerging state. Secondary sources; 18 notes. G. O. Gagnon

1472. Burton, John W. ATUOT ETHNICITY: AN ASPECT OF NILOTIC ETHNOLOGY. *Africa [Great Britain] 1981 51(1): 496-507.* Tradition concerning the Atuot included conflict with the Turks, ability to defend themselves even against superior forces, and a close relationship with the Nuer, with whom they claimed a common origin. Current beliefs agree that the Atuot broke away from the Nuer after a quarrel concerning either cattle or a bead of special significance. The true identity of the Atuot has yet to be established and depends on further research into the history of the Nuer and the Dinka. Fieldwork; 5 notes, biblio. R. L. Collison

1473. Burton, John W. INDEPENDENCE AND THE STATUS OF NILOTIC WOMEN. *Africa Today 1981 28(2): 54-60.* Points out that the traditional parallel power role of Nuer women was ignored by colonial and Arab institutions which has relegated Nuer women to an inferior status. Some changes are occurring. Based on secondary sources; 21 notes. G. O. Gagnon

1474. Burton, John W. PASTORAL NILOTES AND BRITISH COLONIALISM. *Ethnohistory 1981 28(2): 125-132.* The pastoral Nilotic-speaking Atuot of the Southern Sudan, as well as their neighbors, the Nuer and Dinka, responded to the two phases of British colonial rule in the Southern Sudan in two rather different ways. This essay examines the nature of these responses, first to a general lack of administrative policy and then to a policy which could be characterized as one of benign neglect. J

1475. Chaudri, Ahsen. FOREIGN POLICY OF SUDAN UNDER PRESIDENT NUMEIRI. *Pakistan Horizon [Pakistan] 1975 28(4): 19-52.* Sudan's foreign policy under President Jaafar Mohammed Nemery since 1969 has taken into account the nation's Arab and African ethnic groups and its volatile geographical position, and has responded to domestic economic necessity.

1476. Deng, Francis. DYNAMICS OF IDENTIFICATION: A BASIS FOR NATIONAL INTEGRATION IN THE SUDAN. *Africa Today 1973 20(3): 19-28.* Analyzes the disruptive forces in the Sudan, past and present. Recommends free social intercourse between the regions and a conscious effort to develop symbols of unity. 7 notes. G. O. Gagnon

1477. Dyba, Marian. SUDAŃSKA PARTIA KOMUNISTYCZNA 1946-1958 [The Sudanese Communist Party 1946-58]. *Z Pola Walki [Poland] 1974 17(65): 185-213.* Deals with problems connected with the Sudanese Communist Party from 1946 to 17 November 1958 when the reactionary coup d'état changed the conditions of activity of Sudanese Communists. The role played by the Party in the struggle against British colonialism is presented against the social and economic background of the Sudan. J/S

1478. El-Bushra, El-Sayed. SOME DEMOGRAPHIC INDICATORS FOR KHARTOUM CONURBATION, SUDAN. *Middle Eastern Studies [Great Britain] 1979 15(3): 295-309.* Considers the growth, structure, and population distribution of the three cities of Khartoum, Khartoum North, and Omdurman, situated at the confluence of the Blue and White Niles. Internal migration—chiefly males because of social restrictions—rather than a rising birth rate accounts for most of the population increase since the 1830's. The real growth has taken place since World War II; by 1973 it was 800,000. The population is young, male, and with a high percentage of children, reflecting high fertility and mortality. Based mainly on National Population Census of 1955-56, and the Population and Housing Surveys, 1964-65; 4 maps, 6 tables, 2 fig., 12 notes. S

1479. Faaland, Just. POLITIKK OG ØKONOMI I SUDAN [Sudan—politics and economy]. *Internasjonal Politikk [Norway] 1976 (1): 71-88.* Examines Sudan's present central and local political structures within a historical context. Discusses the emerging contours of a strategy for development based on economic potential. J/S

1480. Farah, Abdul-Aziz and Preston, Samuel H. CHILD MORTALITY DIFFERENTIALS IN SUDAN. *Population and Development Rev. 1982 8(2): 365-383.* Based on the 1973 census and an investigation of Khartoum conducted by the Changing African Family Program under the direction of John C. Caldwell, discusses factors influencing child mortality levels in various regions of Sudan, including maternal education, father's occupation, and woman's place of birth.

1481. Fleur-Lobban, Carolyn. SHARI'A LAW IN THE SUDAN: HISTORY AND TRENDS SINCE INDEPENDENCE. *Africa Today 1981 28(2): 69-77.* Traces the use of Shari'a Islamiya [Islamic law] in the Sudan during the precolonial, colonial, and postindependence periods. Concludes that Islamic law is closer to reality than ever but that secularists and non-Moslems oppose an Islamic republic. Secondary sources; 14 notes. G. O. Gagnon

1482. Gabashi, Phillip. GROWTH OF BLACK POLITICAL CONSCIOUSNESS IN NORTHERN SUDAN. *Africa Today 1973 20(3): 29-43.* Describes the evolution of black power organizations among the non-Arab populations of the Northern Sudan and the causes of their discontent. The United Sudanese African Liberation Front (USALF) coalesced the black power groups and attempted two coups in 1969. Calls for continued rebellion. Based on secondary sources and the author's experience; 2 tables, 26 notes. G. O. Gagnon

1483. Grandin-Blanc, Nicole. SOUDAN ARABE—SOUDAN AFRICAIN: LES ORIGINES D'UNE GUERRE CIVILE [Arab Sudan, African Sudan: the origins of a civil war]. *African Perspectives [Netherlands] 1977 (2): 9-42.* Analyzes the conflicting situation in Sudan since its independence in 1956. Although integrated by the Nile, Sudan's northern and southern parts are divided, the Islamic North being favored geographically. This brought civil war until the 1972 Addis Ababa peace accords, made necessary by a conjunction of popular opinion and the critical economic and political situation in the North. Today, the conflict, still latent, might be revived by the aggravation of tense relations with Ethiopia. 25 notes, biblio. G. P. Cleyet

1484. Gruenbaum, Ellen Ruth. MEDICAL ANTHROPOLOGY, HEALTH POLICY AND THE STATE: A CASE STUDY OF SUDAN. *Policy Studies Rev. 1981 1(1): 47-65.* In Sudan medical anthropologists must be concerned with the role of the state, its economic and political institutions, elites' interests, and the dynamic of their development.

1485. Howell, John. HORN OF AFRICA: LESSONS FROM THE SUDAN CONFLICT. *Int. Affairs [Great Britain] 1978 54(3): 421-436.* The southern Sudanese movement emerged in the mid-1950's, although it was constantly weakened by factional rivalries which undermined the leadership of the Anya Nya. In 1969 a coup brought Jaafar Nemery to power; his government, which reflected military and communist influences, conflicted with the Azania Liberation Front and its military wing, the Anya Nya. The changing military situation and international responses hastened the end of the civil war. The attitude of Israel, the Arab states, Uganda, and Ethiopia was significant, while the Anya Nya failed to secure recognition from other African states. The agreement signed at Addis Ababa, February 1972, by the parties to the Sudanese conflict is an example of a pragmatic response to a regional problem in its international setting. Based partly on interviews with those involved in the civil war; 45 notes. P. J. Beck

1486. Ibrahim, Hassan Ahmed. IMPERIALISM AND NEO-MAHDISM IN THE SUDAN: A STUDY OF BRITISH POLICY TOWARDS NEO-MAHDISM, 1924-1927. *Int. J. of African Hist. Studies 1980 13(2): 214-239.* Sir Geoffrey Archer, governor-general of the Sudan, 1925-26, and Sayyid al- Rahman, the leader of the Mahdist organization, attempted to work closely with each other. This temporary alliance was defeated by a coalition of Egyptian interests and lower level civil servants of the Sudan establishment. Based on British government archives; 84 notes. R. T. Brown

1487. Ibrahim, Hassan Ahmed. MAHDIST RISINGS AGAINST THE CONDOMINIUM GOVERNMENT IN THE SUDAN, 1900-1927. *Int. J. of African Hist. Studies 1979 12(3): 440-471.* The Mahdist risings during the years of condominium government in the Sudan failed to command a popular following and, with the exception of the risings of 1908 and 1921, none of the rebellions constituted any real threat to the authority of the government. 106 notes. M. McCarthy

1488. Johnson, Douglas H. THE FIGHTING NUER: PRIMARY SOURCES AND THE ORIGINS OF A STEREOTYPE. *Africa [Great Britain] 1981 51(1): 508-527.* Unfortunate incidents in the initial contacts of merchants and the Egyptian army earned the Nuer a lasting reputation for hostility to foreigners in the 19th century, but most Nuer lived in remote areas in the southern Sudan and had no contact with the West. At the end of the century the government was led to believe in the Nuer's inveterate hostility and continued to intervene against them. Enforcement of cattle tribute brought retaliation from the Nuer in the early 20th century. In the Nuer Settlement, 1928-30, Nuer prophets were suppressed and there was an unsuccessful attempt to separate the Nuer from the Dinka. Pacification and a better understanding of the Nuer were achieved by the time of the independence of the Sudan. Based on Sudan and British archives and fieldwork; map, 20 notes, biblio. R. L. Collison

1489. Johnson, Douglas H. THE FUTURE OF SOUTHERN SUDAN'S PAST. *Africa Today 1981 28(2): 33-41.* Castigates preindependence historians of the southern Sudan for ignoring oral and local sources, thus producing gross historiographical mistakes. The only redress is for historians to consult local sources. Secondary sources; 19 notes. G. O. Gagnon

1490. Johnson, Douglas H. TRIBAL BOUNDARIES AND BORDER WARS: NUER-DINKA RELATIONS IN THE SOBAT AND ZARAF VALLEYS, C.1860-1976. *J. of African Hist. [Great Britain] 1982 23(2): 183-203.* Many Nuer living east of the Nile were originally Dinka, or were descended from Dinka. The development of a common Nuer-Dinka vocabulary and the growth of intermarriage and kinship ties and of intersettlement blurred the distinction between Nuer and Dinka. By the end of the 19th century strong religious leaders deliberately fostered the growth of a Nuer-Dinka community. The Anglo-Egyptian administration's attempt to separate Nuer and Dinka into discrete political units ultimately failed, owing to the strength of the ties linking the two peoples, and the border region became a transitional zone where one system merged into the other, a border without a boundary. Based on interviews and published sources; map, 105 notes. R. L. Collison

1491. Kaikati, Jack G. THE ECONOMY OF SUDAN: A POTENTIAL BREADBASKET OF THE ARAB WORLD? *Int. J. of Middle East Studies [Great Britain] 1980 11(1): 99-123.* Reviews Sudan's recent economic developments and describes its agriculture, emphasizing its determination to become the principal food supplier of Arab oil-producing countries. The Sudan has more arable land than the Arab nations together, but only 10% is under cultivation. Huge sums from Arab states, principally Saudi Arabia and Kuwait, are pouring in to develop the land. 3 tables, 18 notes. R. B. Orr

1492. Kasfir, Nelson. SOUTHERN SUDANESE POLITICS SINCE THE ADDIS ABABA AGREEMENT. *African Affairs [Great Britain] 1977 76(303): 143-160.* The Addis Ababa Agreement of 1972 has resulted in the avoidance of civil war and the successful maintenance of peace in the new Southern Region of the Sudan. The author discusses the political problems which arose in the north and south as a result of implementing the agreement. 56 notes. E. P. Stickney

1493. Kirk-Greene, A. H. M. THE SUDAN POLITICAL SERVICE: A PROFILE IN THE SOCIOLOGY OF IMPERIALISM. *Int. J. of African Hist. Studies 1982 15(1): 21-48.* A statistical examination of the records of the 393 individuals who served in the Sudan Political Service shows that they were not only an elite in their education and their athletic skills, but also, contrary to popular opinion, in their intellectual abilities. They were, as they were reputed to be, the finest colonial service. Based on Sudan Service records; 4 tables, 52 notes. R. T. Brown

1494. Kotlov, L. N. D. R. VOBLIKOV: *RESPUBLIKA SUDAN (1956-MAI 1969).*[D. R. Voblikov, *The Republic of Sudan (1956-May 1969)].Narody Azii i Afriki [USSR] 1980 (1): 197-202.* Reviews D. R. Voblikov's *Respublika Sudan (1956-Mai 1969) [Republic of Sudan (1956-May 1969)],* (Moscow: Nauka, 1978), which studies the main socioeconomic and political problems faced by the independent Sudanese state, especially the arrangement of class and political forces, traditional conflicts in Sudanese society, problems concerning Arab unity in general, the various forms of neocolonialism, and the meaning and results of Sudanese cooperation with socialist states. 2 notes. C. Pichelin

1495. Ladouceur, Paul. THE SOUTHERN SUDAN: A FORGOTTEN WAR AND A FORGOTTEN PEACE. *Int. J. [Canada] 1975 30(3): 406-427.* The Addis Ababa agreement of 1972 brought an end to 17 years of conflict in the Sudan but the ensuing peace has remained fragile. 23 notes. R. V. Kubicek

1496. Loban, Richard A., Jr. THE LAW OF ELEPHANTS AND THE LAW OF MONKEYS: TWO CASES OF IDEOLOGY AND POLITICS. *Africa Today 1981 28(2): 87-95.* Relates two instances of Sudanese resistance to British rule: Mohammed Amin Hodeib, imprisoned for public speeches in 1919, and the Tuti Island "republic," where a whole village successfully resisted British attempts to control them, 1935-46. The two examples symbolize widespread resistance to British rule. Based on court records and secondary sources; 7 notes. G. O. Gagnon

1497. Niblock, Timothy C. A NEW POLITICAL SYSTEM IN SUDAN. *African Affairs [Great Britain] 1974 73(293): 408-418.* Analyzes Sudanese politics since 1971 and interprets the new political system's nature and goals, its assets and weaknesses. Through this process of "new politics," many elements that were hostile to the central government are now its supporters. 20 notes. H. G. Soff

1498. Onwubuemeli, Emeka. AGRICULTURE, THE THEORY OF ECONOMIC DEVELOPMENT, AND THE ZANDE SCHEME. *J. of Modern African Studies [Great Britain] 1974 12(4): 569-587.* An analysis of the process by which economic development moves a nation from agriculture to industry. Emphasizes the Zande scheme of southern Sudan, 1945-56. Zande had been an area of subsistence farming until after World War II. It is suggested that many assumptions dealing with agricultural development be reexamined. 45 notes. H. G. Soff

1499. Osman, Mohammed K. THE RISE AND DECLINE OF THE PEOPLE'S *(AHLIA)* EDUCATION IN THE NORTHERN SUDAN (1927-1957). *Paedagogica Hist. [Belgium] 1979 19(2): 355-371.* Traces the development of *Ahlia* education in the Northern Sudan from the inception of the movement in 1927 to the amalgamation of the schools into the government system after independence and describes the official policy of the government toward the movement, with particular attention to attempts to limit expansion of the schools and improve the quality of their education. Based on archival materials; table, 25 notes. J. M. McCarthy

1500. Ring, Bona M. M. POLITICAL RELATIONSHIPS BETWEEN NORTHERN AND SOUTHERN BLACKS IN THE SUDAN. *Africa Today 1973 20(3): 13-18.* Outlines the major challenges for a united Sudan since the Regional Autonomy Agreement (1972). Urges optimistic caution in predicting a viable Sudan. Based on author's experience; 7 notes. G. O. Gagnon

1501. Roden, David. REGIONAL INEQUALITY AND REBELLION IN THE SUDAN. *Geographical R. 1974 64(4): 498-516.* "Growth-pole strategy has become widely accepted as a basis for investment allocation despite the probability that regional disparities will be accentuated in less-developed economies. The case of the Sudan illustrates some of the problems that may arise. During the colonial period social and economic development was concentrated in the northern riverine districts, where conditions seemed most favorable for rapid growth. This policy was continued after independence in conscious adoption of a growth- pole strategy. The resulting discontent in underprivileged, peripheral regions created a spiral of violence that devastated parts of southern Sudan, necessitated growing expenditures for security, and encouraged further concentration of fresh investment in the more advanced core. A recent agreement that grants local autonomy to southern Sudan may mark a break from the pattern." J

1502. Rondinelli, Dennis A. ADMINISTRATIVE DECENTRALISATION AND ECONOMIC DEVELOPMENT: THE SUDAN'S EXPERIMENT WITH DEVOLUTION. *J. of Modern African Studies [Great Britain] 1981 19(4): 595-624.* Widespread popular opinion of the Sudanese government as corrupt, inefficient, and ineffective supported the revolution of May 1969. The postrevolutionary regime of Jaafar Nemery and his Sudan Socialist Union recognized the need for administrative decentralization and local participation in government. The People's Local Government Act of 1971 provided for the creation of elective provincial councils and appointive provincial commissioners to achieve these goals. While the Sudan since then has shown a tendency toward federalism under semi-autonomous regional governments, the new system is imperiled by a variety of financial and technical limitations, as well as the unwillingness of many bureaucrats in Khartoum to relocate in the provinces. Based on published Sudanese and US Agency for International Development documents and newspapers; 55 notes. L. W. Truschel

1503. Rondot, Pierre. CHRETIENS ET MUSULMANS AU SOUDAN [Christians and Muslims in the Sudan]. *Etudes [France] 1983 358(1): 23-38.* Describes the propagation of Islam throughout Central Africa from the 16th to the 19th century, but concentrates on the history of Sudan, 1881-1981, and clashes between Muslim and Christian elements.

1504. Rondot, Pierre. TRADITIONS ET RÉVOLUTION AU SOUDAN [Traditions and revolution in the Sudan]. *Défense Natl. [France] 1979 35(May): 47-63.* The history of the Sudan from the 16th century to 1979, the 10th anniversary of President Jaafar Nemery's accession to power, with special reference to the importance of religion in the Sudan. 6 notes.

1505. Sanderson, Lilian. THE SUDAN INTERIOR MISSION AND THE CONDOMINIUM SUDAN, 1937-1955. *J. of Religion in Africa [Netherlands] 1976 8(1): 13-40.* The Sudan Interior Mission (SIM) headquartered in Canada, had worked in Nigeria and Ethiopia before entering the Sudan in 1937. A year-by-year account of the SIM's activities is given, including its difficulties with the British government. Of particular importance to the SIM was the development of schools and the role of the British government in the education of Africans. The areas where the SIM went were peopled by Africans who had little interest in missionaries or their schools. 116 notes. H. G. Soff

1506. Sanderson, Lilian Passmore. EDUCATION IN THE SOUTHERN SUDAN: THE IMPACT OF GOVERNMENT-MISSIONARY-SOUTHERN SUDANESE RELATIONSHIPS UPON THE DEVELOPMENT OF EDUCATION DURING THE CONDOMINIUM PERIOD, 1898-1956. *African Affairs [Great Britain] 1980 79(315): 157-169.* By examining the impact of government, missionary, and Southern Sudanese attitudes after the establishment of schools in Southern Sudan, attempts to refute the view that missionary schools imparted the wrong values as an infrastructure for the wrong skills. In the Sudan the government was the most powerful agent influencing educational development and missionary values were to some extent muted by government sponsorship of African values. The missionaries developed the skills which the government allowed them to develop. 47 notes. J. V. Coutinho

1507. Sarkesian, Sam C. THE SOUTHERN SUDAN: A REASSESSMENT. *African Studies R. 1973 16(1): 1-22.* Retraces the development and course of disaffection in the Southern Sudan under colonial and independent governments. S

1508. Shinnie, P. L. CHANGING ATTITUDES TOWARD THE PAST. *Africa Today 1981 28(2): 25-32.* Traces the changing attitudes of Sudanese and foreigners toward archaeology in the Sudan. Aside from steadily increasing interest, the major changes have been greater Sudanese participation and greater numbers and range of countries involved in archaeology. Based on personal experience. G. O. Gagnon

1509. Simon, Rachel. YAHASEI MEMSHELET HASUDAN IM HADAROM B'AIDAN HA'ATZMAUT [Relations between the Sudanese government and the south during the republican era]. *Hamizrah Hehadash [Israel] 1978 27(3-4): 225-269.* Problems in southern Sudan existed long before the establishment of the Sudanese republic in 1956. British colonial aspirations, Mahdist efforts to spread the influence of Islam, and the small role given to southerners contributed to the explosive situation. The military rule of General Ibrahim Abbud (1958-64) drove southern political leaders to form a militant underground. Abbud's regime fell in 1964 and a round table conference was held in 1965. General Jaafar Nemery signed an agreement for southern regional autonomy in February 1972, ending a near civil war. Discusses the development of the Anya Nya (the southern rebel army), and how it achieved regional autonomy through military and civilian political organizations. Based on books, articles, and some official documents; 169 notes. T. Koppel

1510. Stevens, Richard P. THE 1972 ADDIS ABABA AGREEMENT AND THE SUDAN'S AFRO-ARAB POLICY. *J. of Modern African Studies [Great Britain] 1976 14(2): 247-274.* Studies Sudanese developments since the 1972 Addis Ababa agreement which point to the determination of Jaafar Nemery's government to remain an Afro-Arab state in both domestic and foreign policy. Thus Sudan's resolution of its southern problem and of its relations with southern and western neighbors as well as with the Arab world. 90 notes. R. V. Ritter

1511. Suliman, Ali Ahmed. DEFICIT FINANCE AND ECONOMIC DEVELOPMENT IN THE SUDAN. *J. of Modern African Studies [Great Britain] 1973 11(4): 547-558.* A study measuring and analyzing the importance of deficit finance in the economic development of the Sudan during the period 1960-69 and its implications for the Five-Year Plan, 1970-75. Although deficit finance should not be encouraged, it is both necessary and inevitable for the 1970's. However, the maximum amount of such advances should be reduced to within 15 percent of the estimated ordinary revenue of the government. If thus limited it will be an invaluable asset for economic development. Moreover, a progressive rise in the price level may be a stimulus for the increased production of certain goods. Although mild inflation can be a stimulus to the economy, deficit finance can only be helpful if used with care. 4 tables, 17 notes. R. V. Ritter

1512. Tosh, John. THE ECONOMY OF THE SOUTHERN SUDAN UNDER THE BRITISH, 1898-1955. *J. of Imperial and Commonwealth Hist. [Great Britain] 1981 9(3): 275-288.* Deals with the British failure to establish significant links with the world economy for the Southern Sudan before 1955. This failure was in large part due to environmental and human geography, problems that could be solved only by long-term capital investment, well beyond the means of any colonial government in Africa. This underdevelopment continued up to independence. Based on materials in the Sudan Archives, Durham and the Central Records Office, Khartoum; 90 notes. M. C. Rosenfield

1513. Unsigned. SUDAN: JOY OF PEACE, BURDEN OF PIONEERING. *Africa Today 1973 20(3): 44-46.* Summarizes the massive economic problems in the Southern Sudan. Concludes that unity is accepted but the economics of unity bode ill. Reprinted from the *Daily News,* Dar-es-Salaam, Tanzania, 13 April 1973. G. O. Gagnon

1514. Voll, John. EFFECTS OF ISLAMIC STRUCTURES ON MODERN ISLAMIC EXPANSION IN THE EASTERN SUDAN. *Int. J. of African Hist. Studies 1974 7(1): 85-99.* Four aspects of Sudanese Islam—the nature of the frontier, the identification of Arab and Islamic culture, the religious brotherhoods, and the attitude toward the state—operating within the framework of the events of the last century and a half have resulted in only the limited expansion of Islam. The strength of Islam in the North, joined with events of the current century, have created a reaction in the South and an attempt to assert an independent southern identity. Primary and secondary sources; 42 notes. M. M. McCarthy

1515. Voll, John. ISLAM: ITS FUTURE IN THE SUDAN. *Muslim World 1973 63(4): 280-296.* Examines the nature and experiences of

Islamic institutions in the Sudan, and the impact of modernization on them. Modernization has undermined traditional religious institutions in the Moslem world, and traditional institutions are now declining in the Sudan. The *ulama* (religious leaders) formerly played a secondary role to that of the local leaders and religious brotherhoods, but a renewal of pride in Islamic identity as well as the search for practical and realistic solutions to the problems of Sudanese society is emerging. Based largely on secondary sources; 33 notes. P. J. Mattar

1516. Voll, John O. RECONCILIATION IN THE SUDAN. *Current Hist. 1981 80(470): 422-425, 435-436, 488.* Since independence in 1956, the Sudan's leadership has faced the challenges of achieving national unity, creating a sound modern economy, and establishing Sudan's place in the world. The Nemery government's resolution of the southern conflict, its policy of political reconciliation, and the creation of a regional system have created new opportunities for national unity despite the Sudan's social diversity.

1517. Voll, John Obert. UNITY OF THE NILE VALLEY: IDENTITY AND REGIONAL INTEGRATION. *J. of African Studies 1976 3(2): 205-228.* Examines the rise and decline of the nationalist, anti-imperialist ideal of the "unity of the Nile Valley" as an example of the dynamics of regional political integration in the modern world. The function of this ideal in the developing political system is "the key to understanding the success and failure of Nile Valley integration in the first half of the 20th century." The ideal had had a significant psychological place in assisting the young educated Sudanese in their search for personal and national identity. Once that was secured it ceased to have effective significance. 59 notes. R. V. Ritter

1518. Voll, Sarah P. COTTON IN KASSALA: THE OTHER SCHEME. *J. of African Studies 1978 5(2): 205-222.* Analysis of the failure of the Kassala cotton scheme in the Gash River valley of the eastern Anglo-Egyptian Sudan during the 1920's. The Sudanese administration and the directors of the Kassala Cotton Company made grievous errors of judgment in planning irrigation and cotton growing by tenants in the Gash valley. Less than a fifth of the planned acreage could be put under irrigation, the local Hadendowa pastoralists could not be successfully fitted into the scheme as tenants, and the company went under in 1928. The problems encountered by the Kassala scheme, as much as the success of the better known Gezira cotton scheme, should be borne in mind by project planners in contemporary Africa. Based on archival sources; 62 notes. L. W. Truschel

1519. Wai, Dunstan. PAX BRITANNICA AND THE SOUTHERN SUDAN: THE VIEW FROM THE THEATRE. *African Affairs [Great Britain] 1980 79(316): 375-395.* British colonial policy in the Sudan has been held responsible for the division of the Arab North and the African South and for the postcolonial strife in the country. The Anglo-Egyptian Condominium policy of separate administration was essentially right, and the major mistake committed against the Southerners was the abandonment of that separation and the political unification of the two regions on the eve of imperial withdrawal. Partly based on primary material in the Government archives; Khartoum; 57 notes. J. V. Coutinho

1520. Wai, Dunstan M. REVOLUTION, RHETORIC, AND REALITY IN THE SUDAN. *J. of Modern African Studies [Great Britain] 1979 17(1): 71-93.* Analyzes the performance of the autocratic military government of President Jaafar Nemery, who has largely failed to create viable political institutions. He has given regional autonomy to Southern Sudan, but the South remains discriminated against both economically and politically. Laggard implementation of political and economic programs stems from the deficiency of administrative institutions and inefficient civil servants. Secondary sources; 2 tables, 39 notes. A. Sbacchi

1521. Wai, Dunstan M. THE SUDAN: DOMESTIC POLITICS AND FOREIGN RELATIONS UNDER NIMIERY. *African Affairs [Great Britain] 1979 78(312): 297-317.* Under Jaafar Nemery the Sudan's foreign policy has been subjected to frequent changes in character owing to the absence of a unifying ideology. During the first phase, 1969-71, the Soviet Union became the principal source of economic and military aid, trade with Eastern Europe rose a quarter of exports and 18% of imports, and 2,000 Soviet and East European technical advisers were stationed in the Sudan. The 1971 coup and countercoup led to deterioration of relations with the USSR, a purge of Communist sympathizers, and abandonment of the proposed Arab Federation with Libya and Egypt. Diplomatic relations with the United States were resumed and Western investment encouraged. Arab oil producers have financed several projects. 42 notes. R. L. Collison

1522. Warburg, Gabriel. SLAVERY AND LABOUR IN THE ANGLO-EGYPTIAN SUDAN. *Asian and African Studies [Israel] 1978 12(2): 221-245.* Although British public opinion was staunchly abolitionist, the Sudan colonial service recognized the importance of slavery in the political and economic life of the Sudan. As a result, moves against slavery were very cautious and both the slave trade and domestic slavery continued to the end of the colonial era. Based on British and Sudan government archives; 86 notes. R. T. Brown

1523. Warburg, Gabriel. SUDAN NE'EVEKET 'AL 'ATSMA'UTAH, 1952-1956 [Sudan's struggle for independence, 1952-56]. *Hamizrah Hehadash [Israel] 1975 25(1-2): 38-51.* Examines the political influence of Isma'il al-Azhari, Sudan's first prime minister, and Sayyid 'Abd al-Rahman al-Mahdi and Sayyid 'Ali al-Mirgham, heads of the *Ansar* and *Khatmiyyah*religious sects, respectively. The principle of unity with Egypt was dropped during the 1953 election campaign. Political power was held by the religious leaders and an agreement between them led to independence on 1 January 1956. Seven months later a coalition of the two political parties controlled by *Ansar* and *Khatmiyyah* replaced al-Azhari's government. 60 notes. T. Sassoon

1524. Warburg, Gabriel R. FROM ANSAR TO UMMA: SECTARIAN POLITICS IN THE SUDAN, 1914-1945. *Asian and African Studies [Israel] 1973 9(2): 101-153.* Discusses the sectarian politics of the Sudan, 1914-45, showing the dichotomy between the Ansar Party, which stood for traditional tribal society, and the Umma Party, whose slogan became "Sudan for the Sudanese." Demonstrates that the two main characteristics of the Sudanese political scene throughout the period were the strength and flexibility of popular Islam and the inability of the British authorities to formulate policies to suit the situation.

1525. Wilson, R. T. THE INCIDENCE AND CONTROL OF LIVESTOCK DISEASES IN DARFUR, ANGLO-EGYPTIAN SUDAN, DURING THE PERIOD OF THE CONDOMINIUM, 1916-1956. *Int. J. of African Hist. Studies 1979 12(1): 62-82.* During the 40-year period of condominium rule in Darfur, the westernmost province of the republic of the Sudan, the veterinary services were overwhelmingly concerned with the control of rinderpest and contagious bovine pleuropneumonia. The increase in livestock numbers was due to factors not concerned with curative or preventive treatments, such as increased law and order, prevention of intertribal raids, and above all, the introduction of a fixed annual poll tax to replace tribute formerly payable to the Sultan. Based on documents in the Sudan Government Archives; 3 tables, map, 80 notes. M. M. McCarthy

1526. Wilson, R. T. TEMPORAL CHANGES IN LIVESTOCK NUMBERS AND PATTERNS OF TRANSHUMANCE IN SOUTHERN DARFUR, SUDAN. *J. of Developing Areas 1977 11(4): 493-508.* Improved health services and control of epidemic diseases explain an unprecedented increase in the world's human and livestock populations. For centuries disease restricted cattle population, but by 1940 political stability, availability of vaccines, and the increased use of motor transport, which allowed the limited number of veterinarians to cover large areas, resulted in a rapid buildup of cattle. The cattle population soon outstripped available food supplies. Simultaneously, the growing sedentary human population restricted the total area available for traditional migratory movements. Consequently, more goats were raised because they could supply milk and meat and live under harsher range conditions. Donkeys also increased in response to the need to transport cash crops to market. Based on Sudan tax records and oral history; 4 tables, 3 fig., 36 notes. O. W. Eads, Jr.

1527. Woodward, Peter. THE SOUTH IN SUDANESE POLITICS, 1946-1956. *Middle Eastern Studies [Great Britain] 1980 16(3): 178-192.* Analyzes Sudanese politics from 1946, when the British abandoned the policy of isolating the south from the north of Sudan, until the 1955 mutiny among southern troops. The South was unable to exert any effective influence on Sudanese politics, particularly on vital issues such as maintaining indigenous culture, consultation in decisionmaking, and the rapid replacement of the British by northern administrators. The internal discontent helped spark the violence of 1955. Based on British sources and secondary works; 22 notes, 4 ref. P. J. Mattar

1528. Zakaria, Ibrahim. THE STRUGGLE OF THE SUDANESE COMMUNISTS. *World Marxist Rev. 1977 20(4): 55-62.* Sketches the activities of the Sudanese Communist Party, 1946-77.

1529. —. SYMPOSIUM ON THE CHANGING STATUS OF SUDANESE WOMEN: AHFAD UNIVERSITY COLLEGE FOR WOMEN: OMDURMAN, SUDAN, 23 FEBRUARY-1 MARCH 1979. *Resources for Feminist Res. [Canada] 1980 9(1): 81-94.*

Tunisia

1530. Allman, James. LA MOBILITÉ SOCIALE ET L'ÉDUCATION DE MASSE DANS LA TUNISIE INDÉPENDANTE [Social mobility and mass education in independent Tunisia]. *Rev. de l'Occident Musulman et de la Méditerranée [France] 1975 (19): 17-28.* Examines the principal factors affecting social mobility, which increased sharply after independence until the 1960's, and then rapidly diminished. Includes the preliminary results of research into the types of employment pursued by youth in representative Tunisian communities, illustrating the correlation between education and social mobility. 5 tables, 20 notes. R. O. Khan

1531. Amami, S. El; Gachet, J. P.; and Gallali, T. CHOIX TECHNIQUES ET AGRICULTURE MAGHREBINE: LA CAS DE LA TUNISIE [Technical alternatives and agriculture in the Maghreb: the case of Tunisia]. *Peuples Mediterranéens-Mediterranean Peoples [France] 1979 (8): 119-152.* Analyzes agricultural production in Tunisia, 1962-78.

1532. Baduel, Pierre-Robert. ÉMIGRATION ET TRANSFORMATION DES RAPPORTS SOCIAUX DANS LE SUD TUNESIEN [Emigration and transformation of social relations in southern Tunisia]. *Mediterranean Peoples [France] 1981 (17): 3-22.* Examines the effects of emigration in southern Tunisia, describing its impact on traditional modes of agricultural production and social organization and the threat to the region's economic stability.

1533. Bessis, Juliette. LE MOUVEMENT OUVRIER TUNISIEN: DE SES ORIGINES À L'INDÉPENDANCE [The Tunisian workers' movement from its origins to independence]. *Mouvement Social [France] 1974 (89): 85-108.* Presents the main periods of Tunisian trade unionisn, since its birth in the 1920's, to the independence of the country and its integration in the Destour party. Considers the great ambiguity of Tunisian trade unionism, a result of the colonial situation and a working class of different ethnic origins. Trade-unionist development illustrates this ambiguity in two main tendencies: the class struggle and nationalism. Nationalism, victorious in the years after the Second World War, was necessary but also was a reason for the weakness of trade unionism which, as an organization, became a part of the Neo-Destour Party after 1956. J/S

1534. Binsbergen, Wim M. J. van. POPULAR AND FORMAL ISLAM, AND SUPRA-LOCAL RELATIONS: THE HIGHLANDS OF NORTH-WESTERN TUNISIA, 1800-1970. *Middle Eastern Studies [Great Britain] 1980 16(1): 71-91.* Discusses the relations between formal and popular Islam, focusing on the supralocal relations, religious structure, and change in the highlands of Khroumerie, Northwestern Tunisia. For centuries formal Islam was accommodated in local society. Colonialism, 1881-1956, and later independence after 1956 upset the pattern of supralocal relations. The political and economic power shifted from the local communities to bureaucratic organizations outside Khroumerie. The new power structures emphasized formal Islam, which polarized formal and popular Islam in the area. Based on the author's data and Western secondary works; table, 43 notes. P. J. Mattar

1535. Boularès, Habib. LA POLITIQUE ÉTRANGÈRE DE LA TUNISIE OU LA TACTIQUE DES HÉRISSONS [Tunisia's foreign policy or the hedgehog tactic]. *Défense Natl. [France] 1977 33(10): 59-70.* Assesses Tunisia's foreign policy, 1974-77, since the break with Libya and in the light of the new confidence brought about by the discovery of native oil resources.

1536. Bouman, F. J. A. LAND TENURE AND AGRICULTURAL DEVELOPMENT IN LE KEF, TUNISIA. *Middle East J. 1977 31(1): 63-80.* More than 90 percent of the total cultivated area of Le Kef is given over to cereals. Figures show that from 1962 to 1974 the proportion of land under tenancy has decreased on small farms, remained stable on medium-sized farms, and increased for large farms. Land tenure relations have contributed to a gradual degeneration of Tunisia's agriculture. "The encouragement of conversion of eroded land into permanent pasture and the substitution of green crops for temporary fallow—which constitutes a potential danger of further erosion—might" be based on price incentives. Map, 11 tables, 33 notes. E. P. Stickney

1537. Cheriaa, Tahar. LE CINEMA EN TUNISIE [The cinema in Tunisia]. *Africa [Italy] 1973 28(3): 431-438.* Analyzes the importation and distribution of films, the indigenous film industry, commercial control, and government policy, and statistics on the origin, language, and content of films, 1968-73. Discusses problems of the Tunisian cinema, principally high entrance charges and state taxation, ineffectively controlled distribution, and production modelled too closely along foreign lines. Note. R. O. Khan

1538. Deshen, S. AN OUTLINE OF THE SOCIAL STRUCTURE OF THE JEWISH COMMUNITIES IN DJERBA AND SOUTHERN TUNISIA FROM THE END OF THE 19TH CENTURY UNTIL THE 1950'S. *Zion [Israel] 1976 41(1-2): 97-108.* Southern Tunisian Jewry has an uninterrupted and relatively peaceful history going back into antiquity. The general Berber population, particularly of the island of Jerba, has since the late 19th century developed a pattern of migrant merchants, who operate throughout Tunisia and retire in their old age to their homes. In this context, the Jews entered local commerce and filled the major local positions; however, they did not engage in international or in itinerant commerce or trade. Jerban Jewry is therefore extremely sedentary and lacking in geographical mobility. As a consequence, the local community is relatively powerful over its individual members. Social control, particularly in religious matters, is strong because of the high visibility of individuals. Community organs are highly developed in comparison to other Jewish communities in North Africa. Based on rabbinical treatises. J

1539. Diemer, G. and Laan, E. Ch. W. van der. THE INFORMAL SECTOR IN HISTORICAL PERSPECTIVE. THE CASE OF TUNIS. *Cultures et Développement [Belgium] 1981 13(1-2): 161-172.* A study of social stratification within the informal sector of the city's economy, tracing the persistence of its class structure since at least the 15th century.

1540. Entelis, John P. IDEOLOGICAL CHANGE AND AN EMERGING COUNTER-CULTURE IN TUNISIAN POLITICS. *J. of Modern African Studies [Great Britain] 1974 12(4): 543-568.* Analyzes Tunisia's elite political culture, dominated by President Bourguiba. After his death it is anticipated that a newly emerging counterculture, led by university students, will secure control of the nation. 5 tables, 24 notes. H. G. Soff

1541. Entelis, John P. REFORMIST IDEOLOGY IN THE ARAB WORLD: THE CASES OF TUNISIA AND LEBANON. *Rev. of Pol. 1975 37(4): 513-546.* Reformist rather than radical ideologies dominate today's Arab world. Ironically, in the most democratic Arab states, Tunisia and Lebanon, reformist ideology appears to be failing. In Tunisia, conservative forces are largely responsible, whereas in Lebanon, a combination of internal and external factors, primarily the Palestine liberation struggle, has been the major problem. Prospects for the triumph of reformism are greater in Tunisia than in Lebanon, where the continuing crisis may encourage government takeover by "Lebanese zealots whose single objective would be the preservation of the Lebanese political system irrespective of long term social consequences." 82 notes. L. E. Ziewacz

1542. Fontaine, Jean. TABLEAU GÉNÉRAL DE LA LITTÉRATURE TUNISIENNE D'EXPRESSION ARABE DEPUIS L'INDÉPENDANCE, 1956-1974 [A general list of Tunisian literature in Arabic since independence, 1956-74]. *Rev. de l'Occident Musulman et de la Méditerranée [France] 1976 (22): 205-214.* A brief statistical survey of Tunisian literature in Arabic since independence, followed by an author and title list in Arabic. Table, graph. R. O. Khan

1543. Gallico, Loris. FASCISMO E MOVIMENTO NAZIONALE IN TUNISIA [Fascism and the national movement in Tunisia]. *Studi Storici [Italy] 1978 19(4): 863-868.* When Fascism came to power in Italy in 1922, Tunisia had a large Italian minority. The Fascists immediately made every effort to seize control of the institutions of the Italian community in order to press for the cession of Tunisia to Italy. The Fascists also tried to win over the Tunisian Muslim nationalists, led by Habib Ben-Ali Bourguiba's Destour Party. During the war, some Destour leaders did collaborate, but not Bourguiba. The Vichy regime released him from prison as a quid pro quo for a speech on Radio Bari, but in his talk Bourguiba avoided pro-Axis statements. He was allowed to go to Tunis under Italian supervision on 6 April 1943, where he remained until the arrival of the Anglo-American liberators on 7 May 1943. Bourguiba's stance, supported by anti-Fascist Italians in Tunisia and by the local Communists, undermined the Axis's attempt to use Arab nationalism against the Allies, an effort symbolized by the pro-Nazi Hajj Amin al-Husayni, leader of the Palestinian Arabs, whose appeals Bourguiba rejected. 5 notes. J. C. Billigmeier

1544. Gil Benumeya, Rodolfo. LA REALIDAD TUNECINA EN LA EVOLUCIÓN DEL MAGREB [The role of Tunisia in the evolution of the Maghreb]. *Rev. de Política Int. [Spain] 1974 (134): 139-149.* Examines the history of Tunisia, 1887-1974, in the context of the history of the Maghreb as a whole. Emphasizes the importance of local factors and the impact of the European powers.

1545. Gourg, Jean-L. LA TUNISIE DE PIERRE MAC ORLAN [Tunisia seen by Pierre Mac Orlan]. *Cahiers de Tunisie [Tunisia] 1979 27(109-110): 345-358.* A review of the works of French author of adventure tales Pierre Mac Orlan (Pierre Dumarchey, 1882-1970) inspired by his brief stay in Tunisia in 1932.

1546. Gusarov, V. NEKOTORYE ITOGI I PERSPEKTIVY SOTSIAL'NO-EKONOMICHESKOGO RAZVITIIA TUNISA V USLOVIIAKH NEZAVISIMOSTI [Some of results and perspectives of the social and economic development of Tunisia under conditions of independence]. *Archív Orientální [Czechoslovakia] 1977 45(4): 305-317.* Failure of a liberal economic policy led to government regulation in the early 1960's. The author gives a detailed survey of the 10-year economic development program initiated in 1962. J/S

1547. Hamzaoui, Salah. NON-CAPITALIST RELATIONS OF PRODUCTION IN CAPITALIST SOCIETY: THE *KHAMMESSAT* IN SOUTHERN TUNISIA. *J. of Peasant Studies [Great Britain] 1979 6(4): 444-470.* The *khammessat* is one of the most ancient social institutions regulating agricultural labor in the Maghreb. The author discusses the nature of the relationship between agricultural labor and landowner in a society dominated by a noncapitalist mode of production, the impact of capitalism on labor relations, and the possibility of development, within the *khammessat* system, of a labor organization and the demand for rights. J

1548. Hopkins, Nicholas S. THE EMERGENCE OF CLASS IN A TUNISIAN TOWN. *Int. J. of Middle East Studies [Great Britain] 1977 8(4): 453-491.* Applies the Marxist notion of class to recent developments in the social, economic, and political structure of Testour, a small agricultural town in northern Tunisia. Explains the meaning of class, and traces the evolution of Testour society over the last generation from a system of rank to one of class. Explains the implications of this method for social analysis and of the local developments in Testour for national social development. Based on field research in Testour; 26 notes, biblio. R. B. Orr

1549. Hopkins, Nicholas S. TUNISIA: AN OPEN AND SHUT CASE. *Social Problems 1981 28(4): 385-393.* Compares the open door economic policy and peace initiatives developed by Egyptian President Anwar Sadat during the 1970's with the liberal policy created in Tunisia by Prime Minister Hedi Nouira in 1971, and describes how both countries have moved from a period of relative self-sufficiency and consolidation to one of increasing integration into the international division of labor.

1550. Kamelgarn, Daniel. STRATÉGIES DE SELF-RELIANCE ET SYSTÈME ÉCONOMIQUE MONDIAL: L'EXPÉRIENCE TUNISIENNE DES ANNÉES 1960 [Self-reliance strategiés and the world economic system: the Tunisian experience during the 1960's]. *Mediterranean Peoples [France] 1980 (13): 107-126.* Discusses a period in Tunisia's economic development which was heavily dependent on foreign capital, the subsequent insertion of the economy into the international division of labor, and the economic constraints which deterred the socialist movement led by Ahmed Ben Salah.

1551. Kamelgarn, Daniel. TUNISIE (1970-1977): LE DÉVELOPPEMENT D'UN CAPITALISME DÉPENDANT [Tunisia, 1970-77: development of a dependent capitalism]. *Peuples Méditerranéens [France] 1978 4: 113-146.* Ahmed Ben Salah's eviction from the highest position in government in 1969 was the starting point of a new stage in the Tunisian economy. Since then the country has become more and more integrated in the international division of labor. The nature of this integration has changed, so that it leads Tunisia in an ever unequal, outward, dependent, and precarious development style. Its economic development, though more rapid, has become a perverse growth. On the one hand, the export of manufactured goods from tax-free areas has risen significantly, and the exploitation of the working class has become the new basis of Tunisian participation in the international division of labor. On the other hand, the extension of the Tunisian market for consumer goods encourages imports of goods and, in the long run, national and foreign investments. The Tunisian pattern reflects the new international division of labor currently occurring in Western economies. J/S

1552. Kassab, A. L'AGRICULTURE TUNISIENNE SUR LA VOIE DE L'INTENSIFICATION [Tunisian agriculture on the way toward intensification]. *Ann. de Géographie [France] 1981 90(497): 55-86.* Studies Tunisian dry and irrigated arboriculture, truck-farming, and industrial fodder farming. Intensification since independence in 1956 has come through changes and development in techniques, but agricultural production has not increased.

1553. Kassab, Ahmed. LA COLONISATION AGRICOLE EN TUNISIE (1881-1956) [Agricultural colonization in Tunisia, 1881-1956]. *Int. Jahrbuch für Geschichts- und Geographieunterricht [West Germany] 1977-78 18: 237-242.* Discusses the European (primarily French, with some Italian) colonization of Tunisian agriculture from the Treaty of Bardo in 1881 to Tunisian independence in 1956. Europeans owned 25% of the country's agricultural resources and completely dominated commercial agriculture, which resulted in the poverty of the majority of the population, despite the greater productivity and efficiency of European farming methods. Based on a paper presented to the Second German-Tunisian Schoolbook Conference, Tunis, 11-15 April 1977; map. J. L. Colwell

1554. Landau, Jacob M. SOVIET WORKS ON TUNISIA (REVIEW ARTICLE). *Middle Eastern Studies [Great Britain] 1980 16(3): 267-270.* Reviews a dozen Soviet works on Tunisia. Tunisia has not attracted much interest among Soviet experts on the Maghreb, and work is less extensive in range and scope than that on other Arab countries. Yet scholars will find them useful, particularly those books dealing with social and economic development, such as on trade unions and workers. Based on the Soviet works cited; 5 notes. P. J. Mattar

1555. Liauzu, Claude. CHEMINOTS MAJORÉS ET CHEMINOTS GUÉNILLARDS EN TUNISIE JUSQU'EN 1938 [Salaried officials and laborers in the Tunisian railway industry to 1938]. *Rev. de l'Occident Musulman et de la Méditerranée [France] 1977 (24): 171-203.* Studies the evolution of labor unions and organizations in the Tunisian railway industry. Analyzes the nationalities, functions, and salaries of Tunisian railroad workers, 1923-36, in the broader perspective of contemporary French and Algerian workers' movements. Maintains that the French workers worried little about their Tunisian members, who only slowly developed demands for equality. 7 tables, 55 notes. M. Smith

1556. Liauzu, Claude. UN ASPECT DE LA CRISE EN TUNISIE: LA NAISSANCE DES BIDONVILLES [An aspect of the crisis in Tunisia: the birth of slums]. *Rev. Française d'Hist. d'Outre-Mer [France] 1976 63(3-4): 607-621.* During the Great Depression North African peasants moved to the towns in search of work, and they came to live in shantytowns known as *bidonvilles.* The *bidonvilles* grew rapidly, despite the desperate living conditions and high mortality rates. The government attempted to remove slum residents to their places of origin, but this policy failed, as new immigrants took the places of the deportees, who themselves returned after a few months. The phenomenon was part of the general population explosion and the problem of underdevelopment, and was not amenable to administrative resolution. Map, 2 tables, 26 notes, appendix. J. C. Billigmeier

1557. Lowy, Paul. L'ARTISANAT DANS LES MÉDINAS DE TUNIS ET DE SFAX [Handicrafts in the Tunis and Sfax medinas]. *Ann. de Géographie 1976 85(470): 473-493.* Tunis and Sfax medinas have many similarities. The old towns are both located near the harbor from which they are separated by a modern European city. Both towns gather, around their mosques, a great number of various handicraft guilds. The two medinas and their guilds exhibit notable similarities but also show two different ways to adjust to changed economic conditions. J

1558. Micaud, Ellen C. BELATED URBAN PLANNING IN TUNIS: PROBLEMS AND PROSPECTS. *Human Organization 1974 33(2): 123-137.*

1559. Micaud, Ellen C. URBANIZATION, URBANISM, AND THE MEDINA OF TUNIS. *Int. J. of Middle East Studies [Great Britain] 1978 9(4): 431-447.* The history of city planning for the medina of Tunis. In the period of postindependence planning, the medina was seen as an obstacle to be surmounted if Tunisia was to have a modern capital. From the late 1960's, Tunisians reappraised the medina and there followed a three-year period of intellectual ferment. The period since 1973 was one of retrenchment and realism. 41 notes. R. B. Orr

1560. Ogunbiyi, Isaac A. TWENTIETH-CENTURY TUNISIAN ARABIC CREATIVE WRITING AS A STUDY IN THE SOCIAL, CULTURAL AND POLITICAL HISTORY OF THE COUNTRY. *Odu: a J. of West African Studies [Nigeria] 1975 (11): 61-74.* Examines the dominant theme in contemporary Tunisian Arabic creative writing and analyzes the sources from which the writers got their inspiration. Tunisian creative writings during the twentieth century have depicted the pleasures and pains of Tunisian society. However, any reconstruction of political, social, and cultural history based on this source must necessarily have some gaps because of the periods when the quality and quantity of the published stories were insufficient to form a basis for reconstructing the history of the country. 51 notes. M. M. McCarthy

1561. Philipeaux, Jean. L'ÉVOLUTION DE LA POLITIQUE ECONOMIQUE EN TUNISIE [Evolution of economic policy in Tunisia]. *Études [France] 1973 339(10): 353-370.* Outlines the development of the Tunisian economy since the 1960's, explaining the basic ideas of the national industrial policy laid down soon after independence in 1955. Describes the political and technical errors which accompanied the economic rebirth of the nation. Since 1970, the Tunisian government has dropped the system of the previous decade and introduced new economic orientation. Secondary sources; 45 notes. G. E. Pergl

1562. Picard, Élizabeth. TUNISIE: RÉÉVALUATION DE LA POLITIQUE ÉTRANGÈRE [Tunisia: reevaluation of foreign policy]. *Défense Natl. [France] 1975 31(5): 51-63.* Presents a panorama of Tunisian diplomacy over the past five years, showing the continuity of President Habib Bourguiba's policy in international relations and its limitations.

1563. Pirson, Roland. LES PROBLÈMES D'ADAPTATION À LA DYNAMIQUE DU CHANGEMENT SOCIAL: L'EXEMPLE TUNISIEN [The problems of adaptation to the dynamics of social change: the case of Tunisia]. *Rev. de l'Inst. de Sociologie [Belgium] 1975 (3-4): 437-458.* Studies the adaptation to political, economic, and social changes after Tunisia gained its independence in 1956.

1564. Poncet, Jean. LA CRISE DES ANNÉES 30 ET SES RÉPERCUSSIONS SUR LA COLONISATION FRANÇAISE EN TUNISIE [The crisis of the 1930's and its repercussions on French colonization in Tunisia]. *Rev. Française d'Hist. d'Outre-Mer [France] 1976 63(3-4): 622-627.* The Great Depression of the 1930's caused the end of the policy of colonizing European farmers in Tunisia, and the end, too, of the expansion of land area owned by Europeans. This was in large part due to the collapse of the market for primary agricultural products, such as olive oil, wine, and wheat. This situation gave great impetus to the rise of modern Tunisian nationalism, and marked the transition from a traditional colonial economy to an underdeveloped one in the current sense. 3 notes. J. C. Billigmeier

1565. Rondot, Pierre. LA TUNISIE EN MOUVEMENT [Tunisia on the move]. *Études [France] 1981 354(4): 451-465.* Traces the political evolution of Tunisia from the 1930's to the present, emphasizing President Habib Bourguiba's efforts to resist the growing liberal sector's strong trend toward democratization and progress, and examines conflicting political groups' prospects.

1566. Salem, Khalsi. POUVOIR ET SOCIÉTÉ DANS LE TIERS MONDE: LA TUNISIE BOURGUIBIENNE [Power and society in the Third World: Bourguiba's Tunisia]. *Esprit [France] 1973 (12): 836-859.* One of three articles on the problem of the exercise of power in recently decolonized Muslim societies. Analyzes Habib Bourguiba's total dominance of Tunisian affairs. G. F. Jewsbury

1567. Stone, Russell A. RELIGIOUS ETHIC AND THE SPIRIT OF CAPITALISM IN TUNISIA. *Internat. J. of Middle East Studies [Great Britain] 1974 5(3): 260-273.* Discusses the relationship between religious ethics and capitalism among a group of merchants in Tunisia who are members of a distinct religious sect within Islam. Attempts to see if Max Weber's thesis might apply to non-European cultures. Secondary sources; 5 notes, biblio. R. B. Orr

1568. Sulejczak, Ewa and Gudowski, Janusz. LES MIGRATIONS RURALES VERS LES VILLES EN TUNISIE DU NORD [Rural migrations toward the cities in northern Tunisia]. *Africana Bull. [Poland] 1978 (27): 65-103.* Analyzes the socioeconomic, political, and demographic aspects of the rural migration toward cities in northern Tunisia, 1936-75.

1569. Taieb, Jacques. EVOLUTION ET COMPORTMENT DEMOGRAPHIQUES DES JUIFS DE TUNISIE SOUS LE PROTECTORAT FRANÇAIS (1881-1956) [Increase and demographic behavior of Jews in Tunisia under the French protectorate (1881-1956)]. *Population [France] 1982 37(4-5): 952-958.* Shows how the Jewish population more than quadrupled during the period under study, amounting to 37% of the total population by 1950, due partly to improved medical care and a declining rate of emigration.

1570. Tessler, Mark A. and Freeman, Patricia K. REGIME ORIENTATION AND PARTICIPANT CITIZENSHIP IN DEVELOPING COUNTRIES: HYPOTHESES AND A TEST WITH LONGITUDINAL DATA FROM TUNISIA. *Western Pol. Q. 1981 34(4): 479-498.* Examines the impact of government orientation on individual political attitude and behavior patterns in developing countries, describing participant citizenship in Tunisia and its relationship to regime policies, taken as both an independent variable and a specification variable. J/S

1571. Tlili, Béchir. CONTRIBUTION À L'ÉLUCIDATION DES PARADOXES DE LA PENSÉE RÉFORMISTE TUNISIENNE MODERNE ET CONTEMPORAINE (1830-1930) [Contribution to the elucidation of the paradoxes of modern and contemporary Tunisian reformist thought (1830-1930)]. *Africa 1975 30(3): 317-344.* Studies Islamic modernism, a movement which has had a great impact on the cultural, social, and political life of many Islamic countries. The complex terminology used by the modernists was not well-defined and was often a source of misunderstanding. Hence the reactions of the conservatives, who in spite of progress held a strong position. Other modernists were engaged in an attempt to solve historical problems and to harmonize the past with the present. The various aspects of the problem of modernism, particularly with regard to the situation in Tunisia, 1830-1930, are emphasized by the author.

1572. Tlili, Béchir. LA FÉDÉRATION RADICALE-SOCIALISTE DE TUNISIE À LA VEILLE DE LA DEUXIÈME GUERRE MONDIALE (1937-1938) [The Tunisian Radical-Socialist Federation on the eve of World War II, 1937-38]. *Cahiers de Tunisie [Tunisia] 1980 28(111-112): 75-202.* A comprehensive description and analysis of the program and activities of the Radical-Socialist Federation of Tunisia, and the important role it played in the affairs of the government in 1937 and 1938.

1573. Tlili, Bechir. LA PRODUCTION HISTORIQUE ET ARCHÉOLOGIQUE EN TUNISIE (1970-1973) [Historical and archaeological work in Tunisia, 1970-73]. *Africa [Italy] 1974 29(1): 65-80.* Surveys the publications of scholars researching Tunisian history and archaeology at the University of Tunis and the National Institute for Archaeology and Arts, with a comprehensive bibliography indexed by department and author. 6 notes. R. O. Khan

1574. Vandewalle, Dirk. BOURGUIBA, CHARISMATIC LEADERSHIP AND THE TUNISIAN ONE PARTY SYSTEM. *Middle East J. 1980 34(2): 149-159.* Habib Bourguiba, President of Tunisia since 1957, realized early that his charismatic appeal would fade if it was not associated with an ideology which would also attract the elites. Elements of his ideology included reason, education, human dignity, and human solidarity. He sought education and prosperity for his people and maintained control over the party and trade unions, but since 1969 his power has been slowly eroding. Secondary sources; 24 notes. P. J. Mattar

1575. Zevi, Tullia. PRESIDENT BOURGUIBA: THE VIEW FROM TUNIS. *Africa Report 1973 18(3): 24-26.* Interview with Tunisian President Habib Bourguiba, who discusses Arab and African unity. S

1576. Zghal, Abdelkader. THE REACTIVATION OF TRADITION IN A POST-TRADITIONAL SOCIETY. *Daedalus 1973 102(1): 225-238.* Discusses modernization and the tendency toward reactivating tradition in Tunisia, 1960's-70's. S

Western Sahara

1577. Carro Martínez, Antonio. LA DESCOLONIZACIÓN DEL SAHARA [The decolonization of the Sahara]. *Rev. de Política Int. [Spain] 1976 (144): 11-38.* Surveys political developments in Western Sahara from the colonial period, through various stages of governmental experimentation, to Spain's unilateral withdrawal, the Moroccan "Green March," and the Declaration of Madrid, December 1975.

1578. Cerón Ayuso, José Luis. ESPAÑA Y EL SAHARA OCCIDENTAL. ANTECEDENTES DE UNA DESCOLONIZACIÓN [Spain and Western Sahara: background to a decolonization]. *Rev. de Política Int. [Spain] 1977 (154): 9-52.* Outlines the steps toward the independence of the Western Sahara and discusses the acceptance of the Saharan right to self-determination in 1960, the referendum, the verdict of the United Nations and the International Tribunal of Justice in 1975, and Spain's refusal to accept responsibility for later developments.

1579. Chhabra, Hari Sharan. DEVELOPMENTS IN WESTERN SAHARA. *Africa Q. [India] 1980 19(3-4): 326-340.* Explores events since Mauritania withdrew from the Western Sahara and Moroccan forces immediately occupied the evacuated area. Focuses especially on the armed struggle by the Polisario Front, the Sahrawi liberation movement backed by Algeria and Libya, to take control from Morocco.

1580. Dougherty, James E. THE POLISARIO INSURGENCY: WAR AND MINUET IN NORTH-WEST AFRICA. *Conflict 1980 2(2): 93-120.* Discusses the struggle between Morocco and Algerian-backed guerrillas for control of the former Spanish Sahara, emphasizing the complex diplomatic background.

1581. Franck, Thomas M. THE STEALING OF THE SAHARA. *Am. J. of Int. Law 1976 70(4): 694-721.* The claim of Morocco to the Western Sahara on the basis of historical title was specious. The denial of self-determination to the Sahrawi people radically departed from the norms of decolonization established and consistently applied by the UN since 1960. The United States and France successfully resisted all efforts within the UN to order Morocco to stop the annexation. A US policy based on the application of force rather than principle has hurt us both in Vietnam and Angola and has helped us only in the Spanish Sahara. R. J. Jirran

1582. Greco, Andrea. SAHARA OCCIDENTALE: LA DIFFICILE RICERCA DI UNA IDENTITÀ NAZIONALE [Western Sahara: the difficult search for a national identity]. *Riv. di Studi Pol. Int. [Italy] 1977 44(1): 106-114.* A concise overview of the history of Western Sahara, from the time of the Almoravid conquest in the 11th century to the present international crisis. Gives special attention to the historical, juridical, ethnic, economic, and strategic claims of Morocco, Mauritania, and Algeria on the former Spanish Sahara. A. Sbacchi

1583. Lewis, William H. WESTERN SAHARA: COMPROMISE OR CONFLICT? *Current Hist. 1981 80(470): 410-413, 431.* Since the Western Sahara has few agreed boundaries, the last six years have been full of conflict, but now the principle participants in the Western Sahara dispute, Morocco, Mauritania, and Algeria, seem to be heading toward a peaceful resolution of their differences which may result in a choice for the inhabitants of the former Spanish Sahara between independence or unification with Morocco.

1584. Lippert, Anne. EMERGENCE OR SUBMERGENCE OF A POTENTIAL STATE: THE STRUGGLE IN WESTERN SAHARA. *Africa Today 1977 24(1): 41-60.* Describes the resistance of the Democratic Sahrawi Arab Republic (DSAR) to efforts by Morocco and Mauritania to absorb the Western Sahara. The resistance has resulted in atrocities, population displacement, and a ravaged land. Concludes that the struggle will continue despite the diverse support of NATO nations, Senegal, Gabon, and Egypt for Morocco and Mauritania. Based on published sources and author's experience in Sahrawi; map, 53 notes. G. O. Gagnon

1585. Marks, Thomas A. SPANISH SAHARA: BACKGROUND TO CONFLICT. *African Affairs [Great Britain] 1976 75(298): 3-13.* Traces Spain's involvement in northwestern Africa since 1476, with an emphasis on events in the Spanish Sahara in the 1970's. Attempts to indicate why Spain agreed to surrender control of Spanish Sahara and the possible future of the region. 8 notes. H. G. Soff

1586. Mercer, John. CONFRONTATION IN THE WESTERN SAHARA. *World Today [Great Britain] 1976 32(6): 230-239.* Traces Spain, Morocco, and Mauritania's claims in the Western Sahara in 1975-76, and Algeria's support of the Sahrawi's self-determination and independence.

1587. Mercer, John. THE CYCLE OF INVASION AND UNIFICATION IN THE WESTERN SAHARA. *African Affairs [Great Britain] 1976 75(301): 498-510.* Traces the history and political development of the Western Sahara, formerly Spanish Sahara, over the past 2,000 years. Due to the geography of the region, the people never unified and were often conquered, but conquerors were seldom able to maintain control for long. The nomadic Sahrawis led a liberation movement starting in 1973, and by 1976 the Polisario Front was the dominant political force. In February 1976 the new republic was declared as an Islamic state and is seeking African and worldwide recognition. 13 notes. H. G. Soff

1588. Miguez, Alberto. LE SAHARA OCCIDENTAL ET LA POLITIQUE MAGHRÉBINE DE L'ESPAGNE [Western Sahara and Spain's policy toward the Maghreb]. *Pol. Étrangère [France] 1978 43(2): 173-180.* Analyzes Spain's policy toward the Maghreb and the slow and difficult process of decolonization of Western Sahara, open to different interpretations and initiated by the Three-Power Agreement on Western Sahara, signed in November 1975 in Madrid, by which Spain was to transfer to Morocco and Mauritania the administration of Western Sahara.

1589. Orobator, Stanley. WESTERN SAHARA: WILL MOROCCO CRACK? *Contemporary Rev. [Great Britain] 1981 239(1389): 186-190.* Surveys the dispute over the Western Sahara since about 1960.

1590. Riedel, Eibe H. CONFRONTATION IN WESTERN SAHARA IN THE LIGHT OF THE ADVISORY OPINION OF THE INTERNATIONAL COURT OF JUSTICE OF 16 OCTOBER 1975.

A CRITICAL APPRAISAL. *German Y. of Int. Law [West Germany] 1976 19: 405-442.* The Western Sahara, formerly Spanish Sahara, was divided by Morocco and Mauritania in 1976, despite efforts of Polisario guerrillas backed by Algeria. The International Court of Justice, by handing down an ambiguous decision on the matter, failed to define precisely the limits of self-determination for small territories and thus set a valuable precedent.

1591. Smith, Anna H. JACQUES LEBAUDY, EMPEROR OF THE SAHARA. *Africana Notes and News [South Africa] 1976 22(3): 119-125.* Jacques Lebaudy was an eccentric French millionaire who was involved in South Africa, the Spanish Sahara, and the United States. He invaded Rio de Oro in 1903 and proclaimed himself Emperor. Although arrested, he managed to secure his freedom and went to the United States. His wife killed him in self-defense in 1919. H. G. Soff

1592. Triki, Mahmoud. LA CRISI DEL SAHARA OCCIDENTALE [The crisis of the Western Sahara]. *Affari Esteri [Italy] 1978 10(37): 118-134.* Describes the positions of Algeria, Mauritania, and Morocco in threatened hostilities in November 1977. Although war was avoided, the balance that remains is very fragile.

1593. Vellas, Pierre. LA DIPLOMATIE MAROCAINE DANS L'AFFAIRE DU SAHARA OCCIDENTAL [Moroccan diplomacy in the Western Sahara affair]. *Pol. Étrangère [France] 1978 43(4): 417-428.* Analyzes Morocco's very skillful diplomatic actions beginning in 1970 and ending with the Madrid agreement of 1975 by which Western Sahara became integrated in Moroccan and Mauritanian territories.

1594. VonSivers, Peter. NORTHWEST AFRICA AND THE WESTERN SAHARA. *Can. J. of African Studies [Canada] 1981 15(1): 124-127.* Reviews Attilio Gaudio's *Le Dossier du Sahara Occidental*(1978) and Elsa Assidon's *Sahara Occidental. Un Enjeu pour le Nord-ouest Africain* (1978), which discuss the war between Morocco and the Western Saharan Polisario Front. Gaudio asserts that Morocco will win the war in the Western Sahara because the people of this region have always been devout Moroccan patriots. Assidon maintains that the Western Sahara will vanquish Moroccan imperialism because the people of this region oppose the reactionary Moroccan monarchy and the world capitalist system that backs the Moroccan king. J. Powell

1595. Wehner, Günter. DER FALL WESTSAHARA: ZUM SELBSTBESTIMMUNGSRECHT EINES KLEINEN NOMADENVOLKES [The case of Western Sahara: the right of self-determination of a small nomad people]. *Frankfurter Hefte [West Germany] 1981 36(8): 33-42.* Western Sahara had been controlled by Spain only since 1936, though its ports were controlled since the late 15th century. Its importance grew with the discovery of phosphate deposits in 1963, which resulted in the interest of Morocco and the founding of the nationalist Polisario Front in 1973.

1596. Weinstein, Brian. THE WESTERN SAHARA. *Current Hist. 1980 78(455): 110-114, 136-137.* Discusses the clash between Morocco and Polisario guerrillas over the Western Sahara (formerly Spanish Sahara) during the 1970's, and the dilemma facing American foreign policy.

1597. White, C. G. THE GREEN MARCH. *Army Q. and Defence J. [Great Britain] 1976 106(3): 351-358.* Discusses the historical background of 1975 territorial disputes between Morocco, Mauritania and Algeria regarding possession of the Spanish Sahara, 1830-1975, emphasizing recent diplomacy and the role of the UN.

1598. Zartman, I. William. CONFLICT IN THE SAHARA: OPTIONS FOR AN OUTSIDE POWER. *SAIS Rev. 1981-82 (3): 167-184.* Discusses US options in the Western Sahara (Spanish Sahara) from Spain's departure in 1976 to 1982, commenting on various territorial claims in the area.

8. WEST AFRICA

General

1599. Aghaji, J. C. ECOWAS: IS IT A COUNTERVAILING POWER FOR ECONOMIC INDEPENDENCE? *J. of Asian and African Studies [Netherlands] 1979 14(1-2): 109-120.* Examines the formation of the Economic Community of West African States (ECOWAS) in 1975. Paper presented at a 1978 University of Nigeria, Nsukka workshop on dependence. Secondary sources; table, 12 notes, biblio. R. T. Brown

1600. Aguolu, Christian C. BIBLIOGRAPHIC PROBLEMS IN GHANA, NIGERIA AND SIERRA LEONE. *Internat. Lib. R. 1973 5(2): 199-208.* Discusses the development of national research libraries and their current level of sophistication in Ghana, Sierra Leone, and Nigeria. S

1601. Alibert, Jacques. LA BANQUE INTERNATIONALE POUR L'AFRIQUE OCCIDENTALE [The International Bank for Western Africa]. *Rev. Française d'Études Pol. Africaines [France] 1973 (92): 54-64.* Traces the long evolution leading to the formation of the International Bank for Western Africa (BIAO), officially founded in 1965, but provided for as early as 1853, and previously developed as the Bank of Western Africa in 13 countries.

1602. Almeida-Topor, Hélène d'. RECHERCHES SUR L'ÉVOLUTION DU TRAVAIL SALARIÉ EN AOF PENDANT LA CRISE ÉCONOMIQUE 1930-1936 [The development of salaried employment in French West Africa during the Great Depression, 1930-36]. *Cahiers d'Études Africaines [France] 1976 16(1-2): 103-117.* Before the Great Depression Africans in French West Africa were reluctant to take salaried jobs there, preferring to work their own land or to take higher paying jobs in neighboring British territories. In the 1930's the lack of opportunity and declining prices for agricultural commodities encouraged increasing numbers to rely on wage employment, leading to the creation of a proletariat. Based on archival material in Paris and secondary literature; 3 tables, 46 notes. B. S. Fetter

1603. Amegbleame, Simon Agbeko. LA FICTION NARRATIVE DANS LA PRODUCTION LITTÉRAIRE EWE: LA NOUVELLE ET LE ROMAN [Narrative fiction in Ewe literature]. *Africa [Great Britain] 1980 50(1): 25-36.* Ewe literature had its origins in classical English and French literature. Fiction now amounts to about a quarter of all Ewe literary production. Stories, dating from 1914, often took the form of narrative biography, having a mechanical construction in which the hero finally triumphs after numerous adventures where he encounters great difficulties and many enemies. These stories have a strong moral and folk legend background. In 1970 Ewe novels began to appear, modelled on Western detective stories. Their marketing has been made possible by the encouragement of the Bureau of Languages at Accra. 3 notes, biblio. R. L. Collison

1604. Asante, S. K. B. THE ITALO-ETHIOPIAN CONFLICT: A CASE STUDY IN BRITISH WEST AFRICAN RESPONSE TO CRISIS DIPLOMACY IN THE 1930'S. *J. of African Hist. [Great Britain] 1974 15(2): 291-302.* British failure to support Ethiopia during the 1935-36 crisis led race-conscious West African nationalists to believe there was a white plot against the black race. Franco-British refusal to supply Ethiopia with arms, the Hoare-Laval peace pact, and British recognition of Italy's conquests solidified their beliefs. As a result African nationalists rejected the idea of trusteeship and shifted to a more anti-white pan-Africanism. Primary and secondary sources; 40 notes. E. Hopkins

1605. Asiwaju, A. I. and Crowder, Michael. INTRODUCTION [PROTEST AGAINST COLONIAL RULE IN WEST AFRICA]. *Tarikh [Nigeria] 1977 5(3):1-5.* Reviews works on the various kinds of rebellions occurring in West Africa, 1900-47.

1606. Asiwaju, A. I. MIGRATIONS AS AN EXPRESSION OF REVOLT: THE EXAMPLE OF FRENCH WEST AFRICA UP TO 1945. *Tarikh [Nigeria] 1977 5(3): 31-43.* Anticolonialism and opposition to compulsory labor and military conscription led to migration from French West Africa to British held areas, 1914-45.

1607. Asiwaju, A. I. MIGRATIONS AS REVOLT: THE EXAMPLE OF THE IVORY COAST AND THE UPPER VOLTA BEFORE 1945. *J. of African Hist. [Great Britain] 1976 17(4): 577-594.* African resistance to colonial rule was often manifested not in armed conflict, but in protest migrations. This is an examination of peaceful protest migration which was less costly to Africans, but had the same effect on colonial authorities. 92 notes. H. G. Soff

1608. Asiwaju, Anthony I. CONTROL THROUGH COERCION, A STUDY OF THE INDIGENAT REGIME IN FRENCH WEST AFRICAN ADMINISTRATION, 1887-1946. *Bull. de l'Inst. Fondamental d'Afrique Noire. Série B [Senegal] 1979 41(1): 35-71.* The Indigenat Code was a group of provisions of the French Criminal Code introduced into French West Africa in 1887. By this the French colonial administrators had the power to impose summary penalties ranging from fines and imprisonment to deportation for infractions not regularly judged by the native courts. It was introduced both for practical necessity and paternalism and soon became the dominant method of colonial control. Abuses occurred in the overdependence on police powers instead of the judicial process, excessive imprisonment and fines, and irregularities arising from the misappropriation of the disciplinary powers by unauthorized persons. The system was abolished in 1946. Based on records in the Archives of Senegal and the Ivory Coast and the Archives Nationales of France; 124 notes. French summary. H. L. Calkin

1609. Barbag, Anna. SIERRA LEONE AND LIBERIA EXPERIMENT: A HISTORICAL AND LINGUISTIC OVERVIEW. *Africana Bull. [Poland] 1977 (26): 103-112.* Surveys the origins of Sierra Leone and Liberia founded as places of settlement for former slaves and the linguistic developments in each, 1787-1961.

1610. Bernard-Duquenet, Nicole. LE FRONT POPULAIRE ET LE PROBLÈME DES PRESTATIONS EN AOF [The Popular Front and the problem of compulsory labor in French West Africa]. *Cahiers d'Études Africaines [France] 1976 16(1-2): 159-172.* Despite the good will of Leon Blum's Popular Front government and that of Colonial Minister Marius Moutet, the reformist governor-general of French West Africa, Marcel de Coppet, was unable to do much to change prevailing policies. In the matter of forced labor, for example, he was able to diminish government demands and private abuses, but upon Coppet's replacement in 1938 the old abuses returned, and forced labor became even worse until 1946. Based on archival material in Paris and Dakar; 51 notes. B. S. Fetter

1611. Berthelemy, Jean-Claude. L'ECONOMIE DE L'AFRIQUE OCCIDENTALE FRANÇAISE ET DU TOGO: 1946-1960 [The economy of French West Africa and Togo, 1946-60]. *Rev. Française d'Hist. d'Outre-Mer [France] 1980 67(3-4): 301-337.* Togo and the nations of French West Africa achieved relatively good postwar economic performances. Studies the factors that influenced economic activity and the magnitude of the effects of each on global economic results. Based on official statistics; 14 tables, biblio. D. G. Law

1612. Bouche, Denise. LA PARTICIPATION DES MISSIONS AU DÉVELOPPEMENT DE L'ENSEIGNEMENT DANS LES COLONIES FRANÇAISES D'AFRIQUE OCCIDENTALE DE 1817 À 1940 [Mission participation in the development of education in French West African colonies, 1817-1940]. *Études d'Hist. Africaine [Zaire] 1976 8: 173-197.* Christian missions have taken a lesser role in French West Africa in the development of education than elsewhere in Africa. The first public school, under lay direction, opened in Senegal in 1817. Schools directed by Catholics came a few years later. Some were private and some public in nature. A general move to place all schools under lay supervision came in the early 20th century. As a result the number and size of mission schools never became very large by 1940, compared with public schools. 3 maps, 3 tables, 89 notes. H. L. Calkin

1613. Bouche, Denise. L'ÉCOLE RURALE EN AFRIQUE OCCIDENTALE FRANÇAISE DE 1903 À 1956 [Rural schools in French West Africa, 1903-56]. *Hist. Reflections [Canada] 1980 7(2-3): 207-219.* Describes the major phases in the evolution of educational policy in French West Africa. Colonial French educators tried to give natives relevant training in agricultural techniques. These pupils, however, sought access to administrative employment, which would allow them to escape their inferior socioeconomic background. This difference in perspective led to the eventual failure of the rural school system. Based on primary government publications and secondary sources; 44 notes. M. Schumacher

1614. Bourgeot, Andre. NOMADIC PASTORAL SOCIETY AND THE MARKET: THE PENETRATION OF THE SAHEL BY COMMERCIAL RELATIONS. *J. of Asian and African Studies [Netherlands] 1981 16(1-2): 116-127.* The great Sahelian drought encouraged the creation of a "livestock bourgeoisie" who came to understand, for the first time, that there were conditions under which the accumulation of livestock for its own sake, rather than for the money and goods it could bring, was dangerous. Based on secondary sources; biblio. R. T. Brown

1615. Brasseur, Gérard. POUR UN CORPUS DE L'HABITAT RURAL EN AFRIQUE OCCIDENTALE. [For a corpus on the rural habitat of West Africa]. *Bull. de l'Inst. Fondamental d'Afrique Noire [Senegal Republic] 1974 36(4): 833-852.* A bibliographical essay on the need to develop a corpus relating to the West African rural habitat, discussing 12 relevant publications issued between 1968 and 1974. 12 notes. H. L. Calkin

1616. Brown, David. BORDERLINE POLITICS IN GHANA: THE NATIONAL LIBERATION MOVEMENT OF WESTERN TOGOLAND. *J. of Modern African Studies [Great Britain] 1980 18(4): 575-609.* From its emergence in 1972, the National Liberation Movement of Western Togoland (Tolimo) appealed to the Ewe of southeast Ghana to seek an ethnic remedy for their ills: rule by an alien regime in Accra, economic difficulties, and an artificial boundary separating them from their fellow Ewe in Togo. Tolimo, however, failed to achieve substantial success in Ghana, because its leaders were divided and without political influence, while the movement itself was weakened by conflicting divergent irredentist, territorial nationalist, and ethnic nationalist tendencies. The Republic of Togo has sporadically supported Ewe nationalism to achieve irredentist aims againt Ghana, some Ewe have sought restoration of the old boundaries of German Togoland before 1914, which excludes Ewe in the old British Gold Coast colony, and Pan-Ewe nationalism has promoted ethnic unity and the destruction of current boundaries. The conflict between these nationalist tendencies seriously impaired the effectiveness of Tolimo in the 1970's. Based on interviews, local political movement documents, newspapers, and secondary sources; map, table, 82 notes. L. W. Truschel

1617. Charnay, Jean-Paul. EXPANSION DE L'ISLAM EN AFRIQUE OCCIDENTALE [The expansion of Islam in West Africa]. *Arabica [Netherlands] 1980 27(2): 140-153.* Islam is advancing in Sub-Saharan Africa. The former direction of advance from north to south and east to west has been reversed. It is now spreading from the Atlantic ports into the interior forests. Conversion is motivated by migration, social development, avoidance of persecution, and desire for education. The introduction of Islam has brought about fundamental changes in black civilizations. The subsequent passage from a syncretic to a purer form of Islam is also motivated by a number of factors. W. J. Wilson

1618. Charnay, Jean-Paul. ISLAM ET STABILITÉ EN AFRIQUE OCCIDENTALE [Islam and stability in West Africa]. *Défense Natl. [France] 1980 36(10): 107-118.* Islamic influence has grown in West African countries as they have emerged from Western European domination, furthered by the spread of Islamic brotherhoods like the Qaddiriyya and Tijaniyya.

1619. Chazam, Naomi H. THE AFRICANIZATION OF POLITICAL CHANGE: SOME ASPECTS OF THE DYNAMICS OF POLITICAL CULTURES IN GHANA AND NIGERIA. *African Studies Rev. 1978 21(2): 15-38.* A theoretical construct which attempts to Africanize the study of politics by isolating traditional political cultural patterns in the two African states. From these an interpretation of 20th-century history is made. Secondary sources; 38 notes, biblio. R. T. Brown

1620. Cole, Babalola. COCOA POLITICS: INSIGHTS FROM THE "POOL" CRISIS. *Int. Studies Notes 1981 8(2): 20-24.* Analyzes the African resentment that the *West African Pilot*expressed during the period of the cocoa crisis of 1937, when European commercial houses entered into an agreement, the "pool," to stabilize cocoa prices at the expense of farmers of the Gold Coast and Nigeria. Analyzes the views of the American consulate in Lagos on the prospects of American corporations' entering the cocoa market.

1621. Collins, John Davidson. THE CLANDESTINE MOVEMENT OF GROUNDNUTS ACROSS THE NIGER-NIGERIA BOUNDARY. *Can. J. of African Studies [Canada] 1976 10(2): 259-278.* Examines the artificial (for the purposes of inter-tribal trade and economic relations) boundary between Niger and Nigeria and the smuggling of peanuts across this border, 1935-76.

1622. Constantin, François and Coulin, Christian. DES CASERNES AUX CHANCELLERIES: LA VARIABLE MILITAIRE DANS LA POLITIQUE EXTÉRIEURE DE TROIS ÉTATS AFRICAINS: HAUTE-VOLTA, TOGO ET MALI [From barracks to chancelleries: the military variable in the foreign policy of three West African states: Upper Volta, Togo and Mali]. *Can. J. of African Studies [Canada] 1975 9(1): 17-49.* Discusses the link between military power and the international system in Upper Volta, Togo, and Mali. Military takeovers are seen as part of modernization and rationalization by the state. The military variable plays only a secondary role in new diplomatic trends which appear on the African continent. Military governments are generally unable to make African states strong enough to allow them to end their colonial dependency. Based on speeches, government documents, and secondary sources; 4 tables, 58 notes. J

1623. Crowder, Michael. THE BORGU REVOLTS OF 1915-17. *Tarikh [Nigeria] 1977 5(3): 18-30.* Borgu, divided between France and Great Britain, erupted in revolt, 1915-17, for various reasons: heavy-handed administration and disregard of native customs in French-held Dahomey, and District Officer J. C. O. Clarke's replacement of Chief Kitoro Gani with an official named Turaki, who was of slave origin in British Nigeria.

1624. Dare, L. O. THE PATTERNS OF MILITARY ENTRENCHMENT IN GHANA AND NIGERIA. *Africa Q. [India] 1977 16(3): 28-41.* Analyzes reasons why military governments in Ghana and Nigeria having seized power, subsequently have difficulty in relinquishing it.

1625. Davidson, Basil. GUINEA-BISSAU AND THE CAPE VERDE ISLANDS: THE TRANSITION FROM WAR TO INDEPENDENCE. *Africa Today 1974 21(4): 5-20.* Provides personal reflections on the transition from Portuguese to PAIGC rule in Guinea-Bissau and the Cape Verde Islands. Concludes that Guinea-Bissau is in the unique position of having created a government unrelated to colonial institutions and that by expanding its rural base it will be able to solve the problems of a primary export economy and a shortage of technical workers. Based on personal observations. G. O. Gagnon

1626. Derrick, Jonathan. THE GREAT WEST AFRICAN DROUGHT, 1972-74. *African Affairs [Great Britain] 1977 76(305): 537-586.* The Sahel drought of the 1970's was the worst national disaster in 60 years. The author explains the causes as well as the normal economy of the region. Agriculture was devastated as were cattle herds. Relief programs were not properly programmed and implemented. 121 notes. H. G. Soff

1627. Dewitte, Philippe. LA CGT ET LES SYNDICATS D'AFRIQUE OCCIDENTALE FRANÇAISE (1945-1957) [The CGT and the trade unions of French West Africa (1945-57)]. *Mouvement Social [France] 1981 (117): 3-32.* After World War II trade unions of French West Africa fought for "a real French Union." The claim for autonomy was quickly adopted by the General Confederation of Labor (CGT) unions, though they felt themselves prisoners of the platform developed in the mother country. In front of this movement, the French

CGT leaders and their supporters in Africa were divided between the fear of the FFTU, the sincere will to act in favor of African social struggles, but also their tendency of putting African problems on the same footing as in the mother country. So, the organizational reform of coordinating committees was quickly found insufficient, and the first African unions gave themselves autonomy in 1955. Then, freed from French tutelage, the African unions found their unity, but were dependent on the bourgeoisies which were gaining access to power. J

1628. Dodu, Silas R. A. MEETING THE HEALTH NEEDS OF OUR DEVELOPING COUNTRIES. *Universitas [Ghana] 1975 5(1): 3-16.* Traces the early history of medicine in West Africa and outlines 20th-century West African medical services. Identifies poverty, ignorance, and preventable illness as the symptoms of underdevelopment; their cures are economics, education, and health, the inseparable factors of development. Present trends in the West African medical services indicate continuing inadequacies, in doctor-population ratios, in management and organization, in finance, and in health education. From a lecture to the Commonwealth Foundation, published as its Occasional Paper No. 25, 1974; biblio. J. J. N. McGurk

1629. Doi, A. Rahman I. MUSLIM MINORITIES IN WEST AFRICA: PAST PROBLEMS, PRESENT PREDICAMENTS, AND FUTURE HOPE. *Search: J. for Arab and Islamic Studies 1980 1(3-4): 256-279.* West Africa's desire for the benefits of modern civilization—including medicine, education, and weaponry—and Muslim disunity permitted Christian missionaries success among both pagans and Muslims in the colonial era. But the oil power of the Arab states has given Islam greater influence, and Africa, far from being a Christian continent by the year 2000, will instead be solidly Muslim.

1630. Domergue, Danielle. L'ÉCHEC D'UNE CONQUÊTE: LE PAYS LOBI (1900-1926) [The defeat of a conquest: the Lobi country, 1900-26]. *Bull. de l'Inst. Fondamental d'Afrique Noire [Senegal] 1977 39(3): 532-553.* The Lobi country is at the junction of the Ivory Coast, Upper Volta, and Ghana. By a convention of 1898 the area went to France. The Lobi have been hostile to all foreign meddling whether European or African. In 1912 Captain H. Labouret arrived to develop a political plan which included a methodical program of occupation, a rigorous order in occupation operations, and a permanent occupation. There was discord between military and civil forces that were attempting unsuccessfully to conquer the area. The Lobi consistently opposed colonization. A conquest in which the expected result was the submission of a people was in fact a defeat for the French. Based in part on records in the Archives Nationales of the Ivory Coast; map, 93 notes. H. L. Calkin

1631. Echenberg, Myron J. LES MIGRATIONS MILITAIRES EN AFRIQUE OCCIDENTALE FRANÇAISE, 1900-1945 [Military migration in French West Africa, 1900-45]. *Can. J. of African Studies [Canada] 1980 14(3): 429-450.* Describes the enormous scale of French military recruitment in West Africa and the widespread migration it produced. Describes three types of "military migration": migration as resistance to military service; soldiers' migration from villages to larger West African centers and overseas; and return migration of demobilized soldiers. While military migration is part of the general process of integration of West Africa into the world capitalist system, the changing rhythm of this migration helps pinpoint moments of crisis in this process and illuminates the process of class formation. J/S

1632. Echenberg, Myron J. PAYING THE BLOOD TAX: MILITARY CONSCRIPTION IN FRENCH WEST AFRICA, 1914-1929. *Can. J. of African Studies [Canada] 1975 9(2): 171-192.* During the first half of the 20th century thousands of young Africans were drafted for three years service overseas. They were not treated like French citizens. France maintained conscription to support a large colonial army. The system was inefficient in some respects. It was biased against the poor. Although there were draft dodgers there were also many volunteers. The indirect social and economic cost of peacetime conscription was a contributing factor to the stagnation of French West Africa from 1919 forward. Based on documents from the Archives de l'Afrique Occidentale Française and secondary sources; 5 tables, 82 notes, appendix. E. R. Campbell

1633. Ekechi, Felix K. AFRICAN POLYGAMY AND WESTERN CHRISTIAN ETHNOCENTRISM. *J. of African Studies 1976 3(3): 329-350.* Examines the attitude of church and colonial government officials toward polygamy and their attempts to replace the African with the Western marriage system. Efforts of 19th- and 20th-century Christian missionaries to impose monogamy was an attempt to destroy the West African social and economic structure and to Europeanize the Africans. Though less so today, polygamy has met the economic needs of the community while conferring social status on its practitioners and continues as a revered African social institution. E. P. Stickney/S

1634. Fall, Ibrahima. THE SAHEL: AFTER THE DROUGHT. *Africa Report 1975 20(3): 37-40.* The drought in the Sahel is over, but the economies of many affected countries are damaged beyond repair and require new policies for economic rehabilitation. S

1635. Frantz, Charles. FULBE CONTINUITY AND CHANGE UNDER FIVE FLAGS ATOP WEST AFRICA: TERRITORIALITY, ETHNICITY, STRATIFICATION AND NATIONAL INTEGRATION. *J. of Asian and African Studies [Netherlands] 1981 16(1-2): 89-115.* One segment of the pastoral Fulbe known as the Mbororoen have moved into the well-watered mountain grasslands of the border region of Nigeria and Cameroon. Local environmental conditions have caused the sedentarization of this pastoral community and its integration into the town system. Based on fieldwork; 8 notes, biblio. R. T. Brown

1636. Gialdino, Carlo Conti. IL REGIME INTERNAZIONALE DEL BACINO DEL NIGER [The international management of the Niger basin]. *Africa [Italy] 1975 30(1): 71-103.* Discusses the developmental stages in the international management of the Niger basin from the Treaty of Berlin (1885), which discussed the possibilities for navigational utilization, to the three conferences of Niamey (1963-1968), which envisioned organized cooperation among the basin states for economic development based on the principle of "equitable utilization" of the waters. Secondary sources; 95 notes. L. R. Atkins

1637. Gialdino, Carlo Curti and Palmieri, Michele Giovanni. VALORIZZAZIONE INTERNAZIONALE DEL BACINO DEL SENEGAL [International utilization of the basin of the Senegal]. *Comunità Int. [Italy] 1974 29(1/2): 63-80.* Describes the international cooperation in water use among the riparian states of the Senegal River (Guinea, Mali, Mauritania, Senegal).

1638. Hargreaves, J. D. FROM STRANGERS TO MINORITIES IN WEST AFRICA. *Tr. of the Royal Hist. Soc. 1981 31: 95-113.* In West Africa colonial and postcolonial boundaries "turned into aliens communities of people who had previously enjoyed a relatively secure status as strangers, under well-established systems of international customary law." Kinship societies defined the status of strangers in a variety of ways—slavery, enclavement of traders (a position shared by Europeans at first)—and recognised whole stranger communities of commercial intermediaries with a kind of extraterritorial status, as in 19th-century Sierra Leone. Extension of colonial rule resulted in a vacillating policy toward stranger enclaves, until British policy in the 1950's tended to the creation of nation states, where strangers were converted into minorities. 51 notes. D. H. Murdoch

1639. Henriksen, Thomas. PORTUGAL IN AFRICA: A NONECONOMIC INTERPRETATION. *African Studies R. 1973 16(3): 405-416.* Examines patriotism and political stability as factors aside from economic gains in maintaining colonial ties in West Africa. S

1640. Hodder, B. W. A NOTE ON NOT PERPETUATING THE STATUS QUO. *African Affairs [Great Britain] 1974 73(291): 159-161.* Discusses the long-term problem of drought in West Africa. Marginal villages and nomadic enclaves are disappearing as people move to the cities or to other countries along the coast where there is greater economic opportunity. These migrations, coupled with drought, have created a difficult situation. Since there is not enough money to alleviate the problem, it is suggested that current conditions be viewed as an opportunity to encourage rational permanent human settlement, and not encourage populations to exist in the marginal lands of the Sahel. H. G. Soff

1641. Holsoe, Svend E. and Lauer, Joseph. WHO ARE THE KRAN/GUERE AND THE GIO/YACOUBA? ETHNIC IDENTIFICATIONS ALONG THE LIBERIA-IVORY COAST BORDER. *African Studies Rev. 1976 19(1): 139-149.* Identifies the local peoples in eastern Liberia and the western Ivory Coast who have been given names by scholars working in a number of disciplines, 1900-75.

1642. Horton, Robin. ON THE RATIONALITY OF CONVERSION. *Africa [Great Britain] 1975 45(3): 219-235, (4): 373-399.* Part I. Analyzes the indigenous religions of West Africa, as evidence of the expansion of Islam and Christianity in Africa. Part II. Analyzes the history of monotheistic religions, particularly Islam, in their confrontation with local animist cults in West Africa.

1643. Hosmer, Rachel. THE PROPHET HARRIS. *Hist. Mag. of the Protestant Episcopal Church 1979 48(3): 331-356.* Presents the ministry of the native-born African Christian prophet William Waddy Harris (ca. 1850-1929) from the point of view of five groups of people who had dealings with him: British Methodists, French officials and missionaries of the Ivory Coast, American Methodists in Liberia, the Episcopal Mission in Cape Palmas, and the Africans. Most believe Harris was a good man working for good ends, and value his work because of the number, zeal, and perseverance of his converts. His major flaw was his practice of polygyny. Following a description of Harris's work, discusses polygyny as the Christian faith related to it, suggesting that since it was so deeply rooted in African culture, the issue should not have been so hotly pursued by missionaries. Had they not, the Prophet Harris would not be the ambiguous figure he is. Based on administrative records of the Ivory Coast, writings of missionaries, collection of the Liberia Papers in the Archives of the Episcopal Church (Austin, Texas), and two book-length accounts by Africans who knew Harris; 100 notes.
H. M. Parker, Jr.

1644. Igué, Ogunsola John. EVOLUTION DU COMMERCE CLANDESTIN ENTRE LE DAHOMEY ET LE NIGERIA DEPUIS LA GUERRE DU "BIAFRA" [The evolution of clandestine trade between Dahomey and Nigeria since the Biafran war]. *Can. J. of African Studies [Canada] 1976 10(2): 235-257.* Discusses smuggling between Dahomey and Nigeria 1966-74 as it was affected by the war in Biafra; examines the cause of such smuggling, methods used, and the nature of the goods smuggled.

1645. Igue, Ogunsola John. UN ASPECT DES ÉCHANGES ENTRE LE DAHOMEY ET LE NIGERIA: LE COMMERCE DU CACAO [An aspect of exchange between Dahomey and Nigeria: the cacao trade]. *Bull. de l'Inst. Fondamental d'Afrique Noire Série B [Senegal] 1976 38(3): 636-669.* The smuggling of agricultural products across frontiers is a current phenomenon in West Africa, especially between English-speaking and French-speaking countries. The movement of cacao between Dahomey and Nigeria is a good example. The author analyzes the extent of the trade from 1968 to 1974, with details on its origins and organization, and discusses perspectives for the cacao plantations. 4 maps, 8 tables, 17 notes.
H. L. Calkin

1646. Jouve, E. CONSTITUTIONNALISME ET RÉFORME AGRO-FONCIÈRE DANS LES PAYS DU CONSEIL DE L'ENTENTE EN AFRIQUE DE L'OUEST [Constitutionalism and land reform in the Entente Council countries in West Africa]. *African Perspectives [Netherlands] 1979 (1): 21-26.* Studies agrarian reforms in West African countries. Countries governed by a basic agrarian reform law and on the path to a just and efficient reform are the Marxist-Leninist Republic of Benin and Togo. Other members of the Council, Ivory Coast, Niger, and Upper Volta, which adhere to their constitutions and follow a capitalist development, have not solved the agrarian problem. Based on African government documents; 23 notes.
G. P. Cleyet

1647. Kaba, Lansiné. THE POLITICS OF QURANIC EDUCATION AMONG MUSLIM TRADERS IN THE WESTERN SUDAN: THE SUBBANU EXPERIENCE. *Can. J. of African Studies [Canada] 1976 10(3): 409-422.* Examines the decline of Koranic schools and the increase in the number of Western-type educational facilities with the advent of African nationalism and independence movements in Upper Ghana, Mali, and the Ivory Coast using the specific case of the Subbanu (a Wahhabite sect) as an example, 1935-75.

1648. Kaniki, Martin. ECONOMICAL TECHNOLOGY AGAINST TECHNICAL EFFICIENCY IN THE OIL PALM INDUSTRY OF WEST AFRICA. *Development and Change [Netherlands] 1980 11(2): 273-284.* The introduction of high technology extractive mills in the West African oil palm industry failed because less efficient traditional methods and hand presses were actually more economical for the producer.

1649. Killingray, David. THE EMPIRE RESOURCES DEVELOPMENT COMMITTEE AND WEST AFRICA 1916-20. *J. of Imperial and Commonwealth Hist. [Great Britain] 1982 10(2): 194-210.* The idea of government intervention in the British economy having been established during World War I, intervention continued in the relationships within the Empire in the postwar years. Traces the work of the Empire Resources Development Committee in West Africa and the role of Lord Milner as exports came to be subject to imperial direction and control. These activities helped to foster later nationalist politics. Based on Colonial Office papers at the Public Record Office, London, and the Milner Papers at the Bodleian Library, Oxford; 50 notes.
M. C. Rosenfield

1650. Klein, Martin A. THE DECOLONIZATION OF WEST AFRICAN HISTORY. *J. of Interdisciplinary Hist. 1975 6(1): 111-125.* Review of recent writing on the history of West Africa. Until recently, most West African history has been "nation-building history" even though it was in large part written by expatriates. The decolonization of African history has noticeably occurred with the Africanization of history departments in Africa. Although limitations do exist with respect to sources, there is a growing awareness that history must be more than lists of names and dates and become a search for "an understanding of how the present became." 20 notes. R. Howell

1651. Kraus, Jon. FROM MILITARY TO CIVILIAN REGIMES IN GHANA AND NIGERIA. *Current Hist. 1979 76(445): 122-126, 134-136, 138.* In 1978 the military governments of Ghana and Nigeria planned to return to civilian rule.

1652. Kraus, Jon. THE RETURN OF CIVILIAN RULE IN NIGERIA AND GHANA. *Current Hist. 1980 78(455): 115-118, 128-129, 137-138, 144.* Discusses political and economic developments leading to the transition from military to civilian government in 1979 in Nigeria and Ghana and their continuing problems.

1653. Kuznetsova, M. EKONOMICHESKAIA INTEGRATSIIA V ZAPADNOI AFRIKE [Economic integration in West Africa]. *Aziia i Afrika Segodnia [USSR] 1982 (5): 10-12.* Traces the history, achievements, and problems of subregional economic integration in West Africa, focusing on the experiences of the Economic Community of West African States and the West African Economic Community.

1654. Lebedeva, E. ZAPADNAIA AFRIKA: REBOCHII KLASS I PROFSOIUZY [West Africa: the working class and labor unions]. *Mirovaia Ekonomika i Mezhdunarodnye Otnosheniia [USSR] 1974 (1): 67-77.* Analyzes the rapid rise in the number and membership of West African labor unions in the 1960's, and examines their involvement in politics especially in raising class consciousness and illegal strike activity.

1655. Mariñas Otero, Luis. EL CONSEJO DE LA ENTENTE [The Council of the Entente]. *Rev. de Política Int. [Spain] 1975 (142): 175-185.* Discusses the background and development of this international West African organization which evolved from the Union Française and includes the Ivory Coast, Benin, Niger, Togo, and Upper Volta.

1656. Mason, Mary. BIBLIOGRAPHIC SOURCES IN ENGLISH-SPEAKING WEST AFRICA. *Can. J. of African Studies [Canada] 1974 8(2): 417-419.* Discusses difficulties in locating bibliographies in English pertaining to West Africa, especially periodicals, pamphlets, and theses. Discusses a few bibliographies currently available which cover 1860-1974, but most of which have been compiled since 1960.

1657. McNulty, Michael L. and Horton, Frank E. WEST AFRICAN URBANIZATION: PATTERNS OF CONVERGENCE OR DIVERGENCE? *Pan-African J. [Kenya] 1976 9(2): 169-180.* Refutes J. F. Berry's *The Human Consequences of Urbanization,* which states that the processes of urbanization in developing nations differ from those in the West. Suggests that the process of urbanization in West Africa is of global consequence, and that a theory of convergence rather than divergence is more relevant to West African urbanization. Secondary sources; 2 tables, 20 notes. M. Feingold

1658. Meillassoux, Claude. THE SOCIAL ORGANISATION OF THE PEASANTRY: THE ECONOMIC BASIS OF KINSHIP. *J. of Peasant Studies [Great Britain] 1973 1(1): 81-90.* Discusses "traditional" peasant organization in West Africa. The social organization of peasantries is studied as productive units and in terms of relations among these units. Deals more briefly with the transformation of the social organization of agricultural production under the impact of market development and capitalism. A basic contention is that the social organization of the peasantry is built around the relations of production as they grow from the economic constraints of agricultural activities and around the need for reproduction of the productive unit. J

1659. Michel, Marc. UN PROGRAMME RÉFORMISTE EN 1919: MAURICE DELAFOSSE ET LA "POLITIQUE INDIGÈNE" EN AOF [A reform program in 1919: Maurice Delafosse and "native policy" in French West Africa]. *Cahiers d'Études Africaines [France] 1975 15(2): 313-327.* Maurice Delafosse (1870-1926), French administrator in West Africa and professor at the École Coloniale, addressed an Anglo-French conference of merchants and administrators in 1919. In his remarks, reprinted here, Delafosse suggested a division of colonial affairs between those which could be devolved to African elites and those which should be left in the hands of colonial governments. Furthermore, he identified several institutions of the mass of uneducated Africans which he felt should be more extensively used by the colonial administration. Based on materials in the Archives National, Section Outre-Mer, Paris and printed materials; 21 notes. B. S. Fetter

1660. Nordman, Curtis R. THE DECISION TO ADMIT UNOFFICIALS TO THE EXECUTIVE COUNCILS OF BRITISH WEST AFRICA. *J. of Imperial and Commonwealth Hist. [Great Britain] 1976 4(2): 194-205.* The decision to admit African representation in the Executive Councils of British West Africa came from neither nationalist pressures nor weakness in Britain's colonial position, but rather from the insistence of Sir Alan Burns, Governor of the Gold Coast, 1941-42. Based on recently declassified documents.

1661. Nwankwo, Robert L. UTOPIA AND REALITY IN THE AFRICAN MASS MEDIA: A CASE STUDY. *Gazette [Netherlands] 1973 19(3): 171-182.* Examines the *West African Pilot,* a postwar English language nationalist paper read throughout West Africa, for attitudes about traditionalism and modernity and the relationship between mass media and politics. The paper's approach was based on emotion rather than on critical thinking.

1662. Nworah, Kenneth D. THE INTEGRATIVE STRAND IN BRITISH WEST AFRICA, 1868-1940. *Genève-Afrique [Switzerland] 1974 13(1): 5-22.* The contemporary desire for West African integration is rooted in the tradition of educated West African idealism of over a century ago. The author surveys the ideas of those who have upheld this tradition, 1868-1940.

1663. Ojo, Olatunde J. B. NIGERIA AND THE FORMATION OF ECOWAS. *Int. Organization 1980 34(4): 571-604.* In May 1975 15 West African countries (later joined by Cape Verde) signed in Lagos a treaty creating the Economic Community of West African States (ECOWAS). Nigeria played the key role in the intensive three-year diplomatic activities culminating in ECOWAS. Explores the factors that determined Nigeria's commitment to ECOWAS and the strategy and tactics that brought ECOWAS into being. J/S

1664. Okonkwo, Rina Lee. THE GARVEY MOVEMENT IN BRITISH WEST AFRICA. *J. of African Hist. [Great Britain] 1980 21(1): 105-117.* A group of American Garveyites put forward proposals for a branch of the Universal Negro Improvement Association (UNIA), in Freetown in 1920. The most attractive of Garvey's proposals was the Black Star Line Corporation, a shipping line for carrying goods between the West Indies, the United States, and West Africa. Marcus Garvey also advocated freeing Africa from colonial rule and establishing a great African republic. George Osborne Marke (1867-1929) of Sierra Leone was appointed Supreme Deputy Potentate of the UNIA, established the *Liberian Patriot,* and was active internationally in the UNIA's behalf. The UNIA was also active in Senegal, the Gold Coast, and Nigeria, but the total achievement was small. Based on West African newspaper files; 78 notes. R. L. Collison

1665. Oloruntimehin, B. Olatunji. THE ECONOMY OF FRENCH WEST AFRICA BETWEEN THE TWO WORLD WARS. *J. of African Studies 1977 4(1): 51-76.* An examination of officially sanctioned economic practices by European business firms in French West Africa, between the two world wars, a period considered by the author as the "golden age" of colonial economic exploitation. The French government provided a nearly closed market situation for the operation of favored French commercial, agricultural, banking, and shipping firms in West Africa. In addition, French colonial labor and tax practices supplemented the general neomercantilist policy, to the detriment of the West Africans. Based on published reports, statistics, and secondary sources; 69 notes. L. W. Truschel

1666. Ọlọruntimẹhin, B. Ọlatunji. EDUCATION FOR COLONIAL DOMINANCE IN FRENCH WEST AFRICA FROM 1900 TO THE SECOND WORLD WAR. *J. of the Hist. Soc. of Nigeria [Nigeria] 1974 7(2): 347-356.* Studies education as a major instrument in the socialization process during the era of French colonialism in West Africa. French approaches to education in the region are described, and the impact of a rather specialized type of education, which had as its primary objective the perpetuation of colonial dominance, is discussed. This has had a lasting impact in educational systems in postindependence Africa. Primary and secondary sources; 39 notes. J. A. Casada

1667. Omosini, Olufemi. COLONIAL THEORIES AND ADMINISTRATIONS IN BRITISH AND FRENCH WEST AFRICA: A COMPARATIVE ANALYSIS. *Odu: a J. of West African Studies [Nigeria] 1975 (12): 25-39.* Such theories as indirect rule, assimilation, and association, were never crucial in the determination of the actual methods of administration. In spite of theoretical differences in their approaches to colonial government in West Africa, the French and the British responded similarly to identical local situations. Primary and secondary sources; 37 notes. M. M. McCarthy

1668. Osagie, Eghosa. WEST AFRICAN CLEARING HOUSE, WEST AFRICAN UNIT OF ACCOUNT, AND PRESSURES FOR MONETARY INTEGRATION. *J. of Common Market Studies [Great Britain] 1979 17(3): 227-235.* Analyzes the important developments of the West African Clearing House since its establishment in June 1975 to further economic interests of the Economic Community of West African States (ECOWAS), focusing on the role of the West African Unit of Account, an artificial currency created to expedite monetary transactions between member central banks and the clearing house.

1669. Oshuntokun, J. A. ANGLOPHONE WEST AFRICA'S FOREIGN POLICY. *Nigeria Mag. [Nigeria] 1975 (117-118): 36-43.* Traces the development of the British Commonwealth and the relationships of its West African members with the West and other African states, 1830's-1974. Emphasizes Ghana and Nigeria, but Sierra Leone and the Gambia are also included. 22 notes. H. G. Soff

1670. Peel, J. D. Y. URBANIZATION AND URBAN HISTORY IN WEST AFRICA. *J. of African Hist. [Great Britain] 1980 21(2): 269-277.* Reviews six works published between 1974 and 1978. Urban historians of West Africa have much to learn from the example of similar work in Europe and North America. There is no full-length social geography of any single West African town, despite the example of the West Indian urban historians. R. L. Collison

1671. Perinbam, B. Marie. NOTES ON DYULA AND NOMENCLATURE. *Bull. de L'Inst. Fondamental d'Afrique Noire [Senegal] 1974 36(4): 676-690.* A study of the origins of the *dyula,* a group of Western Sudanese itinerant traders that differentiates the class of professional traders from the ethnic and linguistic group classifications. The modern *dyulas* arose during the colonial period in Africa and are Muslim, Mandingo-speaking, long-distance traders who have plied the area west of the Ivory Coast and the Mali River. 23 notes, 2 maps. H. L. Calkin

1672. Rayfield, J. R. THEORIES OF URBANIZATION AND THE COLONIAL CITY IN WEST AFRICA. *Africa [Great Britain] 1974 44(2): 163-185.* The urbanization process is universal, and the West African colonial city represents a most recent, rapid, and conspicuous example of it.

1673. Reid, George W. MISSIONARIES AND WEST AFRICAN NATIONALISM. *Phylon 1978 39(3): 225-233.* Christian missionaries played an important role in the rise of African nationalism, undermining the very colonialism of which they were a part. They educated young Africans in order to make missionaries and preachers of them, but the education they received could and was used for secular, political purposes. Missionaries provided Africans with the knowledge of European languages, facilitating intertribal and international communication and giving Africans access to the great political thinkers of all ages. A sense of Western justice and Judeo-Christian equality instilled by the European and American missionaries formed one of the bases of African nationalism. 47 notes. J. C. Billigmeier

1674. Riddell, J. Barry. THE MIGRATION TO THE CITIES OF WEST AFRICA: SOME POLICY CONSIDERATIONS. *J. of Modern African Studies [Great Britain] 1978 16(2): 241-260.* Tropical Africa is the least urbanized part of the world but recently it has experienced an explosion in urbanization. While population transfer to the cities has increased at a yearly average of 7%, employment has risen half as rapidly. The higher standard of living has attracted rural people to towns and cities even though the prospect for employment has not been as good as in the farmlands. The West African governments, by not changing the colonial laws, have allowed socioeconomic exploitation of the rural population by city-based business and industrial concerns. Secondary sources; 25 notes. A. Sbacchi

1675. Robin, Régis. LA GRANDE DÉPRESSION VUE ET VÉCUE PAR UNE SOCIÉTÉ D'IMPORT-EXPORT EN A.O.F.: PEYRISSAC (1924-1939) [The Great Depression as seen and experienced by an import-export company in French West Africa: Peyrissac, 1924-39]. *Rev. Française d'Hist. d'Outre-Mer [France] 1976 63(3-4): 544-554.* Before the beginning of the Great Depression, the Anciens Établissements Charles Peyrissac, which had become a joint stock company in 1908, had an important share of the rubber and peanut trade in French West Africa. The Great Depression, with the falling prices for raw materials that accompanied it, was disastrous to this firm, which was saved from bankruptcy only by an expansion of peanut production in Senegal and the Sudan. The company survived the Depression, but lost all chance of becoming a dominant factor in West African trade. Moreover, the Peyrissac family lost its controlling interest in the firm to Baron de Nervo and his USINOR. 2 fig., 26 notes. J. C. Billigmeier

1676. Rondos, Alex. FRANCO-AFRICAN SUMMIT AIMS FOR COMMONWEALTH: UNEASY GLANCES AT LIBERIA. *Round Table [Great Britain] 1980 (279): 272-277.* The lack of enthusiasm on the part of most former French colonies in Africa for a francophone commonwealth, despite the linguistic unity, stems from the new demands of economic integration and political liberalization. The threat to the position and lives of the established rulers, as manifested by the fate of Liberia's president, means that to survive the new nations need to adopt a more African approach, rather than tighten ties with France, ties which could be even stronger than past colonial restrictions. E. J. Adams

1677. Rosenthal, Jerry E. DROUGHT: THE CREEPING CATASTROPHE. *Africa Report 1973 18(4): 6-13.* The Sahel, encompassing parts of Senegal, Mauritania, Mali, Upper Volta, Niger, and Chad, is experiencing the worst drought in 60 years. S

1678. Sabatier, Peggy R. AFRICAN CULTURE AND COLONIAL EDUCATION: THE WILLIAM PONTY SCHOOL *CAHIERS* AND THEATER. *J. of African Studies 1980 7(1): 2-10.* The William Ponty School, which served the colonies of French West Africa as a normal school, is usually seen as an instrument of France's assimilationist policy in black Africa. During the years 1933-45, however, the students' African milieu was stressed in two important school activities, the required *cahiers*researched and written on African subjects and the extracurricular plays written and performed in the African theater at Ponty by the students. In seeking to promote the emergence of a Franco-African outlook among an educated indigenous elite, the French directors of the Ponty school sponsored this degree of expression of African culture by their students. Based on French West African archival materials, personal communications, interviews, and secondary sources; 57 notes.

1679. Sanda, A. O. ETHNIC PLURALISM AND INTRA-CLASS CONFLICTS IN FOUR WEST AFRICAN SOCIETIES. *Civilisations [Belgium] 1977 27(1-2): 65-80.* Discusses the nature and source of ethnic conflict in Sierra Leone, Ghana, Benin, and Nigeria, 1950's-60's.

1680. Sarr, Dominique. LA CHAMBRE SPECIALE D'HOMOLOGATION DE LA COUR D'APPEL DE L'A.O.F. ET LES COUTUMES PENALES DE 1903 À 1920 [The Special Approvals Tribunal of the Court of Appeal of French West Africa and customary punishments from 1903 to 1920]. *Ann. Africaines [Senegal] 1974 (1): 101-115.* Describes the functioning of the special colonial court created to oversee administration of traditional laws and native justice in French West Africa from the unification of colonial court systems in 1903 until 1920. French officials would not respect and recognize native law and punishments, applying French legal concepts to African cases, including those involving African Muslims. Examples are given of several cases, showing how French and native law was applied, and the actions of the Special Tribunal in reviewing these cases and developing governing principles for the future. African law and penalties were gradually Gallicized by the colonial courts' decisions in cases appealed to them, usually on the basis that French laws were more "civilized," just, and humane in the matter under consideration. Such changes made possible the relatively easy introduction of the whole French penal code in West Africa after World War II. Based on material in the archives of Senegal; 54 notes. R. Garfield

1681. Sheets, Hal and Morris, Roger. DISASTER IN THE DESERT. *Issue 1974 4(1): 24-43.* Role of planning in disaster relief and other dimensions of US and UN response to the drought in the Sahel in West Africa. S

1682. Sircar, Parbati K. and Epie, Maria Dibo. ECOWAS: THE ECONOMIC COMMUNITY OF WEST AFRICAN STATES. *Africa Q. [India] 1981 20(1-2): 46-62.* Discusses the formation, goals, and gradual growth of the Economic Community of West African States (ECOWAS), established in 1975, and provides data concerning the trading volumes, population, and gross national products of the 16 nations which constitute ECOWAS.

1683. Sircar, Parbati K. REGIONAL DEVELOPMENT THROUGH COOPERATION: TWO EXAMPLES FROM WEST AFRICA. *Africa Q. [India] 1978 18(1): 51-66.* Examines two West African projects from the viewpoint of the development of water resources: the Organization pour le Mise en Valeur de Fleuve Senegal (OMVS) and the Lake Chad Commission Projects in the 1970's.

1684. Spitzer, Leo and Denzer, LaRay. I. T. A. WALLACE-JOHNSON AND THE WEST AFRICAN YOUTH LEAGUE. *Int. J. of African Hist. Studies 1973 6(3): 413-452; (4): 565-601.* Part I. Traces the efforts of Isaac Theophilus Akunna Wallace-Johnson to introduce Marxist ideas and mass-oriented politics to West Africa. Hated and feared by British colonial authorities, he founded and led the West African Youth League which became a major force in colonial politics in English-speaking West Africa. Covers the Gold Coast Period (1933-37), and his efforts in London from March 1937 to April 1938 and especially his appeal to the Privy Council on behalf of the Youth League. 134 notes. Part II: THE SIERRA LEONE PERIOD, 1938-1945. Wallace-Johnson seriously considered withdrawing from African political activism, but his return from London to Freetown, Sierra Leone (his homeland), and the immediate and unwise British response to his presence spurred him on to a new crusade for the laboring classes. He created a militant working class consciousness by capitalizing on the popular frustration with the disparities between the new economic dynamism and the deteriorating living conditions of the masses. Rejected by the local establishment press, he began his own newspaper, the *African Standard.* Convicted of libel, he was not released until 1944. World War II effectively robbed the Youth League of its dynamism and strength, and slowed rather than increased the pace of anticolonial nationalism. 98 notes. R. V. Ritter

1685. Stoller, Paul. SOCIAL INTERACTION AND THE MANAGEMENT OF SONGHAY SOCIO-POLITICAL CHANGE. *Africa [Great Britain] 1981 51(3): 765-780.* The development of the Songhai region, 1591-1898, depended on slavery. The Songhai right to govern was not seriously challenged until money was introduced about 1930, when the economy of the Songhai country gradually fell into the hands of Zerma, Hausa, and other non-Songhai merchants. The political leadership of the Songhai is supported by Islamic ceremonies, but the growing power of the immigrant merchants presents a challenge to the Songhai nobles, who are becoming increasingly dependent on them. The merchants are gaining political influence and reconstructing Songhai political reality. Based on fieldwork, 1976-77; 5 notes, biblio.
R. L. Collison

1686. Sudarkasa, Niara. WOMEN AND MIGRATION IN CONTEMPORARY WEST AFRICA. *Signs: J. of Women in Culture and Soc. 1977 3(1): 178-189.* Describes the composition and characteristics of the migratory population of West Africa, a substantial portion of which is female. Women are especially prominent among Yoruba traders and craftspeople; the majority are first wives and travel with their husbands. They often achieve more status as joint decision-makers in the family as a result of this arrangement. Some young people migrate to cities to receive an education while doing domestic service in a relative's home. Female migrants often are style setters and social interpreters for their rural sisters. 40 notes. L. M. Maloney

1687. Suret-Canale, J. STRIKE MOVEMENTS AS PART OF THE ANTI-COLONIAL STRUGGLE IN FRENCH WEST AFRICA. *Tarikh [Nigeria] 1977 5(3): 44-56.* Strikes were only sporadic manifestations of anticolonialism in French West Africa, 1890-1936, but subsequently played an increasingly important role in independence movements.

1688. White, H. P. TRANSPORT AND DEVELOPMENT IN WEST AFRICA: PRESIDENTIAL ADDRESS TO ASAUK, SEPTEMBER 1980. *African Res. and Documentation [Great Britain] 1980 (24): 2-9.* The president of the African Studies Association of the United Kingdom reports on advances in transportation and economic development in West Africa during the 19th and 20th centuries, focusing on the importance of seaport development for import and export growth since the 1950's.

1689. Yansané, Aguibou Y. SOME PROBLEMS OF MONETARY DEPENDENCY IN FRENCH-SPEAKING WEST AFRICAN STATES. *J. of African Studies 1978-79 5(4): 444-470.* Compares the experience in attaining monetary stability of the former French territories in West Africa. Most joined the franc zone through membership in the West African Monetary Union (UMOA). UMOA membership has apparently brought monetary stability, but it has favored the French Treasury by bringing the African currencies into the Paris exchange market and has communicated to Africa inflationary trends from the French franc and other Western currencies. Guinea and Mali (to 1967) followed independent monetary policies and experienced harsh monetary instability due to lack of domestic savings, failures to increase their exports, and administrative inefficiency. More recently, the Lomé Convention has guaranteed West African states greater stability for their export receipts, while a larger 15-member West African common market has been launched with the signing of the treaty in 1975 creating the Economic Community of the West African States. Based on published official documents and secondary sources; 4 tables, 54 notes.
L. W. Truschel

1690. Yansane, Aguibou Y. THE STATE OF ECONOMIC INTEGRATION IN NORTH WEST AFRICA SOUTH OF THE SAHARA: THE EMERGENCE OF THE ECONOMIC COMMUNITY OF WEST AFRICAN STATES (ECOWAS). *African Studies Rev. 1977 20(2): 63-88.* The development of the Economic Community of West African States (ECOWAS) 1958-76, has shown the extent to which African regional cooperation can assist in building the economic foundations in African states, while still allowing them to retain their sovereignty.

1691. Zidouemba, Dominique Hado. LES SOURCES DE L'HISTOIRE DES FRONTIÈRES DE L'OUEST AFRICAIN [Sources for the history of West African borders]. *Bull. de l'Inst. Fondamental d'Afrique Noire [Senegal] 1977 39(4): 695-835.* Annotated bibliography of printed and archival sources in Dakar, Senegal, for the study of frontiers of countries in West Africa. Indexes of frontiers, ethnic groups, places, authors, and other persons cited. 7 maps.
H. L. Calkin

1692. Zima, Petr. THE ROLE OF LINGUISTICS IN A LITERACY CAMPAIGN IN AFRICA. *Archív Orientální [Czechoslovakia] 1975 43(4): 210-222.* Examines the role of linguistics in the UNESCO adult literacy campaign in the Hausa areas of West Africa in the 1960's and early 1970's, citing the author's field experience in this campaign and stressing the change from use of Arabic script to Roman script and the shifts in lexicon which took place to accommodate new terminologies.

1693. Zinsou-Derlin, Lionel. LA BANQUE DE L'AFRIQUE OCCIDENTALE DANS LA CRISE [The Bank of West Africa in the crisis]. *Rev. Française d'Hist. d'Outre-Mer [France] 1976 63(3-4): 506-518.* The Banque de l'Afrique Occidentale [Bank of West Africa] appeared a solid edifice at the beginning of the Great Depression, but between 1926 and 1936 it passed through three crises: 1) the internal problem of renewal of the bank charter, which once resolved produced closer cooperation between the Central Bank and government; 2) involving the whole banking system, when the colonial credit system was saved only by the BAO's yielding to the authorities and the metropolitan banks; and 3) involving all economic activity, the BAO played a more independent role. After this the BAO, with more resources and government encouragement, helped create a new production system in West Africa. The bank showed amazing resilience during the Great Depression; by 1936, with careful management, the levels of 1929 had been regained. 20 notes. J. C. Billigmeier

1694. —. [BILATERAL RELATIONS BETWEEN CANADA AND FRENCH SPEAKING COUNTRIES IN WEST AFRICA]. *Can. J. of African Studies [Canada] 1981 15(1): 77-93.*

Houndjahoué, Michel. LA COOPÉRATION BILATÉRALE ENTRE LE CANADA ET LES PAYS FRANCOPHONES DE L'AFRIQUE DE L'OUEST: UNE ÉVALUATION DE L'OFFRE ENTRE 1961 ET 1975 [Bilateral cooperation between Canada and French-speaking countries in West Africa: a supply evaluation between 1961 and 1975], *pp. 77-91.* An analysis of the foundations and objectives of Canadian aid to French-speaking West Africa from 1961 to 1975. 3 tables, 18 notes.

Dussault, Paul-Normand. LES RELATIONS BILATÉRALES AVEC L'AFRIQUE FRANCOPHONE [Bilateral relations with French-speaking Africa], *pp. 92-93.* Criticizes the author's failure to explain clearly the effects of bilateral cooperation.
G. P. Cleyet

1695. —. [THE CGT AND FRENCH BLACK AFRICA]. *Mouvement Social [France] 1983 (122): 103-121.*

Delanoue, Paul. LA CGT ET LES SYNDICATS DE L'AFRIQUE NOIRE DE COLONISATION FRANÇAISE, DE LA DEUXIEME GUERRE MONDIALE AUX INDEPENDANCES [The CGT and the labor unions of French colonial black Africa, from World War II to independence], *pp. 103-116.* Replies to an article by Philippe Dewitte (see entry 1627) in which Dewitte criticized the French Confédération Générale du Travail for having downplayed the role of rural workers and underlined its own role in the process of independence. Dewitte also criticized the CGT for a lack of enthusiasm in the anti-colonial struggle.

Dewitte, Philippe. RESPONSE A PAUL DELANOUE [Reply to Paul Delanoue], *pp. 117-121.* The CGT did believe in a French Union and thought of no other imperialism but the American. Its perception of African reality lagged behind the historical evolution. 24 notes. J. V. Coutinho

1696. —. [ECONOMIC HISTORY OF WEST AFRICA]. *African Econ. Hist. 1978 (6): 127-144.*

Hill, Polly. PROBLEMS WITH A. G. HOPKINS' ECONOMIC HISTORY OF WEST AFRICA, *pp. 127-133.* On the basis of her study of the Hausa, Hill criticizes A. G. Hopkins's *An Economic History of West Africa* (London: Longmans, 1973) for its analysis of slave systems, economic inequality, technology, demography, land tenure, craftwork, and distribution system.

Dalton, George. COMMENT: WHAT KINDS OF TRADE AND MARKETS?, *pp. 134-138.* Notes the many variations of African market patterns, especially politically administered mercantilism, state monopolies, king's trade, and guild controls. 7 notes.

Hopkins, A. G. AN ECONOMIC HISTORY OF WEST AFRICA: FURTHER COMMENT, *pp. 139-144.* Accuses Hill of inaccuracies by overgeneralizing from her own narrow research. 14 notes. W. D. Piersen

Benin

1697. Asiwaja, A. I. THE COLONIAL EDUCATION HERITAGE AND THE PROBLEM OF NATION-BUILDING IN DAHOMEY. *Bull. de l'Inst. Fondamental d'Afrique Noire [Senegal] 1975 37(2): 340-357.* There are three aspects to the question of colonial education in Dahomey as it relates to building that country into a nation since the dissolution of French control in 1956. First, there has been an overproduction of trained persons for whom there are no positions, especially since many in neighboring countries have been forced to return home. Secondly, the educational system has been dominant in the south, causing resentment in northern Dahomey. The third problem is the assimilation of the educated people into society throughout the country. The French educational system was adequate for colonials but its goals and machinery are inadequate for an independent nation. H. L. Calkin

1698. Asiwaju, A. I. ANTI-FRENCH RESISTANCE MOVEMENT IN ỌHỌRI-IJE (DAHOMEY). *J. of the Hist. Soc. of Nigeria [Nigeria] 1974 7(2): 255-269.* Examines both the nature and causation of the protracted Ọhọri resistance to French colonial government. The resistance was most intense during 1914-16, when the Ọhọri consistently opposed French cultural and political intrusions. The author focuses on incidents of direct military confrontation. Primary and secondary sources; 99 notes. J. A. Casada

1699. Codo, Bellarmin C. and Anignikin, Sylvain C. POUVOIR COLONIAL ET TENTATIVES D'INTEGRATION AFRICAINES DANS LE SYSTEME CAPITALISTE: LE CAS DU DAHOMEY ENTRE LES DEUX GUERRES [Colonial power and possibilities of African integration in the capitalist system: the case of Dahomey between the two world wars]. *Can. J. of African Studies [Canada] 1982 16(2): 331-342.* Examines the link between the local civil service and European trading companies in their fight to reach their respective aims, and the inability of the Dahomean petite bourgeoisie to oppose colonial strength. On the eve of World War I, both on political and economic levels, colonial power had succeeded in reaffirming its exclusive control over the colony, thus confining the Dahomean petite bourgeoisie to the secondary role of collectors of farm products. J

1700. Decalo, Samuel. REGIONALISM, POLITICS, AND THE MILITARY IN DAHOMEY. *J. of Developing Areas 1973 7(3): 449-478.* A case study of political instability in Dahomey, 1960-72. S

1701. Desmangles, Leslie Gerald. AFRICAN INTERPRETATIONS OF THE CHRISTIAN CROSS IN VODUN. *Sociol. Analysis 1977 38(1): 13-24.* Linguistic, theological, and mythological correlations between Dahomean religions and Haiti's voodoo *(vodun)* resulted from contact between Dahomean religions and English Catholicism, 1492-1804, and inspired voodoo's 20th-century symbolism of the cross, which rather than being connected with Christianity is interpreted in the context of Dahomean mythology.

1702. Genne, Marcelle. LA TENTATION DU SOCIALISME AU BENIN [The temptation of socialism in Benin]. *Etudes Int. [Canada] 1978 9(3): 383-404.* The achievement of scientific socialism as conceived by Charles Bettelheim, Jacques Charrière, and Hélène Marchisio is based on four general principles: the taking of power by a proletarian party, the establishment of the dictatorship of the proletariat, the public ownership and control of the economy, and agricultural reform. Relating the experience of Benin to these fundamental principles shows that there are different paths to socialism. Accordingly, different facts lead to a revision of the theory of scientific socialism. Table, 2 graphs, 49 notes. J. F. Harrington, Jr.

1703. Hackett, Rosalind I. J. THIRTY YEARS OF GROWTH AND CHANGE IN A WEST AFRICAN INDEPENDENT CHURCH: A SOCIOLOGICAL PERSPECTIVE. *J. of Religion in Africa [Netherlands] 1980 11(3): 212-224.* The Celestial Church of Christ was founded in Dahomey, now Benin, in 1947. The church was a sect, a small tightly-knit group, fearful of the trappings of bureaucracy and professionalism. The church prospered, particularly in urban areas, and in 1967 bureaucrats and professionals began to join. In 1972, the church made its first real attempt to examine its own identity. The conflict between the church-like tendencies of compromise with the world and the sect-like tendencies of hostility continue to the present. The matter will probably be resolved with the demise of the founder, Samuel Bileou Oschoffa, a former carpenter of Gun and Yoruba origin. The transfer of power to the new generation will tell the tale. R. J. Jirran

1704. Krasnowolski, Andrzej. AFRO-BRAZULIJCZYCY W PROCESIE PRZEMIAN KULTUROWYCH DAHOMEJU POŁUDNIOWEGO [Afro-Brazilians in the process of cultural change in Southern Dahomey]. Szymański, Edward. *Tradycja i Współczesność w Azji, Afryce i Ameryce Łacińskiej* (Warsaw: Polska Akademia Nauk Zakład Krajów Pozaeuropejskich, 1978): 287-313. Analyzes the role of Brazilians in Dahomean cultural change and distinguishes elements of this group from other "Creole" populations in West Africa, 1850-1978.

1705. Manning, Patrick. PUBLIC FINANCE AND CAPITAL INVESTMENT: A NATIONAL PERSPECTIVE ON COLONIAL DAHOMEY. *Can. J. of African Studies [Canada] 1980 14(3): 519-524.* French colonial policy had disastrous effects on Dahomey which extended into the post-independence period. "Such growth as took place during the colonial era resulted from other influences: autonomous domestic growth, technical change, favorable developments in the world market, and private foreign investment." While independent Dahomey continued the contractive policies to a degree, it inaugurated needed economic expansion. Fig., 19 notes. S

1706. Quenum, Alphonse. LEISURE IN A DEVELOPING COUNTRY: THE CASE OF LOWER-DAHOMEY. *Cultures [France] 1973 1(2): 67-86.* Defines leisure and examines the problems of work and leisure in an industrialized society as they appear to the people of Dahomey. Analyzes the similarities and differences in a developing and industrializing nation. Primary and secondary sources; 3 notes. R. K. Adams

1707. Ronen, Dov. THE COLONIAL ELITE IN DAHOMEY. *African Studies Rev. 1974 17(1): 55-76.* The Brazilian settlers in the coastal regions who formed the core of the Dahomean elite, 1920-67, have distinct attitudes toward education and African tradition.

1708. Staniland, Martin. THE THREE PARTY SYSTEM IN DAHOMEY: II, 1956-1957. *J. of African Hist. [Great Britain] 1973 14(3): 491-504.* Continued from a previous article. Examines the rivalry among the Dahomean political parties, the Parti Républicain (PRD), the Mouvement Démocratique (MDD), and the Union Démocratique (UDD). Although all three were regional parties, the UDD claimed to transcend narrow regional issues and command mass support. In the 1957 elections, however, the PRD forced the UDD to campaign on local rather than national issues. The PRD won the elections due to the greater personal standing of its leader, S. M. Apithy, and its greater skill in calculating and manipulating ethnic support. 4 tables, 51 notes. C. Hopkins

1709. —. EXPÉRIENCES DE LA RÉPUBLIQUE POPULAIRE DU BÉNIN EN MATIÈRE DE RÉFORME AGRO-FONCIÈRE [Experiments of Benin regarding land reform]. *African Perspectives [Netherlands] 1979 (1): 27-43.* A Benin government report on agrarian reform projects in the Lower Benin region. Beginning in 1961, areas of rural development were established with a cooperative system and organized by the Société Nationale de Développement Rural for the cultivation of palm oil, and the Société Nationale d'Aménagement et de Développement de la Vallée de l'Ouémé for the cultivation of rice. Although marked progress has been recorded, serious difficulties remain, particularly about the management of the cooperatives, their financing, and the cooperation of the peasantry. Table. G. P. Cleyet

Cape Verde

1710. Fyfe, Christopher. THE CAPE VERDE ISLANDS. *Hist. Today [Great Britain] 1981 31(May): 5-9.* Traces the history of the Cape Verde Islands from their colonization by the Portuguese in 1460 to their independence in 1975 and discusses the effects of 500 years of colonial government on economy, population, and politics.

1711. Fyfe, Christopher. THE CAPE VERDE ISLANDS. *Tarikh [Nigeria] 1980 6(4): 20-30.* In 1975 the independent Cape Verde Islands voted the African Party of Independence into power ending 500 years of oppressive Portuguese rule.

Gambia

1712. Coulon, Christian. LES PARTIS POLITIQUES GAMBIENS [Gambian political parties]. *Rev. Française d'Études Pol. Africaines [France] 1973 (89): 31-49.* Studies the origin, development, and characteristics of the Gambian political parties, 1951-73, which are based on British models of classical, multi-partisan democracy, stresses the amazing political stability in Gambia today, and the possibility for evolution to a single-party country in the future.

1713. Hughes, Arnold. FROM GREEN UPRISING TO NATIONAL RECONCILIATION: THE PEOPLE'S PROGRESSIVE PARTY IN GAMBIA, 1959-1973. *Can. J. of African Studies [Canada] 1975 9(1): 61-74.* The People's Progressive Party comprised of the rural element in Gambia rose up and sought to gain control of the government. This is an example of what S. P. Huntington terms a "green uprising." They pledged to redistribute the natural resources and employment opportunities to the rural class and its largely Madinka members. This created a problem as to how to balance the needed support of the urban Wollof and the bureaucracy and still keep the rural Madinka support. In the future much will depend on the government's ability to keep both these groups happy. Based on government documents, interviews, and secondary works; 49 notes. J

1714. Hutchison, Alan. GAMBIA: THE FIRST TEN YEARS. *Africa Report 1975 20(4): 11-16.* The first ten years of Gambian independence have been marked by economic prosperity, political stability, and good government, 1965-75. S

1715. Nyang, S. S. TOURISM AND GAMBIA'S VIABILITY PROBLEM. *Afrique et L'Asie [France] 1974 (101): 59-61.* Gambia's viability problem can be traced to the artificial division of the Senegambia region by Great Britain and France, resulting in the formation of two states, Gambia and Senegal. Since the leaders of Gambia prefer independence in a small state to federation in a larger and more viable union, Gambia must achieve viability through other means, such as tourism. European tourists may, however, have an adverse effect on Gambian culture. J. S. Gassner

1716. Weil, Peter M. THE STAFF OF LIFE: FOOD AND FEMALE FERTILITY IN A WEST AFRICAN SOCIETY. *Africa [Great Britain] 1976 46(2): 182-195.* Studies fertility associations among the Mandinka of Gambia. In recent years, Mandinka males have turned almost exclusively to producing cash crops, leaving their wives to grow rice for food in the tidal swamplands. The women thus play a significant role in society, but there are no religious or secular institutions through which they might increase their prestige in consequence. The fertility association consists solely of women who are childless or who have given birth to children who have died. They mimic men, place them in mock subservient positions, and assume male speech and actions. This mock role reversal might mask a desire for status reversal, though proof is lacking, but certainly it enables women to pretend the prestige which they feel is deserved but withheld. 9 notes, ref. V. L. Human

1717. Wiseman, John A. LOCAL ELECTIONS IN THE GAMBIA: WHERE THE MARBLE RINGS THE BELL. *Round Table [Great Britain] 1979 (275): 232-237.* The Gambian local government elections in March 1979, in which the People's Progressive Party (PPP) won a clear majority, were free, open, and peaceful.

Ghana

General

1718. Henige, David P. THE NATIONAL ARCHIVES OF GHANA: A SYNOPSIS OF HOLDINGS. *Int. J. of African Hist. Studies 1973 6(3): 475-486.* Briefly outlines the holdings of the National Archives of Ghana, most of which cover the years after 1840. This rough indication of the scope and value of the material must serve until publication of a more detailed guide. The synopsis is based on the typewritten guides available in 1971 and prepared by the senior archives assistant at that time. Ghana also has several regional archives in addition to the main archival depository in Accra. R. V. Ritter

Economics

1719. Arhin, Kwame. THE PRESSURE OF CASH AND ITS POLITICAL CONSEQUENCES IN ASANTE IN THE COLONIAL PERIOD, 1900-1940. *J. of African Studies 1976 3(4): 453-468.* British colonization of Ashanti increased opportunities for earning and using money until it became the warp of society. As the cash nexus spread, stool debts grew in a complex manner. A stool, *akonnua,* is the physical symbol of a political office. Serious political disputes arose over the raising and use of stool funds that put traditional authority into considerable jeopardy even as British policy sought to buttress that authority. The consequences are still unfolding in Ghana and in many other former British colonies. Based on archival and secondary sources; table, 58 notes. W. R. Hively

1720. Benneh, George. SMALL-SCALE FARMING SYSTEMS IN GHANA. *Africa [Great Britain] 1973 43(2): 134-146.* Distinguishes two broad systems of small-scale farming in Ghana: the bush fallow system; and permanent tillage. On the basis of various 20th-century studies, shows that agriculture programs for small-scale farmers would more likely succeed if they were more uniform.

1721. Bhatia, Rattan J. IMPORT PROGRAMMING IN GHANA, 1966-69. *Afro-Asian Econ. Rev. [Egypt] 1973 15(168-169): 7-13.* Discusses Ghanaian import programming, 1966-69, detailing optimum and minimum import plans, and the implementation of the 1969 program.

1722. Crisp, Jeff. UNION ATROPHY AND WORKER REVOLT: LABOUR PROTEST AT TARKWA GOLDFIELDS, GHANA, 1968-1969. *Can. J. of African Studies [Canada] 1979 13(1-2): 267-293.* Between 1968 and 1970 workers in Ghana's gold mines were involved in a series of large-scale strikes, riots and demonstrations. In the course of these events workers were shot by police, managers and union officials were threatened and severely injured by striking mineworkers, and at Ghana's richest mine the army was asked to intervene to restore order and save the mine from closure. This account of worker protest at Tarkwa Goldfields in 1968-69 delineates the principal features of the mineworkers' political consciousness, examines the process of union atrophy and worker revolt that occurred in Ghana's gold mines between 1956 and 1971, and examines the potentialities and limitations of worker protest in postcolonial states. J

1723. Darkoh, Michael B. K. MANUFACTURING IN GHANA, 1957-1967. *Bull. de l'Inst. Fondamental d'Afrique Noire, Serie B [Senegal] 1973 35(4): 813-853.* The growth and economic development of Ghana have been based traditionally on agriculture, forestry, and mining. Manufacturing became established mostly after World War II, with the government providing the major stimulus. Industrialization 1957-67, was characterized by small enterprises producing consumer goods, timber, and agricultural products. By 1967 public opinion began to shift away from a reliance on industrialization as a major source of economic growth. 11 tables, 10 charts, 75 notes. H. L. Calkin

1724. Darkoh, Michael B. K. AN OUTLINE OF POST-1966 REGIONAL PLANNING AND RURAL DEVELOPMENT IN GHANA. *Pan-African J. [Kenya] 1976 9(2): 153-167.* Ghana's economy has remained neocolonial, 1966-75. Various administrative measures aimed at the decentralization of decisionmaking to promote regional development have not been effective. The author presents a critique of various rural development policies since the fall of President Kwame Nkrumah in 1966, including those of the National Liberation Council, 1966-69, the Busia administration, 1964-72, and the National Redemption Council since January 1972. Also discusses the 1975-80 five-year plan. 44 notes. M. Feingold

1725. Darkoh, Michael B. Kwesi. THE DEVELOPMENT AND PROBLEMS OF MANUFACTURING INDUSTRY IN GHANA DURING THE NKRUMAH ERA. *Odu: a J. of West African Studies [Nigeria] 1977 (16): 3-34.* Demonstrates that Ghana under President Kwame Nkrumah: 1) paid little attention to the manufacturing industries; 2) failed to promote intersectoral and spatial linkages in the economy; 3) encouraged the use of capital-intensive technology thereby successfully creating structural unemployment; and 4) failed to diversify the economy or make any attempt to formulate a rational industrial policy. Ghana, like most other African and developing nation economies, suffers from perverse capitalist industrialization. Based on data of the Central Bureau of Statistics, Accra, development plans for 1951, 1959-64, 1963-64, and 1969-70, financial summary reports, and data from the Food Research Institute, Ghana; 11 tables, 73 notes. M. Mtewa

1726. Der, B. G. COLONIAL LAND POLICY IN THE NORTHERN TERRITORIES OF THE GOLD COAST, 1900-1957. *Universitas [Ghana] 1975 4(2): 127-142.* The British colonial government of the Gold Coast's Northern Territories pursued several contradictory and disruptive policies. Native land tenure was based on corporate ownership of unclaimed lands and on private ownership of cultivated lands. The crown's governor granted mining concessions directly in 1901 without consulting the local chiefs. From 1904 to 1926 colonial ordinances resulted in the virtual ownership of all land by the government. In 1927 the Native Land Rights Ordinance sought to return control to the inhabitants, but the application of the law disrupted ethnic control over uncultivated lands and allowed foreign investors to grab huge chunks of the Northern Territories. Because the colony was divided into three areas, the Gold Coast, Asante, and the Northern Territories, the colonial regime was able to placate the south while disinheriting the north. 74 notes. J. W. Leedom

1727. Dumett, Raymond E. OBSTACLES TO GOVERNMENT-ASSISTED AGRICULTURAL DEVELOPMENT IN WEST AFRICA: COTTON-GROWING EXPERIMENTATION IN GHANA IN THE EARLY TWENTIETH CENTURY. *Agric. Hist. Rev. [Great Britain] 1975 23(2): 156-172.* Analyzes the origins of British involvement in cotton-growing in Ghana, 1902-20, assesses the colonial assistance projects and shows the reasons for their failure. Though British cotton-growing teams understood the environmental problems they lacked adequate information on local labor and its sociocultural context. Most significant was the failure of colonial officials to understand "the extent to which West African farmers were generally motivated in their choice of crops not by yield per acre or total profit over an extended period but by the return per man-hour of labor." Based on official reports and Colonial Office Papers in the Public Record Office, London. D. H. Murdoch

1728. Goody, Jack. RICE-BURNING AND THE GREEN REVOLUTION IN NORTHERN GHANA. *J. of Development Studies [Great Britain] 1980 16(2): 136-155.* Introduction in the 1960's of varieties of high yield rice made farming in northern Ghana more lucrative and drew people into an area of former pasturelands. Immigration combined with strict social differentiation and more stringent land claim record keeping created animosities with the local population leading to rice field burning and machinery destruction.

1729. Gray, Paul S. THE GENESIS OF TRADE UNIONS IN GHANA. *J. of African Studies 1981 8(2): 72-78.* African industrial workers in Great Britain's Gold Coast colony engaged in intermittent work stoppages after 1919 in efforts to improve their wages and working conditions. After many years of resisting these efforts and the development of labor unions, the colonial administration switched in the early 1940's to a policy of attempting to coopt the African labor movement through official regulations and advisors. The new policy failed in the postwar period to halt the movement of the newly-formed unions from joining the anticolonial nationalist sentiment. Based on published colonial reports for the Gold Coast and secondary sources; 28 notes. L. W. Truschel

1730. Grayson, Leslie E. A CONGLOMERATE IN AFRICA: PUBLIC-SECTOR MANUFACTURING ENTERPRISES IN GHANA, 1962-1971. *African Studies R. 1973 16(3): 315-346.* Though not always economically feasible, the use of public-sector enterprises is instructive for developing nations. S

1731. Grayson, Leslie E. THE PROMOTION OF INDIGENOUS PRIVATE ENTERPRISE IN GHANA. *J. of Asian and African Studies [Netherlands] 1974 9(1/2): 17-28.* The National Liberation Council of Ghana decreed the "Ghanaization of business', in 1968. Since then the greatest impediment to business expansion has been the business environment, not foreign presence. 39 notes. R. T. Brown

1732. Greenstreet, D. K. PUBLIC CORPORATIONS IN GHANA (GOLD COAST) DURING THE NKRUMAH PERIOD, 1951-66. *African R. [Tanzania] 1973 3(1): 21-31.* During the last 14 years of Kwame Nkrumah's reign, the size of the public domain grew significantly. Discusses the public corporation and society, the legislature and the public corporation, government and the public corporation, the state enterprises secretariat, and corporations' boards of directors. Assesses public corporations' performance. H. G. Soff

1733. Grier, Beverly. UNDERDEVELOPMENT, MODES OF PRODUCTION, AND THE STATE IN COLONIAL GHANA. *African Studies Rev. 1981 24(1): 21-47.* A bibliographic survey of underdevelopment and a case study of Ghana, showing that "the incorporation of Ghana's rural producers into the expanding world-wide capitalist system did not result in immediate capitalist transformation." Colonial administration designed economic policies to stop native capitalist development in favor of that of expatriates. Secondary sources; 12 notes, biblio. R. T. Brown

1734. Gunnarsson, Christer. APPROACHES TO THE ECONOMIC DEVELOPMENT OF GHANA UNDER COLONIAL RULE. *Econ. and Hist. [Sweden] 1974 17: 116-127.* A review article surveying the literature on the subject, notably the works of A. McPhee, A. G. Hopkins, W. K. Hancock, D. Seers, P. Hill, A. Seidman and G. B. Kay. 27 biblio. notes. A. Blumberg

1735. Hilling, D. THE EVOLUTION OF A PORT SYSTEM—THE CASE OF GHANA. *Geography [Great Britain] 1977 62(2): 97-105.* A number of geographers have used models emphasizing stages of development as a means of examining the evolution of individual ports and the regional and national systems in which they combine. The changing pattern of port activity in Ghana is compared with some of the "ideal-typical" sequences of existing models. Three phases of development, surf-port, lighterage and deep-water port, are identified. The spatial consolidation and rationalization which has been the predominant trend is examined by means of a changing index of concentration. J

1736. Howard, Rhoda. DIFFERENTIAL CLASS PARTICIPATION IN AN AFRICAN PROTEST MOVEMENT: THE GHANA COCOA BOYCOTT of 1937-38. *Can. J. of African Studies [Canada] 1976 10(3): 469-480.* Examines cross-class participation in a cocoa boycott held in Ghana, 1937-38.

1737. Howard, Rhoda. FORMATION AND STRATIFICATION OF THE PEASANTRY IN COLONIAL GHANA. *J. of Peasant Studies [Great Britain] 1980 8(1): 61-80.* Examines the transformation of villagers in colonial Ghana, 1885-1939, into peasants and the eventual stratification of this peasantry in response to Ghana's entry into the world capitalist economy. Retention of traditional land tenure insured that a peasant rather than a plantation-oriented economy arose. Stratification also produced a small class of capitalist farmers which has come to represent a weak commercial and financial sector. Secondary sources; 7 notes. G. Alexander

1738. Hutchful, Eboe. ORGANIZATIONAL INSTABILITY IN AFRICAN MILITARY FORCES: THE CASE OF THE GHANAIAN ARMY. *Int. Social Sci. J. [France] 1979 31(4): 606-618.*

1739. Kofi, Tetteh A. [ECONOMIC DEVELOPMENT IN GHANA]. THE ABIBIRIM STRATEGY OF DEVELOPMENT. *Universitas [Ghana] 1975 4(2): 30-64.* A Marxist view of development and capital accumulation in colonial Ghana (Gold Coast). The people realized only scant benefits from the influx of money, and classical and neoclassical economic models have not been able to account for Ghana's lack of economic development. Into the mid-1960's many of Ghana's leaders, especially Kwame Nkrumah, thought that modernization was possible without a technological revolution, simply by slowly absorbing foreign inventions and investments. But progress was thwarted at every turn, first socially, then technologically. The structural imbalance between the tribal country and the European town were too great to overcome. Fig., 108 notes. TOWARDS THE "ABIBIRIM" STRATEGY OF DEVELOPMENT: A FORMAL ARTICULATION. *Universitas [Ghana] 1975 5(1): 42-67.* Uses the historical, structural, and institutional approach to diagnose the causes of Third World economic underdevelopment. *Abibirimism* advocates a transition to socialism from agrarianism and is a nationalist as well as a socialist ideology. It is a strategy to utilize the productive forces of the population blocked by free trade imperialism and colonialism, thereby freeing Africa from the entanglement of Western capitalism. 9 tables, 37 notes. J. W. Leedom/ J. J. N. McGurk

1740. Kraus, Jon. STRIKES AND LABOUR POWER IN GHANA. *Development and Change [Netherlands] 1979 10(2): 259-286.* Discusses the relationship between African workers and labor organizations, and examines the changing political attitudes of the government of Ghana, 1940's-70's; traces the implications of this relationship in analyzing labor unions and strikes.

1741. Lazzarini-Viti, Veronica. WESTERN FOODS AND TRADITIONAL DIET IN GHANA. *Paideuma [West Germany] 1978 24: 103-109.* In the 1960's and 1970's the consumption of bread and canned milk rose continuously in Ghanaian towns and villages, a development causing great problems because both wheat and milk have to be largely imported.

1742. Libby, Ronald T. EXTERNAL CO-OPTATION OF A LESS DEVELOPED COUNTRY'S POLICY MAKING: THE CASE OF GHANA, 1969-1972. *World Pol. 1976 29(1): 67-89.* The World Bank, the International Monetary Fund, and creditor countries structured the context in which their client, Ghana—a less developed country—formulated its economic policy, 1969-72. The intergovernmental organizations and creditor countries failed to take Ghana's domestic political situation into account, however. When the country became heavily dependent upon the intergovernmental organizations and creditors for financial assistance to enable the government to survive a disastrous shortfall in foreign exchange earnings, it was forced to accept extreme and politically dangerous measures in order to secure assistance. The policies that were adopted were catastrophic, and destroyed what remained of the democratic government's public support. This dramatic change in public climate made the government fatally vulnerable to a military coup d'état. J

1743. McCaskie, T. C. OFFICE, LAND AND SUBJECTS IN THE HISTORY OF THE MANWERE *FEKUO* OF KUMASE: AN ESSAY IN THE POLITICAL ECONOMY OF THE ASANTE STATE. *J. of African Hist. [Great Britain] 1980 21(2): 189-208.* The last of the ten *fekuo* (administrative units) of Kumase to be created was the Manwere, founded by Asantehene Kwaku Dua Panin (reigned 1834-67). He vested its headship in Kwasi Brantuo who, by the time of his death in 1865 had amassed a great personal fortune from his duties as a fiscal agent, from the collection of fines, and from personal investments. Kwaku Dua Panin used his sons as instruments for controlling the political hierarchy: four of them were given senior offices in the Manwere *fekuo,* and became elements in his dynastic policy. After his death the Manwere *fekuo* was retrenched for political reasons, and his personal fortune dissipated. The status of Manwere was diminished. The colonial period (1901-57) saw the renewal of the struggle of the Kumase officeholders to regain their powers, a struggle that continues. Based on personal interviews and official records; 74 notes. R. L. Collison

1744. Meredith, David. THE CONSTRUCTION OF TAKORADI HARBOUR IN THE GOLD COAST 1919-1930: A CASE STUDY IN COLONIAL DEVELOPMENT AND ADMINISTRATION. *Transafrican J. of Hist. [Kenya] 1976 5(1): 134-149.* Takoradi Harbor was the most expensive public works project carried out by the British in tropical Africa during the 1920's. The author analyzes why it was built and its role in Britain's worldwide policy. In addition, several major administrative problems that arose as a result of its construction are discussed, including its failure to show any profit until 1942. 2 tables, 52 notes. H. G. Soff

1745. Morrison, Thomas K. THE POLITICAL ECONOMY OF EXPORT INSTABILITY IN DEVELOPING COUNTRIES: THE CASE OF GHANA. *J. of African Studies 1979 6(3): 159-164.* Connects instability in world commodity prices with disruption of national developmental planning in countries dependent on single export items. Ghana suffered export shortfalls in cacao in 1965-66 and 1971-72, which had extremely harsh effects on government revenues and political stability. Such countries should seek to control current expenditures, shift their tax structures away from foreign trade, and diversify their revenue-earning exports. Based on published documents and secondary sources; 9 notes. L. W. Truschel

1746. Ofori-Atta, Jones. SECTORAL CHANGES IN INCOME DISTRIBUTION IN THE ECONOMIES OF WEST AFRICA: GHANA, 1960-69. *Universitas [Ghana] 1975 5(1): 68-83.* Measures economic growth in Ghana, 1960-69, on the yardstick of sectoral distribution of incomes. The growth of the Ghanaian economy in the 1960's depended on the physical absorption of capital and manpower. Nevertheless, the rapid rate of capital formation and the inability of the economy to supply raw materials for full production brought pressures which led to widespread underutilization of capacities. 3 tables, 19 notes. J. J. N. McGurk

1747. Parys, Jan. PRZEOBRAŻENIA EKONOMICZNE A PROBLEM ROZWOJU SPOLECZEŃSTWA W NIEPODLEGLEJ GHANIE [Economic transformation and social development in independent Ghana]. *Przegląd Socjologiczny [Poland] 1979 31(2): 59-90.* Analyzes the pattern of industrialization introduced in 1957 by the Convention People's Party under Kwame Nkrumah and finds that the deficiencies of Nkrumah's economic approach led directly to the financial crisis which resulted in the overthrow of his government by the army in 1966 and the establishment of a military government which for the next six years struggled to cope with the economic chaos inherited from Nkrumah.

1748. Patterson, K. David. THE VETERINARY DEPARTMENT AND THE ANIMAL INDUSTRY IN THE GOLD COAST, 1909-1955. *Int. J. of African Hist. Studies 1980 13(3): 457-491.* Although underfunded and understaffed, the colonial veterinary department made good progress in controlling cattle diseases and in providing facilities for increased marketable herds in the northern provinces of the Gold Coast during the 20th century. Little was provided in the rest of the colony for cattle or other kinds of animals. Based on the archives of Ghana; 5 tables, 192 notes. R. T. Brown

1749. Plange, Nii-K. "OPPORTUNITY COST" AND LABOUR MIGRATION: A MISINTERPRETATION OF PROLETARIANISATION IN NORTHERN GHANA. *J. of Modern African Studies [Great Britain] 1979 17(4): 655-676.* Orthodox studies of labor migration and its connections with economic development use the concept of "opportunity cost," presuming a rational choice to migrate based on alternative opportunities. But a study of the recruitment of labor for gold and diamond mines in colonial Ghana, 1880-1940, shows that it is inapplicable. A coercive recruitment system, using northern Ghana as a source of labor, provided a proletariat for the mining centers and met with resistance from northerners. This destruction of the traditional economy served to create the underdevelopment of the north, integrated as a labor reserve in a capitalist economy. Based on documents in the Ghana National Archives and printed sources; 74 notes. D. J. Nicholls

1750. Priestley, Margaret. THE GOLD COAST SELECT COMMITTEE ON ESTIMATES: 1913-1950. *Int. J. of African Hist. Studies 1973 6(4): 543-564.* Important insights into the management of public finance in the colonial period in the Gold Coast can be derived from a study of the operations of the Select Committee on Estimates, a mechanism by which the legislature considered and approved the government's budget. It was notable in the colonial period for its long history, the presence of African members from the beginning, and the part it played as a forum for discussion on the annual estimates. The author traces in detail the committee's development in procedure and policy and its general impact. 80 notes. R. V. Ritter

1751. Priestley, Margaret. REORGANIZATION OF COLONIAL TREASURIES, 1936: THE CASE OF GHANA. *Public Administration [Great Britain] 1974 52(4): 395-414.* Discusses Great Britain's Treasury reform policy toward the government administration of Ghana and developing nations in 1936, emphasizing questions of colonialism.

1752. Robertson, Claire. GA WOMEN AND SOCIOECONOMIC CHANGE IN ACCRA, GHANA. Hafkin, Nancy J. and Bay, Edna G., eds. *Women in Africa: Studies in Social and Economic Change*(Stanford, Ca.: Stanford U. Pr., 1976): 111-133. The Ga women of Ussher Town in Accra, Ghana, had been highly successful as traders of fish, vegetables, and small luxury items since the late 19th century. By the 1960's, they exercised greater economic independence from their husbands and were less cooperative in sharing information with them about their business dealings. However, women have not been able to make a success of their independence, and their position in relation to men has worsened as men have begun to earn salaries. Trading conditions have deteriorated due to the growth of monopolies in the fish and cloth trade. Because husbands are less willing to fulfill their support obligations, women have been saddled with the added financial burden of their children's education. Interviews and secondary sources; 2 tables, 16 notes. S. Tomlinson-Brown

1753. Simensen, Jarle. KAKOENS BETYDNING I GHANAS HISTORIE I DET 20 ÅRHUNDRE [The importance of cocoa in Ghana's history in the 20th century]. *Internasjonal Politikk [Norway] 1977 (2B): 395-412.* Cultivation of cocoa began in Ghana in the 1880's and has been a staple of foreign trade since 1906. The cocoa trade was then controlled by British companies, with regional control in the hands of the farmers. The trade organization was complicated, especially in the 1930's when the government intervened in a period of low prices. A boycott in the 1930's failed; however, an anticolonial boycott in 1937 was more successful and was the basis for the independence movement during and after World War II. The victory of the Convention People's party and Kwame Nkrumah's premiership led to the first black cabinet in control in Africa. Cocoa has been used as a base for government revenues. Troubles began in the 1960's with a decline in prices and was responsible for a military coup and the fall of Nkrumah.
R. E. Lindgren/S

1754. Smertin, Iu. UROKI RAZVITIIA [Lessons of development]. *Aziia i Afrika Segodnia [USSR] 1982 (3): 17-19.* Ghana has probably tried more models of development and forms of government than any other African state and today faces another decision, in which the consciousness of the people pushes for more change and social progress.

1755. Southall, Roger J. FARMERS, TRADERS AND BROKERS IN THE GOLD COAST COCOA ECONOMY. *Can. J. of African Studies [Canada] 1978 12(2): 185-212.* Analyzes the Gold Coast economy between the wars. It became a supplier of raw materials by exporting cocoa. The challenge of cocoa farmers to expatriate capital became effective, 1937-38, through a united front of producers and brokers. 61 notes. G. E. Pergl

1756. Steel, William F. FEMALE AND SMALL-SCALE EMPLOYMENT UNDER MODERNIZATION IN GHANA. *Econ. Development and Cultural Change 1981 30(1): 153-165.* Examines the effect of large-scale industrialization on female and small-scale employment in Ghana. Ghana's industrial policies, sectoral absorption of increased female labor supply, and the role of female employment in small-scale manufacturing are discussed in detail. Concludes that "Ghana's industrialization policies favoring large-scale, capital-intensive production clearly worked to the disadvantage of small-scale female employment." 5 tables, 19 notes. J. W. Thacker, Jr.

1757. Stevens, Chris. IN SEARCH OF THE ECONOMIC KINGDOM: THE DEVELOPMENT OF ECONOMIC RELATIONS BETWEEN GHANA AND THE U.S.S.R. *J. of Developing Areas 1974 9(1): 3-26.* Ghana, with large debts even after repudiation of some of the questionable ones incurred by Nkrumah, suffers severe adverse trade movements, the cause of 80% of the national debt. After the first trade agreement with the Soviet Union in 1960, a maximum level of $61 million was reached in 1965, but that still was only 8% of Ghana's total trade that year. Realizing their economic dependence on cocoa, Ghanaian administrators proposed four solutions: increase cocoa demand in traditional markets, control supply, develop new uses for cocoa, or develop new markets. Having met with little success in the first three proposed solutions, the Ghanaians turned to new markets and to the second largest consumer of cocoa. That failed to work satisfactorily since the Soviets expected cocoa contracts based upon the preceding year's price. The Soviets nevertheless provided foreign aid to Ghana in various forms. This aid was criticized as expensive and inefficient and even the quality of Soviet education was questioned. 7 tables, 51 notes.
O. W. Eads, Jr.

1758. Struthers, John. INFLATION IN GHANA (1966-78): A PERSPECTIVE ON THE MONETARIST V STRUCTURALIST DEBATE. *Development and Change [Netherlands] 1981 12(2): 177-214.* Places the monetarist-versus-structuralist debate on inflation in developing nations within the context of a single country, Ghana, and concludes that reliance on traditional demand-management policies to the exclusion of structural change will not rid the Ghanaian system of its financial problems.

1759. Szule, Pwa Ewa. PRODUCTION COOPERATIVES IN GHANA—THE KOMENDA REGION. *Hist. of Agric. [India] 1980 2(2): 68-90.* During the 1960's, a cooperative agricultural movement developed in Ghana. In the Komenda region, the government constructed a sugar refinery and organized cooperatives. The cooperatives dispensed seed, educated farmers about sugar cane cultivation, and provided transportation of the crop to the refinery. In return, the farmers were to develop new lands for cultivation. The cooperatives enabled farmers to benefit economically from a crop which they could not raise individually because of limited resources. Since the cooperative was similar to the social and political organization of the tribe, it became a stable and popular economic organization. Secondary sources; 12 tables, 18 notes. R. D. Hurt

1760. Thomas, Roger G. FORCED LABOUR IN BRITISH WEST AFRICA: THE CASE OF THE NORTHERN TERRITORIES OF THE GOLD COAST 1906-1927. *J. of African Hist. [Great Britain] 1973 14(1): 79-103.* Refutes the argument that forced labor in British West Africa did not extend to recruitment for commercial companies. Between 1906 and 1924 the government associated recruitment for public works with the privately owned mines of the Northern Territories of the Gold Coast due to the reluctance of local labor to work underground. The practice ceased only when Sir William Simpson revealed the high death rate among laborers. Primary and secondary sources; note. C. Hopkins

1761. VanHear, Nick. CHILD LABOUR AND THE DEVELOPMENT OF CAPITALIST AGRICULTURE IN GHANA. *Development and Change [Netherlands] 1982 13(4): 499-514.*

Politics

1762. Ablorh-Odjidja, E. GHANA: THE REVOLUTION THAT NEVER WAS. *Crisis 1982 89(1): 22-25.* In 1957, Ghana became the envy of Africa by declaring independence under Kwame Nkrumah. The first of a series of coups occurred in 1966, replacing Nkrumah's government with corruption, mismanagement, and instability. The latest overthrow in December 1981 will not correct Ghana's problems unless intelligent and committed leaders emerge to promote healing.
A. G. Belles

1763. Abramov, V. and Malysheva, N. GANA NA POROGA SOTSIAL'NYKH PEREMEN [Social changes in Ghana]. *Mirovaia Ekonomika i Mezhdunarodnye Otnosheniia [USSR] 1982 (7): 91-94.* Examines the military coup and its effect on political and economic life in Ghana in 1981.

1764. Adekson, J. 'Bayo. ARMY IN A MULTI-ETHNIC SOCIETY. *Armed Forces and Soc. 1976 2(2): 251-272.* Discusses race relations in the military of Ghana in the 1950's and 1960's, emphasizing the policies of Kwame Nkrumah.

1765. Aluko, Olajide. AFTER NKRUMAH: CONTINUITY AND CHANGE IN GHANA'S FOREIGN POLICY. *Issue 1975 5(1): 55-62.* Though there have been some changes in Ghana's foreign policy since the overthrow of Dr. Kwame Nkrumah's regime in 1966, there have also been elements of continuity. S

1766. Ametewee, Victor. THE ECONOMIC ROOTS OF THE INTER-CLAN STRUGGLE FOR POWER AMONG THE BATTOR-EWE OF GHANA AND THE POLITICS OF COLONIAL AND POST-COLONIAL ADMINISTRATION IN LOCAL GOVERNMENT. *J. of African-Afro-American Affairs 1979 3(1): 91-100.* Traces the conflict between five parti-clan kinship groups within the Battor-Ewe in Ghana, 1907-66, spawned by disagreement over property rights and the involvement of the colonial government and later the national government in these as yet unresolved conflicts.

1767. Asante, S. K. B. THE NEGLECTED ASPECTS OF THE ACTIVITIES OF THE GOLD COAST ABORIGINES RIGHTS PROTECTION SOCIETY. *Phylon 1975 36(1): 32-45.* The Gold Coast Aborigines Rights Protection Society (ARPS) was formed in 1898 as a protest movement against the local government's Lands Bill of 1897, but it then spread its activities outward and became a much broader African political protest movement. This article discusses the extra-Gold Coast activities of the organization, with particular emphasis on its steady contacts with the anti-imperialists and Pan-Africanists abroad and culminating in its participation in the 1945 Pan-African Congress in Manchester, England. At the 1945 Pan-African Congress, the ARPS succeeded in gaining support from Kwame Nkrumah, who eventually became one of the most tenacious fighters for freedom and independence in the Gold Coast. But this alliance was short-lived; the middle class intellectuals who supported the ARPS were not as committed to full-scale revolutionary effort as was Nkrumah, and the society shortly declined as an important political force in the Gold Coast. Based on primary and secondary sources; 46 notes. B. A. Glasrud

1768. Asante, S. K. B. THE POLITICS OF CONFRONTATION: THE CASE OF KOBINA SEKYI AND THE COLONIAL SYSTEM IN GHANA. *Universitas [Ghana] 1977 6(2): 15-38.* A search for the intellectual and political roots of Ghanaian independence in the thought and career of the prolific writer and nationalist Kobina Sekyi (1892-1956). For more than 30 years Sekyi systematically opposed racism, colonial government, and indirect rule and sought to replace them with an indigenous political system. The author emphasizes Seyki's role in challenging the European domination of Ghana's commercial enterprises, in spreading ideas of Pan-Africanism and hence in influencing Nkrumah's ideas and strategies for complete independence in the post-1945 environment. Indeed, by the 1940's many of the prominent intelligentsia in Ghana had accepted Sekyi's views on the Provincial Council system which gave the chiefs a preponderance in real government whereas they should have been purely figureheads in their localities. In 64 crowded years of political life Sekyi laid the foundations of Ghana's independence, an event he did not live to see. 106 notes. J. J. N. McGurk

1769. Baynham, S. J. THE MILITARY IN GHANAIAN POLITICS. *Army Q. and Defence J. [Great Britain] 1976 106(4): 428-439.*

1770. Baynham, Simon. CIVILIAN RULE AND THE COUP D'ETAT: THE CASE OF BUSIA'S GHANA. *J. of the Royal United Services Inst. for Defence Studies [Great Britain] 1978 123(3): 27-33.* Discusses the effect of relations between civilian politicians and the military on Ghanaian politics, 1966-72.

1771. Bening, R. B. LOCATION OF DISTRICT ADMINISTRATIVE CAPITALS IN THE NORTHERN TERRITORIES OF THE GOLD COAST (1897-1951). *Bull. de l'Inst. Fondamental d'Afrique Noire [Senegal] 1975 37(3): 646-666.* In the Northern Territories the selection of district capitals between 1897 and 1951 was made with a view to establishing a network of equally distributed posts to keep in touch with the people and to keep trade from being diverted into French and German territories. Large commercial towns on trade routes and those in the midst of hostile areas were chosen. Other considerations were healthy climate, good water, room for expansion, and central location. Based on records of the Colonial Office in the British Public Records Office; 3 maps, 52 notes. H. L. Calkin

1772. Bening, Raymond B. EVOLUTION OF THE ADMINISTRATIVE BOUNDARIES OF ASHANTI, 1896-1951. *J. of African Studies 1978 5(2): 123-150.* Descriptive analysis of the many changes in the administrative boundaries of Asante made by British colonial authorities in the Gold Coast (Ghana) between the time of the British occupation of Kumasi in 1896 and the advent of modern local government. The author ties his chronological treatment of the subject to major changes in British policy, especially the restoration of the Prempeh dynasty and the Asante Confederation. Based on archival materials, particularly British Colonial Office documents relating to the Gold Coast; 7 maps, 89 notes. L. W. Truschel

1773. Bening, R. B. FOUNDATIONS OF THE MODERN NATIVE STATES OF NORTHERN GHANA. *Universitas [Ghana] 1975 5(1): 116-138.* Discusses how the disintegrating kingdoms of northern Ghana were reconstituted and hitherto independent settlements welded together to form native states under colonial domination. These states are now entrenched as traditional areas. The pre-1933 native states were ruled by the paramount chiefs under the Protectorate and the foundations were then laid for a perfect transition from direct to indirect rule. As petty chiefdoms were consolidated into native and subordinate native authorities, these became the units of local government until 1951. The basic loyalties of the people were still essentially local. The institution of chieftaincy fluctuated with changing regimes and with political and military conditions in Ghana as a whole. Primary sources; 7 maps, 86 notes. J. J. N. McGurk

1774. Bennett, Valerie Plave. THE MOTIVATION FOR MILITARY INTERVENTION: THE CASE OF GHANA. *Western Pol. Q. 1973 26(4): 659-674.* Contrary to current literature on the preconditions and motivations for military intervention, the salient factor leading to the coup d'etat of 1972 was the government's refusal to accede to the financial demands of the military in the face of economic decay.

1775. Brown, David. GHANA: FROM PROTEST TO PARTICIPATION. *Contemporary Rev. [Great Britain] 1979 234(1360): 237-244.* Considers political change and economic conditions in Ghana, 1966-79, and explains why the present military regime is being forced out of office by a civilian government.

1776. Brown, David. THE POLITICAL RESPONSE TO IMMISERATION: A CASE STUDY OF RURAL GHANA. *Genève-Afrique [Switzerland] 1980 18(1): 55-74.* Explains the quiescence of the primarily Ewe peoples of the Volta region in southeastern Ghana despite economic hardship. Instead of creating an ideological response, immiseration brought demands for changes in personnel rather than in political institutions and to an idealization of the Nkrumah regime and the immediate postcolonial past. Based on interviews, election statistics, and secondary literature; 2 maps, 2 tables, 50 notes. B. S. Fetter

1777. Callaway, Barbara. NATIONAL-LOCAL LINKAGES IN GHANA. *African Rev. [Tanzania] 1974 4(3): 407-421.* Political processes or linkages flow between the capital and the outlying areas of Ghana in many subtle ways, slowly creating the consciousness of nation. 33 notes. R. T. Brown

1778. Chazan, Naomi. ETHNICITY AND POLITICS IN GHANA. *Pol. Sci. Q. 1982 97(3): 461-485.* Ghanaian politics are influenced by the ethnic plurality of the nation. While some analysts have underrated the ethnic factor, others have overrated it, attributing every political shift to ethnic causes. An analysis of Ghanaian politics for the years 1972-79 reveals that though a pervasive politicization of ethnicity has taken place, ethnicity has little direct effect on politics or on conflict. Rather, allegiance to a political community is brought about by the mechanism of ethnic politics. Table, 81 notes. J. Powell

1779. Chazan, Naomi. GHANAIAN POLITICAL STUDIES IN TRANSITION: A REFLECTION ON SOME RECENT CONTRIBUTIONS. *Development and Change [Netherlands] 1978 9(3): 479-503.*

Examines past works on Ghanaian politics and reviews recent contributions such as Robert Price's *Society and Bureaucracy in Contemporary Ghana* (U. of California Pr., 1975), David and Audrey Smock's *The Politics of Pluralism: A Comparative Study of Ghana and Lebanon* (New York: Elsevier Sci. Publ. Co., 1975), and *Politicians and Soldiers in Ghana, 1966-1972* (London: Frank Cass, 1975), an anthology edited by Dennis Austin and Robin Luckham.

1780. Chazan, Naomi. POLITICAL CULTURE AND SOCIALIZATION TO POLITICS: A GHANAIAN CASE. *Rev. of Pol. 1978 40(1): 3-31.* In the last 20 years, Ghana has undergone four different regimes. The author presents a micropolitical analysis of Ghana's youth, with insights into the reasons for this instability. Reveals the political sophistication of Ghanaian youth but their political orientation springs from a unique African background which differs from the model of Western political units. Concentration of political involvement at the local level and an evaluation by the population of national regimes by their administrative capabilities results. The inability of civilian regimes to reflect basic political values or respond to "local material demands" have been largely responsible for their downfall. 38 notes.
L. E. Ziewacz

1781. Clarke, John Henrik. KWAME NKRUMAH: HIS YEARS IN AMERICA. *Black Scholar 1974 6(2): 9-16.* Chronicles Kwame Nkrumah's activities 1935-63 including his education in America while he did work with the African Students Association and his years of education in Great Britain while working with the Convention People's Party and helping to organize the Pan-African Congress.

1782. Crook, Richard. COLONIAL RULE AND POLITICAL CULTURE IN MODERN ASHANTI. *J. of Commonwealth Pol. Studies [Great Britain] 1973 11(1): 3-27.* Discusses the effect of colonial government on political values in the Offinso district of Asante as revealed through research in that region, 1969-70.

1783. Duffield, Ian. MAKERS OF THE 20TH CENTURY: MARCUS GARVEY AND KWAME NKRUMAH. *Hist. Today [Great Britain] 1981 31(Mar): 24-30.* Studies the roles played by Marcus Garvey and Kwame Nkrumah in one of the most profound changes in modern history, the transformation of Africa from a continent ruled by white colonial masters to a series of independent political states ruled by blacks taking an active part in both their own and world history.

1784. Ekwelieh, Sylvanus A. THE GENESIS OF PRESS CONTROL IN GHANA. *Gazette [Netherlands] 1978 24(3): 196-206.* In 1893, *The Gold Coast People* published an article critical of the British colonial government and its administrators. The government's response was the Newspaper Registration Ordinance (1893), a mild rejoinder which required newspapers to register vital statistics about their operations. For the next 40 years, government and press occasionally tested each other, but a crisis did not emerge until 1934, when the government passed the Criminal Code (Amendment) Ordinance of 1934 which made the publishers of seditious literature criminally liable. When the ordinance was tested shortly thereafter by Nnamdi Azikiwe and I. T. A. Wallace-Johnson, the government chose not to press the issue. After World War II, however, the colonial government's efforts to suppress the press of Kwame Nkrumah resulted in elevating his popularity and ultimately led to Ghanaian independence. W. A. Wiegand

1785. Eluwa, G. I. C. CASELY HAYFORD AND AFRICAN EMANCIPATION. *Pan-African J. [Kenya] 1974 7(2): 111-118.* Casely Hayford, born in 1866 in the Gold Coast, became a widely known teacher, journalist, and lawyer in West Africa. His books included topics such as traditional African land and legal rights. A Pan-Africanist, he led the struggle in West Africa for an end to colonial rule. 24 notes. H. G. Soff

1786. Folson, B. G. D. THE MARXIST PERIOD IN THE DEVELOPMENT OF SOCIALIST IDEOLOGY IN GHANA. *Universitas [Ghana] 1977 6(1): 3-23.* Explores the political philosophy of Kwame Nkrumah through the pages of the *Spark,* the newspaper founded by Nkrumah in 1962. Nkrumah's paper had set itself the task of supplanting "African socialism," then seen as a product of neocolonialism, in favor of a Marxist-Leninist ideology for the Convention People's Party (CCP), whose main tenet and aim was simply the restructuring of Ghanaian society to achieve socialism. When the CCP was overthrown in February 1966, Nkrumah made his ideology clear in a book, *Consciencism,* a program and philosophy for decolonization and development sometimes called Afro-Marxism and more often than not "Nkrumahism." 95 notes. J. J. N. McGurk

1787. Gupta, Anirudha. KWAME NKRUMAH: A REASSESSMENT. *Internat. Studies [India] 1973 12(2): 207-221.* The rule of Kwame Nkrumah in Ghana has been generally criticized, because of his well-publicized failures. These failures received undue attention because they were exposed at a time when many people of varying ideologies were expecting miracles from Nkrumah. The real reason Nkrumah failed was because he let his quest for a dream override all other priorities. He dreamed of one united African nation and let this goal distract him from the internal affairs of Ghana. He united Ghana with an impoverished Guinea purely for ideological reasons, and then began distributing Ghana's funds to aid freedom fighters in other nations, which had a crippling effect on his already poor nation. The real weakness of Nkrumah lay in his idealism. Based on secondary works; 31 notes. G. R. Hess

1788. Hansen, Emmanuel and Collins, Paul. THE ARMY, THE STATE, AND THE "RAWLINGS REVOLUTION" IN GHANA. *African Affairs [Great Britain] 1980 79(314): 3-23.* Examines the significance of the anticorruption coup and military government led by Flight Lieutenant Jerry Rawlings and other junior officers on the political scene, June-September 1979. Discusses whether the coup ushered in a new era. Lists the reasons why, though recent events did not preclude such a possibility, the authors think the army is not capable of radical initiatives in Ghanaian society. J. V. Coutinho

1789. Henige, David. AKAN STOOL SUCCESSION UNDER COLONIAL RULE: CONTINUITY OF CHANGE. *J. of African Hist. [Great Britain] 1975 16(2): 285-301.* An analysis of the supposed regularity and of the mechanics of succession to high political office among the Akan during the colonial period suggests that in the precolonial era there were fewer normative and unvariegated succession and paramountcy patterns and practices than commonly thought. Colonial rule, therefore, was largely uninfluential in changing earlier practices. 78 notes. H. G. Soff/S

1790. Henige, David. SENIORITY AND SUCCESSION IN THE KROBO STOOLS. *Int. J. of African Hist. Studies 1974 7(2): 203-226.* Discusses evidence for a change of succession pattern of the paramount stool of Manya Krobo, an Adangme stool in eastern Ghana. A change from collateral to lineal succession occurred in the office of *konor,* or at least succession had been collateral in the period before the establishment of the office of *konor.* Both external and internal factors contributed to this change. Traces the development of new Krobo notions regarding earlier succession patterns. Primary sources; 104 notes. M. M. McCarthy

1791. Henige, David P. ABREM STOOL: A CONTRIBUTION TO THE HISTORY AND HISTORIOGRAPHY OF SOUTHERN GHANA. *Int. J. of African Hist. Studies 1973 6(1): 1-18.* That the stool of Abrem has not achieved paramount stool status (except for a brief period, 1961-66) while other stools, or states, have achieved independence with less historical justification suggests there is a need for careful examination of the early records. To this end, the author gathers the more important notices of Abrem in the Portuguese, Dutch, and British records and assesses the traditional accounts of Abrem stool history in the light of these records. The necessity of basing decisions on inadequate accounts and yielding to ambient political exigencies rendered the process dubious for the British. 80 notes, appendix.
R. V. Ritter

1792. Herve, Julia. KWAME NKRUMAH: HIS LAST VIEWS ON AFRICAN STRUGGLE. *Black Scholar 1973 4(10): 24-27.* Analyzes the last message of Kwame Nkrumah prior to his 1972 death in terms of its historical perspective and in light of the achievements of the Organization of African Unity, 1966-72.

1793. Herve, Julia. NKRUMAH'S LAST THOUGHTS ON AFRICAN UNITY. *Afriscope [Nigeria] 1973 3(5): 27-29; 40.* A review of Kwame Nkrumah's (1909-72) posthumous *Revolutionary Path.* Nkrumah indicated that the Organization of African Unity (OAU) was merely an "expression of bourgeois nationalism." A new revolutionary purification is necessary to unify Africa. Illus. G. O. Gagnon

1794. Hettne, Björn. SOLDIERS AND POLITICS: THE CASE OF GHANA. *J. of Peace Res. [Norway] 1980 17(2): 173-193.* The politics of the succession of military coups d'état in Ghana represent an illuminating case of militarization processes in an underdeveloped society. The main reasons Kwame Nkrumah's regime fell in 1966 were to be found in the inner dynamics of Ghanaian political, ethnic, and class contradictions, strengthened by personal rivalries. Foreign interests were more than sympathetic to the overthrow, the new regime more than willing to accommodate them, and the coup thus represented a major change in the ideological Great Power struggle over Africa. With Ghana's decreasing international significance, external factors also came to represent a decreasing influence over successive internal conflicts and repeated military coups. The author refutes the military's reputation as modernizing developers and shows how the distinction between civilian and military becomes blurred in the process of struggle and changing administrations. J/S

1795. Hitchens, Diddy R. M. TOWARDS POLITICAL STABILITY IN GHANA: A REJOINDER IN THE UNION GOVERNMENT DEBATE. *African Studies Rev. 1979 22(1): 171-176.* Plans to create a new constitution for Ghana as a result of the 1972 coup have had little real effect on the issues that led to earlier political turmoil because the problems were economic rather than constitutional. 2 notes, biblio. R. T. Brown

1796. Jeffries, Richard. THE GHANAIAN ELECTIONS OF 1979. *African Affairs [Great Britain] 1980 79(316): 397-414.* The "revolution" of Flight Lieutenant Jerry Rawlings aimed more at a moral than a structural transformation, primarily concerned to reassert the principle of popular accountability in Ghanaian politics and public life. Rawlings therefore did not interfere with the political process, and the success of his party in the elections was only indirectly due to the immense popularity which he and his manner of government enjoyed. The elections were determined as usual by communal identifications rather than ideological differences. 7 notes. J. V. Coutinho

1797. Kwaku, Ken. TRADITION AND COLONIALISM IN RURAL GHANA: LOCAL POLITICS IN HAVE, VOLTA REGION. *Can. J. of African Studies [Canada] 1976 10(1): 71-86.* Traces the dynamics of local politics in a small rural Ghanaian village during the colonial era and discusses the allocation of resources and the emergence of local political conflicts. The decolonization period (1948-56) had an impact on the political structure of the local community. The class structure heightened political rivalries which contributed to the persistence of local underdevelopment. Yet at the same time political rivalries led to reconciliation of internal differences and thus assisted in promoting local development. Based on interviews, theses, Ghana National Archives, government documents, and secondary sources; 44 notes. J/S

1798. Luckham, Robin. IMPERIALISM, LAW AND STRUCTURAL DEPENDENCE: THE GHANA LEGAL PROFESSION. *Development and Change [Netherlands] 1978 9(2): 201-243.* The legal system of Ghana between 1890 and 1970 expresses all the contradictions of colonial subordination and the arrival of international trade and foreign capital.

1799. Manu, Yaw. GHANA'S AFRICAN POLITICS: 1958-1963. *Universitas [Ghana] 1975 4(2): 143-152.* In 1958, just after independence, Kwame Nkrumah said that without rapid decolonization of Africa, Ghana's independence was meaningless. In 1961 he annunciated a corollary, that African unity was essential to the development of the continent. These two ideas were the cornerstones of Ghana's African policy until 1963. Without decolonization, Ghana, overshadowed by the colonial presence of greater powers, would have little security or opportunity for a separate foreign policy; without African unity, few new nations would be able to avoid the encroachment of European powers. The Suez crisis in 1956 and the Franco-Algerian war underscored Nkrumah's point, but it was not until 1963, with the foundation of the Organization of African Unity, that Ghana at last succeeded in creating the framework for executing its policy. 27 notes. J. W. Leedom

1800. Martínez, Aurora Cristina. EL NEOCOLONIALISMO EN KWAME N'KRUMAH [Neocolonialism in the thought of Kwame Nkrumah]. *Investigación Econ. [Mexico] 1981 40(158): 99-117.* A conception of imperialism based exclusively on the phenomenon of neocolonialism as a new form of domination prevented Nkrumah from truly understanding the importance of working-class interests in the process of national liberation, and the correlation of the forces of capitalism and socialism as antagonistic systems. Nkrumah fought against the forces that oppressed his people, but lack of understanding of the true nature of those forces resulted in failure to achieve true liberation. 33 notes. J. V. Coutinho

1801. Martyshin, O. V. O POSLEDNIKH KNIGAKH KVAME NKRUMY [The later works of Kwame Nkrumah]. *Narody Azii i Afriki [USSR] 1973 (3): 157-167.* Considers Nkrumah's political development, from African nationalist leader to fighter for scientific socialism, as shown in his works published after the 1967 coup d'état ended the move toward socialism in Ghana.

1802. McCain, James A. ATTITUDES TOWARD SOCIALISM, POLICY, AND LEADERSHIP IN GHANA. *African Studies Rev. 1979 22(1): 149-169.* Provides results of a social survey to determine attitudes on a variety of political issues. Results suggest that Ghanaians have been little affected by the ideologies of Nkrumah and have sophisticated and somewhat cynical political attitudes. Based on interviews; 20 tables, 16 notes, ref. R. T. Brown

1803. Monfils, Barbara S. A MULTIFACETED IMAGE: KWAME NKRUMAH'S EXTRINSIC RHETORICAL STRATEGIES. *J. of Black Studies 1977 7(3): 313-330.* In the early years of Ghana's independence, Kwame Nkrumah, realizing that Ghanaians had to attain a psychological sense of freedom as well as political independence, set about cultivating symbols of national identity through his dress, his presence at certain traditional ceremonies, and his symbolic associations. Nkrumah was given wide exposure as a heroic leader, a chief, and a warrior; in addition, events in his life were compared to those in Jesus Christ's life. A vague philosophy, Nkrumahism, was also promoted. After the 1960 constitution was adopted, however, Nkrumah relied less on generating political support in this manner. 5 notes, biblio. D. C. Neal

1804. Offiong, Daniel A. GARVEYISM AND NKRUMAHISM: THE QUEST FOR BLACK IRREDENTISM. *Pan-African J. [Kenya] 1975 8(1): 89-102.* Marcus Garvey's philosophy of racial pride and African nationalism is fundamentally related to black irredentism in Africa. Kwame Nkrumah of Ghana was a disciple of Garvey and there are many similarities between Garveyism and Nkrumahism. The author considers in particular their concern with the degradation of the black race by the distortion of its history and their wish for a United States of Africa as an instrument of restoring black pride. Such ideas have had a significant effect on the present generation of black Africans and Americans. 60 notes. S

1805. Okadigbo, Miriam. CONSCIENCISM AS THE KEY TO NKRUMAH. *UMOJA: A Scholarly J. of Black Studies 1978 2(1): 41-52.* Examines Kwame Nkrumah's book *Consciencism* (1964) as a key to the thought which put him at the head of West Africa's anti-imperialist, antiracist and nationalist liberation movement, 1965-72.

1806. Owusu, Maxwell. ECONOMIC NATIONALISM, PAN-AFRICANISM AND THE MILITARY: GHANA'S NATIONAL REDEMPTION COUNCIL. *Africa Today 1975 22(1): 31-50.* Extensive analysis of the National Redemption Council which has ruled Ghana since 1972. The military style of leadership has produced trade surpluses, a sound monetary system, the abolition of "osagyefoism," a campaign against various types of official corruption, and support for economic Pan-Africanism. The only question is whether Ghanaians will accept the necessary sacrifices. Based on Ghanaian sources; table, 37 notes. G. O. Gagnon

1807. Peil, Margaret. GHANA'S ALIENS. *Int. Migration Rev. 1974 8(3): 367-381.* Discusses the roles of economics, skilled labor, and ethnic stereotypes in the immigration policy of Ghana, 1960-70's, emphasizing attitudes toward Nigerians.

1808. Pobee, John S. THE FISH AND THE COCK IN GHANA, 1949-1966: A PROBLEM OF ADJUSTMENT. *Kyrkohistorisk Årsskrift [Sweden] 1978 78: 390-396.* Describes the relationship between the Christian Church of the Gold Coast and the Convention People's Party. The church was slow to accommodate to African culture and rebuked the party for its totalitarian socialism. 9 notes, biblio.

1809. Reeck, Darrell. THE CASTLE AND THE UMBRELLA: SOME RELIGIOUS DIMENSIONS OF KWAME NKRUMAH'S RELIGIOUS LEADERSHIP IN GHANA. *Africa Today 1976 23(4): 7-27.* Analyzes Kwame Nkrumah's efforts to create symbolic legitimation of Ghana. Through an increased appeal to tradition, Nkrumah might have provided an appropriate civil religion but his choice of charismatic and Marxist symbols prevented wide acceptance of normative orientations for Ghana. Secondary sources; 58 notes, biblio.
G. O. Gagnon

1810. Robertson, A. F. ANTHROPOLOGY AND GOVERNMENT IN GHANA. *African Affairs [Great Britain] 1975 74(294): 51-59.* Discusses the relationship between anthropology and government based on references in various textbooks 1705-1971. As anthropological knowledge developed, so too did government expertise. In recent years anthropologists have been reluctant to get involved; they are needed and should not be afraid. 46 notes. H. G. Soff

1811. Robertson, A. F. HISTORIES AND POLITICAL OPPOSITION IN AHAFO, GHANA. *Africa [Great Britain] 1973 43(1): 41-58.* Examines the relation between conflicting historical accounts given by Ahafo chiefs and current political divisions in Ahafo and suggests that the histories are purposive and contingent upon political issues.

1812. Rothchild, Donald and Gyimah-Boadi, E. GHANA'S RETURN TO CIVILIAN RULE. *Africa Today 1981 28(1): 3-16.* Speculates on Ghanaian prospects for stable civilian rule. Concludes that Hilla Limann's government faces the conflict between high expectations and minimal resources with a narrow margin of error. The military and portions of the elite are waiting in the wings. Based on periodical and secondary sources; table, 22 notes. G. O. Gagnon

1813. Rothchild, Donald. MILITARY REGIME PERFORMANCE: AN APPRAISAL OF THE GHANA EXPERIENCE, 1972-78. *Comparative Pol. 1980 12(4): 459-479.* Discusses recent cross-national research of military regime performance focusing on the military government of Colonel (later General) Ignatius K. Acheampong. Regime effectiveness is linked to performance first in relation to social science criteria and then in relation to the regime's ability to achieve its own specified goals of self-reliance and regional reallocation. Based on budget figures of the Accountant and Comptroller General's Department and newspapers; table, 56 notes. M. A. Kascus

1814. Shaloff, Stanley. THE AFRICANIZATION CONTROVERSY IN THE GOLD COAST, 1926-1946. *African Studies Rev. 1974 17(3): 493-506.* Individual cases illuminate the difficulties caused by the Africanization of the civil service in Ghana, 1926-46, and the attempts of the indigenous population to gain equal status with the Europeans.

1815. Shaloff, Stanley. THE CAPE COAST ASAFO COMPANY RIOT OF 1932. *Int. J. of African Hist. Studies 1974 7(4): 591-607.* The *asafo* riot of 1932 was not merely a manifestation of traditional violence between rival military formations in the turbulent precincts of Cape Coast, Ghana. The disagreement within the local elite as to how best to react to the 1925 Order in Council, which authorized the town to elect one municipal representative, gave rise to bitter factional strife. Primary and secondary sources; 59 notes. M. M. McCarthy

1816. Shaloff, Stanley. THE INCOME TAX, INDIRECT RULE, AND THE DEPRESSION: THE GOLD COAST RIOTS OF 1931. *Cahiers d'Études Africaines [France] 1974 14(2): 359-375.* An informal coalition of educated coastal Africans, European merchants, and some lesser chiefs succeeded in blocking the proposed introduction of direct taxes in urban and rural areas by inciting popular violence against the colonial government. Thus, Governor Ransford Slater (1927-32) was unable to impose either the taxes or further indirect rule on the Nigerian model on urban Africans. Based on materials found in the Ghana National Archives (ADM 1 and 12), the Public Records Office (CO 96), printed primary sources, and secondary materials; 63 notes.
B. S. Fetter

1817. Silver, Harry. GOING FOR BROKERS: POLITICAL INNOVATION AND STRUCTURAL INTEGRATION IN A CHANGING ASHANTI COMMUNITY. *Comparative Pol. Studies 1981 14(2): 233-263.* Describes, at the local level, the creation of new positions to perform traditional functions and cooptation of long-established roles in the service of modernization and assesses these local innovations in the context of their articulation with state and national systems over the past century.

1818. Simensen, Jarle. THE ASAFO OF KWAHU, GHANA: A MASS MOVEMENT FOR LOCAL REFORM UNDER COLONIAL RULE. *Int. J. of African Hist. Studies 1975 8(3): 383-406.* The asafo is the best documented of the infrequently studied grass roots movements in the Gold Coast. Originally a military formation of commoners, it was transformed by educated leaders and by the modernization process into a new instrument for mass political action against abuses by Kwahu elders who "capitalized on their traditional privileges under modern conditions." The effort to establish representative democracy was blocked by British colonial support of indigenous custom. Based on Ghana National Archives and secondary sources; 2 tables. 75 notes.
W. R. Hively

1819. Simensen, Jarle. RURAL MASS ACTION IN THE CONTEXT OF ANTI-COLONIAL PROTEST: THE ASAFO MOVEMENT OF AKIM ABUAKWA, GHANA. *Can. J. of African Studies [Canada] 1974 8(1): 25-41.* In times of economic distress and as a result of conflicts resulting from modernization and colonialism in the 1910's-50's, an organized body of commoners under joint leadership protested against their chiefs in their dual role as local exploiters and colonial agents.

1820. Tunteng, P. Kiven. KWAME NKRUMAH AND THE AFRICAN REVOLUTION. *Civilisations [Belgium] 1973-1974 23-24(3/4): 233-247.* Nkrumah envisioned an African revolution as early as 1935. His failure to accomplish it was not due to a lack of determination on his part but to his colleagues' seeing it as a threat to their leadership positions and to the fact that conditions which normally favor revolutions were not present in Africa. 34 notes. H. L. Calkin

1821. Twumasi, Yaw. J. B. DANQUAH: TOWARDS AN UNDERSTANDING OF THE SOCIAL AND POLITICAL IDEAS OF A GHANAIAN NATIONALIST AND POLITICIAN. *African Affairs [Great Britain] 1978 77(306): 73-88.* J. B. Danquah was a traditionalist idealist who was a major political opponent of Kwame Nkrumah during the 1950's. He was a scholar and of royal heritage. The author discusses his ideology, which remained constant for years, in terms of social, religious, and political theory. 21 notes. H. G. Soff

1822. Twumasi, Yaw. PRESS FREEDOM AND NATIONALISM UNDER COLONIAL RULE IN THE GOLD COAST (GHANA). *J. of the Hist. Soc. of Nigeria [Nigeria] 1974 7(3): 499-520.* Analyzes the political protest over the Sedition Ordinance of 1934 in the Gold Coast to show how the press, particularly the newspaper editors and proprietors, attempted to make the nationalist movement more radical.

1823. Verdon, Michel. THE STRUCTURE OF TITLED OFFICES AMONG THE ABUTIA EWE. *Africa [Great Britain] 1979 49(2): 159-171.* Though many have regarded the Ewe people as homogeneous in the 19th and 20th centuries, the author contends that the northern areas were quite distinct from the southern. Concerning the political organization of the Abutia Ewe of Ghana, he discusses chiefship and the titled offices around the village chief. Attention is focused on the religious aspect of stools, enshrined ritual objects embodying the chief's power, and Abutia offices. Secondary sources; fig., biblio.
P. J. Taylorson

1824. Werlin, Herbert H. THE CONSEQUENCES OF CORRUPTION: THE GHANAIAN EXPERIENCE. *Pol. Sci. Q. 1973 88(1): 71-85.* Political corruption in America in the past has not retarded economic development. In view of the American experience, some scholars have minimized the extent to which corruption might retard the development of emerging nations. The case of Ghana, however, suggests that political corruption functions differently in the United States than it does in developing nations. In the United States, illegally gained money generally goes back into internal production, while corrupt profits in Ghana are usually invested abroad or spent on wasteful imports. Further, incentive for profit making under US capitalism may induce corruption, but it also facilitates the performance of work, while in socialist Ghana corrupt practices often result in the loss of goods and services. Finally, while US political machines might be corrupt, they still serve a political function and are based on the legitimacy of the American political system, while in Ghana, corruption undermined the very legitimacy of Kwame Nkrumah's regime and the ideological commitment consistent with the betterment of the public welfare under socialism. 42 notes. B. C. Tharaud

1825. Woronoff, Jon. LE PARTI DE LA CONVENTION DU PEUPLE DU GHANA [The Convention Peoples' Party of Ghana]. *Rev. Française d'Études Pol. Africaines [France] 1973 (86): 34-54.* Studies the theoretical and practical organization and activities of the Convention People's Party (CPP), 1949-66, which has become a model for African political parties today.

1826. Woronoff, Jon. NKRUMAH—THE PROPHET RISEN. *Worldview 1973 16(3): 32-36.* A quasi-obituary of Kwame Nkrumah (1909-72), describing his years of rule in Ghana, 1956-66, his subsequent exile, and the praise evoked from formerly antagonistic Ghanaians by his death. Analyzes his ideology of Pan-Africanism, socialism, and anticolonialism.

1827. Zeff, Eleanor E. NEW DIRECTIONS IN UNDERSTANDING MILITARY AND CIVILIAN REGIMES IN GHANA. *African Studies Rev. 1981 24(1): 49-72.* Through a content analysis of official newspaper editorials in the Ghanaian *Daily Graphic* under two civilian and two military governments, it can be seen that there are significant differences in the policy goals of these two kinds of regimes. Based on the editorials and secondary sources; 14 tables, 7 notes, biblio. R. T. Brown

1828. —. TWO VIEWS ON NKRUMAH'S HERITAGE. *Monthly Rev. 1974 26(6): 39-48.*
Milne, Peter. *pp. 39-41.*
Nwafor, Azinna. *pp. 42-48.* Commentary on Azinna Nwafor (see abstract 116) concerning the position of Kwame Nkrumah in Ghana's history and development.

Society

1829. Bame, K. N. DES ORIGINES ET DU DÉVELOPPEMENT DU "CONCERT-PARTY" AU GHANA [The origin and development of concert-party in Ghana]. *Rev. d'Hist. du Théâtre [France] 1975 27(1): 10-20.* Concert-party is a type of music hall performance whose source is in the tradition of story telling, modified by Western influences. Master Yalley is considered the creator of concert-party in Ghana by his presentations of a one-man show in 1918. The tradition was continued by troupes of traveling actors: the 8 Versatiles in the 1920's, the Deux Bobs et la Fille de la Caroline in the 1930's, the Trio d'Axim from 1937-54, and the Happy Trio from 1937-47, succeeded by the Jovial Jokers until 1952. Two of the most important performers in these troupes were Bob Johnson (real name, Ishmael Johnson) and Bob Cole (real name, Kwasi Axotwe). A second type of concert-party is an outgrowth of popular orchestral groups. Twenty-eight of these guitar orchestras formed the Ghana National Entertainment Association in 1960. 4 notes. H. R. Falk

1830. Bening, R. B. COLONIAL CONTROL AND THE PROVISION OF EDUCATION IN NORTHERN GHANA 1908-1951. *Universitas [Ghana] 1976 5(2): 58-99.* Shows that formal education was innovative and met with many obstacles, and that colonial educational policy was much influenced by political and administrative factors. The author traces the work of the White Fathers in Navrongo. Governor Guggisberg's aim was to attain the educational standards in the government schools already achieved in Asante and the Colony, but standards remained lower than those in the mission schools, where useful craft skills were taught as well as basic English and mathematics. Until 1930 there was increased emphasis on learning through the mother tongue, but organizers felt that Hausa, a lingua franca, should be the medium of instruction. The author then traces the expansion under native administration, 1935-51, giving special emphasis to the White Fathers' ten-year plan, special schools for the sons of chiefs, and the staffing and training of teachers. The real impetus for universal primary education and of advanced secondary schooling came from the native authorities and the Northern Territorial Council. It was not until 1951 that a secondary school was opened at Tamale, when an elected African government politically integrated the protectorate with Asante and the Colony. 221 notes. J. J. N. McGurk

1831. Bonsi, Stephen K. PERSISTENCE AND CHANGE IN TRADITIONAL MEDICAL PRACTICE IN GHANA. *Int. J. of Contemporary Sociol. 1977 14(1-2): 27-38.* The process of reconceiving reality in the effort to make traditional medicine acceptable in a rapidly changing social situation could result in alienating the very tradition which is being preserved, because Western techniques which the new healers are adopting are likely to alienate traditional medicine from the populace.

1832. Breidenbach, Paul S. MAAME HARRIS GRACE TANI AND PAPA NACKABAH: THE INDEPENDENT CHURCH LEADERS IN THE GOLD COAST, 1914-1958. *Int. J. of African Hist. Studies 1979 12(4): 581-614.* The Twelve Apostles Church of Ghana was created out of the Prophet Harris movement of the early 20th century. Maame Tani and Papa Nackabah were traditional spiritualists who, after conversion by Prophet Harris, devoted the rest of their lives to the construction of the largest independent church in West Africa, which successfully blended Western and traditional beliefs. Through skillful dealings with the colonial establishment they preserved their independence. Based on interviews and the Ghana National Archives; 52 notes, appendix. R. T. Brown

1833. Breidenbach, Paul S. "SUNSUM EDWUMA": THE LIMITS OF CLASSIFICATION AND THE SIGNIFICANCE OF AN EVENT. *Social Res. 1979 46(1): 63-87.* Contrasts two forms of inquiry used in a 1970-71 study on the *sunsum edwuma* ("working with spirits") healing ritual of the Ghanaian healing movement begun in 1913, the Church of the Twelve Apostles, whose results demonstrate the inadequacy of simple classificatory inquiry and the importance of an appreciation of events whose interpretations are axiomatic to the participants.

1834. Breidenbach, Paul S. THE TWO ELDERS: MAAME HARRIS "GRACE" TANI AND PAPA KWESI "JOHN" NACKABAH. *Tarikh [Nigeria] 1981 7(1): 33-46.* Traces the religious careers of Maame Harris "Grace" Tani (died 1958) and Papa Kwesi "John" Nackabah (died 1947) in Ghana, focusing on their role in the founding of the Twelve Apostles Church of Ghana in 1918 and their activities until about 1939. Comments on the African experience of Christianity both in independent African churches and in European missionary organizations during the colonial period.

1835. Brydon, Lynne. WOMEN AT WORK: SOME CHANGES IN FAMILY STRUCTURE IN AMEDZOFE-AVATIME, GHANA. *Africa [Great Britain] 1979 49(2): 97-111.* Examines developments in family, child rearing, and residential group structure in the village of Amedzofe-Avatime and outlines the economic and social factors that have resulted in the practice of fostering. Discusses various models that have been proposed to account for women's migration in West Africa in the 20th century and notes similarities between Avatime and West Indian fostering patterns. The Avatime practice indicates the versatility of the formal kin group in adapting to meet new externally imposed socioeconomic conditions. Based mainly on author's field research; 21 notes, biblio., appendix. P. J. Taylorson

1836. Callaway, Barbara J. WOMEN IN GHANA. Iglitzin, Lynne B. and Ross, Ruth, eds. *Women in the World* (Santa Barbara, Calif.: Clio Books, 1976): 189-201. "In Ghana, the superimposition of Western values under the colonial aegis disrupted the whole fabric of traditional societies." Before the British colonization of southern Ghana, women were an important and independent group in the matrilinear society. The division of labor was equal, with no hierarchical constructs imposed on tasks. Outside of certain responsibilities, such as feeding their children,

women were free to earn profits from their labor or trade and to run their households; they were also entitled to inherit property. After the British conquest, Ghanaian men were recruited to work the colonial network, and only boys were sent to colonial schools. Thus, the division of labor was upset; women were isolated from the job market and were forced to depend on the men's earnings. The Convention People's Party (1952-66) formed an auxiliary party to involve women in the political process, the National Council of Ghana Women (NCGW). Ideologically and economically controlled by the CPP, the NCGW did not succeed in restoring many lost rights to women. It concentrated on maintaining traditional marriage laws that would hold men responsible for children they fathered. Primary and secondary sources; 19 notes.
J. Holzinger

1837. Chick, John D. THE ASHANTI TIMES: A FOOTNOTE TO GHANAIAN PRESS HISTORY. *African Affairs [Great Britain] 1977 76(302): 80-94.* A history of the *Ashanti Times,* a corporation newspaper in Ghana. Sir Edward Spears, head of Ashanti Goldfields gold mining company, established the newspaper in 1947 as a house organ. He apparently had dreams of national circulation, but they came to naught. The *Ashanti Times* gave Spears a direct voice in public affairs. His dislike for socialism changed when colonial rule ended and governmental censorship began. Other newspapers collapsed, but Spears rode out the Kwame Nkrumah years. The successor government brought him to his knees and Spears faded away as abruptly as his newspaper. 65 notes. V. L. Human

1838. Ekwelie, Sylvanus A. GHANA: LEGAL CONTROL OF THE NATIONALIST PRESS, 1880-1950. *Transafrican J. of Hist. [Kenya] 1976 5(2): 148-159.* An assessment of colonial government ordinances designed to control the press in the Gold Coast. Although several laws of restriction did exist, the British were lax in their enforcement and Africans had relative journalistic freedom. 36 notes. H. G. Soff

1839. Grindal, Bruce T. ISLAMIC AFFILIATIONS AND URBAN ADAPTATION: THE SISALA MIGRANT IN ACCRA, GHANA. *Africa [Great Britain] 1973 43(4): 333-346.* Explains the high incidence of Islamic affiliation during the 20th century among traditionally non-Islamic Sisala migrants in the community of Mamobi in Accra, Ghana; the religious affiliation is related to alienation in a foreign urban environment and the need to achieve a common identity.

1840. Gutkind, Peter C. W. THE LABOURING POOR AND URBAN CLASS FORMATION. *Int. J. of African Hist. Studies 1979 12(1): 83-95.* Review article on R. R. Sandbrook and J. Arn, *The Labouring Poor and Urban Class Formation: The Case of Greater Accra*(Monograph Series No. 12, Centre for Developing Area Studies, McGill University, Montreal, 1977). Because Sandbrook and Arn have elected not to use a diachronic approach, there is no way to assess the real significance of their survey results. Secondary sources; 13 notes.
M. M. McCarthy

1841. Head, Sydney W. BRITISH COLONIAL BROADCASTING POLICIES: THE CASE OF THE GOLD COAST. *African Studies Rev. 1979 22(2): 39-47.* A history of the creation and growth of radio broadcasting in Ghana under the direction of Governor Sir Arnold Hodson. Radio could have been an important tool for colonial control except that it came into use too late and had too little official support. Based on Colonial Office and Gold Coast records; biblio.
R. T. Brown

1842. Head, Sydney W. and Kugblenu, Hohn. GBC-1: A SURVIVAL OF WIRED RADIO IN TROPICAL AFRICA. *Gazette [Netherlands] 1978 24(2): 121-129.* The Ghana Broadcasting Corporation (GBC) has provided subscribers with a nationwide wired radio system which has broadcasted in six African languages and English. The history of the service goes back to 1935. W. A. Wiegand

1843. Herold, Erich. AFRICKÝ UZEL MOUDROSTI [The African knot of wisdom]. *Umění a Řemesla [Czechoslovakia] 1973 (3): 55-60.* Traces the historical and contemporary occurrence of the ornamental motif of the double loop—the "knot of wisdom"— among the Ghanaian Asante. The double-looped "knot amulet" was used similarly in ancient Egypt. Based on printed sources; 15 illus. G. E. Pergl

1844. Howard, Thomas C. WEST AFRICA AND THE AMERICAN SOUTH: NOTES ON JAMES E. K. AGGREY AND THE IDEA OF A UNIVERSITY FOR WEST AFRICA. *J. of African Studies 1975-76 2(4): 445-466.* A study of the idea of a university for Africans as promoted by James Aggrey of the Gold Coast and North Carolina, foremost African educator and founder in 1924 of the Prince of Wales College at Achimota in the Gold Coast. He undertook the difficult task of working within the restricted framework of colonialism, where education was a tool for promoting the interests of the dominant power. He worked as a promoter of the Tuskegee Institute type of education and in association with the Phelps-Stokes Fund of New York, yet he "operated independently and effectively to promote the vision of a new Africa which would include a system of higher education equal in quality to that anywhere in the world." 65 notes. R. V. Ritter

1845. Kalu, Wilhemina J. MODERN GA FAMILY LIFE PATTERNS: A LOOK AT CHANGING MARRIAGE STRUCTURE IN AFRICA. *J. of Black Studies 1981 11(3): 349-352.* The traditional residence pattern of Ga families in Ghana was patrilocal. Modernization has led to new residence patterns—matrilocal kin (most common), patrilocal nuclear (usually well-educated professionals), matrilocal (the newest form, where the woman is financially dominant), and matrilocal-patrilocal (an unstable form found among some new marriage partners). Biblio. R. G. Sherer

1846. Lammen, A. CHIEF SAM EN ZIJN "BACK-TO-AFRICA"-BEWEGING [Chief Sam and his "back-to-Africa" movement]. *Spiegel Hist. [Netherlands] 1979 14(2): 100-106.* In 1913 Alfred Charles Sam (b. 1881) of the English Gold Coast colony formed an organization to transport American blacks to a new life in the Gold Coast. Sam's scheme was profoundly unrealistic but it created great enthusiasm among blacks in Oklahoma, Texas, Kansas, and Arkansas. As many as 6,000 were in some way involved and an emigration camp in Okfuskee County, Oklahoma became the temporary home of 1,000 people. The British government made it clear from the start that they wanted no new immigrants. The American authorities must be faulted for their lack of interest in protecting black Americans. 60 people arrived in Africa in 1915 before the scheme collapsed. Based upon archival and secondary materials; 5 illus. C. W. Wood

1847. Laue, Theodore H. von. ANTHROPOLOGY AND POWER: R. S. RATTRAY AMONG THE ASHANTI. *African Affairs [Great Britain] 1976 75(298): 33-54.* R. Sutherland Rattray was a colonial officer who compiled the first lengthy anthropological studies of the Asante of Ghana. His works, considered thoroughly authoritative when written in the 1920's, are now viewed in their proper perspective. They are riddled with faults. Following a brief survey of his life, the author diagnoses Rattray's writings as a case study in assessing how the power of contending cultures determines the work of anthropologists. 54 notes.
H. G. Soff

1848. Martin, Charles A. SIGNIFICANT TRENDS IN THE DEVELOPMENT OF GHANAIAN EDUCATION. *J. of Negro Educ. 1976 45(1): 46-60.* Survey of education in Ghana since the 16th century, the Seven-Year Plan for Education of the Nkrumah period, which led to free primary education and compulsory secondary education, and the 1966 report of the Education Review Committee. 14 notes.
B. D. Johnson

1849. McCaskie, T. C. ANTI-WITCHCRAFT CULTS IN ASANTE: AN ESSAY IN THE SOCIAL HISTORY OF AN AFRICAN PEOPLE. *Hist. in Africa 1981 8: 125-154.* The social, economic, and political history of three Asante anti-witchcraft cults is discussed. The cults, *domankama, aberewa,* and *hwe me so,* flourished from the late 1870's to the late 1920's. The historical significance of witchcraft as well as these cults is considered, as is the relationship between social history and social anthropology in Africa. Primary sources; 79 notes.
A. C. Drysdale

1850. Okonkwo, Rina. ADELAIDE CASELY HAYFORD: CULTURAL NATIONALIST AND FEMINIST. *Phylon 1981 42(1): 41-51.* Adelaide Casely Hayford (1868-1960) was a prominent cultural nationalist and feminist in the Gold Coast. She organized a technical training school for girls, headed the Ladies' Division of the Universal Negro Improvement Association, and traveled and spoke to refute the stereotype of African barbarism. She combined feminism and cultural nationalism to improve the lives of African women. A. G. Belles

1851. Oppong, Christine. ATTITUDES TO FAMILY SIZE AMONG UNMARRIED JUNIOR CIVIL SERVANTS IN ACCRA. *J. of Asian and African Studies [Netherlands] 1974 9(1/2): 76 -82.* A test of variables concerning attitudes toward family size in Ghana. 4 tables, 3 notes, biblio. R. T. Brown

1852. Oppong, Christine. FROM LOVE TO INSTITUTION: INDICATIONS OF CHANGE IN AKAN MARRIAGE. *J. of Family Hist. 1980 5(2): 197-209.* In the marriages of traditional Akan society in Ghana, love rather than social or economic roles bound the couple. Modernization has given marriage more social and economic duties and diminished the role of love. Biblio. T. W. Smith/S

1853. Popov, V. PROSVESHCHENIE I POLITIKA [Education and politics]. *Aziia i Afrika Segodnia [USSR] 1982 (3): 20-21.* Examines changes in the educational system of Ghana 1972-80.

1854. Robertson, Claire C. THE NATURE AND EFFECTS OF DIFFERENTIAL ACCESS TO EDUCATION IN GA SOCIETY. *Africa [Great Britain] 1977 47(2): 208-219.* Education for girls in Accra, Ghana, in the 19th century, was largely restricted to Sunday school. Up to World War II, it was uncommon to send girls to school since they were needed to help in the home, and there seemed little practical advantage in girls education. By 1960, 66% of the girls were receiving primary education at Ussher Town, as compared with 79% of the boys, and most women felt that girls and boys should be equally educated. But girls' education still has little relationship to job prospects and is inferior in quality and quantity to that of boys. Based on a survey of 220 market women of Central Accra; 2 tables, fig., 21 notes, biblio. R. L. Collison

1855. Schwimmer, Brian. THE ORGANIZATION OF MIGRANT FARMER COMMUNITIES IN SOUTHERN GHANA. *Can. J. of African Studies [Canada] 1980 14(2): 221-238.* In the early 20th century cocoa farmers in the Suhum area of southern Ghana began expanding their settlements into previously uninhabited areas. The new economic conditions allowed new forms of capital accumulation, land tenure, labor organization, and marketing activity to develop which were derived but distinct from traditional patterns. Traditional villages were formed as political alliances among social groups whereas the new settlements became commercial centers serving various production units. Comparison of community and political organization, location, and composition of old and new settlements provides unique examples for the study of economic and political changes in Ghana. Based on fieldwork in the Suhum area, 1970-72; 15 notes. S

1856. Thomas, Roger G. EDUCATION IN NORTHERN GHANA, 1906-1940: A STUDY IN COLONIAL PARADOX. *Int. J. of African Hist. Studies 1974 7(3): 427-467.* There were three phases in the development of administrative policies toward education in the Northern Territories of Ghana until 1940. In the first phase from 1906 to 1919 education was extremely limited, but in the next phase, with the arrival of Governor F. G. Guggisbery, a definite educational policy for the protectorate was established. Greater emphasis was placed on relating education to the rural economy. In the final phase, schools were linked to the new native administrations, though efforts were made to guarantee that the supply of literates did not exceed new job opportunities. Based on official British documents and documents in the Ghana National Archives; map, 3 tables, 190 notes. M. M. Mccarthy

1857. Tiberini, Elvira Stefania. NOTE SULL'ABORTO E LA CONTRACCEZIONE TRA GLI NZEMA DEL GHANA [Abortion and contraception among the Nzema of Ghana]. *Africa [Italy] 1980 35(2): 159-170.* The practice of abortion and contraception is mainly based on the use of plants. Traditional sociopsychological legitimate motivations to abort—incest or other violations of tribal rules—have gradually been replaced by socioeconomic motivations. J/S

1858. Twumasi, Patrick A. HISTORY OF PLURALISTIC MEDICAL SYSTEMS: A SOCIOLOGICAL ANALYSIS OF THE GHANAIAN CASE. *Issue: A Q. J. of Opinion 1979 9(3): 29-34.* Analyzes the various medical systems which have existed in Ghana, focusing on contemporary society, concluding that traditional practices are of continuing value.

1859. Twumasi, Yaw. THE NEWSPAPER PRESS AND POLITICAL LEADERSHIP IN DEVELOPING NATIONS: THE CASE OF GHANA 1964 to 1978. *Gazette [Netherlands] 1980 26(1): 1-16.* Surveys freedom of the press in Ghana from the colonial period. After enjoying relative freedom under the colonial administration, the press was severely restricted under Kwame Nkrumah. Thereafter, under the successive regimes of the National Liberation Council, K. A. Busia, Ignatius K. Acheampong, and Fred W. K. Akuffo, the press operated under conditions which ranged from relative freedom to tight repression. There is no evidence to suggest that newspapers in Ghana have been used by the government to further the economic development of the country since independence. Secondary sources; 44 notes. J. S. Coleman

1860. Verdon, Michel. POLITICAL SOVEREIGNTY, VILLAGE REPRODUCTION AND LEGENDS OF ORIGIN: A COMPARATIVE HYPOTHESIS. *Africa [Great Britain] 1981 51(1): 465-476.* In what is now Ghana the Abutia (inland Ewe) did not create any new villages within living memory, nor did the impermanent settlements on the edge of the villages develop into new villages. The three existing villages were roughly the same size, the clans localized. In Anlo (coastal Ewe) the groups of villages had political sovereignty and new villages grew more easily, the perimeter settlements achieving permanence as the nuclei of future villages, and the Anlo clans were dispersed. Tradition and legend supported the concepts that the Abutia's origins lay in a particular area, whereas those of the Anlo were of a racial character. Based on fieldwork; map, 3 notes. R. L. Collison

1861. Weis, Lois. ETHNICITY IN GHANAIAN SCHOOLS: A REASSESSMENT. *J. of Asian and African Studies [Netherlands] 1980 15(3-4): 229-241.* Expansion of educational opportunity in Ghana has only slightly improved opportunities for ethnic groups of low status, and it has led to a concentration of ethnic elites in high status schools. Based on surveys of secondary school pupils; 3 tables, 22 notes. R. T. Brown

1862. Weis, Lois. SCHOOLING AND PATTERNS OF ACCESS IN GHANA. *Can. J. of African Studies [Canada] 1981 15(2): 311-322.* A review of school attendance in Ghana and its effects on later access to high-prestige positions within the nation. Using data from the years 1961 to 1974, it is clear that more children are now attending school. This is especially true of girls, but both girls and lower class boys are enrolled in inferior schools. This trend becomes more marked the higher one moves in the educational system. The sons of professionals and semi-professionals dominate the colleges, and more so in 1974 than in 1961, which suggests that the school system, and by extension the higher socioeconomic spheres, are becoming increasingly closed and semi-hereditary. 4 tables, 17 notes. V. L. Human

1863. Weis, Lois. WOMEN AND EDUCATION IN GHANA: SOME PROBLEMS OF ASSESSING CHANGE. *Int. J. of Women's Studies [Canada] 1980 3(5): 431-453.* While girls have been admitted to schools in greater numbers and have benefited from the expansion of the educational system in general, girls have been admitted in disproportionate numbers to low status schools and have had greater difficulty in obtaining jobs than have boys. The content of their education differed from that offered boys.

1864. Weiss, Lois. THE REPRODUCTION OF SOCIAL INEQUALITY: CLOSURE IN THE GHANAIAN UNIVERSITY. *J. of Developing Areas 1981 16(1): 17-29.* While the base of male recruitment in the entire university system broadened considerably during the period 1953 to 1963, the trend toward openness has proved to be transitory in that the evidence for the following decade indicates that the university intake has increasingly come from the privileged sectors of society, and this conclusion supports the thesis that educational systems serve primarily to reproduce systems of structured social inequality. 5 tables, 30 notes. V. Samaraweera

1865. Wyllie, Robert W. PIONEERS OF GHANAIAN PENTECOSTALISM: PETER ANIM AND JAMES MCKEOWN. *J. of Religion in Africa [Netherlands] 1974 6(2): 109-122.* Brief biographical sketches of Peter Anim and James McKeown prior to their meeting in Africa. Anim was born in Ghana, McKeown in Scotland. In their religious work, the issue of faith healing caused a rupture: Anim held firm to the power of faith to cure illness while McKeown believed in the use of medicines. Anim became involved in the Christ Apostolic Church, McKeown with the Church of the Pentecost. 24 notes. H. G. Soff

Guinea

1866. Adamolekun, Ladipo. GUINEA: THAT PORTUGUESE INVASION. *Afriscope [Nigeria] 1975 5(2): 40-46.* Summarizes the observed realities of the 1970 invasion of Guinea announced by President Sekou Touré. Concludes that an invasion occurred involving Portuguese soldiers and Guinean dissidents. Describes the purge which followed. Based on observations and newspapers; illus., 11 notes. Article to be continued. G. O. Gagnon

1867. Brabcová-Chelli, Milena. GUINÉE: ACTION SYNDICALE ET POLITIQUE AVANT JANVIER 1956 [Guinea: the trade union movement and the political situation before January 1956]. *Archív Orientální [Czechoslovakia] 1977 45(4): 319-328.* Studies the historical conditions which permitted the victory of the Democratic Party of Guinea. After a presentation of the economic and social background, the author analyzes the political evolution and especially the trade union movement. The peasantry had been impoverished by taxes and forced labor during World War II. A number of them, especially the youth, searched for work in the towns or on the plantations. Nevertheless, in the 1950's, the working class represented only three percent of the whole population and the majority were temporary argicultural workers. Guinea's production of bananas, pineapples, and coffee increased constantly; mines were opened, but the structure of Guinea's economy made impossible the rise of a strong African bourgeoisie. The political movement for emancipation was started by the administrative employees' trade union movement. The strongest labor unions were those of the CGT (Confédération Générale de Travail) supported by the French Communist Party. The trade unions' activities concerned especially wages and working conditions. There were several strikes, the most important of which was in 1953 when the entire people expressed its solidarity with the strikers. The PDG then understood the importance of national unity in the struggle against French colonialism. Its ideology changed according to African practice. Its influence among the peasant masses was proved in the election of January 1956 when it won an absolute majority. The trade union movement followed the same ideological line, and it broke away from the French centers during 1955-56. J

1868. Camara, Sylvain Soriba. LA GUINÉE ET LA COOPÉRATION ÉCONOMIQUE EN AFRIQUE DE L'OUEST [Guinea and economic cooperation in West Africa]. *Cultures et Développement [Belgium] 1976 8(3): 517-532.* Explains the failure of Guinea's attempts at cooperation with various West African states, 1958-72.

1869. Gavrilov, N. I. RAZVITIE PROMYSHLENNOSTI V GVINEISKOI NARODNOI REVOLIUTSIONNOI RESPUBLIKE [Development of industry in Guinea]. *Narody Azii i Afriki [USSR] 1979 (3): 93-99.* After World War II Guinean industries entered a phase of development. With 1960 came nationalization and compromises with foreign corporations, but there was still lack of effective administration and budgetary control. There was also a need for more specialists, which had to come from or be trained abroad. Solutions to these and other problems were outlined at the Democratic Party Congress in 1978. Table, 15 notes. V. A. Packer

1870. Kaba, Lansiné. THE CULTURAL REVOLUTION, ARTISTIC CREATIVITY, AND FREEDOM OF EXPRESSION IN GUINEA. *J. of Modern African Studies [Great Britain] 1976 14(2): 201-218.* A study of the culture of Guinea where authoritarian rule stifles artistic creativity as does a censoring party bureaucracy and national leader. Traces the early major writings of Guineans in French before 1969, the Cultural Revolution, and finally the rise of Sekou Touré as sole interpreter. Those who criticized have been physically eliminated or imprisoned, hence fear and prudence have become the order of the day. Based on the textual interpretation of Guinean radio broadcasts and records and the writings of Sekou Touré; 23 notes. R. V. Ritter

1871. Kaba, Lansiné. GUINEAN POLITICS: A CRITICAL HISTORICAL OVERVIEW. *J. of Modern African Studies [Great Britain] 1977 15(1): 25-45.* Traces the political development of Guinea since World War II with an emphasis on Sekou Touré. Although claiming to be a socialist state, Guinea is really no more than a tyranny which is only interested in self-image and power. 47 notes. H. G. Soff

1872. Kalinina, I. P. PROBLEMS OF ECONOMIC DEVELOPMENT PLANNING IN THE PEOPLE'S REVOLUTIONARY REPUBLIC OF GUINEA. *Arhív Orientální [Czechoslovakia] 1979 47(4): 292-311.* Examines the implementation of economic planning in Guinea and the development of the state sector.

1873. Lacouture, Jean. LE GUINÉE DE SÉKOU TOURÉ À VINGT ANS [Guinea: 20 years under Sekou Touré]. *Histoire [France] 1978 (3): 80-84.* Discusses the economic and political history of Guinea since it refused to join the French Community in 1958, a period marked by increasing political repression.

1874. Leunda, Xavier. NOUVELLES INSTITUTIONS RURALES EN GUINÉE [New rural institutions in Guinea]. *Civilisations [Belgium] 1973-1974 23-24(1-2): 76-97.* Part I. Agricultural cooperatives among planters in Guinea were established in 1951 to meet the critical situation after World War II and have continued to be successful. After Guinea gained independence the Democratic Party and the government started a wide campaign in 1960 to transform all economic activities, except mining and large industrial enterprise, into a cooperative system, but it had a rapid decline. The socioeconomic environment did not favor cooperatives, but instead the extension of small commercial production, private land ownership, and individual accumulations of wealth. 17 notes. To be continued. H. L. Calkin

1875. Poláček, Josef. GUINEJSKÁ DEMOKRATICKÁ STRANA PDG V BOJI PROTI FRANCOUZSKÉMU KOLONIALISMU 1947-1958 [The Democratic Party of Guinea (PDG) in the struggle against French imperialism, 1947-58]. *Československý Časopis Hist. [Czechoslovakia] 1975 23(5): 733-746.* Describes the role of Guinea's Democratic Party from its establishment in May 1947 to independence, October 1958. The party gradually led all Guinea's anti-imperialist forces. Under its leadership the referendum of 1958 rejected the Gaullist idea of French-African association and chose instead a socialist orientation for independent Guinea. Secondary sources; 31 notes. G. E. Pergl

1876. Quimby, Lucy G. HISTORY AS IDENTITY: THE JAAXANKE AND THE FOUNDING OF TUUBA (SENEGAL). *Bull. de l'Inst. Fondamental d'Afrique Noire [Senegal] 1975 37(3): 604-618.* English translations of two Arabic manuscripts written in the 20th century and belonging to Moslem scholars in the Department of Bokel, Senegal. The manuscripts describe the founding and history of Tuuba from the 15th century in what is now Guinea and the scholarly and pious activities of Karamoxo Baa, founder of Tuuba. Map, 23 notes. H. L. Calkin

1877. Rivière, Claude. PURGES ET COMPLOTS AU SEIN DU PARTI DÉMOCRATIQUE DE GUINÉE [Purges and plots at the heart of the Democratic Party in Guinea]. *Rev. Française d'Études Pol. Africaines [France] 1973 8(95): 31-45.* Studies conspiracies and various plots against the regime of Ahmed Sekou Touré, Guinean President, interprets governmental and political trends, and theories on the major crises of the regime, 1957-73.

1878. Savateev, A. GVINEIA: STANOVLENIE VYSSHEI SHKOLY [Guinea: the establishment of higher education]. *Aziia i Afrika Segodnia [USSR] 1982 (10): 31-32.* Asserts that the new educational policies of the Socialist government of Guinea since 1962 are successful.

1879. Sologubovski, N. and Tiurkin, V. VID S NABEREZHNOI BUL'BINE [A view from an embankment]. *Aziia i Afrika Segodnia [USSR] 1981 (10): 32-35.* Surveys contemporary life in Conakry, capital of the west African nation of Guinea.

1880. Trentadue, Michel. LA SOCIÉTÉ GUINÉENNE DANS LA CRISE DE 1930: FISCALITÉ ET POUVOIR D'ACHAT [Guinean society during the crisis of the 1930's: taxation and buying power]. *Rev. Française d'Hist. d'Outre-Mer [France] 1976 63(3-4): 628-639.* The

Great Depression was disastrous for African farmers; the fall in prices for primary agricultural products occurred at the same time as a rise in taxation, thus causing a tremendous drop in African purchasing power. During the 1930's, the resultant agricultural depression included such phenomena as emigration to avoid taxes and the reappearance of domestic slavery. After 1935 Guinea recovered slowly, but the misery of the rural populace lasted considerably longer. Guinea's recovery was assisted by soaring gold production. 2 tables, graph.
J. C. Billigmeier

1881. Trentadue, Michel. MOUVEMENTS COMMERCIAUX ET ÉVOLUTION ÉCONOMIQUE DE LA GUINÉE FRANÇAISE DE 1928 À 1938: L'ESSOR DE LA SPÉCIALISATION BANANIÈRE [Commercial movements and economic evolution of French Guinea from 1928 to 1938: the rise of banana monoculture]. *Rev. Française d'Hist. d'Outre-Mer [France] 1976 63(3-4): 575-589.* The Great Depression began to make itself felt in French Guinea in the commercial slump of 1928. The worst years were 1931-32, and improvement did not come until 1934. With financial insecurity demand for gold increased, stimulating Guinean gold production. Banana growing likewise expanded greatly, becoming the predominant cash crop. Banana production was subsidized, and legislation favored plantation owners at the expense of African workers. In this period, the foundations for the modern Guinean economy were established. 2 graphs, 32 notes.
J. C. Billigmeier

1882. Yansane, Aguibou Y. MONETARY INDEPENDENCE AND TRANSITION TO SOCIALISM IN GUINEA. *J. of African Studies 1979 6(3): 132-143.* Evaluates the first 20 years of effort by the government of Guinea to establish its financial independence and stability since its dramatic breakaway from the French Community in 1958. Operating under the national plans of 1960-63 and 1964-71, state agencies charged with commercial transactions, distribution of consumer goods, and agricultural development fell somewhat short of targeted goals. Success in the mining sector, with Guinea becoming the world's largest bauxite producer, coupled with growing economic realism point to a bright economic future. Based on published statistics and secondary sources; 4 tables, 47 notes. L. W. Truschel

Guinea-Bissau

1883. Bienen, Henry. STATE AND REVOLUTION: THE WORK OF AMILCAR CABRAL. *J. of Modern African Studies [Great Britain] 1977 15(4): 555-568.* Compares Cabral's thought to that of Frantz Fanon, Regis Debray, and Che Guevara, and discusses Cabral's views of the state, class struggle and ethnicity, class struggle and revolutionary consciousness, and violence. Cabral has received less attention than the other three, possibly because he dealt mainly with the Guinean situation and did not generalize his analyses. 36 notes. H. G. Soff

1884. Cabral, Amilcar. THE STRUGGLE HAS TAKEN ROOT. *Black Scholar 1973 4(10): 28-32.* Discusses the national liberation movement in Guinea-Bissau under the African Party for the Independence of Guinea-Bissau and Cape Verde (PAIGC); examines the progress made within Guinea in light of African liberation.

1885. Cabral, Vasco. THE REPUBLIC'S MOTTO—UNITY, STRUGGLE, PROGRESS. *World Marxist R. [Canada] 1974 17(2): 112-116.* Describes the structure and history of the government of the Republic of Guinea-Bissau and its revolutionary party. S

1886. Chabal, Patrick. THE SOCIAL AND POLITICAL THOUGHT OF AMILCAR CABRAL: A REASSESSMENT. *J. of Modern African Studies [Great Britain] 1981 19(1): 31-56.* The late Amilcar Cabral is widely known as a leading Marxist theorist of national liberation, as well as the leader of an anticolonial movement in two Portuguese African dependencies, Guinea-Bissau and the Cape Verde Islands. Though educated in Marxist theory and speaking and writing from a Marxist perspective, Cabral was essentially a pragmatic African nationalist who went so far in contradicting orthodox Marxism-Leninism as to maintain that only the petty bourgeoisie could organize and lead revolution in his country, since there was no Guinean proletariat to speak of and the peasantry was tribalist and politically unreliable. Cabral held that revolutionary morality would eventually merge ethnic and class lines among Guineans in a new nationalist and socialist order. Based on interviews, Cabral's writings, and secondary sources; 91 notes. L. W. Truschel

1887. Chaliand, Gérard. AMILCAR CABRAL. *Int. J. of Pol. 1977-78 7(4): 3-17.* Evaluates the career of Amilcar Cabral (1924-73), leader in the struggle to free Guinea-Bissau from Portugal. Cabral built a revolutionary party, developed its strategy, trained cadres, and established democratic organizations in liberated areas. He played a prominent role in African and Third World conferences, argued his people's case before UN agencies, and made an original theoretical contribution on the nature of class struggle in African societies. His multiple accomplishments, cut short by assassination on the eve of independence, established him as an "African revolutionary without peer, and leader of the first order in the Third World." Based on Cabral's writings; 3 notes.
R. E. Noble

1888. Chilcote, Ronald. THE STRUGGLE FOR GUINEA-BISSAU. *Africa Today 1974 21(1): 57-62.* Reviews A. J. Ventnor's *Portugal's War in Guinea-Bissau*(Pasadena, California: Munger African Library Notes, 1973) which was written with Portuguese official cooperation. Concludes that the author's scholarship is objective. 7 notes.
G. O. Gagnon

1889. Chilcote, Ronald H. GUINEA-BISSAU'S STRUGGLE: PAST AND PRESENT. *Africa Today 1977 24(1): 31-39.* Summarizes the three phases of Guinea-Bissau's struggle for independence: resistance, liberation, and consolidation. Concludes with a summary of an interview with Luiz Cabral, President of Guinea-Bissau. Based on published sources and an interview with Luiz Cabral; photo., 4 notes.
G. O. Gagnon

1890. Correia, Manuel Gardette. O CONTROLO DO PALUDISMO NA ILHA DE BISSAU—GUINE PORTUGUESA [The control of malaria on the island of Bissau—Portuguese Guinea]. *Boletim Cultural da Guine Portuguesa [Portuguese Guinea] 1973 28(110): 197-212.* Notes the great frequency of malaria in Guinea, due in part to the ideal climate for the Anopheles mosquito. Describes the geography, population, and research on the island of Bissau, along with details of the anti-malaria campaign. Several insecticides have proven useful, especially DDT and Baygon, in combating the disease. 7 tables, 3 graphs, fig., biblio. R. Garfield

1891. Cunningham, James. THE COLONIAL PERIOD IN GUINÉ. *Tarikh [Nigeria] 1980 6(4): 31-46.* The successful military campaigns of João Teixeira Pinto (1913-15) laid the basis for full economic and administrative control in Portuguese Guinea. Continuous hostility to colonization by the African population foreshadowed the outbreak of armed resistance in 1962-63.

1892. Davidson, Basil. CABRAL ON THE AFRICAN REVOLUTION. *Monthly Rev. 1979 31(3): 33-44.* Introduction to Amilcar Cabral's *Unity and Struggle,* a collection of speeches selected by the African Party for the Independence of Guinea and Cape Verde (PAIGC), founded by Cabral in 1956. Stresses Cabral's emphasis on the necessity of integrating the realities of life in Africa with revolutionary theories and plans through the application of Marxism.

1893. Ignat'ev, O. K. AMILKAR KABRAL: SYN AFRIKI, PLAMENNYI BORETS PROTIV KOLONIALIZMA [Amilcar Cabral: Africa's son and ardent fighter against colonialism]. *Novaia i Noveishaia Istoriia [USSR] 1975 (5): 104-121, (6): 85-99.* Describes the life and work of Amilcar Cabral, the revolutionary leader in Portuguese Guinea, retracing his youth, education in Portugal, early struggles against imperialism, and foundation of the African Party for the Independence of Guinea and Cape Verde (PAIGC). Cabral's two visits to Moscow in 1962 and 1972 are highlighted, as is the Portuguese government's plot to liquidate Guinea's rebel leaders, which led to Cabral's assassination in 1973. 2 photos, 57 notes. V. A. Packer

1894. Khazanov, A. M. PUT' GVINEI-BISAU K NEZAVISIMOSTI [Guinea-Bissau's path to independence]. *Voprosy Istorii [USSR] 1981 (9): 93-103.* Guinea-Bissau was the first of the Portuguese colonies to gain independence, in 1973, thanks to the organized and heroic efforts of Amilcar Cabral and the PAIGC. This revolutionary party was set up quite early and easily in the prerevolutionary conditions, because there was no strict class differentiation among the indigenous population and they all united against the colonialist oppressor. Since independence, the Soviet Union has given the country much aid and assistance in its revolutionary-democratic development. 47 notes. V. A. Packer

1895. Kravtsova, T. I. AMILKAR KABRAL (1924-1973) [Amilcar Cabral, 1924-73]. *Narody Azii i Afriki [USSR] 1974 (3): 76-87.* Outlines the life of the Portuguese Guinea national liberation movement leader and later Secretary General of the African Party for the Independence of Guinea and the Cape Verde Islands (PAIGC), Amilcar Cabral, who died shortly before Guinea-Bissau came into being in 1973.

1896. Lobban, Richard. GUINEA-BISSAU: TWENTY-FOUR SEPTEMBER AND BEYOND. *Africa Today 1974 21(1): 15-24.* Summarizes the military, social, and economic progress which prompted the African Party for the Independence of Guinea-Bissau and the Cape Verde Islands (PAIGC) to declare the independence of Guinea-Bissau from Portugal. Predicts continued progress and international recognition of PAIGC. Secondary sources; biblio. G. O. Gagnon

1897. Luke, Timothy W. CABRAL'S MARXISM: AN AFRICAN STRATEGY FOR SOCIALIST DEVELOPMENT. *Studies in Comparative Communism 1981 14(4): 307-330.* Amilcar Cabral, assassinated in 1973, developed, like Gramsci, a special Marxist analysis of imperialism. He saw it as depriving a colonized people of its history but introducing it to modern culture. The task of overturning imperial rule requires leadership by the petite bougeoisie of a nation, their aim to restore national vitality and forge a collective will through education, participation, and action. The goal of the process is modernization and then socialism. Cabral feared that the bourgeoisie would not make themselves dispensable, and his fear seems to have been realized in his homeland, Guinea-Bissau. 97 notes. D. Balmuth

1898. Lyon, Judson. MARXISM AND ETHNO-NATIONALISM IN GUINEA-BISSAU, 1956-76. *Ethnic and Racial Studies 1980 3(2): 156-168.* Analyzes the efforts of Amilcar Cabral and his Partido Africano de Independência da Guiné e Cabo Verde to liberate the West African country from Portuguese control and the conflicting ideological sources in Marxism and ethnic nationalism.

1899. McCollester, Charles. THE POLITICAL THOUGHT OF AMILCAR CABRAL. *Monthly R. 1973 24(10): 10-21.* Discusses the Portuguese Guinean leader's ideas on colonialism, African culture, and independence movements. S

1900. McCulloch, Jock. AMILCAR CABRAL: A THEORY OF IMPERIALISM. *J. of Modern African Studies [Great Britain] 1981 19(3): 503-511.* Amilcar Cabral developed his ideas of history as a civil servant and nationalist in Portuguese Guinea. His conceptualization of history and imperialism centered on his view of the determinative role of productive modes, a related but sharply different theory from the standard Marxist emphasis on the class struggle. Based on Cabral's writings; 8 notes. L. W. Truschel

1901. Robinson, Cedric J. AMILCAR CABRAL AND THE DIALECTIC OF PORTUGUESE COLONIALISM. *Radical Am. 1981 15(3): 39-57.* Amilcar Cabral's life and thought as a representative of the petit bourgeois native middle management in Portuguese Africa (Cape Verde, Angola, Mozambique, and Guinea-Bissau) led to his becoming a leader of the revolutionary struggle in Guinea-Bissau and a theorist who ranks with Fanon, Nyerere, Nkrumah, and Lumumba. Twenty years of work and 10 years of open struggle led to independence for Guinea-Bissau in 1972 and Cabral's assassination by Portuguese agents in 1973. 37 notes, 8 illus. C. M. Hough

1902. Rubio García, Leandro. EL CASO DE GUINEA-BISSAU: UNA DESCOLONIZACIÓN VISTA COMO FENÓMENO CULTURAL [The case of Guinea-Bissau: an example of decolonization as a cultural phenomenon]. *Rev. de Política Int. [Spain] 1975 (139): 169-190.* Studies the intellectual and theoretical, as well as the practical decolonization of Guinea-Bissau.

1903. Rudebeck, Lars. DEVELOPMENT AND CLASS STRUGGLE IN GUINEA-BISSAU. *Monthly Rev. 1979 30(8): 14-32.* Discusses the socialist-oriented development of the new sovereign state Guinea-Bissau, from its declaration of sovereignty in 1973 to 1977.

1904. Shundeyev, Vladimir. OUTLINES OF THE NEW WAY. *World Marxist R. [Canada] 1974 17(3): 105-112.* Reports on interviews held with officials of Guinea-Bissau concerning progress made in education, economic development, and the ideological battle against imperialists and reactionaries. S

1905. Urdang, Stephanie. FIGHTING TWO COLONIALISMS: THE WOMEN'S STRUGGLE IN GUINEA-BISSAU. *African Studies Rev. 1975 18(3): 29-34.* Women's position in Guinea-Bissau has improved with the expulsion of Portuguese colonialism, but the domestic colonialism of traditional hierarchical attitudes remains strong.

1906. Venter, Al J. PORTUGAL'S WAR IN GUINEA-BISSAU. *Munger Africana Lib. Notes 1973 19: 7-202.*

1907. Washington, Shirley. NEW INSTITUTIONS FOR DEVELOPMENT IN GUINEA-BISSAU. *Black Scholar 1980 11(5): 14-23.* Discusses the development of political, economic, and educational institutions in Guinea-Bissau since the end of Portuguese rule in 1974.

1908. —. [GUINEA-BISSAU]. *New World R. 1973 41(2): 36-43.*
Davidson, Basil. GUINEA-BISSAU: BUILDING FOR INDEPENDENCE, pp. 36-43.
—. AMILCAR CABRAL, pp. 43. Report on the military and political situation in Guinea-Bissau and an obituary of Amilcar Cabral. S

1909. —. [GUINEA-BISSAU]. *Africa Report 1973 18(2): 21-24.*
Marcum, John. AMILCAR CABRAL: THE MEANING OF AN ASSASSINATION, pp. 21-23.
Mendy, Justin. "THE STRUGGLE GOES ON," p. 24. Discusses the career of Amilcar Cabral, his recent assassination, and its aftermath. S

Ivory Coast

1910. Alalade, F. O. PRESIDENT FELIX HOUPHOUET-BOIGNY, THE IVORY COAST, AND FRANCE. *J. of African Studies 1979 6(3): 122-131.* Assesses Félix Houphouët-Boigny's relations and attitudes toward France before and after the independence of the Ivory Coast in 1960. Houphouët-Boigny is more a humanist than an ideologue and has consistently put the interest of his people above other considerations. He has long pursued a generally pro-French policy to achieve rapid economic and social development at home but is not inextricably tied to Paris. Secondary sources; 72 notes. L. W. Truschel

1911. Braibant, Patrick. L'ADMINISTRATION COLONIALE ET LE PROFIT COMMERCIALE EN CÔTE D'IVOIRE PENDANT LA CRISE DE 1929 [Colonial administration and commercial profit in the Ivory Coast during the crisis of 1929]. *Rev. Française d'Hist. d'Outre-Mer [France] 1976 63(3-4): 555-574.* At the end of the 1920's, the Ivory Coast appeared to be one of the most dynamic colonies in French Africa. Coffee and cacao were replacing palm oil as primary agricultural products. The coming of the Great Depression and the slump in agricultural and other raw materials prices placed a great strain on colonial economies. Commercial firms exerted themselves to preserve their profits, often against the resistance of civil servants interested in public investment. Other officials were sympathetic to the companies and reduced their taxes. As a result, profits were often maintained and even increased. The African agriculturalists, on the other hand, had scant help in surviving the crisis. 6 graphs, 36 notes.
J. C. Billigmeier

1912. Brayton, Abbott A. STABILITY AND MODERNIZATION: THE IVORY COAST MODEL. *World Affairs 1979 141(3): 235-249.* Focuses on development and modernization in the Ivory Coast during the last two decades, comparing it with the model for modernization proposed by Daniel Lerner.

1913. Campbell, Bonnie. L'IDÉOLOGIE DE LA CROISSANCE: UNE ANALYSE DU PLAN QUINQUENNAL DE DÉVELOPPE-

MENT 1971-1975 DE LA CÔTE D'IVOIRE [The ideology of growth: an analysis of the Five-Year Plan of development of the Ivory Coast, 1971-75]. *Can. J. of African Studies [Canada] 1976 10(2): 211-233.* Examines the Ivory Coast Five Year Plan, outlining the ideological and political character of planned social and economic growth which perpetuates particular economic interests to the detriment of others.

1914. Campbell, Bonnie. SOCIAL CHANGE AND CLASS FORMATION IN A FRENCH WEST AFRICAN STATE. *Can. J. of African Studies [Canada] 1974 8(2): 285-306.* Analyzes social change, political development, and economic change in the Ivory Coast according to the development of elites and new social classes, 1920-65.

1915. Chauveau, J. P.; Dozon, J. P.; and Richard, J. HISTOIRES DE RIZ, HISTOIRES D'IGNAME: LE CAS DE LA MOYENNE CÔTE D'IVOIRE [The changing fortunes of rice and yam: the case of the Central Ivory Coast]. *Africa [Great Britain] 1981 51(2): 621-658.* Farmers throughout the colonial period cultivated rice to the west and yams to the east of the Bandama river. Yams, being hardy and having a high yield, are an attractive crop but are difficult to control by mechanized processes, and supplies cannot be easily organized by the state. Rice, on the other hand, lends itself easily to mechanization throughout its planting, harvesting, and marketing, and is a very suitable foodstuff to provide for mass consumption for growing urban demands. Yams have remained the favorite food of the peasants, and their production is only slightly subject to state control. Based on field work; map, 25 notes, biblio. R. L. Collison

1916. Cohen, Michael A. URBAN POLICY AND THE DECLINE OF THE MACHINE: CROSS-ETHNIC POLITICS IN THE IVORY COAST. *J. of Developing Areas 1974 8(2): 227-234.*

1917. Cola Alberich, Julio. EL DESARROLLO DE COSTA DE MARFIL: LA OBRA DE HOUPHOUËT-BOIGNY, UN ESTADISTA EJEMPLAR [The development of the Ivory Coast: the work of Houphouët-Boigny, an exemplary statesman]. *Rev. de Política Int. [Spain] 1974 (134): 167-173.* Examines the career of Félix Houphouët-Boigny, 1944-74, as a union organizer and politician. The economic and political success of the Ivory Coast has been due mainly to him.

1918. Domergue, D. LA LUTTE CONTRE LA TRYPANOSOMIASE EN CÔTE D'IVOIRE, 1900-1945 [The fight against trypanosomiasis (sleeping sickness) on the Ivory Coast, 1900-45]. *J. of African Hist. [Great Britain] 1981 22(1): 63-72.* The period 1900-37 was one of discovery, that of 1938-45 one of intensive struggle against the disease. The first cases of identification of trypanosomiasis on the Ivory Coast occurred in 1904. A study of 1914 confirmed that the disease spread along caravan routes, particularly in the northern half of the colony, being part of an epidemic affecting much of West Africa. Anxiety concerning the spread of the disease caused the authorities to take intensive measures in the 1930's, culminating in the setting up of a special Trypanosomiasis Service in 1939. During the next six years over a million people were surveyed. The disease was brought under control, but the full force of the epidemic had been transformed from the north to the south of the country. Official documents and records, and other published works; table, 2 maps, 21 notes. R. L. Collison

1919. Ekanza, Simon-Pierre. L'OPPRESSION ADMINISTRATIVE EN CÔTE D'IVOIRE (1908-1920) [Administrative oppression in the Ivory Coast, 1908-20]. *Bull. de l'Inst. Fondamental d'Afrique Noire [Senegal] 1975 37(3): 667-684.* Oppression by French administrators of the inhabitants of the Ivory Coast took the form of penalties for engaging in war, requisitions, and forced labor. They demonstrated the French demand for the submission of the population. Taxes weighed heavily on the people, deprived for the most part of bare necessities. The colonial administration drove the people deeper into poverty and helped to strengthen the underdevelopment faced by the Ivory Coast today. Based on archives of the French West Africa at Dakar; map, 46 notes. H. L. Calkin

1920. Etienne, Mona. WOMEN AND MEN, CLOTH AND COLONIZATION: THE TRANSFORMATION OF PRODUCTION-DISTRIBUTION RELATIONS AMONG THE BAULE (IVORY COAST). *Cahiers d'Études Africaines [France] 1977 17(1): 41-64.* Before colonization in the early 20th century, Baule men and women were interdependent in their production relationships. As a result of colonial demands and the industrialization of the textile-making process, women lost control of the production of cotton cloth and became alienated from the production process, although cloth remained an item of high prestige. Based on field research and secondary literature; 36 notes. B. S. Fetter

1921. Etienne, Mona. WOMEN AND MEN, CLOTH AND COLONIZATION: THE TRANSFORMATION OF PRODUCTION-DISTRIBUTION RELATIONS AMONG THE BAULE (IVORY COAST). Etienne, Mona and Leacock, Eleanor, ed. *Women and Colonization: Anthropological Perspectives* (New York: Praeger, J. F. Bergin Publ., 1980): 214-238. Before colonization of east central Ivory Coast in 1893, the Baule maintained a sexual division of labor in their production activities. Women cultivated yams and cotton and controlled their distribution. Men owned the land and spun and wove cotton. Colonization altered this interdependent relationship and provided new opportunities for cloth production. The appearance of imported European cloth and thread and the establishment of the R. Gonfreville textile factory in Bouaké, 1923, diminished women's economic independence. The development of cotton, cocoa, and coffee into cash crops for export under colonial administration further increased male domination of agriculture. Photo, 24 notes, ref. S

1922. Glasman, Monique. CÔTE D'IVOIRE: UNE SOCIÉTÉ ÉBRANLÉE [Ivory Coast: a disturbed society]. *Esprit [France] 1983 (2): 124-132.* After a historical, political, and economic analysis of the Ivory Coast, examines the character of this African country's society since independence (1960), disturbed by the failure to substitute for traditional culture a new coherent and secure system of values adapted to modern reality.

1923. Haliburton, G. M. MARK CHRISTIAN HAYFORD: A NON-SUCCESS STORY. *J. of Religion in Africa [Netherlands] 1981 12(1): 20-37.* A biography of Mark Christian Hayford (1864-1935), the brother of Joseph Ephraim Casely Hayford, one of the founders of modern Ghana, examining his family and social background, his evangelism and fundraising, his relationship with the Prophet William Wade Harris and his movement, a fundraising scandal in Europe, and his death in London. Based on archives of the Ivory Coast, Senegal, London, and personal letters, conversations, and secondary sources. R. J. Jirran

1924. Hinderink, J. and Tempelman, G. J. RURAL CHANGE AND TYPES OF MIGRATION IN NORTHERN IVORY COAST. *African Perspectives [Netherlands] 1978 (1): 93-108.* Studies economic policy and rural change and their effect on migration in the Ivory Coast area. Perceives three distinct periods: 1) the colonial period with its forced labor and compulsory cropping, 1928-46; 2) the period of incentive premiums, 1946-60; and 3) the period of independence with its accelerated growth, 1960-70, and its crop-development approach after 1970. R. V. Ritter

1925. Kipré, Pierre. LA CRISE ÉCONOMIQUE DANS LES CENTRES URBAINS EN CÔTE D'IVOIRE, 1930-1935 [The depression in urban centers in the Ivory Coast, 1930-35]. *Cahiers d'Études Africaines [France] 1976 16(1-2): 119-146.* The European sector of the economy of the Ivory Coast suffered more from the Great Depression than did the African sector. Many urban merchants went bankrupt as a result of disastrously low prices for export commodities. Urban Africans suffered less, benefiting from the lower prices of consumer goods. Rural Africans were even less severely affected, because they were able to return to production of commodities previously abandoned under the pressure of the colonial regime. Based on archival sources in Paris and secondary sources; map, 5 graphs, 2 tables, 34 notes. B. S. Fetter

1926. Lee, Eddy. EXPORT-LED RURAL DEVELOPMENT: THE IVORY COAST. *Development and Change [Netherlands] 1980 11(4): 607-642.* Economic development in the Ivory Coast was above average for African developing countries, 1960-75, due to increased exports of agricultural products.

1927. Pillet-Schwartz, Anne-Marie. UNE TENTATIVE DE VULGARISATION AVORTÉE: L'HÉVÉACULTURE VILLAGEOISE EN CÔTE D'IVOIRE [An unsuccessful attempt at popularization: the village rubber plantations in the Ivory Coast]. *Cahiers d'Études Africaines [France] 1980 20(1-2): 63-82.* Discusses the plans and execution ending in failure of rubber cultivation in the Ivory Coast using a village plantation system.

1928. Savary, Claude. MISSION ETHNOGRAPHIQUE EN CÔTE-D'IVOIRE [Ethnographic expedition to the Ivory Coast, November-December 1973]. *Musées de Genève [Switzerland] 1974 15(147): 25-30.* After revisiting Dahomey the group made preliminary contact with traditional peoples in the districts of Man and Zuénoula to study their arts and crafts and socioreligious attitudes, before they disappear in the face of modernization. 6 illus. R. K. Adams

1929. Semi-Bi, Zan. LE PARTI DÉMOCRATIQUE DE CÔTE-D'IVOIRE [The Democratic Party in the Ivory Coast]. *Rev. Française d'Études Pol. Africaines [France] 1973 8(94): 61-75.* Studies the hard realities and problems in national integration and socioeconomic and cultural development in the Ivory Coast, where the government has moved toward a single party system, 1958-73.

1930. Semi-Bi, Zan. L'INFRASTRUCTURE ROUTIERE ET FERROVIAIRE COLONIALE, SOURCE DE MUTATIONS SOCIALES ET PSYCHOLOGIQUES: LE CAS DE LA CÔTE D'IVOIRE, 1900-1940 [Colonial road and rail infrastructure, source of social and psychological mutations: the case of the Ivory Coast, 1900-40]. *Cahiers d'Études Africaines [France] 1976 16(1-2): 147-158.* Divides the effects of the creation of modern mechanical transportation into two categories: voluntary migrations by Europeans, assimilated Africans, and unskilled Africans; and involuntary migration connected with local public works. The new social mobility lessened the hold of both the chiefs and the colonial government, facilitating a new way of life. Based on archival materials in Paris and published primary materials; 29 notes. B. S. Fetter

1931. Tice, Robert D. ADMINISTRATIVE STRUCTURE, ETHNICITY, AND NATION-BUILDING IN THE IVORY COAST. *J. of Modern African Studies [Great Britain] 1974 12(2): 211-229.* Traces the colonial history of the Ivory Coast since 1889. Although the French followed a policy of assimilation, even today many people do not identify with the nation, but remain localized. They will become more Ivorian, however, as they look more toward the central government and less to tradition. The Ivory Coast may one day be a multinational country. 3 maps, 44 notes. H. G. Soff

1932. Triaud, Jean-Louis. LA QUESTION MUSULMANE EN CÔTE-D'IVOIRE (1893-1939) [The Moslem question in the Ivory Coast, 1893-1939]. *Rev. Francaise d'Hist. d'Outre-Mer [France] 1974 61(225): 542-571.* Islam spread to the Ivory Coast as a result of the immigration of Senegalese and Sudanese soldiers and merchants. The French were hostile to the faith, 1905-30. Thereafter an accommodation of sorts was reached. Based on documents in the National Archives of the Ivory Coast, France (Overseas Section), and Senegal and secondary works; 86 notes. L. B. Chan

1933. Turcotte, Denis. LA PLANIFICATION LINGUISTIQUE EN CÔTE D'IVOIRE: FAIRE DU FRANÇAIS LE VÉHICULAIRE NATIONAL PAR EXCELLENCE [Linguistic planning in the Ivory Coast: making French the preeminent national means of communication]. *Can. J. of African Studies [Canada] 1980 13(3): 423-439.* The newly independent government of the Ivory Coast chose to maintain French as the official language in all state institutions. Following this decision, it set out to ensure the broadest possible diffusion of French in order, it would seem, to make it the supraethnic language, the preeminent national means of communication. In order to support this premise, the author summarizes the linguistic policy and the motives underlying it; analyzes the methods of application of the policy in the fields of education, communications, administration, justice, the armed forces, and the workplace; and describes linguistics research across the country. Examines the powerful means a developing country has at its disposal to promote a language and a language policy. 26 notes. J

1934. Walker, Sheila S. RELIGION AND MODERNIZATION IN AN AFRICAN CONTEXT: THE HARRIST CHURCH OF THE IVORY COAST. *J. of African Studies 1977 4(1): 77-85.* The Harrist Church movement was established in the Ivory Coast in 1913 by the Prophet William Wade Harris, a Liberian Grebo religious leader who had been imprisoned for treason. The Harrist Church developed as the first multiethnic mass movement in the southern Ivory Coast by advancing literacy and other aspects of modernization, while retaining many features of the traditional Ivorian culture. The Harrist Church has become "an authentically Ivorian religion." Based on field research; biblio. L. W. Truschel

1935. Walker, Sheila S. WITCHCRAFT AND HEALING IN AN AFRICAN CHURCH. *J. of Religion in Africa [Netherlands] 1979 10(2): 127-138.* The Harrist Church of the Ivory Coast represents a Christian institution based on African conceptual and structural principles. John Ahui continued the Christian missionary aspect of church organization and Albert Atcho, a distinguished member of the church, fulfilled the traditional African priest role as healer and protector from witchcraft. Based on the author's unpublished doctoral dissertation; 10 notes. R. J. Jirran

1936. —. NOTE DOCUMENTAIRE SUR LA PRESSE EN CÔTE-D'IVOIRE [Documentary notes on the media in the Ivory Coast]. *Rev. Française d'Études Pol. Africaines [France] 1973 8(96): 64-79.* Studies the mass media in the Ivory Coast, colonialization to independence, including the first journalistic publications (1910-1960), and the appearance of radio (1954) and television (1963). outlines the characteristics of important agencies, and certain newspapers and other media organizations.

Liberia

1937. Asibey, Andrew Osei. LIBERIA: POLITICAL ECONOMY OF UNDERDEVELOPMENT AND MILITARY "REVOLUTION CONTINUITY OR CHANGE?" *Can. J. of Development Studies [Canada] 1981 2(2): 386-407.* Ignoring the needs of the majority of the Liberian people led to the overthrow of the US-backed Liberian leadership in 1980, although this did not lead to fundamental changes in socioeconomic structures.

1938. Beleky, Louis P. THE DEVELOPMENT OF LIBERIA. *J. of Modern African Studies [Great Britain] 1973 11(1): 43-60.* Because of its enormous wealth in natural resources, Liberia has experienced considerable economic growth in the last 20 years. In determining economic development, output per capita is not as important as the capacity to provide. During the 1950's Liberia's rate of growth was among the highest in the world. This is an economic analysis of that development from World War II to 1971. 9 tables, 54 notes. H. G. Soff

1939. Carlisle, Rodney. LIBERIA'S FLAG OF CONVENIENCE: ROUGH WATERS AHEAD. *Orbis 1981 24(4): 881-892.* Examines the effect of the 12 April 1980 coup in Liberia and the growing challenge mounted by the developing nations, through the UN Conference on Trade and Development, on the open-registry system of shipping and flags of convenience. Although the recent coup opened the question of political stability in Liberia, it is primarily the aspiration of Liberia to become a leader of the LDC's, who are opposed to the system of flags of convenience, that presents Liberia with difficult policy choices. 2 tables, 18 notes. J. W. Thacker, Jr.

1940. Chaudhuri, J. Pal. BRITISH REACTION TO THE FIRESTONE INVESTMENT IN LIBERIA. *Liberian Studies J. 1972-74 5(1): 25-46.* As a protest against the British Stevenson Restrictions Act of 1922, Harvey S. Firestone's decision to invest in rubber production in Liberia reflected his desire to free the US rubber industry from its dependence on the British Empire. British reactions to the scheme evolved from those of humorous disbelief to exaggerated fears of anti-British conspiracy. Francis O'Meara, British chargé d'affaires in Monrovia, was instructed by the Foreign Office to secure official protection for British interests in Liberia while simultaneously and covertly attempting to thwart the negotiations between the Firestone Company and the Liberian Government. The US State Department denied O'Meara's accusations that it was backing the Firestone scheme, but despite O'Meara's efforts to frustrate the Firestone negotiations, the United States succeeded in the Firestone agreement in imposing a kind of economic imperialism on Liberia which conflicted with the real or imagined economic, political, and strategic interests of the world's then largest colonial power—Great Britain. Primary and secondary sources; 98 notes. C. Fry

1941. Davis, Ronald W. THE LIBERIAN STRUGGLE FOR AUTHORITY ON THE KRU COAST. *Int. J. of African Hist. Studies 1975 8(2): 222-265.* A history of the controversy between the Liberian government and its Kru coastal area. The Kru were proud of their independence and wished to retain it. The struggling Liberian government was attempting to establish a viable state. Imperial powers, especially Britain, clouded the issue by sometimes supporting the Kru, but in the main, British activities aided the Liberian government. The Kru finally revolted openly, but were put down. Their importance lies in their cosmopolitanism. Contact with advanced states caused them to successfully demand reforms which the conservative interior government would hardly have otherwise initiated. Map, 146 notes. V. L. Human

1942. D'Azevedo, Warren L. HONORABLE S. JANGABA M. JOHNSON: LIBERIAN ETHNOGRAPHER. *Liberian Studies J. 1972-74 5(1): 1-5.* S. Jangaba M. Johnson (1895-) was a self-trained pioneer of Liberian ethnography and ethnohistory, whose work is only now beginning to receive the recognition it deserves. In 1952 Johnson was appointed Administrative Assistant and Research Officer of the Bureau of Folkways, an office established by the late President W. V. S. Tubman to improve Liberians' knowledge of their own country and people. From 1952 until his retirement with honors in 1972, Johnson initiated some of the first systematic cultural studies by Liberians, including work on the Vai (1954), the Denwoin (1955), the Glebo (1957), the Gola (1961), and the Bele. Committed to national unification, Johnson is also known for his role in crucial negotiations between government and ethnic groups in matters of sacred tradition and indigenous rights and has shown an active concern for the development of new understanding between rural and urban Liberians. C. Fry

1943. Dobrowolski, Ryszard. CZYNNIK KULTURY W PERSPEKTYWIE PROCESÓW INTEGRACJI SPOŁECZNEJ W LIBERII [Culture from the perspective of social integration processes in Liberia]. Szymański, Edward. *Tradycja i Współczesność w Azji, Afryce i Ameryce Łacińskiej* (Warsaw: Polska Akademia Nauk Zakład Krajów Pozaeuropejskich, 1978): 267-285. Examines cultural dualism in Liberia from the 1820's to the present.

1944. Dunn, D. Elwood. ANTI-COLONIALISM IN LIBERIAN FOREIGN POLICY: A CASE STUDY. *Liberian Studies J. 1972-74 5(1): 47-66.* Examines the anti-colonial stance of postwar Liberia in the question in the United Nations of the disposal of former Italian colonies of Libya, Italian Somaliland, and Eritrea during a period of little or no African influence in world affairs, 1948-51. Like other Afro-Asian states, the Liberian position on this question reflected the interests of the major powers as well as the individual or collective interests of Afro-Asia. Liberia advocated immediate or eventual independence for the territories concerned. This anti-colonial stance was tempered, however, by Liberia's policy affinity with the West, which helps to explain Liberia's abstention on the final vote on the fate of Somaliland. Based on primary and secondary materials, UN official records, and interviews; 4 tables, 40 notes. C. Fry

1945. Ghoshal, Animesh. THE IMPACT OF FOREIGN RUBBER CONCESSIONS ON THE LIBERIAN ECONOMY, 1966-71. *J. of Modern African Studies [Great Britain] 1974 12(4): 589-599.* Investigates the contributions of the Liberian rubber industry to the nation's economy. The government of Liberia, after years of welcoming foreign investment, is now considering an ill-advised interventionist role. 5 tables, 21 notes. H. G. Soff

1946. Goody, Jack; Cole, Michael; and Scribner, Sylvia. WRITING AND FORMAL OPERATIONS: A CASE STUDY AMONG THE VAI. *Africa [Great Britain] 1977 47(3): 289-304.* Access to the detailed written records of 1926-59 of a Muslim brotherhood in Vai throw light on the organization, financial transactions and functions of such brotherhoods, and on the spread of the Malodi associations from Mende into neighboring Vai. Reproduces a translation into English of the complete text of the *Constitution of the Missila Organization,* which constitutes a code of morals, lays down strict regulations concerning the place of women in the brotherhood, and indicates the influence of Islam on commercial and social welfare organizations of this kind. Primary sources; 10 notes, biblio., 2 appendixes. R. L. Collison

1947. Handwerker, W. Penn. CHANGING HOUSEHOLD ORGANIZATION IN THE ORIGINS OF MARKET PLACES IN LIBERIA. *Econ. Development and Cultural Change 1974 22(2): 229-248.* Examines the effect of government-sponsored marketplaces on Liberian society (1950-70). Originally a government response to the dislocation caused by industrial innovation, the marketplaces have also enabled women to assume more of the responsibility for household subsistence by market selling. Based primarily on a sample of 783 Liberian market sellers; illus., 9 tables, 13 notes. J. W. Thacker, Jr.

1948. Handwerker, W. Penn. DAILY MARKETS AND URBAN ECONOMIC DEVELOPMENT. *Human Organization 1979 38(4): 366-376.* Traces the development of the local market system of food supply in Monrovia, Liberia since the 1940's.

1949. Handwerker, W. Penn. KINSHIP, FRIENDSHIP, AND BUSINESS FAILURE AMONG MARKET SELLERS IN MONROVIA, LIBERIA, 1970. *Africa [Great Britain] 1973 43(4): 288-301.* Discusses "the intertwining of the obligations among close friends and kin and the firms of market sellers in Monrovia, Liberia."

1950. Handwerker, W. Penn. MARKET PLACES, TRAVELLING TRADERS, AND SHOPS: COMMERCIAL STRUCTURAL VARIATION IN THE LIBERIAN INTERIOR PRIOR TO 1940. *African Econ. Hist. 1980 (9): 3-26.* Market places, which require long-distance trade and sufficient buyers and sellers, first appeared in Liberia in the 17th century with the arrival of travelling Mande kola traders from the north. In the 18th century trade in less perishable goods came under the control of chiefs, warriors, and secret societies. Resident merchants appeared in the north by the 1800's, and a century later interior markets encouraged by the state were integrated into trading networks dominated by a Euro-American world economy. Based on field research between 1968-1970; 3 fig., 73 notes. W. D. Piersen

1951. Hlophe, Stephen. RULING FAMILIES AND POWER STRUGGLES IN LIBERIA. *J. of African Studies 1979 6(2): 75-82.* The Liberian political system during the long incumbency of the late President William V. S. Tubman shifted its emphasis from the formerly all-powerful families among the Americo-Liberian population to the presidency itself. President Tubman's moves to expand the Liberian polity by incorporating the hinterland peoples and to develop the economy through his open door policy fostered the rise of African nationalism and young technocrats from the interior. His successor after 1971, William R. Tolbert, sought to advance the public service and economy, while uprooting corruption identified with the older generation of politicians. By 1975, however, the clash between interests of the old families elite and the awakened nationalists of the hinterland had reached a crisis point. Based on fieldwork and printed and secondary sources; 29 notes. L. W. Truschel

1952. Liebenow, J. Gus. THE LIBERIAN COUP IN PERSPECTIVE. *Current Hist. 1981 80(464): 101-105, 131-134.* Gives the historical background to the Liberian coup of 12 April 1980, discusses its significance, and examines the arguments over whether it was reformist or revolutionary in nature.

1953. Nelson, Randle W. and Hlophe, Stephen S. EDUCATION AND POLITICS IN LIBERIA AND THE UNITED STATES: A SOCIO-ECONOMIC COMPARISON OF COLONY AND COLONIZER. *Umoja 1977 1(1): 55-72.* Compares institutional interrelations and social organization based on the growth of higher education and government policy development in Liberia and the United States, 1940's-60's.

1954. Sesay, Amadu. SOCIETAL INEQUALITIES, ETHNIC HETEROGENEITY AND POLITICAL INSTABILITY: THE CASE OF LIBERIA. *Plural Soc. [Netherlands] 1980 11(3): 15-30.* Africans in Liberia are little attached to their usually Eurocentric political institutions. Widely different ethnic groups within the country further complicate the competition for power, already difficult because of economic limitations. The April 1980 coup ended 130 years of dominance by Americo-Liberians and led to the first majority-based government, which has attempted to correct some of the abuses permitted multinational corporations. The coup was made possible by the 1973 permission of legal opposition.

1955. Sundiata, Ibrahim K. DIDWO TWE: LIBERIAN OPPOSITION AND HINTERLAND POLICY IN THE TWENTIETH CENTURY. *Tarikh [Nigeria] 1981 7(1): 47-56.* Discusses political conflict between the indigenous and immigrant populations of Liberia from its independence in 1847 to the 20th century, focusing on Didwo Twe (born 1879), a Liberian politician and spokesman for the Kru tribe, and his role in this conflict especially from the 1930's to 1960.

1956. Syfert, Dwight Nash. THE LIBERIAN NAVY SINCE 1892. *Am. Neptune 1979 39(3): 173-183.* In 1892 Liberia purchased two steel gunboats for use as revenue steamers. Until World War I these, and a few other minor craft, enforced commercial regulations. From 1920 until 1952 Liberia was without a naval force of any kind. Since the 50's Liberia has had a presidential yacht and naval gunboats (organized as the National Coast Guard) which have enforced customs duties, a significant source of governmental income, and served as symbols of national power. Based on newspapers; 16 notes. J. C. Bradford

1957. —. [LIBERIA AND DUAL CITIZENSHIP].

Obatala, J. K. LIBERIA: THE MEANING OF "DUAL CITIZENSHIP." *Black Scholar 1973 4(10): 16-19.* Gives a brief description of Liberia's history, its origin as an American neocolonial experiment and eventually its development as a settler-dominated state. Examines the concept of dual citizenship, as outlined by Jesse Jackson, for Afro-Americans.

Shick, Tom W. LIBERIA RECONSIDERED: A REPLY TO J. K. OBATALA. *Black Scholar 1973 5(2): 53-56.* Reviews the history of Liberia to point out the false premises in the article by J. K. Obatala.

Mali

1958. Amselle, Jean-Loup. LA CONSCIENCE PAYSANNE: LA RÉVOLTE DE OUOLOSSÉBOUGOU (JUIN 1968, MALI) [The peasant consciousness: the revolt of Ouolossébougou, June 1968, Mali]. *Can. J. of African Studies [Canada] 1978 12(3): 339-355.* Relates the development of the Ouolossébougou revolt in Mali, in June 1968, six months before the downfall of the socialist regime. Sets the revolt in its sociohistorical context and analyzes the different visions of this uprising, of the government and the rebels. Examines the ideology behind the revolt and the part played by the chiefdom, as well as by geomancy and magic impersonating power. Places the movement within the class struggle in Mali, considered from the viewpoint of factionalism and relations between peasants, tradesmen, and the government apparatus. 26 notes. J/S

1959. Amselle, Jean-Loup. LE MALI SOCIALISTE (1960-68) [Socialist Mali, 1960-68]. *Cahiers d'Études Africaines [France] 1978 18(4): 631-634.* Reviews William I. Jones's *Planning and Economic Policy: Socialist Mali and its Neighbors* (1976), which provides a critical examination of the socialist regime in Mali, 1960-68, and Klaus Ernst's *Tradition and Progress in the African Village: The Non-capitalist Transformation of Rural Communities in Mali* (1976), which studies the peasantry in Mali, 1960-68.

1960. Bennett, Valerie Plave. MILITARY GOVERNMENT IN MALI. *J. of Modern African Studies [Great Britain] 1975 13(2): 249-266.* Studies the military government in Mali's lack of ideological or broad political ambitions and the alleged short-lived power of such governments lacking political ambitions. This is perhaps due to their inability to solve the economic problems inherited from the civilian regime. 52 notes. R. V. Ritter

1961. Hopkins, Nicholas S. A MANINKA MYTHICAL CHARTER. *J. of African Studies 1979 6(1): 17-26.* A comparative and critical analysis of numerous versions of Maninka oral traditions relating to events in the 13th century that have formed a "mythical charter" endorsing the later social and political order among the Maninka of Mali. The versions of this mythical charter do not purport to be accurate. Instead, they symbolically classify the various Maninka groups and express their dominant political values. Based on interviews, other primary, and secondary sources; 35 notes. L. W. Truschel

1962. Marchal, Jean-Yves. L'OFFICE DU NIGER: ÎLOT DE PROSPÉRITÉ PAYSANNE OU PÔLE DE PRODUCTION AGRICOLE? [The Office du Niger: island of peasant prosperity or center of agricultural production?]. *Can. J. of African Studies [Canada] 1974 8(1): 73-90.* Traces the development programs established in the Office du Niger from the 1920's and analyzes the conditions leading to the conflict between the tillers and the office representatives.

1963. Martin, Guy. SOCIALISM, ECONOMIC DEVELOPMENT AND PLANNING IN MALI, 1960-1968. *Can. J. of African Studies [Canada] 1976 10(1): 23-46.* Examines the socialist experiment of Modibo Keita in Mali, 1960-68. The experiment was hampered by the traditional lifestyles of the people. Based on government documents and secondary works; 58 notes. J

1964. Poláček, Josef. VNITROPOLITICKÁ KRIZE REPUBLIKY MALI V LÉTĚ 1967 [Crisis of domestic policy in Mali in summer of 1967]. *Československý Časopis Hist. [Czechoslovakia] 1976 24(2): 189-208.* Progress toward socialism in Mali was interrupted by a reactionary military coup d'état in November 1968, caused by the 1967 domestic political crisis surrounding devaluation and return to the Franc Zone. 40 notes. G. E. Pergl

1965. Rochegude, A. QUELQUES IDÉES SUR LA MÉTHODOLOGIE D'UNE RÉFORME AGRO-FONCIÈRE: L'EXEMPLE DU MALI [The methodology of agrarian reform: the example of Mali]. *African Perspectives [Netherlands] 1979 (1): 83-96.* Analyzes land reform in Mali, centering on the rural development "operations" initiated in 1972. These have multiplied since and constitute successful elements of a progressive and more practical than legal agrarian reform. They have remedied the inadequacy of the land rules mostly inherited from the colonial period and of the laws which, although perfective, had been enacted by the Mali government. It is hoped that they also will contribute to the country's economic and social revolution. Based on official Mali government documents; 15 notes. G. P. Cleyet

1966. Strizek, Helmut. MALI ZWISCHEN MOSKAU UND PEKING—VOR UND NACH DEM "SOZIALISMUS" [Mali between Moscow and Peking—before and after "socialism"]. *Osteuropa [West Germany] 1976 26(4): 254-261.* Led by Modibo Keita during its first eight years of independence, 1960-68, Mali was socialist and neutralist in orientation; in foreign policy it was torn between Moscow, Peking, and Western nations, especially West Germany.

1967. Sy, Moussa Oumar. PROVINCES, CANTONS ET VILLAGES DU SOUDAN FRANÇAIS, DES ORIGINES À L'INDÉPENDENCE. LA COLONIE DU SOUDAN [Provinces, cantons, and villages of French Sudan from its origins to independence: the colony of Sudan]. *Bull. de l'Inst. Fondamental d'Afrique Noire. Série B [Senegal] 1978 40(3): 489-512.* Discusses the origins and establishment of the colony of French Sudan in 1851, and considers directives and orders which changed its administrative organization and boundaries, 1892-1949. Includes data on population growth, 1929-53, and on the nature and authority of internal administrative subdivisions. Based on the archives of Senegal; 7 tables, 45 notes, biblio. Article to be continued. H. L. Calkin

1968. Wolpin, Miles D. DEPENDENCY AND CONSERVATIVE MILITARISM IN MALI. *J. of Modern African Studies [Great Britain] 1975 13(4): 585-620.* Evaluates conditions necessary for a successful socialist revolution, as exemplified by the failure of the revolutionary attempt in Mali. Mobido Keita's form of government was state capitalism rather than socialism. Keita failed to subdue the army, to develop egalitarianism and self-sacrifice, to suppress corruption and bureaucratic elitism, and to create a class of political ideologists. When his policies threatened the elites and the army which supported them, the latter moved to terminate his leadership. 56 notes. V. L. Human

1969. Wolpin, Miles D. LEGITIMISING STATE CAPITALISM: MALIAN MILITARISM IN THIRD-WORLD PERSPECTIVE. *J. of Modern African Studies [Great Britain] 1980 18(2): 281-295.* The active participation of military elites in the Malian government points to a number of recurring problems in the civil-military relations of developing nations; such problems incude excessive government use of force and coercion, inadequate attention to economic development, and a climate of political instability. S

1970. Zolberg, Vera L. NATIONAL GOALS, SOCIAL MOBILITY AND PERSONAL ASPIRATIONS: STUDENTS IN MALI. *Can. J. of African Studies [Canada] 1976 10(1): 125-142.* Mali, one of Africa's poorest nations, has used education to encourage popular nationalism and economic development. The author compares Mali with the Ivory Coast, a richer, nonsocialist country. As in many other countries, there are now many highly educated Malians who refuse to do manual labor, further burdening an already strained economy. Based on interviews, surveys, government documents, and secondary works; 7 tables, 45 notes. J

1971. —. SOCIALIST MALI AND HER NEIGHBORS. *African Econ. Hist. 1978 (5): 78-84.*
Foltz, William J., *pp. 78-80.*
Amselle, Jean-Loup, *pp. 80-81.*
Stryker, J. Dirck, *pp. 81-84.* Reviews William I. Jones's *Planning and Economic Policy: Socialist Mali and Her Neighbors* (Washington, D.C.: Three Continents Press, 1976), which examines the historical background of Mali's development plan of 1961-65 and evaluates its effectiveness from independence to the military coup of 1965. The plan failed because it underestimated the costs and productivity of public enterprise, because Mali lacked sufficient trained personnel, and because the plan was weakened by naivete and miscalculations. W. D. Piersen

Mauritania

1972. Balans, Jean-Louis. SOCIÉTÉ PLURALE ET INTÉGRATION POLITIQUE EN MAURITANIE [Plural society and political integration in Mauritania]. *African Perspectives [Netherlands] 1977 (2): 63-77.* A historical analysis of the plural society and its integration in Mauritania, whose population, since the 15th century, has consisted mainly of nomadic Moors coexisting with an important minority of settled blacks. The emergence of a Mauritanian nation has resulted in spite of a permanent tension between the Mediterranean Islamic and black Sudanese poles, the former being the more active. After many interethnic conflicts, Mauritania realized its national unity; but the modernization undertaken between 1972 and 1975, involving important social structural changes, might revive the old contradictions. Biblio. G. P. Cleyet

1973. Fessard de Foucault, Bertrand. LE PARTI DU PEUPLE MAURITANIEN [The Mauritanian People's Party]. *Rev. Française d'Études Pol. Africaines [France] 1973 8(94): 33-60; (95): 72-98.* Part I. Studies the development of political unity in Mauritania through the creation of a single-party system, with the goal of economic and human advancement, 1946-66. Part II. Deals with the formation of the single-party political system in Mauritania, describing the process of integration of this system into the country's political life, and the absorption of different organized forces into the party, 1966-73.

1974. Fessard de Foucault, Bertrand. SEIZE ANS DE DIPLOMATIE MAURITANIENNE [Sixteen years of Mauritanian diplomacy]. *Rev. Française d'Études Pol. Africaines [France] 1973 (87): 82-92.* Discusses the vital foreign politics of the Islamic Republic of Mauritania, which since its 1960 independence has demonstrated singular national solidarity in its refusal to yield to demands and claims by neighboring Spanish Sahara, Mali, and Morocco.

1975. Stewart, Charles C. A MAURITANIAN REFORMER: SHAIKH SIDIYYA BABA. *Tarikh [Nigeria] 1981 7(1): 65-70.* Discusses the life and political career of Shaikh Sidiyya Baba (1862-1926) in Mauritania, focusing on his role as a spokesman for the political interests of colonial subjects during the late 19th and early 20th centuries and as an example of Muslim influence on the developing nationalist consciousness of Africa.

1976. Vermeer, Donald E. COLLISION OF CLIMATE, CATTLE, AND CULTURE IN MAURITANIA DURING THE 1970S. *Geographical Rev. 1981 71(3): 281-297.* West-central Mauritania normally receives larger amounts of precipitation than do areas to the west and the east. Transhumant groups and cattle, the least drought-tolerant of the herd animals, are concentrated in this favored corridor. During the 1970's this section of the country experienced greater severity of drought than did areas to the west and the east, the chief factor accounting for a 55% loss of cattle by 1973. If historical and climatic patterns persist, drought may recur in Mauritania during the first years of the 21st century. Planning and development with uncharacteristic imagination and flexibility are required to forestall the effects of droughts in this volatile environment. J

Niger

1977. Baier, Stephen. TRANS-SAHARAN TRADE AND THE SAHEL: DAMERGU 1870-1930. *J. of African Hist. [Great Britain] 1977 18(1): 37-60.* Focusing on the Sahelian region of Damergu (Niger) analyzes reaction to the fluctuating caravan trade, 1890's-1920's, on the Tripoli-Kano route, which traverses the area. Damergu population rose and fell with the trade. After 1900, trans-Saharan trade ended, as Sahelian villagers began to trade staples primarily with the south, forsaking traditional links northward through Agadez. 63 notes. H. G. Soff

1978. Baratov, N. NIGER: NAZVANIIA NA ZHELTOM FONE (OCHERK VTOROI) [Niger: names against a yellow background]. *Aziia i Afrika Segodnia [USSR] 1982 (5): 42-44, (6): 36-38.* Describes the author's tour of Agadez, the largest of Niger's seven regions, ruled by a sultan whose position continues a long tradition but signifies little power today.

1979. Bernus, Edmond. L'ÉVOLUTION DES RELATIONS DE DÉPENDANCE DEPUIS LA PÉRIODE PRE-COLONIALE JUSQU'À NOS JOURS CHEZ LES IULLEMMEDEN KEL DINNIK [The evolution of dependency relationships among the Yullemmeden kel Dinnik from the precolonial period to the present]. *Rev. de l'Occident Musulman et de la Méditerranée [France] 1976 (21): 85-99.* Examines the dependents, free men who are neither overlords nor captives, who constitute the majority of the Yullemmeden kel Dinnik Tuareg. Discusses the nature of dependency relationships, the impact of colonialism, social change, the creation of new chieftaincies, and the role of the overlords. Map, 9 notes, biblio. R. O. Khan

1980. Bernus, S. STRATÉGIE MATRIMONIALE ET CONSERVATION DU POUVOIR DANS L'AIR ET CHEZ LES IULLEMMEDEN [Matrimonial policy and the retention of power in Aïr and among the Yullemmeden]. *Rev. de l'Occident Musulman et de la Méditerranée [France] 1976 (21): 101-104.* Examines how the various strata within the society of the Yullemmeden Tuareg of the Aïr region have guaranteed their privileges through endogamous marriage since the 19th century. The Yullemmeden have preserved endogamy virtually intact until recently, but political conflict has forced other groups to relax this policy in order to survive and preserve their autonomy. Note, biblio. R. O. Khan

1981. Franke, Richard W. and Chasin, Barbara H. PEANUTS, PEASANTS, PROFITS, AND PASTORALISTS: THE SOCIAL AND ECONOMIC BACKGROUND TO ECOLOGICAL DETERIORATION IN NIGER. *Peasant Studies 1979 8(3): 1-30.* Discusses the economic and social processes which influenced the disastrous effects of the Sahelian drought in the 1970's.

1982. Fugelstad, Finn. LES *HAUKA*: UNE INTERPRETATION HISTORIQUE [The Hauka: a historical interpretation]. *Cahiers d'Études Africaines [France] 1975 15(2): 203-216.* Describes the *Hauka,* a politico-religious sect found among Hausa-speaking animists in Niger. Although the sect first appeared in 1925, its roots lay in the disruption of local society caused by the 19th-century Moslem revolution and the early 20th-century French conquest. Spirit possession characterizes the thought of the sect, and the incorporation of French offices into its spiritual hierarchy in 1925-27 later became a means for individuals to express their anxieties about modernization. Based on subprefectural and prefectural achives in Niger and published sources; 71 notes. B. S. Fetter

1983. Fuglestad, Finn. LA GRANDE FAMINE DE 1931 DANS L'OUEST NIGÉRIEN: RÉFLEXIONS AUTOUR D'UNE CATASTROPHE NATURELLE [The great famine of 1931 in western Niger: reflections on a natural catastrophe]. *Rev. Française d'Hist. d'Outre-Mer [France] 1974 61(222): 18-33.* A locust invasion and drought were the main reasons for the 1931 famine in western Niger. The population of the region was reduced by 25 to 50%. The French authorities were more concerned with maintaining law and order than with directly coping with the food shortage. Based on documents in the presidential, prefectural, and subprefectural archives of the Republic of the Niger and secondary works; 69 notes. L. B. Chan

1984. Fuglestad, Finn. LES RÉVOLTES DES TOUAREG DU NIGER (1916-17) [The revolts of the Tuareg of Niger, 1916-17]. *Cahiers d'Études Africaines [France] 1973 13(1): 82-120.* The Saharan regions of Niger had only recently been pacified when World War I forced the withdrawal of many French troops from the colonies. The Tuareg, in alliance with the Sanusi brotherhood headquartered in Libya, took advantage of this to revolt and to extend their sway over much of northern Niger and Chad, as well as southern Libya. The appeal of the Sanusi to the Tuareg seems to have been more practical politics than religious conversion. So successful were the insurgents that the French did not finally "pacify" many regions until 1931. 64 notes.
J. C. Billigmeier

1985. Fuglestad, Finn. UNIS AND BNA: THE ROLE OF "TRADITIONALIST" PARTIES IN NIGER, 1948-60. *J. of African Hist. [Great Britain] 1975 16(1): 113-135.* Interprets political developments in Niger prior to independence. Focuses on the Union Nigérienne des Indépendants et Sympathisants (UNIS) and its successor the Bloc Nigérien d'Action (BNA), termed "traditionalist" parties. Analyzes the distinction between these traditionalist parties and the modern parties that have evolved since 1960. 114 notes. H. G. Soff

1986. Higgott, Richard and Fuglestad, Finn. THE 1974 COUP D'ÉTAT IN NIGER: TOWARDS AN EXPLANATION. *J. of Modern African Studies [Great Britain] 1975 13(3): 383-398.* There were four main causes of the downfall of President Hamani Diori's regime to an army coup d'etat led by Lieutenant Colonel Seyni Kountche on 14 April 1974: 1) The underlying conflicts in Niger prior to independence in 1960 were still of crucial importance. Diori's strength was not at the level supposed. 2) The Government was unwilling or unable to modify French involvement in all aspects of economic and political life. 3) By 1974, the socioeconomic and political pressures on the regime had grown immensely. 4) Army leaders believed that the army needed to protect its "corporate self-interest." That these problems have been solved is not yet evident. 45 notes. R. V. Ritter

1987. Lawless, R. I. URANIUM MINING AT ARLIT IN THE REPUBLIC OF NIGER. *Geography [Great Britain] 1974 59(1): 45-48.* Uranium mining in Arlit, Republic of Niger, since 1968 has been conducted under the auspices of a consortium of the Niger Government, the French Atomic Energy Commission, and other French, German, and Italian companies; the project was designed to pull Niger out of its "least developed nation" status.

1988. Poitou, Danièle. ARLIT, VILLE PIONNIERE DE L'INDUSTRIALISATION NIGERIENNE [Arlit, pioneer city of Niger industrialization]. *Afrique et l'Asie Modernes [France] 1982 (2): 29-47.* Retraces the successive stages of the birth of the Niger mining town of Arlit, discussing its conception and development, its integration into the life of the region, its role in the economic upswing of the country, and the value of the uranium ore it mines.

Nigeria

General

1989. Adejuyigbe, Omolade. EVOLUTION OF INTER-COMMUNITY BOUNDARIES IN AFRICA. *Cahiers de Géographie de Québec 1974 18(43): 83-105.* A model of boundary evolution with examples from Western Nigeria. S

1990. Aguolu, C. C. NATIONAL BIBLIOGRAPHY IN NIGERIA: ITS GROWTH, DEVELOPMENT AND INTERNATIONAL DIMENSIONS. *African Res. and Documentation [Great Britain] 1982 (28): 2-9.* Discusses the history, holdings and international standards of Nigeria's National Bibliography.

1991. Akintoye, S. A. NIGERIA CONTRIBUTIONS TO BLACK HISTORY. *Nigeria Mag. [Nigeria] 1975 (115/116): 116-135.* Although European and American historians denied that Africa had a history until recently, Nigerian writings on Africa date from the 11th century. The author emphasizes Nigerian historians of the past 30 years, such as K. O. Dike and S. O. Biobaku, and includes a brief history of Nigeria from the stone age to the present. The role of Nigerians in the Americas is presented. 51 notes. H. G. Soff

1992. Akintunde, J. O. NIGERIAN NATIONAL CHARACTER: A POLITICAL SCIENCE PERSPECTIVE. *Odu [Nigeria] 1974 (9): 95-112.* There are five elements of Nigerian national characteristics which are significant because of the effect they may have on nation-building, national unity, stability, and economic development. They are: tribalism or ethnic particularism, materialistic individualism, traditionalism, colonial mentality, and optimism. Secondary sources; 52 notes.
M. M. McCarthy

1993. Barth, James L. AS NIGERIA GOES, SO GOES.... *Indiana Social Studies Q. 1977 30(2): 56-61.* Discusses Nigeria's movement toward economic and political independence, 1960-77; examines its influence over other African nations and the economic independence oil affords it.

1994. Bello, S. and Oyedele, E. THE CITY OF KADUNA. *Nigeria Mag. [Nigeria] 1978 (124-125): 63-76.* Describes the location, origins, administration, industry, and culture of Kaduna, an important city of north-central Nigeria, and its urban development, 1913-78.

1995. Brionne, Bernard. LE NIGÉRIA, GRANDE PUISSANCE AFRICAINE [Nigeria, a great African power]. *Défense Natl. [France] 1973 29(12): 63-78.* Follows the evolution of Nigeria since 1945, noting the renewal of internal stability, the strong government, reinforced by careful use of oil revenues, and the formation of a progressive capitalist system very different from governments of neighboring countries.

1996. Farley, Jonathan. NIGERIA: THE TRIBAL STRUCTURE. *World Survey [Great Britain] 1976 (93-94): 17-32.*

1997. Gambari, Ibrahim Agboola. NIGERIA AND THE WORLD: A GROWING INTERNAL STABILITY, WEALTH, AND EXTERNAL INFLUENCE. *J. of Int. Affairs 1975 29(2): 155-169.* Discusses the position of Nigeria in international affairs, reviews internal political and economic developments since the 1960's, analyzes Nigeria's contemporary role in Africa and the world, and comments on its prospects.

1998. Gonyok, C. K. THE CITY OF JOS. *Nigeria Mag. [Nigeria] 1978 (124-125): 83-87.* Describes the urban development and importance of Jos, capital of the Benue-Plateau State, as a communications center, ca. 1900-78.

1999. Grossman, David. IBOLAND'S POPULATION DISTRIBUTION: A GEOGRAPHICAL-HISTORICAL APPROACH TO AN EXPLANATION AND APPLICATION. *J. of Developing Areas 1975 9(2): 253-270.* Tropical Africa's population distribution often displays close adjustment to ecological conditions, though the disruptive elements of the slave trade and insecurity are still in evidence. In Igboland (eastern Nigeria) people are clustered in infertile sandy areas which offer the advantages of better roadways, good drainage, and less mosquito infestation, but they also lack food supply and easily obtainable water. Such infertile areas may not have been valued as sufficiently attractive economically for anyone to expand into. The imbalance between the geographical distribution of the natural resources and of the population still remains. Based on fieldwork in Igboland in 1966; 2 figs., 51 notes.
O. W. Eads, Jr.

2000. Hamman, Mahmoud. THE CITY OF YOLA. *Nigeria Mag. [Nigeria] 1978 (124-125): 97-101.* Describes the location, urban development, industry and agriculture of Yola, capital of Gongola State since 1976, from its foundation in ca. 1841.

2001. Herskovits, Jean. NIGERIA: AFRICA'S NEW POWER. *Foreign Affairs 1975 53(2): 314-333.* Stresses the importance of Nigeria in African affairs and to the United States. The only black African oil-producing country, Nigeria, is the United States' second largest supplier of crude oil. Its military government, headed by General Yakubu Gowon, faces certain problems. Plans are being made to rectify shortages of food and trained manpower as well as to start on an indigenous program of industrialization. Despite the end of the civil war in 1970, internal problems remain to be settled, and a census was held in 1973-74 to aid in planning. 10 notes. C. W. Olson

2002. Hughes, Arnold. THE ARMY AS "SOCIAL ENGINEERS" IN NIGERIA. *Contemporary Rev. [Great Britain] 1977 231(1343): 286-291.* Describes how the Nigerian army engaged in a program of "social engineering," 1965-77, with the aim of transforming an economically underdeveloped and politically divided society into a democratic industrial state.

2003. Jarmon, Charles. INDIGENIZATION AND NATION BUILDING IN NIGERIA. *Can. Rev. of Studies in Nationalism [Canada] 1980 7(2): 259-273.* As a result of colonization, European culture was adopted in sub-Saharan Africa. Since independence, nations have increasingly pursued a policy of indigenization, systematic action to reestablish traditional elements or introduce functional alternatives to European culture. In Nigeria, foreign ownership of firms has been limited, missionary schools have been put under state control, universities have been encouraged to research African culture, and Western customs have come under criticism. 29 notes. R. Aldrich

2004. Nkemdirim, Bernard. SOCIAL CHANGE AND THE GENESIS OF POLITICAL CONFLICT IN NIGERIA. *Civilisations [Belgium] 1975 25(1/2): 84-98.* From 1900 to 1966 Nigeria underwent extensive changes in economy, education, and urbanization. These changes were uneven, leading to a concentration of economic resources and the early emergence of a new middle class in the highly urbanized south of Nigeria. In the long run this stimulated changes in the interior northern provinces and the extension of Western education created a new elite sensitive to the lack of balance. Eventually this led to conflict between northern and southern contenders for power. 6 tables, 1 note, biblio. H. L. Calkin

2005. Onibokun, Adepoju. FORCES SHAPING THE PHYSICAL ENVIRONMENT OF CITIES IN THE DEVELOPING COUNTRIES: THE IBADAN CASE. *Land Econ. 1973 49(4): 424-431.*

2006. Prothero, R. Mansell. SOME PERSPECTIVES ON DROUGHT IN NORTH-WEST NIGERIA. *African Affairs [Great Britain] 1974 73(291): 162-169.* Reviews of the physical conditions of North-West Nigeria (former Sokoto Province) where the federal government has declared a disaster area due to the drought. Mentions earlier drought periods in the 20th century, and discusses the human factor. 2 maps, 22 notes. H. G. Soff

2007. Said, Halil I. ARABIC MANUSCRIPTS IN NORTHERN NIGERIA. *Islamic Q. [Great Britain] 1974 18(3-4): 62-72.* Drawing attention to the importance of Arabic manuscripts as source material for the study and teaching of Nigerian history, the author examines the different categories of manuscripts from the pre-Jihad period to contemporary writings. He also names the centers and institutions currently engaged in collecting and preserving manuscripts in Nigeria, and assesses the extent of Nigerian awareness of the value of this material for historical information. 24 notes, biblio. P. J. Taylorson

2008. Stanley, Janet L. REVIEW ESSAY: YORUBA BIBLIOGRAPHY. *J. of African Studies 1977-78 4(4): 474-483.* A detailed critique of David E. Baldwin and Charlene M. Baldwin's *The Yoruba of Southwestern Nigeria: An Indexed Bibliography* (Boston: G. K. Hall, 1976). The Baldwins fail to arrange their references by subject, correct typographical errors, and include broader works dealing with the Yoruba, and lift entire entries from an earlier Nigerian bibliography. The work is unfinished and of questionable use. 3 notes. L. W. Truschel

Economics

2009. Abalu, G. I. O. THE ROLE OF LAND TENURE IN THE AGRICULTURAL DEVELOPMENT OF NIGERIA. *Odu: a J. of West African Studies 1977 (15): 30-43.* Land tenure may provide a means for either facilitating or restraining the development of land resources. The attitude in Nigeria, 1966-73, of allowing individual ownership to gain ground over communal ownership is not conducive to managing the country's resources in the best interest of society. 2 tables, 4 notes. M. M. McCarthy

2010. Abiodun, Josephine Olu. LOCATIONAL EFFECTS OF THE CIVIL WAR ON THE NIGERIAN PETROLEUM INDUSTRY. *Geographical R. 1974 64(2): 253-263.* "The Nigerian petroleum industry has experienced a dynamic rate of growth, particularly since the outbreak of civil war in 1967. The annual value of crude-oil exports rose significantly, from $219,193,120 in 1967 to $1,448,608,640 in 1971. Accompanying this expansion was a shift in the focus of intensive crude-oil exploitation in Nigeria. By the end of the war, in 1970, the Midwestern State had superseded the former Eastern Region as the premier producer of crude oil in Nigeria. Intensive crude-oil activities in the Midwestern State, coupled with the satellization policy of the companies that exploited crude oil, had a differential impact on the growth of settlements in crude-oil-producing areas of the state." J

2011. Afonja, Simi. CHANGING MODES OF PRODUCTION AND THE SEXUAL DIVISION OF LABOR AMONG THE YORUBA. *Signs 1981 7(2): 299-313.* Modernization theory cannot explain the cause and effect of female subordination in cultures like the Yoruba, where the economy is characterized by a low level of specialization. A multidimensional approach proves that there is some continuity between traditional and modern Africa. Not until the 19th century did long-distance trade patterns change the scale and unit of trade, thereby changing the woman's role. While women engaged actively in trade, their sphere was only the small retail shop. The value structure continued to place the woman's function as biological and social reproduction. Based on interviews and research financed by the Ford Foundation; 33 notes. S. P. Conner

2012. Akeredolu-Ale, E. O. A SOCIOLOGICAL STUDY OF THE DEVELOPMENT OF ENTREPRENEURSHIP AMONG THE IJEBU OF WESTERN NIGERIA. *African Studies R. 1973 16(3): 347-364.* Geographical location and high economic and sociocultural standing have enabled the Ijebu to emerge as entrepreneurs among Yoruba people. S

2013. Allen, Rob. AGRICULTURE AND INDUSTRY: A CASE-STUDY OF CAPITALIST FAILURE IN NORTHERN NIGERIA. *J. of Modern African Studies [Great Britain] 1980 18(3): 427-441.* In an effort to make Nigeria's tomato crop self-sufficient, the Nigerian North-Central state government invited the British Cadbury Schweppes firm into its Zaria area to develop a processing factory in 1968. The project collapsed over the next eight years, as the state and company failed to offer the Nigerian peasant farmers economic incentives that matched the higher prices on the free market for their tomato crops. Based on Cadbury Nigeria Limited reports and secondary sources; table, 38 notes. L. W. Truschel

2014. Aluko, Olajide. NIGERIA AND THE EUROPEAN ECONOMIC COMMUNITY. *Int. Studies [India] 1974 13(3): 465-474.* Discusses Nigeria's role in the African nations' negotiations for improved economic ties and trade with the European Economic Community, 1966-73; asserts that Nigeria has emerged into a dominant role among the developing nations because of its political and economic stability.

2015. Ayaode, J. A. A. FEDERALISM AND WAGE POLITICS IN NIGERIA. *J. of Commonwealth and Comparative Pol. [Great Britain] 1975 13(3): 282-289.* Demands for increased wages have often been attributed to rises in the cost of living. However, this assumes that wage increases exceed the growth of productivity and result in higher unit labor costs; such reasoning cannot explain the cyclical pattern in Nigerian wage demands. Since wages are a political issue, wage increases frequently precede an election. Increases in any one region extend to other regions and to the federal government. 28 notes. R. D. Black/S

2016. Bamisaiye, Anne. BEGGING IN IBADAN, SOUTHERN NIGERIA. *Human Organization 1974 33(2): 197-202.*

2017. Barrett, Stanley R. COMMUNALISM, CAPITALISM AND STRATIFICATION IN AN AFRICAN UTOPIA. *J. of Asian and African Studies [Netherlands] 1978 13(1-2): 112-129.* Yoruba fishermen of Nigeria belonging to a prophetic sect established a communal society which, within a few years, became prosperous. Twenty years after the community was created its structure was changed by the leadership, which had succeeded in gaining control of much of the society's wealth. This religious leadership became a prosperous capitalist class. Based on fieldwork; 2 tables, 7 notes, biblio. R. T. Brown

2018. Berry, Sara S. THE CONCEPT OF INNOVATION AND THE HISTORY OF COCOA FARMING IN WESTERN NIGERIA. *J. of African Hist. [Great Britain] 1974 15(1): 83-95.* Cocoa growing in Western Nigeria spread through the efforts of migrant farmers who relied on such traditional noneconomic institutions as lineage and the ethnic community to amass the economic resources necessary to the establishment of cocoa farms. While cocoa growing strengthened traditional institutions in Ibadan, Ife, and Ondo, it also caused significant changes in the rural economic activity of Western Nigeria. Primary and secondary sources; 37 notes. E. Hopkins

2019. Berry, Sara S. SUPPLY RESPONSE RECONSIDERED: COCOA IN WESTERN NIGERIA, 1909-44. *J. of Development Studies [Great Britain] 1976 13(1): 4-17.* Examines statistical data concerning cocoa plantations in western Nigeria, concluding that annual variations were closely related to farmers' income from sales, and long-term trends were most affected by changing opportunity costs and the institutional structure of rural markets, 1909-44.

2020. Collins, Paul. THE POLITICAL ECONOMY OF INDIGENIZATION: THE CASE OF THE NIGERIAN ENTERPRISES PROMOTION DECREE. *African Rev. [Tanzania] 1974 4(4): 491-508.* In March 1972 Nigeria decreed the indigenization of control of a wide variety of business enterprises. The author outlines legislative features of the decrees and examines several cases of their implementation. The result of Nigerianization has not been as planned but rather "contributed to the articulation of conflicts of interest within Nigerian society." 2 tables, 28 notes. R. T. Brown

2021. Cookey, S. J. S. COLONIALISM AND THE PROCESS OF UNDERDEVELOPMENT IN NIGERIA. *J. of Asian and African Studies [Netherlands] 1979 14(1-2): 19-31.* Paper presented at the 1978 University of Nigeria, Nsukka workshop on dependency. Secondary sources; 18 notes, biblio. R. T. Brown

2022. Coulmas, Peter. BERICHT AUS LAGOS [Report from Lagos]. *Schweizer Monatshefte [Switzerland] 1978 58(10): 745-750.* Analyzes the impact of the Nigerian oil boom on the social, economic, and political situation of Lagos since 1966.

2023. Dangana, L. B. DYNAMIQUE URBAINE DE PORT HARCOURT, NIGERIA [The urban dynamism of Port Harcourt, Nigeria]. *Ann. de Géographie [France] 1980 89(495): 605-613.* Examines the impact of industrial expansion and agglomeration of economies on urban growth through the growth and development of the harbor of Port Harcourt, Nigeria in the past three decades.

2024. Dorward, D. C. AN UNKNOWN NIGERIAN EXPORT: TIV BENNISEED PRODUCTION, 1900-1960. *J. of African Hist. [Great Britain] 1975 16(3): 431-459.* An examination of the socioeconomic factors which influenced the Tiv to commercially develop the sesame (benniseed) industry. The Tiv, previously considered subsistence farmers, were actually not. Although it was an item of trade before colonial times, sesame did not play an important role in the indigenous economy until British intervention. Tiv participation in railway construction and their frivolous spending of money is discussed, and the major role of the British in Tiv sesame production is analyzed. Great Britain became the leading importer during World War II, and then virtually controlled the Tiv economy. Tiv farmers, however, were good businessmen and were capable of adapting to new techniques and procedures. 4 tables, graph, 117 notes, appendix. H. G. Soff

2025. Ebgoh, Edmund O. LEGAL EFFORTS TO CONTROL NIGERIAN FORESTS IN THE INTERESTS OF THE METROPOLITAN ECONOMY, 1897-1940. *Q. Rev. of Hist. Studies [India] 1979-80 19(1-2): 64-90.* The indiscriminate tapping of the rubber trees of Nigeria led the English to recognize that legal regulation of the rubber forests was necessary to protect future supplies. From the Benis Law to the more sophisticated and complex legislation of the late 1930's, the British government sustained a policy of active involvement, typical of the British practice throughout the empire. Primary sources; 137 notes. W. T. Walker

2026. Ekechi, F. K. ASPECTS OF PALM OIL TRADE AT OGUTA (EASTERN NIGERIA), 1900-1950. *African Econ. Hist. 1981 (10): 35-65.* The capital resources, canoes, and adroit political manipulations of Kalabari traders permitted them to displace the indigenous middlemen in the palm oil trade of Oguta. But this commercial dominance and the Kalabari's appeal to Igbo market women aroused intense local hostility which combined with the poor markets of the 1930's to eventually drive them from the area. Based on oral traditions and written colonial sources; table, 131 notes. W. D. Piersen

2027. Fajana, Olufemi. IMPORT LICENSING IN NIGERIA. *Development and Change [Netherlands] 1977 8(4): 509-522.* Though import licensing in Nigeria, 1950-75, was enacted to protect domestic industry, ease port congestion, and conserve foreign exchange, it has resulted in misallocation of resources, aggravation of inflation, and poor distribution of income since import planning has not been integrated into overall economic planning.

2028. Fajana, Olufemi. INTRAINDUSTRY WAGE DIFFERENTIALS IN NIGERIA. *J. of Developing Areas 1975 9(4): 523-538.* Dualism exists between small and large-scale businesses in the modern wage sector. A study of Nigerian establishments indicates there are wage differentials by size of establishment, with workers in larger industries earning more than those in small ones. There is a high positive correlation between establishment size and wage size even when industrial classification and skill-mix factors are considered. Large-scale businesses enjoy technological and pecuniary economies, superior productivity, and usually foreign sources of finance, thus giving them the advantage over small establishments. The organized labor movement is concentrated in large-scale industries, helping to explain the wage differentials. 5 tables, 31 notes. O. W. Eads, Jr.

2029. Fajana, Olufemi. TRENDS AND PROSPECTS OF NIGERIAN-JAPANESE TRADE. *J. of Modern African Studies [Great Britain] 1976 14(1): 127-136.* Nigeria's trade with Japan has generated intense local controversy. Imports from Japan grew from under a million naira in 1947 to over 160 million in 1974. Exports, which were zero until 1952, reached 238 million naira in 1974. This remarkable growth reflects a high degree of commodity complementarity between the two economies. Nigeria has lately restricted the importation of Japanese goods to diversify its economy and to rectify its balance of payments difficulties. Furthermore, Japanese aid to developing countries has been disappointing, and its involvement with South Africa is provocative. However, recent signs of changing Japanese attitudes are encouraging. Based on Nigerian government statistics, industry reports, trade journals, and other sources; 67 notes. W. R. Hively

2030. Famoriyo, Şegun. THE DYNAMICS OF DURATION AND ALIENATION ASPECTS IN NIGERIAN LAND TENURE. *Odu: a J. of West African Studies 1977 (15): 44-61.* Examines the land tenure system in Nigeria, 1950-75, in relation to the problems of modernization and employment opportunities in agriculture. Table, 24 notes. M. M. McCarthy

2031. Fatogun, Dapo. NEW HORIZONS IN NIGERIA. *World Marxist Rev. 1977 20(4): 96-102.* A short history of Nigeria since 1914 as an introduction to economic development plans enacted since 1960.

2032. Freund, W. M. LABOUR MIGRATION TO THE NORTHERN NIGERIAN TIN MINES, 1903-1945. *J. of African Hist. [Great Britain] 1981 22(1): 73-84.* The Niger Company established its first mining camp at the foot of the Jos Plateau in 1903. The extension of the railway and the new mines attracted large numbers of migrant casual laborers. The post-World War I slump of 1921 caused wages to be reduced to a third of former levels and the number of jobs to fall. In 1933 world tin prices recovered rapidly, but wages remained low and unemployment remained high, owing to the increased use of machinery and the installation of hydroelectric power. Throughout the period, mine administrators were divided concerning the relative merits of "voluntary" and "forced" labor, the underlying factor being the necessity for Africans to be able to pay their taxes in cash. Based on official reports and published sources; 41 notes. R. L. Collison

2033. Geveling, L. NIGERIISKIE MENEDZHERY V STRUKTURE EKONOMICHESKOI VLASTI [Managers in the structure of economic power in Nigeria]. *Aziia i Afrika Segodnia [USSR] 1981 (2): 47-49.* The emergence of a contingent of Nigerian managers is a law-governed process, combining both the general trends of a capitalist development and peculiarities of political and socioeconomic shifts in Nigeria. Discusses the economic programs worked out by Shehu Shagari's government, envisaging a greater importance for the local administration in the course of further consolidation of Nigeria's economic base. J

2034. Grossman, David. HATEEY'SHEVOTH S'PONTABIT V'HATEEY'SHEVOTH MITOCHAN'NITH BITS'FON IBOLAND, NEEGERIA [Spontaneous and planned agricultural resettlement in Northern Iboland, Nigeria]. *Hamizrah Hehadash [Israel] 1973 23(2): 168-193.* Impatient with the slow evolutionary approach of the former colonial authorities, African leaders after World War II returned to the idea of ambitious settlement and development schemes. The Eastern Nigeria Project aimed to create seven rural centers for 5,000 settlers, based on the Israeli model of regional development. Resistance of the local population, tension between old and new settlers, refusal to adopt modern agricultural methods, attempted exploitation of tenant farmers, and, finally, demands for their forced evacuation have aggravated rather than alleviated uneven population dispersion. The Biafra war brought this particular project to an end. F. Rosenthal

2035. Henderson, Robert D'A. NIGERIA: FUTURE NUCLEAR POWER? *Orbis 1981 25(2): 409-423.* Examines the prospect of Nigeria's developing a nuclear energy capability, which could be used for military purposes. Although Nigeria ratified the Nuclear Nonproliferation Treaty on 27 September 1968, it has no IAEA safeguards agreement in force and utilizes no nuclear reactors of fissionable materials. In order to ascertain how close Nigeria is to becoming a nuclear power, the author examines the technical expertise, mineral resources, nuclear-energy facilities, the transfer of nuclear technology, and the bureaucratic-intellectual constituencies of that nuclear technology. Based on government documents and published works; 33 notes. J. W. Thacker, Jr.

2036. Hinchliffe, Keith. LABOUR ARISTOCRACY: A NORTHERN NIGERIAN CASE STUDY. *J. of Modern African Studies [Great Britain] 1974 12(1): 57-67.* Questions accuracy and relevance of such ideas as labor aristocracy and rural-urban earning differences in Northern Nigeria. Suggests deeper analysis in rural-urban studies is required. 14 notes. H. G. Soff

2037. Hoogvelt, Ankie. INDIGENIZATION AND TECHNOLOGICAL DEPENDENCY. *Development and Change [Netherlands] 1980 11(2): 257-272.* Nigeria's policy of indigenization, by which foreign-owned businesses have had to sell equity in their firms to Nigerians, has not resulted in significantly improved company policies to benefit the localities. In Kano, for example, the indigenized firms employed more sophisticated forms of technology which did not provide more jobs for the local residents.

2038. Ikime, Obaro. THE BRITISH AND NATIVE ADMINISTRATION FINANCE IN NORTHERN NIGERIA, 1900-1934. *J. of the Hist. Soc. of Nigeria [Nigeria] 1975 7(4): 673-692.* A careful examination "of Native Administration finance and the role of Native Administration in the development" of Nigeria, with particular focus on Northern Nigeria. Taxation was the major source of revenue supporting the British administration, and it also served as a useful means of controlling local officials at the bottom of the ruling hierarchy. It was one means of indirect rule, and excess tax monies as well as the whole format of British control helped develop British resources at the expense of the governed region. A number of avenues of potential further research on Nigerian history are suggested. Based on a wide variety of manuscript material and printed sources. 4 tables, 47 notes, appendix. J. A. Casada

2039. Ladipo, Patricia. DEVELOPING WOMEN'S COOPERATIVES: AN EXPERIMENT IN RURAL NIGERIA. *J. of Development Studies [Great Britain] 1981 17(3): 123-136.* Focuses on two groups of Yoruba women that organized cooperatives, one following government regulations, and another more successful group that formed its own regulations.

2040. Lewis, A. O. A CASE STUDY OF INDIGENOUS ENTREPRENEURSHIP IN NIGERIA'S YABA INDUSTRIAL ESTATE. *Odu [Nigeria] 1974 (9): 45-63.* The Yaba Industrial Estate was set up by the Nigerian government to aid in the development of indigenous business. It provides factory buildings, utility services, and a workshop to give technical services to enterprises set up on the estate. The survey studies the enterprises in the Yaba Estate in 1970, as well as the background, motivations, and problems of the entrepreneurs. Based on a survey by the author and secondary sources; 14 tables, 14 notes. M. M. McCarthy

2041. Lovejoy, Paul E. THE BORNO SALT INDUSTRY. *Int. J. of African Hist. Studies 1978 11(4): 629-668.* Probably more salt was traded within Bornu than anywhere else in precolonial Africa. This study analyzes the role of the salt industry in the economy of Bornu during the late 19th and early 20th centuries and provides a preliminary chronology for the economic disintegration of Bornu in the 18th and 19th centuries. 2 maps, 5 tables, 79 notes. M. M. McCarthy

2042. Madujibeya, S. A. OIL AND NIGERIA'S ECONOMIC DEVELOPMENT. *African Affairs [Great Britain] 1976 75(300): 284-316.* Nigeria has been a commercial oil producer since 1958. In the past two decades income from the petroleum industry has risen dramatically. The author examines oil's contribution to the economic development of Nigeria. 6 tables, 67 notes. H. G. Soff

2043. Marican, Y. Mansoor. THE POLITICS OF DEVELOPMENT PLANNING IN NEW STATES: INDUSTRIAL LOCATION IN INDIA AND NIGERIA. *Philippine J. of Public Administration [Philippines] 1973 17(2): 157-177.* "Development planning in new states has been left to economists whose anti-political bias precludes the formulation of comprehensive and realistic plans—i.e., plans which consider not only quantifiable economic factors but also dynamic political variables. By failing to consider a) the political goals of the regime, b) the regime's will to carry out development plans, c) the regime's authority to implement such plans, and d) the nature and extent of political opposition to them, development plans had minimal chances of success from the beginning. The experience on the politics of selecting a site for a steel and iron industrial complex in India and for a textile mill in Nigeria gives at least six tentative propositions showing how inextricably linked are politics and planning. Failure to consider this reality has reduced development planning to a formal, symbolic exercise." J

2044. Milewski, Jan J. THE GREAT DEPRESSION OF THE EARLY 1930'S IN A COLONIAL COUNTRY: A CASE STUDY OF NIGERIA. *Africana Bull. [Poland] 1975 23: 7-45.* The Depression affected Nigeria very unevenly, with many areas being unaffected because they were outside the money economy, and results of the Depression were not entirely negative, as the economic squeeze prompted petit bourgeois efforts to mount economic anticolonial struggles.

2045. Morrison, J. H. EARLY TIN PRODUCTION AND NIGERIAN LABOUR ON THE JOS PLATEAU, 1906-1921. *Can. J. of African Studies [Canada] 1977 11(2): 205-216.* A study of the development of tin mining in northern Nigeria and the problems that developed both with indigenous labor and production. There was also the problem of safety as the result of the hostility engendered by dispossession of indigenous peoples. Even more significant was the total disruption of traditional trade and livelihood patterns. The government's levying a tax on the local inhabitants intended to force work in the mines had only limited success. 53 notes. R. V. Ritter

2046. Muller, Jean-Claude. COMMENT S'APPAUVRIR EN SE DÉVELOPPANT: IMPÔTS ET CHANGEMENT SOCIAL CHEZ LES RUKUBA (NIGÉRIA CENTRAL) [How they became impoverished while developing: taxes and social change among the Rukuba of Central Nigeria]. *Can. J. of African Studies [Canada] 1980 14(1): 83-96.* Examines the evolution of taxation among the Rukuba of Central Nigeria within a period of about 70 years, during which the means of earning cash to pay taxes changed drastically from the sale of indigenous agricultural produce for purely local consumption to mining work, which they dislike and in the past had been able to avoid. The reason for this change is the increasing taxation rate, indexed to the world inflation rate, to which the Rukuba are subjected. The increase of the inflation rate has been greater than the increase of the price of local food products, thus requiring the Rukuba to increase their grain sales tenfold in order to continue paying their taxes in this way. Since they wish to avoid completely depleting the granaries, on which they must draw for their own consumption as well, the Rukuba have had to look for other sources of income. It is this "differential inflation rate" between taxes and the price of local produce which has transformed the Rukuba from agriculturalists into semiproletarians. J

2047. Nafziger, E. Wayne. AFRICAN ENTREPRENEURS: A CASE STUDY OF NIGERIAN INDUSTRIALISTS, 1964-65. *Res. in Econ. Hist. 1982 (Supplement 2): 101-120.* Based on data for 41 indigenous footwear manufacturing firms in Nigeria for the years 1964-65, discusses Frank Knight's concept of the entrepreneur as the ultimate maker of decisions in a firm. Entrepreneurs in this industry often lacked university education, and those with a secondary or university education were not likely to bring in more profits. Apprentice training and experience were necessary for successful entrepreneurs. There was a positive relationship between paternal economic status and entrepreneurial success. J. Powell

2048. Nafziger, E. Wayne. THE POLITICAL ECONOMY OF DISINTEGRATION IN NIGERIA. *J. of Modern African Studies [Great Britain] 1973 11(4): 505-536.* Analyzes the economic factors contributing to the Nigeria-Biafra civil war and the interrelated coups (with consideration of the colonial economic legacy) based on the assumption that "economic variables and political disintegration are linked in several ways." There were growing contradictions between the economic interests of the various regional elites exacerbated by political enmity and violence in promoting these interests. The low priority placed on the alleviation of poverty and income inequality by the political elite gave impetus to disruptive action. Regional competition for employment, the rapid growth of the petroleum industry, and the interregional allocation of revenue and the distribution of funds were major sources of conflict. 49 notes. R. V. Ritter

2049. Ndoma-Egba, B. THE DEVELOPMENT OF VILLAGE MARKETS IN THE CROSS RIVER BASIN OF NIGERIA. *J. of African Studies 1979 6(1): 3-8.* Local sociocultural forces rather than long-distance external trade routes led to the development of village markets in southeastern Nigeria. Describes the rise and arrangement of markets among Ejagham villages in the Cross River area. Secondary sources; 12 notes. L. W. Truschel

2050. Newbury, Colin. TRADE AND TECHNOLOGY IN WEST AFRICA: THE CASE OF THE NIGER COMPANY, 1900-1920. *J. of African Hist. [Great Britain] 1978 19(4): 551-575.* The Niger Company surrendered its charter in 1900 and was acquired by Lever Brothers Ltd. in 1920. The company attempted to defend its monopoly over river communications through pooling agreements, contracts, and negotiations with colonial governments and shippers. Company agents expanded both the geographical area and the range of commercial activities especially mining in the Bauchi Plateau and in peanuts in northern Nigeria. Expansion placed severe strains on personnel and capital, but the exceptional profitability of raw commodities and tin concentrates during World War I obscured the problem. The company participated in the development of railways, but did not restructure its operations to keep pace with resultant changes, particularly at Lagos and Port Harcourt. 4 tables, 84 notes. A. W. Novitsky

2051. Njoku, O. N. DEVELOPMENT OF ROADS AND ROAD TRANSPORT IN SOUTHEASTERN NIGERIA 1903-1939. *J. of African Studies 1978-79 5(4): 471-497.* The British built roads in West Africa to extend their colonial system, exploit the agrarian economy, and transport troops to quell possible disturbances. Until 1925, road construction in southeastern Nigeria was haphazard and based on unskilled forced labor collected by colonially appointed Warrant Chiefs. During 1925-39, the British tried to construct an integrated road system with free labor and a rational bureaucratic administration. Nevertheless, the roads continued to be poorly constructed and maintained because of low wages and limited use. Based on archival and secondary sources; map, table, 58 notes. L. W. Truschel

2052. Nwaka, Geoffrey I. LAND ADMINISTRATION AND URBAN DEVELOPMENT: A NIGERIAN CASE STUDY. *Civilizations [Belgium] 1980 30(1-2): 73-81.* Discusses the growth of the Nigerian city of Calabar as an example of Nigeria's urban growth patterns since the 19th century.

2053. Nwaka, Geoffrey I. TRADE IN OGUTA, 1885-1945. *Bull. de l'Inst. Fondamental d'Afrique Noire. Série B [Senegal] 1979 41(4): 774-786.* In the 1880's Oguta near the Niger River in Nigeria started to assume an important place in the transportation of colonial trade. Its location attracted the Royal Niger Company as well as middlemen traders. Trade extended even more when colonial rule was established. The volume and value of trade developed rapidly until the end of World War II, when the expansion of rail and road networks undermined the role of waterways and diverted trade from Oguta. Based on records in the National Archives at Enugu; 2 maps, 30 notes. H. L. Calkin

2054. Ofonagoro, Walter I. FROM TRADITIONAL TO BRITISH CURRENCY IN SOUTHERN NIGERIA: ANALYSIS OF A CURRENCY REVOLUTION, 1880-1948. *J. of Econ. Hist. 1979 39(3): 623-654.* Soon after establishing political control, the British colonial administration in southern Nigeria attempted to replace the existing currencies of the country with British currency. The traditional currencies competently discharged the functions of money, however, and it required 50 years before the precolonial currencies, attacked by the colonial authorities and unrecognized as legal tender, gradually lost standing and proved worthless to their last holders. Theoretical implications of these developments are discussed. Table, 113 notes. J

2055. Ofonagoro, Walter Ibekwe. THE ARO AND DELTA MIDDLEMEN OF SOUTHEASTERN NIGERIA AND THE CHALLENGE OF THE COLONIAL ECONOMY. *J. of African Studies 1976 3(2): 143-164.* A study of the precolonial trading system as it operated in southeastern Nigeria under the domination of the Aros in the Igbo hinterland and the Delta middlemen, with their control of trading posts and all river transport routes, and how the introduction of colonial rule affected it. Strategic location, available slave manpower, and monopolistic control of the creek and river systems enabled them to develop large-scale commercial enterprises. Colonial rule led to the loss of dominance by the Aro and Delta middlemen. The establishment of British rule "drastically altered the terms and conditions of commercial life, and generated forces which enhanced the decline of the major precolonial commercial specialists of the region," with no ethnic or kinship groups reaping special benefits. 65 notes. R. V. Ritter

2056. Ogbonna, M. N. TAX EVASIONS IN NIGERIA. *Africa Today 1975 22(1): 53-61.* Blames the minimal tax revenue of Nigeria on tax evasion assisted by inadequate laws and tax collecting machinery. Recommends reform measures. Based on Nigerian and UN sources; 18 notes. G. O. Gagnon

2057. Ohadike, D. C. THE INFLUENZA PANDEMIC OF 1918-19 AND THE SPREAD OF CASSAVA CULTIVATION ON THE LOWER NIGER: A STUDY IN HISTORICAL LINKAGES. *J. of African Hist. [Great Britain] 1981 22(3): 380-391.* Cassava was widely grown in the Niger delta, but prior to 1919 it was hardly cultivated on the Lower Niger, an area that had for long been self-sufficient in foodstuffs and moreover exported its surplus of yams to the delta. The outbreak of the influenza pandemic of 1918-19 caused severe labor and food shortages in the Lower Niger. Cassava cultivation was introduced in the Lower Niger in 1919 and by the early 1930's had spread to most parts of the region. Its advantages over yams were soon recognized, even though it was and is regarded as a secondary food. Its place in recent years has been taken by maize and millet. Based on field work and Colonial Office papers; 55 notes. R. L. Collison

2058. Okpala, Donatus C. I. TOWARDS A BETTER CONCEPTUALIZATION OF RURAL COMMUNITY DEVELOPMENT: EMPIRICAL FINDINGS FROM NIGERIA. *Human Organization 1980 39(2): 161-169.* Based on a study of community development projects in the Anambra State of Nigeria since the mid-1950's, argues that, contrary to public policy, rural development and agricultural development are locally perceived as distinct.

2059. Oni, S. A. and Olayemi, J. K. ACREAGE RESPONSE IN A DEVELOPING AGRICULTURE: A CASE STUDY OF WESTERN NIGERIAN COCOA FARMERS. *African Studies Rev. 1974 17(2): 381-395.* "An econometric model to explain the factors which motivate the cocoa farmers in Western Nigeria to cultivate the crop." 2 tables, 5 notes, biblio. R. T. Brown

2060. Onimode, Bade. IMPERIALISM AND MULTINATIONAL CORPORATIONS: A CASE STUDY OF NIGERIA. *J. of Black Studies 1978 9(2): 207-232.*

2061. Onokerhoraye, A. G. OCCUPATIONAL SPECIALIZATION BY ETHNIC GROUPS IN THE INFORMAL SECTOR OF THE URBAN ECONOMIES OF TRADITIONAL NIGERIAN CITIES: THE CASE OF BENIN. *African Studies Rev. 1977 20(1): 53-69.* Outlines the development of occupations and professions, connected especially with crafts and commerce, in Benin since the 1940's.

2062. Onoura Onah, J. and Iwuji, E. C. URBAN POVERTY IN NIGERIA. *Genève-Afrique [Switzerland] 1975 14(2): 74-82.* Discusses poverty and its causes, and attempts to alleviate it in Nigerian cities, 1960-75.

2063. Onyemelukwe, J. O. C. SOME FACTORS IN THE GROWTH OF WEST AFRICAN MARKET TOWNS: THE EXAMPLE OF PRE-CIVIL WAR ONITSHA, NIGERIA. *Urban Studies [Great Britain] 1974 11(1): 47-60.* "In this article, the development of Onitsha to the ranks of the main market towns of pre-civil war Nigeria is analysed against the theoretical background of comparative advantage and centre-periphery notions. Internal exchange co-ordination by Onitsha market is shown to have involved a greater part of Nigeria and relied extensively on economic and socio-cultural factors. Mainly because of adverse economic consequences of high man/land ratio in most parts of Iboland, large-scale migration to other parts of the country was a major pre-civil war phenomenon. The apparently low opportunity cost of petty trade provided considerable attraction. Trade interrelationships between Onitsha and widespread pockets of Ibo migrants developed on a very large scale, particularly in staple food trade. Multiple regression analysis of foodstuffs trade flows shows a strong positive correlation between size of Ibo migrants and volume of trade flows from Onitsha market." J

2064. Ortiz, Sutti. OBSTACLE TO AGRICULTURAL GROWTH IN HAUSALAND VIEWED THROUGH A VILLAGE STUDY. *Econ. Development and Cultural Change 1974 23(1): 163-168.* Reviews Polly Hill's *Rural Hausa: A Village and a Setting*(Cambridge: Cambridge U. Press, 1973), which is a close examination of the economic system of a village in northern Nigeria. The basic reasons for the slow agricultural growth in Nigeria are technical deficiency, inability to fully utilize resources, shortage of working capital, lack of cost-earning activities, increased dependence on high-cost imports, and social and technical costs of marketing. The study of a small village enables the author to make projections for the larger economy. 8 notes.
J. W. Thacker, Jr.

2065. Otite, Onigu. RURAL MIGRANTS AS CATALYSTS IN RURAL DEVELOPMENT: THE URHOBO IN ONDO STATE, NIGERIA. *Africa [Great Britain] 1979 49(3): 226-234.* Describes the migration of Urhobo workers from their homes in Bendel state (Benin) to Ikaleland in search of seasonal work in palm oil production, 1920's-70's. They rent accommodation in village camps from their Ikale landlords, provision being made for their families, who share in seasonal work such as fishing, shoemaking, weeding, or harvesting. Middlemen handle the sale of products, lend money to the immigrants, and provide credit. The general ambition of immigrants is to save enough money to set up shops in expanding population centers in Bendel state. The author suggests that the Nigerian government should encourage this form of rural development. R. L. Collison

2066. Oyemakinde, Wale. MICHAEL IMOUDI AND THE EMERGENCE OF MILITANT TRADE UNIONISM IN NIGERIA, 1940-1942. *J. of the Hist. Soc. of Nigeria [Nigeria] 1974 7(3): 541-561.* Michael Imoudi's leadership of the Railway Workers' Union brought a change in Nigerian labor unionism; for the first time labor unions became serious industrial movements and began to assert their rights more effectively.

2067. Oyemakinde, Wale. THE NIGERIAN GENERAL STRIKE OF 1945. *J. of the Hist. Soc. of Nigeria [Nigeria] 1975 7(4): 693-710.* Examines the Nigerian General Strike of 1945 as a "classic example of strike action in a colonial setting." The issues in the strike were worker demands for higher wages and reluctance of the government, the single biggest employer, to grant them. Workers cooperated with influential politicians and won press support in a manner which suggests that the strike was "the industrial phase of the nationalist reaction to imperialism." In the end, the strike won the workers some concessions and gave them an opportunity to test their strength, but it also showed that political confrontation could have numerous unpleasant side effects. Based on manuscript and published sources; 90 notes. J. A. Casada

2068. Oyemakinde, Wale. THE NIGERIAN GENERAL STRIKE OF 1964. *Genève-Afrique [Switzerland] 1974 13(1): 53-71.* Describes the events leading to the Nigerian general strike of 1964, its course, and the workers' gains.

2069. Oyemakinde, Wale. THE PULLEN MARKETING SCHEME: A TRIAL IN FOOD PRICE CONTROL IN NIGERIA, 1941-1947. *J. of the Hist. Soc. of Nigeria [Nigeria] 1973 6(4): 413-423.* Shortage of food was one of the most vexing problems for colonial administrators in Nigeria during World War II. The Pullen scheme tried to peg prices in the city of Lagos, but in general it failed. 8 tables, 56 notes.
J. A. Casada

2070. Schatz, Sayre P. NIGERIA'S PETRO-POLITICAL FLUCTUATION. *Issue: A Q. J. of Opinion 1981 11(1-2): 35-40.* Describes the relationship between oil revenues and economic fluctuation in Nigeria, 1973-79.

2071. Shatz, Sayre P. MOVING UP. *Wilson Q. 1980 4(1): 57-69.* Surveys Nigeria's economic history since 1960, especially its petroleum industry, a major US supplier.

2072. Shenton, R. W. and Lennihan, Louise. CAPITAL AND CLASS: PEASANT DIFFERENTIATION IN NORTHERN NIGERIA. *J. of Peasant Studies [Great Britain] 1981 9(1): 47-70.* Reviews definitions of "peasant society" and "peasant economies" and examines the problems of peasant persistence, rural inequality, and rural exploitation in Northern Nigeria from 1850, concentrating on the growth of the British Cotton Growers Association (founded 1902) and its relations with the local cotton industry and the evolution of a cash economy. Rural society became increasingly differentiated between rich and poor peasants as indebtedness forced many peasants to sell their food and labor to survive, and the traditional Hausa household structure was undermined. Based largely on Nigerian Archives, Kaduna; table, 22 notes., ref. M. K. Hogg

2073. Sledzevski, I. EKONOMICHESKOE RAZVITIE I GOSUDARSTVO [Economic development and the state]. *Aziia i Afrika Segodnia [USSR] 1973 (6): 9-11.* Looks at the three spheres of economic development in Nigeria, 1947-73: national private enterprise, foreign business, and state economic activity.

2074. Sullivan, B. C. STRUCTURAL DEPENDENCY: THE NIGERIAN ECONOMY AS A CASE STUDY. *J. of Asian and African Studies [Netherlands] 1979 14(1-2): 44-55.* As economic growth has taken place, Nigeria and other African countries have become more dependent on Western capitalist countries. Secondary sources; table, 20 notes, biblio. R. T. Brown

2075. Turner, Terisa. THE TRANSFER OF OIL TECHNOLOGY AND THE NIGERIAN STATE. *Development and Change [Netherlands] 1976 7(4): 353-390.* Refutes the assumption that poor country governments are attempting to gain technology, using the oil industry in Nigeria as a case study. Examines oil company interests, the nature of the Nigerian state, 1956-74, and its experience in the transfer of production and exploration technology.

2076. Ubah, C. N. ISLAMIC FISCAL SYSTEMS AND COLONIAL INNOVATIONS: THE KANO EXAMPLE. *Islamic Q. [Great Britain] 1979 23(4): 173-185.* Examines the implications of British colonial government for the fiscal system of the Sokoto Caliphate, with special reference to the Emirate of Kano from 1806. Islamic law lays down very detailed regulations concerning admissible forms of taxation, which the reformist Sokoto Caliphate was at pains to implement. Nonetheless the authorized crop, cattle, and land taxes had to be supplemented by uncanonical levies on trade, and by institutionalized bribery. The disposition of the state's revenues was also subject to strict rules. At the British occupation in 1903 there were several attempts to break up this taxation system, though each new scheme met fierce popular and religious opposition. However, by 1927 the British had arrived at a relatively simple taxation system under which Muslims and non-Muslims were treated alike. By that time relatively few subjects cared whether the taxes they paid were sanctioned by Islamic law. Based on colonial administrative records, interviews, and printed sources in Arabic and English; 55 notes. A. K. Dalby

2077. Uchendu, Victor C. STATE, LAND, AND SOCIETY IN NIGERIA: A CRITICAL ASSESSMENT OF LAND USE DECREE (1978). *J. of African Studies 1979 6(2): 62-74.* A critical analysis of Nigeria's recent Land Use Decree, 1978. Nigeria has not had a history of cruel exploitation of its peasantry by great landlords, and the British colonial administrations tended to recognize indigenous communal land rights and tenure. The 1978 decree breaks with tradition in vesting land tenure control in the hands of the state, and is seen as "selective institutional radicalism," subject to a large degree of potential political abuse. Secondary sources; 25 notes. L. W. Truschel

2078. Ukpong, I. I. ECONOMIC RECOVERY IN THE EASTERN STATES OF NIGERIA. *Issue 1975 5(1): 45-53.* Describes the improvement in economic conditions in the years following the civil war of 1966-70. S

2079. Ukpong, Ignatius I. THE IMPACT OF FOREIGN AID ON ELECTRICITY DEVELOPMENT IN NIGERIA. *J. of African Studies 1975 2(2): 275-286.* A study of electrical development in Nigeria in relation to over-all national development and the results of the foreign aid allocated for that purpose. There have been a number of negative aspects: site-bound projects; failures to provide for maintenance of the projects financed; and inadequate provision for training in management and technical skills. As a result, there have been frequent power failures from poor maintenance and inefficient management. 10 notes. R. V. Ritter

2080. Uzozie, L. C. THE CHANGING CONTEXT OF LAND USE DECISIONS: THREE FAMILY FARMS IN THE YAM CULTIVATION ZONE OF EASTERN NIGERIA, 1964-1977. *Africa [Great Britain] 1981 51(2): 678-693.* Three farm units in the Igbo-speaking area of eastern Nigeria were studied in 1977. They differed in crop specialization, the men tending to be more involved in yam production, the women with cassava. The effects of the civil war varied in their impact on the different farms. Ecological conditions no longer favor yam cultivation, but the crop remains popular because it is deeply rooted in the lifestyle of the people. Economic factors, such as market demand and transport cost do not feature as decisionmaking criteria. Farmers' choice of crops and systems of production depends on established wisdom, all fields being classified by one or more criteria that guide the productive use of the land. Based on field work; 6 fig., 3 notes. R. L. Collison

2081. Wallace, Tina. THE CHALLENGE OF FOOD: NIGERIA'S APPROACH TO AGRICULTURE 1975-80. *Can. J. of African Studies [Canada] 1981 15(2): 239-258.* Analyzes several provisions of the Nigerian Third Development Plan pertaining to agriculture, to determine their effectiveness in solving Nigeria's food problem, while increasing productivity and raising the living standard of farmers. High priorities include extensive irrigation projects and large-scale farming, projects that have not proved successful in Africa in the past. Table, 19 notes. V. L. Human

2082. Waterman, Peter. COMMUNIST THEORY IN THE NIGERIAN TRADE UNION MOVEMENT. *Politics and Society 1973 3(3): 283-312.* Examines the Nigerian Trade Union Congress, its leadership and organization, and its relationship to the Socialist Workers and Farmers Party. Presents the descriptive background data and analysis of Nigerian society, economy, politics, and its trade union movements, as well as the theoretical and organizational assumptions of the Nigerian Trade Union Congress. Primary and secondary sources; 89 notes. D. G. Nielson

2083. Weinand, Herbert C. SOME SPATIAL ASPECTS OF ECONOMIC DEVELOPMENT IN NIGERIA. *J. of Developing Areas 1973 7(2): 247-264.*

Politics

2084. Achebe, Ifeanyi. UNITED NATIONS ARBITRATION CONVENTION: IMPLICATIONS FOR NIGERIA. *J. of World Trade Law [Switzerland] 1974 8(4): 420-446.* "Discusses the problems arising from the inadequacy of Nigeria's legal system with respect to commercial disputes. In particular, the author considers that there is a need for implementing the UN Arbitration Convention, which would give the business community an alternative to the courts in settling commercial disputes. The paper concludes with a discussion of the settlement of oil disputes in connection with the Nigerian government's desire to control the oil industry." J

2085. Adebisi, Busari. THE POLITICS OF DEVELOPMENT CONTROL IN A NIGERIAN CITY OF IBADAN. *Pan African J. [Kenya] 1974 7(1): 1-11.* The Western State of Nigeria has been lax in planning the city of Ibadan. The inner city is in decay and prone to epidemics. The refusal of politicians to enforce existing laws aggravates the situation. 36 notes. H. G. Soff

2086. Adejuyigbe, Omolade. THE ALLOCATION OF ETHNIC FRONTIERS IN NIGERIA: THE EXAMPLE OF AKOKO-EDO DIVISION. *Odu: a J. of West African Studies [Nigeria] 1974 (10): 118-132.* The situation of Akoko-Edo, like other frontiers in Nigeria, causes disputes because the frontier area does not fall easily into a single ethnic area. No groupings of the Akoko-Edo area or any other ethnic frontier can be satisfactory to all interested parties, and so any decision acceptable to the people in a frontier area has to be respected by the losing sides. Based on primary and secondary sources; 6 figs., 9 notes. M. M. McCarthy

2087. Adejuyigbe, Omolade. THE SIZE OF STATES AND POLITICAL STABILITY IN NIGERIA. *African Studies 1973 16(2): 157-182.*

2088. Adeniran, Tunde. THE DYNAMICS OF PEASANT REVOLT: A CONCEPTUAL ANALYSIS OF THE AGBEKOYA PARAPO UPRISING IN THE WESTERN STATE OF NIGERIA. *J. of Black Studies 1974 4(4): 363-375.* Discusses the growth and gradual radicalization of the peasants and why the Agbekoya Parapo union and other peasant unions marched on the government in 1969. Examines the changes the rebellion brought about in the government and the lives of the peasants. Biblio. K. Butcher

2089. Afigbo, A. E. INDIRECT RULE IN SOUTHEASTERN NIGERIA: THE ERA OF WARRANT CHIEFS 1891-1929. *Tarikh [Nigeria] 1974 4(4): 11-24.*

2090. Akindele, R. A. ON THE OPERATIONAL LINKAGE OF EXTERNAL AND INTERNAL DIMENSIONS OF BALEWA'S FOREIGN POLICY. *Odu: a J. of West African Studies [Nigeria] 1975 (12): 110-122.* Critically examines Gordon J. Idang's *Nigeria: Internal Politics and Foreign Policy, 1960-1966* (U. of Ibadan Pr., 1973); and A. B. Akinyemi's *Foreign Policy and Federalism: The Nigerian Experience*

(U. of Ibadan Pr., 1974). Neither book is a reference work on Abubakar Balewa's foreign policy, but each has made a significant contribution to our understanding of its domestic structure. M. M. McCarthy

2091. Akindele, R. A. and Varma, S. N. THE PROBLEM AND PROSPECT OF NATIONAL PARTIES IN NIGERIA. *African Rev. [Tanzania] 1974 4(3): 381-406.* A history of the failures of local or regional political parties in Nigeria with comparisons with the experiences of other federal states in Asia and Africa. 95 notes. R. T. Brown

2092. Akinsanya, A. THE MACHINERY OF GOVERNMENT DURING THE MILITARY REGIME IN NIGERIA. *Africa Q. [India] 1977 17(2): 32-54.* Analyzes the government and administrative structure in Nigeria as organized by the military government, 1966-77.

2093. Akinsanya, A. ON LAGOS DECISION TO BREAK DIPLOMATIC RELATIONS WITH ISRAEL. *Int. Problems [Israel] 1978 17(1): 65-79.* Considers the factors influencing the decisions of African states to sever diplomatic relations with outside powers, with particular reference to Nigeria's decision to reject Israel following the October War (1973).

2094. Akinsanya, A. THE OFFICE OF THE NIGERIAN PRESIDENT: EXPERIENCE OF THE 1964-5 CONSTITUTIONAL CRISES. *Indian J. of Pol. Studies [India] 1978 2(2): 146-175.* Discusses the actions and negotiations of Nigerian President Dr. Nnamdi Azikiwe in 1964 following a mass boycott by almost 500 candidates seeking seats in the House of Representatives in the nation's first federal election.

2095. Akinyemi, A. Bolaji. RELIGION AND FOREIGN AFFAIRS: PRESS ATTITUDES TOWARDS THE NIGERIAN CIVIL WAR. *Jerusalem J. of Int. Relations [Israel] 1980 4(3): 56-81.* Religion was the major factor in determining the biases of news coverage of the Nigerian civil war, as determined through analysis of the *Egyptian Gazette, Jerusalem Post, Dawn*of Pakistan, and *Statesman* of India.

2096. Akpan, Moses E. THE 1979 NIGERIAN CONSTITUTION AND HUMAN RIGHTS. *Universal Human Rights 1980 2(2): 23-41.* Assesses human rights in Nigeria from 1957 to 1979 and argues that the 1979 constitution provides a foundation for a democratic and egalitarian Nigeria.

2097. Aluko, Olajide. ISRAEL AND NIGERIA: CONTINUITY AND CHANGE IN THEIR RELATIONSHIP. *African Rev. [Tanzania] 1974 4(1): 43-59.* Outlines Nigerian-Israeli bilateral relations and explains why they have changed since 1973. In that year, Nigeria broke relations with Israel, yet Israeli companies and technical experts remained in Nigeria. Nigeria needs Israeli assistance and aid. This relationship will continue for some time. Israel, however, to improve its position in Africa, must withdraw from Arab lands secured in the 1967 and 1973 wars. 2 tables, 81 notes. H. G. Soff

2098. Aluko, Olajide. NIGERIA AND BRITAIN SINCE GOWON. *African Affairs [Great Britain] 1977 76(304): 303-320.* Traces British-Nigerian relations, particularly since General Yakubu Gowon was overthrown in July 1975. Prior to that date, relations were very cordial. 78 notes. H. G. Soff

2099. Aluko, Olajide. NIGERIA AND THE SUPERPOWERS. *Millennium: J. of Int. Studies [Great Britain] 1976 5(2): 127-141.* Analyzes factors affecting the relationship between Nigeria and the Great Powers since independence (1960). Stresses domestic influences upon events, and especially the effect of such events as the coups of 1966 and 1975, the Biafran War, and Nigeria's growing economic strength. Based on the press and secondary sources; 50 notes. P. J. Beck

2100. Amucheazi, Elochukwu. A DECADE OF CHURCH "REVOLT" IN EASTERN NIGERIA, 1956-1966. *Odu: a J. of West African Studies [Nigeria] 1974 (10): 45-62.* Examines some aspects of the political participation of the church in the Eastern Region of Nigeria. When the government decided to exercise more control over education than the colonial government had done, the churches became involved in the region's political process. The churches attempted only to exert influence which would affect government decisions, but the interdenominational rivalry generated in the process greatly affected the efficiency of governmental processes. Primary and secondary sources; 47 notes. M. M. McCarthy

2101. Asiwaju, A. I. POLITICAL MOTIVATION AND ORAL HISTORICAL TRADITIONS IN AFRICA: THE CASE OF YORUBA CROWNS, 1900-1960. *Africa [Great Britain] 1976 46(2): 113-127.* Considers the problem of too many crowned heads in the Yoruba areas of Nigeria, with a few comments about the French experience in Yoruba Dahomey. Kings were common before the period of colonial rule. Regular warfare gave occasion for many village heads to crown themselves. The British initially accepted this system, which worsened matters, for even more persons rushed to declare themselves kings. Britain eventually demanded proof of royal lineage and some kings were deposed, but this was often an expedient. The coming of independence witnessed another spate of self-crowning which the Nigerian government is only beginning to deal with. 68 notes. V. L. Human

2102. Asobie, H. A. BUREAUCRATIC POLITICS AND FOREIGN POLICY: THE NIGERIAN EXPERIENCE, 1960-1975. *Civilisations [Belgium] 1980 30(3-4): 253-273.* Discusses the relation of bureaucratic politics and foreign policy in Nigeria from 1960 to 1975, focusing on the domestic dimensions of the bureaucratic formulation of Nigeria's foreign policy during this period.

2103. Awa, Eme O. THE PLACE OF IDEOLOGY IN NIGERIAN POLITICS. *African Rev. [Tanzania] 1974 4(3): 359-380.* A variety of ideologies have played significant roles in the 20th-century history of Nigeria but only socialism has grown in significance and can serve to solve Nigeria's economic and political problems. 27 notes. R. T. Brown

2104. Ayandele, E. A. THE IDEOLOGICAL FERMENT IN IJEBULAND, 1892-1943. *Nigerian Historical Studies* (London: Frank Cass, 1979): 270-294. Ijebu political theory in prewar colonial Nigeria encompassed both pressure for greater democracy and support for purist monarchical legitimism. Originally appeared in *African Notes.*

2105. Ayoade, John A. A. ELECTORAL LAWS AND NATIONAL UNITY IN NIGERIA. *African Studies Rev. 1980 23(2): 39-50.* Nigerian election laws were based on the federal structure of the government. Thus, whoever controlled the states modified the electoral laws to their own best political advantage. Changes in the laws, therefore, hindered national unity. Secondary sources; 2 tables. R. T. Brown

2106. Ayoade, John A. A. SECESSION THREAT AS A REDRESSIVE MECHANISM IN NIGERIAN FEDERALISM. *Publius 1973 3(1): 57-74.* Discusses constitutional conflict and the political mechanism of secession threat in relation to Nigerian federalism and national unification, 1950-70, emphasizing economic factors.

2107. Bach, Daniel. LE GÉNÉRAL DE GAULLE ET LA GUERRE CIVILE AU NIGERIA [General Charles de Gaulle and the civil war in Nigeria]. *Can. J. of African Studies 1980 14(2): 259-272.* Describes the background of France's decision to become involved in the Nigerian war and discusses French support for Biafra in the African political context. The principal points of French foreign policy are summarized in three parts: the support for historic African leaders, the maintenance of a francophone community, and the primacy of geopolitical considerations. Nigerian federation represented for de Gaulle a threat to be controlled, but his attitude was modified by the generally hostile reaction of the leaders of francophone Africa. J

2108. Baker, Pauline H. LURCHING TOWARD UNITY. *Wilson Q. 1980 4(1): 70-80.* Traces Nigeria's troubled history from 19th-century colonial days, especially the attempts to unite the many nationalities in the country, and the Biafran movement.

2109. Beer, Christopher E. F. and Williams, Gavin. THE POLITICS OF THE IBADAN PEASANTRY. *African Rev. [Tanzania] 1975 5(3): 235-256.* For the past 80 years the small cocoa farmers of Western Nigeria have expressed their grievances through a series of populist movements which used direct action. They have always failed to work any real changes in their situation. 76 notes. R. T. Brown

2110. Bienen, Henry. MILITARY RULE AND POLITICAL PROCESS: NIGERIAN EXAMPLES. *Comparative Pol. 1978 10(2): 205-226.* Examines the political process in Nigeria since the army coup of 1966. The military gradually was forced to accept civilians as executive members. During 1967-74 Nigeria succeeded in creating a military-civilian relationship based on shared power. 25 notes.
G. E. Pergl

2111. Brier, Alan and Tansey, Stephen. ETHNIC DIVERSITY AND POLITICAL ATTITUDES IN A NIGERIAN UNIVERSITY. *Youth and Soc. 1974 6(2): 151-178.* Presents results of a survey of attitudes of the student population of Nigeria's University of Ife, at the outset of the Nigerian civil war. S

2112. Carter, Helen Marshall. PROSPECTS FOR THE ADMINISTRATION OF JUSTICE IN NIGERIA: COURTS, POLICE, AND POLITICS. *Issue: A Q. J. of Opinion 1981 11(1-2): 29-34.* Traces the history of judicial and law enforcement policy in Nigeria from British control to 1979, focusing on judicial, political, and police reforms since 1960.

2113. Cookey, S. J. S. SIR HUGH CLIFFORD AS GOVERNOR OF NIGERIA: AN EVALUATION. *African Affairs [Great Britain] 1980 79(317): 531-547.* Sir Hugh Clifford was governor of Nigeria, 1919-25, and was probably the greatest colonial ruler of that country. He criticized indirect rule and advocated a policy of allowing indigenous society to be permeated by Western ideas; he believed in the equality of Europeans and Africans and in a humane colonial administration. His introduction of the elective principle encouraged the spread of democratic ideals and the rise of party politics, which hastened the thought of independence and contributed to the transfer of power to Nigerians. Based on primary material in the Colonial Office archives; 52 notes.
J. V. Coutinho

2114. Copley, Anthony R. H. NIGERIAN ACADEMIC YEAR 1974-75: BACKGROUND TO THE JULY COUP 1976. *Civilisations [Belgium] 1978 28(1-2): 140-162.* Discusses the closing of four Nigerian universities (Ibadan, Lagos, Ife, and Benin) as a result of student activism and as a prelude to the July 1976 coup d'etat.

2115. Dare, L. O. ON LEADERSHIP AND MILITARY RULE IN NIGERIA. *Odu: a J. of West African Studies [Nigeria] 1977 (16): 70-84.* Compares the leadership styles of Generals Ironsi and Gowon and that of Brigadier Murtala Muhammed, 1966-79. With the exception of technical difficulties encountered by these leaders in implementing their promises for a return to civilian rule, their respective programs of military disengagement from politics were, however, sound. Based on constitutional documents and secondary literature; 19 notes.
M. Mtewa

2116. Davis, Morris. AUDITS OF INTERNATIONAL RELIEF IN THE NIGERIAN CIVIL WAR: SOME POLITICAL PERSPECTIVES. *Int. Organization 1975 29(2): 501-512.* Information from four audits, or audit-like reviews, of international relief programs in the Nigerian-Biafran war sheds considerable light on the financial sources, scope, timing of flows, and cost-efficiency associated with that complex operation. Beyond their intrinsic interest, which is heightened by two of the documents remaining unpublished, such economic data bear heavily on many political aspects of the relief effort. For example, they permit examination of the relationship, and partial disjunction, between dominance in contributions (which was mainly governmental and particularly American) and leadership in administration (which was chiefly continental European and private). They also facilitate an assessment of the massive or token proportions of these endeavors, their capacity to anticipate rather than just respond tardily to predictable catastrophes, and the extent of their entanglement in the domestic and international power fields that characterized the Nigerian conflict. For all their rather divergent modi operandi, the leading role in the relief process of the two private umbrella organizations is clearly apparent; but so too is the limited ambit of even such comparatively massive relief work within the context of an ongoing civil war. J

2117. Dikshit, R. D. NIGERIA: FROM FEDERATION TO THE CIVIL WAR—A STUDY IN THE DYNAMICS OF FEDERALISM. *Pol. Sci. Rev. [India] 1976 15(1): 27-40.* Traces the administrative history of the British colony of Nigeria and the dynamics of its federal system of government which evolved after independence. The Royal Niger Company established its operations at Lagos in 1861 and expanded as far north as the French would permit and as far to the east as the Germans would yield. In 1900 England revoked the colonial charter and proclaimed a protectorate of Northern and Southern Nigeria and the Colony of Lagos. This produced a hodgepodge of different cultural, religious, and linguistic groups with ethnic ties spilling across arbitrary boundaries. In 1960, when Nigeria gained independence by peaceful means, it had no national heroes, charismatic leaders, or political mentors. Ibo tribesmen, however, dominated the elite administrative positions. Northern resentment of the Ibos' privileged position coupled with discovery of commercial oil operations in the East stirred political factions to violence and finally a civil war. By 1966 widespread corruption, disorder, and violence led to a military coup. The author reviews the changing aspirations, leadership, and successes of the three contending factions in Nigeria during the 1960's. Based on secondary sources; 16 notes.
S. H. Frank

2118. Dudley, Billy J. THE NIGERIAN ELECTIONS OF 1979: THE VOTING DECISION. *J. of Commonwealth and Comparative Pol. [Great Britain] 1981 19(3): 276-298.* Detailed account of the legal and constitutional framework governing the Nigerian federal elections of July-August 1979, the formation of the five contesting political parties, and the conduct of the elections. Examines the geographical and ethnic distribution of the contesting parties' electoral support. The National Party of Nigeria (NPN) owed its victory in the presidential election to its vote in the ethnic minority states. In spite of the continued prevalence of ethnic block voting in the majority states, under the current 19-state structure of regional government established in 1976 no party can hope to win Nigerian elections without attracting substantial support in the minority states. Based on published election results and census data and secondary sources; 9 tables, 35 notes.
M. J. Clark

2119. Egboh, Edmund O. THE NIGERIAN TRADE UNIONS AND POLITICS (1945-1965). *Africa Q. [India] 1976 16(2): 56-68.*

2120. Ekechi, Felix K. THE PRESIDENTIAL SYSTEM OF GOVERNMENT IN AFRICA: THE NIGERIAN CASE. *Indiana Social Studies Q. 1977 30(2): 62-73.* Discusses the acceptance of the presidential system in Nigeria, 1966-77, as a prototype for other African governments.

2121. Emezi, C. E. DEVELOPMENT OF ADMINISTRATION IN NIGERIA. *Africa Q. [India] 1977 16(4): 87-98.* Analyzes public administration as a means to improve the lot of the governed, rather than as an instrument of government policy, and the need for the former in Nigeria, 1960-77.

2122. Enyia, Dike Ogbuefi. ETHNIC POLITICS AND HIGHER EDUCATION IN NIGERIA. *J. of African-Afro-American Affairs 1979 3(1): 70-79.* Ethnic groups' interests in higher education in Nigeria, 1960-79, have been manifest in interregional rivalries and ethnic politics, when emphasis should rather have been placed on reaching goals which profit national society and promote Nigeria's introduction into international affairs.

2123. Fieloux, Michele. "FEMMES INVISIBLES" ET "FEMMES MUETTES": À PROPOS DES ÉVÉNEMENTS IBO DE 1929 ["Invisible women" and "silent women": the Igbo incidents of 1929]. *Cahiers d'Études Africaines [France] 1977 17(1): 189-194.* A bibliographical essay demonstrating that male scholars have failed to understand the feminine role in the Aba riots of 1929 in Nigeria. Three female anthropologists have demonstrated that what has been called the Aba riots might better be called the women's war. Based on the secondary literature; 15 notes. B. S. Fetter

2124. Fishel, Murray. POLITICAL CULTURE IN MOBILIZING SYSTEMS: THE CASE OF NIGERIA. *Genève-Afrique [Switzerland] 1975 14(1): 30-58.* Develops a theoretical approach to the study of non-Western political culture by analyzing elitist and popular attitudes in Nigeria, 1800-1960.

2125. Flint, John E. GOVERNOR *VERSUS* COLONIAL OFFICE: AN ANATOMY OF THE RICHARDS CONSTITUTION FOR

NIGERIA, 1939 TO 1945. *Hist. Papers [Canada] 1981: 124-143.* Traces the process of decolonization in Nigeria. Analyzes how the Richards constitution (1939-45) took shape and came to be imposed upon that country, stressing the constant opposition between Governor Sir Arthur Richards's reactionary philosophy and the more advanced ideas of the Colonial Office. Demonstrates that Richards's resistance destroyed Great Britain's chances to organize and direct the nationalist movement and brought about the appearance of Nigerian nationalist parties. Based on London Colonial Office Archives; 45 notes.
G. P. Cleyet

2126. Glushchenko, E. A. IZ ISTORII POLITICHESKOI BOR'BY NIGERII (1940-1960 GG) [The history of the political struggle in Nigeria, 1940-60]. *Narody Azii i Afriki [USSR] 1979 (4): 43-55.* In distinction from Ghana, Guinea, Mali, and Tanzania, where genuine nationalist revolutionary leaders appeared, in Nigeria there were no such popular leaders. In 1945 the National Council of Nigerian Citizens (NCNC) was founded, taking as its model the Indian National Congress. It included many nationalities, but Ibos made up 49%. A radical rising occurred in 1948. Because there was so much regionalization no great national leader appeared. The British could turn over power to whom they chose in 1960. 38 notes. J. L. Evans

2127. Glushchenko, E. A. NIGERIIA: POLITICHESKIE INSTITUTY RAZVITOGO KAPITALIZMA V USLOVIIAKH RAZVIVAIUSHCHEGOSIA OBSHCHESTVA (1960 GODY) [Nigeria: political institutions of developed capitalism in a developing society (the 1960's)]. *Narody Azii i Afriki [USSR] 1980 (4): 34-45.* In the first five years following its independence in 1960, Nigeria adopted a state structure based on Great Britain's and headed by the emirs (feudal lords of Northern Nigeria). Nigeria's traditional society and its economic and social conditions could not conform to such a system. Severe internal strife laid the ground for a military coup in 1966. 34 notes.
S. J. Talalay

2128. Glushchenko, E. A. PADENIE PERVOI RESPUBLIKI V NIGERII (K ISTORII VOENNOGO PEREVOROTA 15 IANVARIA 1966 G.) [The fall of the first Nigerian republic: the history of the coup of 15 January 1966]. *Narody Azii i Afriki [USSR] 1976 (4): 57-68.* Describes the conditions in Nigeria on the eve of the 15 January 1966 military coup, which ended the first Nigerian republic, and the preparations for the coup by a group of young Ibo officers. The coup was a continuation of the decolonization process that began in 1960 with Nigeria's independence. It was followed by another coup in July 1966 and by a bloody civil war a few months later. 38 notes.
L. Kalinowski

2129. Gordon, Jacob U. WEST AFRICAN CITY-STATE: A STUDY OF SAPELE TOWN COUNCIL AND DEVELOPMENT. *Umoja 1977 1(2): 71-82.* Using the town of Sapele, Nigeria, as a case study, the author examines the implications which the formation of local government institutions have on nation building, 1955-77.

2130. Jinadu, L. Adele. THE CONSTITUTIONAL SITUATION OF THE NIGERIAN STATES. *Publius 1982 12(1): 155-185.* Examines constituent state constitution-making since 1979, the year in which Nigeria designed a new federal constitution which was an important element in the demilitarization process. The return to constitutional government in 1979 ended 13 years of military rule. Though the Nigerian states are legislatively autonomous, their constitutions are derived from the federal constitution, which prescribes the number and type of governmental organs they should have, as well as their powers and functions. Based on primary sources; 52 notes. J. Powell

2131. Johnson, Cheryl. MADAM ALIMOTU PELEWURA AND THE LAGOS MARKET WOMEN. *Tarikh [Nigeria] 1981 7(1): 1-10.* Traces the life of Alimotu Pelewura from 1900 to her death in 1951. Describes her role as a market leader for women in Lagos, Nigeria and discusses her influence along with Herbert Macaulay (died 1946), the father of Nigerian nationalism, on the formation of nationalist political parties, including the Nigerian National Democratic Party and the Nigerian Union of Young Democrats, during the 1920's and 1930's in Nigeria.

2132. Joseph, Richard A. DEMOCRATIZATION UNDER MILITARY TUTELAGE: CRISIS AND CONSENSUS IN THE NIGERIAN 1979 ELECTIONS. *Comparative Pol. 1981 14(1): 75-100.* Discusses the transition from the military rule of General Olusegun Obasanjo to the civilian rule of President Alhaji Shehu Shagari in Nigeria on 1 October 1979, focusing on the analytical perspective of Claude Welch. Welch identifies three factors important to the process of military disengagement: 1) the cohesiveness of the ruling junta, 2) the scope of their political objectives, and 3) the "relative fit" with their successor group. Primary emphasis is given to the third factor in discussing the Nigerian transition. The transition from military to civilian rule according to Welch is the result of a "protracted process of civilianization" and this was abundantly evident in the Nigerian case. Based on election analysis and newspapers; 6 tables, fig., 61 notes.
M. A. Kascus

2133. Joseph, Richard A. THE ETHNIC TRAP: NOTES ON THE NIGERIAN CAMPAIGN AND ELECTIONS, 1978-79. *Issue: A Q. J. of Opinion 1981 11(1-2): 17-23.* The electoral decree of 1977 and the constitution of 1979 attempted to end the ethnic, regional, and religious divisions in Nigeria. The 1978-79 political campaigns and elections are examined.

2134. July, Robert W. THE ARTIST'S CREDO: THE POLITICAL PHILOSOPHY OF WOLE SOYINKA. *J. of Modern African Studies [Great Britain] 1981 19(3): 477-498.* As Nigeria's best known playwright, Wole Soyinka has produced plays and novels since 1960 that depict favorably a unique African culture, complementing but not imitating that of the Western world. Soyinka's works have been extremely critical of modernizing trends borrowed wholesale from the West; his political philosophy opposes corrupt societies and political systems that have appeared in recent Africa, while it praises individual and communal harmony. Based on Soyinka's writings and unpublished correspondence; 22 notes. L. W. Truschel

2135. Koehn, Peter. PRELUDE TO CIVILIAN RULE: THE NIGERIAN ELECTIONS OF 1979. *Africa Today 1981 28(1): 17-45.* Analyzes the process of the 1979 state and local elections which formed the basis for Nigerian transition from military to civilian rule. The military government ignored cultural, economic, and organizational realities in structuring an electoral process, resulting in a cosmetic change that obscures the true fragility of the Second Republic. Chart, 3 tables, map, 83 notes. G. O. Gagnon

2136. Kraus, Jon. NIGERIA UNDER SHAGARI. *Current Hist. 1982 81(473): 106-110, 136.* Analyzes Nigeria's economic and social predicament after thirteen years of military rule, and the policies of the newly elected civilian government under President Shehu Shagari.

2137. Kurtz, Donn M. NIGERIAN MINISTERS AND PARLIAMENTARIANS, 1954-1965. *J. of African Studies 1976 3(1): 101-124.* Proceeding from the assumption of the importance of the unity of the elite as the necessary basis for national unity, examines the structure of one sector of the Nigerian political elite in order to assess its degree of unity. Focuses on 626 members of Federal and Regional legislatures between 1954 and 1965, identifying differences between ministers and parliamentarians, ministers and nonministers and analyzes the differences with respect to regional boundaries. The political elite of Nigeria are "unable to serve as a model of unity." 9 tables, 67 notes.
R. V. Ritter

2138. Laïdi, Zaki. LE NIGÉRIA: L'ÉMERGENCE D'UN NOUVEAU CENTRE DE POUVOIR? [Nigeria: emergence of a new center of power?]. *Afrique et l'Asie Modernes [France] 1979 (3): 50-59.* Analyzes the history of Nigeria since its independence (1960), centering on its buildup of power, 1970-73, and emergence since 1973 as possibly the most important power in Africa.

2139. Lynch, Hollis R. K. O. MBADIWE, 1939-1947: THE AMERICAN YEARS OF A NIGERIAN POLITICAL LEADER. *J. of African Studies 1980-81 7(4): 184-203.* As an effective organizer and publicist of American interest in Africa and support for decolonization, Kingsley Ozuomba Mbadiwe, who had come to the United States in a group of Nigerian foreign students in 1939, was the leading pioneer of Nigerian-American relations in the 1940's. Through speeches, personal contacts, writings, and his pivotal involvement in creating and guiding the African Academy of Arts and Research and its activities, 1943-47, Mbadiwe successfully appealed to an audience of African students and politicians, black Americans, and white liberals, including Wendell Wilkie and Eleanor Roosevelt. Coming from a commercially prominent Ibo family, Mbadiwe espoused independence and philanthropic capitalism for uplifting colonial Africa. Based on university records, private papers and correspondence, newspapers, and secondary sources; 131 notes. L. W. Truschel

2140. Mayall, James. OIL AND NIGERIAN FOREIGN POLICY. *African Affairs [Great Britain] 1976 75(300): 317-330.* Nigeria has been a major producer of oil since 1958. The author attempts to show what effect oil income has had on Nigerian policy and trade. Since the United States is not the leading buyer of oil, there are some questions about future constraints and opportunities based on Nigeria's relationship with the United States. 26 notes. H. G. Soff

2141. Moses, Sibyl E. NIGERIAN GOVERNMENT POSTERS: VISUAL RECORDS OF PEOPLE AND PROGRESS. *Government Publ. Rev. 1980 7A(3): 221-227.* Discusses and categorizes Nigerian government posters and emphasizes their value for Nigerian libraries as examples of visual government publications.

2142. Muffett, D. J. M. LEGITIMACY AND DEFERENCE IN A TRADITION ORIENTED SOCIETY: OBSERVATIONS ARISING FROM AN EXAMINATION OF SOME ASPECTS OF A CASE STUDY ASSOCIATED WITH THE ABDICATION OF THE EMIR OF KANO IN 1963. *African Studies Rev. 1975 18(2): 101-115.* Examines the principles of legitimacy and the practice of succession to the emirate of Kano, Nigeria, ca. 1920-63, with particular reference to the abdication of the last emir in 1963.

2143. Munoz, Louis J. TRADITIONAL PARTICIPATION IN A MODERN POLITICAL SYSTEM: THE CASE OF WESTERN NIGERIA. *J. of Modern African Studies [Great Britain] 1980 18(3): 443-468.* Pursuant to the local Lugardian tradition and the model provided by the House of Lords in Westminister, British colonial authorities in Nigeria long sought to incorporate representation of traditional rulers in devising regional and national bodies to exercise advisory and self-governmental functions. Although at odds with certain features of the traditional role of Yoruba and Edo rulers, the colonial authorities created the Obas' Conference for Western Nigeria in 1937, which they themselves and the Nigerian nationalist parties cultivated to win political support. The obas, in their role as spokesmen and arbitrators, but not autocrats, continued their corporate existence, first in the Western House of Chiefs and later in separate Nigerian state councils. Based on unpublished records of colonial Nigerian political conferences, published Nigerian documents and speeches, and secondary sources; 118 notes. L. W. Truschel

2144. Murray, David J. NIGERIA: THE EXPERIENCE OF MILITARY RULE. *Current Hist. 1975 68(405): 216-219.* Regardless of the direction of the political order in Nigeria, the federal and state governments seem likely to face more difficult conditions in the immediate future than they faced in the recent past. Intractable problems have accumulated, and they must be handled by military governments with declining support, and with a revenue from oil which... is no longer increasing in amount at the rate that it increased each year since 1970. J

2145. Nafziger, E. Wayne and Richter, William L. BIAFRA AND BANGLADESH: THE POLITICAL ECONOMY OF SECESSIONIST CONFLICT. *J. of Peace Res. [Norway] 1976 13(2): 91-109.* The post-independence political and economic ties of Nigeria and Pakistan to Britain and the United States intensified social inequalities by strengthening the dominant elite within each less developed country. Military and economic assistance, and private capital from Great Britain and the United States served also to shield this elite from peripheral groups within its own nation-state. The dominant classes utilized sentiments associated with sub-national identities to promote antagonisms among ethnic groups and regions. Major political elites pursued and implemented economic policies which served their economic advantage. These policies had the effect of increasing interregional discrepancies in Pakistan, and threatening established regional economic interests in Nigeria. Both Biafra and Bangladesh came to view their membership within a federal union as one entailing persistent economic costs. The precipitants of the two political conflicts—the reorganization of the Nigerian federation and the postponement of the Pakistan constituent assembly—were only final steps on the long road to secessionist civil war. J

2146. Nicolson, I. F. NIGERIA: WARS COLD AND HOT, AND LUKEWARM IDEAS. *Australian J. of Pol. and Hist. [Australia] 1976 22(3): 379-393.* Denies cold war influences within Nigeria and suggests outside commentators (American, Russian, and European including British) were ideologically inclined to condemn imperialism and unable to accept that colonial officers were recruited on the understanding that their goal be Nigerian independence. The colonial service represented the spectrum of the British political and social system, except for outright reactionaries or revolutionaries. The author analyzes the three main Nigerian political leaders as archetypal figures with their own motivations: Benjamin Azikiwe, "whose spur was fame and wealth"; Obafemi Awolowo, who feared Azikiwe meant Ibo domination of the Yorubas; and Ahmadu Bello, Sardauna of Sokoto, who cherished the traditional loyalties of the Fulani empire. The tragedy of civil war in the 1960's had to do with nationalities and personalities, not ideologies. Based on memoirs and monographs. W. D. McIntyre

2147. Nkemdiri, Bernard A. THE TIV REBELLION IN NIGERIA 1960: A STUDY OF POLITICAL VIOLENCE. *Mawazo [Uganda] 1975 4(3): 35-52.* Uses the Tiv rebellion of 1960 in Nigeria to illustrate the intimate connection between the political process and collective violence, especially when political violence leads to controversy about the sharing or exercise of power. This analysis of the causes of the rebellion shows that violence and other kinds of force are perennially associated with the exercise of power on the acquisition or retention of rights. 18 notes, biblio. J. J. N. McGurk

2148. Nkpa, Nwokocha K. U. RUMORS OF MASS POISONING IN BIAFRA. *Public Opinion Q. 1977 41(3): 332-346.* Many rumors of mass poisoning circulated in Biafra during the recent Nigerian civil war. The author describes the conditions that bred the rumors and the Biafran customs and beliefs that shaped them. J

2149. Nwachuku, Levi A. NIGERIA: WHY GOWON FELL. *Africa Report 1975 20(5): 8-11.* Discusses political and governmental factors involved in the rise and fall of Nigerian military leader and head of state Yakubu Gowon, 1966-75.

2150. Nwuneli, Onuora. BROADCAST REGULATION AND THE POLITICIANS OF THE FIRST NIGERIAN REPUBLIC. *Pan-African J. [Kenya] 1973 6(1): 57-65.* Records the efforts of the politicians of the Nigerian Republic to control broadcasting, 1951-66, and establish an authoritarian grip over Nigeria's mass media.

2151. Odetola, T. O. NATIONAL INTEGRATION AND THE CREATION OF STATES IN NIGERIA. *J. of Black Studies 1978 9(2): 181-193.* For Nigeria to become one, united nation, the political problem of uniting ethnic groups at the communal level is more serious than the problems of rural-urban or elite-peasant gaps. The military regime's creation of states and its establishment of administrative institutions are beginning to solve these problems as the administrative institutions' actions cut through ethnic-political divisions and promote national integration in technical and administrative areas. It is not yet clear whether these institutions will also be able to resolve political issues. 12 notes, biblio. R. G. Sherer

2152. Ofoegbu, Mazi Ray. NIGERIA AND ITS NEIGHBORS. *Odu: a J. of West African Studies [Nigeria] 1975 (12): 3-24.* Examines Nigeria's relations with its neighbors, Benin, Niger, Cameroon, and Chad, since independence. The first phase, 1960-65, was marked by caution and relative inactivity. The second phase, 1966-69, centered on the extraction of political or diplomatic support for a united Nigeria, or at least for their neutral posture. The third phase, 1970 to the present, has been characterized by personal diplomacy and a higher consciousness of the need for cooperation. Primary and secondary sources; 8 tables, 32 notes, 5 appendixes. M. M. McCarthy

2153. Ogunbadejo, Oye. GENERAL GOWON'S AFRICAN POLICY. *Int. Studies [India] 1977 16(1): 35-50.* The examination of Nigeria's African policy under Yakubu Gowon covers the continental issues, the mechanics of the regional policy, and concludes with an overall assessment up to Gowon's overthrow in 1975. Nigeria, in spite of the possibility of isolation, took its African leadership responsibilities seriously on major issues of continental importance. Nigeria emphasized African unity, but without compromise of national integrity, adhered to a policy of noninterference in the internal affairs of other states, and opposed the use of force to revise external boundaries. 57 notes.
R. V. Ritter

2154. Ogunbadejo, Oye. IDEOLOGY AND PRAGMATISM: THE SOVIET ROLE IN NIGERIA, 1960-77. *Orbis 1978 21(4): 803-830.* Discusses changes in the Soviet stance toward Nigeria, its effect on the internal political situation there, the reaction of Lagos to the USSR, and the political, diplomatic, and economic gains made by the USSR.

2155. Ogunbadejo, Oye. NIGERIA AND THE GREAT POWERS: THE IMPACT OF THE CIVIL WAR ON NIGERIAN FOREIGN RELATIONS. *African Affairs [Great Britain] 1976 75(298): 14-32.* An assessment of the Biafra war on Nigeria's relations with the United States, Soviet Union, Great Britain, France, and China. Since the Western Powers were divided in their support during the war, and the Communist nations were likewise divided, there was no fear that the conflict in Nigeria could be a testing ground for East-West competition. Nigeria, while maintaining a stand of nonalignment, must begin a move toward the Left, not from affection for Russia, but in self-interest—to eliminate the domination of the West, particularly Britain. 52 notes.
H. G. Soff

2156. Ogunbadejo, Oye. NIGERIA'S FOREIGN POLICY UNDER MILITARY RULE 1966-79. *Int. J. [Canada] 1980 35(4): 748-765.* There is an element of continuity in Nigerian foreign policy in that all the various regimes from 1966 to 1979 subscribed to nonalignment at the international level. Various regimes interpreted this principle and the extent to which other intra- and extra-Nigerian events shaped the execution of these policies, in various manners. Alhaji Sir Abubakar Tafawa Balewa and Johnson Aguiyi-Ironsi pursued a pro-Western foreign policy. Yakubu Gowon fraternized with the Soviet Union, and Murtala Ramat Muhammed steered Nigeria's foreign relations on to a more militant path. Secondary sources; 29 notes. J. Powell

2157. Ojigbo, Anthony Okion. CONFLICT RESOLUTION IN THE TRADITIONAL YORUBA POLITICAL SYSTEM. *Cahiers d'Études Africaines [France] 1973 13(2): 275-292.* The social organization of traditional Yoruba society can be divided into two groups: the royal lineage and the nonroyal lineages. Yet the "subjects" have such power that it could be said the *oba* (king) is really their "subject." Many religious and political structures, including secret societies, check the power of the king. Significantly, a candidate for the kingship was once rejected for being too tall; looking down on his subjects, either literally or figuratively, is something a Yoruba king must never do. 2 tables, biblio. J. C. Billigmeier

2158. Ojo, Olatunde J. B. THE IMPACT OF PERSONALITY AND ETHNICITY ON THE NIGERIAN ELECTIONS. *Africa Today 1981 28(1): 47-58.* Post-1979 election analyses overemphasize ethnicity as a factor. Nigerian voters consider not only ethnic affiliation but personality, issue, and class concerns in making electoral choices. Scholars must analyze all factors or continue to distort the reality of Nigerian politics. Secondary sources; 26 notes. G. O. Gagnon

2159. Ojo, Olatunde J. B. NIGERIAN-SOVIET RELATIONS: RETROSPECT AND PROSPECT. *African Studies Rev. 1976 19(3): 43-64.* Since gaining independence in October 1960, Nigeria has accepted limited trade, economic assistance, and armaments from the USSR and other Communist nations, yet its policy toward the Soviet Union remains mistrustful.

2160. Okafor, Francis C. POLITICAL DEVELOPMENT AND THE MODERNIZATION PROCESS IN NIGERIA. *Civilisations [Belgium] 1977 27(1-2): 102-118.* Examines the modernization process in Nigeria, 1880's-1960's, the regional differentiation created by its varying impact, and the effect of these differentiations on regional planning in the 20th century.

2161. Okafor, S. O. IDEALS AND REALITY IN BRITISH ADMINISTRATIVE POLICY IN EASTERN NIGERIA. *African Affairs [Great Britain] 1974 73(293): 459-471.* Prior to the 1930's eastern Nigeria was neglected by the colonial government, although other areas of that colony were being developed. In the years 1947-60, the Native Authority tried and failed to change its policies regarding eastern Nigeria. 36 notes. H. G. Soff

2162. Okolo, Julius Emeka and Langley, Winston E. THE CHANGING NIGERIAN FOREIGN POLICY. *World Affairs 1973 135(4): 309-327.* Discusses political, economic, and military factors which have contributed to a change in Nigerian foreign policy since 1960.

2163. Okonjo, Kamene. THE DUAL-SEX POLITICAL SYSTEM IN OPERATION: IGBO WOMEN AND COMMUNITY POLITICS IN MIDWESTERN NIGERIA. Hafkin, Nancy J. and Bay, Edna G., eds. *Women in Africa: Studies in Social and Economic Change*(Stanford U. Pr., 1976): 45-58. Igbo society on the western side of the Niger in Nigeria can be characterized as a dual-sex political system wherein each sex managed its own affairs and women's interests were represented on all levels. The *omu* was in charge of the female sector of the community, overseeing the community market, the institution of title-taking, and women's rituals, while the *otu omuada* acted as a political pressure group for women's interests. With British colonialism in the 1910's, women's political and religious functions were usurped by Christianity and the colonial government. Although there has been a resurgence of women's social position and traditional roles since 1960, women do not function in national political, status-bearing roles. Based on fieldwork and secondary sources. S. Tomlinson-Brown

2164. Ola, R. O. F. DECENTRALIZATION OR DECONCENTRATION: A THEORETICAL AND FUNCTIONAL APPROACH TO LOCAL GOVERNMENT IN KANO EMIRATE IN THE MILITARY ERA. *Australian J. of Pol. and Hist. [Australia] 1979 25(3): 332-344.* An assessment of the type and effectiveness of decentralization in the Kano emirate of Northern Nigeria from 1966 to 1972. It was decentralization of administration not of representative government, the administrative officer being akin to a French prefect. In 1968 the 12,000-square-mile emirate was divided into five administrative divisions, and three of the five of the district officers were non-Hausa. The purpose of the reforms was efficiency in the provision of services, but the system could be found wanting in democratic ideals, political participation, protective services, infrastructural services, social and economic development, and educational development. Based on government yearbooks and reports and secondary sources; 46 notes.
W. D. McIntyre

2165. Ollawa, P. E. THE NIGERIAN ELECTIONS OF 1979: A FURTHER COMMENT. *J. of Commonwealth and Comparative Pol. [Great Britain] 1981 19(3) 299-308.* An analysis of the differential impact of economic and social issues, the sociocultural profiles presented by parties to the electorate, their past political records and the personalities of their leaders as determinants of party choice respectively in the ethnic minority and majority states in the Nigerian federal elections of 1979. Based on the 1979 election results, and on interviews with politicians, party officials, and voters; 6 notes. M. J. Clark

2166. Olusanya, G. O. JULIUS OJO-COLE: A NEGLECTED NIGERIAN NATIONALIST AND EDUCATIONIST. *J. of the Hist. Soc. of Nigeria [Nigeria] 1973 7(1): 91-101.* A biographical sketch of Julius Ojo-Cole (1903-38) focusing on his education (he was a brilliant student), his thought, and his teaching. A staunch advocate of the importance of African culture and a firm believer in Africans taking pride in themselves and their past, his writings reflect a strong nationalism. Today, the strength of his convictions is apparent in that they presaged views generally accepted by leading figures in present-day Nigeria. Based on oral interviews and printed sources; 29 notes.
J. A. Casada

2167. Oreh, Onuma O. THE BEGINNINGS OF SELF-CENSORSHIP IN NIGERIA'S PRESS AND THE MEDIA. *Gazette [Netherlands] 1976 22(3): 150-155.* The government takeover of Nigeria's formerly independent newspapers and mass media, 1960's-74, seems to indicate the beginning of censorship and the end of freedom of speech.

2168. Osuntokun, Jide. POST-FIRST WORLD WAR ECONOMIC AND ADMINISTRATIVE PROBLEMS IN NIGERIA AND THE RESPONSE OF THE CLIFFORD ADMINISTRATION. *J. of the Hist. Soc. of Nigeria [Nigeria] 1973 7(1): 35-48.* World War I had a profound impact on virtually every phase of Nigeria's development and created numerous problems which necessitated administrative attention in the postwar era. Sir Hugh Clifford (1866-1941) brought a new modernism to Nigeria by giving Africans a say in their own government. Based primarily on Colonial Office records relating to Clifford's administration; 53 notes. J. A. Casada

2169. Otakpor, Nkeonye. PLURALISM AND CONSOCIATIONAL DEMOCRACY IN NIGERIA. *Politico [Italy] 1981 46(1-2): 107-125.* Consociational democracy refines and reformulates the conflict model of society, arguing that democratic government within a pluralistic society such as Nigeria may be difficult but not impossible. Nigeria's pluralistic society has been enforced first by a colonial administration and then by a strong government and a civil war. Discusses various elements such as coalition, mutual veto, proportionality in political representation, and autonomy in the Nigerian case. Secondary sources; 35 notes. J. Powell

2170. Otite, Onigu. SUCCESSION IN TWO URHOBO KINGDOMS: A STUDY IN SOCIO-POLITICAL INTEGRATION. *Odu [Nigeria] 1974 (9): 80-94.* Concerns two of the twenty Urhobo social units of the Mid-Western State of Nigeria: the Okpe kingdom and the Ughelli kingdom. They represent the two current forms of succession to indigenous high political offices approved by the government of the Mid-Western State. These two forms of succession, primogenitural and rotatory, invoke alike kinright, local popular election, and new state government appointment. Primary and secondary sources; 15 notes. M. M. McCarthy

2171. Oyediran, Oyeleye. MODAKEKE IN IFE: HISTORICAL BACKGROUND TO AN ASPECT OF CONTEMPORARY IFE POLITICS. *Odu: a J. of West African Studies [Nigeria] 1974 (10): 63-78.* Discusses the origin of communal compartmentalization between the Ife and Modakeke in the precolonial era and the pattern of its development during the colonial era. Based on documents in the National Archives, Ibadan, and other primary sources; 46 notes. M. M. McCarthy

2172. Oyediran, Oyeleye. REORGANIZATION OF THE NIGERIAN FEDERATION: ITS BACKGROUND AND ADMINISTRATIVE PROBLEMS. *Philippine J. of Public Administration [Philippines] 1974 18(3): 226-244.* The reorganization scheme initiated in Nigeria in 1967 was built on a political rather than on an administrative or doctrinal premise. A glimpse at Nigerian history reveals a maze of arbitrary divisions and amalgamations of area units in a pattern based on ethnic composition and geographical expediency. The resultant structural imbalance in the Nigerian Federation led not only to the physical demarcation of geographic regions into distinct entities, but also to the polarization of cultural interests and purposes among the Nigerian populace. Such polarization obstructs future stability. Despite these problems, the 1967 Nigerian reorganization was a necessary and appropriate move. By and large, it was symptomatic of a strong national awareness of the needed integration in Nigeria. J/S

2173. Oyedrian, Oyeleye. LOCAL GOVERNMENT IN SOUTHERN NIGERIA: THE DIRECTION OF CHANGE. *African Rev. [Tanzania] 1974 4(4): 543-555.* Local government was one of the constitutional structures inherited from the British by independent Nigeria. For a variety of reasons this structure did not fulfill expectations. Consequently, from 1966 on, various reforms were attempted. In the Eastern and Western regions these reforms led to the creation of local administration rather than local government. 31 notes. R. T. Brown

2174. Oyovbaire, S. Egite. NIGERIA. *J. of Modern African Studies [Great Britain] 1973 11(4): 655-658.* A review of *Nigeria: Modernization and the Politics of Communalism,* edited by Robert Melson and Howard Wolpe (Michigan State U. Pr., 1971). The volume attempts to deal with the problems of intergroup conflict in Africa by exploring the political experience of Nigeria, "one country in which the destructive potentialities inherent in all communal confrontations were tragically realized." The purpose is "to identify and clarify more precisely the key dimensions of communal conflict." Its most significant contribution is in its examination of the tragedy of the Nigerian political experience—the supplanting of civil rule by a military regime. R. V. Ritter

2175. Paden, John N. ISLAMIC POLITICAL CULTURE AND CONSTITUTIONAL CHANGE IN NIGERIA. *Issue: A Q. J. of Opinion 1981 11(1-2): 24-28.* Summarizes the Islamic aspect of political culture in Nigeria during the 20th century, noting the distribution of Islamic culture in Nigeria, the ideas of the three Islamic leaders whose thoughts serve as the basis of contemporary Islamic thought, constitutional and political development, and Islamic political culture in the industrializing state of Kano and in Nigeria in general.

2176. Paldam, Martin. NIGERIA EFTER FEM ÅRS FRED [Nigeria after five years of peace]. *Økonomi og politik [Denmark] 1975 49(1): 26-65.* Surveys conditions in Nigeria since the end of the civil war (1970), noting the problems but also the possibilities for material and social growth. Central control with the military in command has succeeded in bringing some reforms and improvements—in education, fiscal stability, control of population growth, delegation of responsibility to federal units, and development of administrative personnel. Attempts to stop corruption, improve communications, transportation, and sanitation have failed, and there is much confusion from attempting too much too quickly, from overlapping projects, and waste of resources. There have been further failures in agricultural development and in developing irrigation facilities. The presence of the military is necessary because of ethnic conflicts that persist despite federalism and reasonable efforts to satisfy local demands. R. E. Lindgren

2177. Pearce, R. D. GOVERNORS, NATIONALISTS, AND CONSTITUTIONS IN NIGERIA, 1935-51. *J. of Imperial and Commonwealth Hist. [Great Britain] 1981 9(3): 289-307.* A study of the colonial governors of Nigeria, 1935-51, Sir Bernard Bourdillon (1883-1948), Sir Arthur Richards, and Sir John Macpherson, and their reaction to the growth of Nigerian nationalism and the rise of the country's first president, Nnamdi Azikiwe. Based on materials at the Colonial Office and Public Records Office, London and secondary sources; 93 notes. M. C. Rosenfield

2178. Peil, Margaret. A CIVILIAN APPRAISAL OF MILITARY RULE IN NIGERIA. *Armed Forces and Soc. 1975 2(1): 34-45.* Discusses public opinion toward civilian and military rule in Nigeria in 1971-72, emphasizing the meaning Nigerians attach to peace, violence and political corruption.

2179. Phillips, Claude S. NIGERIA'S NEW POLITICAL INSTITUTIONS. *J. of Modern African Studies [Great Britain] 1980 18(1): 1-22.* Describes the efforts to institutionalize new political organizations and procedures in Nigeria after the transition from military to civilian government. The entire process was remarkably smooth, mainly because the federal military government pursued policies designed to institutionalize new political behavior. Based on documents and secondary sources; 69 notes. A. Sbacchi

2180. Polhemus, James H. NIGERIA AND SOUTHERN AFRICA: INTEREST, POLICY, AND MEANS. *Can. J. of African Studies [Canada] 1977 11(1): 43-66.* Because Nigeria is the eighth largest producer of oil in the world and the most powerful state of black Africa, the study of the development of its international relations is important. The moral opposition to the colonial regime and minorities of Southern Africa was notably reinforced at the time of the civil war of 1967-70 by the conviction that the white regimes of southern Africa could constitute a direct menace to the security of Nigeria. For Nigeria, the liberation of southern Africa signifies the establishment of really representative national governments. The means adopted by Nigeria to promote the liberation of southern Africa have varied very little in their essence, but the successive Nigerian governments have applied the chosen methods with a growing determination. 90 notes. E. P. Stickney

2181. Pribytkovski, L. OT VOENNOGO PRAVLENIIA—K GRAZHDANSKOMU [From military rule to civil rule]. *Aziia i Afrika Segodnia [USSR] 1973 (6): 4-8.* Recounts the discussion that took place in Nigeria following the lecture delivered by a prominent political figure in 1972 on the country's political development.

2182. Pribytkovski, Lev Naumovich. NIGERIIA V PERIOD VOENNYKH REZHIMOV [Nigeria under military governments]. *Narody Azii i Afriki [USSR] 1980 (6): 45-57.* Examines the positive aspects of reforms introduced by Yakubu Gowon and his successors. Nationalization, trade, taxation of foreign oil revenues, and closer economic ties with the USSR strengthened Nigeria's national economy. However, Gowon's inability to check corruption and refusal to grant political freedom caused his ouster in 1975. The dynamic domestic and foreign policy of Brig. Gen. Murtala Muhammed, treacherously assassinated in 1976, was continued under Lt. Gen. Olusegun Obasanjo who restored a multiparty system and saw a president elected in 1979. 22 notes.
N. Frenkley

2183. Ray, Amal. DECISION-MAKING AND FEDERALISING PROCESS IN INDIA AND NIGERIA. *India Q. [India] 1973 29(4): 319-325.* Examines the operational relationship between federal and regional government in India and Nigeria, 1967-73.

2184. Romanov, Aleksandr I. NIGERIISKII KRIZIS 60-KH GODOV: PRICHINY I POSLEDSTVIIA [The Nigerian crisis of the 1960's: causes and consequences]. *Voprosy Istorii [USSR] 1980 (7): 79-93.* The Nigerian crisis of the 1960's is rooted in the country's colonial past and is closely intertwined with the neocolonialist forms and methods of imperialism which is striving at any cost to retain its positions in the states that have cast off the chains of colonialism and won their independence. During the 1960's a process of political polarization took place in Nigeria. There emerged two camps, the first of which brought together the champions of unity, national development, democracy and socialism, while the second united the proponents and allies of neocolonialism and reaction, who relied on the support of the forces of international imperialism. Nigeria was heading for a division and a protracted internecine war. But in spite of the numerous internal complications and outside imperialist interference, the Nigerian people stood their ground against the machinations of the enemies of unity and defeated the separatists. Their struggle ended in victory for the national patriotic forces.
J

2185. Salamone, Frank A. INDIRECT RULE AND THE REINTERPRETATION OF TRADITION: ABDULLAHI OF YAURI. *African Studies Rev. 1980 23(1): 1-14.* Analyzes the career of Abdullahi, ruler (1923-31) of Yauri, a small state in Northern Nigeria, to show that "indigenous rulers were active participants in colonial rule," manipulating the colonial administrator to achieve their own ends. Entries in a court diary document this dual relationship between ruler and ruled. Based on the Yauri Day Book and other sources in the Nigerian archives; 2 tables, 6 notes, biblio.
R. T. Brown

2186. Salomone, Franck A. ETHNICITY AND THE NIGERIAN CIVIL WAR. *L'Afrique et L'Asie modernes [France] 1976 4(111): 5-12.* Outlines theories of ethnicity and their relationship to the formation of a nation, applying these theories to the Nigerian civil war, 1966-67, in an attempt to discover the causes of the political crises and violence of the Biafran breakaway.

2187. Sambo, Wasihi A. THE AGBEKOYA UPRISING: A STUDY IN POLITICAL AND ECONOMIC CONFLICT. *J. of African Studies 1976 3(2): 247-266.* Describes the farmers' rebellion in the Western State of Nigeria which began on 25 November 1968. Now known as the Agbekoya Uprising, it came as a reaction to the changes that were taking place under the military regime in the Western State. The rebellion was precipitated by a 100% increase in the flat-rate tax, which affected cocoa farmers but not other classes of workers. The uprising illustrates the results in "a society whose rapid rate of social mobilization is not matched by increasing capacity of the government to satisfy the aspirations and expectations thus enhanced." Table, 17 notes.
R. V. Ritter

2188. Spiliotes, Nicholas J. NIGERIAN FOREIGN POLICY AND SOUTHERN AFRICA: A CHOICE FOR THE WEST. *Issue: A Q. J. of Opinion 1981 11(1-2): 41-45.* Discusses Nigeria's foreign policy in Southern Africa since the end of Nigeria's civil war in 1970, focusing on relations of the West, particularly Great Britain and the United States, with Nigeria regarding Southern African foreign policy, which is important because of petroleum exports from Lagos and the latter's ability to influence developments in Southern Africa.

2189. Stewart, Marjorie Helen. TRADITION AND A CHANGING POLITICAL ORDER: A DISPUTE AFFECTING THE CHIEFTAINCIES OF KAIAMA AND KENU IN NIGERIA. *Genève-Afrique [Switzerland] 1979 17(1): 67-87.* Describes the consequences of a colonial decision in which a Nigerian chief was subordinated to a former neighbor. In 1948 an heir to the chieftainship was displaced by a nontraditional candidate, and despite six years of appeal the rightful heir never recovered his position. Based on interviews, materials from the Nigerian National Archives, and secondary sources; 2 photos, 2 maps, 22 notes.
B. S. Fetter

2190. Stouffer, Willard B., Jr. PARTICIPATION IN NORTH-WESTERN NIGERIA: DISTRICT COUNCILS IN ACTION. *J. of Modern African Studies [Great Britain] 1974 12(1): 117-125.* Describes the existence of democratic institutions in North-Western Nigeria (1967-68) despite the military government. Reviews a "typical meeting" of the district council in Sokoto. 12 notes.
H. G. Soff

2191. Ubah, C. N. PRELIMINARIES TO THE 1951 "INDIRECT" ELECTIONS AT KANO. *Africa Q. [India] 1978 17(3): 32-46.* Discusses the development of a constitution in Nigeria, 1949-51, focusing on Kano province.

2192. Udofia, O. E. NIGERIAN POLITICAL PARTIES: THEIR ROLE IN MODERNIZING THE POLITICAL SYSTEM, 1920-1966. *J. of Black Studies 1981 11(4): 435-448.* Examines the role of Nigerian political parties in creating a relationship between government and society, and in involving the masses in the political system. Questions to what extent they performed their proper functions and what gaps they created in the process of modernization. Also explores the relationship between the traditional authorities and the parties in the process of the country's modernization. During the period under study social modernization of Nigeria was not realized by the use of political machinery, but instead the country was plunged into civil war. Ref.
J. V. Coutinho

2193. Utomi, Patrick. HISTORICAL-PHILOSOPHICAL FOUNDATIONS OF GOVERNMENT OWNERSHIP OF NEWSPAPERS IN NIGERIA. *Gazette: Int. J. for Mass Communication Studies [Netherlands] 1981 27(1): 69-72.* The historical-governmental characteristics of three regions in Nigeria help explain the patterns of government ownership of newspapers in that country. The Hausa-Fulani tradition in the north is one of autocracy, owing to the influence of Islam. The constitutional monarchy of the Yorubas in the west led to a system of give and take in government which spawned a freer, more combative press. The east, peopled by the Ibos, had a sort of popular democracy which resulted in its being the last area to get a government paper. Secondary sources; 17 notes.
J. S. Coleman

2194. VanAllen, Judith. "ABA RIOTS" OR IGBO "WOMEN'S WAR"? IDEOLOGY, STRATIFICATION, AND THE INVISIBILITY OF WOMEN. Hafkin, Nancy J. and Bay, Edna G., eds. *Women in Africa: Studies in Social and Economic Change*(Stanford, Ca.: Stanford U. Pr., 1976): 59-85. When thousands of women protested before the native administration centers in the Calabar and Owerri provinces of southeastern Nigeria in 1925, the British found it incomprehensible that women with grassroots leadership could agree on demands and join in concerted action against taxation. In an extension of their traditional methods for settling grievances, the women indicated their dissatisfaction with policies that violated their traditional system of diffuse authority, shared rights of enforcement, and a stable balance of power between men and women. Applying Victorian stereotypes to the Igbo women, the British blamed the men as organizers of the disturbance. Economic and educational reforms spurred by the event applied only to the men. 12 notes.
S. Tomlinson-Brown

2195. Whitaker, C. S., Jr. SECOND BEGINNINGS: THE NEW POLITICAL FRAMEWORK. *Issue: A Q. J. of Opinion 1981 11(1-2): 2-13.* Describes the political framework of Nigeria's second republic, formed in 1979 (the first was formed in 1960, but military rule prevailed from 1966 to 1979), concluding that "institutional architecture is a key to democratic viability."

2196. Wiseberg, Laurie S. AN EMERGING LITERATURE: STUDIES OF THE NIGERIAN CIVIL WAR. *African Studies Rev. 1975 18(1): 117-126.* Reviews Thierry Hentsch's *Face au Blocus: La Croix-Rouge internationale dans la Nigéria au Guerre (1967-70)* (Geneva: Inst. U. de Haut Etudes Int., 1973); Suzanne Gronje's *The World and Nigeria: the Diplomatic History of the Biafran War 1967-70*(London: Sidgwick and Jackson, 1972); Zdenek Cervenka's *The Nigerian War 1967-1970* (Frankfurt am Main: Bernard und Graefe, 1971); John de St. Jorre's *The Nigerian Civil War* (London: Hodder and Stoughton, 1972).

2197. —. YOUTH SERVICE AND NATIONAL DISCIPLINE. *Afriscope [Nigeria] 1973 3(6): 8, 9, 45.* Describes the creation of Nigeria's National Youth Service Corps and summarizes the youth corps experience of other African nations. Illus. G. O. Gagnon

Society

2198. Abiodun, Josephine Olu. URBAN GROWTH AND PROBLEMS IN METROPOLITAN LAGOS. *Urban Studies [Great Britain] 1974 11(3): 341-347.* Discusses problems of increasing urbanization in Lagos, Nigeria, in the 1970's, emphasizing housing, transportation, waste disposal, and general sanitation.

2199. Ada, Mary Juliana and Isichei, Elizabeth. PERCEPTIONS OF GOD AND THE CHURCHES IN OBUDU. *J. of Religion in Africa [Netherlands] 1975 7(3): 165-173.* Traces the impact of Christian missionaries and Christianity in the Obudu Division of Nigeria. Traditionally, the people had secret societies, a belief in magic, but also a supreme God. Catholic missions arrived in 1921, but before that the colonial presence had an effect on transforming the local religion. Catholicism developed strongly, and the majority of converts remain women and children. Traditionalists and Christians, however, both claim a similar concept of God, but traditionalists also believe that they lead a more righteous life than many Christians. 43 notes. H. G. Soff

2200. Adedeji, J. A. THE CHURCH AND THE EMERGENCE OF THE NIGERIAN THEATRE: 1914-1945. *J. of the Hist. Soc. of Nigeria [Nigeria] 1973 6(4): 387-396.* Continued from an earlier article. Examines the general fabric of Nigerian life as it affected "the artistic aims and practices of the period." Particular emphasis is placed on individuals and institutions in their relation to the development of theater. 60 notes. J. A. Casada

2201. Adedeji, Joël. LE CONCERT-PARTY AU NIGÉRIA ET LES DÉBUTS D'HUBERT OGUNDE [The concert-party in Nigeria and the beginnings of Hubert Ogunde]. *Rev. d'Hist. du Théâtre [France] 1975 27(1): 21-25.* The term concert-party denotes a kind of music hall performance or the performance of an itinerant theatrical troupe, first used in 1910 by a group of Europeans in Lagos. The first indigenous use of the term was by the Ebute-Ero Concert-Party which presented an opera in Lagos in 1931. The father of the concert-party genre was, however, Hubert Ogunde whose theatrical career began in Lagos in 1944. Shortly thereafter he organized the African Music Research Party then founded a professional theater company which toured throughout Nigeria, Africa, Europe, and America. Ogunde's success with the concert-party in Nigeria is attributed to his recognition that theater must be the mirror of society. 17 notes. H. R. Falk

2202. Adedeji, Joel. NATIONALISM AND THE NIGERIAN NATIONAL THEATRE. *Munger Africana Lib. Notes 1980 (54): 5-19.* Presents three periods in the development of nationalism in Nigeria and the role of the theater in the sociopolitical changes: 1890-1915, the period of cultural nationalism; 1935-60, the period of political nationalism; and since 1960, the period of regenerative nationalism.

2203. Adegbile, Isaiah. EIGHTY MILLION NIGERIANS AND THEIR FUTURE: A COMMENTARY ON THE 1973 CENSUS. *Africa Today 1975 22(1): 63-65.* The 1973 census must be confirmed because of the radical, unexplained growth of four northern states and the deline of population in two eastern states. These discrepancies are crucial in a state where representation and government funds are based on population. Based on the 1973 census; table, note. G. O. Gagnon

2204. Adejunmobi, S. A. THE NEED FOR SOCIAL STUDIES IN NIGERIAN SECONDARY SCHOOLS. *Indiana Social Studies Q. 1974 27(2): 56-62.*

2205. Adekunle, Modolaji A. MULTILINGUALISM AND LANGUAGE FUNCTION IN NIGERIA. *African Studies R. 1972 15(2): 185-207.* Nigeria has a multiplicity of languages whose function varies with the social and political setting. Includes a new functional classification system for each of these languages. Biblio., appendix. R. T. Brown

2206. Adeloye, Adelola. NIGERIAN PIONEER DOCTORS AND EARLY WEST AFRICAN POLITICS. *Nigeria Mag. [Nigeria] 1976 (121): 2-24.* Nigerian graduates of medical schools often became seriously committed to the sociopolitical development of West Africa. Presents brief biographical sketches of several who helped mold Nigeria into a modern nation. The greatest effort appears to have been in the 19th and early 20th century, and was led by Drs. Nathanial King, J. B. Africanus Horton, Obadiah Johnson, Oguntola Sapara, and John Randle. 59 notes. H. G. Soff

2207. Adenira, Tunde. YOUTH CULTURE IN TRANSITION, NIGERIAN YOUTHS IN THE 1970S. *Youth and Soc. 1975 6(4): 481-494.* Having experienced the failure of the intellectuals in the 1960's to improve society, Nigerian youth feel powerless. They may become a political force in the future. Based on author's observations, primary sources; 5 notes, biblio. J. H. Sweetland.

2208. Adesua, Adeleye. VOCATIONAL EDUCATION IN TWO NIGERIAN SCHOOLS: A CASE STUDY. *J. of Negro Educ. 1980 49(2): 215-219.* Brief summary of the vocational education programs at two Nigerian schools: Ajuwa Grammar School, under Guy Gargiulo; and Mayflower School, under Tai Solarin. Based on participant-observations of the schools; 5 notes. R. E. Butchart

2209. Adewọye, O. LAW AND SOCIAL CHANGE IN NIGERIA. *J. of the Hist. Soc. of Nigeria 1973 7(1): 149-159.* A lengthy review article based on T. O. Elias, ed., *Law and Social Change in Nigeria.* The book is a collection of essays which "attempts to look at various aspects of the law in so far as they affect the development of Nigeria since Independence." Actually little of the book is devoted to social questions, and using this consideration as a point of departure, the author outlines a number of areas where such investigations might be made. 53 notes. J. A. Casada

2210. Adeyinka, A. Ade. LOCAL COMMUNITY EFFORTS IN THE DEVELOPMENT OF SECONDARY GRAMMAR SCHOOL EDUCATION IN THE WESTERN STATE OF NIGERIA, 1925-1955. *J. of Negro Educ. 1976 45(3): 263-274.* The Education Ordinance of 1926 was an incentive for communities to establish secondary schools. Thirteen such schools opened between 1931 and 1950. Public support and financing of such community schools led to a decline in the opening mission schools. The history of several community schools is given. 3 tables, 26 notes. B. D. Johnson

2211. Aguolu, C. C. THE FOUNDATION OF MODERN LIBRARIES IN NIGERIA. *Internat. Lib. Rev. [Great Britain] 1977 9(4): 461-484.* Examines the history of libraries and the printed word as well as Islamic scholarship in Nigeria, 1840's-1975. Chronicles printing and publishing throughout the 19th century, the beginnings of libraries in the 20th century and the increasing number through the 1920's-40's under the influence of the Carnegie Corporation. Discusses the impact of nationalism and decolonization policies within the Nigerian government.

2212. Aguolu, C. C. THE ROLE OF ETHNICITY IN NIGERIAN EDUCATION. *J. of Negro Educ. 1979 48(4): 513-529.* Surveys the history and current status of education and educational opportunity in Nigeria, noting especially the effect of ethnicity on educational attainment and social mobility. Of the three dominant ethnic groups—Ibo, Yoruba, and Hausa-Fulani—the Ibo have benefited most from educational opportunity, the Hausa-Fulani the least. Colonial and Western influences have interacted with ethnic cultural values to create differing patterns of opportunity and achievement. Secondary sources; 2 tables, 46 notes. R. E. Butchart

2213. Ahmed, Akbar S. MULLAH, MAHDI, AND MOSQUE: EMERGENT TRENDS IN MUSLIM SOCIETY. *Arab Studies Q. 1982 4(1-2): 127-137.* Analyzes social and political life in the Muslim world, examining the role of ethnicity and religious leaders in rural societies in South Waziristan, Pakistan and Kano, Nigeria during the 20th century.

2214. Alabi, G. A. A STUDY OF PUBLICATIONS GROWTH IN NIGERIA AND THE IMPORTANCE OF THESE PUBLICATIONS TO THE DEVELOPMENT OF THE COUNTRY. *Government Publ. Rev. 1978 5(4): 455-460.* Discusses the nature of publications in Nigeria, 1950-70, typified by a growth in English language publications as more secondary schools, polytechnics, technical colleges, and universities were established, as Nigeria attained independence, and as free primary education was introduced in some areas during the late 1950's.

2215. Alli, Billiamin A. ACCULTURATIVE FORCES: NIGERIA IN CHANGE. *J. of Black Studies 1974 4(4): 376-395.* Islam and Christianity have had a profound effect on the Yoruba culture of Nigeria, in Yoruba religion, poetry, music, and carving. 3 notes, biblio.
K. Butcher

2216. Amadi, Lawrence E. CHURCH-STATE INVOLVEMENT IN EDUCATIONAL DEVELOPMENT IN NIGERIA, 1842-1948. *J. of Church and State 1977 19(3): 483-496.* Formal education in Nigeria began in 1842 and was introduced and controlled by missionaries until 1901. The author discusses the development of education in the period and the transition period, 1901-48, when the government achieved full control. Emphasizes the church-state relationship in both periods, particularly the establishment of schools with government aid. Also examines education codes of 1916 and 1948. 70 notes.
E. E. Eminhizer

2217. Anigbo, Osmund A. C. THE CHANGING PATTERN OF OSTRACISM IN AN IGBO COMMUNITY. *Africa [Italy] 1978 33(3): 419-425.* A review of the nature of ostracism in a modern Nigerian community, 1955-78. The conversion to Catholicism of many of the villagers left the remainder without sufficient funds to stage the annual feast to the spirits of departed ancestors. When the Catholics refused to contribute, the Elders ostracized four of them. They could not eat with or marry other villagers, nor own land. The scheme backfired because land is no longer so important, and because exclusion from traditional feasts simply made the Catholics realize the importance of Christian feasts. The community was thus split, and has remained so, although the Christians are younger, more numerous, and probably will win through in the end. Ref.
V. L. Human

2218. Anoniyi, Timothy A. THE YORUBA LANGUAGE AND THE FORMAL SCHOOL SYSTEM: A STUDY OF THE COLONIAL LANGUAGE POLICY IN NIGERIA. *J. of Educ. Administration and Hist. [Great Britain] 1975 7(2): 9-19.* Discusses the linguistic impact of the introduction of formal colonial schools among the Yoruba in the 19th century, the movement toward the abandonment of the Yoruba language in favor of English, and the fortunes and misfortunes of the language, 1882-1955.

2219. Asein, Samuel Omo. LITERATURE AND SOCIETY IN LAGOS. *Nigeria Mag. [Nigeria] 1975 (117-118): 22-32.* Traces missionary activity in Nigeria and missionaries' attempt to educate Africans to imitate European culture, in part by means of essay competitions, which led to the development of a new class of African writers, "black Victorians," and new forms of theater and concert. 29 notes.
H. G. Soff

2220. Asiwaju, A. I. THE AJA-SPEAKING PEOPLES OF NIGERIA: A NOTE ON THEIR ORIGINS, SETTLEMENT AND CULTURAL ADAPTATION UP TO 1945. *Africa [Great Britain] 1979 49(1): 15-28.* Advocates a cross-frontier approach in contributing to Adja historiography, regarding the Adja as an important element in the ethnic affinity between Nigeria and Benin. Defines the geographical location of Adja settlements, points out the factors that resulted in migrations, from the 18th to the 20th centuries and demonstrates that the Adja have experienced both cultural stability and change since their settlement among Yoruba-speaking peoples. Fig., 33 notes, biblio.
P. J. Taylorson

2221. Awoniyi, Timothy A. THE YORUBA LANGUAGE AND THE FORMAL SCHOOL SYSTEM: A STUDY OF COLONIAL LANGUAGE POLICY IN NIGERIA, 1882-1952. *Int. J. of African Hist. Studies 1975 8(1): 63-80.* British colonialization of the area now known as Nigeria brought with it an emphasis on the use of the English language in the schools. The missionaries, who had been teaching in Nigeria for decades, were outraged. They fought the new policy vigorously, and although they failed to get it repealed, were successful in winning certain modifications. British language policy was always bound up with matters of political expediency. Great Britain feared that use of the native language would encourage nationalism. This fear gradually faded, but English remained the language of the educated class until the coming of independence. 63 notes.
V. L. Human

2222. Ayandele, E. A. AN AFRICAN CHURCH: A LEGITIMATE BRANCH OF THE CHURCH UNIVERSAL. *African Historical Studies* (Totowa, N.J.: Frank Cass, 1979): 211-229. H. W. Turner's two-volume *African Independent Church*(Oxford: Oxford U. Pr., 1967), a comprehensive study of the Church of the Lord, supports African interpretation of Christian doctrine and practices and affirms its legitimacy as a branch of the universal Christian church.

2223. Ayandele, E. A. LUGARD AND EDUCATION IN NIGERIA, 1900-18. *Nigerian Historical Studies* (London: Frank Cass, 1979): 248-269. The educational policy of Frederick Lugard in Northern Nigeria, 1900-06, and as Governor-General of all Nigeria, 1912-18, was secularist, racist, and elitist, but he was the first to advocate rural education and adult education in Nigeria.

2224. Babayẽmi, S. O. BẼRẼ FESTIVAL IN ỌYỌ. *J. of the Hist. Soc. of Nigeria [Nigeria] 1973 7(1): 121-124.* Describes the ceremonies of the Bere, which is a national festival in Oyo. It has political and economic overtones, but is widely enjoyed because it is a period of relaxation and holidays. It centers on the Alaafin, the head of all Oyo-speaking peoples.
J. A. Casada

2225. Barrett, Stanley R. THE POLITICS OF DEFECTION FROM AN AFRICAN UTOPIA. *Africa [Great Britain] 1979 49(1): 1-14.* Describes the defection and recruitment of members of a utopian community of the Holy Apostles in the Ilaje region of Nigeria, 1947-72 and 1973-74. Suggests that village leaders had a vested interest in encouraging male members to leave and in admitting large members of female recruits so that high status men could claim the latter as their wives. Discusses the change from monogamy to polygyny. Based mainly on author's field research; 3 tables, 7 notes, biblio.
P. J. Taylorson

2226. Bozimo, D. O. COOPERATION AMONG UNIVERSITY LIBRARIES IN NIGERIA: (ORIGINS AND COURSE, 1948-75). *Pakistan Lib. Bull. [Pakistan] 1981 12(1): 1-11.* Describes the history of library cooperation in black Africa since 1953, five years after the establishment of the research library of the University College, Ibadan. Most significant was the formation in 1973 of the Committee of (Nigerian) University Libraries.

2227. Chalifoux, Jean Jacques and Muller, Jean Claude. CHANGEMENTS POLITIQUES ET INNOVATIONS RITUELLES/CÉRÉMONIELLES CHEZ LES ABISI (PITI) ET LES RUKUBA, NIGERIA [Political change and ritual/ceremonial innovations among the Abisi (Piti) and the Rukuba of Nigeria]. *Can. J. of African Studies [Canada] 1976 10(1): 107-124.* Traces the innovations brought about by an outside power in the rites and ceremonies of the Abisi and Rukuba tribes of Nigeria. The Abisi devised a ritual making a scapegoat of the mediator who dealt with the foreign power. Nigeria's attempts to persuade both tribes to participate in new ceremonies are usually boycotted because the people distrust the foreign administration. The traditional tribal definitions of the ingredients of the pageantries conflict with the government's interpretation; thus the tribes refuse to participate. Based on interviews, observations, government documents, and secondary sources; 20 notes.
J

2228. Chappel, T. J. H. THE YORUBA CULT OF TWINS IN HISTORICAL PERSPECTIVE. *Africa [Great Britain] 1974 44(3): 250-265.* An examination of the historical basis for two statements—"There was a time when Yoruba did not have twins" and "Yoruba have always accepted twin-births"—reveals that the contemporary Yoruba cult of twins is a reversal of a former practice of twin infanticide. Transition from nonacceptance to acceptance of twins in Yorubaland involved three stages: 1) a direct challenge (probably from external stimulus) to practice of twin infanticide and its supporting belief-system; 2) a period of ambivalence and adjustment due to time-lag between the acceptance of changed practice and the development of a new or modified belief-system; and 3) adoption of an explanatory model which supports veneration of twins while rationally explaining the earlier practice of twin infanticide. Based on oral history, primary and secondary sources; 61 notes, biblio. C. Fry

2229. Chimezie, Amuzie. ATTITUDES OF NIGERIANS TOWARDS ENGLISH: IMPLICATIONS FOR BLACK-AFRICAN RELATIONS. *J. of Black Studies 1973 4(2): 215-219.* Nigerians use competence in English as a measure of intellectual and social status. Though slang is used in tribal languages, correct English is still the mark of an educated person. Blacks from the United States should keep this in mind when visiting Nigeria or any other former British African colony. K. Butcher

2230. Chukunta, N. K. Onuoha. EDUCATION AND NATIONAL INTEGRATION IN AFRICA: A CASE STUDY OF NIGERIA. *African Studies Rev. 1978 21(2): 67-76.* Nigeria's modern educational system has not served an integrative role. Colonial education was British, not Nigerian, oriented. Independence has continued much of the non-Nigerian orientation. Expansion of the system has ended the colonial policy of mixing ethnic groups and has helped encourage disintegration. Secondary sources; 8 notes, biblio. R. T. Brown

2231. Clark, Ebun. OGUNDE THEATRE: THE RISE OF CONTEMPORARY PROFESSIONAL THEATRE IN NIGERIA 1946-72. *Nigeria Mag. [Nigeria] 1974 (114): 3-14.* Hubert Ogunde formed his professional theater in 1946. He has performed and written opera and modern drama in which the first professional Yoruba actresses have performed. He has travelled widely to learn new techniques of theater. During the colonial period, Ogunde frequently ran afoul of immigration officials due to the criticism of his works by the colonial government. 51 notes. Article to be continued. H. G. Soff

2232. Clarke, Peter B. THE RELIGIOUS FACTOR IN THE DEVELOPMENTAL PROCESS IN NIGERIA: A SOCIOHISTORICAL ANALYSIS. *Genève-Afrique [Switzerland] 1979 17(1): 45-65.* Islamic education in Nigeria dates from the 14th century. Although colonial officials after 1903 attempted to provide schools which met both political and religious needs, the education of Muslims in northern Nigeria fell behind that of non-Muslims in the south. In 1976 the Nigerian government launched the Universal Primary Education (UPE) scheme intended to reach northern Muslims, but parents have continued their resistance to secular education. Based on interviews, 1974-78, and printed primary and secondary sources; photo, map, 71 notes. B. S. Fetter

2233. Dike, Azuka A. GROWTH AND DEVELOPMENT PATTERNS OF AWKA AND NSUKKA, NIGERIA. *Africa [Great Britain] 1979 49(3): 235-245.* Awka and Nsukka are both in Igboland and before the Nigerian civil war Awka remained largely undeveloped. Its residents are well-known for their skill in native medicine, carving, and particularly blacksmithing and toolmaking. After the civil war Awka's population more than doubled, and a large daily market developed. Nsukka, traditionally dependent on farming, cloth and basket weaving, and palm wine production, underwent a transformation from 1960 with the establishment of the university. This brought piped water, electricity supplies, and many small scale industries. Nsukka is now a center of national importance; Awka has grown into a semimodern community. 10 notes. R. L. Collison

2234. Dorward, D. C. ETHNOGRAPHY AND ADMINISTRATION: A STUDY OF ANGLO-TIV "WORKING MISUNDERSTANDING." *J. of African Hist. [Great Britain] 1974 15(3): 479-488.* Points out the numerous "working misunderstandings" with the Tiv which arose from the application of conceptual models gained through experiences with other cultures by British administrators in Nigeria. This led to the development of a symbiotic relationship of paternalism and subservience between the cultures. Primary and seconday sources; 90 notes. E. Hopkins

2235. Duruji, C. A. FORESIGHT AND HINDSIGHT FOR NIGERIAN EDUCATORS AND INSIGHT FOR OTHERS. *J. of Educ. Administration and Hist. [Great Britain] 1981 13(2): 43-50.* Considers the efforts to combat educational inadequacies in Nigeria, 1959-61, and analyzes the findings of three commissions set up during this period to inquire into primary and secondary school systems, including teacher training.

2236. Clark, Ebun. OGUNDE THEATER: THE RISE OF CONTEMPORARY PROFESSIONAL THEATRE IN NIGERIA, 1946-1972, PARTS II, III. *Nigeria Mag. [Nigeria] 1975 (115/116): 9-33.* Continued from an earlier article. Hubert Ogunde was the creator of legitimate theater in Nigeria. During 1945-66, his plays and other theatrical works were comments on political developments within his country. The topics included striking workers, foreign intervention, and the banning of political parties. Many of his plays are noted with brief abstracts. Some Ogunde plays were visions into the future; many came true. Under Ogunde, the theater in Nigeria became a weapon for political commentary. Ogunde has been the mainspring for such theater for the past 30 years. 83 notes. H. G. Soff

2237. Echeruo, Michael J. C. DEVELOPMENTS IN THE NIGERIAN PRESS 1960-71. *Nigeria Mag. [Nigeria] 1974 (110-112): 50-61.* Discusses changes in Nigerian radio, newspapers and magazines, 1960-71. The low quality of both the radio and press reflects the poor quality of journalists. Magazines are rising in quality, but "developments" in newspapers over the last decade have tended to mean deterioration, not growth, particularly because papers are viewed as instruments of the government or the opposition. 12 photos. H. G. Soff

2238. Ejiogu, Aloy M. SEX DIFFERENCES IN THE LEADER BEHAVIOUR OF NIGERIAN COLLEGE PRINCIPALS. *J. of Educ. Administration and Hist. [Great Britain] 1982 14(1): 55-61.* Considers barriers placed to keep women from prestigious positions in organizations, in particular a number of incidents in Nigeria involving the appointment of female principals in secondary schools, and the downgrading of their capabilities, 1977-82.

2239. Ekechi, Felix K. EDUCATION AND SOCIAL STATUS IN AN AFRICAN SOCIETY: THE IGBO EXAMPLE. *Umoja: A Scholarly J. of Black Studies 1980 4(3): 17-33.* Western education radically altered the patterns of status allocation and role relationships among the Ibo (Igbo) from about the turn of the 19th century, but although traditional authority systems were eroded, the Ibo people remained as tradition-minded as many of their neighbors.

2240. Ekpe, F. C. THE COLONIAL SITUATION AND LIBRARY DEVELOPMENT IN NIGERIA. *Int. Lib. Rev. [Great Britain] 1979 11(1): 5-18.* Analyzes the interrelationship of political, educational, and socioeconomic institutions created by the British which affected library development in Nigeria, 1900-60.

2241. Ekwelie, Sylvanus A. THE NIGERIAN PRESS UNDER MILITARY RULE. *Gazette [Netherlands] 1979 25(4): 219-232.* When the army assumed control of Nigeria in 1966, a number of laws already regulated the mass media. However, the three military governments of 1966-78 did not attempt to exercise their censorship powers strenuously. There were cases of harassment and detention of newsmen but throughout the period the media continued to enjoy some freedom. The Nigerian military governments displayed much the same appreciation for and fear of a free press as other governments. Based on newspaper reports and secondary sources; 26 notes. J. S. Coleman

2242. Enaohwo, J. O. UNIVERSITY FINANCING IN NIGERIA AND THE IMPLICATIONS FOR HIGHER EDUCATION. *J. of Educ. Administration and Hist. [Great Britain] 1980 12(1): 46-53.* Assesses the Nigerian government's part in financing Nigerian universities and the effect of this on the "development, governance and control" of universities in Nigeria.

2243. Eze, A. FINANCING EDUCATION IN EASTERN NIGERIA BEFORE THE STATE TAKE-OVER OF SCHOOLS. *J. of Educ. Administration and Hist. [Great Britain] 1978 10(1): 46-53.* Discusses the management and financing of the educational system of eastern

Nigeria, 1846-1970, and traces the growth of secondary schools, 1948-58.

2244. Fajana, A. THE NIGERIAN UNION OF TEACHERS: A DECADE OF GROWTH 1931-40. *Nigeria Mag. [Nigeria] 1974 (110-112): 79-89.* The Nigerian Union of Teachers is the only body in Nigeria concerned with the interests of all teachers. Founded in 1931, it continues to organize and stabilize the teaching profession. 69 notes. H. G. Soff

2245. Frantz, Charles. DEVELOPMENT WITHOUT COMMUNITIES: SOCIAL FIELDS, NETWORKS, AND ACTION IN THE MAMBILA GRASSLANDS OF NIGERIA. *Human Organization 1981 40(3): 211-220.* Studies the social organization of the inaccessible Fulbe people in the grasslands of Mambila, in the Gongola State of Nigeria, as a result of their having moved from the savanna, sudan, and sahel into a vastly different ecological zone, discussing the history of development in Mambila, developmental processes and relationships, and emphasizing that development does not necessarily depend upon communities.

2246. Freund, William. THEFT AND SOCIAL PROTEST AMONG THE TIN MINERS OF NORTHERN NIGERIA. *Radical Hist. Rev. 1982 (26): 68-86.* Tin stealing, at its height during 1960, was an act of social protest against the invasion of capital, neglect of the land, and the resulting social and economic dislocation of the Birom people who did not consider their activities a crime.

2247. Goddard, A. D. CHANGING FAMILY STRUCTURES AMONG THE RURAL HAUSA. *Africa [Great Britain] 1973 43(3): 207-218.* The introduction of a monetary economy, the spread of Islam, and the abolition of slavery have been important factors in limiting the size, social composition, and economic functions of the Hausa family structure since the turn of the century.

2248. Hackett, Rosalind. RECENT DEVELOPMENTS IN THE HEALING CONCEPTS AND ACTIVITIES OF THE ALADURA CHURCHES. *African Notes [Nigeria] 1981 8(2): 55-58.* The Aladura, an African Protestant Church among the Yoruba, uses faith healing in conjunction with modern medicine as a primary religious doctrine. Secondary sources; 10 notes. R. T. Brown

2249. Ifeka-Moller, Caroline. WHITE POWER: SOCIAL-STRUCTURAL FACTORS IN CONVERSION TO CHRISTIANITY, EASTERN NIGERIA, 1921-1966. *Can. J. of African Studies [Canada] 1974 8(1): 55-72.* Examines the social structural factors contributing to the differential rates of conversion in eastern Nigeria, critiquing the intellectualist explanation of conversion set forth by Robin Horton.

2250. Igbafe, Philip A. SLAVERY AND EMANCIPATION IN BENIN, 1897-1945. *J. of African Hist. [Great Britain] 1975 16(3): 409-429.* Analyzes slavery and pawning in Benin and the British colonial response to both. Pawning differed from slavery in that it was a type of voluntary or indentured servitude to pay off a debt or obligation. The British, upon their arrival in Benin, unleashed a crusade to eliminate both systems through use of local native courts, plus colonial proclamations. Analyzes the problems this created and their solutions. 74 notes. H. G. Soff

2251. Ilogu, Edmund. CHANGING RELIGIOUS BELIEFS IN NIGERIA. *Nigeria Mag. [Nigeria] 1975 (117-118): 3-20.* Discusses the history and development of the three major religions in Nigeria: Christianity, Islam, and traditional African religion. Analyzes the role of religion and the relationships among them. 10 plates, 14 notes. H. G. Soff

2252. Irele, Abiola. TRADITION AND THE YORUBA WRITER: D. O. FAGUNWA, AMOS TUTUOLA AND WOLE SOYINKA. *Odu: a J. of West African Studies [Nigeria] 1975 (11): 75-100.* It is only among Yoruba writers that the various levels of this transition from the traditional to the modern can be illustrated to bring out its full implications. In Yorubaland, the vast folk literature, which is alive and vigorously contemporary, provides a constant support for new forms. The works of Fagunwa and Tutuola grow out of a living tradition, and the writings of Wole Soyinka show a personal appropriation and reinterpretation of Yoruba cosmology. 6 notes. M. M. McCarthy

2253. Iwundu, Mataebere. IGBO ANTHROPONYMS: LINGUISTIC EVIDENCE FOR REVIEWING THE IBO CULTURE. *Names 1973 21(1): 46-47.* Igbo personal names frequently express significant attitudes or historical facts. S

2254. Jones, G. I. SOCIAL ANTHROPOLOGY IN NIGERIA DURING THE COLONIAL PERIOD. *Africa [Great Britain] 1974 44(3): 280-289.* Evaluates the work of anthropologists in Nigeria during the colonial period, 1884-1960. With few exceptions, early anthropologists in Nigeria contributed little to the general field of social anthropology due to their amateurishness or excessive adherence to outmoded theories. Nigerian colonial records host a virtually unexplored wealth of historical and anthropological information. The most alarming result of anthropologists' work in Nigeria has been its impact upon Nigerians themselves. Based on personal experiences, official colonial records, and secondary sources; 5 notes, biblio. C. Fry

2255. Kastfelt, Niels. AFRICAN PROPHETISM AND CHRISTIAN MISSIONARIES IN NORTHEAST NIGERIA: A HEALING PROPHET AMONG THE MBULA OF ADAMAWA 1927-C. 1932, AS SEEN BY DANISH MISSIONARIES. *J. of Religion in Africa [Netherlands] 1976 8(3): 175-188.* Traces the rise of the Mbula prophet movement at the end of 1926, the attitude of the Danish missionaries toward the movement, and the eventual decline of the movement a few years later. A healing prophet arose because of classical problems: epidemic and crop failure. The movement had similarities to other healing movements and the prophet, Kulibwui, was similar in background to other prophets among Africans. Based on sources in missionary archives; 58 notes. H. G. Soff

2256. Larson, Charles R. NEW WRITERS, NEW READERS. *Wilson Q. 1980 4(1): 81-92.* Provides a sampling of Nigeria's world-class literature, with an overview of the country's publishing history.

2257. Lerche, C. O. SOCIAL STRIFE IN NIGERIA, 1971-1978. *J. of African Studies 1982 9(1): 2-12.* Nigeria in the years between the end of the Biafran War and the resumption of civilian rule in 1979, was the scene not only of rapid economic growth, but also of low-level but increasing social strife. Most of this occurred in the southern states, in the form of strikes, demonstrations, and riots, and was usually directed toward specific local goals associated with improving the standard of living of those involved. The more traditionalist northern states can be expected to experience future turmoil. Secondary sources; 8 tables, 58 notes. L. W. Truschel

2258. Lindfors, Bernth. THE EARLY WRITINGS OF WOLE SOYINKA. *J. of African Studies 1975 2(1): 64-86.* A survey of the early literary career of Nigerian author Wole Soyinka. He began writing in secondary schools, his productions being uneven. Soyinka emphasized boisterous humor, even clownish buffoonery. He continued to disgorge poems, articles, stories, and plays at colleges in Nigeria and England. The quality improved and became predictable. Returning to Nigeria, he produced tales and plays for radio and television, rather ignoring written works until the publication of three books made him famous. Soyinka has never emphasized racialism, preferring an "exciting dignity" which he considers the hallmark of African authors. 46 notes. V. L. Human

2259. Lindfors, Bernth. POPULAR LITERATURE FOR AN AFRICAN ELITE. *J. of Modern African Studies [Great Britain] 1974 12(3): 471-486.* Literature in English developed in Nigeria over 100 years ago, but it flourished after World War II. Almost all Nigerian authors of note began publishing in university magazines and annuals while they were students. 45 notes. H. G. Soff

2260. Lubeck, Paul M. ISLAMIC NETWORKS AND URBAN CAPITALISM: AN INSTANCE OF ARTICULATION FROM NORTHERN NIGERIA. *Cahiers d'Etudes Africaines [France] 1981 21(1-3): 67-78.* Analyzes the working and function of Koranic schools in the city of Kano from the 19th century to the post-civil war era of the 1980's, when new wealth brought by the petroleum boom has effected urban expansion as well as urban problems, including an accelerating rate of inflation. Examines the possibility of various forms of protest against the political authorities for failing to support Koranic education.

2261. Makinde, Olu. HISTORICAL FOUNDATIONS OF COUNSELING IN AFRICA. *J. of Negro Educ. 1978 47(3): 303-311.* The Nigerian *babalawo,* a counselor and diviner, used techniques closely analogous to the prerequisites for nondirective therapy delineated by Carl Rogers. The author reviews the history and legends of the *babalawo* and their methods and provides suggestions for modern therapists drawn from these traditional and highly successful counselors. 17 notes.
R. E. Butchart

2262. Marenin, Otwin. NATIONAL SERVICE AND NATIONAL CONSCIOUSNESS IN NIGERIA. *J. of Modern African Studies [Great Britain] 1979 17(4): 629-654.* Assesses the impact of the National Youth Service Corps in Nigeria, initiated in 1973, in which youth spend a year of service to the nation after leaving university, on the participants, focusing on changed attitudes and whether these have been conducive to national integration. Contact with other people was more influential than the content of the work itself and has reinforced awareness of ethnic distinctions within Nigeria while also raising the level of positive attitudes toward fellow Nigerians, showing that cultural distinctions are not necessarily detrimental to national unity. Participants have a generally high regard for the NYSC but only on an abstract and impersonal level. Based on survey work; 7 tables, 53 notes.
D. J. Nicholls

2263. Mgbejiofor, Sydney E. THE DILEMMAS OF THE NIGERIAN INTELLECTUALS. *Africa Q. [India] 1977 17(1): 37-48.*

2264. Mwosu, S. N. THE BRITISH IDEA OF THE EDUCABILITY OF THE AFRICAN: 1840-1939. *Études d'Hist. Africaine [Zaire] 1976 8: 149-171.* In spite of expanding educational facilities in Nigeria, the official British concept of education for Nigerians until 1940 was one that would keep them in a subordinate position to Europeans. In spite of the emphasis of missionaries and British officials on industrial and agricultural training, the demand of influential Nigerians was for academic education. In 1948 the British accepted a system of education that was not watered down but was adapted to the Nigerian desire for education that would permit them to have self-government. 5 tables, 43 notes.
H. L. Calkin

2265. Nwagwu, N. A. THE POLITICS OF UNIVERSAL PRIMARY EDUCATION IN NIGERIA, 1955-1977. *J. of Educ. Administration and Hist. [Great Britain] 1979 11(2): 41-47.* Considers the political pressures exerted on elementary education in Nigeria from the 1950's to the launching of the free Universal Primary Education Scheme in September 1976.

2266. Nwaka, Geoffrey I. URBAN CULTURE AND THE PROBLEM OF URBAN DEVELOPMENT IN IMO STATE, NIGERIA, A HISTORIAN'S VIEW. *Civilisations [Belgium] 1978 28(3-4): 307-316.* Discusses characteristics of Igbo communities which have led to the poorly organized urban communities in Nigeria.

2267. Nwuneli, Onuora E. and Udoh, Effiong. INTERNATIONAL NEWS COVERAGE IN NIGERIAN NEWSPAPERS. *Gazette: Int. J. for Mass Communication Studies [Netherlands] 1982 29(1-2): 31-40.* Reports on a study of five Nigerian newspapers' foreign coverage for the period December 1978 through November 1979. Not unexpectedly, these newspapers devoted over one-half of their foreign news coverage to the African region, with another one-fourth going to the rest of the Third World. The United States received more coverage than any other developed nation. Although credit was usually lacking, the newspapers under study relied heavily on foreign news wires for their international news. Local news was emphasized at the expense of foreign events. This situation is reflected in the fact that of the 1,487 items identified in the study only 3% made the front page. Ref., 3 tables. J. S. Coleman

2268. Obanya, P. A. I. THE SECONDARY MODERN SCHOOL IN WESTERN NIGERIA. *J. of Educ. Administration and Hist. [Great Britain] 1976 8(2): 46-50.* Studies the characteristics, organization, and structure of the secondary modern school in the Western State of Nigeria and the extent to which they have fulfilled the role originally assigned to them, 1960-74.

2269. Obanya, Pai. TOWARDS A HISTORY OF HIGHER EDUCATION IN NIGERIA. *Can. J. of African Studies [Canada] 1974 8(1): 159-162.* Reviews Nduka Okafor's *The Development of Universities in Nigeria* (Longman, 1971) and *A History of Nigerian Higher Education* (Macmillan, 1971), A. B. Fafunwa, ed., which discuss Nigerian higher education in its 20th-century social, political, and economic context.

2270. Ojo, J. D. SUPERNATURAL POWERS AND CRIMINAL LAW: A STUDY WITH PARTICULAR REFERENCE TO NIGERIA. *J. of Black Studies 1981 11(3): 327-347.* Since most Africans, even the well-educated, believe in Juju or witchcraft, Nigerian criminal law should punish persons who practice Juju against others if evil subsequently befalls the latter. The Nigerian government should establish research institutes to study traditional medicine and the Nigerian courts should use the findings of these institutes in their decisions instead of relying solely on Western rational legal procedures. Based on 50 interviews and nine court cases in Nigeria; biblio. R. G. Sherer

2271. Okafor, Clement A. A SENSE OF HISTORY IN THE NOVELS OF CHINUA ACHEBE. *J. of African Studies 1981 8(2): 50-63.* An examination of Chinua Achebe's four well-known novels of the 1960's, the trilogy comprised of *Things Fall Apart, No Longer at Ease,* and *Arrow of God* and *A Man of the People.* Although treating different characters and set in different though modern time periods, each of these novels, in dealing with a Nigerian patrimony, the choices made by individuals, and a sense of destiny fulfilled, displays a sense of history. Achebe's writing also adapts successfully the English language to Nigerian linguistic patterns and idiomatic expressions. Based on Achebe's writings and secondary sources; 57 notes. L. W. Truschel

2272. Okafor, S. O. THE PORT HARCOURT ISSUE: A NOTE ON DR. TAMUNO'S ARTICLE. *African Affairs [Great Britain] 1973 72(286): 73-75.* A critical response to Tekena N. Tamuno's article "Patriotism and Statism in the Rivers State, Nigeria." The existence of a Rivers "identity" is questioned and the ownership of Port Harcourt is discussed. 5 notes. S

2273. Okeke, Uche. HISTORY OF MODERN NIGERIAN ART. *Nigeria Mag. [Nigeria] 1979 (128-129): 100-118.* Discusses the influence, ideas, and work of Aina Onabolu, circa 1918, the Murray School, 1928, the final decade of Nigeria's colonial history, and the forging of an African identity in the 1960's.

2274. Okwu, Austine S. O. THE BEGINNING OF THE MAYNOOTH MOVEMENT IN SOUTHERN NIGERIA AND THE RISE OF THE ST. PATRICK'S MISSIONARY SOCIETY, 1920-1930. *J. of Religion in Africa [Netherlands] 1979 10(1): 22-45.* When the Congregation of the Holy Ghost, or Spiritan, missionaries failed to provide an adequate staff, secular priests encroached on their geographical territory. The encroachment was resisted by the Holy Ghost Fathers, but was eventually completed by 1934. The seculars, centered in St. Patrick's College Seminary in Maynooth, Ireland, organized the Society of Saint Patrick which today is becoming a powerful international missionary society. Based on materials in the Archives of the Irish Province, Congregation of the Holy Ghost; 77 notes. R. J. Jirran

2275. Olabimtan, Afolabi. RELIGION AS A THEME IN FAGUNWA'S NOVELS. *Odu: a J. of West African Studies [Nigeria] 1975 (11): 101-114.* In five novels published between 1939 and 1961, Fagunwa successfully used traditional material to suppress some traditional beliefs for the purpose of preaching Christian ideals. 57 notes; biblio.
M. M. McCarthy

2276. Omolewa, Michael. A DECADE OF UNIVERSITY ADULT EDUCATION IN NIGERIA 1945-1955: AN EXAMINATION OF BRITISH INFLUENCE. *British J. of Educ. Studies [Great Britain] 1975 23(2): 153-167.* Examines the origins and development of university adult education in Nigeria, 1945-55, and evaluates the British influence. Despite the stated view that adult education in Africa should be distinctly African and should move in this direction away from the British transplanted system, university adult education in Nigeria scarcely changed in the decade under consideration. This was because of the predominance of British personnel and supervision, because those Africans who participated in establishing adult education in Nigeria were well-versed in British traditions, and because, since adult education in Nigeria was without precedent, there was no other system to supplant, replace or destroy it. 40 notes. L. Brown

2277. Omolewa, Michael. OXFORD UNIVERSITY AND THE PLANTING OF ADULT EDUCATION IN NIGERIA, 1945-50. *J. of Educ. Administration and Hist. [Great Britain] 1975 7(1): 28-39.* Considers the contribution of Oxford University's Delegacy for Extra-Mural Studies in the provision of adult education in Nigeria, 1945-50.

2278. Omolewa, Michael. OXFORD UNIVERSITY DELEGACY OF LOCAL EXAMINATIONS AND SECONDARY EDUCATION IN NIGERIA. *J. of Educ. Administration and Hist. [Great Britain] 1978 10(2): 39-49.* Outlines the work of the Oxford University Delegacy in Nigerian school examinations, 1929-37. Considers how and why the delegacy was introduced; why preference was given to Oxford University; the university's contribution to Nigeria's educational system, social organization, and political development; and its withdrawal in 1937.

2279. Omolewa, Michael. THE PROMOTION OF LONDON UNIVERSITY EXAMINATIONS IN NIGERIA, 1887-1951. *Int. J. of African Hist. Studies 1980 13(4): 651-671.* For many years the only institution offering a university degree to Nigerian students was London University through its external examination. The exam was highly respected by Africans and was supported by the colonial government because of the subjects and attitudes it stressed. Colonial involvement kept the standards high. The opportunities and standards this degree by examination provided have not been replaced by any Nigerian degree. Based on British, Nigerian, and University of London official records; 3 tables, 45 notes. R. T. Brown

2280. Omolewa, Michael. THE TEACHING OF FRENCH AND GERMAN IN NIGERIAN SCHOOLS 1859-1959. *Cahiers d'Études Africaines [France] 1978 18(3): 379-396.* Demonstrates that neither French and German missionaries, their governments, nor Nigerians themselves were much interested in learning European languages other than English. Based on missionary and governmental archives in France, Great Britain, and Nigeria; 55 notes. B. S. Fetter

2281. Onyemaeke Ogum, G. E. FERTILITY DIFFERENTIALS IN NIGERIA. *Genus [Italy] 1980 36(3-4): 203-213.* Surveys numerous fertility studies conducted in Nigeria over the last three decades, showing differing levels of fertility among geographical areas, religious groups, and educational levels.

2282. Ottenberg, Simon. ETHNICITY IN A NIGERIAN TOWN AND ITS ENVIRONS. *Ethnicity 1976 3(3): 275-303.* Traces evolving conceptions of ethnicity among groups in the Abakaliki area of Nigeria, 19th century-1960. Ethnic identity was found to be linked to external contact, especially through trade with other outlying groups and with the British colonial government. Further, ethnicity was affected by growing Nigerian nationalism, political independence, and the eventual division of political parties. Ethnic groups came to be associated with particular occupations, and divisions were exacerbated by religious separatism. Further subdivisions were results of commercial and political interests and existed to a great extent in a psychology of opposites (us/them). The author emphasizes the necessity of understanding ethnic group movement and its impact on the civil unrest in Nigeria both prior to and following the civil war. G. A. Hewlett

2283. Oyemade, Adefunkẹ. THE CARE OF MOTHERLESS BABIES: A CENTURY OF VOLUNTARY WORK IN NIGERIA. *J. of the Hist. Soc. of Nigeria 1974 7(2): 369-371.* Research note on the evolution of care for motherless babies in Nigeria. The author describes the types of care and changes in the precolonial, colonial, and independence eras. Based on the author's MD thesis at the University of Glasgow; biblio. J. A. Casada

2284. Peel, J. D. Y. INEQUALITY AND ACTION: THE FORMS OF IJESHA SOCIAL CONFLICT. *Can. J. of African Studies [Canada] 1980 14(3): 473-502.* Compares precolonial Ilesha society with modern Nigerian social organization, examining the concepts of community and class. By rejecting the notion that traditional societies did not evidence class-type action by the deprived, the author notes the similarities in its occurrence at different levels of the community. Redistribution was spontaneous in Yoruba society because the political leadership needed the support of the community to acquire resources such as slaves. Postcolonial commercial society is much less dependent on the community. In the oil economy of modern Nigeria, effective control is possible at the communal level by those with state connections. It is much less certain for the urban masses. Fig., 54 notes. S

2285. Piłaszewicz, Stanisław. POSTAWY I PROBLEMY SPOŁECZNE W POWOJENNEJ LITERATURZE HAUSA [Social attitudes and social problems in postwar Hausa literature]. Szymański, Edward. *Tradycja i Współczesność w Azji, Afryce i Ameryce Łacińskiej* (Warsaw: Polska Akademia Nauk Zakład Krajów Pozaeuropejskich, 1978): 189-222. Examines the cultural relations between West African, Islamic, and Western European cultures and the resultant changes in moral and ethical norms, social attitudes, and patterns of living as reflected in contemporary creative writing.

2286. Salamone, Frank A. BECOMING HAUSA: ETHNIC IDENTITY CHANGE AND ITS IMPLICATIONS FOR THE STUDY OF ETHNIC PLURALISM AND STRATIFICATION. *Africa [Great Britain] 1975 45(4): 410-424.* The process of assimilation of non-Hausa people to the Hausa majority in northern Nigeria is closely connected with Islamization.

2287. Samuels, J. W. HUMANITARIAN RELIEF IN MAN-MADE DISASTERS: THE INTERNATIONAL RED CROSS AND THE NIGERIAN EXPERIENCE. *Behind the Headlines [Canada] 1975 34(3): 1-44.* Traces the experience of the International Committee of the Red Cross (ICRC) in Nigeria during the conflict with Biafra and shows changes in the standard operating procedure. Explains the problems faced by the ICRC in the first conflict of this nature in which they were involved. Cites mistakes which led to the eventual distrust of the ICRC by the federal military government of Nigeria. August Lindt was in charge of the operation. S. G. Yntema

2288. Ubah, C. N. PROBLEMS OF CHRISTIAN MISSIONARIES IN THE MUSLIM EMIRATES OF NIGERIA, 1900-1928. *J. of African Studies 1976 3(3): 351-371.* Studies the problems involved in the embargo on Christian missionary enterprise, and the case of the local Muslim leaders who mounted a vehement opposition against proselytization. The result has been unwarranted criticism of the emirs and British colonial policy, and an undue amount of sympathy being shown to the missionary cause. The sin of apostacy is treated seriously by the Muslims. Demonstrates that the criticisms generally made of the emirs were groundless, that the position of the British administrators has not been fully examined, and that little attempt has been made to take into consideration the indiscretion and tactical blunders of the missionaries. 79 notes. E. P. Stickney

2289. Uche, Chukwudum. THE CONTEXTS OF MORTALITY IN NIGERIA. *Genus [Italy] 1981 37(1-2): 123-135.* Discusses geographical, residential, sexual, and socioeconomic factors affecting the infant mortality rate and crude death rate in Nigeria since the 1930's, commenting on the major causes of death in Nigeria on the basis of hospital records. Examines the impact of a high mortality rate on several aspects of Nigerian society and culture.

2290. Ume-Nwagbo, Ebele N. POLITICS AND ETHNICITY IN THE RISE OF BROADCASTING IN NIGERIA, 1932-62. *Journalism Q. 1979 56(4): 816-821, 826.* Although broadcasting is today a monopoly of the government, the competition between broadcasting services run by the states and federal broadcasters has allowed for some diversity in programming and information. This mixture of state-federal services evolved as a result of the cultural and ethnic diversity which is reflected in the distinctive characters of the state-regions of the federation. The states did not wish to see the federal government become the principal supplier of information for the country and therefore set up their own radio and television services. Based on news reports and secondary sources; 27 notes. J. S. Coleman

2291. Uyanga, Joseph. ETHNICITY AND REGIONALISM IN NIGERIA. *Plural Soc. [Netherlands] 1980 11(3): 49-56.* Nigeria's divisions are partially geography-related (southern forest and root economy and northern grain and animal economy, eastern palm products and western cacao), which suggest a federal grouping as most efficient. Attitudes and religions (Islamic north, Christian south) also differ, and the seasonal flow of rivers further impairs communications between regions, as does ethnic complexity (between 33 and 250 ethnic groups, depending on definition). In 1967, 12 ethnic-nation states were formed, increased to 19 by 1976, illustrating the difficulty in trying to match ethnic and administrative boundaries.

2292. Wangboje, S. I. FUNCTIONAL ARTS IN THE TRADITIONAL PAST. *Nigeria Mag. [Nigeria] 1976 (119): 39-50.* Traditional African art was essentially functional. The artist was a professional who went through a long apprenticeship. The role of village artist was often hereditary, but a talented youth could also qualify without kinship ties. The greatest cultural contribution that Nigeria has given to the world has been her traditional art dating as far back as 900 B.C. Art centers were located primarily at Nok, Ife, and Benin. All three centers are discussed. 52 notes. H. G. Soff

2293. Wangboje, S. I. WESTERN IMPACT ON NIGERIAN ARTS. *Nigeria Mag. [Nigeria] 1977 (122-123): 100-125.* The Western impact on African art was strong and destructive. Missionaries did more harm than did harsh administrators. Missionary education alienated the people from their culture, but this was also true of Muslim invaders. Contemporary art is experiencing searching pains. 45 plates, 39 notes. H. G. Soff

2294. Wiseberg, Laurie S. CHRISTIAN CHURCHES AND THE NIGERIAN CIVIL WAR. *J. of African Studies 1975 2(3): 297-332.* Analyzes the Biafran relief efforts by Euro-American churches and their relationship to the conclusion of the Nigerian civil war. The evidence suggests a position less moral and somewhat more analytical than the two commonly held but divergent interpretations; that the relief efforts were a manifestation of "pure humanitarian concern," or evidence of the political and institutional interests of the Western churches. The relief efforts did get governments to take a stand on humanitarian issues, and they broadened the options available to governments. Table, 94 notes. R. V. Ritter

2295. Wynter, J. H. SOME PROBLEMS IN NIGERIAN LIBRARY DEVELOPMENT SINCE 1960. *Int. Lib. Rev. [Great Britain] 1979 11(1): 19-44.* Discusses the vicissitudes of Nigerian library development since Nigerian independence in 1960, citing ethnic antagonisms, illiteracy, poor communications, and size of the country as the major obstacles to nationwide library development.

Senegal

2296. Abelin, Philippe. DOMAINE NATIONAL ET DÉVELOPPEMENT AU SÉNÉGAL [National domain and the development of Senegal]. *Bull. de l'Inst. Fondamental d'Afrique Noire. Série B [Senegal] 1979 41(3): 508-538.* Senegalese legislation adopted from 1960 to 1976 places the exploitation of rural communities, the use of lands, and agrarian reforms under government control. The village became the administrative nucleus of governmental structure. These laws were sociological as well as administrative. 44 notes, biblio. H. L. Calkin

2297. Aberger, Peter. LÉOPOLD SENGHOR AND THE ISSUE OF REVERSE RACISM. *Phylon 1980 41(3): 276-283.* Leopold Senghor, President of Senegal, defends a negritude which recognizes the existence of permanent and hereditary characteristics of black people. Though he is firmly rooted in his negritude, Senghor has spoken more recently of a conciliatory accord between blacks and whites. 53 notes. N. G. Sapper

2298. Aire, Victor O. DIDACTIC REALISM IN OUSMANE SEMBENE'S *LES BOUTS DE BOIS DE DIEU.Can. J. of African Studies [Canada] 1977 11(2): 283-294.* A nonliterary study of Sembene's novel. Analyzes his approach to the double task of psychological and political emancipation. Beginning with the *status quo,* Sembene moves into an exercise in its demystification and evolution. That his realism has immortalized the longest strike in African union history (1947-48) is a small contribution compared to his denunciation of regressive practices and colonial imperialism and its many repercussions, but above all his advocacy of human dignity regardless of race. 40 notes. R. V. Ritter

2299. Ba, Abdou Bouri. ESSAI SUR L'HISTOIRE DU SALOUM ET DU RIP [An essay on the history of Saloum and Rip]. *Bull. de l'Inst. Fondamental d'Afrique Noire [Senegal] 1976 38(4): 812-860.* Presents information gained from oral traditions in Saloum and Rip, Senegal, on the provinces, the role of Islam in the country, families, and social and political organization. Includes data on the 49 kings of Saloum from 1493 to 1969. 4 notes. H. L. Calkin

2300. Barker, Jonathan. STABILITY AND STAGNATION: THE STATE IN SENEGAL. *Can. J. of African Studies [Canada] 1977 11(1): 23-42.* Senegal combines political stability with economic stagnation. The state helps a foreign capitalist class to accommodate surplus from the Senegalese economy; it also helps repress political energies for change which underdevelopment generates. "The equation of stability with stagnation is likely to become more and more difficult to maintain without major transformations in the state and in its policies." 38 notes. E. P. Stickney

2301. Behrman, Lucy Creevey. MUSLIM POLITICS AND DEVELOPMENT IN SENEGAL. *J. of Modern African Studies [Great Britain] 1977 15(2): 261-277.* Reexamines the research upon which the author's book, *Muslim Brotherhoods and Politics in Senegal* (Cambridge, Mass., 1970), is based. The position of the *marabouts* in politics has not seriously altered in the last decade and will not alter as long as Leopold Senghor is in power. 2 tables, 41 notes. H. G. Soff

2302. Bernard-Duquenet, Nicole. LES DÉBUTS DU SYNDICALISME AU SÉNÉGAL AU TEMPS DU FRONT POPULAIRE [The beginnings of trade unionism in Senegal]. *Mouvement Social [France] 1977 (101): 37-59.* Trade unions had been active for a long time before the Popular Front gave them legal recognition. But when the Socialist governor general led a policy of discussion with the unions, it brought about a cleavage between conciliation-minded leaders and the rank and file, who were more anxious about their living conditions. Based on archival documents, oral testimonies, and articles in periodicals. J

2303. Chikwendu, E. E. THE RELEVANCE OF NEGRITUDE TO SENEGALESE DEVELOPMENT. *UMOJA: A Scholarly J. of Black Studies 1977 1(3): 43-58.* Provides an evaluation of national development in Senegal, based on the African political thinker Leopold Senghor's philosophy that the concept of Negritude, the rediscovery of the African past and culture, is a sound way to combine the African experience and modern technology for development.

2304. Coninck, J. de. THE LITERARY AND POLITICAL WORKS OF LEOPOLD SEDAR SENGHOR: AN APPRAISAL IN THE LIGHT OF RECENT STUDIES ON MILLENARIAN MOVEMENTS. *Mawazo [Uganda] 1974 4(2): 61-86.* Examines the poetry and politics of Senegalese President Leopold Senghor, 1940's-60's drawing parallels between them and examining his major themes, negritude, universal civilization, and African socialism.

2305. Cottingham, Clement. TRADITIONAL SOCIETY, CHANGE, AND ORGANIZATIONAL DEVELOPMENT. *J. of Modern African Studies [Great Britain] 1973 11(4): 675-681.* A review article covering three studies: Donal B. Cruise O'Brien, *The Mourides of Senegal* (Oxford: Clarendon Pr., 1971); Lucy C. Behrman, *Muslim Brotherhoods and Politics in Senegal* (Harvard U. Pr., 1970); and Cheikh Tidiane Sy, *La Confrérie sénégalaise des Mourides* (Paris: Présence africaine, 1969). All examine the origins and capacity for economic, political and social change of a Sūfī Muslim brotherhood, the Mourides of Senegal. They represent a unique socioeconomic, religious response among the rural Wolof and show the possibility of sociocultural change under colonial rule and of the reconstitution of traditional authority patterns through a multipurpose organizaton with a modernistic, religiously-founded work ethic. R. V. Ritter

2306. Dansoko, Amath. SENEGAL: PROBLEMS AND DIFFICULTIES. *World Marxist R. [Canada] 1973 16(12): 96-100.*

2307. Dianoux, Hugues Jean de. LE CHRISTIANISME AU SÉNÉGAL [Christianity in Senegal]. *L'Afrique et l'Asie Modernes [France] 1981 (4): 3-22.* Traces the Christianization of Senegal since 1455, focusing on the Catholic Church's relatively important influence during the administration of Leopold Sedar Senghor, 1960-81.

2308. Diop, Abdoulaye. JEUNESSES EN DEVELOPPEMENT: MEMENTO D'UNE PERIPHERIE [Young people expanding: remembrance of a periphery]. *Communautés: Arch. de Sci. Sociales de la*

Coopération et du Développement [France] 1982 (62): 108-127. Focuses on the history of a youth cooperative in the village of Ronkh, 1963-72, and the progressive impact it has had on the village's social, educational, and economic structure.

2309. Diop, Abdoulaye. LA FAMILLE RURALE WOLOF: MODE DE RÉSIDENCE ET ORGANISATIONS SOCIO-ÉCONOMIQUE [The rural Wolof household: socioeconomic manner of residence and organization]. *Bull. de l'Inst. Fondamental d'Afrique Noire [Senegal] 1974 36(1): 147-163.* An analysis of the size and nature of rural households in the Wolof area of Senegal, the relationship between members of the family and the chief of the household, and the impact of social and economic factors that affect the organization and locations of the households. 3 tables, 8 notes. H. L. Calkin

2310. Falkeid, Kolbein. LÉOPOLD SÉDAR SENGHOR: STATSMANN OG DIKTER [Leopold Sedar Senghor: statesman and poet]. *Samtiden [Norway] 1976 85(7): 385-395.* Surveys the life and cultural achievements of the Senegalese poet and political leader, Leopold Senghor. Based on Senghor's writings. R. G. Selleck

2311. Filesi, Teobaldo. OMMAGGIO AD ALIOUNE DIOP [Tribute to Alioune Diop]. *Africa [Italy] 1980 35(3-4): 449-459.* The Senegalese writer Alioune Diop (1910-80) was the founder of *Présence Africaine* and the Société Africaine de Culture, and the animating force of the group of African artists who, in the years surrounding World War II, tried to rehabilitate African culture and the dignity of African man, under the sign of Negritude. This is a personal tribute on the occasion of his death. J. V. Coutinho

2312. Gosselin, Gabriel. ORDRES, CASTES ET ÉTATS EN PAYS SÉRÈR (SÉNÉGAL): ESSAI D'INTERPRÉTATION D'UN SYSTÈME POLITIQUE EN TRANSITION [Orders, castes, and estates in Serer country, Senegal: an interpretive essay on a political system in transition]. *Can. J. of African Studies [Canada] 1974 8(1): 135-143.* The balance of power system of the ancient Serer kingdoms in which a system of orders dominated a subsystem of castes was weakened by colonialism and has evolved since the 1960's into a system where estates are ascendant over castes.

2313. Johnson, G. Wesley. LOBBIES AND PRESSURE GROUPS IN COLONIAL SENEGAL DURING THE TIME OF BLAISE DIAGNE. *Pro. of the Ann. Meeting of the Western Soc. for French Hist. 1976 4: 411-418.* Studies aspects of the career of Blaise Diagne, deputy from Senegal (1914-34), related to the development of economic and political pressure groups in the French empire in black Africa. Relations were not simply between rulers and the ruled; an elaborate network of lobbies shaped French colonial policy. Based on correspondence, newspaper articles, and editorials; 18 notes. J. D. Falk

2314. Kamara, Moussa and Ndiaye, Moustapha, transl. and ed. HISTOIRE DE BOUNDOU [History of Boundou]. *Bull. de l'Inst. Fondamental d'Afrique Noire [Senegal] 1975 37(4): 784-816.* An annotated account translated from Arabic of the history of Boundou, a theocratic state in eastern Senegal. The account, written by Sheik Moussa Kamara in 1924, recounts the genealogical origins of the different ethnic groups which populated the area and the rule of the *Almâmi,* the ruling class, from Malik (1681) to Woppa-Bokar (1921). Map, 2 tables, 114 notes. H. L. Calkin

2315. Klei, J. van der and Hesseling, G. ANCIENS ET NOUVEAUX DROITS FONCIERS CHEZ LES DIOLA AU SÉNÉGAL ET LEURS CONSÉQUENCES POUR LA RÉPARTITION DES TERRES [Old and new property rights among the Diola of Senegal and their consequences for land distribution]. *African Perspectives [Netherlands] 1979 (1): 53-65.* Analyzes Diola property rights since the colonial period and their evolution toward increased social inequality. During the precolonial and colonial periods, property was transferred through a patrilineal, then nuclear family system of inheritance, with possibility of land loans within the family. The 1964 land reform law established a national domain and a new land distribution, abolishing the former system. After 1978, redistribution was to bring further changes, especially affecting transfers of ownership. Based on fieldwork in 1973-76 with the Centre d'Études Africaines; table, 10 notes, biblio. G. P. Cleyet

2316. Lakroum, Monique. LES SALAIRES DANS LE PORT DE DAKAR [Salaries in the port of Dakar]. *Rev. Française d'Hist. d'Outre-Mer [France] 1976 63(3-4): 640-653.* The monetary crisis of the Great Depression reached Dakar, Senegal in 1931, marked by a fall in port traffic and of the income derived from such traffic. Examination of wages for European and native workers in the port of Dakar shows that income stayed above the cost of living during the early 1930's for all workers except orderlies and laborers. When prices began to rise again after 1935, all groups, including skilled European labor, were hurt; the cost of living had exceeded income for most groups. 5 tables, 16 graphs, 4 notes. J. C. Billigmeier

2317. LeRoy, E. RÉFORME FONCIÈRE ET STRATÉGIE DU DÉVELOPPEMENT (RÉFLEXIONS À PARTIR DE L'EXEMPLE SÉNÉGALAIS) [Agrarian reform and development strategy: the example of Senegal]. *African Perspectives [Netherlands] 1979 (1): 67-81.* Analyzes the 1964 land reform in Senegal, its conception, innovative spirit and techniques, progressive application, and development institutions. It evolved, particularly between 1965 and 1975, toward administrative normalization and integration into industrial society. Although such reform had been aimed at setting up a new agrarian system promoting African socialism, it did not hinder the extension of the capitalist system, and the new social class it helped create was added to the existing regional and ethnic divisions. 23 notes. G. P. Cleyet

2318. Letnev, Artem. L'ASSIMILATION CULTURELLE VUE PAR LES ASSIMILÉS (D'APRÈS LES CAHIERS WILLIAM PONTY) [Cultural assimilation as seen by the assimilated, based on the William Ponty School notebooks]. *Genève-Afrique [Switzerland] 1979 17(2): 19-26.* Analyzes the attitudes toward colonization on the part of Africans about to graduate from the best high school for Africans in French West Africa. Despite the limitations imposed by the teachers, the students managed to demonstrate considerable reservations regarding their status under colonial rule. Based on the notebooks at the Institut Fondamental de l'Afrique Noire in Dakar and secondary sources; 29 notes. B. S. Fetter

2319. Linares, Olga F. FROM TIDAL SWAMP TO INLAND VALLEY: ON THE SOCIAL ORGANIZATION OF WET RICE CULTIVATION AMONG THE DIOLA OF SENEGAL. *Africa [Great Britain] 1981 51(2): 557-595.* Examination of the agricultural systems and social organizations of three ecologically different Diola villages about 50 miles apart in Senegal, revealed that techniques for growing rice vary considerably. In one village, in the most intensive swamp rice area, labor is equally divided between men and women, and the ownership of the land is controlled by conjugal units. In another, whose population comprises largely recent immigrants, the women grow rice only for subsistence, while the men grow cash crops. In the third village, the men grow cash crops with the aid of their wives, and also help their wives in the preparation of the fields. The three villages differ extensively in their religious practices and beliefs. 3 maps, 6 tables, 6 notes, biblio. R. L. Collison

2320. Lodolini, Elio. L'ARCHIVIO NAZIONALE DEL SENEGAL [The National Archives of Senegal]. *Rassegna degli Archivi di Stato [Italy] 1976 36(1): 131-154.* After giving a brief historical background of Senegal, the author points out that in the National Archives in Dakar there are sources from the French colonial period as well as very recent documents from the postindependence period. The colonial sources come from the central offices for French West Africa (Senegal, French Sudan, Dahomey, Ivory Coast, French Guinea, Niger, Mauritania, Upper Volta), from the office dealing only with the territory that is now Senegal, and even from local offices. Uninterrupted documentation begins in 1816, but there are other isolated documents from the 18th century. The archives have undergone various changes in location and direction. Of special interest is the new headquarters of the National Archives. In an agreement between the government of Senegal and the Italian Foreign Ministry, the headquarters was designed in 1974 by an Italian group, the Studio Technico Ingegneria, with the author of this article acting as archive consultant. Appendix. J/S

2321. Madubuike, G. Ihechukwu. FORM, STRUCTURE, AND ESTHETICS OF THE SENEGALESE NOVEL. *J. of Black Studies 1974 4(3): 345-359.* The novel in Senegal has borrowed some of its structure from the French novel, but its content totally reflects Senegalese culture, particularly in its use of the Senegalese oral tradition. It is a literary form in its own right. 2 notes, biblio. K. Butcher

2322. Madubuike, Ihechukwu. THE POLITICS OF ASSIMILATION AND THE EVOLUTION OF THE NOVEL IN SENEGAL. *African Studies Rev. 1975 18(2): 89-99.* Since the 1920's the Senegalese novels have evolved through three phases, each influenced by prevailing local attitudes toward the French colonial policy of assimilation.

2323. Mark, Peter. URBAN MIGRATION, CASH CROPPING, AND CALAMITY: THE SPREAD OF ISLAM AMONG THE DIOLA OF BOULOUF (SENEGAL), 1900-1940. *African Studies Rev. 1978 21(2): 1-14.* A history of social change in rural Senegal caused by the growth of a cash economy. Financial autonomy, particularly among the young, led to conversion to Islam as a means of achieving a measure of social autonomy not then possible in the traditional society. 2 maps, 39 notes, biblio. R. T. Brown

2324. Niang, Mamadou. RÉGIME DES TERRES ET STRATÉGIE DE DÉVELOPPEMENT RURAL AU SÉNÉGAL (UN EXEMPLE DE LA RÉSISTANCE DU DROIT COUTUMIER AFRICAIN) [Land regime and the strategy of rural development in Senegal: an example of the resistance of African customary law]. *African Perspectives [Netherlands] 1979 (1): 45-51.* Studies African customary law in Senegal, its survival through the colonial period and independence. Stresses its resistance to modern legal and economic currents, particularly since the 17 June 1964 agrarian reform law, by which land is legally owned by the occupant who developed it. Discusses the eight-year litigation ending with a compromise in 1976, between the Peuls (cattle-raisers) and the Mourides (farmers), owners of land in the same zone in the village of Cabugél. Based on various primary sources; 8 notes. G. P. Cleyet

2325. O'Brien, Donal Cruise. A VERSATILE CHARISMA: THE MOURIDE BROTHERHOOD 1967-1975. *European J. of Sociol. [Great Britain] 1977 18(1): 84-107.* In Senegal the Mouride brotherhood has shown remarkable resilience and versatility in national politics. After 1886 it was a charismatic community and vehicle of sacred nationalism; from 1912 on an instrument of a massive land settlement; and finally an electoral broker in national party politics, 1951-66. Now the brotherhood has emerged as a curious and slightly ambivalent form of peasants' trade union. Members have experienced a new collective sense of Mouride power in extracting substantial material concessions from the national government. Based on field work and secondary sources; 17 notes. M. L. Lifka

2326. O'Brien, Rita Cruise. SOME PROBLEMS IN THE CONSOLIDATION OF NATIONAL INDEPENDENCE IN AFRICA. THE CASE OF THE FRENCH EXPATRIATES IN SENEGAL. *African Affairs [Great Britain] 1974 73(290): 85-94.* An analysis of role relationships between French expatriates and Senegalese. Senegal relies heavily on France and it is suggested a similar comparison might be made with Kenya. 17 notes. H. G. Soff

2327. Person, Yves. LE FRONT POPULAIRE AU SÉNÉGAL (MAI 1936-OCTOBRE 1938) [The Popular Front in Senegal, May 1936 to October 1938]. *Mouvement Social [France] 1979 (107): 77-102.* The advent of the Popular Front brought about a disruption of the colonial order in some privileged points of French Africa. It was peculiarly the case in Senegal because of the traditional privileges of the "Four Communes" and of the economic and social improvement centered in Dakar. Although the reforms were limited and the outburst miscarried after little more than two years, lasting consequences were perceptible later, during the thrust toward decolonization after 1945. J/S

2328. Rabemananjara, Jacques. ALIOUNE DIOP, LE CÉNOBITE DE LA CULTURE NOIRE [Alioune Diop, the monk of black culture]. *Africa [Italy] 1980 35(3-4): 470-488.* Tribute to Senegalese writer Alioune Diop (1910-80), recollecting student days in Paris, the founding and editing of the review *Présence Africaine,* and the artistic and literary flowering that followed. J. V. Coutinho

2329. Sarr, Dominique. JURISPRUDENCE DES TRIBUNAUX INDIGÈNES DU SÉNÉGAL (LES CAUSES DE RUPTURE DU LIEN MATRIMONIAL DE 1872 À 1946) [The jurisprudence of the native courts of Senegal: the causes of rupture of matrimonial bonds, 1872-1946]. *Ann. Africaines [Senegal] 1975: 143-178.* Surveys the reasons for divorce in Senegal as argued in the native courts between 1872 and 1946; these include cases in both traditional and Muslim law. In general, four types of divorce action are surveyed: adultery, desertion, ill-treatment, and requests for annulment (due to nonconsent, impotence, nonpayment of brideprice, etc.). Summarizes 75 cases, divided by category, listing the court hearing the matter, date, citation, and presenting the facts, the native law or custom invoked, and the decision of the court. 5 notes. R. Garfield

2330. Squarcini, Marco. LEÓPOLD SÉDAR SENGHOR E LA "VIA AFRICANA DEL SOCIALISMO" [Leopold Sedar Senghor and the "African road to socialism"]. *Storia Contemporanea [Italy] 1977 8(1): 121-144.* Describes Leopold Senghor's first political theories as neither Marxist nor communist, as neither left nor right, but as a moral revolution in which existing cultural and political institutions had no sense. He theorized the concept of negritude: anti-European in form; a rejection of Western rationalism, materialism, and productivism; and an affirmation of alternative values such as intuition, emotion, and spiritualism. The author follows Senghor's career in Senegalese politics and the consequent development and adaptation of his political theory. During the 1960's it became obvious that socialism was not an immediate possibility, particularly in light of problems caused by foreign investments. As a result, he proposed an advanced democracy as a transition phase to socialism and which included acceptance of the formation of a national bourgeoisie. 153 notes. M. T. Wilson

2331. Steins, Martin. LA NÉGRITUDE: UN SECOND SOUFFLE? [Negritude: a second wind?]. *Cultures et Développement [Belgium] 1980 12(1): 3-43.* Analyzes negritude, centering on the views expressed by its protagonist, poet, teacher, and president of Senegal, Leopold Senghor (b. 1906). It is experiencing a revival, thanks to Senghor's work of adaptation to ethnic groups.

2332. Taddia, Irma. IL MURIDISMO SENEGALESE E IL PROBLEMA DELLO SVILUPPO ECONOMICO [Senegalese Mouridism and the problem of economic development]. *Africa [Italy] 1978 33(3): 383-404.* There has been a lengthy discussion on Mouride ideology and on the fact that its development coincided with the spreading of groundnut cultivation during the colonial period in Senegal. The author agrees with the most recent interpretations of Mouridism, and deals with global problems of Mouridism. Mouridism is no longer to be presented only as an heretic choice within the Muslim world, or as a mere religious ideology capable of directly shaping social dynamics. Other factors played a role in determining what is now the most important problem of Senegal: underdevelopment. The question is therefore to be shifted to a different social and political ground, in fact to the colonial situation, in which groundnut monoculture reached its peak. Only the study of the colonial framework can explain the phenomenon and enable us to connect it to other colonial situations. J/S

2333. Thiam, Iba Der. GALANDOU DIOUF ET LE FRONT POPULAIRE [Galandou Diouf and the Popular Front]. *Bull. de l'Inst. Fondamental d'Afrique Noire Série B [Senegal] 1976 38(3): 592-618.* The succession on the Senegalese political scene of Galandou Diouf (1875-1941) opened a new page in the history of Senegal. Closely allied to the masses, Diouf remained in favor with the Senegalese electorate. The author discusses Diouf's role in politics, 1936-41, the elections, the reactions in Africa and Europe, and the place of the Popular Front in the Socialist Republican Party. 60 notes. H. L. Calkin

2334. Thiam, Iba Der. LA TUERIE DE THIÈS DE SEPTEMBRE 1938, ESSAI D'INTERPRÉTATION [The slaughter of Thiès in September 1938, an interpretative essay]. *Bull. de l'Inst. Fondamental d'Afrique Noire [Senegal] 1976 38(2): 300-338.* On 27 September 1938 auxiliary railroad workers waged a strike in Thiès, Senegal. In the confrontation between strikers and police and military forces many were killed or wounded. Using the official version, the version of the strikers, and other sources, the author reconstructs what probably happened during the encounter. Map, 91 notes. H. L. Calkin

2335. Vanderklei, Jos. CUSTOMARY LAND TENURE AND LAND REFORM: THE RISE OF NEW INEQUALITIES AMONG THE DIOLA OF SENEGAL. *African Perspectives [Netherlands] 1978*

(2): 35-44. Studies changes in Senegal's land tenure system which have resulted in class distinctions and material inequalities. Discusses the traditional land tenure system of the Diola of Senegal, reconstructing the precolonial situation. Though there were significant changes during the colonial period, the land tenure system remained virtually intact. The new land tenure system which has been in operation since 1964 has involved major changes, including integration of the Diola in the market economy. R. V. Ritter

2336. Zucarelli, François. DE LA CHEFFERIE TRADITIONELLE AU CANTON: ÉVOLUTION DU CANTON COLONIAL AU SÉNÉGAL, 1855-1960 [From the traditional chiefdom to the canton: evolution of the colonial canton in Senegal, 1855-1960]. *Cahiers d'Études Africaines [France] 1973 13(2): 213-238.* When, around 1855, French holdings in Senegal extended beyond the coastal districts of Saint-Louis and Gorée, the administrative system of direct rule had become overextended. This necessitated reliance on the autochthonous political structures in governing the masses of the population. Traditional chiefdoms were gradually transformed into cantons, with the head of the cantonal government often the leading local chief or notable. 42 notes. J. C. Billigmeier

Sierra Leone

2337. Abraham, Arthur. THE INSTITUTION OF "SLAVERY" IN SIERRA LEONE. *Genève-Afrique [Switzerland] 1975 14(2): 46-57.* Discusses institutions of dependence and servitude in Sierra Leone from 1750 to the abolition of "slavery" by the colonial administration in 1928. These institutions were seen as a part of the extended family system, and their disappearance was due to socioeconomic change.

2338. Bebler, Anton. THE AFRICAN MILITARY, NATIONALISM AND ECONOMIC DEVELOPMENT: THE CASE OF SIERRA LEONE, 1967-1968. *J. of African Studies 1974 1(1): 70-86.* The question of whether direct military rule is harmful or beneficial to developing nations can be studied in the case of Sierra Leone, where a military junta took over briefly. Economic development was excellent, primarily because the military, the Economic Advisory Council, and the International Monetary Fund saw eye to eye on such matters. But the development was also artificial in part, and probably could not have been sustained. Nationalism declined, or was at least pursued in a more sedate fashion. The people were never happy with military rule; charges of self-advancement and corruption were not wholly without foundation. 3 tables, 26 notes. V. L. Human

2339. Brown, Lawrence A.; Schneider, Rita; Harvey, Milton E.; and Riddell, J. Barry. INNOVATION DIFFUSION AND DEVELOPMENT IN A THIRD WORLD SETTING: THE COOPERATIVE MOVEMENT IN SIERRA LEONE. *Social Sci. Q. 1979 60(2): 249-268.* Analyzes innovation diffusion and development of agricultural cooperatives in Sierra Leone. Such diffusion is hardly uniform either between areas or between cooperatives within a given area. Although the cooperative itself acts as innovation diffuser, the government represents a variable which acts either to hasten or to delay diffusion. Local chieftains also exercise some influence, all of which adds up to a pattern of disparity and unevenness. Table, 3 fig., 10 notes, refs. V. L. Human

2340. Clute, Robert E. ATTITUDES OF SIERRA LEONEAN YOUTH TOWARD MODERNIZATION. *J. of Asian and African Studies [Netherlands] 1974 9(1/2): 29-42.* A survey of 571 students in Sierra Leone shows the variables affecting modern attitudes toward national political developments. 5 tables, 27 notes. R. T. Brown

2341. Corby, Richard A. BO SCHOOL AND ITS GRADUATES IN COLONIAL SIERRA LEONE. *Can. J. of African Studies [Canada] 1981 15(2): 323-333.* An analysis of the nature and functioning of a British colonial school in Sierra Leone, and the quality and influence of its graduates. Bo School, started in 1906, was not designed to push Africans into the mainstream of modern society, but rather to provide continuity at the chiefdom level in order to smooth the path of British rule. The school did not entirely succeed, mainly because the students had no intention of remaining servants throughout their lives. Today, all important branches of the government are permeated with the graduates of Bo School, an achievement out of proportion to its size and the quality of its curriculum. 20 notes. V. L. Human

2342. Corby, Richard A. PROGRESSIVE CHIEFTAINCY IN SIERRA LEONE: KENEWA GAMANGA OF SIMBARU. *Tarikh [Nigeria] 1981 7(1): 57-64.* Examines the contributions of Kenewa Gamanga of the Simbaru Chiefdom in Sierra Leone to his region's economic, political, and agricultural development from his emergence as chief in 1941 to 1961 and discusses his role in Sierra Leone's independence movement.

2343. Denzer, LaRay. CONSTANCE A. CUMMINGS-JOHN OF SIERRA LEONE: HER EARLY POLITICAL CAREER. *Tarikh [Nigeria] 1981 7(1): 20-32.* Traces the early life and political career of Constance Agatha Cummings-John (née Horton), founder of the Sierra Leone Women's Movement, from her birth in 1918 in Freetown, Sierra Leone to the 1950's, focusing on her involvement in anticolonial and independence movements in West Africa and on her dealings with other African leaders, including I. T. A. Wallace-Johnson (1894-1965) and H. C. Bankole Bright (1883-1958).

2344. Devis, T. L. F. FERTILITY DIFFERENTIALS AMONG THE TRIBAL GROUPS OF SIERRA LEONE. *Population Studies [Great Britain] 1973 27(3): 501-514.* Estimates of fertility levels have already been made for the administrative districts of Sierra Leone. These made use of conventional techniques and were based on age data from the 1963 Census. As such methods assume the hypothetical situation where a population is closed to migration, an attempt was made to approximate it more closely by using the larger ethnic groups of the country. Distinct differences were found between the two largest groups, the Mende and Temne, and in general groups inhabiting the south and east displayed lower levels than those in the north. Other sources provided some confirmation of these results. In view of the lack of information reasons for such differentials can only be guessed at, but it seems likely that the pattern of development in Sierra Leone is a major contributing factor. Cultural influences and religion probably affect the issue also, but the extent of this cannot be assessed. J/S

2345. Dixon-Fyle, S. R. MONETARY DEPENDENCE IN AFRICA: THE CASE OF SIERRA LEONE. *J. of Modern African Studies [Great Britain] 1978 16(2): 273-294.* African independence did not eliminate dependence on metropolitan currencies. This dependence in turn has influenced the deployment of power, official decisionmaking, and development since 1960. Suggests measures that would lead Sierra Leone to monetary independence. Based on government published documents; 23 notes. A. Sbacchi

2346. Dorjahn, Vernon R. MIGRATION IN CENTRAL SIERRA LEONE: THE TEMNE CHIEFDOM OF KOLIFA MAYOSO. *Africa [Great Britain] 1975 45(1): 29-49.* Establishment of a primary school, medical facilities, and other government services in Mayoso, capital of the small Temne chiefdom of Kolifa Mayoso in central Sierra Leone, has resulted in considerable immigration and its resulting problems.

2347. Harrell-Bond, Barbara. THE INFLUENCE OF THE FAMILY CASEWORKER ON THE STRUCTURE OF THE FAMILY: THE SIERRA LEONE CASE. *Social Res. 1977 44(2): 193-215.* Examines the instrumental role of the public welfare caseworker in encouraging changing attitudes toward the family in Sierra Leone; through these means, social change in Africa led to the introduction of Western institutions during the colonial era, 18th-20th centuries.

2348. Hoogvelt, Ankie M. M. and Tinker, Anthony. THE ROLE OF COLONIAL AND POST-COLONIAL STATES IN IMPERIALISM—A CASE-STUDY OF THE SIERRA LEONE DEVELOPMENT COMPANY. *J. of Modern African Studies [Great Britain] 1978 16(1): 67-79.* The Sierra Leone Development Company was founded in 1929 and voluntarily liquidated in 1975. It was an instrument of British imperialism and exploited Sierra Leone. Over 82% of all economic benefits were returned to Britain. The analysis of this company's operations confirms Marxist theories. 2 tables, 2 diagrams; 15 notes. H. G. Soff

2349. Isaac, Barry L. EUROPEAN, LEBANESE, AND AFRICAN TRADERS IN PENDEMBU, SIERRA LEONE: 1908-1968. *Human Organization 1974 33(2): 111-121.*

2350. Isaac, Barry L. PRICE, COMPETITION, AND PROFITS AMONG HAWKERS AND SHOPKEEPERS IN PENDEMBU, SIERRA LEONE: AN INVENTORY APPROACH. *Econ. Development and Cultural Change 1981 29(2): 353-373.* Using the systematic inventory approach, the author analyzes the petty retailing firms in Pendembu, Sierra Leone from 1966 to 1968. Personnel, facilities, inventories, capitalization, unit prices, profits, and petty trading are examined by the author. It is concluded that petty trading is far more lucrative and makes a larger contribution to the general circulation of goods than previously thought. It was also found that the extension of credit was not an important competitive strategy but pricing policy was. Based on the author's field investigation and published works; 6 tables, 25 notes. J. W. Thacker, Jr.

2351. Johnny, Michael; Karimu, John; and Richards, Paul. UPLAND AND SWAMP RICE FARMING IN SIERRA LEONE: THE SOCIAL CONTEXT OF TECHNOLOGICAL CHANGE. *Africa [Great Britain] 1981 51(2): 596-620.* Rice cultivation in Sierra Leone has a long history, as have cash crops and laboring for cash. Intensive swamp rice cultivation on the southeast Asian pattern, supported by the World Bank, dates from 1945. Its yields proved higher than those of upland farming, and responded to increased urban demand for food, at the same time that it robbed the rural areas of labor. Field work in four locations showed that swamp rice cultivation increased rice output by 50-100%. Labor "companies" have superseded the less efficient efforts provided by scarce casual laborers. Current emphasis is on schemes to introduce peasant farmers to "improved" inland valley swamp farming. Based on field work; 3 maps, 11 tables, biblio. R. L. Collison

2352. Kaniki, M. H. Y. ECONOMIC CHANGE IN SIERRA LEONE DURING THE 1930's. *Transafrican J. of Hist. [Kenya] 1973 3(1/2): 72-95.* In 1926 the government of Sierra Leone sponsored a geological survey for mining possibilities to help overcome the country's dependence on agriculture. The survey discovered platinum, gold, iron, and diamonds. The author analyzes mining's effect on the national economy, employment opportunities, agriculture, trade, transporation, and manufacturing. 2 tables, 65 notes. H. G. Soff

2353. Kaniki, Martin H. POLITICS OF PROTEST IN COLONIAL WEST AFRICA: THE SIERRA LEONE EXPERIENCE. *African Rev. [Tanzania] 1974 4(3): 423-458.* The West African Youth League and its founder, Isaac Akunna Wallace-Johnson, representing a variety of growing social and economic tensions among the creole of Sierra Leone, created a major political protest movement in the late 1930's. 174 notes. R. T. Brown

2354. Ly, Frank. SIERRA LEONE: THE PARADOX OF ECONOMIC DECLINE AND POLITICAL STABILITY. *Monthly Rev. 1980 32(2): 10-26.* Discusses the political and economic policies of Siaka Stevens and the effects of his rule on Sierra Leone since 1967.

2355. Merani, H. V. and Laan, H. L. van der. THE INDIAN TRADERS IN SIERRA LEONE. *African Affairs [Great Britain] 1979 78(311): 240-250.* Traces the growth of Indian traders' activities in Sierra Leone and their success in the importing, wholesaling, retailing, and manufacturing businesses. Homogeneity and cooperation among the Indians, hard work, and a favorable business atmosphere from the 1950's have enabled the Indian traders to expand and diversify their businesses numerically and geographically. 2 tables, 25 notes. S. Lakhan

2356. Riddell, J. Barry. PERIODIC MARKETS IN SIERRA LEONE. *Ann. of the Assoc. of Am. Geographers 1974 64(4): 541-548.*

2357. Roberts, George O. THE ROLE OF FOREIGN AID IN INDEPENDENT SIERRA LEONE. *J. of Black Studies 1975 5(4): 339-373.* Sierra Leone received $155 million in foreign aid, 1961-71. Examines the attitude of Sierra Leoneans to foreign aid and the appropriateness of its use. Biblio., appendixes. K. Butcher

2358. Roberts, George O. SIERRA LEONE: FROM MYTH TO REALITY WITH FOREIGN ASSISTANCE. *J. of African Studies 1976 3(1): 83-100.* A reexamination of Sierra Leone's long road to independence, and the place of foreign aid in bringing it about. "It is unfortunate that the sense of common purpose which achieved independence has disintegrated into conflict among individuals even of the same ethnic group. Ideological differences are often blamed, yet the facts readily suggest sheer lust for power." Great sacrifices have been made and are still being made by the masses, but the results are merely "the symbolic experience of being a nation." Leaders need to correct the internal record of failure and irresponsibility. 14 notes. R. V. Ritter

2359. Sibanda, M. J. M. DEPENDENCY AND UNDERDEVELOPMENT IN NORTHWESTERN SIERRA LEONE, 1896-1939. *African Affairs [Great Britain] 1979 78(313): 481-492.* In Northwestern Sierra Leone peasant farming remained the basis of colonial agricultural development. Palm oil extracted from palm kernels was the basis of export development. Temne farmers were well versed in swamp rice production, and their methods were introduced in other parts of the colony. Parts of Temne country were economically independent of Western enterprise, European and Lebanese, which was motivated only by profit maximization. Northern Karene district has remained outside the mainstream of postcolonial politics. Based on published documents and secondary sources; 66 notes. R. L. Collison

2360. Skinner, David and Harrell-Bond, Barbara E. MISUNDERSTANDINGS ARISING FROM THE USE OF THE TERM 'CREOLE' IN THE LITERATURE ON SIERRA LEONE. *Africa [Great Britain] 1977 47(3): 305-320.* Discusses the origins and meanings of the term 'creole' in Sierra Leone in the 19th and 20th centuries. It was mostly used to describe the descendants of liberated slaves and other westernized inhabitants sometimes nicknamed 'Black Englishmen.' Differences in language and customs divided the creole community and the problem of the use of the term seems to have been one of a quest for identity. Based on personal contacts with Sierra Leone specialists; 16 notes, biblio. R. L. Collison

2361. Skinner, David; Harrell-Bond, Barbara; and Howard, Allen. A PROFILE OF URBAN LEADERS IN FREETOWN, SIERRA LEONE (1905-1945). *Tarikh [Nigeria] 1981 7(1): 11-19.* Examines the characteristics of typical urban community leaders in Freetown, Sierra Leone from 1905 to 1945, providing information about their occupations, religious affiliations, and educational backgrounds. Describes their postwar emergence as organizers of anticolonial movements.

2362. Spencer, Chuku-Dinka R. POLITICS, PUBLIC ADMINISTRATION, AND AGRICULTURAL DEVELOPMENT: A CASE STUDY OF THE SIERRA LEONE INDUSTRIAL PLANTATION DEVELOPMENT PROGRAM, 1964-67. *J. of Developing Areas 1977 12(1): 69-86.* In 1964 the government of Sierra Leone attempted to create industrial plantations in the provinces. The program failed because the motives for the scheme were political, leading to frequent political interference in purely technical matters. 44 notes. J. C. Billigmeier

2363. Steady, Filomina Chioma. PROTESTANT WOMEN'S ASSOCIATIONS IN FREETOWN, SIERRA LEONE. Hafkin, Nancy J. and Bay, Edna G., eds. *Women in Africa: Studies in Social and Economic Change*(Stanford, Ca.: Stanford U. Pr., 1976): 213-237. The Protestant religious organizations of Freetown Creole women have fostered Christian values and have provided financial support to the church, 1960's-70's. At the same time, they have promoted a conservative ideology that has prevented the emancipation of women. By providing an outlet for the development of female religious leadership, the organizations have helped maintain the male-dominated clergy. The organizations support a system of morality based on marriage in which men are granted the double sexual standard. Their opposition to divorce is a form of economic protection for the women, who depend on their husbands as breadwinners. The organizations are a form of manipulation to encourage women to conform to society's standards and do not recognize women's needs or potential. Field research and secondary sources; table, 19 notes. S. Tomlinson-Brown

2364. Swindell, Kenneth. MINING WORKERS IN SIERRA LEONE: THEIR STABILITY AND MARITAL STATUS. *African Affairs [Great Britain] 1975 74(295): 180-190.* A discussion of miners in the mid-1960's in the two areas of diamond mining and metal mining.

Their marital status and service at DIMINCO (Diamond Mining Corporation of Sierra Leone) was stable. Mining offers a principal source of wages and the DELCO (Sierra Leone Development Corporation) and DIMINCO miners are not seasonal migratory laborers. 4 figs.; 8 notes. H. G. Soff

2365. Tangri, Roger. CONFLICT AND VIOLENCE IN CONTEMPORARY SIERRA LEONE CHIEFDOMS. *J. of Modern African Studies [Great Britain] 1976 14(2): 311-321.* A study of the recurring violence in the political life of Sierra Leone among the 148 chiefdoms (elected but also hereditary) of the country. A study of these eruptions since the late 1940's indicates that rural violence is not the result of popular discontent, but is the expression of conflict between elites. Whereas at one time such violence was condoned, especially when the chiefdoms were loyal to the central government, it has been difficult to achieve redress of grievances. Recently there has been a shift toward petitioning and away from violent disorders. 30 notes. R. V. Ritter

2366. Williams, G. J. and Hayward, D. F. THE CHANGING LAND—TRANSPORTATION PATTERNS OF SIERRA LEONE. *Scottish Geographical Mag. [Great Britain] 1973 89(2): 107-118.* "The relative importance of the physical geography and the economy of Sierra Leone in determining the pattern of surface transportation in the country is briefly considered. In turn it is noted that economic growth depends upon a soundly developed transport network. The recent changes that have taken place in order to make the system more effective are outlined. Firstly, the 'running down' of the national railway and the reasons for this are discussed, followed by a description of the expansion and modification of the road network and the increase in motor vehicles. Lastly, the related necessary improvements at the port of Freetown are also described." J

2367. Williams, G. J. and Hayward, D. F. RECENT DEVELOPMENT OF THE SIERRA LEONE AIRWAYS SYSTEM. *Geography [Great Britain] 1973 58(1): 58-61.* Discusses domestic and international air lines service in Sierra Leone, 1950's-72.

2368. Wyse, Akintola J. G. ON MISUNDERSTANDINGS ARISING FROM THE USE OF THE TERM "CREOLE" IN THE LITERATURE ON SIERRA LEONE: A REJOINDER. *Africa [Great Britain] 1979 49(4): 408-417.* Response to David Skinner and Barbara Harrell-Bond's article in an earlier issue [*Africa* 1977 47(3): 305-320]. The term Krio has begun to supersede Creole as a name for the preindependence élite community who had a privileged position in colonial Sierra Leone. "Creole" was indeed used loosely during the 19th century. Among many examples one may cite the Golden Jubilee of Queen Victoria, 1887, when the term "creole" was used officially to describe people born of immigrant parents in the settlement. Evidence for a long Krio history exists in their language, and their intermarriage with settlers and reputation for hard work are also attested. Krio society has included both Muslims and Christians. Their educational and religious background have furthered their Westernization. Secondary sources; 17 notes, biblio. R. L. Collison

2369. Wyse, Akintola J. G. REVIEW ARTICLE: SIERRA LEONE CREOLES, THEIR HISTORY AND HISTORIANS. *J. of African Studies 1977 4(2): 228-239.* A detailed, highly critical review of Leo Spitzer's *The Creoles of Sierra Leone: Responses to Colonialism, 1870-1945.* Wyse makes numerous detailed references to the history and culture of Sierra Leone Creoles and "provincials" in taking Spitzer's book to task. Based on archival, primary, and secondary materials; 24 notes. L. W. Truschel

2370. Wyse, Akintola J. G. THE 1926 RAILWAY STRIKE AND ANGLO-KRIO RELATIONS: AN INTERPRETATION. *Int. J. of African Hist. Studies 1981 14(1): 93-123.* What began as a typical labor dispute developed into the first open clash between the British and the Krio elites in Sierra Leone, who came to the aid of the strikers. Although the workers and their Krio supporters were crushed, the foundations of the nationalist movement were laid. Based on British Colonial Office documents; 115 notes. R. T. Brown

Togo

2371. Amenumey, D. E. K. THE 1956 PLEBISCITE IN TOGOLAND UNDER BRITISH ADMINISTRATION AND EWE UNIFICATION. *Universitas [Ghana] 1976 5(2): 126-139.* In May 1956 the United Nations supervised a plebiscite in Togoland under British administration to test public opinion on that territory's future. The results of that plebiscite and the decision taken on them by the UN did more than decide the future of that territory; it dealt the *coup de grâce* to any prospects of uniting the Ewe, a culturally homogeneous people of over a million occupying the Guinea coast between the rivers Mono in the east and the Volta in the west, a territory divided among the Gold Coast, British Togoland, French Togoland. Based mainly on government sources; statistical table, 27 notes. J. J. N. McGurk

2372. Batsch, Christophe. LE TOGO ET LA CRISE: CONTRASTES RÉGIONAUX ET DÉPENDANCE ACCRUE [Togo and the crisis: regional contrasts and increased dependence]. *Rev. Française d'Hist. d'Outre-Mer [France] 1976 63(3-4): 590-600.* Before the Great Depression, Ewe farmers and traders in southern Togo played a leading role in the Togo economy. With the Depression came a plunge in agricultural prices and a rise in customs duties. These ruined the Ewe, and trade and agricultural export passed into European hands. In the north, an extension of the railroad line opened the area to a money economy, but burdened Togo with an increased public debt. The country as a whole was pushed toward more extreme dependence on France and foreign firms. Map, 4 tables, 2 graphs, 12 notes. J. C. Billigmeier

2373. Brydon, Lynne. RICE, YAMS AND CHIEFS IN AVATIME: SPECULATIONS ON THE DEVELOPMENT OF A SOCIAL ORDER. *Africa [Great Britain] 1981 51(2): 659-677.* The calendar for rice cultivation sets the pattern for the agricultural year and indicates the importance of rice in Avatime, one of the vestigial groups of Togo. Rituals for the cultivation of rice concern the whole village and begin with planting in June, continue with harvesting in November, the giving of new rice to the gods, bush-burning, and purification. Yams have much less ritual specifically associated with them, these being in connection with their cultivation and consumption, and are carried out for kinship groups. Chiefship has become integrated with the other ritual systems and, with its wider scope, is subsuming the rice and yam ritual sets. Being elected, chiefs have links with both cultivating rituals and social organization. Based on field work; table, 40 notes. R. L. Collison

2374. Decalo, Samuel. THE POLITICS OF MILITARY RULE IN TOGO. *Genève-Afrique [Switzerland] 1973 12(2): 62-96.* Discusses the character of the military government in Togo, 1967-73, and the socioeconomic causes for the regime's relative stability.

2375. Delval, Raymond. LES MUSULMANS AU TOGO [The Moslems of Togo]. *Afrique et L'Asie [France] 1974 (100): 4-21.* Muslims make up about 10% of the population of Togo. Islam is relatively new in the country, having been introduced mainly from Ghana and Nigeria, and has been rather superficial because of the lack of education of its adherents. In recent years, however, this weakness is being remedied by a revival movement promoted by the Muslim Union of Togo, under the auspices of which schools are being organized, new mosques constructed, and heretical confraternities suppressed. The Muslim Union is also active in sending Togolese students to Arab countries, attending the meetings of the Islamic Congress in Cairo, and participating in exchange visits with Egypt and the USSR. As a result, Islam has been making tremendous progress in Togo. J. S. Gassner

2376. LeBris, E. MIGRATION AND THE DECLINE OF A DENSELY-POPULATED RURAL AREA: THE CASE OF VO KOUTIME IN SOUTH-EAST TOGO. *African Perspectives [Netherlands] 1978 (1): 109-126.* Studies population growth in Vo Koutime, southeast Togo, and suggests that there is no automatic connection between demographic pressure and migration. The capitalist mode of production as functioning in Ouatchi society involves a mechanism of domination which exacerbates the migratory process which in turn affects the society itself, bringing stagnation and contributing to its impoverishment. 2 tables, 2 fig. R. V. Ritter

2377. LeBris, E. SURPRESSION DÉMOGRAPHIQUE ET ÉVOLUTION FONCIÈRE: LE CAS DU SUD-EST DU TOGO [Demographic pressure and agrarian evolution in southeastern Togo]. *African Perspectives [Netherlands] 1979 (1): 107-126.* Analyzes the complex agrarian situation in southeast Togo, a heavily populated area facing a crisis due to an enormous decrease in land productivity and an important rural emigration. Land ownership has been characterized by a diversity of rights and a vigorous customary law. However, several agricultural areas have shown an increase of land registration after 1945 in accordance with Togo government policy. Social transformations have brought low production and large emigration, due to bad working conditions and lack of profit. 3 tables, graph., 24 notes, biblio. G. P. Cleyet

2378. Ricard, Alain. CONCOURS ET CONCERT: THÉÂTRE SCOLAIRE ET THÉÂTRE POPULAIRE AU TOGO [Pedagogy and performance: educational theater and popular theater in Togo]. *Rev. d'Hist. du Théâtre [France] 1975 27(1): 44-86.* Describes educational theater in Togo which in recent years has performed more plays by African playwrights but is still an essentially French-oriented institution. Evaluates the conflict between popular culture and elite culture as manifest in theatrical production and in the choice of plays derived from French-language authors and African-language authors. Popular theater is characterized by "biblical concerts" or cantatas and by the concert-party. These cabaret or music hall performances are derived from the African experience and utilize the indigenous languages and musical forms of West African countries. 55 notes. H. R. Falk

2379. Ricard, Alain. HUBERT OGUNDE À LOMÉ [Hubert Ogunde at Lomé]. *Rev. d'Hist. du Théâtre [France] 1975 27(1): 26-30.* Describes a 1971 performance of *Ewe n la* in Lomé, Togo, by Ogunde, transcribes a statement by him explaining his theatrical work, and discusses the diversity of sources for and influences on the performances of Ogunde's troupe, the oldest and best-known African theater company. Analyzes the relationship of theatrical forms to the social conditions of the spectators in Ogunde's work. H. R. Falk

2380. Rivière, Claude. DZO ET LA PRATIQUE MAGIQUE CHEZ LES ÉVÉ DU TOGO [Dzo and magic practices among the Ewe in Togo]. *Cultures et Développement [Belgium] 1979 11(2): 193-218.* Describes the traditional magic practices among the Ewe in Togo and examines the two most important magic symbols, Dzo (the symbol of fire) and the knot.

2381. Rouveroy van Nieuwaal, E. A. B. van. TERRE AU NORD-TOGO: QUELQUES ASPECTS SUR LA RELATION ANUFÒ-NGAM NGAM EN MATIÈRE FONCIÈRE [Land in North Togo: aspects of the relations between the Anufo and Ngam Ngam groups in agrarian matters]. *African Perspectives [Netherlands] 1979 (1): 139-151.* An analysis of the agrarian situation in North Togo, centering on problems stemming from the conflict between modern legislation and surviving customary law. Examines the motives for criticizing such law, and, through an example of litigation opposing the Anufo to the Ngam Ngam groups, demonstrates that the creation of a uniform agrarian legislation has only enlivened the diversity of customary law. Based on official Togo government documents; 27 notes. G. P. Cleyet

2382. Tscha-Tokey, J. LE MODE D'ATTRIBUTION DE LA TERRE DANS LES SOCIÉTÉS PRÉCAPITALISTES D'AFRIQUE COMME SYSTÈME DE BLOCAGE À L'ACCUMULATION DU CAPITAL AU DÉVELOPPEMENT [The mode of land assignment in African precapitalistic societies as a system pegging the accumulation of capital necessary to the development]. *African Perspectives [Netherlands] 1979 (1): 127-138.* The precapitalist African society has since the colonial period been converted to a class society with the introduction of individual and exclusive land ownership. The example of Togo shows the inadequacy and social unfairness of the system of land ownership of farm proprietors and sharecroppers, which creates an impossible reconstitution of capital and a decrease of production. Urges action toward an authentically African agrarian system. 5 tables, 2 notes. G. P. Cleyet

2383. Wuffli, Peter A. KARL ROHRBACH: PRAKTISCH ENTWICKLUNGSHILFE IN TOGO [Karl Rohrbach: practical aid for development in Togo]. *Schweizer Monatshefte [Switzerland] 1982 62(2): 107-112.* The Swiss priest Karl Rohrbach (b. 1924) in the 1960's developed a concept of agricultural training in Upper Volta, which he applied in his Centre de Formation Agricole et Économique in Togo in 1972.

Upper Volta

2384. Armagnac, Catherine and Retel-Laurentin, Anne. RELATIONS BETWEEN FERTILITY, BIRTH INTERVALS, FOETAL MORTALITY AND MATERNAL HEALTH IN UPPER VOLTA. *Population Studies [Great Britain] 1981 35(2): 217-234.*

2385. Cordell, Dennis D. and Gregory, Joel W. LABOUR RESERVOIRS AND POPULATION: FRENCH COLONIAL STRATEGIES IN KOUDOUGOU, UPPER VOLTA, 1914 TO 1939. *J. of African Hist. [Great Britain] 1982 23(2): 205-224.* Koudougou, a potentially major source of labor, provided forced day labor betwen 1917 and 1938 estimated at five million person-days. Koudougou's dense population comprised mainly Mossi and depended almost completely on the resources of the land. French attempts to drain off labor for the colonial economy directly conflicted with the needs of the rural sector. Forced day labor was introduced to make the colonies self-supporting. Contract labor was developed to help in government enterprises, railway construction, and to meet the needs of private enterprise. These competitive uses of labor, as well as land colonization and military recruitment, gave rise to various forms of evasion ranging from moving short distances to taking refuge in the neighboring Gold Coast. Based on materials in Upper Volta archives; map, 51 notes. R. L. Collison

2386. Grant, Stephen H., Jr. UPPER VOLTA: GETTING BY WITH NOTHING: HOW THE PRESIDENT SEES IT. *Africa Report 1973 18(3): 29-33.* Discusses the problems and possibilities of Upper Volta, with a statement from President Sangoule Lamizana. S

2387. Gregory, Joel W. LEVEL, RATES, AND PATTERNS OF URBANIZATION IN UPPER VOLTA. *Pan-African J. [Kenya] 1976 9(2): 125-134.* Upper Volta is one of the least urbanized countries of tropical Africa with only seven percent of the population residing in urban centers. During 1960-70 some 14 towns designated as urban centers grew three times as fast as the national average. Unlike most other African countries, Volta lacks a central city and has a regular pattern of urban distribution. 3 tables, 2 fig., 22 notes. M. Feingold

2388. Marchal, J.-Y. À PROPOS DE L'AMÉNAGEMENT DES VOLTA ET DE L'ENCADREMENT SANITAIRE DES COLONS (HTE. VOLTA CENTRALE) [Development of the Volta valleys and the sanitary infrastructure of the settlers in central Upper Volta]. *Travaux & Mémoires de l'Inst. des Hautes Études de l'Amérique Latine [France] 1979 (32): 151-159.* A study of the projects for the development of the Volta valleys, including infrastructural investment and sanitary control.

2389. Saul, Mahir. BEER, SORGHUM AND WOMEN: PRODUCTION FOR THE MARKET IN RURAL UPPER VOLTA. *Africa [Great Britain] 1981 51(3): 746-764.* The beer industry in Upper Volta is a major factor in the economy of the villages. The Manga region exports over 1,800 tons of sorghum as malt each season, thus generating an income of about 116,000,000 francs. Sorghum production is in the hands of the men, but beer production is almost entirely the province of the women. European-style bottled beer is increasingly competitive, particularly as a status symbol. Beer consumption is adversely affected by the rapid growth of Islam, which sees sorghum beer as a symbol of primitive culture. Based on fieldwork; map, 14 notes, biblio. R. L. Collison

2390. Sautter, Gilles. MIGRATIONS, SOCIÉTÉ ET DÉVELOPPEMENT EN PAYS MOSSI [Migrations, society, and development in the Mossi region]. *Cahiers d'Études Africaines [France] 1980 20(3): 215-253.* Examines the effects of population movements in the Mossi region of Upper Volta, discussing the stability of its population, the reasons for migration and its effect on rural society, internal migrations, and the development of the country resulting from migrations.

2391. Savonnet, Georges. QUELQUES NOTES SUR L'HISTOIRE DES DYAN (CERCLES DE DIEBOUGOU ET DE LEO, HAUTE-

VOLTA) [Some notes on the history of the Dyan (the Diebougou and Leo groups, Upper Volta)]. *Bull. de l'Inst. Fondamental d'Afrique Noire [Senegal] 1975 37(3): 619-645.* An account of the Dyan in Upper Volta from 1750 to 1920. During the first 50 years they were established on the left bank of the Black Volta River. This was followed by a period of great instability and migratory movements. During the last half of the 19th century they became stabilized and able to defend themselves. The French colonial period of the 20th century did not bring the satisfaction they hoped for. 2 illus., 3 maps, 44 notes. H. L. Calkin

9. CENTRAL AFRICA

General

2392. Coquery-Vidrovitch, Catherine. LE PILLAGE DE L'AFRIQUE ÉQUATORIALE [The exploitation of Equatorial Africa]. *Histoire [France] 1978 (3): 43-52.* For a long time, French Equatorial Africa simply consisted of trading establishments, providing just enough labor to work the plantations. Later, trade concessions led to the introduction of compulsory labor which, for many, meant death. Paradoxically, such systematic plundering may have laid the foundations for economic progress. J

2393. De Craemer, Willy; Vansina, Jan; and Fox, Renée C. RELIGIOUS MOVEMENTS IN CENTRAL AFRICA: A THEORETICAL STUDY. *Comparative Studies in Soc. and Hist. 1976 18(4): 458-475.* An examination of religious movements in Central Africa, particularly Zaire, which deals with the movements as an integral dimension of the cultures common to the area.

2394. Gardinier, David E. SCHOOLING IN THE STATES OF EQUATORIAL AFRICA. *Can. J. of African Studies [Canada] 1974 8(3): 517-538.* Examines education in Gabon, Congo (Brazzaville), the Central African Republic, and Chad during and following French colonial rule, 1879-1974; includes the impact of the French system and reforms since 1957.

2395. Liniger-Goumaz, Max. GABON-GUINÉE ÉQUATORIALE: PROBLÈME FRONTALIER [Gabon and Equatorial Guinea: the frontier problem]. *Genève-Afrique [Switzerland] 1973 12(1): 99-102.* A bibliography concerning the Gabon-Equatorial Guinea frontier problem from 1884-1973.

2396. M'Bokolo, Elikia. FORCES SOCIALES ET IDÉOLOGIES DANS LA DÉCOLONISATION DE L'A.E.F. [Social forces and ideologies in the decolonization of French Equatorial Africa]. *J. of African Hist. [Great Britain] 1981 22(3): 393-407.* The determinant factors in the independence movements in French Equatorial Africa derived from both metropolitan and local authorities during World War II. Despite the encouragement of government administrators, the complex hierarchy of chiefs remained ineffectual in the progress toward independence. Their finances had been deflected to the direct benefit of the people, and in any case they were usually inadequate. The people themselves were disaffected, and some chiefs were corrupt. Chiefs whose powers were inherited from long before the colonial period and were therefore widely respected emphasized the disastrous nature of the rapid changes in administration. Few educated Africans were available. Based on printed sources; 2 tables, 50 notes. R. L. Collison

2397. Suret-Canale, Jean. DE LA COLONISATION AU GÉNOCIDE. LE SYSTÈME CONCESSIONNAIRE EN AFRIQUE ÉQUATORIALE FRANÇAISE (D'APRÈS C. COQUERY-VIDROVITCH ET P. KALCK) [From colonization to genocide: the concessionary system in French Equatorial Africa according to C. Coquery-Vidrovitch and P. Kalck]. *Pensée [France] 1973 (171): 149-157.* Describes the exploitation system in the French colonies of Africa, notably the Central African Republic, 1899-1972, and their dependence on the trade economy even after independence.

2398. Vellut, J.-L. DIVERSIFICATION DE L'ÉCONOMIE DE CUEILLETTE: MIEL ET CIRE DANS LES SOCIÉTÉS DE LA FORÊT CLAIRE D'AFRIQUE CENTRALE (C. 1750-1950) [Diversification in the economy of the collection of honey and wax in the societies of the Central African dry forests: 1750-1950]. *African Econ. Hist. 1979 (7): 93-112.* Studies the areas, techniques, trade, and social implications regarding the collection of honey and wax in the southern rain forest of Equatorial Africa. The honey collection techniques were extensive in dry forest, and intensive in interlacustrine areas. Honey was used as food and in the preparation of mead. Wax trade emerged only with colonial markets and was exported from Angola in large quantities between 1850 and 1950. The production and collection of wax for trade brought about deforestation and a change in the nature of local societies. Photo, map, 2 tables, graph, 59 notes. G. P. Cleyet

Cameroon

2399. Bayart, Jean François. PRESSE ÉCRITE ET DEVELOPPEMENT POLITIQUE AU CAMEROUN [The press and political development in Cameroon]. *Rev. Française d'Études Pol. Africaines [France] 1973 (88): 48-63.* Studies the contribution of newspapers, especially the *Effort Camerounais,* 1955-72, to the development of Cameroon after independence, concluding that its effectiveness and future are limited due to the lack of political, cultural, and economic autonomy.

2400. Bayart, Jean-François. L'UNION DES POPULATIONS DU CAMEROUN ET LA DÉCOLONISATION DE L'AFRIQUE "FRANÇAISE" [The Union des Populations du Cameroun and the decolonization of French Africa]. *Cahiers d'Études Africaines [France] 1978 18(3): 447-457.* A review of Richard A. Joseph's *Radical Nationalism in Cameroun* with a brief response. The author applauds the analysis of class and ethnicity in Cameroon's overt struggle with the Fourth Republic, 1955-56. Secondary sources; biblio. B. S. Fetter

2401. Booth, Bernard F. WEST CAMEROON: A MICROCOSM OF CULTURE CONFLICT IN EDUCATION. *R. de l'U. d'Ottawa [Canada] 1973 43(3): 353-361.* Stresses that West Cameroon "provides an excellent example of how educational development spawned a Cameroonian leadership which reflected its cultural antecedents and which steered the country into a new political leadership." Secondary sources; 14 notes, biblio. M. L. Frey

2402. Burnham, Philip. 'REGROUPMENT' AND MOBILE SOCIETIES: TWO CAMEROON CASES. *J. of African Hist. [Great Britain] 1975 16(4): 577-594.* An analysis of the effect that French colonial rule had on the Gbaya and Fulani in the Adamawa Plateau of Cameroon. The societies differed: Gbaya were agricultural, the Fulani pastoral. Both, however, were mobile, and despite French efforts, they remained a constant problem. The Gbaya and Fulani remain an administrative problem to the Cameroon government today. Map, 42 notes.
H. G. Soff

2403. Clignet, Remi and Stark, Maureen. MODERNIZATION AND FOOTBALL IN CAMEROUN. *J. of Modern African Studies [Great Britain] 1974 12(3): 409-421.* An analysis of the relationship between football (soccer) team composition and society in Cameroon. The sport is traced from its early introduction by the French to modern clubs in urban and suburban areas. Cameroon society in many aspects is similar to football clubs including the class of membership, race of players, name of the club, and their location within the metropolis. 29 notes.
H. G. Soff

2404. Derrick, Jonathan. THE "GERMANOPHONE" ELITE OF DOUALA UNDER THE FRENCH MANDATE. *J. of African Hist. [Great Britain] 1980 21(2): 255-267.* The number of German-speaking Africans increased in four West African German colonies prior to World War I, many of them having studied in Germany. The Dualas signed a treaty in 1884 placing themselves under German rule. By 1914 the Dualas were converted to Protestantism and educated along Western lines. They provided a large number of clerks to German government offices and firms in Africa; they also supplied clerks to French Cameroon, where they became invaluable. Many of them received higher education and became pastors. Nostalgic "German-thinking" Dualas lasted well on into the 1930's, though they worked loyally under the French colonial administrators. Based on personal interviews, official documents, and secondary sources; 54 notes. R. L. Collison

2405. Genest, Serge and Santerre, Renaud. L'ÉCOLE FRANCO-ARABE AU NORD-CAMEROUN [Franco-Arab schools in Northern Cameroon]. *Can. J. of African Studies [Canada] 1974 8(3): 589-606.* Schools teaching both French and Arabic languages in northern Cameroon following independence in 1960 met with opposition from French officials, because of a colonial policy which sought to discourage modernization of traditional Koranic education.

2406. Geschiere, Peter. THE ARTICULATION OF DIFFERENT MODES OF PRODUCTION: OLD AND NEW INEQUALITIES IN MAKA VILLAGES (SOUTHEAST CAMEROON). *African Perspectives [Netherlands] 1978 (2): 45-68.* Analyzes the economic systems that C. Meillassoux and P-P. Rey envisaged would develop in African communities in relation to capitalist economies. Both concentrated on the articulation of capitalism with the old kinship organizations, and defined the developments in Marxist terms. The author applies these results to Maka villages noting inequalities which develop through the integration of old and new. R. V. Ritter

2407. Guyer, Jane I. THE DEPRESSION AND THE ADMINISTRATION IN SOUTH-CENTRAL CAMEROUN. *African Econ. Hist. 1981 (10): 67-79.* Problems of depression cracked the alliance between the Beti chiefs and the colonial government of south-central Cameroon. Beti personal income declined while colonial taxes did not. Caught in the middle as tax collectors, the chiefs lost power. The government reacted by slowly removing the chiefs' taxing functions while at the same time the small farmers were regaining income. The old paternalistic system was thus shattered. Based primarily on the Cameroun National Archives; 43 notes. W. D. Piersen

2408. Guyer, Jane I. FEMALE FARMING AND THE EVOLUTION OF FOOD PRODUCTION PATTERNS AMONGST THE BETI OF SOUTH-CENTRAL CAMEROON. *Africa [Great Britain] 1980 50(4): 341-356.* In precolonial times the Beti operated a two-field system, large fields *(esep)* cleared and burned by men using axes and small intensively worked plots *(afub owondo)* in the savannah worked by women with hoes. *Esep* crops included plaintain, taro, melon seeds, and sugarcane. *Afub owondo* produced groundnuts, maize, and cassava. Labor mobilization of men in the 1920's upset the existing system, but the spread of cocoa cultivation helped to retain the men and was responsible for a monetarized system. Women are now largely responsible for producing food, the men for cocoa production, which has limited the ground available for *esep*. Urban demand for food gives women the chance to make a regular cash income. Based on field research in Cameroon, 1975-77; table, map, 8 notes. R. L. Collison

2409. Guyer, Jane I. THE FOOD ECONOMY AND FRENCH COLONIAL RULE IN CENTRAL CAMEROUN. *J. of African Hist. [Great Britain] 1978 19(4): 577-597.* French administrative policies in Central Cameroon during the interwar period created indigenous chiefs who mobilized manpower and resources from rural areas for the European economic sector. The institution of a food requisition system led to regulation of production, prices, and the trading network, as well as the use of the *indigénat* to support the rights of chiefs over their subjects. It guaranteed cheap, reliable sources of food for the wage-earning population, permitting stable low wages; it also created a class of wealthy planters who supported the colonial government. The system broke down in the late 1930's and was replaced after 1946 by family-based production units lacking an apropriate institutional framework. 82 notes. A. W. Novitsky

2410. Guyer, Jane I. HEAD TAX, SOCIAL STRUCTURE AND RURAL INCOMES IN CAMEROUN, 1922-1937. *Cahiers d'Études Africaines [France] 1980 20(3): 305-329.* Analyzes the interrelationship of state tax policy, market conditions for export crops, and producers' real incomes in Cameroon in terms of changing economic and political conditions during the interwar period, discussing the background of taxation policy in Cameroon, trends in taxation and export production, and tax rates and social policy.

2411. Joseph, Richard. THE ROYAL PRETENDER: PRINCE DOUALA MANGA BELL IN PARIS, 1919-1922. *Cahiers d'Études Africaines [France] 1974 14(2): 339-358.* The Cameroon prince, Douala Manga Bell (1898-1966), who had been educated in Germany, was given the red carpet treatment in France in order to wean him away from any residual sympathies for his former colonizer. His experience left him with ambivalent attitudes toward the French but with sufficient stature to become one of the first Cameroon national leaders. Based on materials in the Archives Nationales, Section Outre-Mer, AP 11/29-30, and secondary materials; 65 notes. B. S. Fetter

2412. Joseph, Richard A. THE GERMAN QUESTION IN FRENCH CAMEROUN, 1919-1939. *Comparative Studies in Soc. and Hist. [Great Britain] 1975 17(1): 65-90.* Discusses colonialism and nationalism in the Cameroon against the background of Germany's efforts to regain its former colony from France, 1919-39. S

2413. Joseph, Richard A. NATIONAL POLITICS IN POSTWAR CAMEROUN: THE DIFFICULT BIRTH OF THE UPC. *J. of African Studies 1975 2(2): 201-230.* Study of the radical party which emerged in Cameroon provides understanding of the broader panorama of nationalist and colonial politics in the area. The moment the Africans sought to use their new constitutional prerogatives, a crisis was created. The essentials of colonial domination must be preserved even though witnessing the extension of certain political freedoms. Traces the several political movements that preceded the formation of the final crucial one, the Union of the Peoples of the Camerouns. The emergence of this radical nationalist party which was eventually compelled to try to win power by revolutionary means was linked from the outset with the hostility of the French colonial establishment to any group which advocated any measure of autonomy. 86 notes. R. V. Ritter

2414. Joseph, Richard A. RUBEN UM NYOBE AND THE "KAMERUN" REBELLION. *African Affairs [Great Britain] 1973 73(293): 428-448.* In Cameroon following World War II, a strong nationalist movement began which demanded independence from France. Traces the movement, 1948-55, assessing military struggles after 1955 and the role of Nyobe, leader of the rebellion. 39 notes. H. G. Soff

2415. Joseph, Richard A. SETTLERS, STRIKERS, AND *SANS-TRAVAIL:* THE DOUALA RIOTS OF SEPTEMBER 1945. *J. of African Hist. [Great Britain] 1974 15(4): 669-687.* Discusses the politicizing effects of World War II on the white settlers and urban African community in the Cameroon which led to the Douala Riots of 1945.

2416. Marchand, Claude. TENTATIVES D'ADAPTATION DE L'ENSEIGNEMENT AUX REALITÉS CAMEROUNAISES: L'ENSEIGNEMENT AGRICOLE, 1921-1970 [Tentative adaptation of education to Cameroon realities: agricultural education, 1921-70]. *Can. J. of African Studies [Canada] 1974 8(3): 539-552.* Chronicles the development of institutions for agricultural education in Cameroon, 1921-70, highlighting the role of manual labor in general primary education, concluding that the agricultural education adaptation, and its relative importance, are a measure of that society's adaptation to education systems in general; examines difficulties in translating French systems to Cameroon realities.

2417. Mvondo Nyina, Barthélémy. L'ENSEIGNEMENT DANS LA POLITIQUE COLONIALE FRANÇAISE AU CAMEROUN DE 1916 À 1938 [Education in French colonial policy in Cameroon, 1916-38]. *Études d'Hist. Africaine [Zaire] 1976 8: 199-213.* The first schools established by the French in Cameroon from 1916 to 1920 had no precise program, the principal aim being the expansion of the use of the French language. In 1922 the French began to propose an educational system to improve the conditions of those who desired a better life. This was not for the masses because the French apparently doubted the ability of the Blacks in Cameroon to assimilate a great amount of instruction. The system included village and regional schools, a superior school in Yaounde, and a special school to prepare future leaders. The development of schools even by 1938 was very uneven throughout Cameroon. 41 notes. H. L. Calkin

2418. Ndongko, Wilfred A. A COMPARATIVE ANALYSIS OF FRENCH AND BRITISH INVESTMENT POLICIES IN CAMEROON. *Pan-African J. [Kenya] 1974 7(2): 101-109.* The French invested more heavily in East Cameroon than the British did in West Cameroon. As a result, the two provinces progressed at different rates after World War II. Since independence, Cameroon has been trying to equalize the regions. 5 tables, 17 notes. H. G. Soff

2419. Ndongko, Wilfred A. THE EXTERNAL TRADE PATTERN OF CAMEROON: 1957-72. *Africa Q. [India] 1976 16(1): 76-87.* Studies the external trade patterns of Cameroon, 1957-72.

2420. Ndongko, Wilfred A. FINANCING ECONOMIC DEVELOPMENT: THE CAMEROON EXPERIENCE. *J. of African Studies 1981 8(1): 16-30.* Six economic development plans have been implemented in the Cameroon since 1947, the first two by the French colonial administration of East Cameroon and the remainder by the Ahidjo government since independence in 1960. The French concentrated very heavily on the development of economic infrastructure and provided 90% of the developmental funding. Since independence the government has shifted the developmental emphasis to industry, mines, energy, and agriculture and has tried to lessen the dependence on external public and private funds. Based on published Cameroon government documents and secondary sources; 11 tables, 25 notes. L. W. Truschel

2421. Nwosu, Humphrey N. THE CONCEPTS OF NATIONALISM AND RIGHT TO SELF-DETERMINATION: CAMEROON AS A CASE STUDY. *Africa Q. [India] 1976 16(2): 1-26.* Examines the concepts of nationalism, nation, and self-determination, applies them to the peoples of Cameroon, and considers the problems of national development in that country since the late 1940's.

2422. Quinn, Frederick. CHARLES ATANGANA OF YAOUNDÉ. *J. of African Hist. [Great Britain] 1980 21(4): 485-495.* Charles Atangana (1880-1943) rose to great power entirely on his own merit. Son of a Beti headman, Atangana was educated by German missionaries in Cameroon. As interpreter to a German administrator, he learned the skills of a negotiator. In Germany, 1911-13, he edited and translated Beti historical documents. After returning to Africa he became president of the local court and, in 1914, Paramount Chief of some 500,000 people of the Ewondo and Bane tribes. During World War I he remained loyal to the Germans; after the war the French restored his position as Paramount Chief. Based on published sources and interviews; 24 notes. R. L. Collison

2423. Quinn, Frederick. GERMAN AND FRENCH RULE IN THE CAMEROON. *Tarikh [Nigeria] 1974 4(4): 54-69.*

2424. Stark, Frank. FEDERALISM IN CAMEROON: THE SHADOW AND THE REALITY. *Can. J. of African Studies [Canada] 1976 10(3): 423-442.* Examines the period of centralized federalism, 1961-72, under president Ahmadou Ahidjo; examines his cultivation of the elites in West Cameroon and how these elites voiced their opinions on federalism; discusses events which led to the not-surprising federal dissolution in 1972.

2425. Stark, Frank M. PERSUASION AND POWER IN CAMEROON. *Can. J. of African Studies [Canada] 1980 14(2): 273-293.* Analyzes the relationships among persuasion, power, and authority in general and with particular reference to the Republic of Cameroon. Discusses the internal structures of rhetoric, the shaping of political reality by symbols, and the relationship between symbols and politics. Examines the interaction between policies and use of symbols under the leadership of Ahmadou Ahidjo, prime minister of Cameroon since 1958. 46 notes. S

Central African Republic

2426. Eggen, Willy. LE FAUX REFUGE: DIABLE, SORCELLERIE ET RÉSIDENCE CHEZ LES BANDA [The false refuge: the devil, sorcery, and residence among the Banda]. *Cultures et Développement [Belgium] 1979 11(2): 175-192.* Examines the traditional importance assigned to the devil, witchcraft, and evil spirits in Banda society.

2427. Gosselin, G. HISTOIRE D'UN CLAN GBEYA (RÉPUBLIQUE CENTRAFRICAINE): LE POINT DE VUE DU COLONISÉ [History of a Gbaya clan (Central African Republic): the point of view of the colonized]. *Genève-Afrique [Switzerland] 1973 12(1): 19-36.* Traces the development of the Baga clan of the Gbaya people of the northwestern Central African Republic, ca. 1800-1963, describing the socioeconomic change produced by colonization.

2428. Mel'nikov, E. N. RETSEDIV KOLONIALIZMA [Recidivist colonialism]. *Sovetskoe Gosudarstvo i Pravo [USSR] 1981 (3): 94-97.* Criticizes French infringement of the principle of noninterference in internal affairs of the Central African Republic in 1979.

Chad

2429. Azevedo, Mario. THE HUMAN PRICE OF DEVELOPMENT: THE BRAZZAVILLE RAILROAD AND THE SARA OF CHAD. *African Studies Rev. 1981 24(1): 1-19.* Because of French views of the physical capabilities of the Sara of Chad, they were the primary recruits among the 120,000 railroad construction crews. Thousands of them died under the exceptionally harsh working conditions resulting from the corrupt colonial administration. Based on French colonial archives; map, 5 tables, 13 notes, biblio. R. T. Brown

2430. Buijtenhuijs, Robert. LA DIALECTIQUE NORD-SUD DANS L'HISTOIRE TCHADIENNE [The North-South dialectic in Chad's history]. *African Perspectives [Netherlands] 1977 (2): 43-61.* A Hegelian dialectic analysis of the opposition between the North (thesis) and the South (antithesis) in Chad. Born from geographical, political, and especially religious contrasts, the conflict is several centuries old, and the latest insurrection in 1965 is still alive today with no hope for a peaceful settlement. The synthesis of the process could be realized if the Frolinat (National Liberation Front), founded in 1966, were finally successful in persuading the South to forget the past opposition and adopt its nationalist, anti-imperialist, and socialist revolutionary program. Note, biblio. G. P. Cleyet

2431. Decalo, Samuel. CHAD: THE ROOTS OF CENTRE-PERIPHERY STRIFE. *African Affairs [Great Britain] 1980 79(317): 491-509.* The total collapse of central authority in Chad in February 1979 and the events that followed were only stages in the political decay and disintegration of the country. Its origins are to be sought in the abolition of competitive politics and the purges of the 1960's; they are anchored in the very nature of the society, which became a French colony in 1900, and in the weakness of the state apparatus inherited at independence. Chad is neither a nation nor in many respects a viable state, and it must either redefine the dimensions of both state and nation or face total disintegration and chaos. 56 notes. J. V. Coutinho

2432. Decalo, Samuel. REGIONALISM, POLITICAL DECAY, AND CIVIL STRIFE IN CHAD. *J. of Modern African Studies [Great Britain] 1980 18(1): 23-56.* Traces current problems in Chad to interethnic animosities, the incompatibility of regional nationalism, and the absence of a representative government. The core of the conflict concerns the lack of state administration in peripheral areas and primitive state services. Based on government published documents and secondary sources; map, 73 notes. A. Sbacchi

2433. Decaluwe, Bernard. STRUCTURES INDUSTRIELLES ET PAYS EN VOIE DE DÉVELOPMENT LES MOINS AVANCÉS: LE CAS DU TCHAD [Industrial structures and the least advanced developing countries: the case of Chad]. *Can. J. of Development Studies [Canada] 1980 1(2): 242-261.* Describes the economic structure of Chad, evaluates the impact of its industrial policies, and identifies the obstacles to industrial development.

2434. Fedorov, P. K SOBYTIIAM V CHADE [What happens in Chad]. *Aziia i Afrika Segodnia [USSR] 1981 (6): 21-24.* Describes the military coalition between Chad and Libya in 1980-81.

2435. Gervais, Raymond. LA PLUS RICHE DES COLONIES PAUVRES: LA POLITIQUE MONETAIRE ET FISCALE DE LA FRANCE AU TCHAD 1900-1920 [The richest of the poor colonies: France's monetary and fiscal policies in Chad, 1900-1920]. *Can. J. of African Studies [Canada] 1982 16(1): 93-112.* The aggressive fiscal policy of the military administration of Chad from 1900 to 1920 achieved considerable fiscal surpluses. Despite policies of currency scarcity, Chad over-achieved as a "self-financing" colony. This fiscal policy, accompanied by violence and combined with underinvestment, laid the foundations for the underdevelopment of Chad, the richest of France's poorest colonies. J/S

2436. Lemarchand, Rene. CHAD: THE ROOTS OF CHAOS. *Current Hist. 1981 80(470): 414-417, 436-438.* Given the military and political ties between the USSR and Libya, the Libyan presence in Chad, like that of the Cubans in Angola, may become a pawn in an East-West struggle, with France and the United States at odds on how to deal with the situation.

2437. Lemarchand, René. THE POLITICS OF SARA ETHNICITY: A NOTE ON THE ORIGINS OF THE CIVIL WAR IN CHAD. *Cahiers d'Etudes Africaines [France] 1980 20(4): 449-471.* Discusses the sociological phenomena of fission and fusion of ethnic groups in Chad, focusing on the politics of the Sara, their conflict with non-Sara groups, and the politics of their transterritorial affiliations.

2438. Orobator, S. E. CHADIAN CRISIS: THE SEARCH FOR A SOLUTION. *Contemporary Rev. [Great Britain] 1981 238(1380): 1-7, (1381): 86-93.* Part I. Describes the political divisions inside the African republic of Chad since its independence in 1960, with particular reference to the overthrow of President Tombolbaye in April 1975. Part II. Analyzes the serious internal conflicts which continued to divide Chad in the late 1970's.

2439. —. LE TCHAD SECOUÉ PAR UN SÉISME [Chad shaken by an earthquake]. *Études [France] 1979 351(1): 7-12.* Discusses the political events in Chad since February 1979, when an earthquake causing the death of 10,000 people and the displacement of 100,000 occurred at the same time as political conflict between President Malloum and Prime Minister Habre.

Congo

2440. Bonte, Pierre. QUELQUES PROBLÈMES THÉORIQUES DE LA RECHERCHE MARXISTE EN ANTHROPOLOGIE [Some theoretical problems in Marxist research on anthropology]. *Pensée [France] 1973 (171): 86-104.* Critically reviews P. P. Rey's *Colonialisme, néo-colonialisme et transition au capitalisme. Exemple de la COMILOG au Congo-Brazzaville* (Maspero: 1971) which studies the advent of capitalism in three primitive societies, and presents a theory on Marxist transformation and rites of passage in societies with a class structure.

2441. Ul'ianovski, R. MARIAN NGUABI [Marien Ngouabi]. *Aziia i Afrika Segodnia [USSR] 1982 (5): 38-41.* Examines the Marxist views and political career of Marien Ngouabi (1938-77), the founder of the Congolese Labor Party and President of the Congo (Brazzaville), 1969-77, focusing on his attempt to adapt Marxist tenets to Congolese socioeconomic realities.

Equatorial Guinea

2442. Chauleur, P. GUINÉE ÉQUATORIALE [Equatorial Guinea]. *Études [France] 1976 345: 607-616.* Guinea has begun to emerge from a pitiless dictatorship and to experience internal peace and justice because of increasing pressures exerted by the African community as a whole.

2443. Eya Nchama, C. M. LA DECOLONISATION DE LA GUINEE EQUATORIALE ET LE PROBLEME DES REFUGIES [The decolonization of Equatorial Guinea and the refugee problem]. *Genève-Afrique [Switzerland] 1982 20(1): 73-128.* Analytical survey of the history of Equatorial Guinea. The territory (partly on the African mainland and partly islands in the Atlantic) has always been a country of refugees, some coming to the territory, others leaving it because of their opposition to the colonial regime. Describes the bloody regime of Francisco Macias Nguema, 1968-79, as indirect colonialism. Based on government documents and secondary sources; 76 notes, appendix, 3 photos. B. S. Fetter

2444. Fegley, Randall. THE U.N. HUMAN RIGHTS COMMISSION: THE EQUATORIAL GUINEA CASE. *Human Rights Q. 1981 3(1): 34-47.* Discusses the history of human rights violations in Equatorial Guinea from 1968 to 1981, with special attention to the UN Human Rights Commission's difficulty in dealing with them.

2445. Gard, Robert C. EQUATORIAL GUINEA: MACHINATIONS IN FOUNDING A NATIONAL BANK. *Munger Africana Lib. Notes 1974 27: 5-46.* The story of the Spaniard Francisco Paesa Sanchez de Caballer, who sought to exploit newly-independent Equatorial Guinea by founding a bank in 1968-69. S

Gabon

2446. Binet, Jacques. DRUGS AND MYSTICISM: THE BWITI CULT OF THE FANG. *Diogenes [Italy] 1974 (86): 31-54.* Examines the theology, mysticism and individualism of the Bwiti cult among the Fang tribe of central Gabon from the 1950's to the 1970's; considers the assimilation of elements of Catholicism in Bwiti attitudes.

2447. Comte, Gilbert. TREIZE ANNÉES D'HISTOIRE [Thirteen years of history]. *Rev. Française d'Études Pol. Africaines [France] 1973 (90): 39-57.* Studies the 1959-72 period of independence and growing nationalism in Gabon, outlining the important roles of people and political parties such as Jean Hilaire Aubaume and his Union Democratique et Social du Gabon, and Léo M'Ba and his Bloc Democratique Gabonais, as well as the contribution of President Albert Bernard Bongo, in national renovation.

2448. Decraene, Philippe. ESQUISSE D'UNE NOUVELLE POLITIQUE ÉTRANGÈRE GABONAISE [Outline of a new Gabonese foreign policy]. *Rev. Française d'Études Pol. Africaines [France] 1973 (90): 58-66.* Discusses the efforts of President Albert Bernard Bongo following his 25 February 1972 election in strengthening international ties, including the opening of new relations, normalization of US-Gabon ties, the establishment of diplomatic relations with Egypt and Algeria, and a policy of general rapprochement with neighboring countries.

2449. deSchaetzen, Yves. L'ÉCONOMIE GABONAISE [Gabonese economy]. *Rev. Française d'Études Pol. Africaines [France] 1973 (90): 67-94.* Studies the rapid growth, 1960-72, of the Gabon economy, with its amazing growth in the gross national product and success in exportation, attributing a good part of this success to a political stability which attracts foreign investment; also lists national resources.

2450. Gaertner, Henryk. ALBERT SCHWEITZER 1875-1965 [Albert Schweitzer, 1875-1965]. *Życie i Myśl [Poland] 1975 25(9): 30-41.* Albert Schweitzer, Protestant theologian, philosopher, physician, musician, scholar, missionary, prolific writer, and founder of the Lambaréné Hospital in French Equatorial Africa, was justly honored by the title of "genius of the 20th century." He won the Nobel Peace Prize in 1953. Swiss by ancestry, German by birth, French by passport, adopted son of Gabon, he was a citizen of the world. M. A. J. Swiecicka

2451. Pourtier, Roland. LA CRISE DE L'AGRICULTURE DANS UN ÉTAT MINIER: LA GABON [Agricultural crisis in a mining state: Gabon]. *Études Rurales [France] 1980 (77): 39-62.* A cycle of mining industry began in Gabon about 20 years ago. The spectacular growth of the extracting activity was not met with an expansion of agriculture; on the contrary, increasing food dependence and decay of rural areas, worsened by declining population, have been recorded. Three factors paralyzed the rural development which is in other respects running short of human and financial means and for which a true political will is lacking: little affinity of people for tillage, archaism of cultural methods, and disorganized commercialization. To remedy the agricultural crisis, developers have decided in favor of industrialization, highly capitalistic and mechanized; this results in the introduction of wage-earning classes in agriculture, but can not revive an agonizing rural society. J/S

2452. Świderski, S. NZE NDONG JEAN REMY, FONDATEUR DE LA COMMUNAUTE ERENDZI DUMA [Nzé Ndong Jean Rémy, founder of the Erendzi Duma]. *J. of Religion in Africa [Netherlands] 1981 12(3): 178-191.* Traces the life of Nzé Ndong Jean Rémy (1919-79) and the development of the independent Christian church he founded in Gabon in the 1950's, called Erendzi Duma Nsur Mor and representative of spiritual renovation that began in Gabon in the 1920's and peaked in the years 1945-60. Based largely on interviews with Nzé Ndong Jean Rémy and members of his community; 6 illus. R. J. Jirran

São Tomé and Príncipe

2453. Durieux, André. DE L'EVOLUTION DE DIVERS TERRITOIRES DE L'ANCIEN OUTRE-MER PORTUGAIS [On the political evolution of several former Portuguese overseas territories]. *Bull. des Séances de l'Acad. des Sci. d'Outre-Mer [Belgium] 1980 26(3): 357-376.* Traces the political development of four small former Portuguese colonies since the Portuguese revolution of April 1974. Portuguese India (Goa) has been incorporated into India and East Timor into Indonesia, São Tomé and Príncipe are independent, and Macao remains a Portuguese territory. Aspects of Macao's constitution are examined. This final loss of overseas colonies marks the end of the great Portuguese colonial empire begun under Henry the Navigator. Primary and secondary sources; 21 notes. M. Schumacher

Zaire

General

2454. Boute, Joseph. DEMOGRAPHIC TRENDS IN THE REPUBLIC OF ZAIRE. *Munger Africana Lib. Notes 1973 (21): 5-24.* Interview with Joseph Boute, Chief of Research at the National Office of Research and Development, discussing current social, cultural, and political trends in the Republic of Zaire. S

2455. Cahen, Daniel. HISTOIRE DE LA RECHERCHE ARCHÉOLOGIQUE AU ZAÏRE [History of archaeological research in Zaire]. *Études d'Hist. Africaine [Zaire] 1977-78 9-10: 33-36.* Early archaeological research in Zaire was first synthesized in 1899. Important turning points were 1925 and 1947 when the first Pan-African Congress on prehistory was held. With the creation of the Institute of National Museums in 1970 research in Zaire received a new emphasis. H. L. Calkin

2456. Chrétien, J. P. LE ZAÏRE, DE LA COLONIE-MODÈLE A L'AUTHENTICITÉ AFRICAINE [Zaire, from model colony to African authenticity]. *Esprit [France] 1974 (2): 327-335.* An overview of several books on Zaire, from the point of view of the conflict facing the African elites in the choice between modernism and African authenticity. 15 notes. G. F. Jewsbury

2457. Francis, P. G. ZAIRE: THE COUNTRY AND PEOPLE. *World Survey [Great Britain] 1973 (59): 1-18.* Issue primarily describing the politics and economic conditions of Zaire since the 1960's.

2458. Jewsiewicki, Bogumil. LA MATURITE DE L'HISTOIRE [Historical maturity]. *Can. J. of African Studies [Canada] 1982 16(3): 611-616.* Reviews Jan Vansina, *The Children of Woot: A History of the Kuba Peoples* (1978), which describes and analyzes the social, economic, and political organization of a people living in isolation in the Congo since before the period of colonization. Vansina's book is a triumph of monographic analysis and of the use of the oral tradition. 5 notes. J. V. Coutinho

2459. Kanyinda, Lusanga Th. RÉFLEXIONS SUR LE LIVRE DE LAURENT MONNIER [Reflections on the book of Laurent Monnier]. *Rev. Française d'Études Pol. Africaines [France] 1973 8(93): 101-105.* Reflects on a book by Laurent Monnier (Paris: EDICEF, 1971), a study in the sociopolitical reality of Zaire, as a model for future regional study, stressing the importance of this direct, historical method (1971).

2460. Olimpio, Guido. SHABA: LE ORIGINI DELLA CRISI [Shaba: the origin of the crisis]. *Civitas [Italy] 1978 29(7-8): 51-62.* The history of the tormented territory of Shaba (Katanga) from the birth of the Belgian Congo in 1885. J

2461. Saint Moulin, L. de. DE ONTWIKKELING VAN KINSHASA [The development of Kinshasa]. *Spiegel Hist. [Netherlands] 1977 12(4): 210-219.* A history of the development of the city of Kinshasa, the capital of Zaire. The first European contacts were made in 1655 by Portuguese missionaries. The area around Kinshasa was an important trading center in the 18th and 19th centuries. The city grew very rapidly in the 20th century, especially during the last two decades. Since 1959, however, the white population has decreased. A large percentage of the current population consists of recent migrants and is relatively young. Also discusses urban planning, transportation, and public utilities. Illus., biblio. G. D. Homan

Economics

2462. Bawele, Mumbanza mwa and Ensobato, Nyabakombi. LA PRODUCTION ALIMENTAIRE DANS LES MARAIS DE LA HAUTE-NGIRI DU XIXe SIÈCLE À NOS JOURS [Production of articles of food in the Upper Ngiri marshland from the 19th century to the present day]. *African Econ. Hist. 1979 (7): 130-139.* Studies Zaire's food production in the Upper Ngiri river marshland between the Ngiri and Moanda rivers. By the end of the 19th century, the production of bananas, yams, manioc, palm oil, and fish was adequate to local consumption, but the high industrialization and new techniques introduced during the colonial period shifted this production from local needs to foreign markets. Many fishermen had to move to more productive fisheries in the north along the Congo (Zaire) River. Although Upper Ngiri food production is adequate today, the future is uncertain. Based on Zaïrean archival documents; 28 notes. G. P. Cleyet

2463. Bidum, Kuyunsa. CONSIDÉRATIONS SUR L'ÉVOLUTION DES INTERVENTIONS SOCIO-ÉCONOMIQUES POUR LE DÉVELOPPEMENT DU MILIEU RURAL ZAÏROIS [The evolution of socioeconomic interventions for the development of rural Zaire]. *Africa [Italy] 1976 31(4): 475-496.* The author underlines the importance of agriculture and agricultural planning in the economic development of the countries of the Third World. He focuses on the case of Zaire, analyzing the government policy in the rural sector during the colonial period and after independence. A particular mention is made of the action undertaken by the Catholic missionaries in the field of agricultural promotion. J

2464. Bidum, Kuyunsa. L'INDUSTRIE KATANGAISE ET LES PROBLÈMES DE LA MAIN D'OEUVRE INDIGÈNE JUSQU'EN 1940 [Katangese industry and the problems of native manpower up to 1940]. *Africa [Italy] 1977 32(4): 577-591.* When the Belgians colonized the Congo they found great mineral wealth in the southeastern region known as Katanga or Shaba. Labor was a problem; the area was thinly settled by people engaged in subsistence agriculture. The mine operator, the Union Minière du Haut-Katanga (UMHK), recruited laborers from Rwanda-Burundi, the Rhodesias, Angola, and the Congo Luba. The result was an extremely heterogeneous population in the mine belt. In Lubumbashi (Elizabethville), Swahili, Tshiluba, and local tribal languages are spoken. 25 notes. J. C. Billigmeier

2465. Bishikwabo, Chubaka. UN ASPECT DU COLONAT AU CONGO BELGE: LE SORT DES TRAVAILLEURS DU KIVU (1900-1940) [An aspect of colonization in the Belgian Congo: the Kivu workers' fate, 1900-40]. *Genève-Afrique [Switzerland] 1977-78 16(2): 25-44.* Discusses the colonization of Zaire as it affected workers' conditions in the Kivu, 1900-40. This area in eastern Zaire was introduced slowly to Western capitalism, cultivation, and white settlement. The administrative authorities and the colonists joined forces to exploit the native workers. Primary sources; 3 maps, 75 notes. G. P. Cleyet

2466. Cohn, Stanley. WHAT'S GOING UP IN ZAIRE? OTRAG'S ROCKET BASE IN SHABA. *Munger Africana Lib. Notes 1979 (49): 3-27.* Discusses the rocket site in Zaire which was rented as of March, 1976 to a West German corporation called Orbital Transport und Raketen Aktiengesellschaft (OTRAG) for setting up installations and firing rockets.

2467. Drachoussoff, V. MÉCANISATION ET INTENSIFICATION DES MÉTHODES CULTURALES DANS LE BAS-ZAÏRE [Mechanization and intensification of cultivation methods in Lower Zaire]. *African Econ. Hist. 1979 (7): 141-154.* Analyzes the semi-intensive methods of cultivation successfully introduced between 1948 and 1960 in the Cataracts areas of Zaire between Angola and the Congo (Brazzaville) by the Groupe d'Économie Rurale (GER), made up of Belgian and Zaire citizens. Without destroying the fertility of the soil, the crop output increased considerably, the annual revenue more than doubled with a substantial per-day work revenue increase. After 1960, the GER activities decreased because of Zaire's economic and political difficulties, but were not interrupted. Map, 3 tables, 3 notes. G. P. Cleyet

2468. Hulstaert, G. L'ÉVOLUTION DE LA PRODUCTION ALIMENTAIRE DES NKUNDO (XIXe-XXe SIÈCLES): UN BILAN

PARTISAN [The evolution of the food production of the Nkundo (19th and 20th centuries): a partisan evaluation]. *African Econ. Hist. 1979 (7): 171-181.* Relates the economic history of the Mongo-Nkundo people, living west of the Luilaka river and south of the equator. Before the colonial period, these people lived on gathering food, hunting, and fishing. European penetration brought new crops, livestock, and poultry, increased labor demands from these people, interfered with their welfare, neglected the development of a diversified agricultural economy, caused a depletion of food supplies, increased the mortality rate and epidemics, and brought about a recent exodus of agricultural workers. Independence has not solved the crisis. Based on the author's almost 50 years as a Catholic missionary in the area; 12 notes. G. P. Cleyet

2469. Jewsiewicki, B. THE GREAT DEPRESSION AND THE MAKING OF THE COLONIAL ECONOMIC SYSTEM IN THE BELGIAN CONGO. *African Econ. Hist. 1977 (4): 153-176.* In the Belgian Congo, the Great Depression of the 1930's occurred at a critical stage in the development of the colonial system, and that economic crisis remains the dominant economic factor in that part of Africa.

2470. Jewsiewicki, B. LE COLONAT AGRICOLE EUROPÉEN AU CONGO-BELGE, 1910-1960: QUESTIONS POLITIQUES ET ÉCONOMIQUES [The European agricultural colony in the Belgian Congo, 1910-60: political and economic questions]. *J. of African Hist. [Great Britain] 1979 20(4): 559-571.* Colonial farmers were only marginal in the colonial economy of the Belgian Congo, which was based on the exploitation of African labor by industrial and commercial firms. European farmers could not compete with businesses in labor recruitment or with African cultivators in prices. They survived only with the aid of government subsidies and monopolies. White farming was maintained for political reasons until 1960, after which it was rapidly abandoned. 41 notes. A. W. Novitsky

2471. Kaluma, Mathieu. QUELQUES ASPECTS STRUCTURELS DE LA CRISE AGRAIRE AU ZAÏRE [Some structural aspects of the agricultural crisis in Zaire]. *Genève-Afrique [Switzerland] 1979 17(1): 151-163.* Demonstrates the deterioration of the rural agricultural base of Zaire by showing the declining ability of farmers to feed burgeoning urban populations. 11 tables, 16 notes. B. S. Fetter

2472. Kivilu, Sabakinu. LA DYNAMIQUE DE L'ESPACE AU BAS-ZAÏRE: QUELQUES DONNÉES D'ANALYSE SUR LES VOIES DE COMMUNICATION DE 1855 À 1938 [The dynamics of space in Lower Zaire: some analytical data on communication networks, 1855-1938]. *Cultures et Développement [Belgium] 1979 11(2): 247-259.* Considers how the economic development of Lower Zaire was affected by the construction of railroads and roads.

2473. Lederer, A. PROBLÈMES ACTUELS DES TRANSPORTS AU ZAÏRE [Current transportation problems in Zaire]. *Bull. des Séances de l'Acad. Royale des Sci. d'Outre-Mer [Belgium] 1977 (2): 200-214.* Since independence in 1960, the transportation system in Zaire has been disrupted due to internal disturbances, external political developments, and natural catastrophes. It has been necessary to use several different routes to export Zaire's mineral wealth: to Matadi, Beira, Lobito, and Dar-es-Salaam. Tonnage along these routes has fluctuated greatly. To improve conditions, Zaire's port facilities must be developed and peace established. Based on statistics and secondary sources; biblio. M. Schumacher

2474. Leynseele, P. van. LES TRANSFORMATIONS DES SYSTÈMES DE PRODUCTION ET D'ÉCHANGES DE POPULATIONS RIPUAIRES DU HAUT-ZAÏRE [Transformations of production and exchange systems of riparian populations in Upper Zaire]. *African Econ. Hist. 1979 (7): 117-129.* Studies the fishing trade of the large population in the Upper Zaire marshland surrounding the Congo river and its tributaries toward its downstream junction with the Ubangi. Centers on the active trade of the Libinza peoples of the Ngiri River banks during precolonial times, under autonomous and independent units of fishermen and their families. During the colonial period, many Ngiri fisheries were neglected and trade was directed toward large urban centers. Since the independence, the fishing operations have been shifted from the Ngiri banks to the area along the Zaire river. Map, 3 photos, 7 notes. G. P. Cleyet

2475. Mpekesa, Bongoy. ROLE AND STATUS OF ECONOMICS IN ZAIRE: A CRITICAL SURVEY. *Int. Social Sci. J. [France] 1978 30(1): 181-192.* Assesses the role and status of economics in Zaire based on a study of the interrelationship of institutionalized economic thought and economic development within Zaire, 1954-78.

2476. Peemans, J. Ph. THE SOCIAL AND ECONOMIC DEVELOPMENT OF ZAIRE SINCE INDEPENDENCE: AN HISTORICAL OUTLINE. *African Affairs [Great Britain] 1975 74(295): 148-179.* An analysis of the economy of Zaire since 1890 and its future prospects. It is anticipated that during the decade of the 1970's, its uneven growth pattern will continue. 16 tables; 56 notes. H. G. Soff

2477. Perrings, Charles. GOOD LAWYERS BUT POOR WORKERS: RECRUITED ANGOLAN LABOUR IN THE COPPER MINES OF KATANGA, 1917-1921. *J. of African Hist. [Great Britain] 1977 18(2): 237-259.* Angolans were first recruited to work in the Robert Williams Co. copper mines in Katanga in 1917. The most aggressive recruiter was J. C. French who used deception and compulsion to fill his quotas. Deserters were brutalized when caught. The author discusses housing and food as well as health care. By 1921 labor recruitment from Angola was prohibited by the Portuguese government. 113 notes. H. G. Soff

2478. Radmann, Wolf. THE NATIONALIZATION OF ZAIRE'S COPPER: FROM UNION MINIÈRE TO GECAMINES. *Africa Today 1978 25(4): 25-47.* Analyzes the pivotal role of the Union Minière du Haut Katanga (UMHK) and Générale Congolaise des Minerais (GECAMIN) on Zaire's economy after nationalization. The process leading to expropriation of UMHK assets, while politically understandable, produced economic disaster. Based on UMHK and GECAMIN publications and secondary sources; 2 tables, chart, 47 notes. G. O. Gagnon

2479. Raymaekers, Paul. DÉVELOPPEMENT À LA BASE EN SAVANES MARGINALES. MICRO-RÉALISATIONS EN RÉPUBLIQUE DU ZAÏRE [Foundation development in outlying savanna: microfulfillment in the Republic of Zaire]. *Communautés: Arch. Int. de Sociol. de la Coopération et du Développement [France] 1973 (34): 273-291.* Describes two projects undertaken by the Office of Organization of Rural Programs of the National University of Zaire for the development of a farm, 1963, and of a semi-industrial cattle ranch, 1970, in the Kwango savanna with evaluation of their success.

2480. Schaetzen, Yves de. NOTES SUR L'ÉCONOMIE DU ZAÏRE [Notes on the economy of Zaire]. *Rev. Française d'Études Pol. Africaines [France] 1973 8(91): 88-109.* Reports on the economy of Zaire since independence from Belgium, 30 June 1960, through the five-year period of unrest and rebellion, the instability, budgetary disorder, but relative fixed prices of the period following the 1965 coup d'etat of General Joseph Désiré Mobutu, to the adjustment and transition period of 1968-72, after the monetary reform of 1967.

2481. Vanderlinden, J. DEUX ASPECTS DES FINANCES PUBLIQUES COLONIALES [Two aspects of colonial public finance]. *Bull. des Séances de l'Acad. Royale des Sci. d'Outre-Mer [Belgium] 1977 (3): 240-278.* Victor-Félix-Désiré Henquin's (1879-1956) career in Belgian government service spanned 40 years. As colonial bureau chief, he established census procedures which substantially increased tax revenues. His 1912 report on the role of local administrators in tax collection provides insights into problems of fiscal administration in the Congo. In 1935 Henquin worked on modifications of the charter of the Banque du Congo Belge. Henquin is one example of anonymous bureaucrats working to develop feasible fiscal policy. Based on Henquin's personal files (inventory included); 97 notes. M. Schumacher

2482. VanDerSteen, Daniel. LE ZAÏRE MALADE DE SA DÉPENDANCE EXTÉRIEURE: APERÇU HISTORIQUE ET DIAGNOSTIC DE L'ÉCONOMIE ZAÏROISE EN 1978 [Zaire, made sick by its external dependency: a historical overview and diagnosis of the Zairian economy in 1978]. *Genève-Afrique [Switzerland] 1979 17(1): 121-131.* Zaire is fundamentally worse off as an independent state than it was under Belgian colonialism, when colonial authorities diverted state revenues for the development of the infrastructure. Since President Mobutu Sese Seko took power in 1965, exports outside the mineral sector have declined. Although the mineral industry was nationalized, foreign companies have continued to collect a large share of the profits through technical services and interest. 9 tables, 13 notes.

B. S. Fetter

2483. Vellut, Jean-Luc. DÉVELOPPEMENT ET SOUS-DÉVELOPPEMENT AU ZAÏRE: NOTES PRELIMINAIRES POUR UNE PERSPECTIVE HISTORIQUE [Development and underdevelopment in Zaire: preliminary notes for a historical perspective]. *Genève-Afrique [Switzerland] 1979 17(1): 133-139.* Questioning both the liberal assumption of a discontinuity between the colonial Belgian Congo and independent Zaire and the radical assumption of ongoing exploitation by the capitalist metropolis, proposes an alternative explanation of Zaire's economic changes before and after independence. Before 1950, economic policy was predicated on increases in the number of African workers; afterwards the economy became more capital intensive, encouraging not only migration to the cities but increased differentiation between rich and poor in rural areas. The 1960's saw increased migration to the cities and warfare between African classes. Secondary materials.

B. S. Fetter

2484. Vorob'eva, T. A. KREST'IANSKIE INDIVIDUAL'NYE KHOZIAISTVA (PEIZANATY) V BEL'GIISKOM KONGO [Individual peasant farms in the Belgian Congo]. *Narody Azii i Afriki [USSR] 1980 (4): 128-135.* During the entire colonial period the Belgians wanted to use the Congo as a source of cheap agricultural goods. Beginning in the 1930's with the unrest in the Congo and the drop in the farm population, the Belgians saw a need to modernize the traditional agrarian system, and in the 1950's they established special settlements *(paysannats),* where individual use of the land was introduced. Differing one from another in structure, they were an attempt by the Belgians to intensify the African sector in agriculture, a means of resolving economic problems. 2 tables, 27 notes. S. J. Talalay

Politics

2485. Adelman, Kenneth L. THE CHURCH-STATE CONFLICT IN ZAIRE: 1969-1974. *African Studies Rev. 1975 18(1): 102-116.* Shows that, while according to President Mobutu of Zaire, churches should adopt a policy of cooperation and noninterference in state affairs, church-state conflict has grown, 1969-74, concerning education, foreign influence, and popular allegiance.

2486. Adelman, Kenneth L. ZAIRIAN POLITICAL PARTY AS RELIGIOUS SURROGATE. *Africa Today 1976 23(4): 47-58.* Describes the development of the Mouvement Populaire de la Revolution (MPR) by President Mobutu Sese Seko as a conscious effort to create national unity. The MPR has the trappings of religion and appears to be providing viable ideological and religious support for a unified state in Zaire. Based on fieldwork and secondary sources; 36 notes.

G. O. Gagnon

2487. Agyeman, Opoku. KWAME NKRUMAH AND THE CONGO (ZAIRE) REVISITED. *African Rev. [Tanzania] 1974 4(4): 531-542.* Kwame Nkrumah's entry into the Congolese crisis on the side of Patrice Lumumba was a conscious attempt to further the causes of African liberation, unity, and anticolonialism. He failed because the "imperialists were too strong" and because other African leaders feared his dominant leadership in the African unity movement. 53 notes. R. T. Brown

2488. Bekić, Darko. DVADESETGODIŠNJICA "KONGOANSKE KRIZE": PRILOG ZA KOMPLEKSNU ANALIZU [The 20th anniversary of the Congo crisis: toward a comprehensive analysis]. *Politička Misao [Yugoslavia] 1980 17(3): 338-346.* Describes Zaire's accession to independence in 1960 and the events leading up to it. Reviews the subsequent international crisis, particularly the roles of the independent nation's first prime minister, Patrice Lumumba, and Moise Tshombe. Analyzes international reaction to the crisis, especially proceedings at the UN.

2489. Beltrán, Luis. LOS FUNDAMENTOS TRADICIONALES DE LA UNICIDAD DEL PODER EN EL REGIMEN POLITICO DEL ZAIRE [Traditional foundations of the single-power regime in Zaire's political system]. *Rev. de Estudios Pol. [Spain] 1982 (26): 35-56.* In many newly independent African countries the realization of the inadequacy of borrowed political structures and the need to create a state out of heterogeneous populations thrown together by the colonial will has led to a "traditional acculturation" of modern structures tending to legitimize presidential and one-party political regimes. The author attempts to show how this has happened in Zaire and how the single-power system is being justified, using 32 proverbs and sayings from the local languages. 16 notes, list of proverbs. J. V. Coutinho

2490. Bishikwabo, Chubaka. DEUX CHEFS DU BUSHI SOUS LA RÉGIME COLONIAL: KABARE ET NGWESHE (1912-1960) [Two chiefs of the Bushi under the colonial regime: Kabare and Ngweshe, 1912-60]. *Etudes d'Hist. Africaine [Zaire] 1975 7: 89-111.* Biographies of Rugemaninzi of Kabare (1912-36) and Mafundwe of Ngweshe (1895-1937), chiefs of the Bushi in the Congo (now Zaire). Discusses the importance of missionaries, internal Bushi problems, the reigns and conflicts of the two chiefs, their relations with colonial authorities, and events after the end of their reigns. 62 notes. H. L. Calkin

2491. Bly, Viola. *CHALLENGE OF THE CONGO* BY KWAME NKRUMAH. *Pan-African J. [Kenya] 1973 6(2): 244-247.* Reviews Nkrumah's book, which records the first five years of Zaire's independence, 1960-65, exposing the attempts of Western powers to keep Zaire in a state of chaos.

2492. Callaghy, Thomas M. STATE-SUBJECT COMMUNICATION IN ZAIRE: DOMINATION AND THE CONCEPT OF DOMAIN CONSENSUS. *J. of Modern African Studies [Great Britain] 1980 18(3): 469-492.* The government of Mobutu Sese Seko exercises control over the population of Zaire by utilizing the forms and symbols of democracy and African tradition, as well as the rhetoric of Third World political mythology. Beyond the mass meetings, marches, dances, songs, and displays of government symbols, the national army and police forces repress unsanctioned political activity, abuse local populations, and enforce the national *salongo,* or collective labor. The central state in Zaire remains authoritarian and extractive behind the scenes of public rituals mandated by the ruler. Based on Zairian administrative correspondence, reports, and personal observation; 54 notes.

L. W. Truschel

2493. Cola Alberich, Julio. ZAIRE BAJO EL RÉGIMEN PRESIDENCIAL DE MOBUTU [Zaire under Mobutu]. *Rev. de Política Int. [Spain] 1974 (132): 151-166.* Analyzes Mobutu Sese Seko's first year in office, November 1965-November 1966, showing how he effectively consolidated his power, suppressed the Simba and Katanga rebellions, and eliminated his most serious rivals, Joseph Kasavubu and Moise Tshombe. Article to be continued.

2494. Filesi, Cesira. PROGETTI ITALIANI DI PENETRAZIONE ECONOMICA NEL CONGO BELGA (1908-1922) [Italian plans for economic penetration of the Belgian Congo, 1908-22]. *Storia Contemporanea [Italy] 1982 13(2): 251-282.* The Belgian plan to annex the independent kingdom of the Congo in 1907 attracted other European powers which had colonial or commercial interests in the area. Favorable attitudes on the part of Italian politicians were based on economic interests and commercial plans. Few such plans ever materialized; at the end of World War I there existed only three Italian commercial firms in the Congo, all in Leopoldville (Kinshasa). Based on material in the historical archives of the Italian ministries of Foreign and African Affairs; 103 notes. J. V. Coutinho

2495. Franke, Dietrich. STREITKRÄFTE DER VEREINTEN NATIONEN [United Nations forces]. *Archiv des Völkerrechts [West Germany] 1979 18(2): 149-181.* Analyzes problems of international law resulting from the use of UN troops in Korea, the Congo, Cyprus and the Middle East between 1950's and the 1970's.

2496. Gould, David J. and Mushi-Mugumorhagerwa. LA MULTIRATIONALITÉ ET LE SOUS-DÉVELOPPEMENT: ÉCOLOGIE DU PROCESSUS DÉCISIONNEL DANS L'ADMINISTRATION LOCALE ZAÏROISE [Multirationality and underdevelopment: the ecology of the decisionmaking process in local administration in Zaire]. *Can. J. of Pol. Sci. [Canada] 1977 10(2): 261-285.* Examines administrative reform at the local level from the perspective of underdevelopment. Reform in 1973 had the contradictory effect of entrenching iniquities

and privilege and fostering external domination as well. 22 notes.
R. V. Kubicek

2497. Kabwit, Ghislain C. ZAIRE: THE ROOTS OF THE CONTINUING CRISIS. *J. of Modern African Studies [Great Britain] 1979 17(3): 381-407.* Reviews the political, economic, and diplomatic policies that led to widespread disenchantment with the rule of Mobutu Sese Seko in Zaire after 1965. Mobutu's political career was always tightly linked to the United States and the CIA, but between 1965 and 1970, by systematically using the levers of repressive power, he brought a measure of economic development and political stability. Since then massive corruption, violation of human rights, and economic mismanagement have increased political opposition, organized by exile groups in Europe, Angola, and southern Zaire, but he has been consistently supported by Western governments. Based on newspapers, Zaire government publications, and other printed sources; 103 notes.
D. J. Nicholls

2498. Keller, Edmund E. URBANIZATION AND THE EMERGENCE OF THE POLITICS OF INDEPENDENCE: BELGIAN CONGO (ZAIRE). *Mawazo [Uganda] 1974 4(2): 37-52.* Examines events which led up to the 1960 independence of Zaire from Belgium, 1945-60, including increased urbanization following World War II, economic development, the emergence of a bourgeoisie, and growth in political participation.

2499. Kowalak, Władysław. MOBUTYZM—NOWA RELIGIA? [Mobutism, a new religion?]. *Życie i Myśl [Poland] 1975 25(9): 41-50.* Mobutism according to Mobutu Sese Seko, its founder, is above all an inseparable bond between the Republic of Zaire and its leader, a national movement aiming at the unification of the nation toward a better future. It is difficult to say to which degree the cult of Mobutu and Mobutism will find echo among the people of Zaire; there is a difference in what Mobutu preaches about himself and public opinion. It is difficult to foresee whether the cult of Mobutu will reach such proportions as that of Simon Kimbangu or share the lot of the cult of Kwame Nkrumah of Ghana.
M. A. J. Swiecicka

2500. Kristiansen, Rolf. NORSK MILITAER INNSATS FOR DE FORENTE NASJONER. KONGO-KRISEN [The Norwegian military contribution to the United Nations: the Congo Crisis]. *Norsk Militaert Tidsskrift [Norway] 1973 143(4): 175-177, (5): 239-245.* Part I. The Norwegian contribution was considerable and covered a wide field, including high command, and was maintained throughout the crisis. Part II. Norway's contribution included an antiaircraft battalion, military police, aircraft and pilots, medical and veterinary staff, and workshop personnel, a total of 1,173 officers and men.

2501. Laidi, Zaki. LES RAPPORTS INTERNATIONAUX À L'ÉPREUVE DES CONFLITS AFRICAINS: REFLEXIONS A PARTIR DE L'ANALYSE DE LA 2ME CRISE DU SHABA (1) [International relations on trial in African conflicts: reflections on the second Shaba crisis, part 1]. *Afrique et l'Asie Moderne [France] 1979 (1): 25-42.* Studies the recent Shaba crisis as a point of reference for studying the political situation in Africa and the roles of the USSR, Cuba, and the United States. Article to be continued.

2502. Marchand, Jean. LA BELGIQUE ET LE CONGO ZAÏRE [Belgium and Congo (Zaire)]. *Écrits de Paris [France] 1973 (322): 59-75.* Belgium has continued to occupy a privileged position in the Congo (Zaire) since independence, despite external efforts to reinforce the separation.

2503. Newbury, David and Newbury, Catharine. KING AND CHIEF: COLONIAL POLITICS ON IJWI ISLAND (ZAIRE). *Int. J. of African Hist. Studies 1982 15(2): 221-246.* Ijwi island in Lake Kivu, on the border of Zaire, developed two different chieftaincies while under colonial rule. Though the area was small and the population homogeneous, different historical bases led to different attitudes toward alien rule. Based on author-collected oral data and colonial archives; map, fig., 63 notes.
R. T. Brown

2504. Nimer, Benjamin. CONGO POLITICS AND THE PITFALLS OF IDEAL TYPE ANALYSIS. *Internat. J. of African Hist. Studies 1973 6(2): 315-334.* Reviews Jean-Claude Willame's *Patrimonialism and Political Change in the Congo* (Stanford University Press, 1972), which is based on a doctoral dissertation at the University of California, Berkeley, and uses Congolese documents (1962-66) and interviews with Congolese political officials for primary sources. 36 notes.
C. W. Olson

2505. Nzongola-Ntalaja. THE CONTINUING STRUGGLE FOR NATIONAL LIBERATION IN ZAIRE. *J. of Modern African Studies [Great Britain] 1979 17(4): 595-614.* Elucidates the factors underlying the rise of political opposition to the regime of Mobutu Sese Seko in Zaire between 1965 and 1978, clarifying the background to the Shaba wars of 1977-78. The growth of organized opposition may be traced from the ideological split between radicals and moderates in the anticolonial movement, leadership struggles among the moderates, the neocolonial character of the postcolonial state, and Mobutu's autocratic rule. These factors have led to a continuing political crisis within Zaire, uniting the democratic struggle against Mobutu's reign of terror with the popular "second independence" movement that developed in the late 60's on the basis of Lumumbist radicalism. Based on printed sources and secondary works; 51 notes.
D. J. Nicholls

2506. Ogunbadejo, Oye. CONFLICT IN AFRICA: A CASE STUDY OF THE SHABA CRISIS, 1977. *World Affairs 1979 141(3): 219-234.* Examines factors that promote conflict in Zaire, specifically the Angolan invasion of the Shaba in 1977.

2507. Ongenaet, Chr. ZAIRE, POLITIEKE STRUCTUREN VROEGER EN NU [Zaire, former and contemporary political structures]. *Spiegel Hist. [Netherlands] 1974 9(9): 494-499.* Surveys the political structure of Zaire, principally in the precolonial period. Biblio.
G. D. Homan

2508. Pétillon, L. A. PRESENTATION DE SON LIVRE: *COURTS METRAGES AFRICAINS POUR SERVIR A L'HISTOIRE* [Presenting *Courts Metrages Africains pour Servir à l'Histoire*]. *Bull. des Séances de l'Acad. Royale des Sci. d'Outre-Mer [Belgium] 1980 26(2): 105-121.* Much of the history of the Belgian Congo's move toward independence in the years following World War II has been cloaked in silence. This book examines the political background in Belgium and in Africa, reanalyzes events of the late 1950's, and provides new insights into Belgian policy toward its most important colony. Following independence, Zaire could have recovered economically with more Belgian support. 3 notes.
M. Schumacher

2509. Piazza, Calogero. I BAYAKA DEL KWANGO E LA POLITICA COLONIALE BELGA (1880-1960) (II) [The Yaka of the Kwango and the Belgian colonial doctrine, 1880-1960]. *Africa [Italy] 1978 33(3): 405-418.* Continued from previous article (see next abstract). Illustrates the evolution of Belgian colonial doctrine and its practical implementation with particular reference to a historical site of the Congo (Zaire) known as the kingdom of the BaYaka on the right bank of the river Kwango. From 1880 to 1960, six different forms of administration have taken place: bonds, subjection, trusteeship, nationalities, protection, association, and emancipation. The Yaka people, who staunchly resisted Belgian domination, derived from these experiences a conservative political attitude, which reflects itself in the rejection of modern mass nationalism.
J

2510. Piazza, Calogero. I BAYAKA DEL KWANGO E LA POLITICA COLONIALE BELGA (1880-1960) [The Bayaka of the Kwango and Belgian colonial policy, 1880-1960]. *Africa [Italy] 1978 33(2): 187-215.* Treats the course of Belgian colonial policy in the Belgian Congo, now the Republic of Zaire, in its relationship with the Yaka people of the Kwango River basin. The Belgians, with few administrators to rule a vast area, tried indirect government through the chiefs, a policy which often failed due to lack of cooperation from native authorities. Local ethnic distinctions were preserved and encouraged. Only in the 1950's was an attempt made to modernize administration, but by then independence was imminent. Indirect rule and ethnic autonomy left a legacy of ethnic conflict for the newly independent country. Article to be continued (see preceding abstract). 137 notes.
J. C. Billigmeier

2511. Saksena, K. P. HAMMARSKJOLD AND THE CONGO CRISIS—A REVIEW. *India Q. [India] 1978 34(2): 193-210.* Reviews four books on the role of UN Secretary General Dag Hammarskjold during the Congo crisis in the early 1960's: Brian Urquhart's *Hammarskjold,* Rajeshwar Dayal's *Mission of Hammarskjold: The Congo Crisis,* Ram Chandra Pradhan's *The United Nations and the Congo Crisis,* and B. Chakravorty's *The Congo Operation 1960-63.* Gives particular attention to the roles played by President Joseph Kasavubu, Prime Minister Patrice Lumumba, and the secretary general's special representative in the Congo, Rajeshwar Dayal. Secondary sources; 33 notes. S. H. Frank

2512. Salmon, Pierre. UNE CORRESPONDANCE EN PARTIE INÉDITE DE PATRICE LUMUMBA [Unpublished correspondence of Patrice Lumumba]. *Bull. des Séances de l'Acad. Royale des Sci. d'Outre-Mer [Belgium] 1974 (3): 359-368.* Presents the 1956-57 correspondence between Lumumba and Paul Sancke of the Belgian Office of Publicity about the publication of his book, *Le Congo terre d'avenir est-il menacé?* (1961). In his book he explained the evolution of the Congo and of Congolese-Belgian relations. Lumumba's goals were to translate Congolese thought in order to enlighten Belgian authorities about Black hopes for the future and the need for harmony between the groups. Primary sources. H. D. Nycz

2513. Schatzberg, Michael G. THE CHIEFS OF UPOTO: POLITICAL ENCAPSULATION AND THE TRANSFORMATION OF TRADITION IN NORTHWESTERN ZAIRE. *Cultures et Développement [Belgium] 1980 12(2): 235-269.* Relates the history of the Bapoto tribe in Upoto (northwestern Zaire) from the middle 1870's; focuses on changes in tradition and its encapsulated political structure.

2514. Schatzberg, Michael G. FIDELITÉ AU GUIDE: THE J.M.P.R. IN ZAIRIAN SCHOOLS. *J. of Modern African Studies [Great Britain] 1978 16(3): 417-437.* The aim of the Young People's Revolutionary Popular Movement (JMPR), the youth wing of Zaire's political party, has been to educate and mobilize the youth in support of President Mobutu Sese Seko. However the process of indoctrination has been unsuccessful because the teachers have shown skepticism and students and instructors contempt for manual work along with feelings of uncertainty for their future. Based on field work interviews and secondary sources; 41 notes. A. Sbacchi

2515. Schatzberg, Michael G. THE STATE AND THE ECONOMY: THE "RADICALIZATION OF THE REVOLUTION" IN MOBUTU'S ZAIRE. *Can. J. of African Studies [Canada] 1980 14(2): 239-257.* Examines the background, evolution of policy, and effects of President Mobutu Sese Seko's radicalization plan announced on 30 December 1974 as a new phase of the Zairian revolution. Calling for radical social and economic changes, the plan allowed the state to take ownership of many businesses, small plantations, and foreign enterprises, placing directorship of these in the hands of high-ranking government officials. Suffering from ambiguous implementation and failing to carry out policies aimed to benefit the interior rural population, the plan was a failure and merely strengthened the already powerful politico-commercial bourgeoisie. 66 notes. S

2516. Serrano Padilla, Vicente. EFERVESCENCIA POLÍTICA EN EL CONGO [Political turmoil in the Congo]. *Rev. de Política Int. [Spain] 1973 (128): 125-137, (129): 101-110, (130): 113-121; 1974 (131): 157-165.* Traces the political history of the Congo since ca. 1960, concentrating on the political upheavals which have afflicted the country both nationally and regionally.

2517. Singleton, Seth. CONFLICT RESOLUTION IN AFRICA: THE CONGO AND THE RULES OF THE GAME. *Pan-African J. [Kenya] 1975 8(1): 1-18.* A principal problem for the independent African states was to establish rules for conflict resolution. The Congo crisis, 1960-65, was fundamental in establishing how, and by whom, conflict should be resolved. Despite two solutions attempted in the 1960's: 1) that African states as a group should control independence movements, and 2) that conflicts should be decided by African states with international aid: both were rejected. Direct bilateral foreign intervention in Africa without Pan-African sanction was condemned. Moreover, US influence over UN policy prevented the use of the latter as an agency for conflict resolution which would be responsive to African wishes. The Organization for African Unity was shown to be weak and although rules were established through the Congo experience, fundamental disagreements did not change, and this prevented the effective Pan-African resolution of African conflicts. 34 notes. S

2518. Traugott, Mark. THE ECONOMIC ORIGINS OF THE KWILU REBELLION. *Comparative Studies in Soc. and Hist. [Great Britain] 1979 21(3): 459-479.* Due to economic conditions, Pierre Mulele and the rebels in Kwilu province in Zaire sought to radically transform society in 1964.

2519. Turner, Thomas. MOBUTU'S ZAIRE: PERMANENTLY ON THE VERGE OF COLLAPSE? *Current Hist. 1981 80(464): 124-127, 130.* Assesses the performance of Mobutu Sese Seko's regime in Zaire, in power since 1965, focusing on its many political and economic deficiencies, and discusses the reasons for its extensive US support.

2520. Turner, Thomas. PEASANTS REBELLION AND ITS SUPPRESSION IN SANKURU, ZAIRE. *Pan-African J. [Kenya] 1974 7(3): 193-215.* Rebels controlled Sankuru from August to October 1964 before they were driven out by the national army. The author draws a physical picture of Sankuru, outlines conditions leading to rebellion, and provides a chronology of the occupation of Sankuru. Describes actions of rebel leaders, nicknamed the Simba, and the reactions of local people. The rebellion represented a class struggle against the governing elites and national bourgeoisie, yet many leaders were elitists. The inconsistencies in Simba action contributed to their defeat. 40 notes. H. G. Soff

2521. Vanderlinden, J. À PROPOS DE LA CONSTITUTION ZAÏROISE DU 15 FEVRIER 1978 [Zaire's 1978 constitution]. *Bull. des Séances de l'Acad. Royale des Sci. d'Outre-Mer [Belgium] 1978 (3): 334-356.* In July 1977, Mobutu Sese Seko announced a constitutional reform. The author compares the 1978 constitution to its predecessor (1974). The new longer text stabilizes the position of Chief of State, gives enormous power to the President of the Conseil Judiciaire, and limits the powers of the National Legislative Council. No fundamental political changes were made. Zaire remains as undemocratic as before. Based on secondary sources; 15 notes. M. Schumacher

2522. Vellut, Jean-Luc. HEGEMONIES EN CONSTRUCTION: ARTICULATIONS ENTRE ETAT ET ENTREPRISES DANS LE BLOC COLONIAL BELGE (1908-1960) [Hegemonies in construction: articulations between state and enterprises in the Belgian colonial bloc]. *Can. J. of African Studies [Canada] 1982 16(2): 313-330.* The political economy of the Belgian Congo was clearly marked by the interdependence of the state and private enterprise. The latter relied on the state to partition the territory into economic and social areas, giving preference to the priorities of various sectors of the colonial economy; the former was dependent on colonial business for its tax revenue. The agreement between the colonial companies and the state constituted a power bloc which was independent of any effective political control. One can see, in this relative autonomy of colonial powers, a legacy of Léopold's system (Congo State). The structural features of this hegemony can be analyzed in Brussels or at the local level in the Congo. If it is true that each member of the colonial coalition enjoyed a certain degree of autonomy, it is also true that limits were set by big business policy. The colonial state has never been able to take advantage of its position inside the governing bodies of big companies and is unable to participate effectively in the planning of development strategies which will determine the future of the colony. J

2523. Vinokurov, Iu. PATRIS LUMUMBA: CHELOVEK I BORETS [Patrice Lumumba as a person and fighter]. *Aziia i Afrika Segodnia [USSR] 1980 (2): 18-21.* The Congo's national hero was a victim of an imperialist conspiracy that became the main cause of the Congolese crisis. Patrice Lumumba was accused of violating democratic principles and neglecting the national interest. But today Africa and the whole world recall the names of Lumumba's murderers only to hold them up to shame and contempt, and Lumumba is considered a great contributor to the African struggle for independence. Industrial enterprises, streets, and educational establishments are named for him, and memorials have been erected to his memory. J/S

2524. Vinokurov, Iu. POVSTANCHESKOE DVIZHENIE 1963-1965 GG. V KONGO [The rebel movement of 1963-65 in the Congo]. *Narody Azii i Afriki [USSR] 1981 (5): 102-109.* The rebellion launched in the summer of 1963 by the Congolese People's Army of Liberation had as its objective the overthrow of the government and the freeing of the Congo from domination by foreign monopolies. By the second half of 1964 the revolt had encompassed some two-thirds of the national territory containing half the population. Nonetheless, the rebellion was fatally compromised throughout by insufficient political preparation, weak organization, and ethnic and regional divisions. These opened the way to intervention by NATO-backed Belgian and American forces. F. A. K. Yasamee

2525. Weissman, Stephen R. THE CONGO. *J. of Modern African Studies [Great Britain] 1973 11(4): 649-653.* A review article on the following books that examine the political conflicts in the Congo: Jean-Claude Willame, *Patrimonialism and Political Change in the Congo* (Stanford U. Pr., 1972); Cléophas Kamitatu, *La Grande mystification du Congo-Kinshasa: les crimes de Mobutu* (Paris: Maspéro, 1971); Thomas Kanza, *Conflict in the Congo* (Harmondsworth: Penguin Books, 1972); Brian Urquhart, *Hammarskjöld* (London: The Bodley Head, 1973).

2526. Welch, Claude E., Jr. IDEOLOGICAL FOUNDATIONS OF REVOLUTION IN KWILU. *African Studies Rev. 1975 18(2): 116-128.* Investigates the development of radical revolutionary attitudes in the province of Kwilu, Zaire, from the 1930's to the rebellion of 1963.

2527. Willame, Jean-Claude. THE ART OF MISQUOTATION: A REPLY TO BENJAMIN NIMER. *Int. J. of African Hist. Studies 1974 7(1): 120-123.* A reply to Benjamin Nimer's review article of Willame's *Patrimonialism and Political Change in the Congo* (see abstract 2504). 5 notes. M. M. McCarthy

2528. Willame, Jean-Claude. LA SECONDE GUERRE DU SHABA [The second Shaba war]. *Genève-Afrique [Switzerland] 1977-78 16(1): 9-26.* Analyzes the rebellion waged in May 1978 by the Front de Libération Nationale du Congo (FLNC) in Kolwezi, Republic of Zaire, against General Mobutu's regime. Discusses the conditions of the rebellious forces, the preparation of their offensive, the attack and occupation of Kolwezi, Belgian diplomatic action, and French military intervention. Notes that the war weakened both the regime and the FLNC. Based on press and radio information, eyewitnesses' statements, and interviews; 59 notes. G. P. Cleyet

2529. Willame, Jean-Claude. PATRIARCHAL STRUCTURES AND FACTIONAL POLITICS. TOWARD AN UNDERSTANDING OF THE DUALIST SOCIETY. *Cahiers d'Études Africaines [France] 1973 13(2): 326-355.* Describes the patriarchal tradition of ethnic and family structures in the post-independence politics of the Kwango region of Zaire. The local rulers did not suffer from colonial dominion, for the Belgians were never able to impose direct rule. Rural Africans are exploited both by the patriarchs and the urban political élite controlling the central government. 62 notes. J. C. Billigmeier

2530. Zezeze, Kalonji-T. LA DEUXIEME GUERRE DU SHABA DANS LA PRESSE "PRO-INTERVENTIONNISTE" EN FRANCE [The Second Shaba War in the pro-interventionist press in France]. *Genève-Afrique [Switzerland] 1982 20(1): 147-169.* A spatial analysis of the coverage of the French intervention in Zaire (Shaba Two) in 1978 covering two newspapers, *Le Figaro* and *L'Aurore.* Demonstrates how pro-Giscard editors encouraged government intervention by giving the story lots of space and by reducing the issue to one of Communist provocation. Based on a spatial analysis of the two newspapers for the period 15-26 May 1978. Biblio., 9 notes, appendix. B. S. Fetter

2531. —. THE STYLE OF MOBUTU. *Africa Report 1975 20(2): 2-3.* Discusses the seeming cult of personality encouraged by Zaire president Mobutu Sese Seko which has, as its end, not personal glorification but political unity and the improvement of national self-image. S

Society

2532. Adams, Lois. WOMEN IN ZAIRE: DISPARATE STATUS AND ROLES. Lindsay, Beverly, ed. *Comparative Perspectives of Third World Women: The Impact of Race, Sex, and Class* (New York: Praeger, 1980): 55-77. Discusses the conflict between the status of women in Zaire based on the Zairian constitution and its legal code, and their traditional role which results in their dependence on men, tracing women's status in marriage and the family, their opportunities for education, and their position in the labor force and in public life since colonial times, focusing on the 1960's and 1970's. Since historical conditions have changed, women's status and role will change in the future also.

2533. Bernard, Guy. L'AFRICAIN ET LA VILLE [The African and the city]. *Cahiers d'Études Africaines [France] 1973 13(3): 575-586.* Kinshasa (originally Léopoldville), capital of Zaire, was built in a dual fashion: one city, modern and comfortable, for the white colonial administrators and merchants; another, sprawling and poorly built, for the Africans. With the end of Belgian rule and departure of most of the whites, the African bourgeoisie took control of the government and the former European city with all its amenities; the masses of blacks continued to crowd into the slums. The city is growing very fast, and urban life is full of vitality; whatever its problems, it seems to the African people a great improvement over the village. 3 tables, 25 notes. J. C. Billigmeier

2534. Betts, Tristram F. RURAL REFUGEES IN AFRICA. *Int. Migration Rev. 1981 15(1-2): 213-218.* The case of Angolan refugees in Zaire shows that although spontaneous settlement of refugees in areas near their homeland borders mitigates the traumatic shock effect of the refugee experience, it ignores certain vital factors, among which are the dilution of already limited health and education services, the risks of overtaxing the land when such large influxes occur, and the risk of intermittent fighting across the borders of origin.

2535. Blondeel, W. DE "COMMISSION PERMANENTE POUR LA PROTECTION DES INDIGÈNES" EN HET DEMOGRAFISCH PROBLEEM IN BELGISCH KONGO DE ALARMKREET VAN 1919 [The Permanent Commission for the Protection of Natives and the warning of a demographic problem in the Belgian Congo in 1919]. *Bull. des Séances de l'Acad. Royale des Sci. d'Outre-Mer [Belgium] 1976 (3): 272-315.* The commission warned in 1919 of the existence of a demographic problem in the Belgian Congo. The author analyzes the causes of population decline as recognized by the commission, the remedies which it suggested, and the importance of individual members' interventions. 89 notes, 2 appendixes. R. O. Khan

2536. Burke, J. and Mortelmans, J. ROL VAN BELGIË IN DE STRIJD TEGEN DE SLAAPZIEKTE EN DE DIERLIJKE TRYPANOSOMIASES EN HUN STUDIE [Belgium's role in the fight against sleeping sickness and animal trypanosomiasis and in their study]. *Bull. des Séances de l'Acad. Royale des Sci. d'Outre-Mer [Belgium] 1980 Supplement(1): 111-135.* Reports on the pioneering laboratory and fieldwork in Zaire by Belgian medical personnel and Belgium's continuing contributions to the fight against Africa's endemic human and animal trypanosomiasis. First reports of sleeping sickness in the Lower Congo (1885) were quickly followed by the establishment of a bacteriological laboratory in Léopoldville, and other research institutes were founded through the 20th century. Doctors like Jean-Emile Van Campenhout, Alphonse Broden, and Jerôme Rodhain, veterinarians, and colonists interested in stockbreeding, have made important contributions to the diagnosis, treatment, and prevention of trypanosomiasis in humans and animals. G. Herritt

2537. Chakirwa, Mushagasha. NOTE SUR LA DYNAMIQUE D'UNE MISSION DU KIVU: NYANGEZI (1906-1929) [A note on the dynamics of a mission to Kivu: Nyangezi 1906-29]. *Etudes d'Hist Africaine [Zaire] 1975 7: 125-135.* The Catholic mission of Nyangezi was established among the Kivu in central Africa from 1906 to 1929. It established political alliances with the military posts and the local authorities. Through the installation of chapels and schools it sought to combat Protestantism. It operated within the colonial context and its economic and social dimensions, as well as its concepts of life, customs, and mentality. 18 notes. H. L. Calkin

2538. DeCraemer, Willy. A SOCIOLOGIST'S ENCOUNTER WITH THE JAMAA. *J. of Religion in Africa [Netherlands] 1976 8(3): 153-174.* Jamaa is a religious movement in Zaire that began within the Catholic Church in 1953. Although much of the movement has moved underground, it is still flourishing. The author compares it with other central African religious movements and examines its distinctive features. In 1974 the government passed a special decree banning Jamaa, and since that time its activities have been limited. Based on personal experience; 12 notes. H. G. Soff

2539. Depelchin, Jacques. THE BASONGYE VILLAGE OF LUPUPA NGYE: A MERRIAM WORLD. *Int. J. of African Hist. Studies 1976 9(4): 606-617.* A review essay of *An African World: The Basongye Village of Lupupa Ngye* by Alan P. Merriam (Bloomington: Indiana U. Pr., 1974). Merriam's work is one of the most flagrant examples of colonial anthropology to appear in recent years. Colonial anthropology customarily ignores a most important ethnic group, the colonizers. Merriam never confronts the colonial situation in Lupupa Ngye (Zaire) for what it is: in the abstract the subjugation of the precapitalist mode of production to the dominant capitalist method; in concrete historical terms the political subjection of the African population coupled with the expropriation of their land and labor. He resorts to the perspective of the ethnographic present, using it as a method of investigating societies as they existed in the past by means of contemporary observation. 16 notes. M. M. McCarthy

2540. Dimandja, Luhaka. LES RÉSEAUX SCOLAIRES MÉTHODISTES AU SHABA (KATANGA) ET AU KASAI SOUS LA PÉRIODE COLONIALE (1910-1960) [The Methodist scholarly network in Shaba and Kasai during the colonial period, 1910-60]. *Études d'Hist. Africaine [Zaire] 1976 8: 55-85.* Methodism began its program of evangelization and education in the Congo in 1910, several years after the Catholics. Their material means and human resources were not always enough to accomplish the tasks they attempted. In addition they were considered to be a "foreign church." Methodist education, therefore, was not as well organized, diverse or extensive as that of the Catholics. It did make an undeniable contribution to the formation of an African petite bourgeoisie which was the avant-garde of independence in 1960. Map, 2 tables, 87 notes. H. L. Calkin

2541. Fabian, Johannes. KAZI: CONCEPTUALIZATIONS OF LABOR IN A CHARISMATIC MOVEMENT AMONG SWAHILI-SPEAKING WORKERS. *Cahiers d'Études Africaines [France] 1973 13(2): 293-325.* The Jamaa ("family") is a movement among Christian industrial workers (mostly employed by the Union Minière) in the province of Katanga in Zaire. It uses the Katangan dialect of Swahili as its official language. Practically all expressions of Jamaa doctrine are pervaded by the conception of labor *(kazi),*with images and metaphors derived from the experience and life-style of an industrial worker. 22 notes, biblio. J. C. Billigmeier

2542. Fabian, Johannes. POPULAR CULTURE IN AFRICA: FINDINGS AND CONJECTURES. *Africa [Great Britain] 1978 48(4): 315-334.* Discusses the representation, 1950-70's, of the male-female relationship in the towns of Shaba, Zaire in popular songs, the teachings of the Jamaa religious movement, and popular painting. Shows how a central theme appears dispersed in these three fields. Table, 11 notes, biblio., 2 appendixes. P. J. Taylorson

2543. Feltz, Gaëtan. UN ÉCHEC DE L'IMPLANTATION SCOLAIRE EN MILIEU RURAL: LE CAS DE LA LULUA ET DU KATANGA CENTRAL DE 1920 À 1960 [A blow to educational development in a rural environment: the case of Lulua and central Katanga, 1920-60]. *Can. J. of African Studies [Canada] 1980 13(3): 441-459.* The creation and development of a school system for the rural regions of Lulua and Lake Moero in Shaba (formerly Katanga), was hampered during the colonial period by certain factors which kept it from achieving its objectives, which were to stabilize and assure the development of the rural society. This lack of success may be attributed on the one hand to the inadequacy of the structure of the educational system in the face of rapid development of the copper belt of the Haut Katanga and the attractiveness of the industrial and mining centers, and on the other hand to colonial policies which tended to exploit the rural population rather than trying to integrate them within a total social, political, and economic framework for the development of the whole country. This imbalance, indeed the disintegration of the rural way of life, is still an important consideration. Map, 2 fig., 45 notes. J

2544. Feltz, Gaëten. ÉCOLE RURALE ET EXPANSION MISSIONNAIRE AU SHABA (1885-1939) [Rural schools and missionary expansion in Shaba, 1885-1939]. *Études d'Hist. Africaine [Zaire] 1976 8: 9-53.* Religious missions were the first intruders in Africa following the explorers. Their purpose was evangelization of the populations without distinction of age or sex. The Catholic Church in Shaba developed a series of schools, 1882-1939. Education and evangelization were overlapping. The size of the country, the dispersion of the population, the diversity of languages and customs, the resistance of authorities to all evolutionary tendencies, and the passivity of the masses were all difficulties which rural education faced. 2 maps, 2 tables, 118 notes. H. L. Calkin

2545. Geuns, Andre. CHRONOLOGIE DES MOUVEMENTS RELIGIEUX INDÉPENDANTS AU BAS-ZAIRE, PARTICULIÈREMENT DU MOUVEMENT FONDÉ PAR LE PROPHÈTE SIMON KIMBANGU [Chronology of independent religious movements in Bas-Zaire, particularly of the movement founded by the prophet Simon Kimbangu]. *J. of Religion in Africa [Netherlands] 1974 6(3): 187-222.* Outlines the Kimbanguist movement. Although the prophet operated for only six months, his Church of Christ on Earth is an extensive and well-structured organization. Biblio. H. G. Soff

2546. Irvine, Cecilia. THE BIRTH OF THE KIMBANGUIST MOVEMENT IN THE BAS-ZAIRE 1921. *J. of Religion in Africa [Netherlands] 1974 6(1): 23-76.* Simon Kimbangu, a member of the Baptist Church at Ngombe Lutete, became a revolutionary prophet in 1921. He was arrested and sentenced to life imprisonment by the Belgian authorities and was not supported by more conservative Protestants. Events from 11 February 1921 to 3 February 1922 are outlined. 43 notes, appendixes. H. G. Soff

2547. Janzen, John M. DEEP THOUGHT: STRUCTURE AND INTENTION IN KONGO PROPHETISM, 1910-1921. *Social Res. 1979 46(1): 106-139.* A 1964 study relates contemporary Kongo cosmology to the Kongo prophet movement of 1921 in an examination of the intentions of prophetic acts following the hardships of early colonial days between 1880 and 1920.

2548. Jewsiewicki, Bogumil. LA CONTESTATION SOCIALE ET LA NAISSANCE DU PROLÉTARIAT ZAÏRE AU COURS DE LA PREMIÈRE MOITIÉ DU XXe SIÈCLE [Social resistance and the birth of the working class in Zaire at the beginning of the 20th century]. *Can. J. of African Studies [Canada] 1976 10(1): 47-70.* In seeking common expressions of African anticolonialism, the author principally analyzes: 1) African religious movements as manifestations of anticolonialism in Zaire; 2) ethnicity as a new principle of social identification in colonial Zaire, especially in relations between ethnicity and urban life; and 3) the African workers' resistance movement and the formation of the African working class in colonial Zaire. The author emphasizes African traditional religious movements as a major expression of social contestation. Based on government documents and secondary works; 57 notes. J

2549. Kara-Murza, A. A. KIMBANGIZM [Kimbanguism]. *Voprosy Istorii [USSR] 1980 (12): 172-176.* In 1921 Protestant missionaries heard about a strange holiness reigning among Africans in Nkamba. The African Christian Simon Kimbangu (b. 1889) had declared himself a prophet and allegedly performed miracles. He attracted many followers in the Belgian Congo and in neighboring Portuguese and French colonies. Kimbangu died in 1951 having been jailed for his revolutionary associations. Kimbanguism continues to have many followers to this day, although it has lost features of its opposition to colonialism and become solely a religious teaching. Based on E. Andersson, *Messianic Popular Movements in the Lower Congo* (Uppsala, 1958) and other sources; 15 notes. S. J. Talalay

2550. Kuntala, Kina. LES ORIGINES DU KIMBANGUISME [The origins of Kimbanguism]. *Genève-Afrique [Switzerland] 1977-78 16(1): 135-139.* Describes the expansion of the native movement of Kimbanguism, named after its originator, African prophet and evangelist Simon Kimbangu, who preached a Christian doctrine, not bound to colonization, but to divine love and the African's freedom of belief. 4 notes. G. P. Cleyet

2551. MacGaffey, Wyatt. CULTURAL ROOTS OF KONGO PROPHETISM. *Hist. of Religions 1977 17(2): 177-193.* Explores a way of diachronically comparing Kimbanguism, a modern African religious movement, with Antonism, which occurred two centuries earlier among the same peoples, the Bakongo of Western Zaire. The question whether there were in Kongo history figures comparable to modern prophets (healers in the public interest) allows obvious resemblances between modern followers of Simon Kimbangu and those of the prophetess Beatrice of the Antonines in the first decade of the 18th century to be examined. 36 notes. N. A. Williamson

2552. Mobutu Sese-Seko. MOBUTO SPEAKS. *Africa Report 1975 20(2): 4-6.* Text of a speech given by Zaire president Mobutu Sese Seko, sketching Zaire's political goals and Africa's relations with the United States. S

2553. Monnier, Laurent. UNE INTERPRÉTATION ORIGINALE DU KIMBANGUISME: CELLE DE WYATT MACGAFFEY [Kimbanguism's original interpretation: Wyatt MacGaffey]. *Genève-Afrique [Switzerland] 1977-78 16(1): 139-143.* Analyzes anthropologist Wyatt MacGaffey's interpretation of Kimbanguism (named after its originator, prophet Simon Kimbangu), as a messianic movement. Messianism is an element of Zaire's social and cultural system, and Kimbanguism was not a reaction to colonial repression, but to a policy perceived as the expression of "integral anarchy." Based on MacGaffey's reseach work in Lower Zaire in 1964-66; 5 notes. G. P. Cleyet

2554. Mufuka, N. Nyamayaro. AMERICAN PRESBYTERIAN MISSIONARIES IN SOUTH-WEST KASAI (CONGO) 1905-1962. *J. of the Can. Church Hist. Soc. [Canada] 1977 19(3-4): 190-207.* Traces the growing involvement and changing attitude of American Presbyterians in Zaire until it gained independence. Americans first went there in 1871 when the Belgian government employed the American journalist Henry M. Stanley. The missionaries of the American Presbyterian Church acted not in the interests of the government but in those of the Zairean people. They spoke out against the Belgian government's use of forced labor and, compared to European missionaries, were less aloof and bigoted in their relations with the African people. But like most Americans, they feared the loss of order when the Belgians unexpectedly proclaimed Zairean independence in 1960. Despite the initial chaos and turmoil, the American missionaries adjusted well to the new conditions and were determined to continue their work in the very different environment that resulted. Based on secondary as well as published and unpublished primary sources; 53 notes. J. A. Kicklighter

2555. Munzihirwa, Christophe. BASES ÉCONOMIQUES DU POUVOIR MONARCHIQUE DE KABARE. LA VACHE ET LE SOC (1900-1960) [Economic bases of the monarchic power of Kabare: the cow and the plowshare, 1900-60]. *Rev. de l'Inst. de Sociol. [Belgium] 1978 (3): 183-207.* Studies the partly feudal socioeconomic system, 1900-60, of the kingdom of Kabare in a densely populated and entirely agrarian area at the eastern border of what is today the Republic of Zaire.

2556. Rimlinger, Gaston V. ADMINISTRATIVE TRAINING AND MODERNIZATION IN ZAIRE. *J. of Development Studies [Great Britain] 1976 12(4): 364-382.* Analyzes the rise and fall of the Ecole Nationale d'Administration of Kinshasa, 1961-71.

2557. Romaniuk, A. INCREASE IN NATURAL FERTILITY DURING THE EARLY STAGES OF MODERNIZATION: EVIDENCE FROM AN AFRICAN CASE STUDY, ZAIRE. *Population Studies [Great Britain] 1980 34(2): 293-310.* Infertility in premodern civilizations in Central Africa is credited to prolonged breast-feeding, postnatal abstinence, and pathological infertility.

2558. Rymenam, J. CLASSES SOCIALES, POUVOIR ET ÉCONOMIE AU ZAÏRE OU "COMMENT LE SOUS-DÉVELOPPEMENT ENRICHIT LES GOUVERNEMENTS" [Social classes, power, and economics in Zaire: how underdevelopment enriches governments]. *Genève-Afrique [Switzerland] 1980 18(1): 45-53.* The ruling class in Zaire has grown rich despite diminished production. This group, consisting of relatives of President Mobutu and certain government officials, derives its profits from control of economic institutions rather than from direct taxes on production. Secondary materials; 6 notes. B. S. Fetter

2559. Sanders, James. THE VERNON ANDERSON PAPERS. *Hist. in Africa 1981 8: 361-364.* Vernon Anderson was a Presbyterian missionary in Zaire from 1921 until 1946. A collection of his letters, notebooks, and other materials is inventoried here. Primary source; note. A. C. Drysdale

2560. Schyns, C.; Fossa, A.; and Colaert, J. L'ÉPIDÉMIE DE CHOLÉRA DANS LE SUD-KIVU [The cholera epidemic in southern Kivu province, Zaire]. *Bull. des Séances de l'Acad. Royale des Sci. d'Outre-Mer [Belgium] 1979 (3): 451-465.* Cholera appeared in Kivu province, Zaire, in May 1978 in epidemic proportions. Vaccination helped reduce the number of cases and their intensity. Women were the most frequent victims. Secondary sources; biblio. M. Schumacher

2561. Vansina, Jan. MWASI'S TRIALS. *Daedalus 1982 111(2): 49-70.* Discusses the plight of Mwasi, the wife of a student, Mobali, at Lovanium University in Zaire after his abduction into the army on 3 June 1971, in a government crackdown on the intelligentsia.

2562. Wrzesinska, Alicja. CONTEMPORANEOUSNESS OF YOUNG AFRICAN GIRLS' ATTITUDES. *Africa [Italy] 1981 36(2): 183-208.* Examines the influence of schools on the attitudes of female students toward marriage and family in Kinshasa, Zaire. Based on a study done in Zaire from 1969 to 1972. J. Powell

2563. Yates, Barbara A. THE ORIGINS OF LANGUAGE POLICY IN ZAIRE. *J. of Modern African Studies [Great Britain] 1980 18(2): 257-279.* Examines the origins of the decisions taken and the attitudes established during the era of Leopold II, 1879-1908, and that continued to influence language policy throughout the colonial period and after. French was not used as a lingua franca because of Catholic missionary opposition. Protestant missionaries and government alternative plans failed because they were not strong enough to influence colonial policy. Based on published government documents in the Archives of the Belgian Ministry of Colonies, Brussels and secondary sources; 72 notes. A. Sbacchi

10. EAST AFRICA

General

2564. Allen, J. de V. TRADITIONAL HISTORY AND AFRICAN LITERATURE: THE SWAHILI CASE. *J. of African Hist. [Great Britain] 1982 23(2): 227-236.* Reviews Jan Knappert's *Four Centuries of Swahili Verse: A Literary History and Anthology* (1979), and Mohamed H. Abdul-aziz's *Muyaka: Nineteenth-century Swahili Popular Poetry*(1979). These two books attempt the reintegration of the study of East African history and the study of Swahili literature and investigate the date and origin of some Swahili verse forms, with reference to the occasions for which some of them were composed. 48 notes. R. L. Collison

2565. Amey, Alan B. and Leonard, David K. PUBLIC POLICY, CLASS AND INEQUALITY IN KENYA AND TANZANIA. *Africa Today 1979 26(4): 3-41.* Extensive description of the emergence of classes in Tanzania and Kenya. Four economic classes have developed in both countries, reinforced by governmental decisionmaking. Kenyan classes are the rich *(matajuri),* who combine government control with capitalism, the petite bourgeoisie of merchants and lower civil servants, peasants, and workers. Tanzanian classes are the *Watumishi,* who form the bureaucracy, the *wanyonyaji,* kulaks and traders, peasants, and workers. Ethnicity deteriorates as class struggles for control of economic resources intensify. Secondary sources; 3 tables, 74 notes.

G. O. Gagnon

2566. Amiji, Hatim. THE BOHRAS OF EAST AFRICA. *J. of Religion in Africa [Netherlands] 1975 7(1): 27-59.* An historical overview of the role of the Bohra community in East Africa. Originally Hindu, the Bohras converted to Islam centuries ago and migrated from India to Africa in the 19th century. They predominate as merchants. In addition to tracing their history in Africa, an analysis of religious beliefs and customs is presented. 65 notes. H. G. Soff

2567. Asein, Samuel Omo. OKOT P'BITEK: LITERATURE AND THE CULTURAL REVOLUTION IN EAST AFRICA. *J. of African Studies 1978 5(3): 357-372.* A consideration of the role of Okot p'Biket and his *Songs*in the East African literary crusade since 1965 to achieve a harvest of writings tied to the cultural heritage of this African region. Describes p'Bitek's assault on blind reliance on imported Western values and call to East African writers to restore their lost ancestral pride, while not becoming totally atavistic. Concludes that p'Bitek and his writings have had a considerable impact on East African writers. Based on literary sources and commentaries; 23 notes. L. W. Truschel

2568. Baker, S. J. K. A BACKGROUND TO THE STUDY OF DROUGHT IN EAST AFRICA. *African Affairs [Great Britain] 1974 73(291): 170-177.* A geographic and climatic discussion of East Africa. Rainfall, temperature, and terrain are assessed indicating that although drought occurs in East Africa, it is an environment unlike that of West Africa. 23 notes. H. G. Soff

2569. Beck, Ann. THE EAST AFRICAN COMMUNITY AND REGIONAL RESEARCH IN SCIENCE AND MEDICINE. *African Affairs [Great Britain] 1973 72(288): 300-308.* A brief survey of coordinated scientific research in Kenya, Tanzania, and Uganda. Although economically, politically, and educationally divided, the East African states continue to pool resources and manpower in the study and control of disease and other scientific research. 24 notes.

H. G. Soff

2570. Berntsen, John L. THE MAASAI AND THEIR NEIGHBORS: VARIABLES OF INTERACTION. *African Econ. Hist. 1976 (2): 1-11.* Investigates the historical interactions between the Maasai and their neighbors of the Rift Valley by examining their environment, economies, languages, myths, and cultures, 1850-1930.

2571. Bienen, Henry. MILITARY AND SOCIETY IN EAST AFRICA: THINKING AGAIN ABOUT PRAETORIANISM. *Comparative Pol. 1974 6(4): 489-518.* Explains the evolution of civil-military relations in Uganda, Kenya, and Tanzania using Samuel Huntington's concept of praetorianism. S

2572. Calchi Novati, Giampaolo. REVOLUCIÓN Y AUTODETERMINACIÓN EN EL CUERNO DE ÁFRICA [Revolution and self-determination in the Horn of Africa]. *Estudios de Asia y África [Mexico] 1979 14(2): 220-243.* The situation in Ethiopia, Somalia, and Djibouti is important for US-Soviet relations but certain of its aspects have a typical pan-African character. On various levels of the crisis exist the convergence and conflict of revolutionary impulses, centrifugal movements, classic rivalries between nations, the last repercussions of decolonization, and the struggle for influence by the superpowers. Explores these various factors by focusing on the situation in Ethiopia. 14 notes. J. V. Coutinho

2573. Chaise, Christian. LES ÉTATS-UNIS ET LA CORNE DE L'AFRIQUE. UNE NOUVELLE POLITIQUE? [The United States and the Horn of Africa: a new policy?] *Défense Natl. [France] 1981 37(Jun): 97-110.* East Africa occupies a sensitive political position owing to Soviet activity in the region and its proximity to the Arabian peninsula. The signing of a treaty of economic and military cooperation between the United States and Somalia on 24 August 1980 marked a turning point in the move away from America's former neutrality. Based in part on newspaper reports; map, 6 notes.

2574. Chaliand, Gérard. THE HORN OF AFRICA'S DILEMMA. *Foreign Policy 1978 (30): 116-131.* The turmoil in the Horn of Africa derives from conflict between Somali and Eritrean nationalism and a basic principle of the Organization of African Unity: the inviolability of colonial borders. Ethiopia, within whose borders live both Eritreans and Somalis, must win on both fronts or face the probable fall of its government. Although this would represent a severe defeat for Soviet interests, the United States should take no action to encourage it, lest African opinion be alienated. America should remain flexible and allow its regional allies to handle the situation. Map, 3 notes.

T. L. Powers

2575. Chrétien, Jean-Pierre. ÉCHANGES ET HIÉRARCHIES DANS LES ROYAUMES DES GRANDS LACS DE L'EST AFRICAIN [Exchanges and hierarchies in the kingdoms of the Great Lakes in East Africa]. *Ann.: Écon., Soc., Civilisations 1974 29(6): 1327-1337.* The highly stratified Bantu monarchies of the Great Lakes region in East Africa have long invited comparison with European feudalism. Both systems are based on dependence and reciprocity. In the African case the client gives beer and his loyalty to a chief in return for cows and, presumably, protection. Yet the chiefs do not possess the land and their clients as serfs on it as in Europe; land is held by lineages, and, though the chief's lineage will have the lion's share, the dependent clans will have their land too. 31 notes. J. C. Billigmeier

2576. Curtin, Philip D. AFRICAN ENTERPRISE IN THE MANGROVE TRADE: THE CASE OF LAMU. *African Econ. Hist. 1981 (10): 23-33.* The important trade in mangrove poles taken from the Lamu archipelago of Kenya and the Rufiji River in Tanzania and shipped to the Persian Gulf has been neglected. Colonial governments declared the mangrove swamps crown land and granted concessions for harvesting, but Bajuni work crews still did the actual cutting as before. Recent concerns have been overcutting and the cutters' small share in the trade's profits. Based on Forest Department papers; 20 notes, appendix. W. D. Piersen

2577. David, Steven. REALIGNMENT IN THE HORN: THE SOVIET ADVANTAGE. *Int. Security 1979 4(2): 69-90.* Traces US and Soviet involvement in Ethiopia and Somalia and accounts for the eventual Russian success in the Horn of Africa in 1977.

2578. DeWolf, J. J. THE DIFFUSION OF AGE-GROUP ORGANIZATION IN EAST AFRICA: A RECONSIDERATION. *Africa [Great Britain] 1980 50(3): 305-310.* The Kalenjin and the Maasai defeated their Bantu neighbors, and it was believed that the latter adopted their conquerors' age-group organization and associated rituals because they believed that they brought success in warfare. Further

investigations showed that the Terik desperately needed military allies, and for this purpose invited refugees of Luyia lineages to join their warrior groups through initiation into Terik age-groups. This successful move resulted in the Bantu-speaking section outnumbering the Kalenjin speakers. But the Kalenjin retained the right to claim ritual superiority over their refugee recruits. Published sources; map, 6 notes, biblio.
R. L. Collison

2579. Dresang, Dennis L. and Sharkansky, Ira. PUBLIC CORPORATIONS IN SINGLE-COUNTRY AND REGIONAL SETTINGS: KENYA AND THE EAST AFRICAN COMMUNITY. *Internat. Organization 1973 27(3): 303-328.* "Draws from the experience of Kenya and the East African Community to ascertain thc impact of single-country or regional ownership on the commercial performance of public enterprises. The advantages of the larger resources base of a regional community are mooted by the problems of mobilizing those resources. A fledgling public corporation can secure assistance most readily when owned by one state. It is also clear that traits of a corporation independent of its regional or single-country status affect commercial success. The essay concludes with a discussion of the limited contribution public corporations make to further levels of regional integration." J

2580. Dubouays, Jean-Marie. L'UNION SOVIÉTIQUE ET LA CORNE DE L'AFRIQUE [The USSR and the Horn of Africa]. *Défense Natl. [France] 1978 34(5): 43-50.* Soviet-Cuban intervention against President Siad Barre's regime in Somalia was not merely a reversal of alliances, but part of Soviet ambitions for control of both banks of the Red Sea, 1967-78. Similar considerations influence Soviet policy toward the Eritrean rebels in Ethiopia.

2581. Eastman, Carol. THE EMERGENCE OF AN AFRICAN REGIONAL LITERATURE: SWAHILI. *African Studies Rev. 1977 20(2): 53-61.* Describes the rise of national literature during the 1950's and 1960's, when all the genres, including poetry, prose, and drama, took clear shape.

2582. El-Khawas, Mohamed A. ARAB INVOLVEMENT IN THE HORN OF AFRICA: THE OGADEN WAR. *Search: J. for Arab and Islamic Studies 1981 2(3-4): 567-582.* Discusses Arab diplomatic and military support for Somalia during its 1977-78 war with Ethiopia, emphasizing the role of Saudi Arabia in mobilizing pro-Western support in the region and US failure to support the Somalis, and thereby Western interests.

2583. Erlich, Haggai. THE HORN OF AFRICA AND THE MIDDLE EAST: POLITICIZATION OF ISLAM IN THE HORN AND DEPOLITICIZATION OF ETHIOPIAN CHRISTIANITY. Tubiana, Joseph, ed. *Modern Ethiopia, from the Accession of Menilek II to the Present* (Rotterdam: Balkema, 1980): 399-408. The Horn of Africa is, in 1980, a part of the Middle East politically as a result of the recent politicization of Islam in the Horn and the simultaneous depoliticization of Ethiopian Christianity.

2584. Eyckmans, L. LE PROBLÉME DU CHOLÉRA EN AFRIQUE DE L'EST [The cholera problem in East Africa]. *Bull. des Séances de l'Acad. Royale des Sci. d'Outre-Mer [Belgium] 1979 (3): 445-450.* Cholera, an Asiatic disease, first appeared in Africa in 1970. Methods of combatting an outbreak in Burundi in 1978 are discussed. Improvement of sanitary conditions and chemoprophylaxis proved quite effective. Secondary sources; biblio.
M. Schumacher

2585. Francis, Samuel T. CONFLICT IN THE HORN OF AFRICA. *J. of Social and Pol. Studies 1978 2(3): 155-168.* Recent American expulsions (both commercial and military) and slackening of American aid due to the moralistic policy of the Carter Administration portends increased Soviet influence in this strategically vital area.

2586. Gitelson, Susan Aurelia. CAN THE U.N. BE AN EFFECTIVE CATALYST FOR REGIONAL INTEGRATION? THE CASE OF THE EAST AFRICAN COMMUNITY. *J. of Developing Areas 1973 8(1): 65-82.* Discusses the UN as advisor on regional integration to the East African Community (EAC). S

2587. Gitelson, Susan A. POLICY OPTIONS FOR SMALL STATES: KENYA AND TANZANIA REVISITED. *Studies in Comparative Int. Development 1977 12(2): 30-57.* Defines nonalignment as a tactical diplomatic principle and focuses on bargaining options for small and middle-sized states. Compares official statements of Kenyan and Tanzanian leaders to foreign policy activity. Both states continue to proclaim nonalignment, but neither has lived up to the definition in practice. The foreign policy behavior of these states reveals a pattern of maneuverability within the ideological guise of nonalignment. As a result of experiences and an awareness that economic development is necessary for maintaining political independence both states have evolved somewhat similar, though obverse, foreign policy stances. Based on speeches, interviews, other primary and secondary sources; 7 tables, 6 notes, biblio.
S. A. Farmerie

2588. Gould, W. T. S. PATTERNS OF SCHOOL PROVISION IN COLONIAL EAST AFRICA. *Études d'Hist. Africaine [Zaire] 1976 8: 131-148.* Governments in East Africa did little to encourage the building of schools from the 1850's to 1910, but there was considerable expansion with the establishment of educational departments, 1911-25. Since then there has been increasing central control of enrollment, curriculum, and the general aims of education. The spatial patterning of colonial East African schools resulted from complex social and economic factors that varied in time and space from one territory to another and within each territory. Map, 47 notes.
H. L. Calkin

2589. Hakes, Jay E. DIVERGING PATHS IN EAST AFRICA. *Current Hist. 1975 68(405): 202-205.* Domestic differences within the East African Community have inhibited the international cooperation among its members necessary for its success. J

2590. Halliday, Fred. LAS RELACIONES INTERNACIONALES EN EL CONFLICTO DEL CUERNO DE ÁFRICA [International relations in the conflict of the Horn of Africa]. *Estudios de Asia y África [Mexico] 1979 14(3): 524-540.* Studies the impact of the Ethiopian-Somali conflict on the relations between the Western and Eastern blocs, on Chinese-Soviet rivalry, on the Arab-Israeli conflict, and on the various African nations belonging to the Organization of African Unity.
J. V. Coutinho

2591. Hazlewood, Arthur. THE END OF THE EAST AFRICAN COMMUNITY: WHAT ARE THE LESSONS FOR REGIONAL INTEGRATION SCHEMES? *J. of Common Market Studies [Great Britain] 1979 18(1): 40-58.* An attempt at summarizing requirements for successful regional integration schemes, based on an analysis of the founding and breakup of the East African Community, 1967-78.

2592. Healey, Sally. THE PRINCIPLE OF SELF-DETERMINATION: STILL ALIVE AND WELL. *Millennium: J. of Int. Studies [Great Britain] 1981 10(1): 14-28.* Traces the coupling of the principle of self-determination with the phenomenon of decolonization from the 1950's to the 1980's, especially in the African context, with specific reference to the irredentist claims of Somalia and the national liberation movement of Eritrea.

2593. Henze, Paul B. HISTORY AND THE HORN. *Problems of Communism 1983 32(1): 66-75.* A review article of eight recent publications on the Ethiopian revolution, Somalia, Eritrea, and the strategic struggle for the Horn of Africa. Much of the current writing on the subject is colored by an unwarranted anti-Americanism and class analysis which distorts accounts of both internal and international developments in the region. 30 notes.
J. M. Lauber

2594. Horner, Norman A. AN EAST AFRICAN ORTHODOX CHURCH. *J. of Ecumenical Studies 1975 12(2): 221-233.* The African Greek Orthodox Church, organized in the 1930's, has shown significant growth in Kenya, Uganda, and Tanzania since 1952. In 1958, the AGOC churches organized the East African archdiocese of the Alexandrian (Orthodox) Patriarchate. The problems this church faces include recruitment and education of clergy, accommodation of religion to African culture, effect of ethnic membership, tension between nationalism and pan-African movements, and relationships to other world Christian churches.
J. A. Overbeck

2595. Hughes, Anthony. COMMUNITY OF DISINTEREST. *Africa Report 1975 20(2): 37-43.* Explains why the East African Community

(EAC), composed of Uganda, Tanzania and Kenya, has been a failure in its purported dream of East African unity. S

2596. Ingham, Kenneth. SOME REFLECTIONS ON EAST AFRICAN HISTORIOGRAPHY. *Historia [South Africa] 1976 21(2): 138-142.* Advocates an objective reappraisal of East Africa's imperial period up to independence, the reinterpretation of official documents, and the use of European and native oral sources while they are still available.

2597. Kaplan, Marion. IN EAST AFRICA POACHING WORSENS. *Smithsonian 1974 5(6): 88-92.* Sheer demand in Japan, India, and China has forced up the price of ivory, with the result that "the ongoing war between poachers and government in East Africa is escalating." This illegal trade, however, is really a minor factor in the problem of wildlife conservation. Illus. E. P. Stickney

2598. Kappeler, Dietrich. CAUSES ET CONSÉQUENCES DE LA DÉSINTÉGRATION DE LA COMMUNAUTÉ EST-AFRICAINE [Causes and consequences of the East African Community's disintegration]. *Pol. Étrangère [France] 1978 43(3): 319-330.* Examines the causes and consequences of the East African Community's disintegration, minimizes the severity of its effects, and shows that it could be the starting point for a more realistic realignment.

2599. Kenny, Michael G. MIRROR IN THE FOREST: THE DOROBO HUNTER-GATHERERS AS AN IMAGE OF THE OTHER. *Africa [Great Britain] 1981 51(1): 477-495.* The Dorobo, small groups of hunter-gatherers in East Africa, provide the local population with game, information on pasturage, and significant ritual services such as circumcision. Their origins are the subject of many conflicting opinions. Their position in the community is one of independence and isolation, the peoples of East Africa regarding them as representing disorder, incest, and sorcery. Their general reputation as the first inhabitants of the earth and thus the owners of an especially close relationship with God, makes them generally accepted as skilled mediators with the spiritual world. Based on fieldwork and published sources; 24 notes, biblio. R. L. Collison

2600. Kiapi, Abraham. MINISTERIAL RESPONSIBILITY IN EAST AFRICA. *African Rev. [Tanzania] 1974 4(4): 565-582.* A constitutional analysis of the concept of ministerial responsibility in independent Kenya, Uganda and Tanzania through case study of specific incidents. 30 notes. R. T. Brown

2601. Kjølberg, Anders. STRIDEN OM AFRIKAS HORN [The horn of Africa: conflicts and actors]. *Internasjonal Politikk [Norway] 1978 (1): 77-98.* Tracing the historical background of the region, the author then gives a broader survey of the local actors and their traditional conflict of interests as well as recent constellations. He further dwells on the African context, discusses the involvement of the Middle East countries, and the actual and potential role of the great powers, to end up with a general assessment of the East-West influence-seeking vis-à-vis the Third World. J

2602. Lechini, Gladys T. LA COMUNIDAD DE AFRICA ORIENTAL [East African Community]. *Rev. de Política Int. [Spain] 1978 (158): 117-146.* Analyzes how the East African Community, once an example of unity, is now disintegrating because of the different political and economic policies of its members.

2603. LeMelle, Wilbert J. THE CHANGING ROLE OF THE PLANNING ADVISER IN EAST AFRICA. *African R. [Tanzania] 1973 3(2): 309-325.* Traces planning in colonial East Africa including the Royal East Africa Commission (1953-55) and the Uganda Ten Years Development Plan (1946). In the past decade a greater adviser impact could have been accomplished if institution building had been pursued. While the role of the adviser in the 1960's was greater than in the 1970's, there is still a need for planners with specific expertise. The need for the general economic adviser had passed. 14 notes, appendixes. H. G. Soff

2604. Lindfors, Bernth. EAST AFRICAN POPULAR LITERATURE IN ENGLISH. *J. of Popular Culture 1979 13(1): 106-115.* Prior to the mid-1960's, East Africa, where the colonial language, English, became the national language, was barren of popular literature in English. Since then, there has been a flood of popular literature in English based on historical, anti-African, anti-Western, and even pornographic themes. Based on field research and interviews, and other primary and secondary sources; 9 notes. D. G. Nielson

2605. Livingstone, Ian. ECONOMIC IRRATIONALITY AMONG PASTORAL PEOPLES: MYTH OR REALITY? *Development and Change [Netherlands] 1977 8(2): 209-230.* The economic structure of overstocking, especially of cattle, by ethnic groups in East Africa may have social, ritualistic, and even economic benefits which belie the apparent inefficiency of the system as seen by Western administrators and technical experts.

2606. Madavo, Callisto E. URBAN HOUSING IN EAST AFRICA. *Can. J. of African Studies [Canada] 1981 15(1): 121-124.* Reviews Richard E. Stren's *Housing the Urban Poor in Africa: Policy, Politics, and Bureaucracy in Mombasa* (1978) and *Urban Inequality and Housing in Tanzania: The Problem of Squatting*(1975), which analyze the housing issues in Tanzania and Kenya. J. Powell

2607. Mandani, Mahmood. REVIEW ARTICLE. *African R. [Tanzania] 1973 3(4): 635-644.* A review article of E. A. Brett, *Colonialism and Underdevelopment in East Africa: The Politics of Economic Change 1919-1939* (London, 1972), which assesses colonial relations and explains the resulting underdevelopment in East Africa. H. G. Soff

2608. Marchand, Jean. LE JEU SOVIÉTIQUE DANS LA CORNE ORIENTALE DE L'AFRIQUE [The Soviet game in the Horn of Africa]. *Écrits de Paris [France] 1978 (378): 24-33.* Discusses the recent efforts of the USSR to "colonize" various countries in East Africa by offering economic and military aid in the hope of establishing a Marxist-Leninist federation of Ethiopia, Somalia, and South Yemen.

2609. Mariñas Otero, Luis. EL FRACASO DE LA COMUNIDAD DEL AFRICA ORIENTAL [The failure of the East African Community]. *Rev. de Política Int. [Spain] 1977 (154): 159-183.* Studies the process by which the East African Community disintegrated till it ceased to exist on 1 July 1977.

2610. Mariñas Otero, Luis. LA COMUNIDAD DEL AFRICA ORIENTAL [The East African Community]. *Rev. de Pol. Int. [Spain] 1975 (141): 113-148.* Discusses the present importance of the East African Community in the Third World, showing the emergence of East African nations from British rule since 1900 and discussing political and economic institutions of the community.

2611. Matogo, B. W. K. PUBLIC LIBRARY TRENDS IN EAST AFRICA, 1945-65. *Int. Lib. Rev. [Great Britain] 1977 9(1): 67-82.* Discusses the role of colonial and national governments, especially East African regional government, in Kenya, Uganda, and Tanzania in the development of libraries since the founding of the East African Literature Bureau in 1948.

2612. Matson, A. T. and Ofcansky, Thomas. A BIO-BIBLIOGRAPHY OF C. W. HOBLEY. *Hist. in Africa 1981 8: 253-260.* The career of Charles William Hobley in East Africa is outlined. From 1890 until his death in 1947 Hobley worked for British settlement and became involved with the people and environment of East Africa. Primary sources; biblio. A. C. Drysdale

2613. Mazrui, Ali A. LANGUAGE IN MILITARY HISTORY: COMMAND AND COMMUNICATION IN EAST AFRICA. *Mawazo [Uganda] 1974 4(2): 19-36.* Examines the use of language, both its inspirational and organizational qualities, in military life and specifically analyzes the use of Swahili in Kenya, Uganda, Zanzibar, and Tanganyika in anticolonialist and nationalist movements, 1905-71.

2614. Mazrui, Ali A. "RACIAL SELF-RELIANCE AND CULTURAL DEPENDENCY: NYERERE AND AMIN IN COMPARATIVE PERSPECTIVE." *J. of Internat. Affairs 1973 27(1): 105-121.* Former African colonies are beset by a cultural schizophrenia which ranges from the submissive to the aggressive. This is especially true of militants who fail to see Marxism as "the most disguised form of Europe's cultural dominance." Tanzania's Julius Nyerere, began as a socialist and became radical after the West refused economic aid; yet he recognizes an ideological dependency. Idi Amin of Uganda, a soldier, is less intellectual and has a milder, though more aggressive, case of cultural schizophrenia. R. D. Frederick

2615. Mazrui, Ali A. THE SACRED AND THE SECULAR IN EAST AFRICAN POLITICS. *Cahiers d'Études Africaines [France] 1973 13(4): 664-681.* Agrees with Kwame Nkrumah in seeing three religious-cultural strains in African life: the traditional faiths, Christianity (Euro-Christianity), and Islam. Islam is socially conservative, politically radical; Christianity socially radical, politically conservative; the traditionalists socially conservative, politically flexible. Africans today seem generally tolerant of leaders of a different religion, whether Muslim, Christian, or traditionalist. 16 notes. J. C. Billigmeier

2616. Mazrui, Ali A. SOLDIERS AS TRADITIONALIZERS. *J. of Asian and African Studies [Netherlands] 1977 12(1-4): 236-258.* Contrary to most opinions, soldiers in political power are more likely to be conservative and traditional in their programs than supportive of modernizing forces. East African examples since 1960, especially Idi Amin, show the future direction of African assertion of indigenous political values. Secondary sources; 25 notes. R. T. Brown

2617. Mbilinyi, Simon M. EAST AFRICAN EXPORT COMMODITIES AND THE ENLARGED EUROPEAN ECONOMIC COMMUNITY. *African R. [Tanzania] 1973 3(1): 85-110.* Discusses the relationship between the EEC and East Africa, tracing the development of European trade in the 20th century. Describes the structure of the East African economies, the Arusha Agreement, and the future of the EEC and the East African Trade Association. The East African Community should expand to include neighbor states to reduce dependence on European trade. 5 tables, 30 notes. H. G. Soff

2618. Miller, Robert A. THE PARTY-STATE AND BUREAUCRATIC/POLITICAL RELATIONS IN AFRICA. *Comparative Pol. Studies 1975 8(3): 293-317.* Demonstrates statistically that in the 1960's and 1970's there were greater differences in the social background of bureaucrats and politicians in Tanzania than in Uganda.

2619. Moon, Henry Lee. WHAT FUTURE FOR ASIANS IN EAST AFRICA? *Crisis 1973 80(1): 6-10.* Discusses problems in race relations between Asians and blacks in East Africa in the 1960's-70's. S

2620. Moore, Gerald. THE LANGUAGE OF LITERATURE IN EAST AFRICA. *Dalhousie R. 1973/74 53(4): 688-700.* Describes solutions of East African authors to the problem of creating an authentic tone in English, their second language. One of 10 papers read at the Conference on African Literature, Dalhousie U., 1973. S

2621. Mpakati, Attata. L'AFRIQUE ORIENTALE ET L'EXPLOITATION COLONIALE [Eastern Africa and colonial exploitation]. *Rev. Française d'Études Pol. Africaines [France] 1973 (87): 66-71.* Analyzes the formation of independent economic systems in Tanganyika, Kenya, Uganda, and Zanzibar after colonization, especially the creation of marketing and production cooperatives since 1960, in countries where British exploitation led to dependence instead of development.

2622. Mueller, Susanne D. SMALLHOLDER PRODUCTION AND RURAL DEVELOPMENT. *Can. J. of African Studies [Canada] 1982 16(3): 617-627.* Reviews Per Kongstad and Mette Mönsted, *Family, Labour and Trade in Western Kenya* (1980) and Jannik Boesen and A. T. Mohele, *The "Success Story" of Peasant Tobacco Production in Tanzania: The Political Economy of Commodity Producing Peasantry*(1979). Both volumes, written from a materialist persective, study the characteristics of the increasingly stratified African smallholding peasantry, its future directions, and what forms labor processes and labor relations are taking within and outside the household. 25 notes. J. V. Coutinho

2623. Mugomba, Agrippah T. REGIONAL ORGANISATION AND AFRICAN UNDERDEVELOPMENT: THE COLLAPSE OF THE EAST AFRICAN COMMUNITY. *J. of Modern African Studies [Great Britain] 1978 16(2): 261-272.* The Organization of African Unity has a history of failures, and ideological divisions have paralyzed it. It was unable to repair the rift in the now defunct East African Community. The pro-Western policy of Kenya, socialist Tanzania's involvement in the problems of Zimbabwe, South Africa, and Mozambique, and the unpredictable behavior of Idi Amin of Uganda caused the collapse of the community. Secondary sources; 16 notes. A. Sbacchi

2624. Murray, Jocelyn. A BIBLIOGRAPHY ON THE EAST AFRICAN REVIVAL MOVEMENT. *J. of Religion in Africa [Netherlands] 1976 8(2): 144-147.* Brief annotations to 28 sources dealing with religious movements in East Africa, published 1946-76. H. G. Soff

2625. Nanji, Azim. MODERNIZATION AND CHANGE IN THE NIZARI ISMAILI COMMUNITY IN EAST AFRICA: A PERSPECTIVE. *J. of Religion in Africa [Netherlands] 1974 6(2): 123-139.* Analyzes how the Nizari Ismaili sect in East Africa has adapted to the modern world. Relates their life in East Africa as well as the role of the Aga Khan who is the head of the community, and outlines many points in the Nizari constitution. The Ismailis are progressive, integrate with Africans, and are trying to remain in industry in Tanzania. A postscript indicates that since this article was written, the entire Nizari community in Uganda has fled. 52 notes. H. G. Soff

2626. O'Connor, Edmund. CONTRASTS IN EDUCATIONAL DEVELOPMENT IN KENYA AND TANZANIA. *African Affairs [Great Britain] 1974 73(290): 67-84.* Although there are differences in educational philosophies, neither Kenya nor Tanzania has created any radical change since independence. Tanzania has a more planned but restricted approach and is avoiding many problems that Kenya faces. Analyzes educational strategies of both nations since 1963, with key importance given to national language policy. 15 notes. H. G. Soff

2627. Pfeiffer, Steven B. THE ROLE OF THE JUDICIARY IN THE CONSTITUTIONAL SYSTEMS OF EAST AFRICA. *J. of Modern African Studies [Great Britain] 1978 16(1): 33-66.* Analyzes the court system in Kenya, Tanzania, and Uganda in relation to the apportionment of national power. Unlike Great Britain, each state had a written constitution in which the court was included as a key part. Analyzes the role of the three high courts since independence. 102 notes. H. G. Soff

2628. Pollet, Maurice. LES INDIENS EN AFRIQUE ORIENTALE [The Indians of eastern Africa]. *Rev. Française d'Études Pol. Africaines [France] 1973 (87): 72-81.* Views the history of East Indian emigration to East Africa, beginning with early settling in Zanzibar in the 6th century, to increased prosperity under British rule, to continental penetration during the construction of the Uganda Railroad, to disillusionment and the final expulsion of all Indo-Pakistanis with British passports by Uganda in 1972.

2629. Potholm, Christian P. WHO KILLED COCK ROBIN? PERCEPTIONS CONCERNING THE BREAKUP OF THE EAST AFRICAN COMMUNITY. *World Affairs 1979 142(1): 45-56.* Examines different views held in Tanzania, Uganda, and Kenya, the member states of the former East African Community, on the reasons for the EAC's 1977 breakup.

2630. Pouwels, Randall L. SH. AL-AMIN B. ALI MAZRUI AND ISLAMIC MODERNISM IN EAST AFRICA, 1875-1947. *Int. J. of Middle East Studies [Great Britain] 1981 13(3): 329-345.* Discusses the contributions of Sheik Al-Amin bin Ali Mazrui (1890-1947), administrator, author, and educator, to the process of modernization and reform in East Africa. Sheik Al-Amin was convinced of the universality of Islam and its appeal to many varieties of people. Moreover he thought Muslims should become skilled in Western science and technology in order to progress. Based on interviews and other primary sources; 60 notes. R. B. Orr

2631. Qureshi, Yasmin. RECENT DEVELOPMENTS IN THE RED SEA REGION WITH SPECIAL REFERENCE TO THE HORN OF AFRICA. *Pakistan Horizon [Pakistan] 1979 32(1-2): 142-159.* Examines the regional conflicts between the states bordering the Red Sea, especially Ethiopia and Somalia, and the rivalry of the Great Powers in the area.

2632. Ravenhill, John. REGIONAL INTEGRATION AND DEVELOPMENT IN AFRICA: LESSONS FROM THE EAST AFRICAN COMMUNITY. *J. of Commonwealth and Comparative Pol. [Great Britain] 1979 17(3): 227-246.* Examines the causes of the failure of

schemes for regional integration, particularly the economic background, the lack of political authority in the institutional infrastructure, and the increasing economic inequality of regions in cooperation. A strong regional secretariat with the power to plan industrial location, although at present impracticable, is the best long-term solution. A regional scheme requires the leadership of a "core" state to provide side-payments to weaker partners, as ideological leadership is insufficient. Benefits may be maximized if cooperation is confined to limited functional spheres, such as the provision of joint services. 24 notes.
K. Rushton

2633. Rizvi, S. S. A. and King, N. Q. THE KHOJA SHIA ITHNA-ASHERIYA COMMUNITY IN EAST AFRICA (1840-1967). *Muslim World 1974 64(3): 194-204.* Describes the development and organization of the Ithna-asheri communities in East Africa, particularly during the last 90 years. The Ithna-asheri communities were formed from diverse ethnic, historical, and religious backgrounds. The early adherents came from Arabia and Persia, and, in the 19th century, from India. The Indian Shi'a Muslims, who were called Khojas, came to East Africa and converted inhabitants along the coast to Shi'a Islam. Yet the communities in Lamu, Mombasa, and Dar-es-Salaam include a spectrum of beliefs, from something close to their original religions to Shi'a Islam. Nonetheless, they held similar views, and in 1945 formed a federation whose functions included religious, social and educational activities. Based on primary and secondary material, as well as oral evidence; 9 notes.
P. J. Mattar

2634. Rothchild, Donald. FROM HEGEMONY TO BARGAINING IN EAST AFRICAN RELATIONS. *J. of African Studies 1974 1(4): 390-416.* Analyzes the resources available to policy makers who have tried to integrate East African nations into a regional economic market. Colonial economic organization was so advantageous that Prime Minister Julius Nyerere of Tanzania suggested in 1960 that his country's independence be delayed until East Africa achieved freedom as a unit. Nyerere's fears have largely materialized: interests have hardened along territorial lines. Based on primary and secondary sources; 55 notes.
W. R. Hively

2635. Rowe, John A. "PROGRESS AND A SENSE OF IDENTITY": AFRICAN HISTORIOGRAPHY IN EAST AFRICA. *Kenya Hist. Rev. [Kenya] 1977 5(1): 23-34.* Considers examples of historiography in East Africa, such as *Amakuru Ga Kiziba N'Abakama Bamu* [The history of Kiziba and its rulers] as attempts by the newly literate generation of East Africans in the early 20th century to preserve their cultural heritage and historical identity during the modernization of their region.

2636. Sathyamurthy, T. V. NEW STATES AND THE INTERNATIONAL ORDER: THE EXPERIENCE OF EAST AFRICAN STATES; THEORETICAL AND METHODOLOGICAL CONSIDERATIONS. *Genève-Afrique [Switzerland] 1973 12(1): 63-82.* Discusses the foreign relations of independent East African states, 1955-73, outlines some questions arising from them which need study, and provides a postscript on events in Uganda, 1971-73.

2637. Schwab, Peter. COLD WAR ON THE HORN OF AFRICA. *African Affairs [Great Britain] 1978 77(306): 6-20.* An analysis of US and Soviet military influence in northeast Africa, 1930-77. The Soviets have gained influence in Ethiopia and other areas on the Horn. US influence has increased in the states surrounding the Horn. 29 notes.
H. G. Soff

2638. Shams B., Feraidoon. CONFLICT IN THE AFRICAN HORN. *Current Hist. 1977 73(432): 199-204, 225.* Examines the antecedents of political and cultural conflict in East Africa, since the 1930's. The availability of Soviet arms to Somalia and Ethiopia and the continuing hostility on all sides make rapid resolution of the area's political issues absolutely essential if other powers are not to become involved.

2639. Sharkansky, Ira and Dresang, Dennis L. INTERNATIONAL ASSISTANCE: ITS VARIETY, COORDINATION, AND IMPACT AMONG PUBLIC CORPORATIONS IN KENYA AND THE EAST AFRICAN COMMUNITY. *Internat. Organization 1974 28(2): 207-231.* "The diverse interests of donors and the desires of recipients to shop for the best deals mean that coordination of projects in international assistance causes problems along with promises of greater efficiency. Evidence from East Africa indicates that political competition and lack of candor and comparability in donors' reports limit the effectiveness of efforts at donor coordination. On the other hand, the policies of Kenya and the East African Community permitting virtual autonomy to profitable public corporations in their dealings with foreign governments and businessmen compromise the opportunity to optimize the use of assistance available in a multi-donar situation."
J

2640. Shelton, L. G., Jr. THE SINO-SOVIET SPLIT: THE HORN OF AFRICA, NOVEMBER 1977 TO FEBRUARY 1979. *Naval War Coll. Rev. 1979 32(3): 78-87.* Examines the successes and setbacks of China and the USSR in Somalia and Ethiopia.
J/S

2641. Sheriff, A. M. H. INDIANS IN EAST AFRICA: A REVIEW ARTICLE. *Tanzania Notes and Records [Tanzania] 1973 72: 75-80.* Focuses on J. S. Mangat's *A History of the Asians in East Africa, c. 1886 to 1945* (Oxford: Clarendon Press, 1968), and H. S. Morris' *The Indians in Uganda: Caste and Sect in a Plural Society* (London: Wiedenfeld and Nicolson, 1968). Mangat's work is particularly weak in economic and social history, while his political history is marred by naiveté. Morris fails to answer how Indians of peasant background became petty merchants and artisans in East Africa. Secondary sources; 10 notes.
E. C. Hopkins

2642. Sherman, Richard F. MARXISM ON THE HORN OF AFRICA. *Problems of Communism 1980 29(5): 61-64.* A review of Colin Legum and Bill Lee's *Conflict in the Horn of Africa* (New York: Africana Pub. Co., 1977); Colin Legum and Bill Lee's *The Horn of Africa in Continuing Crisis* (New York: Africana Pub., 1979); Tom J. Farer's *War Clouds on the Horn of Africa: The Widening Storm* (New York: Carnegie Endowment for International Peace, 1979); John Markakis and Nega Ayele's *Class and Revolution in Ethiopia* (Nottingham: Spokesman, 1978); and Raúl Valdés Vivó's *Ethiopia's Revolution* (New York: International Publishers, 1978). These books emphasize the introduction of non-native weaponries and ideologies into Ethiopia, Somalia, and Djibouti, resulting in a serious gap between the rhetoric and reality of the area's so-called Marxist movements. 2 notes.
J. M. Lauber

2643. Skurnik, W. A. E. WHITHER EAST AFRICA? *Current Hist. 1977 73(432): 205-208, 226.* The East African Community originally seemed a model of regional cooperation for other African developing nations, but growing political, economic, ideological, and expected goals tensions among its members have all but shattered hope of true cooperation.

2644. Stabler, Ernest. KENYA AND TANZANIA: STRATEGIES AND REALITIES IN EDUCATION AND DEVELOPMENT. *African Affairs [Great Britain] 1979 78(310): 33-56.* In postindependence Tanzania and Kenya education was seen as essential to economic growth, social mobility, character building, and unity. Both countries implemented similar plans for these objectives. Following the Arusha Declaration, 1967, Tanzania enacted a program of socialism and self-reliance, and consequently restructured its educational system to meet the demands of socialism, emphasizing agricultural and adult education. Kenya continued emphasizing the growth of the modern economic sector, and expanded its formal system of education, neglecting agricultural and adult education. Primary sources; 3 tables, 49 notes.
S. Lakhan

2645. Stein, Leslie. EXPORT TRENDS IN EAST AFRICA. *Development and Change [Netherlands] 1977 8(1): 103-116.* Examines the role of economic competition and commodity composition in export growth rates and trade in Uganda, Tanzania and Kenya, 1959-71.

2646. Stren, Richard. URBAN POLICY AND PERFORMANCE IN KENYA AND TANZANIA. *J. of Modern African Studies [Great Britain] 1975 13(2): 267-294.* Faced with rapid urban growth superimposed on a meager resource base, urban planners are being pressured to provide adequate and equitable distribution of urban services. Solutions will be heavily conditioned by two sets of factors: the immediate demands of urban growth and the wider political administrative and social context within which policymaking takes place. The author analyzes how these factors operate by comparing the formulation and

implementation of urban policies in Kenya and Tanzania from independence until 1973, concentrating on three policy areas: land allocation, housing, and planning. In Tanzania the chief weakness has been in performance in relation to need. In Kenya relatively successful performance has covered up problems of equity. 5 tables, 75 notes.
R. V. Ritter

2647. Tidrick, Kathryn. THE MASAI AND THEIR MASTERS: A PSYCHOLOGICAL STUDY OF DISTRICT ADMINISTRATION. *African Studies Rev. 1980 23(1): 15-31.* A study of British attitudes toward the Maasai of Kenya and Tanzania which were characterized by sympathy and personal affinity because the Maasai culture stressed many of the same personality traits as that of the British upper classes. Such sympathy, however, did not greatly affect colonial administration. Based on Kenyan and Tanzanian national archives; 55 notes, biblio.
R. T. Brown

2648. Tignor, Robert L. CONTINUITIES AND DISCONTINUITIES IN EAST AFRICAN EDUCATION. *Hist. of Educ. Q. 1973 13(4): 409-413.* Reviews John Cameron's *The Development of Education in East Africa* (New York: Teachers College Pr., 1970), Margaret MacPherson's *They Built for the Future: A Chronicle of Makerere University College, 1922-1962* (Cambridge: Cambridge U. Pr., 1964), Ernest Stabler's *Education Since Uhuru: The School of Kenya* (Middletown, Connecticut: Wesleyan U. Pr., 1969), and George F. F. Urch's *The Africanization of the Curriculum in Kenya* (Ann Arbor: U. of Michigan, 1968).

2649. Valenta, Jiri. SOVIET-CUBAN INTERVENTION IN THE HORN OF AFRICA: IMPACT AND LESSONS. *J. of Int. Affairs 1980-81 34(2): 353-367.* Discusses Soviet-Cuban intervention in Somalia and Ethiopia, 1970-81 and its implications for the United States. Comments on the proposed US military base at Berbera in Somalia and its probable impact on politics in the region.

2650. Verin, Pierre. UNE NOUVELLE DOCUMENTATION SUR L'HISTOIRE DES CÔTES DE L'OUEST DE L'OCÉAN INDIAN [New documentation for the history of the coasts of the western Indian Ocean] *Études d'Hist. Africaine [Zaire] 1977-78 9-10: 213-216.* Recent archaeological studies in Madagascar, Kenya, and Tanzania have established the sequence of history, and the activities of people from other areas of the world in Eastern Africa from the 9th century to the end of the 19th century. Secondary sources; 3 notes. H. L. Calkin

2651. Weeks, Phillipa. TRADE UNIONS AND ONE PARTY STATES: KENYA AND TANGANYIKA, 1961-1966. *ANU Hist. J. [Australia] 1973-74 (10-11): 50-60.* Defends the premise that the specific environment in which trade unionism operates decides its nature in discussing the conflicts between labor unions and the postcolonial government and ruling political parties in Kenya and Tanzania, in addition to the roles of key individuals in both countries. In the absence of a capitalist class in newly independent states, the government assumes the role of labor union antagonist. Functioning as they do in Western democracies, labor unions hinder economic development in developing nations as well as government efforts to coordinate and direct the process. While unions in both Kenya and Tanzania were forced to submit to government control in 1965, the more pluralistic nature of Kenyan society limited centralization and allowed labor some degree of political autonomy. The lack of ethnic or regional diversity in Tanganyika, however, allowed an earlier and more pervasive imposition of government control over unions. Primary sources; 44 notes.
H. Shields

2652. Westcott, N. J. CLOSER UNION AND THE FUTURE OF EAST AFRICA, 1939-1948: A CASE STUDY IN THE "OFFICIAL MIND OF IMPERIALISM". *J. of Imperial and Commonwealth Hist. [Great Britain] 1981 10(1): 67-88.* Examines changes in colonial policy in East Africa as a consequence of World War II. Before the war policy aimed at Closer Union, but by war's end much opposition had developed as the politics of Africa changed, partly due to the war's effect on the administrative and economic structures in East Africa. Based on materials in the Colonial Office Papers, Public Record Office, London, and various secondary sources; 72 notes. M. C. Rosenfield

2653. Westcott, N. J. AN EAST AFRICAN RADICAL: THE LIFE OF ERICA FIAH. *J. of African Hist. [Great Britain] 1981 22(1): 85-101.* Erica Fiah (ca. 1889-1966), born in Buganda, was educated by missionaries. He served in World War I. In the 1920's he worked as a clerk in various European enterprises in Dar es Salaam, but in 1932 he set up his own business there as a general trader. In 1934 he founded the African Commercial Association (ACA). Inspired by the example of Marcus Garvey, he strove to improve the Africans' economic position. Though Fiah was not personally popular among Africans, his activities drew public support, particularly in the fields of provision for adequate burials and for adult literacy. He published *Kwetu* (1937-51), a journal reflecting African social development which reached a wide audience throughout East Africa. Fiah was a leader who only partly achieved his aims. Based on interviews, published records, and Government archives; 82 notes. R. L. Collison

2654. —. [CUBA IN AFRICA]. *Cuban Studies 1980 10(1): 49-90.*

Valdés, Nelson P. CUBA'S INVOLVEMENT IN THE HORN OF AFRICA: THE ETHIOPIAN-SOMALI WAR AND THE ERITREAN CONFLICT, *pp. 49-79.* Cuba's involvement in Ethiopia is limited to providing aid against the Somali invasion. In Eritrea, the Cubans have been reluctant to provide military assistance to Ethiopia. Yet, as long as the Eritrean conflict continues, the chance of Cuban withdrawal is slight. 2 tables, 143 notes.

Fessehatzion, Tekie. COMMENT: ONE ERITREAN VIEW, *pp. 80-84.* Cuba's actions in the Eritrean question are dictated more by the geopolitical ambitions of the USSR than by the policies of Cuban leaders.

Abdi, Said Yusuf. COMMENT: ONE SOMALI PERSPECTIVE, *pp. 85-90.* In the case of Ogaden, Ethiopia is the imperial aggressor, since this area is historically and ethnically linked to Somalia. J. A. Lewis

2655. —. EAST AFRICA: THE FIRST DECADE OF INDEPENDENCE. *Australian Foreign Affairs Record 1974 45(1): 10-23.* In December 1973, Kenya celebrated its first 10 years as an independent nation, following Tanzania and Uganda, which achieved sovereignty earlier in the 1960's. This article traces the history of the three East African nations, and reviews their progress since independence. Strategically and to a lesser extent economically important, the three East African countries play a prominent political role in African affairs and internationally are active through their membership in the Commonwealth and the United Nations. J

Burundi

2656. Aupens, Bernard. L'ENGRENAGE DE LA VIOLENCE AU BURUNDI [The cogs of violence in Burundi]. *Rev. Française d'Études Pol. Africaines [France] 1973 8(91): 48-69.* A ten-year perspective on ethnic violence in Burundi during and since its independence, including the 29-30 April 1972 Hutu insurrection against the Tutsis, in which 4,000-15,000 died.

2657. Bowen, Michael; Freeman, Gary; and Miller, Kay. U.S. POLICY: NO SAMARITAN: THE U.S. AND BURUNDI. STATE DEPARTMENT REPLY. *Africa Report 1973 18(4): 32-39.* Discusses civil disturbances and genocide in Burundi and U.S. tardiness in forming a policy toward them. Response from the State Department is appended.
S

2658. Chrétien, Jean-Pierre. DU HIRSUTE AU HAMITE: LES VARIATIONS DU CYCLE DE NTARE RUSHATSI, FONDATEUR DU ROYAUME DU BURUNDI [From Hirsute to Hamite: the variations of the cycle of Ntare Rushatsi, founder of the kingdom of Burundi]. *Hist. in Africa 1981 8: 3-41.* Examines the rise of a state on the territory of Burundi in this century. Analyzes Burundi and neighboring areas' oral traditions and reinterprets European accounts of Ntare Rushatsi (nicknamed the Hirsute), founder of the kingdom of Burundi. Examines the geopolitical, ideological, and sociopolitical aspects of the building of the Burundi state, which eventually integrated its traditions into the pattern of Hamite mythology. Based on a paper read at a September 1979 Bujumbura Conference; map, table, 5 appendixes, 81 notes. G. P. Cleyet

2659. Chrétien, Jean-Pierre. ÉGLISE ET ÉTAT AU BURUNDI [Church and state in Burundi]. *Cultures et Développement [Belgium] 1975 7(1): 3-32.* Examines the crucial position of the Church in the life of this developing country, 1879-1972.

2660. DeCarolis, Antonio. CHANGEMENTS SOCIO-ÉCONOMIQUES ET DÉGRADATION CULTURELLE CHEZ LES PYGMOIDES BA-TWA BURUNDI [Socioeconomic changes and cultural degradation in the Ba-Twa pygmoids of Burundi]. *Africa [Italy] 1977 32(2): 201-232.* The ethnic pygmoid group, the Twa, holds a marginal position within the society of Burundi. The customary rules have forced it into a status which recalls that of "pariahs" in the Indian society, excluding its members from the principal sources of production and power. The transition into the monetary economy coupled with ever increasing difficulties in obtaining fertile lands for cultivation is lowering the status of the Twa into a subproletarian position devoid of cultural authenticity and means of subsistence. The author discusses aspects of this degradation. J

2661. Forscher, Romain. THE BURUNDI MASSACRES: TRIBALISM IN BLACK AFRICA. *Int. J. of Pol. 1974-75 4(4): 77-87.* The massacres in Burundi in 1972 reflect the political exacerbation of ethnic divisions, the perpetuation of a policy encouraged during the colonial period.

2662. Greenland, Jeremy. THE TWO OPTIONS NOW FACING BURUNDI. *Issue 1975 5(2): 3-5.* Discusses the power struggle between the Tutsi and the Hutu ethnic groups in Burundi politics in the 1970's.

2663. Karpushina, V. BURUNDI [Burundi]. *Aziia i Afrika Segodnia [USSR] 1982 (11): 54-56.* Describes Burundi's formation, economy, culture, and political system.

2664. Lemarchand, René. ETHNIC GENOCIDE. *Issue 1975 5(2): 9-16.* Discusses the 1972 Burundi civil war between the Hutu and Tutsi ethnic groups, in which there were approximately 80,000 to 100,000 deaths.

2665. Lemarchand, René. ETHNIC GENOCIDE. *Society 1975 12(2): 50-60.* Presents the background and immediate events leading to the 1972 ethnic war between Hutu and Tutsi in Burundi and notes the Western powers' lack of significant concern. S

2666. Melady, Thomas Patrick. AN AMBASSADOR'S REFLECTIONS ON A BLOODBATH. *Worldview 1974 17(5): 5-8.* The 20th century has seen alienation and violence between ethnic groups in a variety of countries, nowhere more bloodily than in Burundi, where the author observed the fighting between the Tutsi and Hutu, 1972-73.

2667. Morris, Roger; Bowen, Michael; Freeman, Gary; and Miller, Kay. THE UNITED STATES AND BURUNDI IN 1972. *Foreign Service J. 1973 50(11): 8-15, 29-30.* Report tracing the reaction of the US government to genocide in Burundi, and a reply by the State Department. S

2668. Rodegem, F. "CENT MOUTONS FONT UN LOUP" [One hundred sheep make a wolf]. *Issue 1975 5(2): 6, 7.* Discusses the ethnolinguistics of Burundian politics in the 1970's.

2669. Rozier, Raymond. STRUCTURES SOCIALES ET POLITIQUES DU BURUNDI [Social and political structures in Burundi]. *Rev. Française d'Études Pol. Africaines [France] 1973 8(91): 70-87.* Describes the slow evolution in Burundi toward a European model of civilization from a social organization based on lineage and tribal hierarchy, and a political system based on the absolute power of the *Mwami,* or king, discussing topics such as myth, mysticism, and the cult of cattle.

2670. Weinstein, Warren. BURUNDI: ALTERNATIVES TO VIOLENCE. *Issue 1975 5(2): 17-21.* Proposes alternatives to violence among ethnic groups in Burundi in the 1970's, emphasizing the need for UN intervention.

2671. Weinstein, Warren. BURUNDI 1972/73: A CASE STUDY OF ETHNIC CONFLICT AND PEASANTS' REPRESSION. *Pan-African J. [Kenya] 1974 7(3): 217-234.* The people of Burundi are divided into major groups: 14-16% are dominant Tutsi, 80-85% are subordinate Hutu. The author analyzes the relationship between these two peoples in both Rwanda and Burundi. Ethnic conflict mounted during the years following independence in 1962. In 1965 a Hutu revolt was launched against the king, who then sanctioned a cruel Tutsi repression. Tutsi then overthrew the king and continued repressive measures. The Hutu revolted again in 1972 and subsequently over 200,000 died. Analyzes the forces that led to this revolt and the role of Westernized Hutu elites. Ethnic violence is now endemic in Burundi and will remain so for some time. 44 notes. H. G. Soff

2672. Weinstein, Warren. THE LIMITS OF MILITARY DEPENDENCY: THE CASE OF BELGIAN MILITARY AID TO BURUNDI, 1961-1973. *J. of African Studies 1975 2(3): 419-431.* A study of what may be expected by a donor state when it grants military aid to a former territorial entity, and the actual capacity the donor has to effect desired outcomes in the recipient state's behavior or development. Belgium was shocked by its own inability to influence Burundi's government and the Belgian-trained and equipped military did not provide a stabilizing element in the midst of Burundi's volatile social and economic problems. 3 tables, 28 notes. R. V. Ritter

Djibouti

2673. Abdi, Said Yusef. INDEPENDENCE FOR THE AFARS AND ISSAS: COMPLEX BACKGROUND: UNCERTAIN FUTURE. *Africa Today 1977 24(1): 61-67.* Highlights the nexus of ethnic, ideological, big power, and irredentist factors which make Djibouti an explosive area. By exercising care in granting independence, France could lessen the centrifugal forces; but a unified country is not guaranteed. Based on published sources; 9 notes. G. O. Gagnon

2674. Guillerez, Bernard. DJIBOUTI, CENTRE NÉVRALGIQUE DE LA CORNE D'AFRIQUE [Djibouti, nerve center of the Horn of Africa]. *Défense Natl. [France] 1976 32(2): 79-87.* Examines the background to the insoluble ethnic conflicts that make East Africa so unstable, and explains how France has held the key to political stability through Djibouti.

2675. Marks, Thomas A. DJIBOUTI: FRANCE'S STRATEGIC TOEHOLD IN AFRICA. *African Affairs [Great Britain] 1974 73(290): 95-104.* The French territory of the Afars and the Issas has a strategic importance due to the military and economic situations in the Middle East. Reviews French policy and historical involvement in Somaliland and Ethiopia. The French are in firm control although the Issas are committed to independence and union with Somalia. 49 notes. H. G. Soff

2676. Milhaud, Bernard. DJIBOUTI: UNE INDÉPENDANCE EXPLOSIVE [Djibouti: an explosive independence]. *Écrits de Paris [France] 1977 (373): 5-13.* Shows that Djibouti, though having recently gained its independence from France, is at present on the brink of civil war due to deep ethnic and political divisions which its neighbors seem intent on exacerbating.

2677. Nolde, André. DJIBOUTI: INDÉPENDANCE, OUI MAIS... [Djibouti: independence, yes but...]. *Défense Natl. [France] 1976 32(2): 69-77.* Reviews the importance and influence of France's presence in Djibouti since the 1880's, the increasingly precarious situation of the Afars and Issas territory in the 1970's, and France's dilemma over the terms of future independence.

2678. Shehim, Kassim and Searing, James. DJIBOUTI AND THE QUESTION OF AFAR NATIONALISM. *African Affairs [Great Britain] 1980 79(315): 209-225.* The most serious problem of the new state of Djibouti, founded in 1977, is the lack of loyalty towards it from its two ethnic communities, the Issas and the Afars. Both seem to be more interested in joining with their tribal brethren in neighboring Ethiopia or Somalia than working within the framework of the new republic. In the past Somalis have been the dissidents, but increasingly their place has been taken by the Afars, who do not wish to suffer the fate of the Kurds, a dismembered ethnic group living under different governments. 56 notes. J. V. Coutinho

2679. Shilling, Nancy A. PROBLEMS OF POLITICAL DEVELOPMENT IN A MINISTATE: THE FRENCH TERRITORY OF THE AFARS AND THE ISSAS. *J. of Developing Areas 1973 7(4): 613-634.*

Ethiopia

General

2680. Baldet, Henry. SEVEN DAYS ON THE ROOF OF AFRICA. *Ethiopia Observer 1973 16(2): 70-75.* Reports a 1972 journey to the Ethiopian highlands, describing its topography, wildlife, and population. R. M. Maxon

2681. Clapham, Christopher. MULTIETHNIC ETHIOPIA. *African Affairs [Great Britain] 1976 75(298): 101-103.* Reviews six recent books on Ethiopia, Donald Levine, *Greater Ethiopia: the Evolution of a Multiethnic Society* (U. of Chicago Pr., 1974); William Shack, *The Central Ethiopians: Amhara, Tigrinya and related Peoples* (London: Int. African Inst., 1974); R. H. Kofi Darkwah, *Shewa, Menilek and the Ethiopian Empire*(London: Heinemann, 1975); Harold Marcus, *The Life and Times of Menelik II, Ethiopia 1844-1913* (Oxford, 1975); Patrick Gilkes, *The Dying Lion* (Julian Friedmann, 1975); and Michael Stahl, *Ethiopia* (Stockholm, 1974). H. G. Soff

2682. Fleming, Harold C. SOCIOLOGY, ETHNOLOGY, AND HISTORY IN ETHIOPIA. *Int. J. of African Hist. Studies 1976 9(2): 248-278.* Review article on Donald N. Levine's *Greater Ethiopia: the Evolution of a Multiethnic Society* (U. of Chicago Pr., 1974). Despite errors, Levine's attempt at integrating many disciplines and hypotheses is formidable. 50 notes. M. M. McCarthy

2683. Garretson, Peter P. SOME AMHARIC SOURCES FOR MODERN ETHIOPIAN HISTORY, 1889-1935. *Bull. of the School of Oriental and African Studies [Great Britain] 1978 41(2): 283-296.* Surveys published and unpublished source materials in Amharic for the study of modern Ethiopian history from the accession of Emperor Menelik II in 1889 to the Italian occupation of 1935. Menelik's reign saw an increase in Amharic sources due to the establishment of printing presses and because Amharic superseded Ga'az as the written language of the court. Published material includes collected documents, chronicles, biographies, autobiographies, and newspapers. Unpublished material is in private hands and sometimes in inaccessible archives. The article is interspersed with notes by Richard Pankhurst. 64 notes. E. M. Sirriyeh

2684. Henze, Paul B. LAKE ZWAY AND ITS ISLANDS. *Ethiopia Observer 1973 16(2): 76-88.* A description of the history and cultural patterns of the people of the islands of Lake Zway, some 100 miles south of Addis Ababa. Here a unique Christian culture has survived for many centuries despite being cut off from the Christian north, first by Muslim and later by Galla invaders. Details the island economy, in which fishing and weaving of cotton have traditionally been important. The community is losing its identity under modern pressures, but it remains a promising area for historical anthropological research. 12 photos. R. M. Maxon

2685. Henze, Paul B. PATTERNS OF CULTURAL SURVIVAL ON ISLANDS IN ETHIOPIAN HIGHLAND LAKES. *Ethiopia Observer 1973 16(2): 89-96.* A physical and ethnographic account of the major lakes of the Ethiopian highlands, including the seven lakes of the southern Rift Valley and Lake Tana. The lakes' inhabited islands present interesting cultural survivals. Lake Tana is extremely important as a center of strong Christian influence and activity and an area of economic importance. Lake Tana has a significant past, as yet only partially understood, and holds considerable agricultural and industrial potential. 3 photos. R. M. Maxon

2686. Holden, David. ETHIOPIA—FORTY YEARS ON. *Encounter [Great Britain] 1973 40(2): 76-87.* Surveys the situation in Ethiopia in 1973. Notes the triple cohesive factors of the army, the emperor, and the Church and describes, from personal reminiscences of a recent visit, the capital, surrounding countryside, and the town of Harar. Progress, however, has been the progress of the half-educated and the half-employable, "with their minds full of irony, disappointment and unfulfillable expectations—that characteristically growing and menacing band throughout the underdeveloped world." D. H. Murdoch

2687. Monteiro, Anthony. THE BRIGHT FUTURE OF THE ETHIOPIAN REVOLUTION. *Freedomways 1978 18(3): 135-150.* Ethiopia's history, economic development, and politics, 1917-78.

2688. Pankhurst, Richard. THE HISTORY OF DÄBRÄ TABOR (ETHIOPIA). *Bull. of the School of Oriental and African Studies [Great Britain] 1977 40(2): 235-266.* Traces the history of Däbrä Tabor, capital of Begemdir in Ethiopia, from its foundation in the 1790's. European travel accounts assist in describing the city's role as a major Ethiopian provincial capital in the 19th century and a market center of considerable population. Its selection as the imperial capital by two emperors increased its importance, but its destruction and abandonment by the emperors resulted in an inevitable decline by the early 20th century. 286 notes. D. H. Murdoch

2689. Schwab, Peter. BIBLIOGRAPHY ON ETHIOPIA. *Genève-Afrique [Switzerland] 1973 12(2): 122-129.* A selective bibliography on Ethiopia, concerning primarily political, economic, and anthropological affairs and excluding Eritrea.

Economics

2690. Baker, J. DEVELOPMENTS IN ETHIOPIA'S ROAD SYSTEM. *Geography [Great Britain] 1974 59(2): 150-154.* Details the development and improvements in Ethiopia's road system from 1951 to 1973. Four highway programs under the control of the Imperial Highway Authority were put into effect in 1951-57, 1957-65, 1965-68, and 1968-73. Few improvements were made in road communications and connections, however, with Kenya, Somalia, or the Sudan. Road traffic to these three countries is severely restricted because of "the uncertainties in the political climate between Ethiopia and its neighbours." Table, 2 figs. D. D. Cameron

2691. Beshah, Teferra-Worq and Harbeson, John W. AFAR PASTORALISTS IN TRANSITION AND THE ETHIOPIAN REVOLUTION. *J. of African Studies 1978 5(3): 249-267.* An introductory analysis of recent problems confronting the Afar pastoralists of the Awash River Valley area of Ethiopia. These difficulties stemmed from public and private efforts under the old regime in Ethiopia to encourage development of agrarian plantations in the area and modernize the life of the pastoralists. Government plans to incorporate the Afar into the area's development by way of its Awash Valley Authority failed by the time of the 1974 revolution. The authors hope the new government will promote "a commonwealth of nationalities coexisting in peace and equality," but see no evidence of its happening. Based on published official documents and secondary sources; 29 notes. L. W. Truschel

2692. Bondestam, Lars. NOTES ON MULTINATIONAL CORPORATIONS IN ETHIOPIA. *African Rev. [Tanzania] 1975 5(4): 535-549.* A history of the growth of foreign investment which has remained small and, except for a few areas of production, has had little influence on the Ethiopian economy. Table, 4 notes. R. T. Brown

2693. Bondestam, Lars. PEOPLE AND CAPITALISM IN THE NORTH-EASTERN LOWLANDS OF ETHIOPIA. *J. of Modern African Studies [Great Britain] 1974 12(3): 423-439.* The Afar people of the Awash Valley have been reduced in number by 25-30 per cent due to a severe famine. The immediate causes of the famine are discussed, but the capitalistic system which emphasized cash crops undermined the indigenous system and is the principal cause. The Afar are pastoralists, but 10 years ago commercial farming of sugar and cotton was forced upon them and their valley. Afar were uprooted and evicted, their rivers were polluted, and the land now reserved for them is overpopulated. The future of the Afar is in the hands of a government which is apparently not concerned. Map, 5 tables, 11 notes. H. G. Soff

2694. Brietzke, Paul H. LAND REFORM IN REVOLUTIONARY ETHIOPIA. *J. of Modern African Studies [Great Britain] 1976 14(4): 637-660.* Examines Ethiopia's traditional land tenure practices in the south, the north, and among the nomadic pastoral population. The system whereby a few landholders practically enslave the peasants demanded major change. The nationalization of rural lands proclamation of 4 March 1975 is a step in that direction, though it is operating upon many centuries of tradition. The conversion of individual to nationally collective ownership is a most revolutionary step. 51 notes. R. V. Ritter

2695. Cohen, John M. EFFECTS OF GREEN REVOLUTION STRATEGIES ON TENANTS AND SMALL-SCALE LANDOWNERS IN THE CHILALO REGION OF ETHIOPIA. *J. of Developing Areas 1975 9(3): 335-358.* Even with rich natural resources, 85% of Ethiopia's people still survive by subsistance agriculture; about half of the farmers are tenants, most of them sharecroppers. The Swedish government in 1967 began an agricultural development program in the Chilalo region, with goals of raising production levels, standards of living, and levels of social awareness and participation. The Chilalo Agricultural Development Unit provided low-interest credit, improved roads, conducted research, helped develop water systems, and provided educational and development support. However, the program did not have the full desired impact since wealthy landowners benefited the most. Tenants still have virtually no protection from eviction and thus are reluctant to make improvements. Land rents and taxes are increasing. 64 notes. O. W. Eads, Jr.

2696. Cohen, John M. PEASANTS AND FEUDALISM IN AFRICA: THE CASE OF ETHIOPIA. *Can. J. of African Studies [Canada] 1974 8(1): 155-157.* Lists studies on 20th-century Ethiopian land tenure, the relation of peasants to agricultural production, and the resulting stratification patterns.

2697. Cohen, John M. RURAL CHANGE IN ETHIOPIA: THE CHILALO AGRICULTURAL DEVELOPMENT UNIT. *Econ. Development and Cultural Change 1974 22(4): 58-614.* Examines the effect of the Chilalo (a subdivision in Arussi province) Agricultural Development Unit (CADU) on the efforts to modernize the Ethiopian economy. Begun in 1967, the project sponsors economic and social development, increased employment, and agricultural modernization in the Chilalo district with hopes that the experiences gained would contribute to the development of the whole country. The organization, administration, plans, and programs of the project are discussed in detail. Based on government reports and secondary sources; 5 illus., 3 tables, 10 notes. J. W. Thacker, Jr.

2698. Collier, Owen P. C. and Perkins, K. M. A. HISTORY OF THE FRANCO-ETHIOPIAN RAILWAY FROM DJIBOUTI TO ADDIS ABABA. *Transport Hist. [Great Britain] 1979 10(3): 220-248.* Describes the construction and administration of the Franco-Ethiopian railroad, and its contribution to the economic development of Ethiopia, 1894-1978.

2699. Gal'perin, G. AGRARNAIA REVOLIUTSIIA V EFIOPII [Agrarian revolution in Ethiopia]. *Aziia i Afrika Segodnia [USSR] 1981 (8): 25-28.* Discusses the role of peasant associations in agrarian reforms in Ethiopia during the 1980's, examines various reactions to reforms, and analyzes the different types of cooperatives that have become popular in Ethiopia.

2700. Halperin, Rhoda and Olmstead, Judith. TO CATCH A FEASTGIVER: REDISTRIBUTION AMONG THE DORZE OF ETHIOPIA. *Africa [Great Britain] 1976 46(2): 146-165.* A study of redistributive feastgiving among the Dorze peoples of Ethiopia. About 10% of the male citizens can be expected to be assigned to positions which compel them, in turn, to both give and receive gifts. These gifts can be considerable: a shrewd operator can become wealthy, lesser mortals may be pauperized. The position carries considerable political power and responsibility. Changes were instituted in 1898, when Ethiopia became a centralized state. Recent years have seen more changes: the feastgivers have turned their eyes to a wider horizon, running for national offices and entering modern commerce on a larger scale. The revolution of 1974 will bring more changes, perhaps even terminate the system, but it may not matter, for fewer and fewer men are willing to undertake the expenses and responsibilities of the position. 9 fig., 6 notes, ref. V. L. Human

2701. Kloos, Helmut. FARM LABOR MIGRATIONS IN THE AWASH VALLEY OF ETHIOPIA. *Int. Migration Rev. 1982 16(1): 133-168.* The Awash Valley, an arid area in eastern Ethiopia that has been developed since the 1950's under the 3d Five-Year Development Plan, has experienced farm labor immigrations from the Ethiopian highlands and some lowland districts because of the availability of irrigation. Based on interviews of residents in 1972-73 and 1975-76.

2702. Krylova, N. L. and Svanidze, I. A. SEL'SKOE KHOZIAISTVO NARODOV EFIOPII [The agriculture of the peoples of Ethiopia]. *Sovetskaia Etnografiia [USSR] 1975 (1): 31-43.* Concentrates on the characteristic features of agriculture in Ethiopia, the oldest state in tropical Africa. They show Ethiopia to be one of those African countries whose economy is most agrarian in character, where the proportion of agriculture in the national income, in the labor force, and in exports is highest. The proportion of market production in agriculture is not high. Farming based on modern technology plays only a small role. The living standard of the population is low. Traditional medieval technology and agricultural methods predominate in the rural economy. Ethiopia's agriculture is below the all-African average in most economic indices. The burning problems of modern Ethiopia, whose solution is a precondition for its further progress, are radical agrarian reform, abolition of the obsolete feudal landholding system, and a complete reconstruction of the technology and economy of agriculture. J

2703. Love, Robert S. ECONOMIC CHANGE IN PRE-REVOLUTIONARY ETHIOPIA. *African Affairs [Great Britain] 1979 78(312): 339-355.* A long-term deterioration in the distribution of income coincided in 1973-74 with a period of inflation caused by unprecedentedly high commodity export prices. This combination of events so affected the standards of living of the ordinary soldier and of certain groups of the urban population that protest became overt and led eventually to the emperor's overthrow. There had been a steady if unremarkable growth in the economy between 1960 and 1974, but peasant farmers, industrial workers, and the armed forces had not benefited as much as other sections of the population. By early 1974 inflation exacerbated the situation. 7 tables, 12 notes. R. L. Collison

2704. McCann, James. ETHIOPIA, BRITAIN, AND NEGOTIATIONS FOR THE LAKE TANA DAM, 1922-1935. *Int. J. of African Hist. Studies 1981 14(4): 667-699.* British desire to regulate the flood waters of the Nile was effectively stalled by Ethiopian political maneuvering which resulted from Haile Selassie's concerns over internal matters. When he was able to deal from a position of strength, the British were no longer interested. Based on British and Ethiopian government documents; 111 notes. R. T. Brown

2705. McClellan, Charles W. LAND, LABOR, AND COFFEE: THE SOUTH'S ROLE IN ETHIOPIAN SELF-RELIANCE, 1889-1935. *African Econ. Hist. 1980 (9): 69-83.* In the late 19th century Ethiopia expanded to the south to assure a supply of ivory. But ivory exploitation soon gave way to a quasi-landlord-tenant system of coffee production. Ethiopian leaders consciously underdeveloped the peripheral south to subsidize national independence and self-development. In so doing they created a buffer zone that checked European colonial and economic expansion. Primary sources; 37 notes. W. D. Piersen

2706. Nuciari, Marina. STRATEGIE DI SVILUPPO RURALE E MUTAMENTO SOCIALE IN ETIOPIA [Strategy of rural development and social change in Ethiopia]. *Africa [Italy] 1978 33(1): 23-51.* Analyzes a peculiar rural development strategy in Ethiopia, the package project approach which reflects a specific ethnocentric point of view, intending social development as an offspring of mere introduction of technical innovations, without taking into account the social, cultural, and political dynamics, and the reaction to innovation. The projects aimed to induce economic and social development in some selected rural areas, but owing to the existing land tenure pattern, the action has caused many social hardships to the very part of rural population to whom efforts were directed, thus reinforcing the situation of underdevelopment. J/S

2707. Ottaway, Marina. LAND REFORM IN ETHIOPIA 1974-1977. *African Studies Rev. 1977 20(3): 79-90.* The ruling military council of Ethiopia created an apparently successful revolution when it declared sweeping land reform in 1975. The peasants rapidly created social and political organizations which have become a counterweight to the military. The military council's action originated from its own weaknesses which necessitated immediate allies. Biblio. R. T. Brown

2708. Pankhurst, Richard. ETHIOPIAN MONETARY HISTORY IN THE PHASE OF POST-WAR RECONSTRUCTION (1941-1945). *Ethiopia Observer [Ethiopia] 1974 17(1): 228-303.* Describes the emergence of Ethiopian currency after the liberation of Ethiopia, 1941. Currency problems existed because several currencies, the old Maria Theresa dollar, and Italian, Indian, and East African currencies, circulated in the country in the wake of Italy's defeat. British officials urged the formation of a new currency based on sterling and controlled by a currency board in London, but Ethiopian authorities resisted this scheme to prevent British influence which would compromise Ethiopia's independence. Eventually Ethiopia turned to the United States for currency assistance. Based on British, American, and Ethiopian government documents, official memoirs, and contemporary newspapers. 476 notes. R. M. Maxon

2709. Pankhurst, Richard. ROAD-BUILDING DURING THE ITALIAN FASCIST OCCUPATION OF ETHIOPIA (1936-1941). *Africa Q. [India] 1976 15(3): 21-63.*

2710. Rulon, Philip Reed. HENRY GARLAND BENNETT: THE FATHER OF THE "GREAT ADVENTURE" IN UNIVERSITY-CONTRACTS ABROAD. *Red River Valley Hist. R. 1975 2(2): 255-272.* Chronicles the efforts of Henry Garland Bennett, particularly his 1950-51 work in Ethiopia, as the first permanent director of the Technical Cooperation Administration, which employed colleges to help developing nations cultivate their resources. S

2711. Seleshi Sisaye. SWEDISH AID TO ETHIOPIA, 1954-1967. *J. of African Studies 1981 8(2): 85-90.* The Swedish government, through a bilateral treaty signed in October 1954, began a program of supplying education and health assistance to Ethiopia. The Swedes built schools and clinics in Ethiopia, but until Sweden began to send green revolution technological aid in 1967, their economic aid program was largely confined to urban areas. Based on correspondence, published reports and treaties, newspapers, and secondary sources; 37 notes. L. W. Truschel

2712. Shack, William A. OCCUPATIONAL PRESTIGE, STATUS, AND SOCIAL CHANGE IN MODERN ETHIOPIA. *Africa [Great Britain] 1976 46(2): 166-181.* A study of occupational prestige in modern Ethiopia. It has often been asserted that the ruling Amhara peoples of northern Ethiopia disdained work, but the present study reveals no significant differences in work prestige among any of the eight groups studied. Modernization has no doubt contributed to this state of affairs; once-despised occupations are no longer frowned upon if they pay good wages or offer job security. Ethiopia has entered the modern world of status-seeking and social change; the old ways are fading and probably never will be significant factors in society again. 6 tables, 23 notes, ref., appendix. V. L. Human

2713. Sisaye, Seleshi and Stommes, Eileen. AGRICULTURAL DEVELOPMENT IN ETHIOPIA: GOVERNMENT BUDGETING AND DEVELOPMENT ASSISTANCE IN THE PRE AND POST 1975 PERIODS. *J. of Development Studies [Great Britain] 1980 16(2): 156-185.* While recognizing the importance of agriculture for economic growth, Ethiopia was forced to rely on donor agencies to fund agriculture due to financial difficulties prior to 1975. Afterward, the government provided more money for agricultural development.

2714. Sisaye, Seleshi and Schutt, Russell K. THE ECONOMIC SIGNIFICANCE OF ETHNICITY: UNIONIZED WORKERS IN ADDIS ABABA, ETHIOPIA. *Ethnicity 1981 8(4): 341-351.* Ethnic differences in economic situation were smallest in the more educated sector of the economy. These white-collar industries are a leading edge for assimilation while blue-collar industries lag behind. 6 tables, fig., ref. T. W. Smith

2715. Sisaye, Seleshi. INDUSTRIAL CONFLICT AND LABOR POLITICS IN ETHIOPIA: A STUDY OF THE MARCH 1974 GENERAL STRIKE. *Plural Soc. [Netherlands] 1977 8(2): 49-76.* Studies the general strike in Ethiopia in March 1974, focusing on its causes, the student-worker-military force which opposed an imperial ruling force, and the effects: mainly the politicization of civil servants and workers.

2716. Sisaye, Seleshi and Stommes, Eileen. PEASANTS AND COMMUNITY DEVELOPMENT: THE ETHIOPIAN EXPERIENCE, 1957-1974. *Peasant Studies 1981 9(1): 54-73.* Examines the success of community development programs in rural Ethiopia during the years 1957 through 1974, especially the role of the elite-dominated economic, political, and social structures at the local and national levels in inhibiting effective implementation of the community development approach as a broad-based, participatory development strategy.

2717. Tolstykh, Vera Evgen'evna. AGRARNAIA POLITIKA REVOLIUTSIONNOI EFIOPII [Agrarian policy of revolutionary Ethiopia]. *Narody Azii i Afriki [USSR] 1980 (6): 24-31.* Discusses reforms enacted since 1975: nationalization of land, creation of peasant associations, cooperatives, and state farms, and settlement of nomads. Natural disasters, sabotage, and the war with Somalia forced the government, in 1977-78, to import foodstuffs, introduce price controls, establish production quotas by province, and resettle peasants from drought-prone areas to fertile virgin tracts. A new economic campaign was launched in 1979 to increase agricultural yields especially of export crops, such as coffee, and improve animal husbandry. 25 notes. N. Frenkley

Politics

2718. Asante, S. K. B. THE CATHOLIC MISSIONS, BRITISH WEST AFRICAN NATIONALISTS, AND THE ITALIAN INVASION OF ETHIOPIA, 1935-36. *African Affairs [Great Britain] 1974 73(291): 204-216.* Although Pope Pius XI criticized Mussolini's intended invasion of Ethiopia in 1935, he never used the power of his office to prevent it. Ethiopia had been a Christian bastion against Islam for 1300 years, but Pius XI felt that it was more important to thwart communism in Europe than to prevent genocide in Africa. West African leaders boycotted Christian missions, and education and evangelical activity suffered. 52 notes. H. G. Soff

2719. Asante, S. K. B. I. T. A. WALLACE JOHNSON AND THE ITALO-ETHIOPIAN CRISIS. *J. of the Hist. Soc. of Nigeria [Nigeria] 1975 7(4): 631-646.* Examines a crucial facet of the Pan-Africanism of Isaac Theophilus Akunna Wallace-Johnson (b. 1890) that has generally been neglected, his reaction to the Italian conquest of Ethiopia in 1935. Particular emphasis is placed on the manner in which it "reinforced his opposition to imperialism and colonialism." His campaign in support of the Ethiopian cause is carefully delineated, as is his growing conviction concerning the evils of European rule in general. Based on manuscript and published sources; 78 notes. J. A. Casada

2720. Baer, George W. SANCTIONS AND SECURITY: THE LEAGUE OF NATIONS AND THE ITALIAN-ETHIOPIAN WAR, 1935-1936. *Internat. Organization 1973 27(2): 165-180.* "The imposition of limited sanctions against Italy was given fair prospect of success by members of the League. Sanctions were to have a twofold purpose. One was to uphold the Covenant and encourage collective security. The other was to end the war by putting pressure on the Italian government so as to make it amenable to a negotiated settlement. It was expected that economic and financial measures (as opposed to military means) would be sufficient, over a period of time, to achieve this. The timetable was upset by unexpected political events and by the collapse of Ethiopian military resistance. Policies are explained, events discussed, and to illuminate some dilemmas a distinction (not then well perceived) is made between politically important 'consumatory' assumptions and diplomatically operative 'instrumentalist' and reconciliationist practices." J

2721. Basler, Werner. DER AGGRESSIONSKRIEG ITALIENS GEGEN ÄTHIOPIEN 1935/36 [Italy's war of aggression against Ethiopia, 1935-36]. *Militärgeschichte [East Germany] 1982 21(6): 688-698.* Investigates the preparation and military course of Italian aggression up to the annexation of Ethiopia. The possibility existed throughout the period of bridling Italy's war policy, but the ruling circles of the Western powers, because of their policy of concessions and encouragement, were significantly responsible for this act of aggression, which was a step toward World War II. 58 notes. J/T (H. D. Andrews)

2722. Beck, Peter J. LOOKING TO GENEVA FOR PROTECTION AGAINST THE GREAT POWERS: THE EXAMPLE OF ETHIOPIA IN 1925-1926. *Genève-Afrique [Switzerland] 1981 19(1): 81-102.* In 1926 the Emperor of Ethiopia (later known as Haile Selassie) protested to the League of Nations against a diplomatic agreement between Great Britain and Italy to further their respective interests in Ethiopia. The possibility of League action brought the British and Italians to rescind their agreement, but the respective governments drew very different conclusions from the matter. The British became committed to League intervention in disputes with smaller states, the Ethiopians thought they could rely on the League for protection, and the Italians were ready to ignore it. Based on materials in the Public Record Office and University of Birmingham Library, printed materials, and secondary sources. B. S. Fetter

2723. Bell, J. Bowyer. ENDEMIC INSURGENCY AND INTERNATIONAL ORDER: THE ERITREAN EXPERIENCE. *Orbis 1974 18(2): 427-450.* Discusses civil disorder in the Ethiopian province of Eritrea since 1941 and its effect on foreign relations. S

2724. Bhardwaj, Raman G. ERITREAN SECESSIONISM. *India Q. [India] 1979 35(1): 83-92.* A study of the continuing problem of the relation of Eritrea to Ethiopia. The current war of liberation has now been in progress for 17 years, a protest against tyranny and oppression, a genuine "people's war." The Eritreans' is a distinctive culture which they consider superior to that of Ethiopia and which has added to the spirit of nationalism strengthened by the feeling that Ethiopia's only desire for maintaining ultimate control is for the sake of taxes. A pawn of power politics, Eritrea is the only former colony not given independence after World War II. 20 notes. R. V. Ritter

2725. Bray, Donald W. ETHIOPIA: DISCOVERY OF A REVOLUTION. *Latin Am. Perspectives 1981 8(1): 126-128.* Evaluative commentary on three books about the Ethiopian revolution published in 1978, including a Cuban account. J. F. Vivian

2726. Caulk, R. A. ARMIES AS PREDATORS: SOLDIERS AND PEASANTS IN ETHIOPIA C. 1850-1935. *Int. J. of African Hist. Studies 1978 11(3): 457-493.* Professional armies in Ethiopia have usually been predators living off their lords' other subjects while raiding his enemies for booty. The peasantry of the late 19th and early 20th century were not without means of resisting the impositions of the soldiers. Attempts at reform, 1916-36 generally failed. After 1941 soldiers were no longer quartered on the population and thus did not prey directly on farmers and traders. Map, 89 notes. M. M. McCarthy

2727. Chauleur, Pierre. LA FIN D'UNE CIVILISATION: LA RÉVOLUTION EN ÉTHIOPIE [The end of a civilization: the revolution in Ethiopia]. *Études [France] 1974 341: 685-702.* Outlines the history leading up to the sudden outbreak of revolution in Ethiopia on 12 September 1973 and its consequences.

2728. Chege, Michael. THE REVOLUTION BETRAYED: ETHIOPIA, 1974-9. *J. of Modern African Studies [Great Britain] 1979 17(3): 359-380.* The Ethiopian revolution of 1974 was spearheaded by the working class, students, and an assortment of petit bourgeois elements dedicated to a democratic future. But faced with the fundamental issues of which class should wield state power and the place of national minorities in Ethiopia, the numerical weakness of the revolutionary classes and political backwardness of the peasantry allowed the rise of a military dictatorship lacking a popular class base and beholden to the Soviet Union. Based on newspapers and other printed sources; 68 notes. D. J. Nicholls

2729. Clapham, Christopher. CENTRALIZATION AND LOCAL RESPONSE IN SOUTHERN ETHIOPIA. *African Affairs [Great Britain] 1975 74(294): 72-81.* Outlines the relationship between the central government of Ethiopia and the southern provinces, 1855-1974. Southern Ethiopia has not revolted against the federal authorities and may not in the future. In order to ensure tranquility, however, the government must be aware of the political needs of southerners. 14 notes. H. G. Soff

2730. Cohen, John M. TRADITIONAL POLITICS AND THE MILITARY COUP IN ETHIOPIA. *African Affairs [Great Britain] 1975 74(295): 222-245.* A review article on *Ethiopia: Anatomy of a Traditional Polity* by John Markakis. Although the volume contains a good deal of solid information and analysis, it is "old wine in new bottles." Since research ended in 1969, the book was five years out of date when published. Instead of trying to analyze the full scope of Ethiopia, scholars should localize their efforts. H. G. Soff

2731. Cola Alberich, Julio. ETIOPIA: FINAL DEL REINADO DE HAILE SELASSIE [Ethiopia: the end of Haile Selassie's reign] *Rev. de Política Int. [Spain] 1974 (135): 109-134, (136): 103-122; 1975 (137): 149-170.* Part I. Discusses the motives behind the coup d'etat which deposed Haile Selassie, suggesting as long-term causes, demands for liberalization, and Eritrean secession, and as a short-term cause, drought. Part II. Examines the guerrilla warfare of the early 1970's, the attempts by both the government and the Eritreans to elicit Arab financial support, and the aid to Ethiopia to avert famine. Part III. Studies the problems created by divisions in the army, autonomist and secessionist forces, and the growth of Soviet influence.

2732. Dascălu, Nicolae and Eggleston, Patricia. RĂZBOIUL ITALO-ETIOPIAN (1935-1936) ÎN ISTORIOGRAFIA UNIVERSALĂ [The Ethiopian war, 1935-36, in world historiography]. *Rev. de Istorie [Rumania] 1978 31(10): 1793-1811.* A critical survey of the principal works on the Ethiopian War, 1935-36. Also examines the part played by the League of Nations Archives in Washington. Asserts that, despite extensive research, certain aspects remain inadequately covered, especially the publication of sources, Ethiopia's attitude, international opinion, and the economics of the war. 124 notes. R. O. Khan

2733. DeFelice, Renzo. LA SANTA SEDE E IL CONFLITTO ITALO-ETIOPIANO NEL DIARIO DI BERNADINO NOGARA [The Holy See and the Italo-Ethiopian War in the diary of Bernadino Nogara]. *Storia Contemporanea [Italy] 1977 8(4): 823-834.* The diary of Bernadino Nogara, a high Vatican official who enjoyed the confidence of Pope Pius XI, throws light on the pope's attitudes to the Italo-Ethiopian war. The pope deplored the possibility of war before it occurred, and after it started he discussed the possibilities of putting Benito Mussolini in contact with the negus. Nogara suggested that Pius XI and Franklin D. Roosevelt unite to achieve peace, but the pope replied that the US State Department had indicated that such a step would be impracticable. The author quotes from the diary, and reproduces four memoranda to Pius XI from Nogara keeping him closely in touch with foreign reactions, the effect of the war on Italy's economy, and related matters. Appendix. A. M. Collieu

2734. Dore, Gianni. GUERRA D'ETIOPIA E IDEOLOGIA COLONIALE NELLA TESTIMONIANZA ORALE DI REDUCI SARDI [The Ethiopian War and colonial ideology in the oral testimony of Sardinian veterans]. *Movimento Operaio e Socialista [Italy] 1982 5(3): 475-487.* Examines the processes and channels by which the official colonial ideology was diffused and eventually absorbed by men who were shepherds, peasants, and artisans at the time of their enlistment, and how these members of the Sardinian lower classes reacted on contact with the African populations subjugated by Italian imperialism. Focuses on their motivations and racial and religious attitudes. Based on oral sources in two rural and one urban area in Sardinia; 25 notes. J. V. Coutinho

2735. Doresse, Jean. ETHIOPIE: 1934-1977 (L'HISTOIRE SE RÉPÈTE-T-ELLE?) [Ethiopia: 1934-77: does history repeat itself?]. *Afrique et l'Asie Modernes [France] 1977 (3): 7-11.* The political argument behind recent secessionist attempts in the Ogaden in Ethiopia are reminiscent of the political myths with which Italy justified its aggression against Ethiopia in 1934.

2736. Dow, Thomas E., Jr. and Schwab, Peter. IMPERIAL LEADERSHIP IN CONTEMPORARY ETHIOPIA. *Genève-Afrique [Switzerland] 1973 12(1): 53-62.* Examines the nature and content of Ethiopian imperial leadership and authority, the character and success of imperial policy, and the problem of succession to the Emperor suggesting that attempts to promote social change have failed.

2737. D'Souza, P. P. THE ETHIOPIAN PARLIAMENT: ORIGINS AND EVOLUTION. *Africa Q. [India] 1981 20(3-4): 19-29.* Discusses Emperor Haile Selassie's establishment in 1931 of the Ethiopian Parliament, a purely advisory body, and its history until 1971.

2738. Eberhard, Paul. ETHIOPIE DÉCHIRÉE [Ethiopia torn]. *Études [France] 1978 348(6): 725-735.* Analyzes the history of the revolutionary events in Ethiopia since Haile Selassie's fall in 1974 and the recent intervention of the Russians and the Cubans.

2739. Edwards, P. G. BRITAIN, FASCIST ITALY AND ETHIOPIA, 1925-8. *European Studies Rev. [Great Britain] 1974 4(4): 359-374.* Shows how the accepted picture of British policy toward the Anglo-Italian exchange of notes in December 1925 and the Italo-Ethiopian treaty of friendship in August 1928 has been distorted by hindsight.

2740. Ellingson, Lloyd. THE EMERGENCE OF POLITICAL PARTIES IN ERITREA, 1941-1950. *J. of African Hist. [Great Britain] 1977 18(2): 261-281.* Traces the political development of Eritrea from 1941 when it came under British military administration to 1962 when the Ethiopian government abrogated a UN resolution by declaring Eritrea a province. This action of 1962 has activated a full-scale Eritrean independence movement. 90 notes. H. G. Soff

2741. Eshete, Aleme. ETHIOPIA AND THE BOLSHEVIK REVOLUTION, 1917-1935. *Africa [Italy] 1977 32(1): 1-27.* The Ethiopian government, a monarchy dominated by a strong Orthodox Church, was understandably hostile to Bolshevism. White Russian refugees began arriving in the 1920's and 1930's after sojourns in Western Europe, where favorable reports of Ethiopian receptivity circulated. Most refugees were military officers; some were nobles; one, "Prince" Amiradjibi, was an imposter. Several refugees were deported in the red scare of 1929, but they were exonerated after Captain Babikhian, who was the chief of the Addis Ababa Security Police and an Armenian exile hostile to Russians, was found to have fabricated their "Bolshevik plot." Based on interviews; 21 notes, appendix. W. R. Hively

2742. Frade, Fernando. EL CONFLICTO DEL CUERNO DE ÁFRICA [The conflict in the Horn of Africa]. *Rev. de Política Int. [Spain] 1978 (156): 161-175.* Describes the conflict in Ethiopia since the downfall of Haile Selassie (1891-1975) considering the influence of the USSR and the United States on the new government.

2743. Garretson, Peter P. FRONTIER FEUDALISM IN NORTHWEST ETHIOPIA: SHAYKH AL-IMAN 'ABD ALLAH OF NUGARA, 1901-1923. *Int. J. of African Hist. Studies 1982 15(2): 261-282.* Shaykh Al-Iman built a small state of mixed population on the frontier of Ethiopia by carefully balancing the stronger forces around him. His bands of elephant hunters and slavers survived as long as the frontier was unstable and collapsed with the advent of central authority. Based on Italian, British, and Ethiopian primary sources; map, 160 notes. R. T. Brown

2744. Garretson, Peter P. *MANJIL* HAMDĀN ABŪ SHŌK (1898-1938) AND THE ADMINISTRATION OF GUBBA. Tubiana, Joseph, ed. *Modern Ethiopia, from the Accession of Menilek II to the Present* (Rotterdam: Balkema, 1980): 197-210. Discusses the Gubba province of Ethiopia from 1900 to 1938, its relations with the Sudan, its status within the Ethiopian Empire, and its internal administration under Hamdān Abū Shōk.

2745. Gat, Moshe. BRITAIN'S POSITION REGARDING THE ISSUE OF THE OIL EMBARGO IN THE ITALO-ETHIOPIAN CRISIS, NOVEMBER 1935-MARCH 1936. Artzi, Pinhas, ed. *Bar-Ilan Studies in History* (Ramat-Gan, Israel: Bar-Ilan U. Pr., 1978): 255-274. Great Britain's position was determined by the Mediterranean military situation, especially by France's failure to promise assistance in a crisis. Britain avoided a conflict with Italy because of possible global repercussions and oil sanctions. However, the British government eventually became more aggressive about an oil embargo, principally to placate the Conservatives. The German occupation of the Rhineland effectively ended plans for imposing the oil embargo. Based on Cabinet minutes, 1935-36, and secondary works; 82 notes. A. Alcock

2746. Gebre-Medhin, Yordanos. ERITREA: BACKGROUND TO REVOLUTION. *Monthly Rev. 1976 28(4): 52-61.* "Ever since Eritrea became a historically definite community its history has been one of confrontation and resistance to colonial adversaries: Italy (prior to 1941), England (during the 1940's), and now Ethiopia." Though the UN declared that Eritrea and Ethiopia would become federated co-equals, the demise of Eritrean self-determination was the inevitable result. Since 1961, the resistance of the Eritrean liberation front has given hope to the beleaguered masses of both countries. 4 notes. M. R. Yerburgh

2747. Getachew, Mekasha. AN INSIDE VIEW OF THE ETHIOPIAN REVOLUTION. *Munger Africana Lib. Notes 1977 39:7-39.* Mekasha Getachew, an Ethiopian diplomat who served both Haile Selassie and the revolutionary Dergue, describes from exile the course and excesses of the Ethiopian Revolution, 1973-77.

2748. Gilkes, Patrick. ETHIOPIA: REAL REVOLUTION? *World Today [Great Britain] 1975 31(1): 15-23.* "The soldiers have overthrown the Emperor and executed many of his ministers, but they will have a harder job getting rid of feudalism—not least because they might find it difficult to stay united." J

2749. Gilkes, Patrick S. ÄTHIOPIEN: REVOLUTION AUF HALBEM WEGE [Ethiopia: revolution half way]. *Europa Archiv [West Germany] 1975 30(17): 529-538.* The unwillingness of Emperor Haile Selassie to reform Ethiopian feudalism and the catastrophic drought of the early 1970's provoked the military coup of 1974 that then slowly turned into a socialist revolution.

2750. Goglia, Luigi. UN ASPETTO DELL'AZIONE POLITICA ITALIANA DURANTE LA CAMPAGNA D'ETIOPIA 1935-1936: LA MISSIONE DEL SENATORE JACOPO GASPARINI NELL'AMHARA [One aspect of Italian political action during the Ethiopian campaign, 1935-36: Senator Jacopo Gasparini's mission to the Amhara]. *Storia Contemporanea [Italy] 1977 8(4): 791-822.* An account of Jacopo Gasparini's role before and during the Ethiopian war. Gasparini was a realistic and successful colonist, governor of Eritrea, and friend of the powerful Amhara chief Aialeu Burrú. Burrú's attitude to the war was complex but he resented the negus and was therefore vulnerable to Italian advances. Benito Mussolini knew this, and Gasparini was requested to go to Amhara with the assistance of the political office of the East African command. In May 1936, after Burrú had formally submitted to the Italian government, General Pietro Badoglio curtly dispensed with Gasparini's services. Reproduces a letter sent by Burrú to Gasparini in May 1936, and Gasparini's summary of conditions in Amhara in that month. 42 notes. A. M. Collieu

2751. Gromyko, A. A. SOVETSKO-EFIOPSKIE SVIAZI [Soviet-Ethiopian relations]. *Narody Azii i Afriki [USSR] 1980 (1): 3-13.* Surveys the history of relations between the USSR and Ethiopia with a brief glance at their historical origins from the fifth and sixth centuries. Emphasizes the support given by the Soviet Union to Ethiopia to solve its economic problems and the various agreements between the two countries during national and world crises since the establishment of diplomatic relations in 1943. Reflects the adherence of both countries to the ideals of the struggle against imperialism and colonialism and for peace and social progress in Africa and the world. 20 notes. English summary. C. Pichelin

2752. Gromyko, A. A. SSSR-EFIOPIIA: TRADITSII I SOVREMENNOST' [USSR-Ethiopia: tradition and the present]. *Aziia i Afrika Segodnia [USSR] 1979 (10): 2-5.* Describes the traditional ties of friendship between the peoples of the Soviet Union and Ethiopia, of the Soviet Union's aid to the fraternal people of Ethiopia who are building a new life, and of the theoretical study by Soviet Africanists of the processes going on in Ethiopia. J

2753. Gupta, Vijay. THE ETHIOPIAN REVOLUTION: CAUSES AND RESULTS. *India Q. [India] 1978 34(2): 158-174.* Explores the costs and results of the Ethiopian revolution of 1974. Supported by the church, feudal lords, and the military elite for over 50 years, Emperor Haile Selassie ruled Ethiopia in a medieval authoritarian manner. Only during Italian occupation, 1935-41, was his rule challenged. After devastating famines in 1971-73, junior army officers overthrew the emperor. Brigadier General Teferi Benti assumed power and proclaimed a socialist program of *Ethiopia Tikdem* (Ethiopia first). The nationalization of transportation and utilities followed shortly thereafter, but pervasive poverty continued in the country, still dependent on foreign aid. Secondary sources; 56 notes. S. H. Frank

2754. Hamilton, David. SCHEDULE OF INTERNATIONAL AGREEMENTS RELATING TO THE BOUNDARIES OF ETHIOPIA. *Ethiopia Observer 1973 16(2): 58-69.* A tabular summary, 1827-1968, of treaties that have affected the boundaries of Ethiopia, including commercial treaties. Based on official British publications, British Foreign Office and Colonial Office documents, and secondary sources. R. M. Maxon

2755. Harbeson, John W. SOCIALISM, TRADITIONS, AND REVOLUTIONARY POLITICS IN CONTEMPORARY ETHIOPIA. *Can. J. of African Studies [Canada] 1977 11(2): 217-234.* Analyzes the ideological formulations and political style of the revolutionary military government of Ethiopia, concentrating on the National Democratic Revolutionary Program and the steps that have been taken toward its implementation. Ethiopia is attempting an introduction of the new ideas and restoration of customs and values "distorted, impugned and/or suppressed by contemporary external pressures. This involves changes in relative political power between regions and/or ethnic groups affected by past imperial influences to varying degrees." The *derg's* use of force to achieve its goals seems to come more naturally to it than its ability to mobilize a revolutionary constituency to the same end. This appears in practical reality to have some similarity to the previous regime. 47 notes. R. V. Ritter

2756. Harbeson, John W. TERRITORIAL AND DEVELOPMENT POLITICS IN THE HORN OF AFRICA: THE AFAR OF THE AWASH VALLEY. *African Affairs [Great Britain] 1978 77(309): 479-498.* Discusses the Provisional Military Government's (PMG) settlement plans for the Afar peoples of the Awash Valley in Ethiopia, 1972.

2757. Hayward, R. J. and Hassan, Mohammed. THE OROMO ORTHOGRAPHY OF SHAYKH BAKRI SAPALŌ. *Bull. of the School of Oriental and African Studies [Great Britain] 1981 44(3): 550-566.* Discusses the indigenous alphabet devised in about 1956 by Shaykh Bakri Sapalō for writing the hitherto exclusively oral language of his native Oromo districts of the Hagar region of Ethiopia. Bakri (1895-1980), a prolific writer in Arabic, poet, teacher, theologian, and historian, was for more than 50 years a leading intellectual and political figure in Oromo society, an ardent nationalist and fierce critic of Ethiopian rule in the Hagar. His Oromo alphabet was intended to stimulate the growth of a sense of separate ethnic identity among the Oromo, and to bring their plight to world attention. Consequently, its diffusion was strenuously opposed by the Amharic-speaking officials of successive imperial and military-Marxist Ethiopian regimes determined to stamp out separatist movements in the region. Based on Shaykh Bakri's letters and political tracts in Oromo, oral information, and secondary sources; plate, 5 fig., 27 notes, ref., appendix. M. J. Clark

2758. Heiden, Linda. THE ERITREAN STRUGGLE FOR INDEPENDENCE. *Monthly Rev. 1978 30(2): 13-28.* Discusses the roots of the conflict between Eritrean and Ethiopian central government forces, the internal politics of both regions, and the international significance of the conflict, 1950's-76.

2759. Henze, Paul B. COMMUNISM AND ETHIOPIA. *Problems of Communism 1981 30(3): 55-74.* Despite Communist rhetoric and some early radical social measures, the regime of Ethiopian leader Mengistu Haile Mariam is finding Marxist solutions and Soviet-bloc influence of decreasing relevance to the domestic and foreign problems facing Ethiopia. Traditional nationalism and resurgent Christianity and Islam are strong obstacles to the Marxist ideology. Furthermore, the military leadership shows no haste to develop a genuine revolutionary party. Based on international newspaper accounts; 62 notes. J. M. Lauber

2760. Iadarola, Antoinette. ETHIOPIA'S ADMISSION INTO THE LEAGUE OF NATIONS: AN ASSESSMENT OF MOTIVES. *Int. J. of African Hist. Studies 1975 8(4): 601-622.* A reassessment of the underlying motives of the European powers in regard to Ethiopia's admission to the League of Nations in 1923, based on hitherto unpublished British documents now available at the Public Records Office together with the Italian records. The scramble for Africa was still on, Ethiopia and Liberia being the only remaining independent states. France espoused Ethiopia's cause for economic reasons and to strengthen its cause against Italy in Northern Africa. Italians supported the application only after they realized they could not muster enough votes to oppose it. Great Britain opposed vigorously, ostensibly shocked at the slavery problem and lack of control of arms and incursions into neighboring British spheres of influence, but actually out of imperialistic and strategic designs. Map, 89 notes. R. V. Ritter

2761. Kane, Thomas. THE NASI-RAS ABBÄBÄ ARÄGAY TRUCE ACCORDING TO TWO AMHARIC SOURCES. *Bull. of the School of Oriental and African Studies [Great Britain] 1976 39(1): 47-61.* Several books have been written about the Ethiopian War 1935-41 and they "represent primary sources from the Ethiopian point of view." The author, however, examines several of the difficulties in using such sources and recounts from two of them a significant event of that war when the Italian failure to crush the patriots' spirit of resistance was implied by the arrangement of a truce agreement between General Nasi, the Italian military governor of Shoa province, and the best known of the guerrillas, Ras Abbäbä Arägay. The author provides an analytical account of the events leading to the truce and the gains both sides hoped to obtain by it. Primary sources; 2 figs., 62 notes. R. G. Neville

2762. Keller, Edmond J. THE REVOLUTIONARY TRANSFORMATION OF ETHIOPIA'S TWENTIETH-CENTURY BUREAUCRATIC EMPIRE. *J. of Modern African Studies [Great Britain] 1981 19(2): 307-335.* Emperor Haile Selassie put together Ethiopia's bureaucratic empire on the foundation of centuries of ties between the crown, the Coptic Church, and the nobility and the work of his three important predecessors since 1855. Fundamental contradictions between the traditionalist-bureaucratic regime and peasants, subordinated ethnic groups, and smaller numbers of industrial workers and Western-educated Ethiopians, together with harsh economic problems, made the country ripe for the revolution that destroyed the imperial structure. The Armed Forces Coordinating Committee, or Derg, oversaw reform in the early months of the revolution and has ruthlessly smashed opposition. But it has been unable to legitimize its authority under a widely accepted new social myth to replace the old imperial tradition. Based on newspapers and secondary sources; 58 notes. L. W. Truschel

2763. Koehn, Peter. ETHIOPIAN POLITICS: MILITARY INTERVENTION AND PROSPECTS FOR FURTHER CHANGE. *Africa Today 1975 22(2): 7-21.* Addresses the prospects of Ethiopia since the 1974 coup. The military junta's campaign against corruption and the elimination of the former elite make significant change possible. Secondary sources; 45 notes. G. O. Gagnon

2764. Kokiev, A. and Vigand, V. NATIONAL DEMOCRATIC REVOLUTION IN ETHIOPIA: ECONOMIC AND SOCIO-POLITICAL ASPECTS. Tubiana, Joseph, ed. *Modern Ethiopia, from the Accession of Menelik II to the Present* (Rotterdam: Balkema, 1980): 417-424. Employs a Marxist perspective to analyze the 1974 Ethiopian revolution, the 1976 Program of the National Democratic Revolution in Ethiopia, and related events.

2765. Kühlein, Conrad. DIE AUSWIRKUNGEN DER REVOLUTION IN ÄTHIOPIEN AUF DIE LAGE AM HORN VON AFRIKA [The effects of the Ethiopian revolution on the situation in the Horn of Africa]. *Europa Archiv [West Germany] 1978 33(5): 135-144.* The increasing influence of the USSR in Ethiopia since 1974 enabled the military leadership to continue its wars against various Ethiopian ethnic minorities and at the same time to threaten neighboring states with war in territorial disputes.

2766. Labrousse, Henri. L'ETHIOPIE ET LE TRAITE DE VERSAILLES (SOURCES DIPLOMATIQUES FRANÇAISES) [Ethiopia and the Treaty of Versailles: French diplomatic sources]. Tubiana, Joseph, ed. *Modern Ethiopia, from the Accession of Menilek II to the Present* (Rotterdam: Balkema, 1980): 283-301. Describes Ethiopia's independence, its role among the allies at the end of World War I, and its admission to the League of Nations in 1923.

2767. Lang, Franz. POLITISCHE STABILITÄT UND RECHTSSICHERHEIT: GARANTEN DES FRIEDENS. EVALUIERUNG VON LEHRERFAHRUNGEN AN DER HAILE-SELLASSI-I-UNIVERSITÄT IN ADDIS ABEBA [Political stability and security of law, guarantees of peace: evaluation of teaching experiences at Haile Selassie I University in Addis Ababa]. *Zeitschrift für Politik [West Germany] 1973 20(2): 198-207.* Outlines the sociopolitical conditions in Ethiopia, and speculates on the prospects and methods of internal political change. Chances for social and political change are limited; the most important factor is the gradual development of a competent class of government officials imbued with the principles of the rule of law. Based on secondary works; 18 notes. J. B. Street

2768. Leitner, David L. BELLIGERENT RECOGNITION IN INTERNATIONAL LAW: ERITREA: A CASE STUDY. *Towson State J. of Int. Affairs 1979 13(2): 77-96.* Survey of international law pertaining to the recognition of belligerents, 1850's-1930's, indicates that Eritrea meets necessary requirements—a permanent population, a defined territory, a civil government administering that territory, and official relations with third states—and should be given belligerent status in its attempts at secession from Ethiopia.

2769. Lobban, Richard. THE ERITREAN WAR: ISSUES AND IMPLICATIONS. *Can. J. of African Studies [Canada] 1976 10(2): 335-346.* Examines the geographic and historical differences between Ethiopia and Eritrea, discussing the recent outbreak in 1975 of guerrilla warfare after Eritrea's 14-year struggle for national recognition, the basis for the Eritreans' claim as a separate nationality, the religious and political issues involved, and the professed goals of the Eritreans.

2770. Loir, Raymond. L'ETHIOPIE ET LES PAYS ARABES [Ethiopia and the Arab countries]. *Ecrits de Paris [France] 1974 (342): 51-55.* Discusses the future of Arab Eritrea with the downfall of Emperor Haile Selassie, who had annexed it over UN opposition. P. Rabineau/S

2771. Lupu, N. Z. CONFLICTUL ITALO-ETIOPIAN ŞI UNELE SCHIMBĂRI ÎN RAPORTUL DE FORŢE PE PLAN INTERNAŢIONAL [The Italian-Ethiopian conflict and changes in the balance of power at international level]. *Rev. de Istorie [Rumania] 1977 30(5): 883-899.* Surveys the most serious international consequences of the Ethiopian war, considering: the reinforcement of the aggressive Nazi policy of arbitrarily violating treaties; the consolidation of Germany's position of influence within and outside Europe; the rapprochement and eventual alliance between Italy and Germany; and the subsequent diminution of power of the League of Nations. Based on documentary evidence including Rumanian archival material; 81 notes. R. O. Khan

2772. Lupu, N. Z. PRELUDII DIPLOMATICE ALE RĂZBOIULUI ITALO-ETIOPIAN [Diplomatic preludes to the Italo-Ethiopian war]. *Rev. de Istorie [Rumania] 1975 28(3): 385-405.* The major international episodes of December 1934 - September 1935 in the Italo-Ethiopian conflict as a prelude to the 1935-36 war. Stresses the appeasement policy of France and Great Britain toward Italy, which favored the outbreak of aggression. RSA (12:1354)

2773. Macconi, Ennio. ERITREA CHIAMA [Eritrea calls]. *Ponte [Italy] 1980 36(2-3): 152-170.* An Italian journalist gives his impressions of the military and political situation in Eritrea, the problems of the refugees and the hopes and problems of the popular liberation army.

2774. Makeev, D. A. SOVETSKO-EFIOPSKIE OTNOSHENIIA V 20-30ᵉ GODY [Soviet-Ethiopian relations in the 1920's and 1930's]. *Narody Azii i Afriki [USSR] 1975 (5): 139-145.* Ethiopia, one of the few independent African states, was first to show an interest in developing better relations with the USSR. The USSR in turn began to develop and strengthen its ties with Ethiopia. The author describes the Soviet Union's unsuccessful attempts to normalize relations and establish trade between the two countries in 1924, 1925, and in the 1930's. Discusses the Italian-Ethiopian War of 1935-36 and the Soviet demands in the League of Nations Assembly for economic sanctions against Italy. Based on primary and secondary sources; 28 notes. L. Kalinowski

2775. Marcus, Harold G. T'SEHAI NEGUS (SUN KING). Tubiana, Joseph, ed. *Modern Ethiopia, from the Accession of Menelik II to the Present* (Rotterdam: Balkema, 1980): 459-468. Discusses Haile Selassie's long career as provincial governor, regent, king, and emperor of Ethiopia, especially the guise of intelligence, modesty, and progressiveness which led many Europeans to view him as Ethiopia's last defense in a world of avaricious imperialism.

2776. McClellan, Charles. PERSPECTIVES ON THE *NEFTENYA-GABBAR* SYSTEM: THE DARASA, ETHIOPIA. *Africa [Italy] 1978 33(3): 426-440.* Ethiopia conquered Darassa 60 years ago, and established a landlord system there that bordered on slavery. The Darassans chafed under this rule but could do little about it. Some fled to the forests, others migrated to unsettled regions, but the majority grudgingly submitted to the new master. The revolt of 1975 must be understood within this framework. Promised land reform, the peasants took matters into their own hands during a period of political changeover. They were reclaiming that which they considered to be rightfully theirs. The former landlords took to the hills and staged guerrilla warfare, but were soon eliminated. 29 notes. V. L. Human

2777. Molyneux, Maxine. ALGUNOS PROBLEMAS EN EL ANÁLISIS DE LA REVOLUCIÓN ETÍOPE [Some problems in the analysis of the Ethiopian revolution]. *Estudios de Asia y África [Mexico] 1979 14(3): 541-564.* Attempts to analyze the Ethiopian revolution, describing the characteristics of the political structures that have emerged since 1974 and the principal problems of the revolutionary process in the country's march toward socialism. 14 notes. J. V. Coutinho

2778. Mori, Renato. DELLE CAUSE DELL'IMPRESA ETIOPICA MUSSOLINIANA [The causes of Mussolini's Ethiopian enterprise]. *Storia e Politica [Italy] 1978 17(4): 663-706.* Benito Mussolini's 1935-36 conquest of Ethiopia was the fulfillment of an old dream of Italian nationalists and imperial planners. These plans were put into operation due to a favorable situation internationally, and economic difficulties in Italy. The Great Depression had hit hard, and the prestige of the regime had suffered. A foreign adventure would put people to work, rally public opinion to the government's side, and eventually provide room for Italian settlers. Another factor determining Mussolini's timing of the invasion was Emperor Haile Selassie's policy of centralization, which threatened to create a strong Ethiopia in the future, one less susceptible to Italian infiltration of its periphery. 98 notes. J. C. Billigmeier

2779. Mulcahy, Edward W. RECENT DEVELOPMENTS IN ETHIOPIA. *Issue 1975 5(1): 43-44.* Explains the recent rise of revolutionary movements in Eritrea and urges continued US aid to Ethiopia. S

2780. Nicolas, Gildas. PEASANT REBELLIONS IN THE SOCIO-POLITICAL CONTEXT OF TODAY'S ETHIOPIA. *Pan-African J. [Kenya] 1974 7(3): 235-262.* Most Ethiopians are peasants and a vast majority are also tenant farmers. Most land is controlled by the Imperial family and the Church. In spite of land reform measures during 1941-72, rebellion erupted in both Gojam and Bale provinces in 1968. Both were social and economic failures, sudden revolts that suddenly quieted. 2 maps, 27 notes. H. G. Soff

2781. Norberg, Viveca Halldin. SWEDES AS A PAWN IN HAILE SELASSIE'S FOREIGN POLICY 1924-1952. Tubiana, Joseph, ed. *Modern Ethiopia, from the Accession of Menelik II to the Present* (Rotterdam: Balkema, 1980): 327-350. Discusses whether Ethiopian-Swedish relations from 1924 to 1952 can be seen as one aspect of Haile Selassie's efforts to keep the Great Powers at a distance, focusing especially on the periods from 1924-36, when missionaries and various categories of Swedish personnel found employment in Ethiopian government service (a recruitment interrupted by the war between Italy and Ethiopia) and the period from 1945 to 1952, when large-scale recruitment of Swedes in Ethiopian civil service took place at the same time as missionary work expanded.

2782. Ottaway, Marina. SOCIAL CLASSES AND CORPORATE INTERESTS IN THE ETHIOPIAN REVOLUTION. *J. of Modern African Studies [Great Britain] 1976 14(3): 469-486.* Studies the factors that led to the breakdown of the old Ethiopian system, to the emergence of new social classes during the last decades of Haile Selassie's reign, and to the role different classes played in the unfolding of the revolution. From among the conflicting undercurrents, the attempt by a small military elite to transform the socioeconomic system of the country and to develop political institutions congruent with the new realities of development has prevailed. 31 notes. R. V. Ritter

2783. Pankhurst, Richard. ABUNA PETROS: AN ETHIOPIAN PATRIOT MARTYR IN THE MODERN AMHARIC THEATRE. *Ethiopia Observer 1973 16(2): 118-124.* Describes the martyrdom of Abuna Petros, Bishop of Dessie, and three theatrical renditions of the cleric's execution. Based on dramatic presentations, Italian memoirs, Ethiopian documents on Italian war crimes, and secondary sources; 10 notes. R. M. Maxon

2784. Pankhurst, Richard. THE ITALO-ETHIOPIAN WAR AND LEAGUE OF NATIONS SANCTIONS, 1935-1936. *Genève-Afrique [Switzerland] 1974 13(2): 5-29.* Describes Italo-Ethiopian foreign relations, 1922-36, and international reactions to the invasion of 1935, and assesses the cost to Italy of League of Nations sanctions.

2785. Pankhurst, Richard. THE SECRET HISTORY OF THE ITALIAN FASCIST OCCUPATION OF ETHIOPIA, 1935-1941. *Africa Q. [India] 1977 16(4): 35-86.* Describes the weakness, brutality, and instability of Italian-occupied Ethiopia, as military and civilian authorities vied for power in an increasingly perilous situation.

2786. Papp, Daniel S. THE SOVIET UNION AND CUBA IN ETHIOPIA. *Current Hist. 1979 76(445): 110-114, 129-130.* Compares the political, military, and economic interests of the USSR and Cuba in Ethiopia, 1967-78, and provides background on the conflict there.

2787. Parker, R. A. C. GREAT BRITAIN, FRANCE, and THE ETHIOPIAN CRISIS, 1935-1936. *English Hist. R. [Great Britain] 1974 89(351): 293-332.* Analyzes the "policies of the British and French governments towards the crisis caused by the Italian attack on Ethiopia" in 1935. Fear of an internal social revolution prevented the French from opposing Mussolini too strongly. Britain feared that should Italy attack the Mediterranean fleet France would stand aside, and therefore would not blame France for the lack of effective measures to halt Italian ambitions. Discusses attempts to prevent the attack, attempts to halt the advance, maneuvers following the Hoare-Laval agreement, and the period following the collapse of Ethiopian arms, with particular focus on the period between the attack in October and the Hoare-Laval agreement in December 1935. While the British Cabinet, Foreign Office, Eden, and Vansittart may have had misgivings about the Hoare-Laval terms, they supported the general principles until adverse public reaction became evident. Reveals some lack of decisiveness by Eden although he emerged from the crisis with a reputation for insight and resistance to fascism. Based on the Cabinet and Foreign Office Papers in the British Public Record Office and French sources; 130 notes. R. J. Gromen

2788. Perret, Michel. L'ERYTHREE, LE FASCISME ET LA CRISE [Eritrea, fascism, and crisis]. Tubiana, Joseph, ed. *Modern Ethiopia, from the Accession of Menelik II to the Present* (Rotterdam: Balkema, 1980): 351-375. Describes the economic exploitation of Eritrea under Italian colonialism, 1885-1934, and its use as an Italian base against Ethiopia.

2789. Peyton, Gary D. THE SOVIET-ETHIOPIAN LIAISON: AIRLIFT AND BEYOND. *Air U. Rev. 1979 31(1): 66-73.* Examines the large-scale military airlift of arms and material by the Soviet Union to support the regime of Lieutenant Colonel Mengistu Haile Mariam in Ethiopia in 1977. Using An-12 and An-22 air transport, as well as cargo vessels, the Soviets delivered an estimated billion dollars in fighter-bombers, tanks, artillery, and ammunition in a very short time. The success of this operation demonstrates the ability of the USSR to project military force abroad in order to achieve foreign policy objectives. Based on periodical litrature; 2 drawings, 19 notes. J. W. Thacker, Jr.

2790. Procacci, Giuliano. LE INTERNAZIONALI E L'AGGRESSIONE FASCISTA ALL'ETIOPIA [The Internationals and the Fascist aggression in Ethiopia]. *Ann. dell'Istituto Giangiacomo Feltrinelli [Italy] 1977 18: 7-170.* When the armies of Fascist Italy invaded Ethiopia in October 1935, beginning the first war involving a European power since 1922, the Socialist International, headquartered in Brussels, and the Comintern, seated in Moscow, were loud in their demands for League of Nations sanctions against Italy. The leadership was unanimous in this stand, but there were many in the rank and file who opposed sanctions. The Communists denounced the invasion as an example of rampant imperialism, while the British Labourites pointed out the precedent that successful Italian aggression would set for similar territorial seizures in Europe. 119 notes, 3 appendixes. J. C. Billigmeier

2791. Richardson, Charles O. THE ROME ACCORDS OF JANUARY 1935 AND THE COMING OF THE ITALIAN-ETHIOPIAN WAR. *Historian 1978 41(1): 41-58.* Explores the so-called "Rome Accords" of 7 January 1935, between French Foreign Minister Pierre Laval and Italy's Benito Mussolini. Especially important were the discussions concerning Ethiopia. The understandings or misunderstandings arising from these records are analyzed, as are the consequences of the Italian-Ethiopian War which sabotaged Laval's European policy and drove Mussolini into the Axis. These agreements shattered Laval's plans for a Franco-Italian alliance, and Italy's Ethiopian adventure nearly ruined Laval's political career. M. S. Legan

2792. Robbs, Peter. BATTLE FOR THE RED SEA. *Africa Report 1975 20(2): 14-17.* History of Eritrea's relationship with Ethiopia, and the 10 years of intermittent guerrilla warfare which became a bloody secessionist war, 31 January 1975. S

2793. Robertson, A. F. PAPER LION: A NOTE ON SOME RECENT WRITING ON ETHIOPIA. *J. of Development Studies [Great Britain] 1977 13(4): 433-436.* Much of the recent literature on Ethiopia capitalizes on the 1974 coup, and, in the process, a harsh picture of Emperor Haile Selassie emerges.

2794. Rochat, Giorgio. LA MISSIONE MALLADRA E LA RESPONSABILITÀ DELLA PREPARAZIONE MILITARE IN AFRICA ORIENTALE NEL 1926 [The Malladra mission and responsibility for military preparation in East Africa in 1926]. *Risorgimento [Italy] 1970 22(3): 135-148.* Describes the conflict between military and colonial administration in Italian East Africa (AOI) during 1925-26 with regard to preparation for war with Ethiopia. Mussolini ordered military, economic, and diplomatic action in Ethiopia, but, mindful of the Italian defeat at Adowa (1896) at the hands of the Abyssinians, forbade giving arms to Abyssinian chiefs. Based on Italian archives and secondary sources; 25 notes, 2 appendixes. C. Bates

2795. Rochat, Giorgio. L'ATTENTATO A GRAZIANI E LA REPRESSIONE ITALIANA IN ETIOPIA NEL 1936-37 [The attempt on Graziani's life and the Italian repression in Ethiopia, 1936-37]. *Italia Contemporanea [Italy] 1975 26(118): 3-38.* On 19 February 1937 seven or eight small fragmentation bombs were hurled at Marshal Rodolfo Graziani, Viceroy of Abyssinia. About 30 persons were wounded but only one seriously. A bloody massacre followed, and for several days hastily organized Fascist units committed innumerable acts of terror. In addition to summary executions (324) over 1,000 people were rounded up and herded into concentration camps. In addition, Graziani ordered the total liquidation of all those associated with sorcery or soothsaying. The severity of the measures reveals the shocking cruelty of Fascist colonial rule. H. W. L. Freudenthal

2796. Sbacchi, Alberto. HAILE SELASSIE AND THE ITALIANS 1941-1943. *African Studies Rev. 1979 22(1): 25-42.* Immediately upon his return to Ethiopia, Haile Selassie established secret contacts with representatives of the defeated Italians. Subsequently he utilized the Italians to insure his own survival against continued opposition from Ethiopians and as a counterweight to imperial designs of the British. Based on Italian archives; 43 notes, biblio. R. T. Brown

2797. Sbacchi, Alberto. I GOVERNATORI COLONIALI ITALIANI IN ETIOPIA: GELOSIE E RIVALITÀ NEL PERIODO 1936-1940 [Italian colonial governors in Ethiopia: jealousy and rivalry, 1936-1940]. *Storia Contemporanea [Italy] 1977 8(4); 835-877.* Italian administration of defeated Ethiopia was chaotic, and the Italians looked upon the country as a source of personal wealth. Benito Mussolini appointed officials more for their loyalty to him, or to establish rivalries, than for administrative ability. Italy had no tradition of colonial administration, nor means of training for it. General Rodolfo Graziani was appointed viceroy in 1936, and Prince Umberto, Duke of Aosta, succeeded him in 1937. Graziani was a good soldier and loyal to

Mussolini, but he was narrow, neurotic, and cruel. The Duke of Aosta was a man of liberal views who had studied foreign colonial administration, but both men suffered from the jealousies and rivalries that seethed around them. 226 notes. A. M. Collieu

2798. Sbacchi, Alberto. ITALIAN MANDATE OR PROTECTORATE OVER ETHIOPIA IN 1935-36. *Riv. di Studi Politici Int. [Italy] 1975 42(4): 559-592.* Examines the Fascist insistence in obtaining Ethiopia, the negotiations between the Italian colonial minister and the French and British foreign offices, the League of Nations' rejection of Italian requests for an Ethiopian protectorate, and the eventual Italian resort to force to secure a mandate in Ethiopia. Appendix.

2799. Sbacchi, Alberto. ITALY AND THE TREATMENT OF THE ETHIOPIAN ARISTOCRACY, 1937-1940. *Int. J. of African Hist. Studies 1977 10(2): 209-241.* During its occupation of Ethiopia, Italy was hindered by the chaotic political and military situation from formulating a stable policy on how best to govern. Italy antagonized its Ethiopian subjects, and the memory of past abuses, particularly among the elite, was strong. Based on documents in the Italian Central State Archives and in the Ministry of Italian Africa; 2 charts, 163 notes. M. M. McCarthy

2800. Sbacchi, Alberto. LEGACY OF BITTERNESS: POISON GAS AND ATROCITIES IN THE ITALO-ETHIOPIAN WAR 1935-1936. *Genève-Afrique [Switzerland] 1974 13(2): 30-53.* Discusses the reasons for Italy's use of chemical warfare in Ethiopia in 1935-36, the extent to which it was used, the reaction of the Ethiopians, and its effect on the outcome of the war.

2801. Sbacchi, Alberto. PATRIOTI, MARTIRI, EROI E BANDITI: APPUNTI SULL'OPPOSIZIONE ETIOPICA ALLA DOMINAZIONE ITALIANA (1935-1940) [Patriots, martyrs, heroes, and bandits: notes on the Ethiopian opposition to Italian domination, 1935-40]. *Storia Contemporanea [Italy] 1982 13(4-5): 821-875.* After an initial period of hesitation and hopeful expectation of possible benefits resulting from the Italian occupation, the Ethiopian people soon revolted against measures of brutal repression and economic exploitation. In their resistance the patriots were aided by the neighboring French and British colonies. The Italians, led by general Rodolfo Graziani, committed the serious mistake of ignoring national patrimony and traditions in their unscrupulous attempt to subjugate the people. Based on primary material in the Italian State archive and the British Foreign Office; 156 notes. J. V. Coutinho

2802. Sbacchi, Alberto. SECRET TALKS FOR THE SUBMISSION OF HAILE SELASSIE AND PRINCE ASFAW WASSEN. *Int. J. of African Hist. Studies 1974 7(4): 668-680.* In an attempt to discourage resisters in Ethiopia, Italy entered into indirect negotiations with the Ethiopian royal family in London. The Italians sought the formal submission of Haile Selassie or his son, Asfaw Wassen, and the recognition by either of the Italian Empire. Based on documents in the Central State Archives of Italy and the archives of the former Ministry of Italian Africa in Rome; 54 notes. M. M. McCarthy

2803. Sbacchi, Alberto. [TOWARD THE RECOGNITION OF THE ITALIAN EMPIRE]. *Africa [Italy] 1975 30(3): 373-392, 30(4): 555-573.* Part I. Describes the diplomatic negotiations in which Italy sought recognition of its possession of Ethiopia and France pursued a course intended to protect its interests in East Africa and counter the German threat in Europe. Part II. ANGLO-ITALIAN NEGOTIATIONS FOR THE RECOGNITION OF THE ITALIAN EMPIRE: AND HAILE SELASSIE VS. THE NATIONAL BANK OF EGYPT AND THE CABLE AND WIRELESS CO., 1937-1938. Examines Italian-British relations before the recognition *de jure* of the Italian Empire, 11 November 1938. Concentrates on two legal questions regarding Haile Selassie's attempt to collect funds due the Ethiopian government for business contracted with the National Bank of Egypt and the Cable and Wireless Company. Discusses the political implications of these questions and the change in British government and public opinion toward the conquest of Ethiopia. 85 notes. J/S

2804. Sbacchi, Alberto. TOWARDS THE RECOGNITION OF THE ITALIAN EMPIRE: PERIOD 1936-37. *Riv. di Studi Politici Int. [Italy] 1975 42(1): 52-63.* Italy's rapid conquest of Ethiopia in 1936 caused Italy to be diplomatically isolated from Great Britain and France, who were not prepared to accept the king of Italy as the "Emperor of Ethiopia." In retaliation Italian authorities limited the diplomatic privileges of foreign diplomats in Addis Adaba. Radio contact of the legations with their capitals was forcibly cut off following the transmission of dispatches that were critical of Italian policies. The League of Nations played its usual role of indecisiveness in regard to the question of recognition of Italian control in Ethiopia. Smaller nations of Europe, however, joined Germany in recognizing the Italian empire to protect their commercial interests in Ethiopia. When the British and French governments recognized the de facto government of Italy over Ethiopia other nations did the same. The United States maintained friendly relations with Italy immediately after the conquest, but did not extend recognition. The isolation of Italy during these years and the willingness of Germany to extend full diplomatic recognition to the Italian Empire led to Mussolini's reluctant alliance with Nazi Germany. Based on documents of the former Italian Ministry of Africa and at the State Central Archives, memoirs, and newspapers; notes. J. Davis

2805. Scholler, Heinrich. VERFASSUNGSRECHT UND VERFASSUNGSPOLITIK IN ÄTHIOPIEN SEIT 1974 [Constitutional law and constitutional politics in Ethiopia since 1974]. *Zeitschrift für Politik [West Germany] 1977 24(4): 402-420.* Compares constitutional developments, and constitutional reality, in Ethiopia since 1974 with the constitutions of 1931 and 1955.

2806. Schwab, Peter. HAILE SELASSIE: LEADERSHIP IN ETHIOPIA. *Plural Societies [Netherlands] 1975 6(2): 19-30.* Discusses Haile Selassie's rule from 1930 to his overthrow in 1974, with special attention to his dual role as representative of the landed elite and Ethiopian political leader.

2807. Schwab, Peter. HUMAN RIGHTS IN ETHIOPIA. *J. of Modern African Studies [Great Britain] 1976 14(1): 155-160.* When the Military Committee executed some 60 officials, military officers, and landowners 24 November 1974, several international spotlights focused on this alleged violation of human rights in Ethiopia. The author examines the moral and legal grounds of this liberal publicity and analyzes the political realities it has obscured. The old regime violated human rights on a massive scale, and the struggle against the Orthodox Church and other large landowners cannot be a liberal, orderly process. If socialism is to uproot feudal society, then a violent revolution is necessary. Based on UN records and secondary sources; 18 notes. W. R. Hively

2808. Scott, William. HUBERT F. JULIAN AND THE ITALO-ETHIOPIAN WAR: A DARK EPISODE IN PAN-AFRICAN RELATIONS. *Umoja 1978 2(2): 77-93.* Hubert F. Julian (b. 1897), a black aviator from New York, enlisted in Haile Selassie's Ethiopian air force because of his strong Pan-Africanism, but following rejection, demotion, and deportation from Ethiopia in 1936, he became a vehement critic of Selassie and his conduct of the Italo-Ethiopian War, 1935-36.

2809. Sergeev, S. EFIOPIIA: REVOLIUTSIONNOE OBNOVLENIE DREVNEI STRANY [Ethiopia: revolutionary renewal of an ancient country]. *Novaia i Noveishaia Istoriia [USSR] 1980 (4): 151-164.* The 1974 national democratic revolution marked the end of a long period of feudal-monarchist repression in Ethiopia. Sketches the early history of the country and discusses events during and after the reign of Emperor Haile Selassie. Although Ethiopia was liberated from Italian occupation, Haile Sellassie returned with the support of British troops. Growing discontent produced an abortive coup d'état in 1960 and, as the emperor continued to obstinately oppose political reform, a successful one in 1974. Since then the revolutionary government has repelled counterrevolutionary attacks and pursued a course toward socialism. 3 notes, biblio. J. S. S. Charles

2810. Serra, Enrico. LA QUESTIONE ITALO-ETIOPICA ALLA CONFERENZA DI STRESA [The Italian-Ethiopian question at the Stresa Conference]. *Affari Esteri [Italy] 1977 9(34): 313-339.* Whether the Stresa Conference of Italian, French, and British foreign ministers, 11-14 April 1935, gave Mussolini a free hand to invade Ethiopia depends upon how one interprets Great Britain's position during the negotiations.

2811. Sisaye, Seleshi. HUMAN RIGHTS AND U.S. AID TO ETHIOPIA: A POLICY DILEMMA. *Africa Q. [India] 1979 18(4): 17-30.* Examines American military and economic aid to Ethiopia from 1951. Assistance continued after 1974, when Emperor Haile Selassie was deposed, because despite US objections to human rights violations in Ethiopia, prudence demands continued support in order to maintain the American presence.

2812. Skurnik, W. A. E. REVOLUTION AND CHANGE IN ETHIOPIA. *Current Hist. 1975 68(405): 206-210.* The new civilian and military forces in Ethiopia have an opportunity to lay the foundations of a more democratic and less friable regime. J

2813. Spencer, Joan H. HAILE SELASSIE: TRIUMPH AND TRAGEDY. *Orbis 1975 18(4): 1129-1152.* Discusses the role of Haile Selassie (1891-1975) in shaping the history of Ethiopia for the past 60 years, his successes and failures in his pragmatic approach to politics, belief in collective security, fight against colonialism, and stance on liberalization.

2814. Tedeschi, Salvatore. RIFLESSI DEL CONFLITTO ITALO-ETIOPICO IN AUSTRALIA (1935-1936) [Reflections of the Italian-Ethiopian conflict in Australia, 1935-36]. Tubiana, Joseph, ed. *Modern Ethiopia, from the Accession of Menelik II to the Present* (Rotterdam: Balkema, 1980): 377-386. Apart from the sizable Italian immigrant community, which was sharply divided on the subject of Italy's invasion of Ethiopia, Australian public opinion and government reacted mainly with profound disillusionment to the League of Nations' incapacity to deal effectively with the conflict.

2815. Thomas, Tony. ETHIOPIA: THE EMPIRE TREMBLES. *Internat. Socialist R. 1973 35(5): 4-11.* Despite continued American support, the regime of Emperor Haile Selassie appears to be crumbling internally, with civil disorder breaking out among students, military personnel, and the Eritreans. S

2816. Triulzi, Alessandro. ITALIAN COLONIALISM AND ETHIOPIA. *J. of African Hist. [Great Britain] 1982 23(2): 237-243.* A review article on six books (five from Italy) that deal principally with the military, political, and diplomatic events leading to the occupation of Ethiopia, during the period 1932 to 1940. 12 notes. R. L. Collison

2817. Trofimov, V. A. AGRESSIIA ITALII V EFIOPII I EE POSLEDSTVIIA [Italy's aggression in Ethiopia and its consequences]. *Voprosy Istorii [USSR] 1976 (8): 63-74.* Discloses the sum and substance of the policy furthered by Italian Fascism in Ethiopia in 1935-40: its military, economic, social, and administrative aspects. Examines the consequences of the Italo-Ethiopian war for both Ethiopia and Italy. Based on a wide range of documents, many of which appear for the first time in scientific literature in Russian translation. J

2818. Trofimov, V. A. ITAL'IANSKII FASHIZM I EFIOPIIA [Italian fascism and Ethiopia]. *Novaia i Noveishaia Istoriia [USSR] 1976 (6): 80-93.* The expansionist aspirations of Italian industrialists, landlords, and bankers are shown as the basis of the aggression of Italian fascism against Ethiopia. The author deals in detail with the elaboration of plans of aggression by the Italian fascists and their efforts to ensure foreign policy conditions for that aggression. J

2819. Warren, Anita and Warren, Herrick. THE U.S. ROLE IN THE ERITREAN CONFLICT. *Africa Today 1976 23(2): 39-53.* Provides a brief history of Eritrea from the Axumite Empire to 1975. Emphasizes the differences between Eritrea and the rest of Ethiopia. Concludes that US foreign policy is in a "no-win" dilemma: if the United States supports Eritrean independence, the Ethiopian government will take measures against the United States. If the United States resupplies the Ethiopian army, the inevitable Eritrean victory will result in loss of the Red Sea ports to the United States. Based on authors' residence in Asmara, primary and secondary sources; 54 notes. G. O. Gagnon

2820. Wiberg, Håkan. THE HORN OF AFRICA. *J. of Peace Res. [Norway] 1979 16(3): 189-196.* Constant turmoil in East Africa in the 20th century has centered in Ethiopia, which resisted the incursions of European powers, Arabs, Turks, and Egyptians. Its own territorial ambitions and poorly defined boundaries have resulted in conflict with Somalia, Eritrea, and Djibouti. The situation is complicated by domestic conflict in each of the Ethiopian border areas. Its strategic position for the control of traffic through the Red Sea makes instability in the Horn a concern to the major powers. The author offers several possible solutions to the problem short of armed intervention. 15 ref., biblio. H. F. Thomson

2821. Wright, Patricia. ITALY'S AFRICAN DREAM. *Hist. Today [Great Britain] 1973 23(4): 256-265, (5): 336-344.* Part II. FATAL VICTORY, 1935-6. Continued from a previous article. An analysis and evaluation of the Italian rationale, political background, and campaign tactics in the conquest of Ethiopia. Part III. NEMESIS IN 1941. Describes Britain's defeat of the ill-prepared Italians in Ethiopia, 1940-41.

2822. Yesus, Hagos Gebre. THE BANKRUPTCY OF THE ETHIOPIAN "LEFT": MEISON-EPRP, A TWO HEADED HYDRA—A COMMENTARY ON THE IDEOLOGY AND POLITICS OF NATIONAL NIHILISM. Tubiana, Joseph, ed. *Modern Ethiopia, from the Accession of Menelik II to the Present* (Rotterdam: Balkema, 1980): 447-457. Comments on the general political disarray and bankruptcy of the so-called Ethiopian left and especially of that particular brand of politics of national nihilism pursued by the two kindred political groupings Me'ei Sone or the All-Ethiopian Socialist Movement (AESM) and the Ethiopian People's Revolutionary Party (EPRP), noting especially that while leftist politics and rhetoric were rampant within the Ethiopian student movement, the movement as a whole was never known for its grasp of sound left politics.

2823. —. REVOLUTION IN ETHIOPIA. *Monthly Rev. 1977 29(3): 46-60.* Examines social and political conditions prior to the Ethiopian coup and describes the problems faced by the military government since 1974, including regional conflicts and threats from rival political factions.

Society

2824. Abélès, Marc. L'ORGANISATION SOCIALE ET LE CHANGEMENT A OCHOLLO (ETHIOPIE MERIDIONALE) [Social organization and change in Ochollo, southern Ethiopia]. Tubiana, Joseph, ed. *Modern Ethiopia, from the Accession of Menelik II to the Present* (Rotterdam: Balkema, 1980): 511-522. Describes nearly a century of upheaval in Ochollo as a result of ideological differences between conservative Coptic and progressive Protestant missionaries, which have led the country on the road to civil war.

2825. Ayalew, Solomon. MACRO EVALUATION OF HEALTH EXPENDITURE IN ETHIOPIA. *Ethiopia Observer 1973 16(3): 204-215.* Describes investment in health services, and their rate of development. Shows that Ethiopia ranks behind other African countries in physicians and hospital beds, and concludes that the national effort is much lower than required. Based on Ethiopian government reports, UN documents, and secondary sources; 16 tables, 47 notes, 9 appendixes. R. M. Maxon

2826. Blackhurst, Hector. ETHNICITY IN SOUTHERN ETHIOPIA: THE GENERAL AND THE PARTICULAR. *Africa [Great Britain] 1980 50(1): 54-65.* The Tulama, Orthodox Christian farmers, began in the early 1940's to migrate south to settle in northwest Bale province. The immigration reached its peak about 1956, and had practically ceased by the 1970's. The Bale highlands had been settled by Moslem Arssi, who were pastoralists, and had been conquered by the Amhara. Tulama and Arssi lived in peace but, owing to the difference in faiths, did not integrate; nor did either group have much to do with the Amhara. The Tulama produced a wide variety of cereal crops which provided the region with new opportunities to barter or earn cash to obtain manufactured goods. The three communities have remained distinct entities, the ethnic barriers never having been lowered. Based on fieldwork; 14 notes, biblio. R. L. Collison

2827. Brown, Robert L. COMPARATIVE STATISTICS ON CRIME: ETHIOPIA AND THE UNITED STATES. *African Studies R. 1973 16(3): 364-403.*

2828. Chauvin, Marcel. POLITIQUE LINGUISTIQUE DU GOUVERNEMENT IMPERIAL ETHIOPIEN (1973-1974) [The Imperial Ethiopian government's linguistic policy, 1973-74]. Tubiana, Joseph, ed. *Modern Ethiopia, from the Accession of Menilek II to the Present* (Rotterdam: Balkema, 1980): 425-446. Describes the promotion of Amharic as the official language to aid political, economic, and social integration, while English takes the place of French as the language of education and international diplomacy.

2829. Cohen, John M. ETHIOPIA: A SURVEY ON THE EXISTENCE OF A FEUDAL PEASANTRY. *J. of Modern African Studies [Great Britain] 1974 12(4): 665-672.* Although there is a large peasant class in rural Ethiopia, most rural Africanists ignore that nation in their studies. This article is an attempt to stop the continued ignoring of the Ethiopian feudal peasantry by noting the existing literature that does exist relative to that subject. 6 notes. H. G. Soff

2830. Ellis, Gene. THE FEUDAL PARADIGM AS A HINDRANCE TO UNDERSTANDING ETHIOPIA. *J. of Modern African Studies [Great Britain] 1976 14(2): 275-296.* A critical discussion of studying Ethiopia by means of the commonly accepted paradigm of feudalism. The paradigm confuses the picture more than it clarifies. It fails to take account of the dynamic of either the political system or the land tenure system. "Modern elites—the educated, the civil service, the military—hold power in Ethiopia, as they have increasingly over the last three decades." 63 notes. R. V. Ritter

2831. Gerdes, Victor. PRECURSORS OF MODERN SOCIAL SECURITY IN INDIGENOUS AFRICAN INSTITUTIONS. *J. of Modern African Studies [Great Britain] 1975 13(2): 209-228.* A study of various indigenous self-help organizations that have operated over many decades in tropical Africa, with emphasis on Ethiopia. These systems, which function more effectively than Western imports, take many forms. Though they may appear primitive, "they have been shown to be highly adaptable to the social needs of the people in the countryside who have been little affected by developments elsewhere." Their flexibility should commend them for consideration in other African countries. 28 notes. R. V. Ritter

2832. Guadagni, Marco. NOTE SULLE FONTI DEL DIRITTO ETIOPICO [Notes on the sources of Ethiopian law]. *Africa [Italy] 1973 28(3): 339-356.* Analyzes the eclectic sources of Ethiopian civil law following the introduction of the new civil code in 1960, with special reference to divorce. Emphasizes the survival of the Islamic *sharia* within Ethiopian traditional law, and stresses rules founded on equity. The *Fetha Negast* (Byzantine-Arabic ecclesiastic law) is insignificant concerning divorce, despite official statements to the contrary. 56 notes. R. O. Khan

2833. Kapeliuk, Olga. LANGUAGE POLICY IN ETHIOPIA SINCE THE REVOLUTION OF 1974. *Asian and African Studies [Israel] 1980 14(3): 269-278.* Contrary to the Emperor Haile Selassie's policy of stressing Amharic, the new revolutionary government of Ethiopia supports a pluralistic view. It has helped develop written forms for minority languages as well as providing printing and broadcasting facilities for the national minorities. Based on Ethiopian government documents; 26 notes. R. T. Brown

2834. Kessler, David. FALASHAS: A PATTERN OF PREJUDICE? *Patterns of Prejudice [Great Britain] 1975 9(1): 2-6.* Discusses the history and present plight of Ethiopia's Falashas.

2835. Levin, Meyer. THE LAST OF THE FALASHAS? *Midstream 1975 21(6): 44-49.* Discusses efforts to allow the Falashas, the black Jews of Ethiopia, to immigrate to Israel. S

2836. Lewis, I. M. THE WESTERN SOMALI LIBERATION FRONT (WSLF) AND THE LEGACY OF SHEIKH HUSSEIN OF BALE. Tubiana, Joseph, ed. *Modern Ethiopia, from the Accession of Menelik II to the Present* (Rotterdam: Balkema, 1980): 409-415. Discusses the role of the cult of Sheikh Hussein of Bale, a multifaceted symbol of local Islamic (and anti-Christian Amhara) identity, in bringing together Oromo, Somali, and Arab elements.

2837. Maibaum, Matthew. PLIGHT OF THE FALASHAS. *Patterns of Prejudice [Great Britain] 1974 8(4): 26-29.* Discusses the plight of the Falashas, the Black Jews of Ethiopia, especially from 1970 to the present, focusing on religious repression and violence, and natural disasters which have caused famine in Falasha communities.

2838. Milkias, Paulos. TRADITIONAL INSTITUTIONS AND TRADITIONAL ELITES: THE ROLE OF EDUCATION IN THE ETHIOPIAN BODY-POLITIC. *African Studies Rev. 1976 19(3): 79-93.* Describes the traditional education given to Ethiopian boys, including Haile Selassie, as it has been practiced ca. 1900-74.

2839. Milkias, Paulos Amaya. THE POLITICAL SPECTRUM OF WESTERN EDUCATION IN ETHIOPIA. *J. of African Studies 1982 9(1): 22-29.* Despite the destruction of the foreign-educated elite during the Italian occupation, 1936-41, Western education gained its adherents in post-liberation Ethiopia. Not the least of these was Emperor Haile Selassie, who accepted British and American influences and materials in the training of the bureaucratic elite whom he wished to see divorced from rival traditional loyalties. None of this, however, was able to survive the revolutionary situation which engulfed Ethiopia by the mid-1970's. Based on official Ethiopian publications and printed documents; 39 notes. L. W. Truschel

2840. Nazarova, N. EFIOPSKAIA TSERKOV' [Ethiopian churches]. *Aziia i Afrika Segodnia [USSR] 1982 (7): 56-59.* Ethiopia's religious groups include Christians of the Orthodox Church, Catholics, Jews, Protestants, Moslems, Greek Orthodox, Armenian Apostle believers, and followers of ancient cults.

2841. Pankhurst, Richard. THE MEDICAL HISTORY OF ETHIOPIA DURING THE ITALIAN FASCIST INVASION AND OCCUPATION. *Ethiopia Observer 1973 16(2): 108-117.* A description of Italian medical activity during the invasion of Ethiopia and the subsequent conquest and occupation. While not very substantial before the Italian occupation, medical facilities were significantly increased only for Europeans in the segregated system of Italian East Africa. While efforts to combat venereal disease did affect the African population to some extent, the Italian medical authorities were for the most part little concerned with the interests of Ethiopians. Little was done for them in the way of provision of facilities, care, or preventive measures. Based on contemporary periodicals, memoirs, secondary sources, Italian government reports, and U.S. State Department papers; 136 notes, appendix. R. M. Maxon

2842. Pankhurst, Richard. OLD TIME ETHIOPIAN CURES FOR SYPHILIS, SEVENTEENTH TO TWENTIETH CENTURIES. *J. of the Hist. of Medicine & Allied Sci. 1975 30(3): 199-216.* Syphilis was widely diffused in Ethiopia from the 17th to the 20th centuries. Physicians attempted to control and cure the disease by using indigenous medicines and European remedies. Upper-class patients were able to use the vapor baths using sarsaparilla and mercury while the masses had to rely on traditional forms of treatment. Illus., 100 notes. M. Kaufman

2843. Pankhurst, Richard. SOME NOTES FOR THE HISTORY OF TYPHUS IN ETHIOPIA. *Medical Hist. [Great Britain] 1976 20(4): 384-393.* Discusses the various outbreaks of typhus in Ethiopia, 1866-1941, and medical practices of colonial and native physicians.

2844. Pokshishievski, V. V. O DINAMIKE CHISLENNOSTI I NEKOTORYKH ETNICHESKIKH POKAZATELIAKH GORODSKOGO NASELENIIA EFIOPII [On the numerical dynamic and certain ethnic indices of the urban population of Ethiopia]. *Sovetskaia Etnografiia [USSR] 1973 4: 140-148.*

2845. Scott, William R. RABBI ARNOLD FORD'S BACK-TO-ETHIOPIA MOVEMENT: A STUDY OF BLACK EMIGRATION, 1930-1935. *Pan-African J. [Kenya] 1975 8(2): 191-202.* An account of the career of Rabbi Arnold Ford, an early advocate of Black Nationalism and leader of the back-to-Ethiopia movement. Accompanied by three other members of his congregation, Rabbi Ford arrived in Addis Ababa in 1930 in an attempt to obtain concessions for the rest of his group who, it was hoped, would follow soon after. The author records the difficulties encountered by those 60 members who made the journey to Addis Ababa, 1930-34. Some 25 members returned soon after their arrival and none remained after Ford's death in 1935 and the outbreak of the Italo-Ethiopian War. 52 notes. M. Feingold

2846. Shack, William A. ETHIOPIA AND AFRO-AMERICANS: SOME HISTORICAL NOTES, 1920-1970. *Phylon 1974 35(2): 142-155.* Afro-Americans have generally focused their attention on West Africa, from which most of them originated, but independent Ethiopia also has played a role. Being Christian, Ethiopia was attractive to Back to Africa advocates. A number of groups of Afro-Americans emigrated to Ethiopia during this period. Few stayed very long, but their contributions in military, economic, and social affairs were significant. Urban American Negroes had difficulty adjusting to primitive rural conditions. 26 notes. V. L. Human

2847. Shelemay, Kay Kaufman. CONTINUITY AND CHANGE IN THE LITURGY OF THE FALASHA. Tubiana, Joseph, ed. *Modern Ethiopia, from the Accession of Menelik II to the Present* (Rotterdam: Balkema, 1980): 479-489. Demonstrates the utility of ethnomusicological analysis in understanding the Falasha liturgical surface, and the potential contribution of this type of analysis in clarifying the dynamics of continuity and change within the Falasha liturgy in modern Ethiopia.

2848. Stommes, Eileen and Sisaye, Seleshi. THE DEVELOPMENT AND DISTRIBUTION OF HEALTH CARE SERVICES IN ETHIOPIA: A PRELIMINARY REVIEW. *Can. J. of African Studies [Canada] 1980 13(3): 487-495.* Discusses the administration of public health services and the training of Ethiopian personnel from 1941 to the present. The first national nursing school was founded in 1949 by the Red Cross. By 1969 there were nine nursing schools which had graduated 1,260 nurses three years later. Until the medical school was established at Addis Ababa University in 1964, Ethiopia depended upon training doctors abroad through fellowships and scholarships. 7 tables, 17 notes. S

2849. Torres, Tereska. THE MOST FORGOTTEN JEWS. *Present Tense 1974 1(2): 69-73.* Describes the Jewish community in Ethiopia. S

2850. Weissleder, W. AMHARA MARRIAGE: THE STABILITY OF DIVORCE. *Can. R. of Sociol. and Anthrop. 1974 11(1): 67-85.* "Marriage, divorce, and remarriage delineate significant status distinctions between the clergy and laity of rural Amhara society. Socioeconomic advantages of one group over the other cannot be held accountable for differential divorce rates between the two groups in view of the far-reaching homogeneity that encompasses both. Psychological gratifications, constraints, and pressures appear to be the same in clergy and in laity. In this paper, the incidence of divorce is related not to deterioration of individual marital bonds, but to the playing-out of the societal rationale upon which marriages are based. Divorce is here treated not as a manifestation of the war of men against women, but as a concomitant of the purposive institution of marriage itself." J

Kenya

General

2851. Gertzel, Cherry. DEVELOPMENT IN THE DEPENDENT STATE: THE KENYAN CASE. *Australian Outlook [Australia] 1978 32(1): 84-100.* A review article on E. A. Brett, *Colonialism and Underdevelopment in East Africa* (1973), D. Rothchild, *Racial Bargaining in Independent Kenya* (1973), M. Howard, *Political Integration of Urban Squatters* (1973), H. Bienen, *Kenya: Politics of Participation and Control* (1974), G. Lamb, *Peasant Politics: Muranga* (1977), R. Wolff, *Economics of Colonialism 1870-1930* (1974) and C. Leys, *Underdevelopment in Kenya*(1975). Suggests that the Marxian critique of inequality in Kenya based on concepts of class and capital, which blames foreign capital for constraints in development, neglects the complexity of the Kenyan case. Kenya's system incorporates many disparate elements. While it became more repressive, it was not unresponsive to the masses. Property is highly cherished. Postwar agricultural changes led to an African bourgeoisie which played a leading role in the nationalist movement. This mainly Kikuyu group retains power, and elements of ethnicity have a role. In face of population growth, unemployment, and growing inequality in the 1970's a strategy of redistribution through growth was adopted. 18 notes. W. D. McIntyre

2852. Lamb, Geoff. THE NEOCOLONIAL INTEGRATION OF KENYAN PEASANTS. *Development and Change [Netherlands] 1977 8(1): 45-59.* Discusses shortcomings in Kenya's political assimilation policy toward peasants, and social class aspects of capitalist economic development and agricultural production, 1960's-70's.

2853. Millman, Roger. PROBLEMS OF THE NATURAL ENVIRONMENT ON THE KANO PLAINS OF WESTERN KENYA. *Cahiers d'Études Africaines [France] 1973 13(2): 181-192.* The Kano Plains of Kenya lie at the head of the Kavirondo Gulf near Kisumu. This small area is one of the most densely settled districts of East Africa, but is plagued by alternating periods of drought and flood. With these problems, which it is proposed to correct by drainage and irrigation projects, the Kano Plains are an interesting case study of rural development found within this type of tropical environment. 3 maps, table, 11 notes. J. C. Billigmeier

2854. Ogot, Bethwell A. TOWARDS A HISTORY OF KENYA. *Kenya Hist. Rev. [Kenya] 1976 4(1): 1-9.* Discusses the problems historians have encountered in their attempt to trace the historical independence of Kenya.

2855. Segal, Aaron. KENYA: AFRICA'S ODD MAN IN. *Current Hist. 1981 80(464): 106-110, 130.* Surveys economic, political, and social development in Kenya since independence in 1963 and its position as an African bastion of capitalism, Western alignment, and civilian rule.

2856. Tamarkin, M. CHANGING SOCIAL AND ECONOMIC ROLE OF NAKURU AFRICANS, 1929-1952. *Kenya Hist. Rev. [Kenya] 1978 6(1-2): 105-125.* Discusses socioeconomic change in Nakuru in the Rift Valley, 1929-52, a center for European settlement, with special references to Kikuyu hostility to the emerging urban elite.

2857. Thurston, Anne. THE KENYA COPYING PROJECT. *African Res. and Documentation [Great Britain] 1981 (27): 15-21.* Describes unofficial institutional archives in Great Britain that provide sources for the study of 20th-century development in Kenya. Includes missionary letters and documents, individual company records, Chamber of Commerce records, cotton producers' minutes, and newspaper accounts of events in Kenya.

Economics

2858. Amsden, Alice H. A REVIEW OF KENYA'S POLITICAL ECONOMY SINCE INDEPENDENCE. *J. of African Studies 1974 1(4): 417-440.* Reliance on private enterprise has allowed Kenya's income to grow at an average annual rate of over 3% per capita, substantially higher than the African or Third World average. But unemployment and poverty have been so problematic that in February 1971 the Kenyatta administration invited a mission of the International Labor Organization to study the situation. The mission concluded that income redistribution must be deliberately promoted, but the government's response has been less than enthusiastic. Based on government documents, the ILO mission report, and secondary sources; table, 36 notes. W. R. Hively

2859. Atieno-Odhiambo, E. S. THE POLITICAL ECONOMY OF THE ASIAN PROBLEM IN KENYA, 1888-1939. *Transafrican J. of Hist. [Kenya] 1974 4(2): 135-149.* Analyzes Asian influence in East Africa. Asians were particularly involved in shopkeeping (dukawallah) in towns and bush country. They did not conspire to keep Africans in low status, but they did exploit Africans. The role of Asians in the political climate is discussed including their conflicts with the white settlers. 26 notes. H. G. Soff

2860. Austen, Ralph. CAPITALISM, CLASS, AND AFRICAN COLONIAL AGRICULTURE: THE MATING OF MARXISM AND EMPIRICISM. *J. of Econ. Hist. 1981 41(3): 657-663.* Reviews Gavin Kitching's *Class and Economic Change in Kenya: The Making of an African Petite-Bourgeoisie* (1980) and Frederick Cooper's *From Slaves to Squatters: Plantation Labor and Agriculture in Zanzibar and*

Coastal Kenya (1980) both of which trace, from a Marxist perspective, the development of African rural economies that have survived colonialism. 15 notes. J. Powell

2861. Barnes, Carolyn. AN EXPERIMENT WITH COFFEE PRODUCTION BY KENYANS, 1933-48. *African Econ. Hist. 1979 (8): 198-209.* Between 1933 and 1948 the Colonial Office fostered an experiment in coffee production among the Gusii of southwest Kenya to increase exports and the taxable wealth of African farmers. Since white settlers severely limited and controlled the program it neither won wide Gusii acceptance nor produced significant exports and wealth. The experiment ended when white control was assured and coffee was no longer so important to Kenya. Based on oral interviews with farmers, and documents from the Colonial Office and Kenya National Archives; 76 notes. W. D. Piersen

2862. Bassino, Aldo. LE COOPERATIVE NEL KENYA [Cooperatives in Kenya]. *Africa [Italy] 1976 31(2): 285-290.* At the end of World War II, all the cooperatives functioning in Kenya were made up of Europeans and Asians; the African presence counted for practically nothing. The colonial government of Kenya then made it a policy to encourage the development of cooperatives, and the government of independent Kenya has continued this. Today there are 900 functioning cooperatives in Kenya, of which 700 are agricultural. There are important associations of cooperatives and cooperative banks. Scandinavian countries, with a long history of cooperative endeavor, have given aid and advice and a Cooperative College of Kenya has been set up. 10 notes. J. C. Billigmeier

2863. Berg-Schlosser, Dirk. SOZIALE DIFFERENZIERUNG UND KLASSENBILDUNG IN KENIA. ENTWICKLUNGEN UND PERSPEKTIVEN [Social differentiation and changes in class structure in Kenya: development and perspectives]. *Politische Vierteljahresschrift [West Germany] 1979 20(4): 313-329.* An analysis of changes in class structure in Kenya before the outbreak of Mau Mau unrest and 10 years after independence, with data for the years 1950, 1960, and 1970, comparing the contributions of the various segments of society to the production of exports. The considerable increases in its main products, tea, coffee and pyrethrum after 10 years of independence represent the output of small holdings and have given rise to a kind of capitalism in the rich agricultural regions. But with only 14% of the land arable and the second highest rate of population growth in the world, Kenya must expect a sharp reduction in productive acreage per person and a vastly increased nonagrarian population. 2 tables, diagram, 5 notes, biblio. S. Bonnycastle

2864. Berman, B. J. and Lonsdale, J. M. CRISES OF ACCUMULATION, COERCION AND THE COLONIAL STATE: THE DEVELOPMENT OF THE LABOR CONTROL SYSTEM IN KENYA, 1919-1929. *Can. J. of African Studies [Canada] 1980 14(1): 55-81.* Discusses controls imposed by the Colonial Office on paid seasonal African laborers hired by Europeans to work their agricultural estates. There was a reaction against the increased use of colonial officials as labor recruiters because this "compromised the visible autonomy of the state and its role as paternal protector of the African and disinterested agent of social order." Settler treatment of Africans, however, had led to the replacement of private oppression with state sanctions. 86 notes. S

2865. Brokensha, David and Glazier, Jack. LAND REFORM AMONG THE MBEERE OF CENTRAL KENYA. *Africa [Great Britain] 1973 43(3): 182-206.* Outlines the effect of governmental land reform on the social organization and the system of land rights, 1959-71.

2866. Bujra, Janet M. WOMEN ENTREPRENEURS OF EARLY NAIROBI. *Can. J. of African Studies 1975 9(2): 213-234.* Focuses on the independent role played by women in the society of early Nairobi, Kenya. Through prostitution and beer brewing many women accumulated savings which they invested in houses. In order to have someone to bury them, that is, some "relatives," these women converted to Islam. Another practice to which these women resorted was "woman to woman" marriages. These landholding women became an important part of the African middle class urban economy, not susceptible to male control. Based on government documents, interviews, and secondary works; 43 notes. E. R. Campbell

2867. Coldham, Simon F. R. LAND-TENURE REFORM IN KENYA: THE LIMITS OF LAW. *J. of Modern African Studies [Great Britain] 1979 17(4): 615-627.* Attempts at reform of land tenure in Kenya, superseding customary law with registration of individual titles to land, date back to 1953 and have been pursued with great vigor since independence in 1963. An examination of two agricultural areas, in Central Province among the Kikuyu and in Nyanza among the Luo, and the experience of group ranches in Narok district, illustrate the limits of the law in inducing changes in people's behavior. A failure in communication between low-level bureaucrats and the people has meant that farmers have not always seen that a balance of advantage lies in the adoption of new modes of behavior. Based on fieldwork and printed sources; 23 notes. D. J. Nicholls

2868. Cole, William E. and Sanders, Richard D. POPULATION GROWTH AND EMPLOYMENT: MEXICO'S PAST AND KENYA'S FUTURE. *African Studies Rev. 1976 19(1): 151-163.* The labor force transformations and associated economic change in Mexico, ca. 1940-70, may anticipate similar developments in Kenya.

2869. Coray, Michael S. THE KENYA LAND COMMISSION AND THE KIKUYU OF KIAMBU. *Agric. Hist. 1978 52(1): 179-193.* Great Britain's policy on land tenure in Kenya was based on the Crown Lands Ordinance of 1902. This ordinance assumed that native Kenyans had no sense of land value other than actual usufruct, and that vacated lands should be sold to Europeans. The lost land contributed to native confusion and insecurity. In 1931 the Secretary of State for Colonies commissioned three men to study the problems of the Kikuyu of Kiambu. The Kikuyu claimed they had rights over lands they bought from the Dorobo prior to European contact. European settlers claimed the Kikuyu had no knowledge of individual land ownership until after European contact. The Kenya Land Commission voted in favor of the settlers, and the problem laid dormant until the Mau Mau revolution of the early 1950's. 42 notes. C. L. Harvey

2870. Cowen, Michael. SOME RECENT EAST AFRICAN PEASANT STUDIES. *J. of Peasant Studies [Great Britain] 1982 9(2): 252-261.* Discusses Torben Bager's *Marketing Cooperatives and Peasants in Kenya* (1980), John Carlsen's *Economic and Social Transformation in Rural Kenya* (1980), and Frederick Cooper's *From Slaves to Squatters: Plantation Labour in Zanzibar and Coastal Kenya, 1890-1925* (1980), which confirm that outside the White Highlands a middle peasantry is preponderant, though Carlsen disagrees. Also some methodological issues are discussed. Table. D. J. Nicholls

2871. Dalleo, Peter T. THE SOMALI ROLE IN ORGANIZED POACHING IN NORTHEASTERN KENYA, C. 1909-1939. *Int. J. of African Hist. Studies 1979 12(3): 472-482.* Organized poaching played an important part in the economic life of the Somali of the Northern Frontier District of Kenya. Somali pastoralists, livestock traders, and shopkeepers were major participants in a network which operated north of the Tana River. Somali perseverance in procuring and trading game trophies brought them into direct conflict with British-imposed game laws, and can be viewed as a form of resistance to the newly established British colonial structure. Based on documents in the Kenya National Archives, and Public Record Office (London), and secondary sources; 57 notes. M. McCarthy

2872. Dresang, Dennis L. and Sharkansky, Ira. SEQUENCES OF CHANGE AND THE POLITICAL ECONOMY OF PUBLIC CORPORATIONS: KENYA. *J. of Pol. 1975 37(1): 163-186.* Notes that governments expect public corporations to operate like commercial enterprises while simultaneously satisfying political demands. The emphasis on one or another of these expectations reflects the configuration and dynamics of politics. Kenya's experience suggests that public corporations will perform well commercially when the dominant political elite consists of those with economic advantages and strong commercial interests. When political power is wielded by those outside the most advantaged economic sectors, on the other hand, commercial performance is sacrificed for political goals. Technical traits of a corporation's activity have an important influence on opportunities for political rewards and contribute to an understanding of how public enterprises respond to political changes. J

2873. Dzięgiel, Leszek. TRADYCYJNA RODZINA CHŁOPA WSCHODNIOAFRYKAŃSKIEGO JAKO ZESPÓŁ PRODUKCYJNY [The traditional East African peasant family as a production team]. *Przegląd Socjologiczny [Poland] 1975 27: 159-178.* Studies the Luo tribe in Kenya, 1946-48. The larger agricultural production unit was the patriarch's extended family, mainly divided into a special assignment team led by the patriarch, and the teams of his wives, who, together with their children, worked their own lots on a regular basis. This stage of development was no longer strictly traditional, but still largely self-sufficient—i.e., primitive. Pressures of overpopulation and the prospects of cash crops, already in evidence then, have continued to make this subsistence economic system increasingly obsolete. From the author's doctoral dissertation. Based on secondary sources. L. A. Krzyzak

2874. Elkan, Walter. IS A PROLETARIAT EMERGING IN NAIROBI? *Econ. Development and Cultural Change 1976 24(4): 695-706.* Examines the question of "whether there are beginning to be substantial numbers in Nairobi who are wholly and permanently dependent upon wage employment and whose ties with their villages of origin have become severed." Although a review of the literature and statistical evidence seem to be in conflict, the author concludes that no permanent proletariat is emerging in Nairobi, but very temporary migration (two to three years) has declined. Based on published sources; table, 27 notes. J. W. Thacker, Jr.

2875. Freeman, Donald B. DEVELOPMENT STRATEGIES IN DUAL ECONOMIES: A KENYAN EXAMPLE. *African Studies Rev. 1975 18(2): 17-34.* Kenya, 1963-70, is used to illustrate that through economic planning the degree of productivity and the interaction between urban industrialized centers and traditional rural areas will improve.

2876. Fumagalli, Carl T. AN EVALUATION OF DEVELOPMENT PROJECTS AMONG EAST AFRICAN PASTORALISTS. *African Studies Rev. 1978 21(3): 49-63.* An evaluation of the design and the reasons for the failure of governmental agricultural development projects among the Maasai and Samburu of Kenya. Under both colonial and nationalist governments, these plans have taken little account of the realities of the culture and geography of the pastoral milieu. 2 maps, 2 notes, biblio. R. T. Brown

2877. Godfrey, E. M. and Mutiso, G. C. M. THE POLITICAL ECONOMY OF SELF-HELP: KENYA'S "HARAMBEE" INSTITUTES OF TECHNOLOGY. *Can. J. of African Studies [Canada] 1974 8(1): 109-133.* Gives the political and economic background to the movement since 1971 of rural self-help (harambee) committees' raising money to establish institutes of technology for secondary school graduates.

2878. Hay, Margaret Jean. LUO WOMEN AND ECONOMIC CHANGE DURING THE COLONIAL PERIOD. Hafkin, Nancy J. and Bay, Edna G., eds. *Women in Africa: Studies in Social and Economic Change*(Stanford U. Pr., 1976): 87-109. Innovations in agriculture and trade by Luo women from Kowe, Kenya, had resulted in increased production and capital investment since the 1890's. With deteriorating conditions in the 1930's, however, their experimentations were crucial to the maintenance of the same level of food production. Because of declining soil fertility, the withdrawal of male labor for wage employment, and increased colonial taxation through the 1940's, women reduced their concentration on agriculture, reinvesting it in trade. Education and long-term employment replaced agriculture and land ownership as the sources of economic security and social status. Based on interviews and secondary sources; 26 notes. S. Tomlinson-Brown

2879. Henley, John S. EMPLOYMENT RELATIONSHIPS AND ECONOMIC DEVELOPMENT—THE KENYAN EXPERIENCE. *J. of Modern African Studies [Great Britain] 1973 11(4): 559-589.* A study of the characteristics and problems facing labor in Kenya. Strategies for attracting and retaining workers in agriculture and industry were very different. Analyzes these differences for the colonial period and for the current employment situation. Compares small-scale enterprises, large-scale enterprises, and public sector organizations in these regards. While large-scale farms, industry, and the public service have increasingly come under the management of Africans, the division of the economy into rich and poor sectors remains comparable to the colonial. "The trend toward the formalisation of employment relationships seems to be an inevitable consequence of having exclusive, relatively affluent enclaves in an otherwise poor agricultural economy." 4 tables, 57 notes. R. V. Ritter

2880. Henley, John S. ON THE LACK OF TRADE UNION POWER IN KENYA. *Industrial Relations [Canada] 1976 31(4): 655-667.* Labor unions in Kenya were weak and lacked effective power, 1960's-70's. This was because of its social structure of strong vertical cleavages on ethnic and geographic lines and lack of strong occupational or class ties. In addition, management and government coopted many labor leaders after independence, and their departure to the "other side" crucially weakened the labor movement. 41 notes. J. C. Billigmeier

2881. Hodd, Michael. INCOME DISTRIBUTION IN KENYA (1963-1972). *J. of Development Studies [Great Britain] 1976 12(3): 221-228.* Computes two measures for Kenya's income distribution, compares this distribution with other countries, and explores possible causes for change in the Kenyan distribution and the effects of these changes on domestic economy, 1950's-60's.

2882. Holmes, R. S. LAND TENURE AND AGRICULTURAL PRODUCTIVITY IN THE TRANS-NZOIA, KENYA. *Geography [Great Britain] 1975 60(267): 137-139.* Small farms tended by Africans, sometimes in cooperation with the government Agricultural Development Corporation, replaced large-scale European farming in Kenya.

2883. House, William J. EARNING-PER-WORKER DIFFERENTIALS IN THE PROVINCES OF KENYA, 1963-1970. *J. of Developing Areas 1975 9(3): 359-376.* Analyzes earnings-per-worker and disparities found from province to province of Kenya for the 25% of the population who are wage earners. Some regions have faster growth rates than others, particularly in the higher salary occupations, thus creating income divergence. The slower-growing regions eventually trend toward greater income equality. Based on economic formulas, equations, and coefficients of variation; 8 tables, fig., 28 notes. O. W. Eads, Jr.

2884. House, William J. MARKET STRUCTURE AND INDUSTRY PERFORMANCE: THE CASE OF KENYA. *Oxford Econ. Papers [Great Britain] 1973 25(3): 405-419.* Relates market structure to the differences in performance of a selection of manufacturing industries in Kenya using statistical data provided by the 1963 Census of Industrial Production in Kenya.

2885. Jackson, R. T. PROBLEMS OF TOURIST INDUSTRY DEVELOPMENT ON THE KENYAN COAST. *Geography [Great Britain] 1973 58(1): 62-65.* Discusses tourist industry problems on the coast of Kenya as tourism rose between 1962 and 1972.

2886. Johnson, G. E. and Whitelaw, W. E. URBAN-RURAL INCOME TRANSFERS IN KENYA: AN ESTIMATED—REMITTANCES FUNCTION. *Econ. Development and Cultural Change 1974 22(3): 473-480.* Discusses the divergence between urban and rural income in Kenya and estimates the exchanges between the two sectors and its effect on the economy. Concludes that such transfers provide a significant increase in rural welfare, that the welfare of the typical individual in Kenya depends rather significantly on the number and closeness of relatives working in the urban sector, and that "the proportion of income remitted to rural areas declines as income increases." Based on material gathered in Kenya; 4 tables, 7 notes. J. W. Thacker, Jr.

2887. Jones, William I. SMALL FARMERS AND THE GREEN REVOLUTION IN KENYA. *African Econ. Hist. 1977 (4): 182-185.* Reviews John Gerhart's *Diffusion of Hybrid Maize in Western Kenya: Abridged by CIMMYT,* (Mexico City: Centro Internacional de Mejoramiento de Maiz y Trigo, 1975), which reports that small-scale farmers adopted hybrids much more readily than had been expected and have been quite successful in raising the new crops since 1964.

2888. Jorgensen, J. J. MULTINATIONAL CORPORATIONS AND THE INDIGENIZATION OF THE KENYAN ECONOMY. *African Rev. [Tanzania] 1975 5(4): 429-450.* Political decolonization also brought Africanization in staffing firms and in their ownership. Yet in the postindependence era Kenya's economy is structurally more dependent. 65 notes. R. T. Brown

2889. Jørgensen, Jan Jelmert. AFRIKANISERING AV DEN KENYANSKE ØKONOMI [The Africanization of the Kenyan economy]. *Internasjonal Politikk [Norway] 1975 (1): 109-123.* Discusses the Africanization of the Kenyan economy on three distinct levels. The first level is the structure and orientation of the economy as a whole. The second is the control of units of production and units of distribution within economic sectors and subsectors of the economy. The third is the division of labor by race within individual firms. By viewing the problem of Africanization of the Kenyan economy from these three separate levels, it can be shown that the process of political decolonization, begun in 1952 and culminating in formal political independence in 1964, has led to 1) a higher percentage of Africans in managerial and technical positions within firms, 2) increased African ownership of units of production in agriculture and units of distribution in commerce, particularly retail trade, but 3) markedly less progress in African control of firms in manufacturing, the import trade, and banking. The structure of the Kenyan economy remains predominantly externally oriented and un-Africanized because of a new coalition between foreign-owned firms and the political and commercial urban African elite, a coalition which has little motivation to transform the structure of the domestic economy to make it more responsive to domestic human needs and less dependent on the external international capitalist economy. J

2890. Kabwegyere, T. B. SMALL URBAN CENTRES AND THE GROWTH OF UNDERDEVELOPMENT IN RURAL KENYA. *Africa [Great Britain] 1979 49(3): 308-315.* The 1970-74 Kenya Development Plan designated four levels of centers to stimulate rural development: urban, rural, market, and local. Small urban centers were seen as the vital interface between the developing rural system and the developing urban system. However, the experiences of the 1970's suggest that this can result in the underdevelopment of the rural areas. The author argues that the rural areas were adjunct, and the small urban centers were mere nodes in the process of the further impoverishment of Kenya. R. L. Collison

2891. King, Kenneth. INDO-AFRICAN SKILL TRANSFER IN AN EAST AFRICAN ECONOMY. *African Affairs [Great Britain] 1975 74(294): 65-71.* Analyzes how Indian patterns of labor training for Africans differ from the model established by the Kenya government. British companies traditionally had apprentice programs, but the slumping economy has resulted in a curtailment of these programs. The government programs included a plan for reimbursement to the companies for the costs of training programs. The Indians, although condemned for years for unfair use of African labor, have in fact produced a system that creates a large number of trained African workers. 3 notes. H. G. Soff

2892. Leo, Christopher. THE FAILURE OF THE "PROGRESSIVE FARMER" IN KENYA'S MILLION-ACRE SETTLEMENT SCHEME. *J. of Modern African Studies [Great Britain] 1978 16(4): 619-638.* Shows evidence that agricultural investments have been misplaced when given to poor and uneducated farmers. Suggests instead that it would be more advantageous to educate potential farmers, assess their needs, study their priorities, before giving financial aid. Present agricultural policy in Kenya follows the British colonial model of land development which was meant to benefit white farmers. Based on Kenyan Agricultural Department archival documents, and secondary sources; 3 tables, 29 notes. A. Sbacchi

2893. Leo, Christopher. WHO BENEFITED FROM THE MILLION-ACRE SCHEME? TOWARD A CLASS ANALYSIS OF KENYA'S TRANSITION TO INDEPENDENCE. *Can. J. of African Studies [Canada] 1981 15(2): 201-222.* An analysis of Great Britain's Million-Acre Settlement Scheme in the 1960's as a prelude to Kenyan independence. Although the project served to satisfy at least some of the demands of potential trouble-causing groups and has been a prime cause of the stability that has characterized Kenyan independence, not much attention has been paid to its benefits to the European landholders whom it replaced. Discusses an earlier plan from the failure of which colonial authorities were to learn many lessons invaluable to the success of the later scheme. 46 notes. V. L. Human

2894. Leys, Colin. DEVELOPMENT STRATEGY IN KENYA SINCE 1971. *Can. J. of African Studies [Canada] 1979 13(1-2): 295-320.* Examines Kenya's development strategy, 1963-71 and attempts to identify the social forces that determined the real scope and effect of official policies. Stresses the work of the International Labor Organization (ILO) mission in 1972, whose strategy was accepted verbally, but rejected in practice. Explains the 1973-76 recession and land policy. Based on Kenya government documents; 2 tables, 3 graphs, 59 notes. G. P. Cleyet

2895. Leys, Colin; Borges, Jane; and Gold, Hyam. STATE CAPITAL IN KENYA: A RESEARCH NOTE. *Can. J. of African Studies [Canada] 1980 14(2): 307-317.* Examines the quantitative significance of state capital in the transition to capitalist production following Kenya's independence in 1963. Immediately following independence foreign capital was largely eliminated as an independent capital sector allowing formation of an African capitalist class. Non-African capital from private and state sources was needed to maintain the rate of expansion, especially in manufacturing, because of the amount of capital and production technology involved. The state has employed a wide range of agencies to shore up existing forms of capital and guarantee foreign investment. Reviewed here are: the Industrial and Commercial Development Corporation, the Development Finance Company, and the Industrial Development Bank. 7 tables, 12 notes. S

2896. Livingstone, Ian. AN EVALUATION OF KENYA'S RURAL INDUSTRIAL DEVELOPMENT PROGRAMME. *J. of Modern African Studies [Great Britain] 1977 15(3): 495-504.* A major aspect of development in Kenya is small-scale and rural industries promoted by either the Kenya Industrial Estates Ltd. or the Rural Industrial Development Programme (RIDP). Distinctions are drawn between household, cottage, dwarf, craft industries, and modern small-scale industries. The RIDP has been primarily concerned with the latter and several centers are examined in terms of training, skill, capital, supplies, management, and assistance. Table, 19 notes. H. G. Soff

2897. MacRae, D. S. THE IMPORT-LICENSING SYSTEM IN KENYA. *J. of Modern African Studies [Great Britain] 1979 17(1): 29-46.* Describes the development and functions of Kenya's import licensing system, from the colonial period to 1972, to regulate import and export and to protect local industries. Licensed imports have grown slower than unlicensed imports while local production of commodities was protected. Based on published government documents and secondary sources; 2 tables, 16 notes. A. Sbacchi

2898. Moore, T. R. LAND USE AND EROSION IN THE MACHAKOS HILLS. *Ann. of the Assoc. of Am. Geographers 1979 69(3): 419-431.* Population growth combined with irresponsible grazing and cultivating techniques have caused the Machakos hills of Kenya to erode severely, 1900-70's.

2899. Muir, J. Douglas and Brown, John L. TRADE UNION POWER AND THE PROCESS OF ECONOMIC DEVELOPMENT: THE KENYAN EXAMPLE. *Industrial Relations [Canada] 1974 29(3): 474-494.* Examines how the Kenyan government has sought to reconcile its economic development objectives with traditional freedoms such as the right to strike, the right to bargain collectively, and the right of free association. Discusses as well the development of labor legislation in Kenya and examines its effects on the strike weapon as a source of union power and the effect of strikes on the Kenya economy. J/S

2900. Muller, Maria. THE NATIONAL POLICY OF KENYANISATION OF TRADE: ITS IMPACT ON A TOWN IN KENYA. *Can. J. of African Studies [Canada] 1981 15(2): 293-301.* A review of the Kenyan policy of eliminating foreigners from the ownership of businesses. In the town of Kitale many Asian entrepreneurs were forced out, though some maintained control behind the scenes and others became nominal citizens. Kitale, once the center of a prosperous area of large farms, declined to the status of a small and obscure town. As such, it has little appeal to big business owners, a situation that has allowed local people to take over. 4 tables, 13 notes. V. L. Human

2901. Oculi, Okello. IMPERIALISM, SETTLERS AND CAPITALISM IN KENYA. *Mawazo [Uganda] 1975 4(3): 113-128.* Traces the origin of transforming African territories and societies into estates for

European joint-stock companies to the German, French and British capitalists' greed for African land. Once started in the 1880's, the momentum of land-grabbing quickly engulfed Kenya and Uganda so that from the very beginning of colonization the African legally owned nothing but his labor. The author sees the relationship between finance capitalism and the settlement of Kenya as the *fons et origo* of colonization. The large capitalists used the settlers in Kenya as a primitive and violent force against the African population, which was forced to exploit land and other resources in the interests of the finance capitalists. When faced with revolution, finance capital made a bargain with the African elite that would protect its own entrenched position in Kenya while sacrificing the interests of the conservative wing of the settler community. Secondary sources; 22 notes. J. J. N. McGurk

2902. Odenyo, Amos O. CONQUEST, CLIENTAGE, AND LAND LAW AMONG THE LUO OF KENYA. *Law and Soc. Rev. 1973 7(4): 767-778.* Discusses the types of conflicts raised over land ownership and status in Kenya due to the passage of the Limitation of Action Act in 1968. Seeking to modernize traditional land ownership and use, the act has produced unintended consequences. H. R. Mahood

2903. Okeyo, Achola Pala. DAUGHTERS OF THE LAKES AND RIVERS: COLONIZATION AND THE LAND RIGHTS OF LUO WOMEN. Etienne, Mona and Leacock, Eleanor, ed. *Women and Colonization: Anthropological Perspectives* (New York: Praeger, J. F. Bergin Publ., 1980): 186-213. Examines the interrelationship between land tenure and social organization in the Luo community in West Kenya. Historically women played a key role in the rural economy in terms of food production and reproduction. British attempts in the early 20th century to create a colonial socioeconomic structure through land tenure reforms changed corporate, lineage-based land tenure systems to individualized ones which altered the interdependent roles of men and women and created disputes within the descent group. Photo, 7 notes, ref. S

2904. Oyugi, W. Ouma. ASSESSING LOCAL ADMINISTRATIVE CAPACITY FOR DEVELOPMENT PURPOSES: A KENYAN CASE. *African Rev. [Tanzania] 1975 5(3): 341-352.* Administrative capacity is the key to successful implementation of economic development plans and in the Migori Division of South Nyanza District that capacity is weak because of lack of resources, poor education and training, and the frequent transfer of personnel. 7 tables, 13 notes. R. T. Brown

2905. Pack, Howard. UNEMPLOYMENT AND INCOME DISTRIBUTION IN KENYA. *Econ. Development and Cultural Change 1977 26(1): 157-168.* Explores the question of income distribution in *International Labour Office, Employment, Incomes and Equality in Kenya* (Geneva: ILO, 1972), a report of an ILO mission to Kenya in 1972 which covers agriculture, industry, education, the problems of women, income distribution, and employment. Recommends policies that insure future growth to improve the living standard of the poorest members of the population. 20 notes. J. W. Thacker, Jr.

2906. Parkin, D. J. NATIONAL INDEPENDENCE AND LOCAL TRADITION IN A KENYA TRADING CENTRE. *Bull. of the School of Oriental and African Studies [Great Britain] 1974 37(1): 157-174.* "The practical aim of this paper is to show how Kenya's independence hastened certain economic changes in one small trading center. The theoretical aim is to give a particular empirical demonstration of a process of role differentiation in which there has developed a tendency for key political, economic, and ritual tasks to be performed by specialists equipped with the appropriate skills now required in a changing social order." Biblio. R. G. Neville

2907. Ruthenberg, Hans. LÄNDLICHE ARMUT IN DER DRITTEN WELT: ANALYSE DES PROBLEMS UND DER LÖSUNGSANSÄTZE AM BEISPIEL KENIAS [Rural poverty in the Third World: analysis of the problem and possible solutions shown in Kenya]. *Stimmen der Zeit [West Germany] 1979 197(9): 631-639.* Although Kenya experienced a small growth in rural incomes, 1961-79, the exploitation of the rural masses, unplanned urbanization, and the unequal distribution of wealth actually increased poverty in rural areas.

2908. Steeves, Jeffrey S. CLASS ANALYSIS AND RURAL AFRICA: THE KENYA TEA DEVELOPMENT AUTHORITY. *J. of Modern African Studies [Great Britain] 1978 16(1): 123-132.* There have been two antagonistic groups in the tea areas of Kenya: landowners and hired laborers. The owners were further divided into absentee large owners and small peasant farmers. The Kenya Tea Development Authority began to issue requirements in 1963 that favored the large capitalists. As a result many small farmers illegally planted tea. By 1972 the class distinction increased and sharpened, due to the tea authority. 21 notes. H. G. Soff

2909. Swainson, Nicola. STATE AND ECONOMY IN POST-COLONIAL KENYA, 1963-1978. *Can. J. of African Studies [Canada] 1978 12(3): 357-381.* Since independence, the government of Kenya has promoted the interests of the indigenous middle classes that developed in the 1920's on African reservations. It quickly reduced the settler's state in which African entrepreneurs worked only in limited regions. It acquired businesses of non-Kenyans for citizens, expanded credit, and strictly regulated foreign corporations. While the government has fostered capitalism, it has become less democratic, replacing the British parliamentary system with a strong executive. Based on interviews and published primary and secondary sources; 54 notes, appendix. S

2910. Van Zwanenberg, Paul. KENYA'S PRIMITIVE COLONIAL CAPITALISM: THE ECONOMIC WEAKNESS OF KENYA'S SETTLERS UP TO 1940. *Can. J. of African Studies [Canada] 1975 9(2): 277-292.* Primitive capitalism refers to the methods used to accumulate capital in the preindustrial phase of the British occupation of Kenya. The Kenya white population included three groups: very wealthy farmers, company farms, and the small-scale settler farmers. The third group was the one hurt most in the Great Depression, and the Depression-spawned Land Bank assisted this group. The settlers would not undertake any manual labor, but depended on the Africans. Many farms were abandoned in the 1930's, but with World War II an injection of capital assisted the remaining farmers to survive. Based on government documents in the Kenya National Archives, Land Office Archives, newspapers, letters, and secondary works; table, 45 notes. E. R. Campbell

2911. Van Zwannenberg, Roger. THE DEVELOPMENT OF PEASANT COMMODITY PRODUCTION IN KENYA 1920-40. *Econ. Hist. R. [Great Britain] 1974 27(3): 442-454.* Indicates factors in Kenya which led people to produce agricultural commodities for the market. Explains the growth of regional economic differentiation. Based on archives in Rhodes House, Oxford, and Archdeacon Owen's private papers. B. L. Crapster

2912. Waters, Alan Rufus. CHANGE AND EVOLUTION IN THE STRUCTURE OF THE KENYA COFFEE INDUSTRY. *Hist. of Agriculture [India] 1974 1(4): 81-105.* Study of surviving colonial institutions in the Kenya coffee industry and their relevance to Kenya's present economic development. Coffee was introduced into Kenya about 1894. Between 1900 and 1945 a control structure developed parallel to the development of large-scale producers and centralized coffee processing. With the end of World War II and Kenyan independence, smallholder coffee growing expanded, organized on the basis of producer cooperatives. The problems facing the existing colonial regulatory institutions and the accommodations made to the new developments between 1945 and 1970 are discussed. M. S. Legan

Politics

2913. Berman, Bruce J. EXPLAINING COLONIALISM IN KENYA: A REVIEW ARTICLE. *J. of Commonwealth and Comparative Pol. [Great Britain] 1977 15(1): 84-88.* Reviewing Richard D. Wolff's *The Economics of Colonialism: Britain and Kenya, 1870-1930* (Yale U. Pr., 1974) and Robert L. Tignor's *The Colonial Transformation of Kenya: the Kamba, Kikuyu and Maasai from 1900 to 1939* (Princeton U. Pr., 1975), the author demonstrates the failure of Tignor to develop a theoretical structure capable of determining whether British colonial rule helped or hindered modernization in Kenya. Wolff, with his Marxist foundation, is able to go beyond Tignor's study of the reactions of the natives to British initiatives, and considers the wider problem of

the structure of the British-Kenyan economic relationship.
R. D. Black

2914. Buijtenhuijs, R. THE KENYA AFRICAN NATIONAL UNION. *Int. J. of Pol. 1974-75 4(4): 58-76.* Although the Kenya African National Union (KANU) has suffered from the weaknesses and lack of organization of tribalism and regionalism, it has served as Kenya's most important political arena, the locus of all major political decisions since the 1960's.

2915. Buijtenhuijs, R. L'ÉVOLUTION DU KENYA APRÈS L'INDÉPENDANCE [The evolution of Kenya after independence]. *Rev. Française d'Études Pol. Africaines [France] 1973 (87): 39-65.* Views the history of Kenya since the Mau Mau Revolt of 1952 in relation to the British colonialism, stressing the formation of a new political structure based on colonial models for an independent Kenya, and studying certain national problems in public law, social change and development, agriculture, and nationalism.

2916. Buijtenhuijs, R. L'UNION NATIONALE AFRICAINE DU KENYA [The African National Union of Kenya]. *Rev. Française d'Études Pol. Africaines [France] 1973 (86): 55-70.* Studies the role of the single Kenyan party, the Kenya African National Union (KANU), in national politics since its 1960 formation, suggesting its dominance in Nairobi is built on slight political strength and support.

2917. Colebatch, Hal. ACCESS TO THE STUDY OF LOCAL SERVICES: A KENYAN CASE. *Development and Change 1975 6(2): 107-118.* Describes the relations between the public and county councils in their concern with primary education, rural health, and roads in Kenya since independence.

2918. Ellis, Diana. THE NANDI PROTEST OF 1923 IN THE CONTEXT OF AFRICAN RESISTANCE TO COLONIAL RULE IN KENYA. *J. of African Hist. [Great Britain] 1976 17(4): 555-575.* An examination of the Nandi protest of 1923 which was caused by high colonial taxes, cattle disease, forced employment in European farms, and loss of land to the British. The organized noncooperation protest ended when the five leaders were arrested. A brief comparison of the Nandi protest with other protests is discussed. 124 notes.
H. G. Soff

2919. Eriksen, Tore Linné and Mikkelsen, Britha. POLITISKE RETTIGHETER OG POLITISK MAKT I U-LAND: EKSEMPLET KENYA [Political rights and political power in developing countries: the example of Kenya]. *Samtiden [Norway] 1979 88(1): 77-85.* Describes the sources of political opposition in Kenya from 1963 through 1978 and the limits placed upon its right of expression.

2920. Evans, Emmit B. SOURCES OF SOCIO-POLITICAL INSTABILITY IN AN AFRICAN STATE: THE CASE OF KENYA'S EDUCATED UNEMPLOYED. *African Studies Rev. 1977 20(1): 37-52.* President Jomo Kenyatta of Kenya had a relatively peaceful rule, 1963-76, but difficulties were caused by his inability to adapt to new demands, particularly by the educated unemployed.

2921. Farrell, Christopher. MAU MAU: A REVOLT OR A REVOLUTION? *Kenya Hist. Rev. [Kenya] 1977 5(2): 187-199.* Outlines Alexis de Tocqueville's and Karl Marx's studies on the nature of revolution, applying their observations to the Mau Mau, particularly drawing on Marx's view of capitalism as a catalyst for social upheaval. Also discusses the Mau Mau's significance in the light of Kenya's history after independence.

2922. Frost, Richard A. SIR PHILIP MITCHELL, GOVERNOR OF KENYA. *African Affairs [Great Britain] 1979 78(313): 535-553.* Sir Philip Mitchell was Governor of Kenya, 1944-52. He had long previous experience of administration in East Africa, and had high ideals of what could be done for the Africans. His policy was one of economic advance, the preservation of the land, the improvement of African agriculture, and the advancement of education. He saw that the prime and basic necessity was to achieve economic progress if the African standards of living were to be improved. Tact was essential if the Legislative Council were to be persuaded to pass the necessary measures. His efforts on behalf of the reorganization of Makerere College were especially important. He was notably impartial in racial matters, but he was not always understood or appreciated. Based mainly on Mitchell's diary; 58 notes.
R. L. Collison

2923. Furedi, Frank. THE SOCIAL COMPOSITION OF THE MAU MAU MOVEMENT IN THE WHITE HIGHLANDS. *J. of Peasant Studies [Great Britain] 1974 1(4): 486-505.* Locates the social basis of the Mau Mau movement in the White Highlands of Kenya. The Mau Mau revolt was an outcome of a prolonged agrarian struggle between Kikuyu squatters and European settlers. In this agrarian struggle, the leading role was assumed by Kikuyu artisans and petty traders. This leadership provided the Mau Mau movement with the type of organization and strategy that could unite the Kikuyu peasantry.
J

2924. Gadsen, Fay. FURTHER NOTES ON THE KAMBA DESTOCKING CONTROVERSY OF 1938. *Int. J. of African Hist. Studies 1974 7(4): 681-687.* Discusses the Gandhian aspects of the Kamba campaign against the British colonial policy of cattle destocking in Kenya. The combination of passive resistance and protest politics contributed to the Kamba's success in reversing the government's policies. Primary sources; 22 notes.
M. M. McCarthy

2925. Goldsworthy, David. KENYAN POLITICS SINCE KENYATTA. *Australian Outlook [Australia] 1982 36(1): 27-31.* The smooth succession of Vice-President Daniel Arap Moi on Jomo Kenyatta's death on 22 August 1978 is accounted for by the cohesive central bureaucracy and network of strong provincial administrations in Kenya. After independence Africans were enabled to purchase European farms at market prices; thus, property values held up, and a landed African bourgeoisie emerged. Subsequent settlement schemes have benefitted nearly a third of Kenya's 1.5 million peasants. Leading politicians are district-based and have a background in local power. Wider participation is facilitated by bodies such as the Gikuyu-Embu-Meru Association, a tribal association founded in 1971 to provide welfare. The Kenyan system is characterized by interlocking political-business-property interests. Moi's succession followed the constitutional rule. He has taken a pro-western stance. Current tensions derive from growing income inequality. 9 notes.
W. D. McIntyre

2926. Gordon, David F. COLONIAL CRISES AND ADMINISTRATIVE RESPONSE: KENYA, 1945-60. *J. of African Studies 1979 6(2): 98-111.* Amends the argument of Gray Wasserman in his *Politics of Decolonization* that the British administration began only in the final years of colonial Kenya to adapt the country's political economy to the impending transition to African rule. Wasserman dates this change to the time of the First Lancaster House Conference of January 1960, which promised a decolonization program for Kenya, while the present author considers that first the British Colonial Office during World War II and later their administration in Kenya embarked on a two-state policy of decolonizing the political economy. During the pre-Mau Mau Emergency years of 1945-52, the economic emphasis remained on the white settlers, while greater productivity was the official goal for the African reserves. During 1953-59 the British promoted a series of economic reforms for the African population in their unsuccessful drive to obtain a multiracial settlement. Based on Kenya archival sources and published documents; 104 notes.
L. W. Truschel

2927. Gordon, David F. MAU MAU AND DECOLONIZATION: KENYA AND THE DEFEAT OF MULTI-RACIALISM IN EAST AND CENTRAL AFRICA. *Kenya Hist. Rev. [Kenya] 1977 5(2): 329-348.* Argues that the main issue in the decolonization process in British African territories, 1952-59, concerned to whom the power would be devolved, with the British attempting to guarantee the privileges of immigrants in multiracial political systems. The author also discusses the Mau Mau's role in preventing the establishment of such a neocolonial arrangement in Kenya.

2928. Greenstein, Lewis J. THE NANDI "UPRISING" OF 1923. *Pan-African J. [Kenya] 1976 9(4): 397-406.* The Nandi uprising in Kenya, 1923, led to the arrest and deportation of the Nandi's *Orkoiyot* (religious leader and prophet). The uprising was not a rebellion at all, but resulted largely from the prejudice and ignorance of the colonial administrator for the Nandi. He not only did not understand the Nandi but also distrusted and suspected them. The incident was probably the result of deliberate misinformation on the part of native informants too. Most important, it shows the misunderstanding which existed between colonizers and colonized in Africa and which embittered colonial relations. 21 notes. R. D. Black

2929. Gupta, Vijay. PORTRAIT OF AN AGENT OF EMPIRE. *Africa Q. [India] 1977 17(2): 55-64.* Reviews an American biography of Eliud Mathu, a native member of the Kenyan Legislative Council during the State of Emergency. The council was dismissed as a tool of the British administration.

2930. Jones, Susan. KENYA AND THE DEVONSHIRE WHITE PAPER OF 1923. *A.N.U. Hist. J. [Australia] 1977 13: 20-40.* Enmity between the British and Asians in Kenya was the basis for a 1923 report which attempted to solve differences by emphasizing the necessity of African paramountcy.

2931. Kamoche, Jidlaph G. AFRICAN RESPONSES TO IMPOSITION OF BRITISH RULE IN CENTRAL PROVINCE, KENYA, 1895-1930. *Umoja 1981 5(2): 1-14.* Discusses the issues of land and labor during the British rule in Central Province, Kenya, 1895-1930, and the resistance and collaboration of the African population.

2932. Kanogo, Tabitha M. J. RIFT VALLEY SQUATTERS AND MAU MAU. *Kenya Hist. Rev. [Kenya] 1977 5(2): 243-252.* Suggests that the Mau Mau provided an ideological basis for the attitude of the Rift Valley squatters and first arose as an expansionist movement among the disinherited Kikuyu poor in that region in the 1940's. The author also provides evidence that the Mau Mau was not an exclusively male affair, but was actively supported by women.

2933. Kauffman, Dick. MAU MAU: PEASANT WAR OR REVOLUTION? *Kenya Hist. Rev. [Kenya] 1977 5(2): 173-186.* Discusses whether the Mau Mau movement should be classified as a peasant war or as a revolution, arguing that neither is a valid categorization. Also outlines the Mau Mau's development from its roots in the 1920's to Kenya's rejection of its extreme methods in the 1960's.

2934. Keller, Edmond J. THE POLITICAL SOCIALIZATION OF ADOLESCENTS IN CONTEMPORARY AFRICA: THE ROLE OF THE SCHOOL IN KENYA. *Comparative Pol. 1978 10(2): 227-250.* Explores the different consequences for citizenship of being educated in schools aided by the Central government and *harambee* schools, which are community controlled. Kenya's schools have only reinforced values and orientations brought by students from outside; ethnicity has been an important factor in determining how students view the political system. 39 notes. G. E. Pergl

2935. Khapoya, Vincent B. KENYA UNDER MOI: CONTINUITY OR CHANGE. *Africa Today 1980 27(1): 17-32.* Searches for continuities and disparities between Jomo Kenyatta's government and that of his successor, Daniel Arap Moi, through an analysis of Moi's cabinet and his domestic and foreign policies. Moi has made no substantive changes. Based on secondary, periodical, and personal sources; 2 tables, 37 notes, 2 appendixes. G. O. Gagnon

2936. Kipkorir, B. E. "MAU MAU" AND THE POLITICS OF THE TRANSFER OF POWER IN KENYA, 1957-60. *Kenya Hist. Rev. [Kenya] 1977 5(2): 313-328.* Argues that the Mau Mau emergency, 1952-57, precipitated important constitutional changes and the dismantling of the colonial collaborative framework within Kenya. It also made Kenya's independence inevitable by bringing into sharper focus the nature of Kenya's political problems and the difficulties of colonialism.

2937. Maina-wa-Kinyatti. MAU MAU: THE PEAK OF AFRICAN POLITICAL ORGANIZATION IN COLONIAL KENYA. *Kenya Hist. Rev. [Kenya] 1977 5(2): 287-311.* Argues that the basic aim of the Mau Mau organizers was to create a nationalist movement which would unite all Kenyans in their struggle against colonial occupation and implement land reform, 1952-60. The author also suggests that the Mau Mau's failure to achieve these aims was due to organizational weaknesses.

2938. Martin, Denis. DÉPENDANCE ET LUTTES POLITIQUES AU KENYA, 1975-1977: LA BOURGEOISIE NATIONALE À L'ASSAUT DU POUVOIR D'ÉTAT [Dependence and political struggles in Kenya, 1975-77, the country's middle class out to win state power]. *Can. J. of African Studies [Canada] 1978 12(2): 233-258.* Recent studies have given the opportunity to reexamine theories on economic as well as political dependence. Some of them, particularly on Kenya, have shown how local middle classes had developed notwithstanding a position of global dependence. If one considers, in the light of events from 1975 until 1977, the place and weight enjoyed by this local middle class within the Kenyan political system, it seems quite clear that by using different means (factional struggles within the party, unions, and associations) it is now out to conquer political power which still escapes it, in order to consolidate its position as a national middle class. This new situation puts into motion a complicated game of oppositions and alliances between the social strata and the political forces which represent them, where the socioeconomic determinants definitely appear to prevail over ethnic solidarities. J

2939. Muriuki, Godfrey. CENTRAL KENYA IN THE NYAYO ERA. *Africa Today 1979 26(3): 39-42.* Describes the success of Daniel Arap Moi in achieving the presidency after the death of Jomo Kenyatta as a victory for the rest of Kenya over the clique based in central Kenya that had dominated patronage, corruption, and power during Kenyatta's life. Concludes that new leadership will distribute benefits to all of Kenya. G. O. Gagnon

2940. Nellis, J. R. EXPATRIATES IN THE GOVERNMENT OF KENYA. *J. of Commonwealth Pol. Studies [Great Britain] 1973 11(3): 251-264.* Discusses the role and status of expatriates in Kenyan government service, with particular reference to the use made of technical advisers in administration.

2941. Newsinger, John. REVOLT AND REPRESSION IN KENYA: THE "MAU MAU" REBELLION, 1952-1960. *Sci. & Soc. 1981 45(2): 159-185.* Analyzes the Mau Mau revolt in Kenya in the 1950's. Hampered by an almost total lack of modern weapons and terrorized by savage counterinsurgency military operations, the Kikuyu rebels and their trade union supporters suffered a crushing military defeat. Yet politically they won by separating the interests of the British government from those of the White settlers. But when the British government deserted these settlers as the price of protecting foreign investments, so much of the fruits of the revolt went to the newly encouraged conservative Black gentry that Kenya is today a classic example of neocolonialism. 46 notes. L. V. Eid

2942. Ng'ang'a, D. Mukaru. MAU MAU, LOYALISTS AND POLITICS IN MURANG'A, 1952-1970. *Kenya Hist. Rev. [Kenya] 1977 5(2): 365-384.* Examines the role and activities of Kikuyu loyalists, who opposed the terrorism and legacy of the Mau Mau, 1952-70, in Murang'a. Also discusses their use by the colonial authorities to fight the Mau Mau, and outlines their later ascendancy over Mau Mau supporters within the newly formed nation of Kenya, 1960-70.

2943. Ogot, Bethwell A. INTRODUCTION. *Kenya Hist. Rev. [Kenya] 1977 5(2): 169-172.* Provides guidelines for a discussion of the role of the Mau Mau movement in the development of Kenyan nationalism and in the Kenyan drive for independence, 1944-60. This article is an introductory essay to a special issue of the *Kenya Historical Review* 1977 5(2) devoted to the Mau Mau.

2944. Ogot, Bethwell A. POLITICS, CULTURE AND MUSIC IN CENTRAL KENYA: A STUDY OF MAU MAU HYMNS, 1951-1956. *Kenya Hist. Rev. [Kenya] 1977 5(2): 275-286.* Analyzes the content of Mau Mau hymns published in the books of freedom songs by the Gakaara Book Service in Nairobi in 1952. Argues that the hymns express Kikuyu tribal aspirations and this exclusiveness prevents them from being considered national freedom songs.

2945. Okumu, John J. SOME THOUGHTS ON KENYA'S FOREIGN POLICY. *African R. [Tanzania] 1973 3(2): 263-290.* Although widely expected to be a leader in the socialist Third World, Kenya since independence has been moderate, often noncommittal, and practiced a quiet diplomacy. Examines the factors that have conditioned Kenya to follow such a policy including local border disputes, a desire to be a "good neighbor," the need for regional peace, and the problem of nonalignment. 5 tables, 64 notes. H. G. Soff

2946. Omosule, Monone. KIAMA KIA MUINGI: KIKUYU REACTION TO LAND CONSOLIDATION IN KENYA, 1955-59. *Transaf-*

rican J. of Hist. [Kenya] 1974 4(1/2): 115-134. Kiama Kia Muingi (Society of the People) was a Kikuyu secret society that emerged into public view during the 1950's. The KKM has been ignored by most scholars, and this is an attempt to determine the extent and nature of the society. It is apparent that KKM was not a branch or an offshoot of Mau Mau, but rather an attempt by Africans to voice criticism of government policies. Government reaction to the KKM is discussed. 81 notes. H. G. Soff

2947. Pavlis, Paul A. THE MAASAI AND THE MAU MAU MOVEMENT: AVENUES FOR FUTURE RESEARCH. *Kenya Hist. Rev. [Kenya] 1977 5(2): 253-273.* Explores the role which other Kenyan tribes, especially the Maasai, played in the Mau Mau. Traces the relationship of the Maasai with the Kikuyu and British colonial authorities, and suggests that the Maasai's general lack of participation in the Mau Mau, due to the movement's Kikuyu base, reveals the fatal weakness in the Mau Mau which prevented it from winning widespread support.

2948. Pochepski, V. A. "KONSTITUTSIONNYE PEREGOVORY" S KENIEI: TAKTICHESKII MANEVR ANGLIISKOGO NEOKOLONIALIZMA [The constitutional talks with Kenya: a tactical maneuver in English neocolonialism]. *Narody Azii i Afriki [USSR] 1978 (4): 127-134.* The constitutional talks which took place 1960-63 between Great Britain and the leaders of Kenya's national liberation movement were conducted by the English to preserve their economic and political position in Kenya and to weaken the liberation movement. The talks undermined the progressive forces for many years. Thus independence limited the Africanization of the country to the bureaucratic and commercial elite which was closely tied to neocolonialism. Secondary sources; 33 notes. J. M. Chambers

2949. Rai, Kauleshwar. BRITISH POLICY TOWARDS INDIANS IN KENYA. *Ravindran, T. K., ed.,* Journal of Indian History: Golden Jubilee Volume *(Trivandrum: U. of Kerala, 1973), pp. 909-914.* Analyzes British colonial policies affecting Indians in Kenya in the first two decades of the 20th century. In a series of increasingly discriminatory legislative acts and decrees, Indians were excluded from the highlands of Kenya, limited in their representation in the legislative council, segregated in both residential and commercial areas of towns, and restricted in their immigration into Kenya. British attitudes toward Indians in Kenya were a part of their imperial policy and practices and were dictated largely by the economic interests of the white settlers. Based on Parliamentary Papers and secondary sources; 29 notes. S. H. Frank

2950. Ross, Marc Howard. TWO STYLES OF POLITICAL PARTICIPATION IN AN AFRICAN CITY. *Am. J. of Pol. Sci. 1973 17(1): 1-22.* "Two independent dimensions of political participation are identified in Nairobi, Kenya. The first is party and electoral activity associated with the independence era, while the second is the more individualistic form of political activity important in the post-independence period. Individuals with more limited and homogeneous social networks had a greater chance of being mobilized during the struggle for political independence, while those with more extensive and diverse ties are the most active in the post-independence setting. During the former period the elite mobilized large numbers to place political pressure on the colonial government, while after independence this mobilization ended and individuals have had to rely on their own resources to remain politically active." J

2951. Rouyer, Alwyn R. POLITICAL RECRUITMENT AND POLITICAL CHANGE IN KENYA. *J. of Developing Areas 1976 9(4): 539-562.* Analyzes 221 elected members and 216 defeated candidates to Kenya's legislature. The mean age at the time of election was 35.5 years (in 1962 77.7% of the nation's population was under age 35). Contrary to expectations, the average age increased only 3.4 years during the 11 years under study. Three women had been candidates but none was elected during the period, nor were women found in high-ranking civil service or national party organization positions. Legislators were better educated than the average Kenyan, and the holding of political party office was a significant channel of upward political mobility. Based on social background data for 437 would-be legislators; 6 tables, 2 figs., 43 notes. O. W. Eads, Jr.

2952. Saberwal, Satish. POLITICAL CHANGE AMONG THE EMBU OF CENTRAL KENYA (1900-1964). *Pol. Sci. Rev. [India] 1973 12(1-2): 35-96.* A review of British colonial rule in Kenya, 1906-63, analyzing its effects on the political organization, awareness, and social relations of the Embu people of central Kenya.

2953. Schilling, Donald G. LOCAL NATIVE COUNCILS AND THE POLITICS OF EDUCATION IN KENYA, 1925-1939. *Int. J. of African Hist. Studies 1976 9(2): 218-247.* Focuses on the interaction between educational development and politics in the work of the local native councils (LNCs). Also explores the degree to which the colonized could manipulate a colonial institution to serve their own ends, and concludes that the LNC cannot be dismissed as a mere tool of an alien authority. 102 notes. M. M. McCarthy

2954. Sergeev, L. V. IZ ISTORII BORBY NARODA KENII ZA NEZAVISIMOST [The history of the Kenyan people's struggle for independence]. *Narody Azii i Afriki [USSR] 1978 (1): 36-47.* Throws new light both on the role of the Mau Mau movement in Kenya's path toward independence, and on the uprisings of 1952-56. Describes the activities of the Kenya African National Union, headed by Jomo Kenyatta, and shows that this was not a Kikuyu party, as is usually thought. Indicates that although the Kikuyu played a leading part, a wide range of tribes and races made up the party's membership. Argues that Kenya's revolt against British rule had important consequences beyond Kenya itself and affected British policy in other African territories, although the geographical isolation of the region did not permit outside help to the guerrillas. 33 notes. E. R. Sicher

2955. Spencer, John. KAU AND "MAU MAU": SOME CONNECTIONS. *Kenya Hist. Rev. [Kenya] 1977 5(2): 201-224.* Traces possible connections between the Kenya African Union (KAU), its predecessor the Kikuyu Central Association (KCA), and the Mau Mau. The author emphasizes the attempt of the militant faction in Nairobi to take over the KAU branch there in 1951 and use it as a front for Mau Mau related activities, the use of oaths common to both groups, and Jomo Kenyatta's attempt to dissociate the KAU from the Mau Mau, despite British suspicions that he was Mau Mau's creator.

2956. Srinivasan, Padma. CONTEMPORARY KENYA: A SELECT CLASSIFIED BIBLIOGRAPHY. *Africa Q. [India] 1979 18(2-3): 67-70.* Lists books and articles under the headings Politics and Society: The Ethos of the Single Party, Ethnicity and Factionalism, Government and Political Participation, Public Administration, and Kenyatta, all published between 1960 and 1978.

2957. Srinivasan, Padma. THE KENYATTA ERA: A CRITICAL STUDY. *Africa Q. [India] 1979 18(2-3): 52-66.* Assessment of the 15-year rule, 1963-78 of Jomo Kenyatta (1894-1978), with emphasis on Kenya's political institutions.

2958. Stamp, Patricia. KENYA: THE ECHOING FOOTSTEPS. *Current Hist. 1982 81(473): 115-118, 130, 137-138.* Examines the impact of intensifying political factionalism in Kenya during the late 1970's, and its potential threat to the unity and stability of the regime.

2959. Stichter, Sharon B. WORKERS, TRADE UNIONS, AND THE MAU MAU REBELLION. *Can. J. of African Studies [Canada] 1975 9(2): 259-275.* Peasants and the wage-earners had a part in middle class-led nationalist movements in both East and West Africa. The political potential of the African working class within the larger nationalist movement pressured the leadership to reform. Three main categories within the Kikuyu formed the Mau Mau. The unions were split into pro- and anti-Mau Mau factions. All African union leaders usually believed that violence was not necessary; if economic conditions remain stable, union rebellions are less likely. Based on government documents in the Kenya National Archives, published official statistics, interviews, and secondary works; 52 notes. E. R. Campbell

2960. Tamarkin, M. FROM KENYATTA TO MOI—THE ANATOMY OF A PEACEFUL TRANSITION OF POWER. *Africa Today 1979 26(3): 21-37.* Attributes Kenya's smooth transition from Jomo Kenyatta to Daniel Arap Moi to several factors: Moi and his supporters won the struggle for succession rights before Kenyatta died, Moi gained control of all bureaucratic military and paramilitary centers of power, potential opponents were maneuvered out of existence and Kenya-wide popularity was gained by populist statements concerning the goals of Moi's presidency. The test of permanency remains to be passed. Periodical sources; 85 notes. G. O. Gagnon

2961. Tamarkin, M. THE LOYALISTS IN NAKURU DURING THE MAU MAU REVOLT AND ITS AFTERMATH, 1953-1963. *Asian and African Studies [Israel] 1978 12(2): 247-261.* Anti-Mau Mau loyalists among the Kikuyu of Kenya were mainly Christians and members of the economic elite who defended their moderate political views and their class interests. Because they represented the leadership elite the loyalists have a greater prominence in the independent government than lower-class Mau Mau. Based on Kenya National Archives and interviews; 63 notes. R. T. Brown

2962. Tamarkin, M. MAU MAU IN NAKURU. *J. of African Hist. [Great Britain] 1976 17(1): 119-134.* Traces the militant, violent, and anticolonial Mau Mau movement in Nakuru, the center of white settlement in Kenya, 1944-55. Although the Kikuyu Central Association tried moderation in Nakuru, that approach was rejected. Mau Mau was anticolonial, but it also created fissures among the Kikuyu and with other black Africans. It is suggested that although much has been written about Mau Mau, the truth will unfold only after more local studies have been made. Based on interviews; 75 notes. H. G. Soff

2963. Tamarkin, M. MAU MAU IN NAKURU. *Kenya Hist. Rev. [Kenya] 1977 5(2): 225-241.* Traces the development of the Mau Mau from within the Kikuyu Central Association (KCA) in the 1940's to its role in Nakuru, capital of Kenya's White Highlands during the 1950's. Suggests that the movement was primarily supported by the displaced poor and resisted by Kenya's black elite, who favored a moderate approach to the anticolonial struggle.

2964. Tamarkin, M. THE ROOTS OF POLITICAL STABILITY IN KENYA. *African Affairs [Great Britain] 1978 77(308): 297-320.* Rejects the interpretation that the political system in Kenya has been stable because of the political leadership of Jomo Kenyatta. Stability has rested on the strong state apparatus and the solid social structure. 132 notes. H. G. Soff

2965. Vermouth, Paul. RURAL REBELS: AUDREY WIPPER AND DINI YA MSAMBWA. *Int. J. of African Hist. Studies 1980 13(2): 313-323.* A review article of Audrey Wipper's *Rural Rebels: A Study of Two Protest Movements in Kenya* (Nairobi: Oxford U. Pr., 1977). The political-religious movement called Dini ya Msambwa was a potent force in the overcrowded reserves of the Kenyan Babukusa. This movement fed on the economic crisis of the 1930's. Based on the Kenyan National archives and oral interviews; 41 notes. R. T. Brown

2966. Wanjala, Chris L. IN SEARCH OF A REVOLUTIONARY HERO: A REVIEW ESSAY. *Kenya Hist. Rev. [Kenya] 1977 5(2): 389-395.* Reviews three Kenyan works of fiction: Ngugi wa Thiong'o and Micere Githae Mugo's *The Trial of Dedan Kimathi* (1976); Kenneth Watene's *Dedan Kimathi* (1975); and Micere Githae Mugo's *The Long Illness of Ex-Chief Kiti* (1977). In their attempts to fashion revolutionary heroes out of Mau Mau leaders, these works seriously distort historical reality.

2967. Wasserman, Gary. EUROPEAN SETTLERS AND KENYA COLONY: THOUGHTS ON A CONFLICTED AFFAIR. *African Studies Rev. 1974 17(2): 425-434.* "The process of decolonization itself may be seen as a painful and never quite completed attempt to divide the farmers' interests from the wider imperial ones." 4 notes, biblio. R. T. Brown

2968. Wasserman, Gary. THE INDEPENDENCE BARGAIN: KENYA EUROPEANS AND THE LAND ISSUE 1960-1962. *J. of Commonwealth Pol. Studies [Great Britain] 1973 11(2): 99-120.* Reviews the period of colonial transition in Kenya preceding independence in 1963, with particular reference to the land issue and the political factions involved in the decolonization process.

2969. Whisson, M. G. and Lonsdale, J. M. THE CASE OF JASON GOR AND FOURTEEN OTHERS: A LUO SUCCESSION DISPUTE IN HISTORICAL PERSPECTIVE. *Africa [Great Britain] 1975 45(1): 50-66.* Tells the story of the rise and fall of Jason Gor as chief of a Luo district along the coast of Lake Victoria in Kenya; through it and 14 other cases, analyzes the intricacies of Luo political life.

2970. Wolf, James B. ASIAN AND AFRICAN RECRUITMENT IN THE KENYA POLICE, 1920-1950. *Int. J. of African Hist. Studies 1973 6(3): 401-412.* An analysis of police force recruitment in Kenya shows a "proto-apartheid" at work in their selection and assignment of responsibility. An examination of the triracial structure of the Kenya police as an instrument of the colonialist government reflected the deep racial divisions within the colony itself. Recruitment and population charts show that there is no way to separate the recruitment, training, and use of the Kenya police from the total colonial experience involving descending levels of responsibility from British to Asian to African. 2 tables, 67 notes. R. V. Ritter

2971. Wylie, Diana. CONFRONTATION OVER KENYA: THE COLONIAL OFFICE AND ITS CRITICS, 1918-1940. *J. of African Hist. [Great Britain] 1977 18(3): 427-447.* Norman Leys and W. McGregor Ross were constant champions of Africans during the colonial era. They wrote articles and letters, and gave speeches and interviews which always stressed the inequality to which Kenyans were subjected. European settlers were often the target of these crusaders, but the Colonial Office was often deaf or became alienated due to constant criticism. In the end, however, Leys and Ross were mainly responsible for preventing Kenya from coming totally under the control of white settlers. 59 notes. H. G. Soff

2972. Yankwich, Richard. CONTINUITY IN KENYA HISTORY: NEGATIVE UNITY AND THE LEGITIMACY OF THE MAU MAU REBELLION. *Kenya Hist. Rev. [Kenya] 1977 5(2): 349-363.* Considers some of the links binding the Mau Mau to Kenya's past and present as an expression of anticolonial sentiment, and as a reminder of the counterproductive aspects of Kenyan unity, specifically ethnic division, which conflict with the premises of contemporary Kenya and still threaten its struggle to mold a unified nation.

2973. Youé, Christopher P. THE THREAT OF SETTLER REBELLION AND THE IMPERIAL PREDICAMENT: THE DENIAL OF INDIAN RIGHTS IN KENYA, 1923. *Can. J. of Hist. [Canada] 1978 12(3): 347-360.* Discusses several questions not yet addressed in the episode of Kenya's history. A tougher anti-Indian stance adopted by the settlers caused the European-owned newspaper to about-face and draw the Crown into the political debate. Kenya's governor, Robert Coryndon, did not support the European planting interest in Uganda (where he had been governor 1917-22) to the detriment of African cotton growers; on the contrary he encouraged both. He thought that the existence of the Indian community in East Africa was an obstacle to the economic advance of settlers. He was the settlers' strongest ally in the 1923 conflict. The 1923 White Paper introduced a calm in the colony although the Indian community boycotted the legislative council elections in the next eight years. 56 notes. E. P. Stickney

Society

2974. Bottignole, Silvana. PANORAMA DELLA LETTERATURA AUTOCTONO KENYOTA [A panorama of autochthonous Kenyan literature]. *Africa [Italy] 1974 29(1): 121-130.* Surveys Kenyan literature since 1950, correlating literary development with historical and social factors, particularly colonialism, religion, independence, and government policy.

2975. Brantley, Cynthia. AN HISTORICAL PERSPECTIVE OF THE GIRIAMA AND WITCHCRAFT CONTROL. *Africa [Great Britain] 1979 49(2): 112-133.* Evaluates the extent to which political, social, and economic conditions underlie the witchcraft control movements of the Giriama in Kenya from the 18th to the 20th centuries. Under the traditional *kaya* system and the subsequent dispersed homestead system, the Giriama relied on their own resources and techniques borrowed from neighbors. Under the British colonial administration, 1912-63, and in the postindependence period, their basic belief in witchcraft was questioned, and they adapted both their interpretations of evil and their methods for dealing with it. 41 notes, biblio. P. J. Taylorson

2976. Collier, Valerie C. and Rempel, Henry. THE DIVERGENCE OF PRIVATE FROM SOCIAL COSTS IN RURAL-URBAN MIGRATION: A CASE STUDY OF NAIROBI, KENYA. *J. of Development Studies [Great Britain] 1977 13(3): 199-216.* Considers the determinants of different levels of private and social costs of internal migration in Nairobi, Kenya, and quantifies major private and social costs to determine the extent of divergence, 1964-68.

2977. de Kay, Ormonde, Jr. OUT OF AFRICA, SOMETHING NEW. *Horizon 1975 42(2): 102-111.* Illustrated biography of Karen Blixen (Isak Dinesen), a writer who lived in Kenya in the early 20th century. S

2978. Doro, Marion E. "HUMAN SOUVENIRS OF ANOTHER ERA": EUROPEANS IN POST-KENYATTA KENYA. *Africa Today 1979 26(3): 43-54.* Reviews the role of Europeans, citizen and noncitizen, as it developed during Kenyatta's rule. The settlers will gradually disappear because Africanization of all facets of Kenyan life leaves no future for Europeans. Although the Europeans will fade away, the economy their ancestors helped create will remain. Secondary and periodical sources; 12 notes. G. O. Gagnon

2979. Duran, James J. THE ECOLOGY OF ETHNIC GROUPS FROM A KENYAN PERSPECTIVE. *Ethnicity 1974 1(1): 43-64.* Ethnicity is a rational response to the competition for scarce resources in modern as well as preindustrial societies. The existence of unrest among people sharing a common language, descent, culture, and geographical origins leads to their mobilization, redefinition, maneuvering for advantage, and boundary maintenance. A representative model is Lumbwa, where the competition for land, jobs, businesses, etc., between the Kikuyu, Kipsigis, Luo, and Luyia has fostered continuing ethnicity, particularly visible in the low rates of intermarriage. Based on observation and secondary sources; 12 notes, biblio. E. R. Barkan

2980. El-Safi, Mahassin Abdel Gadir Hag. THE POSITION OF "ALIEN" SOMALIS IN THE EAST AFRICAN PROTECTORATE AND KENYA COLONY 1916-1963. *J. of African Studies 1981 8(1): 39-45.* The "alien" Somali in colonial Kenya were two groups of Somali emigrants from Great Britain's Somaliland Protectorate, as distinct from the "native" Somali of the northeast region of Kenya, who belonged to different clan-families. The alien Somali resented and resisted, by contesting taxes and land allotments, their assigned colonial status as African natives rather than Arabs and the movement restrictions imposed on them. Based on British colonial and Kenyan archival sources; 40 notes. L. W. Truschel

2981. Furedi, Frank. THE DEVELOPMENT OF ANTI-ASIAN OPINION IN NAKURU DISTRICT. *African Affairs [Great Britain] 1974 73(292): 347-358.* Traces the modern settlement of Nakuru and the racial attitudes of Asians, Africans, and Europeans. Although Asian abuse of Africans was not widespread, the incidence of any case was stretched beyond reason. This led to the "stereotype" of Asians which has prevailed. The experience in Nakuru is similar to the pattern throughout Kenya, and Asians are the scapegoat for political aspirants who do not face Kenya's real problems. 34 notes. H. G. Soff

2982. Gadsden, Fay. THE AFRICAN PRESS IN KENYA, 1945-1952. *J. of African Hist. [Great Britain] 1980 21(4): 515-535.* Only a handful of African-controlled vernacular newspapers appeared in Kenya before 1945. From 1945 to 1952, 57 newspapers and periodicals came into being. The demand for vernacular newspapers was due to a widespread growth in literacy and to the political frustrations experienced by the Africans during this period. The Kenya African Union started its own newspaper and its members were also responsible for several other vernacular journals. Radical newspapers appeared alongside the more moderate nationalist papers but owing to financial problems most papers lasted little longer than a year. Based on material in the Kenya National Archives, and associated documents; table, 85 notes. R. L. Collison

2983. Garst, Ronald D. INNOVATION DIFFUSION AMONG THE GUSII OF KENYA. *Econ. Geography 1974 9(4): 300-312.*

2984. Gupta, Desh Bandhu. REGIONAL IMBALANCE AND MIGRATION IN KENYA. *J. of African Studies 1979 6(1): 38-46.* A quantified analysis of interprovincial disparity in migration and developmental patterns in Kenya since the Mau Mau emergency period. Internal migration and economic development have concentrated disproportionately in Central Province, including Nairobi. The higher level of education of the rural population in the province was the key factor. Based on printed government documents and secondary sources; 5 tables, 70 notes. L. W. Truschel

2985. Hjort, Anders. ETHNIC TRANSFORMATION, DEPENDENCY AND CHANGE: THE ILIGIRA SAMBURU OF NORTHERN KENYA. *J. of Asian and African Studies [Netherlands] 1981 16(1-2): 50-67.* The Iligira are Turkana-speaking peoples who have established an economic dependency relation with their traditional enemies, the Samburu, and have thus become partially Samburu. Within two generations of creating this special relation, they appear to become fully Samburu. Based on a field study; map, 18 notes, biblio. R. T. Brown

2986. Kahana, Yoram. THE CARVED DOORS OF LAMU. *Mankind 1974 4(7): 30-35.* Doors have become a highly refined art in the architecture of Lamu, Kenya. S

2987. Kay, Stafford. AFRICAN ROLES, RESPONSES, AND INITIATIVES IN COLONIAL EDUCATION: THE CASE OF WESTERN KENYA. *Paedagogica Hist. [Belgium] 1976 16(2): 272-293.* Older studies of the history of formal education in Africa either explained educational developments only by what colonial governments or missions attempted in education, or portrayed Africans as dehumanized and brainwashed by colonial schooling. The author demonstrates the process of educational development at the local level in Kenya, showing how local and central forces interacted to shape education at the colony-wide level. Colonialism was a dynamic setting with sufficient leeway to produce both conflict and compromise. 55 notes. J. M. McCarthy

2988. Kay, Stafford. LOCAL PRESSURES ON EDUCATIONAL PLANS IN COLONIAL KENYA: POST-SECOND WORLD WAR ACTIVITY AMONG THE SOUTHERN ABALUYIA. *Int. J. of African Hist. Studies 1978 11(4): 689-710.* African educational initiatives among the Southern Abaluyia illustrate the dynamic process by which schooling spread in colonial Kenya. Throughout the postwar era Southern Abaluyia pressures proved highly influential in determining how large-scale development plans were translated into actual institutional development and growth at the local level. In their role the Southern Abaluyia managed to increase dramatically both the number of schools built and the pace at which they were aided. 70 notes. M. M. McCarthy

2989. Keller, Edmond J. HARAMBEE! EDUCATIONAL POLICY, INEQUALITY, AND THE POLITICAL ECONOMY OF RURAL COMMUNITY SELF-HELP IN KENYA. *J. of African Studies 1977 4(1): 86-106.* A highly critical view of the effects of the local *harambee*schools system in present-day Kenya. Traces the history and functioning of the *harambee* schools and the political factors responsible for their continued growth and importance to local Kenyan communities. Concludes that they augment class and ethnic inequities to the detriment of forging Kenyan national unity. Based on field research and archival and published sources; 34 notes. L. W. Truschel

2990. Kenny, Michael G. THE RELATION OF ORAL HISTORY TO SOCIAL STRUCTURE IN SOUTH NYANZA, KENYA. *Africa [Great Britain] 1977 47(3): 276-288.* Discusses the lineage organization, as revealed by oral history and genealogy of sections of the Basuba peoples from the islands and southern mainland of the Gulf of Kavirondo and compares it to that of the Kenyan Luo. Points to possible explanations of the dynastic struggles in the kingdom of Buganda, and of the history of the Luo. Presents extracts from Basuba folklore which clearly illustrate the close connection between tradition and present-day attitudes, and show that some aspects of genealogy function as charters for and explanations of de facto political and economic relationships. Based on fieldwork; 2 maps, 13 notes, biblio. R. L. Collison

2991. Lindsay, Beverly. EDUCATIONAL TESTING IN KENYA. *J. of Negro Educ. 1980 49(3): 274-288.* Although Kenya adopted universal free primary education in 1980, the use of the Certificate of Primary Education (CPE) examination to monitor access to secondary education "continues to stifle the formal educational opportunities for many Kenyan youth." The author evaluates the CPE examination in relation to teacher education and questions of educational equity. 28 notes. R. E. Butchart

2992. Lindsay, Beverly. ISSUES CONFRONTING PROFESSIONAL AFRICAN WOMEN: ILLUSTRATIONS FROM KENYA. Lindsay, Beverly, ed. *Comparative Perspectives of Third World Women: The Impact of Race, Sex, and Class* (New York: Praeger, 1980): 78-95. Describes the professional woman in a Kenyan context as one who has completed postsecondary formal education and is employed, focusing on factors such as domestic roles, social conditions, and educational and career conditions which affect women's participation in the paid labor force, and examines some policy implications for the future.

2993. Manners, John. MASTERS OF MEN'S TRACK. *Africa Report 1974 19(1): 14-18.* Despite limited athletic infrastructure, Kenya is compiling an enviable record in the Olympics. S

2994. Mayne, Margot. HARAMBEE: LA EXPERIENCIA KENIANA DE FORMACIÓN TÉCNICA *[Harambee:* Kenya's experience in technical education]. *Folia Humanistica [Spain] 1980 18(205): 49-51.* The Harambee [Let us unite] principle, coined during the independence movement, has been successfully applied in the field of education from the community construction of schools to establishing institutes of technology, and has since been exported for application in Southeast Asia.

2995. Moock, Joyce Lewinger. PRAGMATISM AND THE PRIMARY SCHOOL: THE CASE OF A NON-RURAL VILLAGE. *Africa [Great Britain] 1973 43(4): 302-315.* Analyzes the educational needs of the South Maragoli Location of Kakamega District, Western Province, Kenya, in terms of its changing socioeconomic pattern in the 1970's, showing how attitudes toward the school system as a means to employment developed in this environment.

2996. Murray, Jocelyn. THE CHURCH MISSIONARY SOCIETY AND THE "FEMALE CIRCUMCISION" ISSUE IN KENYA, 1929-1932. *J. of Religion in Africa [Netherlands] 1976 8(2): 92-104.* The Church Missionary Society opposed clitoridectomy as a ritual of entry into adulthood. Their activity peaked in Kenya during 1929-30 when the various missions disagreed over the religious justification of such an operation. Based on oral interviews, it was determined that as late as 1972 60% of the girls in one area had undergone circumcision. 38 notes. H. G. Soff

2997. Murray, Jocelyn. THE KIKUYU SPIRIT CHURCHES. *J. of Religion in Africa [Netherlands] 1973 5(3): 198-234.* Traces the history of the *Watu wa Mungu* (People of God) sect in Kenya from its inception in the 1920's. In its early years the religious group fell under governmental suspicion and persecution, but the leadership of the church was able to continue its tradition. In the 1970's the sect is appealing to more and more semieducated Kikuyu who are unable to compete in the world of money and power. 145 notes. H. G. Soff

2998. Musisi, J. S. and Abukutsa, J. L. EVOLUTION OF LIBRARY ASSOCIATIONS IN KENYA. *Int. Lib. Rev. [Great Britain] 1978 10(4): 345-354.* The history, operations, publications, and interrelations of the East African Library Association, the Schools Library Association, the National Library Association, and the Kenya Library Association, 1895-1977.

2999. Nyaggah, Mougo. ASIANS IN EAST AFRICA: THE CASE OF KENYA. *J. of African Studies 1974 1(2): 205-233.* Study of the conflict in East Africa between Asians and native Africans. Explores Asians' arrival into Kenya and their precolonial role, the effect of Asians' high status on interaction with Africans, the development of their high status and its contribution to their present dilemma, and measures taken since independence and the reasons for their failure. The root of the problem is really not racism, as often charged, but economics. 106 notes. R. V. Ritter

3000. Odenyo, Amos O. PROFESSIONALISM AMIDST CHANGE: THE CASE OF THE EMERGING LEGAL PROFESSION. *African Studies Rev. 1979 22(3): 33-44.* A statistical analysis of a data questionnaire and followup interviews with lawyers in Kenya. Since independence there has been a marked change in the nature of the field away from the Western colonial standards of professionalism. Based on field research; 10 tables, 6 notes, biblio. R. T. Brown

3001. Parkin, David J. ALONG THE LINE OF ROAD: EXPANDING RURAL CENTRES IN KENYA'S COAST PROVINCE. *Africa [Great Britain] 1979 49(3): 272-282.* Kenya's coastal zone, traditionally Muslim, has had a growing number of non-Muslim immigrants since independence in 1963. This has resulted in intermarriage and the development of incipient townships and capitalist enterprises. Arab-Swahili patronage extends throughout the Muslim community. Government patronage tends to support the non-Muslim community. A possible solution to the problem created by the conflicting interests of the population of this area may be an alliance between the relatively wealthy Arab shopowners and businessmen and up-country entrepreneurs. 3 notes. R. L. Collison

3002. Schilling, Donald G. THE DYNAMICS OF EDUCATION POLICY FORMATION: KENYA 1928-1934. *Hist. of Educ. Q. 1980 20(1): 51-76.* Examines the dynamics of educational policy formation in colonial Kenya during the administration of Henry S. Scott as director of education. Scott devised a rational plan for augmenting the missionary schools with a British style of graded classes taught by well-trained instructors. Conflicts with missionary forces led by J. H. Oldham on the Advisory Committee for Educational Affairs in the Colonial Office in London and Local Native Councils frustrated Scott's efforts. Secondary sources; 63 notes. S. H. Frank

3003. Scotton, James F. KENYA'S MALIGNED AFRICAN PRESS: TIME FOR A REASSESSMENT. *Journalism Q. 1975 52(1): 30-36.* The African press of pre-independence Kenya has received little direct examination. *Mumenyereri* and other important African newspapers were responsible and moderate, even on the issue of European occupation of land. After 1950 printers refused to publish African newspapers because the government was empowered to seize presses used for seditious literature and extremist mimeographed Kikuyu news sheets appeared. Readers turned to the news sheets. Based on the files of the Colonial Criminal Investigation Division in the Kenya National Archives; 52 notes. K. J. Puffer

3004. Scotton, James F. THE PRESS IN KENYA A DECADE AFTER INDEPENDENCE: PATTERN OF READERSHIP AND OWNERSHIP. *Gazette [Netherlands] 1975 21(1): 19-33.* Discusses four Kenyan newspapers: the *East African Standard*(English) and *Baraza* (Swahili), both owned by Lonrho, a London-based corporation, and the *Daily Nation* (English) and the *Taifa Leo* (Swahili), owned by the Aga Khan through the Nation Newspapers Limited. Compares readership and ownership and assesses the impact of ownership and language on editorial policy.

3005. Strobel, Margaret. FROM *LELEMAMA* TO LOBBYING: WOMEN'S ASSOCIATIONS IN MOMBASA, KENYA. Hafkin, Nancy J. and Bay, Edna G., eds. *Women in Africa: Studies in Social and Economic Change*(Stanford, Ca.: Stanford U. Pr., 1976): 183-211. In the 1930's-50's, Mombasa saw the rise of self-help, community-oriented Muslim women's organizations whose goals were entertainment, prestige, and self-improvement. Though organized for entertainment, the *lelemama* dance associations, 1930's-40's, provided women with organizational and leadership experience. Banned in the 1950's because they inflamed ethnic tensions, they were replaced by the Muslim Women's Institute and the Muslim Women's Cultural Association which were founded partly out of a need for prestige and a sense of inferiority to Indian women's organizations. Although their leadership was experienced in *lelemama* activities and their members reflected *lelemama's* factionalism, their concerns were with social welfare and education. Uninvolved with feminist issues they remain today organizations of, not for, women. Fieldwork and secondary sources; 33 notes. S. Tomlinson-Brown

3006. Swartz, Marc J. RELIGIOUS COURTS, COMMUNITY, AND ETHNICITY AMONG THE SWAHILI OF MOMBASA: AN HISTORICAL STUDY OF SOCIAL BOUNDARIES. *Africa [Great Britain] 1979 49(1): 29-41.* Studies the workings of Koranic courts in

Mombasa, Kenya to demonstrate their role in maintaining the individuality of the Swahili. Considers the relationship between control of legal matters and the existence of social boundaries, and the interaction of ethnicity and community, according to the views of Max Weber and Frederik Barth. 14 notes, biblio. P. J. Taylorson

3007. Thomas, Anthony E. OATHS, ORDEALS, AND THE KENYAN COURTS: A POLICY ANALYSIS. *Human Organization 1974 33(1): 59-70.*

3008. Turton, E. R. THE INTRODUCTION AND DEVELOPMENT OF EDUCATIONAL FACILITIES FOR THE SOMALI IN KENYA. *Hist. of Educ. Q. 1974 14(3): 347-366.* In the period ca. 1930-59 Western educational institutions in Kenya were inevitably Christian rather than Muslim, and cut against the grain of Somali social, religious, and cultural life. This factor, together with geographical isolation, prejudice against the education of pastoral peoples, and the failures of local funding bodies, the Native Councils, led to the slow development of educational facilities for the Somali in Kenya.

3009. Turton, E. R. THE ISAQ SOMALI DIASPORA AND POLL-TAX AGITATION IN KENYA, 1936-41. *African Affairs [Great Britain] 1974 73(292): 325-346.* The Isaq diaspora began on the coast of Somalia in the 19th century and spread to all of East Africa. They maintained an attitude of superiority to the Bantu and rejected their African origin. Unlike most poll tax resistance, the Isaq resisted in order to pay more tax; to be classified as Asian, not African. This attitude spread from the Isaq in Kenya to their East African clansmen. The Isaq campaign involved nonpayment of hut taxes, but since they failed to gain support from other Somali peoples, their movement failed. In 1942, however, they were classified as Asiatic. 67 notes. H. G. Soff

3010. Werlin, Herbert H. NAIROBI'S POLITICS OF HOUSING. *African R. [Tanzania] 1973 3(4): 611-629.* Nairobi has not squarely faced its housing problem partly because of its unnecessarily large bureaucracy. There are distinct sections of the city based on social class; the section inhabited by the poor, one-third of the city, is neglected by the government as "temporary housing." 84 notes. H. G. Soff

3011. Whiting, Beatrice B. CHANGING LIFE STYLES IN KENYA. *Daedalus 1977 106(2): 211-225.* Economics seems to determine all in the changes that have occurred in Kenyan family life. The new cash economy is connected with the demarcation of land into individually owned farms, with the demand for Western education, and with shifts into wage-earning jobs. Polygamy as a marriage system is disappearing. Traditional values—generosity, good-heartedness, respectfulness, obedience, and responsibility—are giving way to cleverness and curiosity. Will the Kenyan family be able to maintain its sociable tradition in these new circumstances or will it become increasingly preoccupied with success and personal achievement? Based on secondary sources; 5 notes.
E. McCarthy

3012. Wilkin, David. REFUGEES AND BRITISH ADMINISTRATIVE POLICY IN NORTHERN KENYA, 1936-1938. *African Affairs [Great Britain] 1980 79(317): 510-530.* Between 1936 and 1938 three types of refugees entered or attempted to enter Northern Kenya from Ethiopia under the impact of Italian colonial aggression. Kenyan administrators under instructions from the Colonial Office dealt with each of them discriminately by following a pragmatic policy based on local conditions, the stage of fighting in Ethiopia, public opinion, legal implications, and the international situation. Some of the refugees reluctantly allowed to resettle in the British colony became Britain's allies when war broke out a few years later. Based on primary material in the Kenya National Archives; 117 notes. J. V. Coutinho

3013. Winans, Edgar V. and Haugerud, Angelique. RURAL SELF-HELP IN KENYA: THE *HARAMBEE* MOVEMENT. *Human Organization 1977 36(4): 334-351.* Examines self-help *(harambee)* movements in rural areas of Kenya to determine to what extent grassroots mobilization for change is operative, the influence of local factors in the success of the movement, and regional inequalities that have emerged, 1963-77.

3014. Wipper, Audrey. THE MAENDELEO YA WANAWAKE MOVEMENT: SOME PARADOXES AND CONTRADICTIONS. *African Studies Rev. 1975 18(3): 99-120.* Discusses the origins and program of the Maendeleo Ya Wanawake [women's progress] organization in Kenya, 1954-74, and the attitudes of the rural people, the national executive, and the central government toward it.

3015. —. [SOCIAL CHANGE AMONG THE TESO OF KENYA]. *Africa [Great Britain] 1981 51(3): 781-786.*

Packard, Randall M. SOCIAL CHANGE AND THE TESO, *pp. 781-785.* In a review of Ivan Karp's *Fields of Change among the Iteso of Kenya* in *Africa* 1980 50(2): 214-216, Paul Spencer challenged Karp's historical account of the emergence of neighborhoods among the Teso during the colonial era. Spencer believed that the transformation of Teso social structures was partly brought about by the gradual adjustment of the Teso to new ecological conditions. Karp suggested that the change was due to the overwhelming impact of the British penetration of western Kenya, 1894-1905. Packard emphasizes the need for additional historical research, a meticulous examination of early anthropological accounts, and additional research into the role of crisis in the sociology of change.

Spencer, Paul. A RESPONSE, *p. 786.* Spencer concurs, emphasizing the importance of using a number of models. 9 ref.
R. L. Collison/S

3016. —. TOWARD THE BIOLOGICAL CONTROL OF INSECT PESTS: THE RISE OF THE INTERNATIONAL CENTER OF INSECT PHYSIOLOGY AND ECOLOGY. *Sci. and Public Affairs 1973 29(3): 10-16.*

Wilson, Carroll L. ACTIVATING A VISION, *pp. 10, 14-16.* The International Center of Insect Physiology and Ecology in Nairobi, Kenya, 1970, was founded to further research in insect-related areas, as well as to develop a local scientific community which could research local health and agricultural problems.

Williams, Carroll M. PRINCIPAL AREAS OF INSECT RESEARCH, *pp. 11-14.* Research projects in insect hormones, antihormones, and pheromones conducted at the International Center of Insect Physiology and Ecology in Nairobi, Kenya, aimed at global control of insects, 1970-73.

Rwanda

3017. Fletz, Gaetan. ÉVOLUTION DES STRUCTURES FONCIÈRES ET HISTOIRE POLITIQUE DU RWANDA (XIXe ET XXe SIÈCLES) [The evolution of landed structures and the political history of Rwanda, 19th and 20th centuries]. *Etudes d'Hist. Africaine [Zaire] 1975 7: 143-154.* The network of power in Rwandan politics at the end of the 19th century manifested itself in a tendency toward centralization of authority to the profit of ideologically homogeneous groups. The evolution of the land-based structures in the 20th century accentuated cleavages between the agriculturalists and pastoralists with a resultant fragmentation of power. 2 charts, 31 notes. H. L. Calkin

3018. Lugan, Bernard. CAUSES ET EFFETS DE LA FAMINE "RUMANURA" AU RWANDA, 1916-1918 [Causes and effects of the Rumanura famine in Rwanda, 1916-18]. *Can. J. of African Studies [Canada] 1976 10(2): 347-356.* The Rumanura famine in Rwanda, 1916-18, brought about by inordinately small rainfalls and hostilities which brought in Belgian troops, was worsened by the fact that the Bugoyi Plain area where it began served as a supply area for other less abundant areas of the kingdom and through the spread of the famine and the concurrent small rainfall in other areas of Rwanda (which in other circumstances would have been depended on to supply food to famine-struck areas) resulted in a major disaster for the inhabitants.

3019. Newbury, David S. THE CLANS OF RWANDA: AN HISTORICAL HYPOTHESIS. *Africa [Great Britain] 1980 50(4): 389-403.* Existing concepts of clientship, ethnicity, caste, and clanship in Rwanda have been subject to scrutiny and challenge during the past 10 years. These aspects did not change randomly, but they were not static features of Rwandan social organization. In eastern Rwanda the original clan identities differed from those prevailing at the present time, being influenced by the royal court. Statistical analysis indicates that clan identities have their own history independent of the other social institutions of Rwanda. Map; table, 22 notes. R. L. Collison

3020. Newbury, M. Catherine. ETHNICITY IN RWANDA: THE CASE OF KINYAGA. *Africa [Great Britain] 1978 48(1): 17-29.* The modern ethnic divisions between the Hutu and the Tutsi in the Kinyaga region of Southwest Rwanda stem from political developments, 1860-1960. In the mid-19th century, Rwandan political control in Kinyaga was limited, but in the reign of Kigeri IV Rwabugiri, (ca. 1860-95), the region was incorporated into the Rwandan kingdom. During German (1898-1916) and Belgian (1916-60) colonial rule, power and wealth came to be controlled by the Tutsi authorities. This reduced the autonomy of local groups; jeopardized their personal security, status, and wealth; and increased their mobility, causing political instability. 29 notes. M. Smith

3021. Novelli, Tina. SISTEMA DOTALE TUTSI E HUTU NEL RWANDA [The Tutsi and Hutu dowry system in Rwanda]. *Africa [Italy] 1974 29(2): 213-224.* Examines the dowry system of these two groups, explaining its ethnological significance, illustrating the three types of marriage still in practice, the development of the institution, and problems arising from the different attitudes of generations to it. 7 notes. R. O. Khan

3022. Sayinzoga, Jean. LES REFUGIES RWANDAIS: QUELQUES REPERES HISTORIQUES ET REFLEXIONS SOCIOPOLITIQUES [The Rwanda refugees: some historical guidelines and sociopolitical reflections]. *Genève-Afrique [Switzerland] 1982 20(1): 49-72.* Belgian deformations of the precolonial regime led to a widening gap between the rulers and ruled of Rwanda, which resulted in a racial war between the Hutu and Tutsi peoples, leading to the exile of over 300,000 of the former Tutsi rulers. Secondary sources; 25 notes, 3 tables, 2 photos. B. S. Fetter

3023. Vidal, Claudine. COLONISATION ET DÉCOLONISATION DU RWANDA: LA QUESTION TUTSI-HUTU [The colonization and decolonization of Rwanda: the Tutsi-Hutu question]. *Rev. Française d'Études Pol. Africaines [France] 1973 8(91): 32-47.* Discusses the political development of Rwanda up to the 1972 coup d'etat of General Juvenal Habyalimana, stressing the importance of the conflict between the former Tutsi ruling class and the majority Hutu people.

3024. Weinstein, Warren. MILITARY CONTINUITIES IN THE RWANDA STATE. *J. of Asian and African Studies [Netherlands] 1977 12(1-4): 48-66.* There was a "direct resurrection of the precolonial warrior tradition and organization" among the Tutsi in 1959 which was utilized to combat both the Belgians and the Hutu nationalist organizations. This revival of tradition was finally crushed in 1963. 13 notes, biblio. R. T. Brown

Somalia

3025. Bell, J. Bowyer. STRATEGIC IMPLICATIONS OF THE SOVIET PRESENCE IN SOMALIA. *Orbis 1975 19(2): 402-411.* Notes USSR naval strategy regarding the visits of naval vessels to port of Berbera, Somalia, stressing the significance of oil in the Persian Gulf and the overall strategic importance of the Indian Ocean region, 1960-75.

3026. Cecchini, Vincenzo. LA PROMOZIONE DELL'AUTO-SVILUPPO: IL "CRASH PROGRAMME" IN SOMALIA [The promotion of self-development: the "crash program" in Somalia]. *Africa [Italy] 1975 30(1): 129-133.* In 1970 the Democratic Republic of Somalia decided to move toward the rapid development of fundamental sectors of the economy, chiefly agrarian and zootechnical. The "crash programs," employing unpaid volunteers, encouraged agricultural diversification, return to the land, a concept of work and social justice, control of illiteracy, and cultivation of the social heritage. Based chiefly on Somalian publications; 11 notes. L. R. Atkins

3027. Chaplin, Dennis. SOMALIA AND THE DEVELOPMENT OF SOVIET ACTIVITY IN THE INDIAN OCEAN. *Military Rev. 1975 55(7): 3-9.* Examines the USSR's efforts to cultivate Somalia as a military base for Soviet naval penetration of the Indian Ocean. These efforts are motivated by a desire to counter American naval activity, accumulate prestige through naval bases, apply pressure on Egypt, acquire tactical advantage with regard to the Persian Gulf, obstruct Chinese activities in Africa, and encircle China through friendlier ties with India. Map. J. K. Ohl

3028. Davidson, Basil. SOMALIA IN 1975: SOME NOTES AND IMPRESSIONS. *Issue 1975 5(1): 18-26.* Describes living conditions and history of Somalia. S

3029. Decraene, Philippe. SOMALIA: SCIENTIFIC SOCIALISM—AFRICAN STYLE. *Africa Report 1975 20(3): 46-51.* Somalia's economy is changing from a pastoral family-based economy to a sedentary collective system. S

3030. FitzGibbon, Louis. SOMALIA: A CALL FOR JUSTICE. *Contemporary Rev. [Great Britain] 1982 240(1394): 137-143.* Discusses the historical origins of current problems in Somalia from the Middle Ages to the present.

3031. Gray, Randal. BOMBING THE "MAD MULLAH"—1920. *J. of the Royal United Services Inst. for Defence Studies [Great Britain] 1980 125(4): 41-46.* From remote strongholds in British Somaliland, Seyid Mohammed Abdullah Hassan (the "Mad Mullah") contested British territorial control from 1899 to 1921. After several failed attempts to stop the Mullah, a renewed effort included a unit of a dozen DeHavilland 9 aircraft and began operations in January 1920. Hampered by a rash of mechanical troubles, the planes usually operated in groups of three to six, but their bombing attacks on forts, strafing attacks on troops and animal herds, and aerial scouting kept the Mullah's forces in disarray, leading to capitulation by the spring of 1920. 2 photos, map. R. E. Bilstein

3032. Laitin, David D. THE POLITICAL ECONOMY OF MILITARY RULE IN SOMALIA. *J. of Modern African Studies [Great Britain] 1976 14(3): 449-468.* Assesses the seven years of military rule of General Mohammed Siad Barre in contrast to the previous civilian regime. Although less than hoped for and often gained at the price of civil liberties, Siad's achievements included the end of imbedded corruption, a new nationalism aimed at reducing ethnic conflict and dependency on foreign states, and the introduction of Somali as the official language and of various socialist goals designed to improve the status of the populace. 5 tables, 27 notes. R. V. Ritter

3033. Luling, Virginia. COLONIAL AND POSTCOLONIAL INFLUENCES ON A SOUTH SOMALI COMMUNITY. *J. of African Studies 1976 3(4): 491-511.* The Italian conquest was only the cutting edge of Westernization on the small community of Geledi. Geledi grew smoothly in response to new market opportunities because it was always heterogeneous. Although the noble elite were deprived of their traditional sources of wealth and thrust into a much larger political unit, they showed themselves open to new ideas and began to restore their status. The revolution of 1969 brought a centralized government and actually represents the heaviest impact of Western ideas, even though it was carried out in the name of Somali nationalism. Based on fieldwork and on secondary sources; 11 notes. W. R. Hively

3034. Novati, Giampaolo Calchi. GLI INCIDENTI DI MOGADISCIO DEL GENNAIO 1948: RAPPORTI ITALO-INGLESI E NAZIONALISMO SOMALO [The January 1948 incidents at Mogadisho: Italian and English relations and Somali nationalism]. *Africa [Italy] 1980 35(3-4): 327-356.* January 1948 riots in Mogadisho caused the death of 52 Italians and 14 Somalis. On the basis of Italian and English documentation the author reconstructs the course of the events, determines responsibility, and analyzes the effects on the diplomatic level. The riots fostered the solution of the situation, especially in Great Britain, to abandon the notion of annexing Somalia. Somali nationalism and the Somali Youth League were important factors in the riots. J/S

3035. Pankhurst, Richard. AN EARLY SOMALI AUTOBIOGRAPHY. *Africa [Italy] 1977 32(2): 159-176.* Publishes and explicates *The Life and Adventures of a Somali* by Ibrahim Ismaa'il. This autobiography was written in English when Eugène Gaspard Marin, a Belgian scholar living in an English anarchist community, encouraged Ibrahim Ismaa'il to write about his life. Although the *Life* was completed in 1928, it was not published because the British had little interest in far-off Somaliland. The *Life* reveals that this previously unknown author deserves a place in African literature as a gifted story-teller and a perceptive observer. 28 notes. Article to be continued. W. R. Hively

3036. Payton, Gary D. THE SOMALI COUP OF 1969: THE CASE FOR SOVIET COMPLICITY. *J. of Modern African Studies [Great Britain] 1980 18(3): 493-508.* Soviet strategic planners decided by 1969 to topple the elective civilian Somali government in Mogadisho, in cooperation with a handful of disaffected Somali military officers. Somalia's "drift to the West" under President Sharmarke and Prime Minister Egal in the late 1960's seemed to be removing Somalia as a strategic Soviet ally in East Africa. The Soviet planners were influenced primarily by the threat of US-Chinese cooperation directed against the USSR, particularly its strategic supply line around Africa to its Vietnamese allies. Based on published American documents, newspapers, and secondary sources; 34 notes. L. W. Truschel

3037. Payton, Gary D. SOVIET MILITARY PRESENCE ABROAD: THE LESSONS OF SOMALIA. *Military Rev. 1979 59(1): 67-77.* States that although the USSR gained certain short-term strategic goals through its arms agreement with Somalia, these goals evaporated when the Soviets chose also to support Ethiopia. Until the Russians establish adequate control mechanisms, the threat of similar consequences are quite possible in countries which accept Soviet arms and advisers. Secondary sources; 19 notes. E. C. Hopkins

3038. Piga De Carolis, Adriana. IL QUADRO ETNICO TRADIZIONALE NELLE PROSPETTIVE DI SVILUPPO DELLA VALLE DEL GIUBA [Traditional ethnic factors and development prospects in the Juba Valley]. *Africa [Italy] 1980 35(1): 17-42.* The Juba Valley in southern Somalia represents a major point in the development policy of the socialist government. The author analyzes the origins of some groups living in that area, in particular the Bon, the last representatives of ancient khoisanoid hunters, the Bantu from the Gosha with their characteristic sociopolitical organization, and the Galla and Somali. Considers the controversial history of the Galla and Somali and the surprisingly modern territorial and political organization of the Digil and Rahanwen groups. Focuses on the aspects of traditional culture that could contribute a reference point for the new social model developing in modern Somalia. J/S

3039. Poláček, Zdeněk. VZNIK SAMOSTATNÉHO SOMÁLSKA A VÝVOJ PANSOMALISMU [The origin of independent Somalia and the development of Pan-Somalism]. *Československý Časopis Hist. [Czechoslovakia] 1982 30(1): 7-18.* The markedly clannish character of Somali social organization explains a compensating centripetal tendency in Somali nationalism. Since the fusion of Italian and British Somalia in 1950 and political independence in 1960, Pan-Somalism has served to overcome internal political atomization. Since roughly 1.2 million Somalis live outside Somalia, this irredentist nationalism has encouraged aggression against other African states. Table, 29 notes. Russian and English summaries. R. E. Weltsch

3040. Sherr, E. SOMALIA: SOCIALIST ORIENTATION. *Int. Affairs [USSR] 1974 (2): 84-88.* Compares Somalia in the early 1970's with Somalia in the 1960's.

3041. Sofinsky, V. SOMALIA ON THE PATH OF PROGRESS. *Int. Affairs [USSR] 1974 (11): 62-66.* Evaluates the success of economic and agricultural development, industry, education, socialism and the state of the working class in Somalia from 1960-74, including its foreign relations with the USSR.

3042. Yodfat, Aryeh. BRIT HA-MO'ATSOT V'SOMALIA [The USSR and Somalia]. *Hamizrah Hehadash [Israel] 1980 29(1-4): 43-65.* Discusses the relations between the USSR and Somalia in the context of overall Soviet policies in the Middle East. Implies that the USSR used its rapport with Somalia to divert attention from Soviet economic and agricultural failures. A Soviet-Somali friendship treaty, signed in 1974, gave the USSR a base from which to make its political presence felt in the region. When Somalia and Ethiopia went to war in 1977, the USSR supported Ethiopia and the 1974 treaty was abrogated. Still, Somalia has remained a client of the USSR because no Western country will sell it arms. Somalian President Siad Barre's trip to China in 1978 is seen as an attempt to escape the Soviet grip. Based on contemporary sources, including newspapers and US government translations of foreign publications (FBIS); 74 notes. T. Koppel

Tanzania

General

3043. Bossema, Wim. GESCHIEDSCHRIJVING IN DAR ES SALAAM: NATIONALISM, SOCIALISM EN GESCHIEDENIS IN TANZANIA: EEN HISTORIOGRAFIES OVERZICHT [Historiography in Dar es Salaam: nationalism, socialism, and history in Tanzania: a historiographical survey]. *Kleio [Netherlands] 1979 20(10): 436-441.* Reviews over 10 books and articles by native Tanzanian historians, mostly on the faculty of Dar es Salaam University, written after independence (1961), that deal with Tanzania's history from precolonial to modern times. Characteristic of Tanzania's native historiography is its dependence on oral tradition, due to the lack of written source material, its emphasis on the history of the masses to counterbalance the colonial historians' history of the elite, and its primary purpose of being relevant to the developmentalism of African socialism (Ujamaa). 3 notes, biblio. G. Herritt

3044. Chekala-Mukha, G. DVE STOLITSY [Two capitals]. *Aziia i Afrika Segodnia [USSR] 1982 (1): 44-46.* Dar es Salaam is scheduled eventually to lose its capital status to the provincial city of Dodoma; traces Dar es Salaam's growth since its founding by the Sultan of Zanzibar in 1862.

3045. Collins, Paul. [HISTORY OF TANZANIA]. RECENT DEVELOPMENTS IN TANZANIA. *Afriscope [Nigeria] 1974 4(5): 36-37.* Analyzes the history of Tanzania and outlines the problems of consolidating gains. TANZANIA'S SOCIALISM. *Afriscope [Nigeria] 1974 4(6): 24-26.* Tanzanian socialism continues to move consistently toward self-sufficiency despite pressures from the radical left to accelerate nationalization and from the urban classes who resent highly paid managers. Some tendencies toward bureaucratic centralization have emerged. G. O. Gagnon

3046. Marzoli, Emanuela. TANZANIA: VENT'ANNI DI INDIPENDENZA [Tanzania: 20 years of independence]. *Riv. di Studi Pol. Int. [Italy] 1982 49(1): 89-105.* Describes the theory and practice of the Ujamaa policy, the 2d Five-Year Plan, internal criticism and consensus, and foreign relations.

3047. Matzke, Gordon. THE DEVELOPMENT OF THE SELOUS GAME RESERVE. *Tanzania Notes and Records [Tanzania] 1976 (79-80): 37-48.* Under the direction of the Game Division, the Selous Game Reserve evolved, 1902-72, to occupy 55,000 square kilometers of southeastern Tanzania. Due to the inadequate facilities to protect game, especially elephants, the Mahenge and Mohoro reserves were consolidated in 1972 and christened the Selous Game Reserve. Thereafter, uncultivable, thinly populated, and tsetse infected areas were annexed, forming a contiguous unit encompassing all of the game estate in southeastern Tanzania. Based on materials found in the Tanzanian National Archives, printed primary and secondary sources; 7 maps, 2 tables, note; biblio. S. Lakhan

3048. Nyerere, Julius. FROM UHURU TO UJAMAA. *Africa Today 1974 21(3): 3-8.* An assessment of Tanzanian progress since independence in 1961. Tanzania "is not a socialist society" but is trying to become one. Mistakes have been made but Tanzania still will "create a society in which all citizens work together in freedom, dignity and equality for their common good." G. O. Gagnon

3049. Spengen, Wim van. STRUCTURAL CHARACTERISTICS OF UNDERDEVELOPMENT IN THE MAFIA ARCHIPELAGO: AN HISTORICAL ANALYSIS. *Cahiers d'Études Africaines [France] 1980 20(3): 331-353.* Analyzes and identifies structural characteristics of underdevelopment that lead to social inequality in a microregional context, illustrated by the example of the Mafia Archipelago, a group of islands in the Indian Ocean belonging to Tanzania, emphasizing power structure and colonial dominance, the Mafian setting and its population's history, pre-Omani Mafia, Omani overlordship and European control, socioreligious hierarchy, and the plantation system as a mode of production.

3050. Urfer, Sylvain. LA LONGUE MARCHE DE LA TANZANIE [The long march of Tanzania]. *Études [France] 1976 344: 839-857.* Presents a portrait of Tanzania since its independence in 1961, studying its original brand of socialism, its effective use of local incentive, and its effort toward true independence in its foreign relations.

3051. —. [A DECADE OF PROGRESS: 1961-1971]. *Tanzania Notes and Records [Tanzania] 1975 (76): 1-202.*
Nyerere, Julius K. TANU TEN YEARS AFTER INDEPENDENCE, *pp. 1-50.* 5 photos.
Hydén, Goran. DEVELOPMENT OF THE COOPERATIVE MOVEMENT IN TANZANIA, *pp. 51-56.* 2 photos, 7 notes.
Aldington, T. J. TANZANIAN AGRICULTURE: A DECADE OF PROGRESS IN CROP PRODUCTION, *pp. 57-66.* Photo, 6 tables.
—. LIVESTOCK DEVELOPMENT AFTER NATIONAL INDEPENDENCE, *pp. 67-70.* Photo.
Singh, S. B. FISHERIES AND MARINE RESOURCES—AN OUTLINE OF PROGRESS, *pp. 71-74.* Photo, table.
Kimambo, R. H. N. and Mahanga, W. L. ACTIVITIES OF THE MINERAL RESOURCES DIVISION: 1961-1971, *pp. 75-81.* Photo.
Mawalla, G. M. S. TOURISM DEVELOPMENT: THE TEN YEARS AFTER INDEPENDENCE, *p. 83.* Photo.
Fosbrooke, H. A. NGORONGORO CONSERVATION AREA, 1961 TO 1971 DEVELOPMENT, *pp. 85-88.* 2 photos, table.
Mence, A. J. COLLEGE OF AFRICAN WILDLIFE MANAGEMENT; TEN YEARS AFTER, *pp. 89-92.* Photo.
Mturi, A. A. PROTECTION, PRESERVATION AND DEVELOPMENT OF TANZANIA'S HERITAGE, *pp. 93-101.* Table.
Masao, F. T. NATIONAL MUSEUM OF TANZANIA: POST-INDEPENDENCE PROGRESS, *pp. 103-112.* 3 photos.
Ntiro, S. J. TRADITIONAL ARTS IN THE POST-INDEPENDENCE ERA, *pp. 113-118.* 2 photos.
Mapunda, O. B. EDUCATIONAL PROGRESS IN THE FIRST TEN YEARS OF INDEPENDENCE, *pp. 119-126.* 4 tables.
—. INFORMATION SERVICES AND RADIO TANZANIA: INFORMING THE NATION, *pp. 127-128.*
Kaungamno, E. E. TANGANYIKA LIBRARY SERVICE: 1961-1971, *pp. 129-131.*
Segal, M. BUSINESS AND INDUSTRIES AFTER TEN YEARS, *pp. 133-139.* Photo, 3 tables.
—. NATIONAL DEVELOPMENT CORPORATION AND ECONOMIC GROWTH, *pp. 141-142.* Chart.
—. PROGRESS IN SMALL SCALE INDUSTRIES IN THE INDEPENDENCE YEARS, *pp. 143-144.*
—. NATIONAL INSURANCE CORPORATION: VITAL TO A SOCIALIST ECONOMY, *pp. 145-148.*
Vuo, T. S. MANPOWER PLANNING AND DEVELOPMENT, *pp. 149-156.* 4 tables.
—. NATIONAL INSTITUTE FOR PRODUCTIVITY: PROGRESS IN MANAGEMENT, *pp. 157-158.*
Jamal, A. H. MINISTRY OF FINANCE: A TEN YEAR SUMMARY, *pp. 159-162.* 2 tables.
Mtei, Edwin. BANK OF TANZANIA—ECONOMIC SELF-RELIANCE, *pp. 163-164.*
—. NATIONAL BANK OF COMMERCE—GROWTH AND PROGRESS, *pp. 165-166.*
—. HISTORY OF LAND REFORMS IN TANZANIA, *pp. 167-170.*
—. LAND AND PUBLIC POLICY AFTER INDEPENDENCE, *pp. 171-174.* Photo.
—. ACTIVITIES OF THE LAND REGISTRY DIVISION FROM 1961-1971, *p. 175.*
—. LAND VALUATION: EXPANSION AND SERVICE, *pp. 177-178.* Photo.
—. TOWN PLANNING REVOLVES AROUND THE PEOPLE: A RECORD OF TEN YEARS, *pp. 179-184.*
Kikenya, J. D. NATIONAL HOUSING CORPORATION—PROGRESS IN HOUSING THE MASSES, *pp. 185-190.* Photo, 3 tables, diagram.
—. WATER SUPPLY—SERVICE TO THE NATION TO SPEED DEVELOPMENT, *pp. 191-192.*
—. TANZANIA POLICE FORCE: LAW AND ORDER SINCE UHURU, *pp. 193-196.* Photo.
—. PRISON SERVICE SINCE INDEPENDENCE, *pp. 197-200.*
—. TANZANIA PEOPLES DEFENCE FORCES: DEVELOPMENT 1961-1971, *pp. 201-202.* A special issue covering progress in various national sectors in Tanzania during the first decade of independence (December 1961-December 1971).

Economics

3052. Anthony, Constance G. PEASANT POWER, STATE POWER: TANZANIAN SOCIALISM REVISITED. *Africa Today 1980 27(4): 51-54.* Reviews Goran Hyden's *Beyond Ujamaa in Tanzania: Underdevelopment And An Uncaptured Peasantry* (1980) and concludes that the author fails to prove his thesis that peasant autonomy prevents effective socialism. G. O. Gagnon

3053. Awiti, Adhu. ECONOMIC DIFFERENTIATION IN ISMANI, IRINGI REGION: A CRITICAL ASSESSMENT OF PEASANT'S RESPONSE TO THE UJAMAA VIJININI PROGRAMME. *African R. [Tanzania] 1973 3(2): 209-239.* Ismani area was sparsely settled until the early 1950's when migrant peasants and workers came and requested land. The colonial government developed a Five Year Development Plan and settlement scheme, yet few migrants intended to remain permanently and did not follow modern farming methods. In 1952 some farmers formed the Ismani Maize Growers Co-operative Society to guarantee better prices, but it failed within a year. Eventually there developed class differentiation and class struggle in Ismani. Asians dominated credit and retail markets, as well as transport. To transform villages in this area into socialist villages, the independent government will have to disseminate a clearer meaning of socialism and self-reliance to African peasants. 5 tables, 8 notes. H. G. Soff

3054. Barongo, S. PETROLEUM DEVELOPMENT IN TANZANIA. *Tanzania Notes and Records [Tanzania] 1976 (79-80): 115-121.* Tanzania's expanding economy made oil indispensable, and the Tanzania Petroleum Development Corporation was created in 1969 to tap indigenous resources, possibly located in the sedimentary basins of Tanzania's numerous lakes and its coastal basins. Oceanic of Denver and Agip Spa of Italy operate in partnership with the Tanzanian government in exploration and financing. Table. S. Lakhan

3055. Bhuyan, M. Sayefullah. CAN TANZANIA MAKE TRANSITION TOWARD SOCIALISM? *Dacca U. Studies Part A [Bangladesh] 1980 (33): 112-124.* The Arusha Declaration of 1967 provided a theoretical framework for a transition from underdevelopment to socialism and self-reliance. Despite some socialist inclinations, Tanzania lacks some preconditions for socialist advance. The author deals with the concept of socialism in the Arusha Declaration and the strategy and tactics being pursued to develop Tanzania into a modern state, comparing it with other socialist states. Based mostly on secondary sources; 49 notes. J. V. Groves

3056. Bienefeld, M. A. TRADE UNIONS, THE LABOUR PROCESS, AND THE TANZANIAN STATE. *J. of Modern African Studies [Great Britain] 1979 17(4): 553-593.* The rapid expansion of trade unionism in colonial Tanganyika between 1930 and 1964 may be seen as an institutional response to changes in the processes of colonial production, requiring new forms of control over labor. Unions were fostered cautiously by the colonial government, seeking at all times to minimize the possibility of their becoming politicized. After independence unions were integrated into the government and TANU party structure and declined in importance. Their status shows internal contradictions arising from the pursuit of incompatible objectives—attempting to reach socialist goals in a capitalist economy and combining socialist rhetoric with bureaucracy and incoherence. Based on newspapers, colonial, Tanzanian government and international agency reports, and other published sources; 83 notes. D. J. Nicholls

3057. Biersteker, Thomas J. SELF-RELIANCE IN THEORY AND PRACTICE IN TANZANIAN TRADE RELATIONS. *Int. Organization 1980 34(2): 229-264.* Tanzania has formulated a number of institutions and policies designed to translate self-reliance into practice in its foreign trade sector, but most of its efforts have been unsuccessful because of the nature of the implementation of policy, the limited break with the international system, and structural limitations common to underdeveloped countries. 12 tables, 52 notes. J/S

3058. Binhammer, H. H. THE DEVELOPMENT OF A FINANCIAL INFRASTRUCTURE FOR A SOCIALIST ECONOMY: TANZANIA. *Rev. Int. d'Hist. de la Banque [Italy] 1975-10: 105-125.* With political independence in the early 1960's, Tanzania inherited a British financial administration and structure largely oriented to the financing of export staples and the importation of European manufactures. The banking structure hindered the Tanzanian government's efforts to secure control over Tanzania's economic development, but in the following years important changes took place. To provide a payments mechanism the government created the Bank of Tanzania; commercial banks were nationalized and the Tanzania Bank of Commerce created in 1965. It also was necessary for the government to establish institutions to encourage savings and use them for productive investment in Tanzania. The Post Office Savings Bank, the National Development Corporation, and the Tanzania Investment Bank were but a few of the institutions created to mobilize the financial resources of Tanzania for economic development. Based on government documents and publications and secondary sources; 36 notes. D. McGinnis

3059. Bomani, Paul and Ensminger, Douglas. TANZANIA'S ROAD TO DEVELOPMENT: BRINGING DEVELOPMENT TO THE PEOPLE. *Int. Development Rev. 1974 16(2): 2-9.* Interview with Tanzanian ambassador to the United States, Paul Bomani about social and economic development in rural settlements of Tanzania in the 1960's-70's.

3060. Brain, James L. THE ULUGURU LAND USAGE SCHEME: SUCCESS AND FAILURE. *J. of Developing Areas 1980 14(2): 175-190.* The Uluguru Land Usage Scheme, designed to prevent soil erosion, improve crop yields, and encourage the production of cash crops, was enforced in the Uluguru Mountainous region of Tanzania, an area whose residents believed in the efficacy of ancestral spirits. From 1949 to mid-1953 the proposals seemed to work, but in 1953 there were riots against the scheme as the project began to change from voluntary terracing to compulsory quotas. The discontent arose from several legitimate factors: extortion by scheme officials, who took bribes to say men had met their quotas; misunderstanding of the burning policy to destroy cutworms traditionally carried out by the Luguru; quotas applied only to men landowners and not to women; and misunderstanding by scheme officials of Luguru traditional values. Based on the author's personal experiences in Tanzania in agricultural extension and community development work; fig., 23 notes. O. W. Eads, Jr.

3061. Briggs, John. VILLAGISATION AND THE 1974-6 ECONOMIC CRISIS IN TANZANIA. *J. of Modern African Studies [Great Britain] 1979 17(4): 695-702.* Reply to Michael F. Lofchie, "Agrarian Crisis and Economic Liberalization in Tanzania," *Journal of Modern African Studies* 1978 16(3): 451-475. The economic crisis of 1974-76 in Tanzania was primarily a result of the villagization campaign, launched in late 1973, under which the rural population was moved into villages without necessarily being provided with any communal production component. The small percentage of the population in ujamaa villages meant that production was relatively unaffected before 1973 but went into decline with the villagization policy, which may be seen as a temporary halt in Tanzania's rural policy. Based on Bank of Tanzania data and other published sources; 3 tables, 15 notes. D. J. Nicholls

3062. Bryceson, Deborah Fahy. CHANGES IN PEASANT FOOD PRODUCTION AND FOOD SUPPLY IN RELATION TO THE HISTORICAL DEVELOPMENT OF COMMODITY PRODUCTION IN PRE-COLONIAL AND COLONIAL TANGANYIKA. *J. of Peasant Studies [Great Britain] 1980 7(3): 281-311.* Explores the dynamic interaction between peasant food production and commodity production under conditions of the increasing penetration of capital and consequent erosion of precapitalist modes of production in Tanganyika. While the law of value inherent in commodity production definitely served to effect more specialization of labor in peasant production, it was bounded by the limits of labor productivity attainable in peasant households. Shortfalls in peasant food production appeared as the most glaring consequence of the labor productivity constraint. The role of the colonial state was critical, not merely in the sense of acting to increase peasant commodity production. The colonial state also intervened strategically to dispense famine relief in times of serious food shortfalls, which guaranteeing peasant subsistence, altered its character from that of unreliability to that of regularity. Since peasant subsistence formed the necessary base for peasant commodity production, state famine relief insured the persistence of peasant commodity production but not its proliferation, the latter again being indicative of the labor productivity constraint. J

3063. Campbell, Horace. SOCIALISM IN TANZANIA: A CASE STUDY. *Black Scholar 1975 6(8): 41-51.* Discusses struggles in Tanzania for national independence from 1890 to 1961 and recent efforts by right-wing elements to entrench a neocolonial economy.

3064. Clayton, Anthony. THE GENERAL STRIKE IN ZANZIBAR, 1948. *J. of African Hist. [Great Britain] 1976 17(3): 417-434.* Mainlander migrant laborers led a general strike in Zanzibar on 20 August 1948. The strike lasted three weeks and eventually encompassed Africans in Zanzibar town. The author traces the history of mainland labor on the island, causes of the unrest, and reaction to the strike. The strike was geared more as a protest to British than Arab policy, and also indicated that mainlanders would demand a greater role in the future of Zanzibar. 48 notes. H. G. Soff

3065. Croll, Elizabeth J. WOMEN IN RURAL PRODUCTION AND REPRODUCTION IN THE SOVIET UNION, CHINA, CUBA, AND TANZANIA: CASE STUDIES. *Signs 1981 7(2): 375-399.* More than half of the workers on Soviet farms are women, yet Communist Party membership is only 23% women. Policy decisions including the birth rate are determined predominantly by men. In China, where 90% of the able-bodied women are employed, agrarian tasks are ranked on the basis of strength, skill, and experience. Women fall behind in wages and in access to power. In Cuba, laws have been enacted to force domestic sharing, and in Tanzania laws encouraging "villagization" attempt unsuccessfully to bring economic equality to women. Either the policies are not being carried out to assist women or the ideology is inherently incorrect. Based on newspaper accounts and secondary sources; 119 notes. S. P. Conner

3066. Croll, Elizabeth J. WOMEN IN RURAL PRODUCTION AND REPRODUCTION IN THE SOVIET UNION, CHINA, CUBA, AND TANZANIA: SOCIALIST DEVELOPMENT EXPERIENCES. *Signs 1981 7(2): 361-374.* Collectivization as a tenet of socialist economic development should free women economically by removing patriarchal authority patterns. While women have been recruited into agriculture, they are paid less, maintaining a strong sexual division of labor. Although they were promised state aid in reducing domestic tasks, women instead have fallen under the "double burden" of domestic work and employment. The women's revolution appears to have been lost within the socialist revolution to the detriment of women. 11 notes. S. P. Conner

3067. Cunningham, G. L. PEASANTS AND RURAL DEVELOPMENT IN TANZANIA. *Africa Today 1973 20(4): 3-18.* Describes the continuing problem of underdevelopment. Concludes that the only possibility for escaping the poverty cycle is to focus on peasant production of international trade commodities. Based on secondary sources and the author's Tanzanian experience; 13 tables, 39 notes. G. O. Gagnon

3068. Desai, Priya Mutalik. UJAMAA VILLAGES: A TANZANIAN EXPERIMENT IN RURAL DEVELOPMENT. *Africa Q. [India] 1976 16(2): 36-55.*

3069. Ellis, Ray. UJAMAA: A PERSONAL ASSESSMENT. *Africa Report 1974 19(6): 42-45.* Ujamaa, Tanzania's form of socialism, depends on the creation of community-controlled farming villages. S

3070. Ergas, Zaki. WHY DID THE UJAMAA VILLAGE POLICY FAIL? TOWARDS A GLOBAL ANALYSIS. *J. of Modern African Studies [Great Britain] 1980 18(3): 387-410.* Tanzania's massive state effort to achieve rural socialism through the Ujamaa villages policy failed badly during the decade 1967-77. Major assumptions behind the Ujamaa policy, that peasants could be persuaded to accept communal

agriculture, that they would participate in running the system, that the bureaucrats were more interested in building a socialist society than in retaining decisionmaking powers, that successful private farmers would not resist or subvert the new system, and that rural self-reliance would be achieved, were all proven facts. A severe food crisis worsened the situation in 1973-75, amid the government's successful but costly move to villagize by coercion the vast majority of the rural population. By 1977 the government had substituted control over the peasants for its failed policy of rural socialist development, to secure much-needed assistance from the World Bank, FAO, and transnational corporations. Based on published reports, unpublished University of Dar-es-Salaam papers, newspapers, and secondary sources; 82 notes.
L. W. Truschel

3071. Feldman, Rayah. CUSTOM AND CAPITALISM: CHANGES IN THE BASIS OF LAND TENURE IN ISMANI, TANZANIA. *J. of Development Studies [Great Britain] 1974 10(3/4): 305-320.* "Customary land tenure rules in Tanzania are incompatible with conditions of land shortage arising from agricultural development within an individual and incipiently capitalist framework. They are not equipped to deal with market land values, nor with individual demands which do not rest on a wider set of social obligations. Gross inequalities in land ownership are growing without controls because government policy has caused customary law to be retained for most rural land. In Ismani where agriculture is relatively developed, commercial land transactions are carried out secretly, and are consequently subject to cheating and insecurity. The only (still inadequate) means of securing title is by taking a dispute to court."
J

3072. Freeman, Linda. CIDA, WHEAT AND RURAL DEVELOPMENT IN TANZANIA. *Can. J. of African Studies [Canada] 1982 16(3): 479-504.* Examines a wheat growing project sponsored by the Canadian International Development Agency in Tanzania to evaluate Canadian contribution to food production in that country and as an example of international technology and capital transfer. The project will in the long run increase Tanzanian dependence on imports and foreign aid. It does not take into account the needs of the majority of the Tanzanian people and is determined by the dominant forces in both countries. 110 notes.
J. V. Coutinho

3073. Gottlieb, Manuel. THE EXTENT AND CHARACTER OF DIFFERENTIATION IN TANZANIAN AGRICULTURAL AND RURAL SOCIETY 1967-1969. *African R. [Tanzania] 1973 3(2): 241-261.* Rural social differentiation in Tanzania has not reached the degree that many people believed it would. Only 8,000 Tanzanian farm households expended over 10,000 shillings in 1969, but since they were concentrated in small areas, they attracted attention. Most differentiation that exists is within families, not between societies. Analyzes the household budget survey of 1968 conducted by the Bureau of Statistics. 3 tables, 25 notes, appendix.
H. G. Soff

3074. Graham, James D. THE TANZAM RAILWAY: CONSOLIDATING THE PEOPLE'S DEVELOPMENT AND BUILDING THE INTERNAL ECONOMY. *Africa Today 1974 21(3): 27-42.* Describes the Tanzam Railway as creating the infrastructure necessary for Tanzanian economic development and independence. Reviews the colonial and post-colonial problems of development and independence. The railway has "enormous political and psychological significance." Primary and secondary sources; 63 notes.
G. O. Gagnon

3075. Green, Reginald Herbold. "A TIME TO STRUGGLE": EXOGENOUS SHOCKS, STRUCTURAL TRANSFORMATION AND CRISIS IN TANZANIA. *Millennium: J. of Int. Studies [Great Britain] 1981 10(1): 29-41.* Analyzes Tanzanian economic development since 1967 from a Tanzanian perspective. Despite the external economic and security shocks, the leadership of President Julius Nyerere and the implementation of a domestic economic management plan have provided the basis for renewed economic vigor.

3076. Hirschbein, Sevin. TANZANIA: THE NON-MARXIST PATH TO SOCIALISM? *Monthly Rev. 1981 32(8): 24-41.* Employs a Marxist framework to analyze the effects and ideology of the 1967 Arusha Declaration, a theoretical and practical charter of the country's unique economic stance, committed to socialism while remaining linked to the world capitalist system and yet ignoring Marxist ideology.

3077. Hogendorn, J. S. and Scott, K. M. THE EAST AFRICAN GROUNDNUT SCHEME: LESSONS OF A LARGE-SCALE AGRICULTURAL FAILURE. *African Econ. Hist. 1981 (10): 81-115.* An enormous East African Groundnut Project was conceived in 1947 as a quasimilitary solution to the global fat shortage, a solution that would demonstrate the efficiency of large-scale capital investment in agriculture and serve as a model of African development. It failed miserably because of faulty intelligence—a pilot project would have shown the difficulties were totally underestimated—and because no economies of scale were realized. Ironically, sufficient groundnuts were already available from Nigeria. Based on annual reports of the Overseas Food Corporation and parliamentary debates; 7 tables, 145 notes.
W. D. Piersen

3078. Honey, Martha. ASIAN INDUSTRIAL ACTIVITIES IN TANGANYIKA. *Tanzania Notes and Records [Tanzania] 1974 (75): 55-69.* European discrimination confined Asian industrial activity in Tanzania to small-scale industries. Although some Asians accumulated sufficient capital to begin larger-scale manufacturing, they found themselves blocked by European plantation owners seeking to start their own enterprises, Kenyan and Ugandan capitalists, and British corporations acting directly or through brnaches in East Africa. As a result, when Tanzania achieved independence in 1961 Asians dominated only the craft and small-scale industries. Primary and secondary sources; 3 tables, 58 notes.
C. Hopkins

3079. Hoyle, B. S. AFRICAN POLITICS AND PORT EXPANSION AT DAR ES SALAAM. *Geographical Rev. 1978 68(1): 31-50.* In 1965 Southern Rhodesia unilaterally and illegally declared political independence; in 1975 a new Chinese-sponsored railway linking the Tanzanian seaport of Dar es Salaam and the Zambian copperbelt was opened. In the intervening years, as a result of changing geopolitical conditions in central and eastern Africa, Zambia severed its transport links with southern Africa and developed new links with Tanzania. These politically stimulated changes have brought particular pressures to bear on the port of Dar es Salaam, where facilities have been expanded and growth has taken place at an unprecedented rate. Examines these developments as an illustration of the complex interrelationships between transport geography and political changes in modern Africa.
J/S

3080. Huizer, Gerrit. THE *UJAMAA* VILLAGE PROGRAM IN TANZANIA: NEW FORMS OF RURAL DEVELOPMENT. *Studies in Comparative Internat. Development 1973 8(2): 183-207.*

3081. Hyden, Goran. PUBLIC POLICY-MAKING AND PUBLIC ENTERPRISES IN TANZANIA. *African Rev. [Tanzania] 1975 5(2): 141-165.* Planning is usually seen as a necessary first step to development, but in Tanzania there is a governmental commitment to utilize shortcuts—a policy of "we-must-run-while-others-walk." This often results in failure but is not necessarily an inappropriate policy so long as safeguards are employed to correct mistakes. 70 notes.
R. T. Brown

3082. Jackson, Dudley. THE DISAPPEARANCE OF STRIKES IN TANZANIA: INCOMES POLICY AND INDUSTRIAL DEMOCRACY. *J. of Modern African Studies [Great Britain] 1979 17(2): 219-251.* Strikes virtually disappeared in Tanzania during the 1970's, continuing a declining trend started in 1963. Three main factors explain this: trade unions were reorganized into one body in 1964 and brought under close political control; the government pursued a policy of giving workers more rights and influence as well as imposing obligations on them; a statutory minimum wage and incremental pay scales were introduced to protect workers from the impact of inflation. Based on official documents and statistics; 7 tables, 30 notes.
D. J. Nicholls

3083. Kajunjumele, B. S. RESHAPING THE COOPERATIVE MOVEMENT FOR SOCIALIST CONSTRUCTION. *Taamuli [Tanzania] 1973 3(2): 3-13.* The cooperative movement in Tanzania began in 1932 and now includes 1,800 societies. Its main purpose is to protect peasants from exploitation. In 1972 the Cooperative Union of Tanganyika (CUT) recommended the government lessen regulation and control and place more power in the hands of the cooperatives.
H. G. Soff

3084. Kim, Kwan S. ENTERPRISE PERFORMANCES IN THE PUBLIC AND PRIVATE SECTORS: TANZANIAN EXPERIENCE, 1970-75. *J. of Developing Areas 1981 15(3): 471-484.* In contrast to private enterprise firms (which showed operating surpluses), Tanzanian government-owned firms in the same industries generally incurred operating deficits. Compared with private enterprise firms, government enterprises as a whole characteristically had lower labor and capital productivities, overemployment of labor, and lower managerial efficiency. 4 tables, fig., 28 notes. V. Samaraweera

3085. Kiva, L. V. TROPICAL AFRICA: CERTAIN PROBLEMS OF REVOLUTIONARY-DEMOCRATIC REFORM IN THE COUNTRYSIDE ("UJAMAA" IN TANZANIA). *Int. J. of Pol. 1976-77 6(4): 87-105.* Assesses the ujamaa villages, agricultural cooperatives organized as production collectives with a high level of socialization of labor. As Tanzania's principal method of agrarian reform, the ujamaa may effectively assist the transition from communal landholding to large-scale modern agriculture. The ujamaa villages have been hampered by inadequate planning, excesses such as occasional forced collectivization, peasant reluctance to abandon old communal ways, weak state finances, and lack of skilled personnel. Their future depends upon skillful planning and coordination and success in motivating peasants away from traditional values and toward conscientious collective labor. Translated from *Narody Azii i Afriki* 1974 (5): 15-25. Secondary sources; 22 notes. R. E. Noble

3086. Kjekshus, Helge. THE TANZANIAN VILLAGIZATION POLICY: IMPLEMENTATIONAL LESSONS AND ECOLOGICAL DIMENSIONS. *Can. J. of African Studies [Canada] 1977 11(2): 269-282.* Analyzes the decision of the Tanganyika African National Union (TANU) National Conference of November 1973 that the entire peasantry should live in ujamaa villages within three years. The distinctive feature distinguishing this movement from previous villagization plans is in its emphasis on self-help rather than dependence on outside aid. The whole is advanced from the point of view of the peasantry, and advances on the basis of a grass-roots democracy. However there were problems in implementation and the movement hangs in suspension. It has been found to "militate against... time-tested peasant answers to advantageous man-land relationships." 37 notes. R. V. Ritter

3087. Kürschner, Frank. UJAMAA VILLAGES IN TANZANIA: THE EXAMPLE OF MALILI. *Int. J. of Pol. 1974-75 4(4): 88-101.* Discusses the achievements and problems in the transformation of the village of Malili in 1969-72 to a Ujamaa village—a collective in which the land and means of production are commonly owned.

3088. Lofchie, Michael F. AGRARIAN SOCIALISM IN THE THIRD WORLD: THE TANZANIAN CASE. *Comparative Pol. 1976 8(3): 479-499.* Review article to bring attention to the crisis in the collective village program jeopardizing the Tanzanian socialist policy of the 1970's. Rural collectivization is not always in the interest of radically inclined nations. 27 notes. R. I. Vexler

3089. Mapolu, Henry. TRADITION AND THE QUEST FOR SOCIALISM. *Taamuli [Tanzania] 1973 4(1): 3-15.* In agricultural societies today, traditional forms of cooperation cannot be used as the foundation for a socialist order. Emphasis is given to ujamaa villages in Tanzania. 29 notes. H. G. Soff

3090. Maro, Paul S. and Mlay, Wilfred F. I. DECENTRALIZATION AND THE ORGANIZATION OF SPACE IN TANZANIA. *Africa [Great Britain] 1979 49(3): 291-301.* Tanzania adopted in 1972 the policy of state-planned development through decentralized institutions as a logical step in the implementation of socialism and self-reliance. The three-tier structure included the village at the lowest level, the ward, district headquarters, and regional headquarters at the intermediate level, and the capital at the apex. These three types of service centers form the nerve centers of social, economic, cultural, and public life in the country. By 1976 two out of every three persons in Tanzania resided in villages. The state aimed at providing all districts with primary education, health centers, and a piped water supply. An expanding network of roads and telecommunications enhances rural-urban interactions. 3 maps, table, 2 charts, 3 notes, appendix. R. L. Collison

3091. Masao, Fidelis T. THE IRRIGATION SYSTEM IN UCHAGGA: AN ETHNO-HISTORICAL APPROACH. *Tanzania Notes and Records [Tanzania] 1974 (75): 1-8.* During the past 400 years the Wachagga people of the Mount Kilimanjaro area have developed an extensive irrigation system which allows them to farm large areas of otherwise barren land. The Mfongo clan dig the furrows by hand using only small sticks to plot the course. The Mfongo also appease the spirits and look for the mythical red ants which show the furrow's direction. The Wachagga have not maintained the traditional irrigation furrows in recent years due to the availability of piped water. Secondary sources; 21 notes. C. Hopkins

3092. McCarthy, Dennis M. P. MEDIA AS ENDS: MONEY AND THE UNDERDEVELOPMENT OF TANGANYIKA TO 1940. *J. of Econ. Hist. 1976 36(3): 645-662.* Suggests a broader approach in studying African underdevelopment, its antecedents, manifestations, and consequences, and emphasizes insights that might come from combining aspects of economic anthropology with analysis of institutions. Sketches some monetary perceptions and policies in Tanzania's colonial bureaucracies (German and British) and their reception by Tanzania's diverse population. Indigenous reaction to alien media was rational within a neoclassical tripartite demand-for-money framework. The combined consequences of all parties' actions for both the territory's underdevelopment and under-growth receive final but not definitive scrutiny in the last section. J/S

3093. McHenry, Dean E., Jr. PEASANT PARTICIPATION IN COMMUNAL FARMING: THE TANZANIAN EXPERIENCE. *African Studies Rev. 1977 20(3): 43-63.* The establishment of Ujamaa villages in Tanzania had two goals, to move people into villages from their scattered homesites and to convince them to farm communally. There has been some success with the first goal but very little with the second. Concludes that the most prosperous, best educated have adapted most quickly to communalism. Based on fieldwork; 8 tables, 15 notes, biblio., appendix. R. T. Brown

3094. McHenry, Dean E., Jr. THE UJAMAA VILLAGE IN TANZANIA: COMPARISON WITH CHINESE, SOVIET AND MEXICAN EXPERIENCES IN COLLECTIVIZATION. *Comparative Studies in Soc. and Hist. [Great Britain] 1976 18(3): 347-370.* Compares traditional forms of collective action, land reform, state motives, the landowner, compulsion, the Communist party, leaders and laws, and the success of collectivism in Tanzania since the 1960's, China since the 1950's, USSR since the 1920's, and Mexico since 1910.

3095. McHenry, Dean E., Jr. THE UNDERDEVELOPMENT THEORY: A CASE-STUDY FROM TANZANIA. *J. of Modern African Studies [Great Britain] 1976 14(4): 621-636.* Analyzes the validity of the underdevelopment theory to test its applicability to African underdevelopment by focusing on the *dagaa* fisheries of Tanzania as a case study of manageable yet significant size. The author's study does not support the theory at this particular and subnational level. Map, 3 tables, 53 notes. R. V. Ritter

3096. Mhina, George A. THE ROLE OF KISWAHILI IN THE DEVELOPMENT OF TANZANIA. *Munger Africana Lib. Notes 1974 25: 7-31.*

3097. Mittelman, James H. INTERNATIONAL MONETARY INSTITUTIONS AND POLICIES OF SOCIALISM AND SELF-RELIANCE: ARE THEY COMPATIBLE? THE TANZANIAN EXPERIENCE. *Social Res. 1980 47(1): 141-165.* The Tanzanian experience with international monetary institutions, primarily the World Bank, shows how easily these institutions can nudge national socialist policies toward those of the capitalist world.

3098. Mittelman, James H. UNDERDEVELOPMENT AND NATIONALIZATION: BANKING IN TANZANIA. *J. of Modern African Studies [Great Britain] 1978 16(4): 597-617.* Banks in Tanzania were colonial institutions, an anachronism within independent Tanzania. The nationalization of banks was made possible by a lack of cooperation among the banks that did not adapt to new realities, failed to promote economic competition, and were not able to forestall the coming of multinational banks. Furthermore, the small commercial banks desired to have a bigger share in the economy of Tanzania. The

nationalization of banks received a thrust from the petite bourgeoisie, who did not wish to further the interests of the London bankers, and from the Tanzanian civil servants and junior bank managers who saw in nationalization an opportunity for promotion. Based on interviews, government published documents, and secondary sources; 28 notes.
A. Sbacchi

3099. Mlambiti, M. E. RURAL DEVELOPMENT: THE TANZANIA TYPE. *Tanzania Notes and Records [Tanzania] 1976 (79-80): 1-12.* Describes Tanzania's current rural development. Some 90% of Tanzanians live in rural areas and depend on agriculture, which also accounts for over half of Tanzania's exports. Tanzania promotes the cooperative Ujamaa village development farming schemes. The Ujamaa system is expected to enhance industrialization, improve rural production, increase prices, and improve the quality of life. Biblio, appendix.
S. Lakhan

3100. Mlay, W. F. I. RURAL TO URBAN MIGRATION AND RURAL DEVELOPMENT. *Tanzania Notes and Records [Tanzania] 1977 (81-82): 1-13.* From case studies on Arusha and Moshi, urbanward migration in Tanzania is directly related to the search for wage-employment. The desire for cash earnings has resulted from limited opportunities in the rural areas and the impact of an education unrelated to rural life. 4 tables, 25 notes. S. Lakhan

3101. Msekwa, Pius. WORKERS' PARTICIPATION IN MANAGEMENT IN TANZANIA: A BACKGROUND. *African Rev. [Tanzania] 1975 5(2): 127-140.* Socialism is predicated on worker participation in industrial decisionmaking, but that has largely failed in Tanzania. The author uses specific cases to examine the reasons why. 29 notes.
R. T. Brown

3102. Mueller, Susanne D. THE HISTORICAL ORIGINS OF TANZANIA'S RULING CLASS. *Can. J. of African Studies [Canada] 1981 15(3): 459-498.* Discusses the historical conditions which prevented the development of a strong capitalist class along the Kenyan lines in Tanzania. A "bureaucratic bourgeoisie" retarded Tanzanian capitalist development. Examines the pre-1967 antecedents of the present Tanzanian ruling class and describes the independence movement and the class specificity of the postcolonial state, a class and a state that follow policies tending to institutionalize a petite bourgeoisie and a petty capitalism. 208 notes. J. V. Coutinho

3103. Mueller, Susanne D. TOWARDS SOCIALISM IN TANZANIA. *Int. J. of African Hist. Studies 1980 13(3): 508-516.* Reviews *Towards Socialism in Tanzania,* edited by Bismarck U. Mwansasu and Cranford Pratt (Toronto: U. Pr., 1979), a selection of papers presented at a 1976 conference at the University of Toronto that concludes Tanzania is moving toward socialism. The reviewer disagrees. 9 notes.
R. T. Brown

3104. Musoke, I. K. S. BUILDING SOCIALISM IN BUKOBA: THE ESTABLISHMENT OF RUGAZI (NYERERE) UJAMAA VILLAGE. *Int. J. of Pol. 1974-75 4(4): 102-118.* Discusses the establishment of an Ujamaa, or collective, village in Tanzania's Bukoba district in 1967-69, including planning, recruitment, the traditionalist resistance, and problems of housing, food, water, transportation, and communication.

3105. Mwapachu, Juma Volter. INDUSTRIAL LABOUR PROTEST IN TANZANIA: AN ANALYSIS OF INFLUENTIAL VARIABLES. *African R. [Tanzania] 1973 3(3): 383-401.* Tanzania has been beset with industrial crises including strikes, petitions, and factory takeovers. Analyzes causes and suggests remedies. Concludes that the final solution is socialism, which will create equality. 45 notes. H. G. Soff

3106. Neersö, Peter. TANZANIA'S POLICIES ON PRIVATE FOREIGN INVESTMENT. *African Rev. [Tanzania] 1974 4(1): 61-78.* Beginning in 1967 with the Arusha Declaration, Tanzania began to nationalize many foreign-owned businesses and banks. The government paid a fair value for the shares of these companies. In order to maintain proper control, parastatal holding corporations were created with government funding. Parastatals are analyzed with a view of their critics, government control, and management contracts. Tanzania desires foreign investments, but on its own terms. 6 notes. H. G. Soff

3107. Nsekela, Amon J. THE ROLE OF COMMERCIAL BANKING IN BUILDING A SOCIALIST TANZANIA. *African Rev. [Tanzania] 1974 4(1): 25-42.* Discusses the function of the National Bank of Commerce (NBC) in outlining the development of socialism in Tanzania. Compares the role of banks under capitalism and socialism, and analyzes NBC's lending policy for 1973-74 with major recipients noted. The role of NBC is not rigidly legalized by law; it will change with circumstances. H. G. Soff

3108. Okakura, Takashi. DOKURITSU GO TANZANIA NI OKERU SHAKAI KEIZAI KŌZŌ NO HENKA: KEIZAI KEIKAKU; KEIZAI KŌZŌ; KAIKYŪ KŌSEI [Changes in the socioeconomic structure of Tanzania since independence]. *Ajia Afurika Kenkyū [Japan] 1978 18(2): 11-30.* Surveys changes in the socioeconomic structure in Tanzania caused by economic planning, 1960-78. Since the Arusha Declaration of 1967 Tanzania has pursued noncapitalist development stressing self-reliance and social equality. While remaining dependent on foreign capital and exports of primary goods, the economy has been diversified. The social structure has also changed, its distinctive features including the rise of the "bourgeois-bureaucrat," and the increase in labor organization. 60 notes. M. Nakayama/S

3109. Omari, C. K. TANZANIA'S EMERGING RURAL DEVELOPMENT POLICY. *Africa Today 1974 21(3): 9-14.* Analyzes the rural development efforts of Tanzania. The process cannot yet be evaluated but Tanzania's commitment to the model augurs well. Based on government studies and secondary sources; table, 21 notes.
G. O. Gagnon

3110. Pavlova, V. TANZANIIA: PLANY SOZIDANIIA [Tanzania: planning experience]. *Aziia i Afrika Segodnia [USSR] 1981 (5): 25-27.* Discusses Tanzania's experiences in economic planning from 1961 to 1981, during which period the rate of literacy rose and the gap between the rich and poor shrank. Comments on the Tanzanian 20-year plan of economic and social development announced in July 1981.

3111. Philip, Kjeld. LANDBOREFORMER I TANZANIA [Rural land reforms in Tanzania]. *Økonomi og Politik [Denmark] 1978 52(1): 48-56.* Contrasts rapid land reform in Tanzania with slower changes in Denmark begun 200 years ago and implemented over several decades. Tanzania has established villages rather than encourage individual cultivation of land because the former facilitates provision of public services such as hospitals, schools, transportation, and communications. There have been some private shops and industries, however. The village has administered the land and its product; cultivation has been primitive and on a subsistence level. Reform has moved with dynamic force in changing the rural face of Tanzania. R. E. Lindgren

3112. Picon, Sophie. ZANZIBAR, TERRE D'ESCLAVES [Zanzibar, land of slaves]. *Histoire [France] 1980 (29): 52-60.* Introduced at the beginning of the 19th century, cloves enabled Arabs from the sheikhdom of Oman who settled in Zanzibar to make a fortune until the 1964 revolution. J

3113. Raikes, Philip. RURAL DIFFERENTIATION AND CLASS FORMATION IN TANZANIA. *J. of Peasant Studies [Great Britain] 1978 5(3): 285-325.* Looks at various specific processes of differentiation in rural Tanzania and attempts to relate these to the overall emergence of classes within the Tanzanian social formation and to its incorporation within the international capitalist system. After a brief introduction and outline of some important aspects of the Tanzanian economy and political structure, and a still briefer discussion of "Chayanovian" proposals about an undifferentiated peasantry, the article outlines the developments of the colonial period and their implications for the patterns of differentiation observed. J

3114. Rodgers, W. A. and Lobo, J. D. ELEPHANT CONTROL AND LEGAL IVORY EXPLOITATION: 1920 TO 1976. *Tanzania Notes and Records [Tanzania] 1980 (84-85): 25-54.* During this century there has been considerable legal destruction of elephants by individual hunters and government departments in charge of crop protection. Describes the history and extent of elephant control in Tanzania from the start of British rule in 1920 to the present. It ends with recommendations for the future. Based on primary material in the files of the Tanzanian Game Division, Government and Customs reports, Tanzania

Government Archives, the Ivory Room records, and interviews; list of references, 13 tables, map. J. V. Coutinho

3115. Rogers, Susan G. THE KILIMANJARO NATIVE PLANTERS ASSOCIATION: ADMINISTRATIVE RESPONSES TO CHAGGA INITIATIVES IN THE 1920'S. *Transafrican J. of Hist. [Kenya] 1974 4(2): 94-114.* The Kilimanjaro Native Planters Association (KNPA) was the predecessor of the Kilimanjaro National Cooperative Union (KNCU), both organizations of the Chagga coffee growers of Tanzania. The KNPA has traditionally been viewed as an organ with poor leadership and unsure goals which caused it to collapse. Evidence shows, however, that the KNPA was dynamic and forceful, a sore point with incompetent governmental administrators who sought its demise. 84 notes. H. G. Soff

3116. Rwegasira, Delphin. CAREER GUIDANCE, CAREER POLICY AND HIGH-LEVEL MANPOWER EFFICIENCY IN TANZANIA. *African Rev. [Tanzania] 1974 4(1): 111-126.* Examines career guidance policies of Tanzania, 1961-74. Career guidance and the attempt to match manpower with demand are discussed, and efficiency and career policies are analyzed. With the exception of science and mathematics, the quantitative aspect of planning is satisfactory, but the qualitative aspect is open to question. 15 notes. H. G. Soff

3117. Rweyemamu, Anthony H. THE PREDICAMENT OF MANAGERS OF PUBLIC ENTERPRISES IN TANZANIA. *African Rev. [Tanzania] 1975 5(2): 119-126.* Parastatal organizations in Tanzania have not functioned as well as expected and the managers have had to bear the public blame. 18 notes. R. T. Brown

3118. Rweyemamu, P. FROM "FEAR DISCIPLINE" TO SOCIALIST SELF-DISCIPLINE: PROBLEMS OF ORGANIZATION AND DEMOCRACY IN TANZANIA. *Taamuli [Tanzania] 1973 3(2): 14-21.* Workers in capitalistic societies are influenced by fear of dismissal for their ideas. In Tanzania, workers have been allowed to participate and, although there are problems, there is a high degree of self-disclipline. Discusses various conditions and steps that have led to the current status of workers and suggests changes. 12 notes. H. G. Soff

3119. Sahu, Sunil K. TANZANIA: THE COLONIAL EXPERIENCE AND DEPENDENT DEVELOPMENT/UNDERDEVELOPMENT. *Africa Q. [India] 1978 17(3): 47-96.* Describes and applies dependency theory to an analysis of problems of underdevelopment in Tanzania, 1900 to the present.

3120. Sakarai, Lawrence. CAPITALISM AND THE PEASANTRY—TANZANIA. *J. of the U. of Bombay [India] 1975-76 44-45(80-81): 375-398.* In precolonial Tanzania, ethnic groups existed at different stages of development. Some evolved from primitive communism to the development of a political elite composed of chiefs, councillors, and priests as a result of the collection of tribute. When the Europeans introduced a cash crop economy, the result was to strengthen the wealthier groups and the elites at the expense of subsistence farming. Some, however, were not directly concerned with cash crops and their lives remained unchanged. Secondary works; 4 tables, 86 notes. J. F. Hilliker

3121. Sharaev, V. A. POLITIKA ANGLISKIKH VLASTEI V DEREVNE KOLONIAL'NOI TANGAN'IKI (1945-1960) [The policy of the British government in the countryside of colonial Tanganyika, 1945-1960]. *Narody Azii i Afriki [USSR] 1975 (6): 75-88.* After World War II, Great Britain found itself in a weakened position. To prevent the complete breakdown of its colonial regime in Africa, British authorities created a social basis for colonial capitalism. Great Britain's demand for raw materials compelled the introduction of social and economic measures to ensure the growth of export production. This was achieved in the postwar period until 1960 through intensive exploitation with the development of a plantation economy up to 1955, and by the growth of export production after 1955. 52 notes. L. Kalinowski

3122. Shivji, Issa G. CAPITALISM UNLIMITED: PUBLIC CORPORATIONS IN PARTNERSHIP WITH MULTI-NATIONAL CORPORATIONS. *African R. [Tanzania] 1973 3(3): 359-381.* Analyzes the relationship of public corporations in developing nations with multinational corporations in developed capitalist countries. Focuses on Tanzania as a case study. A result of partnership is the loss of control by the developing nation of its economic resources. The public corporation, instead of developing the economy, aids its underdevelopment. 6 tables, 60 notes. H. G. Soff

3123. Silver, M. S. OWNERSHIP INDICES OF INDUSTRIAL PRODUCTION FOR TANZANIA: 1965-72. *Studies in Comparative Int. Development 1980 15(1): 61-78.* Describes the real industrial production changes for foreign, state, and local sectors in mainland Tanzania. Tanzania's aim enunciated in the 1967 Arusha Declaration of national ownership of a significant share of the country's manufacturing industries has been achieved. Moreover, control of the economy is now in the hands of the Tanzanian government. 3 tables, note, 10 ref. S. A. Farmerie

3124. Silver, M. S. A REGIONAL ANALYSIS OF INDUSTRIAL PRODUCTION AND LABOR PRODUCTIVITY TRENDS IN TANZANIA, 1965 TO 1972. *Can. J. of African Studies [Canada] 1980 13(3): 479-485.* Describes "real production and labor productivity trends in mainland Tanzania for manufacturing establishments both within and outside Dar-es-Salaam." Based on the *Survey of Industries 1965* and the *Survey of Industrial Production,* 1966-72; 3 tables, 8 notes. S

3125. Singh, Chandra Pal. BANKING AND SOCIALISM IN TANZANIA. *Africa Q. [India] 1979 18(4): 45-58.* With the unification of Tanganyika and Zanzibar to create Tanzania in 1964, the banks, which had been under foreign control, were nationalized and given a mandate to promote social improvements in the economic structure of the rural areas.

3126. Stein, Leslie. TRANSFORMING THE TANZANIAN ECONOMY: A REVIEW COVERING THE FIRST DECADE OF INDEPENDENCE. *African Social Res. [Zambia] 1979: 541-564.* A history of Tanzanian development plans and an analysis of their results. By the end of the first decade of independence, real growth had taken place, but the nation still had serious economic problems. Based on International and Tanzanian economic reports; 10 tables, 21 notes, biblio. R. T. Brown

3127. Swai, Bonaventure. THE POLITICAL ECONOMY OF TANZANIAN PRIMARY SCHOOL LEAVERS: A THEORETICAL CONSIDERATION. *Taamuli [Tanzania] 1978 8(1): 38-49.* School leavers in modern Tanzania have deserted the countryside and migrated to the cities despite the government's efforts to emphasize agriculture in the schools. This migration has occurred because rural areas lack opportunities for employment, and not because school leavers prefer city life and white collar jobs. 55 notes. D. S. Rockwood

3128. Tandon, Yash. THE FOOD QUESTION IN EAST AFRICA: A PARTIAL CASE STUDY OF TANZANIA. *Africa Q. [India] 1978 17(4): 5-45.* The imperialism-caused food crisis of 1973-75, and prospects for Tanzania's self-sufficiency in food.

3129. Thobani, Akbarali H. TANZANIA'S FOREIGN TRADE PATTERN. *Africa Today 1974 21(3): 43-48.* Traces the post-independence international trade patterns of Tanzania. Tanzania has reduced its dependence on Great Britain, reflecting Tanzania's policy of nonalignment. It no longer has a favorable balance of trade, and China has become the major source of imports. Based on UN records and secondary sources; table, 6 notes. G. O. Gagnon

3130. Wayne, Jack. COLONIALISM AND UNDERDEVELOPMENT IN KIGOMA REGION, TANZANIA: A SOCIAL STRUCTURAL VIEW. *Can. Rev. of Sociol. and Anthrop. 1975 12(3): 316-332.* British coercion of the population of Kigoma region to work on plantations led to economic exploitation and a crime-ridden society from 1700 to the 1970's.

Politics

3131. Bailey, Martin. TANZANIA AND CHINA. *African Affairs [Great Britain] 1975 74(294): 39-50.* An analysis of why Tanzania has closer ties with China than with any other non-African nation. Relations began in 1961 and both countries exchanged state visits in 1964. China became the leading military supplier to Tanzania in 1970. Both countries stress self-reliance and rural development. Emphasis is given to Chinese assistance in building the TanZam Railway, and reasons why China is willing to help. 2 tables, 29 notes. H. G. Soff

3132. Bailey, Martin. ZANZIBAR'S EXTERNAL RELATIONS. *Int. J. of Pol. 1974-75 4(4): 35-57.* Although Zanzibar has not maintained an independent foreign policy since its union with Tanzania in 1964, it has pursued an independent line in specific areas of defense, relations with Communist countries, and international economic relations.

3133. Beidelman, T. O. CHIEFSHIP IN UKAGURU: THE INVENTION OF ETHNICITY AND TRADITION IN KAGURU COLONIAL HISTORY. *Int. J. of African Hist. Studies 1978 11(2): 227-246.* Examines the development of the concepts of ethnic unity, political integrity, and heirarchy among the Kaguru of Tanzania in response to the Arab, German, and British influences. Because the chiefship and subchiefship did not rest on a proper Kaguru tradition, the result was a local African government which was unpopular with both the colonial governments and many Kaguru. The idea of a strong Kaguru ethnic unity was in large part a colonial product. Fig. 40 notes.
M. M. McCarthy

3134. Collins, Paul. DECENTRALIZATION AND LOCAL ADMINISTRATION FOR DEVELOPMENT IN TANZANIA. *Africa Today 1974 21(3): 15-25.* In addition to one-party democracy and rural development Tanzania began efforts to decentralize local government in 1972. These national decisions have yet to bear fruit but bureaucratic dominance of local government is being checked; popular participation is being introduced. 4 notes. G. O. Gagnon

3135. Cottingham, Clement. TOWARDS DEMOCRATIC SOCIALISM? *African Rev. [Tanzania] 1974 4(4): 583-599.* A review article of *Socialism and Participation; Tanzania's 1970 National Elections* (Dar es Salaam: Tanzania Publ. House, 1974). 6 notes. R. T. Brown

3136. Dash, Michael E. INROADS INTO EAST AFRICA: THE PEOPLE'S REPUBLIC OF CHINA AND TANZANIA. *Military Rev. 1976 56(4): 58-64.* Examines China's foreign aid to Tanzania, 1960-70's, in the context of assisting national liberation movements in developing nations of East Africa.

3137. Decherf, Dominique. DU NON-ALIGNEMENT AU PAN-SOCIALISME. L'ÉVOLUTION DE LA POLITIQUE ÉTRANGÈRE DE LA TANZANIE [From nonalignment to pan-socialism. The evolution of Tanzanian foreign policy]. *Pol. Étrangère [France] 1975 40(5): 493-524.* In the 1970's, Tanzania has had to modify its nonalignment in the direction of a kind of "pan-socialism" in order to meet the needs of its economic and territorial security.

3138. Decherf, Dominique. LA TANZANIE ENTRE L'OCÉAN INDIEN ET LE CONTINENT SUD-AFRICAIN [Tanzania between the Indian Ocean and the South African continent]. *Défense Natl. [France] 1976 32(2): 115-124.* Geographical and historical contradictions have influenced Tanzania's President Julius K. Nyerere's policies.

3139. Duggan, William R. THE SULTAN AND THE BASEBALL GAME. *Foreign Service J. 1977 54(6): 21-23, 36-37.* Account of a 1959 diplomatic meeting at a baseball game between the author, US consul general in East Africa, and Seyyid Khalifa bin Harub, Sultan of Zanzibar.

3140. Goriachev, Mikhail Konstantinovich. TANZANIIA: CHAMA CHA MAPINDUZI—RUKOVODIASHCHAIA SILA STROITEL'STVA NOVOGO OBSHCHESTVA [Tanzania: Chama Cha Mapinduzi—leading force in building a new society]. *Narody Azii i Afriki [USSR] 1981 (1): 82-92.* The union in 1977 of the TANU and Afro-Shirazi parties under the name Chama Cha Mapinduzi (Revolutionary Party of Tanzania) enjoys mass support and points the way to socialism, as shown in its recent progress. Based on Tanzanian publications, especially Nyerere's, and Russian and Western secondary sources.
E. S. Kirby

3141. Graham, James D. INDIRECT RULE: THE ESTABLISHMENT OF "CHIEFS" AND "TRIBES" IN CAMERON'S TANGANYIKA. *Tanzania Notes and Records [Tanzania] 1976 (77-78): 1-9.* Using Njombe district in southwestern Tanzania as an example, the author shows Governor Sir Donald Cameron's plan for indirect rule to be misconceived. Cameron and his subordinates established chieftainships in regions where no ethnic systems existed in order to create a class of inefficient and often corrupt rulers who could be manipulated by British administrators. Tanzanian authorities abolished indirect rule in 1962. Primary and secondary sources. E. Hopkins

3142. Graham, James D. JULIUS NYERERE: A CONTEMPORARY PHILOSOPHER-STATESMAN. *Africa Today 1976 23(4): 67-73.* A review of two works by Julius Nyerere, *Freedom and Development/Uhuru Na Maendeleo: A Selection of Writings and Speeches 1968-1973* (Dar es Salaam, 1973) and *Man and Development* [Binadamu Na Maendeleo] (Dar es Salaam, 1974). The selections are valuable to Africanists because they convey Nyerere's humanistic, pragmatic approach toward African development. G. O. Gagnon

3143. Hill, Frances. ADMINISTRATIVE DECENTRALIZATION FOR DEVELOPMENT, PARTICIPATION AND CONTROL IN TANZANIA. *J. of African Studies 1979-80 6(4): 182-192.* Examines decentralization of the Tanzanian bureaucracy by the Nyerere regime since 1972 in relation to the official goals of achieving economic development and increased citizen participation in political and economic affairs. The nature and relationships of the Tanzanian bureaucracy and ruling Chama cha Mapinduzi, or Revolutionary Party, perplexing divisions between policymaking and implementing powers at the national, regional, district, and village levels, and curtailing of popular and local influence in developmental efforts have all combined to frustrate attainment of these goals during the 1970's. Against this, administrative decentralization has proven ineffectual. Based on interviews, published documents, newspapers, and secondary sources; 48 notes.
L. W. Truschel

3144. Hutchison, Alan. EXORCISING THE GHOST OF KARUME. *Africa Report 1974 19(2): 46-51.* A review of the first decade of Zanzibar's independence from Britain (1964-74), contrasting the dictatorship of Shiekh Abeid Karume with the rule of his successors. S

3145. Illarionov, N. S. ETNOPOLITICHESKIE PROBLEMY SOVREMENNOGO ZANZIBARA (ETNOS OSTROVNYKH SUAKHILI V 1960-1970 GODY) [Ethnopolitical problems of present-day Zanzibar: the island's Swahili ethnic groups, 1960's-70's]. *Sovetskaia Etnografiia [USSR] 1982 (1): 46-55.* Analyzes the course of ethnopolitical development in Zanzibar between groups of Arab and African origins.

3146. Ishumi, Abel G. POLITICAL ACCULTURATION: A GENERAL APPRAISAL WITH A CASE STUDY. *Taamuli [Tanzania] 1973 3(2): 36-43.* Education is vitally relevant to politics since politics is the tool of society for its preservation. In 1971 a study was made of political education throughout Tanzania. Student and teacher responses are outlined. 6 notes. H. G. Soff

3147. James, R. W. IMPLEMENTING THE ARUSHA DECLARATION: THE ROLE OF THE LEGAL SYSTEM. *African R. [Tanzania] 1973 3(2): 179-208.* In Tanzania's transition to socialism there is a danger of expediency's being substituted for legality. A serious problem is the gap between TANU policies and the laws of the land. Shortcomings in implementation of the Arusha Declaration are highlighted, particularly problems that relate to land. Analyzes the role of law and courts. 117 notes. H. G. Soff

3148. Karioli, James N. SOCIALISM IN AFRICA: THE TANZANIAN EXPERIENCE. *Civilisations [Belgium] 1973-1974 23-24(1-2): 31-50.* Tanzania is still as committed to the humanistic attributes of socialism as in the first decade following independence in 1961. An essay by Julius Nyerere formed the ideological cornerstone and was followed by the Arusha Declaration of 13 February 1967. The declaration stated the broad principles for building socialism, thereby promoting self-reliance, rural development, and good leadership. 31 notes.
H. L. Calkin

3149. Kjekshus, Helge. PARLIAMENT IN A ONE-PARTY STATE: THE BUNGE OF TANZANIA, 1965-1970. *J. of Modern African*

Studies [Great Britain] 1974 12(1): 19-43. A presidential commission in 1965 determined that the National Assembly (Bunge) should emerge as a locus of people's power. In 1965, however, only 52 percent of the members were elected by only 45 percent of the eligible electorate who voted. The Bunge met an average of 48 days and passed an average of 54 bills during each of the next five years. The Bunge initiates no policy, as TANU remains supreme in policy making. Parliament members are severely restricted in their private financial practices, but their salary is many times the national average. 2 tables, 58 notes. H. G. Soff

3150. Landor, Alfred. CLOSE-UP OF JULIUS NYERERE. *Contemporary Rev. [Great Britain] 1979 235(1367): 281-284.* A political profile of Julius Nyerere of Tanzania, 1961-70's.

3151. Lisicka-Lutyk, Hanna. PANAFRIKANIZM PREZYDENTA NYERERE [The Pan-Africanism of President Nyerere]. *Kultura i Społeczeństwo [Poland] 1980 24(3-4): 291-304.* Attempts to characterize and evaluate the Pan-Africanism of Julius K. Nyerere, president of Tanzania who, from 1952-72, published over 20 works on the subject of African unity. His Pan-Africanism is characterized by two trends: Pan-Africanism on a continental scale encompassing all Africa, and regional Pan-Africanism, which forms a part of his continental program of unification. Based on the works of J. K. Nyerere and secondary sources; 56 notes. D. S. Lloyd

3152. Mariñas Otero, Luis. GRAN BRETAÑA Y TANZANIA: EVOLUCIÓN DE UNAS RELACIONES EN LA ERA POSTCOLONIAL [Great Britain and Tanzania: development of a relationship in the postcolonial era]. *Rev. de Estudios Int. [Spain] 1981 2(2): 333-358.* Examines relations between Great Britain and Tanzania after 1961 as a model of postcolonial foreign relations. The particular character of the Tanzanian-British relationship is much determined by the foreign policy posture of Tanzania and by its attitude to the Rhodesian issue. Crises betwen Great Britain and Tanzania since 1961 were due mainly to three sets of problems: the amount and conditions of British economic and technical aid, attitudes toward liberation movements in southern Africa, and the nationalization of British assets in Tanzania. Anglo-Tanzanian relations demonstrate the conceptual differences between them on the nature of the relationship and the meaning of equality in international law. 22 notes. D. Ardia

3153. McCarthy, D. M. P. ORGANIZING UNDERDEVELOPMENT FROM THE INSIDE: THE BUREAUCRATIC ECONOMY IN TANGANYIKA, 1919-1940. *Int. J. of African Hist. Studies 1977 10(4): 573-599.* Discusses the Tanganyika bureaucracy in relation to the problem of stability, describes and analyzes specific modes of control and extraction, and evaluates some implications of the bureaucratic economy for an orchestration of underdevelopment from, by, and for the outside. Current research into the origin of African underdevelopment follows a paradigm which explains Africa's incorporation into a growing macroentity called the European world economy, European world system, then capitalist world system. But at least in the case of interwar Tanganyika, the realities of the colonial presence were too complex and contradictory for simple slotting in any international paradigm. Table, 35 notes. M. M. McCarthy

3154. McCarthy, Dennis M. P. LANGUAGE MANIPULATION IN COLONIAL TANGANYIKA, 1919-40. *J. of African Studies 1979 6(1): 9-16.* A descriptive case study of how colonial officials in Tanganyika under the League of Nations mandate manipulated their use of the official English language to compel obedience from their African subjects in providing labor and taxes and in growing specified cash crops. Colonial authorities resorted to language manipulation in Tanganyika and elsewhere to get around formal prohibitions of the use of forced labor. Based on archival sources; 30 notes. L. W. Truschel

3155. McGowan, Patrick J. and Wacirah, H. K. M. THE EVOLUTION OF TANZANIAN POLITICAL LEADERSHIP. *African Studies Rev. 1974 17(1): 179-204.* Tanzanian ideological emphasis on egalitarianism and socialist self-reliance led to new values in the recruitment of political leaders in the 1960's, but many of the 1970's leaders do not possess corresponding characteristics.

3156. McHenry, D. E., Jr. REORGANIZATION: AN ADMINISTRATIVE HISTORY OF KIGOMA DISTRICT. *Tanzania Notes and Records [Tanzania] 1980 (84-85): 65-76.* Social, political and economic changes in African countries have been closely associated with administrative changes, which are thus a useful indicator of other historical changes. This study focuses on a district in western Tanzania from the early 1920's, when British rule began, to the early 1960's when power was transferred to Tanzanians. Every administrative change in the district tended to improve the ability of the central goverment to implement its policies. However, an ominipotent government did not develop because other circumstances tended to undermine the enhanced authority brought about by reorganization. Map, 75 notes. J. V. Coutinho

3157. McHenry, D. E., Jr. A STUDY OF THE RISE OF TANU AND THE DEMISE OF BRITISH RULE IN KIGOMA REGION, WESTERN TANZANIA. *African R. [Tanzania] 1973 3(3): 403-421.* The Kigoma region is one of the poorest in Tanzania. Although studies have been made of the development of political awareness at the national level, little has been said about the local district level. Examines the origin, development, and success of TANU in the Kigoma region during the pre-independence era. 3 tables, 82 notes. H. G. Soff

3158. Miti, Katabaro. CONTENDING INTERPRETATIONS OF TANZANIA'S POLITICAL DEVELOPMENTS: A REVIEW. *Taamuli [Tanzania] 1978 8(1): 7-13.* A review article based on seven studies of the political development of modern Tanzania.

3159. Mushi, S. S. POPULAR PARTICIPATION AND REGIONAL PLANNING: THE POLITICS OF DECENTRALIZED ADMINISTRATION. *Tanzania Notes and Records [Tanzania] 1978 (83): 63-97.* To mobilize the rural masses and promote participation in decision making, the Tanzanian government instituted, in 1972 and 1977, strategies for popular participation. Previous participatory institutions were too bureaucratic and not adapted to local conditions. Self-management schemes were thus implemented, and these were the beginnings of extensive local government reform, aimed at both the decentralization of administration and the restructuring of rural society. However, due to contradictions between the official ideology and planning framework, popular participation did not lead to any noticeable economic improvement. 9 tables, 99 notes. S. Lakhan

3160. Mutahaba, Gelase. THE EFFECT OF CHANGES IN THE TANZANIAN PUBLIC SERVICE SYSTEM UPON ADMINISTRATIVE PRODUCTIVITY, 1961-72. *African Rev. [Tanzania] 1975 5(2): 201-207.* A short history of the Africanization of the civil service, which did not cause a real decline in efficiency and honesty. 4 tables, 5 notes. R. T. Brown

3161. Mwinyi, Aboud Jumbe. INDIA & TANZANIA. *India Q. [India] 1973 29(1): 1-8.* A general discussion of foreign relations between India and Tanzania, 1947-73.

3162. Neve, Herbert T. THE POLITICAL LIFE OF JULIUS K. NYERERE IN RELIGIOUS PERSPECTIVE. *Africa Today 1976 23(4): 29-45.* Traces the sources of Julius Nyerere's political ideology and concludes that his emphasis on equality plus traditional values created a secular religion that provides the unifying and transcendent value structure for Tanzania. Based on Nyerere's writings and secondary sources; 48 notes, biblio. G. O. Gagnon

3163. Nicholson, M. E. R. CHANGE WITHOUT CONFLICT: A CASE STUDY OF LEGAL CHANGE IN TANZANIA. *Law and Soc. Rev. 1973 7(4): 747-766.* Discusses the Sukuma's positive perceptions of changes in legal institutions and procedures in Tanzania. Instituted by President Julius Nyerere in the early 1960's, these legal changes have largely replaced the methods of the colonial period. H. R. Mahood

3164. Nnoli, Okwudiba. POLITICAL WILL AND THE MARGIN OF AUTONOMY IN TANZANIAN FOREIGN POLICY. *Africa Q. [India] 1977 17(1): 5-36.* Describes Julius Nyerere's conduct of Tanzanian foreign policy since independence, seen as a largely successful attempt to assert economic and political autonomy.

3165. Nyerere, Julius K. PROGRESS COMES WITH PRODUCTION. *African R. [Tanzania] 1973 3(4): 519-539.* According to President Nyerere's report to the 16th Tanganyika African National Union biennial conference, government action resulting from TANU

decisions has created more progress in Tanzania. Although production has increased, so has the population. Therefore, to assure continued progress, everyone must produce more each year. 11 tables.
H. G. Soff

3166. Ole-Saibull, S. A. THE POLICY PROCESS: THE CASE OF CONSERVATION IN THE NGORONGORO CRATER HIGHLANDS. *Tanzania Notes and Records [Tanzania] 1978 (83): 101-115.* Studies the problems encountered in trying to determine the "rightful" owners of the Ngorongoro Crater highlands, analyzing the role of the principal interest groups and the implementation of political and administrative decisions. Legislation, in 1948 and 1954, creating a National Park for wildlife conservation in the Ngorongoro highlands incited community conflicts, undermining hereditary property rights by excluding pastoralists and cultivators. As the conflict escalated into an international controversy, the Tanzanian government intervened and reconciled the dispute, agreeing to conserve the area. Based on a lecture presented to the United Nations Environment Programme Conference, Nairobi, 1974; 19 notes, biblio. S. Lakhan

3167. Othman, Haroub. THE TANZANIAN STATE: WHO CONTROLS IT, WHOSE INTERESTS DOES IT SERVE? *Monthly R. 1974 26(7): 46-57.*

3168. Picard, Louis A. ATTITUDES AND DEVELOPMENT: THE DISTRICT ADMINISTRATOR IN TANZANIA. *African Studies Rev. 1980 23(3): 49-67.* A series of interviews with 73 local administrators around the Tanzanian capital shows that President Julius K. Nyerere's attempts to decentralize administration and to have local authorities concentrate on development problems instead of traditional management tasks has had little impact. Based on field research and government documents; 8 tables, 11 notes, biblio. R. T. Brown

3169. Picard, Louis A. SOCIALISM AND THE FIELD ADMINISTRATOR: DECENTRALIZATION IN TANZANIA. *Comparative Pol. 1980 12(4): 439-457.* Discusses Tanzania's experiment with socialism and examines changes in Tanzania's field administration. In the process of establishing socialism, Tanzania has attempted to decentralize its administrative structure. Between 1967 and 1972, four important decisions affected the administrator in the field: the Arusha Declaration of 1967; the decision to establish Ujamaa villages in 1967-68; the publication of Tanganyika Africa National Union (TANU) party guidelines (Mwongozo) in 1971; and the decision to abolish district councils prior to 1972. Decentralization in Tanzania involved the delegation of authority to make decisions on behalf of the central administration to the field administrator. Based on field work in Tanzania in 1975 and interviews with party officials; 55 notes.
M. A. Kascus

3170. Pratt, Cranford. FOREIGN-POLICY ISSUES AND THE EMERGENCE OF SOCIALISM IN TANZANIA 1961-68. *Int. J. [Canada] 1975 30(3): 445-470.* Discusses the compatibility between Tanzania's foreign policy of positive nonalignment and its domestic policy of socialism under Julius Nyerere; 35 notes. R. V. Kubicek

3171. Pratt, Cranford. NYERERE ON THE TRANSITION TO SOCIALISM IN TANZANIA. *African Rev. [Tanzania] 1975 5(1): 63-76.* Concentrates on Tanzanian President Julius Nyerere's ideas about the transition to socialism and concludes that his commitment to both socialism and democratic institutions is consistent and firmly held. 33 notes. R. T. Brown

3172. Pratt, R. C. FOREIGN SCHOLARSHIP IN TANZANIA. *Can. J. of African Studies [Canada] 1974 8(1): 166-169.* Reviews Clyde R. Ingles's *From Village to State in Tanzania: the Politics of Rural Development* (Cornell U. Pr., 1972) and John R. Nellis's *A Theory of Ideology: A Tanzanian Experience*(Nairobi: Oxford U. Pr., 1972).

3173. Proctor, J. H. THE NATIONAL MEMBERS OF THE TANZANIA PARLIAMENT: A STUDY OF LEGISLATIVE BEHAVIOR. *African R. [Tanzania] 1973 3(1): 1-19.* In addition to duly elected local representatives, the Tanzanian parliament includes members chosen on a national basis. Methods for selection are discussed and individual representatives are noted. The purpose of this program was to secure representatives who owed no special allegiance, but would represent the entire nation. In this respect the project has failed, since no consensus on what the national interest required developed. 41 notes.
H. G. Soff

3174. Renard, Nicolas. LA TANZANIE, UN ESPOIR POUR L'AFRIQUE [Tanzania, a hope for Africa]. *Esprit [France] 1974 (3): 501-512.* Describes the evolution of government in Tanzania, called the most original experience in African socialism. G. F. Jewsbury

3175. Rigby, Peter. LOCAL PARTICIPATION IN NATIONAL POLITICS: UGOGO, TANZANIA. *Africa [Great Britain] 1977 47(1): 89-107.* Discusses the attempt by the Tanzanian central government to expand the field of political participation after national independence, pointing briefly to events in the 1960's by referring in particular to changes in the political structures and "villagization" after 1970 as reflected by the peoples of the Ugogo region. By 1975 almost two-thirds of the Gogo had been moved into 142 planned villages. The traditional elders, headmen and officials of the colonial era were replaced by a structure of cells, and elected representatives, party and local government officials, and production units and ward development committees. The system was frustrated to a certain extent by local politics, and by the lack of experience of the new officials. Based on fieldwork; 11 notes, biblio. R. L. Collison

3176. Ross, Alistair. THE CAPRICORN AFRICA SOCIETY AND EUROPEAN REACTIONS TO AFRICAN NATIONALISM IN TANGANYIKA, 1949-60. *African Affairs [Great Britain] 1977 76(305): 519-535.* Traces the role of the liberal Capricorn Africa Society (CAS) in the creation of an independent Tanganyika. The CAS, although dominated by Europeans, included all races in its membership. Discusses the activities of its leader, David Stirling. Of particular note are the reactions of Europeans, particularly farmers, to CAS; relations were not always cordial. Eventually, CAS members were given high rank in the new independent government of Julius Nyerere. 76 notes.
H. G. Soff

3177. Saleh, Ali. LES PARTIS POLITIQUES DE ZANZIBAR [The political parties of Zanzibar]. *Rev. Française d'Études Pol. Africaines [France] 1973 (89): 50-66.* Outlines the history of three Zanzibari political parties which formed following the 1963 independence from British rule, the Zanzibar National Party (ZNP) 1955-64, the Zanzibar and Pemba Peoples' Party (ZPPP) 1959-64, and the Afro-Shirazi Party (ASP) 1930-72, which became the island's only party following a 1964 military coup.

3178. Salum, Said. THE TANZANIAN STATE: A CRITIQUE. *Monthly Rev. 1977 28(8): 51-57.* A critique of Haroub Othman's essay "The Tanzanian State" (see abstract 3167). In terms of serious Marxist analysis, Othman's comments are disturbingly reformist and revisionist. His implication that Tanzania's bourgeois bureaucracy can somehow transform the nation into a productive socialist state is, historically, totally without basis. M. R. Yerburgh

3179. Samoff, Joel and Samoff, Rachel. THE LOCAL POLITICS OF UNDERDEVELOPMENT. *Pol. and Soc. 1976 6(4): 397-432.* Case study of Tanzania's effort in the early 1970's to deal with the internal power relationships that perpetuate Third World underdevelopment and dependence on the world capitalist economy. Examines the characteristics (organization of production, access to education) of the Kilimanjaro district's elite and their continued link with the external capitalist system, and the tactics employed by the new national leadership in its attempts to alter the structure. Table, 67 notes. D. G. Nielson

3180. Sathyamurthy, T. V. TANZANIA'S NON-ALIGNED ROLE IN INTERNATIONAL RELATIONS. *India Q. [India] 1981 37(1): 1-23.* Africa's newly independent and nonaligned nations were split in the early 1960's between radical and centrist factions. Tanzania and most East African leaders favored peaceful transition and African socialism to class struggle and scientific socialism. Secondary sources; 55 notes. J. Powell

3181. Shengena, Joe J. THE TEACHING OF POLITICAL EDUCATION IN TANZANIAN SCHOOLS. *Taamuli [Tanzania] 1973 3(2): 27-35.* Political education is an important agent of social change. Lists the aims and objectives of political education, outlines main areas of

content, and suggests improvements for teacher training. 7 notes.
H. G. Soff

3182. Temu, Peter E. THE EMPLOYMENT OF FOREIGN CONSULTANTS IN TANZANIA: ITS VALUE AND LIMITATIONS. *African R. [Tanzania] 1973 3(1): 69-84.* Noncitizens occupy many important posts in the civil service, but 1980 is the target for virtual self-sufficiency. There is a shortage, however, in the number of Tanzanians being trained in medicine, engineering, and accounting. Discusses three categories of foreign consultants, the visiting fact-finding mission, resident consultant, and consulting firm. Table, 34 notes. H. G. Soff

3183. Verhagen, Koenraad. CHANGES IN TANZANIAN RURAL DEVELOPMENT POLICY 1975-1978. *Development and Change [Netherlands] 11(2): 285-295.* The Village and Ujamaa Villages (Registration, Designation and Administration) Act of 1975 attempted to require the participation of the rural population in rural administration and development, but control by party and government leaves little room for participation at the base.

Society

3184. Alibaruho, Gloria Lindsey. THE CHAGGA OF TANZANIA: LOCALISM AND NATIONALISM. *San José Studies 1976 2(1): 91-105.* Illustrates Tanzania's problems of ethnic integration with the example of the Chagga, who dwell on the slopes of Mount Kilimanjaro.

3185. Arens, W. ISLAM AND CHRISTIANITY IN SUB-SAHARAN AFRICA: ETHNOGRAPHIC REALITY OR IDEOLOGY. *Cahiers d'Études Africaines [France] 1975 15(3): 443-456.* The factors leading Africans to convert to Islam and Christianity have been misunderstood. Tanzanians in the village studied by the author became Muslims not because it coincided with existing organizational and cosmological patterns but because it provided a standard of community morality. Based on field work in northern Tanzania, a critique of the conversion literature, and other secondary literature; 8 notes.
B. S. Fetter

3186. Brain, James L. IS TRANSFORMATION POSSIBLE? STYLES OF SETTLEMENT IN POST-INDEPENDENCE TANZANIA. *African Affairs [Great Britain] 1977 76(303): 231-245.* Describes two approaches to village settlement in Tanzania in the first few years after independence: "one planned by former colonial service officers, heavily capitalized and bureaucratized; the other a spontaneous people's movement with virtually no capital input but having the advice of one expatriate idealist. The former was a colossal failure, the other a great success." Discusses housing, management, recruitment, and discipline. Describes Liweta, a village of the Ruvuma Development Association (RDA) with its intense interest in politics. 16 notes. E. P. Stickney

3187. Brain, James L. LESS THAN SECOND-CLASS: WOMEN IN RURAL SETTLEMENT SCHEMES IN TANZANIA. Hafkin, Nancy J. and Bay, Edna G., eds. *Women in Africa: Studies in Social and Economic Change*(Stanford, Ca.: Stanford U. Pr., 1976): 265-282. In Ujamaa villages established in the 1960's, settlers' wives were denied the rights exercised in traditional society where they had participated in the choice of a political leader and had rights to land and offspring in cases of divorce. In the settlement all proceeds of labor went to their husbands. Since it was assumed that man and wife should function as two equal working units, women had to work eight hours in the fields as well as perform domestic and childrearing duties. Moreover, no provisions were made for them in the event of their husbands' deaths. Fieldwork and secondary sources; note. S. Tomlinson-Brown

3188. Cameron, John. EDUCATION, INDIVIDUALITY AND COMMUNITY—EDUCATION FOR SELF-RELIANCE IN TANZANIA. *British J. of Educational Studies [Great Britain] 1980 28(2): 100-111.* Tanzanian President Nyerere's Education for Self-Reliance program inaugurated in 1967 is often interpreted as a product of Western influences, particularly the individuality of the J. S. Mill variety. Western influence, although it had made its presence felt for more than 80 years, was uneven, and the program was intended to foster nationalism, maintain independence, and build a tightly knit socialist state. 14 notes. D. G. Nielson

3189. Carthew, John. LIFE IMITATES ART: THE STUDENT EXPULSION IN DAR ES SALAAM, OCTOBER 1966, AS DRAMATIC RITUAL. *J. of Modern African Studies [Great Britain] 1980 18(3): 541-549.* Nearly 400 tertiary level students staged a protest march in Dar es Salaam, Tanzania, in October 1966, against government proposals for compulsory national service by university students. President Julius Nyerere expelled the student demonstrators and compelled them to accept rural labor prerequisite to their reentering the university. Tanzanian society at large and the students themselves are said to have accepted this judgment in a spirit akin to classical or Shakespearean tragic justice to prevent the formation in their country of a Western-style bureaucratic elite. Based on personal observations, Tanzanian newspapers, and secondary sources; 31 notes.
L. W. Truschel

3190. Ergas, Zecki. L'ECONOMIE POLITIQUE DU SYSTEME EDUCATIF EN TANZANIE [The political economy of the educational system in Tanzania]. *Genève-Afrique [Switzerland] 1975 14(2): 58-73.* Discusses the evolution of the Tanzanian educational system as an agent of national development since independence.

3191. Forni, Elisabetta. TANZANIA: ALCUNI PROCESSI DI TRASFORMAZIONE DELLA STRUTTURA SOCIALE NELLE CAMPAGNE [Tanzania: some processes of the transformation of the social structure in the countryside]. *Africa [Italy] 1979 34(3): 243-269.* After a short introduction concerning the colonial period, analyzes some rural areas chosen on account of their ecological and historical peculiarities and tries to determine their present social structure in connection with agricultural production, with particular reference to the ujamaa experience. 9 tables, 33 notes. J

3192. Frankl, P. J. L. ANGLICANISM IN SOUTH-EASTERN TANGANYIKA: 1876-1926. *Tanzania Notes and Records [Tanzania] 1974 (74): 1-9.* Outlines the history of the Universities Mission to Central Africa in southeastern Tanzania. Bishop Edward Steere founded the station at Masasi in 1876. In 1882 the Ngoni attacked the station but were bribed off. Although rebels captured Masasi in 1905 during the Maji Maji revolt, German troops quickly recaptured it. During World War I the Germans interned the British missionaries from 1915 to 1917. Primary and secondary sources; biblio. E. Hopkins

3193. Gallagher, Joseph T. THE EMERGENCE OF AN AFRICAN ETHNIC GROUP: THE CASE OF THE NDENDEULI. *Int. J. of African Hist. Studies 1974 7(1): 1-26.* The Ndendeuli who reside in southwestern Tanzania have undergone two radical changes in the past 150 years. The first is an alteration in their ethnic identity. The application of a common name for these peoples was a consequence of the Ngoni invasion in the 1840's. Secondly, when the modern Ndendeuli were granted separate recognition from the Mshope Ngone, the creation of their state organization brought into being an elemental transformation for these traditionally stateless people. Based on oral data and other primary sources; 77 notes. M. M. McCarthy

3194. Hussein, Ebrahim. THE BEGINNING OF IMPORTED THEATRE IN TANZANIAN URBAN CENTRES. *Wissenschaftliche Zeitschrift der Humboldt Universität zu Berlin [East Germany] 1974 23(3/4): 405-409.* Theater in Tanganyika under the British mandate and as a UN trust territory was tied to educational institutions—European, Black, or Asian. Most plays were produced in schools. In Asian schools traditional Asian plays were performed. In European schools 19th-century drawing room drama tended to predominate. For the relatively few black children going beyond the first school years, plays were in the English language—often Shakespeare or drawing room plays. British officials, quite unaware of indigenous traditional culture, used their authority to promote English traditions in Africa. 28 notes.
M. Faissler

3195. Lisicka, Hanna. ZNACZENIE ROZWOJU OŚWIATY W TANZANII W PIERWSZYCH LATACH NIEPODLEGŁOŚCI (1961-1969) [The significance of the growth of education in Tanzania during the first years of independence, 1961-69]. *Kultura i Społeczeństwo [Poland] 1977 21(3): 179-192.* The educational policies in Tanzania during the first years of independence, 1961-69, attempted to widen the horizons of the average African, break ethnic, cultural, religious, and racial barriers, and propagate national and party ideology.

The government appropriated 15-20% of the general national expense to develop education and encouraged Tanzanians to participate in the African conferences on education in 1961, 1962, and 1963. Unfortunately, the great educational activity in Tanzania still does not meet the pressing demands. M. Swiecicka-Ziemianek

3196. Lucas, Stephen A. THE ROLE OF UTANI IN EASTERN TANZANIAN CLAN HISTORIES. *African Rev. [Tanzania] 1974 4(1): 91-109.* *Utani* is a Swahili term that includes a variety of social customs in East Africa. Its meaning is explained, theories of utani are discussed, and the role of utani is analyzed. Using case studies from the oral traditions of the Doe, Kwere, and Zaramo clans, a further overview of utani is presented. 58 notes. H. G. Soff

3197. Mbilinyi, Marjorie J. EDUCATION, STRATIFICATION AND SEXISM IN TANZANIA: POLICY IMPLICATIONS. *African R. [Tanzania] 1973 3(2): 327-340.* Analyzes the factors used by families to determine school enrollment of their children. Indices included sex, standard of living, education of head of household, children per household, and the community. Parents generally educate their children anticipating an eventual economic "return." Argues that urban and rural education be the same to bridge the gap between rural peasantry and urban dwellers. Outlines proposed changes in the educational system. Fig., 39 notes. H. G. Soff

3198. McHenry, Dean E., Jr. THE USE OF SPORTS IN POLICY IMPLEMENTATION: THE CASE OF TANZANIA. *J. of Modern African Studies [Great Britain] 1980 18(2): 237-256.* Shows how the government used sports in domestic and international policymaking. State-controlled sports failed to achieve domestic political objectives, reflecting national opposition to a role for sports in policy implementation. Equally negative have been the efforts to promote African unity through sports. Tanzania succeeded, however, in banning South Africa and Rhodesia from the Olympic games. Secondary sources; 105 notes. A. Sbacchi

3199. Mutahaba, Belase. LOCAL AUTONOMY AND NATIONAL PLANNING: COMPLEMENTARY OR OTHERWISE? CASE STUDY FROM TANZANIA. *African Rev. [Tanzania] 1974 4(4): 509-530.* An examination of educational policies in Bukoba and Ngara Districts of Tanzania shows that decentralized administration is not compatible with national planning. Between 1964 and 1969 all national educational plans collapsed before the realities of local interests and pressures. Table, 52 notes. R. T. Brown

3200. Mwangosi, T. E. J. THE BACKGROUND OF SOCIAL WELFARE IN TANZANIA. *Tanzania Notes and Records [Tanzania] 1976 (77-78): 89-93.* Examines the history of the Social Welfare and Probation Division. Probation began in 1947 when an experienced British officer started training a staff. Since 1973 probation has been the basic program in the division's services. Since 1970 the division has also handled an increasing number of social welfare cases. Transcript of a speech by the then Commissioner for Social Welfare in May 1971. E. Hopkins

3201. Mwapachu, Juma Volter. OPERATION PLANNED VILLAGES IN RURAL TANZANIA: A REVOLUTIONARY STRATEGY FOR DEVELOPMENT. *African Rev. [Tanzania] 1976 6(1): 1-16.* The initial settlement schemes in Tanzania were failures because the people did not have a proper socialist attitude. With the creation of Ujamaa villages, rural socialism and decentralization of planning have resulted. Both are a necessary first step toward development. 23 notes. R. T. Brown

3202. Nimitz, August H., Jr. ISLAM IN TANZANIA: AN ANNOTATED BIBLIOGRAPHY. *Tanzania Notes and Records [Tanzania] 1973 72: 51-74.* Updates Carl H. Becker's bibliography, originally published in *Der Islam* (1911) and reprinted in *Tanzania Notes and Records.* Includes 340 new entries, approximately 75% of which have short annotations. Materials listed include German and British administration files located in the National Archives of Tanzania (48 entries); official publications (18); books, newspapers, and journal articles in Swahili or Arabic (36); and published and unpublished sources in European languages (238). Primary and secondary sources. E. C. Hopkins

3203. Ohly, Rajmund. LEXICOGRAPHY AND NATIONAL LANGUAGE. *Tanzania Notes and Records [Tanzania] 1976 (79-80): 23-30.* Traces the growth of the Swahili language from colonial times. The Germans used Swahili as the official language and prohibited other languages; the British reduced it to a semiofficial language, and encouraged its development, but permitted the use of others. In 1940 a third of Tanganyikans spoke Swahili; by 1961, half spoke it. The government now promotes it as the official language. The further development of Swahili depends on the coining system which hinges on political and ideological factors, and the several lexicographical schools. 40 notes, biblio. S. Lakhan

3204. Rodgers, W. A. PAST WANGINDO SETTLEMENT IN THE EASTERN SELOUS GAME RESERVE. *Tanzania Notes and Records [Tanzania] 1976 (77-78): 21-26.* The Ngindo probably migrated to southern Tanzania from Mozambique, settling to the south of the Rufiji River. A people of shifting cultivators, hunters, and gatherers, they suffered considerably from Ngoni and Arab slave raids throughout the 19th century due to their inability to conduct communal defense. During the British period agriculture remained at a subsistence level. A sleeping sickness epidemic in 1945 caused the Ngindo to be removed to Njinjo. The article includes a list of botanical names. Primary and secondary sources; photo, appendix. E. Hopkins

3205. Rudengren, Jan. UJAMAA OCH BYPOLITIK I TANZANIA [Ujamaa and village development in Tanzania]. *Internasjonal Politikk [Norway] 1976 (3B): 757-770.* Tanzania is well known for having a national ideology which emphasizes equality, decentralization and the development of ujamaa villages designed to increase production and socialist community on the land. In this study of ujamaa policy the author emphasizes the far more complex reality. In recent years the migration to rural towns has been more the result of state bureaucratic orders from above than political mobilization from below. However, it is too early yet to pass final judgment on the experiment which has begun. J

3206. Samoff, Joel. EDUCATION AND TRANSFORMATION IN TANZANIA. *Issue: A Q. J. of Opinion 1981 11(3-4): 22-26.* Since Tanzania became independent in 1961, the educational system has had the responsibility of reeducating the society from a dependent ethos to a liberated one and providing skilled personnel to replace departing Europeans.

3207. Samoff, Joel. EDUCATION IN TANZANIA: CLASS FORMATION AND REPRODUCTION. *J. of Modern African Studies [Great Britain] 1979 17(1): 47-69.* Education is manipulated to insure power, perpetuates social stratification and class differentiation, and is used in an effort to eradicate poverty. Although the government is committed to the elimination of illiteracy, internal political struggle may delay universal primary education. Based on UN documents, on Tanzania Department of Education documents in the National Archives in Dar es Salaam, government published documents, and secondary sources; 6 tables, 67 notes. A. Sbacchi

3208. Scotton, James F. TANGANYIKA'S AFRICAN PRESS, 1937-1960: A NEARLY FORGOTTEN PRE-INDEPENDENCE FORUM. *African Studies Rev. 1978 21(1): 1-18.* African-owned newspapers in colonial Tanganyika brought nationalist ideas to the masses, but were generally small and cautious. 17 notes, biblio. R. T. Brown

3209. Singleton, Michael. MUSLIMS, MISSIONARIES AND THE MILLENNIUM IN UPCOUNTRY TANZANIA. *Cultures et Développement [Belgium] 1977 9(2): 247-314.* Reviews relations in East and Central Africa among French Catholic missionaries, German administrators, and Arab and Black Muslims, noting the antagonisms that often existed among these groups, especially the enmity and misunderstanding that the Catholic fathers often expressed toward Muslims of whatever race.

3210. Stren, Richard E. UNDERDEVELOPMENT, URBAN SQUATTING, AND THE STATE BUREAUCRACY: A CASE STUDY OF TANZANIA. *Can. J. of African Studies [Canada] 1982 16(1): 67-91.* A case study of squatter housing in Dar es Salaam, which demonstrates that class-related factors and scarcity interact to produce a "bureaucratic culture" that stifles the very form of urban development the regime is committed to promote. World Bank project-oriented intervention tends to reinforce, rather than to reform, the bureaucratic culture, and thus stifles the possibility of positive urban change. Based on governmental documents and surveys and secondary sources; 54 notes. L. J. Klass

3211. Swatman, J. E. D. ACCESS TO EDUCATION: THE CHANGING PATTERN IN THE LOCATION OF SCHOOLS. *Tanzania Notes and Records [Tanzania] 1976 (79-80): 107-114.* In Tanzania, school density has been either much above or much below the average relative to the population. The Arab presence on the coast, slave routes, the attitude and strength of chiefs, the German government's attitude, points of commercial and strategic importance, mission headquarter policies, competition among missions, and availability of property and buildings have affected the establishment of schools. From 1945, however, schools were regionalized, and by 1969, day primary schools closely reflected the distribution of population. Based on Tanzanian Hansard reports and secondary sources; 9 notes. S. Lakhan

3212. Tanner, R. E. S. A NOTE ON CHRISTIANITY AND TRADITIONAL RELIGIOUS PRACTICES IN NGARA, TANZANIA. *J. of Religion in Africa [Netherlands] 1974 6(3): 161-168.* Assesses the extent to which Anglicans and Roman Catholics practice traditional religion and Christianity in the Ngara area of Tanzania where the first Christian missionary arrived in the 1930's. Anglicans still practice traditional rites on many occasions, at a rate twice that of Catholics. 4 tables. H. G. Soff

3213. Vitta, Paul B. PROGRESS AND PROBLEMS IN TANZANIA'S SCIENCE EDUCATION. *Taamuli [Tanzania] 1973 3(2): 22-26.* Assesses science education in Tanzania from primary through secondary school. Primary schools have not met their obligations to the nation and should be carefully watched. The major problem in secondary school is inadequate laboratory facilities. 5 notes. H. G. Soff

3214. Westerlund, David. CHRISTIANITY AND SOCIALISM IN TANZANIA: 1967-1977. *J. of Religion in Africa [Netherlands] 1980 11(1): 30-55.* Tanzanian socialism, or *Ujamaa,* has been elaborated by its Roman Catholic president, Julius Nyerere. Ujamaa is a product of the ruling, anti-Marxist elite. Christian churches have a difficulty implementing it because it is decidedly anticolonial. Based on various sources, including the doctoral dissertation by D. Westerlund, *Ujamaa na Dini: A Study of Some Aspects of Society and Religion in Tanzania, 1961-1977* (Stockholm: Almquist & Wiksell International, 1980); 73 notes. R. J. Jirran

3215. Westerlund, David. FREEDOM OF RELIGION UNDER SOCIALIST RULE IN TANZANIA, 1961-1977. *J. of Church and State 1982 24(1): 87-103.* Discusses tensions created by the separation of church and state in Tanzania from 1961 to 1977. Describes how secularization affected native religion, Islam, and Christianity, and analyzes the socialist government's methods of suppressing religious liberty since independence. 52 notes. E. E. Eminhizer

3216. White, P. F. DIVA: THE SWAHILI AESOP. *Tanzania Notes and Records [Tanzania] 1937 (73): 55-62.* The life of David Edward Diva (1916-69), Tanzanian translator and author of *hadithi* (stories) and school and religious books. Diva was born into an Anglican family in Zanzibar. He worked as a schoolteacher until 1960 when he joined the East African Literature Bureau. His first works were translations of Aesop's fables. 28 notes. E. Hopkins

3217. Wright, Marcia. THE CATHOLIC CHURCH IN EAST CENTRAL AFRICA: REFLECTIONS ON ITS RECEPTIVITY TO CHANGE. *Kyrkohistorisk Årsskrift [Sweden] 1978 78: 397-401.* Describes the development of the Catholic Church in Tanzania with emphasis on the relationship between church and state, 1880's-1970's.

Uganda

3218. Adams, Bert N. and Bristow, Mike. THE POLITICO-ECONOMIC POSITION OF UGANDAN ASIANS IN THE COLONIAL AND INDEPENDENT ERAS. *J. of Asian and African Studies [Netherlands] 1978 13(3-4): 151-166.* Most Asians came to Uganda voluntarily in the 20th century and proceeded to gain a crucial role in the economy. Upon independence most did not become citizens and continued to send money out of the country. Except for the Ismailis, Asians did little to identify with Uganda. Based on interviews; 3 tables, 3 notes, biblio. R. T. Brown

3219. Adams, Bert N.; Pereira, Cecil; and Bristow, Mike. UGANDA ASIANS IN EXILE: HOUSEHOLD AND KINSHIP IN THE RESETTLEMENT CRISIS. *Int. Migration [Netherlands] 1978 16(2): 83-94.* Nearly 90% of the 50,000 East Indians that left Uganda, August-November 1972, were resettled in Great Britain, Canada, and India. The authors examine the composition of Asian families in Uganda and the changes in family composition imposed by their move. One of the principal problems was the fragmentation of families. Based on interviews with 1,259 heads of families in the three countries. S/T

3220. Adams, Bert N. and Bristow, Mike. UGANDAN ASIAN EXPULSION EXPERIENCES: RUMOR AND REALITY. *J. of Asian and African Studies [Netherlands] 1979 14(3-4): 191-203.* Interviews with 1,250 refugee Asian families from Uganda suggest that the conditions of their expulsion were difficult but not as bad as the world press portrayed them. Based on interviews; 3 tables, 31 notes. R. T. Brown

3221. Adekson, J. Bayo. ETHNICITY, THE MILITARY, AND DOMINATION: THE CASE OF OBOTE'S UGANDA, 1962-71. *Plural Soc. [Netherlands] 1978 9(1): 85-110.* Traces the development of ethnic military dominance by the Nilotes in Uganda under Milton Obote's government, 1962-71.

3222. Akinsanya, Adeoye A. THE ENTEBBE RESCUE MISSION: A CASE OF AGGRESSION? *Pakistan Horizon [Pakistan] 1981 34(3): 12-35.* Considers whether the Israeli raid on Entebbe, Uganda to rescue civilian hostages taken by the Popular Front for the Liberation of Palestine (PFLP) in the aircraft hijacking of an Air France Jumbo Jet was an act of aggression under international law and concludes that, while Israel defended the 4 July 1976 raid as a humanitarian act in defense of innocent civilians, such actions are probably illegal by international standards of law.

3223. Atanda, J. A. BRITISH RULE IN BUGANDA. *Tarikh [Nigeria] 1974 4(4): 37-53.*

3224. Balezin, A. S. TRANSFORMATSIIA POZEMEL'NYKII OTNOSHENII V UGANDE 1900-1939 [The transformation of land relations in Uganda, 1900-39]. *Narody Azii i Afriki [USSR] 1978 (4): 135-145.* Uganda is an example of how, during the colonial era, the imperialist bourgeoisie extended native precolonial forms of exploitation to areas where they were previously unknown. In the first half of the 20th century private land ownership became quite common and a quasi-feudal system emerged in the more developed parts of the country. In the less developed parts a system of smallholdings was established. Here, either the traditional system reemerged or the small producers were pauperized. Secondary sources; 54 notes. J. M. Chambers

3225. Bowles, B. D. ECONOMIC ANTI-COLONIALISM AND BRITISH REACTION IN UGANDA, 1936-1955. *Can. J. of African Studies [Canada] 1975 9(1): 51-60.* Discusses cash-crop or export-crop growers in Uganda, especially cotton and coffee growers. These farmers complained about the low price of cotton. The British government investigated these complaints and decided that they should fix agricultural prices because the inhabitants were too backward to do so. This inflamed the growers. Accordingly, the government decided to consider more closely the interests of the growers in the future. Based on government documents and secondary sources; 2 tables, 27 notes. E. R. Campbell

3226. Bunker, Stephen G. CLASS, STATUS, AND THE SMALL FARMER: RURAL DEVELOPMENT PROGRAMS AND THE ADVANCE OF CAPITALISM IN UGANDA AND BRAZIL. *Latin Am. Perspectives 1981 8(1): 89-107.* Comparative study of the Bugisu area, Uganda, and rural Pará, Brazil. Government programs aimed at transforming peasants into small farmers integrated into a market economy have much greater chances of success when local middle classes mediate the interaction, as in Bugisu, than when programs

operate in a bipolar class structure, as in Pará. 2 notes, biblio.
J. F. Vivian

3227. Charsley, S. R. DREAMS IN AN INDEPENDENT AFRICAN CHURCH. *Africa [Great Britain] 1973 43(3): 244-275.* A sociological examination of institutional dream-telling in an independent African church in western Uganda; the church, an offshoot from a Canadian Pentecostal Mission in western Kenya, was the local branch among western Kenyan immigrants to Uganda, 1957-60's.

3228. Cohen, D. L. and Parson, J. THE UGANDA PEOPLES CONGRESS BRANCH AND CONSTITUENCY ELECTIONS OF 1970. *J. of Commonwealth Pol. Studies [Great Britain] 1973 11(1): 46-66.* Examines the Uganda elections of 1970 and their meaning for the development of the Uganda People's Congress, with particular reference to the political system in Uganda.

3229. Doornbos, Martin R. ETHNICITY, CHRISTIANITY, AND THE DEVELOPMENT OF SOCIAL STRATIFICATION IN COLONIAL ANKOLE, UGANDA. *Int. J. of African Hist. Studies 1976 9(4): 555-575.* Examines the effects of colonial arrangements on the formation of sociopolitical groups in Ankole District, Uganda. The divergent social developments among the Bairu had important political consequences. They produced a pecking order which placed the Bahima first, the Protestant Bairu second, and the Roman Catholics third in their access to the advantages of the system. The divisiveness which originated in the ethnic-religious cleavages facilitated external control and produced an administrative establishment that required little manipulation to serve the colonial cause. 32 notes.
M. M. McCarthy

3230. Doornbos, Martin R. FACES AND PHASES OF UGANDAN POLITICS: CHANGING PERCEPTIONS OF SOCIAL STRUCTURE AND SOCIAL CONFLICT. *African Perspectives [Netherlands] 1978 (2): 117-134.* Considers Ugandan perceptions of social structure and social conflict since independence, 1961-78. At the time of Uganda's independence, traditionalism and the maintenance of traditional authority were seen as major issues, and provided protection for established political and administrative elites. This was followed in 1966 by the "politics of ethnicity" when the special privileges of traditional patterns were abrogated in favor of a thoroughly centralized system. A conflict developed between ethnic groups and this quickly led to "class politics," Idi Amin's coup, and the ascendancy of the army. R. V. Ritter

3231. Doornbos, Martin R. LAND TENURE AND POLITICAL CONFLICT IN ANKOLE, UGANDA. *J. of Development Studies [Great Britain] 1975 12(1): 54-74.* In Ankole District, Western Uganda, a serious land problem is developing. Land is increasingly being acquired for commercial and speculative purposes; access to land for the majority of Banyankore becomes problematic. This paper is concerned with the origins of two avenues of land acquisition in Ankole, *mailo*grants and individual freehold titles. Both have contributed to nascent problems, if only through their inducement of interests in land as a commodity. Explores the effects of these policies on Ankole sociopolitical divisions and questions general land policies (especially "individualization") concerned with agricultural growth alone. J

3232. Elam, Yitzchak. NOMADISM IN ANKOLE AS A SUBSTITUTE FOR REBELLION. *Africa [Great Britain] 1979 49(2): 147-158.* Points out the factors that hindered the crystallization of territories and inhabitants in Ankole, Uganda as competitors for the throne confined major upheavals there to periods of interregnum. Argues that there were few rebellions because resentments could be regularly vented through nomadism, and discusses the political implications of movements in search of water and moving away as a means of changing one's master. Fig., 12 notes, biblio. P. J. Taylorson

3233. Elam, Yitzchak. THE RELATIONSHIPS BETWEEN HIMA AND IRU IN ANKOLE. *African Studies [South Africa] 1974 33(3): 159-172.* Examines the nature of social and other relationships between the Iru (peasants) and the Hima (breeders of cattle) in the Ugandan kingdom of Ankole. The Iru have grown both in numbers and political influence, while the Hima have declined owing to the decreasing importance of their traditional, nomadic way of life. Various differentiations between the groups are analyzed. Based on printed sources and field research; 77 notes. J. A. Casada

3234. Gershenberg, Irving. MULTINATIONALS AND DEVELOPMENT: COMMERCIAL BANKING IN UGANDA. *Africa Today 1973 20(4): 19-27.* Describes the continued domination of Uganda by former metropolitan-based banking firms. These firms train Ugandan nationals in essentially passive goals and thereby inhibit dynamic, developmental banking practices which would assist economic development. Based on questionnaires and secondary sources; 2 tables, 15 notes.
G. O. Gagnon

3235. Gertzel, Cherry. UGANDA AFTER AMIN: THE CONTINUING SEARCH FOR LEADERSHIP AND CONTROL. *African Affairs [Great Britain] 1980 79(317): 461-489.* Examines the problems of restoration of civilian rule in Uganda. Idi Amin's eight years of arbitrary personal rule resulted not only in widespread destruction but in serious institutional decline. The state survived but it was a "broken-backed" state, and the primary task of restoration was to restore the legitimacy of the central government institutions. Their internal rivalries and divisions had weakened the ability of politicians to do so. The search for control was a search for a new moral basis for Ugandan society, and the politics of liberation have been unsuccessful in achieving this objective. 141 notes. J. V. Coutinho

3236. Gitelson, Susan Aurelia. AMIN BETWEEN ISRAEL AND THE ARABS. *Midstream 1975 21(9): 29-35.* General Idi Amin of Uganda, who initially turned to Israel after his coup in 1971, has now turned against Israel in favor of support from the Arabs.

3237. Gitelson, Susan Aurelia. MAJOR SHIFTS IN RECENT UGANDAN FOREIGN POLICY. *African Affairs [Great Britain] 1977 76(304): 359-380.* Since Idi Amin wrested control of Uganda from Milton Obote, he has maneuvered in world circles and searched for new friends while alienating old allies. Uganda's place in the world rests on Amin's whims. 87 notes. H. G. Soff

3238. Glentworth, Garth and Hancock, Ian. OBOTE AND AMIN: CHANGE AND CONTINUITY IN MODERN UGANDA POLITICS. *African Affairs [Great Britain] 1973 72(288): 237-255.* Idi Amin's brutal and inconsistent behavior is in many ways an extension of the system he inherited in 1971. Post-independence political maneuvering, the massive role of the military, the 1971 coup, and Amin's violent behavior since taking power may bequeath his successor a pattern of violence in government. 30 notes. H. G. Soff

3239. Good, Charles M. PERIODIC MARKETS AND TRAVELING TRADERS IN UGANDA. *Geographical R. 1975 65(1): 49-72.* "Periodic market systems provide excellent examples of the complex spatial and temporal components present in most development problems. This paper draws particular attention to market location and timing as primary decision variables which influence the observed and potential behavior of one class of market user: the traveling trader. Detailed analysis of the circulation patterns of a sample of traders operating in an extensive system of 154 markets in Uganda serves as a basis for exploring theoretically more efficient alternatives to actual locational decisions. In contrast to the classical traveling salesman dilemma, itinerant market traders are constrained by a time lock inherent in the nature of a periodic market system which precludes a lower-cost solution to their transport problem unless they are willing to relocate, in other words, to change their calling order by choosing a different set of markets. A method used to approximate the minimum aggregate path connecting a set of markets yielded results which effectively demonstrated the gains in operating efficiency that traders could realize." J

3240. Grahame, Iain. UGANDA AND ITS PRESIDENT. *Army Q. and Defence J. [Great Britain] 1974 104(4): 480-490.* A biographical survey of Idi Amin, president of Uganda. Reviews Amin's rise to power and stresses his fundamental loyalty to Britain. Stability in Uganda is threatened most by ethnic conflict, which remains "the ever-smoldering fire." The attempted coup of March 1974 was seriously misreported outside Uganda; the affair was confined to a small section of the army, but it convinced Amin he had overplayed his commitment to Islam. The author, a former commanding officer of Amin, recounts recent discussions with Amin. D. H. Murdoch

3241. Gupta, Anirudha. UGANDAN ASIANS, BRITAIN, INDIA AND THE COMMONWEALTH. *African Affairs [Great Britain] 1974 73(292): 312-324.* The Asian exodus from Uganda received worldwide notice with Asian refugees faring far better than most African refugees within the continent. Discusses the crisis of 1972, British and Indian actions, and the consequences for relations within the Commonwealth. It appears that Britain, by not acting harshly toward Uganda, has helped keep the Commonwealth working, and by accepting numerous refugees has obtained respect from India. 17 notes. H. G. Soff

3242. Hancock, I. R. THE KAKAMEGA CLUB OF BUGANDA. *J. of Modern African Studies [Great Britain] 1974 12(1): 131-135.* Traces origins of the Kakamega Club in the 1940's and its involvement in Uganda politics to the 1960's. The club was organized to entertain and befriend the Kabaka (king) of Buganda. Membership was generally restricted to Protestants born of wealth or high political station. In 1961 the club helped form the strength of the Kabaka Yekka (The King Alone) movement. 15 notes. H. G. Soff

3243. Harbeson, John W. and Rothchild, Donald. REHABILITATION IN UGANDA. *Current Hist. 1981 80(464): 115-119, 134-138.* Evaluates the measures taken to rehabilitate Uganda from near political and economic destruction during Idi Amin's regime.

3244. Hastings, Adrian. GANDA CATHOLIC SPIRITUALITY. *J. of Religion in Africa [Netherlands] 1976 8(2): 81-91.* Recalls major events and personalities encountered as a Catholic priest in Uganda, 1958-66. The Catholic diocese of Masaka was a religious stronghold in the country and was noted for the relative lack of external missionary influence. H. G. Soff

3245. Heyneman, Stephen P. CHANGES IN EFFICIENCY AND IN EQUITY ACCRUING FROM GOVERNMENT INVOLVEMENT IN UGANDAN PRIMARY EDUCATION. *African Studies Rev. 1975 18(1): 51-60.* Examines the various forms of Ugandan government involvement in primary education since the early 1950's.

3246. Isoba, John C. G. THE RISE AND FALL OF UGANDA'S NEWSPAPER INDUSTRY, 1900-1976. *Journalism Q. 1980 57(2): 224-233.* Published by the Anglican Church Missionary Society, the *Mengo Notes* became Uganda's first newspaper with its appearance in 1900. Along with other religious papers, a variety of colonial and Ugandan government journals and independent newspapers appeared later. However, by 1976 the industry had declined significantly because of foreign competition and a lack of educational facilities for training journalists in Uganda. Based on papers of the Church Missionary Society, Annual Reports of the Department of Information (London), and secondary sources; 2 tables, 21 notes. J. S. Coleman

3247. Jacobs, B. L. UGANDA'S SECOND REPUBLIC: THE FIRST TWO YEARS. *Africa Today 1973 20(2): 47-57.* Compares Idi Amin with his predecessor Milton Obote. Predicts that Amin will not remain in power as long as Obote because his desperation alienates larger segments of Uganda's population and antagonizes adjacent nations. Based on author's personal experiences. G. O. Gagnon

3248. Jamal, Vali. ASIANS IN UGANDA, 1880-1972: INEQUALITY AND EXPULSION. *Econ. Hist. Rev. [Great Britain] 1976 29(4): 602-616.* Chronicles the economic role played by Asians in Uganda, 1880-1972, and the constant discrimination and resentment which they met.

3249. Jamal, Vali. TAXATION AND INEQUALITY IN UGANDA, 1900-1964. *J. of Econ. Hist. 1978 38(2): 418-438.* Throughout Uganda's modern history the largest share of government revenue has originated in the agricultural sector, a result not only of its preponderance in the economy but more importantly of its being consistently taxed higher than the nonagricultural sector. Since agricultural incomes were much lower than nonagricultural incomes, the tax burden on farmers was heavier than on other groups. The regressiveness of the tax system was further exacerbated by the bias in government expenditure to urban areas. The author provides various period and population group estimates of tax burden and disbursement of government expenditure to demonstrate the backwardness of Uganda's fiscal system. J

3250. Jamison, Martin. IDI AMIN DADA OF UGANDA: A SELECTED BIBLIOGRAPHY. *Bull. of Biblio. and Mag. Notes 1978 35(3): 105-115.* Describes works on the character and actions of Uganda's President Idi Amin, 1971-78.

3251. Kasfir, Nelson. EXPLAINING ETHNIC POLITICAL PARTICIPATION. *World Pol. 1979 31(3): 365-388.* Most concepts of ethnicity are unsuitable for political analysis because they ignore either subjective or objective aspects, and because they ignore the fluid and situational nature of ethnicity. The approach flowing from the concept proposed here permits the observer to examine empirical variations that tend to be treated as rigid assumptions by modernization analysts on the one hand and class analysts on the other. The concept is applied to a study of the Nubians of Uganda because of the intermixture of class and ethnic features involved in their fall from status at the beginning of the colonial period and their subsequent sudden rise following the 1971 coup d'etat of Idi Amin. The fairly recent creation of the Nubians as an ethnic category and the relative ease with which others can become members illustrate other features of the proposed concept of ethnicity. Finally, this concept is used to examine and criticize overly restrictive notions of ethnicity found in theories based upon both cultural pluralism and consociationalism. J

3252. Kiapi, Abraham. LEGAL OBSTACLES TO RURAL DEVELOPMENT IN COLONIAL UGANDA. *Mawazo [Uganda] 1975 4(3): 101-112.* To some extent the laws passed by the British colonial government were a factor in hindering rural development in Uganda. Such was the case with the Town and Country Planning Ordinance, which appeared to give everything to the towns while the country or rural areas were exploited and starved. The land tenure system remained unreformed by the Protectorate government and hindered the African population from making full use of the land. The African was caught between customary and English land systems. The former allowed him to occupy land on a traditional tenure basis, the other denied him legal title to the land he occupied when he wanted to raise loans on the money market. No efforts were made to extend the tourist industry to rural areas. Mining laws, too, stopped the African from exercising traditional skills in making tools, weapons, and farm implements from native ores. 14 notes. J. J. N. McGurk

3253. Kibedi, Wanume. KIBEDI SPEAKS OUT. *Africa Report 1974 19(4): 45-48.* Wanume Kibedi, Idi Amin's foreign minister from 1971 to 1973, explains his participation in the Uganda military government and evaluates David Martin's *General Amin.* S

3254. Kiwanuka, Semakula. THE DIPLOMACY OF THE LOST COUNTIES AND ITS IMPACT ON FOREIGN RELATIONS OF BUGANDA, BUNYORO AND THE REST OF UGANDA, 1900-1964. *Mawazo [Uganda] 1974 4(2): 111-142.* Examines the foreign relations of Buganda and Bunyoro, the so-called lost counties in Uganda prior to independence; further, examines the political dealings of both the British and the African population in attempting to settle border disputes (which have inevitably affected the internal political structure).

3255. Langlands, Bryan. STUDENTS AND POLITICS IN UGANDA. *African Affairs [Great Britain] 1977 76(302): 3-20.* An eyewitness account of student dissension in Uganda. Little dissension has occurred, and there is no tradition for it. But, in view of the prevalence of violent retribution, even modest dissent assumes significant proportions. Students sided generally with the government of Milton Obote. His successor, Idi Amin, alienated the students almost immediately. They boycotted his visit, but reports of a retaliatory massacre of students seem exaggerated, although hard and firm answers are not yet possible. Increased student antigovernment activities are not expected in the foreseeable future. V. L. Human

3256. Laughlin, Charles D., Jr. and Laughlin, Elizabeth R. AGE GENERATIONS AND POLITICAL PROCESS IN SO. *Africa [Great Britain] 1974 44(3): 266-279.* Compares So and Karamojong systems of age-grading in Northeastern Uganda. Differences in formal aspects and in manifestations of functional behavior are attributed to the modification of the Karamojong system when introduced into the So social setting some time after 1900. Where the imported system corresponded with institutional relations previously present in So (e.g., authority in the hands of the elders, sanction of junior males as warriors), it acted to reinforce them. The imported system was modified to meet So interests when it conflicted with important values or institutional arrangements previously held in So (e.g., nonretirement of political authority, lesser formal significance of male initiation rites). Based on field work among So and secondary sources; 2 tables, 8 notes, biblio. C. Fry

3257. Lofchie, Michael F. THE POLITICAL ORIGINS OF THE UGANDA COUP. *J. of African Studies 1974 1(4): 464-496.* Although the army is not an economic class, the 1971 coup is better explained by class analysis than as a populistic uprising or an ethnic conflict. The government's loss of popularity is merely a facilitating agent in most African coups. The Obote government's "Move to the Left" in 1969 threatened the army's illegitimate methods of accumulating capital, pursued because the two legitimate areas, agriculture and trade, were securely occupied by other groups. The expulsion of West African traders, Asians, and British businessmen cleared a path for the military establishment to become a full-fledged entrepreneurial class. Based on Uganda government documents, statistics, and secondary sources; table, 37 notes. W. R. Hively

3258. Mandeville, Elizabeth. POVERTY, WORK AND THE FINANCING OF SINGLE WOMEN IN KAMPALA. *Africa [Great Britain] 1979 49(1): 42-52.* Examines the financial position of all-female households in a poor area of Kampala, Uganda in the 1960's to indicate the relative standards of living of households of various composition and to decide whether the practice of soliciting money from lovers is better viewed as a preferred alternative to employment or as an essential supplementing of inadequate incomes. Based on author's field research; 6 tables, 3 notes, biblio. P. J. Taylorson

3259. Mazrui, Ali A. BOXER MUHAMMAD ALI AND SOLDIER IDI AMIN AS INTERNATIONAL POLITICAL SYMBOLS: THE BIOECONOMICS OF SPORT AND WAR. *Comparative Studies in Soc. and Hist. [Great Britain] 1977 19(2): 189-215.* Examines the rise of Idi Amin in Uganda and Muhammad Ali in US sports, emphasizing their racial allegiance to blacks and the links between biology and economics which have seemed to affect their individual struggles.

3260. Mazrui, Ali A. THE LUMPEN PROLETARIAT AND THE LUMPEN MILITARIAT: AFRICAN SOLDIERS AS A NEW POLITICAL CLASS. *Pol. Studies [Great Britain] 1973 21(1): 1-12.* Tests three hypotheses about the nature of consolidation of statehood, the diversification of class structure, and the process of modernization in Africa based on the Ugandan coup d'etat of January 1971. African experience vindicates Marx's assumption about the relevance of the means of production as a weapon for military efficacy. M. Harrison

3261. Mazrui, Ali A. POLITICAL SCIENCE AND SOCIAL COMMITMENT IN THE FIRST REPUBLIC OF UGANDA: A PERSONAL INTERPRETATION. *Kenya Hist. Rev. [Kenya] 1978 6(1-2): 63-83.* Personal reminiscences of the political science department at Makerere University, Kampala, during the First Republic of Uganda, ca. 1963-71, before Idi Amin's regime.

3262. Mazrui, Ali A. RELIGIOUS STRANGERS IN UGANDA: FROM EMIN PASHA TO AMIN DADA. *African Affairs [Great Britain] 1977 76(302): 21-38.* Uganda is overwhelmingly Christian, but the long-standing Muslim minority could become dominant. Emin Pasha (Eduard Schnitzer, 1840-92) was the last great Islamic leader; the decline of Islam precipitated conflict between Catholics and Protestants. Idi Amin's use of Sudanese troops is once again bringing the religious issue to public attention. Should Amin, or his successors, prove efficacious in their policies, not only Uganda but the whole of eastern Africa could become Islamized. Much depends on a continuing need for Sudanese troops. 23 notes. V. L. Human

3263. Mazrui, Ali A. THE SOCIAL ORIGINS OF UGANDAN PRESIDENTS: FROM KING TO PEASANT WARRIOR. *Can. J. of African Studies [Canada] 1974 8(1): 3-23.* Uganda's transition from an electoral to a structural democracy whose elite was to be recruited from the underprivileged sectors is discussed in terms of the hereditary privilege, education, and ethnic backgrounds of the three post-independence presidents, Sir Edward Mutesa, Milton Obote, and Idi Amin.

3264. Melady, Thomas and Melady, Margaret. THE EXPULSION OF THE ASIANS FROM UGANDA. *Orbis 1976 19(4): 1600-1620.* On 5 August 1972, General Idi Amin ordered the expulsion of Asians who were without Ugandan citizenship. The Asians were given three months to leave, and the British government was asked "to facilitate the departure of those holding British passports." Although the action came as a surprise to many people, Amin had been "generating antagonism against the Asians" since his advent to power on 25 January 1971. As time went on, Amin's original expulsion order was amended and certain concessions made, although by November 1972 only a few Asians remained in the country. 59 notes. A. N. Garland

3265. Menarchik, E. Douglas. STRIKE AGAINST TERROR! THE ENTEBBE RAID. *Air U. Rev. 1980 31(5): 65-76.* Surveys international terrorist activities and specifically analyzes the Israeli raid on Entebbe.

3266. Miltényi, Károlyi. UGANDA NÉPESEDÉSÉNEK NÉHÁNY JELLEGZETESSÉGE [Some characteristics of Uganda's population]. *Demográfia [Hungary] 1979 (2-3): 228-236.* Measures Uganda's population growth, fertility, and mortality based on the 1969 census and a 1975 survey and projects a population of 25 million by 2000.

3267. Mittleman, James H. THE STATE OF RESEARCH ON AFRICAN POLITICS: CONTRIBUTIONS ON UGANDA. *J. of Asian and African Studies [Netherlands] 1976 11(3-4): 152-165.* A bibliographical essay with comments on 51 works. Table, 5 notes. R. T. Brown

3268. Motani, Nizar A. MAKERERE COLLEGE, 1922-1940: A STUDY IN COLONIAL RULE AND EDUCATIONAL RETARDATION. *African Affairs [Great Britain] 1979 78(312): 357-369.* Technical training, initially for carpenters and mechanics, started at Kampala in 1921. This government technical school was officially renamed Makerere College in 1923, when medical and surveying courses were added to the curriculum. The sole function of Makerere for many years was the training of subordinate civil servants and clerks. By 1925 there were 76 students, admission by the Intermediate School Leaving Certificate being introduced in 1926. In 1928 responsibility for technical education was transferred to Kampala Technical School, and Makerere became a center for vocational training. The Ormsby-Gore Commission of 1925 recommended that Makerere should be developed to satisfy African aspirations, a project largely developed by Sir Philip Mitchell, governor 1935-40. 71 notes. R. L. Collison

3269. Mudoola, Dan. RELIGION AND POLITICS IN UGANDA: THE CASE OF BUSOGA, 1900-1962. *African Affairs [Great Britain] 1978 77(306): 22-35.* Although Protestants, Catholics, and Moslems have influenced various parts of Uganda, in Busoga the Protestants have been dominant since colonization. The British sent young boys to school for training and when independence was granted in 1962, the Protestants were as strongly entrenched as they had always been. Table, 48 notes. H. G. Soff

3270. Mujaju, A. B. THE RELIGIO-REGIONAL FACTOR IN UGANDA POLITICS. *Mawazo [Uganda] 1974 4(2): 143-160.* Examines the religious sentiments (usually fighting factions of Catholics and Protestants) in various regions of Uganda, 1880-1970, and the effect of both of these on the formation of political parties, both colonial and non-colonial.

3271. Mujaju, A. B. THE ROLE OF UPC AS A PARTY OF GOVERNMENT IN UGANDA. *Can. J. of African Studies [Canada] 1976 10(3): 443-468.* Examines the extent to which the Uganda People's Congress (UPC) was prepared, in 1969, to become a tool of socialist reform while continuing as the ruling party of Uganda. Maintains that all the political events, 1966-69, which continued to erode the leadership of Milton Obote combined to create a collective political leadership, 1969.

3272. Mujaju, Akiiki. THE DEMISE OF UPCYL AND THE RISE OF NUYO IN UGANDA. *African R. [Tanzania] 1973 3(2): 291-307.*

Analyzes the role of youth in preindependence activities and postindependence. Focuses on the Uganda People's Congress Youth League (UPCYL) and the period 1960-66 during which the UPCYL and the Uganda People's Congress (UPC) split. In response to a crisis among the nation's youth, in 1963 the UPC created the National Union of Youth Organizations (NUYO) which was controlled by state officials. This indicated a definite break between youth and the party from preindependence to postindependence. This is a feature common to many newly independent states. 29 notes. H. G. Soff

3273. Mujaju, Akiiki B. THE POLITICAL CRISIS OF CHURCH INSTITUTIONS IN UGANDA. *African Affairs [Great Britain] 1976 75(298): 67-85.* An analysis of the extent to which churches in Uganda are linked to the political system for redress of grievances. In Protestant churches, regional cleavages hindered problem solving; the Muslims were divided by less organized local groups; but the Catholics were quite different. While the churches all appear calm, it is only due to the style of Idi Amin, who does not tolerate individual criticism of his regime. 36 notes. H. G. Soff

3274. Mulira, James. THE IMPLICATIONS OF "COLLABORATION" BETWEEN AFRICAN NATIONALISTS AND THE COMMUNIST WORLD—A CASE STUDY OF UGANDA 1945-1962. *Uganda J. [Uganda] 1980 39: 1-17.* In 1948, Semakula Mulumba, head of the Bataka Party—formed just before the end of World War II to defend the traditional prerogatives of clan leaders—obtained Soviet help in the UN against British plans for incorporating Uganda and Tanganyika into an East African Federation. There followed increasing cooperation between the USSR and Ugandan nationalists of the Bataka Party and later of the Uganda National Congress and its successor, the Uganda People's Congress. The colonial authorities, for their own purposes, made much of these ties, and the Catholic clergy and press, the largely Catholic Democratic Party, and the monarchical Kabaka Yekka Party, joined in denouncing any such cooperation as a threat to Uganda's freedom. Based on contemporary Ugandan press sources, a 1972 interview with Mulumba, United Nations records, secondary sources; 45 notes. L. Van Wyk

3275. Mulira, James. SOVIET BLOC: TRADE, ECONOMIC, TECHNICAL AND MILITARY INVOLVEMENT IN INDEPENDENT AFRICA: A CASE STUDY OF UGANDA 1962-1979. *Genève-Afrique [Switzerland] 1981 19(1): 39-79.* Under Milton Obote, 1962-71, most Soviet aid to Uganda was economic, made in loans with low interest (2.5%) but otherwise harsh terms. Under Idi Amin, 1971-79, most aid was military, while most of Uganda's trade continued to be with Western nations. Based on printed materials; 88 notes, 2 photos, 7 tables. B. S. Fetter

3276. Musoke, Okello Kaija. ONZE MILLIONS D'OTAGES EN OUGANDA [Eleven million hostages in Uganda]. *Esprit [France] 1977 (9): 109-117.* Studies Uganda's history since colonial times, but focuses on the rule of Idi Amin. Foreign governments have been ignorant of or unconcerned about the problems of Ugandans.

3277. Mutibwa, Phares M. WHITE SETTLERS IN UGANDA: THE ERA OF HOPES AND DISILLUSIONMENT, 1905-1923. *Transafrican J. of Hist. [Kenya] 1976 5(2): 112-122.* Why European plantation farming was not more successful has not been accurately explained due to faulty and prejudicial scholarship relating to British rule in Uganda. More research is necessary on this topic in order to show the relative importance of immigrant and indigenous farmers prior to World War II. 11 notes. H. G. Soff

3278. Nakabayashi, Nobuhiro. BUGANDA NO ŌKEN TO SHIZOKU [Regal authority and clans in Buganda]. *Redishigaku Kenkyū [Japan] 1978 (462): 61-70.* Discusses the relationship between regal authority and the clan in the Kingdom of Buganda, which forms the most vital political relationship within the Kingdom. Focuses on the Saza chiefs, 13c-20c. The Buganda people, comprising 30 to 40 paternity clans, were ruled by the king or his administrative agents, the Saza chiefs. The chiefs were appointed either by succession or by the king. Since the 17th and 18th centuries the latter method has been predominant and the author argues that this change has been closely connected with militarism. There has been an increase in wars of aggression and rewards in the form of land grants have also increased. Based on surveys and the author's own interviews. M. Nakayama/S

3279. Nayenga, Peter F. B. CHIEFS AND THE "LAND QUESTION" IN BUSOGA DISTRICT, UGANDA, 1895-1936. *Int. J. of African Hist. Studies 1979 12(2): 183-209.* Focuses on the efforts of Basoga chiefs to retain their control over land and shows how they had failed by 1936, instead becoming salaried officials functionally divorced from landownership and the production process. In the 1920's, the British introduced reforms which drastically reduced the feudal powers of the chiefs over their subjects. The colonial authorities compensated the lower chiefs for their loss of salary by allowing them to become central agents in the allocation of land. Because the upper chiefs failed to obtain freehold land titles and their social-cultural lifestyle reduced their economic position, poverty has come to characterize the lot of chiefs who at one time were the symbol of prosperity. Map, table, 97 notes. M. M. McCarthy

3280. Nayenga, Peter F. B. COMMERCIAL COTTON GROWING IN BUSOGA DISTRICT, UGANDA, 1905-1923. *African Econ. Hist. 1981 (10): 175-195.* The adoption of cotton as a cash crop in Busoga, Uganda is credited to the initiative of the colonial government and Indian traders. But Africans played a complementary role. Aided by rich agricultural traditions and a fertile soil and climate, African farmers did not have to give up their food staples to grow cotton. Unfortunately, they were denied access to ginning and the export-import aspects of the trade, thus precluding the emergence of an African commercial elite. Based on Department of Agriculture records and other sources; 3 maps, 3 tables, 95 notes. W. D. Piersen

3281. Nayenga, Peter F. B. MYTHS AND REALITIES OF IDI AMIN DADA'S UGANDA. *African Studies Rev. 1979 22(2): 127-138.* A review essay about three recent books which deal with Uganda. All contemporary accounts of Idi Amin's government lack analysis and focus on sensationalism. These books are current popular literature rather than serious studies of a society in trouble. Biblio. R. T. Brown

3282. Nsibambi, Apolo Robin. POPULISM IN UGANDA, 1959-1961. *Indian J. of Pol. Studies [India] 1978 2(1): 19-37.* Discusses the Ugandan populist movement after 1959 and the role of the general public in decisions concerning Uganda's political and economic independence.

3283. Nsimbambi, A. R. SOME REFLECTIONS ON THE UGANDAN INDEPENDENCE CONSTITUTION OF 1962. *Uganda J. [Uganda] 1980 39: 18-26.* G. W. Kanyeihamba, a Ugandan legal theorist, has supported the view of Milton Obote that the independence constitution, abrogated at Obote's urging in 1966, was imposed on Ugandans. It is true that the British played to some extent on Ugandans' eagerness for independence, encouraging uncritical acceptance of certain British constitutional assumptions (for example in the failure to more realistically institutionalize the army's role in an otherwise divided society) and rushing discussion of matters that merited careful consideration. But the federal status accorded the kingdoms of Buganda, Toro, Ankole, and Bunyoro, and the district of Busoga, resulted from the initiative and insistence of Ugandan leaders, with broad popular support. Secondary sources; 36 notes. L. Van Wyk

3284. Nursey-Bray, Paul. UGANDA: THE RESISTABLE RISE OF IDI AMIN? *Flinders J. of Hist. and Pol. [Australia] 1974 4: 95-116.* Analyzes the events leading to the Ugandan military coup d'etat of January 1971, which inaugurated Idi Amin's military dictatorship. Examines alternative interpretations of the causes of the coup, and argues that it demonstrates the collapse of a weak and stagnating political system, a view justified by subsequent events. Secondary sources; 42 notes. P. J. Beck

3285. Oded, Arye. THE BAYUDAYA OF UGANDA. *J. of Religion in Africa [Netherlands] 1974 6(3): 167-189.* The Bayudaya are a Jewish community located mainly in the Busoga district of Uganda. Its population was over 500 in 1966, an increase of 70% from 1962. Its founder, Semei Kakungulu, broke away from Christianity in the early 1900's. In the early Baganda-British conflict, Kakungulu played a key role. His relationship with the Malaki sect is explored and his religious search is outlined. Finally in the 1920's he converted to Judaism. The center of the Bayudaya community is a synagogue made of wood and plaster. It is a poor community, but its members are striving to be perfect Jews. 22 notes. H. G. Soff

3286. Pankrat'ev, V. P. POLITICHESKIE SILY UGANDY NAKANUNE NEZAVISIMOSTI [Political forces in Uganda on the eve of independence]. *Narody Azii i Afriki [USSR] 1979 (2): 100-107.* Problems of independent Uganda can be foreseen in the play of forces on the eve of independence. Analyzes the different political parties and their policies, as well as class and ethnic conflicts. The bourgeoisie became too powerful and rivalry between ethnic groups intensified. While the colonial authorities were in charge these problems remained beneath the surface, but when they were driven away, the troubles reappeared. Draws parallels with the USSR, but concludes that Uganda chose the wrong path. 28 notes. V. A. Packer

3287. Pirouet, M. Louise. RELIGION IN UGANDA UNDER AMIN. *J. of Religion in Africa [Netherlands] 1980 11(1): 13-29.* In Uganda under Idi Amin Roman Catholics outnumbered Anglicans three to two and Muslims comprised about 5% of the population. Through a very complex relationship with the state, the churches provided alternative structures and foci of loyalty at a time when most structures had broken down. Based on personal communications and media sources; 47 notes. R. J. Jirran

3288. Provizer, Norman W. NATIONAL ELECTORAL PROCESS AND STATE BUILDING: PROPOSALS FOR NEW METHODS OF ELECTION IN UGANDA. *Comparative Pol. 1977 9(3): 305-326.* Examines the electoral process in Ugandan national elections, 1961-62, and the problems which they were thought to cause for state-building. Discusses revisions in the process following the constitutional crisis of 1966 and recent proposals for reform.

3289. Quam, Michael D. CATTLE MARKETING AND PASTORAL CONSERVATISM: KARAMOJA DISTRICT, UGANDA, 1948-1970. *African Studies Rev. 1978 21(1): 49-71.* The Karimojong pastoralists are not economically conservative but rather economic nationalists who have not participated fully in government cattle marketing schemes because of the unreliability of the market and because of government failures to provide incentives. 4 tables, biblio. R. T. Brown

3290. Ravenhill, F. J. THE MILITARY AND POLITICS IN UGANDA. *Africa Q. [India] 1979 19(2): 122-147.* Discusses the background to the military coup which brought Idi Amin to power in 1971 and examines his economic policies up to 1979.

3291. Ravenhill, F. J. MILITARY RULE IN UGANDA: THE POLITICS OF SURVIVAL. *African Studies Rev. 1974 17(1): 229-260.* The Amin coup of 1971 was achieved with great ease, but President Idi Amin of Uganda encountered problems in domestic policy, internal military matters, economic issues, and foreign affairs that weakened his position, 1971-74.

3292. Rogers, Rolf E. and Odwori-Mboko, Mally. BUREAUCRACY AND MODERNIZATION IN UGANDA. *Internat. J. of Contemporary Sociol. 1973 10(2/3): 89-108.*

3293. Rollow, Jonathan. UGANDA'S AMIN'S ECONOMIC REVOLUTION. *Africa Report 1974 19(3): 36-38, 42.*

3294. Rowe, John A. CONTINUITIES AND DISCONTINUITIES IN BUGANDA HISTORY. *Kenya Hist. Rev. [Kenya] 1977 5(1): 134-139.* Reviews Anthony Low's *Buganda in Modern History* (1971) which discusses the rivalry between hereditary chiefs and senior appointed office holders in 20th-century Buganda and the revival of the Kabaka's role as a central figure of authority.

3295. Ryan, Selwyn D. ECONOMIC NATIONALISM AND SOCIALISM IN UGANDA. *J. of Commonwealth Pol. Studies [Great Britain] 1973 11(2): 140-158.* Describes the economic policies pursued by Milton Obote and Idi Amin in Uganda and the emphasis each placed upon nationalism, 1966-71.

3296. Sathyamurthy, T. V. THE SOCIAL BASE OF THE UGANDA PEOPLE'S PARTY, 1958-70. *African Affairs [Great Britain] 1975 74(297): 442-460.* The Uganda People's Party (UPC) was a strong political force during its entire existence. It was formed in the late 1950's and was swept into power during independence. During the coup d'etat of 1971 the Party was removed from power and it has been extinct since that time. The author analyzes the complex political background to the origins and growth of the UPC, and the roles of Milton Obote and Sir Edward Mutesa II, the Kabaka (king of the Baganda). Of key importance to the ultimate role of the UPC was its inability to be a potent factor among the Baganda during the early years of independence. When Obote forced the removal of the Kabaka, his grass roots support fell and this was a key that led to the successful coup that overthrew him in 1971. 34 notes. H. G. Soff

3297. Savitski, Iu. POSLE DOLGOI NOCHI [After a long night]. *Aziia i Afrika Segodnia [USSR] 1981 (4): 11-13.* Discusses the economic problems confronting Uganda after the rule of Idi Amin, which are related to both the process of economic restoration and to domestic religious controversies, and outlines the USSR's attempts to alleviate Uganda's difficulties.

3298. Schwebel, Stephen M. THE MOBILIZATION OF SHAME. *Vista 1973 8(4): 16-19.* Reviews the world's reactions to Uganda's expulsion of Asians in 1972, an act which violated the principles of international law and the norms of human rights fostered by the United Nations. H. M. Evans

3299. Scotton, James F. THE FIRST AFRICAN PRESS IN EAST AFRICA: PROTEST AND NATIONALISM IN UGANDA IN THE 1920S. *Internat. J. of African Hist. Studies 1973 6(2): 211-228.* Examines the earliest nationalist press in East Africa in the 1920's, its contributions, and its social and political response to British colonial government. The landed chiefs, particularly Buganda Prime Minister Sir Apolo Kagwa, were frequently the subject of attack in the press. The British, however, did nothing to counter this until their own position in Uganda was questioned by the Swahili, Kikuyu, and Luganda language papers. Among the significant papers and editors were *Sekanyolya* (later *Gambuze)* founded by Sefanio K. Sentongo and Daudi S. Bassude, *Munyonyozi* published by Joswa Kate Mugema, and *Dobozi lya Buganda* (Voice of Buganda) edited by Yusufu S. Bamuta. Assessment of these newspapers is difficult, and this has perhaps led to an underrating of their influence. 78 notes. C. W. Olson

3300. Shaw, Timothy. UGANDA UNDER AMIN: THE COSTS OF CONFRONTING DEPENDENCE. *Africa Today 1973 20(2): 32-45.* Describes General Idi Amin's expulsion of "foreigners" and elimination of domestic enemies as a populist-militaristic solution to the dependency which characterizes the economies of developing nations. Possibly Amin's actions have substituted a dependency on the Arab bloc supported by the officer corps for the old dependencies. 30 notes. G. O. Gagnon

3301. Short, Philip. AMIN: AN AFRICAN EXPERIMENT LACED WITH "BLUDGEON DIPLOMACY." *Internat. Perspectives [Canada] 1973 (1): 43-46.* Traces the background and effects of the invasion from Tanzania and the expulsion of the Asians from Uganda, both of which helped to restore Amin's credibility. L. S. Frey

3302. Short, Phillip. PUTTING IT IN PERSPECTIVE. *Africa Report 1973 18(2): 34-38.* Discusses the evolution in Uganda's government since the 1971 coup d'etat by which Idi Amin assumed power. S

3303. Southall, Aidan. GENERAL AMIN AND THE COUP: GREAT MAN OR HISTORICAL INEVITABILITY? *J. of Modern African Studies [Great Britain] 1975 13(1): 85-106.* A study of the career of General Haji Idi Amin Dada demonstrating that he is not "a bizarre or maverick intrusion upon the Uganda political scene, but is deeply and significantly entwined in it." He is a Nubi and his a dominantly Nubi regime. The Nubi emerged about 1885, having adopted some Muslim ways and feeling a certain superiority to others, but they were always regarded as alien. A study of Amin's rise to power reveals a man of remarkable, but also often self-contradictory, qualities. The process is "one of dialectical inevitability. To the corrupting effect of absolute power on the army is being added the corrupting power of wealth." 35 notes. R. V. Ritter

3304. Southall, Aidan. SOCIAL DISORGANISATION IN UGANDA: BEFORE, DURING, AND AFTER AMIN. *J. of Modern African Studies [Great Britain] 1980 18(4): 627-656.* Assesses political turmoil and later eventual economic and social chaos in independent Uganda. The marginal role of the Nubi in Ugandan society and the problem of Buganda continued after independence in 1962, leading to the use of violence as public policy by the Obote government and the rise of Idi Amin. The decline and fall of Amin, 1976-79, resulted from the total economic disarray and universal corruption associated with control of Amin's military and police. Its effects have continued to disorient society and prolong violence and political instability in the post-Amin period. Based on personal communications, newspapers, and secondary sources; note. L. W. Truschel

3305. Szupejko, Malgorzata. OD PROTEKTORATU DO RZADÓW WOJSKOWYCH: PROCES PRZEMIAN POLITYCZNYCH W UGANDZIE [From protectorate to military government: the process of political change in Uganda]. *Przegląd Socjologiczny [Poland] 1979 31(2): 91-112.* Provides the background for the successful coup of General Idi Amin in Uganda in 1971, emphasizing the role played by ethnic antagonisms in Uganda's domestic conflicts, in the administration of Uganda under British rule, and in bringing Milton Obote, Amin's immediate predecessor, into power in 1962.

3306. Tawa, Habib. OUGANDA: L'ÉTAT, L'ETHNIE ET LE COLON [Uganda: state, ethnicity, and the colonist]. *Histoire [France] 1981 (39): 84-86.* Examines Uganda and the aftereffects of Idi Amin Dada's rule. Even after President Milton Obote's return to power, social and political confusion persists. Examines Uganda's history to discover the roots of the current impasse.

3307. Taylor, Thomas F. THE STRUGGLE FOR ECONOMIC CONTROL OF UGANDA, 1919-1922: FORMULATION OF AN ECONOMIC POLICY. *Int. J. of African Hist. Studies 1978 11(1): 1-31.* By 1919 it had become apparent that the two officially encouraged economic systems in Uganda, the cultivation of both European plantation and indigenous African crops, were inherently incapable of coexistence. Both the protectorate and colonial governments had acknowledged that African agriculture in Uganda was the dominant mode of production for export by 1922. The encouragement of the African agricultural system was the most expedient and least costly method of increasing the supply of raw cotton to British mills, and was not motivated by interest in the welfare of Africans. 119 notes. M. M. McCarthy

3308. Thobani, Akbarali. POLITICAL DEVELOPMENT IN UGANDA. *Africa Today 1973 20(2): 62-66.* Reviews G. S. K. Ibingira's *The Forging of an African Nation* (Viking Press, 1973) and Peter Gukiina's *Uganda: A Case Study in African Political Development* (Notre Dame U. Press, 1972). G. O. Gagnon

3309. Tosh, John. COLONIAL CHIEFS IN A STATELESS SOCIETY: A CASE STUDY FROM NORTHERN UGANDA. *J. of African Hist. [Great Britain] 1973 14(3): 473-490.* Discusses the problems British colonial administrators had with the highly fragmented Lango people of Uganda. The first new chiefs represented a continuity with the precolonial order but were completely unfamiliar with the range of their extensive executive and judicial powers. From 1920 to 1933 the county chiefs gained extensive power and established patronage systems which led to popular estrangement from the administration. These abuses came to light in 1933, but reforms did not come until the 1950's. Primary and secondary sources; 72 notes. C. Hopkins

3310. Tosh, John. LANGO AGRICULTURE DURING THE EARLY COLONIAL PERIOD: LAND AND LABOUR IN A CASH-CROP ECONOMY. *J. of African Hist. [Great Britain] 1978 19(3): 415-439.* Labor constraints and the attraction of competing crops were of equal significance with administrative pressure, price incentives, and petty trading by immigrant minorities in the adoption of cotton growing by the Lango of Uganda in the early 20th century. Cotton, introduced in 1909, could be cultivated only with the sacrifice of a valuable sesame trade. Only in the 1920's, when the sesame market declined and the price of cotton rose, the threat of famine was alleviated, and traditional dry season occupations were modified, did the Lango make the transition. Output ceased to expand after 1931, due to an extremely rugged environment, a simple technology, and a fully occupied labor force. Map, 145 notes. A. W. Novitsky

3311. Turyahikayo-Rugyema, B. THE BRITISH IMPOSITION OF COLONIAL RULE ON UGANDA: THE BAGANDA AGENTS IN KIGEZI (1908-1930). *Transafrican J. of Hist. [Kenya] 1976 5(1): 111-133.* British administrators in colonial Uganda often used the Baganda as agents to enforce colonial rule. The author assesses local reaction by the Bakiga to Baganda interference in their traditional way of life. Although the Germans and Belgians had entered Kigezi earlier, the British brought stability. The author emphasizes the role of Ssbalijja who was put in charge of the whole colonial administration of Kigezi. The Baganda were withdrawn in 1929, but the preceding years had seen revolts, rebellions, and the Nyabingi cult standing out as a major factor against alien rule. Map, 48 notes. H. G. Soff

3312. Twaddle, Michael. THE OUSTING OF IDI AMIN: REGIME'S SWIFT COLLAPSE TOOK TANZANIA BY SURPRISE. *Round Table [Great Britain] 1979 (275): 216-221.* Although Tanzania had fought against Uganda since 1978, its government was surprised at the speed with which the regime of President Idi Amin Dada was overthrown in 1979.

3313. Usoigwe, G. N. RECORDING THE ORAL HISTORY OF AFRICA: REFLECTIONS FROM FIELD EXPERIENCES IN BUNYORO. *African Studies R. 1973 16(2): 183-201.*

3314. Vincent, Joan. COLONIAL CHIEFS AND THE MAKING OF CLASS: A CASE STUDY FROM TESO, EASTERN UGANDA. *Africa [Great Britain] 1977 47(2): 140-159.* Studies Teso District, Eastern Uganda, 1896-1927, where a group of chiefs emerged having neither the stature of traditional rulers nor a hereditary principle of succession to political office. Traces the bureaucratic and authoritarian growth of client chiefship, the changes in relations between the chiefs and the colonial government, as well as with the people. The chiefs' increasing powers of coercion and patronage led to class interest among them, which crystallized in the mid-1920's when they formed a conservative bloc within a colonial administration geared to change. Based on Teso District Archives and secondary sources; map, 5 tables, 45 notes. M. Smith

3315. Vincent, Joan. VISIBILITY AND VULNERABILITY: THE POLITICS OF PACEMAKERS. *Africa [Great Britain] 1974 44(3): 222-234.* An anthropological case study of a Luo entrepreneur who views two pacemaking groups—the Luo and the salariat (administrators, ginnery owners, and shopkeepers)—as his reference groups in the small trading center of Gondo in Eastern Uganda in 1966. Pacemaking groups are characterized by their success with the authorities, achievements in economic life, and efficient mobilization and organization of supporters. While such groups tend to be highly visible and politically vulnerable, any consideration of relative deprivation and felt resentment against pacemaking groups must be related to a study of the avenues of mobility open to the masses. In the case of Gondo, successful Luo did not organize corporately, politicize their ethnicity, or become visible and resented whereas the salariat became the object of marked grassroots discontent as expressed in violence and mob disorder. Based on field work and secondary sources; 12 notes, biblio. C. Fry

3316. Wallace, Tina. WORKING IN RURAL BUGANDA: A STUDY OF THE OCCUPATIONAL ACTIVITIES OF YOUNG PEOPLE IN RURAL VILLAGES. *African R. [Tanzania] 1973 3(1): 133-178.* Analyzes the concepts of formal and informal employment opportunities in a village 17 miles from Kampala. Everyone from 13-25 years of age was contacted with a questionnaire in 1970, and a second one in 1971. In addition, all young people in the village were personally interviewed. Although there are fewer males than females in the village, they hold 64 percent of the jobs. Those who have a formal secondary-school education occupy over 69 percent of the formal jobs, and on an average earn four times the salary of informal workers. Several case studies are presented, based on the educational achievement of the subject. 12 tables, 59 notes, appendixes. H. G. Soff

3317. Walraet, M. DESTIN D'UNE MINORITÉ: LES INDIENS EN UGANDA [Fate of a minority: the Indians in Uganda]. *Bull. des Séances de l'Acad. Royale des Sci. d'Outre-Mer [Belgium] 1973 (2): 138-169.* A brief history of the East Indian presence in East Africa and the actions of Idi Amin in August 1972. To extend the slave trade in the 19th century, Sa'id Ibn Sultan surrounded himself with Indian counselors and merchants who continued to enrich themselves and became essential to the African economy. This wealth created both jealousy and xenophobia. Following World War II, Africans feared that the Asians would use their economic influence in politics to permanently evict Africans from commerce and industry. Growing African nationalism inevitably altered the friendly relations. Asian commercial supremacy became intolerable to the Africans. Amin expelled all Asians holding foreign passports. Biblio. H. D. Nycz

3318. Weeks, Sheldon G. WHERE ARE ALL THE JOBS? THE INFORMAL SECTOR IN BUGISU, UGANDA. *African R. [Tanzania] 1973 3(1): 111-132.* Analyzes informal occupational activities of rural youth, including farming and cottage industries. Several case studies are presented and the interaction between youth and the local weekly market is discussed. Those in formal jobs are usually males, older, in urban areas, and more educated than rural youth in informal jobs. 6 tables, 25 notes. H. G. Soff

3319. Willetts, Peter. THE POLITICS OF UGANDA AS A ONE-PARTY STATE 1969-1970. *African Affairs [Great Britain] 1975 74(296): 278-299.* Contrary to popular belief, during the year of President Milton Obote's one-party state there was serious political activity at high levels. This is a summary of the events leading to that activity. The author traces politics in Uganda from independence in 1962, the move to the left (Common Man's Charter), and development of the National Service. Following these advances, in late 1969 Obote announced a one-party state, and in 1970 he announced new directives including nationalization of major industries. Opponents claimed that Uganda was a police state. Obote, however, needed the masses of people to maintain power. His greatest fault was his underestimation of Idi Amin, who was stealing, plotting, and murdering his way to power even before the coup of 1971. 75 notes. H. G. Soff

3320. Youé, Christopher P. COLONIAL ECONOMIC POLICY IN UGANDA AFTER WORLD WAR I: A REASSESSMENT. *Int. J. of African Hist. Studies 1979 12(2): 270-276.* Comments on the essay by Thomas Taylor concerning the transition phase of the Ugandan colonial economy from the end of World War I to 1921 (see abstract 3307). Taylor stressed the significance of the international trade depression and the influence of British cotton manufacturers, but has not quite understood the practice of economic policy, nor grasped the concept of the dual economy. 13 notes. M. M. McCarthy

3321. Youé, Christopher P. PEASANTS, PLANTERS AND COTTON CAPITALISTS: THE "DUAL ECONOMY" IN COLONIAL UGANDA. *Can. J. of African Studies [Canada] 1978 12(2): 163-184.* Traces the economic policy of the British colonial government in Uganda from the end of World War I to 1929. The direction of land economics was the responsibility of the governor and of local officials, though the Treasury held a potent veto by simple rule of finances. Plantation agriculture played a secondary role in Uganda's economy; the cotton raised by peasants was the major revenue producer and an important raw material for Britain's economy. 108 notes. G. E. Pergl

3322. —. [BANKING TRENDS IN UGANDA]. *Econ. Development and Cultural Change 1976 24(2): 417-422.*

Abdi, Ali. BANKING IN UGANDA SINCE INDEPENDENCE: COMMENT, *pp. 417-419.* Ugandan banks' poor performance in promoting economic development is due to rudimentary market they operate in rather than force of habit cited by Gershenberg.

Gershenberg, Irving. BANKING IN UGANDA SINCE INDEPENDENCE: REPLY, *pp. 421-422.* Abdi's explanation is in reality the same as that proposed in the original article.

3323. —. BEHIND THE RHETORIC IN UGANDA—THE EXPULSION OF THE ASIANS. *Internat. Perspectives [Canada] 1973 (1): 39-43.* Discusses the emergence of the East African middle class as a prosperous minority that dominated commerce and the civil service. The continuing campaign of Africanization led to General Idi Amin's expulsion of Asians in August 1972. The departure of the Asians produced an acute shortage of skilled manpower and disrupted the economy. Prepared by African Affairs Division, Canadian Department of External Affairs. L. S. Frey

3324. —. [HUMAN RIGHTS IN UGANDA]. *Munger Africana Lib. Notes 1982 (67): 3-27.*

Lule, Yusef. HUMAN RIGHTS VIOLATIONS IN UGANDA UNDER OBOTE, *pp. 3-12.* History of human rights violations including torture, murder, and rape during the past 20 years.

—. OMBACI AND OTHER WEST NILE MASSACRES, *pp. 13-15.* Personal account of group murders in 1981.

Wamala, Bakulu-Mpagi. INSIDE OBOTE'S JAIL, *pp. 16-24.* Personal account of abduction, beating, murder, and rape in March and April 1981.

Nyakato, Evelyn. MY EXPERIENCE IN MAKINDYE MILITARY PRISON, *pp. 25-27.* Personal account of abduction and beating of an elementary school teacher during November and December 1981.

3325. —. INSIDE AMIN'S UGANDA: MORE AFRICANS MURDERED. *Munger Africana Lib. Notes 1973 (18): 11-22.*

3326. —. OPERATION JONATHAN: THE RESCUE AT ENTEBBE. *Military Rev. 1982 62(7): 2-23.* Transcript of an interview with the deputy commander of the 1976 Israeli commando raid on Entebbe, describing the planning and execution of the operation, and the circumstances around the death of the Israeli commander, Lieutenant Colonel Jonathan (Yoni) Netanyahu. Photo, 3 maps; 7 notes. D. H. Cline

3327.Describes the capricious disruption of Uganda by General Idi Amin since 1971. Concludes that Amin rules Uganda like a Chinese warlord, with the support of his unrestrained, pampered army. Opponents just disappear. Uganda will remain a subsistence economy, with future dependence on the Arab bloc. Based on secondary sources and personal observation; 68 notes. G. O. Gagnon

11. SOUTHERN AFRICA

General

(including islands of the Indian Ocean)

3328. Adebisi, Busari. ALLIANCE FOR OPPRESSION: PRE-COUP PORTUGAL, RHODESIA AND SOUTH AFRICA VERSUS BLACKS. *Co-Existence [Great Britain] 1976 13(2): 190-208.* Discusses the racial exploitation of Africans in the apartheid policy of South Africa and Rhodesia and the neocolonialism of Portugal and Great Britain in the 1960's and 70's.

3329. Adebisi, Busari. ALLIANCE FOR OPPRESSION: PRE-COUP PORTUGAL, RHODESIA AND SOUTH AFRICA VERSUS BLACKS. *Africa Q. [India] 1977 16(4): 5-26.* Analyzes political and economic mechanisms for the oppression of Africans in Rhodesia, South Africa, and former Portuguese colonies in Africa, and finds closely similar techniques in a common aim of exploitation.

3330. Adelman, Kenneth. WESTERN POLICY IN SOUTHERN AFRICA. *Current Hist. 1980 78(455): 124-126.* Discusses Western diplomatic activities in colonial Zimbabwe and South Africa during the 1970's.

3331. Ahmad, Naveed. GREAT POWER INVOLVEMENT IN SOUTHERN AFRICA. *Pakistan Horizon [Pakistan] 1978 31(2-3): 57-85.* Discusses the relations of the United States, the USSR, and China with colonial Zimbabwe, South Africa, and Namibia during the 1970's.

3332. Anglin, Douglas G. ZAMBIAN CRISIS BEHAVIOR: RHODESIA'S UNILATERAL DECLARATION OF INDEPENDENCE. *Int. Studies Q. 1980 24(4): 581-616.* Zambia's decision makers perceived Southern Rhodesia's unilateral declaration of independence in 1965 as a threat to their basic values. Their greatest concerns were loss of Zambian influence in Southern Africa, internal security, and economic vulnerability. The conclusions of this study accord in some respects with models described in Michael Brecher's International Crisis Behavior Project. 6 tables, 2 fig., 34 notes. E. S. Palais

3333. Auala, Leonard N. THE OVAMBO: OUR PROBLEMS AND HOPES. *Munger Africana Lib. Notes 1973 (17): 10-32.* Examines the situation of the Ovambo people, the largest ethnic group inhabiting the sparse country near the border of Namibia and Angola. S

3334. Azevedo, Mario J. "A SOBER COMMITMENT TO LIBERATION?" MOZAMBIQUE AND SOUTH AFRICA, 1974-1979. *African Affairs [Great Britain] 1980 79(317): 567-584.* Prior to Mozambican independence in 1975, Mozambique's political, economic, and social ties with South Africa had grown so strong that it was a virtual satellite. Mozambique still cooperates with South Africa in the economic sphere and may give the impression of contributing to the maintenance of apartheid. But cutting all ties would be an economic disaster, which neither country desires. Thus two political adversaries continue to deal with each other and make the best of the present situation. 78 notes. J. V. Coutinho

3335. Baker, Donald G. THE IMPACT OF REGIONAL EVENTS ON WHITES IN RHODESIA AND SOUTH AFRICA. *Plural Soc. [Netherlands] 1979 10(1): 27-58.* Whites in South Africa have responded to black nationalist advances in Southern Africa with ever firmer resistance, but in Rhodesia whites moved toward accommodation.

3336. Baldock, R. W. TOWARDS A HISTORY OF INSURGENCY IN RHODESIA. *Rhodesian Hist. [Zimbabwe] 1974 5: 97-102.* Reviews 11 works which deal specifically or peripherally with guerrilla movements in Zimbabwe and southern Africa published during 1971-75. The withdrawal of Portugal from Angola and Mozambique has heightened the role of these national liberation movements. At the same time it has become more difficult to obtain hard data on questions of size, structure, political orientation, and funding of these groups. Comprehensive accounts await the end of the liberation phase. O. B. Pollak

3337. Barratt, John. DÉTENTE IN SOUTHERN AFRICA. *World Today [Great Britain] 1975 31(3): 120-130.* Deals "with some of the effects of the dramatic change in Mozambique on international relations in Southern Africa and, in particular, the immediate issue of Rhodesia" in 1974. S

3338. Beebe, Lucius. SOUTH AFRICA: SEEDBED OF REVOLUTION. *Rev. Militaire Générale [France] 1973 (2): 266-273.* China is a major source of foreign aid to the black nationalist movements in southern Africa. Both China and the USSR are supporting national liberation movements operating in Angola, Mozambique, Rhodesia, South Africa, and Southwest Africa. Their success has been hindered by ethnic and ideological divisions and the absence of coordination, although steps have been taken to remedy these weaknesses. Warns that southern Africa may be the next area in which Communist expansionism will be opposed. J. S. Gassner

3339. Bowman, Larry W. VESTEN OG DET SØRLIGE AFRIKA: STRATEGISK BETINGET TILNAERMING? [The Nixon doctrine and regional strategic planning in southern Africa]. *Internasjonal Politikk [Norway] 1974 (2): 301-314.* "The author describes the evolution and development of United States foreign policy toward Southern Africa and in this context adaptations in accordance with the Nixon doctrine. He further points to the rapidly growing Western economic ties to Southern Africa, and especially Europe's increasing dependence on raw materials from this region. This, in addition to the growth of the liberation movements and the movements of the Soviet navy into Southern Oceans, has triggered the explosion of interest in strategic matters relating to Southern Africa, whereby the security interests of the white regimes are being embraced by the United States and its major European allies." J

3340. Brionne, Bernard. LE CANAL DE MOZAMBIQUE ET LA SÉCURITÉ DE L'AFRIQUE DU SUD [The Mozambique Channel and the safety of South Africa]. *Défense Natl. [France] 1976 32(2): 125-141.* The history of Mozambique's and Madagascar's colonization explains their domestic politics and political orientation.

3341. Bushin, V. SOTSIALISTICHESKII INTERNATSIONAL I PROBLEMY IUGA AFRIKI [The Socialist International and problems of the south of Africa]. *Aziia i Afrika Segodnia [USSR] 1981 (7): 19-23.* Criticizes the duplicity of the policy of the Socialist International of Western Europe toward southern African countries, 1978-80.

3342. Chanaiwa, David. HISTORIOGRAPHICAL TRADITIONS OF SOUTHERN AFRICA. *J. of Southern African Affairs 1978 3(2): 175-193.* A general discussion of the historiography of Southern Africa. Writers on Southern Africa fall into five camps: the imperial, missionary, African, colonialist, and liberal/revisionist. The imperial, missionary, and colonialist traditions are essentially racist. The African school eventually arrived at a race consciousness and hostility to colonialism but was unresponsive to the African masses until about 1950. The liberal/revisionist outlook is the most promising, but its white liberal architects tend to pose as "intellectual district commissioners" and upholders of a sense of false objectivity to emerging African scholars. 39 notes. L. W. Truschel

3343. Cobbe, James. WAGE POLICY PROBLEMS IN THE SMALL PERIPHERAL COUNTRIES OF SOUTHERN AFRICA, 1967-1976. *J. of Southern African Affairs 1977 2(4): 441-468.* Compares the economies, the labor markets, and wage and employment policies in Botswana, Lesotho, and Swaziland. "The integration into the larger Southern African economy extends . . . into labor markets to a surprising degree." In none of the three countries does the government have the whole-hearted support of all its citizens. South Africa's peculiar wage structure based on racial differentials in wages explains labor market developments in the small peripheral countries. 2 tables, 68 notes. E. P. Stickney

3344. Coetzer, J. van H. BLACK WORKERS FROM ZIMBABWE IN SOUTH AFRICA. *NADA [Zimbabwe] 1980 12(2): 100-109.* Discusses the history in South Africa of legal and illegal labor migrants from three major Zimbabwe African groups, the Kalanga of Matabeleland, Manica and Karanga Shona, and Hlengwe, and official measures adopted in recent years to treat the problems of labor migrations. Legal controls since the 1940's have varied and been generally unsuccessful, due to registration restrictions, removal of immediately disposable income as deferred pay, repatriation fees, and fears of government controls. Table. L. W. Truschel

3345. Coker, Christopher. EAST GERMANY AND SOUTHERN AFRICA. *J. of Social and Pol. Studies 1980 5(3): 231-244.* Examines the converging interests of East Germany and the USSR in southern Africa and suggests that East Germany's role in the conflicts of that region from 1978 to 1980 may have been much more significant than that of Cuba.

3346. Coker, Christopher. THE UNITED STATES AND NATIONAL LIBERATION IN SOUTHERN AFRICA. *African Affairs [Great Britain] 1979 78(312): 319-330.* The most important of US problems in southern Africa since 1976 is the uneasy relationship between American realism and African radicalism. The United States is still trying to prevent national liberation from undermining the economic infrastructure of southern Africa, and continues to see multinational corporations and their marketing operations as vital in linking the region into the international economy. America's Agency for International Development programs have gradually improved. The USSR can provide technical skills but little else. The United States has still not faced up to the responsibilities attaching to the central position it occupies in the national liberation struggle. Based on published speeches and documents; 29 notes. R. L. Collison

3347. Collings, Francis d'A. et al. THE RAND AND THE MONETARY SYSTEMS OF BOTSWANA, LESOTHO, AND SWAZILAND. *J. of Modern African Studies [Great Britain] 1978 16(1): 97-121.* Botswana, Lesotho, and Swaziland began in 1974 to officially use the South African Rand as their domestic currency. The author traces their economic ties to South Africa since the South Africa Act of 1909, analyzes currency agreements, and discusses the Rand Monetary Area (RMA) agreement. Today Lesotho is most dependent on South Africa, Botswana has its own currency, and Swaziland uses both the Rand and its own currency. 5 notes. H. G. Soff

3348. Cooper, Frederick. PEASANTS, CAPITALISTS AND HISTORIANS: REVIEW ARTICLE. *J. of Southern African Studies [Great Britain] 1981 7(2): 284-314.* Reviews the following works on the emergence and decline of African peasantries in relation to capitalist development in South Africa or Angola: Colin Bundy's *The Rise and Fall of the South African Peasantry* (1979), W. G. Clarence-Smith's *Slaves, Peasants and Capitalists in Southern Angola 1840-1926* (1979), and William Justin Beinart's "Production, Labour Migrancy and Chieftaincy: Aspects of the Political Economy of Pondoland, ca. 1860-1930" (Ph. D. Dissertation, University of London). Secondary sources; 56 notes. L. W. Truschel

3349. D'Aguiar, Joaquim António. SITUAÇÃO DA IGREJA CATOLICA NOS ESTADOS DE EXPRESSÃO CULTURAL PORTUGUESA [Situation of the Catholic Church in the states of Portuguese culture]. *Independência [Portugal] 1981 2(3): 40-51.* Describes the rationale of missionary work in the former African colonies in alliance with the colonial powers, acknowledges the ambiguity of such activity and its consequences, and examines the present-day situation of the Catholic Church in Mozambique and Angola.

3350. Dale, Richard. COLONIAL RULERS AND RULED IN SOUTH WEST AFRICA AND THE BECHUANALAND PROTECTORATE, 1884-1966: A FRAMEWORK FOR A COMPARATIVE STUDY. *J. of Southern African Affairs 1976 9(special issue): 95-110.* Suggests ten particular facets of the colonial experience in Namibia and Botswana that could provide the basis for a later, more exhaustive study of comparative rule in southern Africa. Secondary sources; 57 notes. A. W. Howell

3351. Dale, Richard. POLITICAL CHANGES IN NAMIBIA, BOTSWANA, AND SWAZILAND. *Current Hist. 1976 71(411): 161-164, 183.* Examines the current political situations of Namibia (South-West Africa), where the white power structure is still intact, and the sovereign states under African majority rule of Botswana and Swaziland to illustrate the problems of tension and conflict in southern Africa.

3352. Dale, Richard. SOUTH AFRICA AND NAMIBIA: CHANGING THE GUARD AND GUARDED CHANGE. *Current Hist. 1979 76(445): 101-104, 136-137.* Discusses the political change in South Africa and Namibia in 1977 and 1978.

3353. Dale, Richard. SOUTH AFRICA AND NAMIBIA. *Current Hist. 1977 73(432): 209-213, 226-227.* Examines current political affairs in South Africa and Namibia, concluding that the settlement of black-white conflict is dependent on political, diplomatic, and, economic skills rather than military hardware. Namibia, through the cooperation of the South West African Peoples' Organization of Namibia and the Turnhalle group, which attempted in 1976 to draft a constitution for the newly forming government, will successfully reach its 1978 deadline for independence.

3354. Damu, Jean. SOUTHERN AFRICA: FROM ANGOLA TO SOWETO. *Black Scholar 1976 8(1): 2-11.* Discusses foreign intervention, primarily by Great Britain and the United States, in Angola, and in South Africa through continued support of the racist regime, 1961-76.

3355. Dekker, L. D.; Hemson, D.; Kane-Berman, J. S.; Lever, J.; and Schlemmer, L. CASE STUDIES IN AFRICAN LABOUR ACTION IN SOUTH AND SOUTH WEST AFRICA. *African Rev. [Tanzania] 1974 4(2): 205-236.* Analyzes several constraints which prevent Africans from organizing and exerting labor power. The case studies discussed include the Ovambo strike in Namibia during 1971-72, a strike action in Natal during 1973, the National Union of Clothing Workers in South Africa, and the Trade Union Council of South Africa. 62 notes. H. G. Soff

3356. Downey, Tom. CONGRESSIONAL AD HOC MONITORING GROUP ON SOUTHERN AFRICA. *J. of Southern African Affairs 1980 5(2): 171-181.* Describes the formation in 1977 and subsequent work of the Ad Hoc Monitoring Group on Southern Africa within the United States Congress. The AHMG was initiated by a number of Congressional liberals in response to the Steve Biko episode in South Africa, and has since sought to pressure the South African government on its political prisoners, apartheid practices, and involvement in South-West Africa. The AHMG also lobbied in Congress against acceptance of the Southern Rhodesian internal solution in 1979. 2 appendixes, 3 notes. L. W. Truschel

3357. Doxey, Margaret. STRATEGIES IN MULTILATERAL DIPLOMACY: THE COMMONWEALTH, SOUTHERN AFRICA, AND THE NIEO. *Int. J. [Canada] 1980 35(2): 329-356.* During the 1960's and 1970's international organizations became increasingly politicized by developing nations, which combined to focus attention on issues such as majority rule in Southern Rhodesia and South Africa and the call for a New International Economic Order. Pressure by developing nations, especially pressure on Britain within the Commonwealth, was largely successful in forcing sanctions against South Africa and Southern Rhodesia. But developing nations in the UN Conference on Trade and Development have been less successful in getting agreement on changes in the world economic order, perhaps because the issue is more global and less clearly defined. Primary sources; 39 notes. E. L. Keyser

3358. Duly, Leslie Clement and Wadlow, Joan Krueger. A REVIEW OF THE STUDY OF NATIONALISM IN SOUTHERN AFRICA, 1974-1979. *Can. Rev. of Studies in Nationalism [Canada] 1979 6(biblio): 173-194.* An annotated bibliography of works published between 1974-79 on nationalism in Southern Africa. J. Powell

3359. Ebert, James I. COMPARABILITY BETWEEN HUNTER-GATHERER GROUPS IN THE PAST AND PRESENT: MODERNIZATION VERSUS EXPLANATION. *Botswana Notes and Records [Botswana] 1978 10: 19-26.* Earlier descriptions of hunter-gatherer groups in southern Africa emphasized their tendencies toward territoriality; partrilineal organization, low mobility, and relatively high population density, while later reports stress low population density, a high degree of mobility, fluidity of social organization, and a lack of territoriality among the Bushmen groups. These apparently radical changes may be due not so much to adaptive reasons assumed by many anthropologists, but to great physical differences between the areas visited by the observers. The earlier accounts were usually of San groups living in relatively favored geographic areas, while later reports describe groups surviving in the much harsher Kalahari region. Based on fieldwork in Botswana and secondary sources; map, table, 31 notes, biblio. L. W. Truschel

3360. El-Ayouty, Yassin. ALIEN SETTLERISM AND THE REVOLUTIONARY RESPONSE IN SOUTHERN AFRICA: THE SIGNIFICANCE OF RECENT YEARS. *Issue 1975 5(1): 27-32.*

3361. Elkan, Walter. LABOR MIGRATION FROM BOTSWANA, LESOTHO, AND SWAZILAND. *Econ. Development and Cultural Change 1980 28(3): 583-596.* Examines the labor migration from Botswana, Lesotho, and Swaziland to South Africa and its effect on the sending countries, 1972-76. Although the labor migration provided needed jobs and foreign exchange, it also slowed internal economic development and made the three countries more dependent on South Africa. Based on government documents and published sources; 4 tables, 4 notes. J. W. Thacker, Jr.

3362. El-Khawas, Mohamed A. FOREIGN ECONOMIC INVOLVEMENT IN ANGOLA AND MOZAMBIQUE. *African Rev. [Tanzania] 1974 4(2): 299-314.* Liberation movements in Angola and Mozambique beginning in the early 1960's prompted Portugal to deviate from its policy of disinterest in fostering economic development and foreign investment in its African colonies. Since then, investments by European, American, and South African multinational corporations have allowed Portugal to undertake its colonial wars for the maintenance of the status quo in Southern Africa. These investments do not contribute to the welfare of the indigenous population or to the attainment of independence in Portuguese Africa. 49 notes. H. G. Soff/S

3363. El-Khawas, Mohamed A. FOREIGN ECONOMIC INVOLVEMENT IN ANGOLA AND MOZAMBIQUE. *Issue 1974 4(2): 21-28.* Foreign investments in Portuguese Africa have not been responsive to the interests of the African majority, but to Portugal. S

3364. El-Khawas, Mohamed A. SOUTH AFRICA AND THE ANGOLAN CONFLICT. *Africa Today 1977 24(2): 35-46.* Reviews the goals and results of South African intervention in Angola within the context of global great power competition and the African policies of South Africa. Intervention undermined South Africa's detente with other African nations, bolstered Cuban-Soviet influence, and led to the recognition of the Popular Movement for the Liberation of Angola (MPLA) by other African nations. Table, 40 notes. G. O. Gagnon

3365. Figueiredo, Antonio de. MOZAMBIQUE: PORTUGAL'S NEW ROLE. *Africa Report 1975 20(3): 6-9.* Portugal is still deeply involved in Mozambique and Angola, despite granting them independence, and must formulate new policies to deal with these countries. S

3366. Frank, Lawrence. KHAMA AND JONATHAN: LEADERSHIP STRATEGIES IN CONTEMPORARY SOUTHERN AFRICA. *J. of Developing Areas 1981 15(2): 173-198.* Applies Max Weber's three models of legitimacy—traditional, charismatic, and legal-rational—to political events and leadership strategies in Botswana and Lesotho and concludes that the two countries reveal radically contrasting situations. Seretse Khama established political authority on the basis of legal-rationalism in Botswana, but Leabua Jonathan failed to achieve legitimacy in Lesotho. 89 notes. V. Samaraweera

3367. Friedland, Elaine A. THE POLITICAL ECONOMY OF COLONIALISM IN SOUTH AFRICA AND MOZAMBIQUE. *J. of Southern African Affairs 1977 2(1): 61-75.* European settlers had a monopoly of land ownership while the local population existed in total subjugation, as noncitizens whose only role was to produce goods and services for the Europeans. The system thwarted the development of any substantial African petite bourgeoisie. 48 notes. E. P. Stickney

3368. Gann, L. H. PORTUGAL, AFRICA, AND THE FUTURE. *J. of Modern African Studies [Great Britain] 1975 13(1): 1-18.* Examines the outbreak of guerrilla warfare in northern Angola in 1961 and the influence of that revolt on various aspects of Portugal's African interests. Analyzes the colonial economy, the military resources, and the developments since the outbreak of hostilities as they affect the economy and the politics of Portuguese Africa. He explores the possible directions the situation may take and the interests of the USSR. An epilogue brings the situation up to 1975 for both Mozambique and Angola. 18 notes. R. V. Ritter

3369. Gitelson, Susan Aurelia. THE TRANSFORMATION OF THE SOUTHERN AFRICAN SUBORDINATE STATE SYSTEM. *J. of African Studies 1977-78 4(4): 367-391.* An analysis of the changing nature of the subordinate state system in Southern Africa since 1968. While the system has continued to exist largely under South African dominance, internal developments in Portugal and South Africa, and Zambian efforts to assert regional influence, tend to lessen Pretoria's dominant position. Table, 64 notes. L. W. Truschel

3370. Gromyko, A. EKONOMICHESKAIA EKSPANSIIA IMPERIALIZMA NA IUGE AFRIKI [Economic expansion of imperialism in southern Africa]. *Mirovaia Ekonomika i Mezhdunarodnye Otnosheniia [USSR] 1979 (9): 63-75.* Discusses the position of international monopolies of leading capitalist powers and colonial regimes in South Africa and Southern Rhodesia. Tables, biblio.

3371. Gromyko, A. OON I OSVOBODITEL'NAIA BOR'BA NARODOV IUGA AFRIKI PROTIV KOLONIZATOROV I RASISTOV [The UN and the liberation struggle of the peoples of southern Africa against colonialists and racists]. *Novaia i Noveishaia Istoriia [USSR] 1979 (4): 21-36.* Basing himself on the resolutions of the UN General Assembly and the Security Council, the author shows the role of the UN in the struggle against colonialists and racists in southern Africa, and exposes the imperialist powers' attempts to hamper the fulfilment of UN resolutions on this region. Analyzes such problems as Namibia's independence, the situation in Southern Rhodesia, and the UN's struggle against apartheid in the Republic of South Africa. J/S

3372. Henderson, Robert D'A. RELATIONS OF NEIGHBOURLINESS—MALAWI AND PORTUGAL 1964-74. *J. of Modern African Studies [Great Britain] 1977 15(3): 425-455.* Explains the decade of cordial foreign relations between black Malawi and white-controlled Mozambique, including relations with FRELIMO both before and since independence. Map, 4 tables, 95 notes. H. G. Soff

3373. Henriksen, Thomas H. ANGOLA AND MOZAMBIQUE: INTERVENTION AND REVOLUTION. *Current Hist. 1976 71(421): 153-157, 181.* Discusses events since the 1960's in these countries and the transformation of their moderate reformist independence movements into revolutionary governments, opposed to capitalism and the West and assisted by the USSR and China.

3374. Hirschmann, David. SOUTHERN AFRICA: DÉTENTE? *J. of Modern African Studies [Great Britain] 1976 14(1): 107-126.* The term detente, borrowed from superpower relations, has been used uncritically to describe the atmosphere of interstate relations in Southern Africa. The author defines detente, analyzes it into ten components, and applies them to Southern Africa. The early claims of detente were premature. Steadily improving communications brought about the first stage of detente by August, 1975, but only between Zambia and South Africa. This is a probationary phase that is narrowly circumscribed. It rests on the single issue of Zimbabwe and does not yet approach normalization or coexistence. Based on secondary sources; 22 notes. W. R. Hively

3375. Hudson, Derek J. BRIEF CHRONOLOGY OF CUSTOMS AGREEMENTS IN SOUTHERN AFRICA, 1855-1979. *Botswana Notes and Records [Botswana] 1979 11: 89-95.* Provides a chronology, with descriptive notes, of customs agreements and related events among the territories of Southern Africa since 1855, when the Cape Colony enacted its first tariff law. Major customs unions followed in 1889, 1903, 1910, and 1969. Based on Botswana government reports, unpublished theses, and secondary sources. L. W. Truschel

3376. Johnston, Thomas F. FOLKLORE EMPHASIS AMONG IMMIGRANT TSONGA: A UNIFYING MECHANISM? *Western Folklore 1975 34(2): 137-143.* Discusses the role of folksongs and folklore among the Tsonga of Mozambique and the Northern Transvaal "as a means of reducing social stress" and maintaining tribal cohesiveness. Includes a list of outside influences on Tsonga music. Primary and secondary sources; 16 notes. S. L. Myres

3377. Katzenellenbogen, Simon. ZAMBIA & RHODESIA: PRISONERS OF THE PAST. A NOTE ON THE HISTORY OF RAILWAY POLITICS IN CENTRAL AFRICA. *African Affairs [Great Britain] 1974 73(290): 63-66.* Traces the development of railway construction in Central and Southern Africa and the relation of the railway to the mining industry. Since the closure of the Zambia-Southern Rhodesia border, emphasis is given to the need of the Tan-Zam Railway. H. G. Soff

3378. Kiernan, J. P. AFRICAN RELIGIOUS RESEARCH: THEMES AND TRENDS IN THE STUDY OF BLACK RELIGION IN SOUTHERN AFRICA. *J. of Religion in Africa [Netherlands] 1981 12(2): 136-147.*

3379. Kiewiet, C. W. de. SOCIAL AND ECONOMIC TRENDS IN SOUTH AFRICA. *African Econ. Hist. 1976 (2): 33-39.* Reviews *Accelerated Development in Southern Africa* (New York: St. Martin's Pr., 1974) by John Barratt et al., editors, which is a compilation of addresses dealing with the political, economic, social, and racial conditions and development in Southern Africa, and assesses US relations with South Africa in particular.

3380. Kulik, Sergei. "GIGANTSKOE FIASKO" TSRU [The CIA's "gigantic fiasco"]. *Aziia i Afrika Segodnia [USSR] 1982 (5): 16-20.* Discusses the involvement of South Africa and the US Central Intelligence Agency in anti-Angolan and anti-Namibian movements, 1974-81, and comments on the purpose and activities of National Union for the Complete Independence of Angola (UNITA).

3381. Lancaster, C. S. THE ZAMBEZI GOBA ANCESTRAL CULT. *Africa [Great Britain] 1977 47(3): 229-241.* The basic institution among the Goba people from the Zambezi River area was, and is, the ancestral cult of the shades, a complex of relationship and ideas regularly linking deceased elders in a structural relationship to their living followers. This cult creates families and descent groups composed of real and fictitious junior kinsmen subject to the sanctions of deceased elder kinsmen whose wishes can only be satisfied through the intermediacy of senior living kinsmen. The system is a form of social control and helps maintain the village's family solidarity. Nowadays ancestral spirits are most often consulted on marital matters. Based on fieldwork; fig., 9 notes, biblio. R. L. Collison

3382. Landis, Elizabeth S. NOTES ON THE OSLO CONFERENCE ON SOUTHERN AFRICA: 9-14 APRIL 1973. *Africa Today 1972 20(2): 58-60.* The conference did not achieve its goal of providing practical directions for affecting the colonialist regimes of Southern Africa through the UN or governmental and independent organizations. G. O. Gagnon

3383. LeFur, Jean. SITUATION DES PAYS DE L'AFRIQUE AUSTRALE AUTRES QUE L'AFRIQUE DU SUD [The situation in southern Africa other than South Africa]. *Défense Natl. [France] 1980 36(7): 45-52.*

3384. Legum, Colin. "NATIONAL LIBERATION" IN SOUTHERN AFRICA. *Problems of Communism 1975 24(1): 1-20.* Investigates the political orientations of the various black liberation groups in Southern Africa and the factors that bear on their policies since the collapse of the Portuguese colonial empire in 1974. Centers on the liberators of Guinea-Bissau and Mozambique and the future of Angola, Namibia, Rhodesia, and South Africa. Primary and secondary English language sources; map, 31 notes. J. M. Lauber

3385. Low, A. R. C. THE EFFECT OF OFF-FARM EMPLOYMENT ON FARM INCOMES AND PRODUCTION: TAIWAN CONTRASTED WITH SOUTHERN AFRICA. *Econ. Development and Cultural Change 1981 29(4): 741-747.* Compares the effect of increased off-farm earning opportunities in Taiwan with Swaziland and Lesotho between 1960 and 1972. Although the transfer of labor from farming to off-farm employment is similar, Taiwan did not suffer substantial declines in agricultural production as did Swaziland and Lesotho. The author concludes that the production decline in the agricultural sector of the two Southern African countries is due to a labor shortage and less use of technology. Based on government documents and published sources; graph, 14 notes. J. W. Thacker, Jr.

3386. Luke, Timothy W. ANGOLA AND MOZAMBIQUE: INSTITUTIONALIZING SOCIAL REVOLUTION IN AFRICA. *Rev. of Pol. 1982 44(3): 413-436.* Discusses the rise of the Popular Movement for the Liberation of Angola (MPLA) and of FRELIMO in Mozambique, the roles of the guerrilla counterstates formed out of these factions, and the effects of these states on the institutionalization of revolution. Operating from a narrow political base in sparsely settled territory with a small labor force and few resources, the MPLA could never gain countryside support. Internal revolt, foreign threats, and inherent weaknesses in the political structure prevented MPLA forces from making further gains. The invitation of foreign elements into Angola's civil conflict is a manifestation of this weakness. In Mozambique, FRELIMO, although wracked by internal dissension, lacked opposition and effectively resisted the Portuguese. Stressing multiracial, nationalistic goals FRELIMO initiated reform programs in "liberated zones" in the countryside. Reforms have spread to the city, but fear of bureaucratization and elitism exists. Secondary sources; 46 notes. G. A. Glovins

3387. Lundahl, Mats and Ndlela, Daniel. LAND ALIENATION, DUALISM, AND ECONOMIC DISCRIMINATION: SOUTH AFRICA AND RHODESIA. *Econ. and Hist. [Sweden] 1980 23(2): 106-132.* Given that commodity price changes were small, land alienation linked with discrimination created an "unlimited" supply of black labor by gradually flattening the supply curve toward subsistence wage levels. The existence of such an "unlimited" supply of black labor—due to the fact that people were forced out of the traditional (agricultural) sector—is evident both for Southern Rhodesia, where real wages appear to have fallen between 1929 and 1945, and for South Africa, where they remained constant between 1911 and 1966. Based on secondary sources; fig., 116 notes. M. Geyer

3388. Madu, Oliver V. A. SOME PROBLEMS OF URBANIZATION IN CENTRAL AFRICA. *Pan-American J. [Kenya] 1973 6(2): 149-161.* Specifies urban problems which help explain the rise of rural African middle-class workers in Malawi and Zambia.

3389. Makambe, E. P. THE NYASALAND AFRICAN LABOUR "ULENDOS" TO SOUTHERN RHODESIA AND THE PROBLEM OF THE AFRICAN "HIGHWAYMEN," 1903-1923: A STUDY IN THE LIMITATIONS OF EARLY INDEPENDENT LABOUR MIGRATION. *African Affairs [Great Britain] 1980 79(317): 548-566.* Labor migration from Nyasaland to Southern Rhodesia was the object of policy differences between the colonial and native authorities as well as vulnerable to various obstacles en route. These obstacles were the result not only of physical and other general environmental factors but connected with diplomatic and historical aspects associated with the various territories which the *ulendos* or traveling parties had to traverse on their way south of the Zambesi, chief among these being the disagreements between the British and Portuguese colonial authorities. The migrants showed great resilience, but the migration had adverse effects on their home territories. Based on primary material in the Colonial Office archives, London; 84 notes. J. V. Coutinho

3390. Mangope, Lukas. WILL BOPHUTHATSWANA JOIN BOTSWANA? *Munger Africana Lib. Notes 1973 (20): 15-40.* Interview with Chief Minister Lukas Mangope of the Bophuthatswana Bantu Homeland, exploring the possibility of its incorporation with Botswana. S

3391. Matsepe, Ivy. UNDERDEVELOPMENT AND AFRICAN WOMEN. *J. of Southern African Affairs 1977 2(2): 135-143.* Studies the role of southern African women in economic, political and ideological terms. The integration of Africa into the capitalist system has produced underdevelopment, with women the main victims. Women initiated political resistance in the face of racist policies, but they hold no important posts in liberation organizations. The dominant ideology in this patriarchal, traditional society with the internalized socialization of women reinforces feelings of inferiority and subordination. 3 tables, 27 notes. J. Tull

3392. Mazrui, Ali A. MICRO-DEPENDENCY: THE CUBAN FACTOR IN SOUTHERN AFRICA. *India Q. [India] 1981 37(3): 329-345.* Reviews the nature of Latin American influence generally, and Cuban influence specifically, in the affairs of states of Southern Africa. Covers linguistic ties, common racial ancestry, and similarities of economies and natural resources. Cuban presence in Africa has thus far been beneficial, but might result in microdependency, the domination of one underdeveloped nation by another. 14 notes. V. L. Human

3393. McCracken, John. RETHINKING RURAL POVERTY. *J. of African Hist. [Great Britain] 1978 19(4): 611-615.* Review article on Robin Palmer and Neil Parsons, *The Roots of Rural Poverty in Central and Southern Africa* (London, 1977). A major preoccupation of recent Central African historiography is the study of African peasants. This volume presents 10 studies of the disastrous effects of colonialism and capitalism in Central and Southern Africa. The widespread contemporary poverty of the region resulted from colonial undermining of self-sufficiency and has led to an absolute impoverishment against previous standards of living. 8 notes. A. W. Novitsky

3394. Molotsi, Peter H. SOUTHERN AFRICAN REFUGEES AND EXILES. *Pan-African J. [Kenya] 1974 7(2): 119-128.* Discusses refugees from Southern Africa, their life situation and future. Due to cruel and inhuman treatment in Namibia, Zimbabwe, Mozambique, and Angola, Africans have fled to neighboring states for protection. The only solution to these problems is the overthrow of existing governments. 27 notes. H. G. Soff

3395. Moneta, Juan Carlos. LA EMIGRACION BLANCA DESDE SUDAFRICA AL CONO SUR LATINOAMERICANO: SU DIMENSION SOCIAL Y POLITICA [White immigration from South Africa into the Southern Cone of Latin America: its social and political implications]. *Estudios de Asia y Africa [Mexico] 1980 16(3): 385-418.* In recent years the white minorities of South Africa, Southern Rhodesia, Namibia, and Angola have sought to obtain agreements with the governments of Bolivia, Paraguay, Uruguay, Brazil, and Argentina to settle groups of their colonists in those countries. Examines this phenomenon in terms of the distinctive characteristics that emerge in the interaction between central and peripheral or dependent societies, giving special importance to political, ideological and economic factors rather than individual reasons for emigrating. 2 tables, 61 notes. J. V. Coutinho

3396. Mufuka, Kenneth Nyamayaro. BRITAIN AND AMALGAMATION OF THE RHODESIAS, 1937-1941. *Rhodesian Hist. [Rhodesia] 1976 7: 85-89.* Publicly the onset of World War II and privately the diverse racial policies in Northern and Southern Rhodesia were propounded to explain delayed British action in changing the political structure of Northern Rhodesia, Nyasaland, and Southern Rhodesia. The real reason, however, is apparent from a secret 1931 all-party special cabinet committee memo, never communicated to the Southern Rhodesian government. It stipulated the need to keep the copper mines under British control for strategic and economic reasons, and thus restraint in regional restructuring. Based on recently opened Colonial Office files, 1937-41, in the Public Record Office, London, and secondary sources; 18 notes. O. B. Pollak

3397. Mufuka, Kenneth Nyamayaro. BRITAIN AND THE RHODESIAN FEDERATION, 1937-1952: A REVISIONIST VIEW. *J. of African Studies 1977 4(2): 188-197.* Takes issue with the view that Great Britain rejected amalgamation of its colonies in Central Africa prior to 1953 because of the race policy of the settler government of Southern Rhodesia. Most accounts take the Bledisloe Commission Report of 1939 at face value in assigning this motive to the British government, but the author discusses a tripartisan secret cabinet paper in 1931 which enunciated a strategic imperative in retaining imperial control over the mining, labor, and food-producing resources of Northern Rhodesia. This overriding strategic factor remained until the end of World War II, when British governments began giving serious attention to the Southern Rhodesian case for Central African amalgamation. Based on archival, primary, and secondary sources; 28 notes. L. W. Truschel

3398. Nyerere, Julius. THE ROLE AND RESPONSIBILITY OF THE UNITED STATES IN SOUTH AFRICA AND RHODESIA. *Black Scholar 1977 9(2): 40-46.* Presents text of a speech by Julius Nyerere, President of Tanzania, on 6 August 1977, which calls for the United States to support the Southern African countries that are struggling for justice and peace. B. D. Ledbetter

3399. Nzongola-Ntalaja. INTERNAL SETTLEMENT, NEOCOLONIALISM AND THE LIBERATION OF SOUTHERN AFRICA. *J. of Southern African Affairs 1979 4(2): 133-151.* A Marxist-Leninist analysis of liberation movements in Central and Southern Africa and problems and prospects confronting them in recent years. Genuine national liberation movements include only those that oppose "all forms of the dependent capitalist state," whether politically independent states under African regimes performing neocolonial tasks, territories subject to internal political settlements by European settlers and collaborationist classes of Africans, and countries still under white governments. Angola and Mozambique are currently in a position to provide leadership and examples of liberation for revolutionary movements in the other territories, including South Africa. Based on secondary sources; 47 notes. L. W. Truschel

3400. Nzuwah, Mariyawanda. A GUIDE TO CONTEMPORARY RESOURCES AND REFERENCE MATERIALS ON SOUTHERN AFRICA (1961-1978): A SELECTED BIBLIOGRAPHY. *J. of Southern African Affairs 1978 3(3): 353-401.* Bibliography of 800 books and pamphlets in English on southern Africa published during 1961-78, with some listings for Zaire and Tanzania. The academic disciplines represented include history, geography, sociology, economics, and political science. The list omits most South African and Southern Rhodesian publications, but includes an array of pamphlets published or sponsored by African liberation movements and international organizations. Black Africans authored less than 12% of the works. Other bibliographic articles are to follow in this series. Based on library resources; 11 notes, biblio. L. W. Truschel

3401. Nzuwah, Mariyawanda, comp. AN INDEX OF SELECTED RESOLUTIONS, DOCUMENTS, AND DECLARATIONS OF THE UNITED NATIONS ON SOUTHERN AFRICA. *J. of Southern African Affairs 1979 4(2): 187-247.* A listing of UN documents pertaining to Southern African territories and released during the years 1946-79. Contains citations and, in some instances, texts of Security Council and General Assembly declarations and resolutions covering the entire region or any of the single territories of Angola, Mozambique, Zimbabwe, Namibia, South Africa, Lesotho, Botswana, and Swaziland. Also lists UN agency studies and reports on these countries. L. W. Truschel

3402. Oudes, Bruce J. PORTOGALLO E AFRICA: IL MOMENTO DELLA TRATTATIVA [Portugal and Africa: The importance of negotiation]. *Affari Esteri [Italy] 1974 6(23): 56-69.* One of the most complicated and important recent developments in Africa is the granting of independence to the former colonies of Portugal. The strategic positions of Mozambique and Angola as well as their significant natural resources require that the United States and the nations of Western Europe assure themselves a close relationship with these new nations. A. R. Stoesen

3403. Perrings, Charles. THE PRODUCTION PROCESS, INDUSTRIAL LABOUR STRATEGIES AND WORKER RESPONSES IN THE SOUTHERN AFRICAN GOLD MINING INDUSTRY. *J. of African Hist. [Great Britain] 1977 18(1): 129-135.* Comments on three recent works on black labor in the gold fields of southern Africa: Frederick Johnstone, *Class, Race and Gold: A Study of Class Relations and Racial Discrimination in South Africa* (London: Routledge and Kegan Paul, 1976); Francis Wilson, *Labour in the South African Gold Mines 1911-1969*(Cambridge U. Pr., 1972); and Charles van Onselen, *Chibaro: African Mine Labour in Southern Rhodesia 1900-1933* (London: Pluto Press, 1976). 9 notes. H. G. Soff

3404. Phatudi, Cedric and Kapuuo, Clemens. SOUTH AFRICA'S HOMELANDS: TWO AFRICAN VIEWS. *Munger Africana Library*

Notes 1974 (22): 7-37. Interviews with chief minister Cedric Phatudi of Lebowa and Herero Chief Clemens Kapuuo of Namibia. S

3405. Ranger, Terence. GROWING FROM THE ROOTS: REFLECTIONS ON PEASANT RESEARCH IN CENTRAL AND SOUTHERN AFRICA. *J. of Southern African Studies [Great Britain] 1978 5(1): 99-133.* A critical review of *Roots of Rural Poverty in Central and Southern Africa* (1977), a seminal work in the field of African peasant studies in its break with colonial historiography, but one defective for its lack of useful definitions, documentation outside colonial archives, adequate coverage of any era except for that of the height of colonial rule, and appropriate comparative situations. Some exceptional chapters treating the precolonial and late colonial eras and utilizing local fieldwork are exempted from the general criticisms of the work. Secondary sources; 34 notes. L. W. Truschel

3406. Ranger, Terence and Murray, Colin. INTRODUCTION. *J. of Southern African Studies [Great Britain] 1981 8(1): 1-15.* Describes papers presented at the Conference on the Interactions of History and Anthropology in Southern Africa held in Manchester, England, in September 1980 and discussions among participants directed toward formulation of a new radical and history-related outlook for cultural anthropologists dealing with this region. Secondary works; 6 notes. L. W. Truschel

3407. Ranger, Terence. THE PEOPLE IN AFRICAN RESISTANCE: A REVIEW. *J. of Southern African Studies [Great Britain] 1977 4(1): 125-146.* A historiographical examination of recent writings on the theme of African resistance to European colonialism in south central Africa, particularly among the Shona-speaking clans of Zimbabwe and Mozambique. The author's seminal 1967 work on the subject, *Revolt in Southern Rhodesia,* while often praised by African nationalists and anticolonialist writers, has also been attacked for its alleged "continuist" view of African primary resistance from the 1890's to the present. Accepts the argument that the development of African classes to support mass protest and revolution should be examined, along with the continuity of earlier resistance forms and ideas. Allen Isaacman's *The Tradition of Resistance in Mozambique* (1976) is the best study since 1967 of the major facets of African resistance, but Ranger questions the assertion of colonial peasantization presented in Isaacman's 1977 follow-up article. Secondary works; 24 notes. L. W. Truschel

3408. Richardson, Peter. SOUTH AND CENTRAL AFRICAN MINING, C. 1900-1933. *African Affairs [Great Britain] 1977 76(303): 249-258.* A review article of *Class, Race, and Gold: A Study of Class Relations and Racial Discrimination in South Africa,* by Frederick A. Johnstone (London: Routledge and Kegan Paul, 1976) and *Chibaro: African Mine Labor in Southern Rhodesia, 1900-1933,* by Charles van Onselen (London: Pluto Pr., 1976). Both books are published versions of University theses. Johnstone's book deals largely with the white operators of the system of racial discrimination, in strong contrast to van Onselen's "measured incisiveness" as to the plight and response of African workers. Both books are major contributions to historical scholarship. 42 notes. E. P. Stickney

3409. Saul, John S. CANADA AND SOUTHERN AFRICA. *Can. Dimension [Canada] 1977 12(1): 46-51.* Regardless of condemnation by many Canadian political groups, trade with South Africa and Southern Rhodesia was continued, 1960's-76.

3410. Saxena, S. C. MALAWI'S RELATIONS WITH SOUTH AFRICA AND THEIR IMPLICATIONS FOR AFRICAN UNITY. *Indian J. of Pol. [India] 1976 10(2): 39-52.* Malawi's hobnobbing with South Africa is full of ominous implications for African unity. Whereas African states, by and large, have severed links with South Africa over apartheid, her refusal to concede majority rule, and defiance of the international community on the question of Namibia's independence, the Republic of Malawi has not only maintained links with South Africa but also vigorously pleaded for normalisation of relations of black Africa with that country, condemned the call for its boycott, refused to oppose the sale of arms to it and did not support the waging of armed struggle for the liberation of Rhodesia and Namibia. Banda pleads for a policy of accommodation with South Africa instead of one of confrontation. His policy of 'killing apartheid with kindness' has met with disapproval all over Africa. Secondary sources; 54 notes. J

3411. Schlegel, John P. OTTAWA'S ACHILLES HEEL: FORMULATING POLICIES IN SOUTHERN AFRICA. *Round Table [Great Britain] 1979 (274): 142-153.* Canada, influenced by Tanzanian foreign policy, has consistently advocated self-determination for the South African and Zimbabwean peoples. Based on secondary sources and on the author's own work; 35 notes.

3412. Shaw, Timothy M. INTERNATIONAL ORGANIZATIONS AND THE POLITICS OF SOUTHERN AFRICA: TOWARDS REGIONAL INTEGRATION OR LIBERATION? *J. of Southern African Studies [Great Britain] 1976 3(1): 1-19.* Examines the development of international organizations in southern Africa since the independence of Mozambique and Angola in 1973, and assesses their impact on the region's future political economy. Based on newspapers; 3 tables, 69 notes. S. P. Carr

3413. Smith, Earl. BLACK AFRICA AND THE PRESS. *Freedomways 1977 17(3): 143-154.* Reviews press coverage of the civil war in Angola and antiapartheid riots in South Africa and charges that American journalists are fundamentally biased against liberation movements.

3414. Steele, M. C. DIALOGUE AND CLOSER ASSOCIATION IN SOUTHERN AFRICA. *Zambezia [Rhodesia] 1973 3(1): 83-87.* Review essay on L. Marquard, *A Federation of Southern Africa* (London: Oxford U. Pr., 1971), N. J. Rhoodie, ed., *South African Dialogue: Contrasts in South African Thinking on Basic Issues* (Johannesburg: McGraw-Hill, 1972), and C. P. Potholm and R. Dale, eds., *Southern Africa in Perspective: Essays in Regional Politics* (New York: Free Press, 1972). Assesses the state of social sciences in their approach to Southern Africa in the early 1970's and their transient applicability in light of the Portuguese coup of April 1974 and projected decolonization of Mozambique and Angola. South Africa's moves toward dialogue with independent black states to the north and the development of independent homelands within South Africa are now complicated by diminished white strongholds and a changed geopolitical map. O. B. Pollak

3415. Sterkenburg, Jan. AGRICULTURAL COMMERCIALIZATION IN AFRICA SOUTH OF THE SAHARA: THE CASES OF LESOTHO AND SWAZILAND. *Development and Change [Netherlands] 1980 11(4): 573-606.* Examines agricultural commercialization in Lesotho and Swaziland, in light of their integration into the world economic system. Discusses land distribution, the farming system, and agricultural development policy to 1980.

3416. Taapopi, Leonard and Keenleyside, T. A. THE WEST AND SOUTHERN AFRICA: ECONOMIC INVOLVEMENT AND SUPPORT FOR LIBERATION 1960-1974. *Can. J. of African Studies [Canada] 1980 13(3): 347-370.* Foreign investments in Southern Africa by Western nations such as the United States, Great Britain, and France have affected their willingness to support decolonization in the region, while countries such as Denmark and Sweden, with low levels of economic investment, were highly supportive of decolonization. Western investments have steadily increased during the 1960's and 1970's, but the author questions whether this will lead to intervention on the side of minority white governments to protect their economic interests, "especially in light of... political developments in the former Portuguese colonies which Western states seemed powerless to prevent or control, and given the reluctance of the United States in particular to intervene directly in Africa as a result of its Vietnam experience." 5 tables, 95 notes. S

3417. Utete, C. Munhamu Botsio. NATO AND SOUTHERN AFRICA. *Black Scholar 1976 7(8): 36-46.* Although barred by legal restrictions to the contrary, NATO has been involved from its beginning in 1949 in the affairs of southern Africa. Acting in a counterrevolutionary manner, it aids in the maintenance of South Africa's colonialist status, and it tries to control the African nationalist movement in order to consolidate neocolonialism. Primary and secondary sources; map, 20 notes. B. D. Ledbetter

3418. Wall, Patrick. CONFLICT IN SOUTHERN AFRICA. *Conflict 1980 2(1): 57-71.* Reviews political developments in southern African countries and anticipates intensification of American-Russian competition for southern African minerals.

3419. Wallerstein, Immanuel. ON THE INTERPRETATION OF NATIONALISM IN THE PERIPHERY: MARCUM'S ANGOLA. *Africa Today 1979 26(4): 67-71.* Reviews John Marcum's *The Angolan Revolution,* vol. 1, *The Anatomy of An Explosion (1950-1962),* vol. 2, *Exile Politics and Guerrilla Warfare (1962-1976)* (Cambridge, Mass.: M.I.T. Pr., 1969, 1978), an exhaustive, detailed description. Marcum's explanation of Angolan nationalism as a tripolar theme is "fundamentally off base." G. O. Gagnon

3420. Wetherell, H. I. BRITAIN AND RHODESIAN EXPANSIONISM: IMPERIAL COLLUSION OR EMPIRICAL CARELESSNESS? *Rhodesian Hist. [Zimbabwe] 1977 8: 115-128.* Review of Martin Chanock's *Unconsummated Union: Britain, Rhodesia and South Africa, 1900-45* (Manchester U. Pr., 1977). Analyzes the three-way geopolitical relationship in the first half of the 20th century between Great Britain, Southern Rhodesia, and South Africa. The British view of Central Africa as counterpoise to South Africa need not be rejected, but a change of emphasis in favor of local politics and administrative history is in order. O. B. Pollak

3421. Wetherell, H. I. SETTLER EXPANSIONISM IN CENTRAL AFRICA: THE IMPERIAL RESPONSE OF 1931 AND SUBSEQUENT IMPLICATIONS. *African Affairs [Great Britain] 1979 78(311): 210-227.* Chronicles the separate development of settler expansion in Southern and Northern Rhodesia and analyzes the manner in which an informal coalition of British capitalist interests and European settlers succeeded in amalgamating Northern and Southern Rhodesia in 1953. A combination of factors (the need for labor, markets, trade and communications ties) led to the revival of interests in unification in the 1930's. The British government, after 1931, began to accede to settler demands, with the result that Africans were marginalized into impoverished areas. Based on Rhodesian archival records, and other primary sources; 46 notes. S. Lakhan

3422. Whalen, Eileen and Lawrence, Ken. AMERICAN WORKERS AND LIBERATION STRUGGLES IN SOUTHERN AFRICA: THE BOYCOTT OF COAL AND CHROME. *Radical Am. 1975 9(3): 1-16.* Discusses the need for labor reform in the 1960's and 1970's and calls for solidarity of black workers through economic boycotts to rid the United Mine Workers of America of racism and to promote anti-imperialism in Southern Africa.

3423. Wheeler, Douglas L. AMERICAN POLICY TOWARD SOUTHERN AFRICA: CRITICAL CHOICES. *Issue 1974 4(2): 4-8.* Calls for reexamination of passive US foreign policy toward Portugal and Southern Africa. S

3424. Wilkinson, Anthony R. ANGOLA AND MOZAMBIQUE: THE IMPLICATIONS OF LOCAL POWER. *Survival [Great Britain] 1974 16(5): 217-227.* Discusses the political and military implications of national independence movements against Portuguese forces.

3425. Wilson, Francis. INTERNATIONAL MIGRATION IN SOUTHERN AFRICA. *Int. Migration Rev. 1976 10(4): 451-488.* Discusses the economic and labor implications of international migration of migrant workers in Southern African nations from the 1950's forward.

3426. —. [AFTER THE VICTORIES OF THE PEOPLES OF MOZAMBIQUE AND ANGOLA]. *World Marxist Rev. [Canada] 1976 19(6): 91-112.*

Batista, Alves Bernardo. GROUNDWORK FOR PEOPLE'S RULE, *pp. 91-95.* Describes the current status of the People's Movement for the Liberation of Angola (MPLA), focusing on the new administrative system in urban and rural areas of Angola and giving economic goals for Angola's revitalization.

Rebelo, Jorge. FORMATIVE PERIOD, *pp. 95-100.* Discusses the political situation in Mozambique one year after independence, focusing primarily on the Mozambique Liberation Front (FRELIMO) and its accomplishments on the provincial political level and in relation to other socialist nations on the international level.

Nzo, Alfred. VORSTER'S DOUBLE STRATEGY, *pp. 100-103.* Notes political changes in contemporary South Africa, focusing on the ambiguous political position of the Vorster regime and countering with the policies of the African National Congress (ANC) of South Africa.

Moyo, Jason and Silundika, George. DESPITE INTRIGUES, FOR THE UNITY OF FIGHTERS, *pp. 104-108.* Discusses the Zimbabwe liberation movement in Southern Rhodesia since the 1960's, showing that the unity of the former Zimbabwe African People's Union (ZAPU) and Zimbabwe African National Union (ZANU) fighters is more important than their divisions.

Garoeb, Moses. FOR A STATE OF WORKERS AND PEASANTS, *pp. 108-112.* Cites the political position of the South-West African People's Organization (SWAPO), outlining its program for the recognition of Namibia either through negotiation or revolutionary action.

3427. —. THE MILITARY BALANCE 1974/75: SUB-SAHARAN AFRICA. *Air Force Mag. 1974 57(12): 70-72.* Describes the defensive agreements between the Central and Southern African states, particularly the members of the Organization of African Unity and other powers, 1960's-74, and discusses the strength and deployment of their military forces.

3428. —. SOUTHERN AFRICA: ARMED STRUGGLE AGAINST IMPERIALISM. *World Marxist R. [Canada] 1973 16(5): 83-91.* Views of the National Liberation Front leaders in Angola, Mozambique, Namibia, Zimbabwe, and South Africa. S

Angola

3429. Arnold, Anne-Sophie. DER BEWAFFNETE BEFREIUNGSKAMPF DES ANGOLANISCHEN VOLKES. ENTWICKLUNG UND SPEZIFIK [The armed struggle for liberation of the Angolan people: development and details]. *Militärgeschichte [East Germany] 1978 17(6): 656-669.* Describes the development of the anticolonial movement in Angola and its leading force, the Popular Movement for the Liberation of Angola (MPLA). Focuses on the specific conditions of this struggle and especially portrays the role of the armed struggle. Considers the struggle of the young Peoples Republic of Angola, which the socialist states jointly supported, carried on in 1975-76 for the defense of independence against the aggression of imperialist and racist forces. 5 illus., 54 notes. H. D. Andrews

3430. Azevedo, Mario J. ZAMBIA, ZAIRE, AND THE ANGOLAN CRISIS RECONSIDERED: FROM ALVOR TO SHABA. *J. of Southern African Affairs 1977 2(3): 275-293.* Maintains that Zambia's and Zaire's roles in the Angolan crisis were considerable and discusses motives and possible outcome. Evidence shows that Zambia and Zaire actively intervened on behalf of the pro-Western forces to secure a defeat of the Popular Movement for the Liberation of Angola (MPLA), motivated by economic and political factors and assured by US and South African assistance. Rapprochement with the victorious MPLA has been slow and hampered in Zaire by the invasion of Shaba by former Katangese (Shaba) gendarmes, probably with the MPLA's approval. 54 notes. J. Tull

3431. Bender, Gerald J. ANGOLA LEFT, RIGHT & WRONG. *Foreign Policy 1981 (43): 53-69.* Continuing a tradition dating at least to 1960, the vacillating policy of President Ronald Reagan's administration toward Angola has alienated virtually every element involved in the conflict, both in Africa and the United States. All agree that a stable Angolan-American relationship would be to the advantage of the United States, but this cannot come about until America recognizes the Marxist-oriented government in Luanda and encourages South Africa to restrain its activities in the area. T. I. Powers

3432. Bender, Gerald J. and Rader, P. Stanley. WHITES IN ANGOLA ON THE EVE OF INDEPENDENCE: THE POLITICS OF NUMBERS. *Africa Today 1974 21(4): 23-37.* A demographic study which concludes that the white Angolan population "does not exceed 335,000," a figure significantly lower than widely accepted estimates. The whites are largely ill-educated and unskilled which places them in direct economic competition with Africans and reinforces white opposition to independence. Based on Portuguese and other demographic data, and secondary sources; 5 tables, 37 notes. G. O. Gagnon

3433. Birmingham, David. COLONIALISM IN ANGOLA: KINYAMA'S EXPERIENCE. *Tarikh [Nigeria] 1980 6(4): 65-75.* Focuses on the sufferings of a fictional Angolan farmer named Kinyama and his family to illustrate the actual effects of Portuguese colonialism on Angolan society from 1956 through the war of liberation and independence in 1975.

3434. Birmingham, David. PORTUGUESE RULE IN ANGOLA. *Tarikh [Nigeria] 1974 4(4): 25-36.*

3435. Birmingham, David. A QUESTION OF COFFEE: BLACK ENTERPRISE IN ANGOLA. *Can. J. of African Studies [Canada] 1982 16(2): 343-346.* Discusses the coffee industry in Angola from 1830 to 1981. In the 19th century the industry was dominated by the peasant sector, which had some competition from African chiefs. The revival of the industry in the 1940's and 1950's brought, along with increased peasant initiative, white enterprise. White shopkeepers gained domination through rural credit and land ownership. The history of the coffee industry needs further research based on both governmental and private archives. Based on secondary sources; 7 notes. J. Powell

3436. Birmingham, David. THEMES AND RESOURCES OF ANGOLAN HISTORY. *African Affairs [Great Britain] 1974 73(291): 188-203.* Although many volumes on Angolan history exist, they deal primarily with Kongo Christianity in the 15th and 16th centuries and 20th-century colonialism. Recent archival findings will allow more intensive research and several areas are suggested: early indigenous Angolan societies; the slave era; the colonial era from 1836 to 1910; the modern colonial era including a history of agriculture, social history of urban areas, and the study of white colonization. 23 notes, appendix. H. G. Soff

3437. Birmingham, David. THE TWENTY-SEVENTH OF MAY: AN HISTORICAL NOTE ON THE ABORTIVE 1977 *COUP* IN ANGOLA. *African Affairs [Great Britain] 1978 77(309): 554-564.* Discusses the attempted coup in Luanda, Angola, 27 May 1977, about two years after Angola's independence, led by Nito Alves.

3438. Birmingham, David. WAR IN AFRICA: A PROBLEM OF EVIDENCE IN CONTEMPORARY HISTORY. *Contemporary Rev. [Great Britain] 1981 238(1382): 113-119.* Challenges the ethnic explanation of the Angolan civil war, which began in 1975, arguing that the three supposed nationalities had long since disintegrated and that the roots of the conflict really lay in rival urban cultures created in the colonial era.

3439. Burness, Donald. NZINGA MBANDI AND ANGOLAN INDEPENDENCE. *Luso-Brazilian Rev. 1977 14(2): 225-229.* The novel *Nzinga Mbandi,* by the MPLA leader Manuel Pacavira, is a significant step in the evolution of African literature as it relates the past to current history. Ideals and beliefs held by the main characters, Ngola Kiluanji, Ngola Mbandi, and Rainha Ginga in the 17th century are still cherished by many Angolans. Therefore, this chronicle has educational as well as artistic purposes. The extensive use of Kimbundu indicates a repudiation of European culture. 4 notes. J. M. Walsh

3440. Carvalho, Eduardo Cruz de. "TRADITIONAL" AND "MODERN" PATTERNS OF CATTLE RAISING IN SOUTHWESTERN ANGOLA: A CRITICAL EVALUATION OF CHANGE FROM PASTORALISM TO RANCHING. *J. of Developing Areas 1974 8(2): 199-226.*

3441. Clarence-Smith, W. G. REVIEW ARTICLE: CLASS STRUCTURE AND CLASS STRUGGLES IN ANGOLA IN THE 1970S. *J. of Southern African Studies [Great Britain] 1980 7(1): 109-126.* A Marxist class analysis of conflicts in Angola since 1961 that attacks other writers for stressing the apparent ethnic and regional nature of Angolan parties fighting both the Portuguese in the late colonial period and among themselves. The MPLA and its government in Luanda have failed to effectively unite Angola since independence, because its membership of "privileged bureaucratic petty bourgeoisie" in the capital city has been unable to gain a large following among the rural peasantry. 59 notes. L. W. Truschel

3442. Davidson, Basil. COLONIALISM IN ANGOLA: PREFATORY NOTE. *Tarikh [Nigeria] 1980 6(4): 61-64.* Having completed so-called pacification in the late 1920's, Portugal exploited Angola economically, employing a very large number of adult males—an estimated 379,000 in 1954—and even children in a form of slavery scarcely disguised as a contract system until Angolan reaction in 1960-61 to the violence of the Portuguese colonial system.

3443. Dias, Jill R. FAMINE AND DISEASE IN THE HISTORY OF ANGOLA, C. 1830-1930. *J. of African Hist. [Great Britain] 1981 22(3): 349-378.* Describes the relationship between the far-reaching changes occasioned by the gradual substitution of the overseas slave trade by commerce in raw materials and cash crops in Angola and the worsening famine and epidemic crises at the end of the 19th century. Commercial instability and depopulation, contributed to by droughts, irregular rainfall, famine, malnutrition, and smallpox epidemics, hindered Portuguese-sponsored non-slave trade development and stimulated unsuccessful revolts in 1902, 1913-15, 1922, 1961, and 1977. Based on materials in Angolan archives and published sources; 2 maps, table, 185 notes. R. L. Collison

3444. Dingeman, Jim. ANGOLA: PORTUGAL IN AFRICA. *Strategy & Tactics 1976 56: 22-37.* Presents an account of the civil war in Angola, 1974-76.

3445. Ebinger, Charles K. EXTERNAL INTERVENTION IN INTERNAL WAR: THE POLITICS AND DIPLOMACY OF THE ANGOLAN CIVIL WAR. *Orbis 1976 20(3): 669-700.* Although the Popular Movement for the Liberation of Angola (MPLA), led by Agostinho Neto, has seemingly gained the upper hand in Angola and Cabinda, the true situation today in those areas is quite fluid. Involved, to varying degrees, are the United States, the USSR, Communist China, South Africa, Cuba, almost all the African nations, and the rival Angolan and Cabindan nationalist groups. US policy toward Angola thus far has been a failure because it concentrated too much on a US-USSR confrontation and ignored the "larger regional and international context of the Angolan struggle." Both Communist China and the USSR maintain an active presence in Africa and confront each other in many areas on that continent. The Cuban forces apparently balance Soviet influence to some degree in Angola since they support Neto against the Interior Minister, Nito Alves, who has Soviet backing and support. Based largely on interviews conducted by the author in Portugal and southern Africa in late 1974 and early 1975; 53 notes. A. N. Garland

3446. Ferreira, Eduardo de Sousa. LA TRANSFORMACIÓN Y CONSOLIDACIÓN DE LA ECONOMÍA EN ANGOLA, 1930-1974 [The transformation and consolidation of the economy in Angola, 1930-74]. *Estudios de Asia y África [Mexico] 1980 15(3): 571-616.* It is commonly believed that no logical plan presided over the colonial economy of Angola. But recent studies show that during the 1950's local manpower was increasingly integrated in a market economy subordinated to metropolitan interests and that beginning in the 1960's this mode of production was expanded and commercial colonial exploitation was transformed through the penetration of outside capital, which increased the possibilities of local accumulation and strengthened the incipient middle class. 15 tables, 76 notes. J. V. Coutinho

3447. Hallett, Robin. THE SOUTH AFRICAN INTERVENTION IN ANGOLA, 1975-76. *African Affairs [Great Britain] 1978 77(308): 347-386.* Interested in Angola for economic and strategic reasons, South Africa invaded it to prevent a Communist takeover. Failure to prevent the takeover was due primarily to faulty intelligence reports, including those furnished by the United States. Secondary sources; 66 notes. H. G. Soff

3448. Heimer, Franz-Wilhelm. FORMATION SOCIALE, DÉVELOPPEMENT ÉCONOMIQUE ET OPTION SOCIALISTE EN ANGOLA [Social organization, economic development, and the socialist option in Angola]. *Genève-Afrique [Switzerland] 1980 18(1): 31-43.* Between 1850 and 1950 Angola developed a colonial society dominated by a small urban sector, intent on exporting raw materials produced by forced labor. After 1961 the Portuguese government insisted on reinvestment in the local economy and the urban sector increased to 15% of the population, including a sizeable petite bourgeoisie and working class. The major question to be decided by the Popular Movement for the Liberation of Angola (MPLA) government is the relationship between the central sector and the periphery and the question of which class will control development. Biblio.
B. S. Fetter

3449. Holness, Mary. THE POETRY OF AGOSTINO NETO. *Afriscope [Nigeria] 1975 5(5): 32-40.* Brief biography of the Angolan revolutionary leader, Agostinho Neto, and the role that poetry has played in his life and in the struggle against Portuguese colonialism. Based on Neto's poems. Illus. G. O. Gagnon

3450. Ignat'ev, O. K. IMPERIALISTICHESKII ZAGOVOR PROTIV ANGOLY [The imperialist conspiracy against Angola]. *Novaia i Noveishaia Istoriia [USSR] 1978 (6): 112-136.* The campaign led by the Popular Movement for the Liberation of Angola (MPLA) was undermined by the two imperialist groups, the National Liberation Front of Angola (FNLA) and the National Union for the Total Independence of Angola (UNITA). The author details the life of the leader of the Northern Angolan People's Union (UPNA) from the formation of UPNA in Leopoldville, 1954, noting that he later became CIA agent Roberto. The Portuguese intelligence agent and UNITA leader Jonas Savimbi is described as as a second "Judas." In the campaign for independence, 1954-75, China aided the FNLA and UNITA in the summer of 1975, and the United Arab Republic entered the war in August. Angola became an independent People's Republic in November 1975. M. R. Colenso/S

3451. Kaur, Harmala. CHINA AND THE ANGOLAN NATIONAL LIBERATION MOVEMENT. *China Report [India] 1977 13(4): 19-33.* Sketches Portuguese colonialism and early Angolan nationalist movement and examines China's involvement in the struggle for control in Angola, which was consistent with its usual response to Soviet initiatives in the Third World. 94 notes. R. V. Ritter

3452. Khazanov, A. M. ANGOLA: BOR'BA ZA NEZAVISIMOST' [Angola: struggle for independence]. *Voprosy Istorii [USSR] 1978 (8): 115-129.* Describes the struggle for Angolan independence since 1956 when left-wing groups merged to form the Marxist organization, the Popular Movement for the Liberation of Angola (MPLA), under the leadership of Agostino Neto. In 1972 the MPLA began the guerrilla campaign against Portugal. The eventual victory of the MPLA was due to the support of progressive international forces, who helped to defeat other guerrilla groups with Chinese and imperialist backers.
J. P. H. Myers/S

3453. Kiracofe, Clifford A., Jr. THE COMMUNIST TAKEOVER OF ANGOLA. *J. of Social, Pol. and Econ. Studies 1981 6(4): 417-437.* Discusses the background of the takeover of Angola in 1975 by the Popular Movement for the Liberation of Angola (MPLA), with special attention to the role of Soviet and Cuban forces.

3454. Łabno, Anna. KSZTAŁTOWANIE PODSTAW PRAWNYCH USTROJU POLITYCZNEGO LUDOWEJ REPUBLIKI ANGOLI [Development of the legal foundations of the People's Republic of Angola]. *Studia Nauk Pol. [Poland] 1980 (6): 131-143.* Angola gained its independence on 11 December 1975; its new constitution was approved by the Central Committee of MPLA, the Party of Labor, on 10 December 1975. MPLA was the only force capable of taking over after the disintegration of Portuguese rule. The constitution is divided into five major parts and several articles and covers general, i.e. constitutional, topics as well as political issues. Secondary sources; 28 notes.
I. Lukes

3455. Larrabee, Stephen. MOSCOW, ANGOLA AND THE DIALECTICS OF DÉTENTE. *World Today [Great Britain] 1976 32(5): 173-182.* Discusses the changing Soviet foreign policy in Africa since 1955, focusing especially on Soviet interests in Angola since 1975 and giving implications of these interests for the rest of Africa.

3456. Leclercq, Hughes. L'ENJEU ÉCONOMIQUE DE LA DÉCOLONISATION EN ANGOLA [The economic lottery of decolonization in Angola]. *Cultures et Développement [Belgium] 1976 8(1): 43-87.* Discusses characteristic traits of colonial Angola's economic structure and events leading to the province's political and economic collapse in 1974.

3457. Levesque, Jacques. LA GUERRE D'ANGOLA ET LE ROLE DE CUBA EN AFRIQUE [The Angola war and Cuba's role in Africa]. *Etudes Int. [Canada] 1978 9(3): 429-434.* Reviews the positions taken by Russia, China, and several South American and African states toward Cuba's military role in Angola in 1975. Notes Cuba's earlier involvement in Africa and suggests that this activity gives Havana greater latitude to develop its own foreign policy in Latin America. 19 notes. J. F. Harrington, Jr.

3458. Mahajan, Harapreet. ANATOMY OF IMPERIALISM IN ANGOLA. *Africa Q. [India] 1978 17(4): 46-66.* Studies the impact of Portuguese colonial expansion in Angola from the late 15th century, the politics of decolonization during the 1960's-70's, and postindependence developments.

3459. Marcum, John A. ANGOLA: BACKGROUND TO THE CONFLICT. *Mawazo [Uganda] 1976 4(4): 3-25.* Examines the birth of modern Angola amid chaos and civil war by looking for the genesis of present events in Angolan history under Portuguese control. The author asks why there should be so much external intervention in a country of six million inhabitants. By analyzing the cultural, class, and ethnic and racial stratification, the author provides a context to assess the recent impact of power politics in Angola. Presidential address to the 18th annual meeting, African Studies Association of America, San Francisco, 29 October 1975. 91 notes. J. J. N. McGurk

3460. Marcum, John A. THE ANGUISH OF ANGOLA: ON BECOMING INDEPENDENT IN THE LAST QUARTER OF THE TWENTIETH CENTURY. *Issue 1975 5(4): 3-11.* Discusses the resurgence of political nationalism in Angola in 1975 and the end of paternal European rule, 1950's-70's.

3461. Martin, Phyllis M. THE CABINDA CONNECTION: AN HISTORICAL PERSPECTIVE. *African Affairs [Great Britain] 1977 76(302): 47-59.* Reviews the independence movement in Cabinda, an ethnic exclave in northwestern Angola. Cabindans came into contact with European traders early and quickly became an entrepreneurial middle class. Many emigrated to the commercial centers of nearby states, thus forming effective support areas separate from the native region. The independence movement began in the 1950's, becoming fully active only after Angolan independence in 1975. The movement has splintered into several subgroups, reducing their effectiveness and leaving the question of Cabindan independence in the hands of stronger forces in Angola and abroad. Map, 41 notes. V. L. Human

3462. Medeiros, Carlos Alberto. LE PHÉNOMÈNE DE LA COLONISATION ET QUELQUES PROBLÈMES DE LA MISE EN VALEUR DU SUD-OUEST DE L'ANGOLA [The phenomenon of colonization and the development of southwest Angola]. *Can. J. of African Studies [Canada] 1977 11(1): 69-83.* Studies Portuguese colonization of southwestern Angola since its beginnings in the mid-19th century. This colonization was made on an essentially rural basis, even in the arid coastal area (agriculture in the valleys of temporary rivers; but a few years later fishing was already important). In 1970 there were 33,500 white inhabitants in the region; most of them left Angola after independence. The evolution of colonization may suggest some ideas about the possibilities of economic development of the region (enlargement of the irrigated area, principal products cultivated, improvement of livestock breeding and of fishing). J

3463. Minter, William. IMPERIAL NETWORK AND EXTERNAL DEPENDENCY: IMPLICATIONS FOR THE ANGOLAN LIBERATION STRUGGLE. *Africa Today 1974 21(1): 25-39.* Examines the implications of the extensive economic involvement of European,

American, and South African investors in Angola, supervised by Portugal. This network of investment mitigates against the independence movement but can be countered by successful guerrilla warfare. Based on author's monograph; biblio. G. O. Gagnon

3464. Nwafor, Azinna. THE LIBERATION OF ANGOLA. *Monthly Rev. 1976 27(9): 1-12.* Describes how the Popular Movement for the Liberation of Angola (MPLA) gradually became the force directly responsible for Angolan independence. Since the beginning of the anti-Portuguese struggle in 1961, various other factions have attempted to shape the final outcome, but only the MPLA represented a popular broad-based movement capable of coordinating all anti-imperialist forces. Despite considerable Russian assistance, Angola will never become "a subservient satrapy." Angola's future will be one of independent revolutionary socialism under the continued leadership of MPLA. 13 notes. M. R. Yerburgh

3465. Ododa, Harry Otieno. THE DYNAMICS OF DECOLONIZATION IN ANGOLA AND THE IMPACT OF MPLA VICTORY ON THE FUTURE OF WHITE MINORITY RULE IN SOUTH AFRICA. *Pan-African J. [Kenya] 1977 10(1): 73-83.* Traces the development of the Popular Movement for the Liberation of Angola (MPLA) from its foundation in 1956 to the aftermath of the MPLA victory on 11 November 1975, when the Portuguese officially left Angola. Angola was the last Portuguese colony in Africa, and the victory of the radical revolutionary and Pan-African oriented MPLA was likely to influence the future of white minority rule in the rest of southern Africa. Based on secondary sources and newspaper reports; 15 notes. F. P. Tudor

3466. Ogunbadejo, Oye. NON-ALIGNMENT IN AFRICA'S INTERNATIONAL RELATIONS: THE CASE OF ANGOLA. *Jerusalem J. of Int. Relations [Israel] 1981 5(2): 16-45.* Briefly outlines the beginnings and development of the Third World nonaligned movement, 1955-80, and traces the changing interpretation of nonalignment in Angola, which maintains a pro-Soviet political stance while pursuing a genuine economic nonalignment that allows Angola to establish economic ties with Western nations and South Africa.

3467. Ortová, Jarmila. LUANDINO VIEIRA, PROSATEUR DU PEUPLE ANGOLAIS EN COMBAT [Luandino Vieira, people's writer of fighting Angola]. *Archiv Orientální [Czechoslovakia] 1973 41(3): 234-242.* A political and artistic profile of Angolan author Luandino Vieira, whose work is devoted to Angolan liberation from Portugal. Though illiteracy in Angola is very high (96 percent), many nationalist cultural organizations disseminate his work. 20 notes. G. E. Pergl

3468. Pelissier, René. ANGOLA: LA GUERRE DE CENT ANS? [Angola: the Hundred Years War?]. *Études [France] 1978 348(2): 149-166.* Analyzes the impact of civil war, ethnic and ideological rivalries, and economic interest groups in Angola in the 1960's-70's.

3469. Penvenne, Jeanne. ANGOLA UNDER THE PORTUGUESE. *Int. J. of African Hist. Studies 1979 12(1): 96-105.* Reviews Gerald J. Bender's *Angola under the Portuguese: The Myth and the Reality* (U. of California Pr., 1978). The work is full of sensitive insight, fascinating detail, and careful scholarship, but glosses over the centrality of the Anglo-Portuguese conglomerates in fostering and perpetuating the Portuguese presence in Angola. 10 notes. M. M. McCarthy

3470. Poltorak, A. MERCENARISM ON TRIAL. *Int. Affairs [USSR] 1976 (10): 96-104.* Examines the importance of the trial of 13 mercenary troops, 10 Britons and three Americans, who were tried by the government of Angola for their participation in armed actions of the National Front for the Liberation of Angola (FNLA), 1976. Discusses the roles played by the consulates of Great Britain and the United States, as well as the United Nations, the Organization of African Unity, and the government in Luanda.

3471. Rivers, Bernard. ANGOLA: MASSACRE AND OPPRESSION. *Africa Today 1974 21(1): 41-45.* Describes the efforts of the Portuguese to deny support to guerrillas by creating *aldeamentos* (strategic resettlements). Massacres are rare but extensive brutality and deprivation occur in the *aldeamentos.* Based on the author's experience, interviews, and secondary sources. G. O. Gagnon

3472. Rivière, J.-Y. NETO: UN PERSONNAGE INSIGNIFIANT, UNE MORT ÉTRANGE [Neto: an insignificant person, a strange death]. *Écrits de Paris [France] 1979 (396): 37-40.* Traces Agostinho Neto's path from obscure medical doctor and Communist Party member to the presidency of Angola and his mysterious death in Moscow in September 1979.

3473. Semenov, L. and Kokorev, V. AGRESSIIA PROTIV ANGOLY [Aggression against Angola]. *Aziia i Afrika Segodnia [USSR] 1982 (1): 16-18.* South Africa's undeclared war against Angola rages on, and certain US circles are commencing a new, most dangerous stage of the arms race.

3474. Serrano, Carlos Moreira Henriques. ANGOLA (1961-1976) BIBLIOGRAFIA [Angola bibliography, 1961-76]. *J. of Southern African Affairs 1977 2(3): 295-321.* Offers a revised and enlarged edition of this bibliography, incorporating the most significant writing on Angola during the period, 1961-76. Includes, particularly, books, articles, pamphlets, and periodicals relating to Angola's independence in 1975. Limited to works published outside Angola and Portugal. J. Tull

3475. Sofinsky, V. and Khazanov, A. ANGOLAN CHRONICLE OF THE PEKING BETRAYAL. *Int. Affairs [USSR] 1978 (7): 60-69.* Defines China's effort to impose Maoist guidance and isolate the national liberation movement from the anti-imperialist front which was behind Peking's foreign policy toward the national liberation movement in Angola, 1961-76.

3476. Stevens, Christopher. THE SOVIET UNION AND ANGOLA. *African Affairs [Great Britain] 1976 75(299): 137-151.* Analyzes Soviet military aid to the Movimento Popular de Libertacao de Angola (MPLA), comparing Soviet political and military intervention in Angola and Zaire (1960). 30 notes. H. G. Soff

3477. Ul'ianovski, R. AGOSTIN'O NETO [Agostinho Neto]. *Aziia i Afrika Segodnia [USSR] 1982 (2): 24-27.* Discusses the life and political career of Agostinho Neto, the first president of independent Angola, focusing on the formation of his political views and on his role in uniting the people of Angola.

3478. Us, V. ANGOLA V BOR'BE ZA NATSIONAL'NUIU NEZAVISIMOST' [Angola fighting for national independence]. *Aziia i Afrika Segodnia [USSR] 1976 (1): 36-38.* Discusses the struggle, 1956-75.

3479. Valenta, Jiri. THE SOVIET-CUBAN INTERVENTION IN ANGOLA. *US Naval Inst. Pro. 1980 106(4): 51-59.* The Soviet military intervention in Afghanistan was heralded by Soviet actions in 1975 and 1976 in Angola. Confident that US intervention in Angola was unlikely, the Soviets conducted a massive air and sea lift of Cuban military personnel and Soviet supplies to support the Popular Movement for the Liberation of Angola (MPLA) of Agostinho Neto. With Soviet and Cuban help, the MPLA, once in danger of defeat, won control of the country. Map, 4 photos. A. N. Garland

3480. Valenta, Jiri. THE SOVIET-CUBAN INTERVENTION, 1975. *Studies in Comparative Communism 1978 (1-2): 3-33.* Soviet military intervention in Angola was opportunistic, a response to American unwillingness to risk another Vietnam-like war in Angola and Chinese influence in Africa. Cuba acted not as a Soviet pawn but as an ally and gained much as a result. Soviet action demonstrated its ability to undertake large-scale airborne aid, sending $300 million. The Angolan situation is still muddled as a guerrilla war continues. The West's willingness to reduce the opportunities available to the USSR and Cuba may restrict future Soviet efforts in Africa. 72 notes. D. Balmuth

3481. Vodop'ianov, I. and Kokorev, V. ANGOLA STROIT NOVOE OBSHCHESTVO [Angola builds a new society]. *Aziia i Afrika Segodnia [USSR] 1981 (9): 27-29.* Discusses the successes of the Popular Movement for the Liberation of Angola-Party of Labor (MPLA-PT) in Angola and the economic problems still facing the nation, and comments on the program of the First Extraordinary Congress of the MPLA (1980).

3482. Zotov, N. M. EVOLIUTSIIA IDEINO-POLITICHESKIKH VZGLIADOV ANGOL'SKIKH BORTSOV ZA NATSIONAL'NOE OSVOBOZHDENIE [The evolution of ideological and political views of the Angolan fighters for national liberation]. *Narody Azii i Afriki [USSR] 1980 (4): 111-118.* Traces the significant social changes which took place in Angola beginning in the 1940's which made possible the success of the Angolan people in their struggle for national liberation. Success was aided by the support shown to Angola by other countries, particularly the socialist countries. 39 notes. S. J. Talalay

3483. —. [ANGOLA, CUBA, AND THE UNITED STATES]. *Foreign Policy 1978 (31): 3-33.*
Bender, Gerald J. ANGOLA, THE CUBANS, AND AMERICAN ANXIETIES, *pp. 3-30.* The presence of Cuban troops in Angola has unsettled both the Carter administration and many Americans. The author seeks to clarify the background and events leading to the Cuban presence and help allay fears of a Soviet victory over American foreign policy interests in Africa.
Crocker, Chester A. COMMENT: MAKING AFRICA SAFE FOR THE CUBANS, *pp. 31-33.* Bender largely masked the USSR's sinister role in Angola and overly romanticized its entanglement with Cuba. H. R. Mahood

3484. —. ARQUIVO HISTÓRICO MILITAR, 2A DIVISÃO: ULTRAMAR PORTUGUÊS, 2A SECÇÃO—ANGOLA: CATÁLOGO DE DOCUMENTOS [Arquivo Histórico Militar, Division 2; Portuguese Overseas, Section 2—Angola: catalog of documents]. *Bol. do Arquivo Hist. Militar [Portugal] 1977 47: 73-351.* Lists the contents of 84 cases of documents relating to Angola in the Arquivo Histórico Militar, Lisbon. The documents date from the period 1705-1970.

Botswana

3485. Aguda, Akinola. LEGAL DEVELOPMENT IN BOTSWANA FROM 1885 TO 1966. *Botswana Notes and Records [Botswana] 1973 5: 52-63.* Traces the evolution of the legal systems of Botswana, 1885-1966.

3486. Barnard, Alan. NHARO BUSHMAN MEDICINE AND MEDICINE MEN. *Africa [Great Britain] 1979 49(1): 68-80.* Describes the medicine of the Nharo of the Western Ghansi district of Botswana in the central-western Kalahari. Discusses physical medicine, which employs physical substances and is either good or evil; spiritual medicine, which requires the medicine man to enter a trance state and is considered good; divination; individual curing rites; medicine dances; exorcism; the place of medicine men in society; and explanations of Nharo medicine. 5 notes, biblio. P. J. Taylorson

3487. Bell, Morag. RURAL-URBAN MOVEMENT AMONG BOTSWANA'S SKILLED MANPOWER: SOME OBSERVATIONS ON THE TWO SECTOR MODEL. *Africa [Great Britain] 1980 50(4): 404-421.* Independence in Botswana in 1966 brought with it increased educational opportunities, employment, and urbanization, all welcome to a government that needed skilled labor. The government is the major employer, absorbing 90% of the graduates and 71% of students with Junior Certificate. There is widespread movement among Botswana families owing to the need to find work in the towns, but ties with the rural areas remain strong. With the lengthy absence of males, females head a third of all households, with the result that young women increasingly appreciate independence and the inherent social changes. The rural families benefit from having relatives in the towns and from their remittances. Based on fieldwork; 7 tables. R. L. Collison

3488. Benson, Mary. TSHEKEDI KHAMA AS I KNEW HIM. *Botswana Notes and Records [Botswana] 1976 8: 121-128.* A highlighting of the career of a leading Botswana nationalist and Ngwato leader, Tshekedi Khama, by his onetime South African secretary and biographer, Mary Benson. Emphasizes the author's close personal knowledge of Tshekedi Khama in London and Bechuanaland during the 1950's to construct a sympathetic overview of his long struggle against the British colonial administration. L. W. Truschel

3489. Bullock, H. L.; Macmillan, W. M.; and Lipson, D. L. REPORTS OF OBSERVERS ON THE ATTITUDE OF THE BAMANGWATO TRIBE TO THE RETURN OF TSHEKEDI KHAMA TO THE BAMANGWATO RESERVE. *Botswana Notes and Records [Botswana] 1978 10: 137-148.* A three-member team was sent to the Bamangwato Tribal Reserve in 1951 by the British Secretary for Commonwealth Relations to investigate the status of the dispute between Tshekedi Khama, who had served for 22 years as regent for his nephew, Seretse Khama, and the Ngwato authorities who had driven him from power in 1949. The two official reports of the team, reprinted here, discuss the reasons for Tshekedi's unpopularity and recommended the return of Seretse, who had been exiled by the British government, as the means of halting deteriorating conditions within the Ngwato. Note. L. W. Truschel

3490. Chiepe, G. K. T. DEVELOPMENT IN BOTSWANA. *African Affairs [Great Britain] 1973 72(288): 319-322.* Traces the British protectorate and independence. Copper, nickel, and diamonds have been discovered, but Botswana still has a manpower and capital shortage. It is economically linked to South Africa, a reliance that may gradually disappear. Condensed from a talk to the R.A.S., 14 March 1973. H. G. Soff

3491. Cohen, Dennis L. THE BOTSWANA POLITICAL ELITE: EVIDENCE FROM THE 1974 GENERAL ELECTION. *J. of Southern African Affairs 1979 4(3): 347-371.* Assesses the nature of the political elite of Botswana at the time of the 1974 elections from responses to questionnaires by all candidates for seats in the National Assembly and local councils. The political elite turned out to be older, better educated, and wealthier than the general adult population in Botswana and most interested in issues of economic growth within the country. The data on the candidates found no significant differences between the four political parties overall, while the officeholding elite of the dominant Botswana Democratic Party has remained particularly stable since the first national elections in 1965. Based on field research, printed documents, and secondary sources; 12 tables, 63 notes. L. W. Truschel

3492. Dale, Richard. PRESIDENT SIR SERETSE KHAMA, BOTSWANA'S FOREIGN POLICY AND THE SOUTHERN AFRICAN SUBORDINATE STATE SYSTEM. *Plural Societies [Netherlands] 1976 7(1): 69-88.* Assesses the evolution and political development of Botswana following independence, 1966-76, its president Seretse Khama, its place in foreign and international relations, and its niche in Southern African foreign policy.

3493. Dennis, Caroline. THE ROLE OF DINGAKA TSA SETSWANA FROM THE 19TH CENTURY TO THE PRESENT. *Botswana Notes and Records [Botswana] 1978 10: 53-66.* Traditional Tswana medicine centered around varied categories of *dingaka* (doctors) at the individual and group levels, some of whom rose to the position of key advisers to the chiefs. European missionaries were, to a degree, seen as new *dingaka*in the 19th century, and traditional medicine continued to function at a reduced level during the colonial period. Based on Botswana National Archives, published documents, and field research; 14 notes, biblio. L. W. Truschel

3494. Duggan, William. THE KWENENG IN THE COLONIAL ERA: A BRIEF ECONOMIC HISTORY. *Botswana Notes and Records [Botswana] 1977 9: 41-48.* A descriptive analysis of the economy of the Bakwena of the Kweneng district in southeastern Botswana during the years of the Bechuanaland Protectorate, 1885-1966. Only through development of agriculture at home and migrant labor in South Africa were the Bakwena able to diversify their precolonial economy which depended on pastoralism and marginal farming. Based on Botswana National Archives documents and secondary works; 46 notes. L. W. Truschel

3495. Gillett, Simon. THE SURVIVAL OF CHIEFTAINCY IN BOTSWANA. *Botswana Notes and Records [Botswana] 1975 7: 103-108.* During the years of the British protectorate, the chiefs of Botswana received substantial support from the imperial authorities. The Botswana government, in a series of laws passed from 1965 to 1970, has sought to curtail the past extensive rights and prerogatives of the chiefs. They, however, retain extensive support among the masses of peasants in the country and function effectively inside modern autonomous district authorities and political movements. With the possible exception of the minority non-Tswana groups, the government has been able to build national unity in Botswana without destroying the traditional institutions. Based on published documents and secondary sources; 11 notes. L. W. Truschel

3496. Gilmore, Kirby S. AN INVESTIGATION INTO THE DECLINE OF THE YAMBEZI FISHERMAN'S CO-OPERATIVE SOCIETY. *Botswana Notes and Records [Botswana] 1979 11: 97-102.* Fishermen of four Subia villages in the Chobe district of northwestern Botswana established the Yambezi Fisherman's Co-operative Society in 1973 to facilitate netting and marketing of fish from Lake Yambezi. Within two years the cooperative began a marked decline as the Zambian market was closed, the Botswana government curtailed its technical and financial support, authorities in Namibia harassed Botswana fishermen on the lake, and the lake's fish population decreased sharply with the spread of the aquatic Salvinia weed. All along the Subia community was distrustful of the government role in the cooperative and the tax levies it collected. Based on personal communications and field investigation; 3 tables, 2 notes, 2 appendixes. L. W. Truschel

3497. Grant, Sandy. MOCHUDI: THE TRANSITION FROM VILLAGE TO TOWN. *Botswana Notes and Records [Botswana] 1973 5: 2-11.* A history of the town of Mochudi, Botswana, since its foundation in 1871.

3498. Grant, Sandy. THE NON-GOVERNMENT CONTRIBUTION TO DEVELOPMENT IN BOTSWANA, 1962-1980. *Botswana Notes and Records [Botswana] 1980 12: 41-47.* Nonprofit voluntary organizations have initiated aid and development projects in Botswana since 1962, particularly in the areas of education, health, job training, and relief for drought victims and refugees. The Botswana government welcomed these outside programs, although misunderstanding and confusion arose between them and official developmental projects. Since 1974 there has been a concerted effort to consolidate private and public developmental efforts under official control. Based on a talk to the Botswana Society in Gaborone, 10 March 1981. L. W. Truschel

3499. Greenhow, Timothy. THE TRIBAL GRAZING LAND POLICY AND INTEGRATED LAND-USE PLANNING: A DISTRICT VIEW. *Botswana Notes and Records [Botswana] 1978 10: 159-168.* The Botswana Government initiated its Tribal Grazing Land Policy in 1975. By altering the traditional land tenurial system, and by limiting livestock numbers to reduce overuse of grazing lands, the government hoped to obtain improved management of land resources. However, the policy needed to be broadened to involve additional issues of integrated land-use planning to meet its objective effectively. Based on printed government documents and secondary works; 3 notes. L. W. Truschel

3500. Henderson, Willie. INDEPENDENT BOTSWANA: A REAPPRAISAL OF FOREIGN POLICY OPTIONS. *African Affairs [Great Britain] 1974 73(290): 37-49.* A refutation of the theories of C. R. Hill, and of Lord Hailey in *South Africa and the High Commission Territories* (Oxford U. Press, 1963). Both men assert a pessimism of the independence of Botswana and stress her dependence on South Africa. Botswana has, however, recognized the problem of dependence, and has made an effort to solve that problem. 29 notes. H. G. Soff

3501. Hermans, Janet. OFFICIAL POLICY TOWARDS THE BUSHMAN OF BOTSWANA: A REVIEW. *Botswana Notes and Records [Botswana] 1977 9: 55-67.* Descriptive analysis of official policy in Botswana toward the San population since inception of the British Bechuanaland Protectorate over the area in 1885. Argues that colonial era policy on the San up to 1940 lacked overall direction or specific concern apart from maintaining close relations with the Tswana leaders. Based on Botswana National Archives documents, published official reports, and secondary sources; 42 notes. Article to be continued. L. W. Truschel

3502. Holm, John D. LIBERAL DEMOCRACY AND RURAL DEVELOPMENT IN BOTSWANA. *African Studies Rev. 1982 25(1): 83-102.* A study of resource allocation in Botswana. Although 85% of the population lives in rural areas and, with their numbers, control the democratic process, still very little funding is designated for rural development. Democracy does not necessarily bring benefits to the majority. Based on field research and government documents; 11 notes, biblio. R. T. Brown

3503. Hudson, Derek J. THE ESTABLISHMENT OF BOTSWANA'S CENTRAL BANK AND THE INTRODUCTION OF THE NEW CURRENCY. *Botswana Notes and Records [Botswana] 1978 10: 119-135.* The Director of Research for the Bank of Botswana assesses the first four years of the bank's history, beginning with its official creation as a national bank in 1975, and the introduction of Botswana's first national currency, the Pula, in 1976. Botswana has created, through its new Central Bank and currency, a number of economic tools without financial loss, and has made substantial political gains as well. Based on Botswana and Bank of Botswana records; 7 tables, 5 notes, appendix. L. W. Truschel

3504. Johns, Sheridan. BOTSWANA'S STRATEGY FOR DEVELOPMENT: AN ASSESSMENT OF DEPENDENCE IN THE SOUTHERN AFRICAN CONTEXT. *J. of Commonwealth Pol. Studies [Great Britain] 1973 11(3): 214-230.* Considers Botswana's links with both South Africa and Southern Rhodesia and with its black African neighbors, and looks at the attempts to improve its economy, 1960's-70's.

3505. Jones, C. R. and Key, R. M. BOTSWANA'S CONTRIBUTION TO THE INTERNATIONAL GEODYNAMICS PROJECT: A REVIEW OF A SECOND TWO YEARS' PARTICIPATION. *Botswana Notes and Records [Botswana] 1977 9: 123-127.* A descriptive listing of publications compiled for projects undertaken by the Geological Survey at Lobatse, Botswana. During 1974-76, the Geological Survey studied the crustal structure of the Kalahari Desert and the Eastern Geotraverse in Botswana. 2 ref. L. W. Truschel

3506. Jones, Keith F. BRITAIN'S CONTRIBUTION TO BOTSWANA'S PUBLIC DEBT, 1956-1976. *Botswana Notes and Records [Botswana] 1977 9: 109-117.* Discusses British policies and actions with respect to the external debt of Botswana during the final decade of the colonial era and during its first decade after independence in 1966. Concludes that while British lending policy during the late colonial period does not seem generous by later standards, Batswana's colonial administration badly needed the loans and aid received from Great Britain. Also describes the role of British loans in Botswana's development expenditures. Based on official documents; 2 tables, 26 notes. L. W. Truschel

3507. Landell-Mills, J. AN EXTRACT FROM THE DIARIES OF C. F. REY. *Botswana Notes and Records [Botswana] 1973 5: 67-81.* Recounts the journey of Rey, Resident Commissioner of the Bechuanaland Protectorate, 1930-37, across the Kalahari Desert.

3508. Massey, David. A CASE OF COLONIAL COLLABORATION: THE HUT TAX AND MIGRANT LABOUR. *Botswana Notes and Records [Botswana] 1978 10: 95-99.* The Hut Tax was established primarily as a revenue-raising measure in the Bechuanaland Protectorate in 1899. Nevertheless, it came to serve the labor demands of South African mining companies, as well as colonial officials and chiefs who gathered revenues from the tax. In 1933-34 the top colonial administrators actively cooperated with South African labor recruiters in promoting a potentially dangerous scheme of experimenting with Lister vaccine among workers drawn from north of the Tropic of Capricorn, an area previously excluded from labor recruitment. Based on Botswana National Archives and secondary sources; 15 notes. L. W. Truschel

3509. Muzorewa, Basil C. THE ROLE OF LOCAL TREASURIES IN THE UNDER-DEVELOPMENT OF BOTSWANA: 1938-1953. *Botswana Notes and Records [Botswana] 1978 10: 113-118.* Local treasuries were officially established in the Bechuanaland Protectorate in 1938. They collected taxes and even kept funds for lending, but failed to develop as banking firms. Their maintenance of reserve funds is seen as excessive and contractionary on the young rural monetary economy. Based on Botswana National Archives; 3 tables, 13 notes. L. W. Truschel

3510. Osborne, Allan. RURAL DEVELOPMENT IN BOTSWANA: A QUALITATIVE VIEW. *J. of Southern African Studies [Great Britain] 1976 2(2): 198-213.* Describes the rural development program adopted by Botswana since independence in 1966. Traditional cultural factors should no longer be neglected in planning. Based on government reports; 49 notes. S. P. Carr

3511. Parson, Jack. CATTLE, CLASS AND THE STATE IN RURAL BOTSWANA. *J. of Southern African Studies [Great Britain] 1981 7(2): 236-255.* Presents a Marxist critique of the rural sector of Botswana's political economy, particularly since independence in 1966. Traditional and recently emergent classes of cattle-owning and landowning capitalists allegedly have been increasing their wealth at the expense of the rural peasantry. Through control of the national government the capitalist classes have aggrandized their wealth in hidden forms, most recently in the National Policy on Tribal Grazing Land. The Botswana capitalists, however, are depicted as themselves limited by international control over mineral prices and South African control over regional migrant labor and beef prices, key determinants in Botswana's economy. Based on published and unpublished Botswana official documents and reports; 56 notes. L. W. Truschel

3512. Parsons, Q. N. THE ECONOMIC HISTORY OF KHAMA'S COUNTRY IN SOUTHERN AFRICA. *African Social Res. [Zambia] 1974 (18): 643-675.* Khama's Country refers to that area of Botswana ruled by Khama III (1835-1923). This is an analysis of the economy in his kingdom from 1875, when Khama III ascended, to the boom of the 1890's and the eventual underdevelopment in the colonial era. This African state, while developing a trade economy, stagnated and was reduced to a colonial labor reserve. Map, 29 notes. H. G. Soff

3513. Parsons, Q. N. "KHAMA & CO." AND THE JOUSSE TROUBLE, 1910-1916. *J. of African Hist. [Great Britain] 1975 16(3): 383-408.* Khama III was king of the Ngwato Tswana kingdom in colonial east-central Botswana, 1875-1923. He was a friend and ally of the British, and they in turn allowed him considerable economic freedom. In 1919 Khama formed a company, but due to his constant trouble with a white trader, Paul Jousse, the colonial government chose to prevent Khama from continuing his commercial enterprise rather than let him subordinate white settlers and merchants. Map; 100 notes. H. G. Soff

3514. Parsons, Q. N. SHOTS FOR A BLACK REPUBLIC? SIMON RATSHOSA AND BOTSWANA NATIONALISM. *African Affairs [Great Britain] 1974 73(293): 449-458.* The colonial period saw a resurgence, not a reduction, in the threat of revolt by Westernized Africans. Two assassination plots in the period 1916-26 were led by educated Africans, particularly the Ratshosa brothers. The author analyzes the political ideology of Simon Ratshosa after 1926, focusing on his ideas on a unified state, the economic status of peasants, and democratization of local governments. 30 notes. H. G. Soff

3515. Picard, Louis A. DISTRICT COUNCILS IN BOTSWANA: A REMNANT OF LOCAL AUTONOMY. *J. of Modern African Studies [Great Britain] 1979 17(2): 285-308.* In most of Africa the autonomy of local and district councils has been dissipated and authority recentralized, but in Botswana since independence in 1966 district councils have continued to perform important political and administrative functions. This has been due to their strengthening before independence between 1960 and 1966, to their being defended by the Ministry of Local Government in bureaucratic disagreements with the Ministry of Finance and Development Planning, and to the relative openness of politics, since there has been general tolerance of opposition at a local level as long as it provides no serious threat to the Botswana Democratic Party. Based on documents in the Botswana National Archives and printed sources; 3 tables, 64 notes. D. J. Nicholls

3516. Picard, Louis A. INDEPENDENT BOTSWANA: THE DISTRICT ADMINISTRATION. *J. of African Studies 1981 8(3): 98-110.* Botswana's District Administration after independence operated to maintain government control in ways reminiscent of the colonial period in the face of challenges by ethnic minorities, urban radicals, and rural traditionalists. District Commissioners acted to suppress or coopt a variety of dissidents in Ghanzi, Mochudi, Francistown, and Kanye. Oppositionist movements, however, registered gains in the 1969 elections, particularly in the Ngwaketse District. Looking ahead politically, the government switched its emphasis in District Administration from control to fostering rural development, with positive results in the 1974 elections. Based on interviews and official Botswana correspondence and reports; 79 notes. L. W. Truschel

3517. Picard, Louis A. RURAL DEVELOPMENT IN BOTSWANA: ADMINISTRATIVE STRUCTURES AND PUBLIC POLICY. *J. of Developing Areas 1979 13(3): 283-300.* With independence in 1966 Botswana inherited a prefectoral system of district administration and a British-style local government system. Over the study period the administrative system became more centralized. Nearly half of the district committee officials were expatriates, and that figure—and thus localization—has not changed much. Initially government efforts were concentrated on the mining sector, though finally some effort also was being channeled into agriculture. Author recommends significant rural development efforts for newly independent nations. Based on Botswana primary sources, also secondary sources; 43 notes. O. W. Eads, Jr.

3518. Potten, David H. ASPECTS OF THE RECENT HISTORY OF NGAMILAND. *Botswana Notes and Records [Botswana] 1976 8: 63-86.* A broad survey of the 19th- and 20th-century economic development efforts in the Ngamiland region in northwestern Botswana, with particular emphasis on the many proposals made since the 1850's to utilize the water resources of the area. None of the diverse recommendations, involving settlement, irrigation, and diversion of water resources in Ngamiland, had come to realization by 1972, but prospects for future development are promising. Based on published documents and archival and secondary materials; 26 notes, 3 tables. L. W. Truschel

3519. Potten, David H. ETSHA: A SUCCESSFUL RESETTLEMENT SCHEME. *Botswana Notes and Records [Botswana] 1976 8: 105-119.* An account of the entry of 4,000 Angolan refugees into the Ngamiland region of northwestern Botswana during the late 1960's and their successful resettlement at Etsha in the same region during the early 1970's. Some 80% of the refugees, who arrived between the end of 1967 and September 1969, were Hambukushu, closely related to peoples resident since the 18th century in Ngamiland. The Angolans wished to farm and become permanent settlers inside Botswana. The Botswana government and the local Batswana welcomed them and with international agencies assisted their settlement in the Etsha area. By 1971 the resettlement had succeeded at low cost. Based on archival and secondary sources and interviews; 3 tables, biblio. L. W. Truschel

3520. Raseroka, B. H. PAST AND PRESENT DISTRIBUTION OF BUFFALO IN BOTSWANA. *Botswana Notes and Records [Botswana] 1975 7: 131-140.* A historical analysis of the distribution of Cape Buffaloes in Botswana and surrounding areas from the time of the first recorded sighting north of the Orange River in 1783. Changes in climate, ecology, human settlement, and hunting practices extinguished the buffalo from southern and eastern Botswana following 1840. Settlement and other human activity has resulted in redistribution of buffalo herds in northern Botswana during the present century. Based on field research and published sources; 2 maps, biblio. L. W. Truschel

3521. Raseroka, H. K. SOME PROBLEMS IN LIBRARY DEVELOPMENT IN BOTSWANA. *Botswana Notes and Records [Botswana] 1978 10: 91-94.* The Botswana National Library Service developed 15 branch libraries, 1968-78. Few of these were situated in the less populated central and western portions of the country, and 95% of the holdings of the National Library service is beyond the reading level of the majority of citizens. 13 notes. L. W. Truschel

3522. Reiz, Otto. W. H. SITWELL 1860-1932. *Rhodesiana [Rhodesia] 1977 (36): 53-61.* Reproduces three letters of William Sitwell to his mother, during his service with the Bechuanaland Border Police at Macloutsi. Describes his military career particularly his achievements in India and the Dardanelles during World War I. Photo, 25 notes. C. A. McNeill

3523. Richter, Wolfgang von and Butynski, T. HUNTING IN BOTSWANA. *Botswana Notes and Records [Botswana] 1973 5: 191-208.* Examines African and safari hunting in Botswana since 1961.

3524. Russell, Margo. SLAVES OR WORKERS? RELATIONS BETWEEN BUSHMEN, TSWANA, AND BOERS IN THE KALAHARI. *J. of Southern African Studies [Great Britain] 1976 2(2): 178-197.* One government inspectors' report (1971) described the position of the San on the cattle ranches in western Botswana as "voluntary slavery." To examine this allegation the author compares the situation with that which existed in the colonial period. The relationship between the San, the Tswana, and the Boers has changed little, although there have been several attempts to formulate solutions to the problem of coexistence. Any government attempt to change this long-standing relationship could be to the detriment of the San. Based on newspapers and government reports; map, 58 notes. S. P. Carr/S

3525. Schapera, I. and Roberts, Simon. RAMPEDI REVISITED. ANOTHER LOOK AT A KGATLA WARD. *Africa [Great Britain] 1975 45(3): 258-279.* Comparing household censuses by Schapera (1934) and Roberts (1973), the article traces the growth of a Kgatla ward in Botswana over a period of 40 years; shows that the basic agnatic character of kinship has proved durable.

3526. Silitshena, R. M. K. CHIEFLY AUTHORITY AND THE ORGANIZATION OF SPACE IN BOTSWANA: TOWARDS AN EXPLANATION OF NUCLEATED SETTLEMENTS AMONG THE TSWANA. *Botswana Notes and Records [Botswana] 1979 11: 55-67.* The prevalent precolonial pattern of large-scale town settlement among the Tswana peoples of Southern Africa has been explained by theories of ecological and defensive necessity or convenience. These theories are inadequate and fail to account for the continued pattern of nucleated settlement during the 80-year colonial period in Botswana's history or the longtime economic success of Barolong dispersed settlement. The powerful position of the chiefs during precolonial and colonial times provides a more satisfactory explanation. Until a series of laws passed between 1965 and 1970 removed his powers over legislative and administrative affairs as well as taxation and land distribution, the chief in Botswana maintained control over the organization of territorial space, use of resources, and the movements of communities and individuals. Based on Botswana archival sources, interviews, and secondary sources; 62 notes. L. W. Truschel

3527. Silitshena, R. M. K. NOTES ON SOME CHARACTERISTICS OF POPULATION THAT HAS MIGRATED PERMANENTLY TO THE LANDS IN THE KWENENG DISTRICT. *Botswana Notes and Records [Botswana] 1978 10: 149-157.* A 1976 survey of three rural settlements of the Kweneng District of southeast Botswana revealed that many of the poorer Tswana were moving in recent years away from the agricultural towns that have predominated in the country to the outlying rural lands. The economics of farming in eastern Botswana are complicating rural resettlement. Based on a questionnaire survey, and published documents and reports; 9 tables, 13 notes, biblio.
L. W. Truschel

3528. Silitshena, R. M. K. ORAPA: A NEW MINING TOWN AT THE EDGE OF THE KGALAGADI (KALAHARI) DESERT. *Geography 1978 63(1): 45-48.* Discusses the development of Orapa, a diamond mining company town in Botswana. After an extended search for diamonds by DeBeers Company geologists, the Botswana government built an all-weather road, installed telephone connections, and built power and water facilities. The author describes the organization of the Orapa mine, and the company township where the employees live. The town has had limited impact on the local economy. Fig.
J. B. Reed

3529. Spears, John V. AN EPIDEMIC AMONG THE KGATLA: THE INFLUENZA OF 1918. *Botswana Notes and Records [Botswana] 1979 11: 69-76.* The worldwide Spanish influenza epidemic of 1918 affected the Bechuanaland Protectorate harshly in October and November of that year. None of the preventive measures or cures attempted by the Kgatla were effective against the three-day disease, and they suffered a high mortality rate. The strong kinship bonds, traditional culture, and political unity of the Kgatla enabled them to survive this disaster without radical social damage. Based on field interviews and Botswana archival and secondary sources; map, table, 24 notes.
L. W. Truschel

3530. Stevens, Christopher and Speed, John. MULTI-PARTYISM IN AFRICA: THE CASE OF BOTSWANA REVISITED. *African Affairs [Great Britain] 1977 76(304): 381-387.* Reviews John Wiseman's "Multi-partyism in Africa: the Case of Botswana," *African Affairs,* 76(302): pp. 70-79. Wiseman's views and interpretations are misleading, especially his discussion on chiefs and government and the party system, 1965-77. 10 notes. H. G. Soff

3531. Taylor, John. MINE LABOUR RECRUITMENT IN THE BECHUANALAND PROTECTORATE. *Botswana Notes and Records [Botswana] 1978 10: 99-112.* Although assessed as a revenue measure in 1899, the Hut Tax of the Bechuanaland Protectorate particularly after 1912, led to heavy mine labor recruitment by South African labor agencies. Operating at first through local traders, the Native Recruiting Corporation sent an annual average of over 3,000 men to the South African mines during the 1930's, while the Witwatersrand Native Labour Organization began to recruit labor north of the Tropic of Capricorn in 1934. Resultant manpower shortages in the African reserves led to an array of economic and social problems during the remainder of the colonial period. Based on Botswana National Archives, and published reports; 2 maps, 2 tables, 37 notes. L. W. Truschel

3532. Vengroff, Richard. POPULAR PARTICIPATION AND THE ADMINISTRATION OF RURAL DEVELOPMENT: THE CASE OF BOTSWANA. *Human Organization 1974 33(4): 303-309.* The role of the village development committee in decisionmaking. S

3533. Vengroff, Richard. TRADITIONAL POLITICAL STRUCTURES IN THE CONTEMPORARY CONTEXT: THE CHIEFTAINCY IN THE KWENENG. *African Studies 1975 34(1): 39-56.* Considers present efforts to create district councils in Botswana to fulfill the political roles traditionally performed by chiefs. The history of traditional leadership among the Tswana people is examined, with particular reference to chieftaincy in the Kweneng, from the standpoint of "changing relations between the chief and the colonial and later post-independence administrations." Concludes that new governmental structures have done little to alter local patterns of political behavior, but that chiefs have assumed a new role as direct servants of the state. Based on printed sources and manuscript material in the Botswana National Archives. 5 tables, 59 notes. J. A. Casada

3534. Wilson, Brian H. SOME NATURAL AND MAN-MADE CHANGES IN THE CHANNELS OF THE OKAVANGO DELTA. *Botswana Notes and Records [Botswana] 1973 5: 132-153.* Examines changes wrought by man and nature on the course of the Okavango Delta in Botswana since 1800.

3535. Wily, Elizabeth. A STRATEGY OF SELF-DETERMINATION FOR THE KALAHARI SAN (THE BOTSWANA GOVERNMENT'S PROGRAMME OF ACTION IN THE GHANZI FARMS). *Development and Change [Netherlands] 1982 13(2): 291-308.* Details the strategy adopted by the Botswana government in 1974 to encourage self-reliance and self-determination among Kalahari San, focusing on events in the Ghansi region as an example of this strategy.

3536. Wiseman, John A. THE ACHIEVEMENT OF SERETSE KHAMA. *Round Table [Great Britain] 1980 (280): 409-414.* Seretse Khama, founder of the Botswana Democratic Party and President of Botswana, 1966-80, managed to create a party of deep national appeal and a stable political regime. The two main principles of his leadership were to reduce the traditional power of the chiefs and transfer them to a democratically elected government, and to reduce the old ethnic animosities and encourage a sense of nationalism. Under Khama, a democratic, multiparty system was maintained, and Botswana's economic prosperity gradually increased. Secondary sources; 4 notes.
E. J. Adams

Lesotho

3537. Bajan, Pavol. ČIERNY BISKUP V AFRIKE [Black bishop in Africa]. *Kalendár Jednota 1979 (82): 86-88.* A short history of Christianity in Lesotho from the establishment of British protectorate in 1884 to new bishop's installation in 1978.

3538. Haliburton, G. M. WALTER MATITTA AND JOSIEL LEFELA: A PROPHET AND A POLITICIAN IN LESOTHO. *J. of Religion in Africa [Netherlands] 1975 7(2): 111-131.* Provides biographical sketches of two men who helped Lesotho obtain independence. They were both born in 1885 and were friends in adulthood. Walter Matitta was a prophet who broke away from his church in 1921 and formed a new sect in honor of a former ruler, Moshoeshoe. Josie Lefela chose to voice disapproval of colonial life through politics and spent his life denouncing chiefs who acquiesced to the demands of colonial masters. Imprisoned several times for his agitation, Lefela died in 1965, one year before independence. 40 notes, appendix. H. G. Soff

3539. Hirschmann, David. ADMINISTRATION OF PLANNING IN LESOTHO: THE SECOND LAG. *Development and Change [Netherlands] 1978 9(3): 397-414.* Discusses the economic planning machinery of Lesotho, 1960's-70's, and factors contributing to the beginning and ending of the second lag.

3540. Hirschmann, David. CHANGES IN LESOTHO'S POLICY TOWARDS SOUTH AFRICA. *African Affairs [Great Britain] 1979 78(311): 177-196.* Analyzes Lesotho's reformulation of its policy toward South Africa in the 1970's. Due to its clientele status and dependency, Lesotho's policy options are circumscribed by South Africa. South African neglect, apartheid, and Lesotho's support for African unity and antiapartheid movements, explain Lesotho's policy changes—confined in any case largely to verbal platitudes. 2 tables, 65 notes. S. Lakhan

3541. Kunene, Daniel P. *LESELINYANA LA LESOTHO* AND SOTHO HISTORIOGRAPHY. *Hist. in Africa 1977 4: 149-161.* Suggests ways in which the newspaper *Leselinyana La Lesotho,* published since 1863, can be of value to historians of the Sotho. Its published research, compilation of proverbs, historical studies, archival material, and literary works such as Thomas Mofolo's *Chaka* are all important sources. Based on research on microfilm copies of the newspaper at the University of Wisconsin, Madison. G. M. Fishman

3542. Macartney, W. J. A. CASE STUDY: THE LESOTHO GENERAL ELECTION OF 1970. *Government and Opposition [Great Britain] 1973 8(4): 473-494.* Discusses the roles of political parties, religion, Basotho culture and foreign policy issues in the 1970 general election.

3543. Thahane, T. LESOTHO, AN ISLAND COUNTRY: THE PROBLEMS OF BEING LAND-LOCKED. *African Rev. [Tanzania] 1974 4(2): 279-290.* Analyzes the difficulties of landlocked nations, emphasizing the problems of Lesotho. Traces international agreements on this subject to 1919. 8 notes. H. G. Soff

3544. Wallman, Sandra. THE MODERNIZATION OF DEPENDENCE: A FURTHER NOTE ON LESOTHO. *J. of Southern African Studies [Great Britain] 1976 3(1): 102-107.* In 1966 Lesotho gained independence after 130 years of British domination. The author examines the country's degree of political and economic independence from South Africa, 1966-76. Secondary sources; 19 notes. S. P. Carr

3545. Weisfelder, Richard F. THE DECLINE OF HUMAN RIGHTS IN LESOTHO: AN EVALUATION OF DOMESTIC AND EXTERNAL DETERMINANTS. *Issue 1976 6(4): 22-33.* Discusses human rights violations during Lesotho's first decade of independence (1966-76) by the government of Prime Minister J. Leabua Jonathan notwithstanding the similarities between its parliamentary system and the British original.

3546. Weisfelder, Richard F. EARLY VOICES OF PROTEST IN BASUTOLAND: THE PROGRESSIVE ASSOCIATION AND *LEKHOTLA LA BAFO.African Studies Rev. 1974 17(2): 397-409.* The Basutoland Progressive Association, composed of Protestant-educated elites and the *Lekhotla La Bafo* (Council of Commoners), whose membership was from the rural peasantry, were the first 20th-century nationalist organizations in Lesotho. 26 notes, biblio. R. T. Brown

3547. Winai-Stom, Gabriele. THE INFLUENCE OF MULTINATIONAL CORPORATION ON LESOTHO'S POLITICS AND ECONOMICS. *African Rev. [Tanzania] 1975 5(4): 473-497.* Focuses on Lesotho's relations with multinational corporations, whose investment is sought as a counterweight to the pervasive influence of South African investment, but economic realities make the effort futile. 8 tables, 113 notes. R. T. Brown

Madagascar and the Islands

(including Mauritius, the Seychelles, Réunion, and the Comoros)

3548. Althabe, Gérard. LE MONIMA [The National Movement for the Independence of Madagascar (MONIMA)]. *Rev. Française d'Études Pol. Africaines [France] 1973 (86): 71-75.* Reviews the history of the Mouvement National pour l'Indépendance de Madagascar (MONIMA), founded in 1958 by Monja Jaona and centered in the southern city of Tuléar, which experienced vicissitudes under the neocolonialist regime of Philibert Tsiranana (president, 1960-72) and with the change of government of 1972, faces a choice between cooperation with the new nationalist government or becoming an opposition party on the left.

3549. Althabe, Gérard. LES LUTTES SOCIALES A TANANARIVE EN 1972 [The social battles at Tananarive in 1972]. *Cahiers d'Etudes Africaines [France] 1980 20(4): 407-447.* Discusses the conflicts between lingering colonial sentiments, a developing nationalism, and the growth of specific political groups, which culminated in battle in 1972 at Tananarive, Madagascar; and the installation of the Ramanantsoa regime (20 May-8 October 1972).

3550. Berg, Gerald M. RIZICULTURE AND THE FOUNDING OF MONARCHY IN IMERINA. *J. of African Hist. [Great Britain] 1981 22(3): 289-308.* According to Merina tradition, rice cultivation originated in the south of Madagascar, but written documentation seems to indicate that rice techniques were borrowed from the Lake Alaotra area. The complex irrigation system for rice cultivation was introduced in a relatively recent period, and regal control was gradually established in the late 18th century. The basis of the Merina monarchy was, however, the sacredness of land and the control over the water supplies, both of which contributed to the evolution of a rigid social hierarchy. The organization of labor needed for large-scale irrigation and the consequent increase in agricultural surplus concentrated power in the hands of the monarch. Based on fieldwork and published sources; 69 notes, map. R. L. Collison

3551. Bézy, Fernand. LA TRANSFORMATION DES STRUCTURES SOCIO-ÉCONOMIQUES À MADAGASCAR (1960-1978) [The transformation of socioeconomic structures in Madagascar, 1960-78]. *Cultures et Développement [Belgium] 1979 11(1): 83-116.* Examines the political, social, and economic changes that have taken place in Madagascar and considers its geographical, demographic, and ethnographic situation.

3552. Bilevich, B. MADAGASKAR: DESIAT' LET REVOLIUTSII [Madagascar: 10 years since revolution]. *Aziia i Afrika Segodnia [USSR] 1982 (6): 12-15.* The administration of President Dadier Ratsiraka, unlike its predecessor, has upheld economic independence, a strong national sovereignty and a democratic domestic policy.

3553. Bouillon, Antoine. LE M.F.M. MALGACHE [The Madagascan M.F.M.]. *Rev. Française d'Études Pol. Africaines [France] 1973 8(95): 46-71.* Describes the creation of the leftist Movement for Proletarian Power (MFM) in Madagascar, composed of peasants, workers, and intellectuals, and formed out of the national uprising of both underground and official organizations in May 1972. Outlines the party's principles, activities, goals for working class advancement, and defiance of government repression.

3554. Coen, J. THE SEYCHELLES. *Hist. Today [Great Britain] 1974 24(11): 799-804.* A history of the Seychelles, 1601-1971.

3555. Cola Alberich, Julio. NOTAS SOBRE LA EVOLUCIÓN POLÍTICA DE MADAGASCAR [Notes on the political development of Madagascar]. *Rev. de Política Int. [Spain] 1973 (125): 215-228, (126): 199-209, (127): 133-143.* Surveys the political history of Madagascar from independence in 1960 to March 1973.

3556. Delval, Raymond. LES MUSULMANS À MADAGASCAR EN 1977 [Muslims in Madagascar, 1977]. *Afrique et l'Asie Modernes [France] 1977 (4): 28-46.* Shows that a true feeling of Islamic unity exists among the Muslims living today in Madagascar in spite of deep differences in ethnic origin and the presence of many different religious groups. Article to be continued (see following entry).

3557. Delval, Raymond. LES MUSULMANS A MADAGASCAR EN 1977 [Muslims in Madagascar, 1977]. *Afrique et l'Asie Modernes [France] 1978 (1): 5-19.* Continued from an earlier article (see preceding entry). Studies the Muslim population of Madagascar, focusing on the Comorians and the Islamic Malagasy.

3558. Esoavelomandroso, Faranirina. RÉSISTANCE À LA MÉDECINE EN SITUATION COLONIALE: LA PESTE À MADAGASCAR [Resistance to medicine in a colonial situation: the plague in Madagascar]. *Ann.: Écon., Soc., Civilisations [France] 1981 36(2): 168-190.* Even if the reaction of the inhabitants of Madagascar to the plague—a "new" disease that appeared in the Central Highlands in 1921—was in many respects comparable to that of the Europeans in the Middle Ages or in modern times, their colonial circumstances conferred a real originality to their attitude. In addition to the anxiety generated by the prospects of a periodic recurrence of the plague and of epidemics striking at entire families and villages, there was the fear not only of a certain death but also of a painful burial. In effect, the sanitary rules decreed by outsiders without taking local traditions into account, prevented the return of the deceased to the ancestral land. In the eyes of the indigenous population, by a series of severe and often inconsistent prophylactic measures, the oppressive colonial administration was seeking nothing but the perpetuation of French domination. The plague—if it existed at all—was nothing but a pretext for pressure on the indigenous population, and the ineffective antiplague vaccines, nothing but a ruse to destroy them. Nationalist leaders thus found in the plague and the various measures adopted to combat it an excellent theme for propaganda. The indigenous reaction to the antiplague campaign organized by the colonists assumed the character of a veritable political resistance, especially during the period of the Popular Front. J

3559. Gaspart, Claude. THE COMORO ISLANDS SINCE INDEPENDENCE: AN ECONOMIC APPRAISAL. *Civilisations [Belgium] 1979 29(3-4): 293-311.* Examines the continuing economic underdevelopment and agricultural imbalance since the 1974 referendum in which 95% of the voters favored independence from France.

3560. Gérard, Pierre. MADAGASCAR: LES CHANCES DE LA "RÉVOLUTION SOCIALISTE" [Madagascar: chances of "socialist revolution"]. *Études [France] 1976 344: 499-515.* A report on the progress of the social reforms enacted as a result of the May Revolution, 1972, in the Malagasy Republic and based on the model of traditional collective society.

3561. Houbert, Jean. MAURITIUS: INDEPENDENCE AND DEPENDENCE. *J. of Modern African Studies [Great Britain] 1981 19(1): 75-105.* Mauritius is a different kind of Third World country, for this Indian Ocean island was devoid of population and most exploitable resources at the time of European contact. In recent times, Mauritius became independent without going through an anticolonial struggle, and ethnic alliances among the Indians, French creoles, and blacks of the island have cut across class lines, so that the politically dominant movements have continued Mauritius' extreme degree of dependence on European trade and tourism. Without maintaining strong capitalist ties to Europe, Mauritius cannot hope to grow economically or even feed its nearly 1,000,000 inhabitants. Based on Mauritius Legislative Council debates, newspapers, and secondary sources; 98 notes.
L. W. Truschel

3562. Houbert, Jean. RÉUNION: I. FRENCH DECOLONISATION IN THE MASCAREIGNES. *J. of Commonwealth and Comparative Pol. [Great Britain] 1980 18(2): 145-171.* The French practice of decolonization has attempted to achieve the integration of the colony concerned with the colonial power. Describes the international context of French decolonizing policy toward Réunion, in the Indian Ocean. For 25 years after World War II France pursued its policy of departmentalization without external interference. More recently, however, French policy has been influenced by the withdrawal of Britain from the Mascarenes and the development of the Communist Party in Réunion. Based on UN General Assembly resolutions, newspapers, periodicals and a wide range of secondary sources; 94 notes. Article to be continued (see following entry). F. P. Tudor

3563. Houbert, Jean. RÉUNION: II. THE POLITICS OF *DÉPARTEMENTALISATION. J. of Commonwealth and Comparative Pol. [Great Britain] 1980 18(3): 325-347.* Continued from a previous article (see preceding entry). Part II. Surveys political, economic, and social developments in Réunion since 1945. The island became a *Département* of France largely at the instigation of the Communists who were very influential under the Fourth Republic, but politics under the Fifth Republic are dominated by the right and the Communist demand for autonomy has no middle-class support. Although social services and communications have been expanded, the economy is still dependent on sugar, and overpopulation and unemployment are only partially checked by emigration to France. The largest employer in Réunion is the government, with vast numbers of civil servants and an inflated tertiary sector. Based on newspapers and secondary works; 28 notes.
D. J. Nicholls

3564. Hutchison, Alan. THE ISLAND VIEWPOINT. *Africa Report 1975 20(1): 50-52.* Assesses feeling among peoples in the Indian Ocean, especially Mauritius, about the military presence of major world powers in that area. S

3565. Jhaveri, Satyavati and Kala, A. S. ISLANDS OF THE SOUTHWEST INDIAN OCEAN: FINDING THEIR NATIONAL IDENTITY. *Africa Q. [India] 1979 19(2): 182-200.* Discusses the history and national development of the southwestern Indian Ocean islands, emphasizing their enhanced strategic importance in the 1970's.

3566. Koerner, Francis. LE FRONT POPULAIRE ET LA QUESTION COLONIALE À MADAGASCAR: LE CLIMAT POLITIQUE EN 1936 [The Popular Front and the colonial question in Madagascar: the political climate in 1936]. *Rev. Française d'Hist. d'Outre-Mer [France] 1974 61(224): 436-454.* The Malagasy independence movement came into being after World War I. By the 1930's, it was torn between contradictory aspirations for assimilation, autonomy, and independence, and met strong resistance within colonial society. In a climate of political friction the government instituted five legal reforms which it enforced until the eve of World War II. Based on documents in the French National Archives, the archives of Madagascar, and secondary sources; 78 notes. L. B. Chan

3567. Korovikov, V. RESPUBLIKA V OKEANE [Republic in the ocean]. *Aziia i Afrika Segodnia [USSR] 1981 (6): 39-41.* Describes the birth of the Seychelles Islands Republic and its achievements in political, economic, and cultural life.

3568. Leymarie, Philippe. ÎLE MAURICE: LA CONSTITUTION MANIPULÉE [Mauritius Island: the manipulated constitution]. *Rev. Française d'Études Pol. Africaines [France] 1973 8(96): 24-27.* Reflects on the cancellation of four legislative elections on Mauritius, November and January 1973, as part of the repressive actions of the Parliament and of Prime Minister Seewoosagur Ramgoolam.

3569. Leymarie, Philippe. LA PRESSE DE L'ILE MAURICE ET DE L'ILE DE LA RÉUNION [The press in Mauritius and Réunion Islands]. *Rev. Française d'Études Pol. Africaines [France] 1973 (88): 74-89.* Compares the smaller, less developed, more politically-oriented media on Réunion (consisting of just one newspaper and one French ORTF station) with the highly successful, more complex information system in Mauritius, which is based on both French and British traditions and is largely self-controlled, ca. 1830-1973.

3570. Leymarie, Philippe. LES SEYCHELLES: LES "INDÉPENDANTISTES" CONTRE LE "TOURISME SAUVAGE" [The Seychelles: the "independentists" against "wild tourism"]. *Rev. Française d'Études Pol. Africaines [France] 1973 8(95): 21-23.* Studies the steady growth of island tourism, largely due to the work of Prime Minister James R. M. Mancham, and underlines the danger of basing all economic and political evolution on tourism, 1968-73.

3571. Leymarie, Philippe. MADAGASCAR: UNE PRESSE PLUS QUE CENTENAIRE [Madagascar: a press over 100 years old]. *Rev. Française d'Études Pol. Africaines [France] 1973 8(96): 34-48.* Describes the history of the development of the press in Madagascar over more than 100 years, from its beginnings by the London Missionary

Society in 1866, through its first years of political censure, and up to its recent liberalization.

3572. Mariñas Otero, Luis. COMOROS: MACROPROBLEMAS DE LA GÉNESIS DE UN MINIESTADO [Comoros: the maximum problems at the birth of a ministate]. *Rev. de Política Int. [Spain] 1978 (155): 123-148.* Describes the problems posed by overpopulation and scarcity of natural resources faced by the new independent state of Comoros, or the Comoro Islands, since they achieved independence from France in 1975.

3573. Mariñas Otero, Luis. SEYCHELLES: BASES Y COORDENADAS DE LA POLÍTICA EXTERIOR DEL ESTADO MAS PEQUEÑO DE ÁFRICA [Seychelles: basis and coordinates of the foreign policy of the smallest state in Africa]. *Rev. de Política Int. [Spain] 1978 (158): 99-115.* Summarizes the Seychelles's foreign policy which aims to reinforce its independence, to respect international treaties and to maintain a position of nonalignment.

3574. Moine, Jacques. OCÉAN INDIEN ET PROGRESSISME [The Indian Ocean and progressivism]. *Afrique et l'Asie Modernes [France] 1979 4(123): 3-23.* Discusses the determination of the leaders of the island states of the Indian Ocean—Madagascar, Mauritius, Réunion, the Comoro Islands, and the Seychelles—to keep the ocean a zone of peace, free from the intrusions of the United States and the USSR.

3575. Moines, Jacques. LES SEYCHELLES: BEAUCOUP DE BRUIT AUTOUR D'UN SI PETIT PAYS [The Seychelles: so much noise over such a small country]. *Afrique et l'Asie Modernes [France] 1978 (4): 2-23.* Discusses the rapidly changing political situation in the Seychelles, including the overthrow of President James Mancham in 1977 in favor of Prime Minister Albert René.

3576. Molet, Louis. "MADAGASCAR DEPUIS 1972" [Madagascar since 1972]. *Afrique et l'Asie Modernes [France] 1977 (2): 39-51.* Reviews *Madagascar depuis 1972: La Marche d'une révolution* (Paris: Editions de l'Harmattan, 1976) by Robert Archer.

3577. Ostheimer, John M. POLITICAL DEVELOPMENT IN COMOROS. *African R. [Tanzania] 1973 3(3): 491-506.* Traces the colonial history of the Comoros from French involvement in 1854 to 1973. Problems facing the islands are cyclones, poverty, and lack of revenue. Although ruled by a high commissioner of the French government, since 1962 the Comoros have had a territorial legislature and a cabinet of ministers. Examines political parties including the Democratic Assembly of the Comorian People, founded in 1968. 4 tables, 43 notes.
H. G. Soff

3578. Rabearimanana, Lucile. PRESSE D'OPINION ET LUTTES POLITIQUES A MADAGASCAR DE 1945 A 1956 [The critical press and political struggles in Madagascar, 1945-56]. *Rev. Française d'Hist d'Outre-Mer [France] 1980 67(1-2): 99-122.* Even at a time of political repression, the press remained a focus of nationalist sentiment. Based on contemporary newspapers; 31 notes. D. G. Law

3579. Rabesahala, Gisele. MADAGASCAR LOOKS AHEAD. *World Marxist R. [Canada] 1974 17(7): 121-126.* Describes politics and reform in Madagascar since the overthrow of the Philibert Tsiranana administration in May 1972. S

3580. Rodopulo, N. A. IZ ISTORII NATSIONAL'NO-OSVOBODITEL'NOGO DVIZHENIIA NA MADAGASKARE V 1945-1947 [The history of the national liberation movement in Madagascar, 1945-47]. *Narody Azii i Afriki [USSR] 1976 (5): 77-85.* Describes the national liberation movement in Madagascar during 1945-47, when the first legal and national political organizations were established. The strongest and most important among these was the Democratic Movement for Malagasy Renaissance (MDRM), a staunch opponent of French colonialism and the leader of the national liberation movement. The MDRM sought to achieve Madagascar's political independence through legal channels. In order to put an end to MDRM's power, the government of France and colonial authorities in Madagascar falsely accused the MDRM of instigating the 29 March 1947 armed uprising. Authorities quelled the uprising and destroyed the MDRM, but not without first shaking the very foundations of French power on the island. 37 notes.
L. Kalinowski

3581. Saint-Alban, Cédric. LES PARTIS POLITIQUES COMORIENS ENTRE LA MODERNITÉ ET LA TRADITION [Comorian political parties between modernization and tradition]. *Rev. Française d'Études Pol. Africaines [France] 1973 8(94): 76-88.* Outlines the formation of the current government and political party system in the Comoro Islands, a French Protectorate which will gain independence within the next five years.

3582. Simon, Pierre. AU SUJET DE L'UNITÉ CULTURELLE MALAGASY [The cultural unity of Madagascar]. *Afrique et L'Asie [France] 1974 (103): 32-44.* For reasons of expediency, the ideology of French colonialism analyzed the history of Madagascar in terms of the opposition between two racial groups, the Hova and the coastal people. In fact, although Madagascar was populated both by Africans and by Indonesians, the two groups became assimilated, so that, while there is no Malagasy race, there is one language and one culture, the product of African and Indonesian cohabitation. Anthropological research has shown that the people of Madagascar cannot be divided into two groups, one Negroid and the other Mongoloid. The existence of dialects does not disprove the linguistic unity of the people nor can the material culture be divided into an African and an Indonesian. The opposition of the two cultures in Madagascar is simply the result of the colonial episode in the island's history. J. S. Gassner

3583. Szymański, Edward. NIEPODLEGŁOŚĆ SESZELI (SEYCHELLES) [Independence of the Seychelles]. *Przegląd Socjologiczny [Poland] 1977 29: 33-43.* A history of the Seychelles from their first occupation by the French in 1768 to their independence from England in 1976.

3584. Tinker, Hugh. ODD MAN OUT: THE LONELINESS OF THE INDIAN COLONIAL POLITICIAN—THE CAREER OF MANILAL DOCTOR. *J. of Imperial and Commonwealth Hist. [Great Britain] 1974 2(2): 226-243.* Examines the career of Manilal Maganlall Doctor (1881-1956), an Indian who came to Mauritius at the age of 26 at the behest of Mahatma Gandhi. Although individuals of Indian origin comprised two-thirds of the island's population, they were distinctly subordinate to the Franco-Mauritian élite. The author documents Doctor's activities in assisting the island's Indian population, particularly in legal matters, and provides a biographical sketch. Based on manuscript and printed sources; 28 notes. J. A. Casada

3585. VanBeek, H. DE KERKELIJKE EN SOCIO-POLITIEKE SITUATIE OP MADAGASCAR [The religious, social, and political situation in Madagascar]. *Wereld en Zending [Netherlands] 1974 3(2): 91-103.* Analyzes the political and social influences on Christianity's development in Madagascar in the 19th century and examines the churches' attitudes to decolonization and Philibert Tsiranana's overthrow in 1972.

3586. Vasilyev, R. WINDS OF CHANGE OVER THE COMORO ISLANDS. *Int. Affairs [USSR] 1976 (10): 105-109.* Traces the history and examines economic prospects of the Comoro Islands and their present governmental and foreign relations situation.

3587. —. MAI 1972 A MADAGASCAR [May 1972 in Madagascar]. *Esprit [France] 1973 (4): 1007-1024.* Documents and programs from the student movement in Madagascar in 1972, as it rallied the unemployed and other politicized elements to alter local politics with a series of strikes and other demonstrations. Cultural nationalism, anti-French protests, and cosmopolitan intellectual trends were the targets of the student attacks. An outline of events is included.
G. F. Jewsbury

Malawi

3588. Anstey, D. G. A LETTER FROM THE CHIEF GAME WARDEN. *Soc. of Malawi J. [Malawi] 1982 35(1): 8-10.* The chief game warden of Malawi National Parks comments on two recent articles in the *Society of Malawi Journal.* In the 1980 33(1) issue an incorrect statement was made that the Parks Department has tried to prohibit photography within the parks. Anstey contends that those who do not comply with park regulations may be denied access. In the 1981 34(1) issue a statement was made that the Malawi government's expansion of

Nyika National Park during the 1970's to increase tourism and combat poaching forced the Phoka people to resettle. Anstey maintains that important ecological issues prevailed. J. Powell

3589. Baker, Colin. THE CHINDE CONCESSION, 1891-1923. *Soc. of Malawi J. [Malawi] 1980 33(1): 6-18.* The British Government declared a protectorate over British Central Africa (now Malawi) in May 1891 and appointed Harry Hamilton Johnston the first Commissioner and Consul-General. Johnston obtained the Chinde mouth of the Zambezi River as a concession from the Portuguese so that personnel, stores, and equipment could be imported to the landlocked protectorate. By 1894, Chinde was a moderately flourishing transit settlement, where the vice-consulate and the post office were staffed, naval vessels maintained, and goods in transit stored. Following extensive damage caused by a cyclone in 1922, the concession was rendered unnecessary by the opening of weekly railway service from Beira on the Indian Ocean to Chindio upstream on the Zambezi, and its lease was cancelled in 1923. Based on British Foreign Office correspondence, documents from the British Central Africa Protectorate and the Nyasaland Protectorate, and other primary sources; 63 ref. L. S. Guyotte

3590. Baker, Colin. DEPRESSION AND DEVELOPMENT IN NYASALAND 1929-1939. *Soc. of Malawi J. [Malawi] 1974 27(1): 7-26.* Despite the worldwide depression of the 1930's, economic growth continued in Nyasaland in part due to the caliber of the Colonial Development Act (1929). Public revenue was maintained which allowed expanded expenditures in the public domain, particularly the railway, education, medicine, and agriculture. 5 tables, 54 notes. H. G. Soff

3591. Baker, Colin. THE GOVERNMENT MEDICAL SERVICE IN MALAWI: AN ADMINISTRATIVE HISTORY, 1891-1974. *Medical Hist. [Great Britain] 1976 20(3): 296-311.* Through examination of staff, financing, and medical policy, traces the development of the Ministry of Health in Malawi, 1891-1974.

3592. Baker, Colin. TAX COLLECTION IN MALAWI: AN ADMINISTRATIVE HISTORY, 1891-1972. *Int. J. of African Hist. Studies 1975 8(1): 40-62.* A history of taxation in the British protectorate of Malawi. Establishment of the protectorate did not include funds to administer it. The first governor established a hut tax, which became a major source of revenue and remains so to this time. A fine line had to be drawn between taxes sufficiently high to encourage work, but not so high as to increase the wage demands of workers. Few people defaulted at first, but the practice soon grew. Mild coercion was sometimes used, but neither British nor native administrators were happy about it, a fact prospective defaulters soon learned. The primary problem was to secure sufficient revenues without disrupting traditional modes of living. 110 notes. V. L. Human

3593. Brietzke, Paul. THE CHILOBWE MURDERS TRIAL. *African Studies Rev. 1974 17(2): 361-379.* To achieve convictions in a politically explosive murder case in Malawi, the government redesigned the legal system and the court structure. 9 notes, biblio.
R. T. Brown

3594. Chand, H. LAW AS AN INSTRUMENT OF DEVELOPMENT, WITH SPECIAL REFERENCE TO MALAWI. *Africa Q. [India] 1979 18(2-3): 37-51.* A 1977 case before the High Court of Malawi illustrates a discussion of the role of international and municipal legal structures and procedures in developing countries.

3595. Chanock, Martin L. AMBIGUITIES IN THE MALAWIAN POLITICAL TRADITION. *African Affairs [Great Britain] 1975 74(296): 326-346.* Analyzes the development of a Malawian political culture following British colonization. There were two distinctive lines to this political development: the revolutionary tradition stemming from John Chilembwe's 1915 revolt, which surfaced again after World War II, and acculturative tradition which absorbed the values of the British and missionaries in the course of the 20th century. Traditional chiefs and headmen resisted change, but the new order more easily accepted European rule. A major ambiguity occurred in rural areas where farmers resented the colonial pressure but welcomed the economic opportunities it presented. 68 notes. H. G. Soff

3596. Chimango, L. J. TRADITIONAL CRIMINAL LAW IN MALAWI. *Soc. of Malawi J. [Malawi] 1975 28(1): 25-39.* Customary societies dealt with law violators in ways that today are not legal. Old methods of retribution have disappeared. The people are, however, not always able to accept modern court decisions and often wish to revert to ancient custom. It is understandable why court decisions are not always popular. 17 notes. H. G. Soff

3597. Chipeta, W. THE ECONOMICS OF THANDO. *Soc. of Malawi J. [Malawi] 1974 27(2): 6-9.* *Thando* means cooperation in food consumption in the Nsanje District of Malawi. Those who cooperate are families living in close proximity. *Thando* does not exist with non-kin. The major advantage was insurance in time of famine. *Thando* also cements the family together, yet the total number of families involved is small. H. G. Soff

3598. Coleman, G. THE AFRICAN POPULATION OF MALAWI. *Soc. of Malawi J. [Malawi] 1974 27(2): 37-46.* Continued from a previous article (see following abstract). Changes took place from 1921-66 in Malawi in the sex and age of the population primarily as a result of reduced mortality rates, and the population is being redistributed in terms of age groups. 6 tables, 7 notes. H. G. Soff

3599. Coleman, G. THE AFRICAN POPULATION OF MALAWI: CENSUS 1901-1966. *Soc. of Malawi J. [Malawi] 1974 27(1): 27-41.* Analyzes censuses in Malawi and speculates on the reasons for changes in the African population, which include the end to ethnic warfare, elimination of slave-raiding, immigration from Mozambique, natural increase, and migration. It is estimated that the current population, which has doubled since 1945, will double again by 1991. 4 tables, 36 notes. Article to be continued (see preceding abstract). H. G. Soff

3600. Hawken, A. J. THE AIRMAIL HISTORY OF NYASALAND. *Soc. of Malawi J. [Malawi] 1980 33(2): 25-32.* The British protectorate of Nyasaland (now Malawi) suffered from its isolation from other British Empire countries. A military engagement with German forces which took place three days after the World War I armistice illustrates the communications lag. During the early 1930's mail was transported by rail to Salisbury and flown to Cape Town for further destinations. In 1934, a regular air mail service was established between Blantyre and Salisbury; in 1935, direct Beira-Salisbury flights were added. The next three years saw flight link-ups to other British Empire countries.
L. S. Guyotte

3601. Hodder-Williams, Richard. DR. BANDA'S MALAWI. *J. of Commonwealth and Comparative Pol. [Great Britain] 1974 12(1): 91-114.* Traces the course of Malawi politics in the period surrounding the crisis of 1964. Analyzes the internal balance of forces in Malawi, the freedom of choice open to President Hastings Banda in the realm of domestic and foreign policy, and the precise nature and implications of Banda's "populist tactics"—the bonds between leader and people and the methods used to strengthen and maintain them. Malawi in 1973 still showed the effects of the 1964 crisis, primarily in an increased reliance on European skills and a heightened conservatism among the Congress Party. Based on extracts from newspapers and articles; 76 notes.
C. Anstey

3602. Hutson, J. A. AN OUTLINE OF THE EARLY HISTORY OF THE TEA INDUSTRY IN MALAWI. *Soc. of Malawi J. [Malawi] 1978 31(1): 40-46.* Tea as a commercial crop was introduced into Malawi in the mid-1800's, but it was not until 1886 that the plant survived. Malawi, therefore, is home to the oldest continuing tea industry in Africa. By 1976 Malawi had 23 processing factories producing over 62 million pounds of tea. H. G. Soff

3603. Kandawire, J. A. K. THANGATA IN PRE-COLONIAL AND COLONIAL SYSTEMS OF LAND TENURE IN SOUTHERN MALAWI, WITH SPECIAL REFERENCE TO CHINGALE. *Africa [Great Britain] 1977 47(2): 185-191.* In the pre-colonial period the concept of *thangata* in southern Malawi was that of a social institution of reciprocal labor in which landless Africans worked for their village communities in return for occupying some of the communally-owned land. In the colonial period *thangata* implied forced labor by Africans for European planters whose crops were intended mainly for export. This generated political problems and a revolt in 1915, even though the

thangata system had been condemned by the High Court at Blantyre in 1903. The Land Commission of 1921 failed to improve the situation, and the Natives on Private Estates Ordinance of 1928 still allowed exploitation of the Africans and there was another revolt in 1953. Based on official records and personal observation; 11 notes, biblio.
R. L. Collison

3604. Kandawire, J. A. K. VILLAGE SEGMENTATION AND CLASS FORMATION IN SOUTHERN MALAWI. *Africa [Great Britain] 1980 50(2): 125-145.* Population density in Malawi varies, being affected by a rapidly growing population and the attraction of places having good water supplies. Even in sparsely populated areas there is pressure on the distribution of settlements in habitable land. The root of the problem lies in the 1891 distribution of land to settlers which evaded the customary system. As a result, a large proportion of the population became landless laborers who migrated wherever opportunities were greater. Thus classes were created of those who leased land and those who had none. The former were subject to the freehold owners' wishes, which led to domestic husbandry, domestic slavery, and capitalism. R. L. Collison

3605. Lamba, Isaac C. AFRICAN WOMEN'S EDUCATION IN MALAWI, 1875-1952. *J. of Educ. Administration and Hist. [Great Britain] 1982 14(1): 46-54.* Surveys the development of women's education in Malawi, 1875-1952, in particular the assistance of European missionaries and the change in status that came with education.

3606. Leishman, A. D. H. THE STEAM ERA IN MALAWI. *Soc. of Malawi J. [Malawi] 1974 27(1): 46-53.* A brief history of railroad development in Malawi. The first line began in 1903, although proposals for a railway had been made as early as 1892. Describes the purchase of various engines and the closure of trunk lines. The railway system is now controlled by the government. Refs. H. G. Soff

3607. Martin, C. G. C. SURVEY OF INDIA IN MALAWI. *Soc. of Malawi J. [Malawi] 1974 27(1): 54-73.* Traces Indian involvement in Malawi from the arrival of Sikh troops in the 1890's to the training of Malawian surveyors in India in 1972. Indian involvement centered around land surveys, boundary commissions, and maps. Refs.
H. G. Soff

3608. McCracken, John. UNDERDEVELOPMENT IN MALAWI: THE MISSIONARY CONTRIBUTION. *African Affairs [Great Britain] 1977 76(303): 195-209.* While the "Protestant Missions were not responsible for the initial impact of the world economy in Malawi, there can be little doubt that they were instrumental in influencing subsequent patterns of change." There is evidence to suggest that the economic activities of David Livingston's agents contributed to the emergence of a rural slum. From 1915 to the 1960's, colonial and later national governments tended to "regard alien Nyasas as the workers they could most readily dispense with." In the long run, the combination of a large scale economic system with a small scale political one places them at a crippling disadvantage. 58 notes. E. P. Stickney

3609. McCracken, K. J. THE UNIVERSITY OF LIVINGSTONIA. *Soc. of Malawi J. [Malawi] 1974 27(2): 14-23.* The University of Livingstonia never existed, but in the 1920's it was a dream of Robert Laws, who did much to raise the standard of education in colonial Malawi: Old age forced Laws to retire in 1925, and his successor did not have the same educational vision. The plans were scrapped with the result that education in colonial Malawi did not compare favorably with its neighbors. 28 notes. H. G. Soff

3610. Mlia, J. Ngoleka. MALAWI'S NEW CAPITAL CITY: A REGIONAL PLANNING PERSPECTIVE. *Pan-African J. [Kenya] 1975 8(4): 387-401.* In 1965, one year after gaining independence, the new national government decided to move Malawi's capital from Zomba to Lilongwe. By 1974 this decision had been implemented. National pride and personal political considerations played a part in the decision, but the main reasons were directly connected with the requirements of regional planning and economic development. Based on government documents and secondary sources; map, 43 notes. R. G. Neville

3611. Mpakati, Attati. MALAWI: THE BIRTH OF A NEO-COLONIAL STATE. *African R. [Tanzania] 1973 3(1): 33-68.* A discussion of Malawi from precolonial times to the present. Of greatest concern is the economic crisis, coupled with the political crisis. Malawi was "stolen" by the colonizers from inept chiefs, and during independence has again been controlled by those whose interest is not the nation. A leader such as John Chilembwe is needed to "strike a blow for a socialist victory." 3 tables, 85 notes. H. G. Soff

3612. Mtewa, Mekki. A STUDY OF POLITICAL TRADITION AND STRATEGY IN MALAWI FROM THE CHILEMBWE ERA TO THE CONTEMPORARY. *Pan-African J. [Kenya] 1975 8(1): 19-30.* Analyzes the underlying causes of the independence movements in Malawi, 1915-63, suggesting that anticolonialism was stimulated by the oppression of the colonial administration, and the European landed interests. Points out the significance of land as a political issue. Suggests that there is continuity in political aspirations in Malawi from the early 20th century, and that the revolution led by John Chilembwe was the progenitor of mass nationalism in Malawi. 42 notes. S

3613. Mwiyeriwa, Steve S. PRINTING PRESSES AND PUBLISHING IN MALAWI. *Soc. of Malawi J. [Malawi] 1978 31(2): 31-35.* Printing, publishing, bookselling, and libraries are interdependent but in Malawi developed unevenly. The first presses were set up in the 1870's but the Malawi Library Association was only founded in 1976. Much printing and publishing was, and is, carried out by the missionary presses although these developed slowly compared with the Government Printing Office which was founded in 1894. The press had the disadvantage of a strong religious bias in its programs and this affected education in the schools, which used their texts. In addition defects in the written language were introduced by enthusiastic but amateur missionary translators. Based on letters to the author and secondary sources; 33 notes. A. E. Standley

3614. Myambo, Kathleen. MALAWI UNIVERSITY STUDENTS; 1967-1971. *Soc. of Malawi J. [Malawi] 1975 28(1): 40-53.* Analyzes the education and background of students at Chancellor College, opened in 1965 to fill the educational needs of newly independent Malawi. Records student aspirations for the future, with the largest percentage preferring government positions, followed closely by teaching. Based on a student questionnaire; 16 tables, 2 notes. H. G. Soff

3615. Nouvel, Jacques. LE MALAWI [Malawi]. *L'Afrique et l'Asie [France] 1974 (102): 14-30.* Malawi, formerly British Nyasaland, became independent in 1964. A subtropical, mountainous region, it has a population of about five million, relatively homogeneous, except in regard to religion. About half of the people are Christian, the remainder being Muslim and animist. The mainstay of the economy is traditional subsistence farming. Dr. Hastings K. Banda, president of the republic and absolute ruler of Malawi, is attempting to modernize the agricultural system and to introduce industry, which will reduce Malawi's dependence upon imports. In his foreign policy, Dr. Banda has walked a tightrope between his black and his white neighbors, and has succeeded, surprisingly enough, in improving relations with both sets.
J. S. Gassner

3616. Ogbu, John U. ECONOMIC TRANSITION AMONG THE POKA OF NORTHERN MALAWI: FROM SUBSISTENCE TO CASH CROPPING. *J. of African Studies 1978 5(2): 151-172.* Case study of the difficulties of imposing new cash crops and farming methods on traditional African societies. The highly rural Phoka of northern Malawi opposed efforts by the colonial administration to encourage coffee growing among them due to the existing low level of their subsistence margin in food crops, the difficulty of shifting to coffee production, and a shortage of capital. Based on fieldwork and secondary sources; 4 tables, 24 notes. L. W. Truschel

3617. Pachai, B. AFRICAN POLITICS IN TWENTIETH CENTURY COLONIAL MALAWI. *Kleio [South Africa] 1974 6(2): 31-59.* Discusses the rise of African nationalism in Malawi, and the development of the independence movement which achieved its goal in 1964.
G. Hewlett

3618. Pachai, Bridglal. LAND POLICIES IN MALAWI: AN EXAMINATION OF THE COLONIAL LEGACY. *J. of African Hist. [Great Britain] 1973 14(4): 681-698.* Evaluates the Malawi government's efforts to redistribute land to the landless peasants. Although there is land pressure, Malawians have shown little desire for individual titles to land. Also the matrilineal system has tied the women rather than the men to the land. Despite these obstacles the Malawi government hopes to develop a modern land policy which will bring relief to the peasants. 70 notes. C. Hopkins

3619. Palmer, Robin. EUROPEAN RESISTANCE TO AFRICAN MAJORITY RULE: THE SETTLERS AND RESIDENTS ASSOCIATION OF NYASALAND, 1960-63. *African Affairs [Great Britain] 1973 72(288): 256-272.* SARAN was formed in 1960 and led the European resistance against Malawian nationalism. Whites numbered fewer than 10,000 in 1960, and SARAN's chief goal was to slow the blacks' constitutional advance. It failed because its members were ignorant of politics, and they were ignored by both local and metropolitan governments. Former SARAN members have learned that peaceful and profitable coexistence with blacks is possible. 63 notes. H. G. Soff

3620. Parratt, John. Y. Z. MWASI AND THE ORIGINS OF THE BLACKMAN'S CHURCH. *J. of Religion in Africa [Netherlands] 1978 9(3): 193-206.* Yesaya Zerenji Mwasi founded the Blackman's Church during the 1930's in Nyasaland in part because of clashes with the leadership of the Church of Scotland mission over church control and procedure, but mostly because of his desire to establish an indigenous church which perpetuated orthodox Christian doctrine.

3621. Rye, G. P. THE NATIONAL LIBRARY SERVICE. *Soc. of Malawi J. [Malawi] 1976 29(1): 35-44.* The National Library Service of Malawi came into existence in 1968 after 18 years of study and investigation. The 1965 plans for a NLS drawn up by R. A. Flood are outlined and the presidential proclamation of 1967 is included. The supplies and resources of the Library Service are examined and their method of book distribution is clarified including library centers, postal service, and service points. Methods of selecting books to be purchased is discussed and sources of funding are explained. At the time of writing, there were 97 library centers in use. H. G. Soff

3622. Schoffeleers, M. THE NYAU SOCIETIES: OUR PRESENT UNDERSTANDING. *Soc. of Malawi J. [Malawi] 1976 29(1): 59-68.* Nyau, a masked dance dating from the Later Stone Age and performed by Nyau societies on the stage, was traditionally done at funerals and initiations but is now danced at national celebrations as well, a full performance lasting several days. Nyau participants consider their dance a religious institution. The history and organization of the Nyau are presented, as well as the role of Nyau in the political, artistic, and economic life of Malawi where they number over 500 groups. H. G. Soff

3623. Thomas, Simon. ECONOMIC DEVELOPMENTS IN MALAWI SINCE INDEPENDENCE. *J. of Southern African Studies [Great Britain] 1975 2(1): 30-51.* Assesses economic policies in Malawi since 1964. Malawi has achieved considerable economic growth and targets have been met, but little has been done to reduce social inequalities. Based upon government reports and statistics; 7 tables, 39 notes. S. P. Carr

3624. Vail, LeRoy. THE MAKING OF AN IMPERIAL SLUM: NYASALAND AND ITS RAILWAYS, 1895-1935. *J. of African Hist. [Great Britain] 1975 16(1): 89-112.* Nyasaland, more than any area of British Africa, suffered from the decisions of the imperial government made without regard to the colony. The railroad, financed by the colony, created an enormous economic hardship contrary to previous histories which view the railroads as a positive contribution. As a result of a five-million-pound deficit in the 1930's, the government encouraged the emigration of Africans to work in the mines of Southern Africa, an economic distortion that continues to haunt independent Malawi. Map, 100 notes. H. G. Soff

Mozambique

3625. Alpers, Edward A. ETHNICITY, POLITICS AND HISTORY IN MOZAMBIQUE. *Africa Today 1974 21(4): 39-52.* Describes the divide-and-rule policy of Portugal vis-à-vis the several major ethnic groups in Mozambique. Although Portuguese claims are historically fallacious, FRELIMO's rule is threatened by the ethnic competition engendered. Primary and secondary sources; 37 notes. G. O. Gagnon

3626. Arnold, Anne-Sophie. POLITISCHE UND MILITÄRISCHE ASPEKTE DES KAMPFES UM DIE NATIONAL UNABHÄNGIGKEIT MOÇAMBIQUES [Political and military aspects of the struggle for the national independence of Mozambique]. *Militärgeschichte [East Germany] 1977 16(2): 170-182.* Describes the struggle of the people of Mozambique under the leadership of the Front for the Liberation of Mozambique (FRELIMO), 1962-75. Initially a union of smaller nationalist organizations under the leadership of Eduardo Mondlane, FRELIMO developed gradually into a revolutionary party whose political struggle had the goal of creating new social structures. 3 illus., 46 notes. H. D. Andrews

3627. Christie, Iain. MOZAMBIQUE: FRELIMO'S NEW STRUGGLE. *Africa Report 1975 20(3): 10-14.* FRELIMO is attempting to destroy the bases of poverty in Mozambique before the end of the next decade. S

3628. Christie, Iain. MOZAMBIQUE: PORTRAIT OF PRESIDENT MACHEL. *Africa Report 1975 20(3): 15-17.* Biography of Samora Moises Machel, president of Mozambique, concentrating on his political and social views. S

3629. Colin, Jean-Pierre. LE MOZAMBIQUE UN AN APRÈS L'INDÉPENDANCE [Mozambique one year after independence]. *Pol. Étrangère [France] 1976 41(5): 433-458.* Traces the evolution of FRELIMO (Mozambique Liberation Front), its activities from its formation 20 June 1962 through the revolution and independence of the country, and its recent transformation into the New Government Party.

3630. Cox, Idris. LIBERATION MOVEMENT IN MOZAMBIQUE. *World Marxist R. [Canada] 1973 16(12): 101-104.*

3631. Degnan, Michael and Delemos, Virgilio. SOUTHERN AFRICA: THE "THREE WARS" OF MOZAMBIQUE: TWO VIEWS OF "WIRIYAMU". *Africa Report 1973 18(5): 6-13.* Discusses engagements between Portuguese and FRELIMO soldiers in the ninth year of guerrilla warfare. S

3632. El-Khawas, Mohamed A. PROBLEMS OF NATION-BUILDING IN MOZAMBIQUE. *Black Scholar 1980 11(5): 24-36.* Examines the efforts to build a socialist society in Mozambique since the end of Portuguese colonial rule in 1975.

3633. Friedland, Elaine A. MOZAMBICAN NATIONALIST RESISTANCE: 1920-1949. *Civilisations [Belgium] 1977 27(3-4): 332-344.* Due to government repression of the nationalist movement in Mozambique and the country's status as an economic satellite to South Africa, art and sociocultural activities became the predominant mode of organized overt nationalist political protest by the 1940's.

3634. Harris, Laurence. AGRICULTURAL CO-OPERATIVES AND DEVELOPMENT POLICY IN MOZAMBIQUE. *J. of Peasant Studies [Great Britain] 1980 7(3): 338-352.* Examines the problems encountered since independence in an agricultural production cooperative in Mozambique. The problems are related to the complex rural class structure in the context of which the cooperative is being constructed and the distinction between the formal structure of the cooperative and its real relations of production. The development of the cooperative is considered in relation to the postindependence formulation of Mozambican policies toward agricultural cooperatives as an element in the transformation of rural social relations. Based on fieldwork conducted in mid-1978.

3635. Hastings, Adrian. SOME REFLECTIONS UPON THE WAR IN MOZAMBIQUE. *African Affairs [Great Britain] 1974 73(292): 263-276.* Discusses Portuguese-Mozambique relations following the 1974 coup in Portugal, particularly the increased recognition of FRELIMO. Reviews guerrilla warfare since 1964 and the gradual FRELIMO control of areas in Mozambique. Recounts Portuguese difficulty in the Tete area since 1572. Analyzes factors which enabled FRELIMO to succeed but notes that facts should not be interpreted as definitive due to a serious lack of confirmed reports at time of writing. 8 notes. H. G. Soff

3636. Hawley, Edward A. EDUARDO CHIVAMBO MONDLANE (1920-1969): A PERSONAL MEMOIR. *Africa Today 1979 26(1): 19-24.* A testimonial to the assassinated leader of FRELIMO which assesses Eduardo Mondlane's contribution to the struggle against colonialism and racism in Mozambique and throughout the world. Based on author's experience; 2 illus. G. O. Gagnon

3637. Henriksen, Thomas H. MARXISM AND MOZAMBIQUE. *African Affairs [Great Britain] 1978 77(309): 441-462.* Traces the background of the revolution in Mozambique which resulted in the ascendency of the Marxist Frente de Libertacão de Moçambique (FRELIMO) after over 10 years of war, since the formation of FRELIMO in Dar es Salaam, Tanzania in 1962, focusing on FRELIMO'S ideology and its implications for Mozambique and the rest of Africa.

3638. Henriksen, Thomas H. THE REVOLUTIONARY THOUGHT OF EDUARDO MONDLANE. *Genève-Afrique [Switzerland] 1973 12(1): 37-52.* Discusses the career and thought of Eduardo Chivambo Mondlane and considers his role as head of FRELIMO in Mozambique, 1961-69.

3639. Isaacman, Allen et al. "COTTON IS THE MOTHER OF POVERTY": PEASANT RESISTANCE AGAINST FORCED COTTON CULTIVATION IN MOZAMBIQUE, 1938-1961. *Int. J. of African Hist. Studies 1980 13(4): 581-615.* The forced cultivation of cash crops, in particular cotton, drove the peasantry into a variety of forms of resistance against the colonial government. Out of this pool of rebellion FRELIMO ultimately arose. Based on interviews and Mozambique archives; map, 2 tables, 130 notes. R. T. Brown

3640. Isaacman, Allen and Isaacman, Barbara. MOZAMBIQUE DURING THE COLONIAL PERIOD. *Tarikh [Nigeria] 1980 6(4): 47-60.* Colonial abuses, which included forced labor, labor export, and forced agricultural production, caused widespread social dislocation and misery, prompting a series of popular resistance movements, though these met with little success.

3641. Isaacman, Allen F. THE TRADITION OF RESISTANCE IN MOZAMBIQUE. *Africa Today 1975 22(3): 37-50.* Summarizes the extensive resistance to Portuguese rule in Mozambique with emphasis on the Zambezi valley. FRELIMO built upon a tradition of guerrilla war and passive resistance which has been continuous since 1550. Based on oral history, primary sources, and the author's other works; 45 notes. G. O. Gagnon

3642. Jundanian, Brendan F. RESETTLEMENT PROGRAMS: COUNTERINSURGENCY IN MOZAMBIQUE. *Comparative Pol. 1974 6(4): 519-540.*

3643. Kiracofe, Clifford A., Jr. THE COMMUNIST TAKEOVER OF MOZAMBIQUE: AN OVERVIEW. *J. of Social, Pol. and Econ. Studies 1982 7(1-2): 115-128.* The Moscow-guided transformation of the National Liberation Movement into a Marxist-Leninist party, and the 1974-75 armed takeover threatens international mining and access to strategic minerals in South Africa, and hence the world economy.

3644. Lefort, Rene. LIBERATED MOZAMBIQUE. *Monthly Rev. 1976 28(7): 25-39.* Traces the wide range of social and political changes that have taken place since the collapse of Portuguese hegemony. Since September 1974, the Mozambique Liberation Front (FRELIMO) has nationalized health service, manufacturing, commerce, and education, has politicized the masses, and has conducted extensive campaigns to eradicate illiteracy. The FRELIMO leadership is convinced that permanent revolution is a vital component of Mozambique's ongoing process of decolonization. M. R. Yerburgh

3645. Legge, Jerome Stewart and Ododa, Harry. THE POLITICAL THOUGHT OF EDUARDO MONDLANE. *Black Scholar 1974 5(7): 11-15.* Reviews the political activities and ideas of Eduardo C. Mondlane, leader of the Mozambique Liberation Front (FRELIMO) until his death in 1969. Examines his personal experiences and diplomatic thought. Primary and secondary sources; 11 notes. M. M. McCarthy

3646. Leonard, Richard W. FRELIMO'S VICTORIES IN MOZAMBIQUE. *Issue 1974 4(2): 38-46.* Examines the recent military defeat of Portugal in Mozambique and the growing strength of the Mozambique Liberation Front (FRELIMO), and relates these developments to US foreign policy toward Portuguese colonialism. S

3647. Machel, Samora. MOZAMBIQUE: A VICTORY FOR THE PEOPLE. *Black Scholar 1974 6(2): 32-41.* Examines the operation of the liberation group FRELIMO as the transitional government of Mozambique.

3648. Middlemas, Keith. TWENTIETH CENTURY WHITE SOCIETY IN MOZAMBIQUE. *Tarikh [Nigeria] 1979 6(2): 30-45.* Portuguese settlement in Mozambique was slight during the early 20th century, but greatly increased after World War II, only to fall again by 90% at the time of independence in 1976.

3649. Mittelman, James H. MOZAMBIQUE: THE POLITICAL ECONOMY OF UNDERDEVELOPMENT. *J. of Southern African Affairs 1978 3(1): 35-54.* Surveys Mozambique's political economy, concentrating on the last years of Portuguese rule and the dramatic changes undertaken by the FRELIMO government during its first year in power, 1975-76. By allowing foreign investments into the colony and migratory labor into neighboring territories, the Portuguese, particularly from the early 1960's on, practiced a type of surrogate colonialism in Mozambique. The author sympathizes with FRELIMO's announced program of removing class oppression, but makes no effort to assess its economic impact. Based on UN and FRELIMO documents and secondary sources; 23 notes. L. W. Truschel

3650. Mittleman, James H. STATE POWER IN MOZAMBIQUE. *Issue: A Q. J. of Opinion 1978 7(1): 4-11.* Analyzes successful efforts by FRELIMO in this former Portuguese colony to achieve independence, 1973-74.

3651. Morosini, Giuseppe. TRADIZIONE E RIVOLUZIONE CULTURALE IN MOZAMBICO [Tradition and cultural revolution in Mozambique]. *Africa [Italy] 1980 35(1): 43-84.* A first approach to cultural change in Mozambique after independence from Portuguese colonial rule (1975). It describes the traditional cultures of precolonial ethnic groups, and the changes during the ten-year armed struggle for national liberation. Focuses on the cultural policy of FRELIMO, and the declared struggle on two fronts, against westernization and against traditionalism. Based on two years of field work. J/S

3652. Neil-Tomlinson, Barry. THE NYASSA CHARTERED COMPANY: 1891-1929. *J. of African Hist. [Great Britain] 1977 18(1): 109-128.* Traces the Nyassa Chartered Company through several periods. From 1894 to 1898 the supposed aim of the company was the economic development of the Nyassa area of northwest Mozambique, but instead the company speculated for quick returns and lost. In the years 1899-1914 the company became a quasi-military conquering force. In 1919-29 the company gave up its dream of greatness and simply maximized revenue by increasing taxes and abuses as its charter was running out. 79 notes. H. G. Soff

3653. Newitt, M. D. D. TOWARDS A HISTORY OF MODERN MOÇAMBIQUE. *Rhodesian Hist. [Rhodesia] 1974 5: 33-47.* Assesses factors which have delayed the preparation of a cohesive history of Mozambique among which are geographic and economic separation and fragmentation under Portuguese rule and differing types of relationships with neighboring states (white-ruled South Africa and white-ruled and landlocked Southern Rhodesia, for example). African resistance movements and nation building may serve as a unifying force that will result in an integrated state and a history to match. 14 notes. O. B. Pollak

3654. Opello, Walter C., Jr. GUERRILLA WAR IN PORTUGUESE AFRICA: AN ASSESSMENT OF THE BALANCE OF FORCE IN MOZAMBIQUE. *Issue 1974 4(2): 29-37.* Assesses the balance of military forces in Mozambique 1964-74 between the Mozambique Liberation Front (FRELIMO) and Portugal. S

3655. Opello, Walter C., Jr. PLURALISM AND ELITE CONFLICT IN AN INDEPENDENCE MOVEMENT: FRELIMO IN THE 1960S. *J. of Southern African Studies [Great Britain] 1975 2(1): 66-82.* The internal conflicts experienced by the Frente de Libertação de Moçambique (Frelimo), 1962-69, were primarily the result of competition among elite factions for power and status within the party. Based on newspapers and other primary sources; map, 45 notes. S. P. Carr

3656. Radmann, Wolf. ZAMBEZI DEVELOPMENT SCHEME OF THE CABORA BASSA: A CONSPIRACY OF INTERNATIONAL COOPERATION. *Pan-African J. [Kenya] 1974 7(2): 87-100.* Analyzes the Portuguese support for the Cabora Bassa hydroelectric dam in Mozambique and the African opposition to the scheme. The ultimate electric production of the dam, first planned in 1953, will rank it among the world's leading power plants. 43 notes. H. G. Soff

3657. Radmann, Wolf. THE ZAMBEZI DEVELOPMENT SCHEME: CABORA BASSA. *Issue 1974 4(2): 47-54.* Examines the Portuguese scheme to construct the Cabora Bassa dam in Mozambique and the impact of African opposition, 1953-74. S

3658. Roux, Dominique de. LIBRE OPINION: LE MOZAMBIQUE ET LA BATAILLE DE L'AFRIQUE AUSTRALE [Free opinion: Mozambique and the battle of Southern Africa]. *Défense Natl. [France] 1973 29(10): 115-122.* Views the problems of Mozambique, a country struggling for full sovereignty and fidelity to a multiracial and Portuguese background, but which now finds itself a major strategic point in the guerrilla warfare of neighboring Tanzania, Zambia, and Southern Rhodesia, ca. 1964-73.

3659. Saul, John S. FRELIMO AND THE MOZAMBIQUE REVOLUTION. *Monthly R. 1973 24(10): 22-52.* Describes FRELIMO (Mozambique Liberation Front) and its resistance to Portuguese colonialism. S

3660. Saul, John S. PORTUGAL AND THE MOZAMBICAN REVOLUTION. *Monthly R. 1974 26(4): 45-64.* Discusses the effects of recent developments on relations between Portugal and Mozambique. S

3661. Schneidman, Witney. FRELIMO'S FOREIGN POLICY AND THE PROCESS OF LIBERATION. *Africa Today 1978 25(1): 57-67.* Analyzes FRELIMO's efforts to achieve its dual foreign policy goals of winning UN support and isolating Portugal internationally by countering its propaganda. Concludes that these goals were met. Secondary sources; 13 notes. G. O. Gagnon

3662. Serapiao, Luis Benjamin. THE ROMAN CATHOLIC CHURCH AND THE PRINCIPLE OF SELF-DETERMINATION: A CASE STUDY IN MOZAMBIQUE. *J. of Church and State 1981 23(2): 323-335.* The claim by apologists of the Catholic Church that the papacy always supported liberation movements in Africa is examined, using Mozambique as a case study. The bishops there supported anticolonialism because the papacy could not prevent them from doing so. Based on mission correspondence and printed sources; 56 notes. E. E. Eminhizer

3663. Shore, Herb. MONDLANE, MACHEL AND MOZAMBIQUE: FROM REBELLION TO REVOLUTION. *Africa Today 1974 21(1): 3-12.* Reviews the continuing struggle to free Mozambique despite the assassination of Eduardo Mondlane. Based on interviews and secondary sources; photo, 11 notes. G. O. Gagnon

3664. Tobias, Phillip V. A LITTLE KNOWN CHAPTER IN THE LIFE OF EDUARDO MONDLANE *Genève-Afrique [Switzerland] 1977-78 16(1): 119-124.* In a previous *Genève-Afrique* article (1973 12(1): 37-52), Professor Thomas H. Henriksen states that Eduardo Chivambo Mondlane, from Mozambique, later a revolutionary activist, had been expelled from South Africa in 1949 because of the policy of the University of Witwatersrand. The author demonstrates that his expulsion had been due only to South African government policy in refusing the renewal of his residence permit. G. P. Cleyet

3665. Vail, LeRoy. MOZAMBIQUE'S CHARTERED COMPANIES: THE RULE OF THE FEEBLE. *J. of African Hist. [Great Britain] 1976 17(3): 389-416.* An analysis of the Portuguese attempt to develop a solvent colony in Mozambique. Chartered companies, the Nyassa Company and the Mozambique Company, were created in 1890 to take the place of the government, but both failed to achieve an adequate financial situation. Africans were abused and so was Portugal. Finally, the government of Antonio Salazar ended the system in 1930, although the Mozambique Company continued until 1941. Map, 132 notes. H. G. Soff

3666. Vail, Leroy and White, Landeg. "TAWANI, MACHAMBERO!" FORCED COTTON AND RICE GROWING ON THE ZAMBEZI. *J. of African Hist. [Great Britain] 1978 19(2): 239-263.* By 1935 large-scale recruiting of labor for the mines and farms of southern Africa, coupled with mass migrations to escape administrative oppression, resulted in a severe labor shortage in Mozambique. Concurrently, Portugal compelled the colonies to increase cotton production. The Sena Sugar Estate, Ltd., the colony's largest employer, required exclusively female cultivation of cotton, leaving men free to work in the company's sugar fields. This policy was adopted by other companies and led to severe oppression which ended only with the abolition of the system in the late 1950's and early 1960's. Based on primary and secondary sources; map, 103 notes. A. W. Novitsky

3667. Webster, D. MIGRANT LABOR, SOCIAL FORMATIONS AND THE PROLETARIANIZATION OF THE CHOPI OF SOUTHERN MOZAMBIQUE. *African Perspectives [Netherlands] 1978 (1): 157-174.* Considers reasons why southern Mozambique, and Chopiland in particular, has remained underdeveloped, ca. 1866-1974. Suggests that the poor economic development has been partly caused by the high numbers of Chopi migrant laborers who for a century have sought work in South Africa and Zimbabwe, in spite of a kinship system which encouraged attachment to kinship groupings. Based on fieldwork conducted in Chopiland, 1969-74; diagram. R. V. Ritter

3668. White, Susan. WOMEN AND UNDERDEVELOPMENT IN MOZAMBIQUE. *Can. Dimension [Canada] 1980 14(6): 38-41.* Discusses the problems of Mozambican women as defined at the 1976 national conference of the Mozambican Women's Organization (OMM), including illiteracy, unemployment, racism, prostitution, and forced marriage, among numerous others. Traces women's situation in Mozambique since before the Portuguese invaded in the early 1500's.

3669. Wright, Robin. MACHEL'S MARXIST MOZAMBIQUE. *Munger Africana Lib. Notes 1976 34: 1-53.* A collection of articles concerning several aspects of revolutionary organizations, programs, leaders, and artists in Mozambique since 1960.

3670. —. FRELIMO: 1970 AND 1974. *Issue 1974 4(2): 55-59.*
—. CABORA BASSA: WHY WE SAY NO, *pp. 56-57.*
—. STATEMENTS BY THE FRELIMO EXECUTIVE COMMITTEE ON THE EVENTS IN PORTUGAL, *pp. 58-59.* Two documents of the Mozambique Liberation Front (FRELIMO) illustrating the resolve of those people to fight colonialism since the Portuguese coup d'etat in April 1974. S

3671. —. [THE MOZAMBIQUE COMPANY]. *J. of African Hist. [Great Britain] 1977 18(2): 283-286.*
Neil-Thomlinson, Barry. DISCUSSION: THE MOZAMBIQUE COMPANY, *pp. 283-285.* Criticizes LeRoy Vail's earlier article (see abstract 3665). Rejects the contention that there was inadequate economic activity in Mozambique. Note.
Vail, LeRoy. REPLY, *pp. 285-286.* Persists in the view that activity does not mean development. 9 notes. H. G. Soff

Namibia

3672. Araud, Claude. LE DOSSIER "NAMIBIE" [The Namibia file]. *Genève-Afrique [Switzerland] 1980 18(2): 39-44.* Describes humanitarian and legal efforts to free Namibia from the politicians, farmers, and companies who run it. Secondary sources; 4 maps, photo. B. S. Fetter

3673. Araya, Francisco Ghisolfo. SUDÁFRICA Y EL EXPANSIONISMO SOVIÉTICO [South Africa and Soviet expansionism]. *Rev. de Marina [Chile] 1981 98(4): 415-428.* South Africa's mandate to administer Namibia was rescinded in 1966, but the danger of a Communist takeover posed by Angola's South-West Africa People's Organization (SWAPO) and the threats from Mozambique, Zimbabwe, and the UN— prodded by socialist, nonaligned, and African nations— led South Africa to refuse to relinquish control.

3674. Belfiglio, Valentine J. THE ISSUE OF NAMIBIAN INDEPENDENCE. *African Affairs [Great Britain] 1979 78(313): 507-522.* The most important revolutionary group operating within Namibia is the South-West Africa People's Organization (SWAPO), its military arm the People's Liberation Army of Namibia operating from southern Angola. The Democratic Turnhalle Alliance (DTA), representing the majority of the Herero and the Kavango peoples, is SWAPO's only serious rival for control over an independent Namibia. The South African Government refused to yield its trusteeship of South-West Africa to the United Nations in 1946, and has been responsible for a considerable advance in its economy in the postwar years. In 1975 the Turnhalle Conference confirmed that an independence constitution would be formulated within three years. Guerrilla warfare ensued while UN negotiations continued. 23 notes. R. L. Collison

3675. Beri, H. M. L. THE NAMIBIA TANGLE. *Africa Q. [India] 1979 18(2-3): 22-36.* Reviews South Africa's strong opposition from 1946 to 1978 to UN resolutions on Namibian independence and discusses strategies for ending the stalemate.

3676. Bowyer, Mathew J. AIRMAIL! *Aviation Q. 1979 5(4): 338-347.* The history of commercial airmail delivery from 1914 in German South-West Africa to the present era of airmail as the rule rather than the exception with the merger of airmail and surface mail.

3677. Caforio, Giuseppe. IL PUNTO SULLA NAMIBIA [On Namibia]. *Politico [Italy] 1980 45(1): 131-150.* Mineral resources, strategic location, and the long border with South Africa have made the decolonization of Namibia long and internationally controversial. The World Court has three times issued judgments, partly contradicting one another, and the UN in 1966 revoked the South African mandate. More recently, Western powers have moved toward effective mediation of Namibian independence, patching up an agreement (1979) between the UN and Pretoria for new elections with the participation of all movements and of political exiles, depending only on the willingness of Soviet-backed SWAPO guerrillas to cease armed resistance. J/S

3678. Clark, Roger S. THE INTERNATIONAL LEAGUE FOR HUMAN RIGHTS AND SOUTH WEST AFRICA, 1947-1957: THE HUMAN RIGHTS NGO AS CATALYST IN THE INTERNATIONAL LEGAL PROCESS. *Human Rights Q. 1981 3(4): 101-136.* Discusses the efforts of the International League for Human Rights to participate in the process concerning Namibia from 1947 to 1957.

3679. Collet, Sue. ECONOMIA DELL'AFRICA DEL SUD OVEST: CONDIZIONI E PROSPETTIVE [South-West Africa's economy: present conditions and prospects]. *Riv. di Studi Pol. Int. [Italy] 1980 47(3): 381-414.* Discusses the economic activities, aspects of production, gross domestic product, balance of payments, foreign investments, public expenditure, economic integration, regional development, and economic vitality of Namibia.

3680. Dale, Richard. THE ARMED FORCES AS AN INSTRUMENT OF SOUTH AFRICAN POLICY IN NAMIBIA. *J. of Modern African Studies [Great Britain] 1980 18(1): 57-71.* Surveys the political history of the use of South African forces in Namibia and the extent to which armed forces were used as a medium between the military and civilian government, and as a means of coercion. Based on government published documents and secondary sources; 70 notes. A. Sbacchi

3681. Dale, Richard. THE "GLASS PALACE WAR" OVER THE INTERNATIONAL DECOLONIZATION OF SOUTH WEST AFRICA. *Int. Organization 1975 29(2): 535-544.* Discusses recent writings about colonialism and nationalism in Namibia and the role of the UN, 1945-70's.

3682. Dale, Richard. WALVIS BAY: A NAVAL GATEWAY, AN ECONOMIC TURNSTILE, OR A DIPLOMATIC BARGAINING CHIP FOR THE FUTURE OF NAMIBIA? *J. of the Royal United Services Inst. for Defence Studies [Great Britain] 1982 127(1): 31-36.* Walvis Bay, a strategic port on Africa's southwest coast, has been seen as a strategically located naval and military base since World War I. Political cross-currents following World War II have sharpened the concern about the port's future and its importance both for the Republic of South Africa and for the nascent state of Namibia. Based on interviews, Republic of South Africa parliamentary documents, and secondary sources; map, 58 notes. R. E. Bilstein

3683. Danaher, Kevin Drew. NAMIBIA: PROFITS, RACISM, AND THE "SOVIET THREAT." *Monthly Rev. 1982 33(8): 36-47.* The stakes in the control of Namibia are the profits from its mines, racism, and the "Soviet threat" seen by Alexander Haig. In the international arena the Reagan administration is learning that the ideology of the 1950's cannot form the basis of African policy in the 1980's.

3684. Drăghici, Mariana. LE PROCESSUS DE DÉCOLONISATION ET QUELQUES CONSIDÉRATIONS CONCERNANT LE STATUT JURIDIQUE DE LA NAMIBIE [The process of decolonization and some considerations concerning the juridical status of Namibia]. *Rev. Roumaine d'Études Int. [Rumania] 1973 7(2-3): 157-174.* Situated on the shores of the South Atlantic, Namibia became a German colony in 1884. During World War I it was occupied by South African forces. The League of Nations gave it as a mandate to South Africa in 1920. Since the dissolution of the League, South Africa has continued to govern Namibia, submitting reports annually to the UN Commission on Mandates. A 1966 International Court decision ruled that South African rule was legal, but subsequently the UN passed resolutions designed to remove any legal grounds for continued administration from Pretoria. The Rumanian people have expressed in word and deed their solidarity with the people of Namibia in their struggle against racism and imperialism. 47 notes. J. C. Billigmeier

3685. Eriksen, Tore Linné. RÅVARER, GRUVESELSKAPER OG POLITIKK: NAMIBIA SOM EKSEMPEL [Raw materials, mining companies, and politics: the case of Namibia]. *Internasjonal Politikk [Norway] 1981 (2): 237-266.* The mining activities and mineral resources of Namibia are of utmost importance in understanding the interests that South Africa, multinational corporations, and the Great Powers seek to protect there. J/S

3686. Gibson, Gordon D. HIMBA EPOCHS. *Hist. in Africa 1977 4: 67-121.* Presents a 90-year chronology of the Himba and Herero of southwestern Africa, based on important events and conditions in the region. This is the first treatment of the methodological problems of ordered correlation between Himba and European chronology. Based on field data for 1960-61, and 1972-73, and data obtained in 1947-48; map. G. M. Fishman/S

3687. Gordon, Robert J. VARIATIONS IN MIGRATION RATES: THE OVAMBO CASE. *J. of Southern African Affairs 1978 3(3): 261-294.* Analyzes migrant labor from Ovamboland, Namibia, since the late 19th century, noting changes in the migratory labor system since its inception in 1891 and its social, economic, and political effects on the Ovambo homeland. The German colonial government until 1915 and the South African administration since 1919 regarded this northern region as the principal source of manual labor for the territory. The Ovambo laborers consistently resented the migratory labor system imposed upon them. The migratory labor system permitted the establishment in Ovamboland of a powerful new class of government-recognized headmen over the Ovambo, many of whom have turned to Christianity in opposition to local authorities. Changes until 1974 had not reversed adverse effects of the migratory labor system in Ovamboland. Based on printed official documents, newspapers, and secondary accounts; 11 tables, 112 notes. L. W. Truschel

3688. Hasan, Najmul. NAMIBIA: SOUTH-WEST AFRICA. *Pakistan Horizon [Pakistan] 1975 28(3): 61-78.* Namibia, formerly South-West Africa, is under the control of South Africa although resolutions and actions have supported independence for Namibia since 1946. 51 notes. H. M. Evans

3689. Johnston, William. NAMIBIA: FORCES AND FACTIONS. *Africa Today 1979 26(2): 23-28.* Briefly reviews the activities of political factions in Namibia. There are only two political forces in Namibia: South Africa and SWAPO (South-West Africa People's

Organization). Each is actively undermining the other's attempts to gain complete control of Namibia. Secondary sources; 11 notes. G. O. Gagnon

3690. Kooy, Marcelle. THE CONTRACT LABOR SYSTEM AND THE OVAMBO CRISIS OF 1971 IN SOUTHWEST AFRICA. *African Studies R. 1973 16(1): 83-105.*

3691. Leu, Christopher A. THE END OF THE WALDHEIM INITIATIVE. *Africa Today 1974 21(2): 43-59.* Summarizes the history of UN efforts to solve the problem of Namibia and Secretary-General Kurt Waldheim's 1972 plan for recovery. Negotiations with South Africa may be unnecessary because of other pressures in Southern Africa. Based on UN documents and secondary sources; 64 notes. G. O. Gagnon

3692. Loxley, John. NAMIBIA: THE STRUGGLE FOR INDEPENDENCE. *Can. Dimension [Canada] 1977 12(1): 26-31.* Offers a short background of Namibia's occupation by foreign powers, 1884-1907, then assesses the important place which it has held in the economic life of South Africa. Discusses the current national liberation movement in Namibia, 1973-77.

3693. MacBride, Sean. NAMIBIA. *Bull. of the Atomic Scientists 1981 37(6): 22-24.* South Africa, in direct violation of international law and the decisions of the International Court of Justice and the UN has refused to relinquish its illegal occupation of Namibia. Western nations have ignored the potential for war or intervention by the USSR.

3694. McDougall, Harold A. NAMIBIA AND PALESTINE: FOCAL POINTS OF AFRO-ARAB SOLIDARITY. *Freedomways 1982 22(4): 213-222.* Discusses the geographical importance of Palestine and Namibia since 1914, the role of British imperialism and the UN in stabilizing these areas, the establishment of Israel and the Republic of South Africa, and the Afro-Arab resistance to Western influence in Namibia and Palestine.

3695. Moorsom, Richard. LABOUR CONSCIOUSNESS AND THE 1971-72 CONTRACT WORKERS STRIKE IN NAMIBIA. *Development and Change [Netherlands] 1979 10(2): 205-231.* Briefly traces the history of capitalist production and contract labor in Namibia since the early 1900's, and examines the contract workers' strike of 1971-72 in the context of the working-class consciousness.

3696. Moorsom, Richard. UNDERDEVELOPMENT, CONTRACT LABOUR AND WORKER CONSCIOUSNESS IN NAMIBIA, 1915-1972. *J. of Southern African Studies [Great Britain] 1977 4(1): 52-87.* An attempt to explain the growth of worker "class consciousness" among Ovambo migrant laborers from the rural northern portion of Namibia from the inception of South African control over the territory in 1915 to the Ovambo worker strikes at Windhoek, Gross Otavi, and Walvis Bay in 1971-72. Land shortages in Ovamboland, increasingly powerful ethnic elites, and aggressive South African recruitment of labor for farms and mines impelled thousands of Ovambo peasants into the migratory labor system over the years. By 1971-72, many Ovambo laborers were prepared to strike out of a growing revolutionary consciousness against the colonial system maintained in Namibia. Discontented Ovambo peasants and an alienated Ovambo peasantry and intelligentsia were part of the same political protest. Based on printed documents, newspapers, and secondary sources; 9 tables, 96 notes. L. W. Truschel

3697. Pelliccioni, Franco. I TOPNAAR DELLA NAMIBIA [The Topnaar of Namibia]. *Africa [Italy] 1974 29(3): 393-408.* Recent research of an American scholar [Edward S. Ross] on the Topnaar, a Khoikhoi group of Namibia, is pictured by the author in a wider ecological and ethno-anthropological context regarding the Khoikhoi people as a whole. Also deals with the problem of origins and the somatic, cultural and linguistic affinities with some peoples in areas far from Namibia. Briefly analyzes the contribution of Khoisan groups to the settling of the Mapungubwe civilization. J/S

3698. Persaud, Motee. NAMIBIA AND THE INTERNATIONAL COURT OF JUSTICE. *Current Hist. 1975 68(405): 220-225.* Barring a commitment by the major Western powers, as well as by the Security Council of the United Nations, a nonviolent transition in Namibia is not now conceivable. J

3699. Redekop, Clarence G. THE LIMITS OF DIPLOMACY: THE CASE OF NAMIBIA. *Int. J. [Canada] 1979-80 35(1): 70-90.* Reviews the historical background of the dispute between the UN and South Africa over Namibia, a territory administered by the latter, formerly under a League of Nations mandate. Focuses Great Power efforts beginning in April 1977 to work out a compromise settlement. Success appeared near in July 1978, but agreement has proved elusive for a number of reasons, one being a dispute over the status of Walvis Bay, an enclave not originally a part of the mandated territory, but rather recognized by the League as an integral part of South Africa. A settlement does not now appear likely. 7 notes. L. Van Wyk

3700. Saxena, S. C. ROLE OF THE U. N. COUNCIL FOR NAMIBIA. *Africa Q. [India] 1978 17(3): 5-31.* Discusses the 1967 formation of the UN Council for Namibia, and work it has done to the present.

3701. Shepherd, George W., Jr. BREAKING THE NAMIBIA IMPASSE. *Africa Today 1982 29(1): 21-35.* Summarizes the realities of strategic, political, and economic interests which have created an impasse preventing independence for Namibia. Offers a plan to resolve the impasse if a shift by the Western nations from a "primarily strategic bias" to a human rights bias occurs. Develops an accommodation plan for simultaneously recognizing the interests of all parties. Based on UN sources; 42 notes. G. O. Gagnon

3702. Shubin, V. NA PUTI K SVOBODE [On the way to freedom]. *Aziia i Afrika Segodnia [USSR] 1975 (10): 15-17.* The heroic people of Namibia, led by the South-West Africa People's Organization, have fought in the 1960's and 70's to gain their independence and to oust South African colonizers. J

3703. Thomas, Elizabeth Marshall. AMERICAN FAMILY'S POIGNANT SOJOURN WITH THE BUSHMEN. *Smithsonian 1980 11(1): 86-95.* Reflections on the 30 years of association of the Lawrence Marshall family with the San of Namibia. From their periodic visits they have witnessed social changes in San society, particularly the effects of being placed on a reservation in the 1960's. S

3704. Trachtman, Joel. THE SOUTH-WEST AFRICA CASES AND THE DEVELOPMENT OF INTERNATIONAL LAW. *Millennium: J. of Int. Studies [Great Britain] 1976-77 5(3): 292-302.* Examines the background to the legal dispute over Namibia and the nature of the struggle within the International Court of Justice between two rival conceptions of international law, as seen in the litigation of 1962-66 and in the advisory opinion of 1971 on the Namibia dispute. The struggle between the positivist school of thought on the one hand and the sociological on the other is, in effect, over the organization of the world. The 1971 advisory opinion, by continuing sociological jurisprudence, was a defeat for positivist philosophy. Based on World Court reports and secondary sources; 26 notes. P. J. Beck

3705. Ulanovskaia, I. NAMIBIIA BUDET SVOBODNOI! [Namibia will be free!]. *Aziia i Afrika Segodnia [USSR] 1981 (5): 28-30.* South Africa in 1981 is attempting to establish a neocolonialist and racist regime in Namibia. Discusses the struggle of the South-West Africa People's Organization (SWAPO) for Namibian independence.

South Africa

General

3706. Ali, Shanti Sadiq. EVOLUTION OF APARTHEID. *Africa Q. [India] 1979 18(4): 31-44.* Studies the development and maintenance of segregationist policies in South Africa, especially as associated with the Calvinist Dutch Reformed Church, the right-wing Broederbond and other social organizations, the National Party, and individuals such as Cecil Rhodes, Paul Kruger, D. F. Malan, Hendrik Verwoerd and Balthazar Johannes Vorster, from 1806 to the present.

3707. Allibert, Jean-François. L'AFRIQUE DU SUD À LA CROISÉE DES CHEMINS [South Africa at the crossroads]. *Défense Natl. [France] 1975 31(4): 81-93, (5): 65-76, (6): 109-126.* Part I: Presents the historical background to South Africa's present racial problems and places it in its international context. Part II: Stresses the strategic importance of South Africa, which is faced with maritime dangers and difficulties arising from the breakup of the Portuguese empire. Part III: Analyzes the origins and application of apartheid, and evaluates perspectives for the development of South Africa's internal policy.

3708. Biesheuvel, S. and Martin, A. S. SPATIAL IMPLICATIONS OF APARTHEID: THE ROLE OF GROWTH CENTRES IN SOUTH AFRICA. *Pan-African J. [Kenya] 1976 9(1): 1-16.* Examines the nature and objectives of South Africa's regional development policy, and its effect on the country's geographical structure. Its expressed objective is to stimulate development in underdeveloped areas. The author describes it as a tool for keeping unwanted blacks out of metropolitan areas and employing them more cheaply in rural areas. 2 tables, 2 fig., 37 notes. M. Feingold

3709. Buraway, M. RACE, CLASS AND COLONIALISM. *Social and Econ. Studies [Jamaica] 1974 23(4): 521-550.* South African racial policies were created in the context of a colonial feudalism and continued despite a change in the economic base. 75 notes.
E. S. Johnson

3710. Butlitsky, A. KNOT OF APARTHEID CONTRADICTIONS. *Int. Affairs [USSR] 1973 (2): 80-86.* Discusses economic, political, and labor aspects of South Africa's apartheid policy, 1947-70's. Accuses the Vorster government of neocolonialism toward other African nations.

3711. Cornevin, Marianne. LES IMPOSTURES DE L'APARTHEID [The deceptions of apartheid]. *Études [France] 1978 349(2-3): 165-184.* Discusses 20th-century apartheid in South Africa, including the characteristics of Afrikaners, Anglophones, and the nine black linguistic groups, the distribution of land, professional and residential segregation, and recent black revolts.

3712. Dadoo, Yusuf M. THE CRISIS OF APARTHEID. *World Marxist R. 1975 18(2): 104-113.*

3713. Davenport, T. R. H. THE HISTORY OF RACE RELATIONS IN SOUTH AFRICA. *Zambezia [Zimbabwe] 1973 3(1): 5-14.* Traces the transition from easy race relations in mid-17th-century South Africa to the harshness of 20th-century separation. Discusses problems of the frontier, land, and urban policy as the prosperity of an economically developing white society is shored up by cheap black labor. Provides highly personal historical vignettes of contradictions, humaneness, and the insignificance of the opponents of separate development.
O. B. Pollak

3714. Davis, R. Hunt, Jr. THE BURDEN OF THE PRESENT. *Int. J. of African Hist. Studies 1979 12(2): 277-282.* Review of Harrison M. Wright's *The Burden of the Present: Liberal-Radical Controversy over Southern African History* (Cape Town: David Philip, 1977), which assesses the controversy between radical and liberal historians over South African history. The basic interests and premises of the two schools give them underlying similarities. Wright's conclusions are overdrawn, particularly his sharp attack on the radical school. 13 notes.
M. M. McCarthy

3715. Denoon, Donald. LIBERAL HISTORY IN THE LAAGER. *African Affairs [Great Britain] 1978 77(308): 403-408.* A review article of three books on South Africa: *The Journals of the Rev. T. L. Hodgson, Missionary to the Seleka-Rolong and the Griquas, 1821-1831* (Witwatersrand U. Pr., 1977) edited by R. L. Cope; Richard Elphick's *Kraal and Castle: Khoikhoi and the Founding of White South Africa* (Yale U. Pr., 1977); and T. R. H. Davenport's *South Africa. A Modern History*(Macmillan, 1977). Cope has done a fine editorial job on the journals of the Reverend Hodgson; Elphick has written the first major review of Khoikhoi history in decades; and Davenport has defended liberal scholarship against revisionist criticisms. The bulk of the review is a discussion of Davenport's defense. H. G. Soff

3716. Giniewski, Paul. L'AFRIQUE DU SUD APRÈS VINGT-CINQ ANS D'APARTHEID [South Africa after 25 years of apartheid]. *Pol. Étrangère [France] 1973 38(6): 753-764.* Evaluates how the policy of apartheid has satisfied goals and expectations, 25 years after its official inauguration by the nationalist government in South Africa, 1948-73.

3717. Good, Kenneth. SETTLER COLONIALISM: ECONOMIC DEVELOPMENT AND CLASS FORMATION. *J. of Modern African Studies [Great Britain] 1976 14(4): 597-620.* Recognizes certain contrasts between the colon, or settler, state and the general experience of the former colonies of the Third World (as illustrated by Kenya, Algeria, Southern Rhodesia, and South Africa). Explores the important similarities whose development can be studied as a means of better understanding the dynamics of change at work in South Africa today. The roles of military power and industrial capitalism, imperialism and the origins of the settler state, economic development and class formation, the political rigidity of the settler state, and class action and imperialism are analyzed. The author concludes that the South African state today presents a latent threat to imperialism in Africa and the Third World. "Its successful reactions of the past do not indicate its certainty of success in a rapidly changing, more threatening future." 101 notes. R. V. Ritter

3718. Gotō, Tomokuni. MINAMI A NO APARUTOHEITO NO SHITEKI KŌSATSU [A historical study of apartheid in South Africa]. *Shigaku Zasshi [Japan] 1974 83(11): 56-72.*

3719. Grzybowski, Antoni. SPOLECZNE DROGI KSZTALTOWANIA SIE APARTHEIDU W AFRYCE POLUDNIOWEJ [Social roads of formation of apartheid in South Africa]. *Przegląd Socjologiczny [Poland] 1979 31(2): 113-142.* Traces South Africa's policy of apartheid to the Calvinism of the Boer settlers and identifies religion, language, and race as the three principal elements undergirding the social policy of the Nationalist government which came to power in 1948.

3720. Hancock, I. R. and Markus, Andrew. RACE AND CLASS: THE NEO-MARXISTS, SOUTH AFRICA AND AUSTRALIA. *Hist. Studies [Australia] 1978 18(70): 134-141.* Nature, function and future of race discrimination in South Africa, with some comparisons with Australia. Contrasts the liberal-reformist school, who believe that industrialism and discrimination are incompatible, and the neo-Marxists, who suggest economic development depends on white supremacy and cheap black labor. W. D. McIntyre

3721. Hessel, Brad. SOUTH AFRICA: VESTIGE OF COLONIALISM. *Strategy and Tactics 1977 62: 4-14.* Argues that in South Africa the divisions between rich and poor, modern and traditional, North and South, cut across the more commonly attended distinctions of ideology, nationality, race, and religion.

3722. Hirschmann, David. PRESSURES ON APARTHEID. *Foreign Affairs 1973 52(1): 168-179.* In South Africa there exist pressures for change from a variety of sources: economic, political, black, white, foreign, and domestic. The task of assessing the significance and direction of change is an awkward one. Nonetheless, trends of some significance are taking place in three principal areas: increasing criticism and protest by the black leadership of the Bantustans; activity among urban blacks, particularly in the black labor movement; and wide-ranging efforts by outside groups to influence South African racial policy. 13 notes. R. Riles

3723. Johnson, Robert E. INDIAN AND BLACK IN SOUTH AFRICA: ANALYSIS OF THE PAST, PROJECTION FOR THE FUTURE. *Michigan Academician 1975 8(2): 157-166.*

3724. Johnstone, Frederick. "MOST PAINFUL TO OUR HEARTS": SOUTH AFRICA THROUGH THE EYES OF THE NEW SCHOOL. *Can. J. of African Studies [Canada] 1982 16(1): 5-26.* The traditional liberal social analysis of South Africa, emphasizing the racial situation as a starting point for all analysis, was supplanted in the 1970's by a new school of Marxist analysis which saw that country's modern dilemma as the product of an inherent class struggle. At its heart is the superexploitation of the black laboring class by a racially structured capitalism. This new Marxist class analysis of South Africa needs to be coupled with the traditional approach so as to reflect the cultural and subjective diversity of South African history. 28 notes. L. J. Klass

3725. Lacina, Karel. HISTORICKÉ ZDROJE APARTHEIDU [The historical sources of apartheid]. *Československý Časopis Hist. [Czechoslovakia] 1981 29(1): 38-62.* Though apartheid did not achieve its status as official South African policy until 1948, its roots reach back to the original Dutch settlement at the Cape of Good Hope after 1652. While a hardline Dutch Calvinism gave religious sanction to European superiority, the expropriation and exploitation of native tribes translated it into economic fact. The Anglo-Afrikaner rivalry of the 19th century was ended by agreement (1902-10) at the expense of the nonwhite majority, whom the racist legislation marked for permanent segregation and exploitation. Secondary sources; 79 notes. Russian and English summaries. R. E. Weltsch

3726. LaGuma, Alex. WHITHER SOUTH AFRICA? *Black Scholar 1974 5(10): 30-36.* After an introductory explanation of the early Dutch colonization and the British conquest of South Africa, the author describes the development of institutionalized racism and white supremacy and the revolutionary response for national liberation of nonwhites in the 20th century.

3727. Legassick, Martin. LEGISLATION, IDEOLOGY AND ECONOMY IN POST-1948 SOUTH AFRICA. *J. of Southern African Studies [Great Britain] 1974 1(1): 5-35.* Criticizes the belief, part of South African liberalism's "conventional wisdom," that apartheid is an ultimately futile attempt to curtail the working of market forces, which are seen as promoting racial integration. Compares the stands on racial policy of the United Party and the victorious Nationalist Party in the 1948 election, finding only moderate differences between the two. Subsequent government policy sought to exploit black labor to advance economic growth, while simultaneously insuring white employment and preventing the growth of assimilated black populations in white areas. Describes the evolution of theory and practice which culminated in the present policy of "separate development." Based primarily on *House of Assembly Debates,*other government publications, and contemporary newspaper accounts; 104 notes. L. W. Van Wyk

3728. Legassick, Martin. RACE, INDUSTRIALIZATION AND SOCIAL CHANGE IN SOUTH AFRICA: THE CASE OF R. F. A. HOERNLE. *African Affairs [Great Britain] 1976 75(299): 224-239.* An examination of the writings of Alfred Hoernle from 1909 to 1939. Although he was optimistic in 1909 about a liberal policy toward Africans, by 1939 it was apparent that the South African state was an instrument of racial domination. 46 notes. H. G. Soff

3729. Maione, Romeo. EXPLOITATION IN SOUTH AFRICA. *Can. Labour 1974 19(1): 20-22.*

3730. Mehliss, Max. THE DILEMMA OF SOUTH AFRICA. *Blackwood's Mag. [Great Britain] 1977 321(1940): 485-490.* A native-born white South African sketches the history of colonialism in Africa and analyzes the current racial and political situations confronting South Africans.

3731. Molev, V. IUAR... I GRIANET VZRYV [South Africa: the explosion is imminent]. *Aziia i Afrika Segodnia [USSR] 1982 (6): 17-20.* The labor unrest and struggle in the South African mining industry signals an ever more political struggle against the entire apartheid system and the fight for "the liquidation of the colour barrier."

3732. Munger, Edwin S. THE AFRIKANER AS SEEN ABROAD. *Munger Africana Lib. Notes 1974 26: 1-58.*

3733. Omer-Cooper, John. WHOSE BABY IS APARTHEID? *Hist. News [New Zealand] 1982 (45): 1-5.* Examines white landownership in Transvaal and Natal, 1860-1903, and government policies from 1903 to 1960 in South Africa which account for apartheid.

3734. Ralston, Richard D. SOCIAL SCIENCE RESEARCH, THE BLACK SCHOLAR, SOUTH AFRICA, AND OTHER ODD BEDFELLOWS: AN HISTORIAN'S PERSPECTIVE. *J. of Ethnic Studies 1977 5(1): 1-11.* Discusses the barriers to most African researchers in South Africa, and the influence of apartheid on historical studies. Black American scholars have unique opportunities for meaningful investigation in South Africa, once the obstacles of travel permits and access to material and informants are overcome. Informants feel more secure speaking to an American African. The pariah status of the South African government virtually guarantees cooperation due to informants' attitudes toward the regime. The author expresses guarded optimism as to the future of social science research from a nonwhite centered conceptual framework and suggests topics to begin the reconstruction of African black history. Based on the author's own experiences and secondary works; 17 notes. G. J. Bobango

3735. Rich, P. B. MINISTERING TO THE WHITE MAN'S NEEDS: THE DEVELOPMENT OF URBAN SEGREGATION IN SOUTH AFRICA 1913-1923. *African Studies [South Africa] 1978 37(2): 177-191.* Analyzes two contending points of view, the liberal interpretation and the "Stallard doctrine," to account for the development of segregation in South Africa, 1913-23.

3736. Rubin, Leslie. SOUTH AFRICA 1948-1973: APARTHEID AFTER TWENTY-FIVE YEARS. *Issue 1974 4(3): 2.* Introduction to six papers presented at a 1973 symposium of the African Studies Association. S

3737. Schmidl, Erwin. EINIGE BEMERKUNGEN ZUM THEMA: ARCHIVARBEIT IN SÜDAFRIKA [Some remarks on archival work in South Africa]. *Scrinium [Austria] 1981 24: 185-189.* Discusses the contents of the South African State Archive/Transvaal Archives Depot at Pretoria, the Orange Free State Archive Depot at Bloemfontein, and the four regional archives of South Africa and their development since 1910.

3738. Schofield, Victoria. SOUTH AFRICA TODAY. *Blackwood's Mag. [Great Britain] 1977 1935(321): 4-24.* Discusses race relations, social problems, economic conditions, labor, education and political leadership in South Africa in the 1960's and 1970's. Considers the viability of the Homelands Policy, the effort to divide Blacks into ethnic group areas.

3739. Selby, John. SOUTH AFRICA: SOME MISCONCEPTIONS. *Army Q. and Defence J. [Great Britain] 1976 106(2): 204-210.* Justifies the policy of apartheid as a means of maintaining balanced race relations between different groups of black Africans, 1948-70's.

3740. Siegrist, Samuel. SÜDAFRIKA IM WANDEL [South Africa in transition]. *Schweizer Monatshefte [Switzerland] 1980 60(12): 975-987.* Reviews the conflicts between the Dutch and English elements, the conflict between Europeans and Africans, and the attempts to modify apartheid in South Africa since 1945.

3741. Smith, Anna H. JOHANNESBURG 90. *Africana Notes and News [South Africa] 1976 22(3): 89-91.* A brief recollection of some published works about Johannesburg on the occasion of the city's 90th birthday. H. G. Soff

3742. Smith, Anna H. WOMEN AND AFRICANA. *Africana Notes and News [South Africa] 1974 21(2): 45-47.* There is a need for both women and men interested in Africana to prepare manuscripts on topics such as military insignia, forms of transport, needlework, etc. Women have led in the past as collectors of Africana and curators of Africana museums. H. G. Soff

3743. Stasiulis, Daiva K. PLURALIST MARXIST PERSPECTIVES ON RACIAL DISCRIMINATION IN SOUTH AFRICA. *British J. of Sociol. [Great Britain] 1980 31(4): 463-490.* Defends a Marxist analysis of racial discrimination in South Africa, claiming that it is an integral part of the growth of capitalism in that country.

3744. Thompson, Carol B. FORUM: INVESTING IN SOUTH AFRICAN APARTHEID. *Peace and Change 1976 4(2): 53-57.* Examines the apartheid system in South Africa, offering statistics on income, educational, social, political, and economic differences in white and black residents and an overall assessment of race relations, 1971-76.

3745. Varley, D. H. THE MAKING OF SABIB: A LANDMARK IN SOUTH AFRICAN BIBLIOGRAPHY. *African Res. and Documentation [Great Britain] 1980 (22): 13-18.* Discusses the history of the South African Bibliography to 1925 (SABIB) project in South Africa, from its origins in Sidney Mendelssohn's classic, *Mendelssohn's South African Bibliography* (1910).

3746. Winfrey, Dorman H. THE SOUTH AFRICAN FRONTIER EXPERIENCE: SOME PARALLELS WITH TEXAS AND THE AMERICAN WEST. *Texana 1973 11(2): 145-174.* Discusses frontier expansion 1900-50 in South Africa and interprets events there in terms of the American frontier. 112 notes.

3747. Yudelman, David. INDUSTRIALIZATION, RACE RELATIONS AND CHANGE IN SOUTH AFRICA: AN IDEOLOGICAL AND ACADEMIC DEBATE. *African Affairs [Great Britain] 1975 74(294): 82-96.* A critical evaluation of the radical-revisionist view of South African history. The revisionists perpetuate the same myths as the reformists. They do not understand revolution or evolution completely. A full study of urban unemployment is required for those interested in industrialization. 19 notes. H. G. Soff

3748. —. [RACIAL DYNAMICS]. *Can. Dimension [Canada] 1977 12(1): 32-37.*

Segal, Mark D. RACIAL DYNAMICS ON THE PERIPHERY: APARTHEID, *pp. 32-37.* Examines the economic infrastructure of Southern Africa concluding that transnational corporate capitalism supports the system of apartheid in South Africa because that system serves its economic ends.

Loxley, Zeeba. BANTUSTANS, *pp. 32-34.* Examines the system of Bantu Homelands (or Bantustans) set up as reserves for African residence by South African governments since 1925.

Economics

3749. Belcher, Timothy. INDUSTRIAL DECENTRALISATION AND THE DYNAMICS OF FORCED LABOUR IN SOUTH AFRICA. *J. of Modern African Studies [Great Britain] 1979 17(4): 677-686.* Confronted with an organized movement demanding the basic right of economic survival, the South African government in the 1950's decided to modernize the system of labor control by dispersing urban Africans into the underdeveloped Bantustans and moving industry to their borders. But the industrial decentralization program has failed to meet the government's objectives. The political exigencies of maintaining the ruling coalition, by which employers extract high rates of surplus value and the state bears the cost of repression, have come into conflict with the process of accumulation, forcing the government to abandon social engineering in favor of direct coercion. Based on South African Government documents and other published sources; 29 notes. D. J. Nicholls

3750. Bozzoli, Belinda. THE ORIGINS, DEVELOPMENT, AND IDEOLOGY OF LOCAL MANUFACTURING IN SOUTH AFRICA. *J. of Southern African Studies [Great Britain] 1975 1(2): 194-214.* Traces the evolution of the ideologies of the local manufacturing communities in South Africa. They grew from a small group struggling for acceptance and recognition to a major interest group which ideologically dominated society. Argues that the development of group cohesion was made possible by the evolution of a specific middle-class ideology in these communities. Based on industrial publications; 71 notes. S. P. Carr

3751. Bremer, N. VAKBONDEN EN APARTHEID IN ZUID-AFRIKA [Labor unions and apartheid in South Africa]. *Economisch en Sociaal-Historisch Jaarboek [Netherlands] 1977 40: 199-241.* Strict racial separation developed in the late 19th and early 20th centuries. Differentials existed in social status, job classifications, and wages. After the Boer War, labor organizations pressured for the use of more white labor in mines and the exclusion of Chinese and Blacks. In the printing industry racial barriers were lifted only to allow Africans in a special African Workers Section. In the garment workers' unions there were few racial hindrances. Here most labor unions accepted members of all races on an equal basis, although numerical differences continued to exist. 6 tables, 124 notes, 2 appendixes. F. Frankfort

3752. Coker, Christopher. COLLECTIVE BARGAINING AS AN INTERNAL SANCTION: THE ROLE OF U.S. CORPORATIONS IN SOUTH AFRICA. *J. of Modern African Studies [Great Britain] 1981 19(4): 647-665.* An analysis of the relationship between American businesses in South Africa and the emergence of black African labor unions and their effectiveness against official Apartheid policies. The Polaroid experiment of 1970 and the Sullivan program of 1977 did encourage formation and growth of black unions and foster official concessions by way of the Wiehahn Commission on labor policy and the Industrial Conciliation Act of 1979, which authorized the formation of African trade unions. In such ways foreign corporations have helped improve the contractual status of African workers. The unions have also begun to mobilize support outside the factories among urban communities and establish ties to African political organizations in South Africa. Based on American and South African official documents and newspapers; 28 notes. L. W. Truschel

3753. Davies, Robert. CAPITAL RESTRUCTURING AND THE MODIFICATION OF THE RACIAL DIVISION OF LABOUR IN SOUTH AFRICA. *J. of Southern African Studies [Great Britain] 1979 5(2): 181-198.* Applies neo-Marxist theory to changes in South African labor policies, as considered by the government's Wiehahn Commission. The proposed ending of statutory racial job reservation and closed shops in South Africa are seen as a maneuver by the bourgeois state to counter the threat of African revolution posed by the 1976 riots by opening lower-level skilled jobs to a few Africans, without the possibility of any significant African advancement in the middle and upper job levels. The Wiehahn Commission recommendations are seen also as an effort to reattract foreign capital investments in South Africa. White workers will be persuaded to accept the proposed changes, while African workers will continue the class struggle within the country. Based on newspapers and secondary sources; 2 tables, 34 notes. L. W. Truschel

3754. Davies, Robert and Kaplan, David. CAPITALIST DEVELOPMENT AND THE EVOLUTION OF RACIAL POLICY IN SOUTH AFRICA. *Tarikh [Nigeria] 1979 6(2): 46-62.* Discusses the economic exploitation of Africans by Europeans as part of state economic policy directed at the development of South Africa.

3755. Davies, Robert. THE WHITE WORKING CLASS IN SOUTH AFRICA. *New Left R. [Great Britain] 1973 (82): 40-59.* Argues, with reference to history and to statistical evidence, that there is a "labor aristocracy" in South Africa. The white manual workers exist on the surplus value taken from the black workers. This ensures their allegiance to the apartheid government. Concludes that liberation for the blacks means liberation for the proletariat. Based mainly on statistical sources; 6 tables, 40 notes. P. J. Beck

3756. Dekenah, I. SOUTH AFRICAN CIGARETTE MAKERS AND THEIR PRODUCTS. *Africana Notes and News [South Africa] 1974 21(2): 47-50.* Traces the development of cigarette manufacture in South Africa and recommends that more people become interested in the hobby of collecting old cigarette wrappers. 3 plates. H. G. Soff

3757. duPlessis, Esau. DON'T SQUEEZE A SOUTH AFRICAN DRY. *Africa Today 1974 21(2): 59-68.* Describes the boycott of South African oranges in the Netherlands during the summer of 1973. Concludes that its success paves the way for effective pressure against apartheid products. Based on author's experience as a leader of the movement. G. O. Gagnon

3758. DuToit, Darcy. THE WHITE WORKERS IN SOUTH AFRICA. *African Perspectives [Netherlands] 1978 (2): 99-116.* Much misinterpretation has attended the position of the white worker in South Africa. The author attempts to destroy the ambiguities in interpretations of the position of the white worker in South Africa, by surveying the distinctions and definitions proposed by various theorists, and asserts that "a class division is created between the employer and his employees by the ownership of the means of production." The supervisory function of the white worker puts him on the side of the employer to protect his special political and other privileges. Racism is therefore supported at this level. 14 notes. R. V. Ritter

3759. Fourie, J. J. DIE VRAAG NA EN AANBOD VAN DIE AFRIKANER SE ARBEID AS BEPALENDE FAKTOR IN SY SOSIO-EKONOMIESE POSISIE AAN DIE RAND TOT 1924 [The question of demand for the Afrikaner's work as the determining factor for his social-economic position on the Reef until 1924]. *Historia [South Africa] 1981 26(2): 141-154.* Discusses the labor situation for Afrikaners in Johannesburg after the discovery of gold on the Witwatersrand (1886) to its regulation in 1924. Lack of education and industrial skills and a different attitude to life and work kept the rural Afrikaner forced to seek a living in urban Johannesburg from getting any but the lowest paid jobs for unskilled labor in the mining and transportation industries

and slowed his adaptation to the city's economic and social life. Based on newspaper reports and official documents; table, 46 notes.
G. Herritt

3760. Greenberg, Stanley B. ECONOMIC GROWTH AND POLITICAL CHANGE: THE SOUTH AFRICAN CASE. *J. of Modern African Studies [Great Britain] 1981 19(4): 667-704.* Longterm capitalist economic development and official policy in South Africa have created a substantial degree of class differentiation among Africans, alongside a large and growing "surplus" of labor. The ultimate political consequence of this economic growth and government action is difficult to foresee. The government may succeed in coopting a class of settled urban workers as its allies, or this group may join far poorer classes of rural, Homeland, and unemployed workers in a black nationalist movement to topple the white power structure. Based on corporation reports and published South African documents; 6 tables, 113 notes.
L. W. Truschel

3761. Grundy, Kenneth W. ON DOMESTICATING TRANSNATIONAL CORPORATIONS: SOUTH AFRICA AND THE AUTOMOTIVE INDUSTRY. *J. of Commonwealth and Comparative Pol. [Great Britain] 1981 19(2): 157-173.* Examines the status of the automobile industry in South Africa since 1945, a story that combines protectionism for infant industry, mercantilism or economic nationalism, import substitution, and the subtle enlistment of nonstate actors to develop positive protective foreign linkages. The South African government attempted to localize and harness the motor industry as a catalyst for industrialization, but in economic terms the opportunity costs and costs to the consumer seem unacceptable. European South African car ownership is approaching saturation, and South Africa's competitive advantage, a regimented, low-paid labor force, excludes it from larger regional markets. Based on Board of Trade and Industries' Reports and secondary sources; table, 39 notes. M. K. Hogg

3762. Guelke, Adrian. AFRICA AS A MARKET FOR SOUTH AFRICAN GOODS. *J. of Modern African Studies [Great Britain] 1974 12(1): 69-88.* Examines South Africa's economic position in Africa. In the past 20 years, only a small percentage of total exports went to African states outside Southern Africa. Since 1964 South African trade increased with Southern Rhodesia, Zambia, Malawi, Angola, and Mozambique. South African capital expansion outside its borders is largely limited to the Cabora-Bassa project. Discusses effects of the Southern Rhodesian U.D.I. and reviews current trade patterns with Zambia. South Africa has made no political concessions with regard to apartheid in order to improve its foreign trade in Africa. 9 tables, 37 notes.
H. G. Soff

3763. Hemson, David. DOCK WORKERS, LABOUR CIRCULATION, AND CLASS STRUGGLES IN DURBAN, 1940-1959. *J. of Southern African Studies [Great Britain] 1977 4(1): 88-124.* A Marxist analysis of labor unrest among African longshoremen in Durban during the 1940's and 1950's. These migrant laborers were proletarianized to the point of forming a "volatile and class conscious element within the working class in Durban." Zulu Phungula, described as a fiery populist from the Ixcopo area, led the dockworkers from 1939 on in issuing wage and working condition demands and waging periodic strikes against the local companies. After leading a general strike in the city in 1949, Phungula was banished to his rural home area, while, over the next ten years, the South African government and the companies engineered a successful "collective capitalist reaction" to reassert control over the dockworkers. Based on published documents, newspapers, and secondary accounts; 114 notes. L. W. Truschel

3764. Hoagland, Jim. THE DOLLAR'S SHADOW. *Foreign Service J. 1973 50(4): 16-17, 27-28.* Examines US investment in South Africa over the past decade and diplomatic effects. S

3765. Jordaan, Kenneth A. THE BLACK WORKERS' STRUGGLE IN SOUTH AFRICA. *Internat. Socialist R. 1973 35(5): 24-30.* Discusses the mass unemployment and exploitation of black workers, with special attention to South Africa's apartheid policy and the British Trades Union Congress. S

3766. Kantor, B. S. and Kenny, H. F. THE POVERTY OF NEO-MARXISM: THE CASE OF SOUTH AFRICA. *J. of Southern African Studies [Great Britain] 1976 3(1): 20-40.* Critically examines the recent historiography of South Africa and the validity of some neo-Marxist explanations of important aspects of South African economic history. Pays particular attention to the works of Wolpe, Legassick, Trapido, and Johnstone. Secondary sources; 41 notes. S. P. Carr

3767. Kienzle, William. GERMAN-SOUTH AFRICAN TRADE RELATIONS IN THE NAZI ERA. *African Affairs [Great Britain] 1979 78(310): 81-90.* Describes trade relations between South Africa and Germany in the Nazi era, emphasizing their reciprocity. In 1934, the first commercial agreement between the two countries was signed, formalizing a relationship dating back to 1910. Trade so flourished that even after South Africa declared war against Hitler in 1939, the Germans made efforts to continue trade. Based on a 1974 Pennsylvania State University PhD dissertation; 53 notes. S. Lakhan

3768. Koog, Marcelle. BLACK WORKER UNREST IN SOUTH AFRICA 1971-1973 IN ITS HISTORICAL CONTEXT. *Africa Today 1974 21(4): 53-74.* Explains the evolution of the large wage disparity between blacks and whites in South Africa. Although this inequality was based upon the economic needs of an industrializing nation, apartheid has perpetuated it in a developed economy. The Ovambo (1971) and Natal (1973) strikes by Africans serve as symbolic notice to South Africa that the disparities can be reduced. Primary and secondary sources; 72 notes.
G. O. Gagnon

3769. Legassick, Martin and Innes, Duncan. CAPITAL RESTRUCTURING AND APARTHEID: A CRITIQUE OF CONSTRUCTIVE ENGAGEMENT. *African Affairs [Great Britain] 1977 76(305): 437-482.* Merle Lipton has written a series of articles supporting constructive engagement in South Africa, but her research and that of the constructive engagement school is based on faulty premises. Their work is superficial, wrong, or misrepresentative. The authors attempt to refute Lipton's condemnation of Neo-Marxists. 92 notes. H. G. Soff

3770. Lerumo, Anton. THE STRUGGLE OF THE SOUTH AFRICAN WORKING CLASS. *World Marxist R. [Canada] 1973 16(11): 56-63.*

3771. Lipton, Merle. WHITE FARMING: A CASE STUDY OF CHANGE IN SOUTH AFRICA. *J. of Commonwealth and Comparative Pol. [Great Britain] 1974 12(1): 42-61.* With the postwar expansion of South Africa's economy, it has been argued, particularly by neo-Marxist scholars, that the country's economy, built on cheap forced labor, cannot combine capitalist development with a rising standard of living for the masses. The author denies this, arguing that for many groups of nonwhites change has meant an easing of restrictions and more bargaining power, but not increasing "immiseration." Taking agriculture, a backward sector, as a test case, the author shows that real wages of blacks have risen and that pressures for reform have emanated from the self-interest of whites. 2 tables, 72 notes. R. D. Black

3772. MacRae, Phyllis. RACE AND CLASS IN SOUTHERN AFRICA. *African Rev. [Tanzania] 1974 4(2): 237-247.* Apartheid in South Africa has proven a useful tool to promote white racial advantages, especially its economic interests. Capitalism is the cause of racial prejudice. 40 notes. H. G. Soff

3773. Magnusson, Åke. SVERIGES FÖRBINDELSER MED SYDAFRIKA [Sweden's relations with South Africa]. *Internasjonal Politikk [Norway] 1975 (2): 219-240.* Limiting himself to the direct relations between the two countries, the author describes the main economic traits, presents some aspects of wage conditions in six Swedish companies located in South Africa, and assesses some actions now being undertaken in Sweden. J

3774. Mbeki, Moeletsi. CAPITAL AND LABOR IN SOUTH AFRICA: PRELIMINARY REMARKS ON THE WIEHAHN COMMISSION REPORT. *Monthly Rev. 1980 31(10): 10-19.* Briefly discusses the findings of the two-year investigations by the Wiehahn Commission of "the legal framework governing day-to-day relations between capital and labor" from 1977-79, criticizing the commission's recommendations as mere illusions of change which will do little or nothing to end exploitation or oppression of South Africa's black working class. Includes a brief history of South African labor activity in the 1970's.

3775. Mehlman, Maxwell J.; Milch, Thomas H.; and Toumanoff, Michael V. UNITED STATES RESTRICTIONS ON EXPORTS TO SOUTH AFRICA. *Am. J. of Int. Law 1979 73(4): 581-603.* Traces US policy since 1960. Indicates public laws have gone deliberately unenforced. Only in 1977 did the State Department admit that guidelines had been liberalized in 1970. Between 1960 and 1977, the State Department approved more Munitions List items to South Africa than to any other African country. The 1978 level of aircraft and computer-related exports to South Africa was among the very highest for all countries. Recommends policy changes designed to improve enforcement. 94 notes.
R. J. Jirran

3776. Mezger, Dorothea. HOW THE MINING INDUSTRY UNDERMINES LIBERATION MOVEMENTS IN SOUTHERN AFRICA. *J. of Southern African Affairs 1979 4(3): 301-324.* Examines South Africa's gold and other mining industries. South African mineral production is of crucial strategic value to the West, and South African mining corporations have begun intensive mechanization of their mines, developed integrated control of their financing and operations with large foreign firms, and even advocated the end of apartheid. These moves are clever survival tactics by the mining companies designed to stave off truly radical forms of nationalization by a future black socialist regime. Secondary sources; 4 tables, 38 notes. L. W. Truschel

3777. Mhlongo, Sam. BLACK WORKERS' STRIKES IN SOUTHERN AFRICA. *New Left R. [Great Britain] 1973 (83): 41-49.* Examines the development and position of the black working class and its role in industrial militancy in South Africa and Namibia, 1972-73. The action indicates both the possibilities and limitations of the black proletarian struggle. Based on the South African press and on secondary sources; 2 tables, 22 notes. P. J. Beck

3778. Morris, Mike. THE DEVELOPMENT OF CAPITALISM IN SOUTH AFRICA. *J. of Development Studies [Great Britain] 1976 12(3): 280-292.* Reviews H. Hobart Houghton and J. Dagut's *Source Material on the South African Economy, 1860-1970* (Cape Town: Oxford U. Pr., 1972-73).

3779. Nyathi, V. M. SOUTH AFRICAN IMPERIALISM IN SOUTHERN AFRICA. *African Rev. [Tanzania] 1975 5(4): 451-471.* South Africa has long had a classical exploitative economic relationship with neighboring states, but is little more than an economic dependency of European neoimperialism. 6 tables, 35 notes. R. T. Brown

3780. O'Meara, Dan. ANALYSING AFRIKANER NATIONALISM: THE "CHRISTIAN-NATIONAL" ASSAULT ON WHITE TRADE UNIONISM IN SOUTH AFRICA, 1934-1948. *African Affairs [Great Britain] 1978 77(306): 45-72.* The Christian Nationalists were Afrikaners who sought a new type of trade unionism. Since Afrikaans speakers are disadvantaged within the white labor force, it is surprising that the success of Christian Nationalist trade unionism was so limited. 110 notes. H. G. Soff

3781. O'Meara, Dan. THE 1946 AFRICAN MINE WORKERS STRIKE AND THE POLITICAL ECONOMY OF SOUTH AFRICA. *J. of Commonwealth and Comparative Pol. [Great Britain] 1975 13(2): 146-173.* Analyzes the effect of the 1946 miners' strike in terms of its contribution to changes in the class basis of African opposition and the ideology of nationalism in the late 1940's. Examines the implications of South Africa's economic growth during the 1930's-40's for race relations and the labor movement. Based on Labor Department reports and *Union Statistics for Fifty Years*(Pretoria 1960). 65 notes. C. Anstey

3782. Phillips, Earl. STATE REGULATION AND ECONOMIC INITIATIVE: THE SOUTH AFRICAN CASE TO 1960. *Int. J. of African Hist. Studies 1974 7(2): 227-254.* The economic progress of South Africa from 1939 to 1960 was impressive, but the maintenance of a high level of investment was hampered by such supply factors as shortages of skilled and semiskilled workers, productive capacity, and especially, capital. The success of the economy rests largely with the government policy of mobilizing domestic capital. The size of this governmental initiative and its strategic significance for economic growth have both been important factors. Underlying all government activity has been the necessity of providing whites with a high standard of living. Primary and secondary sources; chart, 98 notes.
M. M. McCarthy

3783. Pollock, N. PROBLEMS OF AGRICULTURAL DIFFUSION IN NATAL, SOUTH AFRICA. *Geography [Great Britain] 1974 59(3): 257-260.* In Natal less than five percent of the white population is engaged in agriculture, while the majority of the Africans are subsistence farmers. Acceptance of new farming techniques in the Bantu Homelands is generally slower than in the white farming areas. Since 1950 the Valley Trust has fostered innovation in African agriculture.
D. D. Cameron

3784. Prothero, R. Mansell. FOREIGN MIGRANT LABOUR FOR SOUTH AFRICA. *Int. Migration Rev. 1974 8(3): 383-394.* Discusses the role of apartheid in the politics and economics of South Africa's migrant labor policy in the 1960's and 70's.

3785. Rogerson, C. M. INDUSTRIALIZATION OF THE BANTU HOMELANDS. *Geography [Great Britain] 1974 59(3): 260-264.* An analysis of the problems arising from the establishment in 1969 of nine autonomous Bantu Homelands "wherein all rights could be conferred upon Africans, to coexist alongside one white nation in which all rights would be reserved for whites. The 'independent' Homelands would remain economically dependent satellites of the white state.... If the present South African government is sincere in its stated desire for separate viable Homeland nations in empathy with one another and the white state, the incentive system must be altered to redress the severe cost disadvantage of a Homelands location." 2 tables, fig.
D. D. Cameron

3786. Rogerson, Christian M. GROWTH POINT PROBLEMS: THE CASE OF BABELEGI, BOPHUTHATSWANA. *J. of Modern African Studies [Great Britain] 1974 12(1): 126-130.* Babelegi township, an industrial site north of Pretoria, is designed to bring work to the Africans and ease the problem of overcrowded cities. Most residents are, however, unskilled. The industrialization of this Bantu Homeland is an example of growth without development. 19 notes. H. G. Soff

3787. Samoff, Joel. TRANSNATIONALS, INDUSTRIALIZATION, AND BLACK CONSCIOUSNESS: CHANGE IN SOUTH AFRICA. *J. of Southern African Affairs 1978 3(4): 489-520.* A discussion of principal currents in the political economy of South Africa. The underlying forces at work in South Africa are the operations of multinational corporations and foreign monopoly capital, and resistance by South African agricultural export, mining, industrial, and Afrikaner capitalism. Other forces are the expansion of South African capitalism into other parts of southern and central Africa and local resistance to it, as in revolutionary Mozambique, and lower class resistance within South Africa itself. Views the black power-black consciousness movement in South Africa as an unstable and uncertain factor, since race and ethnicity are seen here to merely reflect the deeper currents at work, and also because the movement is run by members of marginal elements of society. States that all of the same forces would continue to operate under an African government. Based on secondary sources; 18 notes, biblio. L. W. Truschel

3788. Seidman, Ann and Seidman, Neva. UNITED STATES MULTINATIONALS IN SOUTH AFRICA. *J. of Southern African Affairs 1976 1(special issue): 125-166.* A handful of the biggest firms in the United States have provided over three-fourths of US investments in South Africa. They are linked with each other, as well as with most of the nearly 400 other US companies which have invested in South Africa, through their boards of directors. Together, these firms comprised the growing economic interest which, even when it was smaller, apparently helped to convince the US National Security Council in 1969 that the US government should maintain cordial relations with the South African government. These are the interests which Secretary of State Henry Kissinger was seeking to protect by his shuttle-diplomacy designed to prevent major upheavals in South Africa. Secondary sources; 5 tables, 53 notes. A. W. Howell

3789. Simkins, Charles. AGRICULTURAL PRODUCTION IN THE AFRICAN RESERVES OF SOUTH AFRICA, 1918-1969. *J. of Southern African Studies [Great Britain] 1981 7(2): 256-283.* A quantitative analysis of crop and livestock production in South Africa's

African reserves, including state and mission reserves and locations, communal and individually owned farms, state lands occupied by Africans, and African Trust Lands purchased since 1936. While total production did not decline over the whole period 1918-69, per capita output began to fall rapidly after 1954, with sharp increases in the population of the reserves. Based on South African Agricultural Censuses and other official reports; 5 fig., 2 appendixes, 12 notes.
L. W. Truschel

3790. Simson, Howard. THE MYTH OF THE WHITE WORKING CLASS IN SOUTH AFRICA. *African Rev. [Tanzania] 1974 4(2): 189-203.* Refutes the commonly held theory that the working class in South Africa is divided into an elite white and an oppressed black section. From a Marxist perspective it is apparent that particularly in the mining industry there is no white working class. There is a white authoritative class, and a black labor class. The Communist Party, which seeks to unify the two, is in reality trying to unite two groups with contradictory aims. 2 tables, 50 notes. H. G. Soff

3791. Slater, Henry. LAND, LABOUR AND CAPITAL IN NATAL: THE NATAL LAND AND COLONISATION COMPANY 1860-1948. *J. of African Hist. [Great Britain] 1975 16(2): 257-283.* Following their unsuccessful attempts to control Africans in Natal, many settlers sold their land to speculators and left the colony. Schemes were developed to bring in new settlers, but a continuing shortage of labor and capital stagnated the colony. The idea of forced labor was discussed, and in 1860 the Natal Land and Colonization Company was formed with a capital of 225,000 pounds and 250,000 acres. Some land was sold to colonists who in turn rented it to Africans, but the Company itself was a leading landlord. Beginning in 1900 the Company sold rural and bought urban land to supplement the rents paid by African tenants. Urban holdings fit into the developing mining economy of South Africa. The Company became part of Eagle Star Insurance Co. in 1948. 172 notes. H. G. Soff

3792. Smit, Johan. GLASS BOTTLE MANUFACTURE IN SOUTH AFRICA UP TO 1944. *Africana Notes and News [South Africa] 1981 24(8): 265-270.* Describes glass factories in South Africa from the Hatherley factory, founded in 1896, to the Pretoria Glass Works, founded in 1937.

3793. Southall, Roger. AFRICAN CAPITALISM IN CONTEMPORARY SOUTH AFRICA. *J. of Southern African Studies [Great Britain] 1980 7(1): 38-70.* A Marxist analysis of black entrepreneurship and government policy in South Africa and a history of that country's National African Federated Chambers of Commerce since 1964. The South African black petite bourgeoisie is seen in a dependency relationship with white business and the government's separate development policy, so that African businessmen oppose the interest of the mass of African workers to overthrow the white state and its economic and racial system. Based on papers of the South African National African Federated Chambers of Commerce, newspapers, and secondary sources; 86 notes. L. W. Truschel

3794. Stokes, Randall and Harris, Anthony. SOUTH AFRICAN DEVELOPMENT AND THE PARADOX OF RACIAL PARTICULARISM: TOWARD A THEORY OF MODERNIZATION FROM THE CENTER. *Econ. Development and Cultural Change 1978 26(2): 245-269.* Examines the prevailing thesis that universalism progressively increases with industrialization and presents an alternative outline of modernization from the center within societies which began industrialization after the West. This pattern, a sharp break with Western developmental patterns, provides an understanding of why South Africa and other late developing nations have diverged from Western modernization. South Africa's racism is a retention and amplification of traditional patterns which, in turn, are direct consequences of the modernization of Afrikaner society from its center. Based on published works; 39 notes. J. W. Thacker, Jr.

3795. Stokes, Randall G. THE AFRIKANER INDUSTRIAL ENTREPRENEUR AND AFRIKANER NATIONALISM. *Econ. Development and Cultural Change 1974 22(4): 557-579.* Examines the degree to which Afrikaner nationalism has stimulated industrial entrepreneurship in South Africa. "One major key to the rise of Afrikaner industrial entrepreneurship lies in the value transformation brought about by the Afrikaner nationalist movement. By redefining modernizing economic activity as a service to the collectivity, the nationalist movement provided a new and powerful motivational nexus for the seeking out of entrepreneurial roles." Based mainly on secondary sources; 8 tables, 32 notes. J. W. Thacker, Jr.

3796. Svanidze, I. A. AGRARNAIA POLITIKA KOLONIZATOROV V IUZHNOI AFRIKE [The agrarian policy of the South African colonists]. *Voprosy Istorii [USSR] 1982 (5): 77-88.* The agrarian structure of South Africa is characterized by the division of the country into white settlement areas, where modern production is concentrated, and African reserves with primitive subsistence agriculture, and hunger. Describes the history of land dispossession of the indigenous population by white colonialists. The agrarian laws imposed by the racist authorities are aimed at consolidating and intensifying land dispossession, racial discrimination, and segregation in landholding and land usage. J

3797. Tabata, I. B. THE STRIKE WAVE IN SOUTH AFRICA. *Internat. Socialist R. 1973 34(4): 17-23.*

3798. Tostensen, Arne. FAGORGANISERING OG ARBEIDSMARKEDSREGULERING I SØR-AFRIKA [Trade unions and labor legislation in South Africa]. *Internasjonal Politikk [Norway] 1980 (3B): 639-709.* An analysis of proposals from the Wiehahn and Riekert Commissions for change in two key areas: the position of black trade unions in labor market conflict resolution and the mobility of black manpower, including legislation regarding agriculture, mines, and industry. The author assesses what these proposals mean in terms of real liberalization of the apartheid system. J

3799. Väryrnen, Raimo. TRANSNATIONAL CORPORATIONS IN THE MILITARY SECTOR OF SOUTH AFRICA. *J. of Southern African Affairs 1980 5(2): 199-255.* A detailed survey of the involvement of multinational corporations in the military sector of South Africa's political economy since 1960. South Africa has long welcomed foreign investments and technical expertise in its production of military and strategic goods, with emphasis during the 1970's on indigenizing this production. This process has involved large numbers of major Western firms and their South African subsidiaries, including many not directly related to munitions production, such as mining and electronics companies and banks. Based on published company and official reports, newspapers, and secondary sources; 204 notes. L. W. Truschel

3800. Wickens, Peter L. THE ONE BIG UNION MOVEMENT AMONG BLACK WORKERS IN SOUTH AFRICA. *Int. J. of African Hist. Studies 1974 7(3): 391-416.* Discusses the relationship between Clements Kadalie, secretary of the Industrial and Commercial Workers' Union of Africa (ICU) and H. Selby Msimang, a labor leader of the Orange Free State. An attempt to form one big union (the ICWU) was made at the Bloemfontein Conference in 1919, but the ICU of Cape Town, under Kadalie, seceded shortly after it joined. Primary and secondary sources; 128 notes. M. M. McCarthy

3801. —. SOUTH AFRICA. *Africa Report 1973 18(2): 25-31.*
Pogrund, Benjamin. THE DURBAN STRIKES, pp. 25-26.
Thebehali, David. THE LABOR STRUCTURE WHICH CAUSED THE STRIKE, p. 27.
Mafukidze, Takawira S. CHANGE THROUGH REALISM, pp. 28-29. Interview with Tema Sono, former president of South African Students Association.
—. THE ABLEST POLITICIAN: CHIEF GATSHA BUTHELEZI, pp. 30-31. Series of articles dealing with strikes in South Africa and the corresponding racial tensions. S

Politics

3802. Adam, Heribert. CONQUEST AND CONFLICT IN SOUTH AFRICA. *J. of Modern African Studies [Great Britain] 1975 13(4): 621-640.* Whereas cultural racism is generally blamed for South Africa's racial problems and policies, economics is a more significant factor. The government has used coercive, ideological, political, and economic controls to hold down the African majority. The dominant means of control has changed over the years as the reasons for control have changed. Economic control is dominant at present. A black middle class is developing and accommodations must be made to give them a place in the nation. 30 notes. V. L. Human

3803. Adelman, Kenneth L. and Knight, Albion W. CAN SOUTH AFRICA GO NUCLEAR? *Orbis 1979 23(3): 633-647.* Analyzes the technical capabilities and the military, economic, and political factors governing South Africa's capability of producing an atomic bomb. South Africa not only has the technical capabilities to produce a nuclear bomb but also operational aircraft capable of delivering nuclear weapons at ranges appropriate to its defense needs. Possible US policy responses are also discussed. Based on published sources; 28 notes. J. W. Thacker, Jr.

3804. Aleksandrov, L. A. SEKRETNYE SLUZHBY IUAR [The secret service in the Republic of South Africa]. *Narody Azii i Afriki [USSR] 1976 (4): 117-123.* The secret service of the Republic of South Africa is directed against antiracist organizations within the country and in Namibia, those who fight against apartheid outside of South Africa, and independent African states. The head of the secret service is Van der Berg, an active member of the fascist organization of South African racists Ossewa Brandwag and considered second only to Prime Minister John Vorster. In May 1969, the Bureau of State Security was created and given many functions and rights. The author describes the work of this agency and its agents in Africa and throughout the world. Primary sources; 31 notes. L. Kalinowski

3805. Amody, Francis J. THE SABRE TOOTH CHEETAHS OF OSAN. *Am. Aviation Hist. Soc. J. 1980 25(1): 42-44.* South Africa's sole unit in the Korean War, No. 2 Squadron, the Flying Cheetahs, converted from F-51D Mustangs to F-86F Sabres in 1953, becoming the first jet-equipped unit in the South African air force and the first foreign airmen to fly the Sabres in combat under their own flag.

3806. Baker, Ross K. SOUTHERN AFRICA: A CATACLYSM AVERTED? *Worldview 1975 18(11): 11-16.* Discusses politics and racial policies in the regime of John Vorster in South Africa, 1970's.

3807. Baldwin, Alan. MASS REMOVALS AND SEPARATE DEVELOPMENT. *J. of Southern African Studies [Great Britain] 1975 1(2): 215-227.* Examines the transference of thousands of Africans from white areas in South Africa and their resettlement in compounds. Traces the origins of this policy since the Native Land Act (1913), and considers the figures for removals since 1960. Based on government reports and newspapers; table, 34 notes. S. P. Carr

3808. Baldwin, Charlene M. SOUTH AFRICAN POLITICAL EPHEMERA: PAMPHLETS, BROADSIDES, SERIALS, AND MANUSCRIPTS IN THE MUNGER AFRICANA LIBRARY WITH 42 ILLUSTRATIONS. *Munger Africana Lib. Notes 1975 29: 1-124.* A catalog of South African political ephemera in the Munger Africana Library prepared for the Southern African Research Archives Project. Plates. S

3809. Belfiglio, Valentine J. AMERICAN VIEWPOINTS ON MULTI-NATIONAL DEVELOPMENT IN SOUTH AFRICA. *Issues and Studies [Taiwan] 1976 12(12): 55-76.* Examines historical roots of open foreign relations between South Africa and the United States, contrasting differing racial policies of the two nations, 1779-1976. Closely examines recent diplomacy, emphasizing South Africa's need to equalize treatment of blacks to maintain good diplomatic relations with the United States.

3810. Berrada, Abdu. UNE LUTTE ININTERROMPUE [An uninterrupted struggle]. *Genève-Afrique [Switzerland] 1980 18(2): 17-26.* Describes opposition to the South African government since 1906 with particular reference to the African National Congress. Also includes black and white Marxist associations, black liberal associations, and certain groups recognized by the government. 2 notes, photo. B. S. Fetter

3811. Bissell, Richard. SOUTH AFRICA AND INTERNATIONAL OSTRACISM. *World Affairs 1974/75 137(3): 179-185.* Attempts to exclude South Africa from the world community in order to change its racial policies have been unsuccessful and are now unfeasible in light of its growing economic and political power. S

3812. Blo, Sammy Kum. FORTRESS SOUTH AFRICA. *Africa Report 1975 20(1): 11-16.* A look at South Africa's armaments buildup and its role in military strategy in the Indian Ocean, 1960-74. S

3813. Brionne, Bernard. L'AFRIQUE DU SUD, SA VÉRITÉ, SES ILLUSIONS [South Africa, truth and illusions]. *Défense Natl. [France] 1978 34(4): 73-91.* Provides a survey of the Afrikaners in South Africa, 1837-1978, and argues that apartheid is a guarantee of stability. In a multiracial regime, white expulsion would place the government under Soviet influence and seriously endanger mineral and energy sources.

3814. Brown, Trevor. DID ANYBODY KNOW HIS NAME? U.S. PRESS COVERAGE OF BIKO. *Journalism Q. 1980 57(1): 31-38, 44.* A study of indexes for the *New York Times* and the *Washington Post* reveals that although both newspapers gave extensive coverage to the death of Steve Biko (1947-77), the black South African activist, he received little coverage during his lifetime. He was called internationally known in reports of his death; nevertheless, each paper had carried only one substantial article on Biko before his death. The fact that Biko was frequently restricted in his movements hindered the press in evaluating his importance and influence during his life. However, it appears that there was also a lack of perception on the part of many reporters and observers in regard to Biko's influence and the flow of events in South Africa during the 1960's and 1970's. Based on press reports and secondary sources; 17 notes. J. S. Coleman

3815. Bull, Hedley. THE WEST AND SOUTH AFRICA. *Daedalus 1982 111(2): 255-270.* Discusses the USSR's threat to South Africa, the stance of the Reagan administration in countering it, and the reluctance of Western Europe to perceive the Soviet threat in the same way.

3816. Carrington, Walter C. TIME OF TRIAL. *Africa Report 1975 20(2): 7-11.* Reports on the horrors of apartheid in South Africa, urging that the United States keep no detente with South Africa until Prime Minister John Vorster releases pressure on the increasingly radicalized black urban masses. S

3817. Cartwright, M. F. OVER THE WALL INTO POLITICS. *Q. Bull. of the South African Lib. [South Africa] 1981 35(4): 150-153.* Sketches the life of Sister Clare Goodlatte (1866-1942). Irish by birth and educated in London, Goodlatte went to South Africa around 1886 to teach. After teaching at Port Elizabeth and Grahamstown, she retired to Woodstock in 1921, where she engaged in social work among the poor. Becoming interested in Communism and its potential for resolving racial frictions, she left her social work to devote her time to this new cause. Later, she became disenchanted with Communism because of the course of that movement in Stalinist Russia. One of her newspaper articles follows. Based on Goodlatte's letters and secondary sources; illus., 6 notes. J. S. Coleman

3818. Chatterjee, Debi. AFRO-ASIAN ATTITUDE TO APARTHEID. *Africa Q. [India] 1979 19(1): 54-72.* Examines attitudes of African and Asian nations to South Africa's policy of apartheid expressed at nonaligned nations conferences and in the UN, where during 1953-73 all Asian and African nonaligned nations supported every resolution opposing apartheid.

3819. Chettle, John. THE UNITED STATES AND SOUTH AFRICA: BARRIERS TO COMMUNICATION. *Orbis 1981 25(1): 145-163.* Discusses the historical, constitutional, sociological, and psychological barriers to communication between the United States and South Africa. Although South Africa is in the midst of change toward a more liberal racial policy, the United States government has not lessened its criticism. More understanding and less criticism would probably be more effective. Based on published sources; 26 notes. J. W. Thacker, Jr.

3820. Church, W. Lawrence. FREE SPEECH, DEFAMATION AND SOUTH AFRICA: AN AMERICAN LEGAL VIEW. *Issue 1974 4(3): 51-58.* Focuses on freedom of speech in South Africa from a judicial perspective. S

3821. Coker, Christopher. RETREAT INTO THE FUTURE: THE UNITED STATES, SOUTH AFRICA, AND HUMAN RIGHTS, 1976-8. *J. of Modern African Studies [Great Britain] 1980 18(3): 509-524.* The Carter Administration's program for human rights failed to make headway in South Africa for a variety of reasons. The most important of these was American insistence on the extension of political rights to Africans, without an effort to win broader citizenship rights for nonwhites, and the failure to extend any guarantees of survival to the white population in a future nonracial South African state. The Vorster government in Pretoria maintains its policy of developing separate national communities in South Africa. Based on newspapers, speeches, and secondary sources; 48 notes. L. W. Truschel

3822. Coker, Christopher. SOUTH AFRICA'S STRATEGIC IMPORTANCE: A REASSESSMENT. *J. of the Royal United Services Inst. for Defence Studies [Great Britain] 1979 124(4): 22-26.* South Africa's reliance on the West for security interests to the point where the West depends on South Africa's defense, has resulted in South Africa's having to make the relationship less embarrassing for the West by making apartheid more respectable, even at the risk of making the policy less effective. South Africa's dependence on Western markets intensifies the problem. The combination of commercial and security reliance enhances the political pressure that can be brought to bear on South Africa to change its domestic policies. Based on secondary sources and conversations with South African military and government personnel; 16 notes. E. J. Adams

3823. Cuadra, Héctor. EL APARTHEID COMO PATOLOGÍA SOCIAL [Apartheid as social pathology]. *Rev. Mexicana de Ciencia Pol. [Mexico] 1973 19(71): 33-57.* Discusses resolutions against apartheid adopted by the UN and their economic and political effects on South Africa, 1948-70.

3824. Cuthbertson, G. C. JEWISH IMMIGRATION AS AN ISSUE IN SOUTH AFRICAN POLITICS, 1937-39. *Historia [South Africa] 1981 26(2): 119-133.* The primary opposition party in South Africa, the Purified Nationalist Party of Dr. D. F. Malan, grew increasingly anti-Semitic from 1930-39. Many Jews fleeing Europe went to South Africa. The Quota Bill of 1930 established quotas for immigrants, but the Purified National Party felt the need for further legislation in order to maintain the racial integrity of South Africa. The Aliens Bill of 1937 limited the inflow of Jews by almost half. The Nationalist Party's increasing anti-Semitism culminated in Eric Louw's Aliens Amendment Bill of 1939. Primary sources; 62 notes. J. Powell

3825. Cuthbertson, Gregor Craig. RICHARD STUTTAFORD AND THE ANTHEM QUESTION OF 1938. *Historia [South Africa] 1979 24(2): 74-82.* Discusses the part taken by Richard Stuttaford (1870-1945), Minister of the Interior during South Africa's Fusion Government of James Hertzog and Jan Christiaan Smuts, in what almost developed into a cabinet crisis over the question of the national anthem. The addition, at Prime Minister Hertzog's suggestion, of an Afrikaans anthem after the official English one at the opening of the Union's seventh Parliament, and the English anthem's omission on Union Day, caused the English loyalist Stuttaford's resignation which, with Smuts acting as mediator, he withdrew the next day, when he was assured that both anthems would receive equal recognition. Based on Smuts's and Stuttaford's papers and other primary sources; 59 notes. G. Herritt

3826. Dalcanton, David C. VORSTER AND THE POLITICS OF CONFIDENCE 1966-1974. *African Affairs [Great Britain] 1976 75(299): 163-181.* An analysis of new policies developed in South African politics since John Vorster became prime minister in 1966. Discusses the elections of 1970 and 1974 in which the National Party was able to continue to expand its dominance. 56 notes. H. G. Soff

3827. Danaher, Kevin. SOUTH AFRICA, U.S. POLICY, AND THE ANTI-APARTHEID MOVEMENT. *Rev. of Radical Pol. Econ. 1979 11(3): 42-59.* A review of race relations in South Africa, the strength of the apartheid parties, American foreign policy, and what can be done to change matters. Black Africa's refusal to trade with the South African government has caused greater reliance on Western Europe and the United States, resulting in a host of political, economic, and military ties which are hard to break. 5 tables, fig., 57 notes, ref. V. L. Human

3828. Danaher, Kevin. THE U.S. AND SOUTH AFRICA: BUILDING THE BASE FOR SANCTIONS. *Freedomways 1981 21(1): 29-40.* Analyzes US government resistance to the imposition of sanctions against South Africa in the struggle against apartheid and suggests new moves in antiapartheid strategy.

3829. David, Charles. LE CONSEIL NATIONAL DE SECURITE ET LA POLITIQUE SUD-AFRICAINE DES ETATS-UNIS DE 1969 A 1976 [The National Security Council and US foreign policy toward South Africa, 1969-76]. *Études Int. [Canada] 1981 12(4): 657-690.* Examines the performance of the National Security Council (NSC) as a policymaking body vis-à-vis the southern African conflict under the Nixon and Ford administrations. Discusses and verifies the hypothesis that the institutionalized system of the NSC gives the president a way to improve his policies by analyzing the range of options and alternatives free of negative bureaucratic influences. 63 notes. J. F. Harrington

3830. Davidson, Apollon. LENIN O IUZHNOI AFRIKE [Lenin on South Africa]. *Aziia i Afrika Segodnia [USSR] 1982 (4): 5-7.* Shows how seriously Lenin studied the specific reality of South Africa, considering is various aspects, primarily its socioeconomic structure, social struggle, and national liberation movement, striving to learn South African problems as well as possible.

3831. Davidson, Basil. SOUTH AFRICA AND PORTUGAL. *Issue 1974 4(2): 9-20.* Studies South Africa's relationship to Portuguese territories in Africa as well as its relations with the Portuguese regime in Lisbon. S

3832. Davis, R. Hunt, Jr. JOHN L. DUBE: A SOUTH AFRICAN EXPONENT OF BOOKER T. WASHINGTON. *J. of African Studies 1975-76 2(4): 497-529.* A study of the career of John L. Dube and his efforts on behalf of his Zulu countrymen, but especially of the formative influences of his American experience and of Booker T. Washington on his social and educational philosophy. Emphasizes three facets of his career: his work as educator, involving his founding and lifelong association with Ohlange Institute; his role as a political leader; and his attempts at finding a modus vivendi between blacks and whites in South Africa. This involved him in a continuing effort to reach a measure of accommodation with the more progressive and reasonable whites. 119 notes. R. V. Ritter

3833. de Kiewiet, C. W. SOUTH AFRICA AND THE WALLS OF TROY. *Virginia Q. R. 1974 50(4): 515-537.* During the 50's and 60's US foreign policy protected South Africa as the British Commonwealth had previously. However, Nixon's visits to Peking and Moscow and the dénoument in Vietnam indicate "America is a country in search of a new foreign policy." Colonialism in Africa "has not quietly disappeared" and both China and Russia will be more deeply involved in the Indian Ocean. South Africa's strategic position, its race situation, and American disillusionment with foreign intervention will all affect new American foreign policy decisions. O. H. Zabel

3834. Decter, Moshe. THE ARMS TRAFFIC WITH SOUTH AFRICA. *Midstream 1977 23(2): 14-25.* Contrary to Arab propaganda, there is no military collaboration nor any arms trade between Israel and South Africa. South Africa has purchased most of its arms from France, Great Britain, and other nations.

3835. Delius, Antony. ALTERNATIVEN ZUR APARTHEID-POLITIK IN SÜDAFRIKA. DIE POLITISCHEN KRÄFTE UND IHRE KONZEPTE [Alternatives to apartheid in South Africa: the political forces and their concepts]. *Europa Archiv [West Germany] 1978 33(2): 53-62.* Some black exile groups such as the African National Congress and the Pan-African Congress have rejected political negotiation with the South African government since the early 1960's. To the contrary, Stephen Biko's Black Consciousness movement has tried to establish black majority rule without violence by strengthening black political and cultural consciousness. South Africa's progressive white opposition has supported its efforts and has proposed federalism since the 1950's.

3836. Delius, Anthony. SOUTH AFRICAN ALTERNATIVES. *World Today [Great Britain] 1978 34(1): 21-30.* Examines 1977 elections in South Africa which sustained John Vorster in power, on a platform of power for the Afrikaner majority among whites, the protection of white economic interests, and the political exclusion of Africans. Small gains for the Progressive Party, which has traditionally supported a racially balanced government, give some small hope.

3837. deSt. Jorre, John. INSIDE THE LAAGER: WHITE POWER IN SOUTH AFRICA. *Foreign Affairs 1976 55(1): 169-186.* Afrikaner nationalism is the controlling factor in South Africa. Black Africans accept that South Africa must work out its own problems because it is an independent sovereign state. White power is Afrikaner power, since the English speaking make up only about 40 percent of the population, only a minority of which are citizens. At any rate a recent poll showed that the Prime Minister, John Vorster, appeals to the English and has an overall electoral backing of 80 percent. Afrikaners have had 300 years to form their nationalism. They cut themselves off from Europe and established their own traditions, and they have only their land to which to cling. This produced the Afrikaner psyche with its tenacious hold on power. The South African government anticipates slight, slow changes in its domestic policy; this is the one issue on which Afrikaners agree. Nonetheless, detente with black Africa is the foundation of Afrikaner foreign policy. 9 notes. R. Riles

3838. Dickie-Clark, H. E. DO THE SOUTH AFRICAN WHITES NEED RACIAL DISCRIMINATION? *Plural Soc. [Netherlands] 1980 11(1): 47-54.* Discusses differing theories on the potential for modification in South Africa's apartheid system and the continued dominance of the white Afrikaaners.

3839. Dodd, Norman L. SOUTH AFRICA: THE HALF-WAY HOUSE OF THE WORLD. *Army Q. and Defence J. [Great Britain] 1975 105(3): 317-329.* Describes the South African army, navy, and air forces since the 1960's.

3840. Dodd, Norman L. THE SOUTH AFRICAN DEFENCE FORCE. *J. of the Royal United Services Inst. for Defence Studies [Great Britain] 1974 119(4): 36-40.* Describes the armaments industry and military organizations of the Republic of South Africa. Militarily it is virtually impregnable to conventional attack. South Africa will seek recognition of its role in the worldwide struggle with communism, self-sufficiency in production, improved police and armed forces, and development of the Bantu Homelands to permit formation of self-defense units. South Africa needs external aid in defense of the Cape route and surveillance of Soviet forces in the South Atlantic and Indian Oceans—on which the "safety of the free world may depend." D. H. Murdoch

3841. Dory, Emmanuel. LES PARTIS POLITIQUES SUD-AFRICAINS [South African political parties]. *Rev. Française d'Études Pol. Africaines [France] 1973 (89): 67-84.* Studies the three major Afrikaner parties: the Nationalist Party 1914-73, the United Party, 1934-73, and the Progressive Party 1959-73; and four white, liberal, African, or forbidden parties: the Liberal Party 1953-, the Communist Party 1922-50, the African National Congress 1958-73, and the Pan-African Congress 1959-73, also mentioning some very small African movements since 1970.

3842. Dory, Emmanuel. RÉPUBLIQUE SUD-AFRICAINE: NAISSANCE D'UN NOUVEAU PARTI POLITIQUE [Republic of South Africa: the birth of a new political party]. *Rev. Française d'Études Pol. Africaines [France] 1973 8(96): 21-23.* Describes the formation of the Democratic Party, founded by Theo Gerdener in November 1973, and its policy of ending the South African policy of apartheid; expresses doubts concerning its effectiveness.

3843. D'Souza, P. P. NELSON MANDELA. *Indian Horizons [India] 1980 29(2): 25-30.* This article presents a defense of Nelson Mandela's life's work. He was a South African political activist. Even as a youth he exhibited an independent spirit full of social awareness. The increased tempo of his activism in the African National Congress in the 1940's and the Pan-African Freedom Movement in the 1950's and 1960's showed his deep contempt for South Africa's policy of apartheid, the legal separation of the races. His activities led to his arrest and imprisonment. In April 1964, he was sentenced to life imprisonment. The article concludes with a plea for his release. D. J. Wren

3844. Duly, Leslie Clement. THE HISTORIAN AND THE STUDY OF NATIONALISM IN SOUTH AFRICA: A REVIEW OF RECENT LITERATURE. *Can. Rev. of Studies in Nationalism [Canada] 1973 1(1): 126-137.* The literature on the emergence, character, and role of South African black and white nationalism and "identity" movements is disappointing. Most accounts are either superficially descriptive journalistic or moralistic efforts, or they are autobiographies whose main value lies in their function as primary sources for the historian. Even the scholarly literature has been surprisingly devoid of analytical insight, and many of the works dealing with the 20th century have been rigid in form and content, or too easily identified as representing a racial viewpoint. Only in the last few years have several new studies of importance to the historian of nationalism appeared to stress form over content. 16 notes. T. Spira

3845. El-Khawas, Mohamed A. and Hope, Constance Morris. A BIBLIOGRAPHICAL ESSAY ON U.S. DIPLOMATIC RELATIONS WITH SOUTH AFRICA. *J. of Southern African Affairs 1979 4(1): 81-115.* A brief treatment of US-South African relations, centering on attitudes toward South Africa within the executive branch, from the Eisenhower administration through the first years of the Carter administration. Publications on Washington-Pretoria relations are categorized and listed, with those from sources close to the American government discussed in the body of the article. L. W. Truschel

3846. El-Khawas, Mohamed A. PARTNERS IN APARTHEID: U.S. ECONOMIC AND MILITARY LINKAGES WITH SOUTH AFRICA. *J. of Southern African Affairs 1977 2(3): 323-342.* US economic and military ties with South Africa support apartheid. Trade has increased sharply, as has investment, and the arms embargo has been eroded. As a result, white rule has been strengthened, and blacks have made no significant economic or political gains. 4 tables, 19 notes. J. Tull

3847. Enloe, Cynthia H. ETHNIC FACTORS IN THE EVOLUTION OF THE SOUTH AFRICAN MILITARY. *Issue 1975 5(4): 21-28.* Discusses the relationship of the military establishment to politics in South Africa in the 1960's-70's, emphasizing disparities in the manpower distribution of ethnic groups.

3848. Frankel, Philip. THE DYNAMICS OF A POLITICAL RENAISSANCE: THE SOWETO STUDENTS REPRESENTATIVE COUNCIL. *J. of African Studies 1980 7(3): 167-180.* The Soweto Students Representative Council existed for 18 months as a radical political protest organization in South Africa during the period of African unrest, 1976-77. The students who organized it produced a rebellion against the existing African education system, but failed to generate a revolution among the Soweto community at large. Hostility between student radicals and the older African generation, even teachers, the failure of the council to demand broader changes in the areas of pass laws, wages, and political rights, the immature state of the black consciousness ideology in 1976, the willingness of whites to resist, and the marginal economic position of the Soweto workers foredoomed such a revolution. Based on personal communications, newspapers, and secondary sources; 36 notes. L. W. Truschel

3849. Frankel, Philip. MUNICIPAL TRANSFORMATION IN SOWETO: RACE, POLITICS AND MALADMINISTRATION IN BLACK JOHANNESBURG. *African Studies Rev. 1979 22(2): 49-63.* Urban black policy "has never been able to break free of the racial forces determining the working of all facets of South African society." Consequently, the removal of Soweto from Johannesburg city council jurisdiction in 1971 and the assumption of control by the West Rand Bantu Administration Board has only worsened living conditions for Africans. Secondary sources; 29 notes, biblio. R. T. Brown

3850. Frankel, Philip. POLITICAL CULTURE AND REVOLUTION IN SOWETO. *J. of Pol. 1981 43(3): 831-849.* Cross-racial communication in South Africa remains infrequent, ritualized, and laden with tension and suspicion. In Soweto, ethnicity has assumed new, resilient and functionally adaptive forms rather than declining in the urban setting. The boundedness and insecurity of township life and racial structures have crystallized and politicized cultural uniformity. The maintenance of the caste system has depended on blacks internalizing ideologies and racial myths which induce acceptance of low status. Few township residents are happy, secure, or confident, but many see apartheid as a purely Afrikaner, rather than English, creation. The 1976 disturbances indicated that dissatisfaction with the political status quo is strongest among the young, more educated, and urban-born. Many

Soweto residents emphasize security of land tenure over the acquisition of political rights. 74 notes. A. W. Novitsky

3851. Frankel, Philip. THE POLITICS OF PASSES: CONTROL AND CHANGE IN SOUTH AFRICA. *J. of Modern African Studies [Great Britain] 1979 17(2): 199-217.* Discusses the importance of the pass laws and influx policies to the South African political system since the Native Urban Areas Act of 1923 and describes the forces supporting and opposing them. The pass laws reveal in microcosm the problems of social change in South Africa. The laws have influenced political developments in urban areas by helping central government to escape from its social and political obligations to urban blacks, shaping political culture in the black townships, and inhibiting economic self-improvement. White opposition to the system and official response to it has been concerned with rationalizing and humanizing it, not abolishing it, which would involve the dismantling of a vast bureaucracy and prove politically disastrous for the National Party. Based on legal and other official documents, newspapers, and other printed sources; 65 notes. D. J. Nicholls

3852. Frankel, Philip. THE POLITICS OF POVERTY: POLITICAL COMPETITION IN SOWETO. *Can. J. of African Studies [Canada] 1980 14(2): 201-220.* Since 1976 Soweto community policies have been dominated by three organizations: the Soweto Civil Association, supported by students and middle class nationalists; the Soweto Council, established by the South African government to replace the Urban Bantu Council; and the Inkatha movement, established in 1928 to promote the cultural liberation of the Zulu people. The origins of each group and their different social bases contribute to a power struggle which inhibits racial solidarity. In the context of poverty political support is determined by ability to obtain aid from the national government. The author foresees the power struggle narrowing between the Soweto Civil Association and the Inkatha with the ultimate outcome dependent on ability to create a coherent political group out of varied ethnic and political interests. 79 notes. S

3853. Geber, Beryl A. THE LIBERAL DILEMMA IN SOUTH AFRICA. *Patterns of Prejudice [Great Britain] 1973 7(4): 11-14.* Reports of the South African Council of Churches document South African inequality, and offer solutions. Suggestions include decisionmaking for all by those in power. Their reforms, though aimed at gradual change, would in fact probably open the door to unplanned revolutionary change. M. W. Szewczyk

3854. Glass, Humphrey. THE STRUGGLE FOR SOUTH AFRICA. *Monthly Rev. 1976 28(7): 7-24.* Discusses the various political and economic injustices that resulted in the Soweto uprisings of 1976. "The whites are no longer the sole initiators of events. South Africa is fast entering an era in which the struggle between moderate blacks and radical blacks will become more important than the conflict between whites and blacks. The struggle for South Africa, the key to all of Southern Africa and perhaps much more, has begun." 12 notes. M. R. Yerburgh

3855. Gorbunov, Iu. MILITARIZATSIIA IUAR [Militarization in South Africa]. *Aziia i Afrika Segodnia [USSR] 1981 (3): 27-28, 33.* Cites new facts which show that the South African army, dissatisfied with its former role "as an instrument for strengthening the power of the white racist minority,... is increasingly gaining a foothold as a leading military and political force of the South African regime."

3856. Grotpeter, John. CHANGING SOUTH AFRICA. *Current Hist. 1980 78(455): 119-123, 134-136.* Discusses Prime Minister Pieter Botha's campaign to reform apartheid in South Africa during the 1970's.

3857. Grundlingh, A. M. DIE REBELLIE VAN 1914: 'N HISTORIOGRAFIESE VERKENNING [The Rebellion of 1914: a historiographical survey]. *Kleio [South Africa] 1979 11(1-2): 18-30.* Describes and evaluates the most important studies of the South African rebellion of 1914 and identifies the main approaches to its history. The key question in the study of the rebellion is why the Boer generals, who had supported the Afrikaaner fight for freedom from British imperialism so vigorously during the Boer War, opposed the Afrikaaner struggle equally strongly in 1914. 27 notes. M. K. Hogg

3858. Grundy, Kenneth W. THE ASSIGNMENT OF SOUTH AFRICAN ARMED FORCES ABROAD, 1912-1976. *J. of African Studies 1978-79 5(4): 396-413.* Analysis of South Africa's use of armed forces beyond its frontiers from the passage of the Union's first Defence Act in 1912 to the Defence Amendment Act in 1976. The laws of 1912, 1940, and 1957 all specified geographical limits to the obligation of South African Defence Force members to serve abroad, but the Union governments under Louis Botha and Jan Christiaan Smuts extended their definitions to include distant areas of Africa during the two world wars and also sent large numbers of volunteers further afield. Their erstwhile opponents among Afrikaner nationalists endorsed similar measures in the later years of the Union and finally passed the 1976 law during the Angolan crisis to eliminate all restraints of a voluntary or territorial nature to utilization of South African armed forces abroad. Based on published parliamentary debates and official documents, newspapers, and secondary sources; 39 notes. L. W. Truschel

3859. Hackland, Brian. THE ECONOMIC AND POLITICAL CONTEXT OF THE GROWTH OF THE PROGRESSIVE FEDERAL PARTY IN SOUTH AFRICA, 1959-1978. *J. of Southern African Studies [Great Britain] 1980 7(1): 1-16.* An analysis of the history of the South African Progressive Federal Party and its ties to major business interests in South Africa, especially the Anglo-American Group. South African monopoly capital is uncomfortable with the ruling National Party and behind the creation and growth of the Progressive Federal Party, which articulates its political and economic ideology. Based on interviews, Progressive Federal Party documents, newspapers, and secondary sources; 74 notes. L. W. Truschel

3860. Hanf, Theodor and Weiland, Heribert. KONKORDANZDEMOKRATIE FÜR SÜDAFRIKA? ZUR BEDEUTUNG DER NEUEREN VERFASSUNGSPOLITISCHEN DEBATTE [Concordance democracy for South Africa? The importance of the more recent constitutional-political debate]. *Europa Archiv [West Germany] 1978 33(23): 755-770.* Since the early 1970's South African constitutional experts have studied the possibilities of a concordance model of democracy to solve the race problem. The model would not regulate conflicts by majority decision but by negotiated agreements and constant compromises, a decisionmaking process including the participation of all politically significant social groups.

3861. Hudson, Darril. THE WORLD COUNCIL OF CHURCHES AND RACISM IN SOUTHERN AFRICA. *Int. J. [Canada] 1979 34(3): 475-500.* A description of the World Council of Churches activities to combat racism in South Africa. In 1969 the council established the Program to Combat Racism. This became their primary organ in their campaign for racial equality. A special fund of $500,000 for distribution to organizations of oppressed racial groups was the heart of this program. In addition, the program is active in the areas of investments, bank loans, and nuclear proliferation. M. J. Wentworth

3862. Hugo, Maria. DIE ERE-ADRESSE AAN GENL. J. B. M. HERTZOG AS HISTORIESE BRON [The testimonials addressed to General J. B. M. Hertzog as historical source]. *Historia [South Africa] 1977 22(2): 130-140.* Shows the importance of the 642 testimonials, dating from 1895 to 1940, to Hertzog's biographer and to the historian of South Africa.

3863. Hull, Galen. SOUTH AFRICA'S PROPAGANDA WAR: A BIBLIOGRAPHIC ESSAY. *African Studies Rev. 1979 22(3): 79-98.* A historical analysis of the methods and organization of the South Africa lobby effort in Britain and the United States through examination of newspaper articles about that effort. Concentrates on the Muldergate scandal of 1978. Based on newspapers; biblio. R. T. Brown

3864. Humeniuk, B. I. Z ISTORII BOROTBY KOLIOROVOHO NASELENNIA PIVDENNO-AFRYKANSKOI RESPUBLIKY PROTY APARTEIDU I RASYZMU [The Coloureds' struggle against apartheid and racism in South Africa]. *Ukraïns'kyi Istorychnyi Zhurnal [USSR] 1979 (5): 102-105.*

3865. Hunter, Maxine Grace. THE UNITED NATIONS AND THE ANTI-APARTHEID IN SPORT MOVEMENT. *Can. J. of Hist. of Sport and Physical Educ. [Canada] 1980 11(1): 19-35.* Discusses the resolutions of the UN against apartheid in South Africa and the extent of their success in integrating that country's sports teams.

3866. Janosik, Robert J. and Lawrence, Barbara E. SOUTHERN AFRICAN PRESSURE POLITICS IN THE US. *Issue 1974 4(3): 76-80.* Lobbying in the United States for white Southern African interests is done through the South Africa Foundation, Rhodesian Information Office and representatives of South African sugar interests in the United States. S

3867. Johns, Sheridan. THE BIRTH OF THE COMMUNIST PARTY OF SOUTH AFRICA. *Int. J. of African Hist. Studies 1976 9(3): 371-400.* Analyzes the process leading to the formation of the Communist Party in South Africa, with particular attention to the maneuvers of various left-wing socialist groups, especially the International Socialist League (ISL). Describes the South African party's links with the international socialist movement. Based on newspaper accounts and on documents and publications of the Communist International and left-wing socialist groups; 78 notes. M. M. McCarthy

3868. Johns, Sheridan. THE COMINTERN, SOUTH AFRICA AND THE BLACK DIASPORA. *R. of Pol. 1975 37(2): 200-234.* The South African Communist Party by 1928 had become a multiracial party based primarily within the African majority of the country. In 1928, the Comintern dictated that South Africa was part of larger colonial and world black problems. The new Comintern program and its controversial slogan of "an independent native South African republic" weakened the CPSA which only regained its strength in the late 1930's when Moscow's influence was withdrawn. L. E. Ziewacz

3869. Johns, Sheridan. THE THRUST OF PRETORIA'S AFRICAN POLICY OF DIALOGUE. *South Atlantic Q. 1973 72(2): 179-197.* "In mid-1971 white-ruled South Africa appeared on the verge of a diplomatic breakthrough within black Africa." Less than two years later this "outward movement" is stalled. Traces the factors which contributed to this rapid turnabout to developments within black Africa and to the essentially unchanging nature of South African domestic policy, and notes the new currents of African assertion. Pretoria recognized that a policy of dialogue could enhance South Africa's image with key groups in the states of Western Europe, North America, and the "white" Commonwealth countries whose toleration, if not good will, remains the keystone of South Africa's foreign policy. E. P. Stickney

3870. Kallaway, Peter. F. S. MALAN, THE CAPE LIBERAL TRADITION, AND SOUTH AFRICAN POLITICS, 1908-1924. *J. of African Hist. [Great Britain] 1974 15(1): 113-129.* Examines the role of F. S. Malan in determining the nature of South Africa's multiracial society. Although Malan defended the Cape franchise which granted Africans citizenship rights within a limited political context, only for a brief period in 1918 did he attempt a settlement of the country's racial and industrial problems. While Minister of Mines and Industries and effective Minister of Native Affairs, Malan initiated a comprehensive system of labor legislation between 1913 and 1924, though he did not intend to challenge the status quo in South Africa. Primary and secondary sources; 87 notes. E. C. Hopkins

3871. Kaplan, D. E. THE POLITICS OF INDUSTRIAL PROTECTION IN SOUTH AFRICA, 1910-1939. *J. of Southern African Studies [Great Britain] 1976 3(1): 70-91.* The requirements of capitalism rather than racism determined the policy of protectionism in South Africa, 1910-39. The author examines the various interest groups which support the policy, and considers the needs of the state. Based on newspapers, and reports; table, 99 notes. S. P. Carr

3872. Keppel-Jones, A. M. SOUTH AFRICA IN 1998: TRENDS AND DEVELOPMENTS DURING THE NEXT TWENTY-FIVE YEARS. *Issue 1974 4(3): 38-42.* Projects that the South African system of apartheid will be changed by revolution, foreign invasion, or peaceful constitutional means. S

3873. Klare, Michael T. EVADING THE EMBARGO: ILLICIT U.S. ARMS TRANSFERS TO SOUTH AFRICA. *J. of Int. Affairs 1981 35(1): 15-28.* Many US firms, such as Olin-Winchester Corporation, have been deeply involved in the transfer of military hardware and technological knowledge to South Africa, despite the UN embargo on arms sales to that country. Advocates measures to enforce the embargo and restore US credibility by showing its intent to honor its international obligations.

3874. Krasnopetseva, T. I. VOENNO-PROMYSHLENNYI KOMPLEKS IUAR [The military-industrial complex of South Africa]. *Narody Azii i Afriki [USSR] 1980 (2): 109-117.* Describes South Africa's aggression against Angola, Mozambique, Namibia, and Zimbabwe. South Africa, defying a UN decision, refuses to acknowledge the independent governments of Angola and Mozambique. Its total strategy since Pieter Botha became prime minister is shown through the recruitment of women, military propaganda, and the mobilization of the country's resources to achieve its military aims. 5 notes. C. Pichelin

3875. Kreindler, Joshua David. SOUTH AFRICA, JEWISH PALESTINE AND ISRAEL: THE GROWING RELATIONSHIP 1919-1974. *Africa Q. [India] 1981 20(3-4): 48-87.* Discusses the friendship between Jewish Palestine and later Israel, and South Africa 1919-74, despite strong Jewish criticism of apartheid, with special emphasis on political, cultural, and economic cooperation between the two nations.

3876. Lacina, Karel. HOSPODÁŘSKÁ A VOJENSKÁ POLITIKA JIHOAFRICKÝCH RASISTŮ [The economic and military policy of the South African racists]. *Sborník Hist. [Czechoslovakia] 1982 28: 249-298.* The exploitative character of apartheid links the racist regime of South Africa with Western imperialist interests. Commercial and military agreements harness South Africa to the Western global effort to dominate strategic raw materials bases, in exchange for military technology and political support. Progressive forces in Africa and elsewhere uphold the human rights of the nonwhite majority and condemn colonialism, neocolonialism, and racism. Secondary sources; 120 notes. Russian and English summaries. R. E. Weltsch

3877. Lacina, Karel. ÚLOHA JIHOAFRICKÉ REPUBLIKY V GLOBÁLNÍ POLITICE IMPERIALISMU [South Africa in imperialist global politics]. *Československý Časopis Hist. [Czechoslovakia] 1982 30(4): 486-514.* Since the Arab-Israeli War of 1967, the governments of Great Britain, the United States, France, West Germany, Italy, Japan, and Israel have been in continual strategic contact with the racist South African government, to such a point that the Reagan administration could immediately proceed with a political-military partnership with Pretoria. This partnership, which is meant to secure the South Atlantic route for NATO, conflicts with majority opinion at the UN and serves the interests of multinational monopoly capital. Based on the press and secondary sources; 89 notes. Russian and English summaries.
R. E. Weltsch

3878. Lever, Henry. OPINION POLLING IN SOUTH AFRICA: INITIAL FINDINGS. *Public Opinion Q. 1974 38(3): 400-408.* Examines voter opinions on the dominant political issues in South Africa just prior to the general election in 1970. The "Argus Poll" was conducted by the publishers of *The Argus*(Cape Town), *The Daily Star* (Johannesburg), the *Daily News*(Natal), and several other newspapers; the "Dagbreek poll" was conducted by the Afrikaans Sunday newspaper *Dagbreek en Sondagnuus* in December 1969, and February-April 1970. "Political controversy in South Africa is dominated by discussions pertaining to race relations.... There is general support for the view that Africans should be allowed to do more skilled jobs and...should have the opportunity to earn higher wages. Support for both propositions declined as the income level of the respondent declined." 6 tables, 7 notes. D. D. Cameron

3879. Lever, Henry. SOUTH AFRICAN GENERAL ELECTION, 1977. *Social Sci. 1981 56(4): 213-225.* Two important events occurred during the South African general election. The first involved authoritarian action taken by the government against some of its political opponents. This was followed by the United Nations resolution placing an embargo on arms sales to South Africa. It was widely believed that the first event hampered the governing party's electoral prospects, while the second promoted its prospects. Since both took place while opinion surveys were being undertaken, it was possible to assess their impact.
J

3880. Lipton, Merle. SOUTH AFRICA: AUTHORITARIAN REFORM? *World Today [Great Britain] 1974 30(6): 247-258.* Despite the ruling Nationalist Party's 1974 election victory, South African blacks are benefiting from significant economic, political, and social changes already under way. S

3881. Lodge, Tom. THE CAPE TOWN TROUBLES, MARCH-APRIL 1960. *J. of Southern African Studies [Great Britain] 1978 4(2): 216-239.* An examination of the potentially revolutionary situation in Cape Town's two African townships and the politics of the local Pan-African Congress leaders in the immediate post-Sharpeville affair period in 1960. A close relationship existed between the young PAC leaders, especially Philip Kgosana, and a radical Liberal Party group led by Patrick Duncan, editor of the *Contact* publication, which favored the political goals of the PAC. Violence flared at Langa location on 21 March, but the revolutionary potential of the strike failed to develop due to leadership's unwillingness to challenge the authorities. Based on interviews, diaries, and secondary sources; 140 notes. L. W. Truschel

3882. Madzoevski, S. IUZHNOAFRIKANSKII UZEL MIROVOI POLITIKI [South Africa, the center of world politics]. *Mirovaia Ekonomika i Mezhdunarodnye Otnosheniia [USSR] 1977 (7): 10-21.* Discusses the policy of the most important Western Powers toward the white regime in South Africa, and shows how this policy is determined by imperialist interests.

3883. Makarov, A. A. APARTKHEID I POLITIKA PRAVIASH-CHIKH KRUGOV BANTUSTANOV IUAR [Apartheid and the policies of the ruling circles of the Bantu in the South African Republic]. *Narody Azii i Afriki [USSR] 1977 (5): 97-110.* Examines the background of growing discontent among blacks and the white intelligentsia with the racist policies of the South African government in the early 1970's. Dissent also manifested itself among the white rulers. The African leaders had little support among the African population, since they openly collaborated with the South African regime, or accepted separate African development as inevitable. They greatly feared revolutionary tendencies among the African masses. 41 notes. E. R. Sicher

3884. Mandela, Nelson. A LETTER FROM NELSON MANDELA. *Africa Q. [India] 1981 21(1): 67-72.* A letter of acceptance from Nelson Mandela from Robben Island prison, South Africa, upon his receiving the Jawaharlal Nehru Award for International Understanding in 1979.

3885. Mariñas Otero, Luis. TRANSKEI, UN ESTADO INVISIBLE [Transkei, an invisible state]. *Rev. de Estudios Int. [Spain] 1980 1(2): 373-402.* The historical record of Transkei since 1936 shows the emergence of a new independent African state. Though encompassing all the attributes of a sovereign and independent country, Transkei is completely ignored by the international community. The reasons for this situation are to be found in the pattern of the African evolution in these last years: the hostility of the Organization of African Unity, supported by the greater part of the Third World, toward South Africa and its policy of apartheid, of which the creation of Transkei is seen as a corollary. Its heavy economic dependence on South Africa notwithstanding, Transkei has always been seeking an internal and external independent policy. 21 notes. D. Ardia

3886. Marks, Shula. NATAL, THE ZULU ROYAL FAMILY AND THE IDEOLOGY OF SEGREGATION. *J. of Southern African Studies [Great Britain] 1978 4(2): 172-194.* Postulates development in the 1920's of a class alliance in Natal between white capitalists, an African petite bourgeoisie, and the Zulu royal family under the Usuthu ruler Solomon. The three parties feared proletarianization among Natal Africans which had begun in Zululand during the 1880's. George Heaton Nicholls, a leading white planter and politician in Zululand, promoted an ideology of racism through espousing Zulu communalism. His object was to stem growth of working-class militancy among the rural Zulu population. In siding with Nicholls through Solomon's *Inkathaya ka Zulu* organization, the royal family sought to restore its paramount position lost both in the 1879 war with the British and in civil warfare in the 1880's. John Dube and other middle-class Zulus shared the white fear of a revolutionary peasant class. Based on archival and secondary sources; 97 notes. L. W. Truschel

3887. Martin, Denis. SOWETO ENTRE LES LIGNES: QUELQUES LIVRES RÉCENTS SUR L'AFRIQUE DU SUD [Soweto between the lines: recent books on South Africa]. *Rev. Française de Sci. Pol. [France] 1979 29(6): 1090-1107.* Reviews 15 monographs and yearbooks on politics, race relations, and South Africa's place in the international community.

3888. Mayer, Pierre. L'AFRIQUE DU SUD AUX PRISES AVEC LE CHANGEMENT [South Africa grapples with change]. *Défense Natl. [France] 1980 36(7): 35-43.* Discusses South African responses to external and internal pressures for change.

3889. Mbeki, Moeletsi. IS THERE A DIALECTIC BETWEEN RACE AND CLASS? *Freedomways 1981 21(2): 119-122.* Bernard Magubane's *The Political Economy of Race and Class in South Africa* goes beyond the issue of nationalism and addresses the nature of the development of human society toward historical materialism or socialism.

3890. McCormack, Robert L. MAN WITH A MISSION: OSWALD PIROW AND SOUTH AFRICAN AIRWAYS, 1933-1939. *J. of African Hist. [Great Britain] 1979 20(4): 543-557.* Oswald Pirow served as minister of defense and transport in the Hertzog administration for more than a decade, shaping an aggressive South Africa first policy in foreign affairs. Through the South African Airways, he challenged British primacy in the Rhodesias and East Africa, in direct conflict with the British Imperial Airway for routes, service, mail, passengers, and prestige. By 1939, SAA's modern Junkers surpassed Imperial from Kenya southward, declining only with the outbreak of World War II. 105 notes. A. W. Novitsky

3891. Meyer, Lysle E. THE AMERICAN IMAGE OF SOUTH AFRICA IN HISTORICAL PERSPECTIVE. *Social Studies 1976 67(1): 19-27.* Relates incidents illustrating the negative image the majority of Americans have of South Africa. Nevertheless, the two governments have accomplished much in their relations with one another since the mid-19th century. 37 notes. L. R. Raife

3892. Mitchell, Louis D. STEVE BIKO: SOUTH AFRICA'S MODERN SYMBOL. *Crisis 1978 85(4): 123-135.* Steve Biko died but the controversies raised before and after his death continue and in many ways symbolize the struggle for which he was fighting. Prime Minister John Vorster of South Africa was not dismantling apartheid as promised and Biko drew world attention to this fact. Biko began to organize students in December 1968, which represented a black threat in the eyes of the white minority government. Pretoria's massive crackdown in October-December 1977, which included the death of Biko, resulted in strong international protests. The legacy of Steve Biko may be the rapid elimination of apartheid from South Africa. A. G. Belles

3893. Morse, Stanley J. and Peele, Stanton. "COLOURED POWER" OR "COLOURED BOURGEOISIE?" POLITICAL ATTITUDES AMONG SOUTH AFRICAN COLOUREDS. *Public Opinion Q. 1974 38(3): 317-334.* "Why have Coloureds in South Africa—people of mixed racial descent—voiced less opposition to white minority rule than have black Africans? A theoretical analysis suggests that Coloureds feel both 'relatively deprived' in comparison with whites and 'relatively gratified' in comparison with Africans, that they believe they may eventually be accepted by whites, and that individually they have difficulty identifying with the broader Coloured community; in short, seemingly ideal conditions for the emergence of a 'Coloured Bourgeoisie' rather than a 'Coloured Power' ideology." J

3894. Mugomba, Agrippah T. THE MILITARIZATION OF THE INDIAN OCEAN AND THE LIBERATION OF SOUTHERN AFRICA. *J. of Southern African Affairs 1979 4(3): 261-279.* Considers the background and current possibility for the emergence of a Western alliance with South Africa in the interest of controlling Atlantic sea lanes into the Indian Ocean and further development of their mutual nuclear potential. Such ties will hamper the efforts of independence movements within Southern Africa. Based on newspapers and secondary sources; 32 notes. L. W. Truschel

3895. Murapa, Rukudzo. A GLOBAL PERSPECTIVE OF THE POLITICAL ECONOMY OF THE U.S. POLICY TOWARD

SOUTHERN AFRICA. *J. of Southern African Affairs 1977 2(1): 77-98.* American foreign policy is directed largely by multinational corporations. The United States had identified certain countries "critical to its survival and continued world domination," among them, Indonesia, Iran, Israel, and Brazil. South Africa is now being prepared to play a similar role. The United States has become South Africa's third largest supplier of imports, but the critical commodity South Africa lacks is oil. US multinational companies have been highly active in the search for local supplies and have made other contributions to South African manufacturing. Henry Kissinger's policy toward South Africa was part of a plan to construct an extended alliance which links strong middle powers with the West. 52 notes. E. P. Stickney

3896. Ngubane, Jordan K. THE ROAD TO AND FROM SOWETO: A CASE FOR THE COORDINATION OF AFRICAN POLITICS IN SOUTH AFRICA. *J. of Southern African Affairs 1977 2(2): 167-181.* Studies events leading up to the Soweto rebellion of June 1976, beginning with the establishment of South Africa in 1910 and the subsequent evolution of the Afrikaners' desire to dominate the blacks. Blacks are potentially their own liberators, not passive victims of the whites and their allies. 23 notes. J. Tull

3897. Ojo-Ade, Femi. STEPHEN BIKO: BLACK CONSCIOUSNESS, BLACK STRUGGLE, BLACK SURVIVAL. *J. of Modern African Studies [Great Britain] 1981 19(3): 539-546.* Reviews the following books on Biko: Hilda Bernstein's *Steve Biko* (1978), Aelred Stubbs, ed., *Steve Biko—I Write What I Like* (1978), and Donald Woods's *Biko* (1978). These books all support Biko and are hostile to the South African government. L. W. Truschel

3898. O'Meara, Dan. THE AFRIKANER BROEDERBOND, 1927-1948: CLASS VANGUARD OF AFRIKANER NATIONALISM. *J. of Southern African Studies [Great Britain] 1977 3(2): 156-186.* Describes the activities of the Afrikaner Broederbond, the secret society with the professed aim of promoting all of the interests of the Afrikaner nation, and considers the Bond in the wider context of Afrikaner nationalism. It was a united and disciplined body of middle-class nationalist militants. Based on newspapers and other primary sources; 79 notes. S. P. Carr

3899. O'Meara, Patrick. SOUTH AFRICA: THE POLITICS OF CHANGE. *Current Hist. 1981 80(464): 111-114, 134.* Examines recent and proposed modifications of South Africa's apartheid policies and discusses the effect of their implementation on appeasement of the urban African population and possible changes in US policy.

3900. Oppenheimer, H. F. SOUTH AFRICA AFTER THE ELECTION. *African Affairs [Great Britain] 1974 73(293): 399-407.* Discusses the April 1974 election in South Africa, where the National Party increased its majority, and unexpectedly, the Progressive Party elected six members to parliament. Traces the structure and policy of the National Party, the United Party, and the Progressive Party. Analyzes current economic policy and the effect of Bantustan policies. South Africa will survive and solve its problems since goodwill exists. H. G. Soff

3901. Orlik, Peter B. SOUTH AFRICAN BROADCASTING CORPORATION: AN INSTRUMENT OF AFRIKANER POLITICAL POWER. *J. of Southern African Affairs 1978 3(1): 54-64.* Traces efforts by Afrikaner nationalists to gain control of the South African Broadcasting Corporation (SABC) from its inception as a governmental agency in 1936. Afrikaner nationalists began to infiltrate the SABC during World War II and consolidated their control of it following the electoral victory of Daniel François Malan's National Party in 1948. The nationalists' takeover of the SABC and its subsequent use by the government until 1966 was part of a long-standing political and cultural struggle in South Africa between Afrikaners and English-speaking whites. Based on newspaper accounts, interviews, correspondence and secondary sources; 40 notes. L. W. Truschel

3902. Osia, Kunirum. ISRAEL-SOUTH AFRICA CONNECTION: CAUSE OR CONSEQUENCE OF BLACK AFRICAN MIDDLE EAST POLICY. *Search: J. for Arab and Islamic Studies 1981 2(3-4): 543-566.* The cultural, commercial, and military links between Israel and South Africa have been the prime source of anti-Israeli sentiment among black African nations.

3903. Oudes, Bruce. SOUTHERN AFRICA POLICY WATERSHED. *Africa Report 1974 19(6): 46-50.* US foreign policy toward South Africa is turning away from the pro-white stance embodied in Henry Kissinger's 1970 recommendations to Nixon, here reprinted in part. S

3904. Ovendale, Ritchie. THE SOUTH AFRICAN POLICY OF THE BRITISH LABOUR GOVERNMENT, 1947-51. *Int. Affairs [Great Britain] 1982-83 59(1): 41-58.* Discusses the history and development of political and economic relations between Great Britain and South Africa, including policies regarding apartheid, self-governance, federation, roles in international treaties and politics, and economic support.

3905. Peele, Stanton and Morse, Stanley J. ETHNIC VOTING AND POLITICAL CHANGE IN SOUTH AFRICA. *Am. Pol. Sci. Rev. 1974 68(4): 1520-1541.* Immediately prior to the 1970 parliamentary election in the Republic of South Africa, 462 white voters in Cape Town were questioned about their demographic backgrounds, voting intentions, and political attitudes. The study showed that ethnicity is the major determinant of party vote: Afrikaners vote for the National Party, the English-speaking for the United Party. SES-related factors predict party identification only insofar as they covary with ethnicity. While a liberalization of political attitudes with rising SES can be observed, this has no bearing on electoral behavior. Party vote is not related to ideological or issue orientations, but is related to the intensity of the voters' identification with their own ethnic groups and with white South Africans in general. Voters tend to react positively or negatively to the NP, with the UP serving chiefly as a vehicle for protest votes against the government. The slight drop in NP support in 1970 was due to a key group of abstainers who—while basically Nat supporters—were more liberal than those who said they would vote for the NP. It is "Ambiguous Afrikaners" (those who are changing to an "English" identity), and only some of those, who are defecting completely from their traditional political allegiance. They represent the one sign of potential change in South Africa's uniquely stable political system. J

3906. Pelliccioni, Franco. LE ELEZIONI DEL 1974 IN SUD AFRICA: TENTATIVO DI BILANCIO POLITICO GENERALE [The 1974 national elections in South Africa: an attempt at a general political balance]. *Riv. di Studi Politici Int. [Italy] 1975 42(1): 74-84.* Surveys the platforms of the political parties in South Africa, their similar programs, striking differences, and their common concern with future African rebellions and opposition. The National Party advocated the apartheid policy of separate development in South Africa, the creation of autonomous and politically independent peoples economically interdependent with the South African Republic. The United Party proposed to the electorate a federal system based on ethnic and geographic differentiation. The Progressive Party introduced the most striking political program—to give the privilege of suffrage based on merit not on color. A. Sbacchi

3907. Pichon, Roland. L'AFRIQUE DU SUD—ORIGINE ET CONSÉQUENCES DE L'APARTHEID [South Africa—The origin and the consequences of apartheid]. *Études [France] 1976 344: 669-687.* Studies the history and application since 1948 of the separate development doctrine leading up to the current refusal of the South African government to abandon this unjust policy, despite international pressure.

3908. Prudnikov, A. IZRAIL'—IUAR: "NADEZHNYE PARTNERY" [Israel and South Africa: "reliable partners"]. *Aziia i Afrika Segodnia [USSR] 1982 (11): 30-33.* Discusses the history of imperialist influence in South Africa and Palestine and the threats posed by the racist regimes of South Africa and Israel to the peoples of Africa and the Middle East.

3909. Ralston, Richard D. AMERICAN EPISODES IN THE MAKING OF AN AFRICAN LEADER: A CASE STUDY OF ALFRED B. XUMA (1893-1962). *Int. J. of African Hist. Studies 1973 6(1): 72-93.* The American experiences of Alfred Bitini Xuma (1893-1962), who exercised strong leadership in the African National Congress in South

Africa and other facets of African development, illustrate the thesis that "the American experiences of African students were one of the important variables affecting developments in African leadership during the colonial period." He took his degree in medicine, coming under the influence of Booker T. Washington, and returned to Africa in 1927. His historical importance in Africa is comparable with much more heralded leaders. 88 notes. R. V. Ritter

3910. Rathbone, Richard. REVIEW ARTICLE: THE PEOPLE AND SOWETO. *J. of Southern African Studies [Great Britain] 1979 6(1): 124-132.* Presents a comparative assessment of two books treating the Soweto disturbances of 1976, John Kane-Berman's *South Africa: The Method in the Madness* and Baruch Hirson's *Year of Fire, Year of Ash.* Both studies are greatly handicapped by lacking any access to official sources and archives and enjoying only limited cooperation by participants in the disturbances. Neither cites any Afrikaans language sources nor handles disturbances in South Africa in 1976-77 outside Soweto. While both describe the Soweto riots and South Africa's political economy as responsible for the outbreaks, a point of view shared by the reviewer, neither is able to breathe much life into the cultural or personal lives of the African participants. Secondary sources; 11 notes.
L. W. Truschel

3911. Rathbone, Richard. STUDENTS AND POLITICS: SOUTH AFRICA. *J. of Commonwealth and Comparative Pol. [Great Britain] 1977 15(2): 103-111.* Traces the history of the National Union of South African Students (NUSAS) founded in 1924. Examines its reaction to the 1959 University Act which put an end to interracial study, and its part in the student riots which swept the universities in the late 1960's and 70's. Discusses relations between the NUSAS and the South African Students Organization set up by black students in 1969, their respective roles in South African politics, and the degree of government intervention in the organization and activities of each. Based on material from the Survey of Race Relations in South Africa, (Johannesburg, South African Institute of Race Relations); 8 notes.
C. Anstey

3912. Reid, B. L. THE FEDERAL PARTY AND THE NATAL PROVINCIAL ELECTIONS OF 1954 AND 1959. *Kleio [South Africa] 1981 13(1-2): 20-31.* In Natal, South Africa's Federal and United Parties were divided on the issues of education, race, and republicanism during the 1954 elections. The Federal Party was defeated in the 1954 elections, along with their fairly liberal racial policy. By 1959 the Nationalists, who had succeeded in removing the blacks from the election roll, had become increasingly republican. Again in 1959, education and racial issues were paramount, along with the republican issue. Again the Federal Party suffered defeat. Primary sources; 55 notes. J. Powell

3913. Rich, Paul. ADMINISTRATIVE IDEOLOGY, URBAN SOCIAL CONTROL AND THE ORIGINS OF APARTHEID THEORY, 1930-1939. *J. of African Studies 1980 7(2): 70-82.* An investigation of the origins of apartheid in pre-1940's official race policy formation for the cities of the Union of South Africa. The Native Economic Commission Report of 1932 broke with earlier policy in recognizing the permanence of an urban African population, but also endorsed residential racial segregation, a key feature later mandated by the Native (Urban Areas) Amendment Act of 1937. The bureaucrats of the Union and municipal governments thereby created a system of urban segregation for South Africa. Based on published and unpublished South African government reports and private papers; 89 notes.
L. W. Truschel

3914. Rich, Paul. LIBERALISM AND ETHNICITY IN SOUTH AFRICAN POLITICS, 1921-1948. *African Studies [South Africa] 1976 35(3-4): 229-251.* Examines the role of ethnicity in South Africa's political development and suggests that social scientists have failed to understand the true nature of liberalism in a racial ideology just as advocates of liberalism have misunderstood the country's special situation. Certainly liberalism failed, and one explanation of this lies in the fact that "urbanization and industrialism may have been actually promoted by an ideology of racial separatism." Based on printed and manuscript sources; 98 notes. J. A. Casada

3915. Rich, Paul. THE ORIGINS OF APARTHEID IDEOLOGY: THE CASE OF ERNEST STUBBS AND TRANSVAAL NATIVE ADMINISTRATION, C. 1902-1932. *African Affairs [Great Britain] 1980 79(315): 171-194.* Ernest Stubbs was a Native Affairs official who in 1925 wrote a paper on segregation arguing for a radical system of racial partitioning which was in line with the apartheid policy of the South African Bureau of Racial Affairs (SABRA). Stubbs was a member of the anti-Nationalist Dominion Party, but he championed the idea of African residence, as far as possible, in rural areas and he favored larger allocations of land to African peasants and chiefdoms than was allowed at that time. Identifies key aspects of his career and views, which reflected some crucial features of South African industrialization in this century and the development of white capitalist settler agriculture. 107 notes. J. V. Coutinho

3916. Richardson, Henry J., III. SELF-DETERMINATION, INTERNATIONAL LAW AND THE SOUTH AFRICAN BANTUSTAN POLICY. *Columbia J. of Transnational Law 1978 17(2): 185-219.* Questions the legality under international law of the South African policy of granting "independence" to the Bantu Homelands, relying on two recent UN General Assembly resolutions which condemn the Bantustan policy.

3917. Riubin, Neville. LAW, RACE AND COLOR IN SOUTH AFRICA. *Issue 1974 4(3): 6-11.* Under apartheid, law has become the handmaiden of discrimination and repression. S

3918. St. Jorre, John de. SOUTH AFRICA: UP AGAINST THE WORLD. *Foreign Policy 1977 (28): 53-85.* The Republic of South Africa has come under siege both internally as well as externally over apartheid, 1965-77. Most government policies have sought to buy time and succeeded only in perpetuating tension. H. R. Mahood

3919. Saul, John S. and Gelb, Stephen. THE CRISIS IN SOUTH AFRICA: CLASS DEFENSE, CLASS REVOLUTION. *Monthly Rev. 1981 33(3): 1-156.* Analyzes violence against the South African government by angry blacks, which indicate "that the tide has at last begun to turn against South Africa's apartheid system," and outlines political formats to focus revolutionary energy and consolidate the revolutionary class alliance.

3920. Schieber, Michael T. APARTHEID UNDER PRESSURE: SOUTH AFRICA'S MILITARY STRENGTH IN A CHANGING POLITICAL CONTEXT. *Africa Today 1976 23(1): 27-45.* Provides detailed analysis of the development of South Africa's military capability since 1960. Current leadership combined with available military power has made South Africa safe from internal revolution and secure from outside aggression. The complexity of racial economic interdependence and external pressures probably will lead to gradual change. Based on secondary, UN, and South African sources; 6 tables, 72 notes.
G. O. Gagnon

3921. Schroeder, John J. SOUTH AFRICA UNDER PRESSURE. *Indiana Social Studies Q. 1977 30(2): 38-43.* Examines the policies of the South African government and the pressure which has grown steadily 1960-77, from within and without the country, to change its racial policies and eradicate apartheid.

3922. Seidelmann, Raimund. AKTEUR UND INTERESSE ALS ANALYTISCHE KONZEPTE ZUR ERFASSUNG VON BEZIEHUNGEN AM BEISPIEL USA SÜDAFRIKANISCHE REPUBLIK [Actor and interest as analytical concepts in the formulation of relations: the United States and South Africa]. *Politische Vierteljahresschrift [West Germany] 1974 15(3-4): 313-391.* Analyzes the relationship between the United States and South Africa, where the former is the actor and the latter is the interest, or the representative of the United States in the sub-Saharan zone. This view is possible because of the structural compatibility of their interests. In terms of goals, means, and potential the relationship between the two is very fruitful. Statistical and secondary sources; 199 notes. A. Alcock

3923. Seidman, Ann and Makgetla, Neza. TRANSNATIONAL CORPORATE INVOLVEMENT IN SOUTH AFRICA'S MILITARY BUILD-UP. *J. of Southern African Affairs 1979 4(2): 153-173.* A descriptive statement, relying on material presented in testimony to the

UN Anti-Apartheid Committee in New York City on 21 February 1978, of alleged participation by multinational corporations in armaments programs and related activities by the Republic of South Africa since 1960. Based on printed corporate documents, newspapers, and secondary sources; 82 notes. L. W. Truschel

3924. Shubin, V. ANK: GODY PODOL'IA I VOORUZHENNOI BOR'BY [African National Congress: the years of armed underground struggle]. *Aziia i Afrika Segodnia [USSR] 1982 (1): 34-37.* The struggle of the peoples of South Africa has been waged in extremely difficult conditions, given South Africa's economically advanced situation and assistance from imperialist states.

3925. Shubin, V. VOENNO-POLITICHESKOE SOTRUDNICHESTVO STRAN ZAPADA S IUAR [Military and political cooperation of Western nations with South Africa]. *Narody Azii i Afriki [USSR] 1981 (3): 26-37.* The South African region occupies an important place in the global strategy of imperialism. The imperialist powers, particularly the United States, are interested in the natural resources of South Africa, and they are also able to provide it financial aid. Parallel to these economic ties is the sale of arms to South Africa, recently discussed in the UN Security Council. The common interests of imperialism and South African racism continue to bind countries of the West politically to South Africa. Cites South African newspapers and other primary sources; 50 notes. S. J. Talalay

3926. Sibeko, David M. FROM SHARPEVILLE TO SOWETO. *Black Scholar 1978 9(5): 13-20.* Discusses the black liberation movement in South Africa, 1960-77, detailing government measures in response to agitation for equal rights and the formation of black activist organizations.

3927. Sills, H. D. THE BREAKUP OF THE CENTRAL AFRICAN FEDERATION: NOTES ON THE VALIDITY OF ASSURANCES. *African Affairs [Great Britain] 1974 73(290): 50-62.* In 1963 when the Federation of Southern Rhodesia, Northern Rhodesia, and Nyasaland divided, the British government reneged on assurances that it had made to Southern Rhodesia relative to self-government. Southern Rhodesians became resentful and the Unilateral Declaration of Independence was inevitable. Focuses on the Federation Conference (1960), the Victoria Falls Conference (1963), and worldwide sanctions against Southern Rhodesia since 1966. Independence should not have been given to the dissident states of Zambia and Malawi without independence to Southern Rhodesia. 31 notes. H. G. Soff

3928. Simson, Howard. FASCISM IN SOUTH AFRICA. *African R. [Tanzania] 1973 3(3): 423-451.* A Marxist analysis of the class struggle within South Africa, emphasizing the 1940's. Discusses the structure and practice of apartheid, negating common stereotypes. The crisis of the 1940's was resolved by fascist suppression. 120 notes. H. G. Soff

3929. Southall, Roger J. THE BENEFICIARIES OF TRANSKEIAN "INDEPENDENCE." *J. of Modern African Studies [Great Britain] 1977 15(1): 1-23.* When the Transkei was given "independence," many people stated that it was a puppet state with no relevance to the political future of South Africa. There were those, however, who benefitted, particularly a new social and political class in the Transkei. 3 tables, 69 notes. H. G. Soff

3930. Spence, J. E. THE REPUBLIC OF SOUTH AFRICA. *World Survey [Great Britain] 1975 (77): 1-18.* South Africa's foreign policy toward Southern Rhodesia, Angola and Mozambique, 1965-74.

3931. Spence, J. E. SOUTH AFRICAN FOREIGN POLICY: CHANGING PERSPECTIVES. *World Today [Great Britain] 1978 34(11): 417-425.* An examination of current South African views of events in Africa during the past two years, relating changes within the republic to international politics.

3932. Stevens, Richard P. SMUTS AND WEIZMANN. *J. of Palestine Studies [Lebanon] 1973 3(1): 35-59.* The little-publicized relationship, 1917-50, between General Jan Christian Smuts, South Africa's prime minister, and Chaim Weizmann, Zionist leader and first president of Israel, "helps to throw into perspective both the contradictions of Western liberalism and the psychological climate which rationalized the dominant position of a white minority in South Africa on the one hand and of a new European settlement in Palestine on the other."

3933. Stokke, Olav. NORSK POLITIKK OVERFOR DET SØRLIGE AFRIKA [Norwegian policy toward South Africa]. *Internasjonal Politikk [Norway] 1978 (3): 381-426.* Norwegian policy toward Southern Africa is analyzed against the background of recent developments in the region. Examines Norwegian options and boycott policy and the existing economic relations between Norway and South Africa. 57 notes. J

3934. Stokke, Olav. SØR-AFRIKAS DOMINANS-STRATEGI: FRA DIALOG TIL DETENTE [South Africa's dominance strategy: from dialog to detente]. *Samtiden [Norway] 1976 85(5): 271-282.* In 1960 South Africa was being isolated from the various international organizations: the Economic Commission for Africa, UNESCO and ILO. By the middle of the 1960's, a campaign was launched to create good relations with the Western powers emphasizing the importance of a friendly port around the Cape and an outpost among the newly created African nations. After 1972, these so-called dialog politics were temporarily suspended even though the South African government has not given up the outward-looking strategy of which the dialog politics were a part. Concludes with an explanation of the intervention in Angola. B. L. Jeppeson

3935. Strong, A. THE ROLE OF THE ZULUS IN AFRICAN LIBERATION: 1912-1978. *Hist. Teacher [Australia] 1979 (23): 27-43.*

3936. Tambo, Oliver. THE BLACK REACTION. *Issue 1974 4(3): 3-5.* Examines the reaction of the African majority to apartheid in South Africa 1948-73, under the leadership of Albert Luthuli and his successor, Oliver Tambo. S

3937. Tennyson, Brian D. CANADIAN POLICY TOWARDS SOUTH AFRICA. *Africa Today 1982 29(1): 3-20.* Canada's policy toward South Africa has been based on a concern for human rights together with a realization that economic sanctions are not an option. Summarizes Canadian economic involvement and action in the UN and on the Namibia question. Secondary sources; 42 notes. G. O. Gagnon

3938. Ume, Kalu E. THE ORIGIN OF APARTHEID IN SOUTH AFRICA. *J. of African Studies 1981-82 8(4): 176-181.* A survey of the history of racial separatism in South Africa, as reflected in official policy and legislation. The first South African race laws date back to the early period of Dutch East India Company administration in 1682, when slaves and freed slaves were confronted with legal obstacles to emancipation. The British, after occupying the Cape in 1806, were quick to adopt a racially separatist policy, as was the government of the Union following unification in 1910. Concludes that white exclusiveness has always remained inflexible in the face of African opposition. Based on printed South African documents and secondary sources; 12 notes. L. W. Truschel

3939. Urnov, A. AL'IANS VASHINGTON-PRETORIIA I AFRIKA [The Washington-Pretoria alliance and Africa]. *Mirovaia Ekonomika i Mezhdunarodyne Otnosheniia [USSR] 1982 (3): 46-58.* Considers the economic, political, and strategic causes of US-South African rapprochement since the inauguration of Ronald Reagan, explaining that the United States and South Africa base their aggressive and disruptive policies in Angola, South-West Africa, and other areas of southern Africa on the myth of a Soviet threat to the region.

3940. Vandenbosch, Amry. BROWN SOUTH AFRICANS AND THE PROPOSED NEW CONSTITUTION. *J. of Pol. 1979 41(2): 566-588.* South African Coloureds are the product of intermixing of Europeans, Africans, Asians, and Malays, and lack both an independent cultural tradition and language. Classification of Coloureds in the political racial structure has troubled South Africa since the formation of the Union in 1910. In 1951, a bill in the House of Assembly urged a separate voters roll for Coloureds and the division of Cape Province into four districts, each with a White to represent Coloured interests. The bill was invalidated in 1952, but a packed Supreme Court upheld it in 1956. In 1964, a Coloured Persons' Representative Council of limited powers was established, with elections, in 1969. The council has served as a forum for expression of discontent with political, economic, and social status. For both Coloureds and Asians, establishment of separate homelands has been impossible, and a consociational democracy based on ethnic parliaments has been proposed. 37 notes. A. W. Novitsky

3941. Vickery, Kenneth P. "HERRENVOLK" DEMOCRACY AND EGALITARIANISM IN SOUTH AFRICA AND THE U.S. SOUTH. *Comparative Studies in Soc. and Hist. [Great Britain] 1974 16(3): 309-328.*

3942. Weiss, Julian M. SHOULD THE U.S. COLD-SHOULDER TRANSKEI? *Contemporary Rev. [Great Britain] 1979 235(1362): 7-13.* Discusses the development of American attitude toward the Transkei since the 1950's, showing how US foreign policy is governed by the situation in Pretoria, not the Transkei itself.

3943. Weyl, Nathaniel. ISRAEL AND SOUTH AFRICA: TWO BELEAGUERED ELITES. *Mankind Q. [Great Britain] 1973 13(3): 158-165.* Discusses basic similarities between the Israelis and white South Africans. Recalls Africa's initial support of the new state of Israel. Hints at the necessity of preventing revolutionary regimes from breaking Europe's ties with the Middle East and, in turn, penetrating Asia and black Africa. Suggests overt support for Israel and South Africa as an alternative Western policy. Primary and secondary sources; 9 notes. K. Halil

3944. Willan, Brian. THE ANTI-SLAVERY AND ABORIGINES' PROTECTION SOCIETY AND THE SOUTH AFRICAN NATIVES' LAND ACT OF 1913. *J. of African Hist. [Great Britain] 1979 20(1): 83-102.* The Anti-Slavery and Aborigines' Protection Society supported the South African Natives' Land Act of 1913, despite the opposition of Africans, because it was predisposed to accept segregation and because it needed to retain the support of the imperial government in its campaign against the British South Africa Company. The Society's attitude emerged in its handling of the South Africa Native National Congress's deputation to England in 1914, and in its dispute with Sol Plaatje, author of *Native Life in South Africa.* Plaatje supporters Jane Cobden Unwin and Georgiana Solomon were expelled from the Society's executive committee, leading to the foundation in 1918 of the Society for the Protection of Peoples of African Origin and the African Progress Union. 81 notes. A. W. Novitsky

3945. Willan, Brian. SOL PLAATJE, DE BEERS AND AN OLD TRAM SHED: CLASS RELATIONS AND SOCIAL CONTROL IN A SOUTH AFRICAN TOWN, 1918-1919. *J. of Southern African Studies [Great Britain] 1978 4(2): 195-215.* An evaluation of events and personalities surrounding transfer by the De Beers Company in 1918 of an old tram shed to Solomon Tshekisho Plaatje and his Brotherhood Movement for use as their assembly hall in Kimberley. Attacks Plaatje, generally regarded as one of the leading early African nationalists in the Union of South Africa, as a class enemy of African workers during the industrial unrest of 1918-19 and a conscious ally of De Beers. Contends that, as a representative of the African petite bourgeoisie, Plaatje felt threatened by those he called the "black Bolsheviks of Johannesburg" and, in the eyes of the white corporation, "was undoubtedly regarded as a valued agent in the task of keeping South Africa safe for capitalism." Fearing the spread of African industrial worker militancy beyond the Witwatersrand in 1918-19, De Beers and the Union government hastened to lend its support for Plaatje and his movement. Based on De Beers records, newspapers, and secondary sources; 53 notes. L. W. Truschel

3946. Zagajac, Milivoje. SANCTIONS AGAINST SOUTH AFRICA. *Contemporary Rev. [Great Britain] 1982 240(1396): 247-250.* Discusses UN sanctions against South Africa in the context of the development of apartheid in the 20th century.

3947. —. PORTRAIT: ROBERT SOBUKWE OF THE PAC. *Africa Report 1975 20(3): 18-20.* A biography of Robert Sobukwe, leader of the Pan-Africanist Congress, who has been a prisoner of the South African government since 1960. S

3948. —. THE SOUTH AFRICAN AIR FORCE. *Aerospace Hist. 1973 20(2): 62-70.* An official history of the South African Air Force from 1912 to 1968. S

Society

3949. Adler, Taffy. LITHUANIA'S DIASPORA: THE JOHANNESBURG JEWISH WORKERS' CLUB, 1928-1948. *J. of Southern African Studies [Great Britain] 1979 6(1): 70-92.* The Johannesburg Jewish Workers' Club was composed of working-class Jews who had migrated to South Africa's main industrial area from Lithuania. The club was a social as well as political organization; from 1928 to the date of its demise in 1948 it became subordinate to the South African Communist Party, and accepted the Native Republic concept enunciated by the Sixth World Congress of the Comintern in 1928 and other tenets of Stalinism. The club appealed to the most militant Jewish socialists, and gradually died out as more Witwatersrand Jews rose upward into the white middle class. Based on interviews, newspapers, and secondary sources; 75 notes. L. W. Truschel

3950. Alverson, Hoyt S. MINORITY GROUP AUTONOMY AND THE REJECTION OF DOMINANT GROUP RACIAL MYTHOLOGIES: THE ZULU OF SOUTH AFRICA. *African Studies [South Africa] 1974 33(1): 3-24.* Studies the effects of discrimination on the Zulu. The Zulu, by retaining local identity, have maintained a sense of security and personal dignity despite white domination. They have refused to accept the stereotyped image accorded them by those who discriminate against them. 4 tables, 2 figs., biblio., appendix. J.A. Casada

3951. Anthony, David H. *THE BLACK SCHOLAR* INTERVIEWS: MAHOMO. *Black Scholar 1976 7(8): 30-35.* Mahomo is connected with the London-based Morena Films, an organization of black and white South African exiles which has made two documentary films with the assistance of British friends. The films, *Phela Ndaba: End of Dialogue* (1970) and *Last Grave at Dimbaza* (1974), were both secretly filmed inside South Africa. Both have been shown throughout Europe and North America for the purpose of showing the people in the West the truth about conditions in South Africa. In this interview, Mahomo discusses many issues that would be of interest to those sympathetic to the liberation struggle in South Africa. B. D. Ledbetter

3952. Asein, Samuel Omo. THE REVOLUTIONARY VISION IN ALEX LA GUMA'S NOVELS. *Phylon 1978 39(1): 74-86.* Examines the literary ethics and social commitment of black South African author, Alex La Guma. Explores the gradual development of La Guma's radical strategies by analyzing major themes in his four novels. This development is characterized by a shift from political naiveté and the mere evasion of oppression to radical maturity and the militant opposition to oppression. 25 notes. J. Moore

3953. Ballard, Charles. THE DUNN RESERVE, 1895-1948: A CASE STUDY OF SEGREGATION AND UNDERDEVELOPMENT IN A RESERVED LAND CATEGORY. *J. of Southern African Affairs 1978 3(4): 521-537.* An overview of economic and social history of the Dunn Reserve in Natal, South Africa. The Dunns are the descendants of the 19th-century European trader, John Dunn, and his 49 African wives and 114 children. Falling clearly under neither European or Native law in Natal or the Union of South Africa, the Dunns came to be sharply divided between those residing at the Emoyeni and Mangete land blocks set aside for them by the Zululand Lands Delimitation Committee in 1904. Those at Emoyeni were accepted virtually as Europeans and were granted inclusion in the European sugar growing quota established by law and agreement in 1936 and 1943. The darker Dunns at Mangete were excluded from the European quota and were claimed as tribal subjects by the Nguni chief Somshekwe. The Mangete Dunns sought to improve their individual and collective status, eventually with partial success. Based on archival sources, published documents, and newspapers; 69 notes. L. W. Truschel

3954. Balson, C. S. LARKAN AND ST FAITHS TOKENS. *Africana Notes and News [South Africa] 1978 23(3): 109-114.* Discusses tokens minted at Durban in 1906 and used to replace cardboard coinage for farming and trading at the store on Bont Rand farm in the Umzimkulu district, 1906-29.

3955. Becken, H.-J. EKUPHAKAMENI REVISITED: RECENT DEVELOPMENTS WITHIN THE NAZARETHA CHURCH IN SOUTH AFRICA. *J. of Religion in Africa [Netherlands] 1978 9(3):*

161-172. Traces the development of the Nazaretha Church at the church farm, Ekuphakameni, Natal, South Africa, the largest member of the African Independent Church, from its founding in 1910 by Isaiah Shembe to the 1970's and examines the leadership of Londa Shembe.

3956. Bosch, David J. CURRENTS AND CROSSCURRENTS IN SOUTH AFRICAN BLACK THEOLOGY. *J. of Religion in Africa [Netherlands] 1974 6(1): 1-22.* South African black theology has developed from the African independent churches and the writings of James Cone. Jesus and his apostles were seen as Blacks. Emphasis is given to the relationship between black theology and Africa's traditional religions, effectively excluding Christian gospel. Black theology is an attempt to remove the stigma of slavery and tokenism, and it is forcing Western Christianity to evaluate its priorities. 59 notes. H. G. Soff

3957. Brand, C. M. PERSISTENCE AND CHANGE IN SOUTH AFRICAN SOCIETY. *Zambezia [Rhodesia] 1973 3(1): 75-81.* Review essay tracing the changing themes in sociological literature on South Africa from the predictions of imminent collapse from internal contradictions voiced in the late 1950's and the first half of the 1960's to studies in the late 1960's and early 1970's on what holds the divided society together and how it is most likely to change in the future. Assesses the contributions of G. C. Kinloch, *Sociological Study of South Africa* (London: Macmillan, 1972), Heribert Adam, *Modernizing Racial Domination* (Berkeley: U. of California Pr., 1971) and *South Africa: Sociological Perspectives* (London: Oxford U. Pr., 1971), and *A Taste of Power* (1973) published by the Study Project on Christianity in Apartheid Society (SPRO-CAS) to the understanding of the apartheid process. O. B. Pollak

3958. Christenson, Ronald. THE CIVIL RELIGION OF APARTHEID: AFRIKANERDOM'S COVENANT. *Midwest Q. 1979 20(2): 137-146.* The ideology of the Afrikaner was expressed by Paul Kruger in the late 19th century and has continued to find expression in the Nationalist Party. It is a civil religion that portrays the Afrikaners as God's chosen people who have escaped the corruption of the old world to build a civilization in the wilderness. Apartheid was designed by the Nationalists to preserve the Afrikaners' ethnic identity. Biblio.

3959. Clingman, Stephen. HISTORY FROM THE INSIDE: THE NOVELS OF NADINE GORDIMER. *J. of Southern African Studies [Great Britain] 1981 7(2): 165-193.* Between publication of her first novel in 1953 and her seventh in 1979, Nadine Gordimer's perception of South African affairs has undergone substantial change, especially in the area of European-African relationships, which closely reflect the responses of white radicals in South Africa to the major historical developments of these years. The egocentric white liberal fear of the Nationalist victory of 1948 reflected in the first novel has become, step by step, an identification or merger with the black consciousness of the 1970's. Based on an interview with and the writings of Nadine Gordimer; 79 notes. L. W. Truschel

3960. Coplan, David. THE AFRICAN MUSICIAN AND THE DEVELOPMENT OF THE JOHANNESBURG ENTERTAINMENT INDUSTRY, 1900-1960. *J. of Southern African Studies [Great Britain] 1979 5(2): 135-164.* Early in the 20th century, African music began to develop in the Johannesburg area separately among the urban middle class and the unskilled workers from traditional African melodies and a strong influence from black America. By the 1930's these songs had created a distinctive urban African identity. The white recording industry from this time made high profits by recording the *mbqanga* and *kwela* styles of urban songs. Only with the establishment in 1954 of the Union of South African Artists did the musicians begin to demand royalty agreements from the recording companies. Based on newspapers, interviews, and secondary sources; 47 notes. L. W. Truschel

3961. Corrigan, Edward C. SOUTH AFRICA ENTERS THE ELECTRONIC AGE: THE DECISION TO INTRODUCE TELEVISION. *Africa Today 1974 21(2): 15-28.* After 20 years of debate, television will be developed in South Africa. This will be designed to reinforce apartheid but change will come. Primary and secondary sources; 47 notes. G. O. Gagnon

3962. Davis, R. Hunt, Jr. CHARLES T. LORAM AND AN AMERICAN MODEL FOR AFRICAN EDUCATION IN SOUTH AFRICA. *African Studies Rev. 1976 19(2): 87-99.* Outlines Charles T. Loram's effort to create an American-derived model for African schools, especially in South Africa, during the 1920's and 1930's.

3963. DeGruchy, John W. THE RELATIONSHIP BETWEEN THE STATE AND SOME CHURCHES IN SOUTH AFRICA, 1968-1975. *J. of Church and State 1977 19(3): 437-455.* Discusses the relationship between the churches of South Africa and the state, 1968-75. A general review of the relationship of the major religious groups (Dutch Reformed, Roman Catholic, South African Council of Churches, and the Christian Institute) with the state before 1968 is followed by a detailed discussion of their reaction to apartheid since 1968. 43 notes. E. E. Eminhizer

3964. Dekenah, I. CANE SPIRIT. *Africana Notes and News [South Africa] 1980 24(2): 53-56.* The history of this South African product of fermented molasses from 1860 on—its name legalized in 1913—and its brand names and labels, 1954-78.

3965. Dodson, Don. THE FOUR MODES OF *DRUM*: POPULAR FICTION AND SOCIAL CONTROL IN SOUTH AFRICA. *African Studies Rev. 1974 17(2): 317-343.* An analysis of the contents of *Drum,* the popular South African magazine, to show that "literature is both an object and an agent of social control." Note, biblio. R. T. Brown

3966. duToit, Brian M. AFRIKANER BROEDERBOND: SECRET SOCIETY AS CULTURAL AGENT. *Patterns of Prejudice [Great Britain] 1974 8(2): 1-7.* Discusses the sociological phenomenon of secret societies as a means of promoting racism and religious intolerance in South Africa, emphasizing the Afrikaner Broederbond in the 20th century.

3967. DuToit, Brian M. CONTINUITY AND CHANGE IN CANNABIS USE BY AFRICANS IN SOUTH AFRICA. *J. of Asian and African Studies [Netherlands] 1976 11(3-4): 203-208.* A research note concerning cannabis use in traditional African society and South African attempts to suppress its use in modern settings. 3 notes, biblio. R. T. Brown

3968. Edgar, Robert and Saunders, Christopher. A. A. S. LEFLEUR AND THE GRIQUA TREK OF 1917: SEGREGATION, SELF-HELP, AND ETHNIC IDENTITY. *Int. J. of African Hist. Studies 1982 15(2): 201-220.* The Cape Coloureds, also known as Griqua, tried to preserve their identity by allying themselves with the segregationist policies of the white community. To fulfill this program they tried to create economic independence by removing themselves to an isolated farming community. Based on the LeFleur papers in South Africa and government documents; map, 102 notes. R. T. Brown

3969. Edgar, Robert. THE PROPHET MOTIVE: ENOCH MGIJIMA, THE ISRAELITES, AND THE BACKGROUND TO THE BULLHOEK MASSACRE. *Int. J. of African Hist. Studies 1982 15(3): 401-422.* A history of the South African prophet Enoch Mgijima and of his millennial church which was destroyed when some two hundred of his followers were killed in a clash with police in 1921. Based on South African documents and interviews with survivors; 71 notes. R. T. Brown

3970. February, V. THE AFRIKAANS LANGUAGE—AFRIKANERIZING INSTRUMENT. *African Perspectives [Netherlands] 1976 (1): 11-23.* Traces the history of the Afrikaans language movements in South Africa back to the formation of the Genootskap vir regte Afrikaners at Paarl in 1875. Describes the policies of the Nationalist governments since 1948 to control the African population through a policy of retribalization. Official promotion of Afrikaans among Africans is a basic means to manipulate their labor services. Based on newspapers and secondary sources; 4 notes, biblio. L. W. Truschel

3971. February, V. FROM ORDINANCE FIFTY UNTIL THE ERIKA THERON COMMISSION. *African Perspectives [Netherlands] 1976 (1): 24-33.* Traces the history of official policy toward the Coloured population in South Africa, up to the changes recommended by the Theron Commission in 1976. Asserts that the Coloureds will not be content with the reforms already proposed. Based on printed documents and secondary works; biblio. L. W. Truschel

3972. Gaitskell, Deborah. "CHRISTIAN COMPOUNDS FOR GIRLS": CHURCH HOSTELS FOR AFRICAN WOMEN IN JOHANNESBURG, 1907-1970. *J. of Southern African Studies [Great Britain] 1979 6(1): 44-69.* American and British churches opened hostels in Johannesburg from the early 20th century on to provide for the moral, social, recreational, and health needs of African women arriving for labor purposes from rural areas. These hostels grew in the 1910's and 1920's as Europeans replaced male domestic servants with female employees, so that the churches assisted the changing labor demands of South African whites as well as offering services to African women. By the 1950's the hostels were in great demand by African women seeking safe housing, religious guidance, job training, and social activity. Primary sources; 132 notes. L. W. Truschel

3973. Gerold-Scheepers, Thérèse. APPROACHES TO AFRICAN INDEPENDENT CHURCHES IN SOUTH AFRICA: A REVIEW OF RECENT PUBLICATIONS. *African Perspectives [Netherland] 1976 (2): 137-147.* A critical comparative review of five recent books and articles on African independent churches in South Africa. B. Sundkler's *Zulu Zion and Some Swazi Zionists,* J. P. Kiernan's article "Where Zionists Draw the Line," M. West's *Bishops and Prophets in a Black City,* E. Kamphausen's *Anfänge der Kirchlichen Unabhängigkeitsbewegungen in Südafrika,* and C. Hanekom's *Krisis & Kultus.* L. W. Truschel

3974. Giffard, C. A. CIRCULATION TRENDS IN SOUTH AFRICA. *Journalism Q. 1980 57(1): 86-91, 106.* A study of the circulation trends for 23 daily newspapers reveals that although the population grew by 60%, per capita income by 123%, and school enrollment by 150%, circulation increased by only 55%. Circulation gains tended to fluctuate somewhat in relation to economic conditions and the influence of events and the public's interest in those events. 7 notes. J. S. Coleman

3975. Gordimer, Nadine. ENGLISH-LANGUAGE LITERATURE AND POLITICS IN SOUTH AFRICA. *J. of Southern African Studies [Great Britain] 1976 2(2): 131-150.* Traces the development of English-language literature in South Africa since the arrival of Thomas Pringle in 1820, and its relationship with politics. Concentrates on 20th-century works reflecting primarily guilty attitudes toward the color bar. Biblio. S. P. Carr

3976. Gordimer, Nadine. WRITERS IN SOUTH AFRICA: THE NEW BLACK POETS. *Dalhousie R. 1973/74 53(4): 645-664.* Posits that African authors in South Africa use poetry as a last resort to evade official attention in a country which has banned black prose. One of 10 papers read at the Conference on African Literature, Dalhousie U., 1973. S

3977. Gray, Stephen. HERMAN CHARLES BOSMAN AND LAGO CLIFFORD. *Africana Notes and News [South Africa] 1978 23(4): 155-157.* Review article of Valerie Rosenberg, *Sunflower to the Sun*(Human and Rosseau, 1976) that criticizes the thesis that Herman Charles Bosman was actor and writer Lago Clifford. They were two different people writing about their prison experiences at different times.

3978. Grundy, Kenneth W. A REVIEW OF SCHOLARLY LITERATURE ON PRETORIA'S HOMELANDS SCHEME. *J. of Southern African Affairs 1978 3(2): 224-234.* Reviews works appearing since 1961 on South Africa's planning and implementation of the Bantu Homeland's policy, especially the 1977 study of Jeffrey Butler, Robert I. Rotberg, and John Adams, *The Black Homelands of South Africa* (Berkeley: U. of California Pr., 1977). L. W. Truschel

3979. Harington, J. S. and McGlashan, N. D. MIGRANT WORKERS AND CANCER PATTERNS IN SOUTH AFRICA. *J. of South African Studies [Great Britain] 1976 3(1): 92-101.* Areas with a migrant labor population provide an opportunity to study disease in different environments. The author considers the incidence of cancer among migrant workers in South Africa, ca. 1930-75, with particular reference to the 1960's. Based on medical reports; table, 3 fig., 22 notes. S. P. Carr

3980. Heaven, Patrick C. L. AUTHORITARIANISM AMONG AFRIKANERS. *Ethnic and Racial Studies [Great Britain] 1982 5(2): 229-231.* Reviews 20th-century scholarship dealing with the racial views of Afrikaners and discusses the impact of historical, social, and religious factors on the level of authoritarian attitudes, such as *baasskap* (mastership), among the Afrikaner population of South Africa.

3981. Hugo, Pierre J. ACADEMIC DISSENT AND APARTHEID IN SOUTH AFRICA. *J. of Black Studies 1977 7(3): 243-262.* The author's conversations with Afrikaner academics who declined to sign a declaration in 1971 calling for racial reform revealed that some opponents of apartheid feared university or governmental retaliations. Other dissenters preferred to wait for a better vehicle of protest, to attack apartheid more obliquely, or to seek more enlightened racial policies by influencing their students. A third group of academics argued that to involve themselves in a political issue would violate their code of ethics or embarrass their universities. As internal and external pressure on South Africa grows, increased conformist thought will stifle dissent among Afrikaner academics and intellectuals. Primary and secondary sources; biblio. D. C. Neal

3982. Ireland, Ralph R. APARTHEID AND THE EDUCATION OF THE INDIAN COMMUNITY IN THE REPUBLIC OF SOUTH AFRICA. *Plural Societies [Netherlands] 1975 6(2): 3-17.*

3983. Kinloch, Graham C. RACIAL PREJUDICE IN HIGHLY AND LESS RACIST SOCIETIES: SOCIAL DISTANCE PREFERENCES AMONG WHITE COLLEGE STUDENTS IN SOUTH AFRICA AND HAWAII. *Sociol. and Social Res. 1974 59(1): 1-13.* "Inter-societal comparisons using white college students in South Africa and Hawaii highlighted the importance of sex and white-black interaction to racial prejudice in South Africa, and religiosity and conformity to social distance in Hawaii, but social distance in both was related to background characteristics, racial experience and personal attitudes. It is concluded that societal context rather than personality orientations is paramount in the comparative understanding of racial attitudes." J

3984. Kisanga, E. J. THE ORGANIZATION OF AFRICAN UNITY (OAU) AND THE LIBERATION STRUGGLE IN SOUTHERN AFRICA. *Taamuli [Tanzania] 1977 7(2): 32-49.* Since its founding in 1963 the Organization of African Unity has failed to make progress toward the liberation of Africans in South Africa. Poorly financed and loosely organized, the OAU has been split between those advocating a nonviolent policy of patience and those advocating immediate action against South Africa. The OAU's unwillingness to accept a radical, socialist policy toward South Africa has damaged the cause of liberation. 44 notes. D. S. Rockwood

3985. Kotze, Dirk A. THE RISE AND DECLINE OF NATIVE ADMINISTRATION. *Teaching Pol. Sci. 1977 4(2): 235-246.* Discusses the development of Native Administration as an academic discipline and as part of the departmental offerings of South African universities since 1956.

3986. Krige, Eileen Jensen. A LOVEDU PRAYER—THE LIGHT IT THROWS ON THE ANCESTOR CULT. *African Studies [South Africa] 1974 33(2): 91-97.* Investigates a Lovedu prayer which was offered together with a beer offering and cattle sacrifice for rain 1 February 1963, by Queen Modjadji IV. The prayer is analyzed "in the hope of laying bare some of the concepts" underlying the ancestor cult of the Lovedu. The wording of the prayer is carefully examined and shows a warm and intimate relationship with ancestors. Biblio. J. A. Casada

3987. Lapchick, Richard E. SOUTH AFRICA: SPORT AND APARTHEID POLITICS. *Ann. of the Am. Acad. of Pol. and Social Sci. 1979 (445): 155-165.* Despite severe sanctions from the international sports community, including expulsion from the Olympics and the withdrawal of competition, apartheid continues relatively unabated in South Africa. South African sports officials assert that their system is changing and that there are no color barriers. This may be true on paper or in public forums, but it is not true in practice. Both in and outside of South Africa, protesting groups have been active in seeking equality but with no significant results. South Africa's ideological and cultural traditions continue to reinforce secondary citizen status for nonwhites. J

3988. Larson, Charles R. ALAN PATON'S *CRY THE BELOVED COUNTRY* AFTER TWENTY-FIVE YEARS. *Africa Today 1973 20(4): 53-57.* Contrasts the initial critical acclaim for Alan Paton's first novel with the harsh criticism currently in vogue. Concludes that the novel has been dated by a too rapidly changing South Africa and wider world. *Cry the Beloved Country* is "still a beautifully lyrical novel" but its optimism no longer addresses a cynical world. G. O. Gagnon

3989. Lefort, René. THE "BLACK" PRESS IN SOUTH AFRICA. *Int. Social Sci. J. [France] 1981 33(1): 99-121.* South Africa does not enjoy a free press. The "black" press, largely staffed and read by Africans, is owned by Europeans, and in no way contributes to African liberation, nor does the largely English-language opposition press, though it may help to raise the consciousness of its readership, which includes many Africans.

3990. Lodge, Tom. THE DESTRUCTION OF SOPHIATOWN. *J. of Modern African Studies [Great Britain] 1981 19(1): 107-132.* Sophiatown in the early 1950's existed as a prominent African "Black Spot" in Johannesburg's Western Areas, which the South African government sought to eliminate by relocating its population in an area that eventually became a part of Soweto. The antiapartheid African National Congress (ANC) was strongly represented in Sophiatown and led a campaign to resist removal in the years 1953-55. This effort cut across class lines within Sophiatown to include propertyholders and members of criminal tsotsi gangs, but it was unable to mobilize sufficient support and seriously impair, let alone block, the removals. Based on published and unpublished reports and surveys, trial records, interviews, newspapers, and secondary notes; 107 notes. L. W. Truschel

3991. Manganyi, N. C. BIOGRAPHY: THE BLACK SOUTH AFRICAN CONNECTION. Friedson, Anthony M., ed. *New Directions in Biography* (Honolulu, U. Pr. of Hawaii for the Biog. Res. Center, 1981): 52-61. Applies Western criteria to the prospects for autobiography in particular, and biographical writing in general, in cultures such as the black society in South Africa. J

3992. Marable, W. Manning. A BLACK SCHOOL IN SOUTH AFRICA. *Negro Hist. Bull. 1974 37(4): 258-261.* Describes the technical education given Africans, 1900-30's, by John Langalibalela Dube, an American, at his Ohlange Institute in Natal, South Africa.

3993. Marks, Shula. THE AMBIGUITIES OF DEPENDENCE: JOHN L. DUBE OF NATAL. *J. of Southern African Studies [Great Britain] 1975 1(2): 162-179.* The most dramatic grass roots resistance to white rule in the 20th century has come from Natal, where the contradictions between white theory, i.e., paternalism, and white practice, i.e., exploitation, have been most blatant. Examines the role of John L. Dube (b. 1871), whose career as a black leader was akin to that of Booker T. Washington of the United States and reflects some of the complexities of the racial situation. Based on the press and private papers; 92 notes. S. P. Carr

3994. Mechanic, David. APARTHEID MEDICINE. *Society 1973 10(3): 36-44.* Overview of the inequalities of medical care for whites and blacks in South Africa. S

3995. Merwe, D. W. van der. BOCHUM-BLAUBERG: DIE ONTSTAAN, STIGTING EN ONTWIKKELING VAN DIE HELENE FRANZ-HOSPITAAL, 1895-1935 [Bochum-Blauberg: the origin, foundation, and development of the Helene Franz Hospital, 1895-1935]. *Kleio [South Africa] 1978 10(1-2): 2-20.* Discusses the fight against syphilis among Africans in South Africa and the role of Robert Franz (d. 1919) and his wife Helene (1866-1935) of the Berlin Mission Society. Helene's medical training and free treatment at the Frosts' personal expense at the mission station attracted the natives. By 1905, the government financed a syphilis hospital in Bochum, headed by Helene until her death, in which tuberculosis also was treated after syphilis declined, and added a Leper Institute in 1914, all run by the Frost family. Archival and secondary sources; 96 notes. G. Herritt

3996. Merwe, I. J. van der. DIFFERENTIAL URBANIZATION IN SOUTH AFRICA. *Geography [Great Britain] 1973 58(4): 335-339.* The arrival of the first white settlers at the Cape in 1652 provided a stimulus to urbanization in South Africa, a process which occurred along the coast. Rural primary economic activities were predominant until the discovery of diamonds and gold between 1871 and 1886. The intensification of urbanization then occurred, and the first census was taken in 1904 when the total urban population was 23.6 percent; by 1970 it had risen to 47.9 percent—considerably higher than the 21 percent for developing countries but well below the 61 percent of developed countries. The growth rates of the white, Coloured and Asian groups are best compared to the developed countries, while the less urbanized Africans with a higher growth rate should be compared to the developing countries. Table, 2 figs. E. P. Stickney

3997. Meyer, Lysle. A REPORT ON SOUTH AFRICA'S BLACK UNIVERSITIES. *Issue 1974 4(3): 12-18.* Evaluates political and racial abuse in the administration, faculty, curriculum and learning environment of South Africa's separate African colleges. S

3998. Mphahlele, Ezekiel. SOUTH AFRICA: TWO COMMUNITIES AND THE STRUGGLE FOR A BIRTHRIGHT. *J. of African Studies 1977 4(1): 21-50.* A noted South African novelist broadly assesses Afrikaner and African nationalism in South Africa during the past three centuries. He asserts a basic unity of culture, language, and political interests among Bantu-speaking peoples comparable to, though incompatible with, the pronounced sense of community attained by the Afrikaans-speaking group since 1875. Secondary works; 9 notes, biblio. L. W. Truschel

3999. Munger, Ned. POPPIE AND HER BOSWELL. *Munger Africana Lib. Notes 1981 (58): 3-12.* A brief biography of Elsa Joubert, author of *The Long Journey of Poppie Nongena,* a novel that traces the suffering of a black woman and her family in South Africa. Includes an essay on the historical and political significance of this work.

4000. Nicholson, Frederick. FREDERICK NICHOLSON OF HEATHFIELD. *Africana Notes and News [South Africa] 1977 22(5): 201-211.* Extracts from the diary of Frederick Nicholson (1880-1967). Includes his thoughts on his parents, brothers, home, and education. Nicholson was the third member of his family to leave England for South Africa, 1901. The diary covers his early years there with comments on land leases of the 1930's and events during World War II. H. G. Soff

4001. Nkomo, Mokubung O. THE CONTRADICTIONS OF BANTU EDUCATION. *Harvard Educ. Rev. 1981 51(1): 126-138.* Discusses the South African apartheid government's use of higher education as a tool for promoting a policy of separate development, and disturbances in South African universities that might contribute to the demise of the apartheid system.

4002. Nöthling, F. J. DIE VESTIGING VAN NIE-BLANKES IN BRAKPAN 1888-1930 [The settlement of nonwhites in Brakpan, 1888-1930]. *Kleio [South Africa] 1973 5(1): 14-38.* Deals with the necessity of settling the increasing number of nonwhite workers after Brakpan's economic rise through gold production (1903), and the difficulties and delays in acquiring a suitable area outside the city, whose charter allowed whites only to live there. Building finally started in 1927.

4003. Ogunghesan, Kolawole. THE POLITICAL NOVELS OF PETER ABRAHAMS. *Phylon 1973 34(4): 419-432.* Discusses the political novels of Peter Abrahams, a South African novelist living in Jamaica. S

4004. Peart-Binns, John S. AMBROSE REEVES: PRELATE, RECONCILER, REVOLUTIONARY. *Contemporary Rev. [Great Britain] 1973 222(1286): 134-140.* Discusses the role in South African life of Ambrose Reeves (b. 1899) as Anglican Bishop of Johannesburg, 1949-60, and his revolutionary activities.

4005. Preston-Whyte, Eleanor and Sibisi, Harriet. ETHNOGRAPHIC ODDITY OR ECOLOGICAL SENSE? NYUSWA-ZULU DESCENT GROUPS AND LAND ALLOCATION. *African Studies [South Africa] 1975 34(4): 283-316.* Focuses on the "informal yet vital role played by local lineage segments in the process of land allocation in certain Natal Nguni societies" as an example of the differences which occur in the nature "and operation of descent groups in Bantu-speaking societies." A detailed examination of the manner in which lands have been allocated among the Nyuswa-Zulu descent group suggests that descendants of early settlers have dominated land holdings and that this has been ecologically beneficial owing to population density and land scarcity. Based on field research; table, 5 figs, 26 notes, biblio., 3 appendixes. J. A. Casada

4006. Randall, Peter. SPRO-CAS: SOME PUBLISHING PROBLEMS. *Africa Today 1974 21(2): 75-78.* Summarizes the publishing problems of SPRO-CAS I (Study Project on Christianity in an Apartheid Society) and SPRO-CAS II (Special Project for Christian Action in Society) which issued 25 publications for the Christian Institute of South Africa in the South African Council of Churches. The South African government used many means to stop publication. G. O. Gagnon

4007. Reitz, J. F. THE REITZ FAMILY IN SOUTH AFRICA. *Africana Notes and News [South Africa] 1978 23(3): 105-108.* Discusses several members of the Reitz family that originated in Pomerania in the 15th century and then spread to many countries, including South Africa where a centennial has been held at Swellendam to commemorate the 1877 family gathering.

4008. Rotberg, Robert I. TWO SOCIETIES, BOTH UNFREE. *Rev. in Am. Hist. 1982 10(1): 1-6.* Reviews George M. Fredrickson's *White Supremacy: A Comparative Study in American and South African History* (1981), which compares the American South and South Africa and traces the history of race relations in both locations from the 18th to the 20th centuries.

4009. Schauder, D. E. LIBRARIANS AND APARTHEID. *Int. Lib. Rev. [Great Britain] 1978 10(4): 335-344.* Examines the effects of apartheid on libraries in South Africa in terms of racial classification, separate facilities, separate education, and labor laws; and explores ethics, human rights, and political impartiality within the library profession, 1950's-78.

4010. Scher, D. M. THE JEWISH EXPERIENCE IN SOUTH AFRICA, 1910-1967. *Kleio [South Africa] 1981 13(1-2): 46-49.* Reviews G. Shimoni's *Jews and Zionism: The South African Experience 1910-1967* (1980), a history of the post-Union Jewish community in South Africa. J. Powell

4011. Schutte, A. G. DUAL RELIGIOUS ORIENTATION IN AN URBAN AFRICAN CHURCH. *African Studies [South Africa] 1974 33(2): 113-120.* Identifies two spheres of religion—public and private—which African members of a Dutch Reformed Church in Soweto associated with two sets of beliefs and practices. Ancestor worship and cultism had great importance in the private sphere whereas Christianity stood out in the public sphere. The fusion of these two sets of beliefs came in the concept of spirit. The author attempts "to discover the manner and extent to which the idea of the *Spirit* has permitted church members to integrate the private sphere into the public sphere in a meaningful way." Primary and secondary sources; 11 notes. J. A. Casada

4012. Sharp, John. THE ROOTS AND DEVELOPMENT OF *VOLKEKUNDE* IN SOUTH AFRICA. *J. of Southern African Studies [Great Britain] 1981 8(1): 16-36.* The *Volkekunde* school of anthropology dominant in several leading Afrikaans universities in South Africa assigns determinative roles to the ethnic cultures of particular population groups. Associated also with long-standing German romanticist notions concerning the state, South African *Volkekunde* developed within the Afrikaner nationalist movement from the late 1920's and 1930's, becoming a major intellectual pillar of official Separate Development policy in later years. Based on South African university theses in anthropology and unpublished papers; 88 notes. L. W. Truschel

4013. Sheer, Vivienne. ETIENNE LEROUX'S *SEWE DAE BY DIE SILBERSTEINS:* A REEXAMINATION IN THE LIGHT OF ITS HISTORICAL CONTEXT. *J. of Southern African Studies [Great Britain] 1982 8(2): 173-186.* When the Afrikaans novel *Sewe Dae by die Silbersteins*[Seven days with the Silbersteins] appeared in 1962, critics pronounced it a revolutionary breakthrough in an Afrikaner New Left, due to its presentation, in lurid detail, of a liberal-radical alternative to the Christian Nationalist outlook of most Afrikaners. In South Africa, the novel, by its graphic description of immoral life among the decadent Silberstein family and its purposeful spread to morally pure Afrikaners, had the intent and effect of arousing opinion against an alien conspiracy of liberals and Communists to corrupt and finally destroy the Afrikaner and his culture. Based on newspapers and secondary sources; 42 notes. L. W. Truschel

4014. Smith, A. H. EDUCATIONAL FACILITIES IN EARLY JOHANNESBURG. *Africana Notes and News [South Africa] 1976 22(1): 13-22.* Continued from an earlier article. Studies Johannesburg schools dating from 1902. Brief histories are given of several schools including Park Town School, Spes Bona School, and the Troyeville Schools. H. G. Soff

4015. Smith, Anna H. EMBROIDERED SILK POST CARDS. *Africana Notes and News [South Africa] 1982 25(3): 97-101.* Describes 17 embroidered silk postcards now in the Africana Museum of South Africa. The table describing the cards lists the design, message, letter, publisher, and donor of each card. Some were made in France and others in South Africa during the 1930's. J. Powell

4016. Smith, Anna H. JOHANNESBURG MEDALS AND TOKENS. *Africana Notes and News [South Africa] 1974 21(2): 67-72.* Traces the history of medals in Johannesburg including those that honored events such as a boxing championship in 1889, the Jameson Raid of 1895-96, agricultural shows, and the Johannesburg Empire Exhibition of 1936. In addition to official medals, organizations (the Operatic Society) have issued commemorative medals. Address given to the South Africa Numismatic Convention in 1974. H. G. Soff

4017. Stadler, A. W. BIRDS IN THE CORNFIELD: SQUATTER MOVEMENTS IN JOHANNESBURG, 1944-1947. *J. of Southern African Studies [Great Britain] 1979 6(1): 93-123.* Illegal camps of migrant African workers and job-seekers were formed in and around African locations in the Johannesburg area in the mid-1940's. These squatter settlements were generally said to have resulted from the wartime housing shortage that existed in the city and its African locations and were eventually demolished by the municipal authorities. To this actual housing shortage, added factors included the growing land hunger on the African reserves of South Africa, the massive wartime labor influx into the industrial areas, and the high rate of African unemployment and low wages, which resulted in a widespread inability to pay rents demanded by location housing authorities. At the outset, a number of leaders appeared among these incipient squatters. While unable to resist the local authorities in their determination to remove the settlements, these leaders are depicted not as the authoritarian bullies described in official sources, but as political class leaders among their people. Based on published documents; 94 notes. L. W. Truschel

4018. Stadler, Alf. ANXIOUS RADICALS: SPRO-CAS AND THE APARTHEID SOCIETY. *J. of Southern African Studies [Great Britain] 1975 2(1): 102-108.* The Study Project of Christianity in Apartheid Society was established in 1969 to explore the possibilities and problems of creating an alternative social order to apartheid in South Africa. Lists and examines the reports published to date. Biblio. S. P. Carr

4019. Stokes, Randall. RACISM VS. MODERNITY. *Worldview 1974 17(4): 5-12.* Despite the increasing modernization in South Africa in the past decade, race relations have deteriorated and the policy of apartheid has strengthened. This is attributable to the monolithic white Afrikaner culture, religion, National Party, and economic community which insist upon the threat to their survival posed by the African masses since the 1830's.

4020. Stokes, Randall G. AFRIKANER CALVINISM AND ECONOMIC ACTION: THE WEBERIAN THESIS IN SOUTH AFRICA. *Am. J. of Sociol. 1975 81(1): 62-81.* Examines the relationship between traditional Afrikaner religion and worldly action. The specific question addressed is why Afrikaner Calvinism, which is theologically identical to European Calvinism of the 18th century, had a highly conservative impact on economic action, in contrast to the European case. The theoretical position put forward is that any analysis of religion's secular impact must be contextual and focus upon what is here termed "operant religion," meaning religious belief as it has been actualized within the actor's phenomenal world. The major substantive portions of the paper are concerned with an explication of the way in which the social and historical context of Afrikaner Calvinism shaped Afrikaner operant religion, and secondly, with the resulting consequences for economic action. J

4021. Stone, John. THE "MIGRANT FACTOR" IN A PLURAL SOCIETY: A SOUTH AFRICAN CASE STUDY. *Int. Migration Rev. 1975 9(1): 15-28.* Studies British migration to South Africa from 1820 to the present, showing how British immigration heightened both the black-white and English-Afrikaans conflicts in South African society.

4022. Strebel, Elizabeth Grottle. THE VOORTREKKERS: A CINEMATOGRAPHIC REFLECTION OF RISING AFRIKANER NATIONALISM. *Film and Hist. 1979 9(2): 25-32.* Discusses the Afrikaner film, *The Voortrekkers* (1916) which depicts the Great Trek of Boer emigration from the Cape to Natal in 1837, the slaying of Voortrekker leader Piet Retief and his party by Zulus under Dingaan, and the Boer victory over the Zulus in the 1838 Battle of Blood River. The film was designed to promote nationalism in the Afrikaner people, recently defeated in the Anglo-Boer War of 1899-1902.

4023. Terblanche, H. O. DIE TREK VAN DIE AFRIKANER NA PORT ELIZABETH [The Afrikaners' trek to Port Elisabeth]. *Historia [South Africa] 1977 22(2): 90-107.* Discusses the emigration of impoverished white farmers to cities like Port Elisabeth, where between 1904 to 1960 their share in the total white population increased from 3.9% to 41.4%, which caused great unemployment and housing problems.

4024. Terblanche, H. O. LOUISA MEYBURGH: HELDIN VAN DIE STAD [Louisa Meyburgh: town heroine]. *Historia [South Africa] 1979 24(2): 12-20; 1980 25(1): 2-13.* Part I. Relates the life of Louisa Fredericka Meyburgh (1876-1956) and her work in Port Elizabeth on behalf of the Afrikaner minority and the Dutch Reformed Church. After coming to Port Elizabeth from Graaff-Reinet in 1900, Louisa devoted herself to the spiritual education and welfare of the small and poor Afrikaner community that was part of the church district Uitenhage. There she took upon herself many of its minister's duties, thus helping to lay the foundation for the establishment in 1907 of Port Elizabeth's own Dutch Reformed Church, in which she became a salaried assistant. Part II. ARMESORGWERK [Poor relief work]. Deals with the work of Louisa Meyburgh in Port Elizabeth as assistant in the Dutch Reformed Church from 1907 to her official retirement in 1940 and later. Louisa's care for the spiritual, social, and economic welfare of Afrikaners extended to visiting them at home, in hospitals, and in factories, finding them housing and employment, and promoting their social life through church activities. Based on L. Meyburgh's diaries and other primary sources; 112 notes. G. Herritt

4025. Wade, Michael. MYTH, TRUTH AND THE SOUTH AFRICAN REALITY IN THE FICTION OF SARAH GERTRUDE MILLIN. *J. of Southern African Studies [Great Britain] 1974 1(1): 91-108.* Examines the preoccupations and prejudices displayed by Sarah G. Millin in her career as a novelist, which spanned the years 1917-65. She emerges as a spokeswoman for the majority of white English-speaking South Africans. Her relatively narrow repertoire of situations consistently express the most mechanistic racial determinism. In her novels, racially mixed marriages are common, ending always in unhappiness, and the characters consistently feel, act, and develop as Millin's compatriots would expect. England is presented as the source of immature and shallow notions of racial equality which are irrelevant to the South African experience. Discusses the Millin novel *God's Stepchildren* (1924), in detail. 11 notes. L. W. Van Wyk

4026. Walshe, Peter. CHURCH VERSUS STATE IN SOUTH AFRICA: THE CHRISTIAN INSTITUTE AND THE RESURGENCE OF AFRICAN NATIONALISM. *J. of Church and State 1977 19(3): 457-479.* Reviews the development of ecumenical and interracial organizations following the withdrawal of the Dutch Reformed Church from the World Council in 1960. The Christian Institute's formation, policies, and relation to the churches are discussed, as well as its place in the resurgence of African nationalism. 4 notes. E. E. Eminhizer

4027. Wauthier, Claude. LA PRESSE EN AFRIQUE DU SUD [The press in South Africa]. *Rev. Française d'Études Pol. Africaines [France] 1973 (88): 64-73.* Studies the lack of important African newspapers and television programming in South Africa, which symbolizes the apartheid, the strict segregation, and the European repression since colonization, ca. 1900-73, and examines attempts at small publications in African languages, notably those by the African National Congress, after 1912.

4028. West, M. E. INDEPENDENCE AND UNITY: PROBLEMS OF CO-OPERATION BETWEEN AFRICAN INDEPENDENT CHURCH LEADERS IN SOWETO. *African Studies [South Africa] 1974 33(2): 121-129.* The normal approach to the independent church movement in Africa focuses on the divisiveness and leadership disputes which plague it, but this article examines cohesive factors in the movement. Areas where there is cooperation include association for the purpose of presenting a more unified front to authority, in fund raising projects, and in theological education. These considerations are evaluated against leadership struggles and recognition of their social and political implications. Based on field research and printed sources; 13 notes, biblio. J. A. Casada

4029. Wright, George V. RACISM IN SPORT: AN UPDATE. *Africa Today 1974 21(2): 9-14.* Analyzes South Africa's response to the nearly complete ban on international athletic participation imposed by the various amateur athletic associations. Since 1970, nonwhites have been allowed to compete with whites in South Africa but apartheid is enforced in seating, organization, and elsewhere. Readmission of South Africa to international competition is doubtful. Based on secondary sources; 29 notes. G. O. Gagnon

4030. Zungu, Yeyedwa. THE EDUCATION FOR AFRICANS IN SOUTH AFRICA. *J. of Negro Educ. 1977 46(3): 202-218.* African education was instituted by the apartheid government of South Africa in 1954 as an integral part of its Bantustan program and continued a tradition of inadequate schooling for colonized Africans that began in the early 1800's. Both systems sought to maintain a racially stratified society and a pliant black working population. But the resistance of the Africans will doom "Bantu" education to failure. Based on secondary sources; 3 tables, 20 notes. R. E. Butchart

4031. —. EDUCATION AND SOCIAL CONTROL IN SOUTH AFRICA. *African Affairs [Great Britain] 1979 78(311): 228-239.* African education serves to legitimize the prevailing inequalities in South Africa, extend white dominance, and encourage apartheid. The major contradiction in the educational system is the creation of a situation of cultural dependency (wants) on foreign technology, medicine, ideology, and art forms, while simultaneously generating forces (expectations) opposed to the dominance of the groups who live off the system. Such a contradiction has incited conflicts over wants and expectations. Based on a University of Michigan doctoral dissertation; 60 notes. S. Lakhan

Swaziland

4032. Crush, Jonathan S. NATIONAL PARKS IN AFRICA: A NOTE ON A PROBLEM OF INDIGENIZATION. *African Studies Rev. 1980 23(3): 21-32.* A study of the administration of national parks in Swaziland. The parks can survive only if they are able to overcome their image in African minds as playgrounds for foreign elites. Based on Swaziland government documents; 2 maps, chart, 12 notes, biblio. R. T. Brown

4033. Crush, Jonathan S. THE PARAMETERS OF DEPENDENCE IN SOUTHERN AFRICA: A CASE STUDY OF SWAZILAND. *J. of Southern African Affairs 1979 4(1): 55-66.* A radical perspective on the political economy of the kingdom of Swaziland, viewing it as relentlessly bound up with South Africa and South African companies. The neocolonial dependence of Swaziland on South Africa was achieved with British cooperation during the colonial era and that since independence in 1968 the kingdom has been unable to attract overseas capital and aid to achieve a diversified dependence. Secondary sources; table, 34 notes. L. W. Truschel

4034. Funnell, D. C. CHANGES IN FARM INCOMES AND THE RURAL DEVELOPMENT PROGRAM IN SWAZILAND. *J. of Developing Areas 1982 16(2): 271-290.* Assuming that the Rural Development Area Program, the centerpiece of plans to raise the income of the majority of Swaziland's population, is successfully implemented during the project period of 1977-99, the per capita net farm income should rise from approximately $26 to about $36.80. If the program is not implemented or fails, there will be a decline of per capita net farm income to $14.40. About two-thirds of the projected increase would be absorbed in maintaining income levels even with expected population increase. Even if it succeeds the program can only be described as a "holding operation," which will also have little impact on the urban-rural income gap. Map, 3 fig., 8 tables. V. Samaraweera

4035. Potholm, Christian. SWAZILAND UNDER SOBHUZA II: THE FUTURE OF AN AFRICAN MONARCHY. *Round Table [Great Britain] 1974 (254): 219-227.* Discusses the repeal of the Swazi constitution and the temporary assumption of power by the present monarch Ngwenyama Sobhuza II in 1973. This step, taken by an aging king, presents a unique situation in post-colonial Africa. Outlines the pattern of decolonization in Swaziland, the nature of the Swazi monarchy, and the disposition of political forces. Notes that the Swazi economy and society will face a major test of stability on the death of the present king. 10 notes. D. H. Murdoch

4036. Proctor, J. H. TRADITIONALISM AND PARLIAMENTARY GOVERNMENT IN SWAZILAND. *African Affairs [Great Britain] 1973 72(288): 273-287.* The Paramount Chief of the Swazi, in concert with local councils, is the most powerful traditional authority operating in independent Africa. The author analyzes the contrasts between traditional and Westminster models. Sobhuza II on 12 April 1973 repealed the Constitution and dissolved all political associations, claiming they represented alien ideologies. 24 notes. H. G. Soff

4037. Youé, C. P. IMPERIAL LAND POLICY IN SWAZILAND AND THE AFRICAN RESPONSE. *J. of Imperial and Commonwealth Hist. [Great Britain] 1978 7(1): 56-70.* Using the land claim problems in Swaziland as an analogy, investigates the thesis that land claims would have faired better in Southern Rhodesia if it had been possible for them to have been presented directly to the British imperial authorities instead of to the British South Africa Company or, after 1923, to the white settlers themselves. Examines negotiations from the beginning of the century until independence and shows that until 1940 British land policy in Swaziland was as restrictive as that of the British South Africa Company and settler governments in Southern Rhodesia. In the government view Swazi "rights" did not exist, a view which had ultimately to be accepted. Even attempts to buy title rights were largely frustrated. 2 fig., 65 notes. R. V. Ritter

Zambia

4038. Alford, B. W. E. and Harvey, C. E. COPPERBELT MERGER: THE FORMATION OF THE RHOKANA CORPORATION, 1930-1932. *Business Hist. Rev. 1980 54(3): 330-358.* Examines a key 1930 merger of three mining companies in the Zambian Copperbelt. The Rhodesian Congo Border Concession, N'Changa Copper Mines Ltd., and Bwana M'Kubwa Copper Mining Company Ltd. formed the Rhokana Corporation. The facts of this particular merger are measured against former merger theory. The activities of "insider" shareholders, a major factor in the promotion of Rhokana, has been given too little attention by analysts. The Rhokana merger defies the precepts of the formal theory of mergers. Based largely on company records; 4 tables, 70 notes. C. J. Pusateri

4039. Andrews, Loretta Kreider and Andrews, Herbert D. THE CHURCH AND THE BIRTH OF A NATION: THE MINDOLO ECUMENICAL FOUNDATION AND ZAMBIA. *J. of Church and State 1975 17(2): 191-216.* Missionaries established the Mindolo Ecumenical Foundation in Zambia in the 1950's and 1960's.

4040. Anglin, Douglas G. ZAMBIA AND SOUTHERN AFRICAN "DÉTENTE'. *Int. J. [Canada] 1975 30(3): 471-503.* Suggests that Zambia's willingness to negotiate with racist regimes is not founded on acceptance of detente but rather on the belief of Kenneth Kaunda that such contact may minimize racial conflagration in the process of the liberation of black South Africans. Table, 31 notes. R. V. Kubicek

4041. Bates, Robert H. and Bennett, Bruce W. DETERMINANTS OF THE RURAL EXODUS IN ZAMBIA: A STUDY OF INTERCENSAL MIGRATION 1963-1969. *Cahiers d'Études Africaines [France] 1974 14(3): 543-564.* Analyzes factors leading to integral migration, concluding that though there was some regional variation, factors which led to migration tended to affect the country as a whole. These factors were the high ratio of males to females, the number of educated people, and the poverty of the district. Based on statistical analysis of government censuses and published materials; 18 notes. B. S. Fetter

4042. Bates, Robert H. RURAL DEVELOPMENT IN KASUMPA VILLAGE, ZAMBIA. *J. of African Studies 1975 2(3): 333-362.* This study of the response of the members of Kasumpa village to the government's agricultural development programs makes apparent that development, political protest, and rural emigration to urban areas are interdependent phenomena. Rural development largely failed and political protest resulted. Seeking their own solutions by using the urban market for labor and sending family members to the city, rural residents discovered they could thereby provide for themselves a form of social and economic security. 17 tables, 16 notes. R. V. Ritter

4043. Baylies, Carolyn L. and Szeftel, Morris. THE RISE OF A ZAMBIAN CAPITALIST CLASS IN THE 1970S. *J. of Southern African Studies [Great Britain] 1982 8(2): 187-213.* A new class of native capitalists has arisen in Zambia since independence in 1964, able to accumulate capital through association with the government and the ruling United National Independence Party. Some of the new capitalists of Zambia went so far as to challenge the rule of President Kaunda in 1980, but as a class they have thus far been kept from political power. Based on unpublished Zambian documents and newspapers; table, 56 notes. L. W. Truschel

4044. Beveridge, Andrew A. ECONOMIC INDEPENDENCE, INDIGENIZATION, AND THE AFRICAN BUSINESSMAN: SOME EFFECTS OF ZAMBIA'S ECONOMIC REFORMS. *African Studies Rev. 1974 17(3): 477-490.* Considers the economic policies introduced by the Zambian government since the 1960's and the resulting improvements for African businessmen.

4045. Binsbergen, W. M. J. van. RELIGIOUS INNOVATION AND POLITICAL CONFLICT IN ZAMBIA: A CONTRIBUTION TO THE INTERPRETATION OF THE LUMPA RISING. *African Perspectives [Netherlands] 1976 (2): 101-135.* Assesses the conflict which erupted in 1964 between the new nationalist government of Zambia and the Lumpa religious movement of Alice Lenshina. Social and economic change in Zambia by 1964 had brought the Lumpa sect and the nationalist United National Independence Party into conflict over the loyalty of Bemba peasants in the northeastern area of the country. The leaders and adherents of the Lumpa sect became violently opposed to the postcolonial state and as such have been an acute embarrassment to the Zambian authorities. Zambian and outside scholars dependent on official support inside the country have maintained a near silence on the bloody conflict that followed. Based on field research and archival and secondary sources; 29 notes, biblio. L. W. Truschel

4046. Bond, George Clement. NEW COALITIONS AND TRADITIONAL CHIEFTAINSHIP IN NORTHERN ZAMBIA: THE POLITICS OF LOCAL GOVERNMENT IN UYOMBE. *Africa [Great Britain] 1975 45(4): 348-362.* Independence has siphoned off the most able and progressive members of rural chiefdoms, who go to the national government, leaving local authority increasingly in the hands of traditional and conservative elements.

4047. Brown, Richard. PASSAGES IN THE LIFE OF A WHITE ANTHROPOLOGIST: MAX GLUCKMAN IN NORTHERN RHODESIA. *J. of African Hist. [Great Britain] 1979 20(4): 525-541.* From 1939 through 1947, Max Gluckman served as Assistant Anthropologist and Director of the Rhodes-Livingstone Institute, and researched among the Lozi of Barotseland. He shifted from academic aloofness to involvement with the administration as a result of both personal matters and the national unifying effect of World War II. He was successful in organizing social research through local institutes, but not in engaging directly in practical affairs. While his influence on colonial evolution was indirect, his position was in harmony with trends toward decolonization. 86 notes. A. W. Novitsky

4048. Burawoy, Michael. CONSCIOUSNESS AND CONTRADICTION: A STUDY OF STUDENT PROTEST IN ZAMBIA. *British J. of Sociol. [Great Britain] 1976 27(1): 78-98.* Discusses the student demonstrations from the founding of the University of Zambia in 1966 to their peak in 1971 to show both the structural contradictions activated by the student protests and the changes in Zambia in its transition from colonial rule to independence.

4049. Burawoy, Michael. THE HIDDEN ABODE OF UNDERDEVELOPMENT: LABOR PROCESS AND THE STATE IN ZAMBIA. *Pol. & Soc. 1982 11(2): 123-166.* Challenges the conventional theories of underdevelopment on the grounds that they neglect to take into account relations in the modes of production and the social formations that take place at the periphery as the state moves from colonialism to political independence. A historical examination of changing mining practices in South Africa and a case study of mining in Zambia based on participant observer and interview techniques undertaken in 1971 demonstrate that the labor processes and international relations impose limits on the "apparatuses of production and the apparatuses of the state." Based on participant observation and interviews; 66 notes. D. G. Nielson

4050. Burdette, Marcia M. NATIONALIZATION IN ZAMBIA: A CRITIQUE OF BARGAINING THEORY. *Can. J. of African Studies [Canada] 1977 11(3): 471-496.* Examines the 1969-76 nationalization of privately owned industry by the government of Zambia as part of a series of reforms called the Zambian Economic Revolution. Views the history of the cancellation of contracts and the nationalization of the copper industry (1973) at huge governmental expense, and the resulting contribution to the creation of severe economic recession in Zambia. Studies the effect of poor management, powerful external factors, and negotiations between multinational corporations and the Zambian government on the evolution of the political economy. Concludes that Third World countries dependent on metropolitan economies cannot afford to antagonize international corporations that dominate their economies without serious disruption. Secondary sources; 116 notes. S. Sevilla

4051. Calmettes, Jean-Loup. UN CONFLIT POLITICO-RELIGIEUX EN ZAMBIE: LES ENSEIGNEMENTS DE LA CRISE LUMPA [A politico-religious conflict in Zambia: the lessons of the Lumpa crisis]. *Cultures et Développement [Belgium] 1980 12(2): 195-233.* Relates the history of the Lumpa Church founded by Alice Lenshina in 1954 in Zambia; stresses its evolution, its politico-religious conflict in 1964 with the United National Independence Party (UNIP), and its dissolution in 1965.

4052. Chauncey, George, Jr. THE LOCUS OF REPRODUCTION: WOMEN'S LABOUR IN THE ZAMBIAN COPPERBELT, 1927-1953. *J. of Southern African Studies [Great Britain] 1981 7(2): 135-164.* Great Britain's colonial administration and the local Native Authorities in colonial Zambia opposed the migration of African women from rural areas to the industrial copperbelt region, the government fearing proletarianization of rural society and the local elders resenting their loss of authority and labor. The mining companies, however, took positive steps to encourage this migration, since women on the copperbelt made substantial economic and social contributions by providing food, housekeeping, and other supportive services for the miners. Based on official Zambian colonial and company documents and reports and on interviews; 111 notes. L. W. Truschel

4053. Chikulo, B. C. POPULAR PARTICIPATION AND DEVELOPMENT: THE ZAMBIAN MODEL. *Africa Q. [India] 1979 19(2): 170-181.* Examines the organization and character of popular participation in local government in Zambia.

4054. Chuvaeva, M. ZAMBIIA: 15 LET STROITEL'STVA I BOR'BY [Zambia: 15 years of building and fighting]. *Aziia i Afrika Segodnia [USSR] 1979 (10): 6-9.* Traces the main stages of the socioeconomic reforms carried out in the country, the most highly developed in tropical Africa, after the achievement of independence. Pays special attention to the anti-immperialist and anticolonialist stand taken by Zambia in the world arena and to the development of Soviet-Zambian contacts in economics, politics, and culture. J

4055. Cliffe, Lionel. LABOUR MIGRATION AND PEASANT DIFFERENTIATION: ZAMBIAN EXPERIENCES. *J. of Peasant Studies [Great Britain] 1978 5(3): 326-346.* Peasants in Zambia, as elsewhere in Southern Africa, were drawn into the world economy as labour migrants, and even now, when urban employment is more permanent, the rural areas are given over more to the reproduction of labour than to the production of commodities. The resulting general impoverishment has not, however, precluded significant differentiation among the various regional peasantries. Moreover, in these peasantries, where many men are absent, changes in property rights related to kinship and the division of labour between sexes take place. Differentiation and the special position of women have to be taken into account in assessing the political potential in societies whose complexity gives special meaning to the "worker-peasant alliance." J

4056. Colson, Elizabeth. FROM LIVINGSTONE TO LUSAKA, 1948-51. *African Social Res. [Zambia] 1977 (24): 297-306.* The memoirs of Elizabeth Colson, who succeeded Max Gluckman as director of the Rhodes-Livingstone Institute in 1948. The building was then being renovated, though funds were not adequate for proper research or for paying a director's salary. Priority was put on developing a research plan to bolster the institute's appeal for funding. When Colson resigned in 1951, new staff had been hired and research was well underway as was the institute's move to the new headquarters at Lusaka. Appendix. H. G. Soff

4057. Colson, Elizabeth. THE INSTITUTE UNDER MAX GLUCKMAN, 1942-47. *African Social Res. [Zambia] 1977 (24): 285-294.* From 1942, when Max Gluckman became director of the Rhodes-Livingstone Institute, until 1946 he was the only researcher on the staff. He carried out field work on Lozi law and believed that the results of research should be made available to the people of Africa. He therefore encouraged institute publications. He initiated the separation of the museum and the institute and continually planned for the future of the institute. He resigned in 1947 to accept a post at Oxford University. Appendix. H. G. Soff

4058. Cross, Sholto. POLITICS AND CRITICISM IN ZAMBIA: A REVIEW ARTICLE. *J. of Southern African Studies [Great Britain] 1974 1(1): 109-115.* Review article on five recent books on Zambian politics: Jan Pettman, *Zambia: Security and Conflict* (London: Julian Friedman Publishers, 1974), Kenneth Kaunda, *Letter to My Children* (London: Longman, 1973), Henry S. Meebelo, *Main Currents of Zambian Humanist Thought* (Lusaka; Oxford U. Pr., 1973), Anthony Martin *Minding Their Own Business: Zambia's Struggle Against Western Control* (London: Hutchinson, 1972), and Michael Burawoy *The Color of Class on the Copper Mines: From African Advancement to Zambianisation* (Lusaka: Institute for African Studies, 1972). Kaunda, as president, and Meebelo, as permanent secretary in the Ministry for National Guidance, as well as Pettman and Martin, present a generally favorable view of Zambia's new ruling elite, while Burawoy accuses them of often simply stepping into the shoes of the colonialists. L. W. Van Wyk

4059. Curry, Robert L., Jr. ZAMBIA'S ECONOMIC CRISIS: A CHALLENGE TO BUDGETARY POLITICS. *J. of African Studies 1979-80 6(4): 213-217.* Government revenues fell drastically in the Republic of Zambia during the early and mid-1970's, due to problems within the mining sector and the failure of new tax adjustments designed to promote foreign investments. The finance ministry in early 1977 took public recognition of the fiscal crisis, but failed to offer proposals shifting the tax burden onto the Zambian elite or foreign investors. Based on published documents, newspapers, and secondary sources; table, 24 notes. L. W. Truschel

4060. Derricourt, Robin M. ARCHAEOLOGY IN ZAMBIA—AN HISTORICAL OUTLINE. *African Social Res. [Zambia] 1976 (21): 31-50.* A summary of archaeological activity in Zambia since 1905 and prospects for the future. Among the more noteworthy events have been the discovery of *Homo rhodesiensis* (1921), the passage of Ordinance No. 5 (1930), the rock paintings discovered at Nsalu (1936), the appointment of J. Desmond Clark as curator of the museum (1938), and Clark's studies at Kalambo Falls (1953-66). 2 figs, 9 notes, appendix. H. G. Soff

4061. Dixon-Fyle, McSamuel. THE SEVENTH DAY ADVENTISTS (S.D.A.) IN THE PROTEST POLITICS OF THE TONGA PLATEAU, NORTHERN RHODESIA. *African Social Res. [Zambia] 1978 26(2): 453-467.* Seventh-Day Adventists' missions with their African ministers and teachers and schools training in agricultural skills quickly became centers of organized resistance to colonial policies. Adventist farmers of Keemba Hill were especially wealthy and so became leaders in the promotion of various opposition policies. Based on British and Zambian archives and interviews; 28 notes. R. T. Brown

4062. Eriksen, Tore Linné. ZAMBIA: DEN VANSKELIGE VEIEN MOT ØKONOMISK UAVHENGIGHET [Zambia: The difficult road toward economic independence]. *Internasjonal Politikk [Norway] 1975 (4): 557-574.* Focuses on strategies of national independence and control of natural resources as well as on efforts to reduce economic and transportation ties with Southern Africa. J

4063. Erikson, Tore Linné. RÅVARER OG PRODUSENTSAMMENSLUTNINGER: KOPPER OG ZAMBIA SOM EKSEMPEL [Raw materials and producer associations: copper and Zambia as examples]. *Internasjonal Politikk [Norway] 1978 (4): 685-709.* Surveys international copper production as a basis for general assessments of raw material actions and the copper producers situation. Further compares structural relations regarding copper and oil, and discusses trends in the relationships between producer countries and industrialized nations. 3 tables, 37 notes. J

4064. Fielder, Robin J. ECONOMIC SPHERES IN PRE-COLONIAL ILA SOCIETY. *African Social Res. [Zambia] 1979: 617-641.* The Ila are a cattle-keeping people of southern Zambia who have developed a complex system of economic spheres of interchange which allows capital accumulation in the form of cattle. Based on field research; 2 charts, biblio. R. T. Brown

4065. Fielder, Robin J. THE ROLE OF CATTLE IN THE ILA ECONOMY: A CONFLICT OF VIEWS ON THE USES OF CATTLE BY THE ILA OF NAMWALA. *African Social Res. [Zambia] 1973 (15): 327-361.* Zambia needs to market more cattle, but many ethnic groups that have cattle refuse to sell them. Anthropologists have often called this irrational, but the author shows that there is a rational economic justification for Ila resistance to selling which is relevant to herders throughout Africa. 21 notes. H. G. Soff

4066. Fincham, Robin. ECONOMIC DEPENDENCE AND THE DEVELOPMENT OF INDUSTRY IN ZAMBIA. *J. of Modern African Studies [Great Britain] 1980 18(2): 297-313.* Analyzes the reasons for Zambia's decline in industrial and mining output, due to international unstable copper prices and the country's dependence on imported goods. Zambia's economic malaise is accentuated by lack of indigenous skills, a small national market, and frequent disruption of supply routes. Based on published government documents and secondary sources; 4 tables, 2 graphs, 34 notes. A. Sbacchi

4067. Fosbrooke, Henry. FROM LUSAKA TO SALISBURY, 1956-60. *African Social Res. [Zambia] 1977 (24): 319-325.* The memoirs of Henry Fosbrooke, who was director of the Rhodes-Livingstone Institute, 1956-60 in Zambia. His first impression was of the heavy government involvement in the institute. He notes special researchers and their projects and his efforts to interest school children in a possible career in social research. He resigned when the institute was turned over to University College. H. G. Soff

4068. Freshwater, Peter B. THE PERSONAL PAPERS OF WILL FRESHWATER (1872-1936): MISSIONARY IN NORTHERN RHODESIA. *African Res. and Documentation [Great Britain] 1978 (18): 15-20.* Discusses the collection of journals and private papers from the years 1897-1933 which describe the work of Will Freshwater, of the London Missionary School, whose contributions in the field of language and translation enhanced the development of Zambia.

4069. Fyle-Dixon, Mac. AGRICULTURAL IMPROVEMENT AND POLITICAL PROTEST ON THE TONGA PLATEAU, NORTHERN RHODESIA. *J. of African Hist. [Great Britain] 1977 18(4): 579-596.* The Tonga, an agricultural people, came under British South Africa Company rule in 1899. Taxes were introduced in 1904 and African surplus was usually sold to pay the tax. Most land was, however, alienated for settlers and this led to the Native Reserves policy. The resulting racial animosity continued until present times. Problems in maize production and soil erosion on African farms led the government in 1936 to establish extension stations on the plateau to demonstrate better techniques. This became known as the Kanchomba system. The system is described and its spread to other areas is discussed. In some cases it was the missionary effort that insured success, in other areas it was the size of the cash bonus. In many districts, however, the scheme was viewed with hostility and suspicion. In 1946 the Improved Farming Scheme was introduced. This scheme and farmers organizations are analyzed, including their entry into the political arena. Map; 106 notes. H. G. Soff

4070. Garvey, Brian. BEMBA CHIEFS AND CATHOLIC MISSIONS, 1898-1935. *J. of African Hist. [Great Britain] 1977 18(3): 411-426.* The French Catholic White Fathers arrived in Zambia in the early 1890's and immediately began to erode the power of traditional Bemba chiefs. The decline in local authority continued and corresponded with a continual rise in mission influence. By the 1930's the chiefs' spiritual authority had reached its nadir. 88 notes. H. G. Soff

4071. Gertzel, Cherry. LABOUR AND THE STATE: THE CASE OF ZAMBIA'S MINEWORKERS UNION: A REVIEW ARTICLE. *J. of Commonwealth and Comparative Pol. [Great Britain] 1975 13(3): 290-304.* Robert H. Bates's *Unions, Parties and Political Development: A Study of Mineworkers in Zambia* (New Haven: Yale U. Pr., 1971) and Michael Burawoy's *The Colour of Class on the Copper-mines*show that whereas unions and nationalist parties cooperated to oppose colonial government, postindependence governments have subordinated unions to the state to eliminate political opposition. Bates is concerned with the Zambian Mineworkers' Union itself and its relations with the government and the party, whereas Burawoy analyzes the attitudes of mineworkers. Burawoy explains the widening gap between union leadership and rank and file in terms of class, whereas Bates does so in terms of race. 27 notes. R. D. Black

4072. Hansen, Art. REFUGEE DYNAMICS: ANGOLANS IN ZAMBIA 1966 TO 1972. *Int. Migration Rev. 1981 15(1-2): 175-194.* Examines the decisionmaking dynamics of refugee movements in the case of extensive self-settlement in Zambia, and briefly compares the welfare of self-settling refugees and those who are in government programs.

4073. Harvey, Charles. RURAL CREDIT IN ZAMBIA: ACCESS AND EXIT. *Development and Change 1975 6(2): 89-105.* Rural credit from banks and government rural credit agencies has been granted to small-scale businessmen and farmers in Zambia since independence in 1964.

4074. Hatch of Lusby, Baron. ZAMBIA: A SPECIAL THIRD WORLD CASE. *Contemporary Rev. [Great Britain] 1982 240(1392): 1-7.* From the suffering caused to Zambia by the Ian Smith regime in Southern Rhodesia and the struggle for Zimbabwean independence has arisen conflict between the consumer-oriented entrepreneurs and the "humanists" led by President Kenneth Kaunda. A. E. Standley

4075. Heisler, Helmuth. THE PATTERN OF MIGRATION IN ZAMBIA. *Cahiers d'Études Africaines [France] 1973 13(2): 193-212.* General descriptions of internal migration in Africa no longer can be said to apply to Zambia. The traditional pattern was one of oscillation between villages organized on the basis of a subsistence economy, and cities, mines, and commercial farms where migrants could find employment for wages. Now, more and more Zambian migrants to urban districts, such as the Copper Belt, stay there permanently. The sex ratio in the towns is also changing, as more women, particularly from southern and central Zambia, move to the city. 3 tables, 49 notes. J. C. Billigmeier

4076. Henderson, Ian. EARLY AFRICAN LEADERSHIP: THE COPPERBELT DISTURBANCES OF 1935 AND 1940. *J. of Southern African Studies [Great Britain] 1975 2(1): 83-97.* On 29 May 1935 six African miners were killed by police in the copperbelt region of what is now Zambia, and on 3 April 1940 16 miners died in similar circumstances. This was the first sign of African industrial grievances and the first intimation of any form of African protest in an area which was later to be the scene of racial conflict. Based on reports in the national archives of Zambia, and newspapers; 52 notes. S. P. Carr

4077. Henderson, Ian. THE ECONOMIC ORIGINS OF DECOLONISATION IN ZAMBIA, 1940-1945. *Rhodesian Hist. [Zimbabwe] 1974 5: 49-66.* Discusses the relationships among economic development plans, African advancement, World War II, and colonial finances. The war provided the white settlers with an opportunity to retrench. Colonial government cooperation with the mines and white workers generally superseded African interests. The formation of the Federation provided additional political focus to the disadvantaged African economic sector. Employs Zambian government and corporation archives, government reports; 5 tables, 59 notes. O. B. Pollak

4078. Henderson, Ian. THE LIMITS OF COLONIAL POWER: RACE AND LABOUR PROBLEMS IN COLONIAL ZAMBIA, 1900-1953. *J. of Imperial and Commonwealth Hist. [Great Britain] 1974 2(3): 294-307.* Examines various methodological approaches such as Eurocentrism, Afrocentrism, and Marxism in the way they can be applied to a specific problem in African history. Shows how, in keeping with Marxist tenets, there was powerful corporative political influence in colonial Zambia, but also stresses that there were counterforces in the form of African and European populism. These factors are considered in light of the problems which faced the colonial regime, which lacked the knowledge, manpower, and funds to implement Africanization. Based on manuscript and published sources; 3 tables, 38 notes.
J. A. Casada

4079. Heron, Alastair. THE YEARS OF TRANSITION, 1963-67. *African Social Res. [Zambia] 1977 (24): 331-334.* The memoirs of Alastair Heron, who became director of the Rhodes-Livingstone Institute in 1963 and intended to make of it a University of Zambia. During his directorship, Zambia became independent and good ties were established between the institute and the new government.
H. G. Soff

4080. Hulec, Otakar. THE CONCORDANCE AND CONTRADICTIONS OF ZAMBIA'S ECONOMY AND POLITICS. *Archív Orientální [Czechoslovakia] 1980 48(1): 22-33.* Discusses the two most important factors influencing the economy and politics of Zambia: its history of colonial domination and the foreign ownership of much of its immense copper resources.

4081. Illarionov, N. S. SOTSIAL'NO-POLITICHESKIE ISTOKI "ZAMBIISKOGO GUMANIZMA" [The sociopolitical sources of "Zambian humanism"]. *Narody Azii i Afriki [USSR] 1974 (2): 17-27.* Discusses contemporary Zambia's ideological approach to the modernization of traditional society as expressed mainly by Kenneth Kaunda's concept of humanistic democratic socialism, to which there are both progressive and reactionary aspects.

4082. Johnson, Walton R. and Offurum, Tony Pascal. THE AFRICAN DIASPORA: OPPORTUNITY FOR PROFITABLE ECONOMIC LINKAGES. *Pan-African J. [Kenya] 1977 10(1): 39-50.* Examines the opportunities for black American entrepreneurs in the economy of Zambia and traces the latter's development. One of the major objectives of the First National Development Plan, 1966-70, was to diversify the copper-based economy. Following the creation of a number of new industries, the Second National Development Plan, 1972-76, placed the expansion of agricultural production as a top priority for the developing economy. Based on data concerning imports, exports, balance of trade, and planned development and investment; 4 tables, 2 notes. F. P. Tudor

4083. Jules-Rosette, Bennetta. MARRAPODI: AN INDEPENDENT RELIGIOUS COMMUNITY IN TRANSITION. *African Studies Rev. 1975 18(2): 1-15.* Examines the development since the 1930's of Marrapodi, a unique community located north of Lusaka, where several different indigenous religious groups have coexisted in peace.

4084. Kanduza, Ackson M. TEACHERS' STRIKE, 1970: A CHAPTER IN ZAMBIA'S LABOUR HISTORY. *Social Hist. [Canada] 1981 14(28): 485-507.* In June 1970, some 20,000 Zambian teachers went on strike, mainly because of inadequate or expensive housing. The strike might have been averted if the government had heeded the Rogers Report on the 1968 teachers' strike. A settlement was negotiated, but subsequent government action against teachers' leaders caused acrimonious relations with the government and helped create union solidarity in Zambia. Based on the Report of the Soko Board of Inquiry, other primary, and secondary sources; map, 64 notes. D. F. Chard

4085. Libby, Ronald T. and Woakes, Michael E. NATIONALIZATION AND THE DISPLACEMENT OF DEVELOPMENT POLICY IN ZAMBIA. *African Studies Rev. 1980 23(1): 33-50.* The Zambian government nationalized the copper industry in 1969 with the intention of freeing the economy from outside interference and with the purpose of gaining additional development funds. The result has been that the government now finds itself tied to supporting a weak industry during a long period of international recession and forced to follow the same profit based motives of previous foreign owners. Based on Zambian government documents; 4 tables, diagram, 2 fig., 21 notes, biblio.
R. T. Brown

4086. Marks, Stuart A. PROFILE AND PROCESS: SUBSISTENCE HUNTERS IN A ZAMBIAN COMMUNITY. *Africa [Great Britain] 1979 49(1): 53-67.* As part of a study of the hunting ecology of the Bisa of the Luangwa Valley, the author describes the society and the hunting, ceremonial, and other cultural traditions of three generations of hunters in the same community. Attention is drawn to the effects of prevailing social conditions, the role of the government as an agent of social change, and the implications for the future of the Bisa subsistence hunter. Based mainly on author's field research; 2 tables, 5 notes, biblio.
P. J. Taylorson

4087. Martin, P. AN EXAMPLE OF CO-OPERATIVE MIXED FARMING IN THE ZAMBIAN COPPERBELT. *Geography [Great Britain] 1974 59(3): 264-266.* An account of the aims and successes of two projects, located at Kafubu and Kafulafuta in the copperbelt of Zambia, in which, since 1966, cooperative mixed farming has brought about a rapid transition from a subsistence to a market economy under the guidance of Israeli advisers. D. D. Cameron

4088. Mazrui, Ali A. KENNETH KAUNDA: FROM SATYAGRAHA TO DETENTE. *African Social Res. [Zambia] 1976 (22): 155-159.* A review of Fergus Macpherson's *Kenneth Kaunda of Zambia: The Times and the Man* (London, 1974). Macpherson is a friend of Kaunda, but his book is still objective history, though he falls short in his analysis. The reviewer lays particular emphasis on Kaunda's attitude toward violence and detente in southern Africa, questioning whether or not Kaunda's idea of detente had its roots in prenationalist nonviolent resistance. H. G. Soff

4089. Mihalyi, Louis J. ELECTRICITY AND ELECTRIFICATION FOR ZAMBIA. *Geographical Rev. 1977 67(1): 63-70.* Hydroelectric installations provide more than 90 percent of the energy for the electric utility industry in Zambia. This development began in colonial times, but its present status is due to the policies of independent Zambia. The power supply is heavily dependent on two major installations, and the copperbelt represents a single customer of overwhelming importance. In the present decade the country will be able to meet all internal electricity demands from domestic sources, partly because the full electrification of the rural regions cannot be implemented. The large lakes created behind new dams present a number of ecological and environmental issues, most of which still await investigation. J

4090. Mitchell, J. Clyde. THE SHADOW OF FEDERATION, 1952-55. *African Social Res. [Zambia] 1977 (24): 309-318.* The memoirs of J. Clyde Mitchell, who succeeded Elizabeth Colson as director of the Rhodes-Livingstone Institute in 1951. Notes each member of the staff, including their current positions; conflicts with trustees of the RLI; and research projects that should have been accomplished. Appendix of *Central African Post* editorials condemning research along with the institute's response. H. G. Soff

4091. Mtshali, Benedict V. THE ZAMBIAN FOREIGN SERVICE 1964-1972. *African Rev. [Tanzania] 1975 5(3): 302-316.* An analysis of the structure, education, experience, and training of foreign service officers. They have not yet reached acceptable standards for a modern nation. 2 tables, 36 notes. R. T. Brown

4092. Muntemba, Maud Shimwaayi. EXPECTATIONS UNFULFILLED: THE UNDERDEVELOPMENT OF PEASANT AGRICULTURE IN ZAMBIA: THE CASE OF KABWE RURAL DISTRICT, 1964-1970. *J. of Southern African Studies [Great Britain] 1978 5(1): 59-85.* Analyzes the failure by the Zambian government to realize its aim of transforming rural society in Kabwe during the First National Development Plan. Official documents and field interviews reveal a pronounced urban bias and lack of realistic planning and proper implementation of rural development programs by administrators. Zambian officials failed to respond effectively to the expressed desires of farmers to modernize agriculture and increase output. The result was a growth of rural impoverishment in Kabwe and other areas, which was acknowledged by the head of state in 1970. Based on interviews, Zambian archival sources, and published reports; 4 tables, 81 notes.
L. W. Truschel

4093. Musambachime, Mwelwa C. THE SOCIAL AND ECONOMIC EFFECTS OF SLEEPING SICKNESS IN MWERU-LUAPULA 1906-1922. *African Econ. Hist. 1981 (10): 151-173.* Fearing a potential sleeping sickness epidemic, the colonial administration of Zambia imposed unnecessary restrictions on the Mweru-Luapula area that proscribed fishing, disrupted trade and religious rituals, hindered missionary work, and caused labor shortages in neighboring Katanga. Resettlement led to serious hunger, unemployment, and discontent with colonial government incompetence. Based on Colonial Office records and other sources; 2 maps, 2 tables, 136 notes. W. D. Piersen

4094. Nag, Prithvish. ASIAN SETTLEMENT IN ZAMBIA. *Africa Q. [India] 1979 18(4): 59-77.* Reviews the contributions made to Zambian life and culture by Asian (mainly Indian) settlers in the fields of commerce, agriculture, technology, etc. Asians have been successfully settled only in the large towns, and a melding of Asian and African cultures has not yet occurred.

4095. Ng'andwe, Chiselebwe O. M. AFRICAN TRADITIONAL LAND TENURE AND AGRICULTURAL DEVELOPMENT: CASE STUDY OF THE KUNDA PEOPLE IN JUMBE. *African Social Res. [Zambia] 1976 (21): 51-67.* Traditional land tenure systems have not been a hinderance to the Kunda and cotton production. Although freehold has often been suggested as a more useful system, the Kunda land tenure system is free from all the weaknesses of freehold. Based on a two-week field trip. 7 notes. H. G. Soff

4096. Nsugbe, P. O. BRIEF BUT BLACK AUTHORITY, 1968-70. *African Social Res. [Zambia] 1977 (24): 335-340.* The memoirs of P. O. Nsugbe, who as director of Zambia's Rhodes-Livingstone Institute and the Centre for African Studies merged them into the Institute for African Studies in 1970. Some whites resented losing the name Rhodes-Livingstone and others supported the change. Zambians were caught in the middle of the conflict. Nsugbe faced opposition from those who resented a black director. H. G. Soff

4097. Oberschall, Anthony. AFRICAN TRADERS AND SMALL BUSINESSMEN IN LUSAKA. *African Social Res. [Zambia] 1973 (16): 474-502.* Analyzes urban business in Zambia, after the economic reforms of the late 1960's, demonstrating that many theories are invalid when applied to the Zambian economy. Businessmen tend to be individualistic and apparently disinterested in playing national leadership roles. African enterprises range from very small businesses to high volume industries. Case studies are provided which indicate neither wealth nor education is needed to become a successful businessman. 4 tables, 14 notes, biblio. H. Soff

4098. Ohadike, Patrick O. IMMIGRANTS AND DEVELOPMENT IN ZAMBIA. *Int. Migration Rev. 1974 8(3): 395-411.* Discusses the influence of European and Asian immigrants on the economic growth and labor force of Zambia, 1911-69.

4099. Ollawa, Patrick E. POLITICAL PARTICIPATION IN A DEVELOPING SOCIETY: THEORETICAL CONSIDERATIONS AND THE CASE OF ZAMBIA. *J. of Commonwealth and Comparative Pol. [Great Britain] 1978 16(2): 169-189.* The concept of political participation as developed by Max Weber for application to Western industrial democracies is inadequate for a discussion of one-party states in the developing world. A new definition, in which political participation is defined as "those kinds of behavior or activities of the citizens that are functionally relevant for the implementation-process of party-government policies and decisions" is here applied to Zambia since the creation of a one-party state in 1972. The author reveals the contradictions between the official ideology of humanism and socialism and the centralization and patronage system of state capitalism. Based on printed sources and secondary works; 58 notes. D. J. Nicholls

4100. Oxenham, John. COMMUNITY DEVELOPMENT AND VILLAGE EMPLOYMENT IN ZAMBIA, 1948-1962. *African Affairs [Great Britain] 1976 75(298): 55-66.* The colonial government in Zambia introduced Development Area Schools to train village men and women in specific crafts and trades. The author discusses the program, the disenchantment with its ineffectiveness, and its effect on urban employment. 30 notes, appendix. H. G. Soff

4101. Perrings, Charles. CONSCIOUSNESS, CONFLICT AND PROLETARIANIZATION: AN ASSESSMENT OF THE 1935 MINEWORKERS' STRIKE ON THE NORTHERN RHODESIAN COPPERBELT. *J. of Southern African Studies [Great Britain] 1977 4(1): 31-51.* A comparative analysis of three May 1935 strikes at Copperbelt mines by African migrant laborers. The most violent of these occurred at the Roan Antelope Mine, where African police clashed with strikers, killing six and wounding 22. Paradoxically, this mine required substantially higher technical proficiency from its miners than did the other two, while production there had been in recent serious decline. The Roan Antelope miners were more "proletarianized" than the other miners and therefore reacted more violently to conditions producing the strikes. Documented from archival and secondary sources; 117 notes.
L. W. Truschel

4102. Perrings, Charles. A MOMENT IN THE "PROLETARIANIZATION" OF THE NEW MIDDLE CLASS: RACE, VALUE AND DIVISION OF LABOUR IN THE COPPERBELT, 1946-1966. *J. of Southern African Studies [Great Britain] 1980 6(2): 183-213.* A Marxist analysis of how new mining technology and profit-seeking by the mining firms reduced the newly emerging middle class of Africans to the level of "proletarians" in Zambia's Copperbelt under the guise of Africanizing the skilled labor force after the war by eliminating the industrial color bar, which had reserved skilled job categories for Europeans. Based on Northern Rhodesian and Zambian published reports, interviews, and secondary sources; 4 tables, 56 notes.
L. W. Truschel

4103. Pettman, Jan. ZAMBIA'S SECOND REPUBLIC: THE ESTABLISHMENT OF A ONE-PARTY STATE. *J. of Modern African Studies [Great Britain] 1974 12(2): 231-244.* Prior to independence, Zambia was unified mainly through common hatred of the colonial administration. With the enemy removed, national unity suffered. Since 1964 the government has moved steadily toward a one-party state, which was declared in a White Paper in 1972. The United National Independence Party of Kenneth Kaunda has eliminated opposition and centralized the party, 25 notes. H. G. Soff

4104. Phiri, A. I. THE CURRENT SITUATION IN ZAMBIA. *African Affairs [Great Britain] 1973 72(288): 323-325.* Discusses the Southern Rhodesian blockade and analyzes Zambia's one-party participatory democracy. From an R.A.S./R.C.S. talk 15 February 1973.
H. G. Soff

4105. Pilyatskin, B. ZAMBIA: ACHIEVEMENTS AND HOPES. *Int. Affairs [USSR] 1975 (1): 110-116.* A report on the progress of Zambia since achieving independence from Great Britain in 1965. Zambia's most important task is to strengthen political independence to counteract threats from the reactionary activities of the United Progressive Party led by former Vice President, Simon Kapwepwe, and the white regimes of Southern Rhodesia and South Africa. D. K. McQuilkin

4106. Quick, Stephen A. BUREAUCRACY AND RURAL SOCIALISM IN ZAMBIA. *J. of Modern African Studies [Great Britain] 1977 15(3): 379-400.* Following colonial rule, the economies of most African states were unbalanced and vulnerable. There were three choices available to develop and modernize an area: individual capitalism, macrosocialism, and microsocialism. In Zambia, a microsocialist strategy was tried with enthusiasm but the cooperatives failed. The author analyzes the Zambian case with emphasis on government policy. 36 notes. H. G. Soff

4107. Ranger, Terence. MAKING NORTHERN RHODESIA IMPERIAL: VARIATIONS ON A ROYAL THEME, 1924-1938. *African Affairs [Great Britain] 1980 79(316): 349-373.* Reasons, such as coercion, collaborators, confidence and competence, advanced to explain African acquiescence in colonialism are insufficient to explain the achievement of such acquiescence and not merely its continuance. Colonial rule required a shared ideology linking rulers and ruled. In Zambia the colonial government after 1924 sought to create such an ideology around the idea of the imperial monarchy. It was successful at first but it contained within itself contradictions that undermined its effectiveness by the 1940's. Based on primary material in the National Archives, Lusaka; 90 notes. J. V. Coutinho

4108. Rennie, J. K. ZAMBIA: HISTORICAL DRAMA. *Radical Hist. Rev. 1981 (25): 177-179.* Examines the use of historical drama in disseminating radical ideology in Zambia from the British-ruled 1950's through the independent 1960's and 1970's.

4109. Richards, Audrey. THE RHODES LIVINGSTONE INSTITUTE: AN EXPERIMENT IN RESEARCH 1933-38. *African Social Res. [Zambia] 1977 (24): 275-278.* The memoirs of Audrey Richards, who participated in the earliest discussions leading to establishment of the Rhodes-Livingstone Institute in Northern Rhodesia. The institute was not universally popular: the Colonial Office opposed it as did the local Legislative Council. In spite of pessimism, the RLI quickly gained international repute and became the model for similar institutes in Uganda and Nigeria. 5 notes. H. G. Soff

4110. Roberts, A. D. NOTES TOWARDS A FINANCIAL HISTORY OF COPPER MINING IN NORTHERN RHODESIA. *Can. J. of African Studies [Canada] 1982 16(2): 347-359.* Outlines the history of interaction of private and public finance on the Zambian Copperbelt during five periods: 1924-29, initial development and capital formation; 1929-39, world depression and rearmament; 1939-49, World War II and aftermath; 1949-56, sterling devaluation and US stockpiling; 1956-64, price fluctuation and diversification of mining investment. Secondary sources; 70 notes. J. Powell

4111. Scaritt, James R. THE DECLINE OF POLITICAL LEGITIMACY IN ZAMBIA: AN EXPLANATION BASED ON INCOMPLETE DATA. *African Studies Rev. 1979 22(2): 13-38.* An explanation of the decline of postindependence legitimacy in Zambia through the application of 18 specific proposals about the nature of change to the political behavior of specific categories within the population. Change is often undirected; decline in the legitimacy of the ruling elite is inevitable. Secondary sources; 11 notes, biblio. R. T. Brown

4112. Schuster, Ilsa. PERSPECTIVES IN DEVELOPMENT: THE PROBLEM OF NURSES AND NURSING IN ZAMBIA. *J. of Development Studies [Great Britain] 1981 17(3): 77-97.* Traditional Zambian society does not associate the healing process with young women; therefore, young Zambian nurses must act within the area of conflict created by their western medical training and traditional attitudes.

4113. Scott, Ian. MIDDLE CLASS POLITICS IN ZAMBIA. *African Affairs [Great Britain] 1978 77(308): 321-334.* Traces the political climate and the role of the masses and middle classes since Zambian independence in 1964. The elections of 1973 involved less than half of the voting electorate of 1968, partly because politics had moved from mass support to middle-class support. Table, 40 notes. H. G. Soff

4114. Scott, Ian. PARTY FUNCTIONS AND CAPABILITIES: THE LOCAL-LEVEL UNIP ORGANISATION DURING THE FIRST ZAMBIAN REPUBLIC, 1964-1973. *African Social Res. [Zambia] 1976 (22): 107-129.* In the preindependence era, many political parties developed in Africa which were rigid, unbending and thought only of independence. These parties have now lost their vitality and purpose. The United National Independence Party (UNIP) of Zambia, however, never had independence as its only objective and it has, therefore, also been valuable during independence. Examines the regional strongholds of the UNIP in Zambia and the Party's functions and capabilities. 43 notes, biblio. H. G. Soff

4115. Seidman, Ann. THE DISTORTED GROWTH OF IMPORT-SUBSTITUTION INDUSTRY: THE ZAMBIAN CASE. *J. of Modern African Studies [Great Britain] 1974 12(4): 601-631.* Although manufacturing in Zambia has expanded greatly in the 1960's, it has not benefited the overall economy of the nation. Interest groups and a small industrial elite are protected. It is imperative that a long-term industrial strategy be developed to eliminate the distorted manufacturing sector and improve conditions in all sectors of Zambia. 2 tables, 51 notes. H. G. Soff

4116. Seidman, Ann. ENDING DEPENDENCE ON COPPER IN ZAMBIA? *African Social Res. [Zambia] 1973 (15): 381-386.* Review article of Mark Bostock and Charles Harvey, eds., *Economic Independence and Zambian Copper: A Case Study of Foreign Investment* (New York, 1971). Although the book offers valuable information concerning foreign-dominated mines in the developing nations, there are serious flaws. Innovative government policies are not given enough attention, nor are the consequences of reducing the economic dependence on copper considered. Note. H. G. Soff

4117. Shaw, Timothy M. DILEMMAS OF DEPENDENCE AND (UNDER) DEVELOPMENT: CONFLICTS AND CHOICES IN ZAMBIA'S PRESENT AND PROSPECTIVE FOREIGN POLICY. *Africa Today 1979 26(4): 43-65.* Summary of Zambian development and foreign policy since independence. Internal and external crises will continue to impede Zambia's goals of determining its own future and asserting leadership even when South Africa has been freed. Secondary sources; 75 notes. G. O. Gagnon

4118. Shaw, Timothy M. THE FOREIGN POLICY OF ZAMBIA: IDEOLOGY AND INTERESTS. *J. of Modern African Studies [Great Britain] 1976 14(1): 79-105.* Zambia's complicated foreign policy is influenced by the domestic conditions of growing state capitalism and social inequality. Foreign policy values are compatible with an elitist attempt to control Zambian society and resources. Zambia's sophisticated stance toward liberation in South Africa, its nonalignment, and its pan-Africanism reflect the national interest, as does the national ideology of humanism that has yet to become either a revolution or a reality. As a philosopher-king, President Kaunda at times expresses his preference for a more radical policy, but he rules pragmatically. 99 notes. W. R. Hively

4119. Shaw, Timothy M. THE FOREIGN POLICY SYSTEM OF ZAMBIA. *African Studies Rev. 1976 19(1): 31-66.* Discusses the influence of domestic and external politics in Zambia on its foreign policy, 1967-75.

4120. Shaw, Timothy M. and Mugomba, Agrippah T. THE POLITICAL ECONOMY OF REGIONAL DETENTE: ZAMBIA AND SOUTHERN AFRICA. *J. of African Studies 1977-78 4(4): 392-413.* Explains Zambia's regional policies in Southern Africa since independence as the work of a narrow ruling class within the country. The rulers of Zambia have been so enmeshed in a materialist ethic and so tied to interests of foreign capital from white-ruled African states that they have failed to carry out President Kaunda's policy of socialist humanism at home and refused to ally with revolutionary movements seeking to overthrow the white regimes elsewhere in Southern Africa. Based on secondary sources; table, 72 notes. L. W. Truschel

4121. Shaw, Timothy M. THE POLITICAL ECONOMY OF ZAMBIA. *Current Hist. 1982 81(473): 125-128, 144.* Examines the pressures that the transition from war to peace in Zimbabwe and the deepening world recession put on the economic and domestic policies of the Kaunda regime in Zambia.

4122. Simons, H. J. [A PROLOGUE TO DISCUSSION ON THE RHODES-LIVINGSTONE INSTITUTE]. *African Social Res. [Zambia] 1977 (24): 259-273.* Surveys the leadership of Zambia's Rhodes-Livingstone Institute (now the Institute for Social Research) and its problems during 40 years of existence. The author discusses each of the articles appearing in this issue of the journal, the authors of which were outstanding members of the institute. H. G. Soff

4123. Siwale, Donald. AUTOBIOGRAPHICAL SKETCH. *African Social Res. [Zambia] 1973 (15): 362-373.* Brief remembrances of the past 75 years, including schooling, missionary activity, colonial government, and independence. Explains family life, interprets indigenous society, and notes the difficulties of commercial farming for Africans. 8 notes. H. G. Soff

4124. Small, N. J. THE NORTHERN RHODESIAN POLICE AND ITS LEGACY. *African Social Res. [Zambia] 1979: 523-539.* A history of the Zambian police force which, during the colonial era, was primarily used as a military arm to protect the white elite. Secondary sources; biblio. R. T. Brown

4125. Southall, Tony. ZAMBIA: CLASS FORMATION AND GOVERNMENT POLICY IN THE 1970S. *J. of Southern African Studies [Great Britain] 1980 7(1): 91-108.* Economic reforms in Zambia since 1968 have led to the growth of an indigenous class of businessmen and farmers, while most rural Zambians have grown poorer. The new middle class has begun to challenge President Kenneth Kaunda's government, which has led to a decline of the populist style in Zambian politics. Based on published reports, newspapers, and secondary sources; 7 tables, 67 notes. L. W. Truschel

4126. Stabler, John B. NORTHERN RHODESIAN REACTION TO 1948 RESPONSIBLE GOVERNMENT PROPOSALS: ROLE OF SIR STEWART GORE-BROWNE. *J. of Southern African Affairs 1978 3(3): 295-317.* Analyzes the proposals made in Northern Rhodesia's Legislative Council in 1948 by the member for native interests, Sir Stewart Gore-Browne, for responsible government in the colonial territory and federation with Southern Rhodesia. Attacks Robert I. Rotberg's interpretation that Sir Stewart made an honest error in misjudging African public opinion, which condemned the proposals as tantamount to the extension northward of Southern Rhodesian settler rule and racism. Gore-Browne served as a stalking horse for the leader of the white settlers, Roy Welensky, who wanted to amalgamate the two Rhodesias. Gore-Browne was a dyed-in-the-wool aristocratic paternalist who failed to consult African opinion before he made his proposals. He believed African interests would be best safeguarded by a loose federation with Southern Rhodesia along with African political representation at the parliamentary level. Based on newspapers, archives, and secondary sources; 50 notes. L. W. Truschel

4127. Tipple, A. G. SELF-HELP HOUSING POLICIES IN A ZAMBIAN MINING TOWN. *Urban Studies [Great Britain] 1976 13(2): 167-169.* The advent of independence in Zambia opened previously all-white areas to African habitation, though Africans had little money to take advantage of the situation. In the mining town of Kitwe, as elsewhere, extensive squatter settlements rose on the town outskirts. The new government moved to provide low-cost housing, but the squatters naturally preferred their rent-free facilities. The squatters' position was therefore legalized, with the result that they are much more willing to work for living improvements. Local industries and employer-employee relations are developing. 4 notes, biblio. V. L. Human

4128. Tordoff, William. ZAMBIA: THE POLITICS OF DISENGAGEMENT. *African Affairs [Great Britain] 1977 76(302): 60-69.* Analyzes Zambian domestic and foreign policy since 1964. President Kenneth Kaunda set up a one-party system based on humanism, a rejection of capitalism in favor of a moderate socialist system. Rather successful efforts were undertaken to remove foreign landowners and businessmen from positions of power. Zambia's dependence on the copper industry and its landlocked geographical position render full economic independence difficult. Kaunda tried at first to eliminate white-dominated governments in Southern Rhodesia and South Africa by diplomacy, but, this failing, turned to open support of guerrilla movements. 12 notes. V. L. Human

4129. Vail, Leroy. ECOLOGY AND HISTORY: THE EXAMPLE OF EASTERN ZAMBIA. *J. of Southern African Studies [Great Britain] 1977 3(2): 129-155.* The dual impact of expanding capitalism and colonial administration on Eastern Zambian society after 1895 resulted in a major ecological disaster. By the end of the colonial period people living in some of the areas with the most fertile land were impoverished and disease-ridden. The land was barren, and the balance between man and his environment which had existed before 1890 was undermined. The author examines the interaction between colonial land policy and ecological degradation. Based on documents in the Public Record Office, London, the National Archives of Zambia, and field research in Malawi and Zambia; 2 maps, 130 notes. S. P. Carr

4130. Vail, Leroy. THE IMPACT OF MULTINATIONAL FIRMS IN SOUTHERN AFRICA. *African Econ. Hist. 1976 (2): 40-42.* Review essay of Richard L. Sklar's *Corporate Power in an African State: The Political Impact of Multinational Mining Companies in Zambia* (U. of California Pr., 1975), which focuses on relations between the Zambian government and multinational corporations in the mining industry and on the relations between the managerial bourgeoisie, the labor elite of mine workers, and governmental policy.

4131. Vanzetti, N. R. and Bessell, J. E. EDUCATION AND THE DEVELOPMENT OF FARMING IN TWO AREAS OF ZAMBIA. *J. of Development Studies [Great Britain] 1974 11(1): 41-54.* Discusses how education has contributed to modernization of agricultural practices in present-day Zambia.

4132. Velsen, J. van. SOCIAL RESEARCH AND SOCIAL RELEVANCE: SUGGESTIONS FOR A RESEARCH POLICY AND SOME RESEARCH PRIORITIES FOR THE INSTITUTE FOR AFRICAN STUDIES. *African Social Res. [Zambia] 1974 (17): 517-553.* Established in 1937, the Institute for African Studies has done pure, applied, and commissioned research. Proposed and current topics include Zambian culture (language, arts, and religion), legal studies, demography, regional, labor, and economic history, and industrial studies. 31 notes. H. Soff.

4133. White, C. M. N. INTERREGNA, 1955-56 AND 1960-62. *African Social Res. [Zambia] 1977 (24): 327-329.* The memoirs of C. M. N. White who was acting director of the Rhodes-Livingstone Institute on two separate occasions. His own research and study did not suffer since the institute's administration did not require much time. When the university absorbed the institute, White was dismayed and wanted politics kept out of social research. H. G. Soff

4134. Wilson, Monica. THE FIRST THREE YEARS, 1938-41. *African Social Res. [Zambia] 1977 (24): 279-283.* Outlines the contributions of Godfrey Wilson to Zambia's Rhodes-Livingstone Institute as its first director. A key issue during his tenure was urbanization, particularly in the mining areas. Urbanization was counter to official government policy, but Wilson's role as an anthropologist was to provide the government with evidence on which they could make proper policy decisions. His evidence was often not what the administration wanted to hear. He resigned in 1941 in utter frustration. H. G. Soff

4135. Woldring, Klaas. ASPECTS OF ZAMBIAN FOREIGN POLICY IN THE CONTEXT OF SOUTHERN AFRICA. *Australian Outlook [Australia] 1980 34(3): 338-348.* Zambia's foreign policy is influenced by geopolitical and ideological factors. As a landlocked state, it is affected by political turmoil in its neighbors, its position as a host for guerrillas, and its chronic problem of supply routes. Regarding the last, there were great hopes for the TAZARA railway to Dar es Salaam, but it has not fulfilled expectations. Foreign policy is made by the president, who is committed to Pan-Africanism, nonalignment, the interests of the Front Line states, humanism, and the Lusaka Manifesto of 1969 on human equality and national self-determination in Southern Africa. Based on newspapers, pamphlets, and addresses; 27 notes. W. D. McIntyre

4136. —. ONE ZAMBIA. ONE NATION. ONE PARTY: PRESIDENT KAUNDA SPEAKS. *Afriscope [Nigeria] 1973 3(8): 10-18.*

An interview with Kenneth Kaunda, president of Zambia, in which he responds to questions about Zambia's one-party government, sectionalism, relations with South Africa, Southern Rhodesia, economics, and the Organization of African Unity. Illus. G. O. Gagnon

Zimbabwe

General

4137. Bannerman, J. H. TOWARDS A HISTORY OF THE HLENGWE PEOPLE OF THE SOUTH OF RHODESIA. *NADA [Zimbabwe] 1978 11(5): 483-496.* An overview of the history of the Hlengwe people of the southeast Lowveld region of Zimbabwe since the 17th century.

4138. Beach, D. N. THE HISTORIOGRAPHY OF THE PEOPLE OF ZIMBABWE IN THE 1960S. *Rhodesian Hist. [Zimbabwe] 1973 4: 21-30.* Traces the accelerated academic interest in the Great Zimbabwe complex in Zimbabwe. The establishment of chronology through oral tradition, documents, carbon dating, artifacts, and the reconstructed history of surrounding peoples has led to a new shortened chronology. Based on interviews, printed sources, and documents in the National Archives, Harare; 59 notes. O. B. Pollak

4139. Burke, E. E. *NADA:* A BIBLIOGRAPHICAL NOTE. *Heritage [Zimbabwe] 1982 2: 52-56.* A bibliographical note describing the *Native Affairs Department Annual,* published in Zimbabwe between 1923 and 1981.

4140. Cable, Mary. WHO BUILT ZIMBABWE? *Horizon 1976 18(2): 31-37.* Since 1905, archaeologists have concluded that the stone ruins of Great Zimbabwe were built by Africans between the 4th and 13th centuries, but white racist Southern Rhodesians, especially since the advent of Ian Smith's government (1964), refuse to accept this and continue to postulate alternative theories.

4141. Dellar, Geoffrey. LIBRARIES IN A SIEGE ECONOMY. *African Res. & Documentation [Great Britain] 1979 (20): 1-5.* The Uninlateral Declaration of Independence (UDI) in colonial Zimbabwe in 1965 had a detrimental effect on public libraries, but some positive steps accomplished during the period include the retrospective *Rhodesia National Bibliography 1890-1930,*the National Archives' list of periodicals, the Annual Research Index, and catalogs of university Africana collections.

4142. Hayes, M. E. THE NAMBIYA PEOPLE OF WANGE. *NADA [Zimbabwe] 1977 11(4): 385-393.* An overview of the history of the dynasty of the Nambiya people of the Wange region of Zimbabwe since 1737, with comments on social organization and rituals.

4143. Kinloch, Graham C. CHANGING RHODESIAN RACE RELATIONS: A STUDY OF DEMOGRAPHIC AND ECONOMIC FACTORS. *Pro. of the Am. Phil. Soc. 1978 122(1): 18-24.* Reviews sociological literature on race relations in general and in the Zimbabwean context. Presents an analysis of documents published in Zimbabwe between 1893 and 1973. Notes the frequency of references to selected issues and of the advocacy of selected policies related to race by year, race, and occupation. Measures correlations between attitudinal indices and, for example, the white-black population ratio and the occupation of the speaker according to Kendall's Tau (beta) statistic as a measure of association. Those of both races involved in manufacturing and the professions (as opposed to mining and services) tended to express more liberal attitudes on race relations. Discusses this and other findings. 2 tables, 23 ref. L. W. Van Wyk

4144. Masterson, G. M. MEMORIES OF A NATIVE COMMISSIONER'S WIFE. *NADA [Zimbabwe] 1977 11(4): 397-406; 1978 11(5): 510-515.* Recollections of G. M. Masterson, wife of H. B. Masterson, who joined the Native Affairs Department in colonial Zimbabwe in 1925 and served as commissioner of the African population in a number of regions until his death in 1966.

4145. Munjeri, Dawson. THE KORSTEN BASKETMAKERS. *NADA [Zimbabwe] 1978 11(5): 497-509.* A history of the Korsten Basketmakers, a religious movement founded in the Makoni district of Manicaland by Baba Johane Masowe (1914-73) and established in Zimbabwe in 1962 after its expulsion from South Africa.

4146. Osipov, A. ZIMBABVE: STANOVLENIE NOVOI ZHIZNI [Zimbabwe constructing a new life]. *Aziia i Afrika Segodnia [USSR] 1981 (3): 16-18.* Discusses life in Zimbabwe and efforts to build a new future.

4147. Sanger, Clyde. A CHAPTER OF ZIMBABWEAN HISTORY. *Can. J. of African Studies [Canada] 1980 14(3): 546-548.* Review article of Martin Meredith's *The Past is Another Country: Rhodesia 1890-1979* (London: Andre Deutsch, 1979), A. K. H. Weinrich's *Mucheke: Race, Status and Politics in a Rhodesian Community* (Paris: UNESCO, 1976), and Elaine Windrich's *Britain and the Politics of Rhodesian Independence* (New York: Africana Publ., 1978), all of which were written before Southern Rhodesia became Zimbabwe.

4148. Singh, Harjinder. ARMED STRUGGLE AND ZIMBABWEAN INDEPENDENCE. *Africa Q. [India] 1981 20(3-4): 88-106.* Discusses the struggle for independence from British domination in Zimbabwe, 1961-79.

4149. Vladimirov, V. ZIMBABVE: NOVAIA ISTORIIA MOLODOI RESPUBLIKI [Zimbabwe: a new history of a young republic]. *Aziia i Afrika Segodnia [USSR] 1982 (12): 24-27.* Discusses the achievements, difficulties, and daily concerns of the common working people of Zimbabwe, the hostility of South Africa, and the help and concern offered by the USSR.

4150. Warhurst, P. R. THE HISTORY OF RACE RELATIONS IN RHODESIA. *Zambezia [Zimbabwe] 1973 3(1): 15-19.* Traces race relations in Zimbabwe from its conquest in the 1890's through periods of the chartered company, colonial government, federation, and illegal independence. Concludes that race relations are worse when the level of integration is highest. "The tragedy of modern Rhodesia is that the races are so concerned with promoting their own sectional interests that they ignore the hopes and fears of the other groups." O. B. Pollak

4151. White, J. THE VAMHARI. *NADA [Zimbabwe] 1980 12(2): 117-129.* A survey of the history of the VaMhari Shona segment that split off under Chief Mapanzure, 1859-60. The group was on the fringe of Shona-Ndebele and Shona-European conflicts in the latter 19th century. Based on archival sources and annuals; 39 notes. L. W. Truschel

4152. Wilkinson, A. R. THE IMPACT OF THE WAR. *J. of Commonwealth and Comparative Pol. [Great Britain] 1980 18(1): 110-123.* After the Unilateral Declaration of Independence (UDI) in 1965 the white settler government created a highly self-sufficient economy to combat sanctions and successfully defeated moves by nationalist forces. By 1974 Southern Rhodesia faced a hostile government in Mozambique across a long and vulnerable border. The war affected investment and new exploration, and the country's economic position was further afflicted by the rise in oil prices. White emigration threatened the basis of the regime and the administration of the whole nation was disrupted. The war resulted in deep physical and psychological scars and great problems of readjustment to peacetime conditions, especially for the army and the police. Based on printed sources; map, table, 17 notes. E. J. Adams

Economics

4153. Bamber, F. W. THE EARLY HISTORY OF BULAWAYO'S ELECTRICITY UNDERTAKING. *Heritage [Zimbabwe] 1981 (1): 37-41.* Shortly after the establishment of Bulawayo and the opening of the railway lines from Mafeking in 1893, William Napier, Percy Vipont Weir, and Charles Clark set up a company to supply Bulawayo with water and electricity. A. Alcock

4154. Bourdillon, M. F. C. LABOUR MIGRANTS FROM KOREKORE COUNTRY. *Zambezia: the J. of the U. of Zimbabwe [Rhodesia] 1977 5(1): 1-29.* Field research carried out from 1969 to 1973 in Korekore, an economically backward northeast corner of Zimbabwe,

discovered that nearly half the males over 16 are absent at any one time from the homestead. They go to work in mining, agriculture, and in towns. They take outside employment regardless of their local status and "the rural and urban aspects of the lives of circulatory migration can thus be seen as a structured continuity." 18 tables, 26 notes.
O. B. Pollak

4155. Brand, C. M. RACE AND POLITICS IN RHODESIAN TRADE UNIONS. *African Perspectives [Netherlands] 1976 (1): 55-80.* A detailed historical assessment of the strengths and weaknesses of African labor unions in Zimbabwe. Historically, the African unions have exercised little influence over the economy or the determination of industrial working conditions for Africans. The author attributes this to restrictive labor laws, the large numbers of alien migrant and rural migrant laborers, lack of cooperation from European trade unions, and strong schismatic tendencies among the African labor leaders themselves, which stem from regional, ethnic, and personality factors. Recently the African unions have had an appreciable political significance in promoting African nationalism. Based on printed documents and secondary sources; 9 notes, biblio. L. W. Truschel

4156. Bratton, Michael. SETTLER STATE, GUERRILLA WAR, AND RURAL UNDERDEVELOPMENT IN RHODESIA. *Issue: A Q. J. of Opinion 1979 9(1-2): 56-62.* Economic figures and sociopolitical conditions in Zimbabwe for the period 1962-78 indicate that the imbalance of land ownership and discriminatory government agricultural development policies have resulted in a rural decline to beyond the point where self-reliant local governments can meet basic human needs. Thus fertile ground for radical political movements and guerrilla warfare has been prepared.

4157. Bratton, Michael. STRUCTURAL TRANSFORMATION IN ZIMBABWE: COMPARATIVE NOTES FROM THE NEOCOLONIZATION OF KENYA. *J. of Modern African Studies [Great Britain] 1977 15(4): 591-611.* An analysis of the Zimbabwean political economy and an assessment of a possible neocolonial solution to decolonization. Explores key similarities and differences with Kenya at similar times in political development. Two key problems that must be solved are the impoverishment of African trust lands, and whether or not to accept development funding that will tie Zimbabwe to Western influence. 2 tables, 43 notes. H. G. Soff

4158. Cherer Smith, R. THE RENNIE TAILYOUR CONCESSION. *Rhodesiana [Zimbabwe] 1978 38: 35-48.* Considers the development of the Rennie Tailyour Concession in Zimbabwe and provides notes on some of the gold mines once operated on the concession by the London and Rhodesia Mining and Land Company.

4159. Cherer Smith, R. REZENDE MINE. *Rhodesiana [Zimbabwe] 1976 (34): 21-27.* Outlines the development of the gold mine managed on behalf of the Portuguese Mozambique Company by Baron de Rezende. Discusses the effects of the British South Africa Company's shareholding, 1898-1948. 3 photos. C. A. McNeill

4160. Chhabra, Hari Sharan. OIL TO RHODESIA: A WESTERN CONSPIRACY. *India Q. [India] 1978 34(1): 26-38.* In November 1965 the British government imposed an oil embargo on Southern Rhodesia following the Unilateral Declaration of Independence. The author reviews the details of UN sanctions and the means by which the white government of Southern Rhodesia circumvented the restriction of its petroleum supply, and examines the covert transshipments by Portuguese Mozambique and the Republic of South Africa and others including the 16-country network code-named Zophyr. Secondary sources; 41 notes. S. H. Frank

4161. Clarke, D. G. LAND INEQUALITY AND INCOME DISTRIBUTION IN RHODESIA. *African Studies Rev. 1975 18(1): 1-8.* Illustrates how the process of capital accumulation in colonial Zimbabwe, and particularly the land policy, discriminated against blacks in capital markets and impaired their economic advancement, 1946-69.

4162. Clarke, D. G. ZIMBABWE'S INTERNATIONAL ECONOMIC POSITION AND ASPECTS OF SANCTIONS REMOVAL. *J. of Commonwealth and Comparative Pol. [Great Britain] 1980 18(1): 28-54.* Until 1965 Southern Rhodesia recorded a positive growth in GDP and per capita income, although investments were falling and African unemployment increasing. The application of sanctions failed to precipitate massive economic distress, due in part to a successful import substitution strategy. There was a general economic decline after 1974, but this paralleled the rise in oil prices. Trade surpluses were sustained through subordinating domestic policy to balance of payments considerations. The prospects for the post-sanction period lie in changes in the balance of payments and investments which could lead to a recovery beyond past levels of growth and income. Based on UN Reports and secondary material; 4 tables, 22 notes. E. J. Adams

4163. Duggan, William R. THE NATIVE LAND HUSBANDRY ACT OF 1951 AND THE RURAL AFRICAN MIDDLE CLASS OF SOUTHERN RHODESIA. *African Affairs [Great Britain] 1980 79(315): 227-239.* While African peasant agriculture in Southern Rhodesia deteriorated in the first half of this century, the government suddenly shifted its policy in the 1950's by introducing individual tenure in the reserves under government control. This move was viewed as part of an attempt to create a loyal urban and rural middle class among Africans. Writing before the end of the independence struggle in Zimbabwe and taking into account what happened in Kenya before its independence, the author examines under what conditions such an objective could be achieved. 43 notes. J. V. Coutinho

4164. Harris, Peter. INDUSTRIAL WORKERS IN RHODESIA 1946-1972: WORKING CLASS ELITES OR LUMPENPROLETARIAT? *J. of Southern African Studies [Great Britain] 1975 1(2): 139-161.* Examines the social stratification of the Zimbabwean labor force 1946-72 and the impact of industrial increased wages. Changes in wage rates have reflected the supply and demand for labor, and the relationship between the industrial regions and the underdeveloped agrarian regions. Also considers the reasons behind the marked rises in the industrial wages of Africans, 1946-72, and the slower growth after 1963. Based on government reports, censuses, and the press; 4 tables, 87 notes. S. P. Carr

4165. Hoogvelt, Ankie M. M. and Child, David. RHODESIA: ECONOMIC BLOCKADE AND DEVELOPMENT. *Monthly R. 1973 25(5): 41-57.* Examines colonial Zimbabwe's economy 1965-73, demonstrating that the international boycott has spurred economic development. S

4166. Hulec, Otakar. THE POSITION AND ROLE OF AFRICANS IN RHODESIAN AGRICULTURE. *Archiv Orientální [Czechoslovakia] 1974 42(1): 16-32.* Discusses the development of agriculture in Zimbabwe. African farmers, after the arrival of European colonists, achieved fine results in cultivation. It was for this reason that Zimbabwe became not only self-supporting but capable of exporting. Ownership of land and its wealth became one of the important factors in the relationship of Europeans in Zimbabwe toward their African partners.
G. E. Pergl

4167. Kosmin, B. A. "FREEDOM, JUSTICE AND COMMERCE": SOME FACTORS AFFECTING ASIAN TRADING PATTERNS IN SOUTHERN RHODESIA, 1897-1942. *Rhodesian Hist. [Zimbabwe] 1975 6: 15-29.* Attacks the prevailing superficial explanation of Asian commercial success in colonial Zimbabwe, hitherto ascribed to a "happy combination of socially inherited capacity and the fortunes of history." Variables such as the white minority regime's self-interest and the numerical predominance of African labor precluded several economic choices for Asians. Trading in the African market emerged as an occupation of least resistance. Based on official documents in the National Archives, other primary, and secondary sources; 4 tables, 34 notes. O. B. Pollak

4168. Kosmin, Barry A. THE INYOKA TOBACCO INDUSTRY OF THE SHANGWE PEOPLE: A CASE STUDY OF THE DISPLACEMENT OF A PRE-COLONIAL ECONOMY IN SOUTHERN RHODESIA, 1898-1938. *African Social Res. [Zambia] 1974 (17): 554-577.* A test of the hypothesis set forth by G. Arrighi in *The Political Economy of Rhodesia* (New York: Humanities, 1970) relative to the proletarianization of peasants in colonial Zimbabwe. Using the Shangwe as a case study, this analysis supports and confirms Arrighi. Africans are not lazy or backward: their resistance to forced labor in the urban sector

was due to their love of independence. Map, 2 tables, 57 notes.
H. G. Soff

4169. Makgetla, Neva Seidman. TRANSNATIONAL CORPORATIONS IN SOUTHERN RHODESIA. *J. of Southern African Affairs 1980 5(1): 57-88.* Assesses the linkage between Western multinational corporations, European settlers, and the white settler government during the Unilateral Declaration of Independence period, 1965-78. The Ian Smith government "systematized and expanded the exploitative, racist labor system" by encouraging investments from foreign corporations, while keeping African wages low and undermining UN economic sanctions. Until the mid-1970's, agricultural industry, mining, and manufacturing all benefited from this government policy and transnational corporate funding and transactions. Based on company reports, newspaper accounts, and secondary sources; 7 tables, 82 notes.
L. W. Truschel

4170. Moyana, Henry Vusso. LAND AND RACE IN RHODESIA. *African Rev. [Tanzania] 1975 5(1): 17-41.* A history of landowning acts promulgated by the white government and the relationship between the desire for land and the rise of African nationalism. 6 tables, 114 notes.
R. T. Brown

4171. Moyana, J. Kombo. THE POLITICAL ECONOMY OF SANCTIONS AND IMPLICATIONS FOR FUTURE ECONOMIC POLICY. *J. of Southern African Studies 1977 2(4): 493-520.* Southern Rhodesia's Unilateral Declaration of Independence of 1965 was opposed by tobacco farmers dependent on exports for their livelihood, international capital, much of domestic capital, and of course by Africans. In a few days Great Britain imposed economic sanctions and asked the UN to do the same. Contrary to predictions, the economy under sanctions attained a better than average growth performance. Concludes that the more developing countries are integrated into the world system through investment, aid, and trade, the faster they will develop. 61 notes.
E. P. Stickney

4172. Moyana, Tafirenyika. CREATING AN AFRICAN MIDDLE CLASS: THE POLITICAL ECONOMY OF EDUCATION AND EXPLOITATION IN ZIMBABWE. *J. of Southern African Affairs 1979 4(3): 325-346.* Official and mission schools' educational policy in colonial Zimbabwe, 1953-70, reflected shifting class interests among the European settlers ruling the territory. During 1953-62, the dominant upper middle class whites sought to create a narrow African middle class to oppose an emergent hostile African proletariat, while the white workers and farmers dominant in the Rhodesian Front governments after 1962 curtailed the facilities created under the Kerr Commission framework to suppress the rise of rival classes of African skilled laborers and businessmen. In either case, Salisbury's official educational policy is depicted as a conscious effort to promote Western cultural imperialism through both state and mission schools. Based on published reports and secondary sources; 3 tables, 109 notes.
L. W. Truschel

4173. Murapa, Rukudzo. GEOGRAPHY, RACE, CLASS AND POWER IN RHODESIA: 1890 TO THE PRESENT. *J. of Southern African Affairs 1978 3(2): 159-173.* An overview of the development of the colonial economy and social classes among the white and black populations. The territory passed from initial control by international capitalist interests to a rural white settler bourgeoisie in 1923, to a white manufacturing class allied with a newly formed African middle class in 1953, back to the rural white group in 1962, which has been threatened by a revolution of African peasants and proletarians since the Unilateral Declaration of Independence by the Smith government in 1965. The country's landlocked geographical position has assisted its survival against international sanctions since 1966. Secondary sources; 15 notes.
L. W. Truschel

4174. Onselen, Charles van. BLACK WORKERS IN CENTRAL AFRICAN INDUSTRY: A CRITICAL ESSAY IN THE HISTORIOGRAPHY AND SOCIOLOGY OF RHODESIA. *J. of Southern African Studies [Great Britain] 1975 1(2): 228-246.* Examines the customary view of colonial Zimbabwe's industrialization through the work of historians and sociologists. Demonstrates that there are substantial limitations to much of this work; that a more rigorous explanation of "race" and "class" is needed; and that the concepts of laissez faire and tribal backwardness have often impeded studies in this area. A deeper understanding of the process of proletarianization and class formation is required. Secondary sources; 98 notes.
S. P. Carr

4175. Palmer, Robin. AFRICAN MINE LABOUR IN SOUTHERN RHODESIA. *African Social Res. [Zambia] 1976 (22): 147-153.* A review article on Charles van Onselen's *Chibaro: African Mine Labour in Southern Rhodesia, 1900-1933* (London, 1976).
H. G. Soff

4176. Phimister, I. R. MEAT AND MONOPOLIES: BEEF CATTLE IN SOUTHERN RHODESIA, 1890-1938. *J. of African Hist. [Great Britain] 1978 19(3): 391-414.* While Zimbabwe was considered a potentially valuable beef cattle country early in its history, realization of this potential required competition in a market dominated by a few large cold-storage companies, drawing on production based mainly in Argentina. Only one company, Liebigs, was induced to operate in the colony. While land, labor, and stocks of indigenous cattle were cheap and plentiful, the industry suffered from lack of capital, inadequate transport, the poor quality of local cattle, and disease. State support of the industry developed early but remained futile. The Imperial Cold Storage Company, while a major factor in southern Africa, was insignificant on a world scale. In 1938, the local Cold Storage Commission was established. 94 notes.
A. W. Novitsky

4177. Phimister, I. R. PEASANT PRODUCTION AND UNDERDEVELOPMENT IN SOUTHERN RHODESIA, 1890-1914. *African Affairs [Great Britain] 1974 73(291): 217-228.* By the 1920's, three major economic sectors could be identified in Southern Rhodesia: mines and capitalized farms; local production supplying food and services to cities and mines; and peripheral regions supplying migrant labor. Analyzes peasant production and the relationships between peasants and traders, using the Victoria district as a case study. 60 notes.
H. G. Soff

4178. Phimister, Ian. WHITE MINERS IN HISTORICAL PERSPECTIVE: SOUTHERN RHODESIA 1890-1953. *J. of Southern African Studies [Great Britain] 1977 3(2): 187-206.* White miners constituted only 4% of Zimbabwe's industrial labor force, 1890-1953, and yet they monopolized the skilled and supervisory jobs. The structural position of this white working class was one of strength, but paradoxically also one of social insecurity. Based on newspapers; 111 notes.
S. P. Carr

4179. Pollak, Oliver B. BLACK FARMERS AND WHITE POLITICS IN RHODESIA. *African Affairs [Great Britain] 1975 74(296): 263-277.* Traces the availability of land in Zimbabwe for purchase by Africans. The available land was usually inferior, and by 1925 only 45,000 acres had been secured by Africans. New laws were introduced in 1930, and although severe restrictions were involved, there were more Africans desiring land than land made available. In some areas, Africans formed farmers' associations and cooperatives similar to European associations. Government officials, however, viewed this movement as irresponsible, and growth was thwarted through World War II. Following 1945, the African Farmers Union gained concessions and earned new respect. If Africans gain control of this country, those who own freehold may face a problem with a new government that does not recognize freehold land tenure. 64 notes.
H. G. Soff

4180. Porter, Richard C. ECONOMIC SANCTIONS: THE THEORY AND THE EVIDENCE FROM RHODESIA. *J. of Peace Sci. 1978 3(2): 93-110.* Offers an aggregate, static, and neoclassical theory of economic sanctions and examines five alternative theoretical views. Assesses the effectiveness and theoretical implications of the sanctions imposed in Southern Rhodesia.

4181. Riddell, Roger. ZIMBABWE'S LAND PROBLEM: THE CENTRAL ISSUE. *J. of Commonwealth and Comparative Pol. [Great Britain] 1980 18(1): 1-13.* By the 1970's the distribution of land remained very unequal. European farms were larger and included most of the most fertile land. African farms in the Tribal Trust Lands were very small units. In the European sector much land was unused or underutilized, while the problems of the Africans were accompanied by growing overpopulation, landlessness, and land deterioration. Land was vital to the economy as it was the only area capable of absorbing an increasing population and lessening the widening economic differential within the population. But the land issue is a highly political question and one which Zimbabwe will only solve by a commitment to radical reorganization. Secondary sources; 12 notes. E. J. Adams

4182. Schooler, Robert D. and Paul, Robert J. THE RHODESIAN EXPERIENCE ANALYSED AGAINST THE IDEAL CONDITIONS FOR ECONOMIC SANCTIONS. *Int. Studies [India] 1979 18(3): 339-352.* Analyzes the effectiveness of the British boycott against Southern Rhodesia, begun in 1965, and judges it an economic failure. Great Britain underestimated settler willingness to endure hardship and miscalculated South Africa's commitment to support them. The unwillingness of Japan, West Germany, and other nations to honor the economic sanctions was also an important factor in the boycott's failure. 5 tables, 31 notes. T. P. Linkfield

4183. Sharland, J. L. THE OFFICES OF THE MUNICIPALITY OF BULAWAYO. *Heritage [Zimbabwe] 1981 (1): 1-9.* Traces the history of municipal office buildings in Bulawayo from 1894 to the civic center complex currently being built, in which all offices will eventually be accommodated. Based on minutes of Bulawayo Council. A. Alcock

4184. Stocking, M. A. RELATIONSHIP OF AGRICULTURAL HISTORY AND SETTLEMENT TO SEVERE SOIL EROSION IN RHODESIA. *Zambezia: the J. of the U. of Rhodesia [Zimbabwe] 1978 6(2): 129-146.* Traces white settlement, stock, and land use in the Mondoro Reserve-Tribal Trust Land about 60 miles southwest of Harare since 1890. While the erosion, variously termed as *lavaka,arroyos,* and *bocorocas,* is severe it is not linked to the misuse of land resources or overpopulation. Attempts to arrest erosion were mismanaged, ill-conceived or the object of administrative neglect. Based on government archives; 2 tables, 2 maps, 43 notes. O. B. Pollak

4185. Stoneman, Colin. ZIMBABWE'S PROSPECTS AS AN INDUSTRIAL POWER. *J. of Commonwealth and Comparative Pol. [Great Britain] 1980 18(1): 14-27.* The industrial sector of Zimbabwe's economy has been a vital component at least since the Unilateral Declaration of Independence (UDI) in 1965, earning more than agriculture. Zimbabwe possesses a unique diversity of raw materials, a wide range of industry, mining, and manufacturing, and a developed capital market. Since 1965, and particularly as a result of the war and sanctions, its industrial capacity has been hurt through lack of investment and exploration. However, the key to its industrial future lies in the historical foreign ownership of most of its industrial investment. About one fifth of its total capacity is owned by foreigners or white settlers. Zimbabwe's industrial future lies in the attitude of any new government to the foreign owners of this capital. Based on secondary sources; 6 notes. E. J. Adams

4186. Suckling, J. WHAT PRICE BLACK LABOUR IN RHODESIA? *Zambezia: the J. of the U. of Rhodesia [Zimbabwe] 1974 3(2): 113-116.* Reviews two papers by D. G. Clarke, *Domestic Workers in Rhodesia and Contract Workers* and *Underdevelopment in Rhodesia* (Gwelo: Mambo Pr., 1974), and V. S. Cubitt and R. C. Riddell's *The Urban Poverty Datum Line in Rhodesia* (U. of Rhodesia, 1974), P. S. Harris's *Black Industrial Workers in Rhodesia* (Gwelo: Mambo Pr., 1974), and A. J. B. Hughes's *Development in Rhodesian Tribal Areas* (Salisbury: Tribal Areas of Rhodesia Research Foundation, 1974). Analysis of black labor's historical origins indicates that urban-rural migration, low productivity, and employer agreements not to compete for labor have resulted in an artificially depressed wage rate. O. B. Pollak

4187. Wasserman, Ursula. ECONOMIC SANCTIONS—THE RHODESIAN EXPERIENCE. *J. of World Trade Law [Switzerland] 1975 9(5): 590-593.* Comments on the impact, if any, that economic sanctions have had on the economy of Southern Rhodesia. J

Politics

4188. Arnold, Anne-Sophie. DER KAMPF DER PATRIOTISCHEN KRÄFTE SIMBABWES FÜR NATIONALE UNABHÄNGIGKEIT UND DEMOKRATIE [The struggle of the patriotic forces of Zimbabwe for national independence and democracy]. *Militärgeschichte [East Germany] 1980 19(6): 670-684.* Proceeding from the victory of the national liberation movement and the founding of the Republic of Zimbabwe in 1980, the author investigates the role of armed struggle in the contest between Africans and the white minority regime of Southern Rhodesia in the 1960's and 1970's. Zimbabwe nationalists were supported by the "Front States" and the Smith regime by the racist Republic of South Africa. The author interprets the establishment of the operative unity of the Zimbabwe African People's Union (ZAPU) and the Zimbabwe African National Union (ZANU) in the Patriotic Front, which was created with great difficulty, as one of the prime conditions for success. 3 photos, 2 maps, table, 32 notes. J/T (H. D. Andrews)

4189. Arnold, Guy. RHODESIA UNDER PRESSURE. *Africa Report 1975 20(4): 16-20.* The Portuguese coup placed political and military pressures on the Ian Smith regime because of changes in Mozambique and South Africa. S

4190. Bratton, Michael. THE PUBLIC SERVICE IN ZIMBABWE. *Pol. Sci. Q. 1980 95(3): 441-464.* Describes the opportunities and constraints regarding public service reform in Zimbabwe at the time of its political independence. J

4191. Chanaiwa, David. THE PREMIERSHIP OF GARFIELD TODD IN RHODESIA: RACIAL PARTNERSHIP VERSUS COLONIAL INTERESTS, 1953-1958. *J. of Southern African Affairs 1976 1(special issue): 83-94.* The premiership of Garfield Todd in Southern Rhodesia, 1953-58, symbolized an unsuccessful attempt by European and African moderates to settle race relations. It also marked the end of effective African-European cooperation in the country. In spite of his reputation as an ultraliberal and champion of African interests, Todd was essentially opposed to the political, economic, and cultural aspirations of the African people, and thus found universal suffrage and majority rule totally unacceptable. His main concern was for the African elites—such as doctors, lawyers, teachers, and nurses—who had demonstrated the desire to emulate Europeans. The masses, however, commanded little of his sympathy, as revealed in Todd's major pieces of legislation. The author discusses the causes of Todd's political downfall. Secondary sources; 21 notes. A. W. Howell

4192. Chartrand, Philip E. POLITICAL CHANGE IN RHODESIA: THE SOUTH AFRICA FACTOR. *Issue 1975 5(4): 13-20.* Discusses the Southern Rhodesian government's willingness to begin direct negotiations with African liberation movements advocating majority rule in 1974 and the relationship to the current foreign policy of South Africa.

4193. Cheater, Angela. WOMEN AND THEIR PARTICIPATION IN COMMERCIAL AGRICULTURAL PRODUCTION: THE CASE OF MEDIUM-SCALE FREEHOLD IN ZIMBABWE. *Development and Change [Netherlands] 1981 12(3): 349-377.* Examines female participation in production oriented to the national market on medium-scale freehold farms in Zimbabwe and analyzes Zimbabwe's present state of economic evolution from a Marxist perspective.

4194. Clarke, D. G. ECONOMIC AND POLITICAL ASPECTS OF THE RHODESIAN FRANCHISE: A RESEARCH NOTE. *J. of Commonwealth Pol. Studies [Great Britain] 1973 11(1): 67-78.* Analyzes the economic changes in Southern Rhodesia's constitution and the shift toward apartheid, and considers its relations with Great Britain, 1961-71.

4195. Cobb, Charles. ZIMBABWE: A YEAR OF INDEPENDENCE. *Crisis 1981 88(3): 146-152.* After a year of independence some confusion and legacies of old Rhodesia still linger. Robert Mugabe, prime minister of Zimbabwe, bases his new government on the end of white rule, a new nationalism, and a hybrid Marxism. Zimbabwe is transforming its systems, not radically replacing them. Democracy and participation among the masses are increasing. A. G. Belles

4196. Coker, Christopher. DECOLONIZATION IN THE SEVENTIES: RHODESIA AND THE DIALECTIC OF NATIONAL LIBERATION. *Round Table [Great Britain] 1979 (274): 122-136.* The steps taken toward Zimbabwe independence must be seen against the background of the guerrilla war, condoned by the Front Line Presidents (FLPs) in 1969, which will develop into civil war in 1979. Based on secondary sources, mainly newspaper artaicles; 14 notes.

4197. Cunningham, Patsy. A BARGAIN AT ANY PRICE: ZIMBABWE ON THE BLOCK. *Can. Dimension [Canada] 1977 12(1): 22-25.* Examines the white government of Southern Rhodesia, 1931-76, and the growing national liberation movement.

4198. Danaher, Kevin Drew. THE POLITICAL ECONOMY OF HUNGER IN RHODESIA AND ZIMBABWE. *Issue: A Q. J. of Opinion 1981 11(3-4): 33-35.* Discusses Operation Turkey, 1979-81, the colonial government's plan to deprive the rural areas of Zimbabwe of sufficient food so that the guerrillas and their civilian supporters would not have the strength to carry on a war. Even after liberation, the rural population is suffering from the effects of malnutrition.

4199. Day, John. THE CREATION OF POLITICAL MYTHS: AFRICAN NATIONALISM IN SOUTHERN RHODESIA. *J. of Southern African Studies [Great Britain] 1975 2(1): 52-65.* The rapid growth of African nationalism in Southern Rhodesia in the late 1950's created a political atmosphere of unprecedented intensity. The sudden eruption of a radical mass movement produced emotional turbulence which generated powerful myths in both the African and European communities. The Africans believed that self-government was imminent, and the whites claimed that few Africans supported African nationalism. Based on press reports; 32 notes. S. P. Carr

4200. Day, John. THE INSIGNIFICANCE OF TRIBE IN THE AFRICAN POLITICS OF ZIMBABWE RHODESIA. *J. of Commonwealth and Comparative Pol. [Great Britain] 1980 18(1): 85-109.* The political divisions within Southern Rhodesia since the 1960's have been complex, but not due to the hostility between the Shona and the Ndebele. The wars between them are ancient history and mostly forgotten, and in 1896 both groups had rebelled against white rule, showing signs of longstanding coordination. Neither existed as a undifferentiated social unit before the whites arrived and colonial rule eroded traditional groupings and knowledge of English broke down language barriers. Nationalism and other political creeds have transcended ethnic considerations. Based on printed sources, newspapers, and interviews; 63 notes. E. J. Adams

4201. Day, John. RHODESIA, THE POLITICAL PROBLEM. *World Survey [Great Britain] 1976 (86): 1-16.* Discusses the struggle between the races for political control of Zimbabwe since 1888.

4202. Day, John. RHODESIENS SCHWIERIGER WEG ZUR MEHRHEITSHERRSCHAFT. DIE INTERNE REGELUNG ALS VERSUCH EINES FRIEDLICHEN ÜBERGANGES [Rhodesia's difficult road to majority rule: the internal solution as an attempt for a peaceful transition]. *Europa Archiv [West Germany] 1978 33(13): 411-418.* Continuous guerrilla warfare since the early 1960's resulted in the increasing political and economic weakness of Southern Rhodesia. Ian Smith's government rejected negotiations with the black majority until 1974, when the South African government pressed him to adopt a less rigid line.

4203. Day, John. ZIMBABWE DIVIDED. *Contemporary Rev. [Great Britain] 1975 227(1318): 240-245.* Discusses the divisions within the Zimbabwean African nationalist movement, 1961-75.

4204. DeLisle Thompson, J. THE COLOURS OF THE SOUTHERN RHODESIA VOLUNTEERS (WESTERN DIVISION). *Rhodesiana [Zimbabwe] 1977 (36): 23-25.* Describes the disbandment of the Southern Rhodesia Volunteers in 1927 and the laying up of their flags in St. Johns Cathedral, Bulawayo, in 1951. Photo. C. A. McNeill

4205. DeWolf, Shirley. THE RESETTLEMENT AND REHABILITATION OF REFUGEES IN THE UMTALI AREA. *Issue: A Q. J. of Opinion 1981 11(3-4): 27-20.* Discusses the repatriation and resettlement of refugees exiled during the Zimbabwe war of independence as implemented in 1980 by the United Nations High Commission for Refugees, especially the psychological difficulties involved and the response of the receiving communities, with special attention to the Umtali-Fort Victoria area.

4206. Eriksen, Tore Linné. FRA RHODESIA TIL ZIMBABWE [From Rhodesia to Zimbabwe]. *Internasjonal Politikk [Norway] 1976 (3B): 659-688.* Presents the historical background to the Zimbabwe conflict and the emergence of the liberation movements, underlining the obvious weakening of the illegal Smith regime, economically, militarily and politically. Kissinger's diplomacy is an attempt to create a neocolonial transitional solution which may simultaneously stabilize conditions inside South Africa as well. Such an assessment necessarily means that a transitional arrangement based on the premises of the Kissinger/Smith plan will conflict sharply with the aims of the nationalist and guerrilla movements. J

4207. Fynn, A. R. THE NEW ADMINISTRATION. *NADA [Zimbabwe] 1978 11(5): 519-521.* Describes the changes wrought on the conduct of provincial administration in Southern Rhodesia by the guerrilla warfare of 1972-74.

4208. Galic, Camille-Marie. LA RHODÉSIE, D'HIER À DEMAIN [Rhodesia, from yesterday to tomorrow]. *Écrits de Paris [France] 1978 (378): 12-23.* Discusses events leading up to the agreement recently signed in Southern Rhodesia to transfer power from the government of Ian Smith to the black majority and expresses fear for the white minority once the transfer actually takes place.

4209. Gerold-Scheepers, T. AFRICAN RESISTANCE IN RHODESIA: A CONCISE SURVEY OF PUBLICATIONS. *African Perspectives [Netherlands] 1976 (1): 109-134.* Thematic bibliographic essay assessing works devoted to the history of African opposition to European penetration and rule in Zimbabwe during the 19th and 20th centuries. 21 notes, biblio. L. W. Truschel

4210. Good, Kenneth. SETTLER COLONIALISM IN RHODESIA. *African Affairs [Great Britain] 1974 73(290): 10-36.* Discusses the current white settler position in Southern Rhodesia. The military, presently all volunteer, is inadequate and the economy is beset with many weaknesses including a 10 to 1 wage discrepancy based on race. Settlers take full advantage of the constitution and Africans have, in many instances, turned to guerrilla warfare. The settler government has refused to compromise with African citizens. table, 93 notes. H. G. Soff

4211. Gregory, Martyn. THE ZIMBABWE ELECTION: THE POLITICAL AND MILITARY IMPLICATIONS. *J. of Southern African Studies [Great Britain] 1980 7(1): 17-37.* The Zimbabwe elections of 1980 resulted in the coming to power of an unequal coalition of the former guerrilla groups known as the Patriotic Front, consisting of Robert Mugabe's Zimbabwe African National Union and Joshua Nkomo's Zimbabwe African People's Union (whose name was changed to the Patriotic Front for the 1980 elections). Analyzes political and military factors in the settlement and predicts the continuation of multiparty and multiracial politics. Based on interviews, speeches, and newspapers; 61 notes. L. W. Truschel

4212. Gregory, Martyn. ZIMBABWE 1980: POLITICISATION THROUGH ARMED STRUGGLE AND ELECTORAL MOBILISATION. *J. of Commonwealth and Comparative Pol. [Great Britain] 1981 19(1): 62-94.* Conventional criteria of electoral analysis are inappropriate for the study of the transitional period and election campaign and results in Zimbabwe, 1979-80. The victory of Robert Mugabe's Zimbabwe African National Union-Patriotic Front can only be understood by reference to seven years of armed struggle, the establishment of "dual power" in the countryside by the guerrillas, and the systematic mobilization of the peasantry. Their electoral campaign was entirely concerned with getting supporters to the polls, while Bishop Abel Muzorewa's United African National Council was discredited by cooperation with the whites and failure to control the security forces. The chronic misreading of the situation by whites, Great Britain, and South Africa helped to ease Mugabe's road to power. Based on official reports, interviews, newspapers, and other printed sources; map, 9 tables, 88 notes. D. J. Nicholls

4213. Hancock, I. R. THE CAPRICORN AFRICA SOCIETY IN SOUTHERN RHODESIA. *Rhodesian Hist. [Zimbabwe] 1978 9: 41-62.* Colonel David Stirling formed the Capricorn Society in 1952 to combat South African racism, African nationalism and negative sentimentalism. It was neither sufficiently political, nor practical, and its indecisiveness exposed its utopian nature. Its membership was overwhelmingly white and reached a peak of 2,556 members in January 1957, and when Stirling resigned in 1958 the organization disintegrated. Based on

sources in National Archives and Ranche House College, Harare, University of York, several collections of private papers in Zimbabwe and England, interviews and secondary sources; 77 notes.
O. B. Pollak

4214. Hancock, I. R. CONFRONTATION IN THE "LAND OF LOST CONTENT": THE WHITE CONTRIBUTION TO THE PRESENT CONFLICT IN RHODESIA. *Conflict 1979 1(3): 191-209.* Critical view of white supremacists' role in the growing racial discord in Southern Rhodesia, 1960-78.

4215. Hancock, I. R. and Neal, P. V. CONFRONTATION IN THE "LAND OF LOST CONTENT": THE BLACK CONTRIBUTION TO THE PRESENT CONFLICT IN RHODESIA. *Conflict 1980 2(4): 383-399.* Traces the political divisions within the African nationalist movements in Zimbabwe and their ambivalence toward armed conflict until its escalation from 1976 to the end of 1979. Demonstrates the roles of the Zimbabwe African People's Union (ZAPU) and the Zimbabwe African National Union (ZANU) in the rise of African nationalist militancy from the early 1960's.

4216. Hancock, I. R. SANE AND PRAGMATIC LIBERALISM: THE ACTION GROUP IN BULAWAYO, 1955-1965. *Rhodesian Hist. [Zimbabwe] 1976 7: 65-83.* Peter Gibbs formed the Action Group in 1942 in Bulawayo, Zimbabwe's second largest city, with membership limited to 30. Some of its members became members of parliament and cabinet officers. Committed to federation, economic growth, and building African confidence in white intentions, the group never thought that whites would relinquish rule. Not as advanced as the Inter Racial Association or the Capricorn Society, it nevertheless floundered in the face of the right-wing political movement of the 1960's and completely collapsed in 1972. Based on documents in the Zimbabwe National Archives, newspapers, interviews, and secondary sources; 57 notes.
O. B. Pollak

4217. Harris, Peter S. THE RHODESIAN BLOCKADE AND INTERNAL STRUCTURAL CHANGE. *Monthly R. 1974 26(7): 59-62.*

4218. Hull, Richard W. THE CONFLICT IN RHODESIA. *Current Hist. 1976 71(421): 149-152, 185.* Examines the presence of armed conflict in Zimbabwe since the 19th century and the current efforts toward peaceful independence from white regimes, although the Communist-trained Zimbabwe Liberation Army is convinced that true liberation will never be achieved without armed struggle.

4219. Hull, Richard W. THE CONTINUING CRISIS IN RHODESIA. *Current Hist. 1980 78(455): 107-109, 133-134.* Reviews the political developments leading to black majority rule, and projects continuing unrest in Zimbabwe.

4220. Hull, Richard W. RHODESIA IN CRISIS. *Current Hist. 1979 76(445): 105-109, 137-138.* Provides background on the 1972-78 conflict in Zimbabwe between the multiracial transitional coalition government and the guerrilla armies led by Robert Mugabe and Joshua Nkomo.

4221. Hull, Richard W. ZIMBABWE: TIME RUNNING OUT. *Current Hist. 1981 80(464): 120-123, 130-131.* Examines the situation in Zimbabwe after the 1979 cease-fire in the civil war, Robert Mugabe's conciliary policies, attempts to reach economic stability and to forge a national army, and US neglect.

4222. Jokonya, T. J. B. THE EFFECTS OF THE WAR ON THE RURAL POPULATION OF ZIMBABWE. *J. of Southern African Affairs 1980 5(2): 133-147.* A neo-Marxist assessment of disruptive events on African peasants in Zimbabwe during the 1966-79 war. Large numbers became refugees in cities and neighboring countries or were moved into resettlement villages during the fighting, as the rural economy and public facilities collapsed. Many of these peasant refugees were proletarianized by the war and being uprooted from their traditional rural existence. Based on interviews, International Red Cross reports, newspapers, and secondary sources; 40 notes.
L. W. Truschel

4223. Kinloch, G. C. RHODESIA IN THE 1960S. *Zambezia: the J. of the U. of Rhodesia [Rhodesia] 1974 3(2): 121-124.* Review essay on E. Mlambo, *Rhodesia: The Struggle for a Birthright* (London: Hurst, 1972); S. E. Wilmer, ed., *Zimbabwe Now* (London: R. Collings, 1973); M. I. Hirsch, *A Decade of Crisis: Ten Years of Rhodesian Front Rule* (Salisbury: P. Dearlove, 1973); and R. C. Good, *U.D.I.: The International Politics of the Rhodesian Rebellion* (London: Faber, 1973). All these writers focus on the 1960's and the movement toward the 1971 Anglo-Rhodesian settlement proposals. The author wishes to impose an "analytic, process-oriented" model to this period. The studies analyzed are by an African nationalist, Rhodesian Front propagandist, and a former US ambassador to Zambia. The deficiencies of these studies demonstrate the necessity of a multi-dimensional approach to Southern Rhodesian politics.
O. B. Pollak

4224. Kirk, Tony. POLITICS AND VIOLENCE IN RHODESIA. *African Affairs [Great Britain] 1975 74(294): 3-38.* Traces nationalist politics in Zimbabwe from 1963 to the guerrilla raids of 1972 led by the Front for the Liberation of Zimbabwe (FROLIZI). Analyzes the FROLIZI movement which was designed to terrorize white settlers, and the government response to this sabotage. Also refutes several propositions of Kenneth Good (see abstract 4210). Although the blacks might have been just in taking up arms, their leadership was interested in selfish goals and not national deliverance. 39 notes.
H. G. Soff

4225. Kirk, Tony. THE RHODESIAN FRONT AND THE AFRICAN NATIONAL COUNCIL. *Issue 1974 4(1): 14-23.* Discusses the Rhodesian Front, governing party of Southern Rhodesia, and its policy of racial segregation and dialogues with the African National Council.
S

4226. Larsen, Joar Hoel. FRA RHODESIA TIL ZIMBABWE [From Rhodesia to Zimbabwe]. *Samtiden [Norway] 1977 86(4): 223-229.* Traces the origins and emergence of liberation movements in Zimbabwe since the 1920's with particular reference to the activities of the Zimbabwe African People's Union (ZAPU) and the Zimbabwe African National Union (ZANU), 1960's-70's.

4227. Lee, M. Elaine. AN ANALYSIS OF THE RHODESIAN REFERENDUM, 1922. *Rhodesian Hist. [Zimbabwe] 1977 8: 71-98.* Detailed analysis of the referendum that led to the introduction of responsible government in Southern Rhodesia in 1923. The movement was initiated by farmers with the support of white-collar workers and labor. Between 1920 and 1922 there was some diminution of support, but the three sectors merged in a popular party initially called the Rhodesian Responsible Government Party, and later the Rhodesian Party. Based on National Archive Salisbury documents and newspapers; map, 11 tables, 108 notes.
O. B. Pollak

4228. Lee, M. Elaine. THE ORIGINS OF THE RHODESIAN RESPONSIBLE GOVERNMENT MOVEMENT. *Rhodesian Hist. [Rhodesia] 1975 6: 33-52.* Demonstrates the complexity of local politics and economic interests attending opposition to rule by the British South Africa Company in Southern Rhodesia and the desire for responsible government as had become common in the British Empire. While the Chartered Company government was efficient it could not satisfy farmers while being more concerned with mining interests. Based on sources in the Southern Rhodesian National Archives, newspapers, other primary, and secondary sources; 4 tables, 55 notes.
O. B. Pollak

4229. Lemon, Anthony. ELECTORAL MACHINERY AND VOTING PATTERNS IN RHODESIA, 1962-1977. *African Affairs [Great Britain] 1978 77(309): 511-530.* Describes the dual system of voting on A and B rolls in colonial Zimbabwe, 1962-77, with a franchise based on income, property, and educational qualification.

4230. Libby, Ronald T. ANGLO-AMERICAN DIPLOMACY AND THE RHODESIAN SETTLEMENT: A LOSS OF IMPETUS. *Orbis 1979 23(1): 185-211.* Traces internal developments in Southern Rhodesia and Anglo-American diplomacy to reach a peace settlement, 1970's.

4231. MacKenzie, J. M. SOUTHERN RHODESIA AND RESPONSIBLE GOVERNMENT. *Rhodesian Hist. [Zimbabwe] 1978 9: 23-40.* Southern Rhodesia was granted responsible government by Great Britain following a virtually unprecedented referendum in 1923. This victory was the result of the Colonial Office's hostility to the British South Africa Company, whose agent fostered the interests of white populist-oriented labor against commercial interests. Based on documents in the Public Record Office, London, National Archives, Harare, newspapers, and secondary sources; 90 notes. O. B. Pollak

4232. Makambe, E. P. AFRICAN PROTEST MOVEMENTS IN SOUTHERN RHODESIA BEFORE 1930. *Munger Africana Lib. Notes 1982 (65-66): 3-35.* Describes early protest movements in Zimbabwe between 1898 and 1957, which provided a militant political tradition for the nationalist movement of the 1950's and 1960's.

4233. Malinowski, Marek J. THE RISE OF THE AFRICAN NATIONAL-LIBERATION MOVEMENT IN RHODESIA. *Studies on the Developing Countries [Poland] 1975 (7): 88-112.* Chronicles Zimbabwe's African national liberation movement, 1910's-75.

4234. Matthews, Robert O. TALKING WITHOUT NEGOTIATING: THE CASE OF RHODESIA. *Int. J. [Canada] 1979-80 35(1): 91-117.* From the time of Southern Rhodesia's Unilateral Declaration of Independence (UDI) in 1965 to the 1979 London negotiations which brought a temporary return to British rule leading to early majority rule, Prime Minister Ian Smith was frequently engaged in negotiations over Rhodesia's future. Mr. Smith, rather than negotiating in good faith, seems throughout to have been concerned with dividing his opponents, uniting his domestic supporters, pacifying his friends abroad, winning favorable publicity, and above all with assuring the survival of white minority rule for the longest possible time. Based on British government documents and press sources; 41 notes. L. Van Wyk

4235. Maxey, K. THE CONTINUING FIGHT FOR ZIMBABWE. *African Perspectives [Netherlands] 1976 (1): 91-107.* Pro-Zimbabwe nationalist account of phases of guerrilla warfare in Zimbabwe since 1966. Predicts continued fighting and no negotiated political settlement, a situation which will lead inevitably to a guerrilla victory. Based on media and some documentary sources; 54 notes. L. W. Truschel

4236. McAdam, A. RHODESIA'S PHANTOM 'LIBERALISM': IMPERIALISM, FEDERALISM AND REBELLION IN BRITISH CENTRAL AFRICA. *African Perspectives [Netherlands] 1976 (1): 47-54.* A historical assessment of Southern Rhodesian liberalism as mere window dressing on the part of European settlers and their leaders to achieve from Great Britain greater political power within the colony and expansion of their influence and control across British Central Africa. Argues that genuine pro-African white liberals have always been few in Southern Rhodesia. 20 notes. L. W. Truschel

4237. McLaughlin, P. THE THIN WHITE LINE: RHODESIA'S ARMED FORCES SINCE THE SECOND WORLD WAR. *Zambezia: the J. of the U. of Rhodesia [Zimbabwe] 1978 6(2); 175-188.* Reviews six books and several articles which are a mix of official, scholarly, propagandistic prowhite and proguerrilla accounts. Identifies types and numbers of units, financing and manpower, and the strains on the armed forces during the protracted liberation struggle. Objective and accurate study is difficult due to the restricted use of archives on security matters. 54 notes. O. B. Pollak

4238. Mlambo, Eshmael. TENSIONS IN THE WHITE REDOUBT: SOUTHERN RHODESIA. *Africa Today 1974 21(2): 29-37.* Southern Rhodesian stability has been seriously undermined by four traumas: the negative Pearce Commission decision, new guerrilla tactics, closure of the Southern Rhodesian-Zambian border, and the oil embargo. Based on newspapers and secondary sources; 20 notes. G. O. Gagnon

4239. Moyana, Henry V. BRITISH COMPLICITY POLICY ON RHODESIA 1923 TO 1970. *Pan-African J. [Kenya] 1975 8(1): 45-74.* Attempts to show how Great Britain has neglected her responsibilities toward Africans in Southern Rhodesia. Speeches made by British politicians since 1923, and even since the Unilateral Declaration of Independence, have been made to disguise the policy of collaboration with white settlers against the aspirations of the blacks. Based on UN documents, newspaper sources and secondary works; 111 notes. S

4240. Mudariki, P. T. THE ROLE OF EDUCATION IN NATIONAL RECONSTRUCTION IN ZIMBABWE. *Issue: A Q. J. of Opinion 1981 (3-4): 17-21.* Colonial education in Zimbabwe focused on the production of laborers rather than managers and administrators, and during the war of independence many schools were destroyed or shut down. The new government, elected in 1981, has voted to provide free primary education for all children attending government schools and adopted a policy of education that meets cultural and political as well as production needs.

4241. Mufuka, K. Nyamayaro. RHODESIA'S INTERNAL SETTLEMENT: A TRAGEDY. *African Affairs [Great Britain] 1979 78(313): 439-450.* Summarizes Southern Rhodesia's recent history up to Bishop Abel Muzorewa's regime. The constitutional agreement for Southern Rhodesia (1978) was a radical departure from Ian Smith's policy but was designed to produce a pliable black government and a modified form of white supremacy. The ensuing April 1979 election was a victory, in the short term, for Smith's colonial policy. Muzorewa believed that cooperation with the Europeans was a necessary price to be paid for economic development. Collusion between the British Government and the Rhodesian Front existed from the Declaration of Independence in 1965. Muzorewa's election made reconciliation with the Patriotic Front more difficult. 23 notes. R. L. Collison

4242. Mufuka, Kenneth N. RECENT RHODESIAN HISTORY: AN AFRICAN VIEWPOINT. *Africa Today 1977 24(2): 72-74.* Reviews Lawrence Vambe's *From Rhodesia to Zimbabwe* (1976), which is an autobiographical history of the rise of political aspirations among the African population and particularly among the educated Africans who moved from collaboration to revolution. Vambe has provided a valuable insight for Africanists who seek understanding of how some Africans clung to loyalty to Southern Rhodesia. G. O. Gagnon

4243. Mutiti, M. Aaron Benjamin. RHODESIA AND HER FOUR DISCRIMINATORY CONSTITUTIONS. *African Rev. [Tanzania] 1974 4(2): 259-278.* Analyzes each of Southern Rhodesia's four constitutions written since 1923, stressing their differences and Great Britain's involvement in their construction. The discriminatory acts discussed include the Land Apportionment Act of 1930 and the Industrial Conciliation Act of 1934 (under the constitution of 1923); the Declaration of Rights, the Constitutional Council and Voting Rights (under the Constitution of 1961); economic sanctions and their effect (under the constitution of 1965); and the removal of the Common Roll (under the constitution of 1969). Southern Rhodesia is legally a British colony, but Britain has failed to grasp this fact. Each of the four constitutions contain oppressive legislation which Britain should have nullified. 43 notes. H. G. Soff

4244. Ndlovu, Saul. STUDENT PROTEST IN SALISBURY. *Africa Today 1974 21(2): 39-42.* Describes the causes and effects of the University of Rhodesia student demonstrations in August 1974. G. O. Gagnon

4245. Nesuk, M. D. NAROD ZIMBABVE V BOROT'BI ZA SVOBODU [The people of Zimbabwe in their struggle for freedom]. *Ukrains'kyi Istorychnyi Zhurnal [USSR] 1975 (2): 89-97.* Examines the development of the national liberation movement of the African people of Zimbabwe against the white majority regime, 1893-1974.

4246. Niesewand, Peter. WHAT SMITH REALLY FACES. *Africa Report 1973 18(2): 16-20.* Discusses conflict between guerrilla forces and Southern Rhodesia's white government, led by Ian Smith. S

4247. Nzuwah, Mariyawanda. CONFLICT RESOLUTION IN ZIMBABWE: SUPERPOWER DETERMINANTS TO THE PEACE SETTLEMENT. *J. of Southern African Affairs 1979 4(4): 389-400.* Analyzes the peace negotiations held at Lancaster House, London, from 10 September to 17 December 1979, and the settlement agreement signed on 21 December. The author accuses the Western Powers of sabotaging the Zimbabwe revolution by pressuring the Patriotic Front groups to accept Western and anti-Soviet economic, strategic, and ideological interests in the country, and credits the Soviets with promoting wars of genuine liberation in Africa. Based on published documents, newspapers, and secondary sources; 33 notes. L. W. Truschel

4248. Ostapenko, G. S. RODEZIISKAIA PROBLEMA (OBZOR ANGLO-AMERIKANSKOI LITERATURY 60-KH GODOV) [The

Rhodesian problem: a survey of Anglo-American literature of the 1960's]. *Narody Azii i Afriki [USSR] 1975 (2): 157-168.* Liberal authors condemn colonialism and the racist policies of the Southern Rhodesian government, but defend the interests of the British middle classes. Conservatives also condemn racism, but add that it is less dangerous than African nationalism. They also stress the role of the British as civilizers. Openly racist authors defend Ian Smith's regime and European privileges, while considering Africans uncivilized. Based on primary sources; 28 notes. L. Kalinowski/S

4249. Passmore, Gloria C. BEYOND INDEPENDENCE: UNFETTERED COMMUNITY DEVELOPMENT. *Zambezia [Zimbabwe] 1980 8(1): 85-99.* Michael Bratton's pamphlet, *Beyond Community Development*(1978), misrepresents and inaccurately describes the policy of Community Development and Local Government initiated in Zimbabwe in 1962. Failing to recognize its liberal origins or the genuine interest in developing democratic practices and leadership through the African Councils Act of 1957, Bratton wrongly states that African councils acquired few important powers and that emphasis on local government was merely a way for the central government to shun responsibility. The policy had faults, but it was not racist in intent and did provide useful precedents for development of local democratic government. Based on debates and reports of the government of Southern Rhodesia; 41 notes. D. H. Nicely

4250. Patel, H. H. ASIAN POLITICAL ACTIVITY IN RHODESIA FROM THE SECOND WORLD WAR TO 1972. *Rhodesian Hist. [Zimbabwe] 1978 9: 63-82.* Suggests that the aim of Asians in colonial Zimbabwe was to ameliorate the disabilities of a minority community. Describes their social characteristics and internal organization, and analyzes four methods of political interaction: persuasion, demonstration, litigation and alliance. Based on collections of private papers of Indian organizations in Harare and Bulawayo and secondary sources; 52 notes. O. B. Pollak

4251. Peaden, W. R. ASPECTS OF THE CHURCH AND ITS POLITICAL INVOLVEMENT IN SOUTHERN RHODESIA, 1959-1972. *Zambezia [Zimbabwe] 1979 7(2): 191-210.* There is a substantial body of literature on the role of the church in Zimbabwe from early missionary days to contemporary church-state conflicts. The church facilitated white settlement and provided a vehicle for selected African upward mobility. The literature treats the church on a continuum from saint to sinner. The author discusses radical missionaries, education, nationalism, Catholics, Methodists, Dutch Reformed Church, World Council of Churches, reaction to the Unilateral Declaration of Independence, guerrilla activity, and racist legislation. Based on archives in England and Zimbabwe, newspapers, legislation and parliamentary debates, and secondary sources; 71 notes. O. B. Pollak

4252. Peters, J. R. THE FALL OF DINDIKWA, CHIEF MUTAMBARA. *NADA [Zimbabwe] 1974 11(1): 7-10.* Describes the traditional governmental structure of the Vagarwe people in Melsetter District and the usurpation of its chieftainship between 1947 and 1973. Discusses the removal of the usurper, Dindikwa, by the elders and points to the necessity of allowing traditional authorities a major role in enforcing local custom. L. W. Truschel

4253. Phimister, Ian and Onselen, Charles van. THE POLITICAL ECONOMY OF TRIBAL ANIMOSITY: A CASE STUDY OF THE 1929 BULAWAYO LOCATION "FACTION FIGHT." *J. of Southern African Studies [Great Britain] 1979 6(1): 1-43.* In December 1929 a violent disturbance within Bulawayo's African Location involved a few deaths, scores of injuries, and hundreds of arrests. This was one of numerous allegedly interethnic fights that occurred in colonial Zimbabwe's African townships and labor camps. The fighting in Bulawayo is interpreted here as a struggle between an established community of Ndebele workers suffering depredations from a long-term corrupt municipal administration and a sudden decline in employment and a newly arrived underclass of cheap potential laborers, who were Shona from the east and other Africans from the colonial territories north of the Zambezi. The physical violence, stemming from underlying economic causes, took the open form of ethnic animosity when it erupted in 1929. Based on Zimbabwe archival sources; 200 notes. L. W. Truschel

4254. Pollak, Oliver B. ZIMBABWE: REFLECTIONS ON THE DECOLONIZATION OF RHODESIA. *Midwest Q. 1977 18(3): 318-328.* Seventy-five years of rigid social and economic separation during the evolution of Southern Rhodesia may affect the future of independent Zimbabwe. White colonists continuously reinforced the concepts of a superior race and culture and of a highly stratified class-race economy. Land policies discriminated against the Africans, and franchise requirements and representative systems were developed which maintained legislative control in white hands. The 1974 election indicated that 80% of the all-white electorate still preferred to maintain the status quo. The crisis caused by internal pressures combined with sanctions against the country have resulted in even more oppression against the blacks. Zimbabwe has had a bitter past, but it is hoped that rather than perpetuating its problems it can develop a creative and positive future. S. J. Quinlan

4255. Ranger, Terence. THE CHANGING OF THE OLD GUARD: ROBERT MUGABE AND THE REVIVAL OF ZANU. *J. of Southern African Studies [Great Britain] 1980 7(1): 71-90.* Robert Mugabe and his fellow "old guard" leaders within the Zimbabwe African National Union (ZANU) have recently been attacked for abandoning their revolutionary programs during the final years of the conflict and as the new rulers in Zimbabwe. Their actions and speeches since 1974, however, have shown no lessening of their earlier commitments to a revolutionary transformation of society. Based on interviews, correspondence, and speeches of ZANU leaders, newspapers, and secondary sources; 37 notes. L. W. Truschel

4256. Ransford, Oliver. A HISTORY OF RHODESIA BY ROBERT BLAKE. *Rhodesiana [Rhodesia] 1978 38: 19-22.* A review article which examines Robert Blake's *A History of Rhodesia* (London: Methuen, 1977) paying particular attention to the political and constitutional history of Southern Rhodesia.

4257. Raphael, Arnold. ZIMBABWE'S FIRST PRESIDENT? JOSHUA NKOMO AND HIS DETERMINATION TO LEAD AN INDEPENDENT RHODESIA. *Round Table [Great Britain] 1979 (273): 88-91.* Summarizes Joshua Nkomo's career, personality, political ambitions, creation of the Zimbabwe African National Union (ZANU) and support for the Patriotic Front.

4258. Rimanelli, Marco. ZIMBABWE: LA FINE DEL PROBLEMA RHODESIANO? [Zimbabwe: the end of the Rhodesian problem?]. *Africa [Italy] 1980 35(3-4): 387-413.* Observes the political and economic evolution of Zimbabwe from a British colony to an independent state, drawing attention to the effects of unilateral independence declared by the white community to preserve its privileges in the face of the African majority. After 15 years of rebellion, seven years of war with more than 27,000 dead, and a number of unsuccessful negotiations, the solution of the political problem and the daily situation in Zimbabwe are the tasks to be undertaken by the government in power. J

4259. Roberts, R. S. AN HISTORICAL BIBLIOGRAPHY OF VOTERS LISTS IN SOUTHERN RHODESIA. *Rhodesian Hist. [Zimbabwe] 1977 8: 111-114.* Part I. 1899-1922. Available voters lists for the 1899, 1903, 1905, 1908, 1911, 1914, 1917, 1920, and 1922 elections. These lists include the voter's name, place of residence, and occupation, and are crucial source materials for historical and political analysis. 7 notes. Article to be continued. O. B. Pollak

4260. Roberts, R. S. TOWARDS A HISTORY OF RHODESIA'S ARMED FORCES. *Rhodesian Hist. [Zimbabwe] 1974 5: 103-110.* Surveys available literature on the Southern Rhodesian military, noting neglected topics of research such as law enforcement and criminality in a plural society, recruitment problems in which the militant social control apparatus is over two-thirds African staffed, and the quasi-militarist nature of white civilians in a settler society. 23 notes. O. B. Pollak

4261. Rotberg, Robert I. WINNING THE WAR FOR ZIMBABWE. *Orbis 1982 24(4): 1045-1053.* Presents a combined review of Lewis H. Gann and Thomas H. Henrikson's *The Struggle for Zimbabwe: Battle in the Bush*(1981) and David Martin and Phyllis Johnson's, *The Struggle for Zimbabwe: The Chimarenga War* (1981). Itemizes seven lessons of the Zimbabwe struggle that should be studied by South Africa. 2 notes. J. W. Thacker, Jr.

4262. Rustin, Bayard. THE WAR AGAINST ZIMBABWE. *Commentary 1979 68(1): 25-32.* Discusses the recent 1979 election in Zimbabwe from the point of view of the Zimbabweans who viewed it as a positive step in the developing country, and of outside critics who saw it as a staged election.

4263. Saint Brides, Lord. THE LESSONS OF ZIMBABWE-RHODESIA. *Int. Security 1980 4(4): 177-184.* Discusses the move toward independence of Zimbabwe, never governed directly from Britain through the Colonial Office but from the Dominions Office, from 1961 through the breakdown of talks and the declaration of unilateral independence by Ian Smith in 1965, to the final settlement in 1979-80.

4264. Schutz, Barry M. THE COLONIAL HERITAGE OF STRIFE: SOURCES OF CLEAVAGE IN THE ZIMBABWE LIBERATION MOVEMENT. *Africa Today 1978 25(1): 7-27.* Examines the usual explanations of disunity among Zimbabwean independence movements and concludes that the "settler colonial system of education" was decisive. Missionary controlled education reflected divisions between religious idealism and political pragmatism common in white Rhodesia. These cleavages were transmitted to missionary educated Zimbabweans and reinforced by cultural tendencies among the ethnic groups. Secondary sources; 32 notes. G. O. Gagnon

4265. Seidman, Robert B. and Gagne, Martin. THE STATE, LAW, AND DEVELOPMENT IN ZIMBABWE. *J. of Southern African Affairs 1980 5(2): 149-170.* Analysis from a Marxist perspective of how Europeans in Zimbabwe since the early 20th century utilized the country's legal system to attain racial domination of the economy and of the African population. The new revolutionary Zimbabwe will have to transform not only the openly racist laws of the past, but also eliminate the property, contract, and public service laws in order to achieve its aim of creating a socialist state and society. Based on International Labor Organization reports, Rhodesian codes, and secondary sources; 47 notes. L. W. Truschel

4266. Shamuyarira, Nathan M. ZIMBABWE'S LIBERATION THROUGH SELF-RELIANCE. *Alternatives [Netherlands] 1975 1(1): 55-77.* In this era of nuclear stalemate, guerrilla warfare has assumed great importance as a tool for settling national and international disputes and for changing governmental systems. In the South African subcontinent no fewer than eight liberation movements have organized guerrilla activity among a growing section of the 30 million inhabitants against the four million white settlers dominating the present political and economic system. J

4267. Sitole, Masipula. ETHNICITY AND FACTIONALISM IN ZIMBABWE NATIONALIST POLITICS, 1957-79. *Ethnic and Racial Studies [Great Britain] 1980 3(1): 17-39.* A major cause of factionalism in Zimbabwe national politics has been the question of ethnic representation in the political parties.

4268. Smiley, Xan. ZIMBABWE, SOUTHERN AFRICA AND THE RISE OF ROBERT MUGABE. *Foreign Affairs 1980 58(5): 1060-1083.* Traces Robert Mugabe's consolidation of his leadership of the Zimbabwe African National Union after 1974 and the course of negotiations with Margaret Thatcher's conservative government during the transition to independent government in Zimbabwe. Describes Mugabe's organization of the postindependence government and the evolution of foreign relations in southern Africa. 6 notes. A. A. Englard

4269. Smith, Clive G. ZIMBABWE'S FORGOTTEN MAN. *Working Papers for a New Society 1980 7(3): 61-63.* Argues that the political emergence of Robert Mugabe in 1979 was evolutionary rather than unexpected as portrayed by the Western press.

4270. Soames, Lord. FROM RHODESIA TO ZIMBABWE. *Int. Affairs [Great Britain] 1980 56(3): 405-419.* Discusses Great Britain's role in facilitating the transition to majority rule in Zimbabwe.

4271. Stephenson, Glenn V. THE IMPACT OF INTERNATIONAL ECONOMIC SANCTIONS ON THE INTERNAL VIABILITY OF RHODESIA. *Geographical R. 1975 65(3): 377-389.* Southern Rhodesia has been subjected to an economic boycott since 1965, when economic sanctions were placed on the country in an effort to force the small white ruling class to agree to the principles of unimpeded progress toward majority rule and the ending of racial discrimination. However, international political coercion has not essentially altered the position of the white settler government. It has successfully withstood external economic pressures by trading through third-party arrangements and by developing national economic policies favorable to the white minority, thereby increasing economic disparities between the Africans and the Europeans. This study analyzes the differential impact of sanctions on racial economic development patterns and considers various alternative measures that might be taken to encourage national cohesion. J

4272. Strack, Harry R. THE INFLUENCE OF TRANSNATIONAL ACTORS ON THE ENFORCEMENT OF SANCTIONS AGAINST RHODESIA. *Naval War Coll. Rev. 1976 28(4): 52-64.* Economic sanctions have been considered, at least in theory, as the most powerful and most effective means of compelling a government to pursue or to desist from a specific course of action. When the Southern Rhodesian government in November 1965 declared independence from Great Britain, first the British Government and then the United Nations imposed economic sanctions to compel that government "to return to legality." The experience of the past 10 years shows that not only have economic sanctions not brought about the intended political changes, but also that Southern Rhodesia has, in fact, prospered. From the author's forthcoming *Sanctions: The Case of Rhodesia,* to be published by the Syracuse University Press in 1977. J

4273. Thomas, Norman E. THE ETHICS OF BISHOP ABEL MUZOREWA. *Religion in Life 1980 49(2): 178-194.* Traces the life and political activity of United Methodist Bishop Abel Muzorewa, former prime minister of Zimbabwe-Rhodesia, and analyzes the ethical content of his speeches and writings.

4274. Todd, Judith. RHODESIA: GUARDING AGAINST THE "HAPPIEST AFRICANS." *Africa Report 1973 18(4): 40-42.* Describes oppression of the black majority by the white minority in Southern Rhodesia. S

4275. Vambe, Lawrence C. MUGABE FACES A FUTURE OF PROMISES AND PROBLEMS. *Round Table [Great Britain] 1980 (279): 278-282.* The Ndebele, who ruled before the formation of Southern Rhodesia, are now the second ethnic group in Zimbabwe, with the Shona holding the predominance of power. The rivalry between the two will determine the future of Zimbabwe, as will the extent of the divisions within the Shona, which itself consists of four subgroupings. A power struggle between them could threaten the stability of the nation. E. J. Adams

4276. Weinrich, A. K. H. THE AFRICAN NATIONAL COUNCIL'S PAST PERFORMANCE AND PRESENT PROSPECTS IN RHODESIA. *Africa Today 1975 22(1): 5-28.* The African National Council (ANC), established in 1971, represents a center position between guerrilla and rightist white elements in Southern Rhodesia. Based on Southern Rhodesian sources; 35 notes. G. O. Gagnon

4277. Wetherell, H. I. N. H. WILSON: POPULISM IN RHODESIAN POLITICS. *Rhodesian Hist.[Zimbabwe] 1975 6: 53-76.* Traces the career of Neil Housman Wilson from his arrival in Southern Rhodesia in 1906, with special focus on his political activities, 1930's-50's. At various times he espoused the aspirations and grievances of small farmers, miners, shopkeepers, and disillusioned politicians against the incumbent ministry of Godfrey Huggins. Despite repeated electoral failure, the government adopted aspects of the opposition program. The rise of the Rhodesian Front in the 1960's was the culmination of populist movements. Based on government documents in the National Archives, newspapers, and interviews; 71 notes. O. B. Pollak

4278. Wild, N. C. A QUESTION OF SUCCESSION. *NADA [Zimbabwe] 1977 11(4): 415-427.* Describes the controversy surrounding the selection of a successor to Magumbo Mabena, headman of the Maribeha Tribal Trust Land, in 1972, when five men claimed the title as rightfully theirs.

4279. Windrich, Elaine. CONTROLLING THE MEDIA: RHODESIAN STYLE. *J. of Southern African Affairs 1980 5(1): 89-100.* Traces the history of government censorship of newspapers and radio under the rule of the Rhodesian Front from 1962 to 1978 and during the internal settlement period in 1978-79. Official censorship was applied from the Ministry of Information, Immigration, and Tourism, while this same agency and the Rhodesian Broadcasting Corporation promoted the government's view that Southern Rhodesia was under attack by Soviet and Western governments and a variety of domestic liberals and black extremists. Based on newspaper accounts and secondary sources; 22 notes. L. W. Truschel

4280. Windrich, Elaine. RHODESIA AND THE UNITED STATES. *African Affairs [Great Britain] 1977 76(303): 260-261.* A review article of Anthony Lake's *The 'Tar Baby' Option: American Policy Toward Southern Rhodesia*, (New York: Columbia U. Pr., 1976). This is the first study of reversal of American foreign policy from benign neglect to active intervention on the side of the white minority regime. "American actions may well have contributed to the continued suppression of the six million Blacks by the white minority regime" and "to the weakening of international law and institutions by hindering the efforts of the United Nations to deal with Rhodesia as a threat to international peace and security." The author is committed to a reversal of that policy. E. P. Stickney

4281. Windrich, Elaine. RHODESIA: THE CHALLENGE TO DETENTE. *World Today [Great Britain] 1975 31(9): 358-367.* Armed struggle is the only alternative to detente in view of the failure of the Lusaka talks to solve the dilemma of the Ian Smith regime in Southern Rhodesia in 1974.

4282. Windrich, Elaine. RHODESIA: THE ROAD FROM LUANDA TO GENEVA. *World Today [Great Britain] 1977 33(3): 101-110.* Examines the US role in the settlement of the Zimbabwe independence dispute, especially the role played by Henry Kissinger in Geneva, 1976.

4283. Windrich, Elaine. RHODESIAN CENSORSHIP: THE ROLE OF THE MEDIA IN THE MAKING OF A ONE-PARTY STATE. *African Affairs [Great Britain] 1979 78(313): 522-534.* Southern Rhodesia was subject to censorship from 1963 onwards. The aim was to secure complete control of radio and television, and to destroy the credibility of the press. The Argus Press of South Africa, one of whose subsidiaries published Southern Rhodesia's daily and weekly newspapers, was particularly under attack since it was opposed to the illegal declaration of independence by the Rhodesian Front. Extremists in the government's information department packed the newspapers' correspondence columns with letters representing the Rhodesian Front's interests, and censored both news and opinion. The only African daily newspaper was banned in 1964. Many journalists were deported, some of whom have now returned. 16 notes. R. L. Collison

4284. Woolacott, R. C. DISTRICT ADMINISTRATION, 1912 AND 1977. *NADA [Zimbabwe] 1980 12(2): 94-99.* Extracts from the diaries of two Southern Rhodesian administrators patrolling the same area near the Zambezi valley in 1912-13 and 1977, with some analysis. Despite the difference of half a century, many of the petty problems of local administration appear to be similar. Based on diaries of Rhodesian district administrators. L. W. Truschel

4285. Zeliniker, Shimson. SETTLERS AND SETTLEMENT: THE RHODESIA CRISIS 1974-75. *Africa Today 1975 22(2): 23-44.* The apparent vacillations of the Ian Smith government toward the African National Council is prompted by Smith's need to conciliate moderate Europeans when events favored them while appeasing the conservatives of Smith's own party. Based on periodical and secondary sources; 56 notes. G. O. Gagnon

4286. Zvobgo, Chengetai J. RHODESIA'S INTERNAL SETTLEMENT 1977-1979: A RECORD. *J. of Southern African Affairs 1980 5(1): 25-38.* Analyzes the creation and failure of Zimbabwe's brief internal settlement constitution and government, 1977-79. African leaders Chief Jeremiah Chirau, Bishop Abel Muzorewa, and Reverend Ndabaningi Sithole, joined the besieged white settler government in formulating the internal settlement, but with strong entrenchment of European interests and without participation by the armed guerrilla parties of the Patriotic Front, the new government was unable to receive foreign recognition or end the war inside the country. Based on United Nations resolutions and newspaper accounts; 32 notes.
L. W. Truschel

4287. Zvobgo, Chengetai J. M. SOUTHERN RHODESIA UNDER EDGAR WHITEHEAD, 1958-1962. *J. of Southern African Affairs 1977 2(4): 481-492.* Sir Edgar Whitehead (1905-71) the last of the liberal white politicians in Southern Rhodesia, fell from power because of the polarization in race relations, the result of which was that the aspirations of the white minority and those of the African majority had become irreconcilable. The Law and Order Maintenance Act made it virtually impossible for Africans to criticize the government or voice grievances. The campaign to prevent Africans from taking part in the election of 1962 was remarkably successful. The policy of partnership failed because it was incompatible with the political, economic, and social aspirations of the white minority. 40 notes. E. P. Stickney

4288. Zvobgo, Eddison Jonas Mudadirwa. A HERO'S DEATH: HERBERT TAPFUMANEI CHITEPO. *Issue 1975 5(1): 3-4.* Biography of Herbert Tafumanei Chitepo, Chairman of the Zimbabwe African National Union (ZANU), assassinated 18 March 1975. S

4289. —. AFRICAN NAMES OF NATIVE AND DISTRICT COMMISSIONERS. *NADA [Zimbabwe] 1977 11(4): 456-458.* Lists the nicknames given by the Africans of colonial Zimbabwe to the European Native Commissioners, 1892-1948.

4290. —. AMNESTY INTERNATIONAL BRIEFING: RHODESIA/ZIMBABWE. *Issue 1976 6(4): 34-37.* Discusses Amnesty International's concern with human rights violations, capital punishment and the treatment of political prisoners in Southern Rhodesia, and considers the implications of Southern Rhodesia's Law and Order Act (1960) and Emergency Powers Regulations (1966).

4291. —. DOCUMENTS ON THE SOUTHERN RHODESIA CONSTITUTIONAL CONFERENCE HELD AT LANCASTER HOUSE, LONDON, SEPTEMBER-DECEMBER 1979. *J. of Southern African Affairs 1979 4(4): 401-512.* Negotiations at Lancaster House in late 1979 between officials and representatives of the British and Zimbabwe governments and the Zimbabwe Patriotic Front produced an agreement that ended seven years of fighting and the era of white settler rule which began in 1965. The accord also overturned Southern Rhodesia's 1978 internal settlement and the elected government of Bishop Abel Muzorewa and his supporters. The 1979 agreement installed a transitional British administration and prepared for African rule. Includes 14 documents pertaining to the 1979 negotiations and settlement.
L. W. Truschel

4292. —. AN OUTLINE HISTORY OF THE RHODESIAN AIR FORCE. *Aerospace Hist. 1976 23(1): 36-42.* In 1934 the Parliament of Southern Rhodesia appropriated 10,000 pounds which was used to establish an Air Unit. A slow but gradual buildup took place and on 19 September 1939 the Air Unit officially became the Southern Rhodesian Air Force. In April, 1940, the force was absorbed into the RAF. Southern Rhodesian fighter and bomber squadrons served in North Africa and England during World War II. One man in five was killed. After the war the Air Force was disbanded. Pressures by returning ex-Air Force personnel led to the establishment of the Air Force as a permanent unit in November, 1947. Appropriations remained small and expansion slow until the Korean War. With Federation the RRAF expanded its role and took part in RAF operations in the Middle East. In 1965 Southern Rhodesia declared independence and in 1970 the "Royal" prefix was dropped. 17 photos. C. W. Ohrvall

4293. —. SENIOR HONOURS AND AWARDS GRANTED TO THE STAFF OF THE MINISTRY OF INTERNAL AFFAIRS SINCE 1973. *NADA [Zimbabwe] 1978 11(5): 470-482.* Lists persons belonging to the staff of the ministry of internal affairs of Southern Rhodesia who were awarded senior honors and awards 1973-77.

4294. —. UN NOUVEAU LEADER AFRICAIN, ROBERT MUGABE [A new African leader: Robert Mugabe]. *Études [France] 1980 353(2-3): 175-184.* Comments on the political situation in Zimbabwe, centering on the history of the emergence of Robert Mugabe (b. 1928) as a new African leader able to establish a national front but forced to contend with social, political, economic, and military divisions.

4295. —. ZIMBABWE RHODESIA: PROPOSALS FOR INDEPENDENCE. *Africa Q. [India] 1980 19(3-4): 388-433.* Reproduces the independence constitution drafted by the Lancaster House Conference to enable Zimbabwe to proceed to legal independence. At the conference all the contending parties presented their points of view for the future of Zimbabwe and reached agreement on a summary of the independence constitution, arrangements for the preindependence period, and a cease-fire agreement.

Society

4296. Burgess, M. Elaine. ETHNIC SCALE AND INTENSITY: THE ZIMBABWEAN EXPERIENCE. *Social Forces 1981 59(3): 601-626.* The Zimbabwe setting illustrates two of many issues requiring more rigorous sociological examination: 1) changing scale of ethnic boundaries, and 2) the effect of countervailing or coinciding factors on ethnic intensity. Contrary to prevailing expectations, the organizational potential of large-scale modern boundaries can be seen in Zimbabwe's pattern of ethnicity; the main determinants of intensity have tended to diminish ethnic cleavages among the general citizenry. J/S

4297. Burke, E. E. THE CHIEF'S BADGE. *NADA [Zimbabwe] 1977 11(4): 428-431.* A study of the origins of the ornamental badges given to chiefs by European settlers in Southern Rhodesia, 1898-1977.

4298. Coggin, C. THE PIONEER CORPS: A REVIEW ARTICLE. *Rhodesiana [Zimbabwe] 1976 (35): 16-18.* A review of Robert Cary *The Pioneer Corps* (Salisbury: Galaxie Press, 1975), with some addenda by Cary.

4299. Daneel, M. L. INDEPENDENT CHURCH LEADERSHIP SOUTH OF THE ZAMBEZI. *African Perspectives [Netherlands] 1976 (2): 81-99.* Applies B. G. M. Sundkler's chief-prophet-messiah typology to existing African independent churches among the Shona of Zimbabwe. Sundkler's typology, based on evidence from independent religious sects in Natal, does not apply neatly to patterns of leadership found among independent Shona churches. 15 notes.
L. W. Truschel

4300. Fleming, C. J. W. THE CONSTITUTION OF THE INDIGENOUS FAMILY. *NADA [Zimbabwe] 1973 10(5): 56-65.* Provides succinct descriptions of the three traditional extended family systems of Central Africa: the matripotestal, collateral patripotestal, and primogenitary patripotestal. Discusses marriage, succession, and property-holding within these family systems. These family forms continue to exert great influence despite the inevitable modern tendency toward legal, social, and economic independence of individuals. Based on published court cases and secondary works; 4 diagrams, 36 notes, biblio.
L. W. Truschel

4301. Hardwick, P. A. PROGRESS TOWARD TRANSPORTATION-PLANNING IN SALISBURY. *Zambezia: the J. of the U. of Rhodesia [Zimbabwe] 1975 3(1): 77-93.* Salisbury has a population of 490,000. The white population automobile ratios of 3:1 (1948) and 2.5:1 (1969) necessitate transportation and city planning from 1953 to 1974 for parking space in the central business district. The author outlines various commissions, basic proposals, and alternative transportation methods. Based on local government reports. 6 maps, 12 notes.
O. B. Pollak

4302. Hodder-Williams, Richard. AFRIKANERS IN RHODESIA: A PARTIAL PORTRAIT. *African Social Res. [Zambia] 1974 (18): 611-642.* Prior to 1962, Afrikaans-speaking whites and English-speaking whites in Southern Rhodesia were not integrated. Once white supremacy became the key issue, however, whites forgot their past debate and united. The author examines this unity and analyzes how Afrikaners rose from a lowly social status in 1900 to one of esteem in 1970. Although Afrikaners have remained cohesive, British opposition to them has diminished. 45 notes, 2 tables. H. G. Soff

4303. Intaf, Binga. THE BURIAL OF CHIEF SIABUWA: BINGA DISTRICT. *NADA [Zimbabwe] 1977 11(4): 459-461.* Describes the burial in 1976 of Chief Munchunkwe Sigaleta Siabuwa of Binga District.

4304. Johnson, Hazel Cameron. RHODESIA/ZIMBABWE: NO END TO DISCRIMINATION. *J. of African Studies 1979-80 6(4): 218-226.* Examines Zimbabwe-Rhodesia's October 1978 proclamation terminating all forms of racial discrimination in the light of the country's history of racial separatism by law and custom, especially since enactment of the Land Apportionment Act of 1930. The European settlers in Southern Rhodesia benefited from racial legislation and governmental policies regarding land, the wage economy, and education to such an extent that declarations ending racial discrimination will not in themselves produce meaningful integration in Zimbabwe. Based on secondary sources and published documents; 2 tables, 59 notes.
L. W. Truschel

4305. Jordan, T. W. F. THE VICTORIA MASTER FARMERS' ASSOCIATION. *NADA [Zimbabwe] 1978 11(5): 516-518.* A history of the Victoria Master Farmers' Association, founded in 1929 in the Victoria province of Southern Rhodesia to encourage African farmers to adopt new farming techniques.

4306. Katz, A. ASPECTS OF THE HISTORY OF THE RHODESIAN ACCOUNTANTS ACT. *Rhodesian Hist. [Zimbabwe] 1976 7: 991-995.* A critical analysis of the Southern Rhodesian Accountants Ordinances and professional membership practices, 1918-73. Professional requirements and law case challenges indicate that practices are exclusionary and that regulations lag behind the rest of the English-speaking world. Based on National Archives documents and parliamentary debates; 17 notes. O. B. Pollak

4307. Kimberley, Michael J. FREDERICK JOHN VAN DER BYL HOPLEY 1883-1951. *Heritage [Zimbabwe] 1981 (1): 32-36.* Hopley was a distinguished sportsman who took up farming after World War I, became Director of Physical Education briefly in Harare, 1949-51, and is commemorated by the John Hopley Trophy awarded to the best amateur sportsman in Zimbabwe. A. Alcock

4308. Kimberley, Michael J. HAROLD BASIL CHRISTIAN, AN EARLY RHODESIAN BOTANIST. *Rhodesiana [Zimbabwe] 1977 (36): 37-46.* Describes the role of Harold Basil Christian (1871-1950) in the study of Southern Rhodesian botany and particularly his work as President of the Rhodesian Agricultural Union. 2 photos, biblio.
C. A. McNeill

4309. Kimberley, Michael J. WILLIAM MUSGRAVE HOPLEY: RHODESIA'S THIRD JUSTICE. *Rhodesiana [Zimbabwe] 1979 40: 22-28.* Provides a biography of William Musgrave Hopley (1853-1919), the third judge in Southern Rhodesia, 1914-19.

4310. Kinloch, G. C. CHANGING BLACK REACTION TO WHITE DOMINATION. *Rhodesian Hist. [Zimbabwe] 1974 5: 67-78.* Studies 2500 letters to the editor appearing in *Bantu Mirror, African Weekly,* and *African Daily News,* 1930's-1970, with particular reference to economic, social, and racial factors. Racial orientations changed from conformity to colonial caste system to "nationalism and political awareness" in conjunction with increased urban residence. Secondary sources in English; table, 20 notes. O. B. Pollak

4311. Kinloch, G. C. CHANGING INTERGROUP ATTITUDES OF RHODESIAN WHITES AS DEFINED BY THE PRESS: THE PROCESS OF COLONIAL ADAPTATION. *Zambezia: the J. of the U. of Rhodesia (*Zimbabwe] 1975 4(1): 105-117.* Defines changing values based on 2,639 editorials in four major newspapers between 1892 and 1968. Single factors to explain values, and "a more multidimensional and dynamic view of the society's white elite" emerges from a half dozen analytical categories. Based on the larger study *Flame or Lily? Rhodesian Values as Defined by the Press* (Durban: Alpha Graphic, 1970). 14 notes. O. B. Pollak

4312. Linden, Jan and Redmayne, Alison. AFRICAN RELIGIOUS RESEARCH: ZIMBABWE AND THE CATHOLIC CHURCH: THE OXFORD COLONIAL RECORDS PROJECT. *J. of Religion in Africa [Netherlands] 1980 11(1): 67-73.* Reviews *Journey to Gubulawayo. Letters of Frs. H. Depelchin and C. Croonenberghs S. J., 1879-1880, 1881* (Bulawayo: Books of Rhodesia, 1979 edited by R. S. Roberts and translated by Moira Lloyd); Francis C. Barr's *Archbishop Aston Chichester 1879-1962. A Memoir* (Gwelo: Mambo Press, 1978); A. J.

Dachs and W. F. Rea's *The Catholic Church and Zimbabwe, 1879-1979 (Zambeziana 8)* (Gwelo: Mambo Press, 1979); *100 Years, 1879-1979. Centenary of the Catholic Church in Zimbabwe Rhodesia*(Gwelo: Mambo Press, 1979); and *Manuscript Collections of Africana in Rhodes House Library Oxford,* archival indexes that are useful reference books for libraries concerned with Africa and the Commonwealth.
R. J. Jirran

4313. Loewenson, R. and Gelfand, M. CUSTOMARY LAW CASES IN TWO SHONA CHIEFTAINSHIPS. *NADA [Zimbabwe] 1980 12(2): 130-136.* A comparative analysis of criminal statistics emerging from 20th century record case books of the courts of chiefs Nyajina and Chiota. Very similar criminal patterns are found in the records of these geographically separate chiefdoms. Based on Shona tribal court records; 4 fig. L. W. Truschel

4314. Mantzaris, Evangelos A. GREEK RURAL SETTLEMENT IN SOUTHERN RHODESIA, 1890-1930. *J. of the Hellenic Diaspora 1980 7(1): 89-102.* Greeks in Southern Rhodesia after 1915 formed an affluent landowning class but played little role in Southern Rhodesian politics.

4315. McAdam, J. ON WINGS OF FABRIC: EXCERPTS FROM THE LOG-BOOK OF A RHODESIAN AIR PILOT: JULY 1935-APRIL 1937. *Heritage [Zimbabwe] 1982 2: 15-28.* Prints, with a short introduction, excerpts from the author's logbook, which describes the activities of a commercial pilot in Zimbabwe between 1935 and 1937. Based on the author's logbook; 4 photos, 4 notes.

4316. Morris, R. M. MEDICAL PRACTITIONERS OF BULAWAYO IN THE MID 1920'S. *Rhodesiana [Zimbabwe] 1977 37: 26-43, 38: 23-34.* Describes memories of physicians he met in Bulawayo, including Alfred Vigne, Alexander William Forrester, Edward Head, Francis Heygate Ellis, and Robert Standish White.

4317. Morris, R. M. THE UMTALI HOSPITALS. *Rhodesiana [Zimbabwe] 1979 40: 29-33.* Gives a history of the old hospital built in Umtali in 1897 and the building of the new one in 1930.

4318. Orbell, S. F. W. PARTNERSHIP IN TRANSITION AND DEVELOPMENT. *Zambezia [Zimbabwe] 1980 8(1): 27-36.* Traces the origins of the Rhodesian Institute of Education from its founding by Basil Fletcher in 1956 and, while acknowledging its strong debt to the English model of teacher training at the London Institute, praises its emphasis on the need to change with the changing needs of a developing country and the importance of providing training to teachers in service and to adults of diverse qualifications who wish to enhance career prospects. The establishment of an Associate College of Education to expand teacher training is to be encouraged, and in-service workshops as an updating procedure should be emphasized. Based on an inaugural lecture on becoming Director of the Institute of Education, March 1980; 28 notes. D. H. Nicely

4319. Parkinson, D. K. THE PIONEER ROAD: TULI TO FORT VICTORIA IN THE CHIBI DISTRICT 1890-1966. *Rhodesiana [Zimbabwe] 1977 (37): 44-53.* Discusses the pioneer road from the Lundi River to the Towkewe River, describing the graves of pioneers and laager sites along the route and the terrain which it crosses. 4 photos, map. C. A. McNeill

4320. Ranger, Terence. THE MOBILIZATION OF LABOUR AND THE PRODUCTION OF KNOWLEDGE: THE ANTIQUARIAN TRADITION IN RHODESIA. *J. of African Hist. [Great Britain] 1979 20(4): 507-524.* The antiquarian tradition in Southern Rhodesia arose in the context of the coerced mobilization of African labor for industrial employment and task differentiation between blacks and whites, where the idea of racial harmony was extended to make distinctions of race appropriate to employment prospects. Much of the tradition was developed by both the Native Affairs Department and medical doctors who doubled as amateur anthropologists. A prime example was J. Blake-Thompson, who, with his orderly Lino, propounded theories of Oriental and Semitic origins for various ethnic groups and whose theories were accepted without question by most scholars. 47 notes.
A. W. Novitsky

4321. Reid, M. G. FIFTY YEARS: A TRIBUTE TO E. D. ALVORD. *NADA [Zimbabwe] 1977 11(4): 432-435.* A biographical study of E. D. Alvord (1889-1959), an American who in 1918 volunteered for life service as an agricultural Christian missionary in Southern Rhodesia and proceeded to play a vital role in the development and modernization of African farming.

4322. Roberts, R. S. THE SETTLERS. *Rhodesiana [Zimbabwe] 1978 (39): 55-61.* Examines the growth and characteristics of European settlement, 1890-1976, with particular reference to immigration policies and the occupational and racial structure of the settler population.

4323. Sinclair, Michael. EDUCATION IN ZIMBABWE: A BIBLIOGRAPHY OF SOME MAJOR RECENT PUBLICATIONS, REPORTS, AND OTHER REFERENCES. *Issue: A Q. J. of Opinion 1981 11(3-4): 64-67.* Provides a bibliography of sources of information about education in Zimbabwe, including 1) publications prepared by or for the Patriotic Front, 2) Southern Rhodesian government publications, 3) other publications from or generated in Southern Rhodesia, and 4) external publications, reports, etc.

4324. Waddy, Monica. BUILDINGS OF HISTORIC INTEREST: NO. 7. HOUSES IN BULAWAYO. *Rhodesiana [Zimbabwe] 1978 38: 14-18.* Discusses the history of six houses in the Hillside and Suburbs area of Bulawayo.

4325. Waddy, Monica G. SIR PHILIP BOURCHIER SHERARD WREY. *Rhodesiana [Zimbabwe] 1977 (37): 54-58.* Outlines the distinguished career of Philip Bourchier Sherard Wrey (1858-1936), discussing his work in civil engineering, the military, agriculture, and mining. 2 photos, note. C. A. McNeill

4326. Weinrich, A. K. H. THE CLOSED SOCIETY: WHITE SETTLERS IN ZIMBABWE. *Tarikh [Nigeria] 1979 6(2): 13-29.* Discusses briefly the founding of Southern Rhodesia followed by the subsequent settlement of Europeans from the 1920's to the disintegration of settler society beginning in the 1960's.

4327. Weinrich, A. K. H. STRATEGIC RESETTLEMENT IN RHODESIA. *J. of Southern African Studies [Great Britain] 1977 3(2): 207-229.* Discusses the impact of the resettlement of almost 250,000 Africans into consolidated, or protected, villages as a result of the intensification of guerrilla warfare after 1972. Also traces the precursors of these settlements back to the villages of Malawi in the 1940's, and those administered by the Portuguese in Mozambique. Based on newspapers; map, plan. S. P. Carr

4328. Zvobgo, C. J. THE REVD E. T. J. NEMAPARE AND THE AFRICAN METHODIST CHURCH IN SOUTHERN RHODESIA, 1930-1950. *Rhodesian Hist. [Zimbabwe] 1975 6: 83-87.* Discusses the Reverend E. T. J. Nemapare's separatist movement. Tensions that Nemapare felt within the colonial organization of the white-dominated Methodist Church led him to form his own organization in 1947. Based on primary sources in the Methodist Missionary Society Archives, London; 24 notes. O. B. Pollak

4329. Zvobgo, Chengetai J. M. AFRICAN EDUCATION IN ZIMBABWE: THE COLONIAL INHERITANCE OF THE NEW STATE, 1899-1979. *Issue: A Q. J. of Opinion 1981 11(3-4): 13-16.* Reviews the educational system in colonial Zimbabwe, characterized by exploitation of the African majority by offering industrial rather than academic training in black schools, which ended with Zimbabwe's new African government, elected in 1980.

SUBJECT INDEX

Subject Profile Index (SPIndex) carries both generic and specific index terms. Begin a search at the general term but also look under more specific or related terms. This index includes selective cross-references.

Each string of index descriptors is intended to present a profile of a given article; however, no particular relationship between any two terms in the profile is implied. Terms within the profile are listed alphabetically after the leading term. The variety of punctuation and capitalization reflects production methods and has no intrinsic meaning; e.g., there is no difference in meaning between "History, study of" and "History (study of)."

Cities, towns, and other small geographical subdivisions are normally listed in parentheses following their respective countries e.g., "Kenya (Mombasa)." Note that "Africa" is not used as a leading index term; if no country or region is mentioned, the index entry refers to Africa as a whole. However, when an index entry refers to a region of Africa, such as East Africa, it will have that region as a leading index term, e.g. "Africa, East."

Terms beginning with an arabic numeral are listed after the letter Z. Chronology of a particular article appears at the end of the string of index descriptors. In the chronological descriptor, "c" stands for century, e.g., "19c" means "19th century."

The last number in the index string, in italics, refers to the bibliographic entry number.

A

Aba riots. Igbo. Nigeria (Calabar, Owerri). Social Conditions. Women. 1925. *2194*
Abaza, Aziz. Drama. Egypt. Poetry. 1899-1973. *1360*
Abbäbä Arägay. Ethiopia. Guerrillas. Italy. Nasi, General. Truce. 1935-41. *2761*
Abbas II (papers). Egypt. Foreign Policy. Politics. 1914-44. *1246*
'Abd Allah, al-Iman. Boundaries. Ethiopia (Nugara). Feudalism. State Formation. 1901-23. *2743*
Abdel-Fadil, Mahmoud. Agricultural Policy (review article). Egypt. Land reform. 1952-70. *1136*
Abd-el-Krim. Anticolonialism. Morocco. 1908-67. *1451*
—. France. Morocco. Resistance. Rif War. Spain. 1921-26. *1412*
Abdullahi. Colonial Government. Indirect rule. Nigeria (Northern; Yauri). 1923-31. *2185*
Abibirimism. Economic development. Ghana. 20c. *1739*
Abisi. Nigeria. Political change. Rites and ceremonies. Rukuba. ca 1950-76. *2227*
Abolition Movement *See also* Emancipation.
—. Great Britain. Slavery. Sudan. 1877-1960. *1522*
Aborigines Rights Protection Society. Ghana. Pan-Africanism. Political protest. 1897-1948. *1767*
Abortion. Birth Control. Ghana. Nzema. 1973-75. *1857*
Abrahams, Peter. Novels. Race Relations. South Africa. 1945-66. *4003*
Abrem, stool of. Ghana, southern. Historiography. ca 1505-1950. *1791*
Abuna Petros. Ethiopia. Theater. War. 1936. - 1973. *2783*
Academic freedom. African studies. Self-determination. 1973. *311*
—. Apartheid. Colleges and Universities. South Africa. 1870-1973. *3997*
Academy of Sciences. African studies. Communist Party (24th Congress). National liberation movements. USSR. 1971-76. *50*
Academy of Sciences (Africa Institute). African Studies. USSR. 1970-79. *618*
Accountants Ordinances. Zimbabwe. 1918-72. *4306*
Acculturation *See also* Assimilation.
—. Adja. Benin. Nigeria. Settlement. 18c-1945. *2220*
—. Cameroon. Duala. Elites (German-speaking). 1884-1940. *2404*
—. Christianity. Church and State. Convention People's Party. Ghana. Socialism. 1949-66. *1808*
—. Christianity. Islam. Nigeria. Yoruba. 1970's. *2215*
—. Cities. Schools. 1945-74. *894*
—. Colonialism. Islam. Maghreb. Tradition. 1959-75. *918*
—. Education. Political Socialization. Tanzania. 1970's. *3181*
—. Education. Political Socialization. Tanzania. 1971. *3146*
—. Malawi. Political culture. Revolution. 1909-61. *3595*
Acculturation (resistance to). Africa, West. Colonial government. Missions and Missionaries. Polygamy. 19c-20c. *1633*
Acheampong, Ignatius K. Ghana. Military government. 1972-78. *1813*
Achebe, Chinua. Nigeria. Novels. 1963-68. *2271*
Action Group. Liberalism. Political Factions. Zimbabwe (Bulawayo). 1940-72. *4216*
Ad Hoc Monitoring Group on Southern Africa. Africa, Southern. Foreign Relations. USA. 1977-80. *3356*
Adangme. Ghana. Manya Krobo, stool of. Succession. 1800-1939. *1790*
Addis Ababa Agreement. Anya Nya. Civil War. Sudan, Southern. Sudanese African National Union. 1902-74. *1507*
—. Civil War. Nemery, Jaafar. Sudan. 1957-73. *1465*
—. Civil War. Sudan. 1947-74. *1495*
—. Domestic Policy. Foreign policy. Nemery, Jaafar. Sudan. 1972-76. *1510*
—. Politics. Sudan, southern. ca 1972-74. *1492*
Adja. Acculturation. Benin. Nigeria. Settlement. 18c-1945. *2220*
Administrative reform. Decisionmaking. Local Government. Zaire. 1973. *2496*
Adult education. Colleges and Universities. Colonialism. Nigeria. 1945-55. *2276*
—. Nigeria. Oxford University Delegacy. 1945-50. *2277*
—. Theater. 1930-79. *830*
Afar. Agriculture (cash crops). Capitalism. Famine. 1965-73. *2693*
—. Djibouti. Nationalism. 1977-80. *2678*
—. Ethiopia (Awash Valley). Modernization. Pastoralism. ca 1950-75. *2691*
—. Ethiopia (Awash Valley). Settlement. 1972-78. *2756*
Africa, central. Africa, East. Colonial policy. Films. Great Britain. 1920-50. *230*
—. Africa, southern. Collaboration. Imperialism. Resistance. 1850-1920. *183*
—. Colonial Government. Education. Reform. 1879-1974. *2394*
—. Culture. Religious movements. Prehistory-1970. *2393*
—. Forests. Honey. Wax. 1750-1950. *2398*
Africa, East. Africa, central. Colonial policy. Films. Great Britain. 1920-50. *230*
—. African Commercial Association (ACA). Fiah, Erica. Social Movements. 1889-1966. *2653*
—. African Greek Orthodox Church. Religion. 1930-75. *2594*
—. Armies. Europeans. Humor. Smuts, Jan. World War I. 1914-18. *711*
—. Armies (manpower). Great Britain. World War I. 1914-18. *695*
—. Arusha Agreement. East African Community. East African Trade Association. European Economic Community. Exports. 1973. *2617*
—. Asians. Bohras. Islam. 1100-1975. *2566*
—. Asians. Race relations. 1960's-70's. *2619*
—. Asians. Settlement. Uganda. 6c-1972. *2628*
—. Asians (review article). Mangat, J. S. Morris, H. S. 19c-20c. *2641*
—. Assimilation. Kalenjin. Maasai. Social Organization (age groups). 1890-1980. *2578*
—. Authors. English. Literature. 1966-73. *2620*
—. Bibliographies. Hobley, Charles William. Settlement (European). 1890-1947. *2612*
—. Bibliographies. Religious movements. 1946-76. *2624*
—. Brett, E. A. Colonialism. Economic change (review article). Politics. 1919-39. *2607*
—. Burundi. Cholera. Public Health. 1970-79. *2584*
—. Cattle Raising (overstocking). Economic structure. 1961-76. *2605*
—. Christianity. Ethiopia. Islam. Middle East. 1980. *2583*
—. Christianity. Missions and Missionaries. Uganda (Kigezi). World War I. 1914-18. *713*
—. Civil-military relations. Huntington, Samuel. Praetorianism (concept). 1960's-74. *2571*
—. Cold War. Foreign Policy. USA. USSR. 1930-77. *2637*
—. Colonial government. Economic Planning. 1946-73. *2603*
—. Colonial Government. Ghana. Higher Education (development). 1945-67. *672*
—. Colonial Government. Neutrality. World War I. 1914-15. *692*
—. Colonial policy. World War II. 1939-48. *2652*
—. Colonialism. Cooperatives. Economic system. 1960-73. *2621*
—. Colonialism. Education. 1850-1960. *2588*
—. Colonialism. Historiography. Oral history. 19c-20c. *2596*
—. Conflict and Conflict Resolution. 1850-1970's. *2601*
—. Constitutions. Courts. 1920's-73. *2627*
—. Constitutions. Ministerial responsibility. 1961-74. *2600*
—. Developing nations. Fisheries. Lake Victoria. Norway. UN Development Program. 1965-75. *628*
—. Diseases. Germany. Great Britain. Military Operations. World War I. 1914-18. *688*
—. Djibouti. Ethnic conflict. France. Political stability. 1896-1976. *2674*
—. Dorobo. Ethnic Groups. National Characteristics. 20c. *2599*
—. Droughts. 1946-73. *2568*
—. East African Community. International cooperation. ca 1965-75. *2589*
—. East African Community. International Organizations. 20c. *2602*
—. East African Community. Medicine. Research, regional. 1906-73. *2569*
—. East African Community. Regional integration. 1900-70's. *2610*
—. East African Community. Regional integration. 1967-74. *2595*
—. East African Community (dissolution). 1977. *2598*
—. East African Community (dissolution). Organization of African Unity. 1963-77. *2623*
—. East African Community (dissolution). Regional Integration. 1967-77. *2609*
—. Economic competition. Export trends. 1959-71. *2645*
—. Economic Integration. Nyerere, Julius. Regionalism. ca 1920-73. *2634*
—. Education (review article). 1922-62. *2648*
—. English. Literature, popular. 1960's-70's. *2604*
—. Ethiopia. Refugees. Sudan. 1970's. *385*
—. Foreign Policy. Somalia. USA. 1977-80. *2573*
—. Foreign Relations. 1955-73. *2636*
—. Great Britain. Lake Victoria. *Sybil* (vessel). World War I. 1915-16. *720*
—. Historiography. National Self-image. Prehistory-20c. ca 1900-30. *2635*

—. Ethiopia. Language policy. 1973-74. *2828*
Amin, Ahmad. Egypt. Liberalism. Public opinion. 1939-54. *1293*
Amin, Idi. Ali, Muhammad. Racial allegiance. Uganda. USA. 20c. *3259*
—. Arab States. Economic Conditions (dependency). Politics and the Military. Uganda. 1971-73. *3300*
—. Arab states. Foreign Relations. Israel. Uganda. 1971-. *3236*
—. Asians. Economic influence. Politics. Uganda. 1850-1972. *3317*
—. Asians (expulsion). Economic Conditions. Uganda. 1972-73. *3323*
—. Asians (expulsion). Foreign Policy. Tanzania. Uganda. 1972. *3301*
—. Asians (expulsion). Uganda. 1971-72. *3264*
—. Bibliographies. Uganda. 1971-78. *3250*
—. Christianity. Islam. Uganda. ca 1890-1976. *3262*
—. Church and State. Uganda. 1971-79. *3287*
—. Coups d'etat (causes). Uganda. 1960-73. *3284*
—. Cultural dependency. Marxism. Nyerere, Julius. Radicals and Radicalism. 19c-1973. *2614*
—. Economic Policy. Nationalism. Obote, Milton. Socialism. Uganda. 1966-71. *3295*
—. Economic Policy. Politics and the Military. Uganda. 1962-1979. *3290*
—. Economic revolution. Uganda. 1973-74. *3293*
—. Foreign Aid. Obote, Milton. Uganda. USSR. 1962-79. *3275*
—. Foreign policy. Uganda. 1962-76. *3237*
—. Government. Uganda. 1971-73. *3302*
—. Government (collapse). Tanzania. Uganda. 1978-79. *3312*
—. Military Government. Uganda. 1971-74. *3291*
—. Nubi. Politics. Uganda. ca 1885-1975. *3303*
—. Obote, Milton. Politics. Uganda. 1964-73. *3247*
—. Obote, Milton. Uganda. Violence. 1962-72. *3238*
—. Political instability. Uganda. 1962-80. *3304*
—. Political Systems. Uganda. 19c-1979. *3306*
—. Politics and the Military. Uganda. 1962-74. *3240*
—. Politics and the Military. Uganda. 1971-73. *3327*
—. Uganda. 1960's-70's. *3276*
—. Uganda. 1971-73. *3325*
Amin, Idi (review article). Kibedi, Wanume. Martin, David. Uganda. 1971-74. *3253*
—. Uganda. 1969-78. *3281*
Amnesty International. Human rights violations. Zimbabwe. 1960's-70's. *4290*
Anderson, Vernon (papers). Archives. Missions and Missionaries. Presbyterian Church. Zaire. 1921-46. *2559*
Anglicanism. Missions and Missionaries. Steere, Edward. Tanzania. Universities Mission to Central Africa (UMCA). 1876-1926. *3192*
Angola *See also* Africa, Southern.
—. Agriculture. Coffee. Economic structure. 19c-20c. *3435*
—. *Aldeamentos,* (strategic settlements). Guerrilla Warfare. Portugal. 1973. *3471*
—. Algeria. Cuba. Intervention, military. Syria. 1961-76. *411*
—. Anti-Imperialism. National liberation movements. Popular Movement for the Liberation of Angola (MPLA). 1970's. *3429*
—. Archives. Arquivo Histórico Militar. Colonialism. Portugal. 1705-1970. *3484*
—. Auala, Leonard N. Namibia. Ovambo. 1973. *3333*
—. Beinart, William Justin. Bundy, Colin. Capitalism. Clarence-Smith, W. G. Peasants (review article). South Africa. 1900-80. *3348*
—. Bender, Gerald J. Colonial Government (review article). 1500-1970. *3469*
—. Bibliographies. Independence. 1961-76. *3474*
—. Catholic Church. Church and State. Missions and Missionaries. Mozambique. 1975-81. *3349*
—. Cattle raising. 1970's. *3440*
—. Central Intelligence Agency. Independence Movements. Namibia. National Union for the Complete Independence of Angola (UNITA). South Africa. USA. 1974-81. *3380*
—. Central Intelligence Agency. USA. Zaire. 1960-76. *505*
—. China. Foreign Policy. National liberation movements. 1950-76. *3451*
—. China. Foreign policy. National liberation movements. 1961-76. *3475*
—. Civil war. 1960's-70's. *3468*
—. Civil war. 1974-76. *3444*
—. Civil war. Great Powers. Intervention. 1974-76. *3445*
—. Civil war. Historiography. 1975-76. *3438*
—. Civil war. Intervention (foreign). Nigeria. Organization of African Unity. 1960-75. *270*
—. Civil war. Liberation movements. Press coverage. South Africa. USA. 1975-76. *3413*
—. Colonial Government. 1488-1961. *3434*
—. Colonial government. Economic Policy. 1930-74. *3446*
—. Colonial wars. Military Finance. Mozambique. Multinational corporations. Portugal. 1960-73. *3362*
—. Colonialism. 1920-61. *3442*
—. Colonialism. 1956-75. *3433*
—. Colonialism. Guinea-Bissau. Mozambique. Portugal. 1955-73. *193*
—. Communist Parties and Movements. Popular Movement for the Liberation of Angola (MPLA). 1975. *3453*
—. Communist Party. Guinea. Mozambique. 1970-75. *271*
—. Conflict and Conflict Resolution. Zaire. Zambia. 1976-78. *237*
—. Constitutions. 1975-80. *3454*
—. Copper mines and Mining. French, J. C. Labor recruitment. Robert Williams Co. Zaire (Shaba). 1917-21. *2477*
—. Counterinsurgency. Guinea-Bissau. Mozambique. Portugal. 1961-74. *177*
—. Cuba. Ethiopia. Germany, East. Marxism. Mozambique. 1975-78. *528*
—. Cuba. Foreign policy. Intervention. 1966-77. *3457*
—. Cuba. Foreign Policy. Intervention, military. USA. USSR. 1975-77. *3483*
—. Cuba. Intervention, military. USSR. 1975-76. *3479*
—. Cuba. Intervention, military. USSR. 1975-76. *3480*
—. Decolonization. Economic structure. 1970's. *3456*
—. Decolonization. Imperialism. 15c-20c. *3458*
—. Decolonization. Popular Movement for the Liberation of Angola (MPLA). 1956-76. *3465*
—. Demography. Europeans. Independence. 1974. *3432*
—. Diseases. Economic conditions. Famine. 1830-1930. *3443*
—. Economic development. Social organization. 1850-1978. *3448*
—. Foreign Investments. Independence movements. 1970-74. *3463*
—. Foreign investments. Mozambique. Portugal. 1950's-75. *3363*
—. Foreign Policy. Intervention, military. South Africa. USA. 1970's-82. *3473*
—. Foreign Policy. Mozambique. Portugal. 1974-75. *3365*
—. Foreign policy. Mozambique. South Africa. Zimbabwe. 1965-74. *3930*
—. Foreign Policy. Popular Movement for the Liberation of Angola (MPLA). Zaire. Zambia. 1961-77. *3430*
—. Foreign Policy. USA. 1960-81. *3431*
—. Foreign policy. USSR. 1955-75. *3455*
—. Foreign Relations. Independence. Mozambique. Portugal. 1970's. *3402*
—. Foreign Relations. Nonalignment. 1955-80. *3466*
—. FRELIMO. Mozambique. Popular Movement for the Liberation of Angola (MPLA). Revolution. 1970-80. *3386*
—. Guerrilla warfare. Guinea-Bissau. Mozambique. ca 1959-76. *179*
—. Guerrilla warfare. Guinea-Bissau. Mozambique. National liberation. ca 1960's-70's. *181*
—. Guerrilla warfare. Mozambique. Portugal. ca 1961-75. *3368*
—. Guerrillas. Guinea-Bissau. Mozambique. Political control. Portugal. 1940-74. *218*
—. Gulf Oil. Oil Industry and Trade (drilling). Public Relations. 1968-74. *571*
—. Historiography. 1480-1973. *3436*
—. Ideology. Independence Movements. Social change. 1940-79. *3482*
—. Imperialism. Independence Movements. 1954-75. *3450*
—. Imperialism (review article). Independence Movements. Pélissier, René. Portugal. 1845-1975. *167*
—. Independence. Nationalism. 1950's-75. *3460*
—. Independence. Novels. Pacavira, Manuel *(Nzinga Mbandi).* 17c-20c. *3439*
—. Independence. Popular Movement for the Liberation of Angola (MPLA). 1961-75. *3464*
—. Independence Movements. 1956-75. *3478*
—. Independence Movements. Intervention. -1970's. *3459*
—. Independence Movements. Literature. Vieira, Luandino. 1960-73. *3467*
—. Independence movements. Mozambique. Portugal. 1970's. *3424*
—. Independence Movements. Popular Movement for the Liberation of Angola (MPLA). 1956-77. *3452*
—. Independence Movements (review article). Marcum, John. 1950-78. *3419*
—. Intervention. Military Intelligence. South Africa. 1975-76. *3447*
—. Intervention. Mozambique. Revolution. 1960's-70's. *3373*
—. Intervention. South Africa. 1975-77. *3364*
—. Intervention, foreign. South Africa. 1961-76. *3354*
—. Mercenary troops. Trials. 1976. *3470*
—. Military aid. Popular Movement for the Liberation of Angola (MPLA). USSR. 1956-74. *3476*
—. Neto, Agostinho. 1959-79. *3472*
—. Neto, Agostinho. Poetry. Political leadership. ca 1922-75. *3449*
—. Neto, Agostinho. Political Leadership. 1947-82. *3477*
—. Popular Movement for the Liberation of Angola (MPLA; 1st Extraordinary Congress). 1980. *3481*
—. Social Organization (review article). 1961-79. *3441*
Angola (Cabinda). Independence movements. ca 1885-1977. *3461*
Angola (Luanda). Alves, Nito. Coups d'etat. 1977. *3437*
Angola, southwest. Colonization. Development. Portugal. 19c-20c. *3462*
Angolans. Botswana (Etsha). Resettlement. 1967-75. *3519*
—. Refugees. Resettlement. Zaire. 1960's-70's. *2534*
—. Refugees. Resettlement. Zambia. 1966-72. *4072*
Anim, Peter. Ghana. McKeown, James. Pentecostalism. 1890-1974. *1865*
Animal industry. Cattle diseases. Colonial Government. Ghana. Veterinary Medicine. 1909-55. *1748*
Animism. Africa, West. Christianity. Conversion. Islam. -20c. *1642*
Annexation. Green March. Hassan II. Morocco. Western Sahara. 1975. *1455*
Ansar Party. Islam. Politics. Sudan. Umma Party. 1914-45. *1524*
Anthropologists. Nigeria. 1884-1960. *2254*
Anthropology *See also* Acculturation; Archaeology; Language; Linguistics; Race Relations; Social Change.
—. African studies. Functionalism. Historiography. Radcliffe-Brown, A. R. 20c. *33*
—. Asante. Ghana. Rattray, R. Sutherland. 1881-1938. *1847*
—. Capitalism. Congo. Marxism. Neocolonialism (review article). Rey, P. P. 20c. *2440*
—. Decolonization. Gluckman, Max. Rhodes-Livingstone Institute. Zambia. 1939-47. *4047*
—. Ethnic Groups. South Africa. *Volkekunde* school. 1920's-81. *4012*
—. Excavations. Great Zimbabwe. Historiography. Zimbabwe. 1960's-72. *4138*
—. Ghana. Government. 1705-1971. *1810*
Anthropology (colonialist; review article). Colonialism. Merriam, Alan P. Zaire (Lupupa Ngye). ca 1930-60. *2539*
Anthropology, Cultural. Africa, Southern. ca 1850-1980. *3406*
Anthropology, medical. Political Systems. Public Health. Sudan. 1950's-70's. *1484*
Anthropology, social. Philosophy. Popper, Karl. Social thought. Traditionalism. 1945-75. *846*
Anticolonial movements. Africa, Southern. Organization of African Unity. ca 1963-77. *86*
—. Algeria (Aurès). Bandits. Ben Zelmat, Messaoud. 1917-21. *1013*
—. Politics. Religion. ca 1900-50's. *229*
Anticolonialism. Abd-el-Krim. Morocco. 1908-67. *1451*
—. *African Standard* (newspaper). Ghana. Sierra Leone. Wallace-Johnson, I. T. A. West African Youth League. 1930-45. *1684*
—. Africans. Veterans. World War II. 1940-77. *747*

Arabs. Algeria. Camus, Albert. Independence Movements. 1934-60. *1086*
—. Algeria. Literature. Popular culture. Stereotypes. 1891-1920. *1091*
—. Berber Myth (review article). Colonial attitudes. Montagne, Robert. Morocco. 1930-70's. *1438*
—. Cloves. Slaves. Tanzania (Zanzibar). 19c-1964. *3112*
—. Foreign Relations. Israel. 1960-75. *467*
—. Israel. Jews. Minorities. Morocco. Tunisia. 1972-75. *972*
Arbitration. Commercial disputes. 1965-75. *895*
Arbitration Convention. Commercial disputes. Nigeria. Oil industry and Trade. Treaties. UN. 1960's-70's. *2084*
Arbitration, International *See also* Boundaries.
—. International law. Libya. Nationalization. Oil Industry and Trade. USA. 1971-80. *1404*
Archaeology *See also* Anthropology; Excavations.
—. Attitudes. Sudan. 1946-81. *1508*
—. Bibliographies. Historiography. Tunisia. Prehistory-1973. *1573*
—. Clark, J. Desmond. Zambia. 1905-76. *4060*
—. Egypt. Emery, Walter Bryan. 1924-71. *1114*
—. Egypt. Tutankhamen, curse of. 1922. *1352*
—. Great Zimbabwe. Racial theories. Zimbabwe. -20c. *4140*
—. Kenya. Madagascar. Migration. Tanzania. 9c-19c. 20c. *2650*
—. Research. Zaire. 1899-1970. *2455*
—. Sudan. 1817-1980. *1459*
Archer, Geoffrey. Colonial Government. Mahdism. Rahman, Sayyid al-. Sudan. 1924-27. *1486*
Archer, Robert. Madagascar. Revolution (review article). ca 1972-74. *3576*
Architecture. Social needs. 1974. *876*
Architecture (carved doors). Kenya (Lamu). 1450-1974. *2986*
Archives *See also* names of individual archives; Documents; Manuscripts.
—. Anderson, Vernon (papers). Missions and Missionaries. Presbyterian Church. Zaire. 1921-46. *2559*
—. Angola. Arquivo Histórico Militar. Colonialism. Portugal. 1705-1970. *3484*
—. Great Britain. Kenya. 20c. *2857*
—. Missions and Missionaries. St. Joseph's Society for the Missions. 1866-1980. *25*
—. South Africa. 1910-80. *3737*
Archives, international. Art. Folklore. 1975. *802*
Archives, National. French West Africa. Senegal (Dakar). 18c-20c. *2320*
Archives, National (collections). Ghana. 1840-1971. *1718*
Archives, State. Germany, East (Potsdam). Historical sources. 19c-20c. *31*
Aristocracy. Ethiopia. Government. Italy. Military Occupation. 1937-40. *2799*
Armaments. Economic Structure. Foreign investments. Multinational corporations. South Africa. 1945-78. *3799*
—. Indian Ocean. Military strategy. South Africa. 1960-74. *3812*
—. Multinational corporations. South Africa. UN Anti-Apartheid Committee. 1960-77. *3923*
Armaments, conventional. Arms Trade. Domestic Policy. 1964-76. *539*
Armaments industry. Military organizations. South Africa. 1974. *3840*
Armed Forces. *See* Military.
Armies. Africa, East. Europeans. Humor. Smuts, Jan. World War I. 1914-18. *711*
—. Civic action. Civil-Military Relations. -1974. *362*
—. Coups d'etat. Social Classes. Uganda. ca 1962-71. *3257*
—. Economic Policy. Mugabe, Robert. Zimbabwe. 1979-80. *4221*
—. Ethiopia. Peasants. 1850-1935. *2726*
—. Ghana. Military Organization. 1947-70's. *1738*
—. Nigeria. Social Change. 1965-77. *2002*
—. Officer corps. 1970's. *358*
Armies (colonial). Africans. British Empire. 1916-60. *750*
Armies (Historical Section monographs; review article). Africa, North. Historiography. Italy. World War II. 1940-43. 1949-74. *732*
Armies (manpower). Africa, East. Great Britain. World War I. 1914-18. *695*
Armies (native troops). Morocco. Spain. 1300-1966. *1452*
Armies (Supreme Command; documents). Africa, North. Germany. Middle East. Military campaigns. World War II. 1941-45. *753*
Armored Vehicles and Tank Warfare. Africa, North. Italy. World War II. 1940-41. *760*
—. Africa, North. World War II. 1940-42. *755*
—. Foreign Legion *(régiment de marche)*. World War II. 1943-45. *745*
Arms Trade *See also* Armaments Industry.
—. 1970-77. *585*
—. Armaments, conventional. Domestic Policy. 1964-76. *539*
—. Embargo. South Africa. USA. 1978-80's. *3873*
—. Exports (restrictions). South Africa. USA. 1945-78. *3775*
—. Israel. South Africa. 1967-70's. *3834*
—. Politics and the Military (review article). 1960's-73. *374*
Army officers. Egypt. Intelligentsia. Revolutionary Movements. 1849-1952. *1199*
Army Service Corps. Algeria. France. Transportation, Military. 1954-62. *1025*
Army, 2d. Egypt. Ghazala, Mohamed. Military Strategy. October War. Suez Canal (crossing). 1973. *1314*
Aro. Colonial Government. Nigeria (Eastern Delta). Trade, precolonial. 19c-20c. *2055*
Arquivo Histórico Militar. Angola. Archives. Colonialism. Portugal. 1705-1970. *3484*
Arrighi, G. Peasants (proletarianization). Shangwe. Tobacco industry. Zimbabwe. 1898-1938. *4168*
Arslan, Chekib. Maghreb. Nationalism. Pan-Arabism. 1866-1946. *925*
Arssi. Amhara. Ethiopia (Bale province). Ethnic Groups. Tulama. 1890-1974. *2826*
Art *See also* Architecture; Artists; Arts and Crafts; Painting; Sculpture.
—. 1973. *19*
—. Archives, international. Folklore. 1975. *802*
—. Barnes, Albert C. Collectors. Locke, Alain. USA. 1920's. *821*
—. Benin. Europe. Literature. 1897-20c. *862*
—. Culture. Diop, Alioune. 1947-77. *855*
—. Missions and Missionaries. Nigeria. 15c-20c. *2293*
—. Modernism. Nigeria. 1918-60. *2273*
Art and State. Censorship. Guinea. Touré, Sekou. ca 1947-76. *1870*
Art Galleries and Museums *See also* names of particular galleries and museums.
—. Collectors. 1960's-70's. *795*
Artists. Algeria (Sidi Madani). France. Intellectuals. 1948. *1012*
Arts and crafts. Ivory Coast (Man, Zuénoula). Religious attitudes. Social attitudes. 1974. *1928*
—. Medinas. Tunisia (Sfax, Tunis). ca 1970. *1557*
Arts, functional. Nigeria (Benin, Ife, Nok). 900 BC-20c. *2292*
Arusha Agreement. Africa, East. East African Community. East African Trade Association. European Economic Community. Exports. 1973. *2617*
Arusha Declaration. Legal systems. Politics. Socialism. Tanzania. 1967-73. *3147*
—. Nyerere, Julius. Socialism. Tanzania. 1961-73. *3148*
—. Socialism. Tanzania. 1967-77. *3055*
—. Socialism. Tanzania. 1967-77. *3076*
Asafo movement. Colonialism. Ghana. Modernization. Political Protest. 1910's-50. *1819*
—. Ghana. Reform. ca 1905-32. *1818*
—. Ghana (Cape Coast). Riots. 1925-35. *1815*
Asante. Anthropology. Ghana. Rattray, R. Sutherland. 1881-1938. *1847*
—. Folklore. Ghana. Knot of wisdom. -1973. *1843*
—. Ghana. Local Government. Modernization. Political Development. 1881-1981. *1817*
—. Ghana. Sects, Religious. Social Customs. Witchcraft. 1870-1930. *1849*
—. Ghana (Kumase). Manwere *fekuo*. Public Administration. 1834-1970's. *1743*
Asfaw Wassen. Diplomacy (secret negotiations). Ethiopia. Haile Selassie. Italy. 1936-39. *2802*
Ashanti Times (newspaper). Ghana. Newspapers. Spears, Edward. 1947-70. *1837*
Ashraf. Egypt. Elites. Islam. 1650-1952. *1356*
Asia. China. Chou En-Lai. Diplomacy. 1963-64. *410*
—. Communists. Economic development. Political Systems. Public sector. -1973. *641*
—. Development. Peasants. Poverty. 1970-80's. *657*
Asians. Africa, East. Bohras. Islam. 1100-1975. *2566*
—. Africa, East. Race relations. 1960's-70's. *2619*
—. Africa, East. Settlement. Uganda. 6c-1972. *2628*
—. Africans. Kenya. Labor training. 1968-74. *2891*
—. Africans. Kenya. Race Relations. ca 1805-1974. *2999*
—. Africans. Race Relations. South Africa. 1970's. *3723*
—. Amin, Idi. Economic influence. Politics. Uganda. 1850-1972. *3317*
—. Apartheid. Education. South Africa. 20c. *3982*
—. British Commonwealth. Foreign Relations. India. Refugees. Uganda. 1972. *3241*
—. Civil Rights. Colonial government. Coryndon, Robert. Kenya. 1917-33. *2973*
—. Colonial policy. Discrimination. Great Britain. Kenya. 1903-25. *2949*
—. Deportation. Uganda. 1972. *3220*
—. Devonshire White Paper. Kenya. 1923. *2930*
—. Discrimination. Industry, small-scale. Tanzania. 1890-1967. *3078*
—. Discrimination. Kenya (Nakuru). Racial attitudes. 1912-72. *2981*
—. Discrimination. Uganda. 1880-1972. *3248*
—. Doctor, Manilal Maganlall. Mauritius. Politics. ca 1900-56. *3584*
—. Economic Structure. Kenya. 1888-1939. *2859*
—. Exiles. Family composition. Social Surveys. Uganda. 1972-74. *3219*
—. Minorities. Politics. Zimbabwe. 1890-1970. *4250*
—. Occupational segregation. Zimbabwe. 1890-1950. *4167*
—. Sierra Leone. Trade (domestic). 1950-78. *2355*
—. Uganda. 1954-72. *3218*
—. Zambia. 1890's-1970's. *4094*
Asians (expulsion). Amin, Idi. Economic Conditions. Uganda. 1972-73. *3323*
—. Amin, Idi. Foreign Policy. Tanzania. Uganda. 1972. *3301*
—. Amin, Idi. Uganda. 1971-72. *3264*
—. Human rights. Uganda. 1972. *3298*
Asians (review article). Africa, East. Mangat, J. S. Morris, H. S. 19c-20c. *2641*
Assassination. Cabral, Amilcar. Colonialism. Guinea-Bissau. Independence Movements. Portugal. 1953-73. *1901*
—. Cabral, Amilcar. Guinea-Bissau. 1966-72. *1909*
—. Colonial Government. Ethiopia. Graziani, Rodolfo. Italy. Political repression. 1936-37. *2795*
Assidon, Elsa. Gaudio, Attilio. Morocco. Polisario Front. War. Western Sahara (review article). 1976-80. *1594*
Assimilation *See also* Acculturation; Integration.
—. Africa, East. Kalenjin. Maasai. Social Organization (age groups). 1890-1980. *2578*
—. Attitudes. Colonization. Education. Senegal (Dakar). William Ponty School. 1937-45. *2318*
—. Colonial policy. Novels. Senegal. 1920's-60's. *2322*
—. Colonialism. France. 1945-73. *388*
—. Economic Structure. Iligira. Kenya. Samburu. 20c. *2985*
—. Hausa. Islam. Nigeria, northern. 20c. *2286*
Association, right of. Ghana. Tanzania. 1940-65. *339*
Aswan Dam. Decisionmaking. Egypt. Technology. USA. World Bank. 1953-68. *1166*
—. Economic Development. Egypt. 1960-77. *1133*
—. Egypt. 1950's-71. *1141*
—. Egypt. Social problems. 1958-70. *1158*
—. Egypt. USSR. 1959. *1151*
Asylum. Refugees. Resettlement. 1970's. *323*
Atangana, Charles. Beti. Cameroon (Yaoundé). 1911-43. *2422*
Atangana, Karl. Beti. Cameroon (Yaoundé). League of Nations. Mandates. World War I. 1914-22. *714*
Atrocities. Chemical and Biological Warfare (poison gas). Ethiopia. Italy. 1935-36. *2800*
At-Takfir wa al-Higrah (sect). Egypt. Muslims. Pan-Islamism. 1970-78. *1196*
Attitudes *See also* Political Attitudes; Public Opinion; Values.
—. Apartheid. Nonaligned nations. South Africa. 1953-73. *3818*
—. Archaeology. Sudan. 1946-81. *1508*
—. Assimilation. Colonization. Education. Senegal (Dakar). William Ponty School. 1937-45. *2318*
—. Benin. Brazilians. Education. Elites. Tradition. 1920-67. *1707*
—. Civil servants. Family size. Ghana (Accra). 1954-74. *1851*
—. Colonial Government. Kenya. Maasai. Tanzania. 1890-1960. *2647*
—. Colonialism. Ethnic Groups. Social Classes. 1960's-70's. *915*

—. Economic development. Education. Mali. Students. 1950-76. *1970*
—. Education. Missions and Missionaries. 19c-1974. *792*
—. Egypt. Foreign Relations. Intellectuals. Israel. Palestine. Self-determination. 1967-80. *1200*
—. English, competence in. Nigeria. Social status. 1973. *2229*
—. Family. Girls. Marriage. Schools. Zaire (Kinshasa). 1969-72. *2562*
—. Great Powers. Indian Ocean. Mauritius. Military presence. 1965-75. *3564*
—. Guinea-Bissau. Women. 1960's-75. *1905*
—. Intellectuals. Islam. Leadership. Maghreb. 1945-80. *969*
—. Kenya. Maendeleo Ya Wanawake. Women. 1954-74. *3014*
—. Methodology. Nigeria. Political culture. Social Classes. 1800-1960. *2124*
—. Nurses and nursing. Tradition. Zambia. 1981. *4112*
—. USA. 1958-71. *380*
Atuot. Colonialism. Great Britain. Sudan, Southern. 1920's-55. *1474*
—. Ethnicity. Sudan. 18c-20c. *1472*
Auala, Leonard N. Angola. Namibia. Ovambo. 1973. *3333*
Aubaume, Jean Hilaire. Bongo, Albert Bernard. Gabon. M'Ba, Léo. Nationalism. Political parties. 1959-72. *2447*
Auchinleck, Claude. El Alamein (battle). Great Britain. World War II. 1942. *743*
Auden, Maurice (disappearance). Algeria. France. Revolution. 1957-. *1105*
Aurore (newspaper). *Figaro* (newspaper). France. Intervention (military). Journalism. Politics. Zaire. 1978. *2530*
Australia. Economic development. Historiography. Racism (review article). South Africa. 20c. *3720*
—. Ethiopia. Foreign Policy. Italy. Public opinion. War. 1935-36. *2814*
—. Libraries. New Zealand. Office of War Information. South Africa. USA. World War II. 1942. *765*
Authoritarian regimes. Coups d'etat. Political Parties. 1945-77. *262*
Authoritarianism. Afrikaners. South Africa. 20c. *3980*
—. Domestic Policy. Government. Zaire. 1965-80. *2492*
—. Economic Development. ca 1960-75. *304*
—. Egypt. Modernization. Nasser, Gamal Abdel. Political Culture. 1950's. *1252*
Authority. Botswana. Settlement. Tswana. 19c-1978. *3526*
—. Islam (formal, popular). Tunisia (Khroumerie). 1881-1970. *1534*
Authors *See also* names of individual authors; Dramatists; Poets.
—. Africa, East. English. Literature. 1966-73. *2620*
—. Africa, North. Schools, French. 1830-1950's. *942*
—. Blacks. French language. 1930-74. *906*
—. Bosman, Herman Charles. Clifford, Lago. Prisons. Rosenberg, Valerie (review article). South Africa. 20c. *3977*
—. Diop, Alioune. Negritude. Senegal. 1940-80. *2311*
—. Diva, David Edward. Swahili. Tanzania. Translating and Interpreting (Aesop's fables). 1916-69. *3216*
—. Fiction. Orlan, Pierre Mac. Tunisia. 1932. *1545*
—. France. Harlem Renaissance. Literature. Negritude. USA. 1921-39. *852*
—. Literary Criticism. 20c. *801*
—. Literary criticism. Tutuola, Amos. 1950-76. *865*
—. Nigeria. Soyinka, Wole. ca 1952-63. *2258*
—. Politics. 1967-73. *908*
Autobiography and Memoirs *See also* Biography; Diaries.
—. Avriel, Ehud. Diplomacy. Ghana. Israel. Liberia. 1957-73. *393*
—. Borneman, Ernest. England (London). Independence Movements. Student Movement House. 1933-38. *155*
—. Malawi. Sunderland Flying Boat. Wills, K. B. 1950. *584*
Automobile industry and trade. Foreign Investments. South Africa. 1945-80. *3761*
Autonomy. Algeria. Colonial Government. France. 1934-35. *1050*
—. Anya Nya. Civil war. Sudan, southern. 1956-72. *1509*
—. Botswana. District councils. Local Government. 1960-79. *3515*
—. Botswana (Ghansi). San. Social Policy. 1974-82. *3535*
—. Social Classes. South Africa (Transkei). 1956-75. *3929*
Avatime. Rice. Social Customs. Social organization. Togo. Yams. 20c. *2373*
Aviators. Zimbabwe. 1935-37. *4315*
Avriel, Ehud. Autobiography and Memoirs. Diplomacy. Ghana. Israel. Liberia. 1957-73. *393*
Azan, Paul *(Armée Indigène Nord-Africaine)*. Africa, North. Colonialism. France. Military Recruitment. 1925. *932*
Azikiwe, Nnamdi. Constitutional crises. Nigeria. Presidency. 1964-65. *2094*
Azores. *See* Portugal.

B

Baa, Karamoxo. Guinea (Tuuba). Jaaxanke. Manuscripts, Arabic. 15c-20c. *1876*
Babalawo. Counseling. Nigeria. ca 500 BC-1978. *2261*
Badges. Chiefs. Zimbabwe. 1898-1977. *4297*
Badoglio, Pietro. Burrú, Aialeu. Diplomacy. Ethiopia (Amhara). Gasparini, Jacopo. Italy. 1936. *2750*
—. Documents. Graziani, Rodolfo. Italy. Libya (Cyrenaica). Mukhtar, Omar el-. Resistance. 1930-31. *1391*
Baggara. Modernization. Sudan (Darfur, Kordofan). 19c-20c. *1457*
Baines, Thomas. Africa, Southern. Discovery and Exploration. Historiography. Wolfe, Richard. 1973. *5*
Bakri Sapalō. Alphabets. Ethiopia (Hagar). Oromo. Separatist movements. 1875-1980. *2757*
Balance of power. Africa, North. Western Nations. 1950's-73. *947*
—. Ethiopia. Italy. League of Nations. War. 1935-37. *2771*
Baldwin, Charlene M. Baldwin, David E. Bibliographies. Nigeria. Yoruba (review article). 11c-20c. *2008*
Baldwin, David E. Baldwin, Charlene M. Bibliographies. Nigeria. Yoruba (review article). 11c-20c. *2008*
Balewa, Abubakar. Akinyemi, A. B. Foreign Policy (review article). Idang, Gordon J. Nigeria. 1960-66. *2090*
Banana production. Depression. Economic Structure. Guinea. 1929-34. *1881*
Banda. Central African Republic. Witchcraft. 15c-20c. *2426*
Banda, Hastings Kamuzu. Agricultural systems. Economic Development. Foreign policy. Malawi. 1964-74. *3615*
—. Malawi. Political leadership. 1964-74. *3601*
Bandits. Algeria (Aurès). Anticolonial movements. Ben Zelmat, Messaoud. 1917-21. *1013*
Bangladesh. Civil war. Economic policies. Nigeria. Political economy. 20c. *2145*
Bank Misr. Economic structure. Egypt. Federation of Industries. General Agricultural Syndicate. Social Classes. 1880-1940. *1170*
—. Egypt. Foreign Investments. Nationalism. 1919-49. *1306*
—. Egypt. Middle Classes. 1910-50. *1138*
Bank of Botswana. Botswana. Economic Development. Money. 1974-78. *3503*
Banking *See also* Foreign Exchange; Investments; Money.
—. Africa, West. International Bank for Western Africa. 1965-73. *1601*
—. Crime and Criminals (fraud). Equatorial Guinea. Paesa Sanchez de Caballer, Francisco. 1968-69. *2445*
—. Economic development. Uganda. 1966-70's. *3322*
—. Nationalization. Socialism. Tanzania. 1960's. *3125*
—. Nationalization. Tanzania. 1960-70. *3098*
Banking (commercial). Economic development. Multinational Corporations. Uganda. 1961-75. *3234*
—. National Bank of Commerce (NBC). Tanzania. 1973-74. *3107*
Banking (savings institutions). Economic development. Tanzania. 1960-70. *3058*
Banks. Business. Europe. USA. 1972-74. *603*
—. Government. Rural credit. Zambia. 1964-75. *4073*
Banque de l'Afrique Occidentale. Africa, West. Depression. 1926-36. *1693*
Bantu Homelands. Agricultural diffusion. Farmers, subsistence. South Africa (Natal). Valley Trust. 1950-74. *3783*
—. Agricultural production. South Africa. 1918-69. *3789*
—. Apartheid. Economic structure. South Africa. 1925-76. *3748*
—. Botswana. Mangope, Lukas (interview). South Africa (Bophuthatswana). 1973. *3390*
—. Economic Conditions. Industrialization. South Africa. 1969-73. *3785*
—. Economic policy. Elections. Political Parties. South Africa. 1920-74. *3900*
—. International law. Self-determination. South Africa. 1971-78. *3916*
—. Namibia. South Africa. 1974. *3404*
Bantu Homelands policy (review article). Apartheid. Bibliographies. South Africa. 1961-77. *3978*
Bantu Mirror (periodical). *African Daily News* (periodical). *African Weekly* (periodical). Letters to the editor. Race Relations. Zimbabwe. 1930-70. *4310*
Bantustans. *See* Bantu Homelands; individual areas by name, e.g. South Africa (Bophuthatswana).
Bapostolo ritual. Christianity. *Kerek* (ritual). ca 1900-75. *791*
Baptists. Kimbangu, Simon. Religious Movements. Zaire. 1921-22. *2546*
Barnes, Albert C. Art. Collectors. Locke, Alain. USA. 1920's. *821*
Barnes, Leonard. Gibson, Richard. Independence (review article). 1971-72. *212*
Basutoland Progressive Association. *Lekhotla La Bafo* (Council of Commoners). Lesotho. Nationalist organizations. 20c. *3546*
Bataka Party. Nationalism. Uganda. USSR. 1945-62. *3274*
Bates, Robert H. Burawoy, Michael. Copper Mines and Mining. Government. Labor Unions and Organizations (review article). Zambia. 1949-70. *4071*
Battle, Lucius D. Egypt. Foreign Relations. Sadat, Anwar. 1957-81. *1189*
Battles. Gabon (Cocobeach). World War I. 1914. *690*
Baule. Agriculture. Ivory Coast. Labor, division of. Women. 19c-20c. *1921*
—. Colonization. Ivory Coast. Textile Industry. Women. 1875-1975. *1920*
Bay, Edna G. Hafkin, Nancy J. Women (review article). 1700-1975. *916*
Bayudaya. Judaism. Kakungulu, Semei. Malaki sect. Uganda. 1856-1974. *3285*
Beamish, Henry Hamilton. Colonialism. Fascism. Great Britain. ca 1920-48. *192*
Beer. Economic Conditions. Islam. Sorghum. Upper Volta. Women. 1978-80. *2389*
Begging. Hausa. Migration, Internal. Nigeria (Ibadan). 1974. *2016*
Beinart, William Justin. Angola. Bundy, Colin. Capitalism. Clarence-Smith, W. G. Peasants (review article). South Africa. 1900-80. *3348*
Beja (battle). Tunisia. World War II. 1943. *768*
Belgian Congo. *See* Zaire.
Belgium. Burundi. Foreign Relations. Military aid. ca 1960-72. *2672*
—. City Planning. Colonial Government. France. 1960-80. *914*
—. Lumumba, Patrice (correspondence). Sancke, Paul. Zaire. 1956-57. *2512*
—. Medical Research. Public Health. Sleeping sickness. Zaire. 1885-1980. *2536*
—. Zaire. 1961-73. *2502*
Bell, Rudolph Douala Manga. Cameroon. Independence Movements. Political Leadership. 1919-22. *2411*
Belligerent recognition. Ethiopia (Eritrea). International law. 1850's-1979. *2768*
Bemba. Catholic Church. Local government. Missions and Missionaries. Zambia. 1890-1935. *4070*
—. Lenshina, Alice. Lumpa rising. Rebellions. Sects, Religious. Zambia. 1953-68. *4045*
Ben Zelmat, Messaoud. Algeria (Aurès). Anticolonial movements. Bandits. 1917-21. *1013*
Bender, Gerald J. Angola. Colonial Government (review article). 1500-1970. *3469*
Benin *See also* Africa, West; Dahomey; French West Africa.

—. Democracy. Public expenditures. Rural development. 1965-80. *3502*
—. Development. Economic Aid (private). 1962-80. *3498*
—. Dingaka. Medicine. 1820-1970. *3493*
—. District Administration. Local Government. 1965-74. *3516*
—. Economic Development. 1910-73. *3490*
—. Economic History. Khama III. 1875-1923. *3512*
—. Elites (political). 1965-74. *3491*
—. Epidemics. Influenza, Spanish. Kgatla. 1918. *3529*
—. Foreign policy. Khama, Seretse. Political development. South Africa. 1966-76. *3492*
—. Foreign policy. South Africa. 1970's. *3500*
—. Hunting. 1961-73. *3523*
—. Jonathan, Leabua. Khama, Seretse. Lesotho. Political Leadership. 1966-73. *3366*
—. Kalahari Desert. Rey, C. F. (diaries). Travel accounts. 1930-37. *3507*
—. Kgatla. Kinship. 1934-73. *3525*
—. Khama, Seretse. Political Leadership. 1966-80. *3536*
—. Khama, Tshekedi. Nationalism. 1925-59. *3488*
—. Khama, Tshekedi. Ngwato. Politics. 1948-51. *3489*
—. Labor. Migration, Internal. Social Change. 1966-80. *3487*
—. Labor. Mines. South Africa. 1899-1966. *3531*
—. Labor markets. Lesotho. South Africa. Swaziland. 1967-76. *3343*
—. Legal systems. 1885-1966. *3485*
—. Lesotho. Monetary systems. Rand Monetary Area. South Africa. Swaziland. 1909-78. *3347*
—. Libraries. National Library Service. 1968-77. *3521*
—. Namibia. Political change. Swaziland. 20c. *3351*
—. Nationalism. Political ideology. Ratshosa, Simon. 1916-32. *3514*
—. Political Parties (review article). Wiseman, John. 1965-77. *3530*
—. Public Administration. Rural development. 1970-74. *3517*
—. Rural development. 1966-75. *3510*
Botswana (Chobe District). Cooperatives. Fishing. Namibia. Subia. Yambezi Fisherman's Co-operative Society. 1973-77. *3496*
Botswana (Etsha). Angolans. Resettlement. 1967-75. *3519*
Botswana (Ghansi). Autonomy. San. Social Policy. 1974-82. *3535*
—. Medicine. Nharo. 1970's. *3486*
Botswana (Kweneng). Chiefs. District councils. Local Government. 1960's-70's. *3533*
—. Economic history. Kwena. 1885-1966. *3494*
—. Migration. Population. Settlement. 1965-76. *3527*
Botswana (Macloutsi). Police (border patrol). Sitwell, William (letters). 1892-1915. *3522*
Botswana (Mochudi). Towns. 1871-1971. *3497*
Botswana (Ngamiland). Economic development. ca 1800-1972. *3518*
Botswana (Okavango Delta). Environment. 19c-1973. *3534*
Botswana (Orapa). Company towns. DeBeers Company. Diamonds. Mining. 1955-78. *3528*
Botswana, western. Afrikaners. Labor. San. Social Conditions. Tswana. 1900-71. *3524*
Boudjedra, Rashid. Benjelloun, Tahar. Khaïr-Eddine, Mohammed. Maghreb. Novels. 1965-75. *920*
Boumédienne, Houari. Africa, North. Political Leadership. 1978. *948*
—. Algeria. Economy. Foreign policy. Oil industry and Trade. 1965-75. *1027*
—. Algeria. Islam. Political Leadership. Revolution. 1940's-78. *1083*
—. Algeria. Political Leadership. 1952-78. *1078*
—. Algeria. Political Leadership. Revolution. 1946-78. *1048*
—. Algeria. Politics. 1979-80. *1082*
Boundaries *See also* Annexation.
—. 'Abd Allah, al-Iman. Ethiopia (Nugara). Feudalism. State Formation. 1901-23. *2743*
—. Africa, West. Bibliographies. 1977. *1691*
—. Bibliographies. Equatorial Guinea. Gabon. 1884-1973. *2395*
—. Colonial Government. Ghana (Asante). Local government. 1896-1951. *1772*
—. Conflict and Conflict Resolution. Ethiopia. 1870-1979. *2820*
—. Decolonization. Western Sahara. 1975-76. *1586*
—. Dinka. Nuer. Sudan (Sobat, Zaraf valleys). 1860-1976. *1490*
—. Diplomacy. Mauritania. 1960-76. *1974*
—. Egypt. Great Britain. Sinai Peninsula. 1906-47. *1124*
—. Ethiopia. Treaties. 1827-1968. *2754*
—. Ethiopia (Eritrea). Foreign Policy. Somalia. USA. USSR. 1974-77. *2574*
—. Ethnic Groups. Nigeria (Akoko-Edo). 1960-74. *2086*
—. Ewe. Ghana. National Liberation Movement of Western Togoland. Nationalism. Togo. 1943-78. *1616*
—. Foreign relations. Uganda (Buganda; Bunyoro). 1900-64. *3254*
—. Nigeria, Western. 1897-1963. *1989*
Boundaries (concept). Political theory. 19c-20c. *114*
Boundaries (disputes). Conflict and Conflict Resolution. Maghreb. Western Sahara. 20c. *956*
—. Foreign Policy. USA. Western Sahara. 1976-82. *1598*
—. Libya. Military Aid. Sudan (Darfur). USA. 1870-1981. *929*
—. Malawi. Tanzania. ca 1967-73. *448*
Bourgeoisie. *See* Middle Classes.
Bourguiba, Habib. Democratization. Political Leadership. Tunisia. 1969-80. *1565*
—. Elites. Ideology. Political Leadership. Tunisia. 1955-77. *1574*
—. Fascism. Italy. Nationalism. Tunisia. 1922-43. *1543*
—. Foreign policy. Tunisia. 1970-75. *1562*
—. Power, exercise of. Tunisia. 1950's-70's. *1566*
Bourguiba, Habib (interview). Arab unity. Tunisia. 1973. *1575*
Boute, Joseph (interview). Demographic trends. Zaire. 1973. *2454*
Boycott Outspan Action Foundation (BOA). Netherlands. Oranges. South Africa. 1972-73. *3757*
Boycotts. Africa, Southern. Labor reform. Racism. United Mine Workers. USA. 1960's-74. *3422*
—. Cocoa. Ghana. Political Participation. Social Classes. 1937-38. *1736*
—. Colonial government. Economic development. Zimbabwe. 1965-73. *4165*
—. Foreign relations. Norway. South Africa. 1970-77. *3933*
Bratton, Michael. Colonial Government. Community development. Zimbabwe. 1957-73. *4249*
Brazil. Africa, southern. Foreign policy. Portugal. 1970's. *511*
—. Africa, West. Foreign Relations. Trade. 1970's. *549*
—. Foreign Relations. 1970-75. *484*
Brazil (Pará). Gisu. Rural development. Social Classes. Uganda. 1969-78. *3226*
Brazilians. Attitudes. Benin. Education. Elites. Tradition. 1920-67. *1707*
—. Benin. Cultural Change. 1850-1978. *1704*
Brett, E. A. Africa, East. Colonialism. Economic change (review article). Politics. 1919-39. *2607*
British Commonwealth *See also* Great Britain.
—. Africa, Southern. Developing nations. Diplomacy. International organizations. New International Economic Order. 1960-79. *3357*
—. Africa, West. Foreign policy. 1830's-1974. *1669*
—. Asians. Foreign Relations. India. Refugees. Uganda. 1972. *3241*
—. Constitutional law. Nwabueze, B. O. (review article). 1870-1975. *255*
British Commonwealth (Secretariat). 1965-77. *422*
British Empire *See also* Great Britain.
—. Africa, West. Empire Resources Development Committee. Exports. Milner, Alfred. 1916-20. *1649*
—. Africans. Armies (colonial). 1916-60. *750*
—. Independence Movements. Morality. 1919-47. *224*
British Empire (review article). Duignan, Peter. Gann, L. H. 1870-1960. *182*
British South Africa Company. Colonial government. Land policy. Swaziland. Zimbabwe. ca 1900-68. *4037*
—. Gold Mines and Mining. Investments. Mozambique Company. Rezende, Baron de. Zimbabwe. 1887-1948. *4159*
Broederbond. Afrikaners. Nationalism. South Africa. 1927-48. *3898*
—. Secret Societies. Social Organizations. South Africa. 20c. *3966*
Brotherhood Movement. Class Struggle. DeBeers Consolidated Mines. Plaatje, Solomon Tshekisho. South Africa (Kimberley). 1918-19. *3945*
Buffaloes, Cape. Botswana. Wildlife. 1783-1975. *3520*
Bullhoek massacre. Israelites. Mgijima, Enoch. Religion. South Africa. 1868-1921. *3969*
Bundy, Colin. Angola. Beinart, William Justin. Capitalism. Clarence-Smith, W. G. Peasants (review article). South Africa. 1900-80. *3348*
Burawoy, Michael. Bates, Robert H. Copper Mines and Mining. Government. Labor Unions and Organizations (review article). Zambia. 1949-70. *4071*
Bureau of State Security. Secret Police. South Africa. 1969-76. *3804*
Bureaucracies. Colonial Government. Economic Policy. Tanzania. 1919-39. *3153*
—. Decentralization. Local government. Tanzania. 1972. *3134*
—. Economic Growth. Modernization. 1960-74. *675*
—. Egypt. Public Administration. 1973-82. *1182*
—. Ethiopia. Monarchy. Revolution. 1930-80. *2762*
—. Foreign policy. Nigeria. Politics. 1960-75. *2102*
—. Ghana (review article). Historiography. Politics and the Military. 1955-75. *1779*
—. Housing. Squatter settlements. Tanzania (Dar es Salaam). Urbanization. 1965-82. *3210*
—. Modernization. Uganda. -1966. *3292*
Bureaucracies (merging of). Commission for Technical Cooperation. Organization of African Unity. 1950-68. *118*
Bureaucracies (Sudanization). Civil Service (training). Sudan. 1956-73. *1456*
Bureaucrats. Politicians. Social Status (comparative study). Tanzania. Uganda. 1960's-70's. *2618*
Burns, Alan. Africa, West. Colonial Government (Executive Councils). Great Britain. Political Participation. 1941-42. *1660*
Burrú, Aialeu. Badoglio, Pietro. Diplomacy. Ethiopia (Amhara). Gasparini, Jacopo. Italy. 1936. *2750*
Burundi. Africa, East. Cholera. Public Health. 1970-79. *2584*
—. Belgium. Foreign Relations. Military aid. ca 1960-72. *2672*
—. Church and state. 1879-1972. *2659*
—. Civil War. 1962-72. *2656*
—. Civil War. Foreign Policy. Genocide. USA. 1972. *2657*
—. Civil war. Hutu. Tutsi. 1956-72. *2665*
—. Colonialism. Ethnic conflict. Massacres. 1972. *2661*
—. Conflicts and conflict resolution. Ethnic groups. 1970's. *2670*
—. Cultural degradation. Social Change. Twa. 20c. *2660*
—. Culture. Economic Conditions. Political Systems. 1962-81. *2663*
—. Ethnic conflict. Hutu. Tutsi. 1962-75. *2671*
—. Ethnic groups. Hutu. Tutsi. Violence. 1972-73. *2666*
—. Ethnolinguistics. Politics. 1970's. *2668*
—. Genocide. Hutu. Tutsi. 1972. *2664*
—. Genocide. USA. 1964-72. *2667*
—. Historiography. Monarchy. Ntare Rushatsi. 1900-77. *2658*
—. Hutu. Politics. Tutsi. 1970's. *2662*
—. Political systems. Social organization. 20c. *2669*
Bushmen. *See* San.
Business. Aliens. Egypt. Middle Classes. 1920-50. *1168*
—. Banks. Europe. USA. 1972-74. *603*
—. Bibliographies. Company histories. 1836-1973. *559*
—. Collective bargaining. Labor Unions and Organizations. Race Relations. South Africa. USA. 1970-81. *3752*
—. Dependency. Indigenization. Niger (Kano). Technology. 1972-79. *2037*
—. Economic reform. Independence. Zambia. 1960's-74. *4044*
—. Foreign Investments. Kenya (Kitale). Nationalization. 1969-76. *2900*
—. Kenya (Nairobi). Landholding. Women. ca 1900-50. *2866*
—. Progressive Federal Party. Social Classes. South Africa. 1959-78. *3859*
Business community, French. Dubreuil, Lemaigre. Morocco. 1952-55. *1429*
Business environment. Ghana. Ghanaization. National Liberation Council. 1968-. *1731*

Business History. Friendship. Kinship. Liberia (Monrovia). Merchants. 1970. *1949*
—. Historiography. 1867-1973. *27*
Businessmen. Dependency theory. Economic Development. Foreign investments. 1960's-70's. *564*
—. Zambia (Lusaka). 1960's-72. *4097*
Buthelezi, Gatsha. Labor Unions and Organizations. Racial tensions. South Africa (Durban). Strikes. ca 1910-73. *3801*
Bwiti cult. Catholicism. Drugs. Fang. Gabon, central. Mysticism. ca 1950's-70's. *2446*

C

Cabinet *See also* individual names of cabinet members.
—. Civil-Military Relations. Egypt. Military. 1952-77. *1201*
—. Elites (political). Nigeria. Parliaments. 1954-65. *2137*
Cabinet crisis. National Anthems. South Africa. Stuttaford, Richard. 1938. *3825*
Cabora Bassa dam. Colonial Government. Mozambique. Technology. 1953-73. *3656*
—. Colonialism. FRELIMO. Mozambique. Portugal. 1968-75. *3670*
—. Economic Development. Mozambique (Zambezi Valley). Portugal. 1953-79. *3657*
Cabral, Amilcar. Assassination. Colonialism. Guinea-Bissau. Independence Movements. Portugal. 1953-73. *1901*
—. Assassination. Guinea-Bissau. 1966-72. *1909*
—. Cape Verde Islands. Guinea-Bissau. Independence Movements. Marxism. ca 1960-75. *1886*
—. Colonialism. Culture. Guinea-Bissau. Independence movements. Political thought. ca 1920-72. *1899*
—. Cultural models. Fanon, Frantz. Modernization. 1950-75. *629*
—. Ethnicity. Guinea-Bissau. Independence Movements. Marxism. 1930-76. *1898*
—. Fanon, Frantz. Political theory. Revolution. 20c. *4*
—. Guinea-Bissau. Imperialism. Political Theory. 1956-69. *1900*
—. Guinea-Bissau. Independence. 1911-74. *1894*
—. Guinea-Bissau. Independence Movements. 1930's-73. *1893*
—. Guinea-Bissau. Independence Movements. Portugal. 1924-73. *1887*
—. Guinea-Bissau. Marxism. Middle Classes. 1950's-70's. *1897*
—. Guinea-Bissau. National liberation movements. 1924-73. *1895*
—. Guinea-Bissau. Political Theory. Revolution. 1950's-73. *1892*
—. Guinea-Bissau. Political Theory. Revolution. 1960's. *1883*
Cabral, Amilcar (assassination). National liberation. 1973. *160*
Cabral, Amilcar (essay). Imperialism. Revolution. 20c. *209*
Cabral, Amilcar (obituary). Guinea-Bissau. Politics. 1971-73. *1908*
Cabral, Luiz (interview). Guinea-Bissau. Independence Movements. 20c. *1889*
Cadbury Schweppes (firm). Agricultural Industry. Foreign Investments. Nigeria (Zaria). 1968-76. *2013*
Calvinism. Apartheid. Social policy. South Africa. 1948-79. *3719*
Calvinism, Afrikaner. Economic activity. South Africa. 18c-1975. *4020*
Cambon, Pierre Paul. Colonial Government. France. Lyautey, Hubert. Morocco. Tunisia. 1869-1925. *949*
Cameroon *See also* Africa, West.
—. Acculturation. Duala. Elites (German-speaking). 1884-1940. *2404*
—. Agriculture. Beti. Cocoa. Labor, division of. Nigeria. Women. Yoruba. 1950-79. *620*
—. Agriculture. Beti. Economic Structure. Women. 1920-77. *2408*
—. Agriculture. Education. 1921-70. *2416*
—. Ahidjo, Ahmadou. Federalism. 1961-72. *2424*
—. Ahidjo, Ahmadou. Politics. Symbols. 1958-76. *2425*
—. Bell, Rudolph Douala Manga. Independence Movements. Political Leadership. 1919-22. *2411*
—. Beti. Chiefs. Depression. Public Administration. 1929-34. *2407*
—. Colonial Government. Economic Growth. Investment policies. 1945-60. *2418*
—. Colonial Government. Education. 1916-38. *2417*
—. Colonial Government. France. Germany. 1884-1960. *2423*
—. Colonial policy. Language. Schools. 1960-74. *2405*
—. Colonialism. France. Germany. Nationalism. 1919-39. *2412*
—. Decolonization. Joseph, Richard A. (review article). Union des Populations de Cameroun. 1948-56. *2400*
—. Economic development. Public Finance. 1947-81. *2420*
—. *Effort Camerounais* (newspaper). Political development. Press. 1955-72. *2399*
—. France. Great Britain. Military Occupation. Partition, provisional. World War I. 1914-16. *701*
—. Fulbe (Mbororean). Nigeria. Nomads and Nomadism. Sedentarization. Social Change. 20c. *1635*
—. Income, rural. Social Organization. Taxation. 1922-37. *2410*
—. Independence Movements. Nyobe, Ruben Um. 1948-59. *2414*
—. Independence Movements. Politics. Radicals and Radicalism. Union des Populations de Camerouns. ca 1945-48. *2413*
—. Ivory Coast. Social change. Social Status. Women. 1955-71. *800*
—. Modernization. Soccer. Social Organizations. 1880's-1974. *2403*
—. National development. Nationalism. Self-determination. ca 1948-76. *2421*
—. Trade patterns. 1957-72. *2419*
Cameroon (Adamawa Plateau). Colonial Government. Fulani. Gbaya. 1899-1966. *2402*
Cameroon, Central. Colonial government. Food production. 1920-46. *2409*
Cameroon (Douala). Riots. World War II. 1945. *2415*
Cameroon, southeast. Capitalism. Economic Theory. Inequality. Maka. ca 1930-78. *2406*
Cameroon, West. Cultural conflict. Education. Political leadership. 1950's-72. *2401*
Cameroon (Yaoundé). Atangana, Charles. Beti. 1911-43. *2422*
—. Atangana, Karl. Beti. League of Nations. Mandates. World War I. 1914-22. *714*
Camp David Agreement. Economic conditions. Egypt. Foreign policy. Israel. 1970's. *1132*
Campaigns. *See* Military Campaigns.
Campaigns, Political. *See* Political Campaigns.
Camus, Albert. Algeria. Arabs. Independence Movements. 1934-60. *1086*
Canada. Africa, West. Foreign Aid. 1961-75. *1694*
—. Cultural Imperialism. Literature, African. 1973. *831*
—. Education. Great Britain. Missions and Missionaries. Sudan Interior Mission. 1937-55. *1505*
—. Foreign aid. 1961-81. *525*
—. Foreign Aid. Refugees. 1970-80. *526*
—. Foreign aid. Trade. 1970-75. *447*
—. Foreign Policy. Self-determination. South Africa. Zimbabwe. ca 1961-79. *3411*
—. Foreign Policy. South Africa. 1899-1982. *3937*
—. Foreign Policy. South Africa. Trade. Zimbabwe. 1960's-76. *3409*
—. Foreign Relations. 1970-79. *415*
Canadian International Development Agency. Rural development. Tanzania. Wheat. 1979-82. *3072*
Cancer. Epidemiology. Migrant labor. South Africa. 1930-75. *3979*
Cane spirit. Alcoholic Beverages. South Africa. 1860-1978. *3964*
Cannabis, diffusion of. Social Customs. 100-1974. *806*
Cannabis use. South Africa. 20c. *3967*
Cape Verde Islands. Cabral, Amilcar. Guinea-Bissau. Independence Movements. Marxism. ca 1960-75. *1886*
—. Colonial government. Independence. 1460-1975. *1710*
—. Cultural identity. Decolonization. Guinea-Bissau. Mozambique. 1950-81. *779*
—. Guinea-Bissau. Independence. 1970's. *1625*
—. Independence. Partido Africano da Independência da Guiné e Cabo Verde (PAIGC). 1460-1975. *1711*
Capital *See also* Banking; Capitalism; Investments; Labor; Monopolies.
—. Economic structure. Kenya. 1963-76. *2895*
Capital accumulation. Colonialism. Income distribution. Land policy. Zimbabwe. 1946-69. *4161*
—. Economic development. Maghreb. 1960's-70's. *970*
—. Land Ownership. Social Organization. Togo. 1885-1979. *2382*
Capital mobilization. Economic growth. Government policy. South Africa. 1939-60. *3782*
Capital reserves. Algeria. Economic Policy. Government. 1959-73. *1095*
Capitalism *See also* Capital; Socialism.
—. Afar. Agriculture (cash crops). Famine. 1965-73. *2693*
—. Agricultural Policy. Colonial Government. Food production. Tanzania. 1840-1960's. *3062*
—. Agriculture. Child labor. Ghana. 18c-20c. *1761*
—. Agriculture (conference). 20c. *637*
—. Angola. Beinart, William Justin. Bundy, Colin. Clarence-Smith, W. G. Peasants (review article). South Africa. 1900-80. *3348*
—. Anthropology. Congo. Marxism. Neocolonialism (review article). Rey, P. P. 20c. *2440*
—. Apartheid. South Africa. 1841-1974. *3772*
—. Cameroon, southeast. Economic Theory. Inequality. Maka. ca 1930-78. *2406*
—. Colonialism. 1900-50. *184*
—. Colonialism. Economic Development. Ghana. 1800-1957. *1733*
—. Colonization. Kenya. Land. ca 1880's-1920's. *2901*
—. Developing nations. Economic system, international. 1968-74. *683*
—. Development. Kenya. Socialism. Zimbabwe. 1950-81. *617*
—. Economic Structure. Nigeria, northern. Peasants. Social Classes. 1850-1980. *2072*
—. Economic Structure (international). 1500-1960. *389*
—. Elites. Political development. Tanzania. 19c-1960's. *3120*
—. Islam (ethics). Merchants. Tunisia. Weber, Max. 1960's. *1567*
—. Nigeria. Sects, Religious. Social Classes. Yoruba. 1947-74. *2017*
—. Protectionism. Racism. South Africa. 1910-39. *3871*
—. Race Relations. South Africa. 1918-78. *3743*
—. Revolutionary movements. 1960's-70's. *671*
Capitalism (peripheric). Colonialism. Developing Nations. Marxism. 1975. *653*
Capitalism, Primitive. Depression. Europeans. Kenya. Settlers. ca 1900-50. *2910*
Capitalism (review article). Dagut, J. Houghton, H. Hobart. South Africa. 1860-1970. *3778*
Capitalist countries. Technical assistance. 1960-81. *515*
Capitalists. Social Classes. United National Independence Party. Zambia. 1964-81. *4043*
Capot-Rey, Robert. Geography. Institute for Saharan Research. Sahara. 1935-78. *926*
Capricorn Africa Society. Nationalism. Racism. Stirling, David. Zimbabwe. 1945-60. *4213*
—. Nationalism. Tanzania. 1949-67. *3176*
Career choices. Education. Egypt. 1882-1922. *1348*
Career guidance policies. Manpower efficiency. Tanzania. 1961-74. *3116*
Cartels. Cocoa. Economic Crisis. Ghana. Nigeria. *West African Pilot* (newspaper). 1937. *1620*
Cary, Robert. Pioneer Corps (review article). Zimbabwe. 1869-1975. *4298*
Cassava. Influenza. Niger River, lower. Nigeria. 20c. *2057*
Catholic Church *See also* religious orders by name, e.g. White Fathers, etc.; Vatican.
—. Angola. Church and State. Missions and Missionaries. Mozambique. 1975-81. *3349*
—. Anticolonialism. Mozambique. 1868-1979. *3662*
—. Bemba. Local government. Missions and Missionaries. Zambia. 1890-1935. *4070*
—. Bibliographies. *Bibliotheca Missionum*. Missions and Missionaries. 1053-1940. *26*
—. Christianity. Senegal. 1455-1981. *2307*
—. Church and state. Tanzania. 1880's-1970's. *3217*
—. Church and State (review article). Zimbabwe. 1820-1979. *4312*
—. Communism. Goodlatte, Clare. Politics. Social work. South Africa. 1860-1940. *3817*
—. Education, rural. Missions and Missionaries. Zaire (Shaba). 1885-1939. *2544*

—. Colonial Office. Decolonization. Nigeria. Richards, Arthur. 1939-45. *2125*
—. Confederation. Gore-Browne, Stewart. Political Reform. Public opinion. Zambia. 1948. *4126*
—. Confederation. Great Britain. Zambia. Zimbabwe. 1931-52. *3397*
—. Conscription, military. French West Africa. ca 1900-50. *1632*
—. Constitutions. Discriminatory acts. Great Britain. Zimbabwe. 1923-74. *4243*
—. Constitutions. Governors. Nationalism. Nigeria. 1935-51. *2177*
—. Coppet, Marcel de. French West Africa. Labor, forced. Popular Front. 1936-46. *1610*
—. Cotton. Economic policy. Uganda. 1918-29. *3321*
—. Court of Appeal (Special Approvals Tribunal). French West Africa. Law, traditional. 1903-20. *1680*
—. Cultural imperialism. Educational policy. Middle Classes (African). Zimbabwe. 1953-70. *4172*
—. Dahomey (Borgu). Nigeria (Borgu). Rebellions. 1915-17. *1623*
—. Delafosse, Maurice (speech). French West Africa. Public Administration (native policy). 1919. *1659*
—. Dependency. Development. Tanzania. 20c. *3119*
—. Depression. Economic Policy. Ivory Coast. Profits. 1929-35. *1911*
—. Depression. Economic system. Zaire. 1930's-77. *2469*
—. Developing nations. Ghana. Great Britain. Treasury reform. 1936. *1751*
—. District Commissioners. Great Britain. Public Administration. 1900-60. *190*
—. Ecology. Land policy. Zambia, Eastern. 1895-1940. *4129*
—. Economic Conditions. Electoral system. Great Britain. Zimbabwe. 1961-71. *4194*
—. Economic Conditions. Malawi. Railroads. 1895-1935. *3624*
—. Economic Conditions. Public Health. Sleeping sickness. Social Conditions. Zambia (Mweru-Luapula). 1906-22. *4093*
—. Economic development. Ghana (review article). 15c-20c. *1734*
—. Economic development. Ivory Coast. World War I. 1914-19. *712*
—. Economic Development. Money. Tanzania. ca 1880-1940. *3092*
—. Economic Development. Mozambique. Mozambique Company. 1900-32. *3671*
—. Economic development. World War II. Zambia. 1940-45. *4077*
—. Economic Growth. Nigeria, eastern. 1862-1960. *2161*
—. Economic Planning. Geography. Great Britain. 1943-56. *624*
—. Economic sanctions. Great Britain. UN. Zimbabwe. 1965-75. *4272*
—. Economic sanctions. Zimbabwe. 1965. *4171*
—. Economic Structure. Sudan, Southern. 1898-1955. *1512*
—. *Education Policy in British Tropical Africa* (White Paper). Great Britain. 1914-39. *235*
—. Educational Policy. Ghana, northern. Guggisbery, F. G. 1906-40. *1856*
—. Educational policy. Great Britain. 1923-39. *168*
—. Educational policy. Kenya. Scott, Henry S. 1920-34. *3002*
—. Educational policy. Lugard, Frederick. Nigeria. 1900-18. *2223*
—. Embargo. Oil. Unilateral Declaration of Independence (UDI). Zimbabwe. 1965-77. *4160*
—. English. Labor. Language manipulation. Tanzania. 1919-40. *3154*
—. Ethiopia. Graziani, Rodolfo. Umberto, Prince. 1936-40. *2797*
—. Ethiopia. Kenya, northern. Refugees. 1936-38. *3012*
—. Ethiopia. Malladra mission. Military preparation. 1925-26. *2794*
—. Ethnic ranking. Great Britain. Race Relations. 19c-1980. *189*
—. Ethnicity. Kaguru. Political Leadership. Tanzania. 1880-1944. *3133*
—. Ethnicity. Lugard, Frederick. Military Recruitment. 1900-60. *347*
—. Exports. Kenya (Lamu archipelago). Mangrove poles. Tanzania (Rufiji River). 1900-81. *2576*
—. Famine. Law and order. Niger. 1931. *1983*
—. Farming, plantation. Uganda. 1901-23. *3277*
—. Food Shortages. Nigeria (Lagos). Price control. Pullen marketing scheme. World War II. 1941-47. *2069*
—. Forests. Great Britain. Legislation. Nigeria. Rubber. 1897-1940. *2025*
—. France. Labor Unions and Organizations. Popular Front. Senegal. 1919-38. *2302*
—. France. Lyautey, Hubert. Morocco. 1912-25. *1410*
—. France. Lyautey, Hubert. Morocco. Zionism. 1915-25. *1418*
—. French West Africa. Indigenat Code. 1887-1946. *1608*
—. French West Africa. Islam. Nigeria. Rebellions. World War I. 1914-17. *704*
—. Ganda. Kiga. Local Government. Ssbalijja. Uganda (Kigezi). 1908-30. *3311*
—. Ghana. Indirect rule. Riots. Slater, Ransford. Taxation, direct. 1929-44. *1816*
—. Ghana (Asante). Political culture. 1969-70. *1782*
—. Ghana, northern. Local government. Native states. 20c. *1773*
—. Ghana (Northern Territories). Land policy. 1900-57. *1726*
—. Ghana (Takoradi Harbor). Public works. 1919-42. *1744*
—. Government Enterprise. Mozambique. Mozambique Company. Nyassa Company. 1870's-1941. *3665*
—. Governors. Great Britain. 19c-20c. 1930-76. *188*
—. Great Britain. Hodeib, Mohammed Amin. Resistance. Sudan (Tuti Island). 1914-46. *1496*
—. Great Britain. Marxism. Social Customs. Witchcraft. 19c-20c. *173*
—. Great Britain. Muslims. Nigeria. Rebellions. World War I. 1914-19. *705*
—. Great Britain. Nationalism. Press. Uganda. 1920's-30's. *3299*
—. Great Britain. Nigeria. Tiv. 1900-70. *2234*
—. Great Britain. Nigeria, Northern. Public Finance. Taxation. 1900-34. *2038*
—. Great Britain. Sudan. 1899-1952. *1493*
—. Guerrilla Warfare. Independence Movements. Mozambique. 1960-73. *3630*
—. Guinea-Bissau. Independence Movements. 1913-63. *1891*
—. Higher education. Makerere University. Uganda. 1921-40. *3268*
—. Igbo. Nigeria. Political systems, dual-sex. Women. -1970's. *2163*
—. Immigration. Kenya. Social Status. Somalis. 1916-63. *2980*
—. Independence Movements. Mozambique. 1885-1960. *3640*
—. International Labor Organization. Labor policy. 1920-47. *206*
—. Islam. Ivory Coast. 1893-1939. *1932*
—. Islam. Missions and Missionaries. Nigeria (Muslim emirates). Proselytization. 1900-28. *2288*
—. Islam. Nigeria (Kano). Taxation. 1806-1927. *2076*
—. Ivory Coast. Public Health. Sleeping sickness. 1900-45. *1918*
—. Ivory Coast. Repression. 1908-20. *1919*
—. Kenya. Kiama Kia Muingi. Kikuyu. Secret societies. 1953-61. *2946*
—. Kenya. Legislative Council. Mathu, Eliud. 1919-57. *2929*
—. Kenya. Mitchell, Philip. 1944-52. *2922*
—. Kenya. Nandi. Political Protest. 1905-23. *2918*
—. Kenya. Nandi. Rebellions. 1923. *2928*
—. Kenya. Police. Racial structure. 1920-50. *2970*
—. Labor (forced). Malawi. Peasants. Political consciousness. Rwanda. 19c-1962. *207*
—. Labor problems. Race Relations. Zambia. 1900-53. *4078*
—. Lake Kivu. Local government. Zaire (Ijwi Island). 1900-70. *2503*
—. Land policy. Malawi. Peasants. ca 1900-73. *3618*
—. Land tenure. Rural development. Uganda. 1900-66. *3252*
—. Land Tenure. Zaire. 1930-60. *2484*
—. Language policy. Nigeria. Yoruba. 1882-1955. *2218*
—. Libya. 1835-1969. *1376*
—. Local Politics. Nigeria. Political leadership. 1904-54. *2189*
—. Malawi. Tax collection. 1891-1972. *3592*
—. Mali. 1851-1953. *1967*
—. Masterson, G. M. (memoirs). Zimbabwe. 1925-66. *4144*
—. Military (review article). Zimbabwe. 1945-78. *4237*
—. Monarchy. Myths and Symbols. National Self-image. Zambia. 1924-38. *4107*
—. Monarchy. Nigeria. Yoruba. 1900-60. *2101*
—. Nigeria. Strikes, general. 1945. *2067*
—. Nigeria (Benin). Slavery. 1897-1945. *2250*
—. Nigeria (Southeastern). Roads. 1903-39. *2051*
—. Nigeria, southeastern. Warrant chiefs. 1891-1951. *2089*
—. Nigeria, Western. Obas' Conference. Political Participation. 1913-79. *2143*
—. Nuer. Stereotypes. Sudan. 1800-1956. *1488*
—. Permanent Commission for the Protection of Natives. Population decline. Zaire. 1896-1926. *2535*
—. Police. Zambia. 1901-72. *4124*
—. Political economy. Private enterprise. Zaire. 1908-60. *2522*
—. Referendum. Responsible Government Party. Zimbabwe. 1920-23. *4227*
—. Rhodes-Livingstone Institute. Urbanization. Wilson, Godfrey. Zambia. 1938-41. *4134*
—. Schools, Development Area. Zambia. 1948-62. *4100*
—. Tanzania. Theater. 1920-62. *3194*
—. Uganda Agreement of 1900. Uganda (Buganda). 1856-1960's. *3223*
—. Zimbabwe. 1900-30. *4231*
Colonial Government (British, German). Bibliographies. Islam. Tanzania. 1973. *3202*
Colonial Government (cantons). Indirect rule. Senegal. 1855-1960. *2336*
Colonial Government (Executive Councils). Africa, West. Burns, Alan. Great Britain. Political Participation. 1941-42. *1660*
Colonial Government (indirect rule). Tanzania (Njombe). 1919-62. *3141*
Colonial Government (resistance to). Chewa. Labor service. Malawi. World War I. 1914-19. *707*
—. Ideology. Independence movements. 19c-20c. *157*
—. Madagascar. Medicine. Plague. 1921. *3558*
Colonial Government (review article). Angola. Bender, Gerald J. 1500-1970. *3469*
Colonial history. Ethnicity. Ivory Coast. National development. 1889-1969. *1931*
Colonial ideology. Madagascar. Racial groups. 1974. *3582*
Colonial legacy. France. Great Britain. Military dependence. 20c. *354*
Colonial Office. Colonial Government. Decolonization. Nigeria. Richards, Arthur. 1939-45. *2125*
—. Decolonization. Great Britain. Jones, Arthur Creech. 1947. *161*
—. Great Britain. Nationalism. 1947. *216*
—. Kenya. Leys, Norman. Ross, W. McGregor. Senate (European). 1900-40. *2971*
Colonial policy. Africa, central. Africa, East. Films. Great Britain. 1920-50. *230*
—. Africa, East. World War II. 1939-48. *2652*
—. Algeria. France. Resettlement programs. 1954-66. *1103*
—. Amendola, Giovanni. Italy. Libya (Cyrenaica). 1920-25. *1373*
—. Amendola, Giovanni. Italy. Libya (Tripoli). 1922. *1374*
—. Asians. Discrimination. Great Britain. Kenya. 1903-25. *2949*
—. Assimilation. Novels. Senegal. 1920's-60's. *2322*
—. Cameroon. Language. Schools. 1960-74. *2405*
—. Central African Federation (breakup). Federation Conference (1960). Victoria Falls Conference (1963). Zimbabwe. 1953-69. *3927*
—. Concessionary system. French Equatorial Africa. Trade. 1899-1972. *2397*
—. Diagne, Blaise. Pressure groups. Senegal. 1914-34. *2313*
—. Djibouti. France. 1862-1974. *2675*
—. Economic Conditions. Egypt. Great Britain. 1886-1937. *1148*
—. Ethnic conflict. Yaka. Zaire (Kwango basin). 1880-1960. *2510*
—. Ethnic groups. Mozambique. Portugal. 20c. *3625*
—. Ghana. Great Britain. Radio broadcasting. 1927-57. *1841*
—. Great Britain. Sudan. Unification. 1898-1953. *1519*
—. Guerrilla warfare. Italy. Libya. Mukhtar, Omar al-. 1929-31. *1389*
—. Independence. Kenya. Land reform. ca 1950-62. *2893*

—. Angola, southwest. Development. Portugal. 19c-20c. *3462*
—. Assimilation. Attitudes. Education. Senegal (Dakar). William Ponty School. 1937-45. *2318*
—. Baule. Ivory Coast. Textile Industry. Women. 1875-1975. *1920*
—. Blacks. Ghana. Sam, Alfred Charles. USA. 1913-16. *1846*
—. Capitalism. Kenya. Land. ca 1880's-1920's. *2901*
—. Debt. Depression. France. Morocco. 1930-36. *1440*
—. Depression. Farmers, European. France. Nationalism. Tunisia. 1930's. *1564*
—. Domestic politics. Madagascar. Mozambique. ca 1750-1976. *3340*
—. Economic Structure. Ghana. Peasants. 1885-1939. *1737*
—. Educational policy. Lyautey, Hubert. Morocco. 1920's. *1444*
—. Europeans. 20c. *860*
—. Europeans. Zimbabwe. 1920-76. *4326*
—. Exploitation. Working Class. Zaire (Kivu). 1900-40. *2465*
—. French West Africa. Lobi. Resistance. 1898-1926. *1630*
—. Kenya. Land tenure. Luo. Social organization. Women. 20c. *2903*
—. Labor supply. Land. Natal Land and Colonization Company. South Africa. 1838-1948. *3791*
—. Portugal. 15c-20c. *156*
Colonization, attempted. Italy. Libya. Resistance. 1907-32. *1375*
Colonna, F. Algeria. Leca, Jean. Politics (review article). Social Classes. Teachers. Vatin, J.-C. 1883-1975. *1094*
Colons. Algeria. Muslims. Nationalism. 1880-1920. *1008*
Coloureds. Apartheid. South Africa. 1931-62. *3864*
—. Economic Conditions. Ethnic Groups. Griqua trek. LeFleur, A. A. S. South Africa. 1867-1920. *3968*
—. Ideology. Political attitudes. South Africa. 1974. *3893*
—. Political representation. South Africa. 1951-79. *3940*
—. Racial policies. Reform. South Africa. Theron Commission. 20c. *3971*
Colson, Elizabeth (memoirs). Rhodes-Livingstone Institute. Zambia. 1948-51. *4056*
Comintern *See also* national parties by countries.
—. Communist Party. Race Relations. South Africa. 1920's-30's. *3868*
—. Ethiopia. Italy. Socialist International. War. 1935-36. *2790*
Commerce *See also* Banking; Business; International Trade; Monopolies; Prices; Statistics; Trade; Transportation.
—. Botswana. Colonial government. Great Britain. Jousse, Paul. Khama III. Ngwato. 1910-16. *3513*
Commercial disputes. Arbitration. 1965-75. *895*
—. Arbitration Convention. Nigeria. Oil industry and Trade. Treaties. UN. 1960's-70's. *2084*
Commission for Technical Cooperation. Bureaucracies (merging of). Organization of African Unity. 1950-68. *118*
Commodities. Price boom. Trade, terms of. 1960's-70's. *582*
Common Market. *See* European Economic Community.
Commonwealth Prime Ministers Conference (Ottawa, 1973). Colonialism. Foreign Policy. Great Britain. Portugal. 1965-74. *439*
Communal compartmentalization. Modakeke. Nigeria (Ife). Politics. 1820-1966. *2171*
Communal conflict (review article). Civil War. Modernization. Nigeria. 1971. *2174*
Communications *See also* Language; Mass Media; Newspapers.
—. Air mail service. Malawi. 1930-38. *3600*
—. Nigeria (Jos). Urban development. ca 1900-78. *1998*
Communism *See also* Comintern; Leftism; Marxism; Socialism.
—. Catholic Church. Goodlatte, Clare. Politics. Social work. South Africa. 1860-1940. *3817*
—. China. Cuba. Economic conditions. Tanzania. USSR. Women. 1977-78. *3066*
—. Ethiopia. Mengistu Haile Mariam. Public Policy. 1974-81. *2759*
—. Jewish Workers' Club. Jews. South Africa (Johannesburg). 1928-48. *3949*
—. Labor Unions and Organizations. Nigeria. Nigerian Trade Union Congress. Socialist Workers and Farmers Party. 1960's-70's. *2082*
Communist Countries. Historiography. National liberation movements. Symposium of Historians and Africanists of Socialist Countries, 3d. 1970-79. *217*
Communist International. *See* Comintern.
Communist Parties and Movements *See also* specific parties by country.
—. Angola. Popular Movement for the Liberation of Angola (MPLA). 1975. *3453*
—. Economic Development (noncapitalist). 1945-75. *302*
—. Foreign Relations. Mozambique. National Liberation Movements. 1962-75. *3643*
Communist Party. Algeria. 1927-35. *1092*
—. Algeria. Colonialism. Independence Movements. 1935-39. *1066*
—. Algeria. France. Politics. 1935-39. *1090*
—. Algeria. Ideology. Racism. 1920-27. *1093*
—. Angola. Guinea. Mozambique. 1970-75. *271*
—. Colonialism. Sudan. 1946-58. *1477*
—. Comintern. Race Relations. South Africa. 1920's-30's. *3868*
—. France. USSR. 1945-50. *432*
—. International Socialist League. South Africa. 1917-21. *3867*
—. Sudan. 1946-77. *1528*
Communist Party (24th Congress). Academy of Sciences. African studies. National liberation movements. USSR. 1971-76. *50*
Communists. Asia. Economic development. Political Systems. Public sector. -1973. *641*
Community. Bibliographies. Family. 20c. *818*
Community development. Bratton, Michael. Colonial Government. Zimbabwe. 1957-73. *4249*
—. Ethiopia. Peasants. Rural Development. Social Organization. 1957-74. *2716*
Community formation. Squatter settlements. Urbanization. 1960-74. *324*
Comoro Islands. Colonialism. France. Political development. 1854-1973. *3577*
—. Economic Conditions. 1975-79. *3559*
—. Economic Development. Foreign relations. Government. 1960's-75. *3586*
—. Independence. 1975-78. *3572*
—. Political parties. 20c. *3581*
Compagnie Financière de Suez. Egypt. France. Nationalization. Suez Canal. 1956-80. *1219*
Company histories. Bibliographies. Business. 1836-1973. *559*
Company towns. Botswana (Orapa). DeBeers Company. Diamonds. Mining. 1955-78. *3528*
Composers. Darwish, Sayyid. Egypt. 1892-1974. *1325*
Concert-party. Ghana. National Entertainment Association. Theater. 1918-75. *1829*
—. Nigeria (Lagos). Ogunde, Hubert. Theater. 1910-75. *2201*
Concessionary system. Colonial policy. French Equatorial Africa. Trade. 1899-1972. *2397*
Conciliation. Civil War. Sudan. -1972. *1469*
Cone, James. Religion, traditional. South Africa. Theology, African. 1700-1970's. *3956*
Confederation *See also* Political Integration.
—. Colonial government. Gore-Browne, Stewart. Political Reform. Public opinion. Zambia. 1948. *4126*
—. Colonial Government. Great Britain. Zambia. Zimbabwe. 1931-52. *3397*
—. Colonialism. Economic Development. Social Conditions. Zambia. Zimbabwe. 1925-35. *3421*
Conflict and Conflict Resolution. 1943-81. *32*
—. 1950's-70's. *294*
—. Africa, East. 1850-1970's. *2601*
—. Angola. Zaire. Zambia. 1976-78. *237*
—. Boundaries. Ethiopia. 1870-1979. *2820*
—. Boundaries (disputes). Maghreb. Western Sahara. 20c. *956*
—. Egypt. Foreign Relations. Libya. Qadhafi, Muammar. Sadat, Anwar. 1950-77. *965*
—. Land Tenure. Tanzania (Ngorongoro Crater). Wildlife Conservation. 1948-74. *3166*
—. Nigeria. *Oba* (king). Social organization. Yoruba. 19c-20c. *2157*
—. Organization of African Unity. UN. 1950's-70's. *81*
—. Political institutionalization. Social mobilization. 1960-69. *268*
—. UN. Zaire. 1960-65. *2517*
Conflict, armed. Zimbabwe. Zimbabwe Liberation Army. 19c-20c. *4218*
Conflict management, intraregional. Organization of African Unity. Regional organizations. 1963-74. *110*
Conflicts and conflict resolution. Burundi. Ethnic groups. 1970's. *2670*
Congo. Anthropology. Capitalism. Marxism. Neocolonialism (review article). Rey, P. P. 20c. *2440*
—. Congolese Labor Party. Marxism. Ngouabi, Marien. Political Leadership. 1930's-79. *2441*
Congo (Brazzaville). *See* Congo.
Congolese Labor Party. Congo. Marxism. Ngouabi, Marien. Political Leadership. 1930's-79. *2441*
Congregation of the Holy Ghost. Missions and Missionaries. Nigeria. St. Patrick's Missionary Society. 1920-30. *2274*
Congress *See also* Legislation.
—. Black caucus. Foreign policy. USA. 1970-75. *453*
Conscription, Military *See also* Military Recruitment.
—. Africa, West. France. Great Britain. Rebellions. World War I. 1914-18. *706*
—. Colonial Government. French West Africa. ca 1900-50. *1632*
—. France. Guinea. Social Change. World War I. 1906-30. *717*
Conseil de l'Entente. *See* Entente Council.
Conservatism. Cattle. Marketing schemes. Uganda (Karamoja). 1948-70. *3289*
—. Egypt. Nasserism. Sadat, Anwar. 1970-74. *1282*
Constitutional conflict. Economic factors. Federalism. Nigeria. Secession threat. 1950-70. *2106*
Constitutional crises. Azikiwe, Nnamdi. Nigeria. Presidency. 1964-65. *2094*
Constitutional Law *See also* Citizenship; Civil Rights; Democracy; Legislation; Monarchy; Political Science; Referendum.
—. British Commonwealth. Nwabueze, B. O. (review article). 1870-1975. *255*
—. Ethiopia. 1931-77. *2805*
Constitutionalism. Africa, West. Entente Council. Land reform. 1958-76. *1646*
Constitutions. Africa, East. Courts. 1920's-73. *2627*
—. Africa, East. Ministerial responsibility. 1961-74. *2600*
—. Algeria. Arabization. Culture. 1960's. *1088*
—. Angola. 1975-80. *3454*
—. Colonial government. Discriminatory acts. Great Britain. Zimbabwe. 1923-74. *4243*
—. Colonial Government. Governors. Nationalism. Nigeria. 1935-51. *2177*
—. Diplomacy. Great Britain. Independence. Kenya. Neocolonialism. 1960-69. *2948*
—. Documents. Great Britain. Lancaster House Conference. Zimbabwe. 1970-79. *4291*
—. Economic Conditions. Ghana. 1972-77. *1795*
—. Elections. Ethnic Groups. Nigeria. Political campaigns. 1977-79. *2133*
—. Elections. Nigeria (Kano). 1949-51. *2191*
—. Human rights. Nigeria. 1957-79. *2096*
—. Independence. Namibia. South Africa. South West Africa People's Organization (SWAPO). 1970's. *3353*
—. Independence. Uganda. 1962-66. *3283*
—. Independence. Zimbabwe. 1979. *4295*
—. Islam. Maghreb. 1980. *941*
—. Mali. Maninka. Oral tradition. Values. 13c-20c. *1961*
—. Muzorewa, Abel. Zimbabwe. 1965-79. *4241*
—. Nigeria. State government. 1975-78. *2130*
—. Zaire. 1974-78. *2521*
Constructive engagement. Apartheid. Lipton, Merle (review article). South Africa. 1977. *3769*
Consular Reports. Germany. Jews. Libya. Walter, Gebhard. World War II. 1940-43. *722*
Consultants. Civil service. Employment (aliens). Tanzania. 1961-73. *3182*
Consumer goods. Africa, North. Africa, West. France. Lend-Lease. Trade, private. World War II. 1941-46. *735*
Consumption. Economic Policy. Egypt. Exports. Import substitution. 1954-70's. *1129*
Continental unity. Foreign Relations. Israel. October War. 1956-74. *452*
Convention People's Party. Acculturation. Christianity. Church and State. Ghana. Socialism. 1949-66. *1808*
—. Ghana. Political Parties. 1949-66. *1825*
—. Great Britain. Nkrumah, Kwame. Pan-African Congress. USA. 1935-63. *1781*
Conventions, International. *See* Treaties.
Conventions, Political. *See* Political Conventions.

Conversion. Africa, West. Animism. Christianity. Islam. -20c. *1642*
—. Africa, West. Islam. 20c. *1617*
—. Christianity. Islam. Tanzania. 1973. *3185*
—. Christianity. Nigeria, eastern. 1921-66. *2249*
Conversion experience. Apostles. Maranke, John. Rites and Ceremonies. Sects, Religious. 1932-72. *829*
Converts. Catholics. Igbo. Nigeria. Ostracism. ca 1955-78. *2217*
Cooperation. Churches, independent. Leadership. South Africa (Soweto). 1960's-70's. *4028*
Cooperative Union of Tanganyika. Peasants. Tanzania. 1932-72. *3083*
Cooperatives *See also* Agricultural Cooperatives.
—. Africa, East. Colonialism. Economic system. 1960-73. *2621*
—. Botswana (Chobe District). Fishing. Namibia. Subia. Yambezi Fisherman's Co-operative Society. 1973-77. *3496*
—. Economic structure. Senegal. Social Conditions. Youth. 1963-72. *2308*
—. Kenya. 1945-76. *2862*
—. Nigeria. Women. Yoruba. 1972-80. *2039*
Cooperatives, Grazing. Algeria. Livestock production. Rural Development. 1971-74. *1061*
Cooperatives, Multipurpose. Agricultural development. Algeria. Rural life. 1962-72. *1060*
Cope, R. L. Davenport, T. R. H. Elphick, Richard. Hodgson, T. L. Khoi. South Africa (review article). 19c-20c. *3715*
Copper. Economic dependence. Foreign Investments (review article). Zambia. 1970's. *4116*
—. Générale Congolaise des Minerais. Nationalization. Union Minière du Haut-Katanga (UMHK). Zaire. ca 1960-77. *2478*
—. Producer associations. Raw materials. Zambia. 1967-78. *4063*
Copper industry. Economic Conditions. Multinational corporations. Nationalization. Zambia. 1969-73. *4050*
Copper mines and Mining. Angola. French, J. C. Labor recruitment. Robert Williams Co. Zaire (Shaba). 1917-21. *2477*
—. Bates, Robert H. Burawoy, Michael. Government. Labor Unions and Organizations (review article). Zambia. 1949-70. *4071*
—. Economic Policy. Nationalization. Zambia. 1969-78. *4085*
—. Finance. Zambia. 1924-64. *4110*
—. Kenya. Political protest. Strikes. Zambia. 1922-62. *175*
—. Mergers. Rhokana Corporation. Zambia. 1930-32. *4038*
—. Migrant Labor. Women. Zambia. 1927-53. *4052*
—. Mining industry. Multinational Corporations. Nationalization. Zaire. Zambia. 1960's-82. *668*
—. Strikes. Zambia. 1935. *4101*
Coppet, Marcel de. Colonial Government. French West Africa. Labor, forced. Popular Front. 1936-46. *1610*
Coptic Church. Egypt. Politics. 5c-20c. *1344*
—. Ethiopia (Ochollo). Missions and Missionaries. Protestant Churches. Social Change. 1898-1980. *2824*
Copts. Alienation, cultural. Egypt. Musa, Salama. Nationalism. 1909-30's. *1234*
—. Church and state. Egypt. Minorities. 1950-80. *1347*
—. Egypt. Islam. Persecution. 19c-20c. *1318*
—. Egypt. Nationalism. Politics. Wafd Party. 1918-42. *1194*
Corn (review article). Farmers, small. Gerhart, John. Green revolution. Kenya. 1964-75. *2887*
Coryndon, Robert. Asians. Civil Rights. Colonial government. Kenya. 1917-33. *2973*
Cost of Living *See also* Prices; Wages.
—. Depression. Ports. Senegal (Dakar). Wages. 1929-39. *2316*
Cottage industries. Agriculture. Markets. Occupations. Uganda (Bugisu). Youth, rural. 1973. *3318*
Cotton. Agricultural development. Colonial Government. Ghana. 1902-20. *1727*
—. Agricultural Labor. Egypt. Labor. 1882-1940. *1165*
—. Agricultural Policy. FRELIMO. Government, Resistance to. Mozambique. Peasants. 1938-61. *3639*
—. Agriculture. Colonial government. Economic policy. Uganda. 1919-22. *3307*
—. Agriculture. Colonial government. Uganda (Busoga). 1905-23. *3280*
—. Agriculture. Lango. Uganda. 1909-31. *3310*
—. Colonial government. Economic policy. Uganda. 1918-29. *3321*
—. Economic Structure. Egypt. 1805-1930. *1159*
—. Egypt. Land use. Prices. 1944-66. *1175*
—. Irrigation. Kassala Cotton Company. Sudan (Gash River valley). 1922-28. *1518*
—. Labor. Mozambique. Sena Sugar Estate, Ltd. Women. 1935-60. *3666*
Cotton production. Agricultural development. Kunda. Land tenure. Zambia. 1960's-70's. *4095*
Counseling *See also* Social Work.
—. *Babalawo*. Nigeria. ca 500 BC-1978. *2261*
Counterinsurgency *See also* Guerrilla Warfare.
—. Angola. Guinea-Bissau. Mozambique. Portugal. 1961-74. *177*
—. FRELIMO. Mozambique. Resettlement programs. 1960-74. *3642*
—. Kenya. Public Opinion. Sudan. Zimbabwe. 1951-75. *219*
—. Portugal. 1960's-70's. *180*
Counterinsurgency techniques. Algeria. France. Peasants. Psychological warfare. Resettlement, forced. 1954-62. *992*
Counterinsurgency, urban. Algeria (Algiers). France. Massu, Jacques. 1957. *1039*
Coups d'etat. ca 1960-. *367*
—. Algeria. 1960. *1002*
—. Alves, Nito. Angola (Luanda). 1977. *3437*
—. Armies. Social Classes. Uganda. ca 1962-71. *3257*
—. Authoritarian regimes. Political Parties. 1945-77. *262*
—. Bibliographies. 1960's-80's. *352*
—. Bibliographies. Ethiopia. Haile Selassie. 1947-76. *2793*
—. Civil-Military Relations. Ghana. 1966-72. *1770*
—. Colleges and Universities. Nigeria. Student activism. 1974-76. *2114*
—. Developing nations. Foreign Relations. Liberia. Shipping (open registry). 1980-81. *1939*
—. Diori, Hamani. Niger. 1974. *1986*
—. Egypt. Nasser, Gamal Abdel. USSR. 1952-77. *1250*
—. Ethiopia. Historiography. Markakis, John (review article). Politics, traditional. 1960's-70's. *2730*
—. Ethiopia. Military government. Regional conflicts. 1974-76. *2823*
—. Ethiopia (Eritrea). Haile Selassie. Political Factions. 1970-75. *2731*
—. Ethnic Groups. Liberia. Political instability. 1963-80. *1954*
—. Ethnic Groups. Social mobilization. Voting and Voting Behavior. 1960-75. *359*
—. Foreign Relations. Mancham, James. Political Factions. René, Albert. Seychelles. 1964-77. *3575*
—. Free Officers Organization. Libya. Qadhafi, Muammar. 1951-69. *1403*
—. Ghana. Military. Social change. 1981. *1763*
—. Ghana. Military government. Rawlings, Jerry. 1979-80. *1788*
—. Ghana. Political Systems. 1957-81. *1762*
—. Ghana. Politics and the Military. 1972. *1774*
—. Liberia. 1980. *1952*
—. Liberia. Military. Political economy. 1964-80. *1937*
—. Mali. Political crisis. 1960-68. *1964*
—. Military. 1960-75. *375*
—. Military government. 1963-78. *368*
—. Military Government (review article). 1963-71. *355*
—. Morocco. 1971. *1414*
—. Nigeria. 1966. *2128*
—. Political Culture. 1960's. *378*
—. Political Theory. Wells, Alan. 1976. *379*
—. Politics and the Military. 1963-77. *360*
—. Politics and the Military. Social Classes. Uganda. 1971. *3260*
—. Portugal. Smith, Ian. Zimbabwe. 1974. *4189*
—. Somalia. USSR. 1960-69. *3036*
—. Violence, political. 19c-20c. *376*
Coups d'etat (causes). Amin, Idi. Uganda. 1960-73. *3284*
Coups d'etat (review article). African studies. Lofchie, Michael. Social Classes. Uganda. ca 1965-75. *303*
Court of Appeal (Special Approvals Tribunal). Colonial Government. French West Africa. Law, traditional. 1903-20. *1680*
Courts *See also* International Court of Justice; Judges; Judicial Administration.
—. Africa, East. Constitutions. 1920's-73. *2627*
—. Berber dahir. Cities. France. Morocco. 1930. *1428*
—. Islam. Morocco. 1967-78. *1449*
—. Kenya. Social control. 1969-74. *3007*
Courts, Koranic. Ethnicity. Kenya (Mombasa). Social Organization. Swahili. 15c-1970's. *3006*
Courts, native. Divorce. Senegal. 1872-1946. *2329*
Crafts. *See* Arts and Crafts; Home Economics.
Creole (term). Sierra Leone. Social History. 1800-1970. *2360*
Creoles (review article). Sierra Leone. Spitzer, Leo. 1870-1951. *2369*
Crime and Criminals *See also* names of crimes, e.g. Murder, etc.; Criminal Law; Police; Prisons; Riots; Terrorism; Trials; Violence.
—. Chilobwe murders trial. Legal systems. Malawi. 1968-71. *3593*
—. Law, customary. Shona. Statistics. Zimbabwe. 1936-71. *4313*
Crime and Criminals (fraud). Banking. Equatorial Guinea. Paesa Sanchez de Caballer, Francisco. 1968-69. *2445*
Crime and Criminals (statistics). Ethiopia. USA. 1958-74. *2827*
Criminal Code (Amendment) Ordinance of 1934. Censorship. Colonial government. Ghana. Newspaper Registration Ordinance (1893). Nkrumah, Kwame. 1890-1951. *1784*
Criminal Law *See also* Military Offenses; Trials.
—. Law Reform. 1956-72. *911*
—. Malawi. Tradition. 20c. *3596*
—. Nigeria. Witchcraft. 1938-59. *2270*
Cuba. Africa, Southern. Dependency. ca 1945-80. *3392*
—. Algeria. Angola. Intervention, military. Syria. 1961-76. *411*
—. Angola. Ethiopia. Germany, East. Marxism. Mozambique. 1975-78. *528*
—. Angola. Foreign policy. Intervention. 1966-77. *3457*
—. Angola. Foreign Policy. Intervention, military. USA. USSR. 1975-77. *3483*
—. Angola. Intervention, military. USSR. 1975-76. *3479*
—. Angola. Intervention, military. USSR. 1975-76. *3480*
—. China. Communism. Economic conditions. Tanzania. USSR. Women. 1977-78. *3066*
—. China. Socialism. Tanzania. USSR. Women. 1917-81. *3065*
—. Ethiopia. Foreign Relations. USSR. 1967-78. *2786*
—. Ethiopia. Intervention. Revolution. USSR. 1974-78. *2738*
—. Ethiopia. Intervention, military. Somalia. War. 1959-78. *2654*
—. Military. 1959-78. *465*
Cultural Change. Benin. Brazilians. 1850-1978. *1704*
Cultural conflict. Cameroon, West. Education. Political leadership. 1950's-72. *2401*
Cultural degradation. Burundi. Social Change. Twa. 20c. *2660*
Cultural dependence. 1960-74. *776*
Cultural dependency. Amin, Idi. Marxism. Nyerere, Julius. Radicals and Radicalism. 19c-1973. *2614*
Cultural identity. Cape Verde Islands. Decolonization. Guinea-Bissau. Mozambique. 1950-81. *779*
—. Morality. Sex roles. ca 1920-70. *887*
Cultural Imperialism. Canada. Literature, African. 1973. *831*
—. Colonial government. Educational policy. Middle Classes (African). Zimbabwe. 1953-70. *4172*
—. Education. Racism. 16c-20c. *835*
Cultural Imperialism (review article). Great Britain. Lefever, Ernest W. Nigeria. ca 1700-1966. *213*
Cultural interaction. Africa, East (Rift Valley). Maasai. 1850-1930. *2570*
Cultural liberation. Algeria. Male-female relations. Women. 1830's-1970's. *993*
Cultural models. Cabral, Amilcar. Fanon, Frantz. Modernization. 1950-75. *629*
Cultural policy. Morocco. Novels (Arabic). Politics. 1936-65. *1437*
—. Mozambique. Revolution. Tradition. 1964-78. *3651*
Cultural relations. Europe, Western. Hausa. Islam. Literature. Social Attitudes. 1945-78. *2285*
Cultural revolution. Algeria. Industrialization. Land reform. Quadrennial plan, 2d. 1970-74. *986*

Culture *See also* Education; Popular Culture.
—. Africa, central. Religious movements. Prehistory-1970. *2393*
—. Algeria. Arabization. Constitutions. 1960's. *1088*
—. Algeria. Economic Development. Political Change. Revolution. 1976-81. *1110*
—. Algeria. Education. 1962-77. *1075*
—. Algeria. Ethnic groups. Tradition. Tunisia. 5c-20c. *945*
—. Art. Diop, Alioune. 1947-77. *855*
—. Burundi. Economic Conditions. Political Systems. 1962-81. *2663*
—. Cabral, Amilcar. Colonialism. Guinea-Bissau. Independence movements. Political thought. ca 1920-72. *1899*
—. Colonialism. Education. Technology, Western. 1960's-73. *615*
—. Emancipation. Senegal. South Africa. Tanzania. ca 1914-76. *816*
—. Ethnic Groups. South Africa. 1652-1977. *3998*
—. Liberia. Social integration. 19c-20c. *1943*
—. Literature. 20c. *839*
—. Niger (Agadez). Travel accounts. 14c-1982. *1978*
Culture, African. Education, colonial. French West Africa. William Ponty School. 1927-45. *1678*
Culture, elite. Popular culture. Theater, educational. Togo. 1945-75. *2378*
Culture, European. Literature. Missions and Missionaries. Nigeria (Lagos). 1515-1930's. *2219*
Culture (tradition). Literature. 1973. *784*
Cummings-John, Constance Agatha. Africa, West. Independence movements. Politics. Sierra Leone. Women's Movement. 1918-50's. *2343*
Currency. *See* Money.
Curricula. Colleges and Universities. Native Administration. South Africa. 1956-75. *3985*
—. Egypt. Modernization. Textbooks. 1960-79. *1333*
Customary law. Lesotho. Research. 1969-75. *875*
Customs unions. Africa, southern. 1855-1980. *3375*

D

Dagut, J. Capitalism (review article). Houghton, H. Hobart. South Africa. 1860-1970. *3778*
Dahir Barbère (law). Cities. Morocco. Nationalist movements. Rif War. 1920-40. *1415*
Dahomey *See also* Africa, West; Benin.
—. Civil War. Nigeria. Smuggling. 1966-74. *1644*
—. Cocoa. Nigeria. Smuggling. 1968-74. *1645*
Dahomey (Borgu). Colonial Government. Nigeria (Borgu). Rebellions. 1915-17. *1623*
Daily Graphic (newspaper). Editorials (content analysis). Ghana. Government (civilian). Military government. 1957-78. *1827*
Daily Life *See also* Popular Culture.
—. Africa, West. South Africa. 1973. *858*
—. Agricultural production. Colonial Government. Depression. French West Africa. Prices. 1929-36. *150*
—. Egypt (Alexandria, Cairo). Jewish communities. 1970's. *1350*
—. Guinea (Conakry). 1978-80. *1879*
—. Morocco (Cape Juby). Sahara. Saint-Exupéry, Antoine de (reports). 1928-29. *1417*
—. Political Development. Zimbabwe. 1980-81. *4146*
Dairying. Lactose malabsorption. 3000BC-1978. *882*
Dams *See also* names of dams, e.g. Cabora Bassa Dam, etc.
—. Ethiopia. Great Britain. Lake Tana. Negotiations. 1922-35. *2704*
Dance. Malawi. Nyau societies. Prehistory-1975. *3622*
Danquah, J. B. Ghana. Political theory. 1895-1961. *1821*
Darwish, Sayyid. Composers. Egypt. 1892-1974. *1325*
Davenport, T. R. H. Cope, R. L. Elphick, Richard. Hodgson, T. L. Khoi. South Africa (review article). 19c-20c. *3715*
Davidson, Basil. Historiography. 1850-1970's. *16*
—. Historiography. Nationalism (review article). 1890's-1970's. *35*
—. Historiography (review article). 19c-1970's. *44*
DeBeers Company. Botswana (Orapa). Company towns. Diamonds. Mining. 1955-78. *3528*
DeBeers Consolidated Mines. Brotherhood Movement. Class Struggle. Plaatje, Solomon Tshekisho. South Africa (Kimberley). 1918-19. *3945*
Debt. Colonization. Depression. France. Morocco. 1930-36. *1440*
Debt, external. Botswana. Great Britain. Public Finance. 1956-76. *3506*
Decentralization. Algeria. Land reform. 1962-74. *1098*
—. Bureaucracies. Local government. Tanzania. 1972. *3134*
—. Economic development. Political Participation. Tanzania. 1972-78. *3143*
—. Economic development. Sudan. 1969-80. *1502*
—. Local Government (field administrator). Socialism. Tanzania. 1965-80. *3169*
—. Nigeria (Kano). Public Administration. 1966-72. *2164*
—. Public Administration (territorial organization). Tanzania. 1961-78. *3090*
Decisionmaking. Administrative reform. Local Government. Zaire. 1973. *2496*
—. Aswan Dam. Egypt. Technology. USA. World Bank. 1953-68. *1166*
—. Botswana. Local Government. Rural development. 1969-72. *3532*
—. Civil war. Land use. Nigeria, eastern. Yams. 1964-77. *2080*
—. Egypt. Foreign Policy. October War. 1971-73. *1185*
—. Egypt. Israel. UN. 1956. *1295*
—. Egypt. October War. Sadat, Anwar. 1973. *1209*
—. Federalism. India. Nigeria. Regional government. 1967-73. *2183*
—. National Security. Unilateral Declaration of Independence (UDI). Zambia. Zimbabwe. 1965-66. *3332*
Decolonization. Africa, Southern. Foreign investments. Western nations. 1960's-70's. *3416*
—. Agricultural land. Italians. Italo-Libyan Accord (1956). Libya. 1940-64. *1377*
—. Algeria. Fanon, Frantz *(A Dying Colonialism)*. 1953-67. *1023*
—. Algeria. Foreign policy. National development. Political Systems. 1973-77. *984*
—. Angola. Economic structure. 1970's. *3456*
—. Angola. Imperialism. 15c-20c. *3458*
—. Angola. Popular Movement for the Liberation of Angola (MPLA). 1956-76. *3465*
—. Anthropology. Gluckman, Max. Rhodes-Livingstone Institute. Zambia. 1939-47. *4047*
—. Arab states. 1945-78. *471*
—. Boundaries. Western Sahara. 1975-76. *1586*
—. Cameroon. Joseph, Richard A. (review article). Union des Populations de Cameroun. 1948-56. *2400*
—. Cape Verde Islands. Cultural identity. Guinea-Bissau. Mozambique. 1950-81. *779*
—. Colonial Government. Colonial Office. Nigeria. Richards, Arthur. 1939-45. *2125*
—. Colonial Office. Great Britain. Jones, Arthur Creech. 1947. *161*
—. Colonialism. Historiography. Portugal. 1900-73. *174*
—. Colonialism, Portuguese. UN. 1946-74. *384*
—. Demography. Morocco. Urbanization. 1952-71. *1405*
—. Economic Conditions. 1950's-70's. *651*
—. Equatorial Guinea. Nguema, Francisco Macias. Refugees. 1469-1979. *2443*
—. Ethiopia (Eritrea). Irredentism. Self-determination. Somalia. 1950's-80. *2592*
—. Ethnic groups. Political repression. Violence. 1960-78. *250*
—. Europeans. Kenya. Settlers. 1960's. *2967*
—. Foreign policy. USSR. 20c. *454*
—. France. Réunion. 1945-79. *3562*
—. FRELIMO. Mozambique. 1974-76. *3644*
—. French Equatorial Africa. 1940-70. *2396*
—. Goa. Macao. Portugal. São Tomé and Príncipe. Timor, East. 1975-80. *2453*
—. Great Britain. Kenya. Public Administration. 1945-60. *2926*
—. Guerrilla warfare. Zimbabwe. 1969-79. *4196*
—. Guinea-Bissau. 1970's. *1902*
—. International Law. Namibia. South Africa. 1884-1973. *3684*
—. Kenya. Land reform. Mau Mau. Nationalism. 1952-60. *2937*
—. Kenya. Mau Mau. 1957-60. *2936*
—. Kenya. Mau Mau. Multiracialism. 1952-59. *2927*
—. Mauritania. Morocco. Spain. Western Sahara. 1970's. *1588*
—. Morocco. Spain. Western Sahara. 1970-75. *1577*
—. Nationalism. Negritude. 1940's-70's. *844*
—. Organization of African Unity. 20c. *72*
—. Political Change. 1956-74. *252*
—. Portugal. UN. 1950's-60's. *215*
—. Racism. 1956-74. *274*
—. Racism. Zimbabwe. 1900-75. *4254*
—. Refugees. 1970-74. *343*
—. Spain. Western Sahara. 1476-1974. *1585*
—. Spain. Western Sahara. 1960-75. *1578*
Decolonization, consensual. Political Leadership (indigenous). 1945-65. *338*
Decolonization, revolutionary. Algeria. Fanon, Frantz *(The Wretched of the Earth)*. Political systems. 1954-69. *989*
Decorations. Internal Affairs, Ministry of. Zimbabwe. 1973-77. *4293*
Defense Policy *See also* National Security.
—. Apartheid. South Africa. Western Nations. 1970-79. *3822*
—. Legislation. Military Service (geographical limits). South Africa. 1912-76. *3858*
DeGaulle, Charles. Algeria. Rebellions. Sétif incident. 1945. *1014*
—. Civil war. Foreign policy. France. Nigeria. 1967-69. *2107*
—. France. Independence. Judicial systems. 1958-73. *413*
—. Kissinger, Henry A. Nationalism. Nkrumah, Kwame. Nyerere, Julius. Political Leadership. ca 1940's-70's. *308*
Degrees, Academic. Higher Education. London University. Nigeria. 1887-1951. *2279*
Delafosse, Maurice (speech). Colonial government. French West Africa. Public Administration (native policy). 1919. *1659*
Demi-Brigade, 13th. Foreign Legion. France. Morocco. Narvik landing. Norway. World War II. 1940. *727*
Demobilization. Colonialism. Nigeria. Veterans. World War I. 1918-25. *700*
Democracy. Botswana. Public expenditures. Rural development. 1965-80. *3502*
—. Colonies. Independence. UN. ca 1939-76. *153*
—. Government, one-party. Political Parties. 1957-73. *335*
—. *Jamahiriya* (concept). Libya. Political theory. Qadhafi, Muammar *(Green Book)*. Rousseau, Jean Jacques *(Social Contract)*. 1967-79. *1380*
—. Nigeria. Political Systems. 1960-81. *2195*
Democracy, Concordance. Models. South Africa. 1970's. *3860*
Democracy, Consociational. Nigeria. Pluralism. 1967-76. *2169*
Democracy, industrial. Income policy. Tanzania. 1963-79. *3082*
Democracy, parliamentary. Economic Conditions. 1960-73. *319*
Democracy (review article). Socialism. Tanzania. 1967-70. *3135*
Democratic institutions. District councils. Nigeria (Northwestern; Sokoto). 1967-68. *2190*
Democratic Movement for Malagasy Renaissance (MDRM). Madagascar. National liberation movements. Rebellions. 1945-47. *3580*
Democratic Party. Apartheid. Gerdener, Theo. South Africa. 1970's. *3842*
—. France. Guinea. 1947-58. *1875*
—. France. Guinea. Independence Movements. Labor unions and organizations. 1940's-56. *1867*
—. Government, Resistance to. Guinea. Purges. Touré, Sekou. 1957-73. *1877*
—. Ivory Coast. 1958-73. *1929*
Democratic Turnhalle Alliance. Independence Movements. Namibia. South West Africa People's Organization (SWAPO). 1920-79. *3674*
Democratization. Bourguiba, Habib. Political Leadership. Tunisia. 1969-80. *1565*
Demographic trends. Boute, Joseph (interview). Zaire. 1973. *2454*
Demography *See also* Birth Control; Mortality; Population.
—. Angola. Europeans. Independence. 1974. *3432*
—. Apartheid. Regional Planning. South Africa. 1960-73. *3708*
—. Census (1973). Nigeria. 1973. *2203*
—. Decolonization. Morocco. Urbanization. 1952-71. *1405*
—. Economic Development. Food Supply. 20c. *605*
—. Jews. Tunisia. 1881-1956. *1569*
—. Land Tenure. Togo. 1885-1979. *2377*
—. Sudan (Khartoum). Urban Areas. 20c. *1478*
Demonstrations *See also* Riots.
—. Independence movements. Students. Zambia. 1966-71. *4048*

—. National service, compulsory. Students. Tanzania (Dar es Salaam). 1966-67. *3189*
Denmark *See also* Scandinavia.
—. Mbula. Missions and Missionaries. Nigeria (Adamawa). Prophet movement. 1926-35. *2255*
Dependency. Africa, Southern. Cuba. ca 1945-80. *3392*
—. Africa, Southern. Foreign Relations. 1968-75. *3369*
—. Africa, West. Franc Zone. Monetary stability. 1962-75. *1689*
—. Africans. Middle Classes. National African Federated Chambers of Commerce. South Africa. 1964-78. *3793*
—. Agricultural development. Colonial Government. Sierra Leone (northwestern). 1896-1939. *2359*
—. Business. Indigenization. Niger (Kano). Technology. 1972-79. *2037*
—. Colonial Government. Development. Tanzania. 20c. *3119*
—. Colonialism. Economic history. Prehistory-1950. *593*
—. Depression. Ewe. Farmers. Togo. Traders. 1929-38. *2372*
—. Economic aid. Egypt. World Bank. 1970-78. *1161*
—. Economic Conditions. Exports. Mobutu Sese Seko. Zaire. 1960-78. *2482*
—. Economic Development. Socialism. 1962-79. *241*
—. Economic development. Trade. Tunisia. 1970-77. *1551*
—. Education. 1945-80. *798*
—. Egypt. Foreign policy. Oil Industry and Trade. 1967-76. *1152*
—. Elites. Local politics. Tanzania (Kilimanjaro district). 1970's. *3179*
—. Modernization. Women. 1970-. *903*
—. Multinational corporations. 1970's. *669*
Dependency, economic. Economic Conditions. Trade. ca 1965-67. *649*
—. Political Systems. 20c. *238*
Dependency relationships. Colonialism. Niger. Social change. Tuareg, Yullemmeden kel Dinnik. 1800-1974. *1979*
Dependency, structural. Nigeria. 1946-75. *2074*
Dependency theory. Businessmen. Economic Development. Foreign investments. 1960's-70's. *564*
—. Economic development. 1960-82. *643*
—. Economic Development. Egypt. 1920-50. *1169*
—. Periodization of History. 19c-20c. *61*
Deportation. Asians. Uganda. 1972. *3220*
Depression. Africa, North. Economic Crisis. 1929-36. *967*
—. Africa, West. Banque de l'Afrique Occidentale. 1926-36. *1693*
—. Agricultural production. Colonial Government. Daily Life. French West Africa. Prices. 1929-36. *150*
—. Agriculture. Colonialism. France. Maghreb. Nationalism. 1929-36. *955*
—. Algeria. Foreign Exchange. France. Trade, terms of. 1924-38. *1055*
—. Banana production. Economic Structure. Guinea. 1929-34. *1881*
—. Beti. Cameroon. Chiefs. Public Administration. 1929-34. *2407*
—. Capitalism, Primitive. Europeans. Kenya. Settlers. ca 1900-50. *2910*
—. Cities. Economic Conditions. Ivory Coast. 1930-35. *1925*
—. Colonial Government. Economic Policy. Ivory Coast. Profits. 1929-35. *1911*
—. Colonial Government. Economic system. Zaire. 1930's-77. *2469*
—. Colonialism. Economic Structure. France. 1928-35. *163*
—. Colonies. Indochina. Statistics. 1924-38. *151*
—. Colonization. Debt. France. Morocco. 1930-36. *1440*
—. Colonization. Farmers, European. France. Nationalism. Tunisia. 1930's. *1564*
—. Cost of living. Ports. Senegal (Dakar). Wages. 1929-39. *2316*
—. Dependency. Ewe. Farmers. Togo. Traders. 1929-38. *2372*
—. Economic conditions. Morocco. 1926-42. *1425*
—. Economic Conditions. Morocco. 1975-80. *1431*
—. Economic conditions. Nigeria. 1930's. *2044*
—. Economic Development. France. Imperialism. 1930-36. *164*
—. Employment, salaried. French West Africa. Working class (creation of). 1927-36. *1602*
—. Farmers. Guinea. Purchasing power. Social Conditions. Taxation. 1930's. *1880*
—. French West Africa. Peanut production. Peyrissac (firm). Rubber. Trade. 1924-39. *1675*
—. Slums *(bidonvilles)*. Tunisia. 1930's. *1556*
Descent groups. Land allocation. South Africa. Zulu (Nyuswa). ca 1825-1970. *4005*
Desert encroachment. Climatic change. Overgrazing. 1974. *619*
Desertification. Environment. Soil erosion. 1981. *679*
Destour Party. Labor Unions and Organizations. Nationalism. Tunisia. 1920-56. *1533*
Detente *See also* Balance of Power.
—. Africa, Southern. Foreign Relations. ca 1946-76. *3374*
—. Foreign Relations. Kaunda, Kenneth. Racism. South Africa. Zambia. 1964-74. *4040*
—. Foreign Relations. Mozambique. Zimbabwe. 1974. *3337*
—. Kaunda, Kenneth (review article). Macpherson, Fergus. Political leadership. Zambia. 1940's-75. *4088*
—. Lusaka talks. Zimbabwe. 1974. *4281*
Developing Nations *See also* Nonaligned Nations.
—. Africa, East. Fisheries. Lake Victoria. Norway. UN Development Program. 1965-75. *628*
—. Africa, Southern. British Commonwealth. Diplomacy. International organizations. New International Economic Order. 1960-79. *3357*
—. Africa, West. Berry, J. F. Urbanization (review article). 1920-76. *1657*
—. Africa, West. Public Health. 19c-20c. *1628*
—. Algeria. Economic reform. Foreign Relations. 1962-76. *1065*
—. Benin. Leisure. -1973. *1706*
—. Bennett, Henry Garland. Colleges and Universities. Ethiopia. Technical Cooperation Administration. 1950-51. *2710*
—. Capitalism. Economic system, international. 1968-74. *683*
—. Capitalism (peripheric). Colonialism. Marxism. 1975. *653*
—. Colonial Government. Ghana. Great Britain. Treasury reform. 1936. *1751*
—. Coups d'etat. Foreign Relations. Liberia. Shipping (open registry). 1980-81. *1939*
—. Diplomacy. Economic relations. European Economic Community. Lomé Convention. 1957-76. *583*
—. Economic Development. European Economic Community. Lomé Convention. 1975-77. *552*
—. Economic Growth (review article). Modernization. 1960-75. *665*
—. Economic Planning. UN Conference on Human Settlements. 1978. *639*
—. Economics. 1960-80. *387*
—. Ethnic Groups. Mauritius. National Development. 1968-80. *3561*
—. European Economic Community. Foreign Aid. Interdependence. Lomé Convention. 1975. *556*
—. European Economic Community. Nigeria. Trade. 1966-73. *2014*
—. Fanon, Frantz. Political Theory. 1973. *1018*
—. Foreign Relations. Germany, East. Military Aid. 1960-81. *401*
—. Human rights violations. Racism. 1970's. *341*
—. Labor. Political Change. Zambia. 1880-1981. *4049*
—. Library education. Morocco. 1912-73. *1416*
—. Models. Slums. 1956-63. *782*
—. Political institutionalization. 1946-73. *267*
—. Working class. 1970's. *886*
Developing Nations (least developed). Economic Conditions. Economic Structure. 1970-77. *676*
Development *See also* Economic Development; National Development.
—. Angola, southwest. Colonization. Portugal. 19c-20c. *3462*
—. Asia. Peasants. Poverty. 1970-80's. *657*
—. Botswana. Economic Aid (private). 1962-80. *3498*
—. Capitalism. Kenya. Socialism. Zimbabwe. 1950-81. *617*
—. Colonial Government. Dependency. Tanzania. 20c. *3119*
—. Colonialism. Libraries. Nigeria. 1900-60. *2240*
—. Dunn Reserve. Land Tenure. Segregation. South Africa (Natal). 1895-1948. *3953*
—. Economic stagnation. Political stability. Senegal. 1800-1970's. *2300*
—. Education. Kenya. Tanzania. 1961-77. *2644*
—. Foreign policy. Zambia. 1963-78. *4117*
—. Fulbe. Nigeria (Gongola State; Mambila grasslands). Social organization. 1915-74. *2245*
—. Ghana. Port system. 1482-20c. *1735*
—. Guinea-Bissau. Institutions. 1974-79. *1907*
—. Guinea-Bissau. Socialism. 1973-77. *1903*
—. Hyden, Goran (review article). Peasants. Socialism. Tanzania. 1870-1975. *3052*
—. Ivory Coast. Modernization. 1961-75. *1912*
—. Language. Swahili. Tanzania. 1960's-74. *3096*
—. Liberia. Military Strategy. USA. World War II. 1938-45. *725*
—. Modernization. Racism. South Africa. 20c. *3794*
—. Nigeria. Physicians. Politics. 1935-75. *2206*
—. Oil. Tanzania. 1969-74. *3054*
—. Sanitation. Upper Volta. 1960-76. *2388*
Development plans. Economic Conditions. Tanzania. 1961-71. *3126*
Development (review article). Economic history. Historiography. Imperialism. 1919-73. *640*
Development Strategy. Economic Policy. International Labor Organization. Kenya. 1963-77. *2894*
—. Land reform. Senegal. 1964-79. *2317*
Devonshire White Paper. Asians. Kenya. 1923. *2930*
Diagne, Blaise. Colonial policy. Pressure groups. Senegal. 1914-34. *2313*
Dialectical materialism (review article). Marxism. Sik, Endre. Prehistory-1977. *3*
Diamonds. Botswana (Orapa). Company towns. DeBeers Company. Mining. 1955-78. *3528*
Diaries. Egypt. Monasteries. Orthodox Eastern Church. St. Catherine (monastery). Sinai, Mount. 1980. *1123*
—. Local Government. Public Administration. Zimbabwe (Zambezi valley). 1912-13. 1977. *4284*
Diet. *See* Food Consumption.
Diffusion. Intervention, military. Political change. Political Parties (single-party system). 1950's-70's. *258*
Dindikwa. Local government. Vagarwe. Zimbabwe (Melsetter District). 1947-73. *4252*
Dinesen, Isak (Karen Blixen; biography). Kenya. ca 1910-30. *2977*
Dingaka. Botswana. Medicine. 1820-1970. *3493*
Dini ya Msambwa. Kenya. Rebellions (review article). Wipper, Audrey. 1930-49. *2965*
Dinka. Boundaries. Nuer. Sudan (Sobat, Zaraf valleys). 1860-1976. *1490*
—. Gambia. People's Progressive Party. Politics. ca 1950-75. *1713*
Diola. Agricultural systems. Rice. Senegal. Social organization. 20c. *2319*
—. Islam. Modernization. Senegal. 1900-40. *2323*
—. Land reform. Property rights. Senegal. 1918-78. *2315*
—. Land Reform. Senegal. Social Change. ca 1885-1978. *2335*
Diop, Alioune. Art. Culture. 1947-77. *855*
—. Authors. Negritude. Senegal. 1940-80. *2311*
—. Literature. *Présence Africaine* (periodical). Senegal. 1940-80. *2328*
Diori, Hamani. Coups d'etat. Niger. 1974. *1986*
Diouf, Galandou. Elections. Political Leadership. Popular Front. Senegal. Socialist Republican Party. 1936-41. *2333*
Diplomacy *See also* Treaties.
—. Africa, Southern. British Commonwealth. Developing nations. International organizations. New International Economic Order. 1960-79. *3357*
—. Africa, West. Economic Community of West African States. Economic Integration. Nigeria. Regionalism. 1960-75. *1663*
—. Algeria. Economic cooperation. Morocco. Tunisia. 1954-70's. *976*
—. Appeasement policy. Ethiopia. France. Great Britain. Italy. 1934-35. *2772*
—. Arab States. Ethiopia. Somalia. War. 1977-78. *2582*
—. Asia. China. Chou En-Lai. 1963-64. *410*
—. Autobiography and Memoirs. Avriel, Ehud. Ghana. Israel. Liberia. 1957-73. *393*
—. Badoglio, Pietro. Burrú, Aialeu. Ethiopia (Amhara). Gasparini, Jacopo. Italy. 1936. *2750*
—. Boundaries. Mauritania. 1960-76. *1974*
—. Colonialism. Ethiopia. Italy. 1935-36. *2798*
—. Constitutions. Great Britain. Independence. Kenya. Neocolonialism. 1960-69. *2948*
—. Developing nations. Economic relations. European Economic Community. Lomé Convention. 1957-76. *583*
—. Duggan, William R. (memoir). Khalifa bin Harub. Tanzania (Zanzibar). USA. 1959. *3139*

E

—. Apartheid. Asians. South Africa. 20c. *3982*
—. Apartheid. South Africa. 1800-1977. *4030*
—. Apartheid. South Africa. 1976-78. *4001*
—. Assimilation. Attitudes. Colonization. Senegal (Dakar). William Ponty School. 1937-45. *2318*
—. Attitudes. Benin. Brazilians. Elites. Tradition. 1920-67. *1707*
—. Attitudes. Economic development. Mali. Students. 1950-76. *1970*
—. Attitudes. Missions and Missionaries. 19c-1974. *792*
—. Bibliographies. Zimbabwe. 1970's. *4323*
—. Bo School (graduates). Sierra Leone. 1906-80. *2341*
—. Cameroon. Colonial Government. 1916-38. *2417*
—. Cameroon, West. Cultural conflict. Political leadership. 1950's-72. *2401*
—. Canada. Great Britain. Missions and Missionaries. Sudan Interior Mission. 1937-55. *1505*
—. Career choices. Egypt. 1882-1922. *1348*
—. Church and State. Missions and Missionaries. Nigeria. 1842-1948. *2216*
—. Church and State. Nigeria (Eastern Region). 1956-66. *2100*
—. Churches, independent. ca 1900-75. *897*
—. Colleges and Universities. Economic independence. -1975. *647*
—. Colleges and Universities. Nigeria. Public finance. 1960's-70's. *2242*
—. Colonialism. Culture. Technology, Western. 1960's-73. *615*
—. Colonialism. Elites. Social change. ca 1900-76. *863*
—. Colonialism. France. French West Africa. 1900-39. *1666*
—. Colonialism. Kenya. Missions and Missionaries. 1902-32. *2987*
—. Colonialism. Nigeria. 1840-1939. *2264*
—. Colonialism. Zimbabwe. 1899-1979. *4329*
—. Cultural Imperialism. Racism. 16c-20c. *835*
—. Dependency. 1945-80. *798*
—. Development. Kenya. Tanzania. 1961-77. *2644*
—. Economic conditions. Homelands Policy. Race relations. South Africa. 1960's-70's. *3738*
—. Economic development. Egypt. Labor. Lewis, W. A. Models. 1952-67. *1174*
—. Economic development. Guinea-Bissau. Ideology. 1974. *1904*
—. Economic Growth. Islam. Nigeria (Kano). 19c-1981. *2260*
—. Egypt. National integration. Social classes. 1805-1968. *1330*
—. Elites. Ethiopia. Tradition. ca 1900-74. *2838*
—. Elites. Ethiopia. Westernization. 1936-74. *2839*
—. Employment. Kenya (Kakamega). 1970-73. *2995*
—. Ethnic groups. Ghana. Social Status. 1961-74. *1861*
—. Ethnic groups. Independence movements. Missions and Missionaries. Political Factions. Zimbabwe. ca 1880-1977. *4264*
—. Ethnicity. Nigeria. Social mobility. 1840's-1975. *2212*
—. Foreign policy. Foundations. Intervention. USA. 1945-75. *534*
—. French West Africa. Missions and Missionaries. 1817-1940. *1612*
—. Ghana. Politics. 1972-80. *1853*
—. Ghana. Seven-Year Plan for Education. 1529-1966. *1848*
—. Ghana. Social Status. 1961-74. *1862*
—. Ghana. Women. 1961-74. *1863*
—. Ghana (Accra). Sex discrimination. Women. 1850-1972. *1854*
—. Ghana, northern. Native administration. White Fathers. 1908-51. *1830*
—. Government. Missions and Missionaries. Sudan, Southern. Values. 1898-1956. *1506*
—. Igbo. Nigeria. Social status. Westernization. 1800-1956. *2239*
—. Islam. Nigeria. Religion. 1903-78. *2232*
—. Kenya. Local Native Councils. Politics. 1925-39. *2953*
—. Kenya. Local Politics. Luhya (southern). 1930-60. *2988*
—. Kenya. Political instability. Unemployment. 1963-76. *2920*
—. Kenya. Rural self-help (harambee). Technology, institutes of. 1971-74. *2877*
—. Kenya. Somalis. 1930-59. *3008*
—. Liberia. National development. Values. Westernization. 19c-20c. *244*
—. Malawi. Women. 1875-1952. *3605*
—. Mass media. National liberation movements. Propaganda. 1960's-70's. *211*
—. Methodism. Missions and Missionaries. Zaire (Shaba, Kasai). 1910-60. *2540*
—. National Development. Nigeria. 1914-78. *2230*
—. National Development. Tanzania. 1961-81. *3206*
—. National Development. Zimbabwe. 1980-81. *4240*
—. Nigeria. Publishers and Publishing. 1950-70. *2214*
—. Nigeria, eastern. Public finance. Secondary Education. 1846-1970. *2243*
—. Nigeria, northern. Public Administration. Sudan. 1890-1962. *227*
—. Philanthropy. USA. 1920's-77. *516*
—. Social Classes. Tanzania. 1961-79. *3207*
—. Social control. South Africa. 1960-78. *4031*
—. Textbooks (review article). 1960-78. *833*
Education, *Ahlia*. Sudan, Northern. 1927-57. *1499*
Education, colonial. Culture, African. French West Africa. William Ponty School. 1927-45. *1678*
Education, French. Algeria. Colonialism. Islam. 1830-1960. *1036*
Education, mass. Employment. Social mobility. Tunisia. Youth. 1955-74. *1530*
Education Policy in British Tropical Africa (White Paper). Colonial government. Great Britain. 1914-39. *235*
Education (review article). 1830-1940. *834*
—. 1900-76. *793*
—. Africa, East. 1922-62. *2648*
—. King, Kenneth James. Murphy, E. Jefferson. Philanthropy. USA. ca 1900-75. *517*
Education, rural. Catholic Church. Missions and Missionaries. Zaire (Shaba). 1885-1939. *2544*
Educational development. Kenya. Language policy. Tanzania. 1963-74. *2626*
—. Rural areas. Zaire (Shaba). 1920-60. *2543*
Educational planning. Modernization. Social Customs. 1974. *803*
Educational policy. Algeria. Arabization. Social change. 1962-73. *1087*
—. Citizenship. Tanzania. 1967-79. *3188*
—. Colonial government. Cultural imperialism. Middle Classes (African). Zimbabwe. 1953-70. *4172*
—. Colonial Government. Ghana, northern. Guggisbery, F. G. 1906-40. *1856*
—. Colonial Government. Great Britain. 1923-39. *168*
—. Colonial Government. Kenya. Scott, Henry S. 1920-34. *3002*
—. Colonial government. Lugard, Frederick. Nigeria. 1900-18. *2223*
—. Colonization. Lyautey, Hubert. Morocco. 1920's. *1444*
—. Economic Conditions. Rural self-help (harambee). 1960-77. *2989*
—. Elementary Education. 1961-80. *799*
—. Elementary Education. Uganda. 1960-75. *3245*
—. French West Africa. Rural Areas. 1903-56. *1613*
—. Nigeria. 1959-61. *2235*
—. Tanzania. 1961-69. *3195*
—. Tanzania (Bukoba, Ngara). 1961-69. *3199*
Educational Reform *See also* Education.
—. Al-Azhar, University of. Egypt. Maraghi, Muhammad Mustafa al-. Zawahiri, Ahmadi az-. 1895-1929. *1354*
—. School enrollment. Tanzania. 1960's-70's. *3197*
Educational system. Benin. 1956-75. *1697*
—. National development. Political economy. Tanzania. 1961-75. *3190*
Educational Tests and Measurements. Elementary Education. Kenya. 1944-80. *2991*
Effort Camerounais (newspaper). Cameroon. Political development. Press. 1955-72. *2399*
Egypt. Abaza, Aziz. Drama. Poetry. 1899-1973. *1360*
—. Abbas II (papers). Foreign Policy. Politics. 1914-44. *1246*
—. Abdel-Fadil, Mahmoud. Agricultural Policy (review article). Land reform. 1952-70. *1136*
—. Africa, North. Libya. Rommel, Erwin. World War II. 1941-42. *754*
—. Agricultural Labor. Cotton. Labor. 1882-1940. *1165*
—. Agricultural mechanization. 1980's. *1163*
—. Agricultural Policy. 1956-80. *1162*
—. Agricultural Policy. Legislation. Water. 19c-1980. *1143*
—. Agricultural Production. Food Consumption. 1886-87. 1967-68. *1147*
—. Agricultural Technology and Research. Social classes. 1920-40. *1164*
—. Agriculture. Economic Policy. Income Distribution. Prices. 1960-80. *1153*
—. Air Warfare. Israel. Military strategy. Six-Day War. 1967. *1178*
—. Al-Azhar, University of. Educational Reform. Maraghi, Muhammad Mustafa al-. Zawahiri, Ahmadi az-. 1895-1929. *1354*
—. Alienation, cultural. Copts. Musa, Salama. Nationalism. 1909-30's. *1234*
—. Aliens. Business. Middle Classes. 1920-50. *1168*
—. American University. Education. Missions and Missionaries. USA. 19c-20c. *1326*
—. Amin, Ahmad. Liberalism. Public opinion. 1939-54. *1293*
—. Arab League. Foreign policy. Israel. Treaties. 1951-78. *1225*
—. Arab League. Fundamentalism. Islam. Nationalism. 1920-45. *1332*
—. Arab Socialist Union. Nasser, Gamal Abdel. Political parties. 1952-78. *1254*
—. Arab Socialist Union. Political parties. 1952-77. *1255*
—. Arab States. Economic development. Foreign investments. USSR. 1960-72. *1125*
—. Arab states. Economic Development. Foreign Relations. Sadat, Anwar. 1970-74. *1224*
—. Arab states. Foreign Relations. Sadat, Anwar. 1973-78. *1294*
—. Arab States. Socialism. 1950-79. *1220*
—. Arab unity. Israel. Peace. 1940's-70's. *1177*
—. Arab unity. National self-image. 1936-39. *1221*
—. Arab unity. National Self-Image. 1936-39. *1222*
—. Arabic. Fiction. Timor, Mahmud. 1894-1973. *1337*
—. Arabic culture. Foreign policy. 1957-77. *1275*
—. Arab-Israeli conflict. Foreign Policy. Peace Movements. Sadat, Anwar. 1967-77. *1217*
—. Arab-Israeli conflict. Foreign Policy. Sadat, Anwar. 1970-79. *1290*
—. Arab-Israeli conflict. Military capability. Nasser, Gamal Abdel (memoirs). Revolutionary Movements. 1948-52. *1257*
—. Archaeology. Emery, Walter Bryan. 1924-71. *1114*
—. Archaeology. Tutankhamen, curse of. 1922. *1352*
—. Army officers. Intelligentsia. Revolutionary Movements. 1849-1952. *1199*
—. Army, 2d. Ghazala, Mohamed. Military Strategy. October War. Suez Canal (crossing). 1973. *1314*
—. *Ashraf.* Elites. Islam. 1650-1952. *1356*
—. Aswan Dam. 1950's-71. *1141*
—. Aswan Dam. Decisionmaking. Technology. USA. World Bank. 1953-68. *1166*
—. Aswan Dam. Economic Development. 1960-77. *1133*
—. Aswan Dam. Social problems. 1958-70. *1158*
—. Aswan Dam. USSR. 1959. *1151*
—. At-Takfir wa al-Higrah (sect). Muslims. Pan-Islamism. 1970-78. *1196*
—. Attitudes. Foreign Relations. Intellectuals. Israel. Palestine. Self-determination. 1967-80. *1200*
—. Authoritarianism. Modernization. Nasser, Gamal Abdel. Political Culture. 1950's. *1252*
—. Bank Misr. Economic structure. Federation of Industries. General Agricultural Syndicate. Social Classes. 1880-1940. *1170*
—. Bank Misr. Foreign Investments. Nationalism. 1919-49. *1306*
—. Bank Misr. Middle Classes. 1910-50. *1138*
—. Battle, Lucius D. Foreign Relations. Sadat, Anwar. 1957-81. *1189*
—. Bibliographies. Foreign policy. Great Britain. ca 1800-1977. *1283*
—. Birth Control. Social Policy. 1966-77. *1320*
—. Boundaries. Great Britain. Sinai Peninsula. 1906-47. *1124*
—. Bureaucracies. Public Administration. 1973-82. *1182*
—. Cabinet. Civil-Military Relations. Military. 1952-77. *1201*
—. Camp David Agreement. Economic conditions. Foreign policy. Israel. 1970's. *1132*
—. Career choices. Education. 1882-1922. *1348*
—. Censorship. Historiography. Nasser, Gamal Abdel. 1952-64. *1202*
—. Charisma (concept). Nasser, Gamal Abdel. Weber, Max. 1956-76. *1193*
—. *Chihrinimi* (newspaper). Iranians. Settlement. 1904-66. *1357*

—. China. Foreign Relations. 1956-59. *1208*
—. China. Modernization. Political Leadership. Revolution. Sadat, Anwar. 1952-79. *1238*
—. Church and state. Copts. Minorities. 1950-80. *1347*
—. Church and State. Islam. 20c. *1116*
—. Church and State. Islam. Popular Culture. 1952-77. *1334*
—. Colleges and Universities. Elites (military and traditional). Modernization. 1961-67. *1343*
—. Colonial Policy. Economic Conditions. Great Britain. 1886-1937. *1148*
—. Compagnie Financière de Suez. France. Nationalization. Suez Canal. 1956-80. *1219*
—. Composers. Darwish, Sayyid. 1892-1974. *1325*
—. Conflict and Conflict Resolution. Foreign Relations. Libya. Qadhafi, Muammar. Sadat, Anwar. 1950-77. *965*
—. Conservatism. Nasserism. Sadat, Anwar. 1970-74. *1282*
—. Consumption. Economic Policy. Exports. Import substitution. 1954-70's. *1129*
—. Coptic Church. Politics. 5c-20c. *1344*
—. Copts. Islam. Persecution. 19c-20c. *1318*
—. Copts. Nationalism. Politics. Wafd Party. 1918-42. *1194*
—. Cotton. Economic Structure. 1805-1930. *1159*
—. Cotton. Land use. Prices. 1944-66. *1175*
—. Coups d'etat. Nasser, Gamal Abdel. USSR. 1952-77. *1250*
—. Curricula. Modernization. Textbooks. 1960-79. *1333*
—. Decisionmaking. Foreign Policy. October War. 1971-73. *1185*
—. Decisionmaking. Israel. UN. 1956. *1295*
—. Decisionmaking. October War. Sadat, Anwar. 1973. *1209*
—. Dependency. Economic aid. World Bank. 1970-78. *1161*
—. Dependency. Foreign policy. Oil Industry and Trade. 1967-76. *1152*
—. Dependency theory. Economic Development. 1920-50. *1169*
—. Diaries. Monasteries. Orthodox Eastern Church. St. Catherine (monastery). Sinai, Mount. 1980. *1123*
—. Diplomacy. Israel. Sadat, Anwar. 1956-79. *1229*
—. Diplomacy. Military offenses. October War. USA. 1967-73. *1292*
—. Domestic Policy. Economic development. Foreign Policy. Sadat, Anwar. 1970-75. *1274*
—. Drama. 19c-20c. *1340*
—. Drama. Nasser, Gamal Abdel. Political Protest. Sabūr, Salāh 'Abd al-. 1950's-60's. *1287*
—. Drama. Social change. 1919-80. *1341*
—. Economic Conditions. Ethiopia. Politics. Social Conditions. 1970's. *340*
—. Economic conditions. Peace. 1950's-78. *1245*
—. Economic Conditions. Peace. Political Power. Sadat, Anwar. 1970-79. *1289*
—. Economic Conditions. Revolution. Social Conditions. 1952-82. *1307*
—. Economic development. Education. Labor. Lewis, W. A. Models. 1952-67. *1174*
—. Economic Development. Foreign Policy. 1971-80. *1126*
—. Economic Development. Iran. Land reform. 1952-78. *1160*
—. Economic Development. Nasser, Gamal Abdel. Social Change. 1952-62. *1167*
—. Economic Development. New Valley project. Reclamation of Land. 1959-77. *1156*
—. Economic Development (maritime). Navies. USA. 1970's. *1135*
—. Economic growth. Labor force. Migration, internal. Social organization. 1937-70's. *1342*
—. Economic Growth. Political development. 1973-75. *1121*
—. Economic integration. Foreign Investments. Legislation. Middle East. 1974-81. *1145*
—. Economic liberalization. International Monetary Fund. Open Door Policy. 1970-74. *1150*
—. Economic planning. Nationalism. 1922-43. *1171*
—. Economic Policy. Foreign Investments. 1962-76. *1115*
—. Economic Policy. Foreign Policy. Tradition. 1960-80. *1130*
—. Economic policy. Foreign Policy. Tunisia. 1970-80. *1549*
—. Economic Policy. Politics. 1967-71. *1137*
—. Economic Policy. Ten-Year Plan. 1960's-73. *1142*
—. Economic status. Fertility. Modernity. -1970's. *1336*
—. Education. National integration. Social classes. 1805-1968. *1330*
—. Elites. Political Change. 1970-80. *1230*
—. Elites. Political leadership. Women. 1952-79. *1231*
—. Emigration (brain drain). Labor. 1972-77. *1134*
—. Europeans. Minorities. 1805-1961. *1139*
—. Farouk I. Great Britain. Lampson, Miles Wedderburn. Wafd party. 1942. *1310*
—. Farouk I. Great Britain. Wafd Party. 1937-45. *1298*
—. Film industry. 1934-76. *1324*
—. Films. Politics. 1945-72. *1187*
—. Food consumption. Malnutrition. 1959-71. *1157*
—. Foreign investments. 1971-79. *1176*
—. Foreign Investments. Foreign Policy. Sadat, Anwar. 1971-80. *1131*
—. Foreign Policy. Fundamentalism. Islam. 1981. *1248*
—. Foreign Policy. Islam. Political thought. Sadat, Anwar. 1970-80. *1237*
—. Foreign Policy. Israel. Peace. Sadat, Anwar (Knesset speech). 1977-78. *1281*
—. Foreign policy. Middle East. 1948-78. *1228*
—. Foreign Policy. Military aid. Nasser, Gamal Abdel. Sadat, Anwar. USSR. 1960's-72. *1218*
—. Foreign Policy. Nasser, Gamal Abdel. Political Leadership. Sadat, Anwar. 1953-76. *1232*
—. Foreign policy. Oil. 1973-. *1280*
—. Foreign Policy. Palestine. 1922-39. *1278*
—. Foreign Policy. Palestine. 1936-39. *1240*
—. Foreign Policy. Political Leadership. Sadat, Anwar. 1969-81. *1261*
—. Foreign policy. Sadat, Anwar. 1970-79. *1284*
—. Foreign policy. USA. USSR. 1973-75. *1279*
—. Foreign Policy (peace plan). Israel. Sadat, Anwar. 1948-79. *1260*
—. Foreign Relations. Israel. 1956-70. *483*
—. Foreign Relations. Israel. Libya. Political Leadership. Qadhafi, Muammar. 1942-82. *1369*
—. Foreign Relations. Israel. Sadat, Anwar. 1973-78. *1308*
—. Foreign Relations. Libya. 1969-73. *964*
—. Foreign Relations. Military Strategy. October War. 1973. *1273*
—. Foreign Relations. Nasser, Gamal Abdel. USA. 1950-57. *1277*
—. Foreign Relations. Political leadership. USSR. 1947-82. *1262*
—. Foreign Relations. Saudi Arabia. 1811-1975. *1203*
—. Foreign Relations. USA. 1971-77. *1297*
—. Foreign Relations. USA. 1972-75. *1296*
—. Foreign Relations. USA. 1977-80. *1303*
—. Foreign Relations. USSR. ca 1959-76. *1263*
—. Foreign Relations (isolation). Peace. Politics. 1970's. *1197*
—. France. Great Britain. Historiography (collusion controversy). Israel. Suez Crisis. 1956. *1211*
—. France. Husayn, Tāhā. Literature. 1889-1973. *1338*
—. Fundamentalism. Islam. Legislation. 1970-80. *1181*
—. General Desert Development Organization. New towns. Rural development. 1961-78. *1128*
—. Government, Resistance to. Islam. Repentance and Holy Flight group. 1977-79. *1235*
—. Great Britain. Imperialism (review article). Islam. ca 1882-1952. *1355*
—. Great Britain. Lloyd, George Ambrose. Modernization. National Development. 1919-33. *1249*
—. Great Britain. Nationalism. Rebellions. Wafd Party. 1918-21. *1206*
—. Great Britain. World War II. 1936-42. *1259*
—. Halim, Tahia. Painting. 1919-70's. *1317*
—. Haqqī, Yahyā. Literary criticism. Nationalism. 1920-59. *1323*
—. Heikal, Muhammed. Intellectuals. Modernization. Muslim Brotherhood. Social Change. 1914-55. *1353*
—. Historiography. Leftism. Sa'īd, Rif'at as-. 1940-50. *1195*
—. Husayn, Tāhā. Islam. Political Theory. 1889-1961. *1319*
—. Husseini, Muhammed Amin al-. Islamic Conference. 1931-36. *1247*
—. Ideology. Nasserism. Political Factions. Political Leadership. 1952-65. *1253*
—. Independence Movements. Indian National Congress. Wafd party. 1930's. *1243*
—. Industrialization. Islam. Labor markets. Women. 1952-. *1172*
—. Industrialization. Unemployment. 1952-67. *1127*
—. Industry. Labor force. Women. 1816-1975. *1146*
—. Intellectuals. Wafd Party. Working class. 1882-1952. *1198*
—. Intellectuals (attitudes). Nasser, Gamal Abdel. Power, exercise of. 1952-70. *1213*
—. Intelligentsia. Political Factions. Social Classes. 1907-52. *1322*
—. Intervention. Nasser, Gamal Abdel. Yemen. 1962. *1204*
—. Islam. Muslim Brotherhood. Political Reform. 1928-81. *1316*
—. Islam. Muslim Brotherhood. Sadat, Anwar. 1970-82. *1236*
—. Islam. Nasserism. Socialism. 1955-65. *1269*
—. Islam. Nationalism. Salafi movement. 1920-40. *1223*
—. Islam. Political systems. ca 20c. *1179*
—. Islam. Political Theory. Rafii, Mustafa Sadik al-. 1920-40. *1329*
—. Islam. Politics. 1950's-79. *1183*
—. Islam. Politics. 20c. *1184*
—. Islam, militant. Political Theory. Rafii, Mustafa Sadik al-. 1880-1937. *1328*
—. Islamic Movement. Modernization. Women. 1973-80. *1327*
—. Islamic revival. Muslim Brotherhood. Political conflict. 1930-79. *1251*
—. Islamic revival. Muslim Brotherhood. Politics. 1952-80. *1311*
—. Israel. Military intelligence. Military Strategy (surprise). October War. 1971-73. *1304*
—. Israel. Military Occupation. Suez Crisis. 1956-57. *1216*
—. Israel. Military Operations. War. 1948. *1258*
—. Israel. Military policy. Nasser, Gamal Abdel. Six-Day War. Syria. 1948-67. *1285*
—. Israel. Military Strategy. October War. 1973. *1309*
—. Israel. Peace negotiations. 1977-78. *1276*
—. Israel. War. 1967. 1973. *1268*
—. Israel. War (limited). 1968-70. *1212*
—. Labor Movement. Politics. Wafd Party. 1919-39. *1205*
—. Land Reform. Reclamation of land. 1952-78. *1173*
—. Land tenure policy. Nasser, Gamal Abdel. Patrimonialism. Political leadership. Sadat, Anwar. 1954-79. *1300*
—. Left. Politics. 1956-78. *1192*
—. Literary criticism. Mandūr, Muhammad. 1930-65. *1346*
—. Literature. 1967-80. *1315*
—. Literature. National Self-image. 1920-75. *1358*
—. Marei, Sayed. Political clientelism. 1920's-70's. *1302*
—. Marxism. Socialism. 1975. *1180*
—. Mary, Virgin. Social behavior. Zeitoun, apparition of. 1968. *1345*
—. Mass Media. 1798-1970's. *1351*
—. *Maxton* (vessel). Suez Canal (clearing). 1967-74. *1154*
—. Middle Classes. Social Organization. Stock companies. 1900-52. *1140*
—. Middle East. Palestinians. 1971-73. *1214*
—. Military Strategy. October War. Suez City (battle). 1973. *1271*
—. Modernization. 1952-75. *1117*
—. Mubarek, Hosni. Politics. USA. 1981-82. *1264*
—. Nasser, Gamal Abdel. Political leadership. 1952-. *1215*
—. Nasser, Gamal Abdel. Political Leadership. 1952-70. *1305*
—. Nasser, Gamal Abdel. Political leadership. Revolution. 1956-76. *1207*
—. Nasser, Gamal Abdel. Political Leadership. Sadat, Anwar. 1952-75. *1191*
—. Nasser, Gamal Abdel. Political Leadership (review article). 1952-70's. *1186*
—. Nasser, Gamal Abdel. Politics (review article). 1952-74. *1299*
—. Nasser, Gamal Abdel. Power, exercise of. 1952-70. *1233*
—. Nasserism. Sadat, Anwar. 1952-74. *1226*
—. National Bar Association. Politics. Wafd Party. 1912-54. *1266*
—. National Characteristics. 1967-74. *1118*
—. Nationalism. Secret societies. 1870-1924. *1242*
—. Nazism. Radicals and Radicalism. 1930's. *1291*
—. Oil and petroleum products. Suez Canal. 1966-77. *1144*

—. Revolution. Socialism. 1974-78. *2777*
—. Revolution (review article). 1974-78. *2725*
—. Social Organizations (self-help). ca 1900-75. *2831*
—. Versailles, Treaty of. 1917-23. *2766*
Ethiopia (Addis Ababa). Djibouti. Economic development. France. Railroads. 1894-1978. *2698*
—. Ethnic Groups. Labor Unions and Organizations. Standard of Living. 1970's. *2714*
Ethiopia (Amhara). Badoglio, Pietro. Burrú, Aialeu. Diplomacy. Gasparini, Jacopo. Italy. 1936. *2750*
Ethiopia (Awash Valley). Afar. Modernization. Pastoralism. ca 1950-75. *2691*
—. Afar. Settlement. 1972-78. *2756*
—. Agricultural Labor. Irrigation. Migration, internal. 1950's-70's. *2701*
Ethiopia (Bale, Gojam). Peasants. Rebellions. 1968. *2780*
Ethiopia (Bale province). Amhara. Arssi. Ethnic Groups. Tulama. 1890-1974. *2826*
Ethiopia (Begemdir; Däbrä Tabor). Local government. Trade. 1798-1936. *2688*
Ethiopia (Chilalo). Agricultural development. 1967-71. *2697*
—. Agricultural development. Sweden. Tenants. 1967-74. *2695*
Ethiopia (Darassa). Land reform. Peasants. 1970-75. *2776*
Ethiopia (Eritrea). Arab States. Foreign Relations. 1974-. *2770*
—. Belligerent recognition. International law. 1850's-1979. *2768*
—. Boundaries. Foreign Policy. Somalia. USA. USSR. 1974-77. *2574*
—. Central State Archive. Documents. Italy. Libya (Tripolitania). Somalia. 19c-20c. *958*
—. Civil disorder. Foreign relations. 1941-1973. *2723*
—. Civil disorder. Haile Selassie. 1953-73. *2815*
—. Colonialism. Fascism. Italy. 1885-1934. *2788*
—. Colonialism. Self-determination. 1890-1976. *2746*
—. Coups d'etat. Haile Selassie. Political Factions. 1970-75. *2731*
—. Decolonization. Irredentism. Self-determination. Somalia. 1950's-80. *2592*
—. Foreign Aid. Revolutionary movements. USA. 1975. *2779*
—. Foreign Policy. Military Strategy. Somalia. USSR. 1969-78. *2580*
—. Foreign policy. USA. 300-1975. *2819*
—. Independence Movements. 1950's-76. *2758*
—. Independence Movements. 1960-76. *2769*
—. Independence Movements. ca 1961-75. *2792*
—. Independence movements. Political parties. 1941-62. *2740*
—. Organization of African Unity. Secessionist movement. 1963-75. *84*
—. Separatist Movements. 1960-79. *2724*
—. Separatist Movements. 1979. *2773*
Ethiopia (Gubba). Hamdān Abū Shōk. Local government. Sudan. 1900-38. *2744*
Ethiopia (Hagar). Alphabets. Bakri Sapalō. Oromo. Separatist movements. 1875-1980. *2757*
Ethiopia (Lake Tana, highland lakes). Christianity. Ethnography. 1970-72. *2685*
Ethiopia (Lake Zway islands). Christianity. Economy. 11c-20c. *2684*
Ethiopia (Nugara). 'Abd Allah, al-Iman. Boundaries. Feudalism. State Formation. 1901-23. *2743*
Ethiopia (Ochollo). Coptic Church. Missions and Missionaries. Protestant Churches. Social Change. 1898-1980. *2824*
Ethiopia (Ogaden). Italy. Secession. 1934. 1977. *2735*
Ethiopia (Southern). Centralization. Domestic Policy. 1855-1974. *2729*
—. Coffee. Economic Policy. Foreign Relations. Land Tenure. 1895-1935. *2705*
Ethiopia (travel account). 1972. *2680*
Ethiopianism. Literature. Pan-Africanism. USA. ca 1770-1930. *140*
Ethnic competition. Modernization. 1974. *249*
Ethnic conflict. Africa, East. Djibouti. France. Political stability. 1896-1976. *2674*
—. Africa, West. 1950's-60's. *1679*
—. Burundi. Colonialism. Massacres. 1972. *2661*
—. Burundi. Hutu. Tutsi. 1962-75. *2671*
—. Colonial policy. Yaka. Zaire (Kwango basin). 1880-1960. *2510*
—. Ndebele. Shona. Zimbabwe. 10c-20c. *4275*
Ethnic diversity. Civil War. Ife, University of. Nigeria. Political attitudes. Students. 1957-69. *2111*
—. Political instability. 1960's-70's. *248*
Ethnic Groups *See also* Minorities; Nationalities.
—. Africa, East. Dorobo. National Characteristics. 20c. *2599*
—. Algeria. Berbers. Social Policy. 1980-82. *1011*
—. Algeria. Culture. Tradition. Tunisia. 5c-20c. *945*
—. Algeria (Annaba). Colonialism. Segregation, residential. 1872-1954. *1076*
—. Amhara. Arssi. Ethiopia (Bale province). Tulama. 1890-1974. *2826*
—. Anthropology. South Africa. *Volkekunde* school. 1920's-81. *4012*
—. Attitudes. Colonialism. Social Classes. 1960's-70's. *915*
—. Boundaries. Nigeria (Akoko-Edo). 1960-74. *2086*
—. Burundi. Conflicts and conflict resolution. 1970's. *2670*
—. Burundi. Hutu. Tutsi. Violence. 1972-73. *2666*
—. Christianity. Colonial Government. Social Classes. Uganda (Ankole). 1900-25. *3229*
—. Colonial policy. Mozambique. Portugal. 20c. *3625*
—. Colonialism. Political Systems. Refugees. Rwanda. 1853-1980. *3022*
—. Coloureds. Economic Conditions. Griqua trek. LeFleur, A. A. S. South Africa. 1867-1920. *3968*
—. Constitutions. Elections. Nigeria. Political campaigns. 1977-79. *2133*
—. Coups d'etat. Liberia. Political instability. 1963-80. *1954*
—. Coups d'etat. Social mobilization. Voting and Voting Behavior. 1960-75. *359*
—. Culture. South Africa. 1652-1977. *3998*
—. Decolonization. Political repression. Violence. 1960-78. *250*
—. Developing Nations. Mauritius. National Development. 1968-80. *3561*
—. Djibouti. Independence. 1862-1977. *2676*
—. Education. Ghana. Social Status. 1961-74. *1861*
—. Education. Independence movements. Missions and Missionaries. Political Factions. Zimbabwe. ca 1880-1977. *4264*
—. Elections. Nigeria. 1978-80. *2158*
—. Ethiopia. Falasha. Music (liturgical). 1980. *2847*
—. Ethiopia. Foreign Relations. 1974-78. *2765*
—. Ethiopia. Urban population. 20c. *2844*
—. Ethiopia (Addis Ababa). Labor Unions and Organizations. Standard of Living. 1970's. *2714*
—. Federal reorganization. Geography. Nigeria. 1900-74. *2172*
—. Ghana. Politics. 1972-79. *1778*
—. Higher education. Nigeria. 1960-79. *2122*
—. Islam. Separatist Movements. Sudan. 1947-76. *1463*
—. Kamara, Moussa. Political leadership. Senegal, eastern (Boundou). 1681-1921. *2314*
—. Military. Politics. South Africa. 1960's-70's. *3847*
—. Negritude. Senegal. Senghor, Leopold. 1980. *2331*
—. Nigeria. Political Integration. State Government. 1960-78. *2151*
—. Nigeria. Regionalism. 1900-76. *2291*
—. Nigeria (Abakaliki). 19c-1960. *2282*
—. Nigeria (Benin). Occupations. 1940's-77. *2061*
—. Obote, Milton. Politics and the Military. Uganda. 1962-71. *3221*
—. Political change. Uganda. 1962-71. *3305*
—. Political development. Somalia (Juba Valley). 1913-80. *3038*
—. Political development. Tanzania (Zanzibar). 1960-80. *3145*
—. Political Factions. Zimbabwe. 1957-79. *4267*
—. Political Parties (identification). South Africa. 1970. *3905*
—. Politics. 19c-20c. *261*
—. Politics. Religion. 1960-80. *290*
—. Politics. Zimbabwe. 1960-80. *4200*
—. Politics (review article). 20c. *337*
—. Social Change. South Africa. 1945-80. *3740*
—. Zimbabwe. 1940-80. *4296*
Ethnic Groups (review article). Ethiopia. 19c-20c. *2681*
Ethnic identity. Ivory Coast. Liberia, Eastern. ca 1900-75. *1641*
—. Ndendeuli. Tanzania. 1840-1952. *3193*
—. Religious movements. ca 1960-75. *809*
Ethnic integration. Chagga. Tanzania. 1962-76. *3184*
Ethnic ranking. Colonial Government. Great Britain. Race Relations. 19c-1980. *189*
Ethnicity. Atuot. Sudan. 18c-20c. *1472*
—. Cabral, Amilcar. Guinea-Bissau. Independence Movements. Marxism. 1930-76. *1898*
—. Colonial government. Kaguru. Political Leadership. Tanzania. 1880-1944. *3133*
—. Colonial Government. Lugard, Frederick. Military Recruitment. 1900-60. *347*
—. Colonial history. Ivory Coast. National development. 1889-1969. *1931*
—. Courts, Koranic. Kenya (Mombasa). Social Organization. Swahili. 15c-1970's. *3006*
—. Education. Nigeria. Social mobility. 1840's-1975. *2212*
—. Government Ownership. Intergovernmental Relations. Nigeria. Radio. Television. 1932-62. *2290*
—. Hutu. Rwanda (Kinyaga region). Tutsi. 1860-1960. *3020*
—. Kenya (Lumbwa). 1960's-70's. *2979*
—. Liberalism. Political development. South Africa. 1921-48. *3914*
—. Nubians. Political participation. Political Theory. Uganda. 1971. *3251*
Ethnicity, theories of. Civil war. Nigeria. 1966-67. *2186*
Ethnography. Christianity. Ethiopia (Lake Tana, highland lakes). 1970-72. *2685*
—. Johnson, S. Jangaba M. Liberia. National unification. 1895-1973. *1942*
Ethnolinguistics. Burundi. Politics. 1970's. *2668*
Ethnology *See also* Acculturation; Anthropology; Folklore; Language; Race Relations.
—. Khoikhoi (Topnaar). Namibia. -1970's. *3697*
Etienne, B. Algeria. Leca, Jean. Politics (review article). Vatin, J.-C. 1830-1978. *1069*
Europe *See also* Europe, Eastern; Europe, Western.
—. Africa, southern. Imperialism. South Africa. 1900-72. *3779*
—. Algeria. Arab States. Foreign policy. ca 1962-. *985*
—. Art. Benin. Literature. 1897-20c. *862*
—. Banks. Business. USA. 1972-74. *603*
—. Imperialism. Racism. World War I (causes). 1877-1915. *691*
—. Imperialism (review article). 19c-20c. *154*
—. Sculpture. 16c-20c. *788*
Europe, Eastern. Africa, southern. Foreign Policy. USSR. 1960's-70's. *406*
Europe, Western. Africa, southern. Politics. Socialist International. 1978-80. *3341*
—. Cultural relations. Hausa. Islam. Literature. Social Attitudes. 1945-78. *2285*
—. Foreign Investments. 1960-78. *560*
—. National Security. South Africa. USA. USSR. 1980-82. *3815*
European contacts. Social change. 15c-20c. *40*
European Economic Community. 1949-66. *535*
—. 1970's. *537*
—. Africa, East. Arusha Agreement. East African Community. East African Trade Association. Exports. 1973. *2617*
—. Africa, West. Colonial Government. Economic policy. France. 1958-73. *568*
—. Developing nations. Diplomacy. Economic relations. Lomé Convention. 1957-76. *583*
—. Developing Nations. Economic Development. Lomé Convention. 1975-77. *552*
—. Developing Nations. Foreign Aid. Interdependence. Lomé Convention. 1975. *556*
—. Developing nations. Nigeria. Trade. 1966-73. *2014*
—. Economic Development. Lomé Convention. 1975-77. *604*
—. Economic relations. 1957-76. *536*
—. Foreign Policy. Lomé Conventions (review article). 1975-79. *543*
—. Foreign Relations. Intervention. 1975-79. *554*
—. Lomé Convention. 1957-76. *567*
—. Lomé convention. 1976-80. *581*
—. Trade agreements. 1973-74. *553*
European Economic Community (associated states). Trade. 1958-78. *561*
Europeans. Africa, East. Armies. Humor. Smuts, Jan. World War I. 1914-18. *711*
—. Africa, Southern. Emigration. South America. 1967-76. *3395*
—. Africans. Colonial Government. Literature. 1880-1980. *850*
—. Agricultural development. Zimbabwe. ca 1890-1974. *4166*

—. Agricultural Policy. Kenya. Social Organization. World War II. 1939-46. *767*
—. Agriculture. Labor. Zaire. 1910-60. *2470*
—. Angola. Demography. Independence. 1974. *3432*
—. Capitalism, Primitive. Depression. Kenya. Settlers. ca 1900-50. *2910*
—. City planning. Transportation. Zimbabwe (Harare). 1953-74. *4301*
—. Climate. Kenya. Social Customs. Zimbabwe. 1880's-1930's. *185*
—. Colonization. 20c. *860*
—. Colonization. Zimbabwe. 1920-76. *4326*
—. Decolonization. Kenya. Settlers. 1960's. *2967*
—. Economic policy. Racial policies. South Africa. 20c. *3754*
—. Egypt. Minorities. 1805-1961. *1139*
—. Immigration. Settlement. Zimbabwe. 1890-1976. *4322*
—. Independence. Kenya. Land. Political Factions. 1960-63. *2968*
—. Kenya. 1945-79. *2978*
—. Kenya Land Commission. Kikuyu. Land tenure. Settlers. 1902-34. *2869*
—. Nationalism. South Africa. Zimbabwe. 1974-79. *3335*
—. Race Relations. 1960-78. *853*
—. Race Relations. Zimbabwe. 1960-78. *4214*
—. Racism. South Africa. Working Class. ca 1950-78. *3758*
—. Settlement (conference). 20c. *42*
Europeans (conference). 1978. *41*
Ewe. Boundaries. Ghana. National Liberation Movement of Western Togoland. Nationalism. Togo. 1943-78. *1616*
—. Dependency. Depression. Farmers. Togo. Traders. 1929-38. *2372*
—. Dzo. Magic. Myths and Symbols. Togo. 15c-20c. *2380*
—. Fiction. Ghana. Literature. Togo. 20c. *1603*
—. Ghana. Political Attitudes. Poverty. 1957-80. *1776*
—. Ghana. Political Development. Villages. 18c-20c. *1860*
—. Plebiscites. Togo. 1956. *2371*
Ewe, Abutia. Chiefs. Ghana. Political Systems. 19c-20c. *1823*
Ewe (Battor). Ghana. Politics. Property rights. 1907-66. *1766*
Examinations. Nigeria. Oxford University Delegacy. Secondary education. 1929-37. *2278*
Excavations. Anthropology. Great Zimbabwe. Historiography. Zimbabwe. 1960's-72. *4138*
Exiles. Asians. Family composition. Social Surveys. Uganda. 1972-74. *3219*
—. Films, documentary. Mahomo (interview). Morena Films. Propaganda. South Africa. 1960-76. *3951*
—. Literature. 1950-82. *851*
Expansionism *See also* Imperialism.
—. Africa, Southern. Chanock, Martin (review article). Great Britain. 1900-45. *3420*
Expatriates. Government. Kenya. 1970-79. *2940*
Expatriates, French. Senegal. Social Status. 1945-74. *2326*
Exploitation. Colonization. Working Class. Zaire (Kivu). 1900-40. *2465*
—. Land ownership. Uganda. 1900-39. *3224*
Export instability. Cocoa. Ghana. 1961-75. *1745*
Export trends. Africa, east. Economic competition. 1959-71. *2645*
Exporters. Agricultural Policy. Droughts. Famine. Food production. 1960-70. *645*
Exports. Africa, East. Arusha Agreement. East African Community. East African Trade Association. European Economic Community. 1973. *2617*
—. Africa, West. British Empire. Empire Resources Development Committee. Milner, Alfred. 1916-20. *1649*
—. Colonial government. Kenya (Lamu archipelago). Mangrove poles. Tanzania (Rufiji River). 1900-81. *2576*
—. Colonialism. Economic Policy. Great Britain. Tanzania. 1945-60. *3121*
—. Consumption. Economic Policy. Egypt. Import substitution. 1954-70's. *1129*
—. Dependency. Economic Conditions. Mobutu Sese Seko. Zaire. 1960-78. *2482*
—. Ivory Coast. Rural development. 1960-75. *1926*
—. Kenya. Land Tenure. Social Classes. 1950-79. *2863*
Exports (restrictions). Arms trade. South Africa. USA. 1945-78. *3775*

F

Fafunwa, A. B. Higher Education (review article). Nigeria. Okafor, Nduka. 20c. *2269*
Fagunwa, D. O. Christian ideals. Nigeria. Novels. Traditional beliefs. 1939-61. *2275*
—. Literature. Nigeria. Soyinka, Wole. Tradition. Tutuola, Amos. Yoruba. 1945-70's. *2252*
Faith healing. Aladura. Medicine. Nigeria. Sects, Religious. 1950's-80's. *2248*
Falasha. Emigration. Ethiopia. Israel. Jews. 1969-75. *2835*
—. Ethiopia. 1972-73. *2849*
—. Ethiopia. Ethnic Groups. Music (liturgical). 1980. *2847*
—. Ethiopia. Jews. 1970-. *2837*
—. Ethiopia. Jews. Prejudice. 10c BC-1975. *2834*
Family *See also* Divorce; Marriage; Women.
—. Algeria. Values. Women. 1962-81. *1019*
—. Attitudes. Girls. Marriage. Schools. Zaire (Kinshasa). 1969-72. *2562*
—. Bibliographies. Community. 20c. *818*
—. Economic change. Labor. Sierra Leone. ca 1750-1928. *2337*
—. Economic cooperation *(Thando)*. Food consumption. Malawi (Nsanje District). 1970's. *3597*
—. Public welfare. Sierra Leone. Westernization. 18c-20c. *2347*
—. Rural households. Senegal. Wolof. 20c. *2309*
Family composition. Asians. Exiles. Social Surveys. Uganda. 1972-74. *3219*
Family life. Economic Conditions. Kenya. Social Change. 1900-77. *3011*
Family Organization. Government Enterprise. Industrial innovation. Liberia. Markets. Women. 1950-70. *1947*
Family size. Attitudes. Civil servants. Ghana (Accra). 1954-74. *1851*
Family structure. Economic Conditions. Ghana (Amedzofe-Avatime). Women. 20c. *1835*
—. Hausa. Nigeria. Rural areas. Social Change. 20c. *2247*
—. USA. 17c-1979. *892*
Family systems, extended. Zimbabwe. ca 1500-1973. *4300*
Famine. Afar. Agriculture (cash crops). Capitalism. 1965-73. *2693*
—. Africa, West. Foreign Aid. Sahel. USA. 1968-75. *521*
—. Agricultural Policy. Droughts. Exporters. Food production. 1960-70. *645*
—. Angola. Diseases. Economic conditions. 1830-1930. *3443*
—. Bibliographies. Droughts. Economic conditions. Sahel. 1968-73. *677*
—. Colonial Government. Law and order. Niger. 1931. *1983*
—. Droughts. Sahel. ca 1972-74. *616*
—. Foreign Aid. Sahel. ca 1972-74. *614*
—. Rwanda. 1916-18. *3018*
Famine, seasonal. Chakaka Pola. Malawi, Northern. Nigeria, Eastern. Onicha Ibo. 1964-71. *656*
Fang. Bwiti cult. Catholicism. Drugs. Gabon, central. Mysticism. ca 1950's-70's. *2446*
Fanon, Frantz. Algeria. Independence Movements. Political thought. 1945-61. *995*
—. Algeria. Political Theory. 1950's-70's. *1077*
—. Cabral, Amilcar. Cultural models. Modernization. 1950-75. *629*
—. Cabral, Amilcar. Political theory. Revolution. 20c. *4*
—. Colonialism. Nationalism. Revolutionary theory. 1800-1960. *1070*
—. Developing Nations. Political Theory. 1973. *1018*
—. Freedom. Political Philosophy. Revolution. 1952-61. *1030*
—. Historiography. Politics. 1950's-70. *287*
—. Nation, idea of. Political theory. 1950's-60's. *1029*
—. Political theory. Social Classes (analysis). 1950's-60's. *1109*
Fanon, Frantz *(A Dying Colonialism)*. Algeria. Decolonization. 1953-67. *1023*
Fanon, Frantz *(The Wretched of the Earth)*. Algeria. Decolonization, revolutionary. Political systems. 1954-69. *989*
—. Ideas, History of. Political Theory. 1961-75. *998*
Farmers *See also* Peasants.
—. Afrikaners. Migration, Internal. South Africa (Port Elizabeth). Urbanization. 1904-60. *4023*
—. Agricultural prices. Anticolonialism. Great Britain. Uganda. ca 1900-75. *3225*
—. Cocoa. Ghana. Trade. 1918-39. *1755*
—. Cocoa. Ghana (Suhum). Political change. Settlement. 1900-72. *1855*
—. Cocoa. Nigeria, Western. Populism. 1893-1973. *2109*
—. Dependency. Depression. Ewe. Togo. Traders. 1929-38. *2372*
—. Depression. Guinea. Purchasing power. Social Conditions. Taxation. 1930's. *1880*
Farmers, European. Colonization. Depression. France. Nationalism. Tunisia. 1930's. *1564*
Farmers, migrant. Agricultural Development. Cocoa. Innovation (concept). Nigeria (western). 1850-1974. *2018*
Farmers, small. Agricultural Policy. 1970's. *684*
—. Agriculture. Ghana. 20c. *1720*
—. Corn (review article). Gerhart, John. Green revolution. Kenya. 1964-75. *2887*
Farmers, subsistence. Agricultural diffusion. Bantu Homelands. South Africa (Natal). Valley Trust. 1950-74. *3783*
Farming, plantation. Colonial Government. Uganda. 1901-23. *3277*
Farouk I. Egypt. Great Britain. Lampson, Miles Wedderburn. Wafd party. 1942. *1310*
—. Egypt. Great Britain. Wafd Party. 1937-45. *1298*
Fascism *See also* Anti-Fascist Movements.
—. Algeria (Oran). Public opinion. 1936-40. *1045*
—. Beamish, Henry Hamilton. Colonialism. Great Britain. ca 1920-48. *192*
—. Bourguiba, Habib. Italy. Nationalism. Tunisia. 1922-43. *1543*
—. Colonialism. Ethiopia (Eritrea). Italy. 1885-1934. *2788*
—. Ethiopia. Imperialism. Italy. 1930's. *2818*
Federal reorganization. Ethnic Groups. Geography. Nigeria. 1900-74. *2172*
Federal states. Nigeria. Political parties, regional. 1945-66. *2091*
Federalism. Africa, Southern. Nigeria. South Africa. 20c. *30*
—. Ahidjo, Ahmadou. Cameroon. 1961-72. *2424*
—. Civil war. Nigeria. Political factions. 1960-66. *2117*
—. Constitutional conflict. Economic factors. Nigeria. Secession threat. 1950-70. *2106*
—. Decisionmaking. India. Nigeria. Regional government. 1967-73. *2183*
—. Election laws. Nigeria. 1939-66. *2105*
—. Nigeria. Politics. Wages. 1954-75. *2015*
—. Sudan. 1956-81. *1516*
Federation. *See* Confederation.
Federation Conference (1960). Central African Federation (breakup). Colonial policy. Victoria Falls Conference (1963). Zimbabwe. 1953-69. *3927*
Federation of Industries. Bank Misr. Economic structure. Egypt. General Agricultural Syndicate. Social Classes. 1880-1940. *1170*
Federation of Unions of Algerian Workers (USTA). Algeria. France. Labor Unions and Organizations. 1956-59. *1101*
Feminism. Ghana. Hayford, Adelaide Casely. Nationalism, cultural. Universal Negro Improvement Association. Women. 1868-1960. *1850*
Feraoun, Mouloud. Algeria. Ideology. Intellectuals. Nationalism. 1955-62. *1020*
Fernando Póo. Cocoa cultivation. Economic relations. Liberia. Migrant labor. 1860-1930. *580*
Fertility. Economic status. Egypt. Modernity. -1970's. *1336*
—. Migration. Morocco. Social mobility. 1960-69. *1450*
—. Modernization. Zaire. 1960-79. *2557*
—. Mortality. Public Health. Upper Volta. 1971-77. *2384*
—. Nigeria. 1952-80. *2281*
Fertility associations. Food Supply. Gambia. Mandinka. Women. 1965-75. *1716*
Fertility levels. Mende. Sierra Leone. Temne. 1963-73. *2344*
Fertility (review article). Sterility. ca 1950-76. *841*
Feudalism. 'Abd Allah, al-Iman. Boundaries. Ethiopia (Nugara). State Formation. 1901-23. *2743*
—. Ethiopia. Models. Political systems. ca 1800-1976. *2830*
—. Ethiopia. Politics and the Military. Revolution. 1972-75. *2748*

Fiah, Erica. Africa, East. African Commercial Association (ACA). Social Movements. 1889-1966. *2653*
Fiction *See also* Novels.
—. Arabic. Egypt. Timor, Mahmud. 1894-1973. *1337*
—. Authors. Orlan, Pierre Mac. Tunisia. 1932. *1545*
—. Ewe. Ghana. Literature. Togo. 20c. *1603*
—. Heroes. Kenya. Mau Mau. Revolution. ca 1950-57. *2966*
Fiction (adventure stories). Guillot, René. Henty, G. A. Kimenye, Barbara. 1870's-1970's. *879*
Figaro (newspaper). *Aurore* (newspaper). France. Intervention (military). Journalism. Politics. Zaire. 1978. *2530*
Film industry. Egypt. 1934-76. *1324*
Films. 1950's-70's. *849*
—. Africa, central. Africa, East. Colonial policy. Great Britain. 1920-50. *230*
—. Afrikaners. Nationalism. South Africa. *Voortrekkers* (film). 1837-1916. *4022*
—. Egypt. Politics. 1945-72. *1187*
—. Independence. 1950's-70's. *811*
—. Social change. 1926-74. *893*
—. Tunisia. 1968-73. *1537*
Films (directors). 1970's-82. *812*
Films, documentary. Exiles. Mahomo (interview). Morena Films. Propaganda. South Africa. 1960-76. *3951*
Finance *See also* Business; Commerce; Economics; Public Finance.
—. Botswana. Colonial government. Economic structure. Treasuries, local. 1938-53. *3509*
—. Copper Mines and Mining. Zambia. 1924-64. *4110*
Finland *See also* Scandinavia.
—. Mission Society. Namibia. Political Commentary. Tanzania. 1945-75. *836*
Firestone, Harvey S. Great Britain. Imperialism, economic. Liberia. O'Meara, Francis. Rubber industry. USA. 1922-27. *1940*
Fisheries. Africa, East. Developing nations. Lake Victoria. Norway. UN Development Program. 1965-75. *628*
—. Economic Development. Tanzania. Underdevelopment (theory). ca 1953-69. *3095*
Fishing. Botswana (Chobe District). Cooperatives. Namibia. Subia. Yambezi Fisherman's Co-operative Society. 1973-77. *3496*
—. Food production. Zaire, upper. 1900-75. *2462*
—. Libinza. Trade. Zaire, upper. 19c-1973. *2474*
Five-Year Plan. Economic growth. Ivory Coast. 1971-75. *1913*
Flags. Southern Rhodesia Volunteers. Zimbabwe (Bulawayo). 1927. 1951. *4204*
Folklore. Americas (North and South). 17c-1970's. *822*
—. Archives, international. Art. 1975. *802*
—. Asante. Ghana. Knot of wisdom. -1973. *1843*
—. Methodology. 1973. *787*
—. Mozambique. Music. South Africa (Transvaal, Northern). Tsonga. 20c. *3376*
Folklore (review article). Religious studies. 19c-20c. *840*
Food. Population. 1970's. *622*
Food and Agriculture Organization (regional office). Arab States. Egypt (Cairo). Foreign Relations. UN. 1975-79. *1286*
Food Consumption. Agricultural Production. Egypt. 1886-87. 1967-68. *1147*
—. Economic cooperation *(Thando)*. Family. Malawi (Nsanje District). 1970's. *3597*
—. Egypt. Malnutrition. 1959-71. *1157*
—. Ghana. Milk. Wheat. 1960's-70's. *1741*
Food production. Agricultural Policy. Capitalism. Colonial Government. Tanzania. 1840-1960's. *3062*
—. Agricultural Policy. Droughts. Exporters. Famine. 1960-70. *645*
—. Cameroon, Central. Colonial government. 1920-46. *2409*
—. Colonialism. Mongo-Nkundo. Social change. Zaire (Equateur). 19c-20c. *2468*
—. Fishing. Zaire, upper. 1900-75. *2462*
Food Shortages. Colonial Government. Nigeria (Lagos). Price control. Pullen marketing scheme. World War II. 1941-47. *2069*
Food Supply. Africa, West. Ethiopia. Transportation. UNICEF. -1974. *533*
—. Agricultural production. Algeria. 1966-77. *1084*
—. Demography. Economic Development. 20c. *605*
—. Economic Aid. 1970's-82. *611*
—. Fertility associations. Gambia. Mandinka. Women. 1965-75. *1716*
—. Imperialism. Tanzania. 1973-75. *3128*
—. Imports. 1960's-70's. *650*
Ford, Arnold. Blacks. Emigration. Ethiopia. USA. 1930-35. *2845*
Foreign Aid *See also* Economic Aid; Industrialization; Military Aid; Modernization.
—. 1950-81. *513*
—. Africa, southern. China. National liberation movements. USSR. 1960-72. *3338*
—. Africa, West. Canada. 1961-75. *1694*
—. Africa, West. Famine. Sahel. USA. 1968-75. *521*
—. Agricultural Cooperatives. Israel. Zambia. 1966-73. *4087*
—. Amin, Idi. Obote, Milton. Uganda. USSR. 1962-79. *3275*
—. Arab states. Israel. UN. Voting and Voting Behavior. 1958-72. *419*
—. Arab states. Oil. Organization of Petroleum Exporting Countries. Prices. 1975-80. *523*
—. Arab States. Political attitudes. 1973-76. *482*
—. Canada. 1961-81. *525*
—. Canada. Refugees. 1970-80. *526*
—. Canada. Trade. 1970-75. *447*
—. China. Economic Growth. Tan-Zam Railway. Tanzania. 1949-74. *531*
—. China. National liberation movements. Tanzania. 1960-70's. *3136*
—. Cocoa. Ghana. Trade. USSR. 1957-72. *1757*
—. Developing Nations. European Economic Community. Interdependence. Lomé Convention. 1975. *556*
—. Economic development. Sahara. 19c-20c. *632*
—. Electric Power. Nigeria. ca 1958-75. *2079*
—. Ethiopia. Somalia. USSR. 1963-77. *2608*
—. Ethiopia. USA. 1951-70's. *2811*
—. Ethiopia (Eritrea). Revolutionary movements. USA. 1975. *2779*
—. Famine. Sahel. ca 1972-74. *614*
—. Germany, West. 1966-74. *518*
—. Independence. Political Leadership. Sierra Leone. ca 1787-1976. *2358*
—. National liberation movements. USSR. World War II. 1945-75. *490*
—. Political attitudes. USSR. 1970-78. *438*
—. Sierra Leone. 1970's. *2357*
—. USA. 1971-74. *519*
—. USSR. 1950's-70's. *529*
Foreign Aid (coordination). East African Community. International assistance. Kenya. Public corporations. 1974. *2639*
Foreign aid policy. China. Guinea-Bissau. Mozambique. 1960's-70's. *507*
Foreign Exchange. Algeria. Depression. France. Trade, terms of. 1924-38. *1055*
Foreign investments. Africa, Southern. Decolonization. Western nations. 1960's-70's. *3416*
—. Agricultural Industry. Cadbury Schweppes (firm). Nigeria (Zaria). 1968-76. *2013*
—. Angola. Independence movements. 1970-74. *3463*
—. Angola. Mozambique. Portugal. 1950's-75. *3363*
—. Arab States. Economic development. Egypt. USSR. 1960-72. *1125*
—. Armaments. Economic Structure. Multinational corporations. South Africa. 1945-78. *3799*
—. Automobile industry and trade. South Africa. 1945-80. *3761*
—. Bank Misr. Egypt. Nationalism. 1919-49. *1306*
—. Business. Kenya (Kitale). Nationalization. 1969-76. *2900*
—. Businessmen. Dependency theory. Economic Development. 1960's-70's. *564*
—. Colonialism. Zambia. 1964-80. *4080*
—. Diplomacy. South Africa. USA. 1962-72. *3764*
—. Economic Conditions. France. French West Africa. 1919-39. *1665*
—. Economic Conditions. France. Imperialism. 1924-75. *546*
—. Economic Development. ca 1945-70's. *573*
—. Economic Growth. Gabon. Political stability. 1960-72. *2449*
—. Economic integration. Egypt. Legislation. Middle East. 1974-81. *1145*
—. Economic Policy. Egypt. 1962-76. *1115*
—. Economic Policy. Indigenization. Nigeria. 1972-74. *2020*
—. Economic Policy. Zimbabwe. 1965-80. *4162*
—. Economic prospects. Morocco. Politics. 1971-75. *1419*
—. Egypt. 1971-79. *1176*
—. Egypt. Foreign Policy. Sadat, Anwar. 1971-80. *1131*
—. Ethiopia. Multinational corporations. 1910-74. *2692*
—. Europe, Western. 1960-78. *560*
—. Indigenization. Nationalization. 1960-75. *664*
—. Industry. Zimbabwe. 1965-80. *4185*
—. Lesotho. Multinational corporations. 1966-74. *3547*
—. Liberia. Rubber industry. 1966-71. *1945*
—. Morocco. USA. 1960-79. *1432*
—. Multinational corporations. 1975. *572*
—. USA. 1957-73. *579*
Foreign investments, private. Government Enterprise (parastatal holding corporations). Nationalization. Tanzania. 1967-74. *3106*
Foreign Investments (review article). Copper. Economic dependence. Zambia. 1970's. *4116*
Foreign Legion. Africa, North. Bir Hacheim (battle). France. World War II. 1942. *766*
—. Demi-Brigade, 13th. France. Morocco. Narvik landing. Norway. World War II. 1940. *727*
—. France. Military Campaigns. Tunisia. World War II. 1942-43. *734*
Foreign Legion *(régiment de marche)*. Armored Vehicles and Tank Warfare. World War II. 1943-45. *745*
Foreign Policy *See also* Defense Policy.
—. 1963-73. *478*
—. 1965-70's. *412*
—. Abbas II (papers). Egypt. Politics. 1914-44. *1246*
—. Addis Ababa Agreement. Domestic Policy. Nemery, Jaafar. Sudan. 1972-76. *1510*
—. Africa, East. Cold War. USA. USSR. 1930-77. *2637*
—. Africa, east. Somalia. USA. 1977-80. *2573*
—. Africa, North. Cold War. Nationalism, Muslim. USA. 1945-62. *978*
—. Africa, North. Maghreb. USA. 1776-1976. *930*
—. Africa, southern. Brazil. Portugal. 1970's. *511*
—. Africa, Southern. Economic Growth. National Liberation Movements. ca 1960-75. *256*
—. Africa, southern. Europe, Eastern. USSR. 1960's-70's. *406*
—. Africa, southern. Germany, East. USSR. 1978-80. *3345*
—. Africa, southern. National liberation movements. National Security. Nigeria. 1967-70. *2180*
—. Africa, Southern. Nigeria. Oil Industry and Trade. 1970-80. *2188*
—. Africa, Southern. Nixon Doctrine. Strategic planning. USA. 1960's-74. *3339*
—. Africa, Southern. Portugal. USA. 19c-1974. *3423*
—. Africa, West. British Commonwealth. 1830's-1974. *1669*
—. African unity. Gowon, Yakubu. Nigeria. Political leadership. 1967-75. *2153*
—. Agricultural systems. Banda, Hastings Kamuzu. Economic Development. Malawi. 1964-74. *3615*
—. Air Lines. Pirow, Oswald. South Africa. South African Airways. 1933-39. *3890*
—. Algeria. 1962-70. *988*
—. Algeria. Anti-Imperialism. 1962-76. *1089*
—. Algeria. Arab States. Europe. ca 1962-. *985*
—. Algeria. Boumédienne, Houari. Economy. Oil industry and Trade. 1965-75. *1027*
—. Algeria. Chadli, Bendjedid. Political Leadership. Succession. 1975-81. *1064*
—. Algeria. Decolonization. National development. Political Systems. 1973-77. *984*
—. Amin, Idi. Asians (expulsion). Tanzania. Uganda. 1972. *3301*
—. Amin, Idi. Uganda. 1962-76. *3237*
—. Angola. China. National liberation movements. 1950-76. *3451*
—. Angola. China. National liberation movements. 1961-76. *3475*
—. Angola. Cuba. Intervention. 1966-77. *3457*
—. Angola. Cuba. Intervention, military. USA. USSR. 1975-77. *3483*
—. Angola. Intervention, military. South Africa. USA. 1970's-82. *3473*
—. Angola. Mozambique. Portugal. 1974-75. *3365*
—. Angola. Mozambique. South Africa. Zimbabwe. 1965-74. *3930*
—. Angola. Popular Movement for the Liberation of Angola (MPLA). Zaire. Zambia. 1961-77. *3430*
—. Angola. USA. 1960-81. *3431*
—. Angola. USSR. 1955-75. *3455*

—. Berber dahir. Cities. Courts. Morocco. 1930. *1428*
—. Cambon, Pierre Paul. Colonial Government. Lyautey, Hubert. Morocco. Tunisia. 1869-1925. *949*
—. Cameroon. Colonial Government. Germany. 1884-1960. *2423*
—. Cameroon. Colonialism. Germany. Nationalism. 1919-39. *2412*
—. Cameroon. Great Britain. Military Occupation. Partition, provisional. World War I. 1914-16. *701*
—. Central African Republic. Colonialism. Intervention. 1979. *2428*
—. Civil war. DeGaulle, Charles. Foreign policy. Nigeria. 1967-69. *2107*
—. Colonial Government. Labor Unions and Organizations. Popular Front. Senegal. 1919-38. *2302*
—. Colonial Government. Lyautey, Hubert. Morocco. 1912-25. *1410*
—. Colonial Government. Lyautey, Hubert. Morocco. Zionism. 1915-25. *1418*
—. Colonial legacy. Great Britain. Military dependence. 20c. *354*
—. Colonial Policy. Djibouti. 1862-1974. *2675*
—. Colonialism. Comoro Islands. Political development. 1854-1973. *3577*
—. Colonialism. Depression. Economic Structure. 1928-35. *163*
—. Colonialism. Economic development. Investments. Public Finance. 1924-38. *600*
—. Colonialism. Education. French West Africa. 1900-39. *1666*
—. Colonialism. Germany. Great Britain. Togo. World War II. 1939-45. *740*
—. Colonialism. Historiography. 1860-1930. *232*
—. Colonialism. Parti colonial français. 1914-22. *152*
—. Colonialism (Eurafrica concept). Germany. International administration, unified. 1876-1954. *149*
—. Colonization. Debt. Depression. Morocco. 1930-36. *1440*
—. Colonization. Depression. Farmers, European. Nationalism. Tunisia. 1930's. *1564*
—. Communist Party. USSR. 1945-50. *432*
—. Compagnie Financière de Suez. Egypt. Nationalization. Suez Canal. 1956-80. *1219*
—. Conscription, military. Guinea. Social Change. World War I. 1906-30. *717*
—. Decolonization. Réunion. 1945-79. *3562*
—. DeGaulle, Charles. Independence. Judicial systems. 1958-73. *413*
—. Demi-Brigade, 13th. Foreign Legion. Morocco. Narvik landing. Norway. World War II. 1940. *727*
—. Democratic Party. Guinea. 1947-58. *1875*
—. Democratic Party. Guinea. Independence Movements. Labor unions and organizations. 1940's-56. *1867*
—. Depression. Economic Development. Imperialism. 1930-36. *164*
—. Diplomacy. Eden, Anthony. Ethiopia. Great Britain. Italy. War. 1935-36. *2787*
—. Diplomacy. Ethiopia. Great Britain. Italy. Stresa Conference. 1935. *2810*
—. Djibouti. Economic development. Ethiopia (Addis Ababa). Railroads. 1894-1978. *2698*
—. Economic Conditions. Foreign Investments. French West Africa. 1919-39. *1665*
—. Economic Conditions. Foreign investments. Imperialism. 1924-75. *546*
—. Economic Conditions. Intergovernmental Relations. Politics. Réunion. 1945-80. *3563*
—. Economic Policy. Social policy. 1918-39. *162*
—. Egypt. Great Britain. Historiography (collusion controversy). Israel. Suez Crisis. 1956. *1211*
—. Egypt. Husayn, Tāhā. Literature. 1889-1973. *1338*
—. Ethiopia. Italy. Laval, Pierre. Treaties. 1935. *2791*
—. Foreign Legion. Military Campaigns. Tunisia. World War II. 1942-43. *734*
—. Foreign policy. 1960-74. *497*
—. Foreign policy. 1960-79. *440*
—. Foreign Policy. 1970-79. *404*
—. Foreign Policy. Houphouët-Boigny, Félix. Ivory Coast. 1945-72. *1910*
—. Foreign Policy. Intervention. 1970's. *457*
—. Foreign policy. Mobutu Sese Seko. Zaire. 1958-77. *414*
—. Foreign Relations. 1950's-70's. *445*
—. Foreign Relations. Neocolonialism. 1950's-60's. *390*
—. Foreign Relations. South Africa. Zaire. 1974-78. *426*
—. French West Africa. General Confederation of Labor (CGT). Labor Unions and Organizations. 1945-57. *1627*
—. French West Africa. General Confederation of Labor (CGT). Labor Unions and Organizations. 1945-57. *1695*
—. Great Britain. Mers el-Kebir (battle). World War II. 1940. *724*
—. Great Britain. Military Invasion. Togo. World War I (antecedents). 1914. *694*
—. Great Britain. Neocolonialism. 1960's. *502*
—. Independence movements. Middle classes. Morocco. 1912-1960. *1439*
—. Independence movements. Morocco. 1920-60. *1408*
—. Intervention. 1958-78. *399*
—. Intervention (military). 1976-80. *485*
—. Labor unions and organizations. Railroad workers. Tunisia. 1923-38. *1555*
—. Libraries. 1803-1975. *842*
—. Libya. Political change. Qadhafi, Muammar. 1969-73. *1399*
—. Military policy. 1960-70. *458*
—. Neocolonialism. 1920-80. *423*
—. Neocolonialism. 1958-70's. *492*
—. Neocolonialism. 1960-72. *491*
—. World War I. 1914-40. *687*
France (Abbaye de Senanque). Africa, North. Social Organization (colloquium). Tuareg. 1974. *971*
Fredrickson, George M. (review article). Race relations. South Africa. USA (South). 18c-20c. *4008*
Free Officers Organization. Coups d'etat. Libya. Qadhafi, Muammar. 1951-69. *1403*
Free World. *See* Western Nations; Industrialized Countries.
Freedom. Fanon, Frantz. Political Philosophy. Revolution. 1952-61. *1030*
Freedom of Speech. Law. South Africa. 1964. *3820*
Freedom of the Press *See also* Censorship.
—. Ghana. Newspapers. Political leadership. 1964-78. *1859*
—. Newspapers. 1970's. *828*
Freeman-Grenville, G. S. P. (review article). Chronology. 1000 BC-1971. *24*
FRELIMO. Agricultural Policy. Cotton. Government, Resistance to. Mozambique. Peasants. 1938-61. *3639*
—. Angola. Mozambique. Popular Movement for the Liberation of Angola (MPLA). Revolution. 1970-80. *3386*
—. Cabora Bassa Dam. Colonialism. Mozambique. Portugal. 1968-75. *3670*
—. Colonialism. Foreign policy. Mozambique. Portugal. USA. 1960-74. *3646*
—. Colonialism. Mozambique. 1962-72. *3659*
—. Counterinsurgency. Mozambique. Resettlement programs. 1960-74. *3642*
—. Decolonization. Mozambique. 1974-76. *3644*
—. Economic Development. Mozambique. Poverty. 1975. *3627*
—. Elites. Mozambique. Political Factions. 1962-69. *3655*
—. Foreign policy. Independence Movements. Mozambique. Portugal. UN. ca 1957-77. *3661*
—. Foreign relations. Malawi. Mozambique. Portugal. 1960-76. *3372*
—. Government, transitional. Mozambique. 1974. *3647*
—. Guerrilla warfare. Mozambique. 1964-74. *3631*
—. Guerrilla warfare. Mozambique. Portugal. 16c-20c. 1964-74. *3635*
—. Guerrilla Warfare (balance of forces). Mozambique. Portugal. 1962-74. *3654*
—. Independence. Mozambique. 1962-76. *3629*
—. Independence Movements. Machel, Samora. Mondlane, Eduardo. Mozambique. 1969-74. *3663*
—. Independence Movements. Mondlane, Eduardo. Mozambique. 1920-69. *3636*
—. Independence Movements. Mozambique. 1962-75. *3626*
—. Independence Movements. Mozambique. 1973-74. *3650*
—. Marxism. Mozambique. Revolutionary Movements. 1962-78. *3637*
—. Mondlane, Eduardo. Mozambique. Political thought. 1948-69. *3645*
—. Mondlane, Eduardo. Mozambique. Revolutionary Movements. 1920-69. *3638*
—. Mozambique. Political economy. Portugal. ca 1930-76. *3649*
French. Diplomacy. Great Britain. USA. World War II. 1941-42. *764*
—. Ivory Coast. Language policy. 1960-77. *1933*
French Community. Independence. Political Systems. 1958-70. *292*
French Equatorial Africa *See also* successor states by name; Africa, West.
—. Colonial policy. Concessionary system. Trade. 1899-1972. *2397*
—. Colonialism. Labor. 1880-1930. *2392*
—. Decolonization. 1940-70. *2396*
French, J. C. Angola. Copper mines and Mining. Labor recruitment. Robert Williams Co. Zaire (Shaba). 1917-21. *2477*
French language. Authors. Blacks. 1930-74. *906*
French Sudan. *See* Mali.
French West Africa *See also* successor states by name; Africa, West.
—. Agricultural production. Colonial Government. Daily Life. Depression. Prices. 1929-36. *150*
—. Algeria. Education. Elites. 1903-45. *226*
—. Anticolonialism. Independence movements. Strikes. 1890-1960. *1687*
—. Anticolonialism. Migration. 1914-45. *1606*
—. Archives, National. Senegal (Dakar). 18c-20c. *2320*
—. Boisson, Pierre. Giraud, Henri. Political Change. World War II. 1940-43. *728*
—. Colonial Government. Conscription, military. ca 1900-50. *1632*
—. Colonial Government. Coppet, Marcel de. Labor, forced. Popular Front. 1936-46. *1610*
—. Colonial Government. Court of Appeal (Special Approvals Tribunal). Law, traditional. 1903-20. *1680*
—. Colonial government. Delafosse, Maurice (speech). Public Administration (native policy). 1919. *1659*
—. Colonial Government. Indigenat Code. 1887-1946. *1608*
—. Colonial government. Islam. Nigeria. Rebellions. World War I. 1914-17. *704*
—. Colonialism. Education. France. 1900-39. *1666*
—. Colonization. Lobi. Resistance. 1898-1926. *1630*
—. Culture, African. Education, colonial. William Ponty School. 1927-45. *1678*
—. Depression. Employment, salaried. Working class (creation of). 1927-36. *1602*
—. Depression. Peanut production. Peyrissac (firm). Rubber. Trade. 1924-39. *1675*
—. Economic Conditions. Foreign Investments. France. 1919-39. *1665*
—. Economic Conditions. Togo. 1945-60. *1611*
—. Education. Missions and Missionaries. 1817-1940. *1612*
—. Educational policy. Rural Areas. 1903-56. *1613*
—. France. General Confederation of Labor (CGT). Labor Unions and Organizations. 1945-57. *1627*
—. France. General Confederation of Labor (CGT). Labor Unions and Organizations. 1945-57. *1695*
—. Migration. Military recruitment. 1900-45. *1631*
Freshwater, Will (papers). Linguistics. London Missionary School. Missions and Missionaries. Zambia. 1872-1959. *4068*
Friendship. Business History. Kinship. Liberia (Monrovia). Merchants. 1970. *1949*
Front de Libération Nationale du Congo. Rebellions. Zaire (Shaba). 1978. *2528*
Front for the Liberation of Zimbabwe (FROLIZI). Guerrilla Warfare. Zimbabwe. 1963-72. *4224*
Frontier and Pioneer Life (comparative). South Africa. USA. 1900-50. *3746*
Fulani. Cameroon (Adamawa Plateau). Colonial Government. Gbaya. 1899-1966. *2402*
Fulbe. Development. Nigeria (Gongola State; Mambila grasslands). Social organization. 1915-74. *2245*
Fulbe (Mbororean). Cameroon. Nigeria. Nomads and Nomadism. Sedentarization. Social Change. 20c. *1635*
Functionalism. African studies. Anthropology. Historiography. Radcliffe-Brown, A. R. 20c. *33*
Fundamentalism. Arab League. Egypt. Islam. Nationalism. 1920-45. *1332*
—. Egypt. Foreign Policy. Islam. 1981. *1248*
—. Egypt. Islam. Legislation. 1970-80. *1181*
—. Historiography (Egyptian). Islam. 20c. *1339*
Funerals. Chiefs. Siabuwa, Munchunkwe Sigaleta. Zimbabwe (Binga). 1976. *4303*

G

—. *Daily Graphic* (newspaper). Editorials (content analysis). Government (civilian). Military government. 1957-78. *1827*
—. Danquah, J. B. Political theory. 1895-1961. *1821*
—. Development. Port system. 1482-20c. *1735*
—. Economic conditions. Great Britain. World War I. 1900-30's. *698*
—. Economic conditions. Politics and the Military. 1966-79. *1775*
—. Economic development. Industrialization. 1957-67. *1723*
—. Economic development. Nkrumah, Kwame. Political corruption. 1955-68. *1824*
—. Economic growth. Income distribution. 1960-69. *1746*
—. Economic nationalism. Military Government. National Redemption Council. Pan-Africanism. ca 1972-75. *1806*
—. Economic Planning. Imports. 1966-69. *1721*
—. Economic Policy. Employment. Women. 1962-70. *1756*
—. Economic Policy. Industrialization. Nkrumah, Kwame. Social development. 1957-72. *1747*
—. Economic policy. Intergovernmental organizations. Intervention (political). 1969-72. *1742*
—. Economic Policy. Manufacturing. 1958-64. *1725*
—. Economic Theory. Inflation. Monetarism. Structuralism. 1959-79. *1758*
—. Education. Ethnic groups. Social Status. 1961-74. *1861*
—. Education. Politics. 1972-80. *1853*
—. Education. Seven-Year Plan for Education. 1529-1966. *1848*
—. Education. Social Status. 1961-74. *1862*
—. Education. Women. 1961-74. *1863*
—. Elections. Rawlings, Jerry. 1979. *1796*
—. Ethnic Groups. Politics. 1972-79. *1778*
—. Ewe. Fiction. Literature. Togo. 20c. *1603*
—. Ewe. Political Attitudes. Poverty. 1957-80. *1776*
—. Ewe. Political Development. Villages. 18c-20c. *1860*
—. Ewe (Battor). Politics. Property rights. 1907-66. *1766*
—. Feminism. Hayford, Adelaide Casely. Nationalism, cultural. Universal Negro Improvement Association. Women. 1868-1960. *1850*
—. Food Consumption. Milk. Wheat. 1960's-70's. *1741*
—. Foreign policy. Nkrumah, Kwame. 1966-75. *1765*
—. Foreign policy. Nkrumah, Kwame. Organization of African Unity. 1958-63. *1799*
—. Foreign Relations. Israel. Nigeria. 1956-79. *418*
—. Freedom of the press. Newspapers. Political leadership. 1964-78. *1859*
—. Ga. Marriage. Modernization. Social Organization. 1970's. *1845*
—. Ghana Industrial Holding Corporation. Government Enterprise. Industrialization. 1962-71. *1730*
—. Government. Labor, forced. Mines. 1906-27. *1760*
—. Government. Limann, Hilla. Politics and the Military. 1979-81. *1812*
—. Government (civilian). Nigeria. 1970's. *1652*
—. Government Enterprise. Nkrumah, Kwame. Public corporations. 1951-66. *1732*
—. Great Britain. Labor. Military Recruitment. World War II. 1939-46. *751*
—. Great Britain. Military recruitment. World War I. 1914-18. *718*
—. Healing movement. Methodology. Rites and Ceremonies. Twelve Apostles Church. 1913-71. *1833*
—. Ideology. Marxism. Nkrumah, Kwame. 1956-66. *1786*
—. Immigration policy. Nigerians. 1960-70's. *1807*
—. Imperialism. Legal systems. 1890-1970. *1798*
—. Independence Movements. Nationalism. Sekyi, Kobina. 1920's-50's. *1768*
—. Intergovernmental Relations. National Self-image. 1952-74. *1777*
—. Labor Unions and Organizations. Strikes. 1940's-70's. *1740*
—. Medicine. Tradition. Prehistory-1979. *1858*
—. Medicine, traditional. 20c. *1831*
—. Military. Nkrumah, Kwame. Race relations. 1950's-60's. *1764*
—. Military. Politics. 1957-75. *1769*
—. Military Government. Nigeria. 1960-77. *1624*
—. Military government. Nigeria. 1978. *1651*
—. Models. Nigeria. Political change. 20c. *1619*
—. Nackabah, Papa. Sects, Religious. Tani, Maame. Twelve Apostles Church. 1914-58. *1832*
—. National Council of Ghana Women. Women. 19c-1966. *1836*
—. National Self-image. Nkrumah, Kwame. Nyerere, Julius. Tanzania. 1951-60's. *328*
—. National Self-image. Nkrumah, Kwame. Rhetorical strategies. 1957-60. *1803*
—. Nkrumah, Kwame. Pan-Africanism. 1945-57. *1828*
—. Nkrumah, Kwame. Pan-Africanism. 1966-72. *1826*
—. Nkrumah, Kwame. Pan-Africanism. Politics (idealism). 1945-66. *1787*
—. Nkrumah, Kwame. Political Theory. Socialism. 1967-70. *1801*
—. Nkrumah, Kwame. Politics and the Military. 1947-79. *1794*
—. Nkrumah, Kwame. Religion. ca 1947-66. *1809*
—. Nkrumah, Kwame (message). Organization of African Unity. 1966-72. *1792*
—. Padmore, George. 1933-59. *334*
—. Political attitudes. Public Opinion. 1957-73. *1802*
—. Political culture. Youth. 1968-78. *1780*
—. Political Development. 1957-82. *1754*
—. Public finance, management of. Select Committee on Estimates. 1913-50. *1750*
—. Regional planning. Rural development. 1966-75. *1724*
Ghana (Accra). Attitudes. Civil servants. Family size. 1954-74. *1851*
—. Education. Sex discrimination. Women. 1850-1972. *1854*
—. Islam. Migrants. Sisala. Urban adaptation. 20c. *1839*
—. Urbanization. Working Class. 1930-77. *1840*
Ghana (Accra; Ussher Town). Economic change. Ga. Women. 1960's-70's. *1752*
Ghana (Ahafo). History. Political Factions. 1966-69. *1811*
Ghana (Amedzofe-Avatime). Economic Conditions. Family structure. Women. 20c. *1835*
Ghana (Asante). Boundaries. Colonial Government. Local government. 1896-1951. *1772*
—. Colonial Government. Political culture. 1969-70. *1782*
—. Money. Politics. 1900-40. *1719*
Ghana Broadcasting Corporation. Radio, wired. 1935-78. *1842*
Ghana (Cape Coast). Asafo movement. Riots. 1925-35. *1815*
Ghana Industrial Holding Corporation. Ghana. Government Enterprise. Industrialization. 1962-71. *1730*
Ghana (Komenda). Agricultural Cooperatives. Rural Development. Sugar. 1960-76. *1759*
Ghana (Kumase). Asante. Manwere *fekuo*. Public Administration. 1834-1970's. *1743*
Ghana, northern. Colonial Government. Educational Policy. Guggisbery, F. G. 1906-40. *1856*
—. Colonial Government. Local government. Native states. 20c. *1773*
—. Education. Native administration. White Fathers. 1908-51. *1830*
—. Green revolution. Immigration. Rice. Violence. 1965-80. *1728*
—. Labor recruitment. Migration. Mines. 1880-1940. *1749*
Ghana (Northern Territories). Colonial government. Land policy. 1900-57. *1726*
—. Local Government (district capitals, selection of). 1897-1951. *1771*
Ghana (review article). Bureaucracies. Historiography. Politics and the Military. 1955-75. *1779*
—. Colonial Government. Economic development. 15c-20c. *1734*
Ghana, southern. Abrem, stool of. Historiography. ca 1505-1950. *1791*
Ghana (Suhum). Cocoa. Farmers. Political change. Settlement. 1900-72. *1855*
Ghana (Swedru). Hopkins, Nicholas S. Local politics. Mali (Kita). Owusu, Maxwell. Uganda (Gondo). Vincent, Joan. 1960's-. *247*
Ghana (Takoradi Harbor). Colonial Government. Public works. 1919-42. *1744*
Ghana (Tarkwa). Gold mines and Mining. Labor Disputes. 1968-69. *1722*
Ghana (Volta region; Have). Colonialism. Local politics. Tradition. ca 1900-76. *1797*
Ghanaization. Business environment. Ghana. National Liberation Council. 1968-. *1731*
Ghazala, Mohamed. Army, 2d. Egypt. Military Strategy. October War. Suez Canal (crossing). 1973. *1314*
Gibson, Richard. Barnes, Leonard. Independence (review article). 1971-72. *212*
Giornale (newspaper). Anti-Fascist Movements. Tunisia. 1939. *769*
Giraud, Henri. Boisson, Pierre. French West Africa. Political Change. World War II. 1940-43. *728*
Giriama. Kenya. Witchcraft. 18c-1970's. *2975*
Girls. Attitudes. Family. Marriage. Schools. Zaire (Kinshasa). 1969-72. *2562*
Gisu. Brazil (Pará). Rural development. Social Classes. Uganda. 1969-78. *3226*
Glass and Glassmaking. South Africa. 1896-1944. *3792*
Gluckman, Max. Anthropology. Decolonization. Rhodes-Livingstone Institute. Zambia. 1939-47. *4047*
—. Rhodes-Livingstone Institute. Zambia. 1942-47. *4057*
Goa. Decolonization. Macao. Portugal. São Tomé and Príncipe. Timor, East. 1975-80. *2453*
Goba. Africa, Southern. Religion. Social History. Zambezi River. 1200-1970. *3381*
Gogo. Political Participation. Reform. Tanzania (Ugogo). 1960-77. *3175*
Gold *See also* Mineral Resources; Money.
—. Afrikaners. Labor. South Africa (Johannesburg). 1886-1924. *3759*
Gold Coast. *See* Ghana.
Gold Mines and Mining. British South Africa Company. Investments. Mozambique Company. Rezende, Baron de. Zimbabwe. 1887-1948. *4159*
—. Ghana (Tarkwa). Labor Disputes. 1968-69. *1722*
—. Labor (review article). Race Relations. South Africa. Zimbabwe. 1900-69. *3403*
—. London and Rhodesia Mining and Land Company. Rennie Tailyour Concession. Zimbabwe. 1890-1950's. *4158*
Goodlatte, Clare. Catholic Church. Communism. Politics. Social work. South Africa. 1860-1940. *3817*
Goody, Jack (review article). Economic Conditions. Social Change. Technology. Tradition. ca 18c-20c. *330*
Gor, Jason. Kenya. Luo. Succession disputes. 1940's-70's. *2969*
Gordimer, Nadine. Novels. Politics. Race Relations. South Africa. 1953-79. *3959*
Gore-Browne, Stewart. Colonial government. Confederation. Political Reform. Public opinion. Zambia. 1948. *4126*
Government *See also* Cabinet; Civil Service; Constitutions; Local Government; Military Government; Political Science; Politics; Public Administration; Regional Government; State Government.
—. Algeria. Capital reserves. Economic Policy. 1959-73. *1095*
—. Amin, Idi. Uganda. 1971-73. *3302*
—. Anthropology. Ghana. 1705-1971. *1810*
—. Aristocracy. Ethiopia. Italy. Military Occupation. 1937-40. *2799*
—. Authoritarianism. Domestic Policy. Zaire. 1965-80. *2492*
—. Banks. Rural credit. Zambia. 1964-75. *4073*
—. Bates, Robert H. Burawoy, Michael. Copper Mines and Mining. Labor Unions and Organizations (review article). Zambia. 1949-70. *4071*
—. Bibliographies. Social Change. 19c-20c. *299*
—. Blood feuds. Morocco (Rif). Violence. 1850-1920. *1407*
—. Civil-military relations. Mali. 1970-79. *1969*
—. Comoro Islands. Economic Development. Foreign relations. 1960's-75. *3586*
—. Economic bargaining. Multinational Corporations. 1960's-70's. *547*
—. Economic Conditions. Gambia. Political stability. 1965-75. *1714*
—. Economic control. Middle classes (African). Racism. South Africa. 1652-1975. *3802*
—. Economic system. Nigeria. 1945-73. *1995*
—. Education. Missions and Missionaries. Sudan, Southern. Values. 1898-1956. *1506*
—. Expatriates. Kenya. 1970-79. *2940*
—. Foreign Relations. Race Relations. Zimbabwe. 1964-80. *4258*
—. Ghana. Labor, forced. Mines. 1906-27. *1760*

—. Ghana. Limann, Hilla. Politics and the Military. 1979-81. *1812*
—. Islamic Law. Sudan. 1600-1981. *1481*
—. Mass Media. Nigeria. 1951-66. *2150*
—. Methodology. Political Systems. 1956-75. *370*
—. Methodology (typologies). Political systems. 1960-77. *320*
—. Military Government. Nigeria. Shagari, Shehu. 1973-82. *2136*
—. Mobutu Sese Seko. Zaire. 1965-80. *2519*
—. Multinational corporations. Smith, Ian. Zimbabwe. 1965-79. *4169*
—. Nigeria. Posters. 1975-79. *2141*
—. Nigeria. Presidency. 1966-77. *2120*
—. Othman, Haroub. Tanzania. 1967-76. *3178*
—. Political Culture (Western misconceptions). Tribalism (concept). 1960-73. *344*
—. Political Participation. Tunisia. 1967-73. *1570*
—. Responsible Government Movement. South Africa Company. Zimbabwe. 1910-23. *4228*
—. Socialism. 1963-73. *263*
Government (civilian). *Daily Graphic* (newspaper). Editorials (content analysis). Ghana. Military government. 1957-78. *1827*
—. Ghana. Nigeria. 1970's. *1652*
—. Military Government. Nigeria. 1979. *2132*
Government (collapse). Amin, Idi. Tanzania. Uganda. 1978-79. *3312*
Government control. Housing. Squatter Settlements. 20c. *872*
—. Kenya. Labor unions and organizations. Political Systems (single party). Tanzania. 1961-66. *2651*
Government Employees. *See* Civil Service; Public Employees.
Government Enterprise *See also* Nationalization.
—. Colonial Government. Mozambique. Mozambique Company. Nyassa Company. 1870's-1941. *3665*
—. Economic development. Nigeria. 1947-73. *2073*
—. Economic planning. Guinea. 1960-78. *1872*
—. Economic Planning. Public Policy. Tanzania. 1961-74. *3081*
—. Family Organization. Industrial innovation. Liberia. Markets. Women. 1950-70. *1947*
—. Ghana. Ghana Industrial Holding Corporation. Industrialization. 1962-71. *1730*
—. Ghana. Nkrumah, Kwame. Public corporations. 1951-66. *1732*
—. Industrial production. Tanzania. 1965-72. *3123*
—. Managers. Tanzania. 1962-73. *3117*
—. Private enterprise. Tanzania. 1970-75. *3084*
Government Enterprise (parastatal holding corporations). Foreign investments, private. Nationalization. Tanzania. 1967-74. *3106*
Government (majority rule). Guerrilla warfare. Zimbabwe. 1960's-78. *4202*
Government officials. Ethiopia. Law, rule of. Political change. 1973. *2767*
Government, one-party. Democracy. Political Parties. 1957-73. *335*
Government Ownership *See also* Nationalization.
—. East African Community. Economic integration. Kenya. Public Corporations. 1948-73. *2579*
—. Ethnicity. Intergovernmental Relations. Nigeria. Radio. Television. 1932-62. *2290*
—. Newspapers. Nigeria. 1400-1960. *2193*
Government policy. Capital mobilization. Economic growth. South Africa. 1939-60. *3782*
—. Violence. 1964-74. *266*
Government, provisional. Algeria (Algiers). France. World War II. 1940-45. *756*
Government regulation. Economic development. Tunisia. 1956-76. *1546*
—. Economic Structure (international). Multinational corporations. 1970-82. *569*
—. Grain. Marketing. Sahel. 1960's-70's. *558*
Government repression. Mozambique. Nationalism. Political protest. 1920-49. *3633*
Government, Resistance to *See also* Revolution.
—. 20c. *200*
—. African Independence Party of Senegal. Neocolonialism. Senegal. 1958-72. *2306*
—. African National Congress. South Africa. 1906-79. *3810*
—. African National Congress. South Africa. 1960's-82. *3924*
—. Africans. Collaboration. Colonialism. Great Britain. Kenya (Central Province). 1895-1930. *2931*
—. Agricultural Policy. Cotton. FRELIMO. Mozambique. Peasants. 1938-61. *3639*
—. Apartheid. South Africa. 1950's-78. *3835*
—. Apartheid. South Africa. 1973. *3722*
—. Bibliographies. Zimbabwe. 19c-20c. *4209*
—. Democratic Party. Guinea. Purges. Touré, Sekou. 1957-73. *1877*
—. Egypt. Islam. Repentance and Holy Flight group. 1977-79. *1235*
—. Ivory Coast. Migrations, protest. Upper Volta. 1901-45. *1607*
—. Liberia (Kru Coast). Reform. 1822-1935. *1941*
Government, Resistance to (review article). Africa, southern. Colonialism. Historiography. Isaacman, Allen. Social Classes. 1890's-1970's. *3407*
Government, transitional. FRELIMO. Mozambique. 1974. *3647*
Governors. Colonial Government. Constitutions. Nationalism. Nigeria. 1935-51. *2177*
—. Colonial Government. Great Britain. 19c-20c. 1930-76. *188*
Gowon, Yakubu. African unity. Foreign Policy. Nigeria. Political leadership. 1967-75. *2153*
—. Foreign Relations. Great Britain. Nigeria. 1961-75. *2098*
—. Military Government. Nigeria. Politics. 1966-75. *2149*
Gowon, Yakubu (interview). Organization of African Unity. 1963-73. *148*
Grain *See also* Cereals.
—. Government regulation. Marketing. Sahel. 1960's-70's. *558*
Graziani, Rodolfo. Assassination. Colonial Government. Ethiopia. Italy. Political repression. 1936-37. *2795*
—. Badoglio, Pietro. Documents. Italy. Libya (Cyrenaica). Mukhtar, Omar el-. Resistance. 1930-31. *1391*
—. Colonial Government. Ethiopia. Umberto, Prince. 1936-40. *2797*
—. Ethiopia. Italy. Military occupation. Resistance. 1935-40. *2801*
Great Britain *See also* British Commonwealth; British Empire.
—. Abolition Movement. Slavery. Sudan. 1877-1960. *1522*
—. Africa, central. Africa, East. Colonial policy. Films. 1920-50. *230*
—. Africa, East. Armies (manpower). World War I. 1914-18. *695*
—. Africa, East. Diseases. Germany. Military Operations. World War I. 1914-18. *688*
—. Africa, East. Lake Victoria. *Sybil* (vessel). World War I. 1915-16. *720*
—. Africa, Southern. Chanock, Martin (review article). Expansionism. 1900-45. *3420*
—. Africa, West. Aliens. Colonial Government. Law, customary. Minorities. 19c-20c. *1638*
—. Africa, West. Burns, Alan. Colonial Government (Executive Councils). Political Participation. 1941-42. *1660*
—. Africa, West. Colonial government. France. 1880-1960. *1667*
—. Africa, West. Conscription, military. France. Rebellions. World War I. 1914-18. *706*
—. Africa, West. Foreign Relations. Spain. World War I. 1914-18. *702*
—. Africa, West. Military Recruitment. Transportation, Military. World War I. 1914-19. *697*
—. Africans. Collaboration. Colonialism. Government, Resistance to. Kenya (Central Province). 1895-1930. *2931*
—. Agricultural prices. Anticolonialism. Farmers. Uganda. ca 1900-75. *3225*
—. Agricultural production. Nigeria. Sesame. Tiv. Trade. 1900-60. *2024*
—. Air Lines. Imperialism. 1919-32. *201*
—. Air route. Hoare, Samuel. Imperial Airways. South Africa (Cape Town). 1918-32. *202*
—. Air Warfare. Hassan, Mohammed Abdullah (the "Mad Mullah"). Somalia. 1919-21. *3031*
—. Appeasement policy. Diplomacy. Ethiopia. France. Italy. 1934-35. *2772*
—. Archives. Kenya. 20c. *2857*
—. Asians. Colonial policy. Discrimination. Kenya. 1903-25. *2949*
—. Atuot. Colonialism. Sudan, Southern. 1920's-55. *1474*
—. Auchinleck, Claude. El Alamein (battle). World War II. 1942. *743*
—. Beamish, Henry Hamilton. Colonialism. Fascism. ca 1920-48. *192*
—. Bibliographies. Egypt. Foreign policy. ca 1800-1977. *1283*
—. Botswana. Colonial government. Commerce. Jousse, Paul. Khama III. Ngwato. 1910-16. *3513*
—. Botswana. Debt, external. Public Finance. 1956-76. *3506*
—. Boundaries. Egypt. Sinai Peninsula. 1906-47. *1124*
—. Cameroon. France. Military Occupation. Partition, provisional. World War I. 1914-16. *701*
—. Canada. Education. Missions and Missionaries. Sudan Interior Mission. 1937-55. *1505*
—. Catholic Church. Ethiopia. Military government. Missions and missionaries. Vatican. World War II. 1941-43. *731*
—. Cold War. Colonies. Italy. USA. 1947. *479*
—. Colonial Government. Confederation. Zambia. Zimbabwe. 1931-52. *3397*
—. Colonial government. Constitutions. Discriminatory acts. Zimbabwe. 1923-74. *4243*
—. Colonial Government. Developing nations. Ghana. Treasury reform. 1936. *1751*
—. Colonial Government. District Commissioners. Public Administration. 1900-60. *190*
—. Colonial government. Economic Conditions. Electoral system. Zimbabwe. 1961-71. *4194*
—. Colonial Government. Economic Planning. Geography. 1943-56. *624*
—. Colonial government. Economic sanctions. UN. Zimbabwe. 1965-75. *4272*
—. Colonial government. *Education Policy in British Tropical Africa* (White Paper). 1914-39. *235*
—. Colonial Government. Educational policy. 1923-39. *168*
—. Colonial Government. Ethnic ranking. Race Relations. 19c-1980. *189*
—. Colonial Government. Forests. Legislation. Nigeria. Rubber. 1897-1940. *2025*
—. Colonial Government. Governors. 19c-20c. 1930-76. *188*
—. Colonial Government. Hodeib, Mohammed Amin. Resistance. Sudan (Tuti Island). 1914-46. *1496*
—. Colonial Government. Marxism. Social Customs. Witchcraft. 19c-20c. *173*
—. Colonial government. Muslims. Nigeria. Rebellions. World War I. 1914-19. *705*
—. Colonial Government. Nationalism. Press. Uganda. 1920's-30's. *3299*
—. Colonial Government. Nigeria. Tiv. 1900-70. *2234*
—. Colonial Government. Nigeria, Northern. Public Finance. Taxation. 1900-34. *2038*
—. Colonial Government. Sudan. 1899-1952. *1493*
—. Colonial legacy. France. Military dependence. 20c. *354*
—. Colonial Office. Decolonization. Jones, Arthur Creech. 1947. *161*
—. Colonial Office. Nationalism. 1947. *216*
—. Colonial Policy. Economic Conditions. Egypt. 1886-1937. *1148*
—. Colonial policy. Ghana. Radio broadcasting. 1927-57. *1841*
—. Colonial policy. Sudan. Unification. 1898-1953. *1519*
—. Colonial policy (memorandum). Military Strategy. Political Reform (delay of). Zambia. Zimbabwe. 1930-45. *3396*
—. Colonialism. Commonwealth Prime Ministers Conference (Ottawa, 1973). Foreign Policy. Portugal. 1965-74. *439*
—. Colonialism. Economic Policy. Exports. Tanzania. 1945-60. *3121*
—. Colonialism. Economic sanctions. Unilateral Declaration of Independence (UDI). Zimbabwe. 1965-73. *4182*
—. Colonialism. France. Germany. Togo. World War II. 1939-45. *740*
—. Colonialism. Law. National Development. 1960's-80. *667*
—. Colonies. Foreign Relations. Germany. 1920-36. *170*
—. Constitutions. Diplomacy. Independence. Kenya. Neocolonialism. 1960-69. *2948*
—. Constitutions. Documents. Lancaster House Conference. Zimbabwe. 1970-79. *4291*
—. Convention People's Party. Nkrumah, Kwame. Pan-African Congress. USA. 1935-63. *1781*
—. Cultural Imperialism (review article). Lefever, Ernest W. Nigeria. ca 1700-1966. *213*
—. Dams. Ethiopia. Lake Tana. Negotiations. 1922-35. *2704*
—. Decolonization. Kenya. Public Administration. 1945-60. *2926*
—. Diplomacy. Eden, Anthony. Ethiopia. France. Italy. War. 1935-36. *2787*

—. Cape Verde Islands. Cultural identity. Decolonization. Mozambique. 1950-81. *779*
—. Cape Verde Islands. Independence. 1970's. *1625*
—. China. Foreign aid policy. Mozambique. 1960's-70's. *507*
—. Colonial Government. Independence Movements. 1913-63. *1891*
—. Decolonization. 1970's. *1902*
—. Development. Institutions. 1974-79. *1907*
—. Development. Socialism. 1973-77. *1903*
—. Economic development. Education. Ideology. 1974. *1904*
—. Guerrilla Warfare. Independence Movements. Partido Africano da Independência da Guiné e Cabo Verde (PAIGC). 1963-73. *1906*
—. Independence Movements. Partido Africano da Independência da Guiné e Cabo Verde (PAIGC). 1955-74. *1896*
—. National liberation movements. Partido Africano da Independência da Guiné e Cabo Verde (PAIGC). 1970-73. *1884*
—. Partido Africano da Independência da Guiné e Cabo Verde (PAIGC). 1964-73. *1885*
Guinea-Bissau (Bissau Island). Diseases. Malaria control. 20c. *1890*
Guinea-Bissau (review article). Independence Movements. Ventnor, A. J. 1971-73. *1888*
Gukiina, Peter. Ibingira, G. S. K. Obote, Milton. Political development (review essay). Uganda. 1885-1971. *3308*
Gulf of Sidra incident. International law. Libya. Territorial Waters. USA. 1981-83. *1386*
Gulf Oil. Angola. Oil Industry and Trade (drilling). Public Relations. 1968-74. *571*
Gusii. Agricultural Policy. Coffee. Colonial Government. Kenya. 1933-48. *2861*
—. Innovation diffusion. Kenya. 1960-71. *2983*

H

Hafkin, Nancy J. Bay, Edna G. Women (review article). 1700-1975. *916*
Haile Selassie. Asfaw Wassen. Diplomacy (secret negotiations). Ethiopia. Italy. 1936-39. *2802*
—. Bibliographies. Coups d'etat. Ethiopia. 1947-76. *2793*
—. Civil disorder. Ethiopia (Eritrea). 1953-73. *2815*
—. Coups d'etat. Ethiopia (Eritrea). Political Factions. 1970-75. *2731*
—. Diplomatic recognition. Ethiopia. Great Powers. Italy. 1937-38. *2803*
—. DuBois, W. E. B. Pan-Africanism. USA. 1919-73. *132*
—. Ethiopia. 1917-74. *2775*
—. Ethiopia. ca 1915-70's. *2813*
—. Ethiopia. Foreign Relations. Italy. 1940-43. *2796*
—. Ethiopia. Parliaments. 1931-71. *2737*
—. Ethiopia. Political Leadership. 1930-74. *2806*
—. Ethiopia. Revolution. 1896-1980. *2809*
—. Ethiopia. Revolution. Teferi Benti. 20c. *2753*
Haiti. Benin. Myths and Symbols (cross). Voodoo. 1492-20c. *1701*
Halim, Tahia. Egypt. Painting. 1919-70's. *1317*
Hamdān Abū Shōk. Ethiopia (Gubba). Local government. Sudan. 1900-38. *2744*
Hammarskjold, Dag (review article). Independence. UN. Zaire. 1960. *2511*
Handicrafts. *See* Arts and Crafts.
Haqqī, Yahyā. Egypt. Literary criticism. Nationalism. 1920-59. *1323*
Harlem Renaissance. Authors. France. Literature. Negritude. USA. 1921-39. *852*
Harris, William Waddy. Africa, West. Christianity. Missions and Missionaries. Polygyny. 1910-29. *1643*
Harrist Church. Ivory Coast. Missions and Missionaries. Witchcraft. 1913-79. *1935*
—. Ivory Coast. Modernization. Religion. 1910-72. *1934*
Hassan II. Annexation. Green March. Morocco. Western Sahara. 1975. *1455*
—. Morocco. Parliaments. War. 1977. *1443*
—. Morocco. Political Leadership. 1975-80. *1448*
Hassan, Mohammed Abdullah (the "Mad Mullah"). Air Warfare. Great Britain. Somalia. 1919-21. *3031*
Hauka. Modernization. Niger. Sects, politico-religious. 1850-1975. *1982*
Hausa. Africa, West. Droughts. Economic history. Sahel. Tuareg. 1550-1973. *595*
—. Africa, West. Linguistics. Literacy campaign. UNESCO. 1960's-70's. *1692*
—. Assimilation. Islam. Nigeria, northern. 20c. *2286*
—. Begging. Migration, Internal. Nigeria (Ibadan). 1974. *2016*
—. Cultural relations. Europe, Western. Islam. Literature. Social Attitudes. 1945-78. *2285*
—. Family structure. Nigeria. Rural areas. Social Change. 20c. *2247*
Hayford, Adelaide Casely. Africa, West. Pan-Africanism. 1866-1930. *1785*
—. Feminism. Ghana. Nationalism, cultural. Universal Negro Improvement Association. Women. 1868-1960. *1850*
Hayford, Mark Christian. Ivory Coast. Religion. 1864-1945. *1923*
Healing movement. Ghana. Methodology. Rites and Ceremonies. Twelve Apostles Church. 1913-71. *1833*
Health, Ministry of. Malawi. Medical policy. Public Administration. 1891-1974. *3591*
Heikal, Muhammed. Egypt. Intellectuals. Modernization. Muslim Brotherhood. Social Change. 1914-55. *1353*
Helene Franz Hospital. Missions and Missionaries. Public Health. South Africa (Bochum-Blauberg). Syphilis. 1895-1935. *3995*
Henquin, Victor-Félix-Désiré (papers). Civil Service. Colonial Government. Public finance. Zaire. 1901-36. *2481*
Henty, G. A. Fiction (adventure stories). Guillot, René. Kimenye, Barbara. 1870's-1970's. *879*
Herero. Chronology. Himba. Methodology. Namibia. 20c. *3686*
Heroes. Fiction. Kenya. Mau Mau. Revolution. ca 1950-57. *2966*
Heron, Alastair (memoirs). Rhodes-Livingstone Institute. Zambia. 1963-67. *4079*
Hertzog, J. B. M. (testimonials). Historiography. South Africa. 1900-39. *3862*
Hierarchies. Africa, East (Lakes region). Land Tenure. Monarchy. ca 800-ca 1960. *2575*
Higher Education *See also* Adult Education; Colleges and Universities; Technical Education.
—. Aggrey, James. Ghana. Prince of Wales College. USA. 1920's. *1844*
—. Cognition. Islam. Morocco (Marrakech). 1920's-30's. *1422*
—. Colonial Government. Makerere University. Uganda. 1921-40. *3268*
—. Degrees, Academic. London University. Nigeria. 1887-1951. *2279*
—. Ethnic groups. Nigeria. 1960-79. *2122*
—. Guinea. Socialism. 1962-82. *1878*
—. Liberia. Policy development. Politics. Social organization. 1940's-60's. *1953*
Higher Education (development). Africa, East. Colonial Government. Ghana. 1945-67. *672*
Higher Education (review article). Fafunwa, A. B. Nigeria. Okafor, Nduka. 20c. *2269*
Hill, Polly. Agricultural growth. Nigeria (Hausaland). Villages (review article). 20c. *2064*
Hima. Iru. Social Classes. Uganda (Ankole). 1960's-70's. *3233*
Himba. Chronology. Herero. Methodology. Namibia. 20c. *3686*
Historical sources. Amharic. Ethiopia. 1889-1935. *2683*
—. Arabic. Manuscripts. Nigeria. 15c-20c. *2007*
—. Archives, State. Germany, East (Potsdam). 19c-20c. *31*
—. *Leselinyana La Lesotho* (newspaper). Lesotho. 1863-1977. *3541*
Historiography *See also* Periodization of History.
—. 16c-20c. 1978. *48*
—. 1876-1978. *43*
—. Abrem, stool of. Ghana, southern. ca 1505-1950. *1791*
—. Africa, East. Colonialism. Oral history. 19c-20c. *2596*
—. Africa, East. National Self-image. Prehistory-20c. ca 1900-30. *2635*
—. Africa, North. Armies (Historical Section monographs; review article). Italy. World War II. 1940-43. 1949-74. *732*
—. Africa, North. Bibliographies. Foreign Relations. USA. 1785-1975. *977*
—. Africa, Southern. 19c-20c. *3342*
—. Africa, Southern. Baines, Thomas. Discovery and Exploration. Wolfe, Richard. 1973. *5*
—. Africa, southern. Colonialism. Government, Resistance to (review article). Isaacman, Allen. Social Classes. 1890's-1970's. *3407*
—. Africa, West. Nationalism. 1975. *1650*
—. Africa, West. Rebellions (review article). 1900-47. *1605*
—. African studies. Anthropology. Functionalism. Radcliffe-Brown, A. R. 20c. *33*
—. African studies. Radicals and Radicalism. ca 1960-73. *57*
—. African studies. USA. 1960-80. *12*
—. Afrikaners. Rebellions. South Africa. 1914. *3857*
—. Angola. 1480-1973. *3436*
—. Angola. Civil war. 1975-76. *3438*
—. Anthropology. Excavations. Great Zimbabwe. Zimbabwe. 1960's-72. *4138*
—. Apartheid. Scholars, black. South Africa. USA. 1948-75. *3734*
—. Archaeology. Bibliographies. Tunisia. Prehistory-1973. *1573*
—. Australia. Economic development. Racism (review article). South Africa. 20c. *3720*
—. Bureaucracies. Ghana (review article). Politics and the Military. 1955-75. *1779*
—. Burundi. Monarchy. Ntare Rushatsi. 1900-77. *2658*
—. Business history. 1867-1973. *27*
—. Censorship. Egypt. Nasser, Gamal Abdel. 1952-64. *1202*
—. Christianity. Church history. Missions and Missionaries. 19c-20c. *786*
—. Colonialism. Decolonization. Portugal. 1900-73. *174*
—. Colonialism. France. 1860-1930. *232*
—. Colonialism. Ideology. Slavery. 19c-1960's. *196*
—. Colonialism. Imperialism. 1800-1974. *13*
—. Colonialism. Libya (Cyrenaica). Massacres. 1930-31. *1390*
—. Communist Countries. National liberation movements. Symposium of Historians and Africanists of Socialist Countries, 3d. 1970-79. *217*
—. Coups d'etat. Ethiopia. Markakis, John (review article). Politics, traditional. 1960's-70's. *2730*
—. Davidson, Basil. 1850-1970's. *16*
—. Davidson, Basil. Nationalism (review article). 1890's-1970's. *35*
—. Development (review article). Economic history. Imperialism. 1919-73. *640*
—. Economic development. Imperialism. 1832-1971. *682*
—. Economic history. 19c-20c. *38*
—. Economic Theory. Political Theory. Radicals and Radicalism. 1960's-77. *47*
—. Egypt. Leftism. Sa'īd, Rif'at as-. 1940-50. *1195*
—. Ethiopia. Foreign Relations. Great Britain. Italy. 1925-28. *2739*
—. Ethiopia. Foreign Relations. USSR. 1917-79. *2752*
—. Ethiopia. War. 1935-36. *2732*
—. Fanon, Frantz. Politics. 1950's-70. *287*
—. Foreign Relations. USA. 20c. *461*
—. Hertzog, J. B. M. (testimonials). South Africa. 1900-39. *3862*
—. Imperialism (review article). -1973. *158*
—. Independence. Kenya. 1963-75. Prehistory-20c. *2854*
—. Industrialization. Zimbabwe. ca 1900-75. *4174*
—. Kuba (review article). Oral tradition. Vansina, Jan. Zaire. 19c-20c. *2458*
—. Literature. 1976-80. *912*
—. Maghreb. USA. 1776-1974. *979*
—. Military. Political Science. Research, interdisciplinary. 1898-1976. *361*
—. Monnier, Laurent (review article). Politics. Zaire. 1971. *2459*
—. Mozambique. 1800-1970. *3653*
—. Nationalism. 1945-74. *282*
—. Nationalism. 19c-20c. 1960's-70's. *56*
—. Nationalism. Race Relations. South Africa. 1965-72. *3844*
—. Nigeria. -1975. *1991*
—. Scholars, African. 1955-75. *36*
—. South Africa (Johannesburg). 1887-1976. *3741*
—. Sudan, southern. 1821-1980. *1489*
—. Tanzania. 19c-20c. *3043*
—. USSR. 1959-79. *20*
Historiography (Anglo-American). Racism. Zimbabwe. 20c. 1960's. *4248*
Historiography (collusion controversy). Egypt. France. Great Britain. Israel. Suez Crisis. 1956. *1211*
Historiography (Eastern European). Morocco. 1925-79. *1435*
Historiography (Egyptian). Fundamentalism. Islam. 20c. *1339*

Historiography (Marxist). Nationalism. Ranger, T. O. Resistance. 20c. *14*
Historiography (neo-Marxist). Economic history. South Africa. 1960-76. *3766*
Historiography (review article). 1982. *52*
—. ca 1800-1970's. *34*
—. Blake, Robert. Zimbabwe. 1880's-1960's. *4256*
—. Colonialism. 1870-1960. *1*
—. Davidson, Basil. 19c-1970's. *44*
—. Maghreb. ca 9c-20c. ca 1965-75. *931*
—. South Africa. Wright, Harrison M. 1800-1957. *3714*
Historiography (revisionist). Industrialization. Race relations. South Africa. 20c. *3747*
Historiography (Turkish). Bibliographies. Documents. ca 1400-1976. *37*
Historiography (US). Algeria. Independence Movements. 1960-74. *1047*
History *See also* particular branches of history, e.g. business history, oral history, psychohistory, science, history of; Ideas, History of.
—. Ghana (Ahafo). Political Factions. 1966-69. *1811*
Hitler, Adolf. Africa, North. Logistics. Military Strategy. Rommel, Erwin. World War II. 1941-42. *770*
Hlengwe. Zimbabwe (Lowveld). 1600-1977. *4137*
Hoare, Samuel. Air route. Great Britain. Imperial Airways. South Africa (Cape Town). 1918-32. *202*
Hobley, Charles William. Africa, East. Bibliographies. Settlement (European). 1890-1947. *2612*
Hodeib, Mohammed Amin. Colonial Government. Great Britain. Resistance. Sudan (Tuti Island). 1914-46. *1496*
Hodgson, T. L. Cope, R. L. Davenport, T. R. H. Elphick, Richard. Khoi. South Africa (review article). 19c-20c. *3715*
Hoernle, Alfred. Industrialization. Racism. Social change. South Africa. 1900-39. *3728*
Holy Apostles. Nigeria (Ilaje). Religious movements. Utopias (defection, recruitment). 1947-74. *2225*
Homelands Policy. Economic conditions. Education. Race relations. South Africa. 1960's-70's. *3738*
Honey. Africa, Central. Forests. Wax. 1750-1950. *2398*
Hopkins, Nicholas S. Ghana (Swedru). Local politics. Mali (Kita). Owusu, Maxwell. Uganda (Gondo). Vincent, Joan. 1960's-. *247*
Hopley, Frederick John van der Byl. John Hopley Trophy. Sports. Zimbabwe. 1883-1951. *4307*
Hopley, William Musgrave. Judges. Zimbabwe. 1853-1919. *4309*
Horn of Africa. *See* Africa, East; Djibouti; Ethiopia; Somalia.
Horne, Alastair. Algeria. Independence Movements. War. 1954-75. *1037*
Horne, Alistair (review article). Algeria. Colonial Government. France. War. 1954-62. *1026*
Hospitals. Zimbabwe (Umtali). 1897-1930. *4317*
Hostels. Africans. Christianity. Servants. South Africa (Johannesburg). Women. 1907-70. *3972*
Houghton, H. Hobart. Capitalism (review article). Dagut, J. South Africa. 1860-1970. *3778*
Houphouët-Boigny, Félix. Foreign Policy. France. Ivory Coast. 1945-72. *1910*
—. Ivory Coast. National Development. Political Leadership. 1944-74. *1917*
Housing *See also* City Planning.
—. Bureaucracies. Squatter settlements. Tanzania (Dar es Salaam). Urbanization. 1965-82. *3210*
—. Government control. Squatter Settlements. 20c. *872*
—. Kenya (Nairobi). 1960-72. *3010*
—. Zimbabwe (Bulawayo). 19c-20c. *4324*
Housing policies. Zambia (Kitwe). 1964-76. *4127*
Housing (review article). Cities. Kenya. Stren, Richard E. Tanzania. 1960-80. *2606*
Housing shortage. Settlement. South Africa (Johannesburg). Squatters. 1944-47. *4017*
Human rights. 1791-1974. *381*
—. 1948-80. *280*
—. 1970's. *58*
—. Asians (expulsion). Uganda. 1972. *3298*
—. Constitutions. Nigeria. 1957-79. *2096*
—. Equatorial Guinea. UN Human Rights Commission. 1968-81. *2444*
—. Ethiopia. ca 1967-74. *2807*
—. Independence. Namibia. 1950's-82. *3701*
—. International Law. International League for Human Rights. Namibia. 1947-57. *3678*
—. Lesotho. 1966-70's. *3545*
—. Obote, Milton. Personal Narratives. Uganda. 1962-82. *3324*
—. Organization of African Unity. 1963-80. *144*
—. Organization of African Unity. 1970's-80's. *99*
—. Portugal. South Africa. Zimbabwe. 1853-1977. *3329*
—. Race Relations. South Africa. USA. 1973-78. *3821*
—. UN (27th session). 1972. *382*
Human rights violations. Amnesty International. Zimbabwe. 1960's-70's. *4290*
—. Developing nations. Racism. 1970's. *341*
—. UN Commission on Human Rights. 1966-70's. *504*
Humanism. Kaunda, Kenneth. Modernization. Socialism. Zambia. ca 1960's. *4081*
Humanism, Western. Literature. 1870's-1974. *868*
Humor. Africa, West. Armies. Europeans. Smuts, Jan. World War I. 1914-18. *711*
Hunger. Independence, War of. Operation Turkey. Political economy. Zimbabwe. 1979-81. *4198*
Hunters, subsistence. Bisa. Zambia (Luangwa Valley). 20c. *4086*
Hunting. Botswana. 1961-73. *3523*
Huntington, Samuel. Africa, East. Civil-military relations. Praetorianism (concept). 1960's-74. *2571*
Husayn, Tāhā. Egypt. France. Literature. 1889-1973. *1338*
—. Egypt. Islam. Political Theory. 1889-1961. *1319*
Hussein of Bale. Ethiopia. Islam. Western Somali Liberation Front. 1975-80. *2836*
Husseini, Muhammed Amin al-. Egypt. Islamic Conference. 1931-36. *1247*
Hutu. Burundi. Civil war. Tutsi. 1956-72. *2665*
—. Burundi. Ethnic conflict. Tutsi. 1962-75. *2671*
—. Burundi. Ethnic groups. Tutsi. Violence. 1972-73. *2666*
—. Burundi. Genocide. Tutsi. 1972. *2664*
—. Burundi. Politics. Tutsi. 1970's. *2662*
—. Dowry system. Marriage. Rwanda. Tutsi. 1970's. *3021*
—. Ethnicity. Rwanda (Kinyaga region). Tutsi. 1860-1960. *3020*
—. Political development. Rwanda. Tutsi. 1919-72. *3023*
Hyden, Goran (review article). Development. Peasants. Socialism. Tanzania. 1870-1975. *3052*
Hydroelectric installations. Energy. Zambia. 1950's-70's. *4089*
Hymns. Kenya. Kikuyu. Mau Mau. Politics. 1952. *2944*

I

Ibingira, G. S. K. Gukiina, Peter. Obote, Milton. Political development (review essay). Uganda. 1885-1971. *3308*
Idang, Gordon J. Akinyemi, A. B. Balewa, Abubakar. Foreign Policy (review article). Nigeria. 1960-66. *2090*
Idealism. Africa, West. Elites. Integration. 1868-1940. *1662*
Ideal-type analysis. Political Change (review article). Willame, Jean-Claude. Zaire. 1962-66. *2504*
Ideas, History of *See also* Intellectuals.
—. Colonialism. 1950's-70's. *627*
—. Fanon, Frantz *(The Wretched of the Earth)*. Political Theory. 1961-75. *998*
—. Negritude. 1930's-70's. *257*
Ideas, History of (eclecticism). 20c. *848*
Ideological evolution. Pan-Africanism. Socialism. 1945-75. *139*
Ideology. 1970's. *305*
—. Africa, West. Independence Movements. Leadership. Nkrumah, Kwame *(Consciencism)*. 1964-72. *1805*
—. Algeria. Communist Party. Racism. 1920-27. *1093*
—. Algeria. Feraoun, Mouloud. Intellectuals. Nationalism. 1955-62. *1020*
—. Angola. Independence Movements. Social change. 1940-79. *3482*
—. Apartheid. South African Bureau of Racial Affairs. Stubbs, Ernest. 1902-32. *3915*
—. Bibliographies. Religion. 20c. *843*
—. Blyden, Edward Wilmot. Negritude. Senghor, Leopold. 1800-1900's. *810*
—. Bourguiba, Habib. Elites. Political Leadership. Tunisia. 1955-77. *1574*
—. Colonial Government (resistance to). Independence movements. 19c-20c. *157*
—. Colonialism. Historiography. Slavery. 19c-1960's. *196*
—. Coloureds. Political attitudes. South Africa. 1974. *3893*
—. Economic development. Education. Guinea-Bissau. 1974. *1904*
—. Economic Theory. Islam. Libya. Qadhafi, Muammar *(Green Book)*. 1976-79. *1385*
—. Egypt. Nasserism. Political Factions. Political Leadership. 1952-65. *1253*
—. Ethiopia. Italy (Sardinia). Oral History. Propaganda. War. 1935-36. *2734*
—. Foreign Relations. Libya. Qadhafi, Muammar. 1969-74. *1382*
—. Ghana. Marxism. Nkrumah, Kwame. 1956-66. *1786*
—. Interest Groups. Manufacturing. South Africa. 1900-25. *3750*
—. Lebanon. Reformism. Tunisia. 1970's. *1541*
—. Mobutu Sese Seko. Zaire. 1960's-70's. *2499*
—. Monarchy. Morocco. 8c-20c. *1413*
—. Morocco. Rif War. 1921-26. *1441*
—. Nigeria. Socialism. 20c. *2103*
—. Nyerere, Julius. Political Leadership. Socialism. 1960-70. *309*
—. Pan-Africanism. 1970-76. *131*
—. Political culture. Tunisia. 1950's-74. *1540*
—. Rebellions. Revolution. Zaire (Kwilu). 1930's-63. *2526*
—. Socialism. Tradition. ca 1900-73. *889*
Ife, University of. Civil War. Ethnic diversity. Nigeria. Political attitudes. Students. 1957-69. *2111*
Igbo. Aba riots. Nigeria (Calabar, Owerri). Social Conditions. Women. 1925. *2194*
—. Bibliographies. Nigeria (Aba). Riots. Women. 1929-30. *2123*
—. Catholics. Converts. Nigeria. Ostracism. ca 1955-78. *2217*
—. Colonial government. Nigeria. Political systems, dual-sex. Women. -1970's. *2163*
—. Education. Nigeria. Social status. Westernization. 1800-1956. *2239*
—. Kalabari. Nigeria (Oguta). Palm oil. Trade. 1900-50. *2026*
—. Linguistics. Names, personal. Nigeria. -1973. *2253*
—. Nigeria (Imo). Urbanization. 1902-78. *2266*
Ijebu. Entrepreneurship. Nigeria. Yoruba. 1950-74. *2012*
—. Nigeria. Political theory. 1892-1943. *2104*
Ila. Cattle. Economic behavior. Zambia. 20c. *4065*
—. Cattle. Economic Structure. Zambia. 19c-20c. *4064*
Iligira. Assimilation. Economic Structure. Kenya. Samburu. 20c. *2985*
Immigrants. Economic growth. Labor. Zambia. 1911-69. *4098*
Immigrants, Kenyan. Churches, independent. Pentecostal Mission. Rites and Ceremonies (dream-telling). Uganda. 1957-60's. *3227*
Immigration *See also* Assimilation; Demography; Deportation; Emigration; Population; Race Relations; Refugees; Social Problems.
—. Algeria. Foreign Relations. France. Labor. 1962-79. *1063*
—. Anti-Semitism. Jews. Purified Nationalist Party. South Africa. 1937-39. *3824*
—. Colonial Government. Kenya. Social Status. Somalis. 1916-63. *2980*
—. Europeans. Settlement. Zimbabwe. 1890-1976. *4322*
—. Ghana, northern. Green revolution. Rice. Violence. 1965-80. *1728*
Immigration, British. Race Relations. South Africa. 1820-1970's. *4021*
Immigration policy. Ghana. Nigerians. 1960-70's. *1807*
Imoudi, Michael. Labor movement. Nigeria. Railway Workers' Union. 1940-42. *2066*
Imperial Airways. Air route. Great Britain. Hoare, Samuel. South Africa (Cape Town). 1918-32. *202*
Imperial Highway Authority. Ethiopia. Roads. 1951-73. *2690*
Imperialism *See also* Colonialism; Expansionism; Militarism.
—. Africa, central. Africa, southern. Collaboration. Resistance. 1850-1920. *183*
—. Africa, southern. Europe. South Africa. 1900-72. *3779*
—. Air Lines. Great Britain. 1919-32. *201*
—. Angola. Decolonization. 15c-20c. *3458*
—. Angola. Independence Movements. 1954-75. *3450*

Intergovernmental organizations. Economic policy. Ghana. Intervention (political). 1969-72. *1742*
Intergovernmental Relations. Economic Conditions. France. Politics. Réunion. 1945-80. *3563*
—. Ethnicity. Government Ownership. Nigeria. Radio. Television. 1932-62. *2290*
—. Ghana. National Self-image. 1952-74. *1777*
—. Public Administration (reorganization). Tanzania (Kigoma district). 1921-63. *3156*
Intermarriage. Economic conditions. Kenya (Coast Province). Muslims. Urbanization. 1963-78. *3001*
Internal Affairs, Ministry of. Decorations. Zimbabwe. 1973-77. *4293*
Internal Migration. *See* Migration, Internal.
International administration, unified. Colonialism (Eurafrica concept). France. Germany. 1876-1954. *149*
International African Institute. Great Britain. 1926-76. *2*
International assistance. East African Community. Foreign Aid (coordination). Kenya. Public corporations. 1974. *2639*
International Bank for Western Africa. Africa, West. Banking. 1965-73. *1601*
International Center of Insect Physiology and Ecology. Biological control. Insects. Kenya (Nairobi). 1970-73. *3016*
International cooperation. Africa, East. East African Community. ca 1965-75. *2589*
—. Senegal River. Water use. 1962-74. *1637*
International Court of Justice. International law. Namibia. 1919-71. *3704*
—. Namibia. 1945-75. *3698*
—. Polisario Front. Self-determination. Western Sahara. 1970's. *1590*
International Labor Office (review article). Income distribution. Kenya. Unemployment. 1972. *2905*
International Labor Organization. Colonial Government. Labor policy. 1920-47. *206*
—. Development Strategy. Economic Policy. Kenya. 1963-77. *2894*
—. Economic Conditions. Kenya. 1963-74. *2858*
—. Organization of African Unity. Political Cooperation. 1963-73. *119*
International Law *See also* Arbitration, International; Boundaries; International Court of Justice; Refugees; Slave Trade; Treaties; War.
—. Aircraft hijacking. Entebbe raid. Israel. Popular Front for the Liberation of Palestine. Uganda. 1976. *3222*
—. Arbitration, international. Libya. Nationalization. Oil Industry and Trade. USA. 1971-80. *1404*
—. Bantu Homelands. Self-determination. South Africa. 1971-78. *3916*
—. Belligerent recognition. Ethiopia (Eritrea). 1850's-1979. *2768*
—. Decolonization. Namibia. South Africa. 1884-1973. *3684*
—. Domestic jurisdiction. Organization of African Unity. 1963-73. *142*
—. Gulf of Sidra incident. Libya. Territorial Waters. USA. 1981-83. *1386*
—. Human rights. International League for Human Rights. Namibia. 1947-57. *3678*
—. International Court of Justice. Namibia. 1919-71. *3704*
—. Morocco. Treaties. USA. Vienna Convention. 1969-78. *1426*
—. Namibia. South Africa. Western nations. 1966-80. *3693*
—. Organization of African Unity. 1963-82. *102*
—. Peacekeeping Forces. UN. Zaire. 1950-80's. *2495*
International League for Human Rights. Human rights. International Law. Namibia. 1947-57. *3678*
International management. Economic development. Niamey (conferences). Niger River. 1885-1968. *1636*
International Monetary Fund. Economic liberalization. Egypt. Open Door Policy. 1970-74. *1150*
International Organizations *See also* specific organizations by name.
—. Africa, East. East African Community. 20c. *2602*
—. Africa, Southern. British Commonwealth. Developing nations. Diplomacy. New International Economic Order. 1960-79. *3357*
—. Africa, southern. Politics. 1973-75. *3412*
International Relations Institute of Cameroon. Diplomacy. 1960's-75. *460*
International Security *See also* Arbitration, International; Peace.
—. Africa, East. USA. USSR. 1970's. *2585*
International Socialist League. Communist Party. South Africa. 1917-21. *3867*
International system. National Development. 1960-80. *293*
International Trade *See also* Foreign Investments.
—. 1960-70's. *574*
—. Peasants. Rural development. Tanzania. 1940-75. *3067*
Intervention. Africa, southern. Great Powers. Natural Resources. Politics. 1970's. *3418*
—. Angola. Civil war. Great Powers. 1974-76. *3445*
—. Angola. Cuba. Foreign policy. 1966-77. *3457*
—. Angola. Independence Movements. -1970's. *3459*
—. Angola. Military Intelligence. South Africa. 1975-76. *3447*
—. Angola. Mozambique. Revolution. 1960's-70's. *3373*
—. Angola. South Africa. 1975-77. *3364*
—. Central African Republic. Colonialism. France. 1979. *2428*
—. Cuba. Ethiopia. Revolution. USSR. 1974-78. *2738*
—. Education. Foreign policy. Foundations. USA. 1945-75. *534*
—. Egypt. Nasser, Gamal Abdel. Yemen. 1962. *1204*
—. Ethiopia. Great Britain. Italy. League of Nations. 1925-36. *2722*
—. European Economic Community. Foreign Relations. 1975-79. *554*
—. Foreign Policy. France. 1970's. *457*
—. Foreign Policy. USSR. 1945-78. *431*
—. France. 1958-78. *399*
—. Israel. Red Sea. 1970's. *488*
—. USSR. 1960's-70's. *501*
Intervention (foreign). Angola. Civil war. Nigeria. Organization of African Unity. 1960-75. *270*
—. Angola. South Africa. 1961-76. *3354*
Intervention, military. Algeria. Angola. Cuba. Syria. 1961-76. *411*
—. Angola. Cuba. Foreign Policy. USA. USSR. 1975-77. *3483*
—. Angola. Cuba. USSR. 1975-76. *3479*
—. Angola. Cuba. USSR. 1975-76. *3480*
—. Angola. Foreign Policy. South Africa. USA. 1970's-82. *3473*
—. *Aurore* (newspaper). *Figaro* (newspaper). France. Journalism. Politics. Zaire. 1978. *2530*
—. Cuba. Ethiopia. Somalia. War. 1959-78. *2654*
—. Diffusion. Political change. Political Parties (single-party system). 1950's-70's. *258*
—. Ethiopia. Foreign Relations. Great Powers. Somalia. 1970-81. *2649*
—. France. 1976-80. *485*
Intervention (political). Economic policy. Ghana. Intergovernmental organizations. 1969-72. *1742*
Invasion. Guinea. Portugal. Touré, Sekou. 1970. *1866*
Investment policies. Cameroon. Colonial Government. Economic Growth. 1945-60. *2418*
Investments. British South Africa Company. Gold Mines and Mining. Mozambique Company. Rezende, Baron de. Zimbabwe. 1887-1948. *4159*
—. Colonialism. Economic development. France. Public Finance. 1924-38. *600*
Investments (growth-pole strategy). Economic Planning. Rebellions. Regional inequality. Sudan. 1974. *1501*
Iran. Economic Development. Egypt. Land reform. 1952-78. *1160*
Iranians. *Chihrinimi* (newspaper). Egypt. Settlement. 1904-66. *1357*
Irredentism. Decolonization. Ethiopia (Eritrea). Self-determination. Somalia. 1950's-80. *2592*
Irrigation *See also* Dams; Reclamation of Land.
—. Agricultural Labor. Ethiopia (Awash Valley). Migration, internal. 1950's-70's. *2701*
—. Agricultural production. Colonial Government. Economic Development. Mali. Office du Niger. 1920's-50's. *1962*
—. Agriculture. Chagga (Mfongo clan). Tanzania (Uchagga). 16c-20c. *3091*
—. Cotton. Kassala Cotton Company. Sudan (Gash River valley). 1922-28. *1518*
Iru. Hima. Social Classes. Uganda (Ankole). 1960's-70's. *3233*
Isaacman, Allen. Africa, southern. Colonialism. Government, Resistance to (review article). Historiography. Social Classes. 1890's-1970's. *3407*
Isaq diaspora. Kenya. Somalia. Tax resistance. 19c-1942. *3009*
Islam. 1960's-70's. *857*
—. 7c-20c. *797*
—. Acculturation. Christianity. Nigeria. Yoruba. 1970's. *2215*
—. Acculturation. Colonialism. Maghreb. Tradition. 1959-75. *918*
—. Africa, East. Asians. Bohras. 1100-1975. *2566*
—. Africa, East. Christianity. Ethiopia. Middle East. 1980. *2583*
—. Africa, East. Ismaili sect, Nizari. Modernization. 1840-1974. *2625*
—. Africa, East. Mazrui, Al-Amin bin Ali. Modernization. 1875-1947. *2630*
—. Africa, North. 18c-20c. *937*
—. Africa, North. Church and State. Economic development. 20c. *919*
—. Africa, North. Maghreb. Maraboutism. Sufism. ca 1100-1975. *960*
—. Africa, North. Political Leadership. Qadhafi, Muammar. 900-1980. *928*
—. Africa, West. Animism. Christianity. Conversion. -20c. *1642*
—. Africa, West. Conversion. 20c. *1617*
—. Africa, West. Political Stability. ca 1960-80. *1618*
—. Algeria. Boumédienne, Houari. Political Leadership. Revolution. 1940's-78. *1083*
—. Algeria. Civil Law. Sudan. 1960-78. *934*
—. Algeria. Colonialism. Education, French. 1830-1960. *1036*
—. Algeria. Colonialism. Women. 1865-. *1100*
—. Algeria. France. Nationalism. Students. 1912-62. *1073*
—. Algeria. National Identity. 19c-20c. *981*
—. Algeria. Politics. Socialism. 1960's-70's. *1022*
—. Algeria. Social Status. Tradition. Tunisia. Women. 1954-81. *951*
—. Algeria (Ahaggar). Kinship. Social organization. Tuareg, Imuhag. 1680-1974. *997*
—. Amin, Idi. Christianity. Uganda. ca 1890-1976. *3262*
—. Ansar Party. Politics. Sudan. Umma Party. 1914-45. *1524*
—. Arab League. Egypt. Fundamentalism. Nationalism. 1920-45. *1332*
—. Arab states. 8c-20c. *856*
—. Arab states. Foreign Relations. 1960's-70's. *436*
—. Arab unity. Foreign Relations. Libya. Qadhafi, Muammar. 1969-73. *1387*
—. Arab unity. Libya. Qadhafi, Muammar. 1971-75. *1371*
—. *Ashraf.* Egypt. Elites. 1650-1952. *1356*
—. Assimilation. Hausa. Nigeria, northern. 20c. *2286*
—. Attitudes. Intellectuals. Leadership. Maghreb. 1945-80. *969*
—. Beer. Economic Conditions. Sorghum. Upper Volta. Women. 1978-80. *2389*
—. Bibliographies. Colonial Government (British, German). Tanzania. 1973. *3202*
—. Christianity. Conversion. Tanzania. 1973. *3185*
—. Christianity. Missions and Missionaries. 20c. *817*
—. Christianity. Oil Industry and Trade. Political Change. 20c. *306*
—. Christianity. Sudan. 16c-1981. *1503*
—. Church and State. Egypt. 20c. *1116*
—. Church and State. Egypt. Popular Culture. 1952-77. *1334*
—. Cities. Morocco. Social organization. 1960-73. *1423*
—. Cognition. Higher education. Morocco (Marrakech). 1920's-30's. *1422*
—. Colonial government. French West Africa. Nigeria. Rebellions. World War I. 1914-17. *704*
—. Colonial Government. Ivory Coast. 1893-1939. *1932*
—. Colonial Government. Missions and Missionaries. Nigeria (Muslim emirates). Proselytization. 1900-28. *2288*
—. Colonial government. Nigeria (Kano). Taxation. 1806-1927. *2076*
—. Constitutions. Maghreb. 1980. *941*
—. Copts. Egypt. Persecution. 19c-20c. *1318*
—. Courts. Morocco. 1967-78. *1449*
—. Cultural relations. Europe, Western. Hausa. Literature. Social Attitudes. 1945-78. *2285*
—. Diola. Modernization. Senegal. 1900-40. *2323*

—. Great Britain. Libya. Navies. Shipping. World War II. 1940-43. *752*
—. Guerrilla Warfare. Libya (Cyrenaica). Mukhtar, Omar al-. Sanusi. 1923-32. *1397*
—. Imperialism. Zaire. 1908-22. *2494*
—. Independence (review article). Negotiations. Rossi, Gianluigi *(L'Africa Italiana verso l'Indipendenza, 1941-1949).* UN. 1946-49. *233*
—. Libya. Nationalism. Qadhafi, Muammar. 1911-78. *1392*
—. Trade. ca 1950-75. *541*
Italy (Sardinia). Ethiopia. Ideology. Oral History. Propaganda. War. 1935-36. *2734*
Ithna-asheri communities. Africa, East. Islam, Shi'a. 1840-1967. *2633*
Ivory. Africa, East. Poaching. Wildlife conservation. 1973-74. *2597*
—. Elephants. Tanzania. Wildlife management. 1920-76. *3114*
Ivory Coast *See also* Africa, West; French West Africa.
—. Agricultural Mechanization. Regionalism. Rice. Yams. 19c-20c. *1915*
—. Agriculture. Baule. Labor, division of. Women. 19c-20c. *1921*
—. Baule. Colonization. Textile Industry. Women. 1875-1975. *1920*
—. Cameroon. Social change. Social Status. Women. 1955-71. *800*
—. Cities. Depression. Economic Conditions. 1930-35. *1925*
—. Civil-Military Relations. 1968. *373*
—. Colonial Government. Depression. Economic Policy. Profits. 1929-35. *1911*
—. Colonial Government. Economic development. World War I. 1914-19. *712*
—. Colonial Government. Islam. 1893-1939. *1932*
—. Colonial Government. Public Health. Sleeping sickness. 1900-45. *1918*
—. Colonial Government. Repression. 1908-20. *1919*
—. Colonial history. Ethnicity. National development. 1889-1969. *1931*
—. Democratic Party. 1958-73. *1929*
—. Development. Modernization. 1961-75. *1912*
—. Economic growth. Five-Year Plan. 1971-75. *1913*
—. Economic Planning. Plantations. Rubber. Villages. 1968-79. *1927*
—. Ethnic identity. Liberia, Eastern. ca 1900-75. *1641*
—. Exports. Rural development. 1960-75. *1926*
—. Foreign Policy. France. Houphouët-Boigny, Félix. 1945-72. *1910*
—. French. Language policy. 1960-77. *1933*
—. Government, Resistance to. Migrations, protest. Upper Volta. 1901-45. *1607*
—. Harrist Church. Missions and Missionaries. Witchcraft. 1913-79. *1935*
—. Harrist Church. Modernization. Religion. 1910-72. *1934*
—. Hayford, Mark Christian. Religion. 1864-1945. *1923*
—. Houphouët-Boigny, Félix. National Development. Political Leadership. 1944-74. *1917*
—. Mass media. Newspapers. 1910-73. *1936*
—. Migration. Modernization. Public Transportation. Social mobility. 1900-40. *1930*
—. Migration. Social Change. 1928-78. *1924*
—. Modernization. Political Systems. Values. 1960-82. *1922*
—. Politics, cross-ethnic. Urban policy. 1960's-70's. *1916*
—. Social change. Social Classes (formation). 1920-65. *1914*
Ivory Coast (Man, Zuénoula). Arts and crafts. Religious attitudes. Social attitudes. 1974. *1928*

J

Jaaxanke. Baa, Karamoxo. Guinea (Tuuba). Manuscripts, Arabic. 15c-20c. *1876*
Jamaa. Christians. Labor, conceptualizations of. Zaire (Shaba). 1950-60's. *2541*
—. Popular culture. Zaire (Shaba). 1950's-70's. *2542*
—. Religious movements. Zaire. 1953-74. *2538*
Jamahiriya (concept). Democracy. Libya. Political theory. Qadhafi, Muammar *(Green Book).* Rousseau, Jean Jacques *(Social Contract).* 1967-79. *1380*
Janzen, J. M. African studies (review article). Palmer, Robin. Parsons, Neil. 20c. *39*
Jaona, Monja. Madagascar. National Movement for the Independence of Madagascar (MONIMA). 1958-73. *3548*
Japan. Nigeria. Trade. 1947-74. *2029*
Jawaharlal Nehru Award for International Understanding. Mandela, Nelson. South Africa. 1979-80. *3884*
Jewish communities. Daily life. Egypt (Alexandria, Cairo). 1970's. *1350*
Jewish Workers' Club. Communism. Jews. South Africa (Johannesburg). 1928-48. *3949*
Jews *See also* Anti-Semitism; Judaism.
—. Anti-Semitism. Immigration. Purified Nationalist Party. South Africa. 1937-39. *3824*
—. Arabs. Israel. Minorities. Morocco. Tunisia. 1972-75. *972*
—. Communism. Jewish Workers' Club. South Africa (Johannesburg). 1928-48. *3949*
—. Consular Reports. Germany. Libya. Walter, Gebhard. World War II. 1940-43. *722*
—. Demography. Tunisia. 1881-1956. *1569*
—. Emigration. Ethiopia. Falasha. Israel. 1969-75. *2835*
—. Ethiopia. Falasha. 1970-. *2837*
—. Ethiopia. Falasha. Prejudice. 10c BC-1975. *2834*
—. Morocco. 15c-20c. *1427*
—. Social organization. Tunisia (Jerba). 19c-1950's. *1538*
—. South Africa. 1910-67. *4010*
John Hopley Trophy. Hopley, Frederick John van der Byl. Sports. Zimbabwe. 1883-1951. *4307*
Johnson, S. Jangaba M. Ethnography. Liberia. National unification. 1895-1973. *1942*
Johnston, Harry Hamilton. Malawi. Mozambique (Chinde). Ports. 1891-1923. *3589*
Jonathan, Leabua. Botswana. Khama, Seretse. Lesotho. Political Leadership. 1966-73. *3366*
Jones, Arthur Creech. Colonial Office. Decolonization. Great Britain. 1947. *161*
Jones, William I. Economic Planning. Ernst, Klaus. Mali. Peasants. Socialism (review article). 1960-68. *1959*
—. Economic Planning (review article). Mali. 1961-68. *1971*
Joseph, Richard A. (review article). Cameroon. Decolonization. Union des Populations de Cameroun. 1948-56. *2400*
Joubert, Elsa. Novels. South Africa. 1955-80. *3999*
Journalism *See also* Films; Freedom of the Press; Newspapers; Periodicals; Press; Reporters and Reporting.
—. *Aurore* (newspaper). *Figaro* (newspaper). France. Intervention (military). Politics. Zaire. 1978. *2530*
Jousse, Paul. Botswana. Colonial government. Commerce. Great Britain. Khama III. Ngwato. 1910-16. *3513*
Judaism *See also* Anti-Semitism; Jews.
—. Bayudaya. Kakungulu, Semei. Malaki sect. Uganda. 1856-1974. *3285*
Judges *See also* Courts; Lawyers.
—. Hopley, William Musgrave. Zimbabwe. 1853-1919. *4309*
Judicial Administration. Nigeria. 19c-1979. *2112*
Judicial systems. DeGaulle, Charles. France. Independence. 1958-73. *413*
Julian, Hubert F. Ethiopia. Italy. Pan-Africanism. Political Attitudes. War. 1935-36. *2808*
Julin, Alphonse Pierre. Algeria. Algiers (battle). World War II. 1942. *741*

K

Kabaka. Low, Anthony. Public Administration (review article). Uganda (Buganda). 1950-71. *3294*
Kabaka Yekka (The King Alone) movement. Kakamega Club. Politics. Uganda (Buganda). 1940-1961. *3242*
Kadalie, Clements. Bloemfontein Conference. Labor Unions and Organizations. Msimang, H. Selby. South Africa. 1919-25. *3800*
Kaguru. Colonial government. Ethnicity. Political Leadership. Tanzania. 1880-1944. *3133*
Kakamega Club. Kabaka Yekka (The King Alone) movement. Politics. Uganda (Buganda). 1940-1961. *3242*
Kakungulu, Semei. Bayudaya. Judaism. Malaki sect. Uganda. 1856-1974. *3285*
Kalabari. Igbo. Nigeria (Oguta). Palm oil. Trade. 1900-50. *2026*
Kalahari Desert. Botswana. Rey, C. F. (diaries). Travel accounts. 1930-37. *3507*
Kalenjin. Africa, East. Assimilation. Maasai. Social Organization (age groups). 1890-1980. *2578*
Kamara, Moussa. Ethnic groups. Political leadership. Senegal, eastern (Boundou). 1681-1921. *2314*
Kamba. Cattle destocking. Colonial Government. Kenya. Political Protest. 1938. *2924*
Karamojong. Generations. Political authority. So. Uganda. 1900-72. *3256*
Karume, Abeid. Politics. Tanzania (Zanzibar). 1964-74. *3144*
Kassala Cotton Company. Cotton. Irrigation. Sudan (Gash River valley). 1922-28. *1518*
Kaunda, Kenneth. Detente. Foreign Relations. Racism. South Africa. Zambia. 1964-74. *4040*
—. Foreign Relations. USA. Zambia. 1970's. *473*
—. Humanism. Modernization. Socialism. Zambia. ca 1960's. *4081*
Kaunda, Kenneth (interview). Zambia. 1973. *4136*
Kaunda, Kenneth (review article). Detente. Macpherson, Fergus. Political leadership. Zambia. 1940's-75. *4088*
Keino, Kipchoge. Kenya. Olympics. Sports (athletic infrastructure). Track and field. 1966-74. *2993*
Keita, Mobido. Elites. Mali. Militarism. Revolution. 1960-68. *1968*
Keita, Modibo. Foreign policy. Mali. 1960-68. *1966*
Kenya *See also* Africa, East.
—. Africanization. Economic Structure. Employment. 1952-75. *2889*
—. Africanization. Economic structure. Multinational corporations. 1902-74. *2888*
—. Africans. Asians. Labor training. 1968-74. *2891*
—. Africans. Asians. Race Relations. ca 1805-1974. *2999*
—. Agricultural development. Colonialism. Domestic Policy. Zimbabwe. 1900-60. *204*
—. Agricultural development. Maasai. Samburu. 1935-75. *2876*
—. Agricultural Labor. Colonial Government. 1919-29. *2864*
—. Agricultural Policy. Coffee. Colonial Government. Gusii. 1933-48. *2861*
—. Agricultural policy. Economic aid. 1950-75. *2892*
—. Agricultural Policy. Europeans. Social Organization. World War II. 1939-46. *767*
—. Agricultural Production. Luo. Peasant family. 1946-48. *2873*
—. Agricultural production. Peasants. Political assimilation. 1960's-70's. *2852*
—. Agricultural Production. Peasants. Regional economic differentiation. 1920-40. *2911*
—. Agriculture (review article). Colonial Government. Marxism. 1950-80. *2860*
—. Archaeology. Madagascar. Migration. Tanzania. 9c-19c. 20c. *2650*
—. Archives. Great Britain. 20c. *2857*
—. Asians. Civil Rights. Colonial government. Coryndon, Robert. 1917-33. *2973*
—. Asians. Colonial policy. Discrimination. Great Britain. 1903-25. *2949*
—. Asians. Devonshire White Paper. 1923. *2930*
—. Asians. Economic Structure. 1888-1939. *2859*
—. Assimilation. Economic Structure. Iligira. Samburu. 20c. *2985*
—. Attitudes. Colonial Government. Maasai. Tanzania. 1890-1960. *2647*
—. Attitudes. Maendeleo Ya Wanawake. Women. 1954-74. *3014*
—. Bibliographies. 1960-78. *2956*
—. Capital. Economic structure. 1963-76. *2895*
—. Capitalism. Colonization. Land. ca 1880's-1920's. *2901*
—. Capitalism. Development. Socialism. Zimbabwe. 1950-81. *617*
—. Capitalism, Primitive. Depression. Europeans. Settlers. ca 1900-50. *2910*
—. Cattle destocking. Colonial Government. Kamba. Political Protest. 1938. *2924*
—. Church Missionary Society. Clitoridectomy. Missions and Missionaries. 1910-72. *2996*
—. Cities. Housing (review article). Stren, Richard E. Tanzania. 1960-80. *2606*
—. Cities (small). Rural development. 1970's. *2890*
—. City Planning. Tanzania. Urban growth. ca 1960-73. *2646*
—. Civil Rights. Political opposition. 1963-78. *2919*
—. Climate. Europeans. Social Customs. Zimbabwe. 1880's-1930's. *185*
—. Coffee. Economic development. 1894-1970. *2912*

—. Colonial Government. Educational policy. Scott, Henry S. 1920-34. *3002*
—. Colonial Government. Immigration. Social Status. Somalis. 1916-63. *2980*
—. Colonial Government. Kiama Kia Muingi. Kikuyu. Secret societies. 1953-61. *2946*
—. Colonial government. Legislative Council. Mathu, Eliud. 1919-57. *2929*
—. Colonial Government. Mitchell, Philip. 1944-52. *2922*
—. Colonial Government. Nandi. Political Protest. 1905-23. *2918*
—. Colonial Government. Nandi. Rebellions. 1923. *2928*
—. Colonial government. Police. Racial structure. 1920-50. *2970*
—. Colonial Office. Leys, Norman. Ross, W. McGregor. Senate (European). 1900-40. *2971*
—. Colonial policy. Independence. Land reform. ca 1950-62. *2893*
—. Colonialism. Education. Missions and Missionaries. 1902-32. *2987*
—. Colonialism. Embu. Political change. 1906-63. *2952*
—. Colonialism. Political structure. Social Conditions. 1952-73. *2915*
—. Colonialism (review article). Modernization. Tignor, Robert L. Wolff, Richard D. 1870-1939. *2913*
—. Colonization. Land tenure. Luo. Social organization. Women. 20c. *2903*
—. Constitutions. Diplomacy. Great Britain. Independence. Neocolonialism. 1960-69. *2948*
—. Cooperatives. 1945-76. *2862*
—. Copper Mines and Mining. Political protest. Strikes. Zambia. 1922-62. *175*
—. Corn (review article). Farmers, small. Gerhart, John. Green revolution. 1964-75. *2887*
—. Counterinsurgency. Public Opinion. Sudan. Zimbabwe. 1951-75. *219*
—. Courts. Social control. 1969-74. *3007*
—. Decolonization. Europeans. Settlers. 1960's. *2967*
—. Decolonization. Great Britain. Public Administration. 1945-60. *2926*
—. Decolonization. Land reform. Mau Mau. Nationalism. 1952-60. *2937*
—. Decolonization. Mau Mau. 1957-60. *2936*
—. Decolonization. Mau Mau. Multiracialism. 1952-59. *2927*
—. Development. Education. Tanzania. 1961-77. *2644*
—. Development Strategy. Economic Policy. International Labor Organization. 1963-77. *2894*
—. Dinesen, Isak (Karen Blixen; biography). ca 1910-30. *2977*
—. Dini ya Msambwa. Rebellions (review article). Wipper, Audrey. 1930-49. *2965*
—. Earnings-per-worker differentials. Economic Growth. Wages. 1967-70. *2883*
—. East African Community. Economic integration. Government Ownership. Public Corporations. 1948-73. *2579*
—. East African Community. Foreign Aid (coordination). International assistance. Public corporations. 1974. *2639*
—. Economic change. Independence. Local tradition. Social Organization. 1940's-60's. *2906*
—. Economic change. Luo. Women. 1890's-1940's. *2878*
—. Economic Conditions. Family life. Social Change. 1900-77. *3011*
—. Economic Conditions. Income distribution. 1950's-60's. *2881*
—. Economic Conditions. International Labor Organization. 1963-74. *2858*
—. Economic Conditions. Political Systems. 1963-80. *2855*
—. Economic development. Employment relationships. Labor. ca 1950-73. *2879*
—. Economic Development. Foreign Relations. Tanzania. Uganda. 1962-74. *2655*
—. Economic Development. Labor. Mexico. ca 1940-75. *2868*
—. Economic development. Labor Unions and Organizations. Legislation. Strikes. 1960's-73. *2899*
—. Economic development. Migration, Internal. Regionalism. 1954-70. *2984*
—. Economic Development (review article). Social Classes. 1870's-1970's. *2851*
—. Economic planning. 1963-70. *2875*
—. Economic structure. Industry. Manufacturing. 1963. *2884*
—. Education. Local Native Councils. Politics. 1925-39. *2953*
—. Education. Local Politics. Luhya (southern). 1930-60. *2988*
—. Education. Political instability. Unemployment. 1963-76. *2920*
—. Education. Rural self-help (harambee). Technology, institutes of. 1971-74. *2877*
—. Education. Somalis. 1930-59. *3008*
—. Educational development. Language policy. Tanzania. 1963-74. *2626*
—. Educational Tests and Measurements. Elementary Education. 1944-80. *2991*
—. Elites. Kikuyu. Mau Mau. Political Leadership. 1950-63. *2961*
—. Employment. Professions. Women. 1960-76. *2992*
—. Europeans. 1945-79. *2978*
—. Europeans. Independence. Land. Political Factions. 1960-63. *2968*
—. Expatriates. Government. 1970-79. *2940*
—. Exports. Land Tenure. Social Classes. 1950-79. *2863*
—. Fiction. Heroes. Mau Mau. Revolution. ca 1950-57. *2966*
—. Foreign policy. 1960-73. *2945*
—. Foreign policy. Nonalignment. Tanzania. 1960-77. *2587*
—. Giriama. Witchcraft. 18c-1970's. *2975*
—. Gor, Jason. Luo. Succession disputes. 1940's-70's. *2969*
—. Government control. Labor unions and organizations. Political Systems (single party). Tanzania. 1961-66. *2651*
—. Gusii. Innovation diffusion. 1960-71. *2983*
—. Historiography. Independence. 1963-75. Prehistory-20c. *2854*
—. Hymns. Kikuyu. Mau Mau. Politics. 1952. *2944*
—. Import licensing. 1950-79. *2897*
—. Income. Poverty. Rural areas. 1961-79. *2907*
—. Income distribution. International Labor Office (review article). Unemployment. 1972. *2905*
—. Income transfers, urban-rural. 1971-74. *2886*
—. Independence. Mau Mau. Nationalism. 1944-60. *2943*
—. Independence Movements. Labor movement. Mau Mau. ca 1910-60. *2959*
—. Independence Movements. Press, African. 1945-52. *3003*
—. Indigenization. Industry. Nigeria. 1954-80. *594*
—. Industrialization. Rural Development. Rural Industrial Development Programme. 1973-77. *2896*
—. Isaq diaspora. Somalia. Tax resistance. 19c-1942. *3009*
—. Keino, Kipchoge. Olympics. Sports (athletic infrastructure). Track and field. 1966-74. *2993*
—. Kenyatta, Jomo. Moi, Daniel Arap. Politics. Succession. 1978-79. *2960*
—. Kenyatta, Jomo. Moi, Daniel Arap. Succession. 1978-1980. *2935*
—. Kenyatta, Jomo. Political development. 1963-68. *2957*
—. Kenyatta, Jomo. Political stability. 1931-78. *2964*
—. Kikuyu. Mau Mau. 1950's. *2923*
—. Kikuyu. Religion. *Watu wa Mungu.* 1920's-70's. *2997*
—. Labor unions and organizations. 1960's-70's. *2880*
—. Labor unions and organizations. Nigeria. Politics. 1939-66. *210*
—. Land ownership. Limitation of Action Act. Luo. 1968-70's. *2902*
—. Land tenure. Reform. 1953-79. *2867*
—. Language. Lonrho. Nation Newspapers Ltd. Newspapers. 1972. *3004*
—. Lawyers. Professionalism. 1906-75. *3000*
—. Legislators. Political recruitment. 1957-68. *2951*
—. Library associations. 1895-1977. *2998*
—. Literature. Luo. 20c. *847*
—. Literature. National Development. 1950-72. *2974*
—. Local Government. 1960's-70's. *2917*
—. Maasai. Mau Mau. 1900-56. *2947*
—. Marx, Karl. Mau Mau. Political Theory. Revolution. Tocqueville, Alexis de. 1888-1963. *2921*
—. Mau Mau. Political conflict. 1952-77. *2972*
—. Mau Mau. Rebellions. 1952-60. *2941*
—. Mau Mau. Revolution. 1920-60. *2933*
—. Middle classes. Political power. 1975-77. *2938*
—. Moi, Daniel Arap. Political leadership. 1978-79. *2939*
—. Moi, Daniel Arap. Politics. Social Organization. 1960's-70's. *2925*
—. National development. Nigeria. Research. Science. 1970's. *612*
—. Neocolonialism. Political economy. Zimbabwe. 1920's-77. *4157*
—. Nigeria. Scientific Experiments and Research. 1960's-70's. *613*
—. Peasants (review article). ca 1890-1980. *2870*
—. Peasants (review article). Rural development. Social Organization. Tanzania. 1970's. *2622*
—. Political Development. 1963-78. *2909*
—. Political economy. Public corporations. 1930's-70's. *2872*
—. Political Factions. 1975-82. *2958*
—. Political socialization. Schools. 1960's-70's. *2934*
—. Press (African). 1945-52. *2982*
—. Public policy. Social Classes. Tanzania. 1960's-70's. *2565*
—. Rural self-help (harambee). 1963-77. *3013*
—. Rural self-help (harambee). Technical education. 1963-70. *2994*
—. Social change. Teso. 19c-20c. *3015*
—. Social Classes. Tea Development Authority. 1960-72. *2908*
Kenya African National Union. Independence Movements. Kikuyu. Mau-Mau. 1945-63. *2954*
—. Kenyatta, Jomo. Kikuyu Central Association. Mau Mau. 1944-52. *2955*
—. Political Parties (single-party system). 1960-73. *2916*
—. Political Systems. 1960-74. *2914*
Kenya, central. Land reform. Mbeere. Social organization. 1959-71. *2865*
Kenya (Central Province). Africans. Collaboration. Colonialism. Government, Resistance to. Great Britain. 1895-1930. *2931*
Kenya (Coast Province). Economic conditions. Intermarriage. Muslims. Urbanization. 1963-78. *3001*
Kenya (coastal region). Economic Development. Tourism. 1962-72. *2885*
Kenya (Kakamega). Education. Employment. 1970-73. *2995*
Kenya (Kano Plains). Environment. Rural development. 20c. *2853*
Kenya (Kitale). Business. Foreign Investments. Nationalization. 1969-76. *2900*
Kenya (Lamu). Architecture (carved doors). 1450-1974. *2986*
Kenya (Lamu archipelago). Colonial government. Exports. Mangrove poles. Tanzania (Rufiji River). 1900-81. *2576*
Kenya Land Commission. Europeans. Kikuyu. Land tenure. Settlers. 1902-34. *2869*
Kenya (Lumbwa). Ethnicity. 1960's-70's. *2979*
Kenya (Machakos hills). Erosion. Land use. Population. 20c. *2898*
Kenya (Mombasa). Courts, Koranic. Ethnicity. Social Organization. Swahili. 15c-1970's. *3006*
—. *Lelemama* dance associations. Muslim Women's Cultural Association. Muslim Women's Institute. Women. 1930's-70's. *3005*
Kenya (Murang'a). Colonialism. Kikuyu. Loyalists. Mau Mau. 1952-70. *2942*
Kenya (Nairobi). Biological control. Insects. International Center of Insect Physiology and Ecology. 1970-73. *3016*
—. Business. Landholding. Women. ca 1900-50. *2866*
—. Employment. Social Change. Working Class. 1952-69. *2874*
—. Housing. 1960-72. *3010*
—. Migration, internal. Urbanization. 1964-68. *2976*
—. Political participation. 1960's-73. *2950*
Kenya (Nakuru). Asians. Discrimination. Racial attitudes. 1912-72. *2981*
—. Economic Development. Elites (urban). Kikuyu. Social Change. 1929-52. *2856*
—. Independence Movements. Mau Mau. 1940-55. *2963*
—. Mau Mau. 1944-55. *2962*
Kenya, northern. Colonial Government. Ethiopia. Refugees. 1936-38. *3012*
Kenya (Northern Frontier District). Poaching. Somalis. 1909-39. *2871*
Kenya (Nyanza, south). Luo. Oral History. Social Organization. Suba. Uganda (Buganda). 1500-1973. *2990*
Kenya (Rift Valley). Kikuyu. Mau Mau. Squatters. 1937-52. *2932*
Kenya (South Nyanza). Economic development. Public Administration. 1967-71. *2904*

Kenya (Trans-Nzoia). Agricultural productivity. Land tenure. 1960's-70's. *2882*
Kenyatta, Jomo. Kenya. Moi, Daniel Arap. Politics. Succession. 1978-79. *2960*
—. Kenya. Moi, Daniel Arap. Succession. 1978-1980. *2935*
—. Kenya. Political development. 1963-68. *2957*
—. Kenya. Political stability. 1931-78. *2964*
—. Kenya African National Union. Kikuyu Central Association. Mau Mau. 1944-52. *2955*
Kerek (ritual). Bapostolo ritual. Christianity. ca 1900-75. *791*
Kgatla. Botswana. Epidemics. Influenza, Spanish. 1918. *3529*
—. Botswana. Kinship. 1934-73. *3525*
Kgosana, Philip. Duncan, Patrick. Pan-African Congress. South Africa (Cape Town). Strikes. 1953-60. *3881*
Khaïr-Eddine, Mohammed. Benjelloun, Tahar. Boudjedra, Rashid. Maghreb. Novels. 1965-75. *920*
Khalifa bin Harub. Diplomacy. Duggan, William R. (memoir). Tanzania (Zanzibar). USA. 1959. *3139*
Khama III. Botswana. Colonial government. Commerce. Great Britain. Jousse, Paul. Ngwato. 1910-16. *3513*
—. Botswana. Economic History. 1875-1923. *3512*
Khama, Seretse. Botswana. Foreign policy. Political development. South Africa. 1966-76. *3492*
—. Botswana. Jonathan, Leabua. Lesotho. Political Leadership. 1966-73. *3366*
—. Botswana. Political Leadership. 1966-80. *3536*
Khama, Tshekedi. Botswana. Nationalism. 1925-59. *3488*
—. Botswana. Ngwato. Politics. 1948-51. *3489*
Khammessat. Agricultural labor. Tunisia, southern. 19c-20c. *1547*
Khoi. Cope, R. L. Davenport, T. R. H. Elphick, Richard. Hodgson, T. L. South Africa (review article). 19c-20c. *3715*
Khoikhoi (Topnaar). Ethnology. Namibia. -1970's. *3697*
Kiama Kia Muingi. Colonial Government. Kenya. Kikuyu. Secret societies. 1953-61. *2946*
Kibedi, Wanume. Amin, Idi (review article). Martin, David. Uganda. 1971-74. *3253*
Kiga. Colonial Government. Ganda. Local Government. Ssbalijja. Uganda (Kigezi). 1908-30. *3311*
Kikuyu. Colonial Government. Kenya. Kiama Kia Muingi. Secret societies. 1953-61. *2946*
—. Colonialism. Kenya (Murang'a). Loyalists. Mau Mau. 1952-70. *2942*
—. Economic Development. Elites (urban). Kenya (Nakuru). Social Change. 1929-52. *2856*
—. Elites. Kenya. Mau Mau. Political Leadership. 1950-63. *2961*
—. Europeans. Kenya Land Commission. Land tenure. Settlers. 1902-34. *2869*
—. Hymns. Kenya. Mau Mau. Politics. 1952. *2944*
—. Independence Movements. Kenya African National Union. Mau-Mau. 1945-63. *2954*
—. Kenya. Mau Mau. 1950's. *2923*
—. Kenya. Religion. *Watu wa Mungu*. 1920's-70's. *2997*
—. Kenya (Rift Valley). Mau Mau. Squatters. 1937-52. *2932*
Kikuyu Central Association. Kenya African National Union. Kenyatta, Jomo. Mau Mau. 1944-52. *2955*
Kilimanjaro Native Planters Association. Chagga. Coffee growers. Colonial Government. Tanzania. 1919-32. *3115*
Kimbangu, Simon. Antonism. Kongo. Prophets. Religion. Zaire. 18c-20c. *2551*
—. Baptists. Religious Movements. Zaire. 1921-22. *2546*
—. Church of Christ on Earth. Religious movements. Zaire. 1881-1972. *2545*
—. Religious Movements. Zaire. 1921-79. *2549*
Kimbanguism. MacGaffey, Wyatt. Messianism. Zaire. 1921. *2553*
—. Religion. Zaire. 1879-1921. *2550*
Kimenye, Barbara. Fiction (adventure stories). Guillot, René. Henty, G. A. 1870's-1970's. *879*
King, Kenneth James. Education (review article). Murphy, E. Jefferson. Philanthropy. USA. ca 1900-75. *517*
Kinship. Africa, West. Agricultural production. Peasants. Social organization. 1973. *1658*
—. Algeria (Ahaggar). Islam. Social organization. Tuareg, Imuhag. 1680-1974. *997*
—. Botswana. Kgatla. 1934-73. *3525*
—. Business History. Friendship. Liberia (Monrovia). Merchants. 1970. *1949*
Kinship, system of. Algeria (Ahaggar). Alliances, matrimonial. Social organization. Tuareg, Kel Rela. ca 1600-1959. *1021*
Kinship terms. Africa, North. Social organization. Tuareg. 19c-20c. *953*
—. Algeria (Ahaggar). Language. Tuareg. 1968-74. *1005*
Kissinger, Henry A. DeGaulle, Charles. Nationalism. Nkrumah, Kwame. Nyerere, Julius. Political Leadership. ca 1940's-70's. *308*
—. Diplomacy. Independence. USA. Zimbabwe. 1976. *4282*
Kissinger, Henry A. (memorandum). Foreign policy. South Africa. USA. 1967-74. *3903*
Ki-Zerbo, Joseph. Africa (review article). 15c-20c. *45*
Knot of wisdom. Asante. Folklore. Ghana. -1973. *1843*
Kongo. Antonism. Kimbangu, Simon. Prophets. Religion. Zaire. 18c-20c. *2551*
—. Colonialism. Prophetism. Religious movements. Zaire. 1880-1964. *2547*
Korea, North. Diplomatic recognition. Foreign policy. Korea, South. 1960-75. *476*
Korea, South. Diplomatic recognition. Foreign policy. Korea, North. 1960-75. *476*
Korean War. Airplanes, Military (jets; F-86F Sabre). South Africa. 1950-53. *3805*
Korsten Basketmakers. Masowe, Baba Johane. Religion. Zimbabwe (Manicaland; Makoni). 1940-77. *4145*
Krio. Elites. Great Britain. Nationalism. Railroads. Sierra Leone. Strikes. 1919-26. *2370*
—. Elites. Language. Sierra Leone. 1853-1978. *2368*
Kru. Liberia. Political Opposition. Twe, Didwo. 1930's-60. *1955*
Kuba (review article). Historiography. Oral tradition. Vansina, Jan. Zaire. 19c-20c. *2458*
Kufra convoy. Africa, North. Logistics. World War II. 1940. *742*
Kufra Scheme. Droughts. Libya. Sheep raising. Water. 1968-73. *1366*
Kunda. Agricultural development. Cotton production. Land tenure. Zambia. 1960's-70's. *4095*
Kwena. Botswana (Kweneng). Economic history. 1885-1966. *3494*

L

Labor *See also* Agricultural Labor; Capitalism; Child Labor; Collective Bargaining; Communism; Cost of Living; Employment; Industrial Relations; Migrant Labor; Socialism; Strikes; Unemployment; Wages; Working Class; Working Conditions.
—. Afrikaners. Botswana, western. San. Social Conditions. Tswana. 1900-71. *3524*
—. Afrikaners. Gold. South Africa (Johannesburg). 1886-1924. *3759*
—. Agricultural Labor. Cotton. Egypt. 1882-1940. *1165*
—. Agriculture. Europeans. Zaire. 1910-60. *2470*
—. Algeria. Foreign Relations. France. Immigration. 1962-79. *1063*
—. Botswana. Migration, Internal. Social Change. 1966-80. *3487*
—. Botswana. Mines. South Africa. 1899-1966. *3531*
—. Class Struggle. Economic growth. South Africa. 1945-80. *3760*
—. Colonial Government. English. Language manipulation. Tanzania. 1919-40. *3154*
—. Colonialism. French Equatorial Africa. 1880-1930. *2392*
—. Colonialism. Land tenure. Malawi, southern. Rebellions. 15c-20c. *3603*
—. Cotton. Mozambique. Sena Sugar Estate, Ltd. Women. 1935-60. *3666*
—. Developing Nations. Political Change. Zambia. 1880-1981. *4049*
—. Economic change. Family. Sierra Leone. ca 1750-1928. *2337*
—. Economic development. Education. Egypt. Lewis, W. A. Models. 1952-67. *1174*
—. Economic development. Employment relationships. Kenya. ca 1950-73. *2879*
—. Economic Development. Kenya. Mexico. ca 1940-75. *2868*
—. Economic growth. Immigrants. Zambia. 1911-69. *4098*
—. Egypt. Emigration (brain drain). 1972-77. *1134*
—. Ghana. Great Britain. Military Recruitment. World War II. 1939-46. *751*
—. Independence movements. Malawi. World War I. 1914-53. *710*
—. Industrialization. South Africa (Bophuthatswana; Babelegi). 1960's-70's. *3786*
—. Industry. Union Minière du Haut-Katanga (UMHK). Zaire (Shaba). 1890's-1940. *2464*
—. Labor Unions and Organizations (black). South Africa. 1918-73. *3729*
—. Migration. Niger Company. Nigeria, northern. Tin mining. 1903-45. *2032*
—. Migration, Internal. Political protest. Rural development. Zambia (Kasumpa). ca 1960-75. *4042*
—. Migration, internal. Tanzania. Urbanization. 1960-72. *3100*
—. Mining industry. Multinational corporations. Sklar, Richard L. (review article). Zambia. 1920-76. *4130*
—. Mining industry. Political Protest. South Africa. 1980's. *3731*
—. Nigeria (Jos plateau). Tin mining. 1906-21. *2045*
Labor aristocracy. Nigeria (Northern). Rural-urban studies. Wages. 1974. *2036*
Labor, black. Colonialism. Wage rates. Zimbabwe. 1900-75. *4186*
Labor, conceptualizations of. Christians. Jamaa. Zaire (Shaba). 1950-60's. *2541*
Labor, contract. Class consciousness. Namibia. Strikes. 1971-72. *3695*
Labor control. Economic Policy. Industrial decentralization. South Africa. ca 1950-79. *3749*
Labor Disputes *See also* Strikes.
—. Ghana (Tarkwa). Gold mines and Mining. 1968-69. *1722*
—. Namibia. National Labor Association. Ovambo crisis. 1971. *3690*
—. Tanzania. ca 1970-73. *3105*
Labor, division of. Agriculture. Baule. Ivory Coast. Women. 19c-20c. *1921*
—. Agriculture. Beti. Cameroon. Cocoa. Nigeria. Women. Yoruba. 1950-79. *620*
—. Blake-Thompson, J. Race Relations. Scholarship (amateur). Zimbabwe. 1921-62. *4320*
—. Nigeria. Women. Yoruba. 1500-1980. *2011*
Labor, division of, international. Economic conditions. Industrialized countries. 1969-75. *659*
Labor force. Economic growth. Egypt. Migration, internal. Social organization. 1937-70's. *1342*
—. Egypt. Industry. Women. 1816-1975. *1146*
—. Miners, white. Social Status. Zimbabwe. 1890-1953. *4178*
Labor, forced. Colonial Government. Coppet, Marcel de. French West Africa. Popular Front. 1936-46. *1610*
—. Colonial government. Malawi. Peasants. Political consciousness. Rwanda. 19c-1962. *207*
—. Colonial policy. Upper Volta (Koudougou). 1914-39. *2385*
—. Colonialism. Plantations. Tanzania (Kigoma). 1700-1970's. *3130*
—. Ghana. Government. Mines. 1906-27. *1760*
Labor markets. Botswana. Lesotho. South Africa. Swaziland. 1967-76. *3343*
—. Egypt. Industrialization. Islam. Women. 1952-. *1172*
Labor Movement. Egypt. Politics. Wafd Party. 1919-39. *1205*
—. Imoudi, Michael. Nigeria. Railway Workers' Union. 1940-42. *2066*
—. Independence Movements. Kenya. Mau Mau. ca 1910-60. *2959*
—. Miners. South Africa. Strikes. 1930's-40's. *3781*
—. Morocco. Union Marocaine du Travail. 1936-58. *1424*
—. Sudan. Workers' Trade Unions Federation. 1956-69. *1462*
Labor policy. Apartheid. Migrant Labor. South Africa. ca 1960's-70's. *3784*
—. Colonial Government. International Labor Organization. 1920-47. *206*
—. South Africa. Wiehahn Commission. 1977-78. *3753*
Labor problems. Colonial Government. Race Relations. Zambia. 1900-53. *4078*
Labor productivity. Industrial production. Tanzania. 1965-72. *3124*

Labor recruitment. Angola. Copper mines and Mining. French, J. C. Robert Williams Co. Zaire (Shaba). 1917-21. *2477*
—. Ghana (northern). Migration. Mines. 1880-1940. *1749*
—. Social conditions. World War I. 1914-20. *715*
Labor reform. Africa, Southern. Boycotts. Racism. United Mine Workers. USA. 1960's-74. *3422*
Labor (review article). Gold Mines and Mining. Race Relations. South Africa. Zimbabwe. 1900-69. *3403*
—. Mines. Onselen, Charles van. Zimbabwe. 1900-33. *4175*
—. Mining. Racism. South Africa. Zimbabwe. 1900-1933. *3408*
Labor service. Chewa. Colonial Government (resistance to). Malawi. World War I. 1914-19. *707*
Labor supply. Colonization. Land. Natal Land and Colonization Company. South Africa. 1838-1948. *3791*
—. Discrimination, economic. Land Tenure (alienation). South Africa. Zimbabwe. 1920-70. *3387*
Labor training. Africans. Asians. Kenya. 1968-74. *2891*
Labor Unions and Organizations *See also* names of labor unions and organizations, e.g. Nigerian Trade Union Congress, etc.; Collective Bargaining; Strikes.
—. Africa, Southern. Colonialism. Social Change. Tradition. Zaire. ca 1900-73. *225*
—. Africa, West. Working class. 1960's. *1654*
—. Africans. Apartheid. Legislation. South Africa. 1958-79. *3798*
—. Algeria. Federation of Unions of Algerian Workers (USTA). France. 1956-59. *1101*
—. Apartheid. Miners. South Africa. Trades Union Congress. 1970-73. *3765*
—. Apartheid. South Africa. 1882-1973. *3770*
—. Apartheid. South Africa. 1890-20c. *3751*
—. Bibliographies. 20c. *18*
—. Bloemfontein Conference. Kadalie, Clements. Msimang, H. Selby. South Africa. 1919-25. *3800*
—. Business. Collective bargaining. Race Relations. South Africa. USA. 1970-81. *3752*
—. Buthelezi, Gatsha. Racial tensions. South Africa (Durban). Strikes. ca 1910-73. *3801*
—. Christian Nationalists. South Africa. 1933-48. *3780*
—. Colonial Government. France. Popular Front. Senegal. 1919-38. *2302*
—. Colonialism. Ghana. 1900-48. *1729*
—. Communism. Nigeria. Nigerian Trade Union Congress. Socialist Workers and Farmers Party. 1960's-70's. *2082*
—. Democratic Party. France. Guinea. Independence Movements. 1940's-56. *1867*
—. Destour Party. Nationalism. Tunisia. 1920-56. *1533*
—. Economic development. Kenya. Legislation. Strikes. 1960's-73. *2899*
—. Ethiopia (Addis Ababa). Ethnic Groups. Standard of Living. 1970's. *2714*
—. France. French West Africa. General Confederation of Labor (CGT). 1945-57. *1627*
—. France. French West Africa. General Confederation of Labor (CGT). 1945-57. *1695*
—. France. Railroad workers. Tunisia. 1923-38. *1555*
—. Ghana. Strikes. 1940's-70's. *1740*
—. Government control. Kenya. Political Systems (single party). Tanzania. 1961-66. *2651*
—. Kenya. 1960's-70's. *2880*
—. Kenya. Nigeria. Politics. 1939-66. *210*
—. Namibia. South Africa. 1920-74. *3355*
—. Nationalism. Political Participation. Working conditions. Zimbabwe. 20c. *4155*
—. Nigeria. Politics. 1945-65. *2119*
—. Race Relations. South Africa. Strikes. 1973. *3797*
—. Tanzania. 1930-79. *3056*
Labor Unions and Organizations (black). Labor. South Africa. 1918-73. *3729*
Labor Unions and Organizations (review article). 1890's-1970's. *635*
—. Bates, Robert H. Burawoy, Michael. Copper Mines and Mining. Government. Zambia. 1949-70. *4071*
Labour Party. Foreign Relations. Great Britain. South Africa. 1947-51. *3904*
Lactose malabsorption. Dairying. 3000BC-1978. *882*
LaGuma, Alex. Novels. Revolution. South Africa. 1956-72. *3952*
Lake, Anthony. Foreign policy (review article). USA. Zimbabwe. 1969-70's. *4280*
Lake Kivu. Colonial Government. Local government. Zaire (Ijwi Island). 1900-70. *2503*
Lake Tana. Dams. Ethiopia. Great Britain. Negotiations. 1922-35. *2704*
Lake Victoria. Africa, East. Developing nations. Fisheries. Norway. UN Development Program. 1965-75. *628*
—. Africa, East. Great Britain. *Sybil* (vessel). World War I. 1915-16. *720*
Lamizana, Sangoule. Droughts. Upper Volta. 1970-74. *2386*
Lampson, Miles Wedderburn. Egypt. Farouk I. Great Britain. Wafd party. 1942. *1310*
Lancaster House Conference. Constitutions. Documents. Great Britain. Zimbabwe. 1970-79. *4291*
—. Great Powers. Peace. Zimbabwe. 1965-79. *4247*
Land *See also* Agriculture; Land Tenure; Reclamation of Land.
—. Capitalism. Colonization. Kenya. ca 1880's-1920's. *2901*
—. Chilembwe, John. Independence movements. Malawi. Political traditions. 1915-63. *3612*
—. Colonization. Labor supply. Natal Land and Colonization Company. South Africa. 1838-1948. *3791*
—. Europeans. Independence. Kenya. Political Factions. 1960-63. *2968*
Land allocation. Descent groups. South Africa. Zulu (Nyuswa). ca 1825-1970. *4005*
Land, common. Law. -1970. *904*
Land management. Agriculture. Cattle raising. Forestation. Morocco (High Atlas mountains). 1965-72. *1453*
Land Ownership. Capital Accumulation. Social Organization. Togo. 1885-1979. *2382*
—. Exploitation. Uganda. 1900-39. *3224*
—. Kenya. Limitation of Action Act. Luo. 1968-70's. *2902*
Land policy. British South Africa Company. Colonial government. Swaziland. Zimbabwe. ca 1900-68. *4037*
—. Capital accumulation. Colonialism. Income distribution. Zimbabwe. 1946-69. *4161*
—. Colonial Government. Ecology. Zambia, Eastern. 1895-1940. *4129*
—. Colonial government. Ghana (Northern Territories). 1900-57. *1726*
—. Colonial Government. Malawi. Peasants. ca 1900-73. *3618*
Land reform. Abdel-Fadil, Mahmoud. Agricultural Policy (review article). Egypt. 1952-70. *1136*
—. Africa, West. Constitutionalism. Entente Council. 1958-76. *1646*
—. Agrarian Revolution Charter and Decree (1971). Algeria. Social Classes (conflict). 1971-73. *1038*
—. Algeria. 1954-78. *1104*
—. Algeria. 1971-81. *982*
—. Algeria. Cultural revolution. Industrialization. Quadrennial plan, 2d. 1970-74. *986*
—. Algeria. Decentralization. 1962-74. *1098*
—. Algeria. Elites. Peasants. 1954-74. *1043*
—. Algeria. Legislation. Political Change. 1962-78. *1081*
—. Algeria (Chénoua). Colonialism. Resettlement. 1840-1967. *1051*
—. Benin. Rural development. 1961-79. *1709*
—. Colonial policy. Independence. Kenya. ca 1950-62. *2893*
—. Decolonization. Kenya. Mau Mau. Nationalism. 1952-60. *2937*
—. Development strategy. Senegal. 1964-79. *2317*
—. Diola. Property rights. Senegal. 1918-78. *2315*
—. Diola. Senegal. Social Change. ca 1885-1978. *2335*
—. Economic Development. Egypt. Iran. 1952-78. *1160*
—. Egypt. Reclamation of land. 1952-78. *1173*
—. Ethiopia. 1974-77. *2707*
—. Ethiopia. Revolution. 1974-76. *2694*
—. Ethiopia (Darassa). Peasants. 1970-75. *2776*
—. Kenya, central. Mbeere. Social organization. 1959-71. *2865*
—. Maghreb. -1975. *973*
—. Mali. Rural development. 1972-79. *1965*
—. Tanzania. 1950's-70's. *3111*
Land Tenure *See also* Peasants.
—. Africa, East (Lakes region). Hierarchies. Monarchy. ca 800-ca 1960. *2575*
—. African Farmers Union. Africans. Politics. Zimbabwe. 1890-1972. *4179*
—. Agricultural development. Cotton production. Kunda. Zambia. 1960's-70's. *4095*
—. Agricultural Development. Nigeria. 1966-73. *2009*
—. Agricultural development. Tunisia (Le Kef). 1940-77. *1536*
—. Agricultural development policies. Guerrilla Warfare. Zimbabwe. 1962-78. *4156*
—. Agricultural policy. Botswana. 1975-77. *3499*
—. Agricultural productivity. Kenya (Trans-Nzoia). 1960's-70's. *2882*
—. Agriculture. Algeria. Collective farming. Self-management. 1954-72. *1057*
—. Agriculture, commercial. Law, traditional. 20c. *783*
—. Anufo. Law, customary. Legislation. Ngam Ngam. Togo, North. 1960-79. *2381*
—. Apartheid. South Africa (Natal, Transvaal). Whites. 1860-1960. *3733*
—. Bibliographies. Ethiopia. Peasants. Social Classes. 20c. *2696*
—. Chiefs. Uganda (Busoga). 1895-1936. *3279*
—. Coffee. Economic Policy. Ethiopia (southern). Foreign Relations. 1895-1935. *2705*
—. Colonial government. Rural development. Uganda. 1900-66. *3252*
—. Colonial Government. Zaire. 1930-60. *2484*
—. Colonial policy. Legislation. Native Land Husbandry Act. Zimbabwe. 1951-80. *4163*
—. Colonialism. Labor. Malawi, southern. Rebellions. 15c-20c. *3603*
—. Colonization. Kenya. Luo. Social organization. Women. 20c. *2903*
—. Conflict and Conflict Resolution. Tanzania (Ngorongoro Crater). Wildlife Conservation. 1948-74. *3166*
—. Demography. Togo. 1885-1979. *2377*
—. Development. Dunn Reserve. Segregation. South Africa (Natal). 1895-1948. *3953*
—. Ethiopia. Rural development. Social change. 1970's. *2706*
—. Europeans. Kenya Land Commission. Kikuyu. Settlers. 1902-34. *2869*
—. Exports. Kenya. Social Classes. 1950-79. *2863*
—. Kenya. Reform. 1953-79. *2867*
—. Law. National Development. Senegal. 1960-76. *2296*
—. Legislation. Race. Zimbabwe. 1894-1965. *4170*
—. Malawi, southern. Social Classes. 1890-1980. *3604*
—. Nigeria. 1950-75. *2030*
—. Noncapitalist Development. Peasants. 1940-50. *680*
—. Political conflict. Uganda (Ankole). ca 1960's-. *3231*
—. Politics. Rwanda. Social Classes. 1850-1950. *3017*
—. Zimbabwe. 1970-79. *4181*
Land Tenure (alienation). Discrimination, economic. Labor Supply. South Africa. Zimbabwe. 1920-70. *3387*
Land tenure policy. Agricultural development. Tanzania (Ismani). 1960's-70's. *3071*
—. Egypt. Nasser, Gamal Abdel. Patrimonialism. Political leadership. Sadat, Anwar. 1954-79. *1300*
Land use. Africa, West. Droughts. Sahel. 1968-74. *607*
—. Algeria. 19c-20c. *980*
—. Civil war. Decisionmaking. Nigeria, eastern. Yams. 1964-77. *2080*
—. Cotton. Egypt. Prices. 1944-66. *1175*
—. Erosion. Kenya (Machakos hills). Population. 20c. *2898*
Land Use Decree. Nigeria. 1978. *2077*
Landholding. Business. Kenya (Nairobi). Women. ca 1900-50. *2866*
Landlocked nations. Lesotho. Treaties. 1833-1974. *3543*
Landowners. Agricultural revolution. Algeria. 1962-76. *990*
Landownership. Apartheid. Law. South Africa. 1932-71. *3796*
Lango. Agriculture. Cotton. Uganda. 1909-31. *3310*
—. Chiefs. Colonial Government. Uganda, northern. 1895-1955. *3309*
Language *See also* Linguistics; Literature.
—. Africa, East. Military life. Swahili. 1905-71. *2613*
—. Afrikaans. Social control. South Africa. 1875-1976. *3970*

—. Algeria (Ahaggar). Kinship terms. Tuareg. 1968-74. *1005*
—. Cameroon. Colonial policy. Schools. 1960-74. *2405*
—. Development. Swahili. Tanzania. 1960's-74. *3096*
—. Elites. Krio. Sierra Leone. 1853-1978. *2368*
—. English. Nationalism. 1710-1975. *245*
—. Kenya. Lonrho. Nation Newspapers Ltd. Newspapers. 1972. *3004*
—. Politics. -1973. *239*
Language function. Nigeria. 1972. *2205*
Language manipulation. Colonial Government. English. Labor. Tanzania. 1919-40. *3154*
Language policy. Algeria. Morocco. Tunisia. 1960-80. *962*
—. Amharic. Ethiopia. 1973-74. *2828*
—. Colonial Government. Nigeria. Yoruba. 1882-1955. *2218*
—. Colonial policy. Zaire. 1880-20c. *2563*
—. Educational development. Kenya. Tanzania. 1963-74. *2626*
—. Ethiopia. 1974-80. *2833*
—. French. Ivory Coast. 1960-77. *1933*
—. Nigeria. Yoruba. 1882-1952. *2221*
Languages, European. Nigeria. Schools. 1859-1959. *2280*
Languages, national. Linguistics. Swahili. Tanzania. 1900-75. *3203*
Larkin, Bruce. China. Foreign Policy (review article). Legvold, Robert. USSR. 1949-70. *494*
Latin America. Foreign Relations. 1974-78. *499*
Laval, Pierre. Ethiopia. France. Italy. Treaties. 1935. *2791*
Law *See also* Constitutional Law; Courts; Criminal Law; Election Laws; International Law; Judges; Judicial Administration; Lawyers; Legislation; Police.
—. Apartheid. Landownership. South Africa. 1932-71. *3796*
—. Apartheid. South Africa. 1910-71. *3917*
—. Censorship. Colonial government. Ghana. Press. 1880-1950. *1838*
—. Colonialism. Great Britain. National Development. 1960's-80. *667*
—. Elias, T. O. (review article). Nigeria. Social change. 1960-73. *2209*
—. Freedom of speech. South Africa. 1964. *3820*
—. Land, common. -1970. *904*
—. Land Tenure. National Development. Senegal. 1960-76. *2296*
—. Malawi. National Development. 1977. *3594*
—. Racism. Zimbabwe. 1920-79. *4265*
Law and order. Colonial Government. Famine. Niger. 1931. *1983*
Law, customary. Africa, West. Aliens. Colonial Government. Great Britain. Minorities. 19c-20c. *1638*
—. Anufo. Land Tenure. Legislation. Ngam Ngam. Togo, North. 1960-79. *2381*
—. Crime and Criminals. Shona. Statistics. Zimbabwe. 1936-71. *4313*
—. Rural development. Senegal. 1931-79. *2324*
Law, French. Reform. ca 1950-75. *838*
Law Reform. Criminal law. 1956-72. *911*
—. Independence movements. Madagascar. Popular Front. 1929-37. *3566*
Law, rule of. Ethiopia. Government officials. Political change. 1973. *2767*
Law, traditional. Agriculture, commercial. Land Tenure. 20c. *783*
—. Colonial Government. Court of Appeal (Special Approvals Tribunal). French West Africa. 1903-20. *1680*
Laws, Robert. Malawi. University of Livingstonia. 1920's. *3609*
Lawyers *See also* Judges.
—. Kenya. Professionalism. 1906-75. *3000*
Leadership *See also* Political Leadership.
—. Africa, West. Ideology. Independence Movements. Nkrumah, Kwame *(Consciencism)*. 1964-72. *1805*
—. Attitudes. Intellectuals. Islam. Maghreb. 1945-80. *969*
—. Churches, independent. Cooperation. South Africa (Soweto). 1960's-70's. *4028*
—. Churches, independent. Shona. Sundkler, B. G. M. Zimbabwe. 1945-70's. *4299*
—. Nigeria. Secondary Education. Women. 1977-82. *2238*
—. Pan-Africanism. 1924-63. *65*
—. Rhodes-Livingstone Institute. Zambia. 1933-76. *4122*
League of Nations. Atangana, Karl. Beti. Cameroon (Yaoundé). Mandates. World War I. 1914-22. *714*
—. Balance of Power. Ethiopia. Italy. War. 1935-37. *2771*
—. Ethiopia. Foreign relations. Italy. Sanctions. War. 1922-36. *2784*
—. Ethiopia. Great Britain. Intervention. Italy. 1925-36. *2722*
—. Ethiopia. Italy. Sanctions. War. 1935-36. *2720*
League of Nations (admission). Ethiopia. Great Powers. Imperialism. ca 1889-1923. *2760*
Lebanon. Ideology. Reformism. Tunisia. 1970's. *1541*
Lebaudy, Jacques. South Africa. Western Sahara. 1886-1919. *1591*
Leca, Jean. Algeria. Colonna, F. Politics (review article). Social Classes. Teachers. Vatin, J.-C. 1883-1975. *1094*
—. Algeria. Etienne, B. Politics (review article). Vatin, J.-C. 1830-1978. *1069*
Lefela, Josie. Independence movements. Lesotho. Matitta, Walter. ca 1902-65. *3538*
Lefever, Ernest W. Cultural Imperialism (review article). Great Britain. Nigeria. ca 1700-1966. *213*
LeFleur, A. A. S. Coloureds. Economic Conditions. Ethnic Groups. Griqua trek. South Africa. 1867-1920. *3968*
Left. Egypt. Politics. 1956-78. *1192*
—. Ethiopia. Me'ei Sone. Nihilism. People's Revolutionary Party. 1970-79. *2822*
Leftism *See also* Communism; Radicals and Radicalism; Socialism.
—. Egypt. Historiography. Sa'īd, Rif'at as-. 1940-50. *1195*
—. Madagascar. Movement for Proletarian Power (MFM). Political Parties. 1972. *3553*
Legal changes. Sukuma. Tanzania. 1960's-70's. *3163*
Legal systems. Arusha Declaration. Politics. Socialism. Tanzania. 1967-73. *3147*
—. Botswana. 1885-1966. *3485*
—. Chilobwe murders trial. Crime and Criminals. Malawi. 1968-71. *3593*
—. Ghana. Imperialism. 1890-1970. *1798*
Legislation *See also* Law.
—. Africans. Apartheid. Labor Unions and Organizations. South Africa. 1958-79. *3798*
—. Agricultural Policy. Egypt. Water. 19c-1980. *1143*
—. Algeria. Land reform. Political Change. 1962-78. *1081*
—. Anufo. Land Tenure. Law, customary. Ngam Ngam. Togo, North. 1960-79. *2381*
—. Colonial Government. Forests. Great Britain. Nigeria. Rubber. 1897-1940. *2025*
—. Colonial policy. Land Tenure. Native Land Husbandry Act. Zimbabwe. 1951-80. *4163*
—. Defense Policy. Military Service (geographical limits). South Africa. 1912-76. *3858*
—. Economic development. Kenya. Labor Unions and Organizations. Strikes. 1960's-73. *2899*
—. Economic integration. Egypt. Foreign Investments. Middle East. 1974-81. *1145*
—. Egypt. Fundamentalism. Islam. 1970-80. *1181*
—. Industrial Relations. South Africa. Wiehahn Commission. 1970's. *3774*
—. Land Tenure. Race. Zimbabwe. 1894-1965. *4170*
Legislative behavior. National representation. Parliaments. Tanzania. 1965-73. *3173*
Legislative Council. Colonial government. Kenya. Mathu, Eliud. 1919-57. *2929*
Legislators. Kenya. Political recruitment. 1957-68. *2951*
Legvold, Robert. China. Foreign Policy (review article). Larkin, Bruce. USSR. 1949-70. *494*
Leisure. Benin. Developing Nations. -1973. *1706*
Lekhotla La Bafo (Council of Commoners). Basutoland Progressive Association. Lesotho. Nationalist organizations. 20c. *3546*
Lelemama dance associations. Kenya (Mombasa). Muslim Women's Cultural Association. Muslim Women's Institute. Women. 1930's-70's. *3005*
Lend-Lease. Africa, North. Africa, West. Consumer goods. France. Trade, private. World War II. 1941-46. *735*
Lenin, V. I. Colonialism. Independence. Revolution. Socialism. 1907-80. *21*
—. South Africa. 19c-1924. *3830*
Lenshina, Alice. Bemba. Lumpa rising. Rebellions. Sects, Religious. Zambia. 1953-68. *4045*
—. Lumpa Church. Politics. Sects, Religious. United National Independence Party. Zambia. 1954-65. *4051*
Leroux, Etienne *(Sewe Dae by die Silbersteins)*. Afrikaners. Liberalism. South Africa. Values. ca 1948-82. *4013*
Leselinyana La Lesotho (newspaper). Historical sources. Lesotho. 1863-1977. *3541*
Lesotho *See also* Africa, Southern.
—. Agricultural development. Swaziland. Trade. 20c. *3415*
—. Agricultural production. Employment, off-farm. Swaziland. Taiwan. 1960-72. *3385*
—. Basutoland Progressive Association. *Lekhotla La Bafo* (Council of Commoners). Nationalist organizations. 20c. *3546*
—. Botswana. Jonathan, Leabua. Khama, Seretse. Political Leadership. 1966-73. *3366*
—. Botswana. Labor markets. South Africa. Swaziland. 1967-76. *3343*
—. Botswana. Monetary systems. Rand Monetary Area. South Africa. Swaziland. 1909-78. *3347*
—. Christianity. 1884-1978. *3537*
—. Customary law. Research. 1969-75. *875*
—. Economic planning. Public Administration. 1960's-70's. *3539*
—. Elections. 1970. *3542*
—. Foreign investments. Multinational corporations. 1966-74. *3547*
—. Foreign Policy. South Africa. 1965-75. *3540*
—. Historical sources. *Leselinyana La Lesotho* (newspaper). 1863-1977. *3541*
—. Human rights. 1966-70's. *3545*
—. Independence. South Africa. 1966-76. *3544*
—. Independence movements. Lefela, Josie. Matitta, Walter. ca 1902-65. *3538*
—. Landlocked nations. Treaties. 1833-1974. *3543*
Letters. Morocco. Zionism. 1919-26. *1411*
Letters to the editor. *African Daily News* (periodical). *African Weekly* (periodical). *Bantu Mirror* (periodical). Race Relations. Zimbabwe. 1930-70. *4310*
Levine, Donald (review article). Ethiopia. 3000 BC-1970. *2682*
Lewis, D. G. "Tommy". Air Warfare. Richthofen, Manfred von. World War I. Zimbabwe. 1918. *696*
Lewis, George Edward (diary). Africa, East. Military Campaigns. South African Field Artillery (4th Battery). World War I. 1916. *699*
Lewis, W. A. Economic development. Education. Egypt. Labor. Models. 1952-67. *1174*
Leys, Norman. Colonial Office. Kenya. Ross, W. McGregor. Senate (European). 1900-40. *2971*
Liberalism. Action Group. Political Factions. Zimbabwe (Bulawayo). 1940-72. *4216*
—. Afrikaners. Leroux, Etienne *(Sewe Dae by die Silbersteins)*. South Africa. Values. ca 1948-82. *4013*
—. Amin, Ahmad. Egypt. Public opinion. 1939-54. *1293*
—. Apartheid. Economic growth. South Africa. 1948-74. *3727*
—. Ethnicity. Political development. South Africa. 1921-48. *3914*
—. Great Britain. Imperialism. Zimbabwe. 19c-20c. *4236*
—. Malan, F. S. Race Relations. South Africa. 1890-1924. *3870*
—. Race Relations. Social Change. South African Council of Churches. 1970's-. *3853*
Liberation. Organization of African Unity. South Africa. 1963-76. *3984*
Liberation movements. Angola. Civil war. Press coverage. South Africa. USA. 1975-76. *3413*
Liberation (review article). Race Relations. USA. Winston, Henry. 1974. *220*
Liberia *See also* Africa, West.
—. Africa, West. France. Political Integration. 1960-79. *1676*
—. Anticolonialism. Colonies. Foreign policy. Italy. UN. 1948-51. *1944*
—. Autobiography and Memoirs. Avriel, Ehud. Diplomacy. Ghana. Israel. 1957-73. *393*
—. Blacks. Citizenship, dual. USA. 1848-1973. *1957*
—. Cocoa cultivation. Economic relations. Fernando Póo. Migrant labor. 1860-1930. *580*
—. Coups d'etat. 1980. *1952*
—. Coups d'etat. Developing nations. Foreign Relations. Shipping (open registry). 1980-81. *1939*
—. Coups d'etat. Ethnic Groups. Political instability. 1963-80. *1954*

—. Coups d'etat. Military. Political economy. 1964-80. *1937*
—. Culture. Social integration. 19c-20c. *1943*
—. Development. Military Strategy. USA. World War II. 1938-45. *725*
—. Economic development. 1944-71. *1938*
—. Economic Development. Models. Tanzania. 1960-72. *588*
—. Education. National development. Values. Westernization. 19c-20c. *244*
—. Elites. Political systems. Tolbert, William R. Tubman, William V. S. 1944-75. *1951*
—. Ethnography. Johnson, S. Jangaba M. National unification. 1895-1973. *1942*
—. Family Organization. Government Enterprise. Industrial innovation. Markets. Women. 1950-70. *1947*
—. Firestone, Harvey S. Great Britain. Imperialism, economic. O'Meara, Francis. Rubber industry. USA. 1922-27. *1940*
—. Foreign investments. Rubber industry. 1966-71. *1945*
—. Higher education. Policy development. Politics. Social organization. 1940's-60's. *1953*
—. Islam. Sierra Leone. Social organizations. Vai. 1926-59. *1946*
—. Kru. Political Opposition. Twe, Didwo. 1930's-60. *1955*
—. Linguistics. Settlement. Sierra Leone. 15c-1961. *1609*
—. Navies. 1892-1970. *1956*
Liberia, Eastern. Ethnic identity. Ivory Coast. ca 1900-75. *1641*
Liberia (interior). Economic Structure. Trade. 1600-1940. *1950*
Liberia (Kru Coast). Government, Resistance to. Reform. 1822-1935. *1941*
Liberia (Monrovia). Business History. Friendship. Kinship. Merchants. 1970. *1949*
—. Economic development. Markets. 1940's-70's. *1948*
Libinza. Fishing. Trade. Zaire, upper. 19c-1973. *2474*
Libraries *See also* names of individual libraries; Archives.
—. Apartheid. South Africa. 1950's-78. *4009*
—. Australia. New Zealand. Office of War Information. South Africa. USA. World War II. 1942. *765*
—. Bibliographies (national). Nigeria. 1953-80. *1990*
—. Botswana. National Library Service. 1968-77. *3521*
—. Colonialism. Development. Nigeria. 1900-60. *2240*
—. France. 1803-1975. *842*
—. Literacy. 19c-20c. *777*
—. Morocco. National Library (Africa section). Spain (Madrid). Prehistory-1973. *935*
—. Nigeria. 1840's-1975. *2211*
—. Nigeria. 1948-75. *2226*
—. Nigeria. 1960-78. *2295*
—. Oral tradition. 1955-79. *827*
—. Zimbabwe. 1965-79. *4141*
Libraries, development of. Africa, East. Regional government. 1945-65. *2611*
Libraries, research. Bibliography. Ghana. Nigeria. Sierra Leone. 20c. *1600*
Library associations. Kenya. 1895-1977. *2998*
Library education. Developing nations. Morocco. 1912-73. *1416*
Libya *See also* Africa, North.
—. Africa, North. Egypt. Rommel, Erwin. World War II. 1941-42. *754*
—. Agricultural development. Oil income. 1953-74. *1365*
—. Agricultural land. Decolonization. Italians. Italo-Libyan Accord (1956). 1940-64. *1377*
—. Arab unity. Foreign Relations. Islam. Qadhafi, Muammar. 1969-73. *1387*
—. Arab unity. Islam. Qadhafi, Muammar. 1971-75. *1371*
—. Arbitration, international. International law. Nationalization. Oil Industry and Trade. USA. 1971-80. *1404*
—. Bibliographies. 1866-1973. *1401*
—. Bibliographies. Qadhafi, Muammar. USSR. 1910-69. 1960-79. *1381*
—. Boundaries (disputes). Military Aid. Sudan (Darfur). USA. 1870-1981. *929*
—. Chad. Civil War. Foreign Relations. 1970's-80's. *2436*
—. Chad. Military. 1980-81. *2434*
—. Colonial Government. 1835-1969. *1376*
—. Colonial policy. Guerrilla warfare. Italy. Mukhtar, Omar al-. 1929-31. *1389*
—. Colonization, attempted. Italy. Resistance. 1907-32. *1375*
—. Conflict and Conflict Resolution. Egypt. Foreign Relations. Qadhafi, Muammar. Sadat, Anwar. 1950-77. *965*
—. Consular Reports. Germany. Jews. Walter, Gebhard. World War II. 1940-43. *722*
—. Coups d'etat. Free Officers Organization. Qadhafi, Muammar. 1951-69. *1403*
—. Democracy. *Jamahiriya* (concept). Political theory. Qadhafi, Muammar *(Green Book)*. Rousseau, Jean Jacques *(Social Contract)*. 1967-79. *1380*
—. Diplomacy. Independence. Rossi, Gianluigi *(L'Africa Italiana verso l'Indipendenza, 1941-1949)*. 1949. *1361*
—. Domestic Policy. Foreign Policy. Qadhafi, Muammar. 1969-81. *1398*
—. *Dors* (military units). Guerrilla Warfare. Italy. Military Organization. 1911-32. *1368*
—. Droughts. Kufra Scheme. Sheep raising. Water. 1968-73. *1366*
—. Economic Development. Foreign Policy. 1969-76. *1378*
—. Economic development. Modernization. Political Systems. 1959-74. *1372*
—. Economic policy. Italy. 1920-40. *1388*
—. Economic relations. India. 1970's. *1402*
—. Economic Theory. Ideology. Islam. Qadhafi, Muammar *(Green Book)*. 1976-79. *1385*
—. Eden, Anthony (Cyrenaica statement). Foreign Policy. Great Britain. Independence. 1940's. *1396*
—. Egypt. Foreign Relations. 1969-73. *964*
—. Egypt. Foreign Relations. Israel. Political Leadership. Qadhafi, Muammar. 1942-82. *1369*
—. Foreign policy. Qadhafi, Muammar. 1969-80. *1362*
—. Foreign policy. USA. 1908-82. *1367*
—. Foreign Relations. Ideology. Qadhafi, Muammar. 1969-74. *1382*
—. France. Political change. Qadhafi, Muammar. 1969-73. *1399*
—. Great Britain. Italy. Navies. Shipping. World War II. 1940-43. *752*
—. Gulf of Sidra incident. International law. Territorial Waters. USA. 1981-83. *1386*
—. Italy. Nationalism. Qadhafi, Muammar. 1911-78. *1392*
—. Nationalism. Ottoman Empire. Secret Service. *Tashkilati Makhsusa*. 1911-18. *1364*
—. Political change. Qadhafi, Muammar. 1969-79. *1394*
—. Political Conditions. 1969-74. *1400*
—. Political leadership. Qadhafi, Muammar. 1969-76. *1393*
—. Political philosophy. Qadhafi, Muammar. 1973. *1395*
—. Political Systems. Revolution. 1969-80. *1363*
—. Qadhafi, Muammar. 1951-73. *1370*
—. Tobruk (battles). World War II. 1939-43. *763*
Libya (Al-Kufrah). Air Forces. Bomber Reserve Group 1 ("Topic" squadron). World War II. 1941. *729*
Libya (Augila Oasis). Agricultural Production. Economic Development. Oil industry and Trade. Social organization. Tradition. 1969-70. *1383*
—. Qadhafi, Muammar. Revolution. Social Conditions. 1968-80. *1384*
Libya (Cyrenaica). Amendola, Giovanni. Colonial policy. Italy. 1920-25. *1373*
—. Badoglio, Pietro. Documents. Graziani, Rodolfo. Italy. Mukhtar, Omar el-. Resistance. 1930-31. *1391*
—. Colonialism. Historiography. Massacres. 1930-31. *1390*
—. Documents. Great Britain. Italy. Popular Culture, Ministry of. Propaganda. World War II. 1941. *733*
—. Guerrilla Warfare. Italy. Mukhtar, Omar al-. Sanusi. 1923-32. *1397*
Libya (Tripoli). Amendola, Giovanni. Colonial policy. Italy. 1922. *1374*
Libya (Tripolitania). Anti-Semitism. Riots. 1945. *1379*
—. Central State Archive. Documents. Ethiopia (Eritrea). Italy. Somalia. 19c-20c. *958*
Limann, Hilla. Ghana. Government. Politics and the Military. 1979-81. *1812*
Limitation of Action Act. Kenya. Land ownership. Luo. 1968-70's. *2902*
Linguistics *See also* Language.
—. Africa, West. Hausa. Literacy campaign. UNESCO. 1960's-70's. *1692*
—. Freshwater, Will (papers). London Missionary School. Missions and Missionaries. Zambia. 1872-1959. *4068*
—. Igbo. Names, personal. Nigeria. -1973. *2253*
—. Languages, national. Swahili. Tanzania. 1900-75. *3203*
—. Liberia. Settlement. Sierra Leone. 15c-1961. *1609*
—. Literature. Maghreb. Yacine, Kateb. 1980. *936*
Lipton, Merle (review article). Apartheid. Constructive engagement. South Africa. 1977. *3769*
Literacy. Libraries. 19c-20c. *777*
Literacy campaign. Africa, West. Hausa. Linguistics. UNESCO. 1960's-70's. *1692*
Literary Criticism. Authors. 20c. *801*
—. Authors. Tutuola, Amos. 1950-76. *865*
—. Egypt. Haqqī, Yahyā. Nationalism. 1920-59. *1323*
—. Egypt. Mandūr, Muhammad. 1930-65. *1346*
Literary Symbolism. *See* Symbolism in Literature.
Literature *See also* Authors; Autobiography and Memoirs; Biography; Books; Drama; Fiction; Journalism; Language; Novels; Poetry.
—. 1939-74. *867*
—. Africa, East. Authors. English. 1966-73. *2620*
—. Africa, East. P'Biket, Okot. 1964-78. *2567*
—. Africa, East. Swahili. 1950's-60's. *2581*
—. Africans. Colonial Government. Europeans. 1880-1980. *850*
—. Algeria. Arabs. Popular culture. Stereotypes. 1891-1920. *1091*
—. Angola. Independence Movements. Vieira, Luandino. 1960-73. *3467*
—. Arabic. Bibliographies. Tunisia. 1956-74. *1542*
—. Art. Benin. Europe. 1897-20c. *862*
—. Authors. France. Harlem Renaissance. Negritude. USA. 1921-39. *852*
—. Bibliographies. USA. ca 1800-1975. *866*
—. Chad. Maran, René. Negritude. ca 1920-40. *808*
—. Colonialism. Social problems. ca 1900-75. *807*
—. Cultural relations. Europe, Western. Hausa. Islam. Social Attitudes. 1945-78. *2285*
—. Culture. 20c. *839*
—. Culture, European. Missions and Missionaries. Nigeria (Lagos). 1515-1930's. *2219*
—. Culture (tradition). 1973. *784*
—. Diop, Alioune. *Présence Africaine* (periodical). Senegal. 1940-80. *2328*
—. Egypt. 1967-80. *1315*
—. Egypt. France. Husayn, Tāhā. 1889-1973. *1338*
—. Egypt. National Self-image. 1920-75. *1358*
—. Ethiopianism. Pan-Africanism. USA. ca 1770-1930. *140*
—. Ewe. Fiction. Ghana. Togo. 20c. *1603*
—. Exiles. 1950-82. *851*
—. Fagunwa, D. O. Nigeria. Soyinka, Wole. Tradition. Tutuola, Amos. Yoruba. 1945-70's. *2252*
—. Greene, Graham *(Journey without Maps)*. 20c. *864*
—. Historiography. 1976-80. *912*
—. Humanism, Western. 1870's-1974. *868*
—. Ismaa'il, Ibrahim (autobiography). Somalia. 1896-1928. *3035*
—. Kenya. Luo. 20c. *847*
—. Kenya. National Development. 1950-72. *2974*
—. Linguistics. Maghreb. Yacine, Kateb. 1980. *936*
—. Negritude. 1600's-1970's. *890*
—. Nigeria. Political Theory. Soyinka, Wole. 1960-81. *2134*
—. Nigeria. Publishers and Publishing. 1950-80. *2256*
—. Oral tradition. ca 1960-75. *824*
—. Paton, Alan *(Cry the Beloved Country)*. South Africa. 1948-75. *3988*
—. Social Conditions. Tunisia. ca 1900-. *1560*
—. Sudan. 1600-1982. *1471*
Literature, African. Canada. Cultural Imperialism. 1973. *831*
—. Poets. South Africa. 1973. *3976*
Literature and politics. Colonialism. Negritude. Senghor, Leopold. 1906-69. *823*
Literature (English-language). Bibliographies. ca 1950-75. *832*
—. Politics. South Africa. ca 1900-75. *3975*
Literature, popular. Africa, East. English. 1960's-70's. *2604*
—. Elites. Nigeria. 1925-74. *2259*

Literature (review article). Africa, East. Swahili. 1600-1950. *2564*
Literature (themes). 1940-75. *907*
Livestock *See also* Cattle Raising; Dairying; Sheep Raising.
—. Diseases. Sudan (Darfur). 1898-1956. *1525*
—. Population. Sudan (Darfur). 400-1975. *1526*
Livestock production. Algeria. Cooperatives, Grazing. Rural Development. 1971-74. *1061*
Livingstone, David. Economic Development. Malawi. Missions and Missionaries. 1874-1972. *3608*
Lloyd, George Ambrose. Egypt. Great Britain. Modernization. National Development. 1919-33. *1249*
Loans *See also* Investments.
—. Agriculture. Tanzania. Zambia. 1973-76. *609*
Lobbying *See also* Interest Groups; Political Factions.
—. Great Britain. Newspapers. Propaganda. South Africa. USA. 1972-79. *3863*
Lobi. Colonization. French West Africa. Resistance. 1898-1926. *1630*
Local Government *See also* Local Politics; Public Administration.
—. Administrative reform. Decisionmaking. Zaire. 1973. *2496*
—. Asante. Ghana. Modernization. Political Development. 1881-1981. *1817*
—. Autonomy. Botswana. District councils. 1960-79. *3515*
—. Bemba. Catholic Church. Missions and Missionaries. Zambia. 1890-1935. *4070*
—. Botswana. Decisionmaking. Rural development. 1969-72. *3532*
—. Botswana. District Administration. 1965-74. *3516*
—. Botswana (Kweneng). Chiefs. District councils. 1960's-70's. *3533*
—. Boundaries. Colonial Government. Ghana (Asante). 1896-1951. *1772*
—. Bureaucracies. Decentralization. Tanzania. 1972. *3134*
—. Colonial Government. Ganda. Kiga. Ssbalijja. Uganda (Kigezi). 1908-30. *3311*
—. Colonial Government. Ghana, northern. Native states. 20c. *1773*
—. Colonial Government. Lake Kivu. Zaire (Ijwi Island). 1900-70. *2503*
—. Diaries. Public Administration. Zimbabwe (Zambezi valley). 1912-13. 1977. *4284*
—. Dindikwa. Vagarwe. Zimbabwe (Melsetter District). 1947-73. *4252*
—. Economic Development. Political Participation. Zambia. 1967-79. *4053*
—. Elites. Sierra Leone. Violence, rural. ca 1945-76. *2365*
—. Ethiopia (Begemdir; Däbrä Tabor). Trade. 1798-1936. *2688*
—. Ethiopia (Gubba). Hamdān Abū Shōk. Sudan. 1900-38. *2744*
—. Kenya. 1960's-70's. *2917*
—. National Development. Nigeria (Sapele). 1955-77. *2129*
—. Nigeria, southern. 1957-71. *2173*
—. Office buildings. Zimbabwe (Bulawayo). 1894-1980. *4183*
—. Political Leadership. Zambia (Uyombe). 20c. *4046*
—. Political Participation. Reform. Tanzania. 1960-78. *3159*
—. Public Administration. Tanzania. 1972-75. *3168*
Local Government (district capitals, selection of). Ghana (Northern Territories). 1897-1951. *1771*
Local Government (field administrator). Decentralization. Socialism. Tanzania. 1965-80. *3169*
Local Government (local and district councils). Self-government. ca 1960-75. *288*
Local identity. Nigeria (Rivers State, Port Harcourt). Patriotism. Tamuno, Tekena N. 1913-60's. *2272*
Local Native Councils. Education. Kenya. Politics. 1925-39. *2953*
Local Politics *See also* Local Government.
—. Colonial Government. Nigeria. Political leadership. 1904-54. *2189*
—. Colonialism. Ghana (Volta region; Have). Tradition. ca 1900-76. *1797*
—. Dependency. Elites. Tanzania (Kilimanjaro district). 1970's. *3179*
—. Education. Kenya. Luhya (southern). 1930-60. *2988*
—. Ghana (Swedru). Hopkins, Nicholas S. Mali (Kita). Owusu, Maxwell. Uganda (Gondo). Vincent, Joan. 1960's-. *247*
—. Islam. Nigeria (Kano). Pakistan (South Waziristan). Rural Areas. 20c. *2213*
Local tradition. Economic change. Independence. Kenya. Social Organization. 1940's-60's. *2906*
Locke, Alain. Art. Barnes, Albert C. Collectors. USA. 1920's. *821*
Lofchie, Michael. African studies. Coups d'etat (review article). Social Classes. Uganda. ca 1965-75. *303*
Logistics *See also* Military Strategy; Naval Strategy.
—. Africa, North. Hitler, Adolf. Military Strategy. Rommel, Erwin. World War II. 1941-42. *770*
—. Africa, North. Kufra convoy. World War II. 1940. *742*
Lomé Convention. Colonialism. Economic Integration. ca 16c-1975. *105*
—. Developing nations. Diplomacy. Economic relations. European Economic Community. 1957-76. *583*
—. Developing Nations. Economic Development. European Economic Community. 1975-77. *552*
—. Developing Nations. European Economic Community. Foreign Aid. Interdependence. 1975. *556*
—. Economic Development. European Economic Community. 1975-77. *604*
—. European Economic Community. 1957-76. *567*
—. European Economic Community. 1976-80. *581*
Lomé Conventions (review article). European Economic Community. Foreign Policy. 1975-79. *543*
London and Rhodesia Mining and Land Company. Gold Mines and Mining. Rennie Tailyour Concession. Zimbabwe. 1890-1950's. *4158*
London Missionary School. Freshwater, Will (papers). Linguistics. Missions and Missionaries. Zambia. 1872-1959. *4068*
London Missionary Society. Madagascar. Newspapers. 1866-1973. *3571*
London University. Degrees, Academic. Higher Education. Nigeria. 1887-1951. *2279*
Longshoremen. Class struggle. Migrant labor. Phungula, Zulu. South Africa (Durban). 1939-59. *3763*
Lonrho. Kenya. Language. Nation Newspapers Ltd. Newspapers. 1972. *3004*
—. Multinational Corporations. Organization of African Unity. Political involvement. 1890's-1974. *586*
Loram, Charles T. Africans. Education. South Africa. USA. 1920's-30's. *3962*
Lovanium University. Intellectuals. Political Repression. Zaire. 1971. *2561*
Lovedu. Prayer. Rites and Ceremonies (ancestor worship). South Africa. 1963. *3986*
Low, Anthony. Kabaka. Public Administration (review article). Uganda (Buganda). 1950-71. *3294*
Loyalists. Colonialism. Kenya (Murang'a). Kikuyu. Mau Mau. 1952-70. *2942*
Luba. Religion, civil. Social customs. ca 1963-76. *796*
Lugard, Frederick. Colonial government. Educational policy. Nigeria. 1900-18. *2223*
—. Colonial Government. Ethnicity. Military Recruitment. 1900-60. *347*
Luguru. Agricultural Policy. Tanzania. Tradition. Uluguru Land Usage Scheme. 1949-55. *3060*
Luhya (southern). Education. Kenya. Local Politics. 1930-60. *2988*
Lumpa Church. Lenshina, Alice. Politics. Sects, Religious. United National Independence Party. Zambia. 1954-65. *4051*
Lumpa rising. Bemba. Lenshina, Alice. Rebellions. Sects, Religious. Zambia. 1953-68. *4045*
Lumumba, Patrice. Anticolonialism. Nkrumah, Kwame. Zaire. 1958-66. *2487*
—. Independence. Tshombe, Moise. Zaire. 1958-61. *2488*
—. Independence Movements. Zaire. 1960-61. *2523*
Lumumba, Patrice (correspondence). Belgium. Sancke, Paul. Zaire. 1956-57. *2512*
Luo. Agricultural Production. Kenya. Peasant family. 1946-48. *2873*
—. Colonization. Kenya. Land tenure. Social organization. Women. 20c. *2903*
—. Economic change. Kenya. Women. 1890's-1940's. *2878*
—. Elites (pacemakers; salariat). Uganda (Gondo). 1966. *3315*
—. Gor, Jason. Kenya. Succession disputes. 1940's-70's. *2969*
—. Kenya. Land ownership. Limitation of Action Act. 1968-70's. *2902*
—. Kenya. Literature. 20c. *847*
—. Kenya (Nyanza, south). Oral History. Social Organization. Suba. Uganda (Buganda). 1500-1973. *2990*
Lusaka talks. Detente. Zimbabwe. 1974. *4281*
Luthuli, Albert. Apartheid. South Africa. Tambo, Oliver. 1652-1973. *3936*
Lyautey, Hubert. Cambon, Pierre Paul. Colonial Government. France. Morocco. Tunisia. 1869-1925. *949*
—. Colonial Government. France. Morocco. 1912-25. *1410*
—. Colonial Government. France. Morocco. Zionism. 1915-25. *1418*
—. Colonization. Educational policy. Morocco. 1920's. *1444*
—. Morocco. Rif War. 1907-25. *1445*

M

Maasai. Africa, East. Assimilation. Kalenjin. Social Organization (age groups). 1890-1980. *2578*
—. Africa, East (Rift Valley). Cultural interaction. 1850-1930. *2570*
—. Agricultural development. Kenya. Samburu. 1935-75. *2876*
—. Attitudes. Colonial Government. Kenya. Tanzania. 1890-1960. *2647*
—. Kenya. Mau Mau. 1900-56. *2947*
Mabena, Magumbo. Maribeha. Succession. Zimbabwe. 1972. *4278*
Macao. Decolonization. Goa. Portugal. São Tomé and Príncipe. Timor, East. 1975-80. *2453*
MacGaffey, Wyatt. Kimbanguism. Messianism. Zaire. 1921. *2553*
Machel, Samora. FRELIMO. Independence Movements. Mondlane, Eduardo. Mozambique. 1969-74. *3663*
Machel, Samora (biography). Mozambique. 1930-75. *3628*
Macpherson, Fergus. Detente. Kaunda, Kenneth (review article). Political leadership. Zambia. 1940's-75. *4088*
Madagascar. Archaeology. Kenya. Migration. Tanzania. 9c-19c. 20c. *2650*
—. Archer, Robert. Revolution (review article). ca 1972-74. *3576*
—. Christianity. Political Change. Social Change. 1850-1972. *3585*
—. Colonial Government (resistance to). Medicine. Plague. 1921. *3558*
—. Colonial ideology. Racial groups. 1974. *3582*
—. Colonization. Domestic politics. Mozambique. ca 1750-1976. *3340*
—. Democratic Movement for Malagasy Renaissance (MDRM). National liberation movements. Rebellions. 1945-47. *3580*
—. Documents. Nationalism, Cultural. Politics. Student movement. 1972. *3587*
—. Economic Development. Political Change. Social Change. 1960-78. *3551*
—. Independence movements. Law Reform. Popular Front. 1929-37. *3566*
—. Jaona, Monja. National Movement for the Independence of Madagascar (MONIMA). 1958-73. *3548*
—. Leftism. Movement for Proletarian Power (MFM). Political Parties. 1972. *3553*
—. London Missionary Society. Newspapers. 1866-1973. *3571*
—. May Revolution. Social reform. 1972. *3560*
—. Merina. Monarchy. Rice. 19c. *3550*
—. Muslims. 1951-77. *3557*
—. Muslims. 1977. *3556*
—. Nationalism. Press. 1945-60. *3578*
—. Political development. 1960-73. *3555*
—. Political Leadership. Ratsiraka, Dadier. 1972-82. *3552*
—. Politics. Reform. Tsiranana, Philibert. 1972-73. *3579*
—. Settlement. Social Organization. 1958-78. *877*
Madagascar (Tananarive). Political Change. 1900-72. *3549*
Maendeleo Ya Wanawake. Attitudes. Kenya. Women. 1954-74. *3014*
Mafundwe. Chiefs. Rugemaninzi. Shi. Zaire (Kabare, Ngweshe). 1895-1960. *2490*
Magazines. *See* Periodicals.
Maghreb *See also* individual states by name; Africa, North.

—. Acculturation. Colonialism. Islam. Tradition. 1959-75. *918*
—. Africa, North. Foreign policy. USA. 1776-1976. *930*
—. Africa, North. Islam. Maraboutism. Sufism. ca 1100-1975. *960*
—. Agriculture. Colonial Government. Social Change. 1800-1956. *966*
—. Agriculture. Colonialism. Depression. France. Nationalism. 1929-36. *955*
—. Arslan, Chekib. Nationalism. Pan-Arabism. 1866-1946. *925*
—. Attitudes. Intellectuals. Islam. Leadership. 1945-80. *969*
—. Benjelloun, Tahar. Boudjedra, Rashid. Khaïr-Eddine, Mohammed. Novels. 1965-75. *920*
—. Boundaries (disputes). Conflict and Conflict Resolution. Western Sahara. 20c. *956*
—. Capital accumulation. Economic development. 1960's-70's. *970*
—. Colonialism. 1890-1932. *946*
—. Constitutions. Islam. 1980. *941*
—. Economic development. Independence. Politics. 1950-74. *974*
—. Elites (review article). 1970's. *975*
—. Historiography. USA. 1776-1974. *979*
—. Historiography (review article). ca 9c-20c. ca 1965-75. *931*
—. Islam. Mauritania. Politics. 1960's-73. *963*
—. Land Reform. -1975. *973*
—. Linguistics. Literature. Yacine, Kateb. 1980. *936*
—. Modernization. Tradition. 1930's-. *924*
—. Political traditions. 1960's-70's. *943*
—. Tunisia. 1887-1974. *1544*
Magic. Dzo. Ewe. Myths and Symbols. Togo. 15c-20c. *2380*
Magubane, Bernard. Political Economy. Race Relations. Social Classes. South Africa. 1950's-80. *3889*
Mahdism. Archer, Geoffrey. Colonial Government. Rahman, Sayyid al-. Sudan. 1924-27. *1486*
—. Church and State. Islamic revival. Wahhabism. 20c. *905*
Mahdists. Rebellions. Sudan. 1900-27. *1487*
Mahomo (interview). Exiles. Films, documentary. Morena Films. Propaganda. South Africa. 1960-76. *3951*
Maka. Cameroon, southeast. Capitalism. Economic Theory. Inequality. ca 1930-78. *2406*
Makerere University. Colleges and Universities. Mazrui, Ali A. (memoirs). Political science. Uganda (Kampala). 1963-71. *3261*
—. Colonial Government. Higher education. Uganda. 1921-40. *3268*
Malaki sect. Bayudaya. Judaism. Kakungulu, Semei. Uganda. 1856-1974. *3285*
Malan, F. S. Liberalism. Race Relations. South Africa. 1890-1924. *3870*
Malaria control. Diseases. Guinea-Bissau (Bissau Island). 20c. *1890*
Malawi *See also* Africa, Southern.
—. Acculturation. Political culture. Revolution. 1909-61. *3595*
—. African Unity. Apartheid. Foreign Relations. South Africa. 1891-1970. *3410*
—. Agricultural systems. Banda, Hastings Kamuzu. Economic Development. Foreign policy. 1964-74. *3615*
—. Air mail service. Communications. 1930-38. *3600*
—. Autobiography and Memoirs. Sunderland Flying Boat. Wills, K. B. 1950. *584*
—. Banda, Hastings Kamuzu. Political leadership. 1964-74. *3601*
—. Blackman's Church. Mwasi, Yesaya Zerenji. Religion. 1880's-1930's. *3620*
—. Boundaries (disputes). Tanzania. ca 1967-73. *448*
—. Census. Population. 1891-1991. *3599*
—. Census. Population. 1921-66. *3598*
—. Chancellor College. Colleges and Universities. Students. 1965-71. *3614*
—. Chewa. Colonial Government (resistance to). Labor service. World War I. 1914-19. *707*
—. Chilembwe, John. Independence movements. Land. Political traditions. 1915-63. *3612*
—. Chilobwe murders trial. Crime and Criminals. Legal systems. 1968-71. *3593*
—. Colonial Development Act (1929). Economic growth. 1929-39. *3590*
—. Colonial Government. Economic Conditions. Railroads. 1895-1935. *3624*
—. Colonial government. Labor (forced). Peasants. Political consciousness. Rwanda. 19c-1962. *207*
—. Colonial Government. Land policy. Peasants. ca 1900-73. *3618*
—. Colonial government. Tax collection. 1891-1972. *3592*
—. Criminal law. Tradition. 20c. *3596*
—. Dance. Nyau societies. Prehistory-1975. *3622*
—. Economic development. 1964-75. *3623*
—. Economic Development. Livingstone, David. Missions and Missionaries. 1874-1972. *3608*
—. Economic structure. Neocolonialism. 1891-1973. *3611*
—. Education. Women. 1875-1952. *3605*
—. Foreign relations. FRELIMO. Mozambique. Portugal. 1960-76. *3372*
—. Foreign Relations. India. Maps. Surveys, land. 1895-1972. *3607*
—. Health, Ministry of. Medical policy. Public Administration. 1891-1974. *3591*
—. Independence movements. Labor. World War I. 1914-53. *710*
—. Independence movements. Nationalism. 1891-1964. *3617*
—. Independence Movements. Settlers and Residents Association of Nyasaland (SARAN). 1959-63. *3619*
—. Johnston, Harry Hamilton. Mozambique (Chinde). Ports. 1891-1923. *3589*
—. Law. National Development. 1977. *3594*
—. Laws, Robert. University of Livingstonia. 1920's. *3609*
—. Marriage. Nyakusa-Ngonde. Social change. Tanzania. 1875-1971. *913*
—. Middle classes. Urbanization. Zambia. 1920-60. *3388*
—. Migrant labor. Zimbabwe. 1903-23. *3389*
—. National Library Service. 1950-75. *3621*
—. National Parks and Reserves. 1970's-80. *3588*
—. Oral history. World War I. 1916-18. *709*
—. Printing. Publishers and Publishing. 1870-1978. *3613*
—. Railroad development. 1892. *3606*
—. Tea industry. 1818-1976. *3602*
—. World War I. 1914-70's. *708*
Malawi (Lilongwe, Zomba). Economic development. Regional planning. 1965-74. *3610*
Malawi, northern. Agricultural Policy. Coffee. Phoka. 1930-77. *3616*
—. Chakaka Pola. Famine, seasonal. Nigeria, Eastern. Onicha Ibo. 1964-71. *656*
Malawi (Nsanje District). Economic cooperation *(Thando)*. Family. Food consumption. 1970's. *3597*
Malawi, southern. Colonialism. Labor. Land tenure. Rebellions. 15c-20c. *3603*
—. Land Tenure. Social Classes. 1890-1980. *3604*
Male-female relations. Algeria. Cultural liberation. Women. 1830's-1970's. *993*
Mali *See also* Africa, West.
—. Agricultural production. Colonial Government. Economic Development. Irrigation. Office du Niger. 1920's-50's. *1962*
—. Attitudes. Economic development. Education. Students. 1950-76. *1970*
—. Civil-military relations. Government. 1970-79. *1969*
—. Colonial Government. 1851-1953. *1967*
—. Constitutions. Maninka. Oral tradition. Values. 13c-20c. *1961*
—. Coups d'etat. Political crisis. 1960-68. *1964*
—. Economic development. Socialism. 1960-68. *1963*
—. Economic Planning. Ernst, Klaus. Jones, William I. Peasants. Socialism (review article). 1960-68. *1959*
—. Economic Planning (review article). Jones, William I. 1961-68. *1971*
—. Elites. Keita, Mobido. Militarism. Revolution. 1960-68. *1968*
—. Foreign policy. Keita, Modibo. 1960-68. *1966*
—. Foreign policy. Military government. Modernization. Togo. Upper Volta. ca 1950-75. *1622*
—. Land reform. Rural development. 1972-79. *1965*
—. Military government. ca 1968-75. *1960*
Mali Federation. Africa, West. Regionalism. Union Douanière Equatoriale (Equatorial Customs Union). West African Custom Union. 1959-73. *112*
Mali (Kita). Cities (small). Rural development. Tunisia (Testour). 1950's-78. *623*
—. Ghana (Swedru). Hopkins, Nicholas S. Local politics. Owusu, Maxwell. Uganda (Gondo). Vincent, Joan. 1960's-. *247*
Mali (Ouolossébougou). Rebellions. 1968. *1958*
Malladra mission. Colonial government. Ethiopia. Military preparation. 1925-26. *2794*
Malnutrition. Egypt. Food consumption. 1959-71. *1157*
Management *See also* Collective Bargaining; Industrial Relations.
—. Economic Structure. Nigeria. 1956-80. *2033*
Managers. Government Enterprise. Tanzania. 1962-73. *3117*
Mancham, James. Coups d'etat. Foreign Relations. Political Factions. René, Albert. Seychelles. 1964-77. *3575*
Mandates. Atangana, Karl. Beti. Cameroon (Yaoundé). League of Nations. World War I. 1914-22. *714*
Mandela, Nelson. African National Congress. Apartheid. Pan-African Freedom Movement. South Africa. 1918-64. *3843*
—. Jawaharlal Nehru Award for International Understanding. South Africa. 1979-80. *3884*
Mandinka. Fertility associations. Food Supply. Gambia. Women. 1965-75. *1716*
Mandūr, Muhammad. Egypt. Literary criticism. 1930-65. *1346*
Mangat, J. S. Africa, East. Asians (review article). Morris, H. S. 19c-20c. *2641*
Mangope, Lukas (interview). Bantu Homelands. Botswana. South Africa (Bophuthatswana). 1973. *3390*
Mangrove poles. Colonial government. Exports. Kenya (Lamu archipelago). Tanzania (Rufiji River). 1900-81. *2576*
Maninka. Constitutions. Mali. Oral tradition. Values. 13c-20c. *1961*
Manpower efficiency. Career guidance policies. Tanzania. 1961-74. *3116*
Manufacturing. Economic development. 1973. *646*
—. Economic Policy. Ghana. 1958-64. *1725*
—. Economic structure. Industry. Kenya. 1963. *2884*
—. Ideology. Interest Groups. South Africa. 1900-25. *3750*
Manuscripts *See also* Documents.
—. Arabic. Historical sources. Nigeria. 15c-20c. *2007*
Manuscripts, Arabic. Baa, Karamoxo. Guinea (Tuuba). Jaaxanke. 15c-20c. *1876*
Manwere *fekuo*. Asante. Ghana (Kumase). Public Administration. 1834-1970's. *1743*
Manya Krobo, stool of. Adangme. Ghana. Succession. 1800-1939. *1790*
Mapanzure. Shona (Mhari). Zimbabwe. 1859-73. *4151*
Mapping mission. Egypt (Foul Bay). World War II (personal narratives). 1943. *757*
Maps. Foreign Relations. India. Malawi. Surveys, land. 1895-1972. *3607*
Maraboutism. Africa, North. Islam. Maghreb. Sufism. ca 1100-1975. *960*
Marabouts. Muslim brotherhoods. Politics. Senegal. Senghor, Leopold. 1964-76. *2301*
Maraghi, Muhammad Mustafa al-. Al-Azhar, University of. Educational Reform. Egypt. Zawahiri, Ahmadi az-. 1895-1929. *1354*
Maran, René. Chad. Literature. Negritude. ca 1920-40. *808*
Maranke, John. Apostles. Conversion experience. Rites and Ceremonies. Sects, Religious. 1932-72. *829*
Marchetti, Victor. Central Intelligence Agency. Intelligence Service (review article). Marks, John. USA. 1974. *472*
Marcum, John. Angola. Independence Movements (review article). 1950-78. *3419*
Marei, Sayed. Egypt. Political clientelism. 1920's-70's. *1302*
Maribeha. Mabena, Magumbo. Succession. Zimbabwe. 1972. *4278*
Markakis, John (review article). Coups d'etat. Ethiopia. Historiography. Politics, traditional. 1960's-70's. *2730*
Marke, George Osborne. Africa, West. Garvey, Marcus. Universal Negro Improvement Association. West Indies. 1920-23. *1664*
Market town development. Migration, Internal. Nigeria (Onitsha). Trade. 1960-67. *2063*
Marketing. Government regulation. Grain. Sahel. 1960's-70's. *558*
Marketing schemes. Cattle. Conservatism. Uganda (Karamoja). 1948-70. *3289*
Markets. Agriculture. Cottage industries. Occupations. Uganda (Bugisu). Youth, rural. 1973. *3318*
—. Economic development. Liberia (Monrovia). 1940's-70's. *1948*

—. Family Organization. Government Enterprise. Industrial innovation. Liberia. Women. 1950-70. *1947*
—. Nigeria (Cross River Basin). Villages. ca 1500-1970's. *2049*
Markets, periodic. Economic Growth. Sierra Leone. Trade (interregional). 1896-1970. *2356*
—. Traders, itinerant. Uganda. 1972. *3239*
Marks, John. Central Intelligence Agency. Intelligence Service (review article). Marchetti, Victor. USA. 1974. *472*
Marriage *See also* Divorce; Family; Women.
—. Akan. Ghana. Modernization. 1800-1970's. *1852*
—. Attitudes. Family. Girls. Schools. Zaire (Kinshasa). 1969-72. *2562*
—. Dowry system. Hutu. Rwanda. Tutsi. 1970's. *3021*
—. Ga. Ghana. Modernization. Social Organization. 1970's. *1845*
—. Malawi. Nyakusa-Ngonde. Social change. Tanzania. 1875-1971. *917*
Marriage, endogamous. Niger (Aïr). Social Organization. Tuareg, Yullemmeden. 19c-20c. *1980*
Marshall, Lawrence (family). Namibia. San. Social change. 1951-80. *3703*
Martin, David. Amin, Idi (review article). Kibedi, Wanume. Uganda. 1971-74. *3253*
Marx, Karl. Kenya. Mau Mau. Political Theory. Revolution. Tocqueville, Alexis de. 1888-1963. *2921*
Marxism *See also* Class Struggle; Communism; Socialism.
—. Agriculture (review article). Colonial Government. Kenya. 1950-80. *2860*
—. Amin, Idi. Cultural dependency. Nyerere, Julius. Radicals and Radicalism. 19c-1973. *2614*
—. Angola. Cuba. Ethiopia. Germany, East. Mozambique. 1975-78. *528*
—. Anthropology. Capitalism. Congo. Neocolonialism (review article). Rey, P. P. 20c. *2440*
—. Cabral, Amilcar. Cape Verde Islands. Guinea-Bissau. Independence Movements. ca 1960-75. *1886*
—. Cabral, Amilcar. Ethnicity. Guinea-Bissau. Independence Movements. 1930-76. *1898*
—. Cabral, Amilcar. Guinea-Bissau. Middle Classes. 1950's-70's. *1897*
—. Capitalism (peripheric). Colonialism. Developing Nations. 1975. *653*
—. Colonial Government. Great Britain. Social Customs. Witchcraft. 19c-20c. *173*
—. Congo. Congolese Labor Party. Ngouabi, Marien. Political Leadership. 1930's-79. *2441*
—. Dialectical materialism (review article). Sik, Endre. Prehistory-1977. *3*
—. Egypt. Socialism. 1975. *1180*
—. FRELIMO. Mozambique. Revolutionary Movements. 1962-78. *3637*
—. Ghana. Ideology. Nkrumah, Kwame. 1956-66. *1786*
—. Novels. ca 1960's-70's. *861*
—. Racism. Social Theory. South Africa. 1970's. *3724*
Marxism (review article). 1960-79. *307*
—. African studies. 1982. *49*
—. Djibouti. Ethiopia. Somalia. 1974-79. *2642*
Marxism-Leninism. 1960-78. *285*
—. Multinational corporations. 1900-75. *563*
Mary, Virgin. Egypt. Social behavior. Zeitoun, apparition of. 1968. *1345*
Masowe, Baba Johane. Korsten Basketmakers. Religion. Zimbabwe (Manicaland; Makoni). 1940-77. *4145*
Mass Media *See also* Films; Newspapers; Radio; Television.
—. African National Congress. Apartheid. South Africa. 1900-73. *4027*
—. Education. National liberation movements. Propaganda. 1960's-70's. *211*
—. Egypt. 1798-1970's. *1351*
—. Government. Nigeria. 1951-66. *2150*
—. Ivory Coast. Newspapers. 1910-73. *1936*
Massacres. Burundi. Colonialism. Ethnic conflict. 1972. *2661*
—. Colonialism. Historiography. Libya (Cyrenaica). 1930-31. *1390*
Massu, Jacques. Algeria (Algiers). Counterinsurgency, urban. France. 1957. *1039*
Master Farmer's Association. Agricultural Reform. Zimbabwe (Victoria). 1929-78. *4305*
Masterson, G. M. (memoirs). Colonial government. Zimbabwe. 1925-66. *4144*
Mathu, Eliud. Colonial government. Kenya. Legislative Council. 1919-57. *2929*
Matitta, Walter. Independence movements. Lefela, Josie. Lesotho. ca 1902-65. *3538*
Mau Mau. Colonialism. Kenya (Murang'a). Kikuyu. Loyalists. 1952-70. *2942*
—. Decolonization. Kenya. 1957-60. *2936*
—. Decolonization. Kenya. Land reform. Nationalism. 1952-60. *2937*
—. Decolonization. Kenya. Multiracialism. 1952-59. *2927*
—. Elites. Kenya. Kikuyu. Political Leadership. 1950-63. *2961*
—. Fiction. Heroes. Kenya. Revolution. ca 1950-57. *2966*
—. Hymns. Kenya. Kikuyu. Politics. 1952. *2944*
—. Independence. Kenya. Nationalism. 1944-60. *2943*
—. Independence Movements. Kenya. Labor movement. ca 1910-60. *2959*
—. Independence Movements. Kenya (Nakuru). 1940-55. *2963*
—. Kenya. Kikuyu. 1950's. *2923*
—. Kenya. Maasai. 1900-56. *2947*
—. Kenya. Marx, Karl. Political Theory. Revolution. Tocqueville, Alexis de. 1888-1963. *2921*
—. Kenya. Political conflict. 1952-77. *2972*
—. Kenya. Rebellions. 1952-60. *2941*
—. Kenya. Revolution. 1920-60. *2933*
—. Kenya African National Union. Kenyatta, Jomo. Kikuyu Central Association. 1944-52. *2955*
—. Kenya (Nakuru). 1944-55. *2962*
—. Kenya (Rift Valley). Kikuyu. Squatters. 1937-52. *2932*
Mau-Mau. Independence Movements. Kenya African National Union. Kikuyu. 1945-63. *2954*
Mauritania *See also* Africa, West; French West Africa.
—. Algeria. Foreign Relations. Morocco. Western Sahara. 1960-78. *1592*
—. Algeria. Morocco. Nationalism. Polisario Front. Territorial claims. Western Sahara. 1956-79. *923*
—. Boundaries. Diplomacy. 1960-76. *1974*
—. Cattle. Droughts. 1970-79. *1976*
—. Decolonization. Morocco. Spain. Western Sahara. 1970's. *1588*
—. Guerrilla Warfare. Morocco. Western Sahara. 1975-76. *1584*
—. Islam. Maghreb. Politics. 1960's-73. *963*
—. Nationalism. Political Leadership. Sidiyya Baba. 1862-1926. *1975*
—. Political integration. 15c-20c. *1972*
Mauritania People's Party (PPM). Political Parties (single-party system). 1946-73. *1973*
Mauritius. Asians. Doctor, Manilal Maganlall. Politics. ca 1900-56. *3584*
—. Attitudes. Great Powers. Indian Ocean. Military presence. 1965-75. *3564*
—. Developing Nations. Ethnic Groups. National Development. 1968-80. *3561*
—. Elections (cancellation). Ramgoolam, Seewoosagur. 1973. *3568*
—. Press. Réunion. ca 1830-1973. *3569*
Maxton (vessel). Egypt. Suez Canal (clearing). 1967-74. *1154*
May Revolution. Madagascar. Social reform. 1972. *3560*
Mayflower School. Ajuwa Grammar School. Nigeria. Secondary Education. Vocational education. 1956-79. *2208*
Mazrui, Al-Amin bin Ali. Africa, East. Islam. Modernization. 1875-1947. *2630*
Mazrui, Ali A. (memoirs). Colleges and Universities. Makerere University. Political science. Uganda (Kampala). 1963-71. *3261*
M'Ba, Léo. Aubaume, Jean Hilaire. Bongo, Albert Bernard. Gabon. Nationalism. Political parties. 1959-72. *2447*
Mbadiwe, Kingsley Ozuomba. Nigeria. Political Leadership. USA. 1939-47. *2139*
Mbeere. Kenya, central. Land reform. Social organization. 1959-71. *2865*
Mboya, Tom. All-African Trade Union Federation. Nkrumah, Kwame. Political Factions. 1958-64. *62*
Mbula. Denmark. Missions and Missionaries. Nigeria (Adamawa). Prophet movement. 1926-35. *2255*
McGuire, George Alexander. African Orthodox Church. Religious movements. 1921-80. *854*
McKeown, James. Anim, Peter. Ghana. Pentecostalism. 1890-1974. *1865*
Medals, commemorative. Numismatics. South Africa (Johannesburg). 1889-1972. *4016*
Mediation. Arab-Israeli conflict. Organization of African Unity. 1971. *85*
Medical administration. Sudan. 1899-1970. *1467*
Medical policy. Health, Ministry of. Malawi. Public Administration. 1891-1974. *3591*
Medical Research. Belgium. Public Health. Sleeping sickness. Zaire. 1885-1980. *2536*
—. Sudan. Wellcome Tropical Research Laboratories. 1903-52. *1466*
Medicine *See also* headings beginning with the word medical; Hospitals; Nurses and Nursing; Physicians.
—. Africa, East. East African Community. Research, regional. 1906-73. *2569*
—. Aladura. Faith healing. Nigeria. Sects, Religious. 1950's-80's. *2248*
—. Apartheid. South Africa. 1972-73. *3994*
—. Botswana. Dingaka. 1820-1970. *3493*
—. Botswana (Ghansi). Nharo. 1970's. *3486*
—. Colonial Government (resistance to). Madagascar. Plague. 1921. *3558*
—. Ethiopia. Syphilis (cures). 17c-20c. *2842*
—. Ghana. Tradition. Prehistory-1979. *1858*
Medicine (practice of) *See also* Diseases; Nurses and Nursing.
—. Ethiopia. Typhus. 1866-1941. *2843*
Medicine, traditional. Ghana. 20c. *1831*
Medinas. Arts and crafts. Tunisia (Sfax, Tunis). ca 1970. *1557*
Me'ei Sone. Ethiopia. Left. Nihilism. People's Revolutionary Party. 1970-79. *2822*
Memoirs. *See* Autobiography and Memoirs; also individual names with the subdivisions (autobiography) or (memoir).
Mende. Fertility levels. Sierra Leone. Temne. 1963-73. *2344*
Menelik II. Ethiopia. Germany. War Aims. World War I. 20c. *716*
Mengistu Haile Mariam. Communism. Ethiopia. Public Policy. 1974-81. *2759*
Mental health. 1955-73. *837*
Mercenary troops. Angola. Trials. 1976. *3470*
—. Foreign Policy. Military recruitment. *Soldier of Fortune* (periodical). USA. 1970-80. *353*
—. Imperialism. 1940's-70's. *371*
Merchants. Business History. Friendship. Kinship. Liberia (Monrovia). 1970. *1949*
—. Capitalism. Islam (ethics). Tunisia. Weber, Max. 1960's. *1567*
Mergers. Copper Mines and Mining. Rhokana Corporation. Zambia. 1930-32. *4038*
Merina. Madagascar. Monarchy. Rice. 19c. *3550*
Merriam, Alan P. Anthropology (colonialist; review article). Colonialism. Zaire (Lupupa Ngye). ca 1930-60. *2539*
Mers el-Kebir (battle). France. Great Britain. World War II. 1940. *724*
Messianism. Kimbanguism. MacGaffey, Wyatt. Zaire. 1921. *2553*
Methodism. Education. Missions and Missionaries. Zaire (Shaba, Kasai). 1910-60. *2540*
Methodist Church. Nemapare, E. T. J. Separatist Movements. Zimbabwe. 1930-50. *4328*
Methodology *See also* Models; Research.
—. Africana collections. South Africa. Women. 20c. *3742*
—. Attitudes. Nigeria. Political culture. Social Classes. 1800-1960. *2124*
—. Chronology. Herero. Himba. Namibia. 20c. *3686*
—. Folklore. 1973. *787*
—. Ghana. Healing movement. Rites and Ceremonies. Twelve Apostles Church. 1913-71. *1833*
—. Government. Political Systems. 1956-75. *370*
—. Musical heritage. ca 16c-1974. *859*
Methodology (typologies). Government. Political systems. 1960-77. *320*
Mexico. China. Collectivization. Tanzania. Ujamaa villages. USSR. 20c. *3094*
—. Economic Development. Kenya. Labor. ca 1940-75. *2868*
Meyburgh, Louisa Fredericka. Afrikaners. Dutch Reformed Church. South Africa (Port Elizabeth). 1900-50. *4024*
Mgijima, Enoch. Bullhoek massacre. Israelites. Religion. South Africa. 1868-1921. *3969*
Middle Classes. Africa, West. Political Leadership. Social Change. Songhai. 1591-1980. *1685*

Military Invasion. France. Great Britain. Togo. World War I (antecedents). 1914. *694*
Military leadership. Africa, North. Montgomery, Bernard. World War II. 1942-45. *744*
—. Modernization. Retraditionalization. 1970's. *365*
Military life. Africa, East. Language. Swahili. 1905-71. *2613*
Military Occupation *See also* Military Government; Resistance.
—. Aristocracy. Ethiopia. Government. Italy. 1937-40. *2799*
—. Cameroon. France. Great Britain. Partition, provisional. World War I. 1914-16. *701*
—. Egypt. Israel. Suez Crisis. 1956-57. *1216*
—. Ethiopia. Graziani, Rodolfo. Italy. Resistance. 1935-40. *2801*
—. Ethiopia. Italy. 1935-41. *2785*
—. Ethiopia. Italy. Public Health. 1935-41. *2841*
—. Ethiopia. Italy. Road construction. 1936-41. *2709*
—. Germany. Tunisia. World War II. 1942-43. *737*
—. Morocco (Tangier). Spain. World War II. 1940-45. *746*
Military offenses. Diplomacy. Egypt. October War. USA. 1967-73. *1292*
Military Operations. Africa, East. Diseases. Germany. Great Britain. World War I. 1914-18. *688*
—. Egypt. Israel. War. 1948. *1258*
Military Organization. Air Forces. France. Plan VII. World War II. 1943-44. *739*
—. Armies. Ghana. 1947-70's. *1738*
—. *Dors* (military units). Guerrilla Warfare. Italy. Libya. 1911-32. *1368*
—. Social organization. ca 1900-75. *377*
Military organizations. Armaments industry. South Africa. 1974. *3840*
Military policy. Algeria. Rural Settlements. 1954-77. *1102*
—. Economic Policy. South Africa. 1970's. *3876*
—. Egypt. Israel. Nasser, Gamal Abdel. Six-Day War. Syria. 1948-67. *1285*
—. France. 1960-70. *458*
Military preparation. Colonial government. Ethiopia. Malladra mission. 1925-26. *2794*
Military presence. Attitudes. Great Powers. Indian Ocean. Mauritius. 1965-75. *3564*
Military Recruitment *See also* Conscription, Military.
—. Africa, North. Azan, Paul *(Armée Indigène Nord-Africaine).* Colonialism. France. 1925. *932*
—. Africa, West. Great Britain. Transportation, Military. World War I. 1914-19. *697*
—. Benin. World War I. 1914-18. *686*
—. Colonial Government. Ethnicity. Lugard, Frederick. 1900-60. *347*
—. Foreign Policy. Mercenary troops. *Soldier of Fortune* (periodical). USA. 1970-80. *353*
—. French West Africa. Migration. 1900-45. *1631*
—. Ghana. Great Britain. Labor. World War II. 1939-46. *751*
—. Ghana. Great Britain. World War I. 1914-18. *718*
Military (review article). Colonial government. Zimbabwe. 1945-78. *4237*
Military rule. Nigeria. Public opinion. 1971-72. *2178*
Military Service (geographical limits). Defense Policy. Legislation. South Africa. 1912-76. *3858*
Military Strategy *See also* Logistics; Naval Strategy.
—. Africa, North. Hitler, Adolf. Logistics. Rommel, Erwin. World War II. 1941-42. *770*
—. Air Warfare. Egypt. Israel. Six-Day War. 1967. *1178*
—. Apartheid. Foreign Relations. South Africa. ca 1488-1975. *3707*
—. Armaments. Indian Ocean. South Africa. 1960-74. *3812*
—. Army, 2d. Egypt. Ghazala, Mohamed. October War. Suez Canal (crossing). 1973. *1314*
—. Colonial policy (memorandum). Great Britain. Political Reform (delay of). Zambia. Zimbabwe. 1930-45. *3396*
—. Development. Liberia. USA. World War II. 1938-45. *725*
—. Egypt. Foreign Relations. October War. 1973. *1273*
—. Egypt. Israel. October War. 1973. *1309*
—. Egypt. October War. Suez City (battle). 1973. *1271*
—. El Alamein (battle). Great Britain. Montgomery, Bernard. World War II. 1930's-45. *772*
—. Ethiopia (Eritrea). Foreign Policy. Somalia. USSR. 1969-78. *2580*
—. Foreign Relations. Namibia (Walvis Bay). Ports. South Africa. 1914-82. *3682*
—. Foreign Relations. South Africa. Western nations. 1970's. *3925*
—. Indian Ocean. USSR. 1960's-70's. *407*
—. Suez Canal (reopening). 19c-20c. *1188*
Military Strategy (surprise). Egypt. Israel. Military intelligence. October War. 1971-73. *1304*
Military Uniforms. *See* Uniforms, Military.
Military-industrial complex. Botha, Pieter. South Africa. 1960-76. *3874*
Milk. Food Consumption. Ghana. Wheat. 1960's-70's. *1741*
Millenarian movements. Poetry. Politics. Senegal. Senghor, Leopold. 1940's-60's. *2304*
Millin, Sarah G. Novels. Racism. South Africa. 1917-65. *4025*
Milner, Alfred. Africa, West. British Empire. Empire Resources Development Committee. Exports. 1916-20. *1649*
Mindolo Ecumenical Foundation. Missions and Missionaries. Zambia. 1950's-60's. *4039*
Mineral resources. Foreign Relations. Mining. Namibia. South Africa. 1966-81. *3685*
—. Foreign Relations. Uranium. 1940's-82. *634*
—. Transportation. Zaire. 1956-76. *2473*
Miners. Apartheid. Labor Unions and Organizations. South Africa. Trades Union Congress. 1970-73. *3765*
—. Birom. Nigeria (northern). Social protest. Stealing. Tin. 1958-78. *2246*
—. Civil Disturbances. Race Relations. Zambia. 1935-40. *4076*
—. Labor movement. South Africa. Strikes. 1930's-40's. *3781*
—. Sierra Leone. 1935-67. *2364*
Miners, white. Labor force. Social Status. Zimbabwe. 1890-1953. *4178*
Mines. Botswana. Labor. South Africa. 1899-1966. *3531*
—. Ghana. Government. Labor, forced. 1906-27. *1760*
—. Ghana (northern). Labor recruitment. Migration. 1880-1940. *1749*
—. Labor (review article). Onselen, Charles van. Zimbabwe. 1900-33. *4175*
Mining. Botswana (Orapa). Company towns. DeBeers Company. Diamonds. 1955-78. *3528*
—. Cities. 1880-1970. *644*
—. Economic change. Sierra Leone. 1930's. *2352*
—. Economic Conditions. Industrial Production. Zambia. 1960-79. *4066*
—. Foreign Relations. Mineral resources. Namibia. South Africa. 1966-81. *3685*
—. Industrialization. Niger (Arlit). Uranium. 1974-81. *1988*
—. Labor (review article). Racism. South Africa. Zimbabwe. 1900-1933. *3408*
—. Niger (Arlit). Technical assistance. Uranium. 1968-73. *1987*
—. Proletarianization. Social Classes. Technology. Zambia. 1946-66. *4102*
Mining industry. Copper Mines and Mining. Multinational Corporations. Nationalization. Zaire. Zambia. 1960's-82. *668*
—. Economic Structure. Political strategy. South Africa. 1970's. *3776*
—. Labor. Multinational corporations. Sklar, Richard L. (review article). Zambia. 1920-76. *4130*
—. Labor. Political Protest. South Africa. 1980's. *3731*
—. Railway politics. Tan-Zam Railway. Zambia. Zimbabwe. 1895-1970. *3377*
Ministerial responsibility. Africa, East. Constitutions. 1961-74. *2600*
Minorities *See also* Discrimination; Ethnic Groups; Nationalism; Nationalities; Population; Racism; Segregation.
—. Africa, West. Aliens. Colonial Government. Great Britain. Law, customary. 19c-20c. *1638*
—. Africa, West. Muslims. 19c-20c. *1629*
—. Arabs. Israel. Jews. Morocco. Tunisia. 1972-75. *972*
—. Asians. Politics. Zimbabwe. 1890-1970. *4250*
—. Church and state. Copts. Egypt. 1950-80. *1347*
—. Egypt. Europeans. 1805-1961. *1139*
Mission Society. Finland. Namibia. Political Commentary. Tanzania. 1945-75. *836*
Missions and Missionaries. Acculturation (resistance to). Africa, West. Colonial government. Polygamy. 19c-20c. *1633*
—. Africa, East. Christianity. Uganda (Kigezi). World War I. 1914-18. *713*
—. Africa, West. Christianity. Harris, William Waddy. Polygyny. 1910-29. *1643*
—. Africa, West. Nationalism. 19c-20c. *1673*
—. Agricultural development. Alvord, E. D. Zimbabwe. 1889-1959. *4321*
—. American University. Education. Egypt. USA. 19c-20c. *1326*
—. Anderson, Vernon (papers). Archives. Presbyterian Church. Zaire. 1921-46. *2559*
—. Anglicanism. Steere, Edward. Tanzania. Universities Mission to Central Africa (UMCA). 1876-1926. *3192*
—. Angola. Catholic Church. Church and State. Mozambique. 1975-81. *3349*
—. Archives. St. Joseph's Society for the Missions. 1866-1980. *25*
—. Art. Nigeria. 15c-20c. *2293*
—. Attitudes. Education. 19c-1974. *792*
—. Bemba. Catholic Church. Local government. Zambia. 1890-1935. *4070*
—. Bibliographies. *Bibliotheca Missionum.* Catholic Church. 1053-1940. *26*
—. Canada. Education. Great Britain. Sudan Interior Mission. 1937-55. *1505*
—. Catholic Church. Education, rural. Zaire (Shaba). 1885-1939. *2544*
—. Catholic Church. Ethiopia. Great Britain. Military government. Vatican. World War II. 1941-43. *731*
—. Catholic Church. Ethiopia. Italy. Pius XI, Pope. War. 1935-36. *2718*
—. Catholic Church. Zaire (Kivu; Nyangezi). 1906-29. *2537*
—. Christianity. Church history. Historiography. 19c-20c. *786*
—. Christianity. Islam. 20c. *817*
—. Christianity. Nigeria (Obudu). 1900-75. *2199*
—. Church and State. 1950-60. *51*
—. Church and State. Education. Nigeria. 1842-1948. *2216*
—. Church Missionary Society. Clitoridectomy. Kenya. 1910-72. *2996*
—. Colonial Government. Islam. Nigeria (Muslim emirates). Proselytization. 1900-28. *2288*
—. Colonialism. Education. Kenya. 1902-32. *2987*
—. Congregation of the Holy Ghost. Nigeria. St. Patrick's Missionary Society. 1920-30. *2274*
—. Coptic Church. Ethiopia (Ochollo). Protestant Churches. Social Change. 1898-1980. *2824*
—. Culture, European. Literature. Nigeria (Lagos). 1515-1930's. *2219*
—. Denmark. Mbula. Nigeria (Adamawa). Prophet movement. 1926-35. *2255*
—. Economic Development. Livingstone, David. Malawi. 1874-1972. *3608*
—. Education. Ethnic groups. Independence movements. Political Factions. Zimbabwe. ca 1880-1977. *4264*
—. Education. French West Africa. 1817-1940. *1612*
—. Education. Government. Sudan, Southern. Values. 1898-1956. *1506*
—. Education. Methodism. Zaire (Shaba, Kasai). 1910-60. *2540*
—. Freshwater, Will (papers). Linguistics. London Missionary School. Zambia. 1872-1959. *4068*
—. Gabon. Schweitzer, Albert. 1900-65. *2450*
—. Harrist Church. Ivory Coast. Witchcraft. 1913-79. *1935*
—. Helene Franz Hospital. Public Health. South Africa (Bochum-Blauberg). Syphilis. 1895-1935. *3995*
—. Mindolo Ecumenical Foundation. Zambia. 1950's-60's. *4039*
—. Muslims. Race Relations. Religion. Tanzania. 1878-1941. *3209*
—. Political Protest. Seventh-Day Adventists. Zambia (Tonga Plateau). 1903-55. *4061*
—. Presbyterian Church. USA. Zaire (Kasai). 1871-1964. *2554*
—. Social theory. ca 1850-1950. *790*
Missions and Missionaries, Catholic. Agricultural Policy. Economic development. Zaire. 1970's. *2463*
Missions and Missionaries, Dutch (diary). Mozambique (Inhaminga). Portugal. 1974. *199*
Mitchell, J. Clyde (memoirs). Rhodes-Livingstone Institute. Zambia. 1952-55. *4090*
Mitchell, Philip. Colonial Government. Kenya. 1944-52. *2922*

Mobility. *See* Geographic Mobility; Social Mobility.
Mobility, occupational. Morocco (Fez). Weavers. 20c. *1436*
Mobutu Sese Seko. Dependency. Economic Conditions. Exports. Zaire. 1960-78. *2482*
—. Foreign policy. France. Zaire. 1958-77. *414*
—. Government. Zaire. 1965-80. *2519*
—. Ideology. Zaire. 1960's-70's. *2499*
—. National self-image. Political Leadership. Zaire. 1974-75. *2531*
—. Political opposition. Zaire. 1965-78. *2497*
—. Political repression. Zaire. 1965-66. *2493*
—. Radicalization. Zaire. 1974-75. *2515*
Mobutu Sese Seko (speech). Foreign Relations. USA. Zaire. 1975. *2552*
Modakeke. Communal compartmentalization. Nigeria (Ife). Politics. 1820-1966. *2171*
Models *See also* Methodology.
—. Democracy, Concordance. South Africa. 1970's. *3860*
—. Developing nations. Slums. 1956-63. *782*
—. Economic development. Education. Egypt. Labor. Lewis, W. A. 1952-67. *1174*
—. Economic Development. Liberia. Tanzania. 1960-72. *588*
—. Ethiopia. Feudalism. Political systems. ca 1800-1976. *2830*
—. Ghana. Nigeria. Political change. 20c. *1619*
Modernism. Art. Nigeria. 1918-60. *2273*
—. Elites. Tradition (review article). Zaire. 1974. *2456*
—. Islam. Reform. Tunisia. 1830-1930. *1571*
Modernity. Economic status. Egypt. Fertility. - 1970's. *1336*
Modernization *See also* Developing Nations; Economic Theory; Foreign Aid; Industrialization; Social Change; Westernization.
—. Afar. Ethiopia (Awash Valley). Pastoralism. ca 1950-75. *2691*
—. Africa, East. Islam. Ismaili sect, Nizari. 1840-1974. *2625*
—. Africa, East. Islam. Mazrui, Al-Amin bin Ali. 1875-1947. *2630*
—. Agriculture. Education. Zambia. 1970's. *4131*
—. Agriculture. Rice. Sierra Leone. 20c. *2351*
—. Agriculture (cash crops). Peasants. 1890-1930. *681*
—. Akan. Ghana. Marriage. 1800-1970's. *1852*
—. Algeria. Independence. 1965-76. *1080*
—. Algeria. Islamic Revival. Tunisia. 1970's. *950*
—. Algeria (Ahaggar; Kel Ulli). Social Classes (Temazlayt relationship). Social Organization. Tuareg. 1864-1960's. *1040*
—. Asafo movement. Colonialism. Ghana. Political Protest. 1910's-50. *1819*
—. Asante. Ghana. Local Government. Political Development. 1881-1981. *1817*
—. Authoritarianism. Egypt. Nasser, Gamal Abdel. Political Culture. 1950's. *1252*
—. Baggara. Sudan (Darfur, Kordofan). 19c-20c. *1457*
—. Bureaucracies. Economic Growth. 1960-74. *675*
—. Bureaucracies. Uganda. -1966. *3292*
—. Cabral, Amilcar. Cultural models. Fanon, Frantz. 1950-75. *629*
—. Cameroon. Soccer. Social Organizations. 1880's-1974. *2403*
—. China. Egypt. Political Leadership. Revolution. Sadat, Anwar. 1952-79. *1238*
—. Cities. 20c. *794*
—. Civil War. Communal conflict (review article). Nigeria. 1971. *2174*
—. Colleges and Universities. Egypt. Elites (military and traditional). 1961-67. *1343*
—. Colonialism. Economic dependence. Political parties. Women. 16c-. *902*
—. Colonialism (review article). Kenya. Tignor, Robert L. Wolff, Richard D. 1870-1939. *2913*
—. Curricula. Egypt. Textbooks. 1960-79. *1333*
—. Dependency. Women. 1970-. *903*
—. Developing nations. Economic Growth (review article). 1960-75. *665*
—. Development. Ivory Coast. 1961-75. *1912*
—. Development. Racism. South Africa. 20c. *3794*
—. Diola. Islam. Senegal. 1900-40. *2323*
—. Ecole Nationale d'Administration. Public Administration (training). Zaire. 1961-71. *2556*
—. Economic development. Libya. Political Systems. 1959-74. *1372*
—. Educational planning. Social Customs. 1974. *803*
—. Egypt. 1952-75. *1117*
—. Egypt. Great Britain. Lloyd, George Ambrose. National Development. 1919-33. *1249*
—. Egypt. Heikal, Muhammed. Intellectuals. Muslim Brotherhood. Social Change. 1914-55. *1353*
—. Egypt. Islamic Movement. Women. 1973-80. *1327*
—. Ethnic competition. 1974. *249*
—. Fertility. Zaire. 1960-79. *2557*
—. Foreign policy. Mali. Military government. Togo. Upper Volta. ca 1950-75. *1622*
—. Ga. Ghana. Marriage. Social Organization. 1970's. *1845*
—. Harrist Church. Ivory Coast. Religion. 1910-72. *1934*
—. Hauka. Niger. Sects, politico-religious. 1850-1975. *1982*
—. Humanism. Kaunda, Kenneth. Socialism. Zambia. ca 1960's. *4081*
—. Islam. Social Institutions. Sudan. 1900-72. *1515*
—. Ivory Coast. Migration. Public Transportation. Social mobility. 1900-40. *1930*
—. Ivory Coast. Political Systems. Values. 1960-82. *1922*
—. Maghreb. Tradition. 1930's-. *924*
—. Military leadership. Retraditionalization. 1970's. *365*
—. Nigeria. Political development. Regional planning. 20c. *2160*
—. Nigeria. Political parties. Political Systems. 1920-66. *2192*
—. Political Attitudes. Sierra Leone. Youth. 1970's. *2340*
—. Political involvement. Religious organizations. Sects, Religious. 1940's-70. *826*
—. Political Parties. Tradition. 1980-81. *283*
—. Racism. South Africa. 1830's-1973. *4019*
—. Tradition, reactivation of. Tunisia. 1960's-70's. *1576*
Moi, Daniel Arap. Kenya. Kenyatta, Jomo. Politics. Succession. 1978-79. *2960*
—. Kenya. Kenyatta, Jomo. Succession. 1978-1980. *2935*
—. Kenya. Political leadership. 1978-79. *2939*
—. Kenya. Politics. Social Organization. 1960's-70's. *2925*
Monarchy. Africa, East (Lakes region). Hierarchies. Land Tenure. ca 800-ca 1960. *2575*
—. Bureaucracies. Ethiopia. Revolution. 1930-80. *2762*
—. Burundi. Historiography. Ntare Rushatsi. 1900-77. *2658*
—. Cattle Raising. Economic Conditions. Zaire (Kabare). 1900-60. *2555*
—. Clans. Saza chiefs. Uganda (Buganda). 13c-20c. *3278*
—. Colonial Government. Myths and Symbols. National Self-image. Zambia. 1924-38. *4107*
—. Colonial government. Nigeria. Yoruba. 1900-60. *2101*
—. Ethiopia. Political Leadership. ca 1930-73. *2736*
—. Ideology. Morocco. 8c-20c. *1413*
—. Madagascar. Merina. Rice. 19c. *3550*
—. Morocco. Political corruption. 1956-73. *1454*
—. Mutesa II, Edward. Obote, Milton. Uganda. Uganda People's Party. 1945-71. *3296*
—. Nicholls, George Heaton. Racism. Social Classes. Solomon. South Africa (Natal). Zulu (Usuthu). 1879-1933. *3886*
—. Nigeria (Kano). Succession. 1920's-63. *2142*
Monasteries. Diaries. Egypt. Orthodox Eastern Church. St. Catherine (monastery). Sinai, Mount. 1980. *1123*
Mondlane, Eduardo. Colleges and Universities. Racism. South Africa (Johannesburg). Witwatersrand, University of. 1945-49. *3664*
—. FRELIMO. Independence Movements. Machel, Samora. Mozambique. 1969-74. *3663*
—. FRELIMO. Independence Movements. Mozambique. 1920-69. *3636*
—. FRELIMO. Mozambique. Political thought. 1948-69. *3645*
—. FRELIMO. Mozambique. Revolutionary Movements. 1920-69. *3638*
Monetarism. Economic Theory. Ghana. Inflation. Structuralism. 1959-79. *1758*
Monetary crises. Economic Conditions. 1960-70. *551*
Monetary relationships. Africa (Francophone). France. Operations Account system. ca 1955-73. *550*
Monetary stability. Africa, West. Dependency. Franc Zone. 1962-75. *1689*
Monetary systems. Botswana. Lesotho. Rand Monetary Area. South Africa. Swaziland. 1909-78. *3347*
—. Ethiopia. Reconstruction. 1941-45. *2708*
—. Sierra Leone. 1960-77. *2345*
Money *See also* Banking; Capital; Foreign Exchange; Gold.
—. Bank of Botswana. Botswana. Economic Development. 1974-78. *3503*
—. Colonial Government. Economic Development. Tanzania. ca 1880-1940. *3092*
—. Ghana (Asante). Politics. 1900-40. *1719*
Money (precolonial currencies). Colonialism. Nigeria. 1880-1948. *2054*
Money (tokens). South Africa (Durban). Trade. 1906-29. *3954*
Mongo-Nkundo. Colonialism. Food production. Social change. Zaire (Equateur). 19c-20c. *2468*
Monnier, Laurent (review article). Historiography. Politics. Zaire. 1971. *2459*
Monopolies *See also* Capitalism; Railroads.
—. Cattle Raising. Cold-storage companies. Zimbabwe. 1890-1938. *4176*
Montagne, Robert. Arabs. Berber Myth (review article). Colonial attitudes. Morocco. 1930-70's. *1438*
Montgomery, Bernard. Africa, North. Military leadership. World War II. 1942-45. *744*
—. El Alamein (battle). Great Britain. Military strategy. World War II. 1930's-45. *772*
Morale. Civil Service. Colonial Government. Nigeria. World War II. 1941-45. *759*
Morality *See also* Values.
—. British Empire. Independence Movements. 1919-47. *224*
—. Cultural identity. Sex roles. ca 1920-70. *887*
Morena Films. Exiles. Films, documentary. Mahomo (interview). Propaganda. South Africa. 1960-76. *3951*
Morocco *See also* Maghreb; Africa, North.
—. Abd-el-Krim. Anticolonialism. 1908-67. *1451*
—. Abd-el-Krim. France. Resistance. Rif War. Spain. 1921-26. *1412*
—. Air forces. France. 1911-39. *1433*
—. Air Warfare. Rebellions. Rif War. Rockwell, Paul Ayres (memoir). Squadron of the Sultan's Guard. USA. 1925. *1447*
—. Algeria. Anticolonialism. Elites. Nationalist movements. Tunisia. 1900-62. *922*
—. Algeria. Birth Control. Social Policy. Tunisia. 1960's-82. *940*
—. Algeria. Diplomacy. Economic cooperation. Tunisia. 1954-70's. *976*
—. Algeria. Foreign Relations. Mauritania. Western Sahara. 1960-78. *1592*
—. Algeria. Language policy. Tunisia. 1960-80. *962*
—. Algeria. Mauritania. Nationalism. Polisario Front. Territorial claims. Western Sahara. 1956-79. *923*
—. Algeria. Nationalism. Tunisia. 1900-60. *968*
—. Algeria. Polisario Front. Western Sahara. 1956-80. *1579*
—. Annexation. Green March. Hassan II. Western Sahara. 1975. *1455*
—. Anual disaster. Colonial Government. Politics and the Military. 1912-21. *1442*
—. Arabs. Berber Myth (review article). Colonial attitudes. Montagne, Robert. 1930-70's. *1438*
—. Arabs. Israel. Jews. Minorities. Tunisia. 1972-75. *972*
—. Armies (native troops). Spain. 1300-1966. *1452*
—. Assidon, Elsa. Gaudio, Attilio. Polisario Front. War. Western Sahara (review article). 1976-80. *1594*
—. Berber dahir. Cities. Courts. France. 1930. *1428*
—. Business community, French. Dubreuil, Lemaigre. 1952-55. *1429*
—. Cambon, Pierre Paul. Colonial Government. France. Lyautey, Hubert. Tunisia. 1869-1925. *949*
—. Cities. *Dahir Barbère* (law). Nationalist movements. Rif War. 1920-40. *1415*
—. Cities. Islam. Social organization. 1960-73. *1423*
—. Colonial Government. France. Lyautey, Hubert. 1912-25. *1410*
—. Colonial Government. France. Lyautey, Hubert. Zionism. 1915-25. *1418*
—. Colonization. Debt. Depression. France. 1930-36. *1440*
—. Colonization. Educational policy. Lyautey, Hubert. 1920's. *1444*
—. Coups d'etat. 1971. *1414*

N

Nation, idea of. Fanon, Frantz. Political theory. 1950's-60's. *1029*
Nation Newspapers Ltd. Kenya. Language. Lonrho. Newspapers. 1972. *3004*
National African Federated Chambers of Commerce. Africans. Dependency. Middle Classes. South Africa. 1964-78. *3793*
National Anthems. Cabinet crisis. South Africa. Stuttaford, Richard. 1938. *3825*
National Assembly (Bunge). Parliaments. Tanganyika African National Union (TANU). Tanzania. 1965-70. *3149*
National Bank of Commerce (NBC). Banking, commercial. Tanzania. 1973-74. *3107*
National Bar Association. Egypt. Politics. Wafd Party. 1912-54. *1266*
National Characteristics *See also* National Self-image; Nationalism.
—. Africa, East. Dorobo. Ethnic Groups. 20c. *2599*
—. Egypt. 1967-74. *1118*
—. Nigeria. ca 1948-74. *1992*
National Charter. Algeria. Revolution. Socialism. ca 1975-76. *1074*
National Congress of British West Africa. Africa, West. Pan-Africanism. 1920-30. *108*
National Council of Ghana Women. Ghana. Women. 19c-1966. *1836*
National Council of Nigerian Citizens. Nigeria. Political Leadership. 1940-60. *2126*
National culture. Colonies. Portugal. 1974-75. *279*
National Development *See also* Economic Development.
—. Africanization. Civil service. Ghana. 1926-46. *1814*
—. Algeria. Decolonization. Foreign policy. Political Systems. 1973-77. *984*
—. Cameroon. Nationalism. Self-determination. ca 1948-76. *2421*
—. Colonial history. Ethnicity. Ivory Coast. 1889-1969. *1931*
—. Colonialism. Great Britain. Law. 1960's-80. *667*
—. Developing Nations. Ethnic Groups. Mauritius. 1968-80. *3561*
—. Economic Planning. Entrepreneurs. Zambia. 1966-76. *4082*
—. Education. Liberia. Values. Westernization. 19c-20c. *244*
—. Education. Nigeria. 1914-78. *2230*
—. Education. Tanzania. 1961-81. *3206*
—. Education. Zimbabwe. 1980-81. *4240*
—. Educational system. Political economy. Tanzania. 1961-75. *3190*
—. Egypt. Great Britain. Lloyd, George Ambrose. Modernization. 1919-33. *1249*
—. Elections. Uganda. 1961-76. *3288*
—. Foreign Relations. 1970's. *80*
—. Foreign relations. Socialism. Tanzania. 1961-76. *3050*
—. Foreign Relations. South Africa. USSR. Zimbabwe. 1979-82. *4149*
—. Guinea. Touré, Sekou. 1958-78. *1873*
—. Houphouët-Boigny, Félix. Ivory Coast. Political Leadership. 1944-74. *1917*
—. Indian Ocean. Islands. 1600-1977. *3565*
—. International system. 1960-80. *293*
—. Kenya. Literature. 1950-72. *2974*
—. Kenya. Nigeria. Research. Science. 1970's. *612*
—. Land Tenure. Law. Senegal. 1960-76. *2296*
—. Law. Malawi. 1977. *3594*
—. Local government. Nigeria (Sapele). 1955-77. *2129*
—. Mozambique. Socialism. 1975-79. *3632*
—. National Youth Service Corps. Nigeria. 1973-79. *2262*
—. Negritude. Senegal. Senghor, Leopold. 1960's-70's. *2303*
—. Nigeria. Oil Industry and Trade. USA. 1960-80. *2071*
—. Political Theory. ca 1960-70's. *313*
—. Tanzania. 1961-71. *3051*
—. Women. 1960-76. *642*
National Development (review article). 1970-79. *254*
—. Foreign Relations. 1950-80. *28*
National Entertainment Association. Concert-party. Ghana. Theater. 1918-75. *1829*
National Identity. Algeria. Islam. 19c-20c. *981*
—. Nile Valley. Political systems. Regional integration. Sudan. ca 1920-55. *1517*
National Integration. Botswana. Chieftaincy. 1934-72. *3495*
—. Civil War. Nigeria. 19c-20c. *2108*
—. Economic insecurity. Violence. 1950-73. *317*
—. Education. Egypt. Social classes. 1805-1968. *1330*
—. Indigenization. Nigeria. 1960-80. *2003*
National Labor Association. Labor Disputes. Namibia. Ovambo crisis. 1971. *3690*
National liberation. Angola. Guerrilla warfare. Guinea-Bissau. Mozambique. ca 1960's-70's. *181*
—. Cabral, Amilcar (assassination). 1973. *160*
—. Political development. Portugal. 1956-74. *326*
National Liberation Army. Algeria. Independence Movements. *Moudjahid* (journal). Propaganda. 1954-62. *1017*
National Liberation Council. Business environment. Ghana. Ghanaization. 1968-. *1731*
National Liberation Front. Algeria. Political systems. 1962-77. *1059*
—. Algeria. Revolutionary movements. Social Classes. 1920-60. *999*
—. Chad. Regionalism. 1800-1977. *2430*
National Liberation Movement of Western Togoland. Boundaries. Ewe. Ghana. Nationalism. Togo. 1943-78. *1616*
National liberation movements. Academy of Sciences. African studies. Communist Party (24th Congress). USSR. 1971-76. *50*
—. Africa, Southern. 1960's. *3426*
—. Africa, southern. China. Foreign aid. USSR. 1960-72. *3338*
—. Africa, Southern. Economic Growth. Foreign Policy. ca 1960-75. *256*
—. Africa, southern. Foreign Policy. National Security. Nigeria. 1967-70. *2180*
—. Africa, southern. Foreign Relations. USA. 1975-79. *3346*
—. Africa, Southern. Guerrilla Warfare. 1968-73. *3428*
—. Africa, Southern. Guerrilla Warfare (review article). Zimbabwe. 1968-75. *3336*
—. Africa, southern. Neocolonialism. 1945-70's. *3399*
—. Africa, southern. UN. 1940's-70's. *3371*
—. Angola. Anti-Imperialism. Popular Movement for the Liberation of Angola (MPLA). 1970's. *3429*
—. Angola. China. Foreign Policy. 1950-76. *3451*
—. Angola. China. Foreign policy. 1961-76. *3475*
—. Anya Nya. Civil war. Political Leadership. Sudan. 1950's-70's. *1485*
—. Apartheid. National Liberation Movements. South Africa. 20c. *3726*
—. Apartheid. National liberation movements. South Africa. 20c. *3726*
—. Cabral, Amilcar. Guinea-Bissau. 1924-73. *1895*
—. China. Foreign aid. Tanzania. 1960-70's. *3136*
—. Communist Countries. Historiography. Symposium of Historians and Africanists of Socialist Countries, 3d. 1970-79. *217*
—. Communist Parties and Movements. Foreign Relations. Mozambique. 1962-75. *3643*
—. Democratic Movement for Malagasy Renaissance (MDRM). Madagascar. Rebellions. 1945-47. *3580*
—. Economic Conditions. Namibia. 1884-1907. 1973-77. *3692*
—. Education. Mass media. Propaganda. 1960's-70's. *211*
—. Foreign aid. USSR. World War II. 1945-75. *490*
—. Foreign policy. South Africa. Zimbabwe. 1974-75. *4192*
—. Guinea-Bissau. Partido Africano da Independência da Guiné e Cabo Verde (PAIGC). 1970-73. *1884*
—. Neocolonialism. Organization of African Unity. 1963-73. *70*
—. Neocolonialism. Pan-Africanism. Revolution. 1945-73. *116*
—. Organization of African Unity. Zimbabwe. 1960-75. *111*
—. Portugal. 1969-74. *187*
—. Socialism. 1970's. *195*
—. Zimbabwe. 1910's-75. *4233*
—. Zimbabwe. 1931-76. *4197*
—. Zimbabwe. 1957-80. *4188*
National Library (Africa section). Libraries. Morocco. Spain (Madrid). Prehistory-1973. *935*
National Library Service. Botswana. Libraries. 1968-77. *3521*
—. Malawi. 1950-75. *3621*
National Movement for the Independence of Madagascar (MONIMA). Jaona, Monja. Madagascar. 1958-73. *3548*
National Parks and Reserves *See also* Wildlife Conservation.
—. Indigenization. Swaziland. 1972-80. *4032*
—. Malawi. 1970's-80. *3588*
National Redemption Council. Economic nationalism. Ghana. Military Government. Pan-Africanism. ca 1972-75. *1806*
National representation. Legislative behavior. Parliaments. Tanzania. 1965-73. *3173*
National Security *See also* Defense Policy.
—. Africa, southern. Foreign Policy. National liberation movements. Nigeria. 1967-70. *2180*
—. Decisionmaking. Unilateral Declaration of Independence (UDI). Zambia. Zimbabwe. 1965-66. *3332*
—. Europe, Western. South Africa. USA. USSR. 1980-82. *3815*
National Security Council. Foreign policy. South Africa. USA. 1969-76. *3829*
National Self-image *See also* National Characteristics.
—. Africa, East. Historiography. Prehistory-20c. ca 1900-30. *2635*
—. Arab unity. Egypt. 1936-39. *1221*
—. Arab unity. Egypt. 1936-39. *1222*
—. Colonial Government. Monarchy. Myths and Symbols. Zambia. 1924-38. *4107*
—. Egypt. Literature. 1920-75. *1358*
—. Ghana. Intergovernmental Relations. 1952-74. *1777*
—. Ghana. Nkrumah, Kwame. Nyerere, Julius. Tanzania. 1951-60's. *328*
—. Ghana. Nkrumah, Kwame. Rhetorical strategies. 1957-60. *1803*
—. Mobutu Sese Seko. Political Leadership. Zaire. 1974-75. *2531*
—. Western Sahara. 1000-1978. *1582*
National service, compulsory. Demonstrations. Students. Tanzania (Dar es Salaam). 1966-67. *3189*
National unification. Ethnography. Johnson, S. Jangaba M. Liberia. 1895-1973. *1942*
National Union for the Complete Independence of Angola (UNITA). Angola. Central Intelligence Agency. Independence Movements. Namibia. South Africa. USA. 1974-81. *3380*
National Union of South African Students. Race Relations. South Africa. South African Students Organization. Students. 1924-76. *3911*
National Union of Youth Organizations. Uganda People's Congress Youth League. Youth. 1960-69. *3272*
National unity. Mouvement Populaire de la Revolution. Religion. Zaire. ca 1973-76. *2486*
National Youth Service Corps. National Development. Nigeria. 1973-79. *2262*
—. Nigeria. Youth. 1970-73. *2197*
Nationalism *See also* Independence Movements; Minorities; Patriotism; Self-Determination; Separatist Movements.
—. 20c. *314*
—. Afar. Djibouti. 1977-80. *2678*
—. Africa, Southern. Bibliographies. 20c. *3358*
—. Africa, West. Historiography. 1975. *1650*
—. Africa, West. Missions and Missionaries. 19c-20c. *1673*
—. Afrikaners. Broederbond. South Africa. 1927-48. *3898*
—. Afrikaners. Entrepreneurship. Industrialization. South Africa. 1968-69. *3795*
—. Afrikaners. Films. South Africa. *Voortrekkers* (film). 1837-1916. *4022*
—. Afrikaners. Political power. South Africa. South African Broadcasting Corporation. 1935-66. *3901*
—. Afrikaners. South Africa. ca 1676-1976. *3837*
—. Agriculture. Colonialism. Depression. France. Maghreb. 1929-36. *955*
—. Algeria. Arabic. Colonial Government. Education. 1830-1954. *1034*
—. Algeria. Berbers. 1925-80. *1031*
—. Algeria. Colons. Muslims. 1880-1920. *1008*
—. Algeria. Feraoun, Mouloud. Ideology. Intellectuals. 1955-62. *1020*
—. Algeria. France. Islam. Students. 1912-62. *1073*
—. Algeria. Mauritania. Morocco. Polisario Front. Territorial claims. Western Sahara. 1956-79. *923*
—. Algeria. Morocco. Tunisia. 1900-60. *968*
—. Algeria. Muslims. World War II. 1939-42. *748*
—. Alienation, cultural. Copts. Egypt. Musa, Salama. 1909-30's. *1234*
—. Amin, Idi. Economic Policy. Obote, Milton. Socialism. Uganda. 1966-71. *3295*
—. Angola. Independence. 1950's-75. *3460*

—. Arab League. Egypt. Fundamentalism. Islam. 1920-45. *1332*
—. Arslan, Chekib. Maghreb. Pan-Arabism. 1866-1946. *925*
—. Aubaume, Jean Hilaire. Bongo, Albert Bernard. Gabon. M'Ba, Léo. Political parties. 1959-72. *2447*
—. Bank Misr. Egypt. Foreign Investments. 1919-49. *1306*
—. Bataka Party. Uganda. USSR. 1945-62. *3274*
—. Botswana. Khama, Tshekedi. 1925-59. *3488*
—. Botswana. Political ideology. Ratshosa, Simon. 1916-32. *3514*
—. Boundaries. Ewe. Ghana. National Liberation Movement of Western Togoland. Togo. 1943-78. *1616*
—. Bourguiba, Habib. Fascism. Italy. Tunisia. 1922-43. *1543*
—. Cameroon. Colonialism. France. Germany. 1919-39. *2412*
—. Cameroon. National development. Self-determination. ca 1948-76. *2421*
—. Capricorn Africa Society. Racism. Stirling, David. Zimbabwe. 1945-60. *4213*
—. Capricorn Africa Society. Tanzania. 1949-67. *3176*
—. Censorship. Colonial Government. Ghana. Press. 1934. *1822*
—. Christian Institute of South Africa. Church and State. Dutch Reformed Church. South Africa. 1960-75. *4026*
—. Colonial Government. Constitutions. Governors. Nigeria. 1935-51. *2177*
—. Colonial Government. Great Britain. Press. Uganda. 1920's-30's. *3299*
—. Colonial Office. Great Britain. 1947. *216*
—. Colonialism. Fanon, Frantz. Revolutionary theory. 1800-1960. *1070*
—. Colonialism. Guerrilla warfare. Zimbabwe. 1893-1973. *4210*
—. Colonialism. Namibia. UN. 1945-70's. *3681*
—. Colonization. Depression. Farmers, European. France. Tunisia. 1930's. *1564*
—. Copts. Egypt. Politics. Wafd Party. 1918-42. *1194*
—. Decolonization. Kenya. Land reform. Mau Mau. 1952-60. *2937*
—. Decolonization. Negritude. 1940's-70's. *844*
—. DeGaulle, Charles. Kissinger, Henry A. Nkrumah, Kwame. Nyerere, Julius. Political Leadership. ca 1940's-70's. *308*
—. Destour Party. Labor Unions and Organizations. Tunisia. 1920-56. *1533*
—. Diplomacy. Great Britain. Italy. Riots. Somalia (Mogadisho). 1948. *3034*
—. Economic development. Military Government. Sierra Leone. 1967-68. *2338*
—. Economic planning. Egypt. 1922-43. *1171*
—. Egypt. Great Britain. Rebellions. Wafd Party. 1918-21. *1206*
—. Egypt. Haqqī, Yahyā. Literary criticism. 1920-59. *1323*
—. Egypt. Islam. Salafi movement. 1920-40. *1223*
—. Egypt. Secret societies. 1870-1924. *1242*
—. Elites. Great Britain. Krio. Railroads. Sierra Leone. Strikes. 1919-26. *2370*
—. English. Language. 1710-1975. *245*
—. Europeans. South Africa. Zimbabwe. 1974-79. *3335*
—. Foreign Policy. Morocco. USA. 1943-56. *1446*
—. Foreign Policy. Neutralism. 1920-76. *462*
—. Foreign Relations. Political economy. Race relations. 1975. *486*
—. Germany. Morocco. Pan-Islamism. World War I. 1914-18. *689*
—. Ghana. Independence Movements. Sekyi, Kobina. 1920's-50's. *1768*
—. Government repression. Mozambique. Political protest. 1920-49. *3633*
—. Historiography. 1945-74. *282*
—. Historiography. 19c-20c. 1960's-70's. *56*
—. Historiography. Race Relations. South Africa. 1965-72. *3844*
—. Historiography (Marxist). Ranger, T. O. Resistance. 20c. *14*
—. Independence. Kenya. Mau Mau. 1944-60. *2943*
—. Independence movements. Malawi. 1891-1964. *3617*
—. Italy. Libya. Qadhafi, Muammar. 1911-78. *1392*
—. Labor Unions and Organizations. Political Participation. Working conditions. Zimbabwe. 20c. *4155*
—. Libya. Ottoman Empire. Secret Service. *Tashkilati Makhsusa*. 1911-18. *1364*
—. Madagascar. Press. 1945-60. *3578*
—. Mauritania. Political Leadership. Sidiyya Baba. 1862-1926. *1975*
—. Newspapers. Tanzania. 1937-60. *3208*
—. Nigeria. Ojo-Cole, Julius. ca 1920-38. *2166*
—. Nigeria. Theater. 1890-1970's. *2202*
—. Nigeria (Lagos). Pelewura, Alimotu. Political Parties. Women. 1900-51. *2131*
—. Pan-Africanism. Race. 20c. *113*
—. Political Factions. Zimbabwe. 1960-79. *4215*
—. Political Factions. Zimbabwe. 1961-75. *4203*
—. Political Protest. Zimbabwe. 1898-1957. *4232*
—. Politics. 1960-73. *333*
—. Religious movements, messianic. 1920's-70's. *159*
—. Socialism. -1970's. *321*
—. USSR. 1917-76. *449*
—. Zimbabwe. 1956-64. *4199*
Nationalism, African. Industrialization. Multinational corporations. Political economy. South Africa. 1978. *3787*
Nationalism, Cultural. Documents. Madagascar. Politics. Student movement. 1972. *3587*
—. Feminism. Ghana. Hayford, Adelaide Casely. Universal Negro Improvement Association. Women. 1868-1960. *1850*
Nationalism, Muslim. Africa, North. Cold War. Foreign policy. USA. 1945-62. *978*
Nationalism (review article). Davidson, Basil. Historiography. 1890's-1970's. *35*
Nationalist movements. Algeria. Anticolonialism. Elites. Morocco. Tunisia. 1900-62. *922*
—. Cities. *Dahir Barbère* (law). Morocco. Rif War. 1920-40. *1415*
Nationalist organizations. Basutoland Progressive Association. *Lekhotla La Bafo* (Council of Commoners). Lesotho. 20c. *3546*
Nationalist Party. Afrikaners. Apartheid. Civil religion. South Africa. 1898-1970's. *3958*
Nationalities *See also* names of specific national groups, e.g. Ibo; Ethnic Groups.
—. Civil war. Colonial Government. Nigeria. Political Leadership. 1950's-60's. *2146*
Nationalization. 1950's-70's. *591*
—. 1956-75. *590*
—. 1956-75. *674*
—. Agricultural Policy. Algeria. 1963-78. *1108*
—. Algeria. Newspapers. 1962-73. *1004*
—. Arbitration, international. International law. Libya. Oil Industry and Trade. USA. 1971-80. *1404*
—. Banking. Socialism. Tanzania. 1960's. *3125*
—. Banking. Tanzania. 1960-70. *3098*
—. Business. Foreign Investments. Kenya (Kitale). 1969-76. *2900*
—. Compagnie Financière de Suez. Egypt. France. Suez Canal. 1956-80. *1219*
—. Copper. Générale Congolaise des Minerais. Union Minière du Haut-Katanga (UMHK). Zaire. ca 1960-77. *2478*
—. Copper industry. Economic Conditions. Multinational corporations. Zambia. 1969-73. *4050*
—. Copper Mines and Mining. Economic Policy. Zambia. 1969-78. *4085*
—. Copper Mines and Mining. Mining industry. Multinational Corporations. Zaire. Zambia. 1960's-82. *668*
—. Foreign investments. Indigenization. 1960-75. *664*
—. Foreign investments, private. Government Enterprise (parastatal holding corporations). Tanzania. 1967-74. *3106*
Native Administration. Colleges and Universities. Curricula. South Africa. 1956-75. *3985*
—. Education. Ghana, northern. White Fathers. 1908-51. *1830*
Native Affairs Department Annual (periodical). Periodicals. Zimbabwe. 1923-81. *4139*
Native Commissioners. Nicknames. Zimbabwe. 1892-1948. *4289*
Native Land Husbandry Act. Colonial policy. Land Tenure. Legislation. Zimbabwe. 1951-80. *4163*
Native states. Colonial Government. Ghana, northern. Local government. 20c. *1773*
Natives' Land Act. Anti-Slavery and Aborigines' Protection Society. South Africa. 1913-19. *3944*
NATO. Africa, southern. Neocolonialism. South Africa. 1949-76. *3417*
—. Alliances. South Africa. 1967-80. *3877*
Natural Resources *See also* Fishing; Mineral Resources; Reclamation of Land.
—. Africa, southern. Great Powers. Intervention. Politics. 1970's. *3418*
—. Economic development. 1960's-70's. *589*
—. Economic independence. Zambia. 1960-75. *4062*
—. Nigeria (Igboland). Population distribution. 1966. *1999*
—. Oil Industry and Trade. ca 1956-74. *602*
Naval Bases. Indian Ocean. Somalia. USSR. 1970-75. *3027*
Naval strategy. Indian Ocean. Somalia. USSR. 1960-75. *3025*
Navies *See also* headings beginning with the word naval; Military.
—. Economic Development (maritime). Egypt. USA. 1970's. *1135*
—. Great Britain. Italy. Libya. Shipping. World War II. 1940-43. *752*
—. Liberia. 1892-1970. *1956*
Nazaretha Church. Religion. Shembe, Isaiah. South Africa (Natal). 1910-78. *3955*
Nazism. Africa, North. Anti-Semitism. Germany. Propaganda. 1933-45. *954*
—. Africa, North. Germany. Propaganda. World War II. 1935-45. *721*
—. Egypt. Radicals and Radicalism. 1930's. *1291*
Ndebele. Ethnic conflict. Shona. Zimbabwe. 10c-20c. *4275*
Ndendeuli. Ethnic identity. Tanzania. 1840-1952. *3193*
Negotiations. Dams. Ethiopia. Great Britain. Lake Tana. 1922-35. *2704*
—. Independence (review article). Italy. Rossi, Gianluigi *(L'Africa Italiana verso l'Indipendenza, 1941-1949)*. UN. 1946-49. *233*
Negritude. Africa, West. Poetry. USA. 1930-72. *901*
—. Authors. Diop, Alioune. Senegal. 1940-80. *2311*
—. Authors. France. Harlem Renaissance. Literature. USA. 1921-39. *852*
—. Blyden, Edward Wilmot. Ideology. Senghor, Leopold. 1800-1900's. *810*
—. Chad. Literature. Maran, René. ca 1920-40. *808*
—. Colonialism. Literature and politics. Senghor, Leopold. 1906-69. *823*
—. Decolonization. Nationalism. 1940's-70's. *844*
—. Ethnic groups. Senegal. Senghor, Leopold. 1980. *2331*
—. Ideas, History of. 1930's-70's. *257*
—. Literature. 1600's-1970's. *890*
—. National development. Senegal. Senghor, Leopold. 1960's-70's. *2303*
—. Senegal. Senghor, Leopold. 1940-73. *2297*
Nellis, John R. Ingles, Clyde R. Scholarship (foreign; review article). Tanzania. 1960's-74. *3172*
Nemapare, E. T. J. Methodist Church. Separatist Movements. Zimbabwe. 1930-50. *4328*
Nemery, Jaafar. Addis Ababa Agreement. Civil War. Sudan. 1957-73. *1465*
—. Addis Ababa Agreement. Domestic Policy. Foreign policy. Sudan. 1972-76. *1510*
—. Foreign policy. Sudan. 1969-75. *1475*
—. Foreign policy. Sudan. 1969-79. *1521*
—. Military Government. Politics and the Military. Sudan. 1956-71. *1468*
—. Political development. Sudan. 1969-79. *1461*
—. Public Administration. Sudan. 1950-79. *1520*
—. Religion. Revolution. Sudan. Tradition. 16c-1979. *1504*
Neocolonialism *See also* Colonialism.
—. 1960's-70's. *240*
—. Africa, southern. National liberation movements. 1945-70's. *3399*
—. Africa, southern. NATO. South Africa. 1949-76. *3417*
—. African Independence Party of Senegal. Government, Resistance to. Senegal. 1958-72. *2306*
—. Agriculture. 1960-80. *636*
—. Apartheid. South Africa. 1947-73. *3710*
—. Constitutions. Diplomacy. Great Britain. Independence. Kenya. 1960-69. *2948*
—. Diplomacy. Guerrilla movements. Zimbabwe. 1973-77. *4206*
—. Economic Policy. Independence Movements. Socialism. Tanzania. 1890-1975. *3063*
—. Economic structure. Malawi. 1891-1973. *3611*
—. Foreign Relations. France. 1950's-60's. *390*
—. France. 1920-80. *423*
—. France. 1958-70's. *492*
—. France. 1960-72. *491*
—. France. Great Britain. 1960's. *502*

—. Great Britain. Portugal. Racism. South Africa. Zimbabwe. 1960's-70's. *3328*
—. Kenya. Political economy. Zimbabwe. 1920's-77. *4157*
—. National liberation movements. Organization of African Unity. 1963-73. *70*
—. National liberation movements. Pan-Africanism. Revolution. 1945-73. *116*
—. Nkrumah, Kwame. Political Theory. 1950's-72. *1800*
Neocolonialism (review article). Anthropology. Capitalism. Congo. Marxism. Rey, P. P. 20c. *2440*
Netanyahu, Jonathan. Entebbe Raid. Israel. Uganda. 1976. *3326*
Netherlands. Boycott Outspan Action Foundation (BOA). Oranges. South Africa. 1972-73. *3757*
Neto, Agostinho. Angola. 1959-79. *3472*
—. Angola. Poetry. Political leadership. ca 1922-75. *3449*
—. Angola. Political Leadership. 1947-82. *3477*
Neutralism. Foreign Policy. Nationalism. 1920-76. *462*
Neutrality *See also* Nonaligned Nations.
—. Africa, East. Colonial Government. World War I. 1914-15. *692*
—. Indian Ocean. 1970-79. *3574*
New International Economic Order. 1960-80. *555*
—. Africa, Southern. British Commonwealth. Developing nations. Diplomacy. International organizations. 1960-79. *3357*
New towns. Egypt. General Desert Development Organization. Rural development. 1961-78. *1128*
New Valley project. Economic Development. Egypt. Reclamation of Land. 1959-77. *1156*
New York Times. Biko, Steve. Reporters and Reporting. South Africa. USA. *Washington Post*. 1969-77. *3814*
New Zealand. Australia. Libraries. Office of War Information. South Africa. USA. World War II. 1942. *765*
News, international. Newspapers. 1966-76. *880*
—. Newspapers. Nigeria. Reporters and Reporting. 1978-79. *2267*
Newspaper Registration Ordinance (1893). Censorship. Colonial government. Criminal Code (Amendment) Ordinance of 1934. Ghana. Nkrumah, Kwame. 1890-1951. *1784*
Newspapers *See also* Freedom of the Press; Journalism; Periodicals; Press; Reporters and Reporting.
—. Africa, West. *West African Pilot* (newspaper). 1945-63. *1661*
—. Algeria. Nationalization. 1962-73. *1004*
—. *Ashanti Times* (newspaper). Ghana. Spears, Edward. 1947-70. *1837*
—. Elites, white. Values. Zimbabwe. 1890-1970. *4311*
—. Freedom of the Press. 1970's. *828*
—. Freedom of the press. Ghana. Political leadership. 1964-78. *1859*
—. Government ownership. Nigeria. 1400-1960. *2193*
—. Great Britain. Lobbying. Propaganda. South Africa. USA. 1972-79. *3863*
—. Ivory Coast. Mass media. 1910-73. *1936*
—. Kenya. Language. Lonrho. Nation Newspapers Ltd. 1972. *3004*
—. London Missionary Society. Madagascar. 1866-1973. *3571*
—. Nationalism. Tanzania. 1937-60. *3208*
—. News, international. 1966-76. *880*
—. News, international. Nigeria. Reporters and Reporting. 1978-79. *2267*
—. Uganda. 1900-76. *3246*
Newspapers (circulation). South Africa. 1958-77. *3974*
Ngam Ngam. Anufo. Land Tenure. Law, customary. Legislation. Togo, North. 1960-79. *2381*
Ngindo. Settlement. Tanzania, southern. 1840-1945. *3204*
Ngouabi, Marien. Congo. Congolese Labor Party. Marxism. Political Leadership. 1930's-79. *2441*
Nguema, Francisco Macias. Decolonization. Equatorial Guinea. Refugees. 1469-1979. *2443*
Ngwato. Botswana. Colonial government. Commerce. Great Britain. Jousse, Paul. Khama III. 1910-16. *3513*
—. Botswana. Khama, Tshekedi. Politics. 1948-51. *3489*
Nharo. Botswana (Ghansi). Medicine. 1970's. *3486*
Niamey (conferences). Economic development. International management. Niger River. 1885-1968. *1636*
Nicholls, George Heaton. Monarchy. Racism. Social Classes. Solomon. South Africa (Natal). Zulu (Usuthu). 1879-1933. *3886*
Nicholson, Frederick (diary). South Africa. 1834-1965. *4000*
Nicknames. Native Commissioners. Zimbabwe. 1892-1948. *4289*
Niger *See also* Africa, West; French West Africa.
—. Colonial Government. Famine. Law and order. 1931. *1983*
—. Colonialism. Dependency relationships. Social change. Tuareg, Yullemmeden kel Dinnik. 1800-1974. *1979*
—. Coups d'etat. Diori, Hamani. 1974. *1986*
—. Droughts. Economic Conditions. Peasants. Social Conditions. 1968-78. *1981*
—. Hauka. Modernization. Sects, politico-religious. 1850-1975. *1982*
—. Nigeria. Peanuts. Smuggling. 1935-76. *1621*
—. Political Parties (traditionalist). 1946-60. *1985*
—. Rebellions. Sanusi brotherhood. Tuareg. 1916-17. *1984*
Niger (Agadez). Culture. Travel accounts. 14c-1982. *1978*
Niger (Aïr). Marriage, endogamous. Social Organization. Tuareg, Yullemmeden. 19c-20c. *1980*
Niger (Arlit). Industrialization. Mining. Uranium. 1974-81. *1988*
—. Mining. Technical assistance. Uranium. 1968-73. *1987*
Niger Company. Labor. Migration. Nigeria, northern. Tin mining. 1903-45. *2032*
—. Nigeria. Technology. Trade. 1900-20. *2050*
Niger (Damergu). Trade, trans-Saharan. Tripoli-Kano route. 1870-1930. *1977*
Niger (Kano). Business. Dependency. Indigenization. Technology. 1972-79. *2037*
Niger River. Economic development. International management. Niamey (conferences). 1885-1968. *1636*
Niger River, lower. Cassava. Influenza. Nigeria. 20c. *2057*
Nigeria *See also* Africa, West.
—. Abisi. Political change. Rites and ceremonies. Rukuba. ca 1950-76. *2227*
—. Acculturation. Adja. Benin. Settlement. 18c-1945. *2220*
—. Acculturation. Christianity. Islam. Yoruba. 1970's. *2215*
—. Achebe, Chinua. Novels. 1963-68. *2271*
—. Adult education. Colleges and Universities. Colonialism. 1945-55. *2276*
—. Adult education. Oxford University Delegacy. 1945-50. *2277*
—. Africa, Southern. Federalism. South Africa. 20c. *30*
—. Africa, southern. Foreign Policy. National liberation movements. National Security. 1967-70. *2180*
—. Africa, Southern. Foreign policy. Oil Industry and Trade. 1970-80. *2188*
—. Africa, West. Colonial government. Muslims. Rebellions. 1914-18. *703*
—. Africa, West. Diplomacy. Economic Community of West African States. Economic Integration. Regionalism. 1960-75. *1663*
—. Africa, West. Foreign Relations. 1960-75. *2152*
—. African affairs. Economic Growth. Power. 1970-74. *2001*
—. African unity. Foreign Policy. Gowon, Yakubu. Political leadership. 1967-75. *2153*
—. Agricultural Development. Land Tenure. 1966-73. *2009*
—. Agricultural Policy. Economic Development. 1975-80. *2081*
—. Agricultural production. Great Britain. Sesame. Tiv. Trade. 1900-60. *2024*
—. Agriculture. Beti. Cameroon. Cocoa. Labor, division of. Women. Yoruba. 1950-79. *620*
—. Ajuwa Grammar School. Mayflower School. Secondary Education. Vocational education. 1956-79. *2208*
—. Akinyemi, A. B. Balewa, Abubakar. Foreign Policy (review article). Idang, Gordon J. 1960-66. *2090*
—. Aladura. Faith healing. Medicine. Sects, Religious. 1950's-80's. *2248*
—. Angola. Civil war. Intervention (foreign). Organization of African Unity. 1960-75. *270*
—. Anthropologists. 1884-1960. *2254*
—. Arabic. Historical sources. Manuscripts. 15c-20c. *2007*
—. Arbitration Convention. Commercial disputes. Oil industry and Trade. Treaties. UN. 1960's-70's. *2084*
—. Armies. Social Change. 1965-77. *2002*
—. Art. Missions and Missionaries. 15c-20c. *2293*
—. Art. Modernism. 1918-60. *2273*
—. Attitudes. English, competence in. Social status. 1973. *2229*
—. Attitudes. Methodology. Political culture. Social Classes. 1800-1960. *2124*
—. Authors. Soyinka, Wole. ca 1952-63. *2258*
—. Azikiwe, Nnamdi. Constitutional crises. Presidency. 1964-65. *2094*
—. *Babalawo*. Counseling. ca 500 BC-1978. *2261*
—. Baldwin, Charlene M. Baldwin, David E. Bibliographies. Yoruba (review article). 11c-20c. *2008*
—. Bangladesh. Civil war. Economic policies. Political economy. 20c. *2145*
—. Bibliographies (national). Libraries. 1953-80. *1990*
—. Bibliography. Ghana. Libraries, research. Sierra Leone. 20c. *1600*
—. Bureaucracies. Foreign policy. Politics. 1960-75. *2102*
—. Cabinet. Elites (political). Parliaments. 1954-65. *2137*
—. Cameroon. Fulbe (Mbororean). Nomads and Nomadism. Sedentarization. Social Change. 20c. *1635*
—. Capitalism. Sects, Religious. Social Classes. Yoruba. 1947-74. *2017*
—. Cartels. Cocoa. Economic Crisis. Ghana. *West African Pilot* (newspaper). 1937. *1620*
—. Cassava. Influenza. Niger River, lower. 20c. *2057*
—. Catholics. Converts. Igbo. Ostracism. ca 1955-78. *2217*
—. Censorship. Military Government. Press. 1966-78. *2241*
—. Censorship. Press. 1960's-76. *2167*
—. Census (1973). Demography. 1973. *2203*
—. Christian churches. Civil war. Relief efforts. ca 1966-69. *2294*
—. Christian ideals. Fagunwa, D. O. Novels. Traditional beliefs. 1939-61. *2275*
—. Church and State. Education. Missions and Missionaries. 1842-1948. *2216*
—. Cities. Poverty. ca 1960-75. *2062*
—. Civil Service. Colonial Government. Morale. World War II. 1941-45. *759*
—. Civil War. 1960-69. *2184*
—. Civil war. Colonial Government. Nationalities. Political Leadership. 1950's-60's. *2146*
—. Civil War. Communal conflict (review article). Modernization. 1971. *2174*
—. Civil War. Dahomey. Smuggling. 1966-74. *1644*
—. Civil war. DeGaulle, Charles. Foreign policy. France. 1967-69. *2107*
—. Civil war. Economic interests. Politics. Regional competition. ca 1947-67. *2048*
—. Civil War. Ethnic diversity. Ife, University of. Political attitudes. Students. 1957-69. *2111*
—. Civil war. Ethnicity, theories of. 1966-67. *2186*
—. Civil war. Federalism. Political factions. 1960-66. *2117*
—. Civil war. Foreign relations. Great powers. 1967-75. *2155*
—. Civil war. Foreign Relations. Religion. Reporters and Reporting. 1960's. *2095*
—. Civil War. National Integration. 19c-20c. *2108*
—. Civil war. Oil Industry and Trade. 1967-74. *2010*
—. Civil War. Poisoning, rumors of. 1967-70. *2148*
—. Civil War. Red Cross. 1966. *2287*
—. Civil War. Refugees. Relief efforts. Sudan. UN. 1966-72. *524*
—. Civil war. Relief efforts. 1967-70. *2116*
—. Civil War (review article). 1967-70. *2196*
—. Civil-military relations. Ghana. Military education. Uganda. 1960-69. *346*
—. Clifford, Hugh. Colonial Government. 1919-25. *2113*
—. Clifford, Hugh. Colonial Government. 1919. *2168*
—. Cocoa. Dahomey. Smuggling. 1968-74. *1645*
—. Cocoa. Economic Regulations. World War II. 1939-45. *758*
—. Colleges and Universities. Coups d'etat. Student activism. 1974-76. *2114*

—. Colleges and Universities. Education. Public finance. 1960's-70's. *2242*
—. Colonial Government. Colonial Office. Decolonization. Richards, Arthur. 1939-45. *2125*
—. Colonial Government. Constitutions. Governors. Nationalism. 1935-51. *2177*
—. Colonial government. Educational policy. Lugard, Frederick. 1900-18. *2223*
—. Colonial Government. Forests. Great Britain. Legislation. Rubber. 1897-1940. *2025*
—. Colonial government. French West Africa. Islam. Rebellions. World War I. 1914-17. *704*
—. Colonial government. Great Britain. Muslims. Rebellions. World War I. 1914-19. *705*
—. Colonial Government. Great Britain. Tiv. 1900-70. *2234*
—. Colonial government. Igbo. Political systems, dual-sex. Women. -1970's. *2163*
—. Colonial Government. Language policy. Yoruba. 1882-1955. *2218*
—. Colonial Government. Local Politics. Political leadership. 1904-54. *2189*
—. Colonial government. Monarchy. Yoruba. 1900-60. *2101*
—. Colonial Government. Strikes, general. 1945. *2067*
—. Colonialism. Demobilization. Veterans. World War I. 1918-25. *700*
—. Colonialism. Development. Libraries. 1900-60. *2240*
—. Colonialism. Economic Development. 1860-1960. *2021*
—. Colonialism. Education. 1840-1939. *2264*
—. Colonialism. Money (precolonial currencies). 1880-1948. *2054*
—. Communism. Labor Unions and Organizations. Nigerian Trade Union Congress. Socialist Workers and Farmers Party. 1960's-70's. *2082*
—. Conflict and conflict resolution. *Oba* (king). Social organization. Yoruba. 19c-20c. *2157*
—. Congregation of the Holy Ghost. Missions and Missionaries. St. Patrick's Missionary Society. 1920-30. *2274*
—. Constitutional conflict. Economic factors. Federalism. Secession threat. 1950-70. *2106*
—. Constitutions. Elections. Ethnic Groups. Political campaigns. 1977-79. *2133*
—. Constitutions. Human rights. 1957-79. *2096*
—. Constitutions. State government. 1975-78. *2130*
—. Cooperatives. Women. Yoruba. 1972-80. *2039*
—. Coups d'etat. 1966. *2128*
—. Criminal law. Witchcraft. 1938-59. *2270*
—. Cultural Imperialism (review article). Great Britain. Lefever, Ernest W. ca 1700-1966. *213*
—. Decisionmaking. Federalism. India. Regional government. 1967-73. *2183*
—. Degrees, Academic. Higher Education. London University. 1887-1951. *2279*
—. Democracy. Political Systems. 1960-81. *2195*
—. Democracy, Consociational. Pluralism. 1967-76. *2169*
—. Dependency, structural. 1946-75. *2074*
—. Depression. Economic conditions. 1930's. *2044*
—. Developing nations. European Economic Community. Trade. 1966-73. *2014*
—. Development. Physicians. Politics. 1935-75. *2206*
—. Diplomatic Relations. Israel. 1950-73. *2093*
—. Economic Conditions. Oil Industry and Trade. 1973-79. *2070*
—. Economic development. 1960's. *2083*
—. Economic development. Foreign Relations. Politics. 1962-75. *1997*
—. Economic development. Government Enterprise. 1947-73. *2073*
—. Economic development. Oil. 1958-74. *2042*
—. Economic Development. Oil. 1960-77. *1993*
—. Economic development plans. 1914-77. *2031*
—. Economic planning. Import licensing. 1950-75. *2027*
—. Economic Planning. India. Industrial location. Political variables. 1973. *2043*
—. Economic Policy. Foreign Investments. Indigenization. 1972-74. *2020*
—. Economic Structure. Management. 1956-80. *2033*
—. Economic system. Government. 1945-73. *1995*
—. Education. Ethnicity. Social mobility. 1840's-1975. *2212*
—. Education. Igbo. Social status. Westernization. 1800-1956. *2239*
—. Education. Islam. Religion. 1903-78. *2232*
—. Education. National Development. 1914-78. *2230*
—. Education. Publishers and Publishing. 1950-70. *2214*
—. Educational Policy. 1959-61. *2235*
—. Election laws. Federalism. 1939-66. *2105*
—. Elections. 1966-79. *2165*
—. Elections. Ethnic Groups. 1978-80. *2158*
—. Elections. Military government. 1978-80. *2135*
—. Elections. Voting and Voting Behavior. 1959-79. *2118*
—. Electric Power. Foreign aid. ca 1958-75. *2079*
—. Elementary education. Politics. 1955-77. *2265*
—. Elias, T. O. (review article). Law. Social change. 1960-73. *2209*
—. Elites. Literature, popular. 1925-74. *2259*
—. Entrepreneurs. 1964-65. *2047*
—. Entrepreneurship. Ijebu. Yoruba. 1950-74. *2012*
—. Entrepreneurship. Yaba Industrial Estate. 1958-70. *2040*
—. Ethnic Groups. Federal reorganization. Geography. 1900-74. *2172*
—. Ethnic groups. Higher education. 1960-79. *2122*
—. Ethnic groups. Political Integration. State Government. 1960-78. *2151*
—. Ethnic groups. Regionalism. 1900-76. *2291*
—. Ethnicity. Government Ownership. Intergovernmental Relations. Radio. Television. 1932-62. *2290*
—. Examinations. Oxford University Delegacy. Secondary education. 1929-37. *2278*
—. Fafunwa, A. B. Higher Education (review article). Okafor, Nduka. 20c. *2269*
—. Fagunwa, D. O. Literature. Soyinka, Wole. Tradition. Tutuola, Amos. Yoruba. 1945-70's. *2252*
—. Family structure. Hausa. Rural areas. Social Change. 20c. *2247*
—. Federal states. Political parties, regional. 1945-66. *2091*
—. Federalism. Politics. Wages. 1954-75. *2015*
—. Fertility. 1952-80. *2281*
—. Foreign policy. 1960-72. *2162*
—. Foreign policy. Military Government. 1966-79. *2156*
—. Foreign policy. Oil. 1958-75. *2140*
—. Foreign Policy. Political Power. 1960-73. *2138*
—. Foreign Policy. USSR. 1960-77. *2154*
—. Foreign Relations. Ghana. Israel. 1956-79. *418*
—. Foreign Relations. Gowon, Yakubu. Great Britain. 1961-75. *2098*
—. Foreign Relations. Great Powers. Politics. 1960-75. *2099*
—. Foreign Relations. Israel. 1960-73. *2097*
—. Foreign Relations. South Africa. 1960-75. *391*
—. Foreign Relations. Tanzania. 1963-79. *468*
—. Foreign Relations. USSR. 1960-73. *2159*
—. Ghana. Government (civilian). 1970's. *1652*
—. Ghana. Military Government. 1960-77. *1624*
—. Ghana. Military government. 1978. *1651*
—. Ghana. Models. Political change. 20c. *1619*
—. Government. Mass Media. 1951-66. *2150*
—. Government. Military Government. Shagari, Shehu. 1973-82. *2136*
—. Government. Posters. 1975-79. *2141*
—. Government. Presidency. 1966-77. *2120*
—. Government (civilian). Military Government. 1979. *2132*
—. Government ownership. Newspapers. 1400-1960. *2193*
—. Gowon, Yakubu. Military Government. Politics. 1966-75. *2149*
—. Historiography. -1975. *1991*
—. Ideology. Socialism. 20c. *2103*
—. Igbo. Linguistics. Names, personal. -1973. *2253*
—. Ijebu. Political theory. 1892-1943. *2104*
—. Imoudi, Michael. Labor movement. Railway Workers' Union. 1940-42. *2066*
—. Imperialism. Multinational corporations. 1960-78. *2060*
—. Indigenization. Industry. Kenya. 1954-80. *594*
—. Indigenization. National integration. 1960-80. *2003*
—. Industry. Wage differentials. 1964-70. *2028*
—. Infants. Orphans. Voluntary work. 19c-20c. *2283*
—. Intellectuals. 1961-77. *2263*
—. Islam. Political culture. 20c. *2175*
—. Japan. Trade. 1947-74. *2029*
—. Judicial Administration. 19c-1979. *2112*
—. Kenya. Labor unions and organizations. Politics. 1939-66. *210*
—. Kenya. National development. Research. Science. 1970's. *612*
—. Kenya. Scientific Experiments and Research. 1960's-70's. *613*
—. Labor, division of. Women. Yoruba. 1500-1980. *2011*
—. Labor Unions and Organizations. Politics. 1945-65. *2119*
—. Land Tenure. 1950-75. *2030*
—. Land Use Decree. 1978. *2077*
—. Language function. 1972. *2205*
—. Language policy. Yoruba. 1882-1952. *2221*
—. Languages, European. Schools. 1859-1959. *2280*
—. Leadership. Secondary Education. Women. 1977-82. *2238*
—. Libraries. 1840's-1975. *2211*
—. Libraries. 1948-75. *2226*
—. Libraries. 1960-78. *2295*
—. Literature. Political Theory. Soyinka, Wole. 1960-81. *2134*
—. Literature. Publishers and Publishing. 1950-80. *2256*
—. Mbadiwe, Kingsley Ozuomba. Political Leadership. USA. 1939-47. *2139*
—. Military Capability. Nuclear power. 1968-81. *2035*
—. Military government. 1960's-70's. *349*
—. Military Government. 1966-77. *2092*
—. Military government. 1966-79. *2182*
—. Military government. 1970-75. *2144*
—. Military Government. Political development. 1970-73. *2181*
—. Military Government. Political Leadership. 1966-79. *2115*
—. Military Government. Public Administration. 1966-77. *2110*
—. Military government. Reform. 1945-74. *2176*
—. Military Government. USSR. 1965-70. *456*
—. Military rule. Public opinion. 1971-72. *2178*
—. Modernization. Political development. Regional planning. 20c. *2160*
—. Modernization. Political parties. Political Systems. 1920-66. *2192*
—. Mortality. 1930's-80. *2289*
—. National characteristics. ca 1948-74. *1992*
—. National Council of Nigerian Citizens. Political Leadership. 1940-60. *2126*
—. National Development. National Youth Service Corps. 1973-79. *2262*
—. National Development. Oil Industry and Trade. USA. 1960-80. *2071*
—. National Youth Service Corps. Youth. 1970-73. *2197*
—. Nationalism. Ojo-Cole, Julius. ca 1920-38. *2166*
—. Nationalism. Theater. 1890-1970's. *2202*
—. News, international. Newspapers. Reporters and Reporting. 1978-79. *2267*
—. Niger. Peanuts. Smuggling. 1935-76. *1621*
—. Niger Company. Technology. Trade. 1900-20. *2050*
—. Occupations. Rukuba. Social Change. Taxation. 1905-70's. *2046*
—. Ogunde, Hubert. Political commentary. Theater. 1945-75. *2236*
—. Ogunde, Hubert. Theater. 1946-72. *2231*
—. Oil industry and Trade. Technology transfer. 1956-74. *2075*
—. Political conflict. Regionalism. Social change. 1900-. *2004*
—. Political Development. 1960-80. *2179*
—. Political stability. States, size of. 1964-67. *2087*
—. Political Systems. 1960-79. *2127*
—. Politics. Rebellions. Tiv. 1960. *2147*
—. Politics. Youth. 1970's. *2207*
—. Press. Radio. 1960-71. *2237*
—. Public Administration. 1960-77. *2121*
—. Religion. 15c-1975. *2251*
—. Secondary Education. Social studies. 1950's-74. *2204*
—. Social conflict. 1971-78. *2257*
—. Social customs. Twins, cult of. Yoruba. 1750-1850. *2228*
—. Social organization. 1960-70's. *1996*
—. Strikes, general. 1963-64. *2068*
—. Tax evasion. ca 1973-75. *2056*
Nigeria (Aba). Bibliographies. Igbo. Riots. Women. 1929-30. *2123*
Nigeria (Abakaliki). Ethnic groups. 19c-1960. *2282*
Nigeria (Adamawa). Denmark. Mbula. Missions and Missionaries. Prophet movement. 1926-35. *2255*
Nigeria (Akoko-Edo). Boundaries. Ethnic Groups. 1960-74. *2086*
Nigeria (Anambra). Agricultural development. Rural development. 1955-85. *2058*

Nigeria (Awka, Nsukka). Urbanization. 1960-76. *2233*
Nigeria (Bendel state, Ikaleland). Migrant Labor. Rural development. Urhobo. 1920-76. *2065*
Nigeria (Benin). Colonial Government. Slavery. 1897-1945. *2250*
—. Ethnic groups. Occupations. 1940's-77. *2061*
Nigeria (Benin, Ife, Nok). Arts, functional. 900 BC-20c. *2292*
Nigeria (Borgu). Colonial Government. Dahomey (Borgu). Rebellions. 1915-17. *1623*
Nigeria (Bornu). Economic Development. Salt industry. 1750-1936. *2041*
Nigeria (Calabar). Urbanization. 1895-1978. *2052*
Nigeria (Calabar, Owerri). Aba riots. Igbo. Social Conditions. Women. 1925. *2194*
Nigeria (Cross River Basin). Markets. Villages. ca 1500-1970's. *2049*
Nigeria, Eastern. Chakaka Pola. Famine, seasonal. Malawi, Northern. Onicha Ibo. 1964-71. *656*
—. Christianity. Conversion. 1921-66. *2249*
—. Civil war. Decisionmaking. Land use. Yams. 1964-77. *2080*
—. Colonial government. Economic Growth. 1862-1960. *2161*
—. Education. Public finance. Secondary Education. 1846-1970. *2243*
Nigeria (Eastern Delta). Aro. Colonial Government. Trade, precolonial. 19c-20c. *2055*
Nigeria (Eastern Region). Church and State. Education. 1956-66. *2100*
Nigeria (Eastern states). Civil war. Economic recovery. 1966-75. *2078*
Nigeria (Gongola State; Mambila grasslands). Development. Fulbe. Social organization. 1915-74. *2245*
Nigeria (Hausaland). Agricultural growth. Hill, Polly. Villages (review article). 20c. *2064*
Nigeria (Ibadan). Begging. Hausa. Migration, Internal. 1974. *2016*
—. Cities. Environment, physical. 1973. *2005*
Nigeria (Ife). Communal compartmentalization. Modakeke. Politics. 1820-1966. *2171*
Nigeria (Igboland). Natural resources. Population distribution. 1966. *1999*
Nigeria (Igboland, Northern). Agriculture. Eastern Nigeria Project. Regional development. Settlement schemes. 1945-67. *2034*
Nigeria (Ilaje). Holy Apostles. Religious movements. Utopias (defection, recruitment). 1947-74. *2225*
Nigeria (Ilesha). Social organization. 16c-19c. 1920-75. *2284*
Nigeria (Imo). Igbo. Urbanization. 1902-78. *2266*
Nigeria (Jos). Communications. Urban development. ca 1900-78. *1998*
Nigeria (Jos plateau). Labor. Tin mining. 1906-21. *2045*
Nigeria (Kaduna). Urban development. 1913-78. *1994*
Nigeria (Kano). Colonial government. Islam. Taxation. 1806-1927. *2076*
—. Constitutions. Elections. 1949-51. *2191*
—. Decentralization. Public Administration. 1966-72. *2164*
—. Economic Growth. Education. Islam. 19c-1981. *2260*
—. Islam. Local Politics. Pakistan (South Waziristan). Rural Areas. 20c. *2213*
—. Monarchy. Succession. 1920's-63. *2142*
Nigeria (Lagos). Colonial Government. Food Shortages. Price control. Pullen marketing scheme. World War II. 1941-47. *2069*
—. Concert-party. Ogunde, Hubert. Theater. 1910-75. *2201*
—. Culture, European. Literature. Missions and Missionaries. 1515-1930's. *2219*
—. Nationalism. Pelewura, Alimotu. Political Parties. Women. 1900-51. *2131*
—. Oil Industry and Trade. 1966-78. *2022*
—. Urbanization. 1970's. *2198*
Nigeria (Mid-Western State). Political Systems. State government. Succession, forms of. Urhobo kingdoms. 1952-63. *2170*
Nigeria (Muslim emirates). Colonial Government. Islam. Missions and Missionaries. Proselytization. 1900-28. *2288*
Nigeria, northern. Assimilation. Hausa. Islam. 20c. *2286*
—. Birom. Miners. Social protest. Stealing. Tin. 1958-78. *2246*
—. Capitalism. Economic Structure. Peasants. Social Classes. 1850-1980. *2072*
—. Colonial Government. Great Britain. Public Finance. Taxation. 1900-34. *2038*
—. Education. Public Administration. Sudan. 1890-1962. *227*
—. Labor. Migration. Niger Company. Tin mining. 1903-45. *2032*
—. Labor aristocracy. Rural-urban studies. Wages. 1974. *2036*
Nigeria (Northern; Yauri). Abdullahi. Colonial Government. Indirect rule. 1923-31. *2185*
Nigeria, North-West. Droughts. 1913-73. *2006*
Nigeria (Northwestern; Sokoto). Democratic institutions. District councils. 1967-68. *2190*
Nigeria (Obudu). Christianity. Missions and Missionaries. 1900-75. *2199*
Nigeria (Oguta). Igbo. Kalabari. Palm oil. Trade. 1900-50. *2026*
—. Trade. Transportation. Waterways. 1885-1945. *2053*
Nigeria (Onitsha). Market town development. Migration, Internal. Trade. 1960-67. *2063*
Nigeria (Oyo). Bēre festival. -1973. *2224*
Nigeria (Port Harcourt). Urbanization. 1950-79. *2023*
Nigeria (Rivers State, Port Harcourt). Local identity. Patriotism. Tamuno, Tekena N. 1913-60's. *2272*
Nigeria (Sapele). Local government. National Development. 1955-77. *2129*
Nigeria (Southeastern). Colonial Government. Roads. 1903-39. *2051*
—. Colonial Government. Warrant chiefs. 1891-1951. *2089*
Nigeria, southern. Local government. 1957-71. *2173*
Nigeria (Western). Agbekoya Parapo. Peasants. Rebellions. 1968-69. *2088*
—. Agbekoya Uprising. Cocoa farmers. Military Government. Taxation. 1968-69. *2187*
—. Agricultural Development. Cocoa. Farmers, migrant. Innovation (concept). 1850-1974. *2018*
—. Agriculture. Cocoa. 1964-74. *2059*
—. Boundaries. 1897-1963. *1989*
—. Cocoa. Economics (supply response). 1909-44. *2019*
—. Cocoa. Farmers. Populism. 1893-1973. *2109*
—. Colonial Government. Obas' Conference. Political Participation. 1913-79. *2143*
—. Schools, community. Secondary Education. 1925-55. *2210*
—. Secondary Education. 1960-74. *2268*
Nigeria (Western; Ibadan). City Planning. Politics. 1958-73. *2085*
Nigeria (Yola). Agriculture. Industry. Urban development. ca 1841-1978. *2000*
Nigeria (Zaria). Agricultural Industry. Cadbury Schweppes (firm). Foreign Investments. 1968-76. *2013*
Nigerian Trade Union Congress. Communism. Labor Unions and Organizations. Nigeria. Socialist Workers and Farmers Party. 1960's-70's. *2082*
Nigerian Union of Teachers. Teachers. 1931-40. *2244*
Nigerians. Ghana. Immigration policy. 1960-70's. *1807*
Nihilism. Ethiopia. Left. Me'ei Sone. People's Revolutionary Party. 1970-79. *2822*
Nile Valley. National identity. Political systems. Regional integration. Sudan. ca 1920-55. *1517*
Nixon Doctrine. Africa, Southern. Foreign policy. Strategic planning. USA. 1960's-74. *3339*
Nixon, Richard M. (speech). Foreign Policy. USA. 1973. *459*
Nkomo, Joshua. Guerrilla Warfare. Mugabe, Robert. Zimbabwe. 1972-78. *4220*
—. Political leadership. Zimbabwe. 1917-79. *4257*
Nkrumah, Kwame. All-African Trade Union Federation. Mboya, Tom. Political Factions. 1958-64. *62*
—. Anticolonialism. Lumumba, Patrice. Zaire. 1958-66. *2487*
—. Black nationalism. Garvey, Marcus. Pan-Africanism. USA. 1920's-75. *1804*
—. Censorship. Colonial government. Criminal Code (Amendment) Ordinance of 1934. Ghana. Newspaper Registration Ordinance (1893). 1890-1951. *1784*
—. Convention People's Party. Great Britain. Pan-African Congress. USA. 1935-63. *1781*
—. DeGaulle, Charles. Kissinger, Henry A. Nationalism. Nyerere, Julius. Political Leadership. ca 1940's-70's. *308*
—. Economic development. Ghana. Political corruption. 1955-68. *1824*
—. Economic Policy. Ghana. Industrialization. Social development. 1957-72. *1747*
—. Foreign policy. Ghana. 1966-75. *1765*
—. Foreign policy. Ghana. Organization of African Unity. 1958-63. *1799*
—. Garvey, Marcus. Independence Movements. 1920-65. *1783*
—. Ghana. Government Enterprise. Public corporations. 1951-66. *1732*
—. Ghana. Ideology. Marxism. 1956-66. *1786*
—. Ghana. Military. Race relations. 1950's-60's. *1764*
—. Ghana. National Self-image. Nyerere, Julius. Tanzania. 1951-60's. *328*
—. Ghana. National Self-image. Rhetorical strategies. 1957-60. *1803*
—. Ghana. Pan-Africanism. 1945-57. *1828*
—. Ghana. Pan-Africanism. 1966-72. *1826*
—. Ghana. Pan-Africanism. Politics (idealism). 1945-66. *1787*
—. Ghana. Political Theory. Socialism. 1967-70. *1801*
—. Ghana. Politics and the Military. 1947-79. *1794*
—. Ghana. Religion. ca 1947-66. *1809*
—. Neocolonialism. Political Theory. 1950's-72. *1800*
—. Nyerere, Julius. Pan-Africanism. ca 1960-69. *63*
—. Organization of African Unity. 1963-73. *129*
—. Revolution, African. 1935-66. *1820*
Nkrumah, Kwame *(Challenge of the Congo)*. Independence. Zaire. 1960-65. *2491*
Nkrumah, Kwame *(Consciencism)*. Africa, West. Ideology. Independence Movements. Leadership. 1964-72. *1805*
Nkrumah, Kwame (message). Ghana. Organization of African Unity. 1966-72. *1792*
Nkrumah, Kwame *(Revolutionary Path)*. Organization of African Unity. Pan-Africanism. ca 1945-71. *1793*
Nogara, Bernadino (diary). Diplomacy. Ethiopia. Italy. Pius XI, Pope. Vatican. 1935-36. *2733*
Nomadic enclaves. Africa, West. Droughts. Economic opportunity. Migrations. Villages, marginal. 1973. *1640*
Nomads and Nomadism. Cameroon. Fulbe (Mbororean). Nigeria. Sedentarization. Social Change. 20c. *1635*
—. Droughts. Economic Structure. Sahel. Social Customs. 1964-74. *1614*
—. Rebellions. Uganda (Ankole). 20c. *3232*
Nonaligned nations. Apartheid. Attitudes. South Africa. 1953-73. *3818*
—. Great Powers. 1955-76. *291*
Nonalignment. Angola. Foreign Relations. 1955-80. *3466*
—. Foreign policy. Kenya. Tanzania. 1960-77. *2587*
—. Foreign Policy. Tanzania. 1961-79. *3180*
Noncapitalist Development. Land Tenure. Peasants. 1940-50. *680*
Noncapitalist development (symposium). Socialism. USSR. 20c. 1977. *631*
Norway *See also* Scandinavia.
—. Africa, East. Developing nations. Fisheries. Lake Victoria. UN Development Program. 1965-75. *628*
—. Boycotts. Foreign relations. South Africa. 1970-77. *3933*
—. Demi-Brigade, 13th. Foreign Legion. France. Morocco. Narvik landing. World War II. 1940. *727*
—. Peacekeeping Forces. UN. Zaire. 1960-64. *2500*
Northern Rhodesia. *See* Zambia.
Novels. 1973. *774*
—. Abrahams, Peter. Race Relations. South Africa. 1945-66. *4003*
—. Achebe, Chinua. Nigeria. 1963-68. *2271*
—. Algeria. Anticolonialism. Muslims. Truphémus, Albert. 1930-35. *1107*
—. Algeria. Colonialism. Wattar, Attahar *(L'as)*. 1950's-60's. *987*
—. Angola. Independence. Pacavira, Manuel *(Nzinga Mbandi)*. 17c-20c. *3439*
—. Assimilation. Colonial policy. Senegal. 1920's-60's. *2322*
—. Benjelloun, Tahar. Boudjedra, Rashid. Khaïr-Eddine, Mohammed. Maghreb. 1965-75. *920*
—. Christian ideals. Fagunwa, D. O. Nigeria. Traditional beliefs. 1939-61. *2275*
—. Colonialism. Sembene, Ousmane *(Les bouts de bois de Dieu)*. Senegal. Strikes. 1947-48. *2298*
—. Gordimer, Nadine. Politics. Race Relations. South Africa. 1953-79. *3959*
—. Joubert, Elsa. South Africa. 1955-80. *3999*

—. LaGuma, Alex. Revolution. South Africa. 1956-72. *3952*
—. Marxism. ca 1960's-70's. *861*
—. Millin, Sarah G. Racism. South Africa. 1917-65. *4025*
—. Oral tradition. Senegal. 1970's. *2321*
Novels (Arabic). Cultural policy. Morocco. Politics. 1936-65. *1437*
Nsugbe, P. O. (memoirs). Institute for African Studies. Zambia. 1968-70. *4096*
Ntare Rushatsi. Burundi. Historiography. Monarchy. 1900-77. *2658*
Nubi. Amin, Idi. Politics. Uganda. ca 1885-1975. *3303*
Nubians. Ethnicity. Political participation. Political Theory. Uganda. 1971. *3251*
Nuclear Arms. Military Capability. South Africa. 1979. *3803*
Nuclear power. Military Capability. Nigeria. 1968-81. *2035*
Nuer. Boundaries. Dinka. Sudan (Sobat, Zaraf valleys). 1860-1976. *1490*
—. Colonial Government. Stereotypes. Sudan. 1800-1956. *1488*
—. Social Status. Sudan. Women. 1930-80. *1473*
Numismatics. Medals, commemorative. South Africa (Johannesburg). 1889-1972. *4016*
Nurses and Nursing. Attitudes. Tradition. Zambia. 1981. *4112*
Nwabueze, B. O. (review article). British Commonwealth. Constitutional law. 1870-1975. *255*
Nyakusa-Ngonde. Malawi. Marriage. Social change. Tanzania. 1875-1971. *913*
Nyasaland. *See* Malawi.
Nyassa Company. Colonial Government. Government Enterprise. Mozambique. Mozambique Company. 1870's-1941. *3665*
—. Mozambique (Nyassa). 1890-1929. *3652*
Nyau societies. Dance. Malawi. Prehistory-1975. *3622*
Nyerere, Julius. Africa, East. Economic Integration. Regionalism. ca 1920-73. *2634*
—. Amin, Idi. Cultural dependency. Marxism. Radicals and Radicalism. 19c-1973. *2614*
—. Arusha Declaration. Socialism. Tanzania. 1961-73. *3148*
—. Black studies. DuBois, W. E. B. Garvey, Marcus. Pan-Africanism. 1905-71. *128*
—. Christianity. Socialism. Tanzania. 1967-80. *3214*
—. DeGaulle, Charles. Kissinger, Henry A. Nationalism. Nkrumah, Kwame. Political Leadership. ca 1940's-70's. *308*
—. Foreign policy. Socialism. Tanzania. 1961-68. *3170*
—. Foreign Policy. Tanzania. 1961-77. *3164*
—. Ghana. National Self-image. Nkrumah, Kwame. Tanzania. 1951-60's. *328*
—. Ideology. Political Leadership. Socialism. 1960-70. *309*
—. Nkrumah, Kwame. Pan-Africanism. ca 1960-69. *63*
—. Pan-Africanism. Tanzania. 1960-77. *3151*
—. Political ideology. Tanzania. Value structure. ca 1955-75. *3162*
—. Political Leadership. Tanzania. 1961-70's. *3150*
—. Socialism, transition to. Tanzania. 1962-71. *3171*
—. Tanzania. 1964-76. *3138*
Nyerere, Julius (progress report). Population. Production. Tanganyika African National Union (TANU). Tanzania. 1969-72. *3165*
Nyerere, Julius (review article). Economic Development. Tanzania. ca 1968-73. *3142*
Nyerere, Julius (speech). Africa, Southern. Tanzania. USA. 1977. *3398*
—. Apartheid. Colonialism. Portugal. South Africa. UN. 20c. *386*
—. Pan-African Congress, 6th. 1900-74. *121*
—. Pan-African Congress, 6th. 1945-74. *122*
—. Pan-Africanism. 20c. *123*
Nyobe, Ruben Um. Cameroon. Independence Movements. 1948-59. *2414*
Nzema. Abortion. Birth Control. Ghana. 1973-75. *1857*

O

Oba (king). Conflict and conflict resolution. Nigeria. Social organization. Yoruba. 19c-20c. *2157*
Obas' Conference. Colonial Government. Nigeria, Western. Political Participation. 1913-79. *2143*
Obote, Milton. Amin, Idi. Economic Policy. Nationalism. Socialism. Uganda. 1966-71. *3295*
—. Amin, Idi. Foreign Aid. Uganda. USSR. 1962-79. *3275*
—. Amin, Idi. Politics. Uganda. 1964-73. *3247*
—. Amin, Idi. Uganda. Violence. 1962-72. *3238*
—. Ethnic Groups. Politics and the Military. Uganda. 1962-71. *3221*
—. Gukiina, Peter. Ibingira, G. S. K. Political development (review essay). Uganda. 1885-1971. *3308*
—. Human rights. Personal Narratives. Uganda. 1962-82. *3324*
—. Monarchy. Mutesa II, Edward. Uganda. Uganda People's Party. 1945-71. *3296*
—. Political leadership. Uganda People's Congress. 1966-69. *3271*
—. Politics. Uganda. 1962-71. *3319*
Occupational prestige. Ethiopia. Social change. 1958-68. *2712*
Occupational segregation. Asians. Zimbabwe. 1890-1950. *4167*
Occupations. 1954-74. *845*
—. Agriculture. Cottage industries. Markets. Uganda (Bugisu). Youth, rural. 1973. *3318*
—. Ethnic groups. Nigeria (Benin). 1940's-77. *2061*
—. Nigeria. Rukuba. Social Change. Taxation. 1905-70's. *2046*
October War. Army, 2d. Egypt. Ghazala, Mohamed. Military Strategy. Suez Canal (crossing). 1973. *1314*
—. Continental unity. Foreign Relations. Israel. 1956-74. *452*
—. Decisionmaking. Egypt. Foreign Policy. 1971-73. *1185*
—. Decisionmaking. Egypt. Sadat, Anwar. 1973. *1209*
—. Diplomacy. Egypt. Military offenses. USA. 1967-73. *1292*
—. Diplomatic relations. Israel. 1973. *512*
—. Egypt. Foreign Relations. Military Strategy. 1973. *1273*
—. Egypt. Israel. Military intelligence. Military Strategy (surprise). 1971-73. *1304*
—. Egypt. Israel. Military Strategy. 1973. *1309*
—. Egypt. Military Strategy. Suez City (battle). 1973. *1271*
Office buildings. Local Government. Zimbabwe (Bulawayo). 1894-1980. *4183*
Office du Niger. Agricultural production. Colonial Government. Economic Development. Irrigation. Mali. 1920's-50's. *1962*
Office of War Information. Australia. Libraries. New Zealand. South Africa. USA. World War II. 1942. *765*
Officer corps. Armies. 1970's. *358*
Ogunde, Hubert. Concert-party. Nigeria (Lagos). Theater. 1910-75. *2201*
—. Nigeria. Political commentary. Theater. 1945-75. *2236*
—. Nigeria. Theater. 1946-72. *2231*
—. Theater. Togo (Lomé). 1944-71. *2379*
Ogunsanwo, Alaba. China. Foreign Policy (review article). 1958-71. *498*
Ohlange Institute. Dube, John L. Political Leadership. Race Relations. South Africa. Washington, Booker T. ca 1885-1925. *3832*
—. Dube, John L. South Africa (Natal). Technical education. 1900-30's. *3992*
Ọhọri. Benin. Colonial government. Resistance. 1914-16. *1698*
Oil. Arab states. Foreign aid. Organization of Petroleum Exporting Countries. Prices. 1975-80. *523*
—. Colonial government. Embargo. Unilateral Declaration of Independence (UDI). Zimbabwe. 1965-77. *4160*
—. Development. Tanzania. 1969-74. *3054*
—. Economic development. Nigeria. 1958-74. *2042*
—. Economic Development. Nigeria. 1960-77. *1993*
—. Egypt. Foreign policy. 1973-. *1280*
—. Embargo. Ethiopia. Great Britain. Italy. War. 1935-36. *2745*
—. Foreign policy. Nigeria. 1958-75. *2140*
—. Foreign policy. Tunisia. 1974-77. *1535*
Oil and Petroleum Products *See also* Oil Industry and Trade.
—. Arab States. Organization of African Unity. Prices. 1970's. *124*
—. Egypt. Suez Canal. 1966-77. *1144*
Oil income. Agricultural development. Libya. 1953-74. *1365*
Oil industry and trade. Africa, North. Middle East. Western nations. 1970's. *961*
—. Africa, Southern. Foreign policy. Nigeria. 1970-80. *2188*
—. Agricultural Production. Economic Development. Libya (Augila Oasis). Social organization. Tradition. 1969-70. *1383*
—. Algeria. Boumédienne, Houari. Economy. Foreign policy. 1965-75. *1027*
—. Arbitration Convention. Commercial disputes. Nigeria. Treaties. UN. 1960's-70's. *2084*
—. Arbitration, international. International law. Libya. Nationalization. USA. 1971-80. *1404*
—. Christianity. Islam. Political Change. 20c. *306*
—. Civil war. Nigeria. 1967-74. *2010*
—. Dependency. Egypt. Foreign policy. 1967-76. *1152*
—. Economic Conditions. Inflation. 1970-82. *562*
—. Economic Conditions. Nigeria. 1973-79. *2070*
—. Economic Development. 1950-77. *596*
—. National Development. Nigeria. USA. 1960-80. *2071*
—. Natural Resources. ca 1956-74. *602*
—. Nigeria. Technology transfer. 1956-74. *2075*
—. Nigeria (Lagos). 1966-78. *2022*
Oil Industry and Trade (drilling). Angola. Gulf Oil. Public Relations. 1968-74. *571*
Oil palm industry. Africa, West. Technology. 1911-60. *1648*
Ojo-Cole, Julius. Nationalism. Nigeria. ca 1920-38. *2166*
Okafor, Nduka. Fafunwa, A. B. Higher Education (review article). Nigeria. 20c. *2269*
Olympics. Keino, Kipchoge. Kenya. Sports (athletic infrastructure). Track and field. 1966-74. *2993*
Ombudsman. Civil rights. 1960's-74. *284*
O'Meara, Francis. Firestone, Harvey S. Great Britain. Imperialism, economic. Liberia. Rubber industry. USA. 1922-27. *1940*
Onicha Ibo. Chakaka Pola. Famine, seasonal. Malawi, Northern. Nigeria, Eastern. 1964-71. *656*
Onselen, Charles van. Labor (review article). Mines. Zimbabwe. 1900-33. *4175*
Open Door Policy. Economic liberalization. Egypt. International Monetary Fund. 1970-74. *1150*
Operation Crossroads Africa. Robinson, James H. Students. 1958-73. *601*
Operation Turkey. Hunger. Independence, War of. Political economy. Zimbabwe. 1979-81. *4198*
Operations Account system. Africa (Francophone). France. Monetary relationships. ca 1955-73. *550*
Oral history. Africa, East. Colonialism. Historiography. 19c-20c. *2596*
—. Algeria. Colonialism. Independence Movements. ca 1830-1950's. *996*
—. Ethiopia. Ideology. Italy (Sardinia). Propaganda. War. 1935-36. *2734*
—. Kenya (Nyanza, south). Luo. Social Organization. Suba. Uganda (Buganda). 1500-1973. *2990*
—. Malawi. World War I. 1916-18. *709*
—. Uganda (Bunyoro-Kitara). 1967-71. *3313*
Oral tradition. Constitutions. Mali. Maninka. Values. 13c-20c. *1961*
—. Historiography. Kuba (review article). Vansina, Jan. Zaire. 19c-20c. *2458*
—. Islam. Senegal (Rip, Saloum). Social Organization. 1493-1969. *2299*
—. Libraries. 1955-79. *827*
—. Literature. ca 1960-75. *824*
—. Novels. Senegal. 1970's. *2321*
Oranges. Boycott Outspan Action Foundation (BOA). Netherlands. South Africa. 1972-73. *3757*
Orbital Transport und Raketen Aktiengesellschaft (OTRAG). Rockets, launching. Zaire (Shaba). 1976. *2466*
Organisation Commune Africaine et Malgache (OCAM). Economic Integration. Independence movements. ca 1965-70's. *106*
Organization Commune Africaine et Malgache (OCAM). 1965-73. *90*
Organization of African Unity. 1963-73. *75*
—. 1963-73. *93*
—. 1963-73. *97*
—. 1963-73. *133*
—. 1963-73. *135*
—. 1963-74. *101*
—. 1963-76. *76*
—. Africa, East. East African Community (dissolution). 1963-77. *2623*
—. Africa, Southern. Anticolonial movements. ca 1963-77. *86*

—. Africa, Southern. Military Capability. 1960's-74. *3427*
—. Angola. Civil war. Intervention (foreign). Nigeria. 1960-75. *270*
—. Apartheid. South Africa. 1963-74. *127*
—. Arab states. 1960's-75. *109*
—. Arab States. Oil and Petroleum Products. Prices. 1970's. *124*
—. Arab States. Pan-Africanism. 1963-76. *67*
—. Arab-Israeli conflict. 1958-81. *71*
—. Arab-Israeli Conflict. Foreign Relations. 1955-77. *430*
—. Arab-Israeli conflict. Mediation. 1971. *85*
—. Arab-Israeli conflict. Senghor, Leopold. UN. 1971. *94*
—. Bureaucracies (merging of). Commission for Technical Cooperation. 1950-68. *118*
—. Conflict and Conflict Resolution. UN. 1950's-70's. *81*
—. Conflict management, intraregional. Regional organizations. 1963-74. *110*
—. Decolonization. 20c. *72*
—. Diplomacy. 1963-73. *66*
—. Domestic jurisdiction. International law. 1963-73. *142*
—. Economic Conditions. Politics. 1962-75. *73*
—. Ethiopia (Eritrea). Secessionist movement. 1963-75. *84*
—. Foreign Policy. 1963-80. *91*
—. Foreign policy. 1963-82. *68*
—. Foreign policy. Ghana. Nkrumah, Kwame. 1958-63. *1799*
—. Foreign Relations. 1961-73. *98*
—. Ghana. Nkrumah, Kwame (message). 1966-72. *1792*
—. Gowon, Yakubu (interview). 1963-73. *148*
—. Human rights. 1963-80. *144*
—. Human rights. 1970's-80's. *99*
—. International Labor Organization. Political Cooperation. 1963-73. *119*
—. International law. 1963-82. *102*
—. Liberation. South Africa. 1963-76. *3984*
—. Lonrho. Multinational Corporations. Political involvement. 1890's-1974. *586*
—. National liberation movements. Neocolonialism. 1963-73. *70*
—. National Liberation Movements. Zimbabwe. 1960-75. *111*
—. Nkrumah, Kwame. 1963-73. *129*
—. Nkrumah, Kwame *(Revolutionary Path)*. Pan-Africanism. ca 1945-71. *1793*
—. Pan-Africanism. 1829-1975. 1963-75. *141*
—. Pan-Africanism. 1958-77. *107*
—. Pan-Africanism. 1960-75. *103*
—. Political crisis. 1964-81. *69*
—. Refugees. 1951-74. *325*
—. Refugees. 1960's-70's. *78*
—. Refugees. 1973. *145*
—. UN. 1963-66. *117*
—. Unilateral Declaration of Independence (UDI). Zimbabwe. 1922-74. *92*
Organization of African Unity (Provisional Secretariat). 1963-64. *130*
Organization of African Unity (10th Summit meeting). Arab-African alliance. 1972-73. *77*
Organization of Petroleum Exporting Countries. Arab states. Foreign aid. Oil. Prices. 1975-80. *523*
Organizational Theory *See also* Public Administration.
—. Socialist self-discipline. Tanzania. Working class. 1973. *3118*
Organizations, professional. Egypt. Professions. 1870's-1970's. *1349*
Orlan, Pierre Mac. Authors. Fiction. Tunisia. 1932. *1545*
Oromo. Alphabets. Bakri Sapalō. Ethiopia (Hagar). Separatist movements. 1875-1980. *2757*
Orphans. Infants. Nigeria. Voluntary work. 19c-20c. *2283*
Orthodox Eastern Church. Diaries. Egypt. Monasteries. St. Catherine (monastery). Sinai, Mount. 1980. *1123*
—. Egypt. Papaioannou, Daniel. Sinai, Mount. 1852-1930. *1321*
Oschoffa, Samuel Bileou. Benin. Celestial Church of Christ. Sects, Religious. 1947-80. *1703*
Oslo conference. Africa, southern. Colonialism. UN. 1973. *3382*
Ostracism. Catholics. Converts. Igbo. Nigeria. ca 1955-78. *2217*
Othman, Haroub. Government. Tanzania. 1967-76. *3178*
Ottoman Empire. Libya. Nationalism. Secret Service. *Tashkilati Makhsusa*. 1911-18. *1364*
Oufkir, Mohamed. Independence. Morocco. 1941-65. *1406*
Ovambo. Angola. Auala, Leonard N. Namibia. 1973. *3333*
—. Class consciousness. Migrant labor. Namibia. Political protest. 1915-72. *3696*
Ovambo crisis. Labor Disputes. Namibia. National Labor Association. 1971. *3690*
Overgrazing. Climatic change. Desert encroachment. 1974. *619*
Owusu, Maxwell. Ghana (Swedru). Hopkins, Nicholas S. Local politics. Mali (Kita). Uganda (Gondo). Vincent, Joan. 1960's-. *247*
Oxford University Delegacy. Adult education. Nigeria. 1945-50. *2277*
—. Examinations. Nigeria. Secondary education. 1929-37. *2278*

P

Pacavira, Manuel *(Nzinga Mbandi)*. Angola. Independence. Novels. 17c-20c. *3439*
Padmore, George. Ghana. 1933-59. *334*
Paesa Sanchez de Caballer, Francisco. Banking. Crime and Criminals (fraud). Equatorial Guinea. 1968-69. *2445*
PAIGC. *See* Partido Africano da Independência da Guiné e Cabo Verde (PAIGC).
Painting. Egypt. Halim, Tahia. 1919-70's. *1317*
Pakistan (South Waziristan). Islam. Local Politics. Nigeria (Kano). Rural Areas. 20c. *2213*
Palestine *See also* Israel.
—. Algeria. Guerrillas. Propaganda. 1954-75. *1009*
—. Attitudes. Egypt. Foreign Relations. Intellectuals. Israel. Self-determination. 1967-80. *1200*
—. Egypt. Foreign Policy. 1922-39. *1278*
—. Egypt. Foreign Policy. 1936-39. *1240*
—. Egypt. Press. Public opinion. 1920-40. *1239*
—. Imperialism. Namibia. UN. 1914-82. *3694*
Palestinians. Egypt. Middle East. 1971-73. *1214*
—. Foreign Relations. Israel. 1947-79. *464*
Palm oil. Igbo. Kalabari. Nigeria (Oguta). Trade. 1900-50. *2026*
Palmer, Robin. Africa, Southern. Colonialism. Parsons, Neil. Peasants. Poverty (review article). 1800's-1970's. *3393*
—. African studies (review article). Janzen, J. M. Parsons, Neil. 20c. *39*
Pan-African Congress. Convention People's Party. Great Britain. Nkrumah, Kwame. USA. 1935-63. *1781*
—. Duncan, Patrick. Kgosana, Philip. South Africa (Cape Town). Strikes. 1953-60. *3881*
—. Sobukwe, Robert. South Africa. 1975. *3947*
Pan-African Congress, 6th. Nyerere, Julius (speech). 1900-74. *121*
—. Nyerere, Julius (speech). 1945-74. *122*
—. Politics. 1974. *125*
Pan-African Freedom Movement. African National Congress. Apartheid. Mandela, Nelson. South Africa. 1918-64. *3843*
Pan-Africanism *See also* African Unity.
—. 1776-1970. *88*
—. 1964-80. *126*
—. 20c. *104*
—. Aborigines Rights Protection Society. Ghana. Political protest. 1897-1948. *1767*
—. Africa, West. Hayford, Adelaide Casely. 1866-1930. *1785*
—. Africa, West. National Congress of British West Africa. 1920-30. *108*
—. Africans, dispersal. ca 8000 BC-1970's. *82*
—. Anticolonialism. DuBois, W. E. B. NAACP. USA. 20c. *143*
—. Arab States. Organization of African Unity. 1963-76. *67*
—. Black nationalism. Garvey, Marcus. Nkrumah, Kwame. USA. 1920's-75. *1804*
—. Black Nationalism. Garvey, Marcus. USA. 1920-75. *95*
—. Black Nationalism. Innes, Roy (interview). 1974. *74*
—. Black studies. DuBois, W. E. B. Garvey, Marcus. Nyerere, Julius. 1905-71. *128*
—. Blyden, Edward Wilmot. 1776-1963. *89*
—. Blyden, Edward Wilmot. Garvey, Marcus. 1893-1927. *87*
—. Diplomacy. Ethiopia. Great Britain. Italy. 1935-36. *1604*
—. DuBois, W. E. B. Haile Selassie. USA. 1919-73. *132*
—. Economic development. 1961-73. *147*
—. Economic nationalism. Ghana. Military Government. National Redemption Council. ca 1972-75. *1806*
—. Elites. Zionism. 20c. *134*
—. Ethiopia. Italy. Julian, Hubert F. Political Attitudes. War. 1935-36. *2808*
—. Ethiopia. Italy. Wallace-Johnson, I. T. A. War. 1935. *2719*
—. Ethiopianism. Literature. USA. ca 1770-1930. *140*
—. Ghana. Nkrumah, Kwame. 1945-57. *1828*
—. Ghana. Nkrumah, Kwame. 1966-72. *1826*
—. Ghana. Nkrumah, Kwame. Politics (idealism). 1945-66. *1787*
—. Ideological evolution. Socialism. 1945-75. *139*
—. Ideology. 1970-76. *131*
—. Industrial education. Racism. USA (South). 1879-1940. *231*
—. Islam. 1975. *120*
—. Leadership. 1924-63. *65*
—. National liberation movements. Neocolonialism. Revolution. 1945-73. *116*
—. Nationalism. Race. 20c. *113*
—. Nkrumah, Kwame. Nyerere, Julius. ca 1960-69. *63*
—. Nkrumah, Kwame *(Revolutionary Path)*. Organization of African Unity. ca 1945-71. *1793*
—. Nyerere, Julius. Tanzania. 1960-77. *3151*
—. Nyerere, Julius (speech). 20c. *123*
—. Organization of African Unity. 1829-1975. 1963-75. *141*
—. Organization of African Unity. 1958-77. *107*
—. Organization of African Unity. 1960-75. *103*
—. Touré, Sekou (speech). 19c-20c. *138*
—. USA. 1854-1974. *115*
—. USA. 1880-1973. *79*
Pan-Africanism (international). Politics. 20c. *64*
Pan-Africanism (review article). Geiss, Imanuel. 1860's-1945. *83*
—. Geiss, Imanuel. 19c-20c. *136*
Pan-Arabism *See also* Arab Unity.
—. Arslan, Chekib. Maghreb. Nationalism. 1866-1946. *925*
—. Egypt. Sadat, Anwar. 1956-75. *1256*
—. Egypt. Society of the Eastern Union. 1922-31. *1335*
Pan-Islamism. At-Takfir wa al-Higrah (sect). Egypt. Muslims. 1970-78. *1196*
—. Germany. Morocco. Nationalism. World War I. 1914-18. *689*
Pan-Somalism. Foreign Relations. Social Organization. Somalia. 1950-77. *3039*
Papaioannou, Daniel. Egypt. Orthodox Eastern Church. Sinai, Mount. 1852-1930. *1321*
Paratroopers. Algeria. France. Public Opinion. Revolution. 1954-78. *1106*
Parliamentary government. Swaziland. Traditionalism. 1967-73. *4036*
Parliaments. Cabinet. Elites (political). Nigeria. 1954-65. *2137*
—. Ethiopia. Haile Selassie. 1931-71. *2737*
—. Hassan II. Morocco. War. 1977. *1443*
—. Legislative behavior. National representation. Tanzania. 1965-73. *3173*
—. National Assembly (Bunge). Tanganyika African National Union (TANU). Tanzania. 1965-70. *3149*
—. Tanzania. Totalitarianism. Zambia. ca 1960-77. *332*
Parsons, Neil. Africa, Southern. Colonialism. Palmer, Robin. Peasants. Poverty (review article). 1800's-1970's. *3393*
—. African studies (review article). Janzen, J. M. Palmer, Robin. 20c. *39*
Parti colonial français. Colonialism. France. 1914-22. *152*
Partido Africano da Independência da Guiné e Cabo Verde (PAIGC). Cape Verde Islands. Independence. 1460-1975. *1711*
—. Guerrilla Warfare. Guinea-Bissau. Independence Movements. 1963-73. *1906*
—. Guinea-Bissau. 1964-73. *1885*
—. Guinea-Bissau. Independence Movements. 1955-74. *1896*
—. Guinea-Bissau. National liberation movements. 1970-73. *1884*
Partition, provisional. Cameroon. France. Great Britain. Military Occupation. World War I. 1914-16. *701*
Pass laws. Political culture. South Africa. 1923-79. *3851*
Pastoralism. Afar. Ethiopia (Awash Valley). Modernization. ca 1950-75. *2691*

Paton, Alan *(Cry the Beloved Country)*. Literature. South Africa. 1948-75. *3988*
Patrimonialism. Egypt. Land tenure policy. Nasser, Gamal Abdel. Political leadership. Sadat, Anwar. 1954-79. *1300*
—. Political Systems. ca 1960-80. *297*
Patriotic Front. Elections. Military. Political Factions. Zimbabwe. 1979-80. *4211*
Patriotism. Local identity. Nigeria (Rivers State, Port Harcourt). Tamuno, Tekena N. 1913-60's. *2272*
P'Biket, Okot. Africa, East. Literature. 1964-78. *2567*
Peace *See also* Arbitration, International; International Security; War.
—. Arab unity. Egypt. Israel. 1940's-70's. *1177*
—. Economic conditions. Egypt. 1950's-78. *1245*
—. Economic Conditions. Egypt. Political Power. Sadat, Anwar. 1970-79. *1289*
—. Egypt. Foreign Policy. Israel. Sadat, Anwar (Knesset speech). 1977-78. *1281*
—. Egypt. Foreign Relations (isolation). Politics. 1970's. *1197*
—. Great Powers. Lancaster House Conference. Zimbabwe. 1965-79. *4247*
Peace Movements. Arab-Israeli conflict. Egypt. Foreign Policy. Sadat, Anwar. 1967-77. *1217*
Peace negotiations. Egypt. Israel. 1977-78. *1276*
Peacekeeping Forces. International law. UN. Zaire. 1950-80's. *2495*
—. Norway. UN. Zaire. 1960-64. *2500*
Peanut production. Depression. French West Africa. Peyrissac (firm). Rubber. Trade. 1924-39. *1675*
Peanuts. Niger. Nigeria. Smuggling. 1935-76. *1621*
Peasant associations. Agricultural Cooperatives. Ethiopia. 1980-81. *2699*
Peasant family. Agricultural Production. Kenya. Luo. 1946-48. *2873*
Peasant production. Zimbabwe. 1890-1930. *4177*
Peasants *See also* Agricultural Labor; Farmers; Land Tenure; Working Class.
—. Africa, Southern. Colonialism. Palmer, Robin. Parsons, Neil. Poverty (review article). 1800's-1970's. *3393*
—. Africa, West. Agricultural production. Kinship. Social organization. 1973. *1658*
—. Agbekoya Parapo. Nigeria (Western). Rebellions. 1968-69. *2088*
—. Agricultural Policy. Cotton. FRELIMO. Government, Resistance to. Mozambique. 1938-61. *3639*
—. Agricultural production. Kenya. Political assimilation. 1960's-70's. *2852*
—. Agricultural Production. Kenya. Regional economic differentiation. 1920-40. *2911*
—. Agriculture (cash crops). Modernization. 1890-1930. *681*
—. Agriculture (review article). 1950-79. *606*
—. Algeria. Colonialism. France. 1830-1954. *991*
—. Algeria. Counterinsurgency techniques. France. Psychological warfare. Resettlement, forced. 1954-62. *992*
—. Algeria. Elites. Land Reform. 1954-74. *1043*
—. Armies. Ethiopia. 1850-1935. *2726*
—. Asia. Development. Poverty. 1970-80's. *657*
—. Bibliographies. Ethiopia. 20c. *2829*
—. Bibliographies. Ethiopia. Land tenure. Social Classes. 20c. *2696*
—. Capitalism. Economic Structure. Nigeria, northern. Social Classes. 1850-1980. *2072*
—. Civil War. Zimbabwe. 1966-79. *4222*
—. Colonial government. Labor (forced). Malawi. Political consciousness. Rwanda. 19c-1962. *207*
—. Colonial Government. Land policy. Malawi. ca 1900-73. *3618*
—. Colonization. Economic Structure. Ghana. 1885-1939. *1737*
—. Community development. Ethiopia. Rural Development. Social Organization. 1957-74. *2716*
—. Cooperative Union of Tanganyika. Tanzania. 1932-72. *3083*
—. Development. Hyden, Goran (review article). Socialism. Tanzania. 1870-1975. *3052*
—. Droughts. Economic Conditions. Niger. Social Conditions. 1968-78. *1981*
—. Economic Planning. Ernst, Klaus. Jones, William I. Mali. Socialism (review article). 1960-68. *1959*
—. Egypt. Political Change. Turkey. 16c-1950's. *1119*
—. Ethiopia (Bale, Gojam). Rebellions. 1968. *2780*
—. Ethiopia (Darassa). Land reform. 1970-75. *2776*
—. Independence movements. 1896-1963. *208*
—. International trade. Rural development. Tanzania. 1940-75. *3067*
—. Land Tenure. Noncapitalist Development. 1940-50. *680*
—. Migrant Labor. Social Organization. Women. Zambia. 1930's-78. *4055*
—. Rebellions. 1960's-70's. *165*
—. Rebellions. 1970's. *336*
—. Rebellions. Simba. Zaire (Sankuru). 1964. *2520*
—. Social Classes. Tanzania. 14c-20c. *3113*
—. Tanzania. Ujamaa villages. 1973-77. *3086*
Peasants (participation). Agriculture. Tanzania. Ujamaa villages. 1967-75. *3093*
Peasants (proletarianization). Arrighi, G. Shangwe. Tobacco industry. Zimbabwe. 1898-1938. *4168*
Peasants (review article). Africa, Southern. Colonial Government. Poverty. 1971-78. *3405*
—. Angola. Beinart, William Justin. Bundy, Colin. Capitalism. Clarence-Smith, W. G. South Africa. 1900-80. *3348*
—. Kenya. ca 1890-1980. *2870*
—. Kenya. Rural development. Social Organization. Tanzania. 1970's. *2622*
Pelewura, Alimotu. Nationalism. Nigeria (Lagos). Political Parties. Women. 1900-51. *2131*
Pélissier, René. Angola. Imperialism (review article). Independence Movements. Portugal. 1845-1975. *167*
Pentecostal Mission. Churches, independent. Immigrants, Kenyan. Rites and Ceremonies (dream-telling). Uganda. 1957-60's. *3227*
Pentecostalism. Anim, Peter. Ghana. McKeown, James. 1890-1974. *1865*
People's Democratic Republic of Yemen. *See* South Yemen.
People's Progressive Party. Dinka. Gambia. Politics. ca 1950-75. *1713*
People's Revolutionary Party. Ethiopia. Left. Me'ei Sone. Nihilism. 1970-79. *2822*
Periodicals *See also* Freedom of the Press; Newspapers; Press.
—. Africa, southern. Bibliographies. -1976. *29*
—. *Native Affairs Department Annual* (periodical). Zimbabwe. 1923-81. *4139*
Periodization of history. Prehistory-20c. *17*
—. Colonialism. 1875-1970's. *221*
—. Dependency theory. 19c-20c. *61*
Permanent Commission for the Protection of Natives. Colonial government. Population decline. Zaire. 1896-1926. *2535*
Persecution *See also* Anti-Semitism; Apartheid; Civil Rights; Religious Liberty.
—. Copts. Egypt. Islam. 19c-20c. *1318*
Personal Narratives. Human rights. Obote, Milton. Uganda. 1962-82. *3324*
Personality (definition). Africans. 1950-75. *909*
Peshkov, Aleksei Maksimovich. *See* Gorky, Maxim.
Peyrissac (firm). Depression. French West Africa. Peanut production. Rubber. Trade. 1924-39. *1675*
Phallic symbols. Politics. War. ca1800-1970. *363*
Philanthropy. Education. USA. 1920's-77. *516*
—. Education (review article). King, Kenneth James. Murphy, E. Jefferson. USA. ca 1900-75. *517*
Philosophy *See also* Mysticism.
—. Anthropology, social. Popper, Karl. Social thought. Traditionalism. 1945-75. *846*
—. Colleges and Universities. 1945-78. *22*
Phoka. Agricultural Policy. Coffee. Malawi, northern. 1930-77. *3616*
Photographs. Geography. Great Britain. Textbooks. 1951-77. *59*
Phungula, Zulu. Class struggle. Longshoremen. Migrant labor. South Africa (Durban). 1939-59. *3763*
Physicians. Development. Nigeria. Politics. 1935-75. *2206*
—. Morris, R. M. (memoirs). Zimbabwe (Bulawayo). 1920-30. *4316*
Pied noirs. Algeria. Independence Movements. Secret Army Organization (OAS). 1954-61. *1052*
Pioneer Corps (review article). Cary, Robert. Zimbabwe. 1869-1975. *4298*
Pioneers. Roads. Zimbabwe (Chibi District). 1890's-1960's. *4319*
Pirow, Oswald. Air Lines. Foreign Policy. South Africa. South African Airways. 1933-39. *3890*
Pius XI, Pope. Catholic Church. Ethiopia. Italy. Missions and Missionaries. War. 1935-36. *2718*
—. Diplomacy. Ethiopia. Italy. Nogara, Bernadino (diary). Vatican. 1935-36. *2733*
Plaatje, Solomon Tshekisho. Brotherhood Movement. Class Struggle. DeBeers Consolidated Mines. South Africa (Kimberley). 1918-19. *3945*
Plague. Colonial Government (resistance to). Madagascar. Medicine. 1921. *3558*
Plan VII. Air Forces. France. Military Organization. World War II. 1943-44. *739*
Plantations. Colonialism. Labor, forced. Tanzania (Kigoma). 1700-1970's. *3130*
—. Economic Planning. Ivory Coast. Rubber. Villages. 1968-79. *1927*
Plantations, industrial. Agricultural development. Economic Planning. Politics. Sierra Leone. 1964-67. *2362*
Plebiscites. Ewe. Togo. 1956. *2371*
Pluralism. Democracy, Consociational. Nigeria. 1967-76. *2169*
Poaching. Africa, East. Ivory. Wildlife conservation. 1973-74. *2597*
—. Kenya (Northern Frontier District). Somalis. 1909-39. *2871*
Poetry. Abaza, Aziz. Drama. Egypt. 1899-1973. *1360*
—. Africa, West. Negritude. USA. 1930-72. *901*
—. Angola. Neto, Agostinho. Political leadership. ca 1922-75. *3449*
—. Millenarian movements. Politics. Senegal. Senghor, Leopold. 1940's-60's. *2304*
Poets. Literature, African. South Africa. 1973. *3976*
—. Political Leadership. Senegal. Senghor, Leopold. 1930's-75. *2310*
Poisoning, rumors of. Civil War. Nigeria. 1967-70. *2148*
Poland. Africa, West. Trade. 1950's-60's. *548*
—. African Studies. Bibliographies. 1960-75. *60*
—. Radio. 1967-78. *825*
Police *See also* Crime and Criminals; Criminal Law; Prisons; Secret Police; Secret Service.
—. Colonial government. Kenya. Racial structure. 1920-50. *2970*
—. Colonial Government. Zambia. 1901-72. *4124*
Police (border patrol). Botswana (Macloutsi). Sitwell, William (letters). 1892-1915. *3522*
Policy development. Higher education. Liberia. Politics. Social organization. 1940's-60's. *1953*
Policymaking. Sports. Tanzania. 1970-79. *3198*
Polisario Front. Algeria. Mauritania. Morocco. Nationalism. Territorial claims. Western Sahara. 1956-79. *923*
—. Algeria. Morocco. Western Sahara. 1956-80. *1579*
—. Assidon, Elsa. Gaudio, Attilio. Morocco. War. Western Sahara (review article). 1976-80. *1594*
—. Guerrilla Warfare. Morocco. Western Sahara. 1970's. *1596*
—. Guerrilla Warfare. Morocco. Western Sahara. 1975-80. *1580*
—. International Court of Justice. Self-determination. Western Sahara. 1970's. *1590*
Political assimilation. Agricultural production. Kenya. Peasants. 1960's-70's. *2852*
Political attitudes. Arab States. Foreign aid. 1973-76. *482*
—. Civil War. Ethnic diversity. Ife, University of. Nigeria. Students. 1957-69. *2111*
—. Coloureds. Ideology. South Africa. 1974. *3893*
—. Ethiopia. Italy. Julian, Hubert F. Pan-Africanism. War. 1935-36. *2808*
—. Ewe. Ghana. Poverty. 1957-80. *1776*
—. Foreign Aid. USSR. 1970-78. *438*
—. Ghana. Public Opinion. 1957-73. *1802*
—. Modernization. Sierra Leone. Youth. 1970's. *2340*
—. Social conflict. Working class. 1950-81. *276*
Political authority. Generations. Karamojong. So. Uganda. 1900-72. *3256*
Political awareness. Colonialism (demise). Tanganyika African National Union (TANU). Tanzania (Kigoma). 1927-60. *3157*
Political Campaigns. Constitutions. Elections. Ethnic Groups. Nigeria. 1977-79. *2133*
Political change. 1970's. *246*
—. Abisi. Nigeria. Rites and ceremonies. Rukuba. ca 1950-76. *2227*
—. Africa, Southern. Social Sciences (review article). 1960-. *3414*
—. Algeria. Culture. Economic Development. Revolution. 1976-81. *1110*
—. Algeria. Land reform. Legislation. 1962-78. *1081*
—. Algeria (Algiers). Riots. 1958. *1079*
—. Apartheid. South Africa. 1896-1998. *3872*

—. Boisson, Pierre. French West Africa. Giraud, Henri. World War II. 1940-43. *728*
—. Botswana. Namibia. Swaziland. 20c. *3351*
—. Christianity. Islam. Oil Industry and Trade. 20c. *306*
—. Christianity. Madagascar. Social Change. 1850-1972. *3585*
—. Christianity. Social Change. 19c-20c. *815*
—. Cocoa. Farmers. Ghana (Suhum). Settlement. 1900-72. *1855*
—. Colonialism. Embu. Kenya. 1906-63. *2952*
—. Decolonization. 1956-74. *252*
—. Developing Nations. Labor. Zambia. 1880-1981. *4049*
—. Diffusion. Intervention, military. Political Parties (single-party system). 1950's-70's. *258*
—. Droughts. 1970's. 1973. *608*
—. Economic Development. Madagascar. Social Change. 1960-78. *3551*
—. Egypt. 1945-52. *1122*
—. Egypt. Elites. 1970-80. *1230*
—. Egypt. Peasants. Turkey. 16c-1950's. *1119*
—. Equatorial Guinea. 1970's. *2442*
—. Ethiopia. Government officials. Law, rule of. 1973. *2767*
—. Ethiopia. Military Government. ca 1974. *2763*
—. Ethnic Groups. Uganda. 1962-71. *3305*
—. France. Libya. Qadhafi, Muammar. 1969-73. *1399*
—. Ghana. Models. Nigeria. 20c. *1619*
—. Independence. ca 1955-75. *273*
—. Libya. Qadhafi, Muammar. 1969-79. *1394*
—. Madagascar (Tananarive). 1900-72. *3549*
—. Namibia. South Africa. 1977-78. *3352*
—. Political Systems. Socialism. 1976-80. *310*
—. Port development. Tanzania (Dar es Salaam). Transportation, Commercial. Zambia. 1960's-70's. *3079*
—. Social conflict. Uganda. 1961-78. *3230*
—. Zaire. 1960's. *2527*
—. Zimbabwe. 1922-79. *4208*
Political Change (review article). Ideal-type analysis. Willame, Jean-Claude. Zaire. 1962-66. *2504*
Political Change (time horizons). 1945-74. *265*
Political clientelism. Egypt. Marei, Sayed. 1920's-70's. *1302*
Political Commentary. Finland. Mission Society. Namibia. Tanzania. 1945-75. *836*
—. Nigeria. Ogunde, Hubert. Theater. 1945-75. *2236*
Political conditions. 1960-80. *345*
—. 1961-76. *301*
—. Libya. 1969-74. *1400*
—. Zaire (Shaba). 1885-1970's. *2460*
Political conflict. East African Community. Regional integration. 1967-77. *2643*
—. Egypt. Islamic revival. Muslim Brotherhood. 1930-79. *1251*
—. Ethiopia. Foreign relations. USA. USSR. 1974-78. *2742*
—. Ethiopia. Somalia. USSR. 1930's-77. *2638*
—. Great Powers. Zaire (Shaba). 1970's. *2501*
—. Kenya. Mau Mau. 1952-77. *2972*
—. Land tenure. Uganda (Ankole). ca 1960's-. *3231*
—. Morocco. Western Sahara. 1960's-81. *1589*
—. Nigeria. Regionalism. Social change. 1900-. *2004*
Political conflict (review article). Ethiopia. Somalia. 1974-82. *2593*
—. Zaire. 1961-73. *2525*
Political consciousness. Colonial government. Labor (forced). Malawi. Peasants. Rwanda. 19c-1962. *207*
—. Sudan, northern. United Sudanese African Liberation Front. 1924-72. *1482*
Political control. Angola. Guerrillas. Guinea-Bissau. Mozambique. Portugal. 1940-74. *218*
Political Cooperation. International Labor Organization. Organization of African Unity. 1963-73. *119*
Political Corruption. Economic development. Ghana. Nkrumah, Kwame. 1955-68. *1824*
—. Monarchy. Morocco. 1956-73. *1454*
Political crisis. Coups d'etat. Mali. 1960-68. *1964*
—. Organization of African Unity. 1964-81. *69*
Political culture. Acculturation. Malawi. Revolution. 1909-61. *3595*
—. Attitudes. Methodology. Nigeria. Social Classes. 1800-1960. *2124*
—. Authoritarianism. Egypt. Modernization. Nasser, Gamal Abdel. 1950's. *1252*
—. Colonial Government. Ghana (Asante). 1969-70. *1782*
—. Coups d'etat. 1960's. *378*
—. Ghana. Youth. 1968-78. *1780*
—. Ideology. Tunisia. 1950's-74. *1540*
—. Islam. Nigeria. 20c. *2175*
—. Pass laws. South Africa. 1923-79. *3851*
—. Political Protest. South Africa (Soweto). 1976-81. *3850*
—. Racism. South Africa. USA (South). 19c-20c. *3941*
—. Values. Warrior tradition. ca 1840-1975. *364*
Political Culture (Western misconceptions). Government. Tribalism (concept). 1960-73. *344*
Political development. American Committee on Africa. 1950's-70's. *424*
—. Asante. Ghana. Local Government. Modernization. 1881-1981. *1817*
—. Botswana. Foreign policy. Khama, Seretse. South Africa. 1966-76. *3492*
—. Cameroon. *Effort Camerounais* (newspaper). Press. 1955-72. *2399*
—. Capitalism. Elites. Tanzania. 19c-1960's. *3120*
—. Chad. Regionalism. 1960-80. *2432*
—. Colonialism. Comoro Islands. France. 1854-1973. *3577*
—. Daily Life. Zimbabwe. 1980-81. *4146*
—. Djibouti. 1958-73. *2679*
—. Economic Growth. Egypt. 1973-75. *1121*
—. Ethnic Groups. Somalia (Juba Valley). 1913-80. *3038*
—. Ethnic Groups. Tanzania (Zanzibar). 1960-80. *3145*
—. Ethnicity. Liberalism. South Africa. 1921-48. *3914*
—. Ewe. Ghana. Villages. 18c-20c. *1860*
—. Ghana. 1957-82. *1754*
—. Hutu. Rwanda. Tutsi. 1919-72. *3023*
—. Independence. Western Sahara. 5c-1976. *1587*
—. Kenya. 1963-78. *2909*
—. Kenya. Kenyatta, Jomo. 1963-68. *2957*
—. Madagascar. 1960-73. *3555*
—. Military Government. Nigeria. 1970-73. *2181*
—. Modernization. Nigeria. Regional planning. 20c. *2160*
—. National liberation. Portugal. 1956-74. *326*
—. Nemery, Jaafar. Sudan. 1969-79. *1461*
—. Nigeria. 1960-80. *2179*
—. Political Leadership. 1970's. *318*
—. Rites and Ceremonies. 1960's-70's. *272*
Political development (review article). Tanzania. 1967-78. *3158*
Political development (review essay). Gukiina, Peter. Ibingira, G. S. K. Obote, Milton. Uganda. 1885-1971. *3308*
Political development theory. 1974. *331*
Political Economy. Bangladesh. Civil war. Economic policies. Nigeria. 20c. *2145*
—. Botswana. Cattle Raising. Economic Structure. 1966-80. *3511*
—. Colonial Government. Private enterprise. Zaire. 1908-60. *2522*
—. Colonialism. Mozambique. South Africa. 1890's-1960's. *3367*
—. Coups d'etat. Liberia. Military. 1964-80. *1937*
—. Educational system. National development. Tanzania. 1961-75. *3190*
—. Foreign Relations. Nationalism. Race relations. 1975. *486*
—. FRELIMO. Mozambique. Portugal. ca 1930-76. *3649*
—. Hunger. Independence, War of. Operation Turkey. Zimbabwe. 1979-81. *4198*
—. Industrialization. Multinational corporations. Nationalism, African. South Africa. 1978. *3787*
—. Kenya. Neocolonialism. Zimbabwe. 1920's-77. *4157*
—. Kenya. Public corporations. 1930's-70's. *2872*
—. Magubane, Bernard. Race Relations. Social Classes. South Africa. 1950's-80. *3889*
—. South Africa. Swaziland. 1968-79. *4033*
Political Economy (review article). ca 1880-20c. *23*
Political Factions. Action Group. Liberalism. Zimbabwe (Bulawayo). 1940-72. *4216*
—. All-African Trade Union Federation. Mboya, Tom. Nkrumah, Kwame. 1958-64. *62*
—. Chad. Earthquakes. 1979. *2439*
—. Civil war. Federalism. Nigeria. 1960-66. *2117*
—. Coups d'etat. Ethiopia (Eritrea). Haile Selassie. 1970-75. *2731*
—. Coups d'etat. Foreign Relations. Mancham, James. René, Albert. Seychelles. 1964-77. *3575*
—. Education. Ethnic groups. Independence movements. Missions and Missionaries. Zimbabwe. ca 1880-1977. *4264*
—. Egypt. Ideology. Nasserism. Political Leadership. 1952-65. *1253*
—. Egypt. Intelligentsia. Social Classes. 1907-52. *1322*
—. Elections. Military. Patriotic Front. Zimbabwe. 1979-80. *4211*
—. Elites. FRELIMO. Mozambique. 1962-69. *3655*
—. Ethnic Groups. Zimbabwe. 1957-79. *4267*
—. Europeans. Independence. Kenya. Land. 1960-63. *2968*
—. Ghana (Ahafo). History. 1966-69. *1811*
—. Independence Movements. Uganda. 1950-69. *3286*
—. Inkatha movement. South Africa (Soweto). Soweto Civil Association. 1976-79. *3852*
—. Kenya. 1975-82. *2958*
—. Namibia. South Africa. 1960-79. *3689*
—. Nationalism. Zimbabwe. 1960-79. *4215*
—. Nationalism. Zimbabwe. 1961-75. *4203*
—. Social Organization. Zaire (Kwango). 1960-73. *2529*
Political ideology. Botswana. Nationalism. Ratshosa, Simon. 1916-32. *3514*
—. Nyerere, Julius. Tanzania. Value structure. ca 1955-75. *3162*
Political instability. Amin, Idi. Uganda. 1962-80. *3304*
—. Coups d'etat. Ethnic Groups. Liberia. 1963-80. *1954*
—. Education. Kenya. Unemployment. 1963-76. *2920*
—. Ethnic diversity. 1960's-70's. *248*
—. Zaire. ca 1960-73. *2516*
Political institutionalization. Conflict and Conflict Resolution. Social mobilization. 1960-69. *268*
—. Developing Nations. 1946-73. *267*
Political Integration *See also* Confederation.
—. Africa, West. France. Liberia. 1960-79. *1676*
—. Civil War. Regionalism. Sudan. 1859-1972. *1476*
—. Ethnic groups. Nigeria. State Government. 1960-78. *2151*
—. Mauritania. 15c-20c. *1972*
Political involvement. Lonrho. Multinational Corporations. Organization of African Unity. 1890's-1974. *586*
—. Modernization. Religious organizations. Sects, Religious. 1940's-70. *826*
Political Leadership. 1952-74. *242*
—. Africa, North. Boumédienne, Houari. 1978. *948*
—. Africa, North. Islam. Qadhafi, Muammar. 900-1980. *928*
—. Africa, West. Akan. Succession. 17c-20c. *1789*
—. Africa, West. Middle Classes. Social Change. Songhai. 1591-1980. *1685*
—. African National Congress. Education. South Africa. USA. Xuma, Alfred Bitini. ca 1914-27. *3909*
—. African unity. Foreign Policy. Gowon, Yakubu. Nigeria. 1967-75. *2153*
—. Algeria. Boumédienne, Houari. 1952-78. *1078*
—. Algeria. Boumédienne, Houari. Islam. Revolution. 1940's-78. *1083*
—. Algeria. Boumédienne, Houari. Revolution. 1946-78. *1048*
—. Algeria. Chadli, Bendjedid. Foreign policy. Succession. 1975-81. *1064*
—. Angola. Neto, Agostinho. 1947-82. *3477*
—. Angola. Neto, Agostinho. Poetry. ca 1922-75. *3449*
—. Anya Nya. Civil war. National liberation movements. Sudan. 1950's-70's. *1485*
—. Banda, Hastings Kamuzu. Malawi. 1964-74. *3601*
—. Bell, Rudolph Douala Manga. Cameroon. Independence Movements. 1919-22. *2411*
—. Botswana. Jonathan, Leabua. Khama, Seretse. Lesotho. 1966-73. *3366*
—. Botswana. Khama, Seretse. 1966-80. *3536*
—. Bourguiba, Habib. Democratization. Tunisia. 1969-80. *1565*
—. Bourguiba, Habib. Elites. Ideology. Tunisia. 1955-77. *1574*
—. Cameroon, West. Cultural conflict. Education. 1950's-72. *2401*
—. Charisma. Succession. 1956-78. *329*
—. China. Egypt. Modernization. Revolution. Sadat, Anwar. 1952-79. *1238*
—. Civil war. Colonial Government. Nationalities. Nigeria. 1950's-60's. *2146*

—. Colonial government. Ethnicity. Kaguru. Tanzania. 1880-1944. *3133*
—. Colonial Government. Local Politics. Nigeria. 1904-54. *2189*
—. Congo. Congolese Labor Party. Marxism. Ngouabi, Marien. 1930's-79. *2441*
—. DeGaulle, Charles. Kissinger, Henry A. Nationalism. Nkrumah, Kwame. Nyerere, Julius. ca 1940's-70's. *308*
—. Detente. Kaunda, Kenneth (review article). Macpherson, Fergus. Zambia. 1940's-75. *4088*
—. Diouf, Galandou. Elections. Popular Front. Senegal. Socialist Republican Party. 1936-41. *2333*
—. Dube, John L. Ohlange Institute. Race Relations. South Africa. Washington, Booker T. ca 1885-1925. *3832*
—. Economic Conditions. Sierra Leone. Stevens, Siaka. 1967-80. *2354*
—. Egypt. Elites. Women. 1952-79. *1231*
—. Egypt. Foreign Policy. Nasser, Gamal Abdel. Sadat, Anwar. 1953-76. *1232*
—. Egypt. Foreign Policy. Sadat, Anwar. 1969-81. *1261*
—. Egypt. Foreign Relations. Israel. Libya. Qadhafi, Muammar. 1942-82. *1369*
—. Egypt. Foreign Relations. USSR. 1947-82. *1262*
—. Egypt. Ideology. Nasserism. Political Factions. 1952-65. *1253*
—. Egypt. Land tenure policy. Nasser, Gamal Abdel. Patrimonialism. Sadat, Anwar. 1954-79. *1300*
—. Egypt. Nasser, Gamal Abdel. 1952-. *1215*
—. Egypt. Nasser, Gamal Abdel. 1952-70. *1305*
—. Egypt. Nasser, Gamal Abdel. Revolution. 1956-76. *1207*
—. Egypt. Nasser, Gamal Abdel. Sadat, Anwar. 1952-75. *1191*
—. Egypt. Revolution. 1952-64. *1270*
—. Egypt. Sadat, Anwar. 1952-73. *1241*
—. Egypt. Sadat, Anwar. 1970-75. *1312*
—. Egypt. Sadat, Anwar. 1970-80. *1272*
—. Elites. Kenya. Kikuyu. Mau Mau. 1950-63. *2961*
—. Ethiopia. Haile Selassie. 1930-74. *2806*
—. Ethiopia. Monarchy. ca 1930-73. *2736*
—. Ethnic groups. Kamara, Moussa. Senegal, eastern (Boundou). 1681-1921. *2314*
—. Foreign aid. Independence. Sierra Leone. ca 1787-1976. *2358*
—. Foreign relations. Mugabe, Robert. Zimbabwe. 1974-80. *4268*
—. Freedom of the press. Ghana. Newspapers. 1964-78. *1859*
—. Gamanga, Kenewa. Independence Movements. Sierra Leone. 1941-61. *2342*
—. Hassan II. Morocco. 1975-80. *1448*
—. Houphouët-Boigny, Félix. Ivory Coast. National Development. 1944-74. *1917*
—. Ideology. Nyerere, Julius. Socialism. 1960-70. *309*
—. Independence Movements. Sierra Leone (Freetown). 1905-45. *2361*
—. Kenya. Moi, Daniel Arap. 1978-79. *2939*
—. Libya. Qadhafi, Muammar. 1969-76. *1393*
—. Local government. Zambia (Uyombe). 20c. *4046*
—. Madagascar. Ratsiraka, Dadier. 1972-82. *3552*
—. Mauritania. Nationalism. Sidiyya Baba. 1862-1926. *1975*
—. Mbadiwe, Kingsley Ozuomba. Nigeria. USA. 1939-47. *2139*
—. Military Government. Nigeria. 1966-79. *2115*
—. Mobutu Sese Seko. National self-image. Zaire. 1974-75. *2531*
—. Mozambique. Revolution. 1960-75. *3669*
—. Mugabe, Robert. Zimbabwe. 1950-80. *4294*
—. Mugabe, Robert. Zimbabwe. 1979-80. *4269*
—. National Council of Nigerian Citizens. Nigeria. 1940-60. *2126*
—. Nkomo, Joshua. Zimbabwe. 1917-79. *4257*
—. Nyerere, Julius. Tanzania. 1961-70's. *3150*
—. Obote, Milton. Uganda People's Congress. 1966-69. *3271*
—. Poets. Senegal. Senghor, Leopold. 1930's-75. *2310*
—. Political Development. 1970's. *318*
—. Political Systems. Uganda. 1979-80. *3235*
—. Tanzania. 1962-68. *3155*
—. Todd, Garfield. Zimbabwe. 1953-58. *4191*
Political Leadership (indigenous). Decolonization, consensual. 1945-65. *338*
Political Leadership (review article). Egypt. Nasser, Gamal Abdel. 1952-70's. *1186*
Political Leadership (succession). Elites. 1945-74. *298*
Political legitimacy. Elites. Zambia. 1964-78. *4111*
Political opposition. Civil Rights. Kenya. 1963-78. *2919*
—. Kru. Liberia. Twe, Didwo. 1930's-60. *1955*
—. Mobutu Sese Seko. Zaire. 1965-78. *2497*
—. Morocco. Social conditions. 1980. *1430*
—. Zaire. 1963-78. *2505*
Political participation. 1958-78. *260*
—. Africa, West. Burns, Alan. Colonial Government (Executive Councils). Great Britain. 1941-42. *1660*
—. Boycotts. Cocoa. Ghana. Social Classes. 1937-38. *1736*
—. Colonial Government. Nigeria, Western. Obas' Conference. 1913-79. *2143*
—. Decentralization. Economic development. Tanzania. 1972-78. *3143*
—. Economic development. 1960's-73. *621*
—. Economic Development. Local government. Zambia. 1967-79. *4053*
—. Ethnicity. Nubians. Political Theory. Uganda. 1971. *3251*
—. Gogo. Reform. Tanzania (Ugogo). 1960-77. *3175*
—. Government. Tunisia. 1967-73. *1570*
—. Independence. Populism. Uganda. 1959-61. *3282*
—. Kenya (Nairobi). 1960's-73. *2950*
—. Labor Unions and Organizations. Nationalism. Working conditions. Zimbabwe. 20c. *4155*
—. Local government. Reform. Tanzania. 1960-78. *3159*
—. Mourides. Muslim brotherhoods. Senegal. 1967-75. *2325*
—. Working class. 1960's-77. *251*
—. Working Class. ca 1958-78. *275*
—. Zambia. 1972-78. *4099*
Political Participation (departicipation). 1955-74. *289*
Political Parties *See also* names of political parties, e.g. United National Independence Party; Elections; Political Campaigns.
—. Apartheid. Elections. South Africa. 1970-74. *3906*
—. Arab Socialist Union. Egypt. 1952-77. *1255*
—. Arab Socialist Union. Egypt. Nasser, Gamal Abdel. 1952-78. *1254*
—. Aubaume, Jean Hilaire. Bongo, Albert Bernard. Gabon. M'Ba, Léo. Nationalism. 1959-72. *2447*
—. Authoritarian regimes. Coups d'etat. 1945-77. *262*
—. Bantu Homelands. Economic policy. Elections. South Africa. 1920-74. *3900*
—. Benin. Elections. 1956-57. *1708*
—. Chama Cha Mapinduzi (CCM). Tanzania. 1977-80. *3140*
—. Colonialism. Economic dependence. Modernization. Women. 16c-. *902*
—. Comoro Islands. 20c. *3581*
—. Convention People's Party. Ghana. 1949-66. *1825*
—. Democracy. Government, one-party. 1957-73. *335*
—. Egypt. Sadat, Anwar. 1970-80. *1288*
—. Ethiopia (Eritrea). Independence movements. 1941-62. *2740*
—. Gambia. 1951-73. *1712*
—. Independence. Sects, religious. Sudan. 1952-56. *1523*
—. Institutionalization. 1958-74. *322*
—. Leftism. Madagascar. Movement for Proletarian Power (MFM). 1972. *3553*
—. Modernization. Nigeria. Political Systems. 1920-66. *2192*
—. Modernization. Tradition. 1980-81. *283*
—. Nationalism. Nigeria (Lagos). Pelewura, Alimotu. Women. 1900-51. *2131*
—. South Africa. 1914-73. *3841*
—. Tanzania (Zanzibar). 1930-72. *3177*
—. United National Independence Party. Zambia. 1964-73. *4114*
Political Parties (identification). Ethnic groups. South Africa. 1970. *3905*
Political parties, regional. Federal states. Nigeria. 1945-66. *2091*
Political Parties (review article). Botswana. Wiseman, John. 1965-77. *3530*
Political Parties (single-party system). Diffusion. Intervention, military. Political change. 1950's-70's. *258*
—. Egypt. 1952-68. *1227*
—. Kenya African National Union. 1960-73. *2916*
—. Mauritania People's Party (PPM). 1946-73. *1973*
Political Parties (traditionalist). Niger. 1946-60. *1985*
Political Philosophy. Fanon, Frantz. Freedom. Revolution. 1952-61. *1030*
—. Libya. Qadhafi, Muammar. 1973. *1395*
Political power. Afrikaners. Nationalism. South Africa. South African Broadcasting Corporation. 1935-66. *3901*
—. Economic Conditions. Egypt. Peace. Sadat, Anwar. 1970-79. *1289*
—. Economic Conditions. Race. Social classes. Zimbabwe. 1890-1970's. *4173*
—. Foreign Policy. Nigeria. 1960-73. *2138*
—. Kenya. Middle classes. 1975-77. *2938*
Political Protest *See also* Civil Disturbances; Demonstrations; Revolution; Riots.
—. Aborigines Rights Protection Society. Ghana. Pan-Africanism. 1897-1948. *1767*
—. Agricultural Development. Tonga. Zambia. 1899-1964. *4069*
—. Apartheid. Biko, Steve. South Africa. 1978. *3892*
—. Asafo movement. Colonialism. Ghana. Modernization. 1910's-50. *1819*
—. Cattle destocking. Colonial Government. Kamba. Kenya. 1938. *2924*
—. Class consciousness. Migrant labor. Namibia. Ovambo. 1915-72. *3696*
—. Colonial Government. Kenya. Nandi. 1905-23. *2918*
—. Copper Mines and Mining. Kenya. Strikes. Zambia. 1922-62. *175*
—. Drama. Egypt. Nasser, Gamal Abdel. Sabūr, Salāh 'Abd al-. 1950's-60's. *1287*
—. Government repression. Mozambique. Nationalism. 1920-49. *3633*
—. Labor. Migration, Internal. Rural development. Zambia (Kasumpa). ca 1960-75. *4042*
—. Labor. Mining industry. South Africa. 1980's. *3731*
—. Missions and Missionaries. Seventh-Day Adventists. Zambia (Tonga Plateau). 1903-55. *4061*
—. Nationalism. Zimbabwe. 1898-1957. *4232*
—. Political culture. South Africa (Soweto). 1976-81. *3850*
—. Race Relations. South Africa. 1960-77. *3926*
—. Rhodesia, University of. Students. Zimbabwe. 1974. *4244*
—. Sierra Leone. Wallace-Johnson, I. T. A. West African Youth League. 1892-1939. *2353*
—. South Africa. Soweto Students Representative Council. Students. 1976-77. *3848*
—. Students. Uganda. 1952-75. *3255*
Political recruitment. Kenya. Legislators. 1957-68. *2951*
Political Reform. Colonial government. Confederation. Gore-Browne, Stewart. Public opinion. Zambia. 1948. *4126*
—. Egypt. Islam. Muslim Brotherhood. 1928-81. *1316*
Political Reform (delay of). Colonial policy (memorandum). Great Britain. Military Strategy. Zambia. Zimbabwe. 1930-45. *3396*
Political relationships. Regional Autonomy Agreement (1972). Sudan (North and South). 1972-73. *1500*
Political representation. Coloureds. South Africa. 1951-79. *3940*
Political repression. Assassination. Colonial Government. Ethiopia. Graziani, Rodolfo. Italy. 1936-37. *2795*
—. Decolonization. Ethnic groups. Violence. 1960-78. *250*
—. Intellectuals. Lovanium University. Zaire. 1971. *2561*
—. Mobutu Sese Seko. Zaire. 1965-66. *2493*
Political Science *See also* Constitutional Law; Democracy; Government; Imperialism; Law; Legislation; Monarchy; Nationalism; Politics; Public Administration; Revolution.
—. Colleges and Universities. Makerere University. Mazrui, Ali A. (memoirs). Uganda (Kampala). 1963-71. *3261*
—. Historiography. Military. Research, interdisciplinary. 1898-1976. *361*
Political Socialization. Acculturation. Education. Tanzania. 1970's. *3181*
—. Acculturation. Education. Tanzania. 1971. *3146*
—. Kenya. Schools. 1960's-70's. *2934*
Political stability. Africa, East. Djibouti. Ethnic conflict. France. 1896-1976. *2674*
—. Africa, West. Islam. ca 1960-80. *1618*

—. Ethiopia. Military government. Socialism. 1974-77. *2755*
—. Ethiopia. Somalia. USA. USSR. 1977. *2577*
—. Ethiopia. Strikes, general. 1974. *2715*
—. Ethnic groups. 19c-20c. *261*
—. Ethnic Groups. Ghana. 1972-79. *1778*
—. Ethnic groups. Military. South Africa. 1960's-70's. *3847*
—. Ethnic groups. Religion. 1960-80. *290*
—. Ethnic groups. Zimbabwe. 1960-80. *4200*
—. Ewe (Battor). Ghana. Property rights. 1907-66. *1766*
—. Fanon, Frantz. Historiography. 1950's-70. *287*
—. Federalism. Nigeria. Wages. 1954-75. *2015*
—. Foreign Relations. Great Powers. Nigeria. 1960-75. *2099*
—. Foreign Relations. Race Relations (review article). South Africa. 1974-79. *3887*
—. Ghana. Military. 1957-75. *1769*
—. Ghana (Asante). Money. 1900-40. *1719*
—. Gordimer, Nadine. Novels. Race Relations. South Africa. 1953-79. *3959*
—. Gowon, Yakubu. Military Government. Nigeria. 1966-75. *2149*
—. Guinea. Touré, Sekou. 1946-74. *1871*
—. Higher education. Liberia. Policy development. Social organization. 1940's-60's. *1953*
—. Historiography. Monnier, Laurent (review article). Zaire. 1971. *2459*
—. Hymns. Kenya. Kikuyu. Mau Mau. 1952. *2944*
—. Independence. Zambia. 1965-75. *4105*
—. Independence. Zimbabwe (review article). 1950-79. *4147*
—. Independence movements. Zimbabwe. 1977-79. *4286*
—. Islam. Maghreb. Mauritania. 1960's-73. *963*
—. Kabaka Yekka (The King Alone) movement. Kakamega Club. Uganda (Buganda). 1940-1961. *3242*
—. Karume, Abeid. Tanzania (Zanzibar). 1964-74. *3144*
—. Kenya. Kenyatta, Jomo. Moi, Daniel Arap. Succession. 1978-79. *2960*
—. Kenya. Labor unions and organizations. Nigeria. 1939-66. *210*
—. Kenya. Moi, Daniel Arap. Social Organization. 1960's-70's. *2925*
—. Labor Unions and Organizations. Nigeria. 1945-65. *2119*
—. Land Tenure. Rwanda. Social Classes. 1850-1950. *3017*
—. Language. -1973. *239*
—. Lenshina, Alice. Lumpa Church. Sects, Religious. United National Independence Party. Zambia. 1954-65. *4051*
—. Literature, English-language. South Africa. ca 1900-75. *3975*
—. Madagascar. Reform. Tsiranana, Philibert. 1972-73. *3579*
—. *Marabouts.* Muslim brotherhoods. Senegal. Senghor, Leopold. 1964-76. *2301*
—. Military. 1960's-74. *350*
—. Military Government. Togo. 1967-73. *2374*
—. Military intervention. 1960-69. *366*
—. Millenarian movements. Poetry. Senegal. Senghor, Leopold. 1940's-60's. *2304*
—. Nationalism. 1960-73. *333*
—. Nigeria. Rebellions. Tiv. 1960. *2147*
—. Nigeria. Youth. 1970's. *2207*
—. Obote, Milton. Uganda. 1962-71. *3319*
—. Pan-African Congress (6th). 1974. *125*
—. Pan-Africanism (international). 20c. *64*
—. Phallic symbols. War. ca1800-1970. *363*
—. Populist movements. Wilson, Neil Housman. Zimbabwe. 1920-60. *4277*
—. Public Finance. Zambia. 1970-77. *4059*
—. Race relations. Whitehead, Edgar. Zimbabwe. 1957-62. *4287*
—. Race Relations. Zimbabwe. 1888-1975. *4201*
—. Religion. Uganda. 1880-1970. *3270*
—. Riots. South Africa (Soweto). 1910-77. *3896*
—. Sobhuza II. Swaziland. 1972-74. *4035*
—. Social Classes. Zambia. 1960-76. *4113*
—. South Africa. Vorster, John. 1966-74. *3826*
—. Sudan (Southern). 1946-56. *1527*
Politics and the Military. Africa, East. Tradition. 1960-75. *2616*
—. Amin, Idi. Arab States. Economic Conditions (dependency). Uganda. 1971-73. *3300*
—. Amin, Idi. Economic Policy. Uganda. 1962-1979. *3290*
—. Amin, Idi. Uganda. 1962-74. *3240*
—. Amin, Idi. Uganda. 1971-73. *3327*
—. Anual disaster. Colonial Government. Morocco. 1912-21. *1442*
—. Benin. Regionalism. 1960-72. *1700*
—. Bureaucracies. Ghana (review article). Historiography. 1955-75. *1779*
—. Civil-Military Relations. 1966-76. *348*
—. Coups d'etat. 1963-77. *360*
—. Coups d'etat. Ghana. 1972. *1774*
—. Coups d'etat. Social Classes. Uganda. 1971. *3260*
—. Economic conditions. Ghana. 1966-79. *1775*
—. Ethiopia. Feudalism. Revolution. 1972-75. *2748*
—. Ethnic Groups. Obote, Milton. Uganda. 1962-71. *3221*
—. Ghana. Government. Limann, Hilla. 1979-81. *1812*
—. Ghana. Nkrumah, Kwame. 1947-79. *1794*
—. Military aid. 1960's. *357*
—. Military Government. Nemery, Jaafar. Sudan. 1956-71. *1468*
Politics and the Military (review article). Arms Trade. 1960's-73. *374*
Politics, cross-ethnic. Ivory Coast. Urban policy. 1960's-70's. *1916*
Politics (idealism). Ghana. Nkrumah, Kwame. Pan-Africanism. 1945-66. *1787*
Politics (review article). Algeria. Colonna, F. Leca, Jean. Social Classes. Teachers. Vatin, J.-C. 1883-1975. *1094*
—. Algeria. Etienne, B. Leca, Jean. Vatin, J.-C. 1830-1978. *1069*
—. Economic development. Social change. 1968-72. *6*
—. Egypt. Nasser, Gamal Abdel. 1952-74. *1299*
—. Elites. Zambia. 1972-74. *4058*
—. Ethnic Groups. 20c. *337*
—. Foreign Relations. Zimbabwe (review article). 1960-71. *4223*
Politics, traditional. Coups d'etat. Ethiopia. Historiography. Markakis, John (review article). 1960's-70's. *2730*
Polygamy. Acculturation (resistance to). Africa, West. Colonial government. Missions and Missionaries. 19c-20c. *1633*
Polygyny. Africa, West. Christianity. Harris, William Waddy. Missions and Missionaries. 1910-29. *1643*
Popper, Karl. Anthropology, social. Philosophy. Social thought. Traditionalism. 1945-75. *846*
Popular Culture *See also* Daily Life; Social Conditions.
—. Algeria. Arabs. Literature. Stereotypes. 1891-1920. *1091*
—. Church and State. Egypt. Islam. 1952-77. *1334*
—. Culture, elite. Theater, educational. Togo. 1945-75. *2378*
—. Jamaa. Zaire (Shaba). 1950's-70's. *2542*
Popular Culture, Ministry of. Documents. Great Britain. Italy. Libya (Cyrenaica). Propaganda. World War II. 1941. *733*
Popular Front. Colonial Government. Coppet, Marcel de. French West Africa. Labor, forced. 1936-46. *1610*
—. Colonial Government. France. Labor Unions and Organizations. Senegal. 1919-38. *2302*
—. Diouf, Galandou. Elections. Political Leadership. Senegal. Socialist Republican Party. 1936-41. *2333*
—. Independence movements. Law Reform. Madagascar. 1929-37. *3566*
—. Reform. Senegal. 1936-38. *2327*
Popular Front for the Liberation of Palestine. Aircraft hijacking. Entebbe raid. International law. Israel. Uganda. 1976. *3222*
Popular Movement for the Liberation of Angola (MPLA). Angola. Anti-Imperialism. National liberation movements. 1970's. *3429*
—. Angola. Communist Parties and Movements. 1975. *3453*
—. Angola. Decolonization. 1956-76. *3465*
—. Angola. Foreign Policy. Zaire. Zambia. 1961-77. *3430*
—. Angola. FRELIMO. Mozambique. Revolution. 1970-80. *3386*
—. Angola. Independence. 1961-75. *3464*
—. Angola. Independence Movements. 1956-77. *3452*
—. Angola. Military aid. USSR. 1956-74. *3476*
Popular Movement for the Liberation of Angola (MPLA; 1st Extraordinary Congress). Angola. 1980. *3481*
Population *See also* Birth Control; Census; Demography; Fertility; Migration, Internal; Mortality.
—. 10c-20c. *15*
—. Algeria. 1966-77. *1085*
—. Botswana (Kweneng). Migration. Settlement. 1965-76. *3527*
—. Census. Malawi. 1891-1991. *3599*
—. Census. Malawi. 1921-66. *3598*
—. Colonialism. Economic Conditions. 20c. *171*
—. Economic growth. Employment. 1973. *660*
—. Erosion. Kenya (Machakos hills). Land use. 20c. *2898*
—. Food. 1970's. *622*
—. Livestock. Sudan (Darfur). 400-1975. *1526*
—. Nyerere, Julius (progress report). Production. Tanganyika African National Union (TANU). Tanzania. 1969-72. *3165*
Population decline. Colonial government. Permanent Commission for the Protection of Natives. Zaire. 1896-1926. *2535*
Population distribution. Natural resources. Nigeria (Igboland). 1966. *1999*
Population growth. Droughts (social causes). Economic Growth. 1948-72. *888*
—. Migration. Togo (Vo Koutime). ca 1925-75. *2376*
—. Uganda. 1969-75. *3266*
—. Urbanization. 1960's-70's. *773*
Population (growth rates). South Africa. Urbanization, differential. 1652-1970. *3996*
Populism. Cocoa. Farmers. Nigeria, Western. 1893-1973. *2109*
—. Independence. Political Participation. Uganda. 1959-61. *3282*
Populist movements. Politics. Wilson, Neil Housman. Zimbabwe. 1920-60. *4277*
Port development. Political Change. Tanzania (Dar es Salaam). Transportation, Commercial. Zambia. 1960's-70's. *3079*
Port system. Development. Ghana. 1482-20c. *1735*
Ports. Africa, West. Economic development. Transportation. 19c-20c. *1688*
—. Cost of living. Depression. Senegal (Dakar). Wages. 1929-39. *2316*
—. Foreign Relations. Military Strategy. Namibia (Walvis Bay). South Africa. 1914-82. *3682*
—. Johnston, Harry Hamilton. Malawi. Mozambique (Chinde). 1891-1923. *3589*
Portugal. Africa, southern. Brazil. Foreign policy. 1970's. *511*
—. Africa, Southern. Foreign policy. USA. 19c-1974. *3423*
—. Africa, West. Colonial Government. 1415-1974. *1639*
—. *Aldeamentos,* (strategic settlements). Angola. Guerrilla Warfare. 1973. *3471*
—. Angola. Archives. Arquivo Histórico Militar. Colonialism. 1705-1970. *3484*
—. Angola. Colonial wars. Military Finance. Mozambique. Multinational corporations. 1960-73. *3362*
—. Angola. Colonialism. Guinea-Bissau. Mozambique. 1955-73. *193*
—. Angola. Counterinsurgency. Guinea-Bissau. Mozambique. 1961-74. *177*
—. Angola. Foreign investments. Mozambique. 1950's-75. *3363*
—. Angola. Foreign Policy. Mozambique. 1974-75. *3365*
—. Angola. Foreign Relations. Independence. Mozambique. 1970's. *3402*
—. Angola. Guerrilla warfare. Mozambique. ca 1961-75. *3368*
—. Angola. Guerrillas. Guinea-Bissau. Mozambique. Political control. 1940-74. *218*
—. Angola. Imperialism (review article). Independence Movements. Pélissier, René. 1845-1975. *167*
—. Angola. Independence movements. Mozambique. 1970's. *3424*
—. Angola, southwest. Colonization. Development. 19c-20c. *3462*
—. Apartheid. Colonialism. Nyerere, Julius (speech). South Africa. UN. 20c. *386*
—. Assassination. Cabral, Amilcar. Colonialism. Guinea-Bissau. Independence Movements. 1953-73. *1901*
—. Cabora Bassa Dam. Colonialism. FRELIMO. Mozambique. 1968-75. *3670*
—. Cabora Bassa dam. Economic Development. Mozambique (Zambezi Valley). 1953-79. *3657*
—. Cabral, Amilcar. Guinea-Bissau. Independence Movements. 1924-73. *1887*
—. Colonial policy. Ethnic groups. Mozambique. 20c. *3625*
—. Colonialism. 1400-1921. *166*
—. Colonialism. 19c-20c. 1937-76. *176*

Q

R

—. Decolonization. Equatorial Guinea. Nguema, Francisco Macias. 1469-1979. *2443*
—. Organization of African Unity. 1951-74. *325*
—. Organization of African Unity. 1960's-70's. *78*
—. Organization of African Unity. 1973. *145*
—. Repatriation. War. Zimbabwe (Umtali). 1980-81. *4205*
Regional Autonomy Agreement (1972). Civil War. Foreign policy. Sudan. 1966-73. *1470*
—. Political relationships. Sudan (North and South). 1972-73. *1500*
Regional competition. Civil war. Economic interests. Nigeria. Politics. ca 1947-67. *2048*
Regional conflicts. Coups d'etat. Ethiopia. Military government. 1974-76. *2823*
Regional development. Africa, West. Water. 1970's. *1683*
—. Agriculture. Eastern Nigeria Project. Nigeria (Igboland, Northern). Settlement schemes. 1945-67. *2034*
Regional economic differentiation. Agricultural Production. Kenya. Peasants. 1920-40. *2911*
Regional government. Africa, East. Libraries, development of. 1945-65. *2611*
—. Decisionmaking. Federalism. India. Nigeria. 1967-73. *2183*
Regional inequality. Economic Planning. Investments (growth-pole strategy). Rebellions. Sudan. 1974. *1501*
Regional integration. Africa, East. East African Community. 1900-70's. *2610*
—. Africa, East. East African Community. 1967-74. *2595*
—. Africa, East. East African Community (dissolution). 1967-77. *2609*
—. Africa, West. Entente Council. 1960's. *1655*
—. East African Community. 1967-78. *2591*
—. East African Community. Economic Development. 1963-72. *96*
—. East African Community. Economic development. 1965-76. *2632*
—. East African Community. Political conflict. 1967-77. *2643*
—. East African Community. UN. 1960's-71. *2586*
—. East African Community (dissolution). 1967-78. *2629*
—. National identity. Nile Valley. Political systems. Sudan. ca 1920-55. *1517*
Regional organizations. Conflict management, intraregional. Organization of African Unity. 1963-74. *110*
Regional Planning. Apartheid. Demography. South Africa. 1960-73. *3708*
—. Economic development. Malawi (Lilongwe, Zomba). 1965-74. *3610*
—. Ghana. Rural development. 1966-75. *1724*
—. Modernization. Nigeria. Political development. 20c. *2160*
Regionalism *See also* Political Integration.
—. Africa, East. Economic Integration. Nyerere, Julius. ca 1920-73. *2634*
—. Africa, West. Diplomacy. Economic Community of West African States. Economic Integration. Nigeria. 1960-75. *1663*
—. Africa, West. Mali Federation. Union Douaniére Equatoriale (Equatorial Customs Union). West African Custom Union. 1959-73. *112*
—. Agricultural Mechanization. Ivory Coast. Rice. Yams. 19c-20c. *1915*
—. Benin. Politics and the Military. 1960-72. *1700*
—. Chad. National Liberation Front. 1800-1977. *2430*
—. Chad. Political Development. 1960-80. *2432*
—. Civil War. Political Integration. Sudan. 1859-1972. *1476*
—. Economic development. Kenya. Migration, Internal. 1954-70. *2984*
—. Ethnic groups. Nigeria. 1900-76. *2291*
—. Nigeria. Political conflict. Social change. 1900-. *2004*
Reitz family. Migration. South Africa. 1877-1977. *4007*
Relief efforts. Christian churches. Civil war. Nigeria. ca 1966-69. *2294*
—. Civil war. Nigeria. 1967-70. *2116*
—. Civil War. Nigeria. Refugees. Sudan. UN. 1966-72. *524*
Religion *See also* Christianity; Church History; Clergy; Missions and Missionaries; Mysticism; Sects, Religious.
—. Africa, East. African Greek Orthodox Church. 1930-75. *2594*
—. Africa, East. Politics. 20c. *2615*
—. Africa, Southern. Goba. Social History. Zambezi River. 1200-1970. *3381*
—. Africa, southern. Research. 1961-80. *3378*
—. Anticolonial movements. Politics. ca 1900-50's. *229*
—. Antonism. Kimbangu, Simon. Kongo. Prophets. Zaire. 18c-20c. *2551*
—. Bibliographies. Ideology. 20c. *843*
—. Blackman's Church. Malawi. Mwasi, Yesaya Zerenji. 1880's-1930's. *3620*
—. Bullhoek massacre. Israelites. Mgijima, Enoch. South Africa. 1868-1921. *3969*
—. Civil war. Foreign Relations. Nigeria. Reporters and Reporting. 1960's. *2095*
—. Colonialism. Politics. Protestants. Uganda (Busoga). 1900-62. *3269*
—. Dutch Reformed Church. South Africa (Soweto). 1970's. *4011*
—. Education. Islam. Nigeria. 1903-78. *2232*
—. Ethiopia. 325-1981. 20c. *2840*
—. Ethnic groups. Politics. 1960-80. *290*
—. Ghana. Nkrumah, Kwame. ca 1947-66. *1809*
—. Harrist Church. Ivory Coast. Modernization. 1910-72. *1934*
—. Hayford, Mark Christian. Ivory Coast. 1864-1945. *1923*
—. Kenya. Kikuyu. *Watu wa Mungu*. 1920's-70's. *2997*
—. Kimbanguism. Zaire. 1879-1921. *2550*
—. Korsten Basketmakers. Masowe, Baba Johane. Zimbabwe (Manicaland; Makoni). 1940-77. *4145*
—. Missions and Missionaries. Muslims. Race Relations. Tanzania. 1878-1941. *3209*
—. Mouvement Populaire de la Revolution. National unity. Zaire. ca 1973-76. *2486*
—. Nazaretha Church. Shembe, Isaiah. South Africa (Natal). 1910-78. *3955*
—. Nemery, Jaafar. Revolution. Sudan. Tradition. 16c-1979. *1504*
—. Nigeria. 15c-1975. *2251*
—. Politics. Uganda. 1880-1970. *3270*
—. Rites and Ceremonies (ancestor worship). Urbanization. 1960's-70's. *870*
—. Social change. 1910's-70's. *874*
—. Zambia (Marrapodi). 1930's-75. *4083*
Religion, civil. Luba. Social customs. ca 1963-76. *796*
Religion (review article). 16c-20c. *891*
—. Churches, independent. South Africa. 1945-70's. *3973*
Religion, traditional. Cone, James. South Africa. Theology, African. 1700-1970's. *3956*
Religious attitudes. Arts and crafts. Ivory Coast (Man, Zuénoula). Social attitudes. 1974. *1928*
Religious change. Christianity. 1881-1960's. *814*
Religious Liberty *See also* Church and State; Persecution.
—. Socialism. Tanzania. 1961-77. *3215*
Religious movements. ca 1500-20c. *899*
—. Africa, central. Culture. Prehistory-1970. *2393*
—. Africa, east. Bibliographies. 1946-76. *2624*
—. African Orthodox Church. McGuire, George Alexander. 1921-80. *854*
—. Anticolonialism. Working class. Zaire. 1900-50. *2548*
—. Baptists. Kimbangu, Simon. Zaire. 1921-22. *2546*
—. Church of Christ on Earth. Kimbangu, Simon. Zaire. 1881-1972. *2545*
—. Colonialism. Kongo. Prophetism. Zaire. 1880-1964. *2547*
—. Ethnic identity. ca 1960-75. *809*
—. Holy Apostles. Nigeria (Ilaje). Utopias (defection, recruitment). 1947-74. *2225*
—. Jamaa. Zaire. 1953-74. *2538*
—. Kimbangu, Simon. Zaire. 1921-79. *2549*
Religious movements, messianic. Nationalism. 1920's-70's. *159*
Religious organizations. Modernization. Political involvement. Sects, Religious. 1940's-70. *826*
Religious studies. Folklore (review article). 19c-20c. *840*
Relocation. African National Congress. Apartheid. South Africa (Johannesburg; Sophiatown). 1933-55. *3990*
Rémy, Nzé Ndong Jean. Christianity. Erendzi Duma Nsur Mor. Gabon. Sects, Religious. 1940's-70's. *2452*
René, Albert. Coups d'etat. Foreign Relations. Mancham, James. Political Factions. Seychelles. 1964-77. *3575*
Rennie Tailyour Concession. Gold Mines and Mining. London and Rhodesia Mining and Land Company. Zimbabwe. 1890-1950's. *4158*
Repatriation. Refugees. War. Zimbabwe (Umtali). 1980-81. *4205*
Repentance and Holy Flight group. Egypt. Government, Resistance to. Islam. 1977-79. *1235*
Reporters and Reporting *See also* Journalism; Press.
—. Biko, Steve. *New York Times*. South Africa. USA. *Washington Post*. 1969-77. *3814*
—. Civil war. Foreign Relations. Nigeria. Religion. 1960's. *2095*
—. News, international. Newspapers. Nigeria. 1978-79. *2267*
Repression. Colonial Government. Ivory Coast. 1908-20. *1919*
Research *See also* Methodology.
—. 20c. *55*
—. Africa, southern. Religion. 1961-80. *3378*
—. Archaeology. Zaire. 1899-1970. *2455*
—. Bibliographies. Colonial government. Military. Zimbabwe. 1890-1975. *4260*
—. Customary law. Lesotho. 1969-75. *875*
—. Kenya. National development. Nigeria. Science. 1970's. *612*
Research, interdisciplinary. Historiography. Military. Political Science. 1898-1976. *361*
Research policy. Institute for African Studies. Zambia. 1930's-70's. *4132*
Research, regional. Africa, East. East African Community. Medicine. 1906-73. *2569*
Resettlement. Africans. Guerrilla warfare. Zimbabwe. 1972-75. *4327*
—. Algeria (Chénoua). Colonialism. Land Reform. 1840-1967. *1051*
—. Angolans. Botswana (Etsha). 1967-75. *3519*
—. Angolans. Refugees. Zaire. 1960's-70's. *2534*
—. Angolans. Refugees. Zambia. 1966-72. *4072*
—. Asylum. Refugees. 1970's. *323*
Resettlement, forced. Algeria. Counterinsurgency techniques. France. Peasants. Psychological warfare. 1954-62. *992*
Resettlement policy. Africans. South Africa. 1913-72. *3807*
—. Colonialism. Portugal. 1930-74. *172*
Resettlement programs. Algeria. Colonial policy. France. 1954-66. *1103*
—. Counterinsurgency. FRELIMO. Mozambique. 1960-74. *3642*
Resistance *See also* Military Occupation.
—. Abd-el-Krim. France. Morocco. Rif War. Spain. 1921-26. *1412*
—. Africa, central. Africa, southern. Collaboration. Imperialism. 1850-1920. *183*
—. Anticolonialism. Mozambique. ca 1500-1972. *3641*
—. Badoglio, Pietro. Documents. Graziani, Rodolfo. Italy. Libya (Cyrenaica). Mukhtar, Omar el-. 1930-31. *1391*
—. Benin. Colonial government. Ọhọri. 1914-16. *1698*
—. Colonial Government. Great Britain. Hodeib, Mohammed Amin. Sudan (Tuti Island). 1914-46. *1496*
—. Colonialism. Portugal. Vietnam. 1862-1975. *186*
—. Colonization. French West Africa. Lobi. 1898-1926. *1630*
—. Colonization, attempted. Italy. Libya. 1907-32. *1375*
—. Dube, John L. Racism. South Africa (Natal). 1871-ca 1940. *3993*
—. Ethiopia. Graziani, Rodolfo. Italy. Military occupation. 1935-40. *2801*
—. Historiography (Marxist). Nationalism. Ranger, T. O. 20c. *14*
Responsible Government Movement. Government. South Africa Company. Zimbabwe. 1910-23. *4228*
Responsible Government Party. Colonial government. Referendum. Zimbabwe. 1920-23. *4227*
Restoration. American Legation. Morocco (Tangier). 1821-1975. *1421*
Retraditionalization. Military leadership. Modernization. 1970's. *365*
Réunion. Decolonization. France. 1945-79. *3562*
—. Economic Conditions. France. Intergovernmental Relations. Politics. 1945-80. *3563*
—. Mauritius. Press. ca 1830-1973. *3569*
Revolution *See also* Civil Disturbances; Coups d'Etat; Government, Resistance to; Independence Movements; Radicals and Radicalism; Rebellions; Riots.
—. Acculturation. Malawi. Political culture. 1909-61. *3595*

—. Algeria. Auden, Maurice (disappearance). France. 1957-. *1105*
—. Algeria. Boumédienne, Houari. Islam. Political Leadership. 1940's-78. *1083*
—. Algeria. Boumédienne, Houari. Political Leadership. 1946-78. *1048*
—. Algeria. Colonialism. 1920-54. *1097*
—. Algeria. Culture. Economic Development. Political Change. 1976-81. *1110*
—. Algeria. France. Paratroopers. Public Opinion. 1954-78. *1106*
—. Algeria. National Charter. Socialism. ca 1975-76. *1074*
—. Angola. FRELIMO. Mozambique. Popular Movement for the Liberation of Angola (MPLA). 1970-80. *3386*
—. Angola. Intervention. Mozambique. 1960's-70's. *3373*
—. Bureaucracies. Ethiopia. Monarchy. 1930-80. *2762*
—. Cabral, Amilcar. Fanon, Frantz. Political theory. 20c. *4*
—. Cabral, Amilcar. Guinea-Bissau. Political Theory. 1950's-73. *1892*
—. Cabral, Amilcar. Guinea-Bissau. Political Theory. 1960's. *1883*
—. Cabral, Amilcar (essay). Imperialism. 20c. *209*
—. China. Egypt. Modernization. Political Leadership. Sadat, Anwar. 1952-79. *1238*
—. Collaboration. Vambe, Lawrence. Zimbabwe. ca 1950-75. *4242*
—. Colonialism. Independence. Lenin, V. I. Socialism. 1907-80. *21*
—. Cuba. Ethiopia. Intervention. USSR. 1974-78. *2738*
—. Cultural policy. Mozambique. Tradition. 1964-78. *3651*
—. Djibouti. Ethiopia. Self-determination. Somalia. 1974-78. *2572*
—. Economic Conditions. Egypt. Social Conditions. 1952-82. *1307*
—. Egypt. Nasser, Gamal Abdel. Political leadership. 1956-76. *1207*
—. Egypt. Political Leadership. 1952-64. *1270*
—. Elites. 1960-78. *253*
—. Elites. Keita, Mobido. Mali. Militarism. 1960-68. *1968*
—. Ethiopia. 1960's-74. *2749*
—. Ethiopia. 1973. *2727*
—. Ethiopia. 1974-75. *2812*
—. Ethiopia. 1974-76. *2764*
—. Ethiopia. Feudalism. Politics and the Military. 1972-75. *2748*
—. Ethiopia. Getachew, Mekasha. 1973-77. *2747*
—. Ethiopia. Haile Selassie. 1896-1980. *2809*
—. Ethiopia. Haile Selassie. Teferi Benti. 20c. *2753*
—. Ethiopia. Land reform. 1974-76. *2694*
—. Ethiopia. Military Government. Social Classes. 1974-79. *2728*
—. Ethiopia. Social classes. 1941-74. *2782*
—. Ethiopia. Socialism. 1974-78. *2777*
—. Fanon, Frantz. Freedom. Political Philosophy. 1952-61. *1030*
—. Fiction. Heroes. Kenya. Mau Mau. ca 1950-57. *2966*
—. Ideology. Rebellions. Zaire (Kwilu). 1930's-63. *2526*
—. Kenya. Marx, Karl. Mau Mau. Political Theory. Tocqueville, Alexis de. 1888-1963. *2921*
—. Kenya. Mau Mau. 1920-60. *2933*
—. LaGuma, Alex. Novels. South Africa. 1956-72. *3952*
—. Libya. Political Systems. 1969-80. *1363*
—. Libya (Augila oasis). Qadhafi, Muammar. Social Conditions. 1968-80. *1384*
—. Mozambique. Political Leadership. 1960-75. *3669*
—. National liberation movements. Neocolonialism. Pan-Africanism. 1945-73. *116*
—. Nemery, Jaafar. Religion. Sudan. Tradition. 16c-1979. *1504*
Revolution, African. Nkrumah, Kwame. 1935-66. *1820*
Revolution (review article). Archer, Robert. Madagascar. ca 1972-74. *3576*
—. Ethiopia. 1974-78. *2725*
Revolutionaries. Algeria. Social Status. 1950's-60's. *1041*
Revolutionary activities. Clergy. Reeves, Ambrose. South Africa (Johannesburg). 1949-60. *4004*
Revolutionary movements *See also* Anticolonial Movements; Independence Movements.
—. Africa, southern. Settlers, European. Zimbabwe African People's Union (ZAPU). 1974-75. *3360*
—. Algeria. 1954-62. *1003*
—. Algeria. National Liberation Front. Social Classes. 1920-60. *999*
—. Arab-Israeli conflict. Egypt. Military capability. Nasser, Gamal Abdel (memoirs). 1948-52. *1257*
—. Army officers. Egypt. Intelligentsia. 1849-1952. *1199*
—. Capitalism. 1960's-70's. *671*
—. Ethiopia (Eritrea). Foreign Aid. USA. 1975. *2779*
—. FRELIMO. Marxism. Mozambique. 1962-78. *3637*
—. FRELIMO. Mondlane, Eduardo. Mozambique. 1920-69. *3638*
—. Mozambique. Portugal. 1961-74. *3660*
—. Mugabe, Robert. Zimbabwe. Zimbabwe African National Union (ZANU). 1974-79. *4255*
Revolutionary theory. Colonialism. Fanon, Frantz. Nationalism. 1800-1960. *1070*
Rey, C. F. (diaries). Botswana. Kalahari Desert. Travel accounts. 1930-37. *3507*
Rey, P. P. Anthropology. Capitalism. Congo. Marxism. Neocolonialism (review article). 20c. *2440*
Rezende, Baron de. British South Africa Company. Gold Mines and Mining. Investments. Mozambique Company. Zimbabwe. 1887-1948. *4159*
Rhetorical strategies. Ghana. National Self-image. Nkrumah, Kwame. 1957-60. *1803*
Rhodesia. *See* Zimbabwe.
Rhodesia, University of. Political Protest. Students. Zimbabwe. 1974. *4244*
Rhodesian Front. African National Council. Colonial government. Segregation. Zimbabwe. 1961-73. *4225*
—. Censorship. Press. Zimbabwe. 1964-79. *4283*
Rhodesian Information Office. Pressure Groups. South Africa Foundation. Sugar interests. USA. 1934-72. *3866*
Rhodes-Livingstone Institute. Anthropology. Decolonization. Gluckman, Max. Zambia. 1939-47. *4047*
—. Colonial government. Urbanization. Wilson, Godfrey. Zambia. 1938-41. *4134*
—. Colson, Elizabeth (memoirs). Zambia. 1948-51. *4056*
—. Fosbrooke, Henry (memoirs). Zambia. 1956-60. *4067*
—. Gluckman, Max. Zambia. 1942-47. *4057*
—. Heron, Alastair (memoirs). Zambia. 1963-67. *4079*
—. Leadership. Zambia. 1933-76. *4122*
—. Mitchell, J. Clyde (memoirs). Zambia. 1952-55. *4090*
—. Richards, Audrey (memoirs). Zambia. 1933-38. *4109*
—. White, C. M. N. (memoirs). Zambia. 1955-62. *4133*
Rhokana Corporation. Copper Mines and Mining. Mergers. Zambia. 1930-32. *4038*
Rice. Agricultural Mechanization. Ivory Coast. Regionalism. Yams. 19c-20c. *1915*
—. Agricultural systems. Diola. Senegal. Social organization. 20c. *2319*
—. Agriculture. Modernization. Sierra Leone. 20c. *2351*
—. Avatime. Social Customs. Social organization. Togo. Yams. 20c. *2373*
—. Ghana, northern. Green revolution. Immigration. Violence. 1965-80. *1728*
—. Madagascar. Merina. Monarchy. 19c. *3550*
Richards, Arthur. Colonial Government. Colonial Office. Decolonization. Nigeria. 1939-45. *2125*
Richards, Audrey (memoirs). Rhodes-Livingstone Institute. Zambia. 1933-38. *4109*
Richthofen, Manfred von. Air Warfare. Lewis, D. G. "Tommy". World War I. Zimbabwe. 1918. *696*
Rif War. Abd-el-Krim. France. Morocco. Resistance. Spain. 1921-26. *1412*
—. Air Warfare. Morocco. Rebellions. Rockwell, Paul Ayres (memoir). Squadron of the Sultan's Guard. USA. 1925. *1447*
—. Cities. *Dahir Barbère* (law). Morocco. Nationalist movements. 1920-40. *1415*
—. Ideology. Morocco. 1921-26. *1441*
—. Lyautey, Hubert. Morocco. 1907-25. *1445*
Riots *See also* Civil Disturbances; Demonstrations; Strikes.
—. Algeria (Algiers). Political Change. 1958. *1079*
—. Anti-Semitism. Libya (Tripolitania). 1945. *1379*
—. Asafo movement. Ghana (Cape Coast). 1925-35. *1815*
—. Bibliographies. Igbo. Nigeria (Aba). Women. 1929-30. *2123*
—. Cameroon (Douala). World War II. 1945. *2415*
—. Colonial government. Ghana. Indirect rule. Slater, Ransford. Taxation, direct. 1929-44. *1816*
—. Diplomacy. Great Britain. Italy. Nationalism. Somalia (Mogadisho). 1948. *3034*
—. Politics. South Africa (Soweto). 1910-77. *3896*
—. Race Relations. South Africa (Soweto). -1976. *3854*
—. Zimbabwe (Bulawayo). 1919-30. *4253*
Rites and ceremonies. Abisi. Nigeria. Political change. Rukuba. ca 1950-76. *2227*
—. Apostles. Conversion experience. Maranke, John. Sects, Religious. 1932-72. *829*
—. Christian sects. Music. 1960-75. *785*
—. Christianity. Tanzania (Ngara). Tradition. 1930's-70's. *3212*
—. Ghana. Healing movement. Methodology. Twelve Apostles Church. 1913-71. *1833*
—. Nambiya. Social organization. Zimbabwe (Wange). 1737-1977. *4142*
—. Political Development. 1960's-70's. *272*
Rites and Ceremonies (ancestor worship). Lovedu. Prayer. South Africa. 1963. *3986*
—. Religion. Urbanization. 1960's-70's. *870*
Rites and Ceremonies (dream-telling). Churches, independent. Immigrants, Kenyan. Pentecostal Mission. Uganda. 1957-60's. *3227*
Road construction. Ethiopia. Italy. Military Occupation. 1936-41. *2709*
Roads. Colonial Government. Nigeria (Southeastern). 1903-39. *2051*
—. Economic development. Railroads. Zaire, lower. 1855-1938. *2472*
—. Ethiopia. Imperial Highway Authority. 1951-73. *2690*
—. Pioneers. Zimbabwe (Chibi District). 1890's-1960's. *4319*
Robert Williams Co. Angola. Copper mines and Mining. French, J. C. Labor recruitment. Zaire (Shaba). 1917-21. *2477*
Robinson, James H. Operation Crossroads Africa. Students. 1958-73. *601*
Rockets, launching. Orbital Transport und Raketen Aktiengesellschaft (OTRAG). Zaire (Shaba). 1976. *2466*
Rockwell, Paul Ayres (memoir). Air Warfare. Morocco. Rebellions. Rif War. Squadron of the Sultan's Guard. USA. 1925. *1447*
Rodney, Walter. Colonialism. Westernization. 1972. *10*
Rohrbach, Karl. Agriculture. Economic Development. Togo. 1960's-70's. *2383*
Roman Catholic Church. *See* Catholic Church.
Rommel, Erwin. Africa, North. Egypt. Libya. World War II. 1941-42. *754*
—. Africa, North. Hitler, Adolf. Logistics. Military Strategy. World War II. 1941-42. *770*
Rosenberg, Valerie (review article). Authors. Bosman, Herman Charles. Clifford, Lago. Prisons. South Africa. 20c. *3977*
Ross, W. McGregor. Colonial Office. Kenya. Leys, Norman. Senate (European). 1900-40. *2971*
Rossi, Gianluigi *(L'Africa Italiana verso l'Indipendenza, 1941-1949).* Diplomacy. Independence. Libya. 1949. *1361*
—. Independence (review article). Italy. Negotiations. UN. 1946-49. *233*
Rousseau, Jean Jacques *(Social Contract).* Democracy. *Jamahiriya* (concept). Libya. Political theory. Qadhafi, Muammar *(Green Book).* 1967-79. *1380*
Rubber. Colonial Government. Forests. Great Britain. Legislation. Nigeria. 1897-1940. *2025*
—. Depression. French West Africa. Peanut production. Peyrissac (firm). Trade. 1924-39. *1675*
—. Economic Planning. Ivory Coast. Plantations. Villages. 1968-79. *1927*
Rubber industry. Firestone, Harvey S. Great Britain. Imperialism, economic. Liberia. O'Meara, Francis. USA. 1922-27. *1940*
—. Foreign investments. Liberia. 1966-71. *1945*
Rugemaninzi. Chiefs. Mafundwe. Shi. Zaire (Kabare, Ngweshe). 1895-1960. *2490*
Rukuba. Abisi. Nigeria. Political change. Rites and ceremonies. ca 1950-76. *2227*
—. Nigeria. Occupations. Social Change. Taxation. 1905-70's. *2046*

Rural areas. Educational development. Zaire (Shaba). 1920-60. *2543*
—. Educational policy. French West Africa. 1903-56. *1613*
—. Employment. Migration. Tanzania. Youth. 1969-79. *3127*
—. Family structure. Hausa. Nigeria. Social Change. 20c. *2247*
—. Income. Kenya. Poverty. 1961-79. *2907*
—. Islam. Local Politics. Nigeria (Kano). Pakistan (South Waziristan). 20c. *2213*
Rural Areas (review article). Africa, North. Middle East. 16c-20c. 1975-78. *939*
Rural credit. Banks. Government. Zambia. 1964-75. *4073*
Rural Development. Agricultural Cooperatives. Ghana (Komenda). Sugar. 1960-76. *1759*
—. Agricultural Cooperatives. Tanganyika African National Union (TANU). Tanzania. Ujamaa villages. 1932-70. *3080*
—. Agricultural cooperatives. Tanzania. ca 1960's-70's. *633*
—. Agricultural development. Nigeria (Anambra). 1955-85. *2058*
—. Agricultural Policy. Social Classes. Tanzania (Iringi; Ismani). Ujamaa villages. 1950-72. *3053*
—. Agriculture. Colonial government. East African Groundnut Project. Tanzania. 1947-54. *3077*
—. Algeria. Cooperatives, Grazing. Livestock production. 1971-74. *1061*
—. Benin. Land reform. 1961-79. *1709*
—. Botswana. 1966-75. *3510*
—. Botswana. Decisionmaking. Local Government. 1969-72. *3532*
—. Botswana. Democracy. Public expenditures. 1965-80. *3502*
—. Botswana. Public Administration. 1970-74. *3517*
—. Brazil (Pará). Gisu. Social Classes. Uganda. 1969-78. *3226*
—. Canadian International Development Agency. Tanzania. Wheat. 1979-82. *3072*
—. Cities (small). Kenya. 1970's. *2890*
—. Cities (small). Mali (Kita). Tunisia (Testour). 1950's-78. *623*
—. Colonial government. Land tenure. Uganda. 1900-66. *3252*
—. Community development. Ethiopia. Peasants. Social Organization. 1957-74. *2716*
—. Egypt. General Desert Development Organization. New towns. 1961-78. *1128*
—. Environment. Kenya (Kano Plains). 20c. *2853*
—. Ethiopia. Land tenure. Social change. 1970's. *2706*
—. Exports. Ivory Coast. 1960-75. *1926*
—. Ghana. Regional planning. 1966-75. *1724*
—. Income, rural. Swaziland. 1860-1982. *4034*
—. Industrialization. Kenya. Rural Industrial Development Programme. 1973-77. *2896*
—. International trade. Peasants. Tanzania. 1940-75. *3067*
—. Kenya. Peasants (review article). Social Organization. Tanzania. 1970's. *2622*
—. Labor. Migration, Internal. Political protest. Zambia (Kasumpa). ca 1960-75. *4042*
—. Land reform. Mali. 1972-79. *1965*
—. Law, customary. Senegal. 1931-79. *2324*
—. Migrant Labor. Nigeria (Bendel state, Ikaleland). Urhobo. 1920-76. *2065*
—. Socialism. Zambia. 1964-77. *4106*
—. Tanzania. Ujamaa villages. 1960's. *3068*
—. Tanzania. Ujamaa villages. 1960-75. *3099*
Rural development policy. Public Administration. Tanzania. 1975-78. *3183*
—. Tanzania. 1960's-70's. *3109*
Rural development programs. Agriculture. Zambia (Kabwe). 1929-70. *4092*
Rural habitat. Africa, West. Bibliographies. 1968-74. *1615*
Rural households. Family. Senegal. Wolof. 20c. *2309*
Rural Industrial Development Programme. Industrialization. Kenya. Rural Development. 1973-77. *2896*
Rural Life. Agricultural development. Algeria. Cooperatives, Multipurpose. 1962-72. *1060*
Rural self-help (harambee). Economic Conditions. Educational policy. 1960-77. *2989*
—. Education. Kenya. Technology, institutes of. 1971-74. *2877*
—. Kenya. 1963-77. *3013*
—. Kenya. Technical education. 1963-70. *2994*
Rural Settlements *See also* Settlement; Villages.
—. Algeria. Military policy. 1954-77. *1102*
—. Bomani, Paul (interview). Economic development. Tanzania. ca 1960's-70's. *3059*
—. Economic Planning. Tanzania. Ujamaa villages. 1967-75. *3201*
—. Greeks. Zimbabwe. 1890-1930. *4314*
Rural society. Social differentiation. Tanzania. 1967-69. *3073*
Rural-urban studies. Labor aristocracy. Nigeria (Northern). Wages. 1974. *2036*
Russian Revolution. Emigres. Ethiopia. 1917-35. *2741*
Ruvuma Development Association. Settlement. Tanzania. 1960's. *3186*
Rwanda. Clans. Social organization. 19c-20c. *3019*
—. Colonial government. Labor (forced). Malawi. Peasants. Political consciousness. 19c-1962. *207*
—. Colonialism. Ethnic Groups. Political Systems. Refugees. 1853-1980. *3022*
—. Dowry system. Hutu. Marriage. Tutsi. 1970's. *3021*
—. Famine. 1916-18. *3018*
—. Hutu. Political development. Tutsi. 1919-72. *3023*
—. Land Tenure. Politics. Social Classes. 1850-1950. *3017*
—. Military. Tradition. Tutsi. 1500-1973. *3024*
Rwanda (Kinyaga region). Ethnicity. Hutu. Tutsi. 1860-1960. *3020*

S

Sabūr, Salāh 'Abd al-. Drama. Egypt. Nasser, Gamal Abdel. Political Protest. 1950's-60's. *1287*
Sadat, Anwar. Arab states. Economic Development. Egypt. Foreign Relations. 1970-74. *1224*
—. Arab states. Egypt. Foreign Relations. 1973-78. *1294*
—. Arab-Israeli conflict. Egypt. Foreign Policy. 1970-79. *1290*
—. Arab-Israeli conflict. Egypt. Foreign Policy. Peace Movements. 1967-77. *1217*
—. Battle, Lucius D. Egypt. Foreign Relations. 1957-81. *1189*
—. China. Egypt. Modernization. Political Leadership. Revolution. 1952-79. *1238*
—. Conflict and Conflict Resolution. Egypt. Foreign Relations. Libya. Qadhafi, Muammar. 1950-77. *965*
—. Conservatism. Egypt. Nasserism. 1970-74. *1282*
—. Decisionmaking. Egypt. October War. 1973. *1209*
—. Diplomacy. Egypt. Israel. 1956-79. *1229*
—. Diplomacy. Egypt (Cairo). Property (gift). USA. 1964-67. *1190*
—. Domestic Policy. Economic development. Egypt. Foreign Policy. 1970-75. *1274*
—. Economic Conditions. Egypt. Peace. Political Power. 1970-79. *1289*
—. Egypt. 1936-74. *1313*
—. Egypt. Foreign Investments. Foreign Policy. 1971-80. *1131*
—. Egypt. Foreign policy. 1970-79. *1284*
—. Egypt. Foreign Policy. Islam. Political thought. 1970-80. *1237*
—. Egypt. Foreign Policy. Military aid. Nasser, Gamal Abdel. USSR. 1960's-72. *1218*
—. Egypt. Foreign Policy. Nasser, Gamal Abdel. Political Leadership. 1953-76. *1232*
—. Egypt. Foreign Policy. Political Leadership. 1969-81. *1261*
—. Egypt. Foreign Policy (peace plan). Israel. 1948-79. *1260*
—. Egypt. Foreign Relations. Israel. 1973-78. *1308*
—. Egypt. Islam. Muslim Brotherhood. 1970-82. *1236*
—. Egypt. Land tenure policy. Nasser, Gamal Abdel. Patrimonialism. Political leadership. 1954-79. *1300*
—. Egypt. Nasser, Gamal Abdel. Political Leadership. 1952-75. *1191*
—. Egypt. Nasserism. 1952-74. *1226*
—. Egypt. Pan-Arabism. 1956-75. *1256*
—. Egypt. Political Leadership. 1952-73. *1241*
—. Egypt. Political Leadership. 1970-75. *1312*
—. Egypt. Political Leadership. 1970-80. *1272*
—. Egypt. Political parties. 1970-80. *1288*
—. Egypt. *Problèmes Politiques et Sociaux* (periodical). 1970-78. *1112*
—. Egypt. Siraj al-Din, Fu'ad. Wafd Party. 1952-78. *1267*
Sadat, Anwar (autobiography). Egypt. 1940-78. *1244*
Sadat, Anwar (Knesset speech). Egypt. Foreign Policy. Israel. Peace. 1977-78. *1281*
Sahara. Algeria, southern. Colonialism. France. 1818-1959. *917*
—. Capot-Rey, Robert. Geography. Institute for Saharan Research. 1935-78. *926*
—. Daily Life. Morocco (Cape Juby). Saint-Exupéry, Antoine de (reports). 1928-29. *1417*
—. Economic development. Foreign aid. 19c-20c. *632*
—. Salt. Social organization. Trade. Tuareg. 19c-20c. *938*
Sahel. Africa, West. Droughts. Economic history. Hausa. Tuareg. 1550-1973. *595*
—. Africa, West. Droughts. Land use. 1968-74. *607*
—. Africa, West. Famine. Foreign Aid. USA. 1968-75. *521*
—. Bibliographies. Droughts. Economic conditions. Famine. 1968-73. *677*
—. Climatic change. Droughts. 1974. *661*
—. Disaster relief. Droughts. 1960-74. *1681*
—. Droughts. 1968-74. *520*
—. Droughts. 1969-74. *1677*
—. Droughts. 1970's. *1626*
—. Droughts. Economic rehabilitation. 1966-75. *1634*
—. Droughts. Economic Structure. Nomads and Nomadism. Social Customs. 1964-74. *1614*
—. Droughts. Famine. ca 1972-74. *616*
—. Droughts. Sheep raising. 1969-74. *599*
—. Droughts (review article). 1977-79. *678*
—. Famine. Foreign Aid. ca 1972-74. *614*
—. Government regulation. Grain. Marketing. 1960's-70's. *558*
Sa'id, Rif'at as-. Egypt. Historiography. Leftism. 1940-50. *1195*
St. Catherine (monastery). Diaries. Egypt. Monasteries. Orthodox Eastern Church. Sinai, Mount. 1980. *1123*
St. Joseph's Society for the Missions. Archives. Missions and Missionaries. 1866-1980. *25*
St. Patrick's Missionary Society. Congregation of the Holy Ghost. Missions and Missionaries. Nigeria. 1920-30. *2274*
Saint-Exupéry, Antoine de (reports). Daily Life. Morocco (Cape Juby). Sahara. 1928-29. *1417*
Salafi movement. Egypt. Islam. Nationalism. 1920-40. *1223*
Salaries. *See* Wages.
Salt. Sahara. Social organization. Trade. Tuareg. 19c-20c. *938*
Salt industry. Economic Development. Nigeria (Bornu). 1750-1936. *2041*
Sam, Alfred Charles. Blacks. Colonization. Ghana. USA. 1913-16. *1846*
Samburu. Agricultural development. Kenya. Maasai. 1935-75. *2876*
—. Assimilation. Economic Structure. Iligira. Kenya. 20c. *2985*
San. Africa, Southern. Geographic Mobility. Social change. ca 1700-1978. *3359*
—. Afrikaners. Botswana, western. Labor. Social Conditions. Tswana. 1900-71. *3524*
—. Autonomy. Botswana (Ghansi). Social Policy. 1974-82. *3535*
—. Botswana. Colonial Government. Domestic Policy. 1835-1940. *3501*
—. Marshall, Lawrence (family). Namibia. Social change. 1951-80. *3703*
Sancke, Paul. Belgium. Lumumba, Patrice (correspondence). Zaire. 1956-57. *2512*
Sanctions *See also* Economic Sanctions.
—. Apartheid. South Africa. UN. 1899-1982. *3946*
—. Apartheid. South Africa. USA. 1950-79. *3828*
—. Economic Conditions. Politics. Zimbabwe. 1904-74. *4217*
—. Ethiopia. Foreign relations. Italy. League of Nations. War. 1922-36. *2784*
—. Ethiopia. Italy. League of Nations. War. 1935-36. *2720*
—. Political systems. Zambia. Zimbabwe. 1973. *4104*
Sanitation *See also* Public Health.
—. Development. Upper Volta. 1960-76. *2388*
Sanusi. Guerrilla Warfare. Italy. Libya (Cyrenaica). Mukhtar, Omar al-. 1923-32. *1397*
Sanusi brotherhood. Niger. Rebellions. Tuareg. 1916-17. *1984*
São Tomé and Príncipe. Decolonization. Goa. Macao. Portugal. Timor, East. 1975-80. *2453*
Sara. Chad. Civil war. Politics. 1930-78. *2437*
—. Chad. Colonial Government. Railroads. Working Conditions. 1921-34. *2429*

—. Methodist Church. Nemapare, E. T. J. Zimbabwe. 1930-50. *4328*
Serer. Political systems. Senegal. Social Classes. 1960's-74. *2312*
Servants. Africans. Christianity. Hostels. South Africa (Johannesburg). Women. 1907-70. *3972*
Sesame. Agricultural production. Great Britain. Nigeria. Tiv. Trade. 1900-60. *2024*
Sétif incident. Algeria. DeGaulle, Charles. Rebellions. 1945. *1014*
Settlement *See also* Colonization; Resettlement; Rural Settlements; Squatter Settlements.
—. Acculturation. Adja. Benin. Nigeria. 18c-1945. *2220*
—. Afar. Ethiopia (Awash Valley). 1972-78. *2756*
—. Africa, East. Asians. Uganda. 6c-1972. *2628*
—. Africans. South Africa (Brakpan). 1903-27. *4002*
—. Agriculture. Soil erosion. Zimbabwe (Mondoro Reserve). 1890-1978. *4184*
—. Algeria. Colonialism. Economic Structure. Social Organization. 1830-1962. *1067*
—. Authority. Botswana. Tswana. 19c-1978. *3526*
—. Botswana (Kweneng). Migration. Population. 1965-76. *3527*
—. *Chihrinimi* (newspaper). Egypt. Iranians. 1904-66. *1357*
—. Cocoa. Farmers. Ghana (Suhum). Political change. 1900-72. *1855*
—. Europeans. Immigration. Zimbabwe. 1890-1976. *4322*
—. Housing shortage. South Africa (Johannesburg). Squatters. 1944-47. *4017*
—. Liberia. Linguistics. Sierra Leone. 15c-1961. *1609*
—. Madagascar. Social Organization. 1958-78. *877*
—. Mozambique. Portuguese. 20c. *3648*
—. Ngindo. Tanzania, southern. 1840-1945. *3204*
—. Ruvuma Development Association. Tanzania. 1960's. *3186*
Settlement (conference). Europeans. 20c. *42*
Settlement (European). Africa, East. Bibliographies. Hobley, Charles William. 1890-1947. *2612*
Settlement schemes. Agriculture. Eastern Nigeria Project. Nigeria (Igboland, Northern). Regional development. 1945-67. *2034*
Settlers. Capitalism, Primitive. Depression. Europeans. Kenya. ca 1900-50. *2910*
—. Decolonization. Europeans. Kenya. 1960's. *2967*
—. Europeans. Kenya Land Commission. Kikuyu. Land tenure. 1902-34. *2869*
Settlers and Residents Association of Nyasaland (SARAN). Independence Movements. Malawi. 1959-63. *3619*
Settlers, European. Africa, southern. Revolutionary movements. Zimbabwe African People's Union (ZAPU). 1974-75. *3360*
Seventh-Day Adventists. Missions and Missionaries. Political Protest. Zambia (Tonga Plateau). 1903-55. *4061*
Seven-Year Plan for Education. Education. Ghana. 1529-1966. *1848*
Sex discrimination. Education. Ghana (Accra). Women. 1850-1972. *1854*
Sex roles. Cultural identity. Morality. ca 1920-70. *887*
Seychelles. 1601-1971. *3554*
—. Coups d'etat. Foreign Relations. Mancham, James. Political Factions. René, Albert. 1964-77. *3575*
—. Foreign Policy. 20c. *3573*
—. Independence. 1768-1976. *3583*
—. Independence. 1977-80. *3567*
—. Tourism. 1968-73. *3570*
Shagari, Shehu. Government. Military Government. Nigeria. 1973-82. *2136*
Shangwe. Arrighi, G. Peasants (proletarianization). Tobacco industry. Zimbabwe. 1898-1938. *4168*
Sheep raising. Agricultural Development. Algeria (high plain). 1973. *1058*
—. Droughts. Kufra Scheme. Libya. Water. 1968-73. *1366*
—. Droughts. Sahel. 1969-74. *599*
Shembe, Isaiah. Nazaretha Church. Religion. South Africa (Natal). 1910-78. *3955*
Shi. Chiefs. Mafundwe. Rugemaninzi. Zaire (Kabare, Ngweshe). 1895-1960. *2490*
Shipping. Great Britain. Italy. Libya. Navies. World War II. 1940-43. *752*
Shipping (open registry). Coups d'etat. Developing nations. Foreign Relations. Liberia. 1980-81. *1939*
Shona. Churches, independent. Leadership. Sundkler, B. G. M. Zimbabwe. 1945-70's. *4299*
—. Crime and Criminals. Law, customary. Statistics. Zimbabwe. 1936-71. *4313*
—. Ethnic conflict. Ndebele. Zimbabwe. 10c-20c. *4275*
Shona (Mhari). Mapanzure. Zimbabwe. 1859-73. *4151*
Siabuwa, Munchunkwe Sigaleta. Chiefs. Funerals. Zimbabwe (Binga). 1976. *4303*
Siad Barre, Mohammed. Civil rights. Military government. Reform. Somalia. 1969-76. *3032*
Sidiyya Baba. Mauritania. Nationalism. Political Leadership. 1862-1926. *1975*
Sierra Leone *See also* Africa, West.
—. Africa, West. Cummings-John, Constance Agatha. Independence movements. Politics. Women's Movement. 1918-50's. *2343*
—. *African Standard* (newspaper). Anticolonialism. Ghana. Wallace-Johnson, I. T. A. West African Youth League. 1930-45. *1684*
—. Agricultural cooperatives. Innovation diffusion. 1948-67. *2339*
—. Agricultural development. Economic Planning. Plantations, industrial. Politics. 1964-67. *2362*
—. Agriculture. Modernization. Rice. 20c. *2351*
—. Air lines. 1950's-72. *2367*
—. Asians. Trade (domestic). 1950-78. *2355*
—. Bibliography. Ghana. Libraries, research. Nigeria. 20c. *1600*
—. Bo School (graduates). Education. 1906-80. *2341*
—. Creole (term). Social History. 1800-1970. *2360*
—. Creoles (review article). Spitzer, Leo. 1870-1951. *2369*
—. Economic change. Family. Labor. ca 1750-1928. *2337*
—. Economic change. Mining. 1930's. *2352*
—. Economic Conditions. Political Leadership. Stevens, Siaka. 1967-80. *2354*
—. Economic development. Military Government. Nationalism. 1967-68. *2338*
—. Economic growth. Geography. Transportation patterns. 20c. *2366*
—. Economic Growth. Markets, periodic. Trade (interregional). 1896-1970. *2356*
—. Elites. Great Britain. Krio. Nationalism. Railroads. Strikes. 1919-26. *2370*
—. Elites. Krio. Language. 1853-1978. *2368*
—. Elites. Local Government. Violence, rural. ca 1945-76. *2365*
—. Family. Public welfare. Westernization. 18c-20c. *2347*
—. Fertility levels. Mende. Temne. 1963-73. *2344*
—. Foreign aid. 1970's. *2357*
—. Foreign aid. Independence. Political Leadership. ca 1787-1976. *2358*
—. Gamanga, Kenewa. Independence Movements. Political Leadership. 1941-61. *2342*
—. Islam. Liberia. Social organizations. Vai. 1926-59. *1946*
—. Liberia. Linguistics. Settlement. 15c-1961. *1609*
—. Miners. 1935-67. *2364*
—. Modernization. Political Attitudes. Youth. 1970's. *2340*
—. Monetary Systems. 1960-77. *2345*
—. Political protest. Wallace-Johnson, I. T. A. West African Youth League. 1892-1939. *2353*
Sierra Leone Development Company. Great Britain. Imperialism. 1929-76. *2348*
Sierra Leone (Freetown). Independence Movements. Political Leadership. 1905-45. *2361*
—. Protestant Churches. Women's associations. 1960's-70's. *2363*
Sierra Leone (Mayoso). Migration. Temne. 1950's-70's. *2346*
Sierra Leone (northwestern). Agricultural development. Colonial Government. Dependency. 1896-1939. *2359*
Sierra Leone (Pendembu). Economic structure. Traders. 1966-68. *2350*
—. Traders. 1908-68. *2349*
Sik, Endre. Dialectical materialism (review article). Marxism. Prehistory-1977. *3*
Simba. Peasants. Rebellions. Zaire (Sankuru). 1964. *2520*
Sinai, Mount. Diaries. Egypt. Monasteries. Orthodox Eastern Church. St. Catherine (monastery). 1980. *1123*
—. Egypt. Orthodox Eastern Church. Papaioannou, Daniel. 1852-1930. *1321*
Sinai Peninsula. Boundaries. Egypt. Great Britain. 1906-47. *1124*
Siraj al-Din, Fu'ad. Egypt. Sadat, Anwar. Wafd Party. 1952-78. *1267*
—. Egypt. Wafd Party. 1910-77. *1265*
Sisala. Ghana (Accra). Islam. Migrants. Urban adaptation. 20c. *1839*
Sitwell, William (letters). Botswana (Macloutsi). Police (border patrol). 1892-1915. *3522*
Siwale, Donald (autobiography). Zambia. 1890's-1964. *4123*
Six-Day War. Air Warfare. Egypt. Israel. Military strategy. 1967. *1178*
—. Egypt. Israel. Military policy. Nasser, Gamal Abdel. Syria. 1948-67. *1285*
Sklar, Richard L. (review article). Labor. Mining industry. Multinational corporations. Zambia. 1920-76. *4130*
Slater, Ransford. Colonial government. Ghana. Indirect rule. Riots. Taxation, direct. 1929-44. *1816*
Slave trade. Foreign relations. Imperialism. Portugal. 15c-20c. *203*
Slavery *See also* Abolition Movement; Emancipation.
—. Abolition Movement. Great Britain. Sudan. 1877-1960. *1522*
—. Colonial Government. Nigeria (Benin). 1897-1945. *2250*
—. Colonialism. Historiography. Ideology. 19c-1960's. *196*
Slaves. Arabs. Cloves. Tanzania (Zanzibar). 19c-1964. *3112*
Sleeping sickness. Belgium. Medical Research. Public Health. Zaire. 1885-1980. *2536*
—. Colonial government. Economic Conditions. Public Health. Social Conditions. Zambia (Mweru-Luapula). 1906-22. *4093*
—. Colonial Government. Ivory Coast. Public Health. 1900-45. *1918*
Slums. Developing nations. Models. 1956-63. *782*
Slums *(bidonvilles).* Depression. Tunisia. 1930's. *1556*
Smith, Ian. African National Council. Zimbabwe. ca 1972-74. *4285*
—. Coups d'etat. Portugal. Zimbabwe. 1974. *4189*
—. Diplomacy. Zimbabwe. 1965-79. *4234*
—. Government. Multinational corporations. Zimbabwe. 1965-79. *4169*
—. Guerrilla warfare. Zimbabwe. 1973. *4246*
—. Independence Movements. Zambia. Zimbabwe. 1953-82. *4074*
—. Race Relations. Zimbabwe. 1971-74. *4274*
Smuggling. Civil War. Dahomey. Nigeria. 1966-74. *1644*
—. Cocoa. Dahomey. Nigeria. 1968-74. *1645*
—. Niger. Nigeria. Peanuts. 1935-76. *1621*
Smuts, Jan. Africa, East. Armies. Europeans. Humor. World War I. 1914-18. *711*
—. Israel. South Africa. Weizmann, Chaim. 1917-50. *3932*
—. South Africa. World War II. 1939. *771*
So. Generations. Karamojong. Political authority. Uganda. 1900-72. *3256*
Sobhuza II. Politics. Swaziland. 1972-74. *4035*
Sobukwe, Robert. Pan-African Congress. South Africa. 1975. *3947*
Soccer. Cameroon. Modernization. Social Organizations. 1880's-1974. *2403*
Social attitudes. Arts and crafts. Ivory Coast (Man, Zuénoula). Religious attitudes. 1974. *1928*
—. Cultural relations. Europe, Western. Hausa. Islam. Literature. 1945-78. *2285*
Social behavior. Egypt. Mary, Virgin. Zeitoun, apparition of. 1968. *1345*
Social Change *See also* Economic Growth; Industrialization; Modernization.
—. Africa, Southern. Colonialism. Labor unions and organizations. Tradition. Zaire. ca 1900-73. *225*
—. Africa, Southern. Geographic Mobility. San. ca 1700-1978. *3359*
—. Africa, West. Middle Classes. Political Leadership. Songhai. 1591-1980. *1685*
—. Agriculture. Colonial Government. Maghreb. 1800-1956. *966*
—. Algeria. Arabization. Educational policy. 1962-73. *1087*
—. Algeria. Colonization. France. 1830-1962. *1015*
—. Algeria. Women. ca 1830-1974. *1032*
—. Angola. Ideology. Independence Movements. 1940-79. *3482*
—. Armies. Nigeria. 1965-77. *2002*
—. Bibliographies. Government. 19c-20c. *299*
—. Botswana. Labor. Migration, Internal. 1966-80. *3487*
—. Burundi. Cultural degradation. Twa. 20c. *2660*

—. Cameroon. Fulbe (Mbororean). Nigeria. Nomads and Nomadism. Sedentarization. 20c. *1635*
—. Cameroon. Ivory Coast. Social Status. Women. 1955-71. *800*
—. Christianity. Madagascar. Political Change. 1850-1972. *3585*
—. Christianity. Political Change. 19c-20c. *815*
—. Colonialism. Dependency relationships. Niger. Tuareg, Yullemmeden kel Dinnik. 1800-1974. *1979*
—. Colonialism. Education. Elites. ca 1900-76. *863*
—. Colonialism. Food production. Mongo-Nkundo. Zaire (Equateur). 19c-20c. *2468*
—. Colonialism. Urbanization. 1910-81. *805*
—. Conscription, military. France. Guinea. World War I. 1906-30. *717*
—. Coptic Church. Ethiopia (Ochollo). Missions and Missionaries. Protestant Churches. 1898-1980. *2824*
—. Coups d'etat. Ghana. Military. 1981. *1763*
—. Diola. Land Reform. Senegal. ca 1885-1978. *2335*
—. Drama. Egypt. 1919-80. *1341*
—. Economic Conditions. Family life. Kenya. 1900-77. *3011*
—. Economic Conditions. Goody, Jack (review article). Technology. Tradition. ca 18c-20c. *330*
—. Economic Conditions. Migration. 1940's-70's. *775*
—. Economic Development. Egypt. Nasser, Gamal Abdel. 1952-62. *1167*
—. Economic Development. Elites (urban). Kenya (Nakuru). Kikuyu. 1929-52. *2856*
—. Economic Development. Madagascar. Political Change. 1960-78. *3551*
—. Economic development. Politics (review article). 1968-72. *6*
—. Economic Development. Women. 19c-20c. *652*
—. Egypt. Heikal, Muhammed. Intellectuals. Modernization. Muslim Brotherhood. 1914-55. *1353*
—. Elias, T. O. (review article). Law. Nigeria. 1960-73. *2209*
—. Employment. Kenya (Nairobi). Working Class. 1952-69. *2874*
—. Ethiopia. Land tenure. Rural development. 1970's. *2706*
—. Ethiopia. Occupational prestige. 1958-68. *2712*
—. Ethnic Groups. South Africa. 1945-80. *3740*
—. European contacts. 15c-20c. *40*
—. Family structure. Hausa. Nigeria. Rural areas. 20c. *2247*
—. Films. 1926-74. *893*
—. Hoernle, Alfred. Industrialization. Racism. South Africa. 1900-39. *3728*
—. Ivory Coast. Migration. 1928-78. *1924*
—. Ivory Coast. Social Classes (formation). 1920-65. *1914*
—. Kenya. Teso. 19c-20c. *3015*
—. Liberalism. Race Relations. South African Council of Churches. 1970's-. *3853*
—. Malawi. Marriage. Nyakusa-Ngonde. Tanzania. 1875-1971. *913*
—. Marshall, Lawrence (family). Namibia. San. 1951-80. *3703*
—. Nigeria. Occupations. Rukuba. Taxation. 1905-70's. *2046*
—. Nigeria. Political conflict. Regionalism. 1900-. *2004*
—. Religion. 1910's-70's. *874*
—. Socialism. Tanzania. 1961-74. *3048*
—. Somalia. 1950-75. *3028*
—. South Africa. 1975-80. *3888*
—. Tunisia. 1956-70's. *1563*
Social Change (review article). Mourides. Muslim brotherhoods. Senegal. 1969-71. *2305*
Social Classes *See also* Class Struggle; Elites; Middle Classes; Social Mobility; Social Status; Working Class.
—. ca 1960-79. *884*
—. Africa, southern. Colonialism. Government, Resistance to (review article). Historiography. Isaacman, Allen. 1890's-1970's. *3407*
—. African studies. Coups d'etat (review article). Lofchie, Michael. Uganda. ca 1965-75. *303*
—. Agricultural cooperatives. Economic Policy. Mozambique. 1975-78. *3634*
—. Agricultural Policy. Rural Development. Tanzania (Iringi; Ismani). Ujamaa villages. 1950-72. *3053*
—. Agricultural Technology and Research. Egypt. 1920-40. *1164*
—. Algeria. 1950-80. *1046*
—. Algeria. Colonna, F. Leca, Jean. Politics (review article). Teachers. Vatin, J.-C. 1883-1975. *1094*
—. Algeria. National Liberation Front. Revolutionary movements. 1920-60. *999*
—. Armies. Coups d'etat. Uganda. ca 1962-71. *3257*
—. Attitudes. Colonialism. Ethnic Groups. 1960's-70's. *915*
—. Attitudes. Methodology. Nigeria. Political culture. 1800-1960. *2124*
—. Autonomy. South Africa (Transkei). 1956-75. *3929*
—. Bank Misr. Economic structure. Egypt. Federation of Industries. General Agricultural Syndicate. 1880-1940. *1170*
—. Bibliographies. Ethiopia. Land tenure. Peasants. 20c. *2696*
—. Boycotts. Cocoa. Ghana. Political Participation. 1937-38. *1736*
—. Brazil (Pará). Gisu. Rural development. Uganda. 1969-78. *3226*
—. Business. Progressive Federal Party. South Africa. 1959-78. *3859*
—. Capitalism. Economic Structure. Nigeria, northern. Peasants. 1850-1980. *2072*
—. Capitalism. Nigeria. Sects, Religious. Yoruba. 1947-74. *2017*
—. Capitalists. United National Independence Party. Zambia. 1964-81. *4043*
—. Chiefs. Colonial government. Uganda (Teso). 1896-1927. *3314*
—. Christianity. Colonial Government. Ethnic Groups. Uganda (Ankole). 1900-25. *3229*
—. Cities. Economic Structure. Tunisia (Tunis). 15c-20c. *1539*
—. Coups d'etat. Politics and the Military. Uganda. 1971. *3260*
—. Economic Conditions. Political power. Race. Zimbabwe. 1890-1970's. *4173*
—. Economic Development. Ethiopia. Inflation. 1960-74. *2703*
—. Economic Development. Migration. Zaire. 1908-78. *2483*
—. Economic Development (review article). Kenya. 1870's-1970's. *2851*
—. Economic Structure. Tanzania (Mafia Islands). 1518-1975. *3049*
—. Education. Egypt. National integration. 1805-1968. *1330*
—. Education. Tanzania. 1961-79. *3207*
—. Egypt. Intelligentsia. Political Factions. 1907-52. *1322*
—. Elites. Socialism. 1960-78. *883*
—. Ethiopia. Military Government. Revolution. 1974-79. *2728*
—. Ethiopia. Revolution. 1941-74. *2782*
—. Exports. Kenya. Land Tenure. 1950-79. *2863*
—. Hima. Iru. Uganda (Ankole). 1960's-70's. *3233*
—. Kenya. Public policy. Tanzania. 1960's-70's. *2565*
—. Kenya. Tea Development Authority. 1960-72. *2908*
—. Land Tenure. Malawi, southern. 1890-1980. *3604*
—. Land Tenure. Politics. Rwanda. 1850-1950. *3017*
—. Magubane, Bernard. Political Economy. Race Relations. South Africa. 1950's-80. *3889*
—. Mining. Proletarianization. Technology. Zambia. 1946-66. *4102*
—. Monarchy. Nicholls, George Heaton. Racism. Solomon. South Africa (Natal). Zulu (Usuthu). 1879-1933. *3886*
—. Peasants. Tanzania. 14c-20c. *3113*
—. Political systems. Senegal. Serer. 1960's-74. *2312*
—. Politics. Zambia. 1960-76. *4113*
—. Presidents. Uganda. 1962-74. *3263*
—. Tunisia (Testour). 1971-74. *1548*
Social Classes (analysis). Fanon, Frantz. Political theory. 1950's-60's. *1109*
Social Classes (conflict). Agrarian Revolution Charter and Decree (1971). Algeria. Land Reform. 1971-73. *1038*
Social Classes (formation). Ivory Coast. Social change. 1920-65. *1914*
Social Classes (Temazlayt relationship). Algeria (Ahaggar; Kel Ulli). Modernization. Social Organization. Tuareg. 1864-1960's. *1040*
Social Conditions *See also* Cities; Cost of Living; Daily Life; Economic Conditions; Family; Labor; Marriage; Migration, Internal; Popular Culture; Social Classes; Social Mobility; Social Problems; Social Reform; Social Surveys; Standard of Living.
—. Aba riots. Igbo. Nigeria (Calabar, Owerri). Women. 1925. *2194*
—. Africa, Southern. Economic Development (review article). 1902-76. *3379*
—. Afrikaners. Botswana, western. Labor. San. Tswana. 1900-71. *3524*
—. Algeria. Economic growth. 1967-73. *1111*
—. Apartheid. Race relations. South Africa. 1971-76. *3744*
—. Colonial government. Economic Conditions. Public Health. Sleeping sickness. Zambia (Mweru-Luapula). 1906-22. *4093*
—. Colonialism. Confederation. Economic Development. Zambia. Zimbabwe. 1925-35. *3421*
—. Colonialism. Economic Development. 1865-1975. *673*
—. Colonialism. Kenya. Political structure. 1952-73. *2915*
—. Cooperatives. Economic structure. Senegal. Youth. 1963-72. *2308*
—. Depression. Farmers. Guinea. Purchasing power. Taxation. 1930's. *1880*
—. Droughts. Economic Conditions. Niger. Peasants. 1968-78. *1981*
—. Economic Conditions. Egypt. Ethiopia. Politics. 1970's. *340*
—. Economic Conditions. Egypt. Revolution. 1952-82. *1307*
—. Economic Conditions. Uganda. USSR. 1981. *3297*
—. Labor recruitment. World War I. 1914-20. *715*
—. Libya (Augila oasis). Qadhafi, Muammar. Revolution. 1968-80. *1384*
—. Literature. Tunisia. ca 1900-. *1560*
—. Morocco. Political opposition. 1980. *1430*
Social conflict. Nigeria. 1971-78. *2257*
—. Political attitudes. Working class. 1950-81. *276*
—. Political Change. Uganda. 1961-78. *3230*
Social control. Afrikaans. Language. South Africa. 1875-1976. *3970*
—. Courts. Kenya. 1969-74. *3007*
—. *Drum* (periodical). South Africa. 1951-. *3965*
—. Education. South Africa. 1960-78. *4031*
Social Customs. Asante. Ghana. Sects, Religious. Witchcraft. 1870-1930. *1849*
—. Avatime. Rice. Social organization. Togo. Yams. 20c. *2373*
—. Cannabis, diffusion of. 100-1974. *806*
—. Church and society. Theater. 1914-45. *2200*
—. Clan histories. Tanzania. Utani. 1960's-70's. *3196*
—. Climate. Europeans. Kenya. Zimbabwe. 1880's-1930's. *185*
—. Colonial Government. Great Britain. Marxism. Witchcraft. 19c-20c. *173*
—. Droughts. Economic Structure. Nomads and Nomadism. Sahel. 1964-74. *1614*
—. Ecological code. Myths and Symbols. -1973. *910*
—. Educational planning. Modernization. 1974. *803*
—. Luba. Religion, civil. ca 1963-76. *796*
—. Nigeria. Twins, cult of. Yoruba. 1750-1850. *2228*
Social Customs (gift-giving). Dorze. Ethiopia. Wealth (redistribution). 1800-1974. *2700*
Social Customs (veil). Africa, North. Tuareg, Southern. 1920-76. *944*
Social democracy. Economic Structure (international). Scandinavia. 1960-80. *538*
Social development. Economic Policy. Ghana. Industrialization. Nkrumah, Kwame. 1957-72. *1747*
Social differentiation. Rural society. Tanzania. 1967-69. *3073*
Social distance. Racism. South Africa. Students. USA (Hawaii). 1974. *3983*
Social History. Africa, Southern. Goba. Religion. Zambezi River. 1200-1970. *3381*
—. Creole (term). Sierra Leone. 1800-1970. *2360*
Social Institutions. Islam. Modernization. Sudan. 1900-72. *1515*
Social integration. Culture. Liberia. 19c-20c. *1943*
Social Mobility. Colleges and Universities. Ghana. 1948-74. *1864*
—. Education. Ethnicity. Nigeria. 1840's-1975. *2212*

—. Apartheid. Law. 1910-71. *3917*
—. Apartheid. Libraries. 1950's-78. *4009*
—. Apartheid. Luthuli, Albert. Tambo, Oliver. 1652-1973. *3936*
—. Apartheid. Medicine. 1972-73. *3994*
—. Apartheid. National liberation movements. National Liberation Movements. 20c. *3726*
—. Apartheid. Neocolonialism. 1947-73. *3710*
—. Apartheid. Organization of African Unity. 1963-74. *127*
—. Apartheid. Political Change. 1896-1998. *3872*
—. Apartheid. Race relations. Social Conditions. 1971-76. *3744*
—. Apartheid. Racial policies formation. 1923-39. *3913*
—. Apartheid. Sanctions. UN. 1899-1982. *3946*
—. Apartheid. Sanctions. USA. 1950-79. *3828*
—. Apartheid. Social Organization (review article). 1950-70's. *3957*
—. Apartheid. Sports. 1940's-70's. *3987*
—. Apartheid. Sports. UN. 1955-80. *3865*
—. Apartheid. Strikes. Wage disparity. Working Class. 1971-73. *3768*
—. Apartheid. Television. 1953-70's. *3961*
—. Apartheid. UN. 1948-70. *3823*
—. Apartheid. Vorster, John. 1965-75. *3816*
—. Apartheid. Working class, white. 20c. *3755*
—. Apartheid. World Council of Churches. 1969-70's. *3861*
—. Arab states. Foreign Relations. 1973-77. *396*
—. Archives. 1910-80. *3737*
—. Armaments. Economic Structure. Foreign investments. Multinational corporations. 1945-78. *3799*
—. Armaments. Indian Ocean. Military strategy. 1960-74. *3812*
—. Armaments. Multinational corporations. UN Anti-Apartheid Committee. 1960-77. *3923*
—. Armaments industry. Military organizations. 1974. *3840*
—. Arms Trade. Embargo. USA. 1978-80's. *3873*
—. Arms trade. Exports (restrictions). USA. 1945-78. *3775*
—. Arms trade. Israel. 1967-70's. *3834*
—. Australia. Economic development. Historiography. Racism (review article). 20c. *3720*
—. Australia. Libraries. New Zealand. Office of War Information. USA. World War II. 1942. *765*
—. Authors. Bosman, Herman Charles. Clifford, Lago. Prisons. Rosenberg, Valerie (review article). 20c. *3977*
—. Automobile industry and trade. Foreign Investments. 1945-80. *3761*
—. Bantu Homelands. Economic Conditions. Industrialization. 1969-73. *3785*
—. Bantu Homelands. Economic policy. Elections. Political Parties. 1920-74. *3900*
—. Bantu Homelands. International law. Self-determination. 1971-78. *3916*
—. Bantu Homelands. Namibia. 1974. *3404*
—. Bibliographies. Foreign Relations. USA. 1950's-78. *3845*
—. Bibliographies. Munger Africana Library. Politics. 1881-1974. *3808*
—. Biko, Steve. *New York Times*. Reporters and Reporting. USA. *Washington Post*. 1969-77. *3814*
—. Biko, Steve (review article). 1948-77. *3897*
—. Bloemfontein Conference. Kadalie, Clements. Labor Unions and Organizations. Msimang, H. Selby. 1919-25. *3800*
—. Botha, Pieter. Military-industrial complex. 1960-76. *3874*
—. Botswana. Foreign policy. 1970's. *3500*
—. Botswana. Foreign policy. Khama, Seretse. Political development. 1966-76. *3492*
—. Botswana. Labor. Mines. 1899-1966. *3531*
—. Botswana. Labor markets. Lesotho. Swaziland. 1967-76. *3343*
—. Botswana. Lesotho. Monetary systems. Rand Monetary Area. Swaziland. 1909-78. *3347*
—. Boycott Outspan Action Foundation (BOA). Netherlands. Oranges. 1972-73. *3757*
—. Boycotts. Foreign relations. Norway. 1970-77. *3933*
—. Broederbond. Secret Societies. Social Organizations. 20c. *3966*
—. Bullhoek massacre. Israelites. Mgijima, Enoch. Religion. 1868-1921. *3969*
—. Bureau of State Security. Secret Police. 1969-76. *3804*
—. Business. Collective bargaining. Labor Unions and Organizations. Race Relations. USA. 1970-81. *3752*
—. Business. Progressive Federal Party. Social Classes. 1959-78. *3859*
—. Cabinet crisis. National Anthems. Stuttaford, Richard. 1938. *3825*
—. Calvinism, Afrikaner. Economic activity. 18c-1975. *4020*
—. Canada. Foreign Policy. 1899-1982. *3937*
—. Canada. Foreign Policy. Self-determination. Zimbabwe. ca 1961-79. *3411*
—. Canada. Foreign Policy. Trade. Zimbabwe. 1960's-76. *3409*
—. Cancer. Epidemiology. Migrant labor. 1930-75. *3979*
—. Cannabis use. 20c. *3967*
—. Capital mobilization. Economic growth. Government policy. 1939-60. *3782*
—. Capitalism. Protectionism. Racism. 1910-39. *3871*
—. Capitalism. Race Relations. 1918-78. *3743*
—. Capitalism (review article). Dagut, J. Houghton, H. Hobart. 1860-1970. *3778*
—. Catholic Church. Communism. Goodlatte, Clare. Politics. Social work. 1860-1940. *3817*
—. Censorship. Christian Institute of South Africa. Study Project on Christianity in an Apartheid Society. 1970's. *4006*
—. Christian Institute of South Africa. Church and State. Dutch Reformed Church. Nationalism. 1960-75. *4026*
—. Christian Nationalists. Labor Unions and Organizations. 1933-48. *3780*
—. Churches, independent. Religion (review article). 1945-70's. *3973*
—. Cigarette manufacture. 1882-1961. *3756*
—. Civil-Military Relations. 1945-81. *3855*
—. Class Struggle. 1972-81. *3919*
—. Class Struggle. Economic growth. Labor. 1945-80. *3760*
—. Colleges and Universities. Curricula. Native Administration. 1956-75. *3985*
—. Colonialism. 19c-20c. *3721*
—. Colonialism. Imperialism. Zimbabwe. 1960-79. *3370*
—. Colonialism. Mozambique. Political economy. 1890's-1960's. *3367*
—. Colonialism. Politics. Race Relations. 18c-1970's. *3730*
—. Colonialism. Racial policies. 1800-1972. *3709*
—. Colonialism, settler. Economic development. 1830-1976. *3717*
—. Colonies. Foreign Relations. Portugal. 1948-74. *3831*
—. Colonization. Labor supply. Land. Natal Land and Colonization Company. 1838-1948. *3791*
—. Coloureds. Economic Conditions. Ethnic Groups. Griqua trek. LeFleur, A. A. S. 1867-1920. *3968*
—. Coloureds. Ideology. Political attitudes. 1974. *3893*
—. Coloureds. Political representation. 1951-79. *3940*
—. Coloureds. Racial policies. Reform. Theron Commission. 20c. *3971*
—. Comintern. Communist Party. Race Relations. 1920's-30's. *3868*
—. Communist Party. International Socialist League. 1917-21. *3867*
—. Cone, James. Religion, traditional. Theology, African. 1700-1970's. *3956*
—. Constitutions. Independence. Namibia. South West Africa People's Organization (SWAPO). 1970's. *3353*
—. Culture. Emancipation. Senegal. Tanzania. ca 1914-76. *816*
—. Culture. Ethnic Groups. 1652-1977. *3998*
—. Decolonization. International Law. Namibia. 1884-1973. *3684*
—. Defense Policy. Legislation. Military Service (geographical limits). 1912-76. *3858*
—. Democracy, Concordance. Models. 1970's. *3860*
—. Descent groups. Land allocation. Zulu (Nyuswa). ca 1825-1970. *4005*
—. Detente. Foreign Relations. Kaunda, Kenneth. Racism. Zambia. 1964-74. *4040*
—. Development. Modernization. Racism. 20c. *3794*
—. Diplomacy. Foreign Investments. USA. 1962-72. *3764*
—. Discrimination. Racism. Zulu. -1974. *3950*
—. Discrimination, economic. Labor Supply. Land Tenure (alienation). Zimbabwe. 1920-70. *3387*
—. Domestic policy. Foreign policy. 1964-73. *3869*
—. *Drum* (periodical). Social control. 1951-. *3965*
—. Dube, John L. Ohlange Institute. Political Leadership. Race Relations. Washington, Booker T. ca 1885-1925. *3832*
—. Economic conditions. Education. Homelands Policy. Race relations. 1960's-70's. *3738*
—. Economic control. Government. Middle classes (African). Racism. 1652-1975. *3802*
—. Economic history. Historiography (neo-Marxist). 1960-76. *3766*
—. Economic policy. Europeans. Racial policies. 20c. *3754*
—. Economic Policy. Industrial decentralization. Labor control. ca 1950-79. *3749*
—. Economic Policy. Military policy. 1970's. *3876*
—. Economic relations. Foreign Relations. Mozambique. 1974-79. *3334*
—. Economic Structure. Mining industry. Political strategy. 1970's. *3776*
—. Education. Social control. 1960-78. *4031*
—. Elections. 1977. *3836*
—. Elections. 1977. *3879*
—. Elections, general. Public Opinion. Race relations. 1969-70. *3878*
—. Elites. Israel. 1930's-70's. *3943*
—. Ethnic groups. Military. Politics. 1960's-70's. *3847*
—. Ethnic groups. Political Parties (identification). 1970. *3905*
—. Ethnic Groups. Social Change. 1945-80. *3740*
—. Ethnicity. Liberalism. Political development. 1921-48. *3914*
—. Europe, Western. National Security. USA. USSR. 1980-82. *3815*
—. Europeans. Nationalism. Zimbabwe. 1974-79. *3335*
—. Europeans. Racism. Working Class. ca 1950-78. *3758*
—. Exiles. Films, documentary. Mahomo (interview). Morena Films. Propaganda. 1960-76. *3951*
—. Foreign Policy. 1960-76. *3934*
—. Foreign policy. 1960-78. *3931*
—. Foreign Policy. Imperialism. Western Nations. 1975-77. *3882*
—. Foreign Policy. Israel. 1948-80. *3902*
—. Foreign policy. Kissinger, Henry A. (memorandum). USA. 1967-74. *3903*
—. Foreign Policy. Lesotho. 1965-75. *3540*
—. Foreign policy. Multinational corporations. USA. 1960-70's. *3895*
—. Foreign policy. National Liberation movements. Zimbabwe. 1974-75. *4192*
—. Foreign policy. National Security Council. USA. 1969-76. *3829*
—. Foreign policy. USA. 1950's-74. *3833*
—. Foreign Policy. Western Nations. Zimbabwe. 1970's. *3330*
—. Foreign Relations. France. Zaire. 1974-78. *426*
—. Foreign Relations. Great Britain. Labour Party. 1947-51. *3904*
—. Foreign Relations. Independence movements. Indian Ocean. Western Nations. 1955-70's. *3894*
—. Foreign Relations. Israel. 1919-74. *3875*
—. Foreign Relations. Military Strategy. Namibia (Walvis Bay). Ports. 1914-82. *3682*
—. Foreign Relations. Military Strategy. Western nations. 1970's. *3925*
—. Foreign Relations. Mineral resources. Mining. Namibia. 1966-81. *3685*
—. Foreign Relations. Multinational Corporations. USA. 1964-76. *3788*
—. Foreign Relations. National Development. USSR. Zimbabwe. 1979-82. *4149*
—. Foreign Relations. Nigeria. 1960-75. *391*
—. Foreign Relations. Politics. Race Relations (review article). 1974-79. *3887*
—. Foreign relations. Racial policies. USA. 1779-1976. *3809*
—. Foreign Relations. Sweden. 1960-74. *3773*
—. Foreign Relations. USA. 1970's. *3922*
—. Foreign Relations. USA. 1976-80. *3819*
—. Foreign Relations. USA. 1981. *3939*
—. Fredrickson, George M. (review article). Race relations. USA (South). 18c-20c. *4008*
—. Freedom of speech. Law. 1964. *3820*
—. Frontier and Pioneer Life (comparative). USA. 1900-50. *3746*
—. Germany. Trade. 1931-39. *3767*
—. Glass and Glassmaking. 1896-1944. *3792*
—. Gold Mines and Mining. Labor (review article). Race Relations. Zimbabwe. 1900-69. *3403*

—. Gordimer, Nadine. Novels. Politics. Race Relations. 1953-79. *3959*
—. Great Britain. Lobbying. Newspapers. Propaganda. USA. 1972-79. *3863*
—. Great Britain. Neocolonialism. Portugal. Racism. Zimbabwe. 1960's-70's. *3328*
—. Hertzog, J. B. M. (testimonials). Historiography. 1900-39. *3862*
—. Historiography. Nationalism. Race Relations. 1965-72. *3844*
—. Historiography (review article). Wright, Harrison M. 1800-1957. *3714*
—. Historiography (revisionist). Industrialization. Race relations. 20c. *3747*
—. Hoernle, Alfred. Industrialization. Racism. Social change. 1900-39. *3728*
—. Human rights. Portugal. Zimbabwe. 1853-1977. *3329*
—. Human rights. Race Relations. USA. 1973-78. *3821*
—. Ideology. Interest Groups. Manufacturing. 1900-25. *3750*
—. Immigration, British. Race Relations. 1820-1970's. *4021*
—. Independence. Lesotho. 1966-76. *3544*
—. Independence. Namibia. UN. 1946-78. *3675*
—. Independence Movements. 1970's. *54*
—. Independence movements. Namibia. USSR. 1966-77. *3673*
—. Independence Movements. Zulu. 1912-78. *3935*
—. Industrial Relations. Legislation. Wiehahn Commission. 1970's. *3774*
—. Industrialization. Multinational corporations. Nationalism, African. Political economy. 1978. *3787*
—. International Law. Namibia. Western nations. 1966-80. *3693*
—. Israel. Racism. 1960's-82. *3908*
—. Israel. Smuts, Jan. Weizmann, Chaim. 1917-50. *3932*
—. Jawaharlal Nehru Award for International Understanding. Mandela, Nelson. 1979-80. *3884*
—. Jews. 1910-67. *4010*
—. Joubert, Elsa. Novels. 1955-80. *3999*
—. Labor. Labor Unions and Organizations (black). 1918-73. *3729*
—. Labor. Mining industry. Political Protest. 1980's. *3731*
—. Labor movement. Miners. Strikes. 1930's-40's. *3781*
—. Labor Policy. Wiehahn Commission. 1977-78. *3753*
—. Labor (review article). Mining. Racism. Zimbabwe. 1900-1933. *3408*
—. Labor Unions and Organizations. Namibia. 1920-74. *3355*
—. Labor Unions and Organizations. Race Relations. Strikes. 1973. *3797*
—. LaGuma, Alex. Novels. Revolution. 1956-72. *3952*
—. Lebaudy, Jacques. Western Sahara. 1886-1919. *1591*
—. Lenin, V. I. 19c-1924. *3830*
—. Liberalism. Malan, F. S. Race Relations. 1890-1924. *3870*
—. Liberation. Organization of African Unity. 1963-76. *3984*
—. Literature. Paton, Alan *(Cry the Beloved Country)*. 1948-75. *3988*
—. Literature, African. Poets. 1973. *3976*
—. Literature, English-language. Politics. ca 1900-75. *3975*
—. Lovedu. Prayer. Rites and Ceremonies (ancestor worship). 1963. *3986*
—. Magubane, Bernard. Political Economy. Race Relations. Social Classes. 1950's-80. *3889*
—. Marxism. Racism. Social Theory. 1970's. *3724*
—. Migrant labor. Zimbabwe. 1940-79. *3344*
—. Migration. Reitz family. 1877-1977. *4007*
—. Military. 1960's-75. *3839*
—. Military. Namibia. 1900-80. *3680*
—. Military capability. ca 1960-76. *3920*
—. Military Capability. Nuclear Arms. 1979. *3803*
—. Millin, Sarah G. Novels. Racism. 1917-65. *4025*
—. Modernization. Racism. 1830's-1973. *4019*
—. Namibia. Political change. 1977-78. *3352*
—. Namibia. Political factions. 1960-79. *3689*
—. Namibia. UN. Waldheim, Kurt. 1966-73. *3691*
—. National Union of South African Students. Race Relations. South African Students Organization. Students. 1924-76. *3911*
—. Newspapers (circulation). 1958-77. *3974*
—. Nicholson, Frederick (diary). 1834-1965. *4000*
—. Pan-African Congress. Sobukwe, Robert. 1975. *3947*
—. Pass laws. Political culture. 1923-79. *3851*
—. Political Culture. Racism. USA (South). 19c-20c. *3941*
—. Political economy. Swaziland. 1968-79. *4033*
—. Political parties. 1914-73. *3841*
—. Political Protest. Race Relations. 1960-77. *3926*
—. Political protest. Soweto Students Representative Council. Students. 1976-77. *3848*
—. Politics. Vorster, John. 1966-74. *3826*
—. Population (growth rates). Urbanization, differential. 1652-1970. *3996*
—. Public opinion. USA. 1846-1976. *3891*
—. Race relations. 17c-20c. *3713*
—. Race Relations. Social Reform. 1970's. *3880*
—. Racial policies. Vorster, John. 1970's. *3806*
—. Racism. Social distance. Students. USA (Hawaii). 1974. *3983*
—. Racism. Sports. 1970's. *4029*
—. Smuts, Jan. World War II. 1939. *771*
—. Social Change. 1975-80. *3888*
—. Strikes. Working class. 1960's-73. *3777*
—. Working class, white (myth). 1830-1974. *3790*
—. World War I. 1914-18. *693*
South Africa (Bochum-Blauberg). Helene Franz Hospital. Missions and Missionaries. Public Health. Syphilis. 1895-1935. *3995*
South Africa (Bophuthatswana). Bantu Homelands. Botswana. Mangope, Lukas (interview). 1973. *3390*
South Africa (Bophuthatswana; Babelegi). Industrialization. Labor. 1960's-70's. *3786*
South Africa (Brakpan). Africans. Settlement. 1903-27. *4002*
South Africa (Cape Town). Air route. Great Britain. Hoare, Samuel. Imperial Airways. 1918-32. *202*
—. Duncan, Patrick. Kgosana, Philip. Pan-African Congress. Strikes. 1953-60. *3881*
South Africa Company. Government. Responsible Government Movement. Zimbabwe. 1910-23. *4228*
South Africa (Durban). Buthelezi, Gatsha. Labor Unions and Organizations. Racial tensions. Strikes. ca 1910-73. *3801*
—. Class struggle. Longshoremen. Migrant labor. Phungula, Zulu. 1939-59. *3763*
—. Money (tokens). Trade. 1906-29. *3954*
South Africa Foundation. Pressure Groups. Rhodesian Information Office. Sugar interests. USA. 1934-72. *3866*
South Africa (Johannesburg). Africans. Christianity. Hostels. Servants. Women. 1907-70. *3972*
—. Afrikaners. Gold. Labor. 1886-1924. *3759*
—. Clergy. Reeves, Ambrose. Revolutionary activities. 1949-60. *4004*
—. Colleges and Universities. Mondlane, Eduardo. Racism. Witwatersrand, University of. 1945-49. *3664*
—. Communism. Jewish Workers' Club. Jews. 1928-48. *3949*
—. Historiography. 1887-1976. *3741*
—. Housing shortage. Settlement. Squatters. 1944-47. *4017*
—. Medals, commemorative. Numismatics. 1889-1972. *4016*
—. Music. Recording industry. Union of South African Artists. 1900-60. *3960*
—. Schools. 1902-68. *4014*
South Africa (Johannesburg; Sophiatown). African National Congress. Apartheid. Relocation. 1933-55. *3990*
South Africa (Johannesburg, Soweto). Africans. City Politics. West Rand Bantu Administration Board. 1971-78. *3849*
South Africa (Kimberley). Brotherhood Movement. Class Struggle. DeBeers Consolidated Mines. Plaatje, Solomon Tshekisho. 1918-19. *3945*
South Africa (Natal). Agricultural diffusion. Bantu Homelands. Farmers, subsistence. Valley Trust. 1950-74. *3783*
—. Development. Dunn Reserve. Land Tenure. Segregation. 1895-1948. *3953*
—. Dube, John L. Ohlange Institute. Technical education. 1900-30's. *3992*
—. Dube, John L. Racism. Resistance. 1871-ca 1940. *3993*
—. Monarchy. Nicholls, George Heaton. Racism. Social Classes. Solomon. Zulu (Usuthu). 1879-1933. *3886*
—. Nazaretha Church. Religion. Shembe, Isaiah. 1910-78. *3955*
—. Voting and Voting Behavior. 1954-59. *3912*
South Africa (Natal, Transvaal). Apartheid. Land Tenure. Whites. 1860-1960. *3733*
South Africa (Port Elizabeth). Afrikaners. Dutch Reformed Church. Meyburgh, Louisa Fredericka. 1900-50. *4024*
—. Afrikaners. Farmers. Migration, Internal. Urbanization. 1904-60. *4023*
South Africa (review article). Cope, R. L. Davenport, T. R. H. Elphick, Richard. Hodgson, T. L. Khoi. 19c-20c. *3715*
South Africa (Soweto). Churches, independent. Cooperation. Leadership. 1960's-70's. *4028*
—. Dutch Reformed Church. Religion. 1970's. *4011*
—. Inkatha movement. Political Factions. Soweto Civil Association. 1976-79. *3852*
—. Political culture. Political Protest. 1976-81. *3850*
—. Politics. Riots. 1910-77. *3896*
—. Race Relations. Riots. -1976. *3854*
—. Rebellions (review article). 1976. *3910*
South Africa (Transkei). Autonomy. Social Classes. 1956-75. *3929*
—. Foreign policy. USA. 1950-79. *3942*
—. Foreign Relations. 1936-80. *3885*
South Africa (Transvaal, Northern). Folklore. Mozambique. Music. Tsonga. 20c. *3376*
South African Airways. Air Lines. Foreign Policy. Pirow, Oswald. South Africa. 1933-39. *3890*
South African Bibliography (SABIB). Bibliographies. Publishers and Publishing. 1904-79. *3745*
South African Broadcasting Corporation. Afrikaners. Nationalism. Political power. South Africa. 1935-66. *3901*
South African Bureau of Racial Affairs. Apartheid. Ideology. Stubbs, Ernest. 1902-32. *3915*
South African Council of Churches. Liberalism. Race Relations. Social Change. 1970's-. *3853*
South African Field Artillery (4th Battery). Africa, East. Lewis, George Edward (diary). Military Campaigns. World War I. 1916. *699*
South African Native Labor Contingent. Africans. World War I. 1916-19. *719*
South African Students Organization. National Union of South African Students. Race Relations. South Africa. Students. 1924-76. *3911*
South America. Africa, Southern. Emigration. Europeans. 1967-76. *3395*
South West Africa. *See* Namibia.
South West Africa People's Organization (SWAPO). Constitutions. Independence. Namibia. South Africa. 1970's. *3353*
—. Democratic Turnhalle Alliance. Independence Movements. Namibia. 1920-79. *3674*
—. Independence Movements. Namibia. 1981. *3705*
Southern Rhodesia. *See* Zimbabwe.
Southern Rhodesia Volunteers. Flags. Zimbabwe (Bulawayo). 1927. 1951. *4204*
Soweto Civil Association. Inkatha movement. Political Factions. South Africa (Soweto). 1976-79. *3852*
Soweto Students Representative Council. Political protest. South Africa. Students. 1976-77. *3848*
Soyinka, Wole. Authors. Nigeria. ca 1952-63. *2258*
—. Fagunwa, D. O. Literature. Nigeria. Tradition. Tutuola, Amos. Yoruba. 1945-70's. *2252*
—. Literature. Nigeria. Political Theory. 1960-81. *2134*
Spain. Abd-el-Krim. France. Morocco. Resistance. Rif War. 1921-26. *1412*
—. Africa, West. Foreign Relations. Great Britain. World War I. 1914-18. *702*
—. Algeria. Foreign relations. 1954-74. *1024*
—. Algeria (Oran). Civil war. 1936-39. *1044*
—. Armies (native troops). Morocco. 1300-1966. *1452*
—. Decolonization. Mauritania. Morocco. Western Sahara. 1970's. *1588*
—. Decolonization. Morocco. Western Sahara. 1970-75. *1577*
—. Decolonization. Western Sahara. 1476-1974. *1585*
—. Decolonization. Western Sahara. 1960-75. *1578*
—. Military occupation. Morocco (Tangier). World War II. 1940-45. *746*
Spain (Madrid). Libraries. Morocco. National Library (Africa section). Prehistory-1973. *935*
Spanish Sahara. *See* Western Sahara.
Spears, Edward. *Ashanti Times* (newspaper). Ghana. Newspapers. 1947-70. *1837*

Special Interest Groups. *See* Interest Groups; Pressure Groups; Lobbies; Political Factions.
Spinola, António de. Portugal. Race Relations (review article). 1960's-70's. *222*
Spitzer, Leo. Creoles (review article). Sierra Leone. 1870-1951. *2369*
Sports. Apartheid. South Africa. 1940's-70's. *3987*
—. Apartheid. South Africa. UN. 1955-80. *3865*
—. Hopley, Frederick John van der Byl. John Hopley Trophy. Zimbabwe. 1883-1951. *4307*
—. Policymaking. Tanzania. 1970-79. *3198*
—. Racism. South Africa. 1970's. *4029*
Sports (athletic infrastructure). Keino, Kipchoge. Kenya. Olympics. Track and field. 1966-74. *2993*
Squadron of the Sultan's Guard. Air Warfare. Morocco. Rebellions. Rif War. Rockwell, Paul Ayres (memoir). USA. 1925. *1447*
Squatter settlements. Bureaucracies. Housing. Tanzania (Dar es Salaam). Urbanization. 1965-82. *3210*
—. Community formation. Urbanization. 1960-74. *324*
—. Government control. Housing. 20c. *872*
Squatters. Housing shortage. Settlement. South Africa (Johannesburg). 1944-47. *4017*
—. Kenya (Rift Valley). Kikuyu. Mau Mau. 1937-52. *2932*
Ssbalijja. Colonial Government. Ganda. Kiga. Local Government. Uganda (Kigezi). 1908-30. *3311*
Standard of Living *See also* Cost of Living.
—. Agriculture. Race Relations. South Africa. 1945-70's. *3771*
—. Ethiopia (Addis Ababa). Ethnic Groups. Labor Unions and Organizations. 1970's. *2714*
State Formation. 'Abd Allah, al-Iman. Boundaries. Ethiopia (Nugara). Feudalism. 1901-23. *2743*
State Government. Constitutions. Nigeria. 1975-78. *2130*
—. Ethnic groups. Nigeria. Political Integration. 1960-78. *2151*
—. Nigeria (Mid-Western State). Political Systems. Succession, forms of. Urhobo kingdoms. 1952-63. *2170*
States, size of. Nigeria. Political stability. 1964-67. *2087*
Statistics *See also* Social Surveys.
—. Colonies. Depression. Indochina. 1924-38. *151*
—. Crime and Criminals. Law, customary. Shona. Zimbabwe. 1936-71. *4313*
Status-field theory. Foreign policy. 1964-66. *495*
Stealing. Birom. Miners. Nigeria (northern). Social protest. Tin. 1958-78. *2246*
Steere, Edward. Anglicanism. Missions and Missionaries. Tanzania. Universities Mission to Central Africa (UMCA). 1876-1926. *3192*
Stereotypes. Algeria. Arabs. Literature. Popular culture. 1891-1920. *1091*
—. Colonial Government. Nuer. Sudan. 1800-1956. *1488*
—. Tourism. 1945-78. *557*
Sterility. Fertility (review article). ca 1950-76. *841*
Stevens, Siaka. Economic Conditions. Political Leadership. Sierra Leone. 1967-80. *2354*
Stirling, David. Capricorn Africa Society. Nationalism. Racism. Zimbabwe. 1945-60. *4213*
Stock companies. Egypt. Middle Classes. Social Organization. 1900-52. *1140*
Strategic planning. Africa, Southern. Foreign policy. Nixon Doctrine. USA. 1960's-74. *3339*
Strategy. *See* Military Strategy; Naval Strategy.
Stren, Richard E. Cities. Housing (review article). Kenya. Tanzania. 1960-80. *2606*
Stresa Conference. Diplomacy. Ethiopia. France. Great Britain. Italy. 1935. *2810*
Strikes *See also* Civil Disturbances; Collective Bargaining; Labor Unions and Organizations.
—. Anticolonialism. French West Africa. Independence movements. 1890-1960. *1687*
—. Apartheid. South Africa. Wage disparity. Working Class. 1971-73. *3768*
—. Buthelezi, Gatsha. Labor Unions and Organizations. Racial tensions. South Africa (Durban). ca 1910-73. *3801*
—. Class consciousness. Labor, contract. Namibia. 1971-72. *3695*
—. Colonialism. Novels. Sembene, Ousmane *(Les bouts de bois de Dieu)*. Senegal. 1947-48. *2298*
—. Copper Mines and Mining. Kenya. Political protest. Zambia. 1922-62. *175*
—. Copper Mines and Mining. Zambia. 1935. *4101*
—. Duncan, Patrick. Kgosana, Philip. Pan-African Congress. South Africa (Cape Town). 1953-60. *3881*
—. Economic development. Kenya. Labor Unions and Organizations. Legislation. 1960's-73. *2899*
—. Elites. Great Britain. Krio. Nationalism. Railroads. Sierra Leone. 1919-26. *2370*
—. Ghana. Labor Unions and Organizations. 1940's-70's. *1740*
—. Labor movement. Miners. South Africa. 1930's-40's. *3781*
—. Labor Unions and Organizations. Race Relations. South Africa. 1973. *3797*
—. Railroad workers. Senegal (Thiès). 1938. *2334*
—. South Africa. Working class. 1960's-73. *3777*
—. Teachers. Zambia. 1968-70. *4084*
Strikes, general. Colonial Government. Nigeria. 1945. *2067*
—. Ethiopia. Politics. 1974. *2715*
—. Migrant labor. Tanzania (Zanzibar). 1923-48. *3064*
—. Nigeria. 1963-64. *2068*
Structuralism. Economic Theory. Ghana. Inflation. Monetarism. 1959-79. *1758*
Stubbs, Ernest. Apartheid. Ideology. South African Bureau of Racial Affairs. 1902-32. *3915*
Student activism. Colleges and Universities. Coups d'etat. Nigeria. 1974-76. *2114*
Student movement. Documents. Madagascar. Nationalism, Cultural. Politics. 1972. *3587*
Student Movement House. Autobiography and Memoirs. Borneman, Ernest. England (London). Independence Movements. 1933-38. *155*
Students *See also* Colleges and Universities; Schools.
—. Algeria. France. Islam. Nationalism. 1912-62. *1073*
—. Attitudes. Economic development. Education. Mali. 1950-76. *1970*
—. Chancellor College. Colleges and Universities. Malawi. 1965-71. *3614*
—. Civil War. Ethnic diversity. Ife, University of. Nigeria. Political attitudes. 1957-69. *2111*
—. Demonstrations. Independence movements. Zambia. 1966-71. *4048*
—. Demonstrations. National service, compulsory. Tanzania (Dar es Salaam). 1966-67. *3189*
—. Emigration (brain drain). USA. 1974. *804*
—. National Union of South African Students. Race Relations. South Africa. South African Students Organization. 1924-76. *3911*
—. Operation Crossroads Africa. Robinson, James H. 1958-73. *601*
—. Political Protest. Rhodesia, University of. Zimbabwe. 1974. *4244*
—. Political protest. South Africa. Soweto Students Representative Council. 1976-77. *3848*
—. Political Protest. Uganda. 1952-75. *3255*
—. Racism. Social distance. South Africa. USA (Hawaii). 1974. *3983*
Study Project of Christianity in an Apartheid Society (reports). Apartheid. Bibliographies. Christianity. South Africa. 1969-75. *4018*
Study Project on Christianity in an Apartheid Society. Censorship. Christian Institute of South Africa. South Africa. 1970's. *4006*
Stuttaford, Richard. Cabinet crisis. National Anthems. South Africa. 1938. *3825*
Suba. Kenya (Nyanza, south). Luo. Oral History. Social Organization. Uganda (Buganda). 1500-1973. *2990*
Subbanu Association. Africa, West. Education. Schools, Koranic. 1935-75. *1647*
Subia. Botswana (Chobe District). Cooperatives. Fishing. Namibia. Yambezi Fisherman's Co-operative Society. 1973-77. *3496*
Succession. Adangme. Ghana. Manya Krobo, stool of. 1800-1939. *1790*
—. Africa, West. Akan. Political Leadership. 17c-20c. *1789*
—. Algeria. Chadli, Bendjedid. Foreign policy. Political Leadership. 1975-81. *1064*
—. Charisma. Political Leadership. 1956-78. *329*
—. Kenya. Kenyatta, Jomo. Moi, Daniel Arap. 1978-1980. *2935*
—. Kenya. Kenyatta, Jomo. Moi, Daniel Arap. Politics. 1978-79. *2960*
—. Mabena, Magumbo. Maribeha. Zimbabwe. 1972. *4278*
—. Monarchy. Nigeria (Kano). 1920's-63. *2142*
Succession disputes. Gor, Jason. Kenya. Luo. 1940's-70's. *2969*
Succession, forms of. Nigeria (Mid-Western State). Political Systems. State government. Urhobo kingdoms. 1952-63. *2170*
Sudan *See also* Africa, East.
—. Abolition Movement. Great Britain. Slavery. 1877-1960. *1522*
—. Addis Ababa agreement. Civil War. 1947-74. *1495*
—. Addis Ababa Agreement. Civil War. Nemery, Jaafar. 1957-73. *1465*
—. Addis Ababa Agreement. Domestic Policy. Foreign policy. Nemery, Jaafar. 1972-76. *1510*
—. Africa, East. Ethiopia. Refugees. 1970's. *385*
—. Agriculture. Economic development. 1970-79. *1491*
—. Algeria. Civil Law. Islam. 1960-78. *934*
—. Ansar Party. Islam. Politics. Umma Party. 1914-45. *1524*
—. Anthropology, medical. Political Systems. Public Health. 1950's-70's. *1484*
—. Anya Nya. Civil war. National liberation movements. Political Leadership. 1950's-70's. *1485*
—. Archaeology. 1817-1980. *1459*
—. Archaeology. Attitudes. 1946-81. *1508*
—. Archer, Geoffrey. Colonial Government. Mahdism. Rahman, Sayyid al-. 1924-27. *1486*
—. Atuot. Ethnicity. 18c-20c. *1472*
—. Bureaucracies (Sudanization). Civil Service (training). 1956-73. *1456*
—. Child Mortality. 1973. *1480*
—. Christianity. Islam. 16c-1981. *1503*
—. Cities (market towns). Urbanization. 1930's-70's. *1460*
—. Civil war. 1956-77. *1483*
—. Civil War. Conciliation. -1972. *1469*
—. Civil War. Foreign policy. Regional Autonomy Agreement (1972). 1966-73. *1470*
—. Civil War. Nigeria. Refugees. Relief efforts. UN. 1966-72. *524*
—. Civil War. Political Integration. Regionalism. 1859-1972. *1476*
—. Colonial Government. Great Britain. 1899-1952. *1493*
—. Colonial Government. Nuer. Stereotypes. 1800-1956. *1488*
—. Colonial policy. Great Britain. Unification. 1898-1953. *1519*
—. Colonialism. Communist Party. 1946-58. *1477*
—. Communist Party. 1946-77. *1528*
—. Counterinsurgency. Kenya. Public Opinion. Zimbabwe. 1951-75. *219*
—. Decentralization. Economic development. 1969-80. *1502*
—. Economic Conditions. Politics. 1970's. *1479*
—. Economic Development. 1950-80. *1464*
—. Economic development. Public Finance (deficits). ca 1960-75. *1511*
—. Economic planning. 1962-70's. *1458*
—. Economic Planning. Investments (growth-pole strategy). Rebellions. Regional inequality. 1974. *1501*
—. Education. Nigeria, northern. Public Administration. 1890-1962. *227*
—. Ethiopia. Foreign Relations. War. 1945-77. *342*
—. Ethiopia (Gubba). Hamdān Abū Shōk. Local government. 1900-38. *2744*
—. Ethnic groups. Islam. Separatist Movements. 1947-76. *1463*
—. Federalism. 1956-81. *1516*
—. Foreign policy. Nemery, Jaafar. 1969-75. *1475*
—. Foreign policy. Nemery, Jaafar. 1969-79. *1521*
—. Government. Islamic Law. 1600-1981. *1481*
—. Independence. Political parties. Sects, religious. 1952-56. *1523*
—. Islam. Modernization. Social Institutions. 1900-72. *1515*
—. Labor movement. Workers' Trade Unions Federation. 1956-69. *1462*
—. Literature. 1600-1982. *1471*
—. Mahdists. Rebellions. 1900-27. *1487*
—. Medical administration. 1899-1970. *1467*
—. Medical research. Wellcome Tropical Research Laboratories. 1903-52. *1466*
—. Military Government. Nemery, Jaafar. Politics and the Military. 1956-71. *1468*
—. National identity. Nile Valley. Political systems. Regional integration. ca 1920-55. *1517*
—. Nemery, Jaafar. Political development. 1969-79. *1461*
—. Nemery, Jaafar. Public Administration. 1950-79. *1520*
—. Nemery, Jaafar. Religion. Revolution. Tradition. 16c-1979. *1504*

—. Nuer. Social Status. Women. 1930-80. *1473*
—. Political systems. 1969-74. *1497*
—. Political Systems. Voblikov, D. R. (review article). 1956-69. *1494*
—. Social Status. Women (conference). 20c. *1529*
Sudan (Darfur). Boundaries (disputes). Libya. Military Aid. USA. 1870-1981. *929*
—. Diseases. Livestock. 1898-1956. *1525*
—. Livestock. Population. 400-1975. *1526*
Sudan (Darfur, Kordofan). Baggara. Modernization. 19c-20c. *1457*
Sudan, eastern. Islam, expansion of. 20c. *1514*
Sudan (Gash River valley). Cotton. Irrigation. Kassala Cotton Company. 1922-28. *1518*
Sudan Interior Mission. Canada. Education. Great Britain. Missions and Missionaries. 1937-55. *1505*
Sudan (Khartoum). Demography. Urban Areas. 20c. *1478*
Sudan (North and South). Political relationships. Regional Autonomy Agreement (1972). 1972-73. *1500*
Sudan, Northern. Education, *Ahlia*. 1927-57. *1499*
—. Political consciousness. United Sudanese African Liberation Front. 1924-72. *1482*
Sudan (Sobat, Zaraf valleys). Boundaries. Dinka. Nuer. 1860-1976. *1490*
Sudan, Southern. Addis Ababa Agreement. Anya Nya. Civil War. Sudanese African National Union. 1902-74. *1507*
—. Addis Ababa Agreement. Politics. ca 1972-74. *1492*
—. Anya Nya. Autonomy. Civil war. 1956-72. *1509*
—. Atuot. Colonialism. Great Britain. 1920's-55. *1474*
—. Colonial Government. Economic Structure. 1898-1955. *1512*
—. Economic problems. 1972. *1513*
—. Education. Government. Missions and Missionaries. Values. 1898-1956. *1506*
—. Historiography. 1821-1980. *1489*
—. Politics. 1946-56. *1527*
Sudan (Tuti Island). Colonial Government. Great Britain. Hodeib, Mohammed Amin. Resistance. 1914-46. *1496*
Sudan (Zande). Agriculture. Economic development. 1920-55. *1498*
Sudanese African National Union. Addis Ababa Agreement. Anya Nya. Civil War. Sudan, Southern. 1902-74. *1507*
Suez. Egypt. 1453-1975. *1120*
Suez Canal. Compagnie Financière de Suez. Egypt. France. Nationalization. 1956-80. *1219*
—. Egypt. Oil and petroleum products. 1966-77. *1144*
—. Egypt. Profitability. 1858-1960. *1149*
Suez Canal (clearing). Egypt. *Maxton* (vessel). 1967-74. *1154*
Suez Canal (crossing). Army, 2d. Egypt. Ghazala, Mohamed. Military Strategy. October War. 1973. *1314*
Suez Canal (reopening). Indian Ocean (demilitarization). USA. USSR. ca 1975. *1210*
—. Military Strategy. 19c-20c. *1188*
Suez City (battle). Egypt. Military Strategy. October War. 1973. *1271*
Suez Crisis. Egypt. France. Great Britain. Historiography (collusion controversy). Israel. 1956. *1211*
—. Egypt. Israel. Military Occupation. 1956-57. *1216*
Sufism. Africa, North. Islam. Maghreb. Maraboutism. ca 1100-1975. *960*
Sugar. Agricultural Cooperatives. Ghana (Komenda). Rural Development. 1960-76. *1759*
Sugar interests. Pressure Groups. Rhodesian Information Office. South Africa Foundation. USA. 1934-72. *3866*
Sukuma. Legal changes. Tanzania. 1960's-70's. *3163*
Sunderland Flying Boat. Autobiography and Memoirs. Malawi. Wills, K. B. 1950. *584*
Sundkler, B. G. M. Churches, independent. Leadership. Shona. Zimbabwe. 1945-70's. *4299*
Surveys, land. Foreign Relations. India. Malawi. Maps. 1895-1972. *3607*
Swahili. Africa, East. Language. Military life. 1905-71. *2613*
—. Africa, East. Literature. 1950's-60's. *2581*
—. Africa, East. Literature (review article). 1600-1950. *2564*
—. Authors. Diva, David Edward. Tanzania. Translating and Interpreting (Aesop's fables). 1916-69. *3216*
—. Courts, Koranic. Ethnicity. Kenya (Mombasa). Social Organization. 15c-1970's. *3006*
—. Development. Language. Tanzania. 1960's-74. *3096*
—. Languages, national. Linguistics. Tanzania. 1900-75. *3203*
Swaziland. Agricultural development. Lesotho. Trade. 20c. *3415*
—. Agricultural production. Employment, off-farm. Lesotho. Taiwan. 1960-72. *3385*
—. Botswana. Labor markets. Lesotho. South Africa. 1967-76. *3343*
—. Botswana. Lesotho. Monetary systems. Rand Monetary Area. South Africa. 1909-78. *3347*
—. Botswana. Namibia. Political change. 20c. *3351*
—. British South Africa Company. Colonial government. Land policy. Zimbabwe. ca 1900-68. *4037*
—. Income, rural. Rural development. 1860-1982. *4034*
—. Indigenization. National Parks and Reserves. 1972-80. *4032*
—. Parliamentary government. Traditionalism. 1967-73. *4036*
—. Political economy. South Africa. 1968-79. *4033*
—. Politics. Sobhuza II. 1972-74. *4035*
Sweden *See also* Scandinavia.
—. Agricultural development. Ethiopia (Chilalo). Tenants. 1967-74. *2695*
—. Economic aid. Ethiopia. 1954-78. *2711*
—. Foreign Relations. South Africa. 1960-74. *3773*
Swedes. Civil service. Ethiopia. Foreign policy. 1924-52. *2781*
Sybil (vessel). Africa, East. Great Britain. Lake Victoria. World War I. 1915-16. *720*
Symbols. Ahidjo, Ahmadou. Cameroon. Politics. 1958-76. *2425*
Symposium of Historians and Africanists of Socialist Countries, 3d. Communist Countries. Historiography. National liberation movements. 1970-79. *217*
Syncretism. Sects, religious. 19c-20c. *885*
Syphilis. Helene Franz Hospital. Missions and Missionaries. Public Health. South Africa (Bochum-Blauberg). 1895-1935. *3995*
Syphilis (cures). Ethiopia. Medicine. 17c-20c. *2842*
Syria. Algeria. Angola. Cuba. Intervention, military. 1961-76. *411*
—. Egypt. Israel. Military policy. Nasser, Gamal Abdel. Six-Day War. 1948-67. *1285*

T

Taiwan. Agricultural production. Employment, off-farm. Lesotho. Swaziland. 1960-72. *3385*
Tambo, Oliver. Apartheid. Luthuli, Albert. South Africa. 1652-1973. *3936*
Tamuno, Tekena N. Local identity. Nigeria (Rivers State, Port Harcourt). Patriotism. 1913-60's. *2272*
Tanganyika. *See* Tanzania.
Tanganyika African National Union (TANU). Agricultural Cooperatives. Rural development. Tanzania. Ujamaa villages. 1932-70. *3080*
—. Colonialism (demise). Political awareness. Tanzania (Kigoma). 1927-60. *3157*
—. National Assembly (Bunge). Parliaments. Tanzania. 1965-70. *3149*
—. Nyerere, Julius (progress report). Population. Production. Tanzania. 1969-72. *3165*
Tani, Maame. Christianity. Ghana. Nackabah, Papa. Sects, Religious. Twelve Apostles Church. 1918-39. *1834*
—. Ghana. Nackabah, Papa. Sects, Religious. Twelve Apostles Church. 1914-58. *1832*
Tan-Zam Railway. China. Economic Aid. 1970-75. *514*
—. China. Economic Growth. Foreign Aid. Tanzania. 1949-74. *531*
—. China. Tanzania. Zambia. 1965-75. *532*
—. Economic development. Railroads. Tanzania. 1960's-70's. *3074*
—. Mining industry. Railway politics. Zambia. Zimbabwe. 1895-1970. *3377*
Tanzania *See also* Africa, East.
—. Acculturation. Education. Political Socialization. 1970's. *3181*
—. Acculturation. Education. Political Socialization. 1971. *3146*
—. Africa, Southern. Nyerere, Julius (speech). USA. 1977. *3398*
—. Africanization. Civil service. Public Administration (productivity). 1961-72. *3160*
—. Agricultural cooperatives. Rural Development. ca 1960's-70's. *633*
—. Agricultural Cooperatives. Rural development. Tanganyika African National Union (TANU). Ujamaa villages. 1932-70. *3080*
—. Agricultural Policy. Capitalism. Colonial Government. Food production. 1840-1960's. *3062*
—. Agricultural Policy. Luguru. Tradition. Uluguru Land Usage Scheme. 1949-55. *3060*
—. Agricultural Policy. Ujamaa villages. 1967-77. *3070*
—. Agricultural Policy (review article). Socialism. Ujamaa villages. 1950's-70's. *3088*
—. Agricultural production. Social Organization. Ujamaa villages. 1960's-70's. *3191*
—. Agricultural Reform. Collectivization. Ujamaa villages. 1963-74. *3085*
—. Agriculture. Colonial government. East African Groundnut Project. Rural Development. 1947-54. *3077*
—. Agriculture. Loans. Zambia. 1973-76. *609*
—. Agriculture. Peasants (participation). Ujamaa villages. 1967-75. *3093*
—. Amin, Idi. Asians (expulsion). Foreign Policy. Uganda. 1972. *3301*
—. Amin, Idi. Government (collapse). Uganda. 1978-79. *3312*
—. Anglicanism. Missions and Missionaries. Steere, Edward. Universities Mission to Central Africa (UMCA). 1876-1926. *3192*
—. Archaeology. Kenya. Madagascar. Migration. 9c-19c. 20c. *2650*
—. Arusha Declaration. Legal systems. Politics. Socialism. 1967-73. *3147*
—. Arusha Declaration. Nyerere, Julius. Socialism. 1961-73. *3148*
—. Arusha Declaration. Socialism. 1967-77. *3055*
—. Arusha Declaration. Socialism. 1967-77. *3076*
—. Asians. Discrimination. Industry, small-scale. 1890-1967. *3078*
—. Association, right of. Ghana. 1940-65. *339*
—. Attitudes. Colonial Government. Kenya. Maasai. 1890-1960. *2647*
—. Authors. Diva, David Edward. Swahili. Translating and Interpreting (Aesop's fables). 1916-69. *3216*
—. Banking. Nationalization. 1960-70. *3098*
—. Banking. Nationalization. Socialism. 1960's. *3125*
—. Banking, commercial. National Bank of Commerce (NBC). 1973-74. *3107*
—. Banking (savings institutions). Economic development. 1960-70. *3058*
—. Bibliographies. Colonial Government (British, German). Islam. 1973. *3202*
—. Bomani, Paul (interview). Economic development. Rural settlements. ca 1960's-70's. *3059*
—. Boundaries (disputes). Malawi. ca 1967-73. *448*
—. Bureaucracies. Colonial Government. Economic Policy. 1919-39. *3153*
—. Bureaucracies. Decentralization. Local government. 1972. *3134*
—. Bureaucrats. Politicians. Social Status (comparative study). Uganda. 1960's-70's. *2618*
—. Canadian International Development Agency. Rural development. Wheat. 1979-82. *3072*
—. Capitalism. Elites. Political development. 19c-1960's. *3120*
—. Capricorn Africa Society. Nationalism. 1949-67. *3176*
—. Career guidance policies. Manpower efficiency. 1961-74. *3116*
—. Catholic Church. Church and state. 1880's-1970's. *3217*
—. Chagga. Coffee growers. Colonial Government. Kilimanjaro Native Planters Association. 1919-32. *3115*
—. Chagga. Ethnic integration. 1962-76. *3184*
—. Chama Cha Mapinduzi (CCM). Political Parties. 1977-80. *3140*
—. China. Collectivization. Mexico. Ujamaa villages. USSR. 20c. *3094*
—. China. Communism. Cuba. Economic conditions. USSR. Women. 1977-78. *3066*
—. China. Cuba. Socialism. USSR. Women. 1917-81. *3065*
—. China. Economic Growth. Foreign Aid. Tan-Zam Railway. 1949-74. *531*
—. China. Foreign aid. National liberation movements. 1960-70's. *3136*
—. China. Foreign Relations. 1961-74. *3131*
—. China. Tan-Zam Railway. Zambia. 1965-75. *532*
—. Christianity. Conversion. Islam. 1973. *3185*

—. Nigeria. Occupations. Rukuba. Social Change. 1905-70's. *2046*
Taxation, direct. Colonial government. Ghana. Indirect rule. Riots. Slater, Ransford. 1929-44. *1816*
Tea Development Authority. Kenya. Social Classes. 1960-72. *2908*
Tea industry. Malawi. 1818-1976. *3602*
Teacher Training. Institute of Education. Zimbabwe. 1956-80. *4318*
Teachers *See also* Teaching.
—. Algeria. Colonna, F. Leca, Jean. Politics (review article). Social Classes. Vatin, J.-C. 1883-1975. *1094*
—. Nigerian Union of Teachers. 1931-40. *2244*
—. Strikes. Zambia. 1968-70. *4084*
Teaching *See also* Education; History Teaching; Schools; Teachers.
—. Algeria. Arabic. Radio. 1969-76. *1054*
Technical assistance. Capitalist countries. 1960-81. *515*
—. Mining. Niger (Arlit). Uranium. 1968-73. *1987*
Technical Cooperation Administration. Bennett, Henry Garland. Colleges and Universities. Developing nations. Ethiopia. 1950-51. *2710*
Technical Education *See also* Vocational Education.
—. Dube, John L. Ohlange Institute. South Africa (Natal). 1900-30's. *3992*
—. Economic development. Multinational corporations. 20c. *597*
—. Kenya. Rural self-help (harambee). 1963-70. *2994*
Technology *See also* Agricultural Technology and Research; Science; Technical Education.
—. Africa, West. Oil palm industry. 1911-60. *1648*
—. Aswan Dam. Decisionmaking. Egypt. USA. World Bank. 1953-68. *1166*
—. Business. Dependency. Indigenization. Niger (Kano). 1972-79. *2037*
—. Cabora Bassa dam. Colonial Government. Mozambique. 1953-73. *3656*
—. Economic Conditions. Goody, Jack (review article). Social Change. Tradition. ca 18c-20c. *330*
—. Mining. Proletarianization. Social Classes. Zambia. 1946-66. *4102*
—. Niger Company. Nigeria. Trade. 1900-20. *2050*
Technology, institutes of. Education. Kenya. Rural self-help (harambee). 1971-74. *2877*
Technology transfer. Nigeria. Oil industry and Trade. 1956-74. *2075*
Technology, Western. Colonialism. Culture. Education. 1960's-73. *615*
Teferi Benti. Ethiopia. Haile Selassie. Revolution. 20c. *2753*
Television. Apartheid. South Africa. 1953-70's. *3961*
—. Ethnicity. Government Ownership. Intergovernmental Relations. Nigeria. Radio. 1932-62. *2290*
Temne. Fertility levels. Mende. Sierra Leone. 1963-73. *2344*
—. Migration. Sierra Leone (Mayoso). 1950's-70's. *2346*
Tenants. Agricultural development. Ethiopia (Chilalo). Sweden. 1967-74. *2695*
Ten-Year Plan. Economic Policy. Egypt. 1960's-73. *1142*
Territorial claims. Algeria. Mauritania. Morocco. Nationalism. Polisario Front. Western Sahara. 1956-79. *923*
Territorial disputes. Green March. UN. Western Sahara. 1830-1975. *1597*
Territorial Waters. Gulf of Sidra incident. International law. Libya. USA. 1981-83. *1386*
Terrorism *See also* Assassination; Crime and Criminals; Guerrilla Warfare.
—. Entebbe raid. Israel. Uganda. 1968-77. *3265*
Teso. Kenya. Social change. 19c-20c. *3015*
Textbooks. Curricula. Egypt. Modernization. 1960-79. *1333*
—. Geography. Great Britain. Photographs. 1951-77. *59*
Textbooks (review article). Education. 1960-78. *833*
Textile Industry. Baule. Colonization. Ivory Coast. Women. 1875-1975. *1920*
Theater *See also* Drama; Films.
—. Abuna Petros. Ethiopia. War. 1936. -1973. *2783*
—. Adult education. 1930-79. *830*
—. Algeria. Dramatists. Théâtre de la Mer (company). Yacine, Kateb. 1970-72. *983*
—. Church and society. Social Customs. 1914-45. *2200*
—. Colonial Government. Tanzania. 1920-62. *3194*
—. Concert-party. Ghana. National Entertainment Association. 1918-75. *1829*
—. Concert-party. Nigeria (Lagos). Ogunde, Hubert. 1910-75. *2201*
—. Nationalism. Nigeria. 1890-1970's. *2202*
—. Nigeria. Ogunde, Hubert. 1946-72. *2231*
—. Nigeria. Ogunde, Hubert. Political commentary. 1945-75. *2236*
—. Ogunde, Hubert. Togo (Lomé). 1944-71. *2379*
Theater, educational. Culture, elite. Popular culture. Togo. 1945-75. *2378*
Théâtre de la Mer (company). Algeria. Dramatists. Theater. Yacine, Kateb. 1970-72. *983*
Theology, African. Cone, James. Religion, traditional. South Africa. 1700-1970's. *3956*
Theron Commission. Coloureds. Racial policies. Reform. South Africa. 20c. *3971*
Thierry d'Argenlieu, Admiral (review article). Germany. Senegal (Dakar). 1940. *723*
Third World. *See* Developing Nations, Non-aligned Nations.
Tignor, Robert L. Colonialism (review article). Kenya. Modernization. Wolff, Richard D. 1870-1939. *2913*
Timor, East. Decolonization. Goa. Macao. Portugal. São Tomé and Principe. 1975-80. *2453*
Timor, Mahmud. Arabic. Egypt. Fiction. 1894-1973. *1337*
Tin. Birom. Miners. Nigeria (northern). Social protest. Stealing. 1958-78. *2246*
Tin mining. Labor. Migration. Niger Company. Nigeria, northern. 1903-45. *2032*
—. Labor. Nigeria (Jos plateau). 1906-21. *2045*
Tiv. Agricultural production. Great Britain. Nigeria. Sesame. Trade. 1900-60. *2024*
—. Colonial Government. Great Britain. Nigeria. 1900-70. *2234*
—. Nigeria. Politics. Rebellions. 1960. *2147*
Tobacco industry. Arrighi, G. Peasants (proletarianization). Shangwe. Zimbabwe. 1898-1938. *4168*
Tobruk (battles). Africa, North. World War II. 1942. *761*
—. Libya. World War II. 1939-43. *763*
—. World War II. 1941-42. *762*
Tocqueville, Alexis de. Kenya. Marx, Karl. Mau Mau. Political Theory. Revolution. 1888-1963. *2921*
Todd, Garfield. Political leadership. Zimbabwe. 1953-58. *4191*
Togo *See also* Africa, West.
—. Agriculture. Economic Development. Rohrbach, Karl. 1960's-70's. *2383*
—. Avatime. Rice. Social Customs. Social organization. Yams. 20c. *2373*
—. Boundaries. Ewe. Ghana. National Liberation Movement of Western Togoland. Nationalism. 1943-78. *1616*
—. Capital Accumulation. Land Ownership. Social Organization. 1885-1979. *2382*
—. Colonialism. France. Germany. Great Britain. World War II. 1939-45. *740*
—. Culture, elite. Popular culture. Theater, educational. 1945-75. *2378*
—. Demography. Land Tenure. 1885-1979. *2377*
—. Dependency. Depression. Ewe. Farmers. Traders. 1929-38. *2372*
—. Dzo. Ewe. Magic. Myths and Symbols. 15c-20c. *2380*
—. Economic Conditions. French West Africa. 1945-60. *1611*
—. Ewe. Fiction. Ghana. Literature. 20c. *1603*
—. Ewe. Plebiscites. 1956. *2371*
—. Foreign policy. Mali. Military government. Modernization. Upper Volta. ca 1950-75. *1622*
—. France. Great Britain. Military Invasion. World War I (antecedents). 1914. *694*
—. Islam. Muslim Union. 1962-72. *2375*
—. Military Government. Politics. 1967-73. *2374*
Togo (Lomé). Ogunde, Hubert. Theater. 1944-71. *2379*
Togo, North. Anufo. Land Tenure. Law, customary. Legislation. Ngam Ngam. 1960-79. *2381*
Togo (Vo Koutime). Migration. Population growth. ca 1925-75. *2376*
Tolbert, William R. Elites. Liberia. Political systems. Tubman, William V. S. 1944-75. *1951*
Tonga. Agricultural Development. Political protest. Zambia. 1899-1964. *4069*
Totalitarianism *See also* Communism; Fascism.
—. Colonialism. Political Systems. ca 1870's-1970's. *286*
—. Parliaments. Tanzania. Zambia. ca 1960-77. *332*
Touré, Sekou. Art and State. Censorship. Guinea. ca 1947-76. *1870*
—. Democratic Party. Government, Resistance to. Guinea. Purges. 1957-73. *1877*
—. Guinea. Invasion. Portugal. 1970. *1866*
—. Guinea. National Development. 1958-78. *1873*
—. Guinea. Politics. 1946-74. *1871*
Touré, Sekou (speech). Pan-Africanism. 19c-20c. *138*
Tourism. Economic Development. 1970's. *570*
—. Economic Development. Kenya (coastal region). 1962-72. *2885*
—. Economic Planning. 1963-73. *630*
—. Economic viability. Gambia. 1970's. *1715*
—. Seychelles. 1968-73. *3570*
—. Stereotypes. 1945-78. *557*
Towns. Botswana (Mochudi). 1871-1971. *3497*
Track and field. Keino, Kipchoge. Kenya. Olympics. Sports (athletic infrastructure). 1966-74. *2993*
Trade *See also* Exports; Imports; International Trade.
—. Africa, Southern. South Africa. 1955-73. *3762*
—. Africa, West. Brazil. Foreign Relations. 1970's. *549*
—. Africa, West. Poland. 1950's-60's. *548*
—. Agricultural development. Lesotho. Swaziland. 20c. *3415*
—. Agricultural production. Great Britain. Nigeria. Sesame. Tiv. 1900-60. *2024*
—. Apartheid. Foreign policy. South Africa. USA. 1974-79. *3827*
—. Benin. Colonialism. Economic Conditions. 1921-41. *1699*
—. BenSalah, Ahmed. Economic development. Socialism. Tunisia. 1960-69. *1550*
—. Canada. Foreign aid. 1970-75. *447*
—. Canada. Foreign Policy. South Africa. Zimbabwe. 1960's-76. *3409*
—. Cocoa. Farmers. Ghana. 1918-39. *1755*
—. Cocoa. Foreign aid. Ghana. USSR. 1957-72. *1757*
—. Cocoa. Ghana. 1880-1970. *1753*
—. Colonial policy. Concessionary system. French Equatorial Africa. 1899-1972. *2397*
—. Dependency. Economic development. Tunisia. 1970-77. *1551*
—. Dependency, economic. Economic Conditions. ca 1965-67. *649*
—. Depression. French West Africa. Peanut production. Peyrissac (firm). Rubber. 1924-39. *1675*
—. Developing nations. European Economic Community. Nigeria. 1966-73. *2014*
—. Economic Structure. Liberia (interior). 1600-1940. *1950*
—. Egypt. USSR. 1922-39. *1155*
—. Ethiopia (Begemdir; Däbrä Tabor). Local government. 1798-1936. *2688*
—. European Economic Community (associated states). 1958-78. *561*
—. Fishing. Libinza. Zaire, upper. 19c-1973. *2474*
—. Foreign Relations. Italy. 1960's-70's. *544*
—. Germany. South Africa. 1931-39. *3767*
—. Igbo. Kalabari. Nigeria (Oguta). Palm oil. 1900-50. *2026*
—. Italy. ca 1950-75. *541*
—. Japan. Nigeria. 1947-74. *2029*
—. Market town development. Migration, Internal. Nigeria (Onitsha). 1960-67. *2063*
—. Money (tokens). South Africa (Durban). 1906-29. *3954*
—. Niger Company. Nigeria. Technology. 1900-20. *2050*
—. Nigeria (Oguta). Transportation. Waterways. 1885-1945. *2053*
—. Sahara. Salt. Social organization. Tuareg. 19c-20c. *938*
—. Self-reliance. Tanzania. 1967-76. *3057*
—. USA. 1973-81. *566*
Trade agreements. European Economic Community. 1973-74. *553*
Trade (domestic). Asians. Sierra Leone. 1950-78. *2355*
Trade (interregional). Economic Growth. Markets, periodic. Sierra Leone. 1896-1970. *2356*
Trade patterns. Cameroon. 1957-72. *2419*
—. Tanzania. 1960's-70's. *3129*
Trade, precolonial. Aro. Colonial Government. Nigeria (Eastern Delta). 19c-20c. *2055*

U

—. China. Collectivization. Mexico. Tanzania. USSR. 20c. *3094*
—. Collectivization. Tanzania (Bukoba). 1967-69. *3104*
—. Economic Conditions. Tanzania. 1973-76. *3061*
—. Economic Planning. Rural Settlements. Tanzania. 1967-75. *3201*
—. Peasants. Tanzania. 1973-77. *3086*
—. Rural development. Tanzania. 1960's. *3068*
—. Rural development. Tanzania. 1960-75. *3099*
—. Socialism. Tanzania. Tradition. 20c. *3089*
—. Tanzania. 1967-74. *3069*
—. Tanzania. 1970's. *3205*
—. Tanzania. Women. 1960's. *3187*
—. Tanzania (Malili). 1969-72. *3087*
Uluguru Land Usage Scheme. Agricultural Policy. Luguru. Tanzania. Tradition. 1949-55. *3060*
Umberto, Prince. Colonial Government. Ethiopia. Graziani, Rodolfo. 1936-40. *2797*
Umma Party. Ansar Party. Islam. Politics. Sudan. 1914-45. *1524*
UN. 1945-78. *416*
—. Africa, southern. Colonialism. Oslo conference. 1973. *3382*
—. Africa, Southern. Documents (index). 1946-79. *3401*
—. Africa, southern. National Liberation Movements. 1940's-70's. *3371*
—. Anticolonialism. Colonies. Foreign policy. Italy. Liberia. 1948-51. *1944*
—. Anti-Zionism. Foreign relations. Israel. 1958-75. *408*
—. Apartheid. Colonialism. Nyerere, Julius (speech). Portugal. South Africa. 20c. *386*
—. Apartheid. Racism. Zionism. 1975. *481*
—. Apartheid. Sanctions. South Africa. 1899-1982. *3946*
—. Apartheid. South Africa. 1948-70. *3823*
—. Apartheid. South Africa. Sports. 1955-80. *3865*
—. Arab States. Egypt (Cairo). Food and Agriculture Organization (regional office). Foreign Relations. 1975-79. *1286*
—. Arab states. Foreign Aid. Israel. Voting and Voting Behavior. 1958-72. *419*
—. Arab-Israeli conflict. Organization of African Unity. Senghor, Leopold. 1971. *94*
—. Arbitration Convention. Commercial disputes. Nigeria. Oil industry and Trade. Treaties. 1960's-70's. *2084*
—. Civil War. Nigeria. Refugees. Relief efforts. Sudan. 1966-72. *524*
—. Colonial government. Economic sanctions. Great Britain. Zimbabwe. 1965-75. *4272*
—. Colonialism. Namibia. Nationalism. 1945-70's. *3681*
—. Colonialism, Portuguese. Decolonization. 1946-74. *384*
—. Colonies. Democracy. Independence. ca 1939-76. *153*
—. Conflict and Conflict Resolution. Organization of African Unity. 1950's-70's. *81*
—. Conflict and Conflict Resolution. Zaire. 1960-65. *2517*
—. Decisionmaking. Egypt. Israel. 1956. *1295*
—. Decolonization. Portugal. 1950's-60's. *215*
—. Diplomacy. Great Powers. Namibia. 1977-79. *3699*
—. East African Community. Regional integration. 1960's-71. *2586*
—. Foreign policy. FRELIMO. Independence Movements. Mozambique. Portugal. ca 1957-77. *3661*
—. Green March. Territorial disputes. Western Sahara. 1830-1975. *1597*
—. Hammarskjold, Dag (review article). Independence. Zaire. 1960. *2511*
—. Imperialism. Namibia. Palestine. 1914-82. *3694*
—. Independence. Namibia. 1946-75. *3688*
—. Independence. Namibia. South Africa. 1946-78. *3675*
—. Independence (review article). Italy. Negotiations. Rossi, Gianluigi (*L'Africa Italiana verso l'Indipendenza, 1941-1949*). 1946-49. *233*
—. International law. Peacekeeping Forces. Zaire. 1950-80's. *2495*
—. Morocco. Western Sahara. 1954-76. *1581*
—. Namibia. South Africa. Waldheim, Kurt. 1966-73. *3691*
—. Norway. Peacekeeping Forces. Zaire. 1960-64. *2500*
—. Organization of African Unity. 1963-66. *117*
UN Anti-Apartheid Committee. Armaments. Multinational corporations. South Africa. 1960-77. *3923*
UN Commission on Human Rights. Human rights violations. 1966-70's. *504*
UN Conference on Human Settlements. Developing nations. Economic Planning. 1978. *639*
UN Council for Namibia. Namibia. 1967-78. *3700*
UN Development Program. Africa, East. Developing nations. Fisheries. Lake Victoria. Norway. 1965-75. *628*
UN Human Rights Commission. Equatorial Guinea. Human rights. 1968-81. *2444*
UN (Trusteeship system). Independence Movements. 1945-62. *214*
UN (27th session). Human rights. 1972. *382*
Underdevelopment (theory). Economic Development. Fisheries. Tanzania. ca 1953-69. *3095*
Unemployment *See also* Employment.
—. Education. Kenya. Political instability. 1963-76. *2920*
—. Egypt. Industrialization. 1952-67. *1127*
—. Income distribution. International Labor Office (review article). Kenya. 1972. *2905*
UNESCO. Africa, West. Hausa. Linguistics. Literacy campaign. 1960's-70's. *1692*
UNICEF. Africa, West. Ethiopia. Food Supply. Transportation. -1974. *533*
Unification. Colonial policy. Great Britain. Sudan. 1898-1953. *1519*
Unilateral Declaration of Independence (UDI). Colonial government. Embargo. Oil. Zimbabwe. 1965-77. *4160*
—. Colonialism. Economic sanctions. Great Britain. Zimbabwe. 1965-73. *4182*
—. Decisionmaking. National Security. Zambia. Zimbabwe. 1965-66. *3332*
—. Economic Conditions. War. Zimbabwe. 1973-80. *4152*
—. Organization of African Unity. Zimbabwe. 1922-74. *92*
Union des Populations de Cameroun. Cameroon. Decolonization. Joseph, Richard A. (review article). 1948-56. *2400*
Union des Populations de Camerouns. Cameroon. Independence Movements. Politics. Radicals and Radicalism. ca 1945-48. *2413*
Union Douaniére Equatoriale (Equatorial Customs Union). Africa, West. Mali Federation. Regionalism. West African Custom Union. 1959-73. *112*
Union Marocaine du Travail. Labor movement. Morocco. 1936-58. *1424*
Union Minière du Haut-Katanga (UMHK). Copper. Générale Congolaise des Minerais. Nationalization. Zaire. ca 1960-77. *2478*
—. Industry. Labor. Zaire (Shaba). 1890's-1940. *2464*
Union of South African Artists. Music. Recording industry. South Africa (Johannesburg). 1900-60. *3960*
Unions. *See* Labor Unions and Organizations.
United Mine Workers. Africa, Southern. Boycotts. Labor reform. Racism. USA. 1960's-74. *3422*
United National Independence Party. Capitalists. Social Classes. Zambia. 1964-81. *4043*
—. Lenshina, Alice. Lumpa Church. Politics. Sects, Religious. Zambia. 1954-65. *4051*
—. Political parties. Zambia. 1964-73. *4114*
—. Political Systems (single party). Zambia. 1964-72. *4103*
United Sudanese African Liberation Front. Political consciousness. Sudan, northern. 1924-72. *1482*
Universal Negro Improvement Association. Africa, West. Garvey, Marcus. Marke, George Osborne. West Indies. 1920-23. *1664*
—. Feminism. Ghana. Hayford, Adelaide Casely. Nationalism, cultural. Women. 1868-1960. *1850*
Universities Mission to Central Africa (UMCA). Anglicanism. Missions and Missionaries. Steere, Edward. Tanzania. 1876-1926. *3192*
University of Livingstonia. Laws, Robert. Malawi. 1920's. *3609*
Upper Volta *See also* Africa, West.
—. Beer. Economic Conditions. Islam. Sorghum. Women. 1978-80. *2389*
—. Development. Sanitation. 1960-76. *2388*
—. Droughts. Lamizana, Sangoule. 1970-74. *2386*
—. Dyan. 1750-1920. *2391*
—. Fertility. Mortality. Public Health. 1971-77. *2384*
—. Foreign policy. Mali. Military government. Modernization. Togo. ca 1950-75. *1622*
—. Government, Resistance to. Ivory Coast. Migrations, protest. 1901-45. *1607*
—. Migration, internal. Mossi. 1960-73. *2390*
—. Urbanization. 1960-70. *2387*
Upper Volta (Koudougou). Colonial policy. Labor, forced. 1914-39. *2385*
Uranium. Foreign Relations. Mineral Resources. 1940's-82. *634*
—. Industrialization. Mining. Niger (Arlit). 1974-81. *1988*
—. Mining. Niger (Arlit). Technical assistance. 1968-73. *1987*
Urban adaptation. Ghana (Accra). Islam. Migrants. Sisala. 20c. *1839*
Urban Areas. Demography. Sudan (Khartoum). 20c. *1478*
Urban development. Agriculture. Industry. Nigeria (Yola). ca 1841-1978. *2000*
—. Communications. Nigeria (Jos). ca 1900-78. *1998*
—. Nigeria (Kaduna). 1913-78. *1994*
Urban growth. City Planning. Kenya. Tanzania. ca 1960-73. *2646*
Urban policy. Ivory Coast. Politics, cross-ethnic. 1960's-70's. *1916*
Urban population. Ethiopia. Ethnic Groups. 20c. *2844*
Urbanization *See also* City Planning; Modernization; Rural-Urban Studies.
—. Africa, West. Migration, Internal. 1930-77. *1674*
—. Afrikaners. Farmers. Migration, Internal. South Africa (Port Elizabeth). 1904-60. *4023*
—. Algeria. Industrial development. 1974. *1099*
—. Bureaucracies. Housing. Squatter settlements. Tanzania (Dar es Salaam). 1965-82. *3210*
—. Cities (market towns). Sudan. 1930's-70's. *1460*
—. Colonial government. Rhodes-Livingstone Institute. Wilson, Godfrey. Zambia. 1938-41. *4134*
—. Colonialism. Social Change. 1910-81. *805*
—. Community formation. Squatter settlements. 1960-74. *324*
—. Decolonization. Demography. Morocco. 1952-71. *1405*
—. Economic conditions. Intermarriage. Kenya (Coast Province). Muslims. 1963-78. *3001*
—. Economic development. 1965-79. *638*
—. Economic Development. Migration. 1962-1976. *587*
—. Ghana (Accra). Working Class. 1930-77. *1840*
—. Igbo. Nigeria (Imo). 1902-78. *2266*
—. Independence. Zaire. 1945-60. *2498*
—. Kenya (Nairobi). Migration, internal. 1964-68. *2976*
—. Labor. Migration, internal. Tanzania. 1960-72. *3100*
—. Malawi. Middle classes. Zambia. 1920-60. *3388*
—. Migration, internal. Zambia. 1964-73. *4075*
—. Nigeria (Awka, Nsukka). 1960-76. *2233*
—. Nigeria (Calabar). 1895-1978. *2052*
—. Nigeria (Lagos). 1970's. *2198*
—. Nigeria (Port Harcourt). 1950-79. *2023*
—. Population growth. 1960's-70's. *773*
—. Religion. Rites and Ceremonies (ancestor worship). 1960's-70's. *870*
—. Social Organization. 1950-75. *869*
—. Upper Volta. 1960-70. *2387*
Urbanization, differential. Population (growth rates). South Africa. 1652-1970. *3996*
Urbanization (review article). Africa, West. 1801-1978. *1670*
—. Africa, West. Berry, J. F. Developing nations. 1920-76. *1657*
Urbanization, theories of. Africa, West. Cities. Colonialism. 18c-20c. *1672*
Urhobo. Migrant Labor. Nigeria (Bendel state, Ikaleland). Rural development. 1920-76. *2065*
Urhobo kingdoms. Nigeria (Mid-Western State). Political Systems. State government. Succession, forms of. 1952-63. *2170*
USA. Ad Hoc Monitoring Group on Southern Africa. Africa, Southern. Foreign Relations. 1977-80. *3356*
—. Africa, East. Cold War. Foreign Policy. USSR. 1930-77. *2637*
—. Africa, east. Foreign Policy. Somalia. 1977-80. *2573*
—. Africa, East. International Security. USSR. 1970's. *2585*
—. Africa, North. Bibliographies. Foreign Relations. Historiography. 1785-1975. *977*

V

W

X

Y

Z

—. Mineral Resources. Transportation. 1956-76. *2473*
—. Mobutu Sese Seko. National self-image. Political Leadership. 1974-75. *2531*
—. Mobutu Sese Seko. Political opposition. 1965-78. *2497*
—. Mobutu Sese Seko. Political repression. 1965-66. *2493*
—. Mobutu Sese Seko. Radicalization. 1974-75. *2515*
—. Mouvement Populaire de la Revolution. National unity. Religion. ca 1973-76. *2486*
—. Norway. Peacekeeping Forces. UN. 1960-64. *2500*
—. Political Change. 1960's. *2527*
—. Political conflict (review article). 1961-73. *2525*
—. Political instability. ca 1960-73. *2516*
—. Political opposition. 1963-78. *2505*
—. Political structure. -20c. *2507*
—. Political Systems. Tradition. 1960's-70's. *2489*
—. Propaganda. Schools. Young People's Revolutionary Popular Movement (JMPR). 1974-78. *2514*
—. Rebellions. 1963-65. *2524*
—. Social Status. Women. 1960-79. *2532*
Zaire (Equateur). Colonialism. Food production. Mongo-Nkundo. Social change. 19c-20c. *2468*
Zaire (Ijwi Island). Colonial Government. Lake Kivu. Local government. 1900-70. *2503*
Zaire (Kabare). Cattle Raising. Economic Conditions. Monarchy. 1900-60. *2555*
Zaire (Kabare, Ngweshe). Chiefs. Mafundwe. Rugemaninzi. Shi. 1895-1960. *2490*
Zaire (Kasai). Missions and Missionaries. Presbyterian Church. USA. 1871-1964. *2554*
Zaire (Kinshasa). Attitudes. Family. Girls. Marriage. Schools. 1969-72. *2562*
—. Cities. 17c-20c. *2461*
—. City Life. 1960-73. *2533*
Zaire (Kivu). Cholera. Public Health. 1978-79. *2560*
—. Colonization. Exploitation. Working Class. 1900-40. *2465*
Zaire (Kivu; Nyangezi). Catholic Church. Missions and Missionaries. 1906-29. *2537*
Zaire (Kwango). Political Factions. Social Organization. 1960-73. *2529*
Zaire (Kwango basin). Colonial policy. Ethnic conflict. Yaka. 1880-1960. *2510*
Zaire (Kwango savanna). Agricultural experimentation. 1963-70. *2479*
Zaire (Kwilu). Ideology. Rebellions. Revolution. 1930's-63. *2526*
Zaire (Kwilu province). Economic conditions. Mulele, Pierre. Rebellions. 1964. *2518*
Zaire, lower. Agricultural Development. 1948-60. *2467*
—. Economic development. Railroads. Roads. 1855-1938. *2472*
Zaire (Lupupa Ngye). Anthropology (colonialist; review article). Colonialism. Merriam, Alan P. ca 1930-60. *2539*
Zaire (Sankuru). Peasants. Rebellions. Simba. 1964. *2520*
Zaire (Shaba). Angola. Copper mines and Mining. French, J. C. Labor recruitment. Robert Williams Co. 1917-21. *2477*
—. Catholic Church. Education, rural. Missions and Missionaries. 1885-1939. *2544*
—. Christians. Jamaa. Labor, conceptualizations of. 1950-60's. *2541*
—. Educational development. Rural areas. 1920-60. *2543*
—. Front de Libération Nationale du Congo. Rebellions. 1978. *2528*
—. Great Powers. Political conflict. 1970's. *2501*
—. Industry. Labor. Union Minière du Haut-Katanga (UMHK). 1890's-1940. *2464*
—. Jamaa. Popular culture. 1950's-70's. *2542*
—. Orbital Transport und Raketen Aktiengesellschaft (OTRAG). Rockets, launching. 1976. *2466*
—. Political conditions. 1885-1970's. *2460*
—. War (antecedents). 1960's-70's. *2506*
Zaire (Shaba, Kasai). Education. Methodism. Missions and Missionaries. 1910-60. *2540*
Zaire (Upoto). Political Systems. Poto. 1870-1980. *2513*
Zaire, upper. Fishing. Food production. 1900-75. *2462*
—. Fishing. Libinza. Trade. 19c-1973. *2474*
Zakaria, Moufdi. Algeria. Independence Movements. 1920's-60's. *1006*
Zambezi River. Africa, Southern. Goba. Religion. Social History. 1200-1970. *3381*
Zambia *See also* Africa, Southern.
—. Agricultural Cooperatives. Foreign Aid. Israel. 1966-73. *4087*
—. Agricultural development. Cotton production. Kunda. Land tenure. 1960's-70's. *4095*
—. Agricultural Development. Political protest. Tonga. 1899-1964. *4069*
—. Agriculture. Education. Modernization. 1970's. *4131*
—. Agriculture. Loans. Tanzania. 1973-76. *609*
—. Angola. Conflict and Conflict Resolution. Zaire. 1976-78. *237*
—. Angola. Foreign Policy. Popular Movement for the Liberation of Angola (MPLA). Zaire. 1961-77. *3430*
—. Angolans. Refugees. Resettlement. 1966-72. *4072*
—. Anthropology. Decolonization. Gluckman, Max. Rhodes-Livingstone Institute. 1939-47. *4047*
—. Archaeology. Clark, J. Desmond. 1905-76. *4060*
—. Asians. 1890's-1970's. *4094*
—. Attitudes. Nurses and nursing. Tradition. 1981. *4112*
—. Banks. Government. Rural credit. 1964-75. *4073*
—. Bates, Robert H. Burawoy, Michael. Copper Mines and Mining. Government. Labor Unions and Organizations (review article). 1949-70. *4071*
—. Bemba. Catholic Church. Local government. Missions and Missionaries. 1890-1935. *4070*
—. Bemba. Lenshina, Alice. Lumpa rising. Rebellions. Sects, Religious. 1953-68. *4045*
—. Business. Economic reform. Independence. 1960's-74. *4044*
—. Capitalists. Social Classes. United National Independence Party. 1964-81. *4043*
—. Cattle. Economic behavior. Ila. 20c. *4065*
—. Cattle. Economic Structure. Ila. 19c-20c. *4064*
—. China. Tan-Zam Railway. Tanzania. 1965-75. *532*
—. Civil Disturbances. Miners. Race Relations. 1935-40. *4076*
—. Colonial government. Confederation. Gore-Browne, Stewart. Political Reform. Public opinion. 1948. *4126*
—. Colonial Government. Confederation. Great Britain. Zimbabwe. 1931-52. *3397*
—. Colonial government. Economic development. World War II. 1940-45. *4077*
—. Colonial Government. Labor problems. Race Relations. 1900-53. *4078*
—. Colonial Government. Monarchy. Myths and Symbols. National Self-image. 1924-38. *4107*
—. Colonial Government. Police. 1901-72. *4124*
—. Colonial government. Rhodes-Livingstone Institute. Urbanization. Wilson, Godfrey. 1938-41. *4134*
—. Colonial government. Schools, Development Area. 1948-62. *4100*
—. Colonial policy (memorandum). Great Britain. Military Strategy. Political Reform (delay of). Zimbabwe. 1930-45. *3396*
—. Colonialism. Confederation. Economic Development. Social Conditions. Zimbabwe. 1925-35. *3421*
—. Colonialism. Foreign Investments. 1964-80. *4080*
—. Colson, Elizabeth (memoirs). Rhodes-Livingstone Institute. 1948-51. *4056*
—. Copper. Economic dependence. Foreign Investments (review article). 1970's. *4116*
—. Copper. Producer associations. Raw materials. 1967-78. *4063*
—. Copper industry. Economic Conditions. Multinational corporations. Nationalization. 1969-73. *4050*
—. Copper Mines and Mining. Economic Policy. Nationalization. 1969-78. *4085*
—. Copper Mines and Mining. Finance. 1924-64. *4110*
—. Copper Mines and Mining. Kenya. Political protest. Strikes. 1922-62. *175*
—. Copper Mines and Mining. Mergers. Rhokana Corporation. 1930-32. *4038*
—. Copper Mines and Mining. Migrant Labor. Women. 1927-53. *4052*
—. Copper Mines and Mining. Mining industry. Multinational Corporations. Nationalization. Zaire. 1960's-82. *668*
—. Copper Mines and Mining. Strikes. 1935. *4101*
—. Decisionmaking. National Security. Unilateral Declaration of Independence (UDI). Zimbabwe. 1965-66. *3332*
—. Demonstrations. Independence movements. Students. 1966-71. *4048*
—. Detente. Foreign Relations. Kaunda, Kenneth. Racism. South Africa. 1964-74. *4040*
—. Detente. Kaunda, Kenneth (review article). Macpherson, Fergus. Political leadership. 1940's-75. *4088*
—. Developing Nations. Labor. Political Change. 1880-1981. *4049*
—. Development. Foreign policy. 1963-78. *4117*
—. Domestic Policy. Foreign policy. 1964-76. *4128*
—. Drama, historical. Radicals and Radicalism. 1950's-70's. *4108*
—. Economic Conditions. Industrial Production. Mining. 1960-79. *4066*
—. Economic Conditions. Industrialization. 1965-72. *4115*
—. Economic Conditions. Politics. 1981-82. *4121*
—. Economic Development. Foreign Relations. USSR. 1964-79. *4054*
—. Economic Development. Local government. Political Participation. 1967-79. *4053*
—. Economic growth. Immigrants. Labor. 1911-69. *4098*
—. Economic independence. Natural resources. 1960-75. *4062*
—. Economic Planning. Entrepreneurs. National Development. 1966-76. *4082*
—. Economic reform. Middle Classes. Politics. 1968-80. *4125*
—. Elites. Political legitimacy. 1964-78. *4111*
—. Elites. Politics (review article). 1972-74. *4058*
—. Energy. Hydroelectric installations. 1950's-70's. *4089*
—. Foreign policy. 1930's-70's. *4135*
—. Foreign Policy. 1964-76. *4120*
—. Foreign policy. 1967-75. *4119*
—. Foreign policy. ca 1963-75. *4118*
—. Foreign Relations. Kaunda, Kenneth. USA. 1970's. *473*
—. Foreign service. 1964-72. *4091*
—. Fosbrooke, Henry (memoirs). Rhodes-Livingstone Institute. 1956-60. *4067*
—. Freshwater, Will (papers). Linguistics. London Missionary School. Missions and Missionaries. 1872-1959. *4068*
—. Gluckman, Max. Rhodes-Livingstone Institute. 1942-47. *4057*
—. Heron, Alastair (memoirs). Rhodes-Livingstone Institute. 1963-67. *4079*
—. Humanism. Kaunda, Kenneth. Modernization. Socialism. ca 1960's. *4081*
—. Independence. Politics. 1965-75. *4105*
—. Independence Movements. Smith, Ian. Zimbabwe. 1953-82. *4074*
—. Institute for African Studies. Nsugbe, P. O. (memoirs). 1968-70. *4096*
—. Institute for African Studies. Research policy. 1930's-70's. *4132*
—. Kaunda, Kenneth (interview). 1973. *4136*
—. Labor. Mining industry. Multinational corporations. Sklar, Richard L. (review article). 1920-76. *4130*
—. Leadership. Rhodes-Livingstone Institute. 1933-76. *4122*
—. Lenshina, Alice. Lumpa Church. Politics. Sects, Religious. United National Independence Party. 1954-65. *4051*
—. Malawi. Middle classes. Urbanization. 1920-60. *3388*
—. Migrant Labor. Peasants. Social Organization. Women. 1930's-78. *4055*
—. Migration, integral. 1963-69. *4041*
—. Migration, internal. Urbanization. 1964-73. *4075*
—. Mindolo Ecumenical Foundation. Missions and Missionaries. 1950's-60's. *4039*
—. Mining. Proletarianization. Social Classes. Technology. 1946-66. *4102*
—. Mining industry. Railway politics. Tan-Zam Railway. Zimbabwe. 1895-1970. *3377*
—. Mitchell, J. Clyde (memoirs). Rhodes-Livingstone Institute. 1952-55. *4090*
—. Parliaments. Tanzania. Totalitarianism. ca 1960-77. *332*
—. Political Change. Port development. Tanzania (Dar es Salaam). Transportation, Commercial. 1960's-70's. *3079*
—. Political Participation. 1972-78. *4099*
—. Political parties. United National Independence Party. 1964-73. *4114*

—. Political systems. Sanctions. Zimbabwe. 1973. *4104*
—. Political Systems (single party). United National Independence Party. 1964-72. *4103*
—. Politics. Public Finance. 1970-77. *4059*
—. Politics. Social Classes. 1960-76. *4113*
—. Rhodes-Livingstone Institute. Richards, Audrey (memoirs). 1933-38. *4109*
—. Rhodes-Livingstone Institute. White, C. M. N. (memoirs). 1955-62. *4133*
—. Rural Development. Socialism. 1964-77. *4106*
—. Siwale, Donald (autobiography). 1890's-1964. *4123*
—. Strikes. Teachers. 1968-70. *4084*
Zambia, Eastern. Colonial Government. Ecology. Land policy. 1895-1940. *4129*
Zambia (Kabwe). Agriculture. Rural development programs. 1929-70. *4092*
Zambia (Kasumpa). Labor. Migration, Internal. Political protest. Rural development. ca 1960-75. *4042*
Zambia (Kitwe). Housing policies. 1964-76. *4127*
Zambia (Luangwa Valley). Bisa. Hunters, subsistence. 20c. *4086*
Zambia (Lusaka). Businessmen. 1960's-72. *4097*
Zambia (Marrapodi). Religion. 1930's-75. *4083*
Zambia (Mweru-Luapula). Colonial government. Economic Conditions. Public Health. Sleeping sickness. Social Conditions. 1906-22. *4093*
Zambia (Tonga Plateau). Missions and Missionaries. Political Protest. Seventh-Day Adventists. 1903-55. *4061*
Zambia (Uyombe). Local government. Political Leadership. 20c. *4046*
Zanzibar. *See* Tanzania (Zanzibar).
Zawahiri, Ahmadi az-. Al-Azhar, University of. Educational Reform. Egypt. Maraghi, Muhammad Mustafa al-. 1895-1929. *1354*
Zeitoun, apparition of. Egypt. Mary, Virgin. Social behavior. 1968. *1345*
Ziegler, Jean. African studies (review article). 1971. *296*
Zimbabwe. Accountants Ordinances. 1918-72. *4306*
—. Africa, Southern. Guerrilla Warfare (review article). National liberation movements. 1968-75. *3336*
—. *African Daily News* (periodical). *African Weekly* (periodical). *Bantu Mirror* (periodical). Letters to the editor. Race Relations. 1930-70. *4310*
—. African Farmers Union. Africans. Land tenure. Politics. 1890-1972. *4179*
—. African National Council. 1971-75. *4276*
—. African National Council. Colonial government. Rhodesian Front. Segregation. 1961-73. *4225*
—. African National Council. Smith, Ian. ca 1972-74. *4285*
—. Africans. Guerrilla warfare. Resettlement. 1972-75. *4327*
—. Afrikaners. Social status. 1900-70. *4302*
—. Agricultural development. Alvord, E. D. Missions and Missionaries. 1889-1959. *4321*
—. Agricultural development. Colonialism. Domestic Policy. Kenya. 1900-60. *204*
—. Agricultural development. Europeans. ca 1890-1974. *4166*
—. Agricultural development policies. Guerrilla Warfare. Land tenure. 1962-78. *4156*
—. Agricultural production. Women. 1973-74. *4193*
—. Agricultural Union. Botany. Christian, Harold Basil. 1900-50. *4308*
—. Air Forces. Colonial government. 1934-75. *4292*
—. Air Warfare. Lewis, D. G. "Tommy". Richthofen, Manfred von. World War I. 1918. *696*
—. Amnesty International. Human rights violations. 1960's-70's. *4290*
—. Angola. Foreign policy. Mozambique. South Africa. 1965-74. *3930*
—. Anthropology. Excavations. Great Zimbabwe. Historiography. 1960's-72. *4138*
—. Archaeology. Great Zimbabwe. Racial theories. -20c. *4140*
—. Armies. Economic Policy. Mugabe, Robert. 1979-80. *4221*
—. Arrighi, G. Peasants (proletarianization). Shangwe. Tobacco industry. 1898-1938. *4168*
—. Asians. Minorities. Politics. 1890-1970. *4250*
—. Asians. Occupational segregation. 1890-1950. *4167*
—. Aviators. 1935-37. *4315*
—. Badges. Chiefs. 1898-1977. *4297*
—. Bibliographies. Colonial government. Military. Research. 1890-1975. *4260*
—. Bibliographies. Education. 1970's. *4323*
—. Bibliographies. Government, Resistance to. 19c-20c. *4209*
—. Bibliographies. Voters (lists). 1899-1922. *4259*
—. Blake, Robert. Historiography (review article). 1880's-1960's. *4256*
—. Blake-Thompson, J. Labor, division of. Race Relations. Scholarship (amateur). 1921-62. *4320*
—. Boycotts. Colonial government. Economic development. 1965-73. *4165*
—. Bratton, Michael. Colonial Government. Community development. 1957-73. *4249*
—. British South Africa Company. Colonial government. Land policy. Swaziland. ca 1900-68. *4037*
—. British South Africa Company. Gold Mines and Mining. Investments. Mozambique Company. Rezende, Baron de. 1887-1948. *4159*
—. Canada. Foreign Policy. Self-determination. South Africa. ca 1961-79. *3411*
—. Canada. Foreign Policy. South Africa. Trade. 1960's-76. *3409*
—. Capital accumulation. Colonialism. Income distribution. Land policy. 1946-69. *4161*
—. Capitalism. Development. Kenya. Socialism. 1950-81. *617*
—. Capricorn Africa Society. Nationalism. Racism. Stirling, David. 1945-60. *4213*
—. Cary, Robert. Pioneer Corps (review article). 1869-1975. *4298*
—. Catholic Church. Church and State (review article). 1820-1979. *4312*
—. Cattle Raising. Cold-storage companies. Monopolies. 1890-1938. *4176*
—. Censorship. 1962-79. *4279*
—. Censorship. Press. Rhodesian Front. 1964-79. *4283*
—. Central African Federation (breakup). Colonial policy. Federation Conference (1960). Victoria Falls Conference (1963). 1953-69. *3927*
—. Chitepo, Herbert Tapfumanei (biography). Zimbabwe African National Union (ZANU). 1922-75. *4288*
—. Church and State. 1959-72. *4251*
—. Churches, independent. Leadership. Shona. Sundkler, B. G. M. 1945-70's. *4299*
—. Civil engineering. Wrey, Philip Bourchier Sherard. ca 1900-1936. *4325*
—. Civil Service. 1965-80. *4190*
—. Civil War. Peasants. 1966-79. *4222*
—. Civil War (review article). 1981. *4261*
—. Climate. Europeans. Kenya. Social Customs. 1880's-1930's. *185*
—. Collaboration. Revolution. Vambe, Lawrence. ca 1950-75. *4242*
—. Colonial Government. 1900-30. *4231*
—. Colonial Government. Confederation. Great Britain. Zambia. 1931-52. *3397*
—. Colonial government. Constitutions. Discriminatory acts. Great Britain. 1923-74. *4243*
—. Colonial government. Cultural imperialism. Educational policy. Middle Classes (African). 1953-70. *4172*
—. Colonial government. Economic Conditions. Electoral system. Great Britain. 1961-71. *4194*
—. Colonial government. Economic sanctions. 1965. *4171*
—. Colonial government. Economic sanctions. Great Britain. UN. 1965-75. *4272*
—. Colonial government. Embargo. Oil. Unilateral Declaration of Independence (UDI). 1965-77. *4160*
—. Colonial government. Masterson, G. M. (memoirs). 1925-66. *4144*
—. Colonial government. Military (review article). 1945-78. *4237*
—. Colonial government. Referendum. Responsible Government Party. 1920-23. *4227*
—. Colonial policy. Land Tenure. Legislation. Native Land Husbandry Act. 1951-80. *4163*
—. Colonial policy (memorandum). Great Britain. Military Strategy. Political Reform (delay of). Zambia. 1930-45. *3396*
—. Colonialism. Confederation. Economic Development. Social Conditions. Zambia. 1925-35. *3421*
—. Colonialism. Economic sanctions. Great Britain. Unilateral Declaration of Independence (UDI). 1965-73. *4182*
—. Colonialism. Education. 1899-1979. *4329*
—. Colonialism. Guerrilla warfare. Nationalism. 1893-1973. *4210*
—. Colonialism. Imperialism. South Africa. 1960-79. *3370*
—. Colonialism. Labor, black. Wage rates. 1900-75. *4186*
—. Colonization. Europeans. 1920-76. *4326*
—. Conflict, armed. Zimbabwe Liberation Army. 19c-20c. *4218*
—. Constitutions. Documents. Great Britain. Lancaster House Conference. 1970-79. *4291*
—. Constitutions. Independence. 1979. *4295*
—. Constitutions. Muzorewa, Abel. 1965-79. *4241*
—. Counterinsurgency. Kenya. Public Opinion. Sudan. 1951-75. *219*
—. Coups d'etat. Portugal. Smith, Ian. 1974. *4189*
—. Crime and Criminals. Law, customary. Shona. Statistics. 1936-71. *4313*
—. Daily Life. Political Development. 1980-81. *4146*
—. Decisionmaking. National Security. Unilateral Declaration of Independence (UDI). Zambia. 1965-66. *3332*
—. Decolonization. Guerrilla warfare. 1969-79. *4196*
—. Decolonization. Racism. 1900-75. *4254*
—. Decorations. Internal Affairs, Ministry of. 1973-77. *4293*
—. Detente. Foreign Relations. Mozambique. 1974. *3337*
—. Detente. Lusaka talks. 1974. *4281*
—. Diplomacy. Guerrilla movements. Neocolonialism. 1973-77. *4206*
—. Diplomacy. Independence. Kissinger, Henry A. USA. 1976. *4282*
—. Diplomacy. Smith, Ian. 1965-79. *4234*
—. Discrimination. Race Relations. 1930-78. *4304*
—. Discrimination, economic. Labor Supply. Land Tenure (alienation). South Africa. 1920-70. *3387*
—. Economic Conditions. Political power. Race. Social classes. 1890-1970's. *4173*
—. Economic Conditions. Politics. Sanctions. 1904-74. *4217*
—. Economic Conditions. Unilateral Declaration of Independence (UDI). War. 1973-80. *4152*
—. Economic Policy. Foreign Investments. 1965-80. *4162*
—. Economic sanctions. 1965-73. *4271*
—. Economic sanctions. 1966-77. *4180*
—. Economic sanctions. 1968-74. *4187*
—. Education. Ethnic groups. Independence movements. Missions and Missionaries. Political Factions. ca 1880-1977. *4264*
—. Education. National Development. 1980-81. *4240*
—. Elections. 1979. *4262*
—. Elections. Guerrilla Warfare. Mugabe, Robert. 1979-80. *4212*
—. Elections. Military. Patriotic Front. Political Factions. 1979-80. *4211*
—. Elections. Voting and Voting Behavior. 1962-77. *4229*
—. Elites, white. Newspapers. Values. 1890-1970. *4311*
—. Ethics. Muzorewa, Abel. 1960's-70's. *4273*
—. Ethnic conflict. Ndebele. Shona. 10c-20c. *4275*
—. Ethnic Groups. 1940-80. *4296*
—. Ethnic Groups. Political Factions. 1957-79. *4267*
—. Ethnic groups. Politics. 1960-80. *4200*
—. Europeans. Immigration. Settlement. 1890-1976. *4322*
—. Europeans. Nationalism. South Africa. 1974-79. *3335*
—. Europeans. Race Relations. 1960-78. *4214*
—. Family systems, extended. ca 1500-1973. *4300*
—. Foreign Investments. Industry. 1965-80. *4185*
—. Foreign Policy. Great Britain. Racism. 1923-70. *4239*
—. Foreign Policy. Great Britain. USA. 1970's. *4230*
—. Foreign policy. National Liberation movements. South Africa. 1974-75. *4192*
—. Foreign Policy. South Africa. Western Nations. 1970's. *3330*
—. Foreign policy (review article). Lake, Anthony. USA. 1969-70's. *4280*
—. Foreign Relations. Government. Race Relations. 1964-80. *4258*
—. Foreign relations. Mugabe, Robert. Political Leadership. 1974-80. *4268*
—. Foreign Relations. National Development. South Africa. USSR. 1979-82. *4149*
—. Front for the Liberation of Zimbabwe (FROLIZI). Guerrilla Warfare. 1963-72. *4224*

—. Gold Mines and Mining. Labor (review article). Race Relations. South Africa. 1900-69. *3403*
—. Gold Mines and Mining. London and Rhodesia Mining and Land Company. Rennie Tailyour Concession. 1890-1950's. *4158*
—. Government. Multinational corporations. Smith, Ian. 1965-79. *4169*
—. Government. Responsible Government Movement. South Africa Company. 1910-23. *4228*
—. Government (majority rule). Guerrilla warfare. 1960's-78. *4202*
—. Great Britain. Imperialism. Liberalism. 19c-20c. *4236*
—. Great Britain. Independence. 1979-80. *4270*
—. Great Britain. Neocolonialism. Portugal. Racism. South Africa. 1960's-70's. *3328*
—. Great Powers. Lancaster House Conference. Peace. 1965-79. *4247*
—. Greeks. Rural Settlements. 1890-1930. *4314*
—. Guerrilla warfare. 1966-76. *4235*
—. Guerrilla Warfare. Mugabe, Robert. Nkomo, Joshua. 1972-78. *4220*
—. Guerrilla warfare. Public Administration. 1972-74. *4207*
—. Guerrilla warfare. Smith, Ian. 1973. *4246*
—. Historiography. Industrialization. ca 1900-75. *4174*
—. Historiography (Anglo-American). Racism. 20c. 1960's. *4248*
—. Hopley, Frederick John van der Byl. John Hopley Trophy. Sports. 1883-1951. *4307*
—. Hopley, William Musgrave. Judges. 1853-1919. *4309*
—. Human rights. Portugal. South Africa. 1853-1977. *3329*
—. Hunger. Independence, War of. Operation Turkey. Political economy. 1979-81. *4198*
—. Independence. 1980-81. *4195*
—. Independence Movements. 1893-1974. *4245*
—. Independence Movements. 1961-79. *4148*
—. Independence Movements. 1961-80. *4263*
—. Independence Movements. 1970's. *4219*
—. Independence movements. Politics. 1977-79. *4286*
—. Independence Movements. Smith, Ian. Zambia. 1953-82. *4074*
—. Independence Movements. Zimbabwe African National Union (ZANU). Zimbabwe African People's Union (ZAPU). 1960's-70's. *4226*
—. Institute of Education. Teacher Training. 1956-80. *4318*
—. Kenya. Neocolonialism. Political economy. 1920's-77. *4157*
—. Labor force. Miners, white. Social Status. 1890-1953. *4178*
—. Labor (review article). Mines. Onselen, Charles van. 1900-33. *4175*
—. Labor (review article). Mining. Racism. South Africa. 1900-1933. *3408*
—. Labor Unions and Organizations. Nationalism. Political Participation. Working conditions. 20c. *4155*
—. Land Tenure. 1970-79. *4181*
—. Land Tenure. Legislation. Race. 1894-1965. *4170*
—. Law. Racism. 1920-79. *4265*
—. Libraries. 1965-79. *4141*
—. Mabena, Magumbo. Maribeha. Succession. 1972. *4278*
—. Malawi. Migrant labor. 1903-23. *3389*
—. Mapanzure. Shona (Mhari). 1859-73. *4151*
—. Methodist Church. Nemapare, E. T. J. Separatist Movements. 1930-50. *4328*
—. Migrant labor. South Africa. 1940-79. *3344*
—. Mining industry. Railway politics. Tan-Zam Railway. Zambia. 1895-1970. *3377*
—. Mugabe, Robert. Political Leadership. 1950-80. *4294*
—. Mugabe, Robert. Political Leadership. 1979-80. *4269*
—. Mugabe, Robert. Revolutionary Movements. Zimbabwe African National Union (ZANU). 1974-79. *4255*
—. National Liberation Movements. 1910's-75. *4233*
—. National liberation movements. 1931-76. *4197*
—. National Liberation Movements. 1957-80. *4188*
—. National Liberation Movements. Organization of African Unity. 1960-75. *111*
—. Nationalism. 1956-64. *4199*
—. Nationalism. Political Factions. 1960-79. *4215*
—. Nationalism. Political Factions. 1961-75. *4203*
—. Nationalism. Political Protest. 1898-1957. *4232*
—. *Native Affairs Department Annual* (periodical). Periodicals. 1923-81. *4139*
—. Native Commissioners. Nicknames. 1892-1948. *4289*
—. Nkomo, Joshua. Political leadership. 1917-79. *4257*
—. Organization of African Unity. Unilateral Declaration of Independence (UDI). 1922-74. *92*
—. Peasant production. 1890-1930. *4177*
—. Political Change. 1922-79. *4208*
—. Political leadership. Todd, Garfield. 1953-58. *4191*
—. Political Protest. Rhodesia, University of. Students. 1974. *4244*
—. Political stability. 1970's. *4238*
—. Political systems. Sanctions. Zambia. 1973. *4104*
—. Politics. Populist movements. Wilson, Neil Housman. 1920-60. *4277*
—. Politics. Race Relations. 1888-1975. *4201*
—. Politics. Race relations. Whitehead, Edgar. 1957-62. *4287*
—. Quantitative Methods. Race relations. 1893-1973. *4143*
—. Race relations. 1890-1970. *4150*
—. Race Relations. Smith, Ian. 1971-74. *4274*
—. Social Organization. Wages. 1946-72. *4164*
Zimbabwe African National Union (ZANU). Chitepo, Herbert Tapfumanei (biography). Zimbabwe. 1922-75. *4288*
—. Independence Movements. Zimbabwe. Zimbabwe African People's Union (ZAPU). 1960's-70's. *4226*
—. Mugabe, Robert. Revolutionary Movements. Zimbabwe. 1974-79. *4255*
Zimbabwe African People's Union (ZAPU). Africa, southern. Revolutionary movements. Settlers, European. 1974-75. *3360*
—. Independence Movements. Zimbabwe. Zimbabwe African National Union (ZANU). 1960's-70's. *4226*
Zimbabwe (Binga). Chiefs. Funerals. Siabuwa, Munchunkwe Sigaleta. 1976. *4303*
Zimbabwe (Bulawayo). Action Group. Liberalism. Political Factions. 1940-72. *4216*
—. Electric Power. Public Utilities. 1890's-1920's. *4153*
—. Flags. Southern Rhodesia Volunteers. 1927. 1951. *4204*
—. Housing. 19c-20c. *4324*
—. Local Government. Office buildings. 1894-1980. *4183*
—. Morris, R. M. (memoirs). Physicians. 1920-30. *4316*
—. Riots. 1919-30. *4253*
Zimbabwe (Chibi District). Pioneers. Roads. 1890's-1960's. *4319*
Zimbabwe (Harare). City planning. Europeans. Transportation. 1953-74. *4301*
Zimbabwe (Korekore). Employment. Migration, Internal. 1930-70. *4154*
Zimbabwe Liberation Army. Conflict, armed. Zimbabwe. 19c-20c. *4218*
Zimbabwe (Lowveld). Hlengwe. 1600-1977. *4137*
Zimbabwe (Manicaland; Makoni). Korsten Basketmakers. Masowe, Baba Johane. Religion. 1940-77. *4145*
Zimbabwe (Melsetter District). Dindikwa. Local government. Vagarwe. 1947-73. *4252*
Zimbabwe (Mondoro Reserve). Agriculture. Settlement. Soil erosion. 1890-1978. *4184*
Zimbabwe (review article). Foreign Relations. Politics (review article). 1960-71. *4223*
—. Independence. Politics. 1950-79. *4147*
Zimbabwe (Umtali). Hospitals. 1897-1930. *4317*
—. Refugees. Repatriation. War. 1980-81. *4205*
Zimbabwe (Victoria). Agricultural Reform. Master Farmer's Association. 1929-78. *4305*
Zimbabwe (Wange). Nambiya. Rites and Ceremonies. Social organization. 1737-1977. *4142*
Zimbabwe (Zambezi valley). Diaries. Local Government. Public Administration. 1912-13. 1977. *4284*
Zionism *See also* Jews.
—. Apartheid. Racism. UN. 1975. *481*
—. Colonial Government. France. Lyautey, Hubert. Morocco. 1915-25. *1418*
—. Egypt. 1900-48. *1359*
—. Elites. Pan-Africanism. 20c. *134*
—. Letters. Morocco. 1919-26. *1411*
Zulu. Discrimination. Racism. South Africa. -1974. *3950*
—. Independence Movements. South Africa. 1912-78. *3935*
Zulu (Nyuswa). Descent groups. Land allocation. South Africa. ca 1825-1970. *4005*
Zulu (Usuthu). Monarchy. Nicholls, George Heaton. Racism. Social Classes. Solomon. South Africa (Natal). 1879-1933. *3886*

AUTHOR INDEX

A

Aballea, François 980
Abalu, G. I. O. 2009
Abate, Yohannis 773
Abdalla, Nazem 1125
Abdel-Khalek, Gouda 1126
Abdel-Malek, Anouar 1177
Abdel-Rahim, Muddathir 1456
Abdi, Ali 3322
Abdi, Said Yusuf 2654 2673
Abed, George T. 1127
Abélès, Marc 2824
Abelin, Philippe 2296
Aberger, Peter 2297
Abiodun, Josephine Olu 2010 2198
Ablorh-Odjidja, E. 1762
Abou-Zeid, Ahmed M. 1128
Abraham, Arthur 2337
Abramov, V. 1763
Abu-Aziz, Yahya 917
Abukutsa, J. L. 2998
Abu-Lughod, Janet 1405
Abun-Nasr, Jamil M. 981
Abusedra, Fathi S. 1372
Achebe, Chinua 774
Achebe, Ifeanyi 2084
Ada, Mary Juliana 2199
Adair, Philippe 982
Adam, Andre 918
Adam, Heribert 3802
Adamolekun, Ladipo 390 1866
Adams, Bert N. 3218 3219 3220
Adams, Lois 2532
Adams, Martin 1457 1458
Adams, William Y. 1459
Ade Ajayi, J. F. 786
Adebisi, Busari 391 2085 3328 3329
Adedeji, Joel 2200 2201 2202
Adegbile, Isaiah 2203
Adejunmobi, S. A. 2204
Adejuyigbe, Omolade 1989 2086 2087
Adekson, J. 'Bayo 346 347 348 1764 3221
Adekunle, Modolaji A. 2205
Adelman, Kenneth L. 237 2485 2486 3330 3803
Adeloye, Adelola 2206
Adenira, Tunde 2088 2207
Adepoju, Aderanti 587 775
Adesua, Adeleye 2208
Adewoye, O. 2209
Adeyinka, A. Ade 2210
Adler, Taffy 3949
Afigbo, A. E. 2089
Afonja, Simi 2011
Ageron, Charles Robert 149 721
Aghaji, J. C. 1599
Agrell, Wilhelm 1178
Aguda, Akinola 3485
Aguolu, C. C. 1600 1990 2211 2212
Agwah, A. 1129
Agwani, M. S. 1179
Agyeman, Opoku 62 63 2487
Ahmad, Muhammad 64
Ahmad, Naveed 3331
Ahmed, Abdel Ghaffar M. 1460
Ahmed, Akbar S. 2213
Aire, Victor O. 2298
Ajala, Adekunle 65
Ake, Claude 238
Akeredolu-Ale, E. O. 2012
Akhavi, Shahrough 1180
Akindele, R. A. 66 2090 2091
Akinsanya, Adeoye 67 535 536 537 2092 2093 2094 3222
Akintoye, S. A. 1991
Akintunde, J. O. 1992
Akinyemi, A. Bolaji 68 69 2095
Akpan, M. B. 588
Akpan, Moses E. 2096
Alabi, G. A. 2214
Alalade, F. O. 1910
Albright, David E. 392
Aldington, T. J. 3051
Aleksandrov, L. A. 3804
Aleksandrovskaia, L. 589 590 591 592
Alessandrini, Adolfo 1361
Alexander, Nathan 1362 1363
Alexandre, Pierre 239 776
Alford, B. W. E. 4038
Al-Harir, 'Abd-al-Muali Salih 1364
Ali, Shanti Sadiq 3706
Alibaruho, Gloria Lindsey 3184
Alibert, Jacques 1601
Alimov, Y. 70
Allan, J. A. 1365 1366
Allen, J. de V. 2564
Allen, Neil 858
Allen, Rob 2013
Allen, Roger 1315
Alli, Billiamin A. 2215
Allibert, Jean-François 3707
Allman, James 1530
Allum, Percy 1461
Almeida-Topor, Hélène d' 150 151 686 1602
Alpers, Edward A. 3625
Althabe, Gérard 3548 3549
Altman, Israel 1181
Aluko, Olajide 1765 2014 2097 2098 2099
Alverson, Hoyt S. 3950
Aly, Abd al-Monein Said 1316
Amadi, Adolphe O. 777
Amadi, Lawrence E. 2216
Amami, S. El 1531
Amegbleame, Simon Agbeko 1603
Amenumey, D. E. K. 2371
Ametewee, Victor 1766
Amey, Alan B. 2565
Amiji, Hatim 2566
Amin, Galal A. 1130
Amin, Samir 593
Amody, Francis J. 3805
Amsden, Alice H. 2858
Amselle, Jean-Loup 1958 1959 1971
Amucheazi, Elochukwu 2100
Amvrosova, M. 538
Anderson, Gwen 778
Anderson, Lisa 1367
Andrade, Mario de 779
Andrew, C. M. 152 687
Andrews, Herbert D. 4039
Andrews, Loretta Kreider 4039
Angelelli, J. P. 1406
Anglin, Douglas G. 3332 4040
Anifowose, Remi 594
Anigbo, Osmund A. C. 2217
Anignikin, Sylvain C. 1699
Anise, Ladun 240 241 242 380 780
Anoniyi, Timothy A. 2218
Anstey, D. G. 3588
Anthony, Constance G. 3052
Anthony, David H. 3951
Anyanwu, K. Chukwulozie 153
Aran, Esther 722
Araud, Claude 3672
Araya, Francisco Ghisolfo 3673
Aref'ev, A. L. 781
Arens, W. 3185
Arhin, Kwame 1719
Arkoun, Muhammad 919
Armagnac, Catherine 2384
Arnaud, Jacqueline 920 983
Arnold, Anne-Sophie 3429 3626 4188
Arnold, Guy 513 4189
Artzi, Pinhas 2745
Asante, S. K. B. 71 1604 1767 1768 2718 2719
Asein, Samuel Omo 2219 2567 3952
Aseto, D. O. 782
Asibey, Andrew Osei 1937
Asiwaju, A. I. 1 1605 1606 1607 1608 1697 1698 2101 2220
Askarova, D. A. 1462
Asobie, H. A. 2102
Atanda, J. A. 3223
Atieno-Odhiambo, E. S. 2859
Atimomo, Emiko 243
Auala, Leonard N. 3333
Ault, David E. 783
Auma-Osolo, Agola 349
Aupens, Bernard 2656
Auphan, Admiral 723
Austen, Ralph 2860
Avery, William P. 539
Avriel, Ehud 393
Awa, Eme O. 2103
Awiti, Adhu 3053
Awoniyi, Timothy A. 2221
Awoonor, Kofi 784
Axelson, O. E. 785
Ayache, Germain 1407
Ayalew, Solomon 2825
Ayandele, E. A. 244 786 2104 2222 2223
Ayoade, John A. A. 2015 2105 2106
Ayubi, Nazih N. M. 1182 1183 1184
Azar, Edward E. 1200
Azéma, Jean-Pierre 724
Azevedo, Mario J. 2429 3334 3430
Aziz, M. A. 1185

B

Ba, Abdou Bouri 2299
Baatz, Wolfgang 394
Babayēmi, S. O. 2224
Bach, Daniel 2107
Badal, R. K. 1463
Badeau, John S. 1186
Badran, Margot Farranto 921
Baduel, Pierre-Robert 1532
Baer, George W. 2720
Baier, Stephen 595 1977
Bailey, Martin 514 3131 3132
Bajan, Pavol 3537
Baker, Colin 3589 3590 3591 3592
Baker, Donald G. 3335
Baker, J. 2690
Baker, Jonathan 596
Baker, Pauline H. 2108
Baker, Raymond William 1131 1187
Baker, Ross K. 3806
Baker, S. J. K. 2568
Balans, Jean-Louis 1972
Baldet, Henry 2680
Baldock, R. W. 3336
Baldwin, Alan 3807
Baldwin, Charlene M. 3808
Balezin, A. S. 3224
Balkovac-Kreškenji, Branka 1112
Ballard, Charles 3953
Balson, C. S. 3954
Balta, Paul 984 985 986
Bamber, F. W. 4153
Bame, K. N. 1829
Bamisaiye, Anne 2016
Bamya, Aïda 987
Banks, F. E. 597
Bannerman, J. H. 4137
Baratelli, F. Micali 1188
Baratov, N. 1978
Barbag, Anna 245 1609
Barbour, K. M. 1464
Baregu, Mwesiga L. 540
Barghathi, Yusuf Salim al- 1368
Barkai, Haim 1132
Barker, Jonathan 2300
Barnard, Alan 3486
Barnes, Carolyn 2861
Barnes, Sandra T. 246
Barongo, S. 3054
Barratt, John 3337
Barrett, Stanley R. 2017 2225
Barrows, Walter L. 247 248
Barth, James L. 1993
Barton, Nathalie 1465
Bascom, William 787
Baskin, V. S. 515
Basler, Werner 2721
Bassani, Ezio 788
Bassino, Aldo 2862
Basu, Anup Ranjan 922 988
Bates, Robert H. 249 4041 4042
Batista, Alves Bernardo 3426
Batsch, Christophe 2372
Battle, Lucius D. 1189 1190
Bawele, Mumbanza 2462
Bay, Edna G. 652 1752 2163 2194 2363 2878 3005 3187
Bayart, Jean-François 2399 2400
Baylies, Carolyn L. 4043
Baynham, S. J. 350 1769
Baynham, Simon 1770
Bayoumi, Ahmed 1466 1467
Ba-Yunus, Ilyas 379
Beach, D. N. 4138
Bebey, Francis 789
Bebler, Anton 2338
Bechtold, Peter K. 1468
Beck, Ann 2569
Beck, Peter J. 2722
Becken, H.-J. 3955
Beckett, Paul A. 989
Beebe, Lucius 3338
Beecher, Lloyd, Jr. 725
Beer, Christopher E. F. 2109
Beeson, Irene 1191
Behrman, Lucy Creevey 2301
Beidelman, T. O. 790 3133
Bekić, Darko 2488
Belcher, Timothy 3749
Beleky, Louis P. 1938
Belfiglio, Valentine J. 3674 3809
Bell, J. Bowyer 1469 1470 2723 3025
Bell, Morag 3487
Bello, S. 1994
Belloncle, Guy 598
Bellot, Jean-Marc 599
Bellot-Couderc, Béatrice 599
Beltrán, Luis 2489
Benabdelkrim, Ahmed 990
Benaerts, Pierre 395
Benani, Ahmed 923
BenBarka, Mehdi 1408 1409
Bender, Gerald J. 3431 3432 3483
Ben-Dor, Gabriel 1009
Benedick, Richard Elliot 1133
Bening, R. B. 1771 1772 1773 1830
Benneh, George 1720
Bennett, Bruce W. 4041
Bennett, Norman Robert 154
Bennett, Valerie Plave 1774 1960
Bennetta, Jules-Rosette 791
Bennoune, Mahfoud 991 992
Benoist-Méchin 1410
Ben-Shalom, Arye 396
Bensimon, Doris 1411
Benson, Mary 3488
Berg, Gerald M. 3550
Berg-Schlosser, Dirk 2863
Beri, H. M. L. 3675
Berkley, Constance E. 1471
Berman, B. J. 2864 2913
Berman, Edward H. 516 517 534 792 793
Bermingham, Jack 397
Bernard, Guy 2533
Bernard-Duquenet, Nicole 1610 2302
Bernardi, Bernardo 2 250
Bernstein, Henry 3
Berntsen, John L. 2570
Bernus, Edmond 1979
Bernus, S. 1980
Berque, Jacque 924
Berrada, Abdu 3810
Berry, Sara S. 2018 2019
Berthelemy, Jean-Claude 1611
Beshah, Teferra-Worq 2691
Bessell, J. E. 4131
Bessis, Juliette 925 1533
Béthouart, Emile 726
Betts, Tristram F. 2534
Beveridge, Andrew A. 4044
Bézy, Fernand 3551
Bhardwaj, Raman G. 2724
Bhatia, Rattan J. 1721
Bhuyan, M. Sayefullah 3055
Bidum, Kuyunsa 2463 2464
Bienefeld, M. A. 3056
Bienen, Henry 351 398 1883 2110 2571
Biersteker, Thomas J. 3057
Biesheuvel, S. 3708
Bilevich, B. 3552
Billops, Camille 1317
Binaisa, Godfrey L. 72
Binder, Leonard 1192
Binet, Jacques 794 2446
Binhammer, H. H. 3058
Binsbergen, W. M. J. van 1534 4045
Birks, J. S. 1134
Birmingham, David 3433 3434 3435 3436 3437 3438
Bishikwabo, Chubaka 2465 2490
Bissell, Richard 73 3811
Bisson, Jean 926
Blackey, Robert 4
Blackhurst, Hector 2826
Blanc, Marcel 727
Bleuchot, Hervé 1369
Blo, Sammy Kum 3812
Block, Peter F. 1135
Blondeel, W. 2535
Blumenthal, Susan 795
Bly, Viola 2491
Boals, Kay 993 994
Bobrie, François 600
Bomani, Paul 3059
Bon, Daniel L. 399
Bond, George Clement 4046
Bondestam, Lars 2692 2693
Bondy, François 995
Bono, Salvatore 541 996
Bonsi, Stephen K. 1831
Bonte, Pierre 2440
Booth, Bernard F. 2401
Booth, Newell S. 796
Borges, Jane 2895
Borneman, Ernest 155
Borrmans, Maurizio 797
Bosch, David J. 3956
Bossema, Wim 3043
Bosworth, William 798
Botoran, Constantin 1412
Bottignole, Silvana 2974
Bouche, Denise 728 1612 1613
Boudroua, Ahmed 1413
Bouillon, Antoine 3553
Boularès, Habib 1535
Bouman, F. J. A. 1536
Bourdillon, M. F. C. 4154
Bourgeot, Andre 997 1614
Boute, Joseph 2454

I

J

K

L

M

T

U

V

W

Y

Z

LIST OF PERIODICALS

A

Action Nationale [Canada]
Administration & Society
Aerospace Historian
Affari Esteri [Italy]
Africa [Great Britain]
Africa [Italy]
Africa Quarterly [India]
Africa Report
Africa Today
African Affairs [Great Britain]
African Economic History
African Historical Studies (see International Journal of African Historical Studies)
African Notes [Nigeria]
African Perspectives [Netherlands]
African Research and Documentation [Great Britain]
African Review [Tanzania]
African Social Research [Zambia]
African Studies [South Africa]
African Studies Review
Africana Aantekeninge en Nuus (see Africana Notes and News = Africana Aantekeninge en Nuus) [South Africa]
Africana Bulletin [Poland]
Africana Notes and News = Africana Aantekeninge en Nuus [South Africa]
Afrique et l'Asie (see Afrique et l'Asie Modernes) [France]
Afrique et l'Asie Modernes [France]
Afriscope [Nigeria]
Afro-Asian Economic Review [Egypt]
Agricultural History
Agricultural History Review [Great Britain]
Air Force Magazine
Air University Review
Ajia Afurika Kenkyū [Japan]
al-Adib [Lebanon]
al-Arabi [Kuwait]
Almenara (IHE) [Spain]
Alternatives: A Journal of World Policy
American Aviation Historical Society Journal
American Behavioral Scientist
American Journal of International Law
American Journal of Political Science
American Journal of Sociology
American Neptune
American Political Science Review
Annales Africaines [Senegal]
Annales Canadiennes d'Histoire (see Canadian Journal of History = Annales Canadiennes d'Histoire) [Canada]
Annales de Géographie [France]
Annales: Economies, Sociétés, Civilisations [France]
Annali dell'Istituto Giangiacomo Feltrinelli [Italy]
Annals of the American Academy of Political and Social Science
Annals of the Association of American Geographers
ANU Historical Journal [Australia]
Arab Studies Quarterly
Arabica [Netherlands]
Archiv des Völkerrechts [German Federal Republic]
Archív Orientální [Czechoslovakia]
Archives Européennes de Sociologie (see European Journal of Sociology = Archives Européennes de Sociologie = Europäisches Archiv für Soziologie) [Great Britain]
Armed Forces and Society
Army Quarterly and Defence Journal [Great Britain]
Asian and African Studies [Israel]
Asian Forum (ceased pub 1981)
Australian Foreign Affairs Record [Australia]
Australian Journal of Politics and History [Australia]
Australian Outlook [Australia]
Aviation Quarterly
Aziia i Afrika Segodnia [Union of Soviet Socialist Republic]

B

Behind the Headlines [Canada]
Belfagor: Rassegna di Varia Umanità [Italy]
Black Scholar
Blackwood's Magazine (ceased pub 1980) [Great Britain]
Boletim Cultural da Guiné Portuguesa (ceased pub 1973) [Guinea Bissau]
Boletim do Arquivo Histórico Militar [Portugal]
Botswana Notes and Records [Botswana]
British Heritage [Great Britain]
British Journal of Educational Studies [Great Britain]
British Journal of Sociology [Great Britain]
Bulletin de la Société d'Histoire Moderne [France]
Bulletin de l'Institut Fondamental d'Afrique Noire. Série B [Senegal]
Bulletin des Séances de l'Académie Royale des Sciences d'Outre-mer [Belgium]
Bulletin of the Atomic Scientists (briefly known as Science and Public Affairs)
Bulletin of the School of Oriental and African Studies [Great Britain]
Business History Review

C

Cahiers de Clio [Belgium]
Cahiers de Géographie de Québec [Canada]
Cahiers de Tunisie [Tunisia]
Cahiers d'Etudes Africaines [France]
Cahiers d'Histoire [France]
Canadian Dimension [Canada]
Canadian Journal of African Studies = Revue Canadienne des Etudes Africaines [Canada]
Canadian Journal of Development Studies = Revue Canadienne d'Etudes du Développement [Canada]
Canadian Journal of History = Annales Canadiennes d'Histoire [Canada]
Canadian Journal of History of Sport = Revue Canadienne de l'Histoire des Sports [Canada]
Canadian Journal of History of Sport and Physical Education (see Canadian Journal of History of Sport = Revue Canadienne de l'Histoire des Sports) [Canada]
Canadian Journal of Political Science = Revue Canadienne de Science Politique [Canada]
Canadian Labour [Canada]
Canadian Review of Sociology and Anthropology = Revue Canadienne de Sociologie et d'Anthropologie [Canada]
Canadian Review of Studies in Nationalism = Revue Canadienne des Etudes sur le Nationalisme [Canada]
Centennial Review
Center Magazine
Československý Časopis Historický [Czechoslovakia]
China Report [India]
Civilisations [Belgium]
Civitas [Italy]
Clio Medica [Netherlands]
Co-Existence [Great Britain]
Colby Library Quarterly
Columbia Journal of Transnational Law
Commentary
Communautés: Archives de Sciences Sociales de la Coopération et du Développement [France]
Communautés: Archives Internationales de Sociologie de la Coopération et du Développement (see Communautés: Archives de Sciences Sociales de la Coopération et du Développement) [France]
Communications Historiques (see Historical Papers = Communications Historiques) [Canada]
Comparative Political Studies
Comparative Politics
Comparative Studies in Society and History [Great Britain]
Comunità [Italy]
Comunità Internazionale [Italy]
Conflict
Contemporary French Civilization
Contemporary Review [Great Britain]
Crisis
Cuban Studies
Cuban Studies Newsletter (see Cuban Studies)
Cultures: Dialogue Between the Peoples of the World [France]
Cultures et Développement: Revue Internationale des Sciences du Développement [Belgium]
Current History

D

Dacca University Studies Part A [Bangladesh]
Daedalus
Dalhousie Review [Canada]
Défense Nationale [France]
Demográfia [Hungary]
Development and Change [Netherlands]
Diogenes [Italy]
Diplomatic History
Dissent

E

Eastern Horizon [Hong Kong]
Economic Development and Cultural Change
Economic Geography
Economic History Review [Great Britain]
Economisch- en Sociaal-Historisch Jaarboek [Netherlands]
Economy and History (merged with Scandinavian Economic History Review 1981) [Sweden]
Ecrits de Paris [France]
Encounter
English Historical Review [Great Britain]
Epetēris Hetaireias Stereoelladikōn Meletōn [Greece]
Esprit [France]
Estudios de Asia y Africa [Mexico]
Ethiopia Observer (suspended pub 1973) [Ethiopia]
Ethnic and Racial Studies [Great Britain]
Ethnicity (ceased pub 1981)
Ethnohistory
Etudes [France]
Etudes d'Histoire Africaine [Zaire]
Etudes Internationales [Canada]
Etudes Polémologiques (suspended pub 1978) [France]
Etudes Rurales [France]
Europa Archiv [German Federal Republic]
Europäisches Archiv für Soziologie (see European Journal of Sociology = Archives Européennes de Sociologie = Europäisches Archiv für Soziologie) [Great Britain]
European Journal of Sociology = Archives Européennes de Sociologie = Europäisches Archiv für Soziologie [Great Britain]
European Studies Review [Great Britain]

F

Film and History
Flinders Journal of History and Politics [Australia]
Folia Humanística [Spain]
Foreign Affairs
Foreign Policy
Foreign Service Journal
Foro Internacional [Mexico]
Francia [France]
Frankfurter Hefte [German Federal Republic]
Freedom at Issue
Freedomways
French Historical Studies

G

Gazette: International Journal for Mass Communication Studies [Netherlands]
Geneva-Africa = Genève-Afrique [Switzerland]
Genève-Afrique (see Geneva-Africa = Genève-Afrique) [Switzerland]
Genus [Italy]
Geographical Review
Geography [Great Britain]
German Yearbook of International Law [German Federal Republic]
Government and Opposition [Great Britain]
Government Publications Review: An International Journal of Issues and Information Resources

H

Hamdard Islamicus [Pakistan]
Hamizrah Hehadash [Israel]
Harvard Educational Review
Heritage [Zimbabwe]
Histoire [France]
Histoire Sociale (see Social History = Histoire Sociale) [Canada]
Historia [South Africa]

Historian
Historical Magazine of the Protestant Episcopal Church
Historical News [New Zealand]
Historical Papers = Communications Historiques [Canada]
Historical Reflections = Réflexions Historiques [Canada]
Historical Studies [Australia]
Historisk Tidsskrift [Norway]
History in Africa
History of Agriculture [India]
History of Education [Great Britain]
History of Education Quarterly
History of Religions
History Teacher
History Today [Great Britain]
Horizon
Human Organization
Human Rights Quarterly

I

Iberian Studies [Great Britain]
IDOC Middle East Quarterly (suspended pub)
Independência: Revista de Cultura Lusiada [Portugal]
India Quarterly: Journal of International Affairs [India]
Indian Horizons [India]
Indian Journal of Political Studies [India]
Indian Journal of Politics [India]
Indian Political Science Review [India]
Indiana Social Studies Quarterly
Industrial Relations = Relations Industrielles [Canada]
Internasjonal Politikk [Norway]
International Affairs [Great Britain]
International Affairs [Union of Soviet Socialist Republic]
International Development Review
International Journal [Canada]
International Journal of African Historical Studies
International Journal of Contemporary Sociology
International Journal of Middle East Studies [Great Britain]
International Journal of Politics
International Journal of Women's Studies [Canada]
International Library Review [Great Britain]
International Migration = Migrations Internationales = Migraciones Internacionales [Netherlands]
International Migration Review
International Organization
International Perspectives [Canada]
International Problems [Israel]
International Review of History and Political Science [India]
International Security
International Social Science Journal [France]
International Social Science Review
International Socialist Review
International Studies [India]
International Studies Notes
International Studies Quarterly
Internationales Jahrbuch für Geschichtsunterricht (see Internationales Jahrbuch für Geschichts- und Geographieunterricht) [German Federal Republic]
Internationales Recht und Diplomatie [German Federal Republic]
Investigación Económica [Mexico]
Islamic Quarterly [Great Britain]
Issue: A Quarterly Journal of Opinion
Issues & Studies [Taiwan]
Italia Contemporanea [Italy]
Izvestiia na Instituta po Istoriia na BKP [Bulgaria]

J

Jahrbuch des Instituts für Deutsche Geschichte [Israel]
Jerusalem Journal of International Relations [Israel]
Jerusalem Quarterly [Israel]
Jewish Social Studies
Journal for the Scientific Study of Religion
Journal of African History [Great Britain]
Journal of African Studies
Journal of African-Afro-American Affairs
Journal of American Folklore
Journal of American Studies [Great Britain]
Journal of Asian and African Studies [Netherlands]
Journal of Black Studies
Journal of Church and State
Journal of Common Market Studies [Great Britain]
Journal of Commonwealth and Comparative Politics [Great Britain]
Journal of Commonwealth Political Studies (see Journal of Commonwealth and Comparative Politics) [Great Britain]
Journal of Comparative Administration (see Administration and Society)
Journal of Conflict Resolution
Journal of Contemporary History [Great Britain]
Journal of Developing Areas
Journal of Development Studies [Great Britain]
Journal of Economic History
Journal of Educational Administration and History [Great Britain]
Journal of Ethnic Studies
Journal of Forest History
Journal of Imperial and Commonwealth History [Great Britain]
Journal of Interamerican Studies and World Affairs
Journal of Interdisciplinary History
Journal of International Affairs
Journal of Law & Economics
Journal of Library History, Philosophy, & Comparative Librarianship
Journal of Modern African Studies [Great Britain]
Journal of Negro Education
Journal of Negro History
Journal of Palestine Studies [Lebanon]
Journal of Peace Research [Norway]
Journal of Peace Science
Journal of Peasant Studies [Great Britain]
Journal of Political and Military Sociology
Journal of Politics
Journal of Popular Culture
Journal of Religion in Africa = Religion en Afrique [Netherlands]
Journal of Social and Political Studies (see Journal of Social, Political and Economic Studies)
Journal of Social, Political and Economic Studies
Journal of Southern African Affairs
Journal of Southern African Studies [Great Britain]
Journal of Strategic Studies [Great Britain]
Journal of the Canadian Church Historical Society [Canada]
Journal of the Hellenic Diaspora: Critical Thoughts on Greek and World Issues
Journal of the Historical Society of Nigeria [Nigeria]
Journal of the History of Medicine and Allied Sciences
Journal of the Royal United Services Institute for Defence Studies [Great Britain]
Journal of the Society of Architectural Historians
Journal of the United Service Institution of India [India]
Journal of the University of Bombay [India]
Journal of World Trade Law [Switzerland]
Journalism Quarterly

K

Kalendar Jednota
Kenya Historical Review [Kenya]
Kleio [Netherlands]
Kleio [South Africa]
Kultura i Społeczeństwo [Poland]
Kungliga Krigsvetenskaps Akademiens Handlingar och Tidskrift [Sweden]
Kyrkohistorisk Årsskrift [Sweden]

L

Land Economics
Latin American Perspectives
Law & Society Review
Liberian Studies Journal
Library Quarterly
Luso-Brazilian Review

M

Magazin Istoric [Romania]
Majallat al-Buhūth al-Tārīkhīya (Journal of Historical Researches) [Libya]
Mankind
Mankind Quarterly
Manuscripts
Marine Rundschau [German Federal Republic]
Mawazo [Uganda]
Medical History [Great Britain]
Mediterranean Peoples = Peuples Méditerranéens [France]
Michael: On the History of the Jews in the Diaspora [Israel]
Michigan Academician
Middle East Journal
Middle Eastern Studies [Great Britain]
Midstream
Midwest Quarterly
Migraciones Internacionales (see International Migration = Migrations Internationales = Migraciones Internacionales) [Netherlands]
Migrations Internationales (see International Migration = Migrations Internationales = Migraciones Internacionales) [Netherlands]
Militärgeschichte [German Democratic Republic]
Military Affairs
Military Review
Millennium: Journal of International Studies [Great Britain]
Minerva: A Review of Science, Learning and Policy [Great Britain]
Mirovaia Ekonomika i Mezhdunarodnye Otnosheniia [Union of Soviet Socialist Republic]
Monthly Review
Mouvement Social [France]
Movimento di Liberazione in Italia (see Italia Contemporanea) [Italy]
Movimento Operaio e Socialista [Italy]
Munger Africana Library Notes
Musées de Genève [Switzerland]
Muslim World

N

NADA (ceased pub 1980) [Zimbabwe]
Names
Narody Azii i Afriki [Union of Soviet Socialist Republic]
Naval War College Review
Negro History Bulletin
New Left Review [Great Britain]
New World Review
New York University Journal of International Law and Politics
Nigeria Magazine [Nigeria]
Norsk Militaert Tidsskrift [Norway]
Nouvelle Revue des Deux Mondes (see Revue des Deux Mondes) [France]
Novaia i Noveishaia Istoriia [Union of Soviet Socialist Republic]
Nuova Rivista Storica [Italy]
Nyasaland Journal (see Society of Malawi Journal) [Malawi]

O

Odu: a Journal of West African Studies [Nigeria]
Økonomi og Politik [Denmark]
Oral History Review
Orbis
Oriente Moderno [Italy]
Osteuropa [German Federal Republic]
Oxford Economic Papers [Great Britain]

P

Paedagogica Historica [Belgium]
Paideuma. Mitteilungen zur Kulturkunde [German Federal Republic]
Pakistan Horizon [Pakistan]
Pakistan Library Bulletin [Pakistan]
Pan-African Journal [Kenya]
Państwo i Prawo [Poland]
Parameters
Párttörténeti Közlemények [Hungary]
Patterns of Prejudice [Great Britain]
Peace and Change
Peace Research Reviews [Canada]
Peasant Studies
Peasant Studies Newsletter (see Peasant Studies)
Pensée [France]
Peuples Méditerranéens-Mediterranean Peoples (see Mediterranean Peoples = Peuples Méditerranéens [France]
Philippine Journal of Public Administration [Philippines]

Phylon
Plural Societies [Netherlands]
Policy Studies Review
Political Science Quarterly
Political Science Review [India]
Political Studies [Great Britain]
Politička Misao [Yugoslavia]
Politico [Italy]
Politics [Australia]
Politics & Society
Politique Etrangère [France]
Politische Vierteljahresschrift [German Federal Republic]
Ponte [Italy]
Population [France]
Population and Development Review
Population Studies [Great Britain]
Present Tense
Problemi di Ulisse [Italy]
Problems of Communism
Proceedings of the American Philosophical Society
Proceedings of the Annual Meeting of the Western Society for French History
Proceedings of the Michiana Area Historians (ceased pub 1975)
Przegląd Socjologiczny [Poland]
Przegląd Zachodni [Poland]
Public Administration [Great Britain]
Public Opinion Quarterly
Publius

Q

Quarterly Bulletin of the South African Library [South Africa]
Quarterly Journal of the Library of Congress
Quarterly Review of Historical Studies [India]

R

Radical America
Radical History Review
Rassegna degli Archivi di Stato [Italy]
Recherche Sociale [France]
Red River Valley Historical Review
Réflexions Historiques (see Historical Reflections = Réflexions Historiques) [Canada]
Rekishigaku Kenkyū [Japan]
Relations Industrielles (see Industrial Relations = Relations Industrielles) [Canada]
Relations Internationales [France]
Religion en Afrique (see Journal of Religion in Africa = Religion en Afrique) [Netherlands]
Religion in Life (ceased pub 1980)
Research in Economic History
Resources for Feminist Research = Documentation sur la Recherche Féministe [Canada]
Review of Politics
Review of Radical Political Economics
Reviews in American History
Revista de Estudios Internacionales (supersedes Revista de Política Internacional) [Spain]
Revista de Estudios Políticos [Spain]
Revista de Historia Militar [Spain]
Revista de Istorie [Romania]
Revista de Marina (IHE) [Chile]
Revista de Política Internacional (superseded by Revista de Estudios Internacionales) [Spain]
Revista Mexicana de Ciencia Política (see Revista Mexicana de Ciencias Políticas y Sociales) [Mexico]
Revista Mexicana de Ciencias Políticas y Sociales [Mexico]
Revue Canadienne de l'Histoire des Sports (see Canadian Journal of History of Sport = Revue Canadienne de l'Histoire des Sports) [Canada]
Revue Canadienne de Science Politique (see Canadian Journal of Political Science = Revue Canadienne de Science Politique) [Canada]
Revue Canadienne de Sociologie et d'Anthropologie (see Canadian Review of Sociology and Anthropology = Revue Canadienne de Sociologie et d'Anthropologie) [Canada]
Revue Canadienne des Etudes Africaines (see Canadian Journal of African Studies = Revue Canadienne des Etudes Africaines) [Canada]
Revue Canadienne des Etudes sur le Nationalisme (see Canadian Review of Studies in Nationalism = Revue Canadienne des Etudes sur le Nationalisme) [Canada]
Revue Canadienne d'Etudes du Développement (see Canadian Journal of Development Studies = Revue Canadienne d'Etudes du Développement) [Canada]
Revue de l'Institut de Sociologie [Belgium]
Revue de l'Occident Musulman et de la Méditerranée [France]
Revue de l'Université d'Ottawa (see University of Ottawa Quarterly = Revue de l'Université d'Ottawa) [Canada]
Revue des Deux Mondes [France]
Revue d'Histoire de la Deuxième Guerre Mondiale [France]
Revue d'Histoire du Théâtre [France]
Revue d'Histoire et de Philosophie Religieuses [France]
Revue d'Histoire Moderne et Contemporaine [France]
Revue Française de Science Politique [France]
Revue Française d'Etudes Politiques Africaines [France]
Revue Française d'Histoire d'Outre-Mer [France]
Revue Historique [France]
Revue Historique de Droit Français et Etranger [France]
Revue Historique des Armées [France]
Revue Internationale d'Histoire de la Banque [Italy]
Revue Militaire Générale (suspended pub 1973) [France]
Revue Roumaine d'Etudes Internationales [Romania]
Rhodesian History [Zimbabwe]
Rhodesiana (superseded by Heritage) [Zimbabwe]
Risorgimento [Italy]
Rivista di Studi Politici Internazionali [Italy]
Rivista Marittima [Italy]
Rivista Militare [Italy]
Rocky Mountain Social Science Journal (see Social Science Journal)
Round Table (ceased pub 1981-82) [Great Britain]

S

SAIS Review
Samtiden [Norway]
San José Studies
Sborník Historický [Czechoslovakia]
Scandinavian Journal of History [Sweden]
Schweizer Monatshefte [Switzerland]
Science and Public Affairs (see Bulletin of the Atomic Scientists)
Science and Society
Scottish Geographical Magazine [Great Britain]
Scrinium; Zeitschrift des Verbandes Österreichischer Archivare [Austria]
Search: Journal for Arab and Islamic Studies
Shigaku Zasshi [Japan]
Signs: Journal of Women in Culture and Society
Smithsonian
Social and Economic Studies [Jamaica]
Social Education
Social Forces
Social History [Great Britain]
Social History = Histoire Sociale [Canada]
Social Problems
Social Research
Social Science (see International Social Science Review)
Social Science Journal
Social Science Quarterly
Social Studies
Society
Society of Malawi Journal [Malawi]
Sociological Analysis
Sociology and Social Research
South Atlantic Quarterly
Southern Exposure
Southern Folklore Quarterly
Southern Quarterly
Sovetskaia Etnografiia [Union of Soviet Socialist Republic]
Sovetskoe Gosudarstvo i Pravo [Union of Soviet Socialist Republic]
Soviet Military Review [Union of Soviet Socialist Republic]
Spiegel Historiael [Netherlands]
Stimmen der Zeit [German Federal Republic]
Storia Contemporanea [Italy]
Storia e Politica [Italy]
Strategy and Tactics
Studi Storici [Italy]
Studia Nauk Politycznych [Poland]
Studies in Comparative Communism
Studies in Comparative International Development
Studies on the Developing Countries (ceased pub 1979) [Poland]
Survey [Great Britain]
Survival [Great Britain]
Századok [Hungary]

T

Taamuli [Tanzania]
Tanzania Notes and Records [Tanzania]
Tarih Enstitüsü Dergisi [Turkey]
Tarikh [Nigeria]
Teaching Political Science
Texana (ceased pub 1974)
Tijdschrift voor Geschiedenis [Netherlands]
Towson State Journal of International Affairs
Transactions of the Royal Historical Society [Great
Transafrican Journal of History [Kenya]
Transport History [Great Britain]
Travaux & Mémoires de l'Institut des Hautes Etudes de l'Amérique Latine [France]
Trends in History
Twentieth Century Studies [Great Britain]

U

Uganda Journal [Uganda]
Ukrains'kyi Istorychnyi Zhurnal [Union of Soviet Socialist Republic]
Umění a Řemesla [Czechoslovakia]
Umoja: A Scholarly Journal of Black Studies
United States Naval Institute Proceedings
Universal Human Rights (see Human Rights Quarterly)
Universitas [Ghana]
University of Ottawa Quarterly = Revue de l'Université
Urban Studies [Great Britain]

V

Virginia Quarterly Review
Vista (ceased pub 1973)
Voenno-Istoricheskii Zhurnal [Union of Soviet Socialist Republic]
Voprosy Istorii [Union of Soviet Socialist Republic]

W

Welt des Islams [Netherlands]
Wereld en Zending [Netherlands]
Western Folklore
Western Political Quarterly
Wiener Library Bulletin [Great Britain]
Wilson Library Bulletin
Wilson Quarterly
Wissenschaftliche Zeitschrift der Humboldt Universität zu Berlin. Gesellschafts- und Sprachwissenschaftliche Reihe [German Democratic Republic]
Wissenschaftliche Zeitschrift der Karl-Marx Universität Leipzig. Gesellschafts- und Sprachwissenschaftliche Reihe [German Democratic Republic]
Women's Studies
Working Papers for a New Society (see Working Papers Magazine)
Working Papers Magazine
World Affairs
World Marxist Review [Canada]
World Politics
World Survey [Great Britain]
World Today [Great Britain]
Worldview
Wort und Wahrheit (ceased pub 1973) [German Federal Republic]

Y

Yalkut Moreshet Periodical [Israel]
Youth and Society

Z

Z Pola Walki [Poland]
Zambezia: The Journal of the University of Zimbabwe [Zimbabwe]
Zeitgeschichte [Austria]
Zeitschrift für Politik [German Federal Republic]
Zion [Israel]
Życie i Myśl [Poland]

LIST OF ABSTRACTERS

A

Adams, E. J.
Adams, R. K.
Alcock, A.
Aldrich, R.
Alexander, G.
Alltmont, R. C.
Altmann, B.
Andrews, H. D.
Anstey, C.
Ardia, D.
Atkins, L. R.
Auffenberg, T. L.

B

Bailor, K. M.
Balmuth, D.
Barkan, E. R.
Bartels, U.
Bates, C.
Bauhs, T. H.
Beck, P. J.
Belles, A. G.
Benfield, S. F.
Billigmeier, J. C.
Bilstein, R. E.
Black, R. D.
Bleaney, C. H.
Blethen, H. T.
Blumberg, A.
Bobango, G. J.
Bolton, G. A.
Bonnycastle, S.
Bradford, J. C.
Brown, L.
Brown, R. T.
Butchart, R. E.
Butcher, K.

C

Calkin, H. L.
Cameron, D. D.
Campbell, E. R.
Canavero, A.
Carr, S. P.
Casada, J. A.
Chambers, J. M.
Chan, L. B.
Chard, D. F.
Charles, J. S. S.
Clark, M. J.
Clements, F. A.
Cleyet, G. P.
Cline, D. H.
Coleman, J. S.
Colenso, M. R.
Collieu, A. M.
Collison, R. L.
Collon, C.
Colwell, J. L.
Conner, S. P.
Coutinho, J. V.
Crapster, B. L.

D

Dalby, A. K.
Davis, G. H.
Davis, J.
Drysdale, A. C.
Dubay, R. W.

E

Eads, O. W.
Eid, L. V.
Eminhizer, E. E.
Englard, A. A.
English, J. C.
Estes, K. W.
Evans, H. M.
Evans, J. L.

F

Faissler, M.
Falk, H. R.
Falk, J. D.
Farmerie, S. A.
Feingold, M.
Fetter, B. S.
Fishman, G. M.
Forgus, S. P.
Frank, S. H.
Frankfort, F.
Franz, D. A.
Frederick, R. D.
Frenkley, N.
Freudenthal, H. W. L.
Frey, L. S.
Frey, M. L.
Fry, C.
Fulton, R. T.

G

Gagnon, G. O.
Garfield, R.
Garland, A. N.
Gassner, J. S.
Geyer, M.
Glasrud, B. A.
Glovins, G. A.
Gromen, R. J.
Groves, J. V.
Gudgin, S. R.
Guyotte, L. S.

H

Halil, K.
Harahan, J. P.
Harrington, J. F.
Harrison, M.
Harvey, C. L.
Held, C. H.
Herritt, G.
Herstein, S. R.
Hess, G. R.
Hetzron, R.
Hewlett, G.
Hilliker, J. F.
Hively, W. R.
Hogg, M. K.
Holmes, L. E.
Holzinger, J.
Homan, G. D.
Hopkins, C.
Hopkins, E.
Hough, C. M.
Howell, A. W.
Howell, R.
Human, V. L.
Hurt, R. D.

J

Jackson, S. G.
Jeppeson, B. L.
Jewsbury, G. F.
Jirran, R. J.
Johnson, B. D.
Johnson, E. S.
Johnson, W. R.
Jones, M. K.

K

Kalinowski, L.
Kascus, M. A.
Kaufman, M.
Keyser, E. L.
Khan, R. O.
Kicklighter, J. A.
Kirby, E. S.
Klass, L. J.
Koppel, T.
Krompart, J. A.
Krzyzak, L. A.
Krzyzaniak, M.
Kubicek, R. V.
Kuner, T.

L

Lakhan, S.
Lambert, D. K.
Lauber, J. M.
Law, D. G.
Layton, R. V.
Ledbetter, B. D.
Lederer, N.
Leedom, J. W.
Legan, M. S.
Lewis, J. A.
Lifka, M. L.
Lindgren, R. E.
Linkfield, T. P.
Lloyd, D. S.
Lovin, H. T.
Lukes, I.

M

Mahood, H. R.
Makin, L.
Makino, E.
Maloney, L. M.
Mattar, P. J.
Maxon, R. M.
Maxted, L. R.
McCarthy, E.
McCarthy, J. M.
McCarthy, M.
McDonald, D. R.
McGinnis, D.
McGurk, J. J. N.
McIntyre, W. D.
McNeill, C. A.
McQuilkin, D. K.
Mendel, R. B.
Menicant, A.
Moore, J.
Mtewa, M.
Murdoch, D. H.
Myers, J. P. H.
Myres, S. L.

N

Nakayama, M.
Neal, D. C.
Neville, G. L.
Neville, R. G.
Newhouse, N. A.
Nicely, D. H.
Nicholls, D. J.
Nielson, D. G.
Noble, R. E.
Novitsky, A. W.
Nycz, H. D.

O

Ohl, J. K.
Ohrvall, C. W.
Olson, C. W.
Orr, R. B.
Osur, A. M.
Overbeck, J. A.
Oxley, A. P.

P

Packer, V. A.
Palais, E. S.
Papalas, A. J.
Parker, H. M.
Pergl, G. E.
Pichelin, C.
Piersen, W. D.
Pollak, O. B.
Powell, J.
Powers, T. I.
Powers, T. L.
Puffer, K. J.
Pusateri, C. J.

Q

Quinlan, S. J.

R

Rabineau, P.
Raife, L. R.
Read, C. J.
Reed, J. B.
Riles, R.
Ritter, R. V.
Rockwood, D. S.
Rosenfield, M. C.
Rosenthal, F.
Rushton, K.

S

Samaraweera, V.
Sanderson, J. M.
Sapper, N. G.
Sarna, J. D.
Sassoon, T.
Sassoon, Y.
Sbacchi, A.
Schumacher, M.
Selleck, R. G.
Sevilla, S.
Sherer, R. G.
Shields, H.
Sicher, E. R.
Sirriyeh, E. M.
Smith, L. C.
Smith, M.
Smith, S. R.
Smith, T. W.
Smoot, J. G.
Soff, H. G.
Souby, A. R.
Spira, T.
Stack, R. E.
Standley, A. E.
Stickney, E. P.
Stoesen, A. R.
Street, J. B.
Stromberg, R.
Sweetland, J. H.
Swiecicka-Ziemianek, M. A. J.
Szewczyk, M. W.

T

Talalay, S. J.
Taylorson, P. J.
Thacker, J. W.
Tharaud, B. C.
Thomas, J. R.
Thomson, H. F.
Tomlinson-Brown, S.
Trauth, M. P.
Travis, P.
Truschel, L. W.
Tudor, F. P.
Tull, J.

V

Valliant, R. B.
Vexler, R. I.
Vivian, J. F.

W

Wagnleitner, R.
Walker, W. T.
Walsh, J. M.
Weltsch, R. E.
Wentworth, M. J.
White, G. M.
Wiegand, W. A.
Williamson, N. A.
Wilson, M. T.
Wilson, W. J.
Wood, C. W.
Wren, D. J.
Wyk, L. W. Van

Y

Yanchisin, D. A.
Yasamee, F. A. K.
Yerburgh, M. R.
Yntema, S. G.

Z

Zabel, O. H.
Ziewacz, L. E.